Human. ~~Geography~~

Noel Castree is Professor of Human Geography at
Manchester University and has a wide range of expertise
in the subject. He has authored and edited several books,
including *Nature, Remaking Reality* (with Bruce Braun),
and *David Harvey: A Critical Reader* (with Derek Gregory).
He is also a senior editor of the recent *International
Encyclopedia of Human Geography* and the forthcoming
International Encyclopedia of Geography.

 Rob Kitchin is a Professor of Human Geography and
Director of the National Institute for Regional and Spatial
Analysis (NIRSA) at the National University of Ireland,
Maynooth. He has published widely across the social
sciences, including twenty books. He is an editor of the
international journals *Progress in Human Geography* and
Dialogues in Human Geography, and for eleven years was
the editor of *Social and Cultural Geography*. He was
an editor-in-chief of the twelve-volume *International
Encyclopedia of Human Geography*.

 Alisdair Rogers is a Fellow of Keble College, Oxford
University, where he teaches geography. He has written
and contributed to textbooks at all levels of education,
from primary school to advanced degree courses. He is
the founding and chief editor of the international journal,
Global Networks: A Journal of Transnational Affairs.

(⊕) SEE WEB LINKS

Many entries in this dictionary have recommended
web links. When you see the above symbol at the end
of an entry go to the dictionary's web page at
http://www.oup.com/uk/reference/resources/
humangeography, click on **Web links** in the Resources
section and locate the entry in the alphabetical list,
then click straight through to the relevant websites.

Oxford Paperback Reference

The most authoritative and up-to-date reference books for both students and the general reader.

Accounting
Animal Behaviour
Archaeology
Architecture and Landscape Architecture
Art and Artists
Art Terms
Arthurian Literature and Legend
Astronomy
Battles
Bible
Biology
Biomedicine
British History
British Place-Names
Business and Management
Card Games
Chemistry
Christian Church
Classical Literature
Classical World
Computing
Construction, Surveying, and Civil Engineering
Contemporary World History
Cosmology
Countries of the World
Critical Theory
Dance
Dentistry
Earth Sciences
Ecology
Economics
Education
Encyclopedia
English Etymology
English Grammar
English Literature
English Surnames
Environment and Conservation
Euphemisms
Everyday Grammar
Film Studies
Finance and Banking
First Names
Food and Nutrition
Foreign Words and Phrases
Forensic Science
Geography
Hinduism
Humorous Quotations
Idioms
Irish History
Islam

Kings and Queens of Britain
Law
Law Enforcement
Linguistics
Literary Terms
London Place-Names
Mathematics
Marketing
Mechanical Engineering*
Media and Communication
Medical
Medicinal Drugs
Modern and Contemporary Art
Modern Quotations
Modern Slang
Music
Musical Terms
Nursing
Opera Characters
Philosophy
Physics
Plant Sciences
Plays
Pocket Fowler's Modern English Usage
Political Quotations
Politics
Popes
Proverbs
Psychology
Quotations
Quotations by Subject
Rhymes
Rhyming Slang
Saints
Science
Scientific Quotations
Scottish History
Shakespeare
Slang
Social Work and Social Care
Sociology
Sports Studies
Statistics
Superstitions
Synonyms and Antonyms
Theatre & Performance
Weather
Weights, Measures, and Units
World History
Word Origins
Zoology

*forthcoming

Many of these titles are also available online at
www.Oxfordreference.com

A Dictionary of

Human
Geography

NOEL CASTREE, ROB KITCHIN,
and ALISDAIR ROGERS

OXFORD
UNIVERSITY PRESS

OXFORD
UNIVERSITY PRESS

Great Clarendon Street, Oxford, OX2 6DP,
United Kingdom

Oxford University Press is a department of the University of Oxford.
It furthers the University's objective of excellence in research, scholarship,
and education by publishing worldwide. Oxford is a registered trade mark of
Oxford University Press in the UK and in certain other countries

British Library Cataloguing in Publication Data

Data available

ISBN 978-0-19-959986-8

Printed in Great Britain by
Clays Ltd, St Ives plc

Preface

The study of geography can be traced back to ancient Greece. It became a formal school and university discipline in the late 19th century and since then it has developed and diversified both conceptually and methodologically. In this volume we provide concise, straightforward definitions of the terms, concepts, and methods that comprise human geography's contemporary lexicon. It is designed to be used by students of the subject at all levels, and by their teachers. But it's also intended to appeal to others who, for whatever reason, are curious about human geography and how it seeks to make sense of the extraordinary world we live in. It is not an encyclopedia, but it offers more breadth and depth concerning the large and diverse body of knowledge of human geography than one finds in most dictionaries of geography, which try to cover both the human and physical aspects of the subject.

In the following pages we have sought to present the debates and insights of our peers in the world of university geography, even as we have included entries on subjects more commonly associated with a geographical reference work. Consequently, readers will find entries for Afghanistan, Mecca, and Tokyo alongside entries for terms such as placelessness, spatial autocorrelation, and Tobler's first law of geography. We have also included other kinds of entry that will, we hope, be of interest. For instance, there are biographical entries about the intellectual contributions of leading human geographers past and present, entries about key books that have influenced geographical thought, and key events, political agreements, and organizations that have shaped the world and the discipline of geography. In the appendices at the back of the book you will find lists of peer-review human geography journals, geographical societies, and human geographers whose research has been recognized as outstanding by their peers, plus maps that show the location of place entries. We have been selective in our coverage of places, countries, events, organizations, and agreements, only including entries on those that, in our view, were or are iconic or important in economic, cultural, or political terms. Some readers may wish for a larger and wider selection, but this book is not intended to be a gazetteer. Many entries direct readers to websites where they can learn more. In other cases, further reading and references are listed at the end of many entries. The majority of entries contain cross-references to other ones, allowing readers to follow their own paths through the dictionary. We hope these cross-references allow you to widen and deepen your understanding of human geography—even if your initial intention was to get clued-up on just one or two of our 2100 headwords. These cross-references are signalled by an asterisk (for example, *planning), or by 'see', 'see also' or 'compare', followed by the headword (for example, *see* PLANNING). Finally, not a few entries offer considerable detail on the subjects in question because of their importance or complexity.

Just a few minutes dipping into this work will reveal that human geography is porous in two senses. First, its subject matter intersects with virtually every social science and humanities subject, from anthropology to philosophy to sociology, and human geographers are engaged in routine exchanges with their academic neighbours. In each case we try to show their relevance to human geography and how our understanding of them benefits from taking a geographical perspective. Secondly, human geography is in many senses an everyday phenomenon. Many of its key concerns are daily news—for instance, urbanization, deindustrialization, and international migration. Likewise, its concepts are everyday ones, even if professional geographers utilize them in ways that lay actors might not readily recognize (for example, landscape, nature, and place). These aspects make a dictionary of human geography relevant to many readers in ways that, say, dictionaries of physics or ancient history are not. We hope readers who study the subject formally and those who hold a more general interest will better understand their own human geographies by perusing the entries.

We wish to thank Joanna Harris, Vicki Donald, and Judith Wilson of Oxford University Press for helping us initiate this project. Joanna remained especially patient as deadlines were renegotiated. Nick Scarle at Manchester University did an exemplary job designing the book's visual aids and we thank him warmly.

Noel Castree, Rob Kitchin, and Alisdair Rogers
February 2013

Contents

AAG *See* ASSOCIATION OF AMERICAN GEOGRAPHERS.

Abler, Ronald F. (1939–) An influential American human geographer who co-authored a pioneering text on the *spatial science approach (*Spatial Organization: The Geographer's View of the World*, 1971). He went on to conduct research into the practical effects of telecommunications' ability to collapse time–space distances. He also examined the effects on people's perceptions of terrestrial space and sense of time. Abler took on important professional leadership roles later in his career, notably in the *Association of American Geographers and the *International Geographical Union.

aboriginal The first or earliest known inhabitants of a *place or *region. Aboriginals are often called *indigenous people. Today, their descendants can be found in Australia, New Zealand, the Pacific Islands, Indonesia, Africa, the Arctic Circle, and in North and Latin America. Often cast as primitive or 'backwards', with in-migration through colonization, aboriginal societies were systematically persecuted and marginalized. Recent geographical investigations, overlapping with the research of anthropologists, have sought to understand these societies in their own terms, to document the ways in which they have (and continue to be) marginalized by settlers, and to chart their struggles for self-determination. *See also* RACE; RACISM.

absolute space *See* SPACE.

abstraction The act or process of isolating a phenomenon and removing it from its real context of existence. It has a mental and a material aspect. The former involves carving the world up into categories or units (*see* ANALYSIS) in order to focus on some aspects perceived to be interesting or important at the expense of others. *Critical realism pays scrupulous attention to abstraction in geographical research. The latter involves the physical delimitation and extraction of something from its social or biogeochemical environment. *Marxist geography has scrutinized how *capitalism entails the 'violent abstraction' of things in the interests of making money from their sale as commodities.

academic capitalism A description of universities, academics, and academic knowledge that suggests these are increasingly being driven by commercial values and goals. The term was popularized by American education analysts Slaughter and Rhoades. It challenges the long-held belief that higher education is—or should be—a public good, not a commodity for purely private purchase and benefit. In human geography it is especially associated with discussions about the pedagogic and wider role of *critical human geography.

Further reading Slaughter, S. and Rhoades, G. (2004), *Academic Capitalism and the New Economy*.

accessibility The ease with which goods and services in one location can be accessed by people living in another location. Transportation and communications media are key infrastructures in this regard, with availability, distance, time, and cost being principal constraints, along with structural barriers such as age, gender, disability, and class. Access to goods and services is often viewed as a key measure of social equity—that is, the greater access one has, the better off one is.

accumulation The process of creating, controlling, moving, and using surplus economic *capital. According to Marxist geographers, who have inquired into the way that accumulation is organized across space and through time, accumulation of a capitalist sort has come to dominate over all others. It involves the production, distribution, sale, and disposal of myriad commodities for the single aim of accumulating more wealth at the end of the process than was laid out by capitalists at the start. The most 'liquid' form in which economic capital can be accumulated is as *money (*see* FINANCE CAPITAL). In the incessant search for sources of new and greater profitability, capitalists can deploy their capital in new locations, in new ventures, and in major new infrastructural investments (perhaps overseas). The financial services industry is usually at the heart of this 'capital switching' process because it can concentrate capital surpluses from multiple investors (*see* FINANCIAL MARKETS). This industry is also in the business of capital accumulation itself, but in a way that is parasitic upon accumulation in the so-called 'real economy'. Marxist geographer David *Harvey argues that early 21st-century *capitalism has relied heavily on 'accumulation by dispossession'. This is a form of accumulation that, unlike its 'classical' counterpart, does not rely on exploiting wage workers so that they are paid less than the value of the commodities they collectively make. Instead, it relies on privatizing the gains of enclosing what were previously open access, common, or communal resources (such as the atmosphere, public forests, or Antarctica).

Further reading Harvey, D. (2003), *The New Imperialism*.

accumulation by dispossession *See* ACCUMULATION; HARVEY, DAVID.

action research An approach that seeks to apply the research tools and knowledge of academia to the practical resolution of social and environmental problems. In addition to producing knowledge about the world, action research explicitly seeks to enact change by addressing specific issues facing people and places. In contrast to *applied geography, wherein academia seeks to aid the state in drafting and evaluating policy or businesses to more effectively compete locally and globally, action research is community focused, working with local stakeholders to achieve outcomes to the benefit of that community. However, unlike *activist geography, action research is not necessarily underpinned by a radical politics, but is guided by a pragmatism to address a particular issue, whether that be helping to more effectively conserve and manage water resources or to make a built environment more accessible to all citizens. This is not to say that action research is ideologically neutral; indeed, as detailed by Ernest Stringer, it is underpinned by a set of broad social values: it seeks to be democratic, equitable, liberating, and life enhancing. It seeks to enact these values and address problems by bringing together all stakeholders, which can include community groups, *non-governmental organizations (NGOs), and state bodies, into a process of investigation. These stakeholders engage in a collectivized process of generating and interpreting data in order to attempt to come to a common understanding of the issue and an agreed plan of resolution. This solution is then enacted and its outcome evaluated. The role of the researcher in this process is one of facilitator, bringing people together, mediating debate, communicating knowledge and best practice elsewhere, and explaining appropriate theory and methodologies, and how to utilize them. In geography, action research has often been framed as *participatory action research. *See also* ADVOCACY GEOGRAPHY.

Further reading Pain, R. (2003), 'Social geography: on action oriented research'. *Progress in Human Geography* 27, 649–57.
Stringer, E. (1999), *Action Research*.

activism The actions of a group of citizens, usually volunteers, who work together to try and redress what they consider to be an unfair or unjust situation. Their activities include campaigning (such as letter writing, marching, and picketing), peaceful marching, civil disobedience, sabotage, or other militant forms of protest. Although usually local in scale, activism can occur at national and supra-national levels, as in the *anti-globalization movement. *See also* ACTIVIST GEOGRAPHY; ADVOCACY GEOGRAPHY.

activist geography The use of a geographer's academic position and expertise in order to influence events beyond the university world. Some geographers not only study *activism, but are activists themselves. While their activism may have no direct relation to their professional work, in many cases the link is organic. Such activist geographers seek to challenge the status quo not only through their research and teaching, but also by using their expertise to effect social, economic, political, cultural, or environmental change in the world. Such practices are ideologically driven and break with traditional notions of the academic as a neutral, objective, and passive scientist. *See also* ADVOCACY GEOGRAPHY; ACTION RESEARCH; OBJECTIVITY.

Further reading Blomley, N. K. (1994), 'Activism and the academy'. *Environment and Planning D: Society and Space* 12: 383–5.

Actor-Network Theory (ANT) An approach to understanding stability and change in the world that situates human *agency in wider networks of non-human actors and materials. From the late 19th century many came to believe that the world of humans was different in kind from the world of non-human entities and processes. This presumed ontological cleavage was reflected in the different subject matter and methods of the social sciences and humanities as compared to the physical, medical, engineering, mathematical, computational, and environmental sciences. In academic geography after 1945 this 'two-worlds' perspective was reflected in the growing schism between human and physical geography. However, in the early 1990s the *Science and Technology Studies scholar Bruno *Latour argued that this perspective was flawed. While humans possess unique attributes and are able to construct their own linguistic, symbolic, and physical worlds, Latour insisted they are also continually dependent on a myriad of non-human 'actants' for their daily survival and for new ventures. Such actants range from the mundane (e.g. a door) to the special (e.g. nuclear rods in a power station). While humans may marshall these actants into various networks—short and long, temporary and enduring—they cannot do without these actants. Latour and like-minded analysts eschew the dualistic language of 'nature' and 'society', 'people' and 'environment', and so on. In British human geography, Actor-Network Theory (ANT) has inspired a large body of research into human relations with non-human entities—be they technical, emotional, aesthetic, auditory, aural, or tactile. Sarah Whatmore's monograph *Hybrid Geographies* (2001) was a pioneering contribution. Physical geographers have been less enamoured and the long-standing division between human and physical geographers has not been significantly reduced because of ANT's prominence in contemporary geography. Meanwhile, Nigel Clark's book *Inhuman Nature* (2011) argues that ANT is too fixated on placid, malleable, or close-at-hand entities, forgetting that much of *nature threatens to overwhelm and overpower humanity. As such, ANT might—ironically—carry its own traces of *anthropocentrism. *See also* ASSEMBLAGE; HYBRIDITY.

Further reading Latour, B. (1993), *We Have Never Been Modern*.

advocacy geography A form of *activist geography and *participatory action research wherein a geographer becomes an advocate for a disadvantaged group or community, working on its behalf to address issues of social and spatial *justice. The approach was pioneered by William *Bunge and co-workers in the late 1960s in their

a

*Detroit Geographical Expedition and Institute where they worked with deprived communities to campaign on issues of poverty and state provision of services. *See also* ACTIVISM.

aerial photography The photographing of the Earth from above the ground and from within the atmosphere. The camera is usually attached to an aeroplane, helicopter, or balloon, rather than a ground-based structure. Photographs can either be vertical (shot from directly overhead), producing a map-like image, or taken from an oblique angle. The first aerial photographs were taken from a balloon in the mid-19th century, but grew enormously in use during the First World War for identifying enemy positions. Subsequently, aerial photographs became important for surveying vast tracts of unmapped land for cartographic purposes. They are an important source of information for a range of activities including photogrammetric surveys, environmental monitoring, and general surveillance. *See also* PHOTOGRAPHY; PHOTOGRAPHY AND GEOGRAPHY; REMOTE SENSING.

affect 1. Conventionally, the influence of one thing on another.
2. In psychology, the generation of instinctive feelings or emotions in relation to some external stimulus.
3. In philosophical discourse and in contemporary human geography, a process in which the immaterial (dreams, intuition, imagination, precognitive thoughts) prestructures responses to physical experiences and social discourses. More generally, affect refers to the wide range of registers—beyond sight, image, and word—in which humans interact with, make sense of, and experience the world. Geographer J. D. Dewsbury explains that it is useful to think of affect in four different ways, respectively: a material thing, a force, a theory, and a mode of expression. First, affect is the medium through which the body relates to the materiality of the world in a manner that is outside conscious thought and intentionality. Second, affect is a sensation, a kind of invisible presence, something felt, and known to be there, but at the same time intangible and not quite there; an emotive predisposition for, and response to, a particular set of conditions. Both as a material phenomenon and force, affect concerns *embodiment and how corporeality is choreographed in the world in largely subconscious ways. Third, as a *theory used by human geographers and other scholars, affect is a critique of several dominant strands of research in geographic research. These strands focus either on social institutions and social relations, or on various social discourses and modes of social *representation. They tend to ignore affect and focus on the conscious, cognitive aspects of human thought and practice. As a theory, affect is most clearly articulated through *non-representational approaches and its focus on human embodiment, practice, and performance, and its politics centred on how bodily capacity can affect others or be affected. Finally, as a mode of human expression, affect concerns how emotional responses are manifested through an event and how situations unfold in action. *See also* EMOTIONAL GEOGRAPHIES; PERFORMATIVITY; PHENOMENOLOGY.

Further reading Dewsbury, J. D. (2009), 'Affect', in *International Encyclopedia of Human Geography*.

Afghanistan A landlocked country located between the Middle East, South Asia, and Central Asia. Afghanistan is often considered to be a *failed state because of internecine struggles between rival political, religious, and ethnic groups since at least the 1970s. The country has long been subject to strong external political and economic influence—some would say interference. Most recently, American and British troops spent several years trying to capture members of the Taliban and al-Quaeda as part of the 'War on Terror' begun in 2001. Afghanistan remains politically unstable, despite being notionally a democracy governed by a single, elected executive. Though it has many valuable untapped natural resources, the country remains very poor and is considered among the least developed in the world.

Africa The world's second largest and second most heavily populated continent after *Asia. It is comprised of 54 internationally recognized nation states, is bisected by the equator, and surrounded by the Mediterranean Sea, Indian Ocean, and Atlantic Ocean. The continent is extraordinarily diverse ethnically, politically, economically, socially, culturally, and in religious terms. The same can be said of its physical geography. Africa is the birthplace of *homo sapiens* and was home to one of the first modern civilizations (Ancient Egypt). Slavery was widespread in Africa prior to the 15th century but European explorers escalated the slave trade, transporting an estimated seven to twelve million Africans to the New World (that is, South, Central, and North America, plus the Caribbean) by 1900. By this year the major European imperial powers of the period—including Britain, France, and Germany—had taken control of large parts of Africa. Between 1945 and the 1980s the various African colonies achieved independence, by peaceful or violent means. During this period several countries took sides in the *Cold War, with encouragement from either the United States or the former USSR. At the same time South Africa became the most internationally visible African state because its ruling parties—descendent from Dutch and British colonists—enforced a policy of racial *apartheid. This policy separated 'whites', 'blacks', and 'coloureds' in all areas of life to the advantage of the former.

Despite containing a wealth of natural resources, Africa remains the world's poorest continent. Most of its countries are considered to have achieved low levels of *development, while many are also considered to be *failed states. The reasons are many and complex and include the following: political and economic corruption, ethnic and linguistic divisions, the hoarding of wealth by elites, endemic diseases, *natural hazards, civil wars, and famines. Many Africa countries are said to suffer from the *'resource curse' (or paradox of plenty). Resources that are internationally valued (such as copper or oil) seem rarely to produce high levels of economic growth and development in Africa. In recent years, wars in the Congo, Somalia, Zimbabwe, and Liberia have commanded considerable international attention, and so too the 1994 genocide of Tutsis in Rwanda at the hands of the majority Hutu population. Likewise, serious crises of food supply—often involving the displacement of people (*see* REFUGEES)—have become global issues (notably those in the Sahel and the Horn of Africa). In spite of this, Africa contains several countries that have enjoyed political stability, economic growth, and above-average levels of economic and social development. Chief among them are South Africa and Egypt. In 2011 the popular protests against authoritarian political leaders in Egypt, Libya, and Tunisia made headline news as part of the wider so-called 'Arab Spring'.

Despite its size and diversity, outside perceptions of Africa continue to be simplistic, even stereotypical. Arguably, many of the prejudices contained in Western *geographical imaginations of Africa during the period of pre-20th-century imperialism survived today in more polite forms. For instance, in Britain the annual fundraising event Red Nose Day—organized by the charity Comic Relief—has, for all its good work, reproduced ideas that Africa is essentially an unruly (even chaotic) continent perpetually in need of a hand-up. *See also* ORIENTALISM.

Further reading Binns, T. et al. (2011), *Africa*.

African Union Established in 2002 to replace the Organization for African Unity, it unites 53 African countries, (all those in Africa bar Morocco), into a set of shared supra-national political and administrative bodies. The objectives of the African Union are to foster political and economic development, cooperation, and integration across the continent; combat poverty and war; promote and defend African common interests; promote democracy, good governance, and human rights.

(((●))) **SEE WEB LINKS**

• Official website of the African Union.

ageing In population terms, the growth in the number and/or proportion of elderly people. It is generally caused by a combination of longer *life expectancy, falling birth rates, and net migration. The study of ageing populations, also known as gerontology, has become increasingly important in human geography because of its significance at international, national, and sub-national scales. It has implications for the planning and provision of health and welfare services, as well as impacts on pensions systems. Where ageing results in an increased *dependency ratio, there will be relatively fewer people of working age to support the non-working population. The UN projects that the proportion of people over 65 in the world will increase from 5.2 per cent in 1950 to 15.6 per cent in 2050.

Further reading Andrews, G. J. and Phillips, D. R. (eds.) (2005) *Ageing and Place: Perspectives, Policy and Practice.*
United Nations Population Division (2001), *World Population and Ageing: 1950–2050.*

agency The potential and actual ability of individuals and institutions to affect the circumstances that structure their thought and action. Geographically speaking, all agents are place based: even the most mobile, cosmopolitan person has roots as well as routes. To what extent, and how, are individuals with different resources at their disposal (economic, cultural, political, or environmental) able to negotiate the more-or-less favourable circumstances into which they are born and raised? Since the 1970s, in reaction to the so-called 'structuralism' of early *Marxist geography, several human geographers have sought to answer this question. Initially they drew upon the work of environmental psychologists and humanistic philosophers (*see* BEHAVIOURAL GEOGRAPHY; HUMANISTIC GEOGRAPHY). Later they drew upon the theoretical works of British sociologist Anthony Giddens, who sought to resolve the so-called *agency-structure debate. Only the poorest and most vulnerable people have little agency, while others exercise their own considerable freedom so as to structure the life chances of millions of others. This uneven socio-spatial distribution of agency remains a major research concern in human geography. In recent years, the long-standing interest in human agency has been complemented—and complicated—by a focus on the agency of non-humans (*see*, for example, ACTOR-NETWORK THEORY).

Further reading Blij, H. de (2010), *The Power of Place.*

agency-structure debate A long-running discussion about how the thoughts and actions of countless individuals and organizations (agents) together comprise large-scale rules, norms, habits, and processes that serve to govern those self-same agents. One of the major contributions of *Marxist geography was to focus attention on how agents—living and working in different locations on the Earth's surface—were circumscribed by both local and global realities over which they appeared to have little control. In reaction to this perceived '*structuralism', advocates of *humanistic geography paid close attention to agents' personal perspectives, feelings, and actions. From the early 1980s, human geographers sought to move beyond this 'structure versus agency' impasse by citing Anthony Giddens' sociological writings on *structuration. Giddens provided a conceptual vocabulary and a set of logical arguments designed to give socio-spatial and historical researchers the ability to take structure and agency equally seriously. The structure-agency debate is not as visible today as it was twenty years ago, though arguably continues in different guises because it focuses on fundamental questions of human existence in a world where even the wealthiest agents cannot ultimately control the grand forces of geography or history. Equally, one might argue that the structure-agency debate has morphed into one more concerned about how non-human agency affects human agency. This is linked to a move away from the idea of 'structure'—which connotes rigidity and fixity—towards a more fluid notion of actors existing within 'networks'. *See also* ACTOR-NETWORK THEORY; AGENCY.

agent-based models (ABM) A class of computational *models that seek to represent and simulate behaviour in time and space at an individual rather than aggregate level. The models work from the bottom up, with wider spatial and temporal patterns emerging from the interactions of individual agents. At their heart, agent-based models enact a kind of *social physics in which ideas such as potential energy and gravitational force are applied to social behaviour, with people and goods being attracted to certain phenomena, with this attraction shaped by factors such as distance, time, and cost. They are important tools in urban, land-use, transportation, and disaster modelling where different scenarios can be observed. The model consists of an environment where individual features such as buildings and roads are assigned certain characteristics. This environment is then populated with agents that are ascribed particular qualities. When the model is run, the agents seek to solve a task, reacting to the environment and other agents in relation to their ascribed characteristics. In this way, the model can examine, for example, how people might behave in an enclosed space such as a stadium if a fire breaks out at a particular location and is therefore useful in helping to determine evacuation plans. The largest agent-based models seek to model *spatial interaction across whole cities. A particular class of agent-based models are *cellular automata that work on a two-dimensional lattice grid, where the state of any cell is related to that of its neighbours. *See also* CHOICE MODELLING; REPRESENTATION; SPATIAL INTERACTION MODELS.

age structure The shape of a population shown by the distribution of age groups. A national population may be youthful, with a high proportion of people in age groups below twenty or conversely, ageing with numbers more concentrated in older age groups. *See also* POPULATION PYRAMID.

agglomeration The process and outcome of concentrating in one location a set of interlinked and interdependent economic activities. The word 'agglomeration' functions as both a verb and a noun. Large and/or dense agglomerations are sometimes known as 'growth clusters'. Studies by economic and development geographers have practical implications because governments, among others, are keenly interested in having successful agglomerations in their territories. These not only enjoy sustained growth but are also in locations that, for whatever reason, are deemed to be strategically important. *See also* AGGLOMERATION ECONOMIES; CLUSTERS.

agglomeration economies The economic advantages that accrue to existing and new firms, and to other economic agents, from concentrating commodity production in a single location. Once agglomeration reaches a certain density, the per capita costs of certain activities or functions may decrease to the advantage of many or most spatially propinquitous economic agents. For instance, while a new road or light rail system may be far too expensive to build in the early years of a blossoming city-region, it becomes both cost effective and necessary later on. Equally, real but uncosted economies can accrue to firms from co-location, such as the ability of their senior employees to interact face-to-face and share information. *See also* AGGLOMERATION.

aggregation In order to make sense of very large data sets about individual entities it is common to aggregate *data into classes and to compare those classes through either *descriptive or *inferential statistics. By aggregating the data a more generalized account of a phenomenon can be observed, one that also addresses concerns over confidentiality. One of the possible effects of aggregation is *ecological fallacy. *See also* MODIFIABLE AREAL UNIT PROBLEM.

Agnew, John (1949–) An English-American political geographer who has shown the key importance of both local and global scales to the conduct of modern politics. Agnew is a professor at the University of California, Los Angeles. His early research focused on the importance of place and region—as much as nation—in the actions of voters, political parties, and political leaders. He has also been an important analyst of the global political scene and the links between America's economic and political power on the world stage. Most recently, he has challenged conventional notions of state sovereignty and sought to rethink the nature and importance of political *borders and boundaries. *See also* POLITICAL GEOGRAPHY.

agoraphobia A fear of places or situations in which a person perceives him- or herself to have little control over events or to be vulnerable Such places might include wide-open, confined, or crowded ones, or places where events are unpredictable, or open to change. Agoraphobia sufferers experience panic attacks when confronted with such locations and, as such, try to avoid public and unfamiliar places.

Agrarian Question, The An ongoing debate about the relationship between peasant agriculture and capitalist economic development. Although the issue was raised by Marx and Engels, the Agrarian Question can best be traced back to Karl Kautsky in a book of that name published in 1899 in Germany. Written in the context of a Europe-wide rural and agrarian crisis and falling farm incomes, Kautsky was concerned with three main problems: what was the impact of capitalism on small-scale or family farming?; how important was agriculture to capitalist development in general?; and what was the role of the peasantry in the political struggle for socialism and democracy? Contrary to Lenin's argument, Kautsky argued that small farmers might persist rather than be swallowed up by capital-intensive farm enterprises. In part this was because they could draw upon family labour, but he also theorized the peculiar dependence of farming on natural cycles and conditions, which made it less attractive for capitalist investment. For Marxists such as Lenin, the key question was whether peasants would support revolutionary politics led by urban working classes, or whether they would prove to be conservative and so reactionary. Lenin was sceptical about the peasantry, but his views were challenged by A. V. Chayanov in the 1930s, who conceived of peasant farmers as an independent form of socialism (*see* PEASANTRY). The Agrarian Question continued to surface into the late 20th century, notably in the context of the US farm crisis in the 1970s. Sociologists Mann and Dickinson suggested that small family farms had a future because the slow turnover of farming did not suit capitalist investment, though others disagreed (Henderson 1998). Given that the conditions of late 19th-century European agriculture, including capitalist penetration, technological change, and rural transformation, are being experienced around the developing world, the debates between Kautsky and others continue to interest human geographers.

Futher reading Henderson, G. (1998), 'Nature and fictitious capital: the historical geography of the agrarian question', *Antipode* 30: 73–118.

agribusiness Firms involved in the systematic integration of food production processes, from inputs (seeds, fertilizer, etc.), growing crops, and raising livestock, processing (e.g. canning), distribution to insurance, and finance. This kind of vertically integrated system was pioneered in the 1950s in such sectors as the US poultry (broiler) and grain industries. *See also* AGRO-FOOD SYSTEM.

agricultural geography The branch of geography concerned with the study of spatial variations in agricultural activity. Given that farming in the developed world occupies an increasingly smaller percentage of the workforce, and that food production is largely integrated into economic, cultural, and regulatory networks beyond farms themselves, the study of agriculture has become closely linked with the human geography of food systems more generally. As a result, a distinct agricultural geography is less prominent than in the period between the 1940s and 1980s: for instance in the *Association of American Geographers, agriculture falls within the remit of the Rural Geography Specialty Group.

Even in 1900 the populations of the USA and France and elsewhere remained predominantly rural, and the study of farming and land use was central to geography. A distinct agricultural geography took shape in the USA from the 1920s, focused in particular on the identification and classification of agricultural regions. Derwent Whittlesey's paper on major agricultural regions of the Earth exemplified this interest. After the Second World War, the focus shifted away from the relations between physical geography and agriculture, to a more statistical analysis of the variation in farm activity, structure, and income. John Weaver's studies of the US Mid-West cast doubt on the homogeneity of agricultural regions. A turn to *spatial science came with the adoption of von Thünen's agricultural land-use model (originally set out in 1826), which sought to explain crop patterns and intensity by distance from markets (*see* VON THÜNEN MODEL). Behavioural studies of farm decision-making qualified these spatial models of agricultural activity. From the 1990s approaches drawing on *political economy, *political ecology, and *Actor-Network Theory (Goodman and Watts 1997) served to bring the study of agriculture in line with industrial and economic geography (*see* AGRO-FOOD SYSTEMS). But, insofar as agriculture involves an irreducible natural element, it is likely to be theorized and understood in terms distinct from manufacturing and services.

Further reading Goodman, D. and Watts, M. J. (eds.) (1997), *Globalising Food: Agrarian Questions and Global Restructuring*.
Robinson, G. (2004), *Geographies of Agriculture*.
Singh, J. and Dhillon, S. S. (3rd ed. 2004), *Agricultural Geography*.
Whittlesey, D. (1936), 'Major agricultural regions of the Earth', *Annals of the Association of American Geographers* 26: 199–240.

Agricultural Revolution A set of transformations in British farming variously dated from the 16th, 17th, or 18th centuries to the 19th century, which resulted in significantly higher levels of agricultural productivity. In the absence of comprehensive statistical data, historians and historical geographers are not agreed on when these processes began, or whether they were gradual or more sudden. There are also questions about its geography, where changes began, and how they diffused. There is some agreement that there were important changes in farming from the 1700s that enabled more food to be grown on less land with fewer farmworkers. These included selective breeding of livestock and the use of turnips, clover, and other fodder crops in rotation, thereby fixing nitrogen in the soil and maintaining its fertility. The pastures freed by mixing fodder and food crops could be converted to arable farming, as could areas cleared of woodland or drained through land reclamation. Towards the end of the period, new machinery for harvesting and threshing grain was introduced, further increasing productivity.

Alongside such technological changes were important social and economic developments, which were both a precondition for the revolution and a consequence of it. Common lands were enclosed, removing communal rights to animal grazing, wood collecting, and other activities in the privatization of land ('enclosure'). Much farming was carried out by tenants leasing land from large estates, making use of landless and relatively mobile wage farmworkers. There was an associate shift towards more commercial agriculture, meeting the needs of urban markets.

Whether there was a single revolution or a series of more local transformations accumulating over time, the outcome was a tripling of grain productivity between 1750 and 1850, sustaining high levels of population growth (*see* DEMOGRAPHIC TRANSITION;

HISTORICAL DEMOGRAPHY). The reduction in the number of agricultural workers encouraged higher levels of manufacturing employment. In these two ways, the Agricultural Revolution may have laid the foundations for the *Industrial Revolution. *See also* GREEN REVOLUTION.

Further reading Overton, M. (1996), *Agricultural Revolution in England: the Transformation of the Agrarian Economy 1500–1800.*

agriculture The farming of crops and livestock to meet human needs. Agriculture involves the manipulation of natural food chains to a greater degree than *hunter-gathering but also includes the production of new organisms through *genetic modification. The result of combining human and natural elements is an agro-ecosystem. The two basic forms of agriculture involve the cultivation of crops on land (arable farming) and the management of animals through herding, breeding, and domestication (including ranching). Fishing and forestry are generally not regarded as part of agriculture, although in practice many agricultural concerns combine them with farming.

Agriculture is arguably the most ubiquitous form of human economic activity, and it occupies up to a third of the world's land surface and engages just under 40 per cent of the world's population, slightly less than services. In more developed countries, agricultural employment is only 2–3 per cent, but in the developing world it can reach 30–40 per cent of the population (China, Morocco, and Thailand, for example). The geography of agricultural activity is governed by a range of physical (e.g. climate, soils, relief) and human factors (e.g. population density, market demand, cultural preference) (*see* AGRICULTURAL GEOGRAPHY). Where soil fertility and market demand are appropriate, agriculture can take *intensive and highly industrial forms (*see* AGRIBUSINESS; AGRICULTURE, INDUSTRIALIZED). Elsewhere, where population density is lower or natural conditions less conducive, more *extensive forms of farming such as ranching may prevail. At one extreme, farming activity is vertically integrated into capital-intensive *agro-food systems, involving large inputs of capital, labour, chemicals, and machinery. An example is the US broiler chicken industry. At the other extreme, *subsistence farmers may produce sufficient for their family but little more. The majority of people involved in agriculture can be classed as peasants, small-scale family producers who may be wholly or partly involved in markets (*see* PEASANTRY). In recent years the interest in alternative, less capital-intensive, and exploitative agriculture has risen (*see* AGRICULTURE, ORGANIC; AGRICULTURE, SUSTAINABLE). Although farming is typically associated with rural areas, urban agriculture is common in Africa, Asia, and other regions of the developing world.

Further reading Robinson, G. (2004), *Geographies of Agriculture.*

agriculture, industrialized The application of industrial techniques, technologies, and labour relations to farming. The farm is regarded as a factory, with inputs of capital, machinery, chemicals, and labour, producing outputs; the aim is to maximize yields, productivity, and profits, so providing relatively cheap food and farm products. Industrial agriculture may involve: monoculture (i.e. concentration on one crop or animal); the standardization of crop and animal varieties; and dependence on chemicals at the expense of the environment and workers' well-being. Farm production may also be integrated with distribution and consumption, organized through transnational corporations. Although industrial agriculture is usually capitalist, it has taken more socialist forms, for example, in the former *Soviet Union. *See also* AGRIBUSINESS; AGRO-FOOD SYSTEM.

agriculture, organic Farming based on holistic principles that seeks to minimize the harm done to agricultural ecosystems by restricting the use of artificial inputs. In practice this means avoiding synthetic fertilizers, pesticides, and other manufactured chemicals, and using instead forms of crop rotation, natural manure, and compost to safeguard crops. In livestock farming it includes restricting the use of antibiotics and drugs, and keeping animals in healthy conditions. Although all farming is, to some degree, organic in that it involves the manipulation of nature, there are codes of regulation and systems of accreditation that classify some practices and products as 'organic'.

agriculture, sustainable Farming that seeks to balance social, economic, and environmental factors thereby producing safe, healthy, and affordable farm products without causing long-term damage to ecosystems, while also providing decent conditions for agricultural workers. Sustainable farming is not a single, well-defined set of practices or codes, but an orientation to agriculture that seeks to reverse many of the supposed harms of industrialized agriculture. It includes *organic farming and farming geared to serving local markets in order to minimize *food miles, but does not rule out the appropriate use of technology and synthetic products. *See also* AGRI-ENVIRONMENT SCHEMES; AGROBIODIVERSITY.

agri-environment schemes Government programmes to encourage more sustainable agriculture. Such policies have become more widespread in the European Union in the past two decades and are associated with *post-productivist agriculture.

agrobiodiversity That part of biodiversity related to the intervention of farmers in processes of natural selection over long periods of time. Included in the crops, livestock, insects, and soil organisms implicated in agriculture, there are many breeds and varieties generated by human agency. An important element of agrobiodiversity is therefore local or *indigenous knowledge.

agroecology The scientific study of agriculture as ecosystems, or agro-ecosystems, with a view to designing and managing them along more ecologically sustainable lines. Agro-ecosystems include human activity, and are generally simplified, more open to inputs from elsewhere (energy, nutrients, chemicals), and with less biodiversity than more natural ecosystems.

agro-food system The totality of actors involved in the production, distribution, and consumption of food, the relations between them, and the regulatory apparatus governing these arrangements. Also referred to as agri-food systems, the concept emerged from political economy approaches to agricultural geography in the 1980s. It responded to at least two developments. Firstly, food production and consumption were becoming increasingly globalized and managed through *transnational corporations. Secondly, farmers and farming organizations themselves were progressively losing control over food production. A narrow focus on *agricultural geography (farms, fields, livestock, and crops) therefore neglected the role of wholesalers, retailers, marketing, food-processing industries, agricultural science and technology, and other agents. At the same time, new regulatory bodies at local, state, regional, and international scales complicated the governance of food chains, for example, in the form of new standards and accreditation agencies. Analysing farming as part of an agro-food system identifies the pattern of forwards and backwards linkages, and the connections between actors, revealing the power relations involved. Some authors prefer the term agro-food network, inspired by *Actor-Network Theory.

Further reading Robinson, G. (2004), *Geographies of Agriculture.*

aid Assistance given to countries in the form of financial, material, or other transfers. Aid may take monetary forms, such as loans and grants, or non-monetary forms such as debt relief, scholarships, and training programmes. It may be bilateral, i.e.

country-to-country, or multilateral, i.e. disbursed by international organizations such as the World Bank or United Nations from funds provided by member states. A third category is philanthropic aid provided by individuals and foundations. The Bill and Melissa Gates Foundation, for example, provided $26 billion of funds between 1994 and 2010. Finally, a distinction can be made between development aid, intended for longer-term structural improvements to economy, society, or environment, and humanitarian or emergency aid, related to disaster relief or conflict situations.

In practice, the distinction between monetary and non-monetary aid is blurred, and the exact definition of aid is complicated. The Organisation for Economic Co-operation and Development (*OECD)'s *Development Assistance Committee (DAC) consists of 24 countries and three international organizations that account for over 90 per cent of the world's development aid. DAC donors agree on common accounting and transparency rules to define aid or Official Development Assistance (ODA). Critics note that ODA can include such things as debt-relief where there may be no actual transfer of money involved. Hence the OECD is advocating a new measure of what it calls 'core aid' termed Country Programmable Aid (CPA) which tries to identify aid over which a recipient country has some measure of control. CPA is typically half the level of ODA. In recent decades a number of significant non-DAC donors have emerged including China, India, Brazil, and the Gulf states. Because they do not abide by the same accounting rules and classifications, their contributions are often not included in estimates of world aid levels and patterns (Mawdsley, 2012).

Aid transfers are sometimes subject to conditions set by donors or multilateral organizations. Input conditionalities describe procurement rules or accounting and reporting procedures that must be met before aid is provided. 'Tied aid' is restricted in its usage, for example, requiring that a country use the aid to purchase goods or services from the donor country. Output conditionalities require a change in regulations, policy, or behaviour from the recipient country, and formed part of *Structural Adjustment Programmes. They have been criticized for undermining state sovereignty.

The USA is the world's largest source of aid, followed by Germany and France. In proportional terms, the most generous countries are from northwestern Europe, including Sweden, Norway, and Luxembourg. In 2010 the largest recipients were Iraq and Afghanistan. Critics argue that aid sustains relations of dependency between the Global North and South, and that it is more often linked with geopolitical or ideological aims than need. Increasing amounts of aid are transferred via *NGOs, outside the control of states. Although there is good evidence of its positive impact in such fields as health, the effects on poverty reduction are more ambiguous. *See also* DEVELOPMENT; MILLENNIUM DEVELOPMENT GOALS; POVERTY REDUCTION STRATEGIES.

Further reading McCormick, D. (2008), 'China and India as Africa's new donors: the impact of aid on development', *Review of African Political Economy* 115: 73–92.

Mawdsley, E. (2012), 'The changing geographies of foreign aid and development cooperation: contributions from gift theory', *Transactions of the Institute of British Geographers* 37: 256–72.

Aid for Trade An initiative of the *World Trade Organization launched in 2005 in order to build up the capacity of developing countries to trade internationally. Around half the funding ($40 billion in 2009) is directed at infrastructure such as road and ports, but it also supports training in how to understand and negotiate complex trading regulations. *See also* AID.

AIDS (Acquired Immune Deficiency Syndrome) A collection of medical conditions arising from a compromised immune system due to the Human Immunodeficiency Virus (HIV). Initially isolated in 1983, there are two types of HIV virus; HIV-1, which is found around the world and HIV-2, which is concentrated in West Africa. Of the estimated 39 million people living with HIV/AIDS 95 per cent are found in developing countries where HIV-infected individuals are more likely to develop associated AIDS conditions due to general poverty and poorer health, and where access to treatments and preventive measures are limited, subject to resource, and educational constraints. Due to these structural factors, AIDS tends to spread through already vulnerable communities. In the developed world, AIDS is much more constrained in its spread through sexual and drug education and preventive programmes such as condom distribution and needle exchanges. Usually stereotyped as a gay male, prostitution, or intravenous drug user disease, HIV/AIDS cases are, in fact, distributed across Western societies, with higher-than-average concentrations in prison inmates and immigrant communities. Geographers have contributed to the study of HIV/AIDS in two main ways:. first, through epidemiological analyses that have sought to map the spatial diffusion of the HIV virus; and second, by studying the *lifeworlds of individuals affected by HIV/AIDS and the communities they live in, and examining the response, organization, and effectiveness of associated health care and related institutions. *See also* HEALTH AND DEVELOPMENT; HEALTH INEQUALITY.

Further reading Gould, P. (1993), *The Slow Plague: Geography of the AIDS Pandemic.*

(⊕) SEE WEB LINKS
• UNAIDS, Joint United Nations Programme on HIV/AIDS.

airports The nodes and hubs in the *network of air travel. They act as key infrastructure in terms of landing, boarding, deplaning, refuelling, immigration, and connecting passengers into ground transportation networks (*see* HUB-AND-SPOKE NETWORK). Given their status as key entry points into a country and their targeting by terrorist organizations, international airports are subject to intense security and surveillance and are highly ordered spaces. *See also* AIR TRAVEL.

Further reading Adey, P. (2010), *Aerial Life.*

air travel The movement between two places by air transportation. Since the Wright Brothers first took to the air in 1903 there has been a massive growth in air travel for commercial, military, and leisure purposes. It is presently estimated that approximately 1.5 million people are in the air at any one time and that air travel is a multi-billion dollar industry governed by a raft of safety and security measures. Air travel has led to enormous *time-space compression and had significant impacts on migration, the organization of businesses, logistical supply chains, and tourism. *See also* AIRPORTS; AUTOMOBILITY.

Alliance of Small Island States (AOSIS) A supra-national coalition of small island and low-lying coastal countries that share developmental challenges and the threat of rising sea levels. Established in 1990 it has 38 member states and four observer states from around the world. AOSIS has been particularly vocal in debates concerning global warming and climate change.

Alonso model A model of urban land use formulated by William Alonso in 1964. Applying and extending the insights of *Von Thünen's model of agricultural land use, Alonso applied *bid-rent curves to account for the patterned relationships between land use, rent, intensity of land use, and distance from the centre of the city. Although the price of land theoretically declines with distance from the centre, the costs of commuting rise. Alonso reasoned that wealthy households would live at lower densities at the edge of the city and poorer households would live at higher densities near the centre.

a

alternative economic geographies Some forms of economic activity pursued as alternatives to those that currently dominate peoples' lives, notably *capitalism. Economic activity in the 21st century is materials intensive, involving massive biophysical transformations at both the 'input' and 'output' ends of the production–consumption chain; it is global, involving long-distance trade, transnational rules and regulations, and hyper-mobile finance and investment; and it is consumerist, with customers incited to ceaselessly purchase ever more commodities ever more quickly. Alternative economic geographies comprise the sites at which different, new forms of economic activity occur, usually with the goals of greater environmental sustainability and social justice in mind.

These geographies aim to be less materials intensive, less global in scale, and less consumerist than their mainstream counterpart. They emphasize the *embeddedness of all economic activity in important non-economic matters, such as peoples' physical and mental well-being, and the quality of the physical environments in which they work, rest, and play. Alternative economic geographies have increased in number and diversity since the 1990s, often as part of the *anti-globalization movement. They comprise everything from 'alternative currency' experiments (where a community may use its own unit and measure of money) to 'slow food' and 'local food' cooperatives. Some alternative economic geographies are less determinedly 'alternative' than others. For instance, though they seek to inject more robust environmental and social values into consumer behaviour, *fair trade advocates have tended to work within the confines a capitalist economic system that many regard as socially unjust and ecologically destructive. *See also* ANTI-CAPITALISM; CIVIL SOCIETY; CONSUMER SOCIETY.

Further reading Fuller, D., Jonas, A., and Lee, R. (eds.) (2011), *Interrogating Alterity: Alternative Economic and Political Spaces.*

alternative food networks Associations of food producers, distributors, and retailers self-consciously positioned outside mainstream and commercial food systems. They involve organic farm products, locally sourced food, *Fair Trade, and other specialized or niche market goods, where ethical consumption is encouraged. Networks may operate through cooperatives, farmers' markets, and other sites outside the mainstream, although commercial retailers are increasingly selling their products. *See also* AGRO-FOOD SYSTEM; ETHICAL TRADING INITIATIVE.

Amazon A river, river basin, and tropical forest ecosystem found in South America and covering parts of Bolivia, *Brazil, Colombia, Ecuador, Guyana, Peru, and Venezuela. The region is exceedingly large (over five and a half million square kilometres), very biodiverse, and its vegetation is an important carbon sink. For these three reasons the Amazon has become a key focus for global attempts to halt environmental degradation and future climate change. Brazil, in particular, has been prevailed upon to halt further legal and illegal logging in the Amazon. Even so, remotely sensed data and information gathered in ground surveys suggests that the area of rainforest may have continued to shrink, most recently because of a major drought in 2010. However, the rate of shrinkage has been reduced, and legislation to protect forests has been passed and enforced in Brazil. Indeed, there may be some overall stabilization of the remaining forest area, although the *conservation of Amazon rainforest depends on effective *environmental policy among the seven relevant nation states, not just Brazil. Though often thought be a realm of pure *nature that is being destroyed by a careless, consumer-driven society, long-term *fieldwork suggests that the Amazon has, in fact, been a humanly modified landscape for a very long time. In this light, the challenge of managing the Amazon's natural resources is not so much to keep people out as to alter their relationships with those resources. *See also* DEFORESTATION; FORTRESS CONSERVATION.

Further reading Raffles, H. (2002), *In Amazonia: a Natural History.*

America *See* UNITED STATES OF AMERICA.

American Geographical Society (AGS) An organization established in 1851, it is the oldest professional *geographical society in the United States. Its mission is to link the work of geographers with the interests of state and business, to create and apply geographic knowledge and techniques to address economic, social, and environmental problems, and to present and interpret geographical knowledge so that it can be understood more broadly, especially by policy makers. It was a pioneer organization in championing exploration and cartography and has an extensive geographical research library. It publishes the journal *Geographical Review*.

Amin, Ash (1955-) A British-Ugandan economic and political geographer based at Cambridge University who is known internationally for his research into *regional inequality, regional identity, and economic *agglomeration. His early work focused on industrial decline and growth in Western Europe during the recessions of the 1970s and 1980s, leading into the so-called era of *globalization. His later work, based on the goals of greater social solidarity and respect among otherwise different social groups, has addressed the potentials of the *social economy on more inclusive forms of urban life, and on the idea of a *cosmopolitan (rather than homogenous) Europe.

analysis The process of making sense of an issue, place, situation, or other phenomena by identifying its key components. All people are routinely analytical but researchers and teachers try to take especial care in justifying their analytical decisions. When confronted with something concrete that needs to be understood—such as a global *commodity chain—geographers seek to achieve synthesis by first analysing what may be a multifaceted phenomenon. Analysis is the search for what some call 'rational abstractions': these aim to 'cut reality at the joints' rather than impose categories that make distinctions between what are, in fact, indissociable or functionally coherent phenomena. *See also* ABSTRACTION.

anarchist geography A branch of geographical work informed by the political philosophy of anarchism, which is opposed to the state and any form of authority, hierarchy, and domination. Anarchists advocate self-government or collective forms of organization, the decentralization of economy and settlement, and federal forms of cooperation. These respond to and realize the human capacities for mutual assistance and responsibility. The philosophy is opposed to violence, which is a form of domination. Hence, it is inaccurate to see 'anarchism' as a synonym for violent lawlessness or chaos. Anarchism, which emerged in 19th-century Europe, takes both social and individualist forms, and has often been spliced with communism, feminism, and pacifism.

Anarchist geography stems from the work of two men, Russian Peter *Kropotkin (1842–1921) and Frenchman Élisée *Reclus (1830–1905). Based on his geographical expeditions to Siberia, Kropotkin drew the opposite lesson from nature to *Social Darwinism—cooperation, not competition, characterized ecological relations in his view. His book *Fields, Factories and Workshops Tomorrow* (1899) set out a radical antimodern vision for a decentralized economic and social life. Kropotkin's ideas may have influenced many of the key figures of the town-planning movement, including Patrick Geddes and Ebenezer Howard. Reclus's main contribution, the six-volume *l'Homme et la Terre* (1905–8), spelled out a more sustainable or non-exploitative relationship between society and the environment. Like Kropotkin, his views were echoed by later Greens and environmentalists. Both men also stressed the significance of a geographical education to oppose imperialism, racism, and exploitation.

There was a brief revival of interest in Kropotkin and Reclus during the early years of *radical geography in the 1960s and 1970s, but no sustained elaboration of anarchist geography to compare with Marxist or feminist geography. The influence of anarchism on human geography is probably more indirect, woven into current concerns for grass-roots activism and alternative politics. In this sense the spirit of anarchism animates currents within *critical human geography today even if the word is rarely used in debates and academic activism.

Further reading Blunt, A. and Wills, J. (2000), *Dissident Geographies*.

Anderson, Benedict (1936-) Author of the influential book *Imagined Communities: Reflections on the Origin and Spread of Nationalism* (1983). Anderson, a Professor Emeritus of International Studies at Cornell University, sought to understand how and why modern, democratic nation states sprang up during the 17th and 18th centuries. Political and cultural geographers have been influenced by Anderson's argument that national communities are imaginative constructs authored not by 'the people', but by a selection of institutions and actors, some of whom wield power over the populations they purport to represent. *See also* GEOGRAPHICAL IMAGINATIONS; NATION; NATIONALISM.

Anglo-American geography A descriptive label for geographical scholarship that is produced in the United Kingdom and the United States and which, it is argued, shares a common intellectual heritage and overlaps in terms of theoretical underpinnings, conceptual development, methodology, and topical foci. This argument is most clearly set out by Ron Johnston and James Sidaway in their book *Geography and Geographers: Anglo-American Geography since 1945*. The label is often extended to include geographical scholarship in other English-speaking countries such as Australia, Canada, Ireland, and New Zealand, and thus is used synonymously with 'English language' geography. As Lawrence Berg and Robin Kearns have noted, this conflation fails to recognize the hegemonic position of the UK and US as gatekeepers to key peer-review journals that are marketed as being international, but whose editorial boards are dominated by UK and US academics. The result is geographical research concerning these two countries is seen as being universal and especially valuable, whereas research focused on other countries is seen as being somewhat parochial and of less merit and worth. This effect is even more pronounced for scholars from non-English-speaking countries. Whilst the professional activities of UK and US geographers are similar in many respects, and there is much cross-fertilization of ideas, they do also have some differences. For example, geography is much more firmly established at both school and university level in the UK and the curricula are more likely to contain elements of both human and physical geography.

Further reading Berg, L. D. and Kearns, R. A. (1998), 'America Unlimited'. *Environment and Planning D: Society and Space* 16(2): 128–32.

Johnston, R. J. and Sidaway, J. (6th ed. 2004), *Geography and Geographers: Anglo-American Geography since 1945*.

animal geographies The geographical study of non-human animals in ways that seek to counter *anthropocentrism for both political and ethical reasons. One aim of scholars in this field is to include animals in their analyses without reducing them to objects or placing them in the background of human lives. This is one way to challenge the nature-culture *dualism pervading Western thought (*see* NATURE). How to accomplish this incorporation of animals without lapsing back into anthropocentric thinking is one of the major challenges of animal geographies, one which has been met by a high degree of theoretical and methodological inventiveness.

In the 19th century the systematic study of animal distributions was known as zoogeography. Similar in methods and goals to what was later termed 'biogeography', it mapped regional variations in species, so contributing to evolutionary biology and the work of Charles *Darwin and Alfred Russell Wallace. The study of plant and animal domestication was a theme of 20th-century cultural geography and *cultural ecology, notably in the work of Carl *Sauer on agricultural origins and dispersals. But an explicit systematic focus on animal geography never developed, possibly lost between the two stools of human and physical geography. In 1995, a key paper by Wolch and Emel introducing a journal special issue declared the intention of 'bringing the animals back in'. Two subsequent edited collections, *Animal Geographies* and *Animal Spaces, Beastly Places*, mapped out the field of 'new animal geographies'. Whereas studies of domestication treated animals as objects of human labour, establishing the cultural distance between humans and other species, these new inquiries sought to overcome or displace such distinctions.

As new animal geographies have grown they have formed around three main approaches (Wilbert, 2009). Political-economic approaches share much in common with agricultural geography for a concern with *agro-food systems involving livestock such as cattle and chickens. They chart the fate of animals drawn into ever more global networks of production and consumption. More social and cultural geographic approaches address the role animals play in relations of human difference such as 'race', class, and gender. Different categories of persons have been variously marginalized or empowered through their close associations with particular animals. Relations with animal species are often time- and place-specific, involved with patterns of inclusion and exclusion. Pets or companion species may be drawn into human family lives, while other species are feared and excluded, such as suburban cougars. The significance of pets as objects of human affection and love, generating a multi-billion dollar industry of support and provision, led Heidi Nast to call for 'critical pet studies'. Humans and animals meet in specific places, from abattoirs to laboratories and zoos, mutually constructing their meanings. Certain landscapes acquire many of their cultural associations from the presence of key and charismatic species.

The third strand of new animal geographies is the most theoretically inventive. Influenced by various *non-representational theories, scholars are trying to engage with animals in ways that accord them more agency, either as a species or as individuals (*see* ACTOR-NETWORK THEORY; POST-HUMANISM). Often infused with strong ethical concerns for animal rights, this work examines how animals share and co-constitute the practices of human-animal relationships. A major interest is in nonhuman difference, i.e. recognizing that not all members of a taxonomic group or species are alike. An elephant raised in a zoo need not be considered the same as a wild or domesticated elephant, for example. There are also a number of studies of individual named creatures. Although much of new animal geographies concerns mammals, there are attempts to understand non-mammalian species such as fish and birds. Insects and micro-organisms do not feature strongly.

Animal geographies proceed from a strong belief that humans and animals are increasingly inter-dependent, in material, symbolic, emotional, and affective ways. But scholars working in this field have also observed that animals are all too often overlooked or taken for granted. They sense greater opportunities for collaboration with natural scientists, as well as the extension of inquiry beyond a few selected species.

References Nast, H. J. (2006), 'Critical pet studies', *Antipode* 38: 894–906.

Philo, C. and Wilbert, C. (eds.) (2000), *Animal Spaces, Beastly Places: New Geographies of Human-Animal Relations*.

Wilbert, C. (2009), 'Animal geographies', in Kitchin, R., Thrift, N. et al. (eds.) *The International Encyclopedia of Human Geography*.

Wolch, J. and Emel, J. (1995), 'Bringing animals back in', *Environment and Planning D: Society and Space* 13: 632–36.

Wolch, J. and Emel, J. (eds.) (1998), *Animal Geographies: Place, Politics and Identity in the Nature-Culture Borderlands*.

Annales School A group of French historians named after a journal, *Annales d'Histoire économique et Sociale* (now *Annales. Histoires, Sciences Sociales*), founded in 1929 by Marc Bloch and Lucien Febvre. The historiography they promoted focused on the social over the political, and rejected Marxist *historical materialism because of its supposed fixation on economic processes. They were influenced by French geographer Paul *Vidal de la Blache among others, and Annaliste histories paid close attention to geographical processes and to regional distinctiveness. This is most evident in the work of the school's most notable historian, Fernand Braudel (1902–85), on Mediterranean history, and two volumes entitled *The Identity of France* (1988–90).

Antarctica An ice-bound continent covering the South Pole. Because it is mostly dry Antarctica is, in effect, a desert. The underlying land is overlaid by an ice sheet with an average thickness of 1.6 km. The possible future melting of this ice sheet because of global climate change has made Antarctica an iconic region in discussions of the negative impact of humanity upon the natural environment. Relatedly, the continent became known as an environmental 'hot spot' in the 1980s because of satellite images of ozone-layer thinning in the upper atmosphere. The continent has no permanent residents and is not a sovereign *territory. Instead, the Antarctic Treaty System (initiated in 1959) allows different countries access to the continent, for research and other purposes. It is believed that large reserves of valuable *natural resources lie beneath the Antarctic ice sheet.

Anthropocene A unit of geological time referring to the period in which human activities have had a tangible impact on the Earth's ecosystems. The term was proposed by Nobel Prize winner Paul Crutzen who argued that anthropogenic environmental change was comparable to natural changes that normally occur over several millennia. The Anthropocene marks a break with the Holocene period that followed the last ice age. There is some dispute as to when the Anthropocene period starts. For some it begins with the rise of agriculture 2000 years ago. For others it is the beginning of the *Industrial Revolution in the early 19th century, when *industrialization led to wide-scale, distributed effects on ecosystems beyond localized sites.

anthropocentrism 1. The habit of viewing the world exclusively in terms of human needs, wants, and aspirations.
   2. The belief that this habit is not only inevitable but also desirable. Anthropocentrism is opposed to ecocentrism, which aims to place the needs, wants, and rights of non-humans on a par with, or even at the forefront of, human thinking and action. It is a version of *anthropomorphism. *See also* OTHER, THE

anthropogenic Something caused by intended or unintended human agency, as opposed to other causes such as natural forces. Global *climate change is the most widely recognized anthropogenic phenomenon.

Anthropogeography A definition of the aims and focus of human geography based on the works of German geographer Friedrich *Ratzel. In the two volumes of *Anthropogeographie* (1882–91) he defined the subject as a systematic study of human interaction with the environment distinct from the methods and ideas of the natural sciences. Volume 1 addressed the effect of physical features on history and Volume II stressed the independent role of human societies and culture.

anthropomorphism The attribution of supposedly human qualities to non-humans, such as animals, objects, and gods. Anthropomorphism can be either metaphorical or

literal, though they are connected. In human geography, one example is the 'anthropo-
morphic map', when a body of a person (real or fictional) is superimposed on a land map
in order to dramatize, entertain, or inform. *See also* ANIMAL GEOGRAPHIES.

anti-capitalism A series of political ideas, their associated activities, and organizations opposed to *capitalism. In a general sense this includes *anarchism, *communism,
*ecofeminism, *socialism, and other *ideologies. In recent years it has been used more
narrowly to describe the *anti-globalization movement. Anti-capitalist thinkers and
activists wish to see serious changes to capitalism in the interests of greater social
and environmental justice. Some argue that a revolution is required that would spell
the end of capitalism, once and for all.

anti-development Opposition to mainstream development thinking and policy,
particularly its tendency to incorporate local or small-scale economies into more globalized ones. This position draws on the ideas of Mohandas Gandhi, E. F. Schumacher,
and more recently, Walden Bello. *See also* DEVELOPMENT; POST-DEVELOPMENT.

anti-globalization movement A worldwide *network of *new social movements,
*non-governmental organizations, and *civil society groups who oppose policies that
permit unrestricted trade and investment. Unlike traditional political movements, it
does not have an appointed leader, a headquarters, a fee-paying membership, and so
on. As with the *anti-capitalism movement with which it is almost synonymous, it is
known as 'a movement of movements' because it is a dynamic, never-complete web of
organizations that choose to affiliate. The anti-globalization movement first found its
voice in the 1999 meeting of the *World Trade Organization (WTO) in Seattle. However,
the 1994 struggles by the *Zapatistas in southern Mexico has set a precedent for stren-
uously opposing neo-liberal trade and investment policies. The 'Battle in Seattle', as
it became known, was one of several high-profile attempts by anti-globalization protestors to tell the WTO and the leaders of *First World countries that *globalization has
serious, negative consequences. As detailed by the movement's intellectuals—notably
Naomi Klein, Vandana Shiva, and Noam Chomsky—these include the displacement
of peasants and indigenous farmers, the crowding out of local entrepreneurs by *transnational corporations, and the '*race to the bottom' in labour and environmental
standards. Anti-globalization protestors aim to protect the well-being of individuals,
families, and communities that lack the means to make neo-liberal globalization work
in their favour. The protestors also aim to reverse the processes of Westernization
and *cultural imperialism in the name of locally and regionally distinctive ways of
life. *See also* ALTERNATIVE ECONOMIC GEOGRAPHIES; *CITTASLOW*; GLOBAL JUSTICE MOVE-
MENT; NON-GOVERNMENTAL ORGANIZATION.

anti-humanism A critique of the idea that all humans possess a single, common set of
attributes irreducible to their shared biology as set out in *humanism. Anti-humanists
reject the idea that all humans possess a universal 'essence' beyond their genetic
commonalities. They argue that all human values, beliefs, habits, goals, and practices
are contingent upon the changing contexts into which people are born, raised, and
socialized. Since these contexts are plural, so too is our 'humanity'. In human geography,
anti-humanists criticize the beliefs of humanistic geographers and reject universal moral
arguments predicated on the idea of 'human nature'. Anti-humanists are usually anti-
naturalist (they oppose the idea that arguments about all humans can be derived from
facts about their biology) and inspired by *social constructivism. *See also* HUMANISTIC
GEOGRAPHY; IDENTITY.

antipodes Places on the Earth's surface that are, geographically speaking, positioned opposite to others when a straight line is driven (metaphorically) through the Earth's core. In Anglophone societies, the antipodes typically refers to Australia and New Zealand as seen from the British Isles.

anti-politics These are practices and agents that seek to limit or close down the scope of politics, in the sense of disagreement among individuals. Andrew Barry makes a distinction between conventional 'politics', the institutions and practices of government at a variety of scales, and 'political', meaning situations that allow for dissent and debate. In his view, much of what passes for contemporary politics is, in fact, anti-political. For example, *neoliberalism often involves the replacement of collective decision-making by market mechanisms. In place of public debate, one finds either scientific or technocratic regulation by experts, government by charismatic individuals, or guided by a moral absolutism that does not recognize the possibility of alternatives. Erik *Swyngedouw uses the term 'post-political' to describe what has happened to Western politics in the past few decades. In the place of national-scale debates animated by values, principles, and genuinely opposed viewpoints, he detects the rise of government by technocratic, managerial, and entrepreneurial elites. Thus, for example, the issue of climate change is reduced to discussions about technical and personal solutions rather than the core values of society. In a slightly different context, the anthropologist James Ferguson has described how the 'anti-political machine' of development programmes in Lesotho has, though failing to produce intended results, nonetheless had the unintended consequence of expanding the power of the bureaucratic state and its experts.

References Barry, A. (2002), 'The anti-political economy', *Economy and Society* 31: 268–84.
Ferguson, J. (1994), *The Anti-Politics Machine: Development, Depoliticization, and Bureaucratic Power in Lesotho.*
Swyngedouw, E. (2009), 'The antinomies of the postpolitical city: in search of a democratic politics of environmental production', *International Journal of Urban and Regional Research* 33: 601–20.

apartheid A political system based on the ethno-racial categorization of people and their geographical separation. This system existed between 1948 and 1994 in *South Africa. Anglo-Dutch colonizers tried to partition South Africa socially and spatially according to a three-fold categorization of 'whites', 'coloureds', and 'blacks'. Rules covering everything from marriage to place of residence were designed to ensure limited mixing between the three groups. This institutionalized white privilege and formalized ethno-racial discrimination. Apartheid was widely opposed within and beyond South Africa, with leading dissident Nelson Mandela the country's first post-apartheid president. In other countries, more piecemeal apartheid policies were, at one time, enacted (for instance, in the southern states of the USA prior to that country's civil rights protests of the 1960s). *See also* RACISM; SEGREGATION; SOCIAL EXCLUSION.

applied geography Geographical knowledge and techniques purposefully directed at pin-pointing and resolving immediate human, environmental, and physical problems. Although one could argue that almost all geographical work is potentially applicable in some way, there have been many attempts to demarcate a distinct field or approach of applied geography, through degree programmes, academic courses, conferences, and publications. There is an Applied Geography Specialty Group of the Association of American Geographers.

Applied geography has emerged out of a set of distinctions that, although often presented as non-competing, in practice are often regarded hierarchically. In the mid-20th century, 'applied' geography was contrasted with geographical work for educational ends. The term described knowledge of practical use, exemplified by the land-use surveys supervised by Carl *Sauer in the USA and Sir L. Dudley Stamp in the

UK. During the 1970s geographers made comparisons between 'relevant' knowledge addressing poverty, racism, and imperialism, and the (by implication) irrelevant work of modelling or abstract *spatial science (*see* RADICAL GEOGRAPHY; RELEVANCE). In the late 20th century, the contrast was more likely to be with pure or basic geography, understood as theory-building. Whereas 'pure' science might be regarded as progressing the discipline through novel understandings of the world, applied science was often dismissed as more artisanal and mundane. The fact that much applied geographical work was and still is carried out through contracts with the public and private sectors, and often results in reports and publications that are not peer-reviewed, compromised its credibility under national academic review programmes (*see* RESEARCH ASSESSMENT). In recent years, the emphasis placed on research having an 'impact' has, however, drawn more human geographers into consultancy and expert assessment.

Michael Pacione, introducing an edited collection featuring ongoing research in applied geography, defended it as an approach rather than a sub-discipline, and stressed that it lies on a continuum with pure geography rather than in opposition. It can be shown that pure and applied research feed back to one another, and applied geography can be at the cutting edge. Alan *Wilson's pioneering work using locational models in health care and retailing is a good example. Pacione's book *Applied Geography* (1999) included research on hazards, environmental change and management, and urban social issues such as transport and poverty. The onus was on practical, technical, or managerial solutions rather than institutional change or societal transformation. The journal *Applied Geography*, founded in 1981, also emphasizes the importance of techniques such as *Geographical Information System (GIS) to tackle land use and related environmental problems. *See also* POLICY, GEOGRAPHY AND; PUBLIC GEOGRAPHY.

Further reading Johnston, R. J. and Sidaway, J. (6th ed. 2004), 'Chapter 9' of *Geography and Geographers: Anglo-American Human Geography Since 1945*.

SEE WEB LINKS
• Website of the Applied Geography Specialty Group of the American Association of Geographers.

appropriate technology The technologies that are suited to the immediate socio-economic, cultural, and environment contexts in which they are introduced. Such technologies were strongly advocated by the environmentalist E. F. Schumacher in his best-seller *Small is Beautiful* (1973). Schumacher argued that for *development to occur, especially in the so-called *Third World, it was essential to introduce affordable technologies that were small in scale and useable by a great many people. Schumacher was a critic of state-bureaucratic, large-scale technologies (such as concrete and steel dams).

Arab Spring The revolutionary uprisings in predominantly Arab countries, starting in December 2010, that sought to overthrow dictatorships and install democratic societies. The initial protests took place in Tunisia and spread to countries across North Africa and the Middle East. The tactics adopted include marches, rallies, and strikes, and in the case of Libya, civil war. They were organized internally and communicated externally through *social networking. The uprisings were met with violence, repression, and counter-demonstrations by government forces and supporters. By the end of summer 2012, regime change had occurred in Tunisia, Egypt, and Libya, with an ongoing uprising in Syria, suppressed uprisings in Bahrain and Yemen, and major protests in a number of other countries.

architecture 1. The expertise or profession of designing and constructing buildings. 2. The product of such practices.

a

3. The style of buildings, commonly classified by historical period, place, and/or culture. By its focus on designing buildings and spaces, architecture shapes the look and function of a place. Much architecture is vernacular, reflecting local cultures (*see* VERNACULAR LANDSCAPE) or is functionally homogenous such as big-box retail units or warehouses. Some other architecture is signature in design, seeking to create an iconic statement (*see* ICONIC ARCHITECTURE). Given the role of architecture in planning and its effect on the *landscape, geographers have long taken an interest in its practices and forms. For example, they have examined the role of architecture in shaping the relationship between people and place, in the sense of dwelling and attachment, but also in relation to senses of inclusion and exclusion from public space. This may mean the ways in which architecture and design manipulate the flow of people through malls and airports, the contribution of architectural ideas to urban crime and incivility, or the affective dimension of interior spaces (Adey 2008). This has most notably developed into the idea of 'space syntax', that buildings and their surroundings can be designed in ways that explicitly shape *spatial behaviour and design out issues such as street crime. Alternately, the design of buildings can exclude certain individuals. Rob Imrie, for example, has argued that the routine practices of architects and designers lead to 'disablist spaces' that marginalize people with disabilities (*see* DISABILITY).

Cultural geographers have studied the architecture and design of buildings as symbols of ways of life or local cultures. Fred Kniffen's research into US folk housing in the 1960s exemplifies the early work in this vein. Later cultural geographers switched from a focus on rural landscapes to urban settings, concentrating more on iconic buildings and monuments than on vernacular dwellings. Much of the initial interest in *postmodernism centred on key buildings such as New York's AT&T (now Sony) building or architects such as Michael Graves. The mix of architectural styles or grammar, variously described as parody or pastiche, came to encapsulate the eclectic spirit of postmodernism in the most public of art forms (Jencks 1984). Geographers have also focused on the role of architects as actors in the built environment, and the process of building itself (Lees 2001). In the past 30 years a small number of superstar architects such as Norman Foster, Richard Rogers, and Frank Gehry have been involved in signature projects in global cities, for example. *See also* BUILT ENVIRONMENT.

References and further reading Adey, P. (2008), 'Airports, mobility and the calculative architecture of affective control', *Geoforum* 39: 438–91.
Imrie, R. (1996), *Disability and the City*.
Jencks, C. (4th ed. 1984), *The Language of Post-Modern Architecture*.
Kniffen, F. (1965), 'Folk housing: key to diffusion'. *Annals of the Association of American Geographers* 55, 549–77.
Lees, L. (2001), 'Towards a critical geography of architecture', *Cultural Geographies* 8: 51–85.

areal differentiation The variable character of the Earth's human and physical geography. In its early years as a university subject, many people associated geography with the study of areal differentiation (*see* CHOROLOGY). Where the so-called 'systematic' disciplines were devoted to *analysis and *abstraction, and where the 'chronological' disciplines focused on change through time, geography was seen as a discipline devoted to synthesis. Its role was to describe and explain the way that human and physical phenomena interacted differently at different points on the Earth's surface. In his influential manifesto for academic geography, Richard *Hartshorne emphasized areal differentiation as the subject's focus and *raison d'être*. Decades later many commentators argued that areal differentiation was a thing of the past because *globalization was facilitating inter-place exchange and mixing. However, writing at the end of the 20th century, Doreen *Massey argued that areal differentiation—while it had altered in the detail—was no less evident than in Hartshorne's day. Massey's contention was that new forms of areal differentiation were, paradoxically, being wrought out of new forms of global connectivity (for example, *Foreign Direct Investment). An areally differentiated world should thus be seen less as a metaphorical mosaic comprised of separate pieces, and more as a *network with points that are connected by lines along which goods, people, and information travel—ultimately altering their destinations.

Area Studies Interdisciplinary programmes specializing in research and teaching on specific regions of the world. Although specialized study of countries and regions has a long history, a distinct Area Studies emerged in the USA and certain other countries after the *Second World War. In the USA, the federal government and philanthropic foundations joined forces to support a series of academic departments in universities focusing on regions of strategic interest. These included Europe initially, and later the *Middle East and other parts of the developing world. There was a perceived lack of expertise in such areas, which had not only hindered the US war effort, but had also compromised the country's ambitions for post-war global leadership. Area Studies assembled experts from across the social sciences, but also included physical scientists and linguists. It generated a large number of regionally focused journals and scholarly associations. Critics regarded Area Studies as an extension of the USA's Cold War intelligence effort, although the programmes did harbour opponents to the Vietnam War.

From the late 1980s, Area Studies entered a period of crisis (Wesley-Smith and Goss 2009). The collapse of the USSR redrew the geopolitical map and undermined some of the basis for Soviet and East European Studies. Globalization eroded the significance of sovereign states as units of scholarship (*see* METHODOLOGICAL NATIONALISM). Foundations channelled their funds into more transnational concerns. In some cases, funding from the countries themselves helped restore Area Studies. Nissan Corporation supported an Institute of Japanese Studies at Oxford University in 1981, for example.

Within geography, area studies has long been a specialism without being as formally institutionalized as Area Studies (*see* REGIONAL GEOGRAPHY). Compared with five decades ago, area studies is less something human geographers practise and more something they subject to critical scrutiny. Farish's recent book on the *Cold War and how geographical knowledge entered into it is a fine example.

References Farish, M. (2010), *Contours of the American Cold War*.
Wesley-Smith, T. and Goss, J. (eds.) (2012), *Remaking Area Studies*.

art and geography **1.** Works of art in a range of genres that focus on geographical themes such as *place or *nature.

2. The analysis of the meaning and significance of such works. Art, in its various forms (e.g. sculpture, painting, or photography), can challenge a society to look at its conventions with fresh and often critical eyes. Equally, it can embody in an aesthetic medium a society's (or a particular social group's) most taken-for-granted beliefs or most cherished values. For these reasons, and because geographical phenomena are routinely the subject of artistic reflection (e.g. picturesque landscapes), geographers have scrutinized the work of diverse artists—some who have been embraced by mainstream *culture and others who are more *avant-garde. Such scrutiny has utilized concepts such as the *gaze, *iconography, and *ways of seeing to *deconstruct art work in order to contextualize and analyse its explicit and hidden meanings. Geographers have also examined the lives and works of artists and their working environments in order to trace out the genealogies of artistic endeavour and their embodied sites and practices. In addition, some geographers act as curators of exhibitions and work with artists on collaborative projects exploring how art can reveal elements of the human spatial condition and be used as an active, community intervention in locales.

Further reading Daniels, S. (2011), 'The art studio', in Agnew, J. and Livingstone, D. (eds), *The Handbook of Geographical Knowledge*.
Miles, M. (1997), *Art, Space and the City*.

ASEAN *See* ASSOCIATION OF SOUTHEAST ASIAN NATIONS.

Asia The world's largest and most populous continent, covering some 30 per cent of global land area and home to four billion people. Its largest economies are those of *Japan, *China, *India, *South Korea, and *Indonesia. These economies account for a large share of global manufacturing and export commodities to the rest of the world, as well as within Asia itself. They have risen to prominence since the 1960s, aside from Japan whose economic success began earlier. China and India have the biggest national populations and land areas in Asia. Japan has been considered to be among *First World nations for decades; so too the city-state of Singapore. However, the rest of Asia is comprised of states with variable levels of economic and social development. Though China is nominally communist, most countries in the continent are now nominally (or actually) democratic and have capitalist economies. Asia is multiethnic, multilingual, and highly diverse in a physical geographic sense. Mainland Asia comprises most of the continent but there are many islands (notably in Indonesia) and peninsulas. The continent became embroiled in the *Cold War after 1945, but more recently has become known for religious and national conflicts (notably in *Afghanistan, Nepal, *Pakistan, Sri Lanka, South Korea, and North Korea). Asia combines extraordinary *poverty among hundreds of millions of its people with equally extraordinary wealth, a disparity repeated across the developing world. The continent contains several *mega-cities such as Shanghai, Mumbai, and Beijing.

Asian Miracle A term used to describe the rapid economic growth of selected East Asian countries between *c.*1965 and *c.*1997. A 1993 World Bank Report attributed the 'East Asian miracle' to *neoliberalism and technological diffusion, arguing that other regions should emulate the policies of Japan and the Four 'Asian Tigers' (Hong Kong, Singapore, Taiwan, and South Korea) (*see* NEWLY INDUSTRIALIZING COUNTRIES). Critics, including Paul *Krugman, countered that the levels of growth were not unprecedented, that the growth was simply a function of increased inputs of capital and labour, that state intervention and repression were key factors, and that there was much variation between countries in the region.

Asiatic Mode of Production A system of producing goods and services supposedly characteristic of Asian societies in the precapitalist era. Unlike the capitalist *mode of production, the Asiatic mode did not depend upon workers selling their capacity to work for others (capitalists) in return for a wage. According to Karl *Marx, it involved the transfer of goods and services from notionally independent peasant households to a political and economic elite. This elite monopolized the means of violence (e.g. they could mobilize a large army) and were thus able to exact tribute from their subjects. The Marxist Karl Wittfogel finessed Marx's thesis to analyse 'Oriental Despotism', whereby large-scale state bureaucracies oversaw the construction of major hydrological projects necessary for ordinary arable farmers in arid environments to grow crops. The bureaucracies, Wittfogel argued, were too powerful for ordinary people to challenge or oppose. *See also* HYDRAULIC SOCIETY; POWER; WATER.

assemblage The contingent, non-necessary coming together of various phenomena, actors, institutions, or processes to form a temporarily stable bundle of relationships and capacities. Human geographers influenced by *Actor-Network Theory and the philosophical writings of Manuel De Landa, Gilles *Deleuze, and Felix Guattari have used the

term critically, in opposition to two dominant ontological doctrines. One (often associated with *spatial science) sees the world as comprised of discrete parts whose relations
to other parts are external. This has been called a Cartesian or 'billiard ball' ontology. The
other (often associated with *Marxist geography) sees the world as a structured totality of
relations that govern the parts according to definite rules or logics. The first approach
sees assemblage as a 'bricks-and-mortar' process akin to house construction, and the
second sees it as a closed, integral system of indissociable parts and relations. De Landa,
Deleuze, and Guattari, by contrast, see the world as a complex, changing, and emergent
product of interactions that are only partly planned, ordered, or controlled. *See also*
ONTOLOGY.

assimilation The process by which newcomers (usually immigrants) become more
like other members of the host society, especially culturally and socially. It is often
contrasted with *social exclusion or segregation (in which newcomers are denied access
to society) on the one hand, and *pluralism or *multiculturalism (in which some cultural
differences are maintained) on the other. Assimilation may be government policy, where
immigrants are expected or required to adopt national culture (France is an example), as
well as a social scientific concept that can be measured by behavioural and attitudinal
variables. Geographers have noted the sometimes close relationship between the social
process of assimilation and the spatial pattern of declining residential *segregation.
See also DIASPORA; IMMIGRATION.

Association of American Geographers (AAG) A non-profit scientific and
educational society, founded in 1904, which promotes the discipline of geography
and geographical analysis in the United States of America. As well as publishing two
leading journals, *Annals of the Association of American Geographers* and *The Professional
Geographer*, the AAG actively contributes to a number of global programmes, such as
My Community, Our Earth, aimed at advancing geographical research, teaching, and
literacy around the world.

( ) SEE WEB LINKS
• Website of the American Association of Geographers.

Association of Southeast Asian Nations (ASEAN) A supra-national political
organization founded in 1967 that represents the political, economic, and social interests
of ten Southeast Asian countries. The aims of ASEAN are to accelerate economic growth,
social progress, and cultural development in Southeast Asia, to promote peace and
stability in the region, and to foster collaboration between member states with respect
to education, agriculture, and trade.

( ) SEE WEB LINKS
• Official website of the Association of Southeast Asian Nations.

asylum Sanctuary given to an individual fleeing persecution by a state or (more rarely)
a religious institution. The conditions for political asylum are set out in the United
Nations *Declaration of Human Rights and the 1951 convention on *refugees; they are
binding under international law.

asylum seeker A *refugee who requests a government to grant them protection
according to the provisions of international human rights law (*asylum). States
are required to assess all such claims under the provisions of international law, although
the exact administrative practices are at their discretion. In countries where there is
a high level of hostility towards immigration in general, governments may make it

practically difficult to seek or obtain asylum by, for example, attaching work- and welfare-related conditions. In some cases applicants are detained in the country of claim or held in third countries awaiting a decision.

Further reading Mountz, A. (2010), *Seeking Asylum: Human Smuggling and Bureaucracy at the Border.*

atlas A collection of *maps presented using a uniform design and common scale. The maps usually relate to the earth, or a portion of the earth such as a region or nation state, although they can focus on domains at other scales such as the wider solar system or universe (*see* CARTOGRAPHY). Atlases can also be themed in relation to a specific phenomenon such as wildlife, health, literature, or war. The first modern atlas was produced by the Dutch cartographer Abraham Ortelius in 1570, though it lacked a uniform mapping frame. The term 'atlas', however, was first used by Gerardus Mercator in 1595. From the 17th century onwards, atlases became more common with the rise of modern cartography. Today, paper atlases are complemented by *virtual globes.

Australia The world's sixth-largest country by area, including Tasmania and many smaller islands adjacent to the Australian mainland. A former British colony, Australia has been an independent *nation state since 1901. Today it is a multiethnic, multilingual society, though English remains the official language. In recent years Australia has begun to recognize the historic rights of *aboriginal peoples to territory, resources, and cultural artefacts that were taken away from them by British and Dutch settlers from the 17th century. Australia's 23 million inhabitants are governed by a democratically elected executive, while its six states are also governed by elected bodies. The country is highly developed, with an *economy based primarily on the export of primary commodities and related manufactured goods (such as steel).

autobiography *See* BIOGRAPHICAL APPROACH.

autoethnography A form of ethnography that is highly self-referential wherein the researcher is partially the focus of analysis. Like *ethnography, autoethnography involves *participant observation and embedding within a community, however, the division between ethnographer and community is blurred with the researcher writing autobiographically about their experiences, ethnographically about their own culture and their place within it, or about their experiences of being the subject of an ethnographic project. It is a reflexive approach aimed at exposing the *positionality of the researchers and situatedness of the analysis. *See also* SITUATED KNOWLEDGE.

automobile industry The family of firms involved in producing, marketing, selling, maintaining, and disposing of automobiles. Narrowly defined, the automobile industry includes firms such as General Motors, BMW, and Nissan, which manufacture cars, lorries and trucks, and motorbikes. Broadly defined, it includes all businesses directly involved in the extended, complex *commodity chains associated with automobiles. The family metaphor is only partly accurate since many of the firms involved compete with one another for market share. Even narrowly defined, the automobile industry remains one of the world's most important. It is a leading employer in many city-regions, a major corporate taxpayer to governments at all levels, and a major consumer of energy, metals, plastics, electronic components, and tyres (all of which are themselves products of large industries). The industry has undergone significant geographical restructuring since the 1970s, when it was largely concentrated in Western capitalist democracies. Today, automobile production is far more global, with automobile manufacturers and their suppliers located across Eastern Europe, Asia, and Central and South America as much as North America and Western Europe. Similarly, the market for automobiles is no longer concentrated in the latter regions. The automobile industry has recently been subject to political pressure from national governments and environmental *non-governmental organizations, among others, as part of a broader project of *ecological modernization. This has led it to develop more fuel-efficient and lighter vehicles, and also battery-powered vehicles. *See also* CORPORATE SOCIAL RESPONSIBILITY.

automobility The capacity of people to move across space using mechanical and/or computer-aided vehicles. Automobility's capacity to 'collapse' space means that it reduces the time people otherwise spend on overcoming the *friction of distance. The analysis of automobility extends beyond issues such as congestion, commuting, *suburbanization, and environmental impacts to also consider the role of driving in cultural identity formation, social standing and status.

autophotography *See* PHOTOGRAPHY.

avant-garde A French phrase used to refer to people or actions that are novel or experimental, particularly with respect to philosophy, the arts, and culture. In human geography it is sometimes used to refer to various thinkers, writers, artists, and iconoclasts who have proposed radically new ways of conceiving *landscape, *nature, *place, *region, *space, and *urbanism. An example is the work of the *Situationists.

B

back-officing The process of moving selected elements of a company's operations from their current locations to cheaper or more strategic sites. Typical activities that are back-officed include IT support, human resource management, and accounting. Back-officing might be quite local, with activities moving from city centre to suburban sites, but can also be global with activities being located in a different country. For instance, many North American *transnational corporations have their back-offices in the Caribbean and those from Europe in South Asia. Many firms—notably several transnational corporations—have contracted out back-office activities to other specialist service providers. Because back-officing usually involves the dispersal of a firm's units and functions, information and communication technologies (*ICTs) are vital to their coordination across *space and through *time. *See also* OFFSHORING; SERVICES.

Baghdad The *capital city of *Iraq, sited on the Tigris river. With a present population of over seven million it is the largest city in the region. In Persian, Baghdad translates as 'God's gift' and the city's history dates back to the late 8th century AD. From 1932 the city became capital of the newly independent nation state of Iraq. From 1979 it was the home of the autocratic government of Saddam Hussein. Following the invasion and occupation of Iraq by foreign armies in 2003 and Hussein's demise, the city was engulfed in fighting between various factions.

balanced development A policy popularized by the *OECD in the first decade of the new millennium. It aims to create equal opportunities for people to benefit from economic development in all parts of a country, especially in both urban and rural areas.

balance of trade The relationship between the value of a country's imports and exports, generally expressed in monetary terms. A country has a net trade surplus if the total value of its exports exceeds the total value of imports, or a net trade deficit if imports exceed exports.

Balkans A region between the *Middle East and *Eastern Europe and bounded geographically by the Adriatic Sea to the west, the Mediterranean Sea (including the Ionian and Aegean seas) and the Marmara Sea to the south, and the Black Sea to the east. The word 'Balkan' originally referred to a chain of wooded mountains in Bulgaria and Serbia, but today denotes Albania, Greece, Bosnia and Herzegovina, Kosovo, Macedonia, Montenegro, and Serbia. The region has experienced a great deal of internecine strife since at least the mid-19th century. Several of its countries came under Soviet influence during the *Cold War, while today most are—or aspire to be—members of the *European Union. Levels of social and economic *development within the region vary quite significantly: for instance, income levels in Albania are markedly lower than elsewhere in the region.

banal nationalism *See* NATIONALISM.

banking *See* FINANCE.

Barnes, Trevor (1956–) A British-Canadian economic geographer who has promoted *political economy and post-structural approaches to his subfield, and utilized *Science and Technology Studies to understand the subfield's history. A professor at the University of British Columbia, Barnes (writing with Eric *Sheppard) showed why—at the level of *theory, not only *empirical investigations—geographical distance and unevenness have a fundamental effect on how the capitalist economy operates. Most economic theory assumes that the world's geography is homogenous whereas Barnes (with Sheppard) conceptualized the effects of spatial separation and differentiation on fundamental economic processes. He has also been important in reinterpreting the history of economic geography. For Barnes, the subfield has always absorbed the values and goals of the surrounding socio-economic and political environment, a fact that alters its claims to be a *social science in the conventional sense of the latter term. For instance, Barnes shows how in the 1950s several economic geographers' research reflected the geopolitical goals of the USA during the Cold War against the former USSR.

Batty, Michael (1945–) A geographer and urban planner known for his theoretical and modelling work on cities as highly complex systems, and for showing the wide cross-disciplinary applications of *Geographic Information Systems (GIS) and spatial statistics and modelling. He is a professor at University College, London, and directs its Centre for Advanced Spatial Analysis. *See also* CHAOS, CATASTROPHE, AND COMPLEXITY THEORY; URBAN MODELLING.

Bayesian statistics A type of *inferential statistical method, derived from the theorem of Thomas Bayes (1763). Rather than simply using observed data to test a hypothesis, it takes into account prior knowledge or beliefs as well as freshly observed data to evaluate the probability of a hypothesis being true. In other words, it enables already-established probabilities to be used in the calculation of new probabilities, thus allowing a consolidation of a hypothesis or a model to be calibrated as evidence is accumulated. In a sense then, Bayesian methods are inductive in that a theory is built up from prior analysis that is reused in subsequent calculations.

Bebbington, Anthony (1962–) A development geographer who has advanced understanding of poverty, inequality, and social vulnerability among low-income households in Latin America. He is particularly well known for his research into the role of development *non-governmental organizations (NGOs), the different forms of *capital involved in development, and the particular role of *social capital.

behavioural geography The study of human spatial activity as the outcome of decisions made by individuals within the constraints set by society and the environment, and according to their perception and understanding of the situation. Behavioural geographers focus on what people do and why they do it, rather than on what they might be expected to do based on abstract models of rational behaviour. They recognize that people live simultaneously in an objective, physical world and a more subjective world of values, meanings, and perceptions. To the extent that people base their behaviour on the world as they perceive it, then spatial models based only on an objective, rational world are likely to be inaccurate or misleading.

Although the term 'behavioural geography' can be used to describe a broad, cross-disciplinary field of study, it generally refers to work by human and environmental geographers who flourished between the 1960s and 1980s. Their studies reflected a range of influences, including psychology (especially child or development psychology), cognitive behaviouralism, architecture, anthropology, and environmental design, and also drew upon traditions of *cultural geography.

According to John Gold (2009) there have been three main clusters of research within behavioural geography. The first addresses spatial decision-making and behaviour, including how spatial knowledge is obtained, retained, accessed, and acted upon. The central problem is often why people behave in ways other than what might be expected if they acted on the basis of profit-maximization or least-effort. A common finding is that individuals were 'satisficers' rather than 'optimizers'. The subject of analysis might be an individual shopper, a family searching for a new residential neighbourhood to live in, or the managers of a company deciding where to locate. A key concept is *cognitive mapping, how people construct and organize their spatial knowledge in a relatively stable manner. Much of this work centres on how children acquired their spatial knowledge in interaction with their environment. Reg *Golledge pioneered studies of how visually impaired and other special populations relate to their spatial environments, feeding into ideas for improving urban design. Following the ideas of urban planner Kevin *Lynch, other geographers sought to understand how people make the urban built environment legible through the images they construct of it. Peter *Gould and colleagues examined systematic patterns on people's preference for places and regions through the method of *mental maps. The core concerns of this strand of behavioural geography are travel, retailing behaviour, migration, residential location, and the spatial behaviour of visually impaired, disabled, and elderly people.

The second cluster brought together physical and human geography around the study of natural *hazards. Here the problem is why people chose to live in areas subject to drought, flooding, earthquakes, or other climatic and geological risks. Heavily influenced by Gilbert F. *White's studies of flood risk in the USA, such studies have established that people act on the basis of a 'bounded rationality', i.e. they only take account of high frequency, low magnitude, and thus low-risk events because to do otherwise would involve too much behavioural disruption.

Gold's third theme in behavioural geography is attachment to *place, where the influence of humanistic ideas has been strongest. Exemplified by Edward *Relph's *Place and Placelessness* and Yi-Fu *Tuan's *Topophilia*, such studies sought to capture or even rescue the significance of deep engagement with places in the face of mass suburbanization and cultural homogenization.

Although the description 'behavioural geography' is less common than it was up to the 1990s, especially outside North America, a concern for decision-making, the acquisition of spatial knowledge, risk, environmental perception, hazards, and related problems thrives within human geography. More recently the field has become closely associated with environmental perception, forming a single speciality group of the Association of American Geographers. Although once regarded as rooted within *positivist methodology, current behavioural approaches include both qualitative and quantitative methods, and are informed by a range of post-positivist epistemologies. *See also* COGNITIVE GEOGRAPHY.

Reference and further reading Gold, J. (2009), 'Behavioural Geography', in *The International Encyclopedia of Human Geography*.
Golledge, R. and Stimson, R. (1997), *Spatial Behavior: A Geographic* Perspective.

(((⊕))) SEE WEB LINKS

• Environmental Perception and Behavioral Geography Specialty Group of the American Association of Geographers.

Beijing Conference Convened by the *United Nations, the Fourth World Conference on Woman was held in Beijing in September 1995 and set out a declaration and a platform for action aimed at addressing discrimination and human rights abuses against women, and achieving greater equality and opportunity for women. The United Nations and national governments agreed collectively to prioritize the *empowerment of women and gender mainstreaming in their policies and programmes.

Beijing consensus A *development model supposedly encapsulating China's post-1978 economic growth and framed in contrast with the *Washington consensus. As first outlined by journalist Joshua Romo in 2004, it has constant innovation and experimentation, sustainability and equality, and national self-determination as its core features. Other writers suggested authoritarianism, mixed property systems, and planning flexibility as principles. There is much written inside and outside China about what constitutes, if anything, the distinct Chinese path to development, and whether other countries should follow it rather than *neoliberalism. The Chinese premier Zhao Ziyang did reiterate five principles of international cooperation in 1981, which included respect for national *sovereignty and opposition to conditions being attached to *aid, but the country's authorities have never formally acknowledged a consensus.

Further reading Li, X., Brødsgaard, K., and Jacobsen, M. (2010), 'Redefining the Beijing consensus', *China Economic Journal* 2: 297–311.

belonging A person's sense of attachment to, and rootedness in, a specific community, neighbourhood, place, region, or country. Belonging is subjective and usually reflects a person's long immersion (through childhood to adulthood) in a particular milieu. Through such immersion people internalize the norms, values, and customs of a *nation, *locality, subculture, or *culture. However, their sense of belonging may also involve highly singular attachments that reflect a person's unique biography. *Humanistic geographers focused on how *place attachment formed an important part of people's identity, and were sometimes critical of the *placelessness produced by the homogenous landscapes some associated with *modern architecture. Critical human geographers subsequently examined how belonging is engendered through local, regional, and national customs and institutions. These customs and institutions are shown to cultivate *nationalism, *ethnocentrism, and even *racism among citizens in often (though not always) subtle ways. Because of *globalization and what some regard as a related process of *McDonaldization, many people are today looking for ways to strengthen people's sense of belonging to the places and countries they hail from. This links with calls for a process of *deglobalization.

Berkeley School A group of scholars associated with the Department of Geography at the University of California, Berkeley, known mainly for its contribution to *cultural geography and *landscape studies. The school enjoyed considerable prominence and influence, especially within US academic geography, between the 1920s and the 1960s. Its talisman was Carl *Sauer, whose many PhD students went on to occupy senior positions in other American university geography departments. The school's major interest was in anthropogenic landscapes, especially those created in the past by rural populations in the Caribbean and Latin America. Through detailed field observations and archival work into all facets of a modified landscape (plants, field systems, buildings, water courses, etc.) Berkeley geographers sought to describe and explain the cultural, economic, social, and political practices that were imprinted on the face of the Earth. Typically, Berkeley School geographers were committed to local or regional scale study (both field and archival) within the tradition of *chorology and valued the skill of synthesis. *See also* CULTURAL ECOLOGY; CULTURAL GEOGRAPHY; CULTURAL LANDSCAPE.

Berlin The capital city of *Germany, located in the north near the Polish border. Berlin was bifurcated after 1945 when Germany was split into a western half and an eastern half as part of the *Cold War division of Europe into two political-economic spheres (one capitalist and democratic, the other communist and more autocratic). During the 1930s and early 1940s it was home to the ruling Nazi Party and the scene of national rallies and parades designed to engender public commitment to *fascism. Since the fall of the Berlin Wall the city has undergone a major physical revival, with significant new building projects at all points of the compass. It is now an international destination city for tourists as much as a capital city for Germany.

Berlin Conference (1884–85) A meeting of the main European imperialist countries (and the Ottoman Empire) at which they agreed the rules for claiming and possessing territory in Africa (*see* IMPERIALISM). At the time, imperial powers asserted control over much of the continent's coastal regions only. Among the agreements of its General Act were: regulations of free trade between colonies; prohibition of international slavery; and a procedure for making new claims to territory based on effective control. The parties agreed 'spheres of influence'—regions in which each country could exclusively attempt to subdue or make treaties with African rulers. This led to the so-called Scramble for Africa. By 1902, 90 per cent of Africa was under European control, creating many of the national boundaries that still exist today and to which many of the continent's problems are attributed. *See also* BORDER; BOUNDARY.

Further reading Griffiths, I. (1986), 'The scramble for Africa: inherited political boundaries', *The Geographical Journal* 152: 204–16.

Berlin Wall A fortified physical barrier constructed from 1961 onwards by the German Democratic Republic (East Germany) separating the parts of the city under GDR control from those governed by the Federal Republic of Germany (West Germany). It symbolized the sharp divisions between the capitalist West and the communist *Eastern Bloc during the *Cold War. Its physical demolition by citizens of the two Germanies in 1989 was hailed as a sign that democracy and the market had triumphed over autocracy and state economic planning. The term 'Berlin Wall' is still used as a metaphor for seemingly absolute borders and divisions.

Berry, Brian J. L. (1934–) An English-American urban geographer and planner who helped pioneer the *spatial science approach to analysing human activities in cities. Berry, who initially trained as an economist, was among the first to use numerical data and statistical techniques as part of a search for geographical patterns common to systems of cities and individual cities. He is particularly known for his early research using *Central Place Theory and his work on urbanization and long wave rhythms in economic development. He is currently a professor at the University of Texas, Dallas.

bias The conscious or unconscious act of failing to be objective in one or more aspects of the research process. The term is usually understood pejoratively in *science and by those human geographers who consider their research to be scientific. Bias can occur in the way research questions are phrased, data are collected, data are analysed, and results interpreted. Many human geographers now believe that *objectivity in research is unattainable, and that what some call 'bias' should be seen more positively as a synonym for *situated knowledge. *See also* ECOLOGICAL FALLACY; MODIFIABLE AREAL UNIT PROBLEM; OBJECTIVITY.

bid-rent curve A graphical representation of the relationship between land or property rental costs and distance from the centre of a city or town. *Rent is the charge levied by a land or property owner to use that land or property by others. In a *free market such rent is supposedly determined by the balance between supply and demand in different rental markets. Potential renters bid for land and property until a price is set. Typically, similar sorts of renters will occupy specific parts of a townscape or cityscape. For instance, very expensive land and property is to be found in large retail centres because big companies compete to attract large numbers of consumers. In reality bid-rent curves are affected by other things (such as government rent controls on residential property). *See also* ALONSO MODEL; VON THÜNEN MODEL.

big data Enormous, dynamic, interconnected digital data sets relating to people, objects, interactions, transactions, and territories. *Software is becoming ever more embedded into everyday life and infrastructures, much of which generates data on its own use in real-time. For example, surveillance cameras, sensors embedded within trains, and transponder-enabled ticketing ('Oyster Cards') provide a constant stream of data concerning the use of the London Underground. Similarly, telecommunications companies can track the location and use of all mobile phones on the network. The result is big data that provides very detailed views of large systems in flux. Given that most big data are spatially and temporally referenced this enables sophisticated geographical *modelling. The challenge of big data is not simply volume, but also variety and velocity; to deal with huge, diverse, complex, dynamic data sets.

biodiversity The variety of non-human genes, species, and/or ecosystems past and present. The term was coined in the late 1980s by a cohort of mostly American conservation biologists concerned about the environmental degradation caused by modern agriculture, industry, and transportation. The *United Nations Convention on Biological Diversity has encouraged many national governments to better *map and conserve biodiversity, in both settled and unsettled areas. In settled areas it is recognized that biodiversity is linked to the presence of ethnocultural diversity: for instance, *indigenous peoples and peasant farmers have, over the millennia, been important contributors to plant biodiversity. Hence some argue that we need to conserve 'biocultural diversity'.

biofuels Fuels that are derived from organic matter, notably (but not exclusively) crops. Because of spikes in fossil fuel prices since 2000, and because of the *climate change risks associated with continued fossil fuel use, biofuels have been championed by some as a 'cleaner' alternative. Fuel types include biogas, bioether, biodiesel, and vegetable oil. Fuel sources include landfill waste, manure, sawdust, grass clippings, and much more besides. Some have questioned the 'green' credentials of biofuels (arguing that they still produce significant greenhouse gas emissions). Others have pointed out that, in many countries, increasing biofuel production reduces national *food security by reducing the land devoted to conventional farming. The geography of biofuel production, export, and consumption is such that, if biofuel production did increase significantly in the 21st century, then many developing countries would become major suppliers to many currently developed countries. *See also* RENEWABLE ENERGY.

biographical approach A way of understanding the relationships between people and place that focuses on an individual's life course. Related approaches include life histories or *life course research. Such approaches from a geographical perspective focus on the spaces and times that individuals flow through and the role of biographical history, identity, culture, and social structures shaping such events and transitions. While biographical approaches have application across the discipline, they have most widely been adopted in migration and gender studies. In the case of migration, they are used to examine the trajectories of people's movement and settlement (e.g., residential location, workplace, family, leisure, and work travel) at different points in their life course (e.g., nest-leaving, separation, retirement), within the context of wider family and structural constraints. The approach thus seeks to find a middle path between approaches that prioritize individual agency and those that provide structural accounts of migration decision-making, while also recognizing that moves are not made in isolation but form part of a larger biography and personal or familial history. In the case of gender, they are used to examine the lifeworlds and spatial behaviour of men and women over or at specific points in the life cycle. Methodologically, biographical approaches can use a range of techniques to gather data including interviews, oral histories, case studies, autobiographies, and story-telling. Biographical approaches are also becoming popular in tracing the history of the discipline by focusing on the individual careers of scholars in order to better understand the production of geographical knowledge.

Further reading Halfacree, K. and Boyle, P. (1993), 'The challenge facing migration research: the case for a biographical approach', *Progress in Human Geography* 17: 333–58.
Hubbard, P. and Kitchin, R. (eds.) (2nd ed. 2011), *Key Thinkers on Space and Place*.
Katz, C. and Monk, J. (eds.) (1993), *Life Worlds: Geographies of Women Over the Life Course*.

biopiracy The theft of biological *resources and/or knowledge about those resources possessed by farmers and communities, including *indigenous peoples. The title of a 1998 book by Indian environmentalist and social justice campaigner Vandana Shiva, the term has been used repeatedly to describe the *bioprospecting activities of Western multinational corporations in various developing countries worldwide.

biopolitics The administration and regulation of human and non-human life at the levels of the population and the individual body. Biopower is therefore a form of *power that targets the population. Both terms are closely associated with the writings of Michel *Foucault, and are best understood as part of a family of concepts—alongside discipline and *governmentality—introduced as part of his analysis of the modern era in Europe. Whereas the archetypal form of premodern power, *sovereignty, was concerned with territory, by the 18th century a new constellation of powers addressed people individually and collectively. The state sought to manage conditions of birth and death, health and disease, race and sexuality, and other dimensions of human well-being in order to foster life. To do so required the proliferation of new kinds of knowledge such as demography, epidemiology, and statistics, which also constituted 'the population' as an object of biopolitical concern. The object of biopower was therefore not the legal subject (the focus of sovereignty), but the biological and physical aspects of human beings separately and as a social body. As an example, human geographers have inquired into how governments and various expert communities have created or reproduced norms and standards that pertain to the 'right' and 'proper' disposition of non-humans or human bodies. Rather than seeing these norms and standards as simply 'necessary', 'efficient', or 'objective', they have shown them to be politics by other means. That is to say, the expert prescriptions of animal welfare officials or of public health authorities are shown to be shot through with values that often reproduce asymmetrical relations of power in a society. But in addition to the health and well-being of the population, biopolitics also covers more violent forms of intervention into the processes of life, such as eugenics, genocide, and racial control.

Biopolitics constitutes a very broad terrain of interest, and its meaning has been extended by subsequent thinkers. Georgio Agamben stressed that there was more continuity between sovereignty and biopolitics than sometimes supposed; the struggle to claim, establish, and exercise sovereignty through biopower is a feature of both colonial history and contemporary conflicts such as the pacification of Iraq, for example. Michael Hardt and Antonio Negri emphasize the possibilities of a biopolitical counterpoint to biopower arising from the body and its forces (*see* MULTITUDE). Human geographers are engaging with biopolitics in a number of ways, including: the geography of war, terrorism, and violence; biometric techniques at political borders; colonial government; famine; and environmental disasters. *See also* BIOSECURITY.

Further reading Legg, S. (2007), *Spaces of Colonialism: Delhi's Urban Governmentalities*.
Schlosser, K. (2008), 'Bio-political geographies', *Geography Compass* 2/5: 1621–34.

bioprospecting The systematic search for little-understood or hitherto unknown biological phenomena (for instance, genes or odours) that might inspire practically useful and commercially profitable commodities. Bioprospecting has been pursued by numerous pharmaceutical, biomedical, cosmetics, and agro-foods firms around the world, with a particular focus on *biodiversity 'hotspots' (such as Costa Rica). It has been criticized as a form of *biopiracy. *See also* BIOTECHNOLOGY; COMMON POOL RESOURCES; INDIGENOUS KNOWLEDGE; INTELLECTUAL PROPERTY RIGHTS.

bioregionalism An environmentalist belief that human societies should adapt to living harmoniously within bioregions. These are territories defined by natural rather than political conditions. A bioregion can be defined as an area in which topography, soils, plant and animal life, climate, weather, and human culture are relatively homogeneous and integrated. It may correspond with a watershed. The concept was formulated by environmentalist Peter Berg and ecologists Raymond Dasmann in 1970s northern California, but has not been taken up much beyond North America. Although bioregions share many of the ideas of classical *regional geography, human geographers have not developed the idea.

biosecurity The security of a country's human population, flora, and fauna against the unwanted introduction of various biological phenomena (such as viruses, toxins, insects, plant species, and mammals). Though the term 'biosecurity' is relatively new, it has long been a concern of national governments. However, a number of major incidents—such as the terrorist attacks on the World Trade Center in 2001, and foot-and-mouth disease in Britain around the same time—conspired to focus the attention of many governments on how adequate their biosecurity measures were. These measures are many and varied, involving everyone from customs officials at international borders to laboratory technicians taking receipt of biological materials from overseas suppliers. Many human geographers have begun to investigate biosecurity, seeing it as far more than a technical issue of getting the 'right' preventative measures. They have inquired into how the *regulation of the movement of biological materials is linked with the *governance of national populations and the identification (and demonization) of 'enemies' and 'threats' at home and abroad. *See also* BIOPOLITICS.

biotechnology A field of applied biological science in which natural processes and organisms are altered intentionally by scientists and technicians in order to achieve specific results. Biotechnology covers human biology, plant biology, animal and insect biology, and microbiology. It is proof positive of economist Eric Zimmerman's famous adage that 'resources are not, they become' (*see* NATURAL RESOURCES). Natural phenomena can become resources for humans for the first time, and existing resources can become useful in new ways because of the opportunities biotechnology presents.

Though often thought to be a recent development in the applied life sciences, biotechnology is, in fact, rather old. For instance, agricultural scientists in the 1910s and 1920s, drawing on the pioneering research of Gregor Mendel, learned how to cross-breed corn plants in order to produce higher-yielding and more hardy varieties (*see* GENETIC MODIFICATION). This hybridization (as it became known) formed the basis of the so-called *Green Revolution in the Global South after 1945. This revolution involved vast acreages of hybrid crops being grown with the aid of specialized pesticides and herbicides. The resulting yields were prodigious, though the ecological effects of agro-chemicals on human health and water quality were harmful.

Today, biotechnology can call upon more invasive methods for altering the character of living organisms. These include genetic cloning, gene splicing, and the creation of artificial life forms (so-called 'synthetic biology'). Because these procedures allow scientists to 'play God' in the eyes of many, they have proven to be controversial. For instance, environmental *non-governmental organizations such as *Greenpeace have opposed genetically modified farming on ecological and moral grounds. Yet others argue that in a world where hunger and crop failure remain rife, such farming can help to save lives.

Biotechnology has a number of geographical aspects. First, it involves actual or potential transformations of farming landscapes and wider *rural ecosystems. Second, its rise to prominence has sparked a counter-movement in agriculture and food consumption focused on promoting organic farming and so-called slow food (*see* ALTERNATIVE FOOD NETWORKS). Third, because several *transnational corporations (such as Monsanto) have actively promoted cutting-edge biotechnologies (such as genetically modified crops), important questions arise about who has rights over living organisms and cultivated landscapes. For instance, as Gary Nabhan details, for millennia *indigenous peoples in countries such as Mexico have exchanged seeds and, on this basis, created biodiverse landraces of corn and other important crops. By *bioprospecting these landraces, so-called 'agrobiotech' companies have appropriated *indigenous knowledge and privatized the commercial gains arising from biotechnological commodities that partly embody this knowledge. Many consider this unjust, an act of *biopiracy. Finally, biotechnology has implications for understandings of self and other, as with the use of genetic tests to discover one's geographical and biological ancestors.

These and other important geographical issues implicate local, national, and supranational state bodies because of these bodies' responsibilities for regulating biotechnology. They also raise fundamental moral questions about whether, how, and to what extent living organisms (include our own bodies) ought to be mined or altered to meet human needs (*see* ANTHROPOCENTRISM). More particularly, we might ask whose needs are being met each time a new biotechnology is applied in farming, cosmetics, or biomedicine? This question is asked by bioethicists, among others. Some environmentalists believe that the latest round of biotechnologies—if applied on a large scale and developed still further—will bring about the end of *nature. Those who believe in *ecological modernization, by contrast, argue that if their use is suitably regulated, biotechnologies can assist in efforts to reduce humanity's *ecological footprint and remove 'imperfections' in our bodies.

References and further reading Nabhan, G. (2002), *Enduring Seeds: Native American Agriculture and Wild Plant Conservation*.
Smith, J. (5th ed. 2004), *Biotechnology*.

black economy An exchange of goods and services outside the legal, financial, and customary practices prevailing in the mainstream (or 'formal') *economy. The black economy has long been the focus of politicians and law enforcement agencies because, among other things, it trades counterfeit and stolen goods (*see* TRAFFICKING), and denies the state access to import duty and taxes. However, while often demonized, the black economy can help people on low incomes secure the money, goods, and services they cannot secure in the formal economy. *See also* ALTERNATIVE ECONOMIC GEOGRAPHIES; SOCIAL ECONOMY.

Blaikie, Piers (1942–) A British geographer who pioneered the *political ecology approach along with sometime co-author Harold Brookfield. Blaikie's best-known work was the *Political Economy of Soil Erosion in Developing Countries* (1985). Influenced in part by Marxist *political economy, the book set out to explain the causes of soil erosion among smallholders in the Global South. Based on his fieldwork in Nepal, Blaikie rejected the idea that farmers were incompetent or working their land harder to feed more family members. Instead, he showed how micro-level farming practices could only be understood with reference to the national and global forces bearing down on small-holders. This approach balanced a focus on farmer *agency with a focus on the wider socio-economic and political structures governing that agency. Blaikie later co-authored a key book about *natural hazards, their human effects, and how to ameliorate those effects. *At risk* (1994) presented an analytical framework with practical policy implications (*see* RISK). It argued that the negative effects of natural hazards tend to be suffered by the poor and disadvantaged, and it suggested socio-economic solutions as much as technical-engineering ones (such as building flood defences).

Blaut, James (1924–2000) An American geographer best known for his writings about *eurocentrism in geographical research and teaching. Blaut's books *The Colonizer's Model of the World: Geographical Diffusionism and Eurocentric History* (1993) and *Eight Eurocentric Historians* (2000) continued Edward *Said's critique of *Orientalism. His other important research focused on *cognitive mapping, where he forwarded the nativist position that people are born with an innate ability to understand maps.

body The physical matter—flesh, bones, organs—of an individual. The body is sometimes referred to as the material form through which people interact with the world. How the body is theorized is a contested terrain. For some quantitative geographers seeking to model *spatial behaviour, the body is little more than a unit of inquiry; encounters with the world are abstracted into generalized disembodied interactions. In contrast, others argue that the body cannot be treated as obvious and taken for granted; they understand the body as shaping geographical encounters of the world in three predominant ways.

First, the physiology of the body and its ability to move, sense, touch, and manipulate, mediates how environments are encountered and experienced (*see* SENSUAL GEOGRA-PHIES). For example, the impaired body (such as one that has to use a wheelchair to navigate a landscape) interacts with and comes to know a place in different ways from someone who can walk (*see* DISABILITY). The impaired or 'unhealthy' body might not be able to access some spaces or will have limited access or have to gain entry in ways different from healthy, unimpaired bodies, or they might be confined to *segregated spaces such as special schools and landscapes of *care.

Second, bodies through their appearance (skin colour, disfigurements, size or the fashions with which they are adorned), or through their physiology (such as sex), are markers of difference and *otherness and the sites of social and cultural inscription (*see* SOCIAL CONSTRUCTION). Varying discursive understandings and material practices are associated with bodily forms and shapes how people are treated and how they experience *place. For example, *feminist geographers have detailed how the female body is sexualized and gendered, framed through a male *gaze of desire, and how this shapes expectations as to a woman's place in the world and how she should behave and act in public space (*see* GENDER; SEXUALITY). Robyn *Longhurst, for example, has shown the ways in which the socio-spatial lives of pregnant women are framed by *normative notions of how the pregnant body should act in public and the spaces it should occupy. Similarly, research has examined how black bodies are marked by *racism that works to figure the socio-spatial lives of black people and underpins processes of *marginalization, *social exclusion, and *segregation.

Third, bodies are expressions of *identity and *subjectivity, a means through which people act in the world and take part in social and familial life—whether that is to dance, play, shop, flirt, eat, etc. They are groomed, styled, clothed, pierced, tattooed, exercised and posed, used to signal identification and group belonging. In other words, the body is self-inscribed as well as being externally inscribed, shaping personal *social capital and socio-spatial encounters (*see* BUTLER, JUDITH).

Encounters with the world and how we come to know the world are embodied (*see* EMBODIED KNOWLEDGE) and the body is a site of contestation, regulation, and resistance. Moreover, it has been argued that bodies are shaped and framed by space, with environments, places, and their associated socio-spatial relations being active ingredients in the constituting of bodies. Bodies and spaces thus construct each other in complex ways, with how bodies perform and are disciplined not simply taking place in space, but through it. How the body and these processes of embodiment are understood varies depending on the theoretical lens used. For example, a variety of approaches have been used in geographical research including *psychoanalytic (the unconscious body), *phenomenological (the lived body), social construction (the inscribed body), and the *poststructural (the performed body). To take the latter, bodies are theorized as being *performative, that is, not defined by their *ontological status but rather by the acts that they perform. From this perspective, being a woman is not defined by biological sex (what the body is), or by gender (how the body is inscribed), but by acting as a woman (what the body does). Such a formulation enables a different kind of *identity politics framed around practices.

References and further reading Duncan, N. (ed.) (1996), *Bodyspace: Destabilizing Geographies of Gender and Sexuality*.

Longhurst, R. (2000), '"Corporeographies" of pregnancy', *Environment and Planning D: Society and Space* 18: 453–72.

Longhurst, R. (2001), *Bodies: Exploring Fluid Boundaries*.

Nast, H. and Pile, S. (eds.) (1998), *Places Through the Body*.

body work Labour in which the human body is central to the accomplishment or understanding of tasks and transactions. One form, common in consumer-oriented service work (e.g. retailing) involves the co-presence of worker or employee and customer; the employee's appearance and deportment is essential to the exchange. Other work is directly on the body, for example, hairdressing, personal fitness trainers. In a third form, e.g. *sex work, workers use their own bodies in the course of the transaction. Such body work usually reproduces and reinforces highly gendered notions of how men and women should dress and act in the workplace and other sites where labour takes place (such as the home). Body work is thus both gendered and sexualized, commodifying and exploiting the body as a site of desire. Linda McDowell argues that such work is increasingly common (although it has always been undertaken in one form or another), at some cost to employees. *See also* EMOTIONAL LABOUR.

Further reading McDowell, L. (2009), *Working Bodies: Interactive Service Employment and Workplace Identities*.

border 1. The line separating two jurisdictions or territories, generally nation states but sometimes also subnational administrative districts.

2. The edge or limit of a *territory. In the first sense, 'border' is often synonymous with *boundary. In the second sense, the term borderland is also sometimes used, although it may also describe the region either side of a political boundary (*see* FRONTIER).

In both senses, as well as referring to physical lines, borders can describe cultural, social, virtual, or metaphorical divisions.

In geography, political boundaries and borders have long been of interest. Until the early 20th century many believed that 'natural boundaries' (such as rivers and coastlines) should be favoured when dividing *territory into national and subnational parcels. However, in areas where no major natural boundaries existed or where different linguistic, religious, or ethnic groups had spilled over such boundaries, other criteria for dividing territory had to be utilized. The distinction between 'natural' and 'artificial' boundaries proved illusory, as all boundaries are in some sense contrived: later geographers, notably Richard *Hartshorne, elaborated typologies of boundaries. Political geographers have also examined the reasons for and effects of particular boundaries and borders being established. This was a topic of practical concern during the colonial and post-colonial periods, during which boundary disputes were rife (*see* BERLIN CONFERENCE). Study of the functional impact of boundaries on populations either side revealed their paradoxical nature: boundaries divide people but also unite them over common concerns such as the environment; borders repel activities but they also attract activities, for example, retailing outlets taking advantage of tax and price differentials. The key cases are the USA–Mexico boundary, and the internal and external borders of the *European Union. Finally, political geographers have taken issue with the proposition, generally attributed to Japanese author Kenichi Ohmae, that we live in a 'borderless world'. The idea that the cumulative impact of economic *globalization renders state boundaries as variously irrelevant or outmoded is challenged by detailed studies of the continued impact of borders on human activity, their *biopolitical function in differentiating flows of people according to their levels of wealth, power, and status, and their symbolic function in maintaining a sense of national identity.

In recent years borders and boundaries have become a chief concern of many other researchers outside political geography. It has been realized that 'bordering' and 'bounding' are practices that occur in all walks of social life. For instance, in his book *Geographies of Exclusion* David *Sibley explores the cultural and spatial confinement of Romany travellers in Western societies, while Nick Blomley (in several works) has examined how the law divides up urban space according to particular cultural values (for example, it is 'right' for individuals to own a home) and dichotomies (such as public versus private). Bordering and bounding are seen to be processes of physical and semantic inclusion/exclusion, with implications for individual and group *identity.

This broader field of inquiry into borders and boundaries is thus still very germane to the classic concerns of political geographers. These geographers are today not only interested in helping policy makers determine the 'right' boundaries and borders in any given dispute or reorganization of political space. They are often also concerned to raise critical questions about the inclusions and exclusions attending boundaries and borders. These questions remind us that the 'right' political divisions are very much dependent on which institutions and groups have the power to determine which criteria of inclusion and exclusion will apply in any given case. *See also* PAASI, ANSSI; POLITICAL GEOGRAPHY.

Further reading Jones, R. (2009), 'Categories, borders and boundaries', *Progress in Human Geography* 33: 174–89.

Newman, D. (2006), 'The lines that continue to separate us: borders in our "borderless" world', *Progress in Human Geography* 30: 143–61.

SEE WEB LINKS
- Nijmegen Centre for Border Research, Netherlands.
- International Boundaries Research Unit, University of Durham.

Boserup thesis An argument advanced by Danish economist Ester Boserup (1910–99), that population pressure drives change in agricultural practices, such that growing numbers of people do not lead to *Malthusian crises. In *The Conditions of Agricultural Growth* (1965) she surveyed different land-use systems across the developing world, and concluded that population and technological change were inter-related, not opposed. In the long run, the intensification of *agriculture and growing population fuelled economic development.

boundary A line indicating the limit of an area and/or separating one area from another. In human geography the term is often used synonymously with *border to refer to the lines separating nation states; it may also apply to other scales, such as fields, properties, municipalities, counties, and other administrative areas. Rarely are boundaries regarded as natural: most human geographers seek to explain how and why they are human creations imposed on a *landscape or area of water.

Bourdieu, Pierre (1930–2002) A French anthropologist, sociologist, and public *intellectual known for his theoretical and empirical research into *social reproduction, social inequality, education, and aesthetics. His early work in Kabylia, Algeria was influential in ideas of *structuration (in *Outline of a Theory of Practice* 1972/1977). In *Distinction* (1979/1984) he showed how class, power, and taste are closely implicated, suggesting that class struggles could take cultural forms (*see* HABITUS). In *Reproduction in Education, Society and Culture* (with J-C. Passeron, 1990) he argued that education systems tend to reproduce class inequality, contrary to those who saw education as the key to social mobility and *development. Bourdieu's proposition that there are various forms of capital—symbolic, *cultural, economic, social—and that they are, to some degree, interchangeable, has influenced much geographical work on migrants, *gentrification, and *consumption.

Further reading Bourdieu, P. (1999), *The Weight of the World: Social Suffering in Contemporary Society.*

Bowman, Isaiah (1878–1950) A Canadian-American political geographer who served as a central government advisor during the presidencies of Woodrow Wilson and Franklin Roosevelt. Bowman was educated at Harvard and Yale universities and authored *The *New World: Problems in Political Geography* (1921). He became president of the Johns Hopkins University and director of the *American Geographical Society.

Further reading Smith, N. (2004), *American Empire.*

Bracero Program A *guestworker programme administered by the United States between 1942 and 1964 that recruited Mexican manual labourers to work on railways and farms. It enabled the USA to fill labour shortages during the Second World War. Its effects included establishing a remittance trail back to Mexico, encouraging illegal immigration into the same sectors once quotas were met, cultivating a backlash from farming unions that felt the programme kept wages low and conditions poor, and transforming the communities of border towns.

brain drain/gain The departure of a country's high-skilled or well-trained individuals through *emigration, commonly understood as a transfer of human capital from developing to developed countries. 'Brain gain' refers to the widely recorded phenomenon of such individuals eventually returning to their country of origin, bringing new skills or capital with them; also known as 'brain circulation'.

branch plant economies Subnational or national economies characterized by a large number of branch plants. The latter are industrial facilities that belong to a larger, usually overseas firm. Many *transnational corporations create a functional and physical separation between their component units. Branch plants are where intermediate or final assembly of a firm's products occur. Their geographical location may be far distant from a firm's headquarters. Branch plant economies have been criticized for exploiting assembly-line workers and for leaving places vulnerable to 'capital flight' when branch plant owners decide to relocate their facilities. *See also* EXPORT PROCESSING ZONE; *MAQUILADORA.*

branding The process of attaching a name, design, symbol, or other feature to something a seller wishes to promote through repeated marketing. Branding is conventionally thought to involve the promotion of particular goods and services, but place branding also occurs, too. In addition, goods and services can be branded in geographical ways, as with drinks or food that are sold on the basis of where they are made or originate (such as Newcastle Brown Ale). *See also* PLACE MARKETING.

Brandt Commission A non-governmental body founded in 1977 to address issues of global inequality and development, chaired by Willy Brandt (1913–92), former German Chancellor. It produced two reports, *North-South: A Program for Survival* (1980) and *Common Crisis: North-South Cooperation for World Recovery* (1983), calling for greater recognition of the interdependence of rich and poor countries and advocating steps to reduce inequality, poverty, hunger, etc. It made famous the Brandt Line, a line on the world map dividing the rich north from the poor south, although this is now generally regarded as over-simplified. *See also* DEVELOPMENT.

Brazil A South American country that is the world's fifth largest by land area and population. Brazil was part of the so-called New World that Spanish and Portuguese explorers colonized from the 15th century onwards. It became independent of Portugal in 1822, though remains the only country in the Americas where Portuguese is the official language. For over a century its economy was largely based on agriculture. Today it is a major exporter of agricultural goods, such as soybeans and corned beef, but it also has a large manufacturing sector, again largely export-orientated. Brazil's economy is one of the world's largest and has enjoyed strong rates of economic growth since the mid-1990s, interrupted by the need for an *International Monetary Fund (IMF) loan. The country has attracted considerable *foreign direct investment (FDI) and is one of the so-called *BRIC countries. Its political system is democratic and, like that of the *United States of America, federal. Large parts of the *Amazon are found in Brazil.

Bretton Woods Agreement An agreement between 44 nations to establish a stable international financial system to govern and facilitate *trade and financial exchanges in the post-*Second World War era. The agreement was negotiated in July 1944 in Bretton Woods, New Hampshire, United States. It obliged each country to consult and agree on monetary policy that would affect other nations, to assist nations that had short-term exchange difficulties, and to alter their monetary policy so that its exchange rate was tied to a common gold standard. The agreement also established the *International Monetary Fund (IMF) and the International Bank for Reconstruction and Development (IBRD, part of the World Bank), and led to the *General Agreement of Tariffs and Trade (GATT). The Bretton Woods exchange rate mechanisms stayed in place until 1971. By then the agreement had had the effect of creating a stable, highly interconnected international financial system to underpin international trade and commerce.

BRIC An acronym for Brazil, Russia, India, and China, large countries with fast-growing economies that are predicted to rival the USA and other *G8 countries in global economic importance. It was coined in 2001 by Goldman Sachs analyst Jim O'Neill. More recently an S has been added to include South Africa (hence BRICS).

bricolage An entity that is built out of whatever materials happen to be available. Places, such as *shanty towns, might be described as bricolage; they are built out of a diverse set of materials and seem to lack order, appearing somewhat ramshackle. Similarly *postmodern architecture that draws together diverse styles, forms, and building materials, or *postmodern thought that draws on a diverse set of intellectual ideas and melds them together, constitutes a form of bricolage.

broken windows theory A theory developed by James Wilson and George Kelling, which argued that areas showing signs of criminal activity propagate further crime, leading to the area's eventual decline. The theory's name is derived from the observation that a building with a couple of broken windows that are not repaired in a timely fashion attracts vandals who will smash the other windows. This will escalate into breaking into the building and squatting, or undertaking other illegal behaviour such as taking drugs, or cause other damage. The proposed solution is to maintain a certain level of crime fighting and repair/maintenance to establish a social norm and discourage additional criminal activity. In many cities this has led to a policy of *zero-tolerance policing. *See also* CRIME.

brown agenda The recognition that many important environmental problems are associated with urban and industrial life, and with people's physical health. The so-called 'green agenda' has long fixated on reducing the human impact on the non-human world for several reasons: because that world provides us with irreplaceable resources; because that world is seen to have rights; and because changing that world can ultimately harm humanity. However, it tended—implicitly—to ignore the created ecosystems of towns and cities, even though these ecosystems are the immediate physical and experiential environment in which most people today live. The brown agenda was developed from the late 1980s, first in large cities in the so-called *Third World. It drew attention to the need to ensure good quality green spaces, eco-friendly buildings, good environmental health standards, and so on.

brownfield sites Land or buildings not currently in use, either vacant, abandoned, and/or contaminated. The term usually refers to former industrial sites in urban areas that may need cleaning up before they can be redeveloped. In the USA, the Environmental Protection Agency's 'Superfund' exists to help recover such sites. *Compare* GREENFIELD DEVELOPMENT.

Brundtland Report An intergovernmental report published in 1987 by the United Nations World Commission on Environment and Development, founded in 1983 and chaired by Gro Harlem Brundtland, former prime minister of Norway. Entitled *Our Common Future*, the report made two key claims: problems of environmental impact, resource depletion, and development were linked at the global scale; and the solution lay in *sustainable development, famously defined in the report as 'development that meets the needs of the present without compromising the ability of future generations to meet their own needs'. *See also* DEVELOPMENT.

(SEE WEB LINKS)
• Report of the World Commission on Environment and Development: Our Common Future.

Buchanan Report (*Traffic in Towns*) An influential inquiry into the development of the UK's road network written by Professor Sir Colin Buchanan and published in 1963. The context for the report was a rapidly growing number of cars, rising population, increasing congestion, planned shrinkage in the rail network, and declining use of public transport. The report recognized that the growth of car use in the absence of good planning would rapidly become counterproductive as congestion increased. At the same time, road building had to be sensitive to heritage, sense of place, safety, quality of life, and the environmental effects of the automobile. The report had a significant impact on urban and *spatial planning and how urban areas evolved subsequently, leading to urban clearways and flyovers, one-way systems, pedestrian shopping areas, multistorey carparks, and traffic and parking restrictions. Many of the ideas in the Buchanan Report have been translated into use in other countries.

buffer zone/state A piece of land that separates and thus acts as a barrier between two or more areas. The idea is to create a cushion or neutral space to keep entities apart. Such zones might include protective zones around hazardous waste facilities, containment zones along borders or around prisons, demilitarized zones between warring factions, and green belts between urban developments. A particular kind of buffer zone, a buffer state is a nation state that sits between two rival states, such as Poland between Germany and Russia prior to the *Second World War. Such states often take on strategic importance and are vulnerable to occupation or being subsumed by neighbouring states.

built environment A physical environment designed, built, and maintained by people, and typically made from brick, stone, metals, plastics, and glass. The built environment is different from the *natural environment, even where the latter is partly *anthropogenic (as with *genetically modified foods). For many years the two environments were seen as almost the antithesis of each other. However, all built environments are necessarily connected with the wider natural environment, sometimes in complementary, sometimes in contradictory ways. Recently, the desire to create 'green buildings' means that built environments are contributing towards a reduction in humanity's *ecological footprint.

Bunge, William (1928–) An American geographer who helped pioneer the *spatial science approach but then went on to reject it in favour of *radical geography. Bunge authored the influential book *Theoretical Geography* (1962), which was a manifesto for geography's post-1945 *Quantitative Revolution. By 1968, however, he argued for a more political form of scholarship devoted to bettering the lives of the poor and disadvantaged. His Detroit (1968) and Toronto (1973) geographical expeditions were designed to dispel the ignorance (as he and co-expeditionists saw it) that most North Americans had about poor inner-city neighbourhoods (*see* DETROIT GEOGRAPHICAL EXPEDITION AND INSTITUTE).

Business Improvement District (BID) An area of a city in which the businesses pay a tax, fee, or levy in order to finance the area's maintenance, improvements, and/or promotion. Although known by different names in different cities, BIDs are usually public–private partnerships designed to make downtown commercial districts more attractive to customers. BIDs can be characterized as a form of *neoliberal governance and have been criticized for compromising urban *public space in pursuit of profit.

Butler, Judith (1956–) An American feminist philosopher known internationally for her attempt to retheorize *gender and *sexuality. Her book *Gender Trouble* (1990) argued (contrary to many feminists) that female identities (like all identities) are socially constituted by what she called 'regulatory discourses'. Identities get routinely acted out ('performed) and thereby naturalize their own arbitrariness. In *Bodies That Matter* (1993) Butler extended this anti-essentialist argument (*see* ESSENTIALISM) to argue that even sex (which appears to be a biological given) is, in fact, constructed through regulatory discourses. Gender identities and roles are thus not, Butler argued, overlaid onto a substratum of pre-existing, natural sex differences. Geographers interested in how people's identities are constructed and performed in specific places, sites, and cultures have drawn heavily on Butler's thinking. *See also* BODY; FOUCAULT, MICHEL; POST-STRUCTURALISM.

Buttimer, Anne (1936–) An Irish geographer who helped to pioneer the humanistic approach to research in her discipline (*see* HUMANISTIC GEOGRAPHY). Buttimer criticized *spatial science for its tendency to assume that humans could be studied like rocks or soil profiles (*see* OBJECTIVITY). She argued for research methods that could help understand people's highly personal '*lifeworld'. Her book *Geography and the Human Spirit* (1993) was an exploration of what she saw as the essence of human existence on the Earth, namely the search for meaning and attachment. *See also* VALUES.

cadastral mapping The mapping of the ownership, administration, and boundaries between land parcels. Cadastral maps are legal documents that set out in precise terms the bounds of land ownership, usually accompanied by other information such as land use, tenure, and taxation value, and the extent of administrative responsibility.

Canada The world's second largest country by land area. It shares a continuous political border with the USA to the south and west (Alaska), and stretches from the Atlantic Ocean (to the east) to the Pacific Ocean (to the west). To the north is the Arctic Ocean and Alaska (one of America's non-contiguous states). A former British colony, it merged with the French colony of Quebec and achieved confederation in 1867, notwithstanding some vestigial ties to Britain as a member of the Commonwealth. It is a wealthy country that has long exported primary commodities such as timber, but which also has a large manufacturing sector (e.g. automobile production). Canada is a federal democracy, with a national government based in Ottawa (the capital city) and each of its ten provinces and three territories governed by elected executives. Quebec separatists have, at times agitated for *secession, while *First Nations Canadians have been struggling to have their historic rights to land, resources, and cultural artefacts recognized.

capabilities approach A perspective on economic development that emphasizes individuals' freedom to live the life that they choose according to their values. Whereas conventional economics is centred on ideas of utility, resources, and income, the capabilities (or capability) approach addresses the obstacles to realizing 'substantive freedoms' such as the ability to participate in politics and other non-economic functionings. It identifies several different but related 'capabilities' that humans possess which, when realized, can produce fulfilment. If people have little or no opportunity to realize their capabilities then, according to Amartya *Sen, they lack freedom and independence. The capabilities approach is *normative because, in a world where poverty and inequality are writ large, it can be used to criticize the current socio-spatial maldistribution of those things necessary for all people to be truly 'capable'. The approach is closely associated with both Sen and philosopher Martha Nussbaum, and informs the *Human Development Index. *See also* UTILITARIANISM

Reference Sen, A. (1999), *Development as Freedom*.

cap and trade An *environmental policy, usually designed to reduce pollution, in which the level of permitted emissions is capped and a market in emissions created up to or above the cap. The European Emissions Trading Scheme is currently the world's largest cap-and-trade scheme. Large atmospheric polluters (such as power stations) must purchase 'emissions credits' from other polluters who do not exceed the emissions cap. They can also purchase 'compensation credits' as a way of off-setting their emissions. *See also* CARBON OFF-SETTING; CARBON TRADING; ECOLOGICAL MODERNIZATION; EMISSIONS TRADING.

capital 1. A city that is the seat of national government (*capital city).

2. In mainstream economics and business studies a stock of liquid (monetary) and illiquid assets existing at the level of individual firms or groups of firms and investors.

3. In Marxist geography and Marxist thinking more widely, a crisis-prone process specific to *capitalism in which one set of commodities (such as machines, factories, and workers) are put to work in order to create others with the overriding aim of making more money at the end than was spent at the beginning.

4. In social science a term describing the different assets that individuals, families, and communities can develop and deploy to enhance their lives or distinguish themselves from others (*see* BOURDIEU, PIERRE; CAPABILITIES APPROACH; HABITUS; SOCIAL CAPITAL).

capital city A city that is home to the government of a country. While some capital cities are the largest in a country in terms of population size (such as London in the UK), many are not (for example, Brasilia in Brazil).

capitalism An economic system in which commodity producers compete for market share in a quest to make profits, which are then reinvested in order to make yet more profitable commodities. Capitalism is the world's dominant economic system but was virtually non-existent three hundred years ago. The 19th-century political economist Karl *Marx famously argued that capitalism was an unjust and crisis-prone system of commodity production, distribution, sale, and consumption. It was unjust, he argued, because the ultimate source of the profits pocketed by the owners and shareholders of capitalist firms is the work performed by those firms' employees. Furthermore, Marx maintained that the system was crisis-prone because growth periods produce excess profits (what he called surplus value) that exceed available opportunities for productive investment. During an economic crisis, jobs are lost, wages are frozen (or cut), firms go bankrupt, money lenders become more risk-averse, and so the capitalist economy shrinks until opportunities open up for a new round of investment in existing or new sites of capital *accumulation. Marx argued that because inter-firm competition, the compulsion to innovate, and the quest for profits were part of capitalism's *raison d'être* it was destined to repeat boom-and-bust cycles in perpetuity. Similarly, he argued that working-class people in all parts of the *labour market—even those who are relatively well paid—can never, in a capitalist system, enjoy true freedom. For Marx the formal freedom of the wage relation—wherein a worker volunteers to work for a certain period for a certain sum of money—conceals an endemic inequity because workers as a whole are exploited by capitalists. In contrast to this critical interpretation of capitalism, mainstream economists tend to take as givens what Marx identified as problems. They seek to improve the way capitalism operates in order to better realize certain goals, such as economic efficiency, better working conditions for employees, less extreme economic crises, and so on. While some of these economists utilize highly abstract models and theories, often assisted by computers and mathematics, others focus on real events, past and present. From the mid-1970s mainstream economic thinking eclipsed more critical thinking about capitalism in many parts of the world. This is especially true in countries that embraced *neoliberalism as an approach to economic, social, and environmental affairs. Some were forced to do so as part of policies of *structural adjustment imposed by the *International Monetary Fund (IMF). However, since the late 1990s critical interpretations of capitalism have resurfaced in academia and the public sphere, notably those indebted to Marx and his acolytes and, more recently, to Karl *Polanyi and John Maynard Keynes (*see* KEYNESIAN). These interpretations have been revived in two phases. The first was as part of the worldwide *anti-capitalist movement that began life in Seattle during the 1999 meeting of the *World Trade Organization. The second was as part of the diagnosis of the global financial crisis of 2007–2009 when even mainstream economists were forced to ask how such a calamity had occurred without many people predicting it.

From the early 1970s, Marxist geographers sought to understand how capitalism was created and affected by the geography of production, transportation, telecommunication, selling, and consumption (*see* MARXIST GEOGRAPHY). They looked, too, at struggles between capitalists and workers in different places and countries as part of what later became the subfield of *labour geography. Meanwhile, more mainstream economic geographers took a less critical perspective. They inquired into the locational require- ments of firms, into the geography of government industrial policy, into the spatial effects of new international trade agreements, and so on. Where this research was *normative it rarely, if ever, extended to calls for revolution and the end of capitalism sounded by David *Harvey, among others.

Ironically, because Marxist geography and other critical currents of geographical political economy are less prominent than a generation ago, human geography is less well placed than it could be to contribute to the critique of capitalism post-Seattle and post the 2007–2009 global financial crisis. David Harvey, though, has been at pains to use Marxist theory to make sense of current affairs, most recently in *The Enigma of Capital* (2010). Relatedly, several human geographers have drawn on Polanyi's writings to criticize *neoliberalism.

carbon footprint The amount of carbon dioxide and other greenhouse gases that are discharged into the atmosphere as a result of economic activities of all kinds. Because contemporary forms of commodity production, distribution, sale, consumption, and disposal are so dependent on the utilization of fossil fuels (*see* PETROCAPITALISM), all people leave a carbon footprint of some sort. *Carbon off-setting is one attempt to reduce that footprint, along with myriad of other environmental policies geared towards *sus- tainable development.

carbon off-setting An *environmental policy where emitters of carbon dioxide and other greenhouse gases pay others to invest in compensatory schemes (such as reforestation projects) that will remove greenhouse gases from the atmosphere. Carbon off-setting is part of *cap-and-trade schemes, but can also be undertaken voluntarily by organizations and individuals. It requires careful regulation, especially of the com- pensatory schemes designed to 'lock up' greenhouse gases for the long term.

carbon tax An obligatory monetary payment imposed by governments that is designed to reduce the *carbon footprint of commodity producers or consumers. A carbon tax, despite its name, can cover greenhouse gases other than CO_2. It is an example of so-called 'command-and-control *environmental policy.

carbon trading An *environmental policy in which atmospheric polluters pay for their emissions by purchasing 'emissions credits' from other polluters. Carbon trading is made possible by pollution caps set by governments and enforced by regulatory authorities (*see* CAP AND TRADE; EMISSIONS TRADING). Though it normally involves polluting firms, carbon trading can also involve individuals who wish to pay for any 'excess pollution' attaching to their consumption or travel activities. The principle of carbon trading is that anthropogenic global warming is the outcome of market failure, i.e., not pricing the negative *externalities of greenhouse gas emissions adequately (*see* STERN REVIEW). The solution is to create 'carbon markets'. These were initially developed within the *Kyoto Protocol, which recognized two systems: cap and trade and a credit or offset market in which actors can undertake activities to reduce greenhouse gas emis- sions from an agreed baseline and then sell the credits or offsets to consumers wishing to reduce their emissions. But attempts to create a single, global centralized market have given way to a proliferation of regional, inter-urban, and private initiatives. The actual creation of a market is difficult because it requires the establishment of agreed systems for measuring, verifying, and tracking credits, and monitoring the actors claiming to reduce their emissions.

Further reading Bumpus, A. G. and Liverman, D. M. (2008), 'Accumulation by decarbonization and the governance of carbon offsets'. *Economic Geography* 84(2): 127–56.
Hoffman, M. J. (2011), *Climate Governance at the Crossroads*.

care The act of looking after dependents such as children or people with health conditions to ensure their well-being. Care can be delivered individually or through a diverse range of health and social supports. The types of care provided can include feeding, bathing, toileting, dressing, communicating, social interaction, and transporting. These practices can be delivered in an individual's home, school, workplace, or an institutional setting such as hospital, mental health facility, and nursing home. Home care is usually practised by family members, usually female, often supported by professional services. Institutional care is provided by a team of dedicated health and social care professionals. The provision of care is inherently geographical because it is organized spatially (locally, nationally, and globally) and it recasts domains such as the home in new ways. Over the past few decades there has been a massive reorganization of health care systems in most Western countries, with large-scale deinstitutionalization and the rise of care-giving in the community. Care can vary geographically with respect to the health care policies and funding priorities of local and national organizations and governments. What this means is that two individuals with the same condition living near to each other but in different administrative areas can receive quite different services, an effect sometimes dubbed 'the postcode lottery'. Geographers have reflected on the question 'how far should we care?' as part of their wider argument that all morality has a geography (as evidenced by the maxim 'nearest is dearest'). *See also* HEALTH GEOGRAPHY; HEALTH INEQUALITY; MENTAL HEALTH.

Further reading Milligan, C. (2001), *Geographies of Care*.

Caribbean A region comprised of a crescent-shaped group of islands more than 3000 km long separating the Gulf of Mexico and the Caribbean Sea to the west and south, and from the Atlantic Ocean to the east and north. The original *indigenous peoples who inhabited the region were displaced by various European immigrants during successive waves of empire-building from the 16th century (involving Spain, Portugal, France, Holland, Denmark, and Britain). Many Caribbean islands were made into plantation colonies, exporting sugar (among other agricultural commodities) to Europe. Most contemporary Caribbeans are descended from slaves imported by colonists from West Africa. With few exceptions, Caribbean countries are economically dependent on tourism and agriculture.

Caribbean Community (CARICOM) A supra-national political organization founded in 1973 that represents the political, economic, and social interests of fifteen Caribbean countries. As well as forming a common economic market, CARICOM seeks to promote better living standards amongst members, develop economic activity and trade, and coordinate foreign policy.

(())) SEE WEB LINKS
• Official website of the Caribbean Community.

carnival A festive season of masked, costumed, and public parades that take place before Lent, typically in Roman Catholic societies. Carnival is a social expression that often subverts and parodies the conventions of society. Such subversion, parody, and satire, when applied to other realms of everyday life such as literature, is sometimes called 'carnivalesque', wherein the world is turned on its head and seen in a fresh, humorous way thus exposing and mocking the flawed practices and decrees of officialdom.

carrying capacity The maximum number of individual organisms that can be supported by the resources of an area. Although in population-resource debates it is often taken to mean the number of people that can be supported by the land they live on, it has recently been applied to a planetary scale. The Worldwide Fund for Nature (WWF) suggests that humanity would need three Earths to sustain the whole world's population at current Western levels of resource consumption. The carrying capacity idea has been criticized because of its neo-*Malthusian overtones and reliance on the idea that *nature places fixed limits on economic growth.

cartel A consortium of companies, political parties, or countries that collude to form an alliance to limit competition or to fix an outcome within an industry or market. Industrial cartels work to create market monopolies by restricting competition, fixing prices, restricting supply, and carving up market territories between cartel members. In so doing, they stifle competition and force other companies out of business. Cartels thus distort normal market conditions and are generally understood as unfair trading and commercial law seeks to restrict their formation.

Cartesianism A world view associated with the 17th-century French polymath René Descartes. In his philosophical writing Descartes made a number of distinctions that came to be seen as ontological. These include mind–body, reason–sensation, subject–object, subjective–objective, and human–animal. In geography, Cartesian thinking permeated the discipline despite its holistic intellectual ambitions when founded as a Western university subject (*see* CHOROLOGY). However, more relational thinkers such as David *Harvey and Doreen *Massey challenged the geographical dualisms, for example, local–global and place–space, which have since been rethought through metaphors such as *networks and neologisms such as 'glocalization'. *Non-representational theories, including *affect, also frequently seek to reconnect the mind and the body. *See also* LINEAR PERSPECTIVE.

cartogram A type of map in which the size of the areal units is scaled to a thematic variable such as population or economic output. Such a scaling leads to a distortion in the shape and size of each unit. It is a particularly effective technique for illustrating the uneven distribution of phenomena across land parcels. (See Fig. 1.)

cartography 1. The practice of making *maps.

2. The study of the ontological and epistemological bases of maps and the history of map making and use. People have been producing and using maps for thousands of years. Some academics have even argued that mapping processes are culturally universal, an innate human activity evident across all societies (e.g., Blaut, et al. 2003), although the resulting cartographic representations are very diverse. It was only in the *Renaissance, however, that cartography as a codified form of knowledge emerged. Prior to this, knowledge of the geographical world was parochial and documented from multiple perspectives to no formal, universal standards. Areas that were unknown were literally off the map, filled with religious cosmology and figures of myth and imagination. Maps were understood more as reminders or as spatial stories, than as scientific representations of the world based on surveyed data. Replacing the piecemeal frameworks of medieval cartography was the adoption of a single universal system of measuring and representing the world that utilized *linear perspectivism and *Cartesian rationality, underpinned by notions of *objectivity, functionality, and ordering. The resulting transformation in cartographic thinking made the world knowable, navigable, and claimable

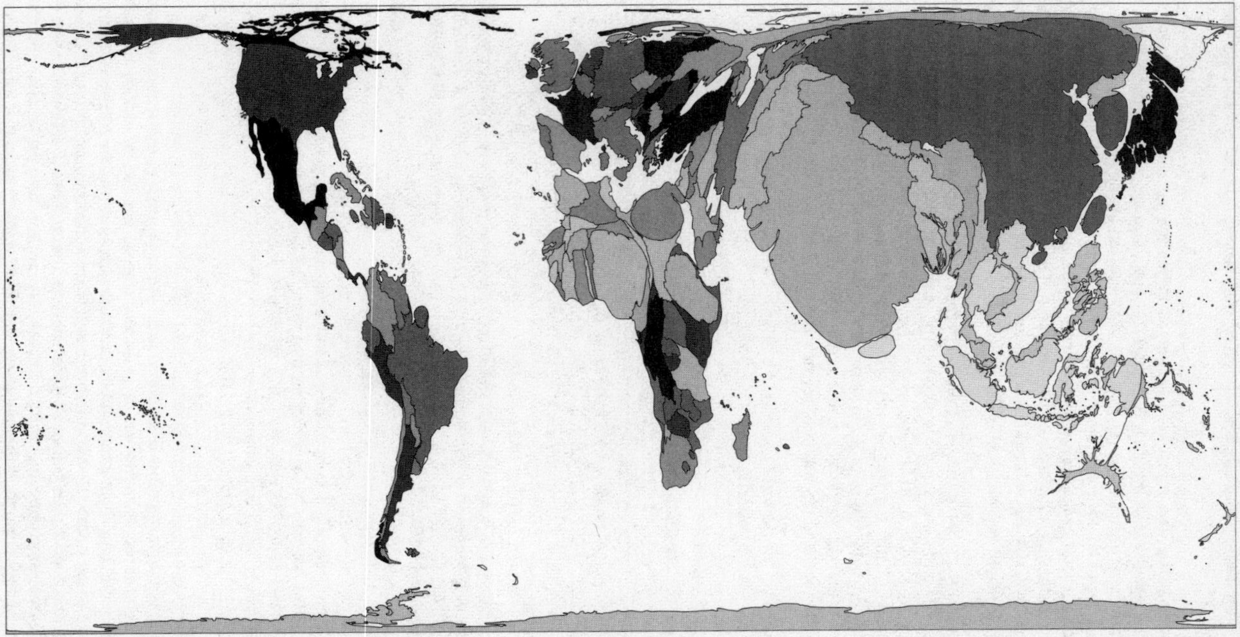

Fig. 1 A cartogram of world population (source: Worldmapper.org)

through a shared framework of scientific endeavour that was translatable across peoples and places. In the centuries that followed, the science of cartography was refined through improvements in surveying and mapping techniques, and the development of a set of established principles of design and aesthetics.

In the late 20th century two important drivers reshaped and energized both professional cartography (the production of maps) and academic cartography (how to think about maps): technological and conceptual advances. In relation to technology, there have been significant advances in terms of data capture (satellite imagery, photogrammatry, GPS, laser ranging tools, etc.), the handling and processing of data (e.g., CAD, *Geographical Information System [GIS], and desktop publishing applications), and the efficient storage and rapid distribution of vast quantities of mapping data (database software, hard drives, servers, data networks, the *Internet, etc.) and the delivery, presentation, and interactive uses of maps (high-resolution display screens, laser printing, multimedia documents, streaming 'live' to location-aware mobile devices). Data are increasingly accurate, dynamic, and accessible, and their collection is no longer the preserve of national mapping agencies or commercial companies but is also *crowdsourced. Software such as GIS has ever more functionality and tools such as Google Earth makes cartographic data and tools available to everyone.

Conceptually, there has been a vibrant debate about how to think about maps ontologically and epistemologically. Initially, this consisted of an engagement with mathematics and psychology in order to develop formalized, scientific rules and principles of map design. Arthur Robinson (1952), for example, sought to advance a communications model approach that cast cartography as a science of communication (as opposed to simply representation). In contrast, French academics such as Jacques Bertin (1967), advocated semiology—the study of signs and symbols—for map design, arguing that maps were complex sign systems. A different challenge to cartographic theory emerged at the end of the 1980s, with Brian *Harley contending that far from presenting the truth of the world, maps were social constructions presenting subjective versions of reality. Maps, he argued, are the product of power and they exert power. Cartography as a science of communication, sign systems, or social constructions are still rooted, however, in representational ways of thinking. Since the early 2000s, a small number of cartographic theorists such as Kitchin and Dodge (2007) have started to rethink maps from a post-representational perspective. Rather than focusing on what maps represent and mean, the post-representational approach focuses more on how maps work and their effects on the world. It casts cartography as a processual science, focusing on the practices of making and using maps.

References and further reading Bertin, J. (1967), *Sémiologie Graphique*.
Blaut, J. M., Stea, D., Spencer, C., and Blades, M. (2003), 'Mapping as a cultural and cognitive universal', *Annals of the Association of American Geographer* 93(1): 165–85.
Crampton, J. (2010), *Mapping: A Critical Introduction to Cartography and GIS*.
Dodge, M., Kitchin, R., and Perkins, C. (eds.) (2011), *The Map Reader*.
Harley, J. B. (1989), 'Deconstructing the map', *Cartographica* 26(2): 1–20.
Kitchin, R. and Dodge, M. (2007), 'Rethinking maps', *Progress in Human Geography* 31(3): 331–44.
Robinson, A. H. (1952), *The Look of Maps*.

case study The investigation of a specific site, community, or event as a means of understanding a wider issue, process or trend. By focusing on a particular case it can be studied in depth. Often, several interacting processes, institutions, or people are studied rather than just one or two. In general a range of different methods of data generation and analysis are used to build up a detailed understanding. Five different types of case study are used in geography: descriptive (an overview of the key elements); exploratory (to gather and analyse foundational data); explanatory (seeking causal relationships and model building); collective (focusing on a set of interrelated cases, perhaps compara-tively); and intrinsic (where the researcher is an insider in the case: *see* PARTICIPANT OBSERVATION). *See also* INTENSIVE RESEARCH.

cash crop Vegetative matter grown for sale to others rather than for consumption by a farmer and his or her family. Though it covers food and non-food crops, the term originally arose in discussions of how peasant farmers supplemented their household income by selling a portion of their produce locally. In turn, the money earned could be used to purchase food, goods, and services that the farmers were not able to produce themselves.

Castells, Manuel (1942–) A Catalan and Spanish sociologist known for his contri-butions to urban theory and *social theory. Castells' early research was influenced by *Marxism. His book *The *Urban Question* (1972/1977) suggested that in modern capital-ist societies, class conflict in the workplace had to some extent been displaced by new conflicts over 'collective consumption' goods such as public housing. Castells argued that urban *social movements were legitimate political actors on the political Left just as much as trades unions were. His later trilogy of books known as *The Information Age: Economy, Society and Culture* (published 1996–98) presented an overarching theory of modern life. It placed particular emphasis on the role of *information and communica-tion technologies (ICT) in facilitating the exercise of *power over space and through time, but also *resistance to that power. Castells argues that the Marxist emphasis on capital-ism and class inequality is no longer sufficient to make sense of an increasingly complex world. Castells' career is a highly international one; he holds posts at the Open University of Catalonia and the Annenberg School of Communication, University of Southern California, Los Angeles.

casualization *See* FLEXIBLE LABOUR.

categorical data analysis A suite of techniques for analysing nominal and ordinal data. Nominal data have unordered scales, for example, names. Ordinal data are orga-nized in an order, for example, by rank. Such data are referred to as categorical, as opposed to data that are continuous in nature, such as age. Statistical analysis of nominal and ordinal data is undertaken using *non-parametric tests. *See also* CHI-SQUARE TEST; LOG-LINEAR MODELLING.

causation The process whereby something changes or occurs through human action, natural events, or a combination of the two. The study of causation is virtually synony-mous with the ability to offer explanations as well as descriptions of the world. Under-standing what causes things to occur can also help with *forecasting and prediction. Because only effects are visible, rather than the decisions or processes causing the effects, most investigations of causation rely on some combination of inference, deduction, and educated guess work on the part of an investigator. For those who argue that geography's proper role is synthesis, understanding causation (and achieving faithful description) is very difficult. Even a small-scale phenomenon, such as a single household, can be seen as an open system in which a multitude of events occur and corelate. Conceptual *abstraction, hypothesis formation, and data gathering (permitting testing) are necessary. Since 1945 many human geographers have favoured the *analysis of a single phenom-enon in a single location in order to make description and explanation more tractable endeavours. However, global climate change and its likely effects are leading many geographers to grapple with complex, coupled human–environment *systems in which causation is multifactoral, dynamic, and often non-linear. *See also* CRITICAL REALISM; EXTENSIVE RESEARCH; INTENSIVE RESEARCH.

CCTV *See* SURVEILLANCE.

cellular automata A particular kind of *agent-based model that works on a two-dimensional lattice grid, where the state of any cell is related to that of its neighbours. In human geography they are often used to simulate and model land change and urban growth.

census A comprehensive survey of an area and its population, usually conducted at regular time intervals. Many nations conduct a census every five or ten years in order to track changes in the population, its demographic characteristics, and social and economic status. It is particularly useful because it is universal and periodic, that is every person is covered and the data are collected regularly. The data provide a state-of-the-nation overview and allows for the evidence-informed planning of state services. *See also* CENSUS GEOGRAPHY.

census geography The spatial organization of conducting a *census and the geographical analysis and *thematic mapping of census data. Census data provide a rich source of spatially referenced data on a nation's population. In order to generate and make sense of the data, the census is organized with respect to a census geography consisting of enumerator areas or census tracts. These are tightly defined, bounded areas, which can be aggregated to provide analysis at different scales and across different kinds of administrative boundaries. By undertaking spatial and longitudinal analysis of the data it is possible to identify spatial and temporal patterns. Because the data are universal and outputted into defined, bounded areas, they provide ideal inputs into spatial models concerning population demographics, housing, migration, transportation, social deprivation, health, and economy. As a result, the geographical analysis of census forms an important input into policy development and planning across sectors and scales of government.

Further reading Rees, P., Martin, D., and Williamson, P. (eds.) (2002), *The Census Data System*.

Central Asia A region within Asia centred on the vast expanse of semi-arid grassland (steppe) and desert stretching between the Caspian Sea in the west and China in the east. Various authorities have defined its boundaries differently, although all regard it as land-locked, i.e. without direct access to the world's oceans. Central Asia is now usually identified with the five former republics of the *USSR: Kazakhstan, Uzbekistan, Tajikistan, Kyrgyzstan and Turkmenistan. Its central location, abutting Russia, China and Afghanistan among other countries, is associated with *geopolitical significance (*see* HEARTLAND).

Central Business District (CBD) The commercial centre of a city. The CBD is a geographically concentrated set of retailers, wholesalers, banks, business services, insurers, legal firms, and other commercial organizations. The precise balance between and spatial arrangement of these commercial activities varies and has been the subject of sustained research by urban geographers. The CBD is abutted by the *inner city.

Central Place Theory A *theory designed to describe and explain the number, size, and relative location of settlements. The theory was first proposed by Walter *Christaller in 1933. Working from first principles, and focusing on commodity producers and consumers, Christaller argued that settlement systems displayed a hierarchical and ordered geography. This geography, he maintained, was the product of rational decision-making by firms (sellers) and their customers (buyers): together they ensured that over time the right number, size, and location of settlements arose. Christaller's theory was one of the inspirations for the embrace of a *spatial science approach in Anglophone geography after 1950.

centre of calculation A site where the accumulation, synthesis, and analysis of observations may generate greater understanding. The concept derives from Bruno *Latour's *sociology of science, in which he stresses the importance of material forms—notebooks, specimens, diagrams—being assembled together. Centres are also sites where new standards and techniques are devised, which can then be further circulated. Felix Driver uses the term with reference to the *Royal Geographical Society in *Geography Militant* (2001). *See also* ACTOR-NETWORK THEORY.

certification schemes Sets of standards and criteria according to which something is judged in order to ensure its quality. Certification schemes have risen to prominence in recent years as part of attempts to reduce humanity's *ecological footprint. Many producers and retailers voluntarily abide by certification schemes in order to ensure greater environmental and/or social responsibility in the *commodity chains in which they participate. These schemes exist for the forestry, poultry, fishing, and other industries worldwide.

chain migration The process by which the migration of one individual to a new place of settlement leads to the migration of others to the same locale via family or *social networks. It is often a characteristic of migration from rural and agrarian regions to cities, and can lead to persons from the same village or district living in the same urban neighbourhood.

chaos, catastrophe, and complexity theory Three sometimes connected, sometimes discrete bodies of theory that highlight the non-linear and often unpredictable behaviour of environmental or social systems. Chaos theory's roots are in mathematics, where it was shown that certain systems are sensitive to small changes, leading to large effects that can change system behaviour. It has filiations with catastrophe theory, which was developed by French mathematician René Thom in the 1970s. Thom showed that systems can cross 'thresholds' that produce qualitative not merely quantitative change. Both theories are interested in sharp discontinuities in system behaviour and the causes of the move to a new phase of system operation. They are often now considered to be part of a wider body of complexity theory. Complexity theory is interested in environmental and/or social phenomena that contain a myriad of relations. It seeks to understand linear and non-linear feedbacks (positive and negative), scale-specific behaviour, inter-scalar links (temporal and spatial), part–whole connections, emergent properties and 'self-organizing' changes. Complexity theory has a strong mathematical base, and now features strongly in the design and application of a range of *models (including computational ones) used in the natural sciences.

Given their strong interest in what are called 'open systems', human geographers might be expected to have applied and developed ideas from chaos, catastrophe, and complexity theory. However, these theories have been used sparingly and selectively. For example, Mike *Batty has utilized them to represent the structure of cities, which are eminently complex entities. But aside from Batty and a few other economic, urban, and regional geographers, the theories have functioned more as metaphors than as formal descriptions of system behaviour. This may reflect the analytical and computational difficulties of representing even approximately the full set of relations and relata in any complex socio-spatial system.

Reference Batty, M. (2005), *Cities and Complexity*.

Chernobyl The site of the world's worst nuclear accident to date, caused by a series of explosions in April 1986. Located in northern Ukraine, the radioactive contamination of the atmosphere by the explosions spread across much of the eastern part of the former *Soviet Union and Europe. Some 350,000 people from Belarus, Ukraine, and Russia were evacuated and since the accident the city of Pripyat has remained abandoned. *See also* DISASTER; NUCLEAR POWER.

Chicago The USA's third most populous city, located on Lake Michigan in the state of Illinois. In the late 19th century Chicago became iconic of American industrialization in the way that Manchester had been emblematic of British industrialization half a century earlier. Initially Chicago was a centre for exchanging, distributing, and processing agricultural produce from the city's huge rural *hinterland. Later it developed a manufacturing base and became a major centre for banking and financial services.

Chicago School 1. A group of sociologists based at the University of Chicago who pioneered the systematic study of the *social ecology of large Western cities. By combining theory with ethnographic *fieldwork, the Chicago School showed cities such as Chicago to be a set of distinct, juxtaposed communities. The ecological metaphor was borrowed from biologists studying ecosystems. These ideas were strongly influential in *urban and *social geography. The Chicago School view of urban communities was later criticized for marginalizing issues of power and inequality (political and economic) that were said to determine people's residential 'choices'.
2. A group of economists at the University of Chicago best known for advocating neoclassical economics and often credited with advancing the ideas of *neoliberalism in contradiction to Keynesian approaches. The school was first recognized in the 1950s and has since produced a very large number of Nobel Prize winning economists, including Milton Friedman.

children's geographies A subdiscipline of human geography concerned with research on, with, and for children. It emerged in the 1990s from the recognition that children were systematically overlooked in geographical study, coinciding with the UN Convention on the Rights of the Child and a general move towards greater rights for children. There were, however, pioneering works by geographers, including William *Bunge's studies of the risk faced by children in Detroit and Toronto, and Jim *Blaut's work on mental mapping and child psychology. Others, including Hugh Matthews and Roger Hart, mapped children's use of space in homes and urban neighbourhoods.
The field is characterized by a number of common themes. Firstly, childhood is regarded as not simply a biological stage, but equally a cultural, legal, and social construction. The meanings and experiences of childhood differ considerably from place to place, particularly between the Global North and Global South. Cindi *Katz's comparative study of children's play in Sudan and New York, published in *Growing Up Global* (2004), was an important contribution to the subject. Secondly, childhood is understood in relation to 'race', class, gender, and other forms of social difference. Thirdly, children are regarded as social actors in their own right, not simply as adults-in-waiting, but as agents capable of transforming their worlds.
Children's geographies embrace a wide range of subject matter, including poverty, development, child labour, globalization, migration, urban and rural livelihoods, and cultural life. There is an understandable focus on the home as a site of experience and personal development, but also the school, neighbourhood, field, street, park, and playground (Hörschelmann and van Blerk 2012). Geographers have also focused on cyberspace which, much like the urban environment, has become a focus for parental fears over safety (Valentine and Holloway 2001). The field is also notable for

its methodological innovativeness, including play, mapping, and *autophotography, although researchers have to be especially mindful of the ethics of researching on and with minors. *See also* YOUTH.

References Hörschelmann, K. and van Blerk, L. (2012), *Children, Youth and the City*.

Valentine, G. and Holloway, S. (2001), 'Online dangers?: geographies of parents' fears for children's safety in cyberspace', *Professional Geographer* 53: 71–83.

China The second largest country in the world by area and the most populous, with an estimated 1.3 billion inhabitants. It is nominally communist and has been ruled by the same political party for decades (*see* COMMUNISM). However, its economy and society have become ever more capitalist since the mid-1970s. This means that greater market freedoms (in the realms of commodity production and consumption) have become available even as democracy remains stymied by the Chinese Communist Party (CCP). China is one of the world's leading manufacturing economies, though it also produces significant volumes of agricultural produce (most of it for domestic consumption). China's prodigious rates of economic growth have allowed it to run huge trade and budget surpluses, to invest heavily in infrastructure, and to pay better wages to many of its workers. However, restrictions on free speech along with low wages and difficult working conditions for many have led to several domestic protests in recent years. It is a member of the *WTO. Despite being ruled by the CCP since 1949, China was not as active on the world stage in the *Cold War as its communist neighbour, the *Soviet Union.

Chipko Movement An Indian socio-ecological movement to protect local livelihoods and associated traditional rights from commercial forestry; also known as Chipko Ando-lan. Although there are many precedents in history, the modern movement was triggered in 1974 when peasant women in a village in (then) Uttar Pradesh in India's Himalayas, embraced trees to stop them being logged. It spread across India and achieved clear-felling bans throughout the country. Commentators around the world have interpreted the movement in many different ways; as an expression of *environmentalism, *ecofem-inism, land rights, peasant resistance, *subaltern politics, and non-violent protest.

Further reading Guha, R. (2nd ed. 2000), *The Unquiet Woods: Ecological Change and Peasant Resistance in the Himalayas*.

chi-square test A *non-parametric test for establishing whether there is a significant difference in the distribution of two or more nominal *variables. The test compares observed frequencies of data with the expected frequencies if chance was the only factor operating. *See also* CATEGORICAL DATA ANALYSIS.

choice modelling A method of analysis for *modelling and predicting the way people make spatial choices and decisions amongst discrete alternatives. Data are generated by asking people about their stated preferences in particular scenarios. Choice modelling works on the premise that people are rational actors who have the opportunity to make decisions, have the ability to trade-off considerations, and will seek to maximize utility when doing so (in terms of distance, price, time, etc.) (*see* RATIONAL CHOICE THEORY). Choice models, if finely calibrated, are used to predict how people will react to a given situation.

chorology The study of how and why there are variations from place to place on the earth's surface (*see* AREAL DIFFERENTIATION). Originating from Greek geographers such as Strabo and Ptolemy, the concept was well understood by European *Renaissance scholars who distinguished between cosmography, geography, and chorography. Cosmography is the study of the earth-centred universe; geography, the study of the larger-scale patterns of land, sea, and climate; and chorography is the study of parts of the earth's surface. In the late 19th century, German geographers debated this further. Ferdinand von Richtofen identified the subject with chorology, the *method* of studying parts or regions as a path to formulating hypotheses and finding causal interrelations, while Otto Schlüter sought a definite *object* of study, the landscape (*see* LANDSCHAFT). These debates were brought into US geography in the 1940–50s by Richard *Hartshorne who defined it as a chorological subject, distinct from chronological subjects (such as history and geology), and systematic subjects (such as physics and economics).

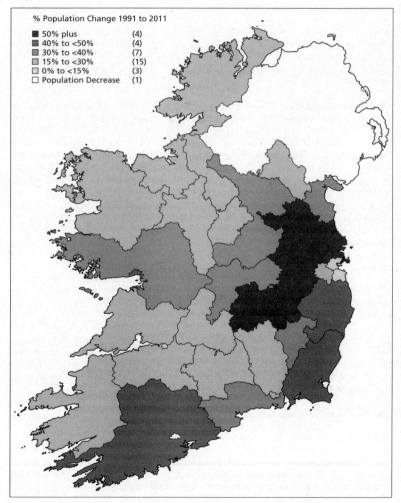

Fig. 2   A choropleth map of population change per local authority in Ireland 1991–2011

choropleth map A thematic *map where areas are shaded according to the value of a variable, such as population characteristics or political voting behaviour. The data displayed are aggregated for defined areal units such as wards or counties, and colour-coded using a progressive scale to denominate high and low values. Choropleth maps are useful because they reveal how a particular phenomenon varies spatially. However, because the data are aggregated, choropleth maps suffer from *ecological fallacy issues such as the *modifiable areal unit problem and failing to normalize data that can lead to false conclusions. (See Fig. 2.)

Christaller, Walter (1893–1969) A German urban and regional planner notable for his formulation of *Central Place Theory. Christaller believed that the spatial organization of human activities should reflect reasoned decision-making, where it did not already. While working for the German Nazi government in the 1940s, Christaller embodied the ideals of rational central government planning so as to improve the lives of citizens. His involvement in politics also revealed the ties between academic knowledge and government policy.

Christian geography The study of the geography of *Christianity and/or the practice of geography underpinned by Christian beliefs, moral values, and faith. On the one hand, Christian geography seeks to understand the spatial distribution and organization of the Christian religion and how Christian doctrine has shaped society. On the other, it concerns how the Christian faith shapes the geographical thought, praxis, and ethics of geographers who profess to be Christian. For example, Paul Cloke and Justin Beaumont have explored how Christian faith-by-praxis has fuelled increased voluntary activity in the public sphere in the UK. *See also* RELIGION.

Cloke, P. and Beaumont, J. (2012), 'Geographies of postsecular rapprochement in the city', *Progress in Human Geography*.

Christianity A collection of inter-related religious faiths and belief systems, which posit that the universe and all it contains was created by God, with its tenets based on the life and teachings of his son Jesus Christ. It is the world's most popular *religion practised by over two billion people. Its organized churches have been important in shaping the cultural identity, social organization, and political views of society, being key drivers in developing education, health care, and welfare systems. They were also an important agent in colonization and in 'civilizing' indigenous populations.

chronic disease An illness that is long lasting with few or no periods of remission. Examples include heart disease, stroke, cancer, and diabetes. The illness usually gets progressively more debilitating over time. Such diseases can radically reshape human spatial behaviour by limiting mobility and making the sufferer reliant on care services, itself shaped by the spatial organization of the health system.

chronotope The inseparability of time and space in life and representations of life. It was developed by literary theorist Mikhail Bakhtin to describe the temporal and spatial matrix within narratives through which subjectivity is organized. Stories, Bakhtin argued, are organized within a *time–space, where how the temporal (e.g. night-time) is conjoined with the spatial (e.g. a dark alley), providing the contextual framing for events and the subjectivity of characters. Bakhtin suggests that carnivalesque is one such chronotope amongst many used in literary representation (*see* CARNIVAL).

cinema *See* FILM.

citation geography The geographical analysis of citation data. Citations are references in an article or a book to other scholarly works. They comprise one measure of academic influence. Citations are monitored and compiled in databases such as the ISI indexes or Google Scholar. By mining these databases it is possible to map and rank key sites of geographical knowledge production and to also construct citation networks of the inter-relationships between authors, places, and ideas.

Cities A book written in 2002 by Ash *Amin and Nigel *Thrift in which the authors challenge conventional views of cityscapes, urban order, and urban futures. Amin and Thrift argue that cities are normally seen as complex but ordered, in large part because of the coordinating activities of governments and the presence of large businesses. Against this they enjoin readers to focus on everyday practices in households, public spaces, communal enterprises, and so on, as well as the non-cognitive elements of urban life.

citizenship **1.** The bundle of *rights and responsibilities of a person by virtue of their membership of a sovereign *nation state or, less commonly, another political community.

2. The way a person practises these rights and responsibilities in their daily life. Chief among these rights is the right of abode, meaning that a state cannot refuse a citizen entry to or expel them from national territory. The rights to vote, hold property, and claim entitlements are also part of citizenship, while responsibilities may include service in the military.

Citizenship rights and responsibilities have changed historically and geographically. It is common to distinguish between civic republican models, in which citizens are expected to actively participate in the political life of their community, and liberal models, which stress the rights of the individual to such things as autonomy, property, and liberty. Most discussions of citizenship also recognize the important distinction made by British sociologist T. H. Marshall in the 1950s between: civil rights (e.g. property); political rights (e.g. voting); and social rights (e.g. entitlements to pensions and social benefits). From this perspective, citizenship is expanding and universalizing on the one hand, but bound to a well-defined cultural community (e.g. a nation), on the other. But human geographers and others have argued that citizenship status is increasingly differentiated, in both positive and negative respects. The idea of 'multicultural citizenship' suggests that certain group rights are necessary and desirable, as argued by Will Kymlicka. Yasmin Soysal postulates the emergence of 'post-national citizenship' founded on international human rights. Migration studies focus on how states differentiate the status accorded to types of migrant, for example, temporary *guestworkers and high-skilled professionals, restricting the rights of those persons deemed less valuable (*see* MIGRATION; REFUGEES). While some individuals are *stateless persons as the result of conflict or displacement, others possess rights in more than one country at a time, known as dual or multiple citizenship (*see* DUAL CITIZENSHIP; FLEXIBLE CITIZENSHIP). Political *boundaries are therefore sites of the construction of variegated citizenship.

While Marshall linked citizenship to the nation state, geographers have tracked the formation of other sites and spaces. For instance, Don *Mitchell and Lynn Staehli have looked at how *public locations (e.g. city squares and parks) are key ingredients in citizen protest and its policing. Others are examining 'transnational citizenship', wherein states accord selected rights to non-residents (*see* DIASPORA). The *European Union represents a form of 'supra-national citizenship'. More radical geographers, often informed by *post-structuralism and *feminism, have critiqued the notions of the autonomous individual and the political community that are central assumptions of most mainstream models, regardless of scale.

References and further reading Ho, E. (2008), 'Citizenship, migration and transnationalism: a review and critical interventions', *Geography Compass*, 2/5: 1286–1300.

Kofman, E. (2003), 'Rights and citizenship' in Agnew, J., Mitchell, K., and Toal, G. (eds.) *A Companion to Political Geography* 393–407.

Mitchell, D. and Staeheli, L. (2005), 'Permitting protest: constructing—and dismantling—the geography of dissent in the United States', *International Journal of Urban and Regional Research* 29: 796–813.

Cittaslow A social movement aimed at enhancing the quality of urban life by emphasizing local foods and traditions, slowing down the pace of urban life, e.g. traffic, and resisting cultural homogenization. It was founded in 1999 in Italy by organizers of the Slow Food movement and has spread to around 150 member cities in 24 countries, mostly in the developed world.

city An agglomeration of people, businesses, and governmental institutions whose activities service a wider region and which, in the 21st century, is normally connected to international flows of information, goods, money, and people. Many cities are governed by a local state body responsible for some or all of the urban area. In rare cases, such as *Washington, DC or Brasilia, politics becomes a city's *raison d'être*. There are no internationally agreed criteria for identifying cities, for example, by extent or population size; each country or, in the case of the USA each state, designates cities according to its own rules, which usually include legal or jurisdictional elements. A city has some power, for example, over taxation, planning, or control over schools, not possessed by other districts. Although English-speaking countries generally refer to cities as places with more inhabitants than towns, in other languages—German and French for example—there is no such distinction. In China, by contrast, there is a threefold hierarchy of municipal-, prefecture- and county-level cities, the minimum size for which is set at 100,000 non-agricultural workers. Canadian cities may possess fewer than 10,000 inhabitants.

Viewed more historically, cities have undergone a number of transformations in form, function, and meaning. Although there is some debate, it is commonly agree that cities first emerged with the Neolithic revolution in Mesopotamia, the Indus Valley, China, and Egypt. A combination of agricultural surplus, classes not directly engaged in agriculture, writing, and organized religion consolidated in cities. Cities also developed as centres of trade, around marketplaces, and political power (*see* PRE-INDUSTRIAL CITY). With the Industrial Revolution, urban areas were increasingly characterized by *agglomeration, the dense and inter-dependent concentration of labour and factories famously described by Friedrich Engels in Manchester, UK.

The spread of cities through *suburbanization or *urban sprawl, the creation of *conurbations (*see* MEGALOPOLIS), and the emergence of so-called *mega-cities with populations of 10–40 million have made it increasingly difficult for urban geographers to delimit a distinct object of inquiry. It might be said that we are witnessing *urbanization without cities. The search for a common and identifiable set of social relations corresponding with a definite territory or urban area, pioneered by late 19th-century sociologists and continued by the *Chicago School of urban ecology, has proved elusive (*see* URBAN GEOGRAPHY). Cities are no more the sites of social disorganization, relations with strangers, or sensory overload than other places. In the early 21st century, cities are understood in terms of two contrasting perspectives. On the one hand, they are regarded as sites of exploitation, poverty, pollution, and instability (Davis 2006). On the other, they are seen as places of ideas, creativity, and opportunity (Saunders 2010). The reality is that cities are usually complex, Janus-faced entities whose inhabitants live in the same place but inhabit overlapping but sometimes separate micro-worlds of movement and experience. *See also* GLOBAL CITY.

References Davis, M. (2006), *Planet of Slums*.
Saunders, D. (2010), *Arrival City: How the Largest Migration in History Is Reshaping our World*.

(⊕) SEE WEB LINKS

• Official website of UN-Habitat, the UN agency for settlements.

city marketing The promotional activities undertaken on behalf of urban governments to either enhance the city's attractiveness to outside investors and tourists, and/or sustain or revive civic pride among inhabitants. 'Civic boosterism' was widespread in the USA throughout the 20th century, but became more pressing with the onset of *deindustrialization. Former manufacturing cities had to reinvent themselves and many chose to do so around themes of culture, quality of life, and enterprise. Acquiring prestigious projects, such as Bilbao's Guggenheim Museum, or hosting major cultural and sporting events, such as the Olympic Games, are two marketing strategies. Many places also engage in city branding; for example, Hong Kong sought to designate itself as 'Asia's World City'.

city-region A geographical unit consisting of a *city and its surrounding region, or hinterland, defined by a single administration, access to services, and/or *commuting patterns. The concept recognizes that the functional city often extends beyond the boundaries of the formal jurisdiction of a city. The idea of a 'global city-region' has been promulgated by Allen J. *Scott and colleagues. Such places are the motors of the global economy, centred either on one major metropolis (e.g. London), or increasingly, polycentric (e.g. the *Pearl River Delta). *See also* EDGE CITY; MEGALOPOLIS.
Reference Scott, A. J. (ed.) (2001), *Global City-Regions*.

civil society The totality of voluntary social relationships, communities, and institutions that lie between the private realm, the market, and the state. The term took on its modern meaning during the European *Enlightenment when feudalism, monarchical rule, and the power of religion were on the wane. Civil society was seen as the real and metaphorical space where citizens could discuss matters of common concern, free from undue interference by the state, and the compulsions of work and *social reproduction. Numerous *NGOs and NSMs (new *social movements) are said to be an index of a strong civil society, so too, high levels of *social capital. With the decline in the membership and political power of national trades unions on most Western countries, civil society is often said to be the contemporary basis for centre- and left-political movements, although critics also point out that there is nothing necessarily progressive about civil associations. To have civil society, citizens need to have civil rights recognized and defended by the *state (such as the right of free speech). Some believe the civil society has been eroded by the spread of *neoliberalism worldwide, though others point to the prevalence of *protest movements since the fall of the *Berlin Wall in 1989. In *development geography, there is a debate as to whether civil society can substitute for or form a bulwark against the state. The World Bank, for example, encourages the growth of civil society organizations by directing *aid through them rather than government. Critics, however, suggest that NGOs are often dominated by Western interests and personnel, and are not accountable to local communities. A second critique is that in many colonized countries, civil society emerged and continues as an elite phenomenon only. Other scholars have identified the growth of transnational migrant organizations as an alternative to outside influence (*see* MIGRATION-DEVELOPMENT NEXUS). Human geographers have inquired into nature and influence of civil society organizations at a range of geographical scales, but especially those at the level of neighbourhoods, towns, and cities. Other social scientists have begun to speculate on the existence of a 'global civil society', constituted by international NGOs, social movements, and transnational advocacy networks.

Further reading McIlwaine, C. (2007), 'From local to global to transnational civil society: re-framing development perspectives on the non-state sector', *Geography Compass* 1/6: 1252–81.

Clark, Gordon L. (1950–) An economic geographer and director of the Smith School of Enterprise and the Environment at Oxford University. His research has been influential within and beyond human geography. He helped to pioneer *labour geography and the geography of *law. In recent years he has focused on pension funds as part of a wider inquiry into financial investments in conditions of risk and uncertainty.

Clash of Civilizations, The A book and thesis by US political scientist Samuel P. Huntington predicting that future conflicts would be between large-scale 'civilizations' rather than nation states. It was published in 1996, based on a 1993 article in the magazine *Foreign Affairs*. Civilizations are based on ethnic, religious, or broadly cultural grounds rather than ideologies such as communism and capitalism. Examples include the West, Islam, the orthodox Christian world, and Latin America. Human geographers have been generally critical of the idea for ignoring connections between these hypothetical civilizations and essentializing the cultural differences on which they are supposedly founded.

Further reading Kearns, G. (2009), *Geopolitics and Empire: The Legacy of Halford Mackinder*.

class, social A dimension of social differentiation based on how people are positioned relative to the distribution of social goods, including land, property, money, and housing, or located within the *division of labour. A class is therefore a social group that shares a similar income and/or position in the economic hierarchy of its society. Class position is both a cause and consequence of power relations, and closely associated with relative degrees of well-being.

Class is one of the key concepts in sociology, but geographers have largely ignored much of that discipline's mainstream contributions. Geographical uses of class can be categorized under four broad headings. First, classes can be understood as aggregates of individuals or households who share one or more attributes such as income, education, and occupation, data for which is readily available from census and related sources. Such groupings can be ranked, and class here is regarded as a form of social stratification. They can be mapped at a variety of scales to reveal, for example, patterns in urban social geography or *spatial inequality. By contrast to stratification approaches, Marxist theories of class are more relational; class is a social relation of power and class struggle is one of the forces driving social change. David *Harvey, for example, argues that capitalist societies had a basic two-class structure in which working-class people were obliged to sell their capacity to work to capitalists, who owned the 'means of production' (factories, machines, distribution networks, etc.). One class is defined in relation to the other and they are inter-dependent. But he also went beyond this schematic representation to identify class fractions and tiers, notably in his study of the revolutionary Paris Communards of 1871. A third approach regards class more as a matter of lifestyle and consumption patterns, sometimes drawing on *Bourdieu's concepts of various forms of capital (economic, cultural, social, etc.). This treatment of class shades into the kind of analysis conducted by marketing firms and political parties into the different kinds of household or consumer with a view to targeting them. *Geodemographics makes a major contribution to this style of analysis. Finally, human geographers are interested in class processes and how they are bound up with space and place. Class relations are not simply given, they must be reproduced (*see* SOCIAL REPRODUCTION). In his Marxist geographical analysis, Harvey's concern was how 'class in itself', defined 'structurally' by the social relations in which people find themselves, is linked to 'class for itself', this being the consciousness of a class fraction of its own and others' class position. He showed how the internal geography of Paris—partially and purposefully reworked by Emperor Napoleon II—was a key factor in inhibiting working-class consciousness and a focus of Communard militancy (as when they toppled the Vendome Column). In a different vein, interest in *kinetic elites reveals how different classes possess contrasting degrees of mobility and possibly attachment to place (*see* ELITES).

The specific analysis of class and its various geographies fell somewhat out of favour in geography after the mid-1980s, coincident with the declining influence of Marxist approaches in the discipline. Where it appears, it does so in two main forms. One is somewhat rhetorical, pronouncing on the polarized nature of capitalist societies. In the other, class is considered alongside other dimensions of social difference, such as gender and race, to examine the complex differentiation of society and constructions of identity (*see* INTERSECTIONALITY). *See also* CREATIVE CLASS; GENTRIFICATION; LABOUR GEOGRAPHY; UNDERCLASS.

Reference and further reading Gibson-Graham, J. K., Resnick, S. A., and Wolff, R. D. (eds.) (2000), *Class and its Others*.
Harvey, D. (1985), *Consciousness and the Urban Experience*.

Claval, Paul (1932–) A prolific French human geographer who has made contributions across the discipline, including regional, cultural, social, political, and urban geography. He has also written extensively on geographical thought. Claval, who spent most of his academic career at the University of Paris IV–Sorbonne, was a key figure in the post-war shift of French geography towards *spatial science.

climate change 1. The natural alteration of regional and global climate patterns occurring over millennia.
2. The unintended alteration of the world's climatic system by humans. Climate change in this sense is perhaps the defining feature of the *Anthropocene (Ruddiman 2005). The release of so-called 'greenhouse gases' (such as carbon dioxide and methane) through the combustion of fossil fuels (among other things) has led to an increase in global mean temperatures since meteorological records began. So-called climate change sceptics argue that it is a hoax played on politicians, businesses, and the public by environmentalists. However, the research of thousands of scientists worldwide—reviewed periodically by the United Nations' *Intergovernmental Panel on Climate Change (IPCC)—suggests that climate change is no hoax. Governments worldwide have, accordingly, been paying increasing attention to how the effects of climate change can be mitigated and adapted to in the years ahead. A series of periodic intergovernmental meetings since the first *Earth Summit have sought to create a legally binding agreement in reducing greenhouse gas emissions and assisting countries seeking a 'greener' path to future economic development.

Reference Ruddiman, W. F. (2005), *Plows, Plagues and Petroleum: How Humans Took Control of Climate*.

climate policy A set of strategic objectives and associated *environmental policies, designed by national and other governments, as well as intergovernmental bodies, to meet the challenges of *climate change and variability. If, as most climate scientists anticipate, climate change profoundly alters the world's environments, then societies worldwide will need to undertake two kinds of action. One is mitigation—the absolute or relative reduction in greenhouse gas emissions (*see* LOW CARBON ECONOMY). Given that some climate change beyond the rate and scale of recent history is inevitable, regardless of what mitigation is achieved, the other policy is adaptation—reducing *vulnerability and enhancing *resilience to environmental change.

Because climate change and variability is, by definition, a transnational issue, climate policy has been pursued through intergovernmental means. The *United Nations

Framework Convention on Climate Change (UNFCCC) is responsible for the *Kyoto Protocol and the annual 'Conferences of the Parties' (COP) through which global policy is negotiated. This framework, described as 'mega-multilateralism' by Hoffmann has had mixed success. National policies, and in the case of the European Union, regional ones, are designed within its parameters. Developing within its shadow, and to some degree complementing or even replacing it, is a growing number of policy experiments at subnational, inter-urban, corporate, and individual levels. These include important municipal networks such as the Cities for Climate Protection (CCP) scheme that links over one hundred cities around the world. Climate policy necessarily intrudes into many other policy domains (e.g. housing and energy), raising complex issues of policy coordination and integration. *See also* ENVIRONMENTAL GOVERNANCE; GOVERNANCE.

Further reading Bailey, I. and Maresh, S. (2009), 'Scales and networks of neoliberal climate governance: the regulatory and territorial logics of European Union emissions trading', *Transactions of the Institute of British Geographers* 34 (4): 445–61.
Bulkeley, H. (2011), 'Cities and sub-national governments', in Dryzek, J. S., et al. (eds.), *The Oxford Handbook of Climate Change and Society*.
Hoffman, M. J. (2011), *Climate Governance at the Crossroads*.

Cloke, Paul (1956–) A professor of Human Geography at Exeter University, England, who has made formative contributions to the study of rural societies, homelessness, and ethical consumption. His research is characterized by a strong interest in moral questions, notably the connective imperative between the research topics he focuses on and his own ethical commitments.

cluster analysis The detection and analysis of clusters in the spatial distribution of data. Generally the detection method seeks to determine the extent to which the pattern of a phenomenon varies from a random pattern. Such analysis is useful for identifying possible hotspots of a particular disease such as cancer and possible underlying causes. A range of different techniques exists that vary by scale and scope of a search and the search method. *See also* CLUSTERS.

clusters The non-random spatial grouping of phenomena. It is commonly observed that phenomena that are alike often cluster together to form spatial concentrations. These phenomena thus display a high degree of *spatial auto-correlation. For example, companies within a specific sector, such as banking or automobile manufacture, will locate close to each other to be able to trade with each other and share knowledge, expertise, and labour. Such business clusters are thought to be important because they foster competition, productivity, innovation, and stimulate the development of new aligned and service businesses. As a result, states often try to encourage the *agglomeration of similar businesses to create clusters. Other kinds of clusters relate to diseases and other health conditions. The detection of such clusters to try and determine their causes is undertaken using *cluster analysis.

codified knowledge A body of knowledge that is recorded in a specific medium (such as a book, manual, or computer program) and makes explicit that which is either tacit or manifest only through practical activities (such as when a craftsperson makes a violin by hand). The contrast between codified and *tacit knowledge is central to economic geographers' analyses of the spatial patterns of economic activity. It is sometimes assumed that codified knowledge travels more easily and is therefore less place-bound than tacit knowledge, although many now question the simplicity of this distinction.

cognitive geography The study of how humans and animals think about space, place, and environment. The approach emerged in the late 1960s and is strongly connected to *behavioural geography and environmental psychology. In essence, it is the application of psychological theory to understanding spatial thinking, learning, and behaviour. Most research has focused on how people learn and remember spatial data, and perceive and understand different environments, though some work has examined the ability of animals to remember local and migratory routes. *See also* COGNITIVE MAPPING; ENVIRONMENTAL PERCEPTION.

Reference Kitchin, R. and Blades, M. (2001), *The Cognition of Geographic Space.*

cognitive mapping The study of how people learn, store, process, and use spatial information about a place and how this shapes human spatial behaviour. The term 'cognitive map' is suggestive of the notion that people hold a map-like database in their minds to which they can add and use to tackle geographical tasks. Research tends to use psychologically derived tests in both natural and laboratory settings to evaluate cognitive map knowledge. *See also* COGNITIVE GEOGRAPHY.

cohort analysis A method of *longitudinal analysis to track a cohort of individuals over time. A cohort shares some common characteristics, usually age. For example, a programme of research might track a sample of children from when they are born through to adulthood, measuring their health, well-being, and social development every couple of years. Such data allow an analysis of how child well-being varies across time, space, life conditions, and opportunities. *See also* BIOGRAPHICAL APPROACH.

Cold War The aggressive ideological stand-off between Western allies and the *Soviet Union and its satellites that operated from the end of the *Second World War until the fall of the Soviet Union in 1991 (*see* WEST). As the Second World War ended, divergent visions for post-war Europe emerged. The Western allies sought reconstruction within a framework of democracy and capitalism, which sought to limit the rise of *communism, both in Europe and around the world. The Soviet Union wanted to advance socialism, propagate communist ideology, and to foster states that took their political, social, and economic lead from Moscow. Each side engaged in political and military manoeuvres and countermoves to shape the wider geopolitical landscape and became embroiled in a battle waged on several fronts including technological and economic development, nuclear arms and space race, and the promotion of culture and ideology. At several points the Cold War threatened to become hot between the two main protagonists, for example, the Cuban missile crisis of 1962. However, military engagement between the superpowers was largely played out indirectly through other conflicts (such as those in Korea, Vietnam, Cambodia, Afghanistan, and Nicaragua where they each backed opposing regimes), or consisted of attempts to undermine particular political regimes by sponsoring opposition groups in Central America, Africa, the *Middle East, and *Southeast Asia. The legacy of the Cold War is still evident in the wider geopolitical world order and in the economies of those countries most directly affected. *See also* DOMINO THEORY; GEOPOLITICS; POLITICAL GEOGRAPHY.

Further reading Agnew, J. and Corbridge, S. (1995), *Mastering Space.*

colonialism The control over one territory and its peoples by another, and the ideologies of superiority and *racism often associated with such domination. Control may be incomplete or contested although fully established colonialism generally involves some measure of formal political and legal rule. Colonialism is often, but not necessarily, accompanied by the settlement of the subordinated territory, a process known as colonization. In turn, the settlement might be referred to as a colony. The term 'colonialism' is often used interchangeably with *imperialism and there is no rigorous or consistent distinction between them. Imperialism can describe a system of domination by one geographical area over others in the form of an empire, and need not involve settlement.

The spread and formation of colonies was widespread within the classical Mediterranean and medieval worlds; the English colonized Wales in the 13th century, and Germans settled throughout Central and Eastern Europe, for example. But it is usual to reserve the term colonialism for a particular historical period from around 1500 to around 1950, during which European countries spread their networks of trade, production, and political power across the world. Portugal, Spain, Holland, France, Britain, Germany, and other European countries extended their control in three main forms: *settler societies, generally where climate and soils suited the transfer of peoples from temperate environments (*see* ECOLOGICAL IMPERIALISM); dependencies, where small colonial elites ruled larger populations; and enclaves or outposts to protecting maritime trade routes. In the former case, colonialism sometimes involved the extermination or displacement of *indigenous peoples (*see* PLANTATION SOCIETY); elsewhere, colonized peoples could be coerced into labour to extract minerals or work land. By common agreement, the process of *decolonization, the extirpation of colonial powers from their territories, began with the USA and Haiti in the 18th century and continued until the post-Second World War decades. From Latin American in the 1820s to North Africa in the 1950s, this was often the result of anticolonial resistance movements.

Understanding colonialism in terms of a European-centred colonial era implies that colonizer and colonized were geographically separated, usually by seas and oceans. But some authors have argued that colonial relations of economic, political, and cultural domination can take place within states, a condition known as *internal colonialism. Examples might include Brittany, Catalonia, and Scotland. Others have suggested that relations between the US federal state and its geographically defined racial and ethnic minorities can also be described as colonialism or occupation. Russia's expansion eastwards into Siberia from the 16th century was also an example of colonization. In more recent times, China's treatment of Tibet is regarded by critics as colonialism.

The notion of a colonial era suggests that colonialism is finished, but this too is contested. Kwame Nkrumah, the first president of independent Ghana, used the term 'neocolonialism' to describe the continued domination of his and other African countries by Western powers and multinational corporations even after formal independence. It is implied that the terms of world trade, the media industry, and the conduct of international affairs continue to embody colonial relations, not least through the privilege accorded to a few European languages (*see* LAND GRAB). In addition, there are territories still effectively governed by former occupying powers, such as Guam and St Helena. Beyond this, the human and environmental geography of the modern world was profoundly transformed by centuries of colonial rule.

Human geographers have gained from, participated in, and actively promoted colonialism in the past, while also trying to study and, increasingly, critique it. Officers and members of the major national *geographical societies took advantage of the opportunities for research and exploration provided by colonies, while also extolling the virtues of colonialism as a 'civilizing mission'. In France, Germany, and elsewhere there were also separate societies for colonization advocating further expansion and settlement. A branch of colonial geography, or the study of contacts between peoples, was established among French geographers; Albert Demangeon's *L'Empire britannique* (1925) was the first major geographical study of an empire and its colonial dimensions. Not all geographers were committed to colonialism: the US geographer Isaiah *Bowman played a significant part in bringing about decolonization by negotiating the dismantling of the British and French empires post-Second World War. In recent decades human geographers have sought a more critical understanding of colonialism, often aligned with the intellectual project of post-colonial studies (*see* POST-COLONIALISM). A leading voice has been Derek *Gregory, whose book *The *Colonial Present* argues that the colonial mix of power, knowledge, and geography, far from having faded into history, has been revived through conflicts in Israel, Afghanistan, and Iraq. *See also* BLAUT, JAMES; EUROCENTRISM; ORIENTALISM.

Further reading Godlewksa, A. and Smith, N. (eds.) (1994), *Geography and Empire.*

Colonial Present, The An influential monograph by Derek *Gregory (2004) on the enduring legacy of colonial thinking about the non-Western world, even in supposedly 'post-colonial' times. Heavily influenced by theorists of power who emphasized the role of knowledge rather than of armies or police forces (such as Edward *Said and Michel *Foucault), Gregory explores the way wars have been waged by Western societies on 'Oriental' peoples in Afghanistan, Iraq, and Palestine. He shows how colonial thinking circulates between the realms of ordinary culture, high politics, and military strategizing. The book highlights the constructedness and consequentiality of *geographical imaginations, and shows the naivety of *empiricism as a way of supposedly 'correcting' false beliefs. *See also* COLONIALISM; ORIENTALISM.

commercial geography A predecessor of *economic geography, concerned with how, what, and where commodities are produced, with close attention paid to the distribution of raw materials and the economic possibilities afforded by colonies. It flourished in the USA and Germany up to the mid-20th century and reflected early academic geography's roots in mapping, surveying, and inventorying territory. British geographer George Chisholm's *Handbook of Commercial Geography* was published in seven editions between 1889 and 1908 such was the popularity of the subject.

commodification The process of turning something into a *commodity that can be exchanged, usually for money. A commodity is a phenomenon (an idea, symbol, or artefact) that has both a use-value for buyers and an exchange-value for sellers. It will also often have a sign-value for buyers, meaning that it 'speaks' to them and others in symbolic ways. Some human geographers regard the *globalization process as one in which the frontiers of commodification have spread outwards and inwards leading to a world in which almost everything is for sale. However, they have challenged the assumption that commodification necessarily leads to a loss of authenticity and place distinctiveness as its effects wash over the globe.

commodity A useful good, service, symbol, or idea that is sold by its maker to a consumer, usually in return for *money. Commodities have been exchanged in markets of various kinds for centuries. However, in the 21st century most commodities are made in order to realize a profit (*see* CAPITALISM) and there is often a considerable physical distance between the makers and buyers of commodities (*see* GLOBALIZATION; COMMODITY CHAIN).

commodity chain The entire range of firms and activities involved in the design, production, distribution, and marketing of any particular *commodity. Each enterprise, labour force, household, and related activity can be seen as one link in a metaphorical chain. In our era of economic *globalization, a great many commodity chains are transnational, crossing several political *borders. The term 'global commodity chain' was developed by US sociologists (including Immanuel *Wallerstein and Gary Gereff) to capture these inter-organizational networks. Questions arise about who coordinates any given commodity chain and who reaps most of the economic rewards. Producer-driven commodity chains are those in which one or more large manufacturers dominate over the distribution, wholesale, and/or retail companies further along the chain. Technology-intensive industries such as automobiles, aircraft, computers, semiconductors, and heavy machinery normally tend to have producer-driven commodity chains. Buyer-driven commodity chains, on the other hand, are those in which large retailers and branded goods sellers set up decentralized production networks in a variety of exporting countries, typically located in the developing world. Such chains are common in labour-intensive consumer goods industries such as garments, footwear, and toys.

Analysts of commodity chains have inquired into the geography of wealth and economic development characteristics of different chains; they have also studied whether and how countries and regions can capture more of the economic gains from the chains they are part of—a process known as upgrading. Their analyses speak to the issue of *uneven development geographically and spatial competition between countries whose economies are linked by commodity chains. *See also* GLOBAL VALUE CHAIN; GLOBAL PRODUCTION NETWORK; WORLD-SYSTEMS APPROACH.

Further reading Gereffi, G. (1996), 'Global commodity chains: new forms of coordination and control among nations and firms in international industries', *Competition and Change* 1(4): 427–439.

commodity fetishism The habit of treating a *commodity as a thing in itself rather than as the product of social and natural relations. *Marxist geographers have long argued that *consumers routinely fetishize commodities. Once purchased, a commodity is private property and comes to seem like a thing rather than the phenomenal form in which complex, often long-distance relationships are maintained (*see* COMMODITY CHAINS). These relationships may sustain various forms of social and environmental injustice, yet these injustices are not advertised in the phenomenal appearance of commodities, nor are they 'costed' in the price of most commodities. It is argued that commodity fetishism conceals the systemic exploitation of both workers and the non-human world by *capitalism.

Common Agricultural Policy (CAP) A *European Union programme of agricultural subsidies, with associated import tariffs and quotas. It is the largest single budgetary activity of the EU. The aim of CAP is to promote and protect agricultural activity in Europe and to make it a viable business and way of life for farmers given the global variations in the price of agricultural production, to create stable and sustainable markets, and to ensure affordable food supply. CAP subsidizes farm activity, providing farmers with a guaranteed minimum price for produce, as well as incentives for land stewardship aimed at enhancing environmental protection and preserving rural heritage. CAP has a major influence on the rural and agricultural geography of Europe, slowing rural decline, and depopulation. It is the recipient of much criticism including that it has led to over-production, maintains artificially high food prices, is iniquitous between farms of different sizes and between states, and has negative environmental impacts. It is presently undergoing significant reform in terms of its vision, activities, and budget. *See also* AGRICULTURAL GEOGRAPHY.

(((•))) SEE WEB LINKS
• European Commission document explaining the Common Agricultural Policy.

common pool resources Materials, goods, and services of various kinds that are open to be used by many people because there is no means of, or reason for, restricting access (i.e. they are 'non-excludable'). Further, use by one individual or group comes at the expense of another (i.e. they are 'rivalrous'). This distinguishes them from 'pure public goods', such as defence, which can be enjoyed or used by everyone equally. Common pool resources exist at all geographical scales, from a European village's grazing common to the global atmosphere. Classic examples include irrigation systems, pastures, and fisheries. They may be owned by governments, communities, corporations, or private individuals, or not owned by anyone at all, in which case they are termed 'open access resources'.

common property resources Materials, goods, and services of various kinds that are managed or owned by a community. Not to be confused with open access resources, common property has identifiable managers or owners who may decide to utilize the resources according to agreed goals and values. The term '*commons' is often synonymous with common property resource.

commons A physical space or natural resource that provides materials, goods, or services that benefit most or all members of a community or the wider public. Commons can assume many physical forms and exist at all geographical scales, from the local to the global. The original sense of commons derives from medieval Europe. Common fields, pastures, wastes, and woodlands were accessible to all in a village community according to local customary arrangements. Such commons were progressively converted into private property through enclosure. In England and Wales, for example, this was both informal and formal, based on parliamentary acts, especially throughout the 18th century. The transfer of land and resources from communal to private control was, according to many historians, one of the foundations of *capitalism (*see* POLANYI, KARL). More recently, such things as the atmosphere and oceans have been conceived as global commons because they are resources upon which humanity depends but which have no clear ownership. *See* TRAGEDY OF THE COMMONS.

Further reading Giordano, M. (2003), 'The geography of the commons: the role of scale and space', *Annals of the Association of American Geographers* 93(2): 365–76.

Commonwealth of Nations An intergovernmental organization of 54 member states, all of whom bar two (Mozambique and Rwanda), were part of the British Empire. Sixteen of the members share a common head of state, Queen Elizabeth II. It is not a political or economic union, but rather an organization through which members share and promote common values and views. Not all former nations of the British Empire are members. Member states compete in the Commonwealth Games held every four years.

commune A group of people who elect to live and work together in a non-hierarchical way according to values of democracy, inclusion, and participation. Given the prevalence of individualism and private ownership in capitalist societies, communes are seen as an 'alternative' way of working and living. Communes can be formed to produce goods and services, to deliver public goods, or to raise children and socially reproduce. Analysts of *alternative economic geographies have examined the formation and operation of communes.

communications and geography Communication concerns the exchange or broadcast of information. Geographers have long been interested in how people communicate, especially over distance, as a means of maintaining connections, exerting political influence, and shaping trade and enterprise. Along with transportation, communication technologies such as postal services, the telegraph, telephone, and the *Internet, are key agents in increasing *time-space compression. In sequence, each of these technologies have sped up the time it takes to communicate between locations, at the same time as increasing the range and volume of information that can be exchanged. As such, they allow for the radical transformation of how social, political, and economic relations are organized spatially. For example, the telegraph network made the governance and control of colonial states by imperial powers more efficient and effective by allowing the quick exchange of information and decisions across vast distances. The telephone and the Internet have enabled businesses to stretch their production systems over ever-larger distances while being in instantaneous contact across the whole company regardless of location. Modern communication technologies, such as mobile phones, are enabling personal and business contact to be conducted on the move, becoming even more flexible and dynamic, and altering patterns of spatial behaviour. As well as technologies of information exchange, communication can be in the form of broadcast through newspapers and television. Here, there are a small number of communicators and many readers/listeners, and the message is highly prescribed and managed (*see* MEDIA). *See also* TELECOMMUNICATIONS; TRANSPORT GEOGRAPHY.

communism A system of political decision-making and economic production in which all citizens enjoy equality and manage their affairs in the collective interest through debate and consensus formation. Communism was strongly advocated by Karl *Marx among others, in response to the appalling inequality he witnessed in Western Europe during the early decades of industrial *capitalism. Later, communism went from ideal to reality in the former USSR and the so-called 'Eastern bloc' countries after 1945. However, critics noted that 'actually existing communism' departed from the ideals of Marx and others. It was ended in 1989–90 by civil revolutions, though continues in name in Cuba, North Korea, and various political parties, notably in India. *See also* POST-SOCIALISM; SOVIET UNION.

communitarianism A way of life that is critical of a certain strand of liberalism and which places value on the benefits that individuals derive from being embedded in a community. Communitarians take issue with the idea that individual freedom is opposed to social relations, institutions, and customs. Rather than acting as a restraint to individual freedom, communitarians see the latter as enabling and enriching for individuals. 'Mild' communitarians emphasize the importance of *social capital. 'Strong' communitarians emphasize the importance of shared cultural values, norms, and habits among individuals, such that a person's freedom is more constrained than in mild communitarianism. The social ties that communitarians value often involve geographical proximity between individuals, who are bound—to a greater or lesser degree—by the ties of *community, *place, and *locality.

communities of practice A group—not necessarily physically proximate—that possesses a shared profession, vocation, or role that has a practical or applied element to it. Such groups are bound together by common training, experience, and expertise (such as doctors or computer programmers). Economic geographers have been interested in how communities of practice feature in the creation and success of industrial clusters, 'new' industrial districts, and growth poles. Despite the prevalence of *ICTs, sustained face-to-face interactions remain vital to the formation and reproduction of communities of practice.

community A form of social, and often spatial, organization centred on common interests and/or a locale. Although its definition is often disputed within academia and amongst policy makers, it is generally recognized that community consists of a grouping of people. The extent to which this grouping consists of an active social network is a source of debate. For some, a community has a common set of customs or shared circumstances. For example, everybody living within a village, although they might not form a coherent, active social network, nevertheless form a community because they are united through shared history, custom, and culture. Here, community is very much culture- and place-specific, although it should be recognized that community and neighbourhood are not always synonymous. For others, community is defined through practice and interaction, based around common interests and values which are actively sustained. Such interactions might be shaped by cultural identity related to religion, ethnicity, race, sexuality, or age. While such communities might be place-based, they can also be virtual, with people who are dispersed across space but who interact collectively and regularly through the *Internet especially social networking sites, considered to form a community. Belonging to a community brings benefits of mutual aid and support in return for reciprocal sharing of time, effort, and broadly defined resources (e.g., money, knowledge). Interest in communities in human geography can be traced back to the *Chicago School of urban sociology and the study of communities remains an important part of social, urban, and rural geography. *See also* COMMUNITARIANISM.

Further reading Aitken, S. C. (1998), *Family Fantasies and Community Space*.
Herbert, S. (2005), 'The trapdoor of community', *Annals of Association of American Geographers* 88: 50–72.

community-based natural resource management (CBNRM) A programme for *sustainable development that tries to combine the *empowerment of local communities—mostly rural and/or indigenous—with nature *conservation. Its main principle is that people will help conserve their natural environment if doing so strengthens their security and increases their social and economic well-being. CBNRM gained momentum from the 1980s, arising from criticisms of top-down, state-led natural resource management. It has been taken up by intergovernmental organizations and NGOs in the *development field.

community forestry The management of forests by including local communities in decision-making and action. Also termed community-based forestry, it originated in the Himalayas in the 1970s and spread throughout much of the tropical developing world as well as North America. The aim of such schemes is usually to combine conservation, commercial exploitation, and local land rights. In England, community forests are also woodlands in cities linked with urban regeneration.

community mapping Collaborative or participatory cartography by residents of a community or urban neighbourhood, often as a prelude for local action on planning or environment. Such mapping includes a diverse range of practices, from hand-drawn maps to *GIS, often designed to map the area's assets and needs.

community planning The strategic provision of public services at a local level, either by local government alone or in consultation with individuals and organizations from a particular community. The degree of input and control accorded to residents and other non-governmental bodies varies considerably, but may extend to actively shaping the way public services are delivered.

commuting The journeying to and from *work. With the rise of public transportation, and especially the growth in the use of the private car, there has been an increasing spatial separation between home and work. This has had a radical effect on the pattern of urban development and the need to develop and maintain large road and rail infrastructures. It has also significantly altered time-space patterns of spatial behaviour with some commuters spending large portions of each working day travelling to and from work. This has knock-on consequences with regards to quality of life and home/work life balances. Given the scale of commuting and issues such as congestion, it has become a key concern of transportation and urban planners. These planners often use large, complex transportation models to predict and manage traffic flow and public transport timetables. *See also* TRANSPORT GEOGRAPHY.

comparative advantage A concept used by economists and economic geographers that describes the relative cost advantages of producing certain goods and services for overseas trade. For instance, if two countries can both produce corn and laptop computers, it may not make economic sense for both of them to produce these commodities for their domestic markets. Instead, it may be relatively cheaper for one to specialize in corn and the other in laptops and trade them for the income required to purchase the other. When this logic is applied to a range of goods and services it means that if pure economic rationality prevailed, countries would specialize in producing and exporting a select range of commodities at any given point in their development. In development geography, the *normative aspects of the concept were criticized during the 1970s and 1980s. It was argued that less developed countries might simply focus on exporting low-value primary commodities (such as vegetable oil) and not seek to compete with overseas countries for 'value-added' commodities such as processed foods, let alone 'high-end' goods and services.

comparative research Analysis that compares phenomena across two or more areas or populations. By comparing data it is possible to identify shared and divergent patterns and to examine the reasons for such commonalities or differences. In *quantitative research, comparison is undertaken using statistical testing to determine if differences are significant. In *qualitative research, comparison is usually through description.

competitive advantage The relative economic gains a firm (or group of similar firms) enjoy over their business rivals at home or overseas. The term derives from business economics and is most associated with Michael *Porter. Competitive advantage can be cost based, where a firm or group of firms are able to produce commodities for less money than it costs their rivals (*see* COMPARATIVE ADVANTAGE). It can also be non-cost based or 'differential'. Here a firm produces a better version of an existing commodity and thus outperforms its rivals by capturing more market share. In a capitalist world, the search for competitive advantage is incessant and a driving force of business innovation in all economic sectors.

complementary and alternative medicine Medicines, therapies, and treatments that are not considered part of mainstream, conventional medicine and health-care practices. They can often trace their roots to premodern times and accordingly are often weakly associated with the global pharmaceutical and medicine industry. Complementary medicines and treatments are used alongside conventional medicine, whereas alternative medicines and treatments are used instead of conventional medicine. Geographers investigating health and well-being are starting to investigate how complementary and alternative medicines feature in new geographies of subjectivity and the *body.

complex emergency A life-threatening situation arising from a combination of factors and so necessitating responses from a mix of outside agencies, including humanitarian aid and peacekeeping forces. War, civil disorder, the breakdown of authority, population *displacement, criminal activity, and even natural disasters may come together to constitute such an emergency. Typically, humanitarian responses such as *aid, medical, or refugee agencies are obstructed by local powers, and must therefore seek the help of military forces to maintain security. Examples include the Rwandan genocide of 1994, Kosovo war 1998–99, the Iraq war of 2003–2011, and the Darfur crisis starting in 2007. These situations challenged conventional approaches to development and humanitarian aid. David Kean points out, however, that most emergencies involve multiple agencies and defining some in this way risks confusing the problem with the solution.

Reference Kean, D. (2008), *Complex Emergencies.*

complexity theory *See* CHAOS, CATASTROPHE, AND COMPLEXITY THEORY.

concentrated deconcentration The movement of people, jobs, and services from a large urban centre to reconcentrate in smaller urban centres elsewhere. It is a planning and growth management tool for redistributing resources, but which retains concentration in order to maintain critical mass, to provide a focus for growth, and to avoid a pattern of sprawl.

concentric zone models Some stylized descriptions of urban form deriving from the work of sociologist Ernest Burgess in the 1920s (*see* CHICAGO SCHOOL; URBAN ECOLOGY). Based on the idea of a *bid-rent curve, Burgess's original described a core *central business district surrounded in turn by a zone of transition, a zone of working-class suburbs, a zone of middle-class suburbs, and an outer commuting zone. Later urban theorists altered and adapted the model. Hoyt, for example, stressed the supply-side of housing provision, proposing the addition of sectors to the rings. Others extended it to suit regions and contexts beyond North America. *See also* ALONSO MODEL; PRE-INDUSTRIAL CITY; URBAN MODELLING.

concept An *abstraction used in everyday language or, more formally, in the theories and *models used by researchers. Often researchers will critically analyse the way concepts are used in everyday life, will seek to redefine them, or will seek to use them in their *analysis of the world. Many concepts have this quality of being ordinary (used by lay actors) and yet also very technical (used by researchers). Examples include rights, justice, *landscape, *nature, and *time. In human geography, there is a small set of key concepts that attracts considerable discussion in both teaching and research.

Further reading Kitchin, R. et al. (eds.) (2009), *Key Concepts in Geography*.

conditional credit transfer (CCT) A poverty-reduction programme in which beneficiaries receive money in return for demonstrating the required behaviour, for example, sending children to school or attending health centres. Most benefit systems are based on eligibility criteria; for example, unemployment benefit goes to people who are unemployed. CCTs, by contrast, seek to alter behaviour by monetary incentives. These *neoliberal programmes began in Latin America in the 1990s and spread to India and elsewhere, including the USA in a reversal of the conventional geography of policy transfer.

Reference Peck, J. and Theodore, N. (2010), 'Recombinant workfare across the Americas: transnationalizing "fast" social policy', *Geoforum* 41(2): 195–208.

Condition of Postmodernity, The A best-selling book by David *Harvey published in 1989 that offered a comprehensive and critical explanation of the rise of postmodern culture during the 1980s. Many commentators celebrated the turn to postmodern styles in architecture, literature, fashion, and other cultural domains from the late 1970s. However, Harvey was not only critical of *postmodernism; he also linked its rise to major changes in Western *capitalism and the shift to a more globalized economy after the economic crises of *Fordism. For Harvey, postmodern culture was the metaphorical clothing worn by the capitalist economy in the attempt to set *accumulation on new profitable paths yet without reducing the *exploitation of workers or environmental degradation. 'Postmodernity' was thus an historical period marked by profound economic restructuring (a move towards *flexible accumulation) with a corresponding attempt to make postmodern *culture a new means for money-making.

congestion charge *See* ROAD PRICING.

Consciousness and the Urban Experience A 1985 book by David *Harvey exploring the influence of *urbanization on people's perceptions of the world and on political activism and consciousness. As a *Marxist, Harvey was especially interested in how cities affect *class identity and class politics. His argument centres on the rise and fall of Second Empire Paris and the subsequent Paris Commune, 1850–72. This episode allows him to uncover the contradictory relations between social and spatial transformation through detailed empirical inquiry. A companion book, *The *Urbanization of Capital*, provides more theoretical foundations.

conservation 1. The maintenance of resources for future use, commonly by protecting species, habitats, natural resources, and human-made objects such as buildings or historic districts from uses that would diminish or even eliminate them.
   2. The associated ideas and practices, variously expressed as a conservation ethic, the conservation movement, or sciences such as conservation biology. It can be contrasted with preservation, in which resources are withheld from use altogether.
   Conservation seeks to address two main problems. Firstly, it is a response to the perceived depletion of resources such as timber, fish, or game (*see* NATURAL RESOURCES). The development of scientific forestry in Europe and many European colonies in the 19th century was a recognition that timber was not a limitless resource (*see* FORESTS AND FORESTRY). A related concern was the supposed loss of *wilderness areas to the encroachments of civilization, which led to the creation of national parks in the USA and then elsewhere. Secondly, and more recently, it addresses anxieties about species loss and extinction (*see* BIODIVERSITY). The listing of, and prohibition of trade in, endangered species at national and international levels is one major response. The Convention on International Trade in Endangered Species of Wild Fauna and Flora (CITES) was first signed in 1973 and now has 175 participating countries.
   The aims of conservation were carried forward by local, national, and from the mid-20th century, by international NGOs: for example, the International Union for the Conservation of Nature (IUCN), the largest such body, was founded in 1948. But conservationists have had to contend with sometimes conflicting sets of ideas, with aesthetic, ethical, economic, and ecological roots. There is a growing critique of conservation ideals, based on their origins in Western and/or colonial conceptions of *nature, as well as the ongoing history of population displacement associated with the creation of protected areas (*see* FORTRESS CONSERVATION). In recent decades there has been a tendency to see people as part of the solution rather than the problem in habitat and species conservation, while the potential profitability of protected areas has drawn conservation efforts closer to capitalist priorities (*see* ECOLOGICAL MODERNIZATION; ECOTOURISM).

consociation A form of national government based on power-sharing between ethnic, religious, or other socially defined groups, all of whom have guaranteed representation at the executive level of government. There are many variations of consociationalism, but they are generally found in situations where communal conflict might otherwise threaten national stability, for example, Lebanon, Northern Ireland, and Bosnia-Herzegovina.

constructivism An approach to understanding knowledge and, in some cases, the physical world that emphasizes the power of human perception, cognition, intention, and action. Constructivists take issue with the epistemological belief that while 'fictional' knowledge is a construct, 'factual' knowledge is like a mirror held up to *nature. Some also question the idea that the material world can somehow exist separately from human action upon it. In both its epistemological and more ontological versions, constructivism shines a light on the why and how of the construction process. Who constructs what, in what ways, and to what ends? This question engenders a degree of suspicion towards those in society who claim to represent or act in accordance with the requirements of nature, 'truth', and 'reality'. Constructivism throws into question aspects of the world often said to be natural and to possess fixed or innate qualities.

In human geography, constructivism first made an impact courtesy of Marxist geographers. *Harvey's critique of 'natural limits to population growth' arguments and Neil *Smith's concept of the *production of nature, both pointed to the ideological role of authoritative claims made about the world. For Harvey and Smith, 'ideology' constituted a one-sided representation of reality that from another's perspective, might be said to be false (or *mis*representations). Later the 'new *cultural geography' set about examining various representations of *landscape and *place (*see* REPRESENTATION). Geographers influenced by *Science and Technology Studies extended constructivist arguments to the conduct of science, but have so far done little to influence the thinking of their physical geography counterparts in this regard. Geographers inspired by *Actor-Network Theory have criticized constructivism for ignoring the materiality and agency of the non-human world. Nigel Clark argues that constructivists have forgotten the Earth's enormous capacity to destroy our symbolic and physical constructions, and our own bodies and communities. This is not a resurrection of *environmental determinism decades after it was discredited intellectually, but rather an insistence that there are always limits to what humans can 'construct' in imagination and practice.

References and further reading Clark, N. (2011), *Inhuman Nature*.
Demeritt, D. (2001), 'Being constructive about nature', in Castree, N. and Braun, B. (eds.) *Social Nature*.
Harvey, D. (1974), 'Population, resources and the ideology of science', *Economic Geography* 50, 2: 256–77.
Smith, N. (1984), *Uneven Development*.

consumer society A society in which the consumption of goods and services is a highly significant aspect of peoples' lives. In a consumer society, *consumption is more than simply purchasing something out of necessity (such as bread or milk). It is also a leisure activity and a means by which people define who they are and distinguish themselves from others. Consumer society depends upon the manufacture of consumer needs, wants, and desires by marketing professionals. *See also* BOURDIEU, PIERRE; BRANDING.

consumption The act of using something to meet the needs and wants of a person, community, or society. Most personal consumption occurs outside the workplace, in the domain of the household, tourism, shopping, and leisure. In a capitalist world, it typically involves the purchase and utilization of commodities: for example, most people consume food and information produced by others rather than by themselves. While some human geographers have sought to defetishize consumption in order to criticize *capitalism (*see* COMMODITY FETISHISM), others have seen it as one way in which people achieve a sense of personal identity and well-being. A focus on 'collective consumption' is less prevalent in human geography than a generation ago, perhaps reflecting the rise of *neoliberalism worldwide and the apparent decline in government-provided (or maintained) public goods and services.

containerization The use of large, standardized, interlocking steel containers for the transportation of goods. Developed after the Second World War, container-based *logistics greatly improved the efficiency and productivity of freight shipping, enabling faster loading and unloading of ships, the swapping between modes of transport with containers fitting onto both trucks and rail cars, and improving security of goods.

Containerization was therefore an important development in accelerating the *time-space compression of *supply chains and furthering processes of *globalization.

contaminated land Land once built upon or used for industrial, agricultural, governmental, or military purposes, and that now contains harmful substances. In order to be reused contaminated lands must be subject to remediation. *See also* BROWN AGENDA.

content analysis An analysis of text with respect to its content, message, and audience. Content analysis seeks to make sense of the diverse range of written texts through which people communicate—letters, newspapers, policy documents, novels, etc. It does this by systematically breaking down the text into component parts and coding them with respect to their content. By grouping similar pieces of text together inferences can be made about the producers of a text, its message, and its audience. Content analysis can be both *quantitative, using descriptive statistics to investigate patterns in the text, and *qualitative using a *hermeneutic reading.

content cloud A way of visualizing *text by using variations in font size to displaying the relative frequency of words or terms. The more frequently a word occurs in a text, the larger it appears in the diagram. It is similar to tag clouds used in blogs, and there is a growing number of software applications to generate them. Contents clouds can be used to represent at a glance where the focus of current interest is among a group of interlocutors.

contextuality A contextual account attempts to understand objects and events in relation to their specific spatial and temporal settings, emphasizing their mutual associations. It is a synthetic way of understanding social life, in contrast with more analytical approaches which either *abstract formal categories from any situation or regard space and time as backdrops to human action rather than constitutive of it. In human geography, the idea is closely associated with Torsten *Hägerstrand.

contiguous zone A zone extending for twelve nautical miles beyond a state's territorial sea or 24 nautical miles from its coastal baseline (taken as the mean low-water mark). It is not considered to be sovereign territory as set out in the United Nations Convention on the *Law of the Sea, but a state can exert limited controls with respect to customs, fiscal, immigration, and sanitary laws. *See* TERRITORIAL SEA.

continent A large, contiguous landmass usually bounded by a significant geographical barrier such as a sea or mountain range. It is generally accepted that there are seven continents on earth—Asia, Africa, Antarctica, Australia, Europe, North America, and South America.

contraction and convergence A proposed strategy for managing global greenhouse gas emissions by lowering them to a safe level ('contraction') through the gradual convergence of national-scale emissions on a single agreed per capita entitlement. There is some support for contraction and convergence within the *United Nations Framework Convention for Climate Change, but considerable disagreement about the appropriate levels and rates of convergence.

conurbation A group of settlements geographically close enough together to be considered a single, larger metropolitan region. Ostrava in the Czech Republic is a good example, comprised as it is of some 30 previously separate townships that have merged over time. *See also* CITY.

coordinates A method of precisely locating a point in a grid or globe by a scaled number system. A number of coordinate systems exist for different shapes. The most common system for locating a point on the earth's surface uses *Cartesian geometry, where the X axis is known as longitude (east/west) and Y axis latitude (north/south).

Corbridge, Stuart (1957–) A leading development geographer known for his writing on theories of *development, on the global *debt crisis, and on the geography of money. He also has long-term field experience in rural India looking at agrarian change and *modernization. He is a professor at the London School of Economics.

core-periphery A binary geographical relation between a centre and it margins. The centre may be where economic activity, population, and/or political power are concentrated, at the expense of the margins, which may supply labour, raw materials, or surplus product. Although in abstract, core and periphery may describe relations at any scale, in practice the distinction is used at either national or international (global) scales. The contrast is also applied to *labour markets, differentiating between a core of secure and well-remunerated jobs and a periphery of insecure employment.

John Friedmann devised a core-periphery model in the 1960s to describe the development of urban systems through four stages. The pre-industrial stage consists of dispersed and relatively self-sufficient settlements, but in the transitional stage a single core emerges as the site of intense capital accumulation, for example, through export trade. In the second two stages, industrial and pre-industrial, Friedmann envisaged a process of convergence. The urban system would be fully integrated through transport and communication links, leading to local specialization but also greater equality of development. At a global scale, Immanuel *Wallerstein's *world-system approach proposed an unequal relation between core and peripheral regions. The latter supplied the commodities for the higher value-added activities of the former. He added the concept of semi-peripheral states, where there was a mix of high and low value-added processes (*see* DEPENDENCY THEORY; DEVELOPMENT THEORY). Neither theory is currently much in vogue, although the World Bank recognizes a distinction between leading areas, possessing a higher economic density, and lagging areas, characterized by distance from such density (World Bank 2009). Two of the main limitations of core-periphery models are that they obscure a more complex *uneven development and that they fetishize spatial relations at the expense of social relations.

Reference World Bank (2009), *World Development Report 2009: Reshaping Economic Geography*.

Corporate Social Responsibility (CSR) The attempt by large firms to make a wider contribution to society, often in recognition of the impact their business activities have on communities, localities, and citizens. It can be described as a form of ethical capitalism. CSR arose in the 1980s, when R. E. Freeman argued that big businesses needed to pay attention to the needs of stakeholders as well as shareholders. Stakeholders are those who have a significant interest in a firm's activities, such as residents living near a steel mill. With the rise of *neoliberalism in many countries worldwide, CSR has become an important way in which the regulation of business activity now works. It is a form of self-regulation in that, so long as a firm's activities do not break domestic or international law, it is not obliged to adopt robust CSR policies. These policies are wide-ranging, and cover everything from providing recreational or educational opportunities for a firm's workers, to making charitable donations to local organizations, to doing pro-bono work for a vulnerable social group. Some firms have made CSR central to their business objectives, as in manufacturers of *Fair Trade food and clothing. Others have made their CSR activities highly visible to consumers and the public as part of an attempt to show they are not interested in making money at the expense of everything else. Critics from the left argue that CSR policies are often window-dressing used by otherwise exploitative and careless corporations to improve their image (*see* GREENWASH). Critics from the business world sometimes argue that companies should merely abide by the law, and leave everything else to governments. Others point out that these policies are necessary to fill the regulatory vacuum created by neoliberalism; they further argue that many left-leaning *new social movements and *non-governmental organizations deserve credit for pressurizing firms to take CSR seriously. Even so, to the extent that CSR policies are voluntary and not mandatory, questions arise about how effective and enduring they are likely to be. *See also* CORPORATION.

Reference and further reading Barry, A. (2004), 'Ethical capitalism', in Larner, W. and Walters, W. (eds.) *Global Governmentality*.

Freeman, R. E. (1984), *Strategic Management*.

Sadler, D. and Lloyd, S. (2009), 'Neo-liberalising corporate social responsibility: A political economy of corporate citizenship', *Geoforum* 40: 613–22.

corporation 1. An association of individuals, recognized by law or other public regulations, that exists over and above the specific people who comprise it at any one time.

2. A firm, whose owners, shareholders, and senior managers together 'incorporate' their resources, rights, and duties.

3. A public body responsible for representing and attending to the various interests and needs of citizens in its geographical domain.

Economic geographers have analysed corporations in the second sense for decades, aiming to understand their locational decisions and how—in the case of *transnational corporations (TNCs)—they integrate research, design, production, distribution, and marketing over large distances and between many countries.

correlation A statistical calculation which measures the probability that there is a potential dependence between two or more *variables. That is, there appears to be a potential causal relationship between the variables, be it direct or indirect. For example, we might expect the cost of travel and distance to be related, where cost is the dependent variable, with people travelling further distances paying substantially more than those travelling shorter journeys. The correlation determines the extent to which such a dependency varies from randomness. While there might be a statistically significant correlation between variables, it does not necessarily mean that a causal relationship exists, but rather that the two sets of data have an alignment which has a non-random pattern (*see* SIGNIFICANCE TEST). *See also* REGRESSION.

corridor A type of economic development zone that stretches along a transportation corridor between two or more principal economic nodes. An example is the Dublin–Belfast motorway/rail corridor in Ireland, where smaller towns along the route seek to take advantage of trade between the two larger nodes by attracting inward investment by companies seeking to service both locales and take advantage of the enhanced transport network. The corridor thus acts as a site of *agglomeration for a linearly aligned *cluster.

Cosgrove, Denis (1949–2008) A leading British cultural geographer who helped alter prevailing views of the nature and study of *landscape. Cosgrove regarded landscapes as the material expression of relations of *power, control, and resistance among dominant and subordinate social groups. Landscapes, he argued (along with co-author Stephen Daniels), invite a critical reading, just as other cultural phenomena such as paintings and novels do. In his later work he explored different ways in which the Earth has been visualized through history. He was Alexander von Humboldt Professor of Human Geography at the University of California, Los Angeles, at the time of his death. *See also* ICONOGRAPHY OF LANDSCAPE, THE.

cosmopolitanism The ethic and practice of being open to and respecting ways of life that may vary significantly from one's own. To be 'cosmopolitan' is to be 'well-travelled' and genuinely curious about the world beyond one's doorstep. It is to have experienced and been enriched by all manner of other people, places, customs, and norms. Cosmopolitanism was advocated by the German philosopher Immanuel Kant in the 18th century. Kant wrestled with the question of how we should respond when confronted by ways of life that, because they are so removed from our own, might strike us as uncivilized, cruel, or simply baffling. He argued that we should treat all people as ends in themselves not simply means to our own ends, thus offering an early criticism of unthinking *ethnocentrism. Over two centuries on, many in the humanities and social sciences—including human geographers—have sought to revisit Kant's cosmopolitan ideal in an enormously changed world. A layering of colonialism, imperialism, international trade, foreign direct investment, mass migration, intergovernmental initiatives, and much more has produced a world in which near is far and the far is near. Yet the globe is not a 'melting pot' in which differences between people have been dissolved into new hybrid formations. Instead, variations in dress, language, religious belief, cuisine, manners, and so on have been brought closer together in time and space. The so-called 'War on Terror' prosecuted by the USA and its allies from 2002–12 showed how some of these differences can be essentialized and demonized. As Derek *Gregory demonstrates in his book *The *Colonial Present*, stereotyped or one-dimensional *geographical imaginations can cause real harm to people whose differences from us deserve to be better understood. Given that we live in a world in which inequality looms large and in which grievances often find military expression, the question arises—how can we foster a rich form of cosmopolitanism that changes us as much as it changes our views of people very different from us? Urban geographers such as Ash *Amin have been asking this question in their inquiries into how to create more cosmopolitan cities that are less scarred by class, ethnic, and other divisions (*see* SUPERDIVERSITY).

cost-benefit analysis (CBA) A procedure that seeks to identify and quantify the relative costs and benefits of major public sector or state-promoted projects, such as a new nuclear power facility, a new railway line, or a new airport. Originating in the USA five decades ago, CBA has become increasingly comprehensive, technical, and contested over time. It involves three stages. First, the full range of costs and benefits in any given case must be identified, ranging from jobs created, to public health risks, to environmental amenities lost. Second, these various costs and benefits must, as far as possible, be measured according to a common denominator, such as money values. This is technically challenging because some costs are arguably priceless (e.g. the loss of a rare bird species), while some benefits are speculative (e.g. will future generations value the electricity supplied by a nuclear power plant as much as present ones might?). Third, once all costs and benefits have been weighed, a decision about whether and how to proceed with a planned project is taken. CBA is highly contentious, especially when assessing large-scale problems, opportunities, or plans. Critics argue that it lends an air of false precision to decisions that are intrinsically political and tries to finesse important differences in how people attach value to a range of social, economic, cultural, and environmental phenomena.

counter-culture A social group or movement whose values and way of life are opposed to the mainstream of society to some degree. The term is often used specifically to refer to the mix of alternative lifestyles and practices that spread through the USA and other Western countries in the 1960s. These embraced commitments to peace and civil rights on the one hand, and experimentation with drugs, mystical practices, and communal living on the other, animated by the decade's popular music.

counter-globalization *See* ANTI-GLOBALIZATION MOVEMENT.

counter-mapping The production of *maps by a *community that seeks to challenge the maps produced and used by a state, administrative body, or commercial company. Counter-maps reveal the ways in which official maps often omit important information in order to justify particular political actions. For example, omitting indigenous villages from areas designated for forestry disenfranchises those villages. Counter-maps are thus useful for inserting local peoples' voices into political debate. *See* CARTOGRAPHY; INDIGENOUS MAPPING.

Further reading Peluso, N. L. (1995), 'Whose woods are these? Counter-mapping forest territories in Kalimantan, Indonesia', *Antipode* 27(4): 383–406.

counter-urbanization A pattern of population change in which smaller towns and villages grow at a faster rate than larger cities within a national settlement system. It is usually a process of population deconcentration, where people move out of cities into rural areas. Since the 1970s, counter-urbanization has been observed in many countries around the world, although in some cases it now appears to be receding.

Further reading Champion, A. (1991), *Counterurbanization*.

countryside A *rural landscape in which there is limited *urbanization and in which settlement is geographically contained to small towns or villages. The country-side is a landscape resource, an amenity, and a working environment. Population is usually small, spatially concentrated, or scattered in one-off houses or farms. The area has limited development and economic activity is largely restricted to small enter-prises, farms, and primary resource extraction. In many nations, countryside areas are protected by zonings aimed at preserving its character and environment. *See also* RURAL GEOGRAPHY.

coupled human-environment systems An analytical perspective that regards human systems (social, political, economic) and environmental systems (biosphere, atmosphere, hydrosphere) as being interlinked in complex inter-dependent relation-ships. The study of coupled human-environment systems focuses on understanding the relations of stability and change between human and environment systems in order to determine how best to manage these interconnections.

Further reading Moran, E. (2011), *Environmental Social Science*.
Turner II, B. L., Clark, W.C., Kates, R.W., Richards, J., Mathews, J. T., and Meyer, W. (eds.) (1990), *The Earth as Transformed by Human Action*.

Cox, Kevin (1938–) A noted political geographer and Distinguished University Professor of Geography at the University of Ohio. His work has sought to put the 'politics' into political geography. His early writings focused on neighbourhood change and conflict in Western cities. Influenced by Marxism, his subsequent work into local economic development showed how political identity and government action were profoundly structured by the economic imperatives of *capitalism. This is linked to his wider interest in the *politics of geographical scale and tensions between local commit-ments and a more global, inclusive political agenda.

creative city *See* CREATIVE CLASS.

creative class A group of professionals, usually possessed of a post-secondary edu-cation, whose work involves creating novel solutions, designs, or technologies. The term was popularized by the US economic geographer Richard *Florida. Florida studied *deindustrialization in the USA during the 1980s and wondered how new centres of economic prosperity, such as those in California's *Silicon Valley, came about. He identified a particular class of people as central to 'post-industrial' economic success. For him, these comprise a 'super creative core' of innovators who, like the inventors of Facebook, devote themselves to producing 'game-changing' goods and services in their respective domains (the arts, engineering, ITCs, etc.). Outside this core Florida identified 'creative professionals', most of whom apply knowledge to solve problems or improve current goods and services in everything from finance to healthcare to marketing. The creative class is the dominant class in society and the bow wave of a new age of creativity, i.e. its impact is epochal in Florida's analysis.

In his several books on the subject, Florida has used official data sources and his own research to map the geography of the creative class in America, with significant consequences for urban policy. His ideas have particular relevance to cities, which can chart their changing levels of relative creativity through various indices. 'Creative cities' have a high concentration of the creative class. In this sense his ideas fuel a form of inter-place competition endemic to *capitalism (*see* URBAN ENTREPRENEURIALISM). His arguments also envisage the creative class as a mobile section of the population, willing and able to uproot in order to find the best jobs and lifestyles.

Florida's work has come in for heavy criticism on both evidential and analytical grounds, and from across the political spectrum (Peck 2011). Some argue that his two-tier creative class concept simplifies a far more complex and messy occupational picture that belies the idea of a unified 'class' of creative people at all. Others argue that his evidential sources are selective and that the inferences he draws from them about 'creative people' are logically unsound. He is also attacked for not stressing tax cuts and other *neoliberal solutions to urban decline. His work has therefore generated a wide response, including empirical challenges to some of the core propositions.

References Florida, R. (2002), *The Rise of the Creative Class*.
Peck, J. (2011), *Constructions of Neoliberalism*.

creative destruction The destruction of the fabric of a community, place, or region in order to create the conditions for future prosperity. The term is closely associated with Karl Marx and later in the 1940s, with Austrian economist Joseph Schumpeter who used it to describe the disruptive nature of innovation in capitalist societies. In human geography, David *Harvey theorized how *capitalism compulsively builds a physical landscape and society to serve its purposes only to find both an eventual impediment in need of restructuring. Change is thus the only geographical constant in capitalist societies.

creative industries Economic activities in which knowledge is applied to create designs, goods, or services that customers perceive to be in some way 'creative' or beyond the range of 'ordinary' commodities. They are sometimes called cultural industries. The creative industries include video-game design, website design, cinema, TV, radio, the various visual and non-visual arts, magazines, advertising, music, fashion, crafts, and signature furnishings. People working in the creative industries are often said to comprise *communities of practice, many of which involve work as a vocation not simply a 'job'. The attraction of the creative industries is that they are often well paid and offer rewarding, non-routine employment. These industries are populated by members of the *creative class, according to Richard *Florida. Human geographers have inquired into the factors that lead creative industries to cluster in specific locations and generate wealth. Many deindustrializing cities, such as Ostrava in the Czech Republic or Buffalo in the USA, have tried to attract such industries in order to set themselves on a 'cleaner' growth path less dependent on heavy industry and manual jobs.

credit crunch The sudden and large reduction in the availability of money available to borrowers in the commercial or residential sectors. The term was coined during the global financial crisis of 2007–2009 when numerous banks, especially in Britain and the USA, hoarded money and made loans to individuals, companies, and governments more difficult to get and more costly after years of low-interest rates.

creolization The formation of a hybridized culture between African cultures and indigenous and European settlers in the New World. In essence, creolization is a process of blending old traditional inherited African culture with other social and political formations to produce new identities that retain the essence of the old culture but are recognizably different. Principally it refers to new creolized cultures in the Caribbean, but also North, Central, and Latin America, and the Indian Ocean. *See also* CULTURE; IDENTITY.

Cresswell, Tim (1965–) A British cultural geographer known internationally for his research into how dominant norms and values get expressed in everyday landscapes and are used to police people's thinking and action. His book *In Place/Out of Place* (1995) examined how people who are 'different' from mainstream society used geography and had it used against them as they struggled to be seen and heard. Later work, notably *On the Move* (2006) was instrumental in the *mobilities turn (*see* MOBILITY).

crime A violation of the law. Crimes are cultural, geographical, and historical constructs and vary between jurisdictions and across time. For example, while prostitution is a crime in some countries, it is not in others, although it might have been at some point in the past. In all territories criminal acts range from relatively benign legal violations through to extreme violence and all have a spatiality and geographical effects. Geographers have studied four related areas of crime. First, they have examined the geography of criminal behaviour by mapping the locations of crimes, seeking to determine their causes and their spatial effects in terms of shaping the mobility of drugs, people, and money; restricting the mobility of victims and staking claims to territory; and shaping perceptions about a place. Research reveals that many crimes have strong spatial patterns and geographical profiling is now regularly used by police forces in an attempt to identify and apprehend criminals. Second, geographers have studied the *fear of crime and its effects on spatial behaviour. Third, they have examined how the *law produces and reinforces certain spatial relations, especially with respect to issues such as *property rights. Fourth, they have investigated how states seek to combat crime, especially through policing and the use of *surveillance technologies such as CCTV.

Further reading Evans, D. and Herbert, D. (eds.) (1989), *The Geography of Crime*.

crisis An emergency event that threatens to destabilize or does destabilize the status quo. Crises can take many forms—economic, financial, social, political, environmental—but all share the effect of causing great anxiety due to how they challenge, or radically and negatively alter the usual way of life (e.g., making people poorer, homeless, victims of violence). While some crises can be anticipated and might have been building for a while (such as political posturing and argument before a war), others can be sudden and unanticipated (such as an earthquake). Geographers are interested in crises because these affect the social and spatial relations between people, place, and environment. Analysis focuses on the factors that caused a crisis, how the crisis was manifested, the geographical effects of the crisis, and potential solutions to militate against similar future events. For example, there is a long tradition of research focusing on environmental hazards, *disaster management, *geopolitics, and *war, economic *recession, and financial crashes. *See also* DEBT CRISIS; FINANCIAL CRISIS; FISCAL CRISIS.

Further reading Larner, W. (2011), 'C-change? Geographies of crisis', *Dialogues in Human Geography* 1(3): 319–35.
Smith, K. and Petley, D. (5th ed. 2009), *Environmental Hazards: Assessing Risk and Reducing Disasters*.

Critical Cartography/GIS A mode of analysing the production and use of paper and computer-based maps that recognizes the politics and subjective dimensions of their creation. Maps, it is argued, are not neutral, objective representations of the world, but are shaped by the worldviews and intentions of those that make them. Critical cartography can be traced to the work of Brian *Harley and his use of the ideas of Michel *Foucault and Jacques Derrida to deconstruct the ideology bound up in the production of maps. Critical GIS extends such thinking to how GIS databases and representations are structured, and how they are used in practice to inform decision-making. *See also* CARTOGRAPHY.

Further reading Harley, J. B. (1989), 'Deconstructing the map', *Cartographica* 26(2): 1–20.
Pickles, J. (ed.) (1995), *Ground Truth: the Social Implications of Geographic Information Systems*.

critical geopolitics The study of how geographical discourses, practices, and models represent the world with a view to uncovering the relationships between space, power, and knowledge. It can be thought of as the application of *post-structuralism to *geopolitics, intended to challenge conservative models of world politics and strategic relations. In *Critical Geopolitics*, Gearóid *Ó Tuathail outlined the important differences between this approach and more traditional perspectives. Conventional geopolitics is founded on an objective view of the world, often in the form of the 'big picture', i.e. a synoptic statement of the role of geographical factors such as territory and resources in the balance of power between states. It is state-centred, not recognizing other political actors and downplaying the significance of economic relations. It is characterized by what Klaus Dodds calls 'a propensity to divide the world into discrete spaces', i.e. a way of mapping allies and enemies and ascribing essential characteristics to regions and their inhabitants (*see* ORIENTALISM). Lastly, it is generally partisan, keen to influence national politicians, and further what they deem to be the national interest. By contrast, critical geopolitics does not assume the observer is detached or neutral, but regards all understandings as *situated knowledge. Rather than treat geopolitical accounts as descriptions of the world, they are regarded as scriptings of the world, ways of representing reality in the interests of power. *Deconstruction is an appropriate method therefore, and critical geopolitics is particularly attentive to the role and technologies of visualization in geopolitical representations. It also considers texts other than those of formal policy documents, including speeches, films, and cartoons. Rather than accept that the world is divided into discrete spaces, it aims to uncover the processes which 'fold distance into difference', as Derek *Gregory puts is.

Further reading Dodd, K. (2005), *Global Geopolitics*.
Gregory, D. (2004), *The Colonial Present*.

Critical Geopolitics A foundational text in the field of *critical geopolitics written by Gearóid *Ó Tuathail and published in 1996. Subtitled 'the politics of writing global space', it feature a series of essays on how national governments have attempted to remap the globe in their own image. The examples include British imperialist, German, and US geopolitics in the mid-20th century, as well as more recent events in Bosnia and Ireland. Although highly regarded, critiques have questioned the focus on discourse and representation at the expense of *affect, *performativity, and the production of political knowledge.

critical (human) geography A range of research and teaching aimed at promoting social change in the form of greater justice, freedom from oppression and exploitation, and the positive recognition of various forms of human difference. At its most radical, critical geography advocates emancipation, rather than managing things according to current norms or piecemeal problem-solving, as the purpose of geography. It seeks change within the academy itself, by challenging styles of research and university practices that are seen to contribute to unfairness or harm, but also in the relations between academics and others outside universities. To some degree, critical geography is a renaming of *radical geography and is closely aligned with the political *left. But its breadth of political commitments and internationalism distinguish it from earlier left movements in the discipline. Inevitably, what counts as 'critical' is a matter of perspective and discussion, but to a large extent 'critical' thinking (in the sense of left-wing) is now dominant in academic human geography as a whole. The online mailing list Critical Geography Forum began in 1996, the first International Conference of Critical Geography was held in Vancouver in 1997 and *ACME: an International E-Journal for Critical Geographies* was launched in 2002.

Critical Legal Studies (CLS) A body of research that takes a critical perspective on the formulation and implementation of the various branches of modern law. CLS emerged in the 1970s in the United States and was inspired by a combination of *Marxism and *Critical Theory in the academy, and the feminist, environmental, and anti-war movements in the wider American society. By the early 1990s it had become an established approach—or rather family of approaches—within many law schools and not a few branches of other social science and humanities subjects. CLS rests on two precepts: first, all law is politics by other means (rather than 'standing above' politics in splendid neutrality); second, law—in both its formulation and implementation—frequently reproduces inequality and injustice, even though it is supposed to redress both. CLS is a creature of the political left but it is not 'anti-law'. Instead, it seeks to improve the law so that it may better serve the diverse interests and needs of people who inhabit societies marked by complex patterns of power, subordination, inclusion, and exclusion.

CLS has had a large impact on those human geographers who study the law. In part, this is because *legal geography developed just a few years after CLS became prominent. In part it is because legal geography grew at a time when critical approaches in the discipline were diversifying and enlarging. The influence of CLS on legal geographers' thinking is evident in the research of Nick Blomley and Don *Mitchell. Both, in different ways, inquire into the ways the law partitions territory and makes impossible certain behaviours and occupancy within the partitions. *See* LAW.

References Blomley, N. (2004), *Unsettling the City.*
Mitchell, D. (2003), *The Right to the City.*

critical rationalism An approach to research that emphasizes relentless criticism as the key to rigour and the achievement of truthful, accurate knowledge of the world. The approach is closely associated with the philosopher of science Karl Popper (1902–94). Popper argued that a good scientist always looks to refute rather than simply verify a hypothesis, model, or theory. In theory, one negative result trumps one hundred positive results of a scientific test or experiment. In geography, David Harvey's *Explanation in Geography* highlighted critical rationalism. However, in practice, it is a less a 'method' than a sensibility used as part of a mix of research practices in the discipline.

critical realism A philosophy applicable to both the social and natural worlds that offers guidance on how best to research these. There are many forms of realism, and they entail a belief that the world exists and acts independently of any one person's knowledge of or beliefs about it. Critical realism takes issue with other forms of realism, such as *empiricism. It posits an ontology and perspective on cause and effect that highlights non-visible processes, a stratified reality, complexity, and *emergence. It also recognizes that humans constitute the social worlds they study, whereas the biophysical world exists regardless of our ideas about it. Critical realism had a notable impact on human geographers' understanding of how to do research in the 1980s, courtesy of Andrew *Sayer. *See also* EXTENSIVE RESEARCH; INTENSIVE RESEARCH.

Critical Theory A family of approaches to understanding advanced capitalist societies that built upon the work of Karl *Marx but adapted it to the changed socio-economic, cultural, and political conditions of the post-1945 West. Sometimes known as the Frankfurt School, Critical Theory's most famous and influential figures were Max Horkheimer, Herbert Marcuse, and Theodore Adorno, followed by Jurgen Habermas. Derek Gregory's book *Ideology, Science and Human Geography* made formal use of Critical Theory and considered how space entered into its constituent claims. Gregory went on to explore the links of Habermas's writings to the concerns of human geographers. However, few others followed his lead and have preferred, instead, more piecemeal engagements with Critical Theory.

criticism and critique The act of identifying problems, weaknesses, or contradictions in the philosophies, theories, models, methods, evidential claims, and prescriptions of others. Criticism is an everyday term, whereas critique is not. The latter signifies formal and sustained criticism, and is used frequently in academic circles. It also signifies criticisms that come to light or seem especially relevant when a moment of crisis occurs. For instance, during the global financial crisis of 2008–2009 many *Marxist geographers pointed to their prescient analyses of *capitalism, which had fallen out of favour in human geography after 1990 or so. For some, critique should avoid the moral condemnation of something and focus instead on that something's own *internal* problems, weaknesses, potentialities, or contradictions. Critique thus locates genuine possibilities for improvement on the basis of what currently exists, not on the basis of utopian plans about a future that may never eventuate. It is immanent not 'external' to its object. In human geography the terms 'criticism' and 'critique' tend to be used interchangeably, with only a minority defining the latter with reference to crisis moments and internal evaluation. Some, influenced by Bruno Latour's recent writings, argue that critique and criticism have for too long sought to 'uncover' and 'disclose' hidden 'truths'. They argue that critics must now seek to be more positive and to help create a better world, not simply point to the current world's maladies.

Reference Latour, B. (2004), 'Why has critique run out of steam? From matters of fact to matters of concern', *Critical Inquiry* 30, 2: 225–48.

cross-border cooperation and trade Agreements by two or more countries to exchange goods, services, and other things (e.g. technology or expertise) for their mutual benefit. Such agreements usually have an economic rationale, but often politics or ethnicity are important too. For instance, in the former communist bloc there was a great deal of international cooperation and trade between socialist countries.

cross-cultural research The comparison of the same phenomenon in different cultural contexts. Much geographical research is cross-cultural in nature, comparing how different human systems are structured and work in different places, and the influence of factors such as culture, social norms, political and religious beliefs, and economic systems. In such research, extra care is needed to take account of and be sensitive to differences in language and cultural practices. *See also* CULTURE; ETHICS OF RESEARCH.

---

crowd-sourcing 86

crowd-sourcing The generation and harvesting of data and ideas produced voluntarily by many people. Many online and mobile technologies allow such data to be automatically generated as these track and trace their own usage and location. The project OpenStreetMap is an example of a crowd-sourced project, wherein detailed map data are produced by people pooling *GPS and metadata.

SEE WEB LINKS
• Website for OpenStreetMap, a free wiki world map

Cuba One of the last remaining countries that is officially socialist and a leading communist country during the *Cold War (see COMMUNISM). Cuba is an island state in the *Caribbean and was (until 1898) a Spanish colony. In 1959 the communist Fidel Castro and his associates staged a coup, and in 1965 Cuba became a one-party state and ally of the former USSR. Because of its close proximity to the USA, Cuba was on the front line of the Cold War, as evidenced by the Cuban missile crisis of the early 1960s that threatened a 'hot war' between Cuba and America. Since the collapse of the Soviet Union and the Eastern bloc of communist states in 1989, Cuba's geopolitical significance on the world stage has declined markedly. Politically, economically, and socially it is more egalitarian than its capitalist neighbours in the Caribbean, though in GDP terms it is considered a 'developing country'.

cultural capital The non-financial assets of an individual used to position and forward that person within a social system of exchange. The concept is most closely associated with the work of Pierre *Bourdieu who initially used it to explain the social mobility of children and the reproduction of *class relations. For Bourdieu, cultural capital is one of a number of capital exchanges that affect class along with social, symbolic, and economic. It exists in three principal states: through corporeality (physique, dress, accent); through cultural artefacts such as possessing valuable or desirable material artefacts; and through institutionalized signifiers such as academic qualifications.

cultural circuit of capital A discursive apparatus comprised of business schools, management consultants, management gurus, and related media that functions to constantly critique and therefore refine capitalism through generating new theories about it. The concept was elaborated by Nigel *Thrift in the context of his cultural-economic analysis of capitalism at the turn of the century, set out on Knowing Capitalism (2005).

cultural ecology The study of the relations between humans and their environment, paying particular attention to processes of adaptation through cultural means. It developed out of US anthropology in the 1950s, notably from the work of Julian Steward, author of Theories of Culture Change. Cultural ecology combines anthropologists' interest in the ethnographic study of non-industrial societies with an understanding of key ecological concepts such as resilience, stability, and biodiversity. Within geography, it is now generally included under *political ecology, signalling an interest in power, conflict, and situations beyond small-scale, non-industrial societies.

cultural economy 1. The name for that part of an economy comprised of *creative and cultural industries.
2. An approach to the study of the economy that highlights the ways in which *culture, in the broadest sense of the term, bleeds into and out of all aspects of economic life. According to Amin and Thrift, this involves the centrality of passions, moral sentiments, and knowledge, while concepts such as evolution, complexity, and *consumption are

central devices for understanding cultural economy (*see* TACIT KNOWLEDGE). Lee and Wills who edited *Geographies of Economies* (1997) did much to kick-start the cultural economy approach in human geography.

Reference Amin, A. and Thrift, N. (eds.) (2004), *The Blackwell Cultural Economy Reader.*

cultural geography The study of the relationship between *culture and *place. In broad terms, cultural geography examines the cultural values, practices, discursive and material expressions and artefacts of people, the cultural diversity and plurality of society, and how cultures are distributed over space, how places and identities are produced, how people make sense of places and build senses of place, and how people produce and communicate knowledge and meaning. Cultural geography has long been a core component of the discipline of geography, though how it has been conceived, its conceptual tools, and the approach to empirical research has changed quite markedly over time.

In the late 19th century, cultural geography sought to compare and contrast different cultures around the world and their relationship to natural environments. This approach has its roots in the *anthropogeography of Friedrich *Ratzel and, in common with anthropology, it aimed to understand cultural practices, social organizations, and indigenous knowledges, but gave emphasis to people's connections with and use of place and *nature (*see* LANDSCHAFT). This form of cultural geography was adopted, extended, and promoted in North American geography in the early 20th century, especially through the *Berkeley School and Carl *Sauer. They were particularly interested in how people adapted to environments, but more particularly how people shaped the *landscape through *agriculture, engineering, and building, and how the landscape was reflective of the people who produced it.

While this form of cultural geography is still practised, it was challenged in the 1980s by new thinking that created what has been termed '*new cultural geography', which led to a broader *cultural turn in the discipline. During this period, cultural geographers started to engage with new theoretical ideas within social theory, including *humanism, *structuralism, *post-structuralism, *postmodernism, and *post-colonialism, recasting cultural geography in a number of significant ways. Most crucially, culture itself was conceived as a fluid, flexible, and dynamic process that actively constructs society, rather than simply reflecting it.

From the perspective of new cultural geography, landscape was not simply a material artefact that reflected culture in straightforward ways, but was laden with symbolic meaning that needed to be decoded with respect to social and historical context, using new techniques such as *iconography. Similarly, it was contended that other cultural practices, artefacts, and representations needed to be theorized and analysed in much more contextual, contingent, and relational ways, sensitive to the workings of difference and *power. Here, new cultural geographers argued that cultural identities are not essentialized and *teleological, but rather need to be understood as constitutive of complex *power geometries giving rise to all kinds of *hydridity and diversity (*see* ESSENTIALISM; TELEOLOGY).

As a result, since the 1980s cultural geography has developed to examine the broad range of ways in which culture evolves and makes a difference to everyday life and places. Studies have examined the *cultural politics of different social groups with respect to issues such as *disability, *ethnicity, *gender, *race, *sexuality, and how the processes and practices of *othering, *colonialism, *imperialism, *nationalism, and *religion shape the lives of people in different locales and contexts fostering senses of *belonging and *exclusion. Others have looked at how culture is reflected and mediated through *representations such as *art, *photography, *music, *film, and mass *media, and material cultures such as fashion, *food, heritage, and *memorials/monuments, as well as the practices of creating knowledge and communicating through *language. More recently still, a move towards non-representational theory has developed the focus beyond representations. Through the cultural turn, there has also been a move to explore how culture intersects with other forms of geographical inquiry such as the economic and political, arguing that these domains are deeply inflected and shaped by cultural processes (*see* CULTURAL ECONOMY). Consequently, cultural geography is one of the most vibrant fields in human geography today.

Further reading Anderson, K., Domosh, M., Pile, S., and Thrift, N. (2002), *Handbook of Cultural Geography.*
Crang, M. (1998), *Cultural Geography.*
Duncan, J. S., Johnson, N., and Schein, R. H. (2004), *A Companion to Cultural Geography.*
Mitchell, D. (2000), *Cultural Geography.*

cultural industries *See* CREATIVE INDUSTRIES.

cultural landscape The material influence of a culture on its natural landscape. Until the *cultural turn, the examination of cultural landscapes was the key pursuit of an older style of *cultural geography. Important in shaping how cultural landscapes were interrogated was the work of Carl *Sauer and the *Berkeley School. Sauer argued, 'The cultural landscape is fashioned from a natural landscape by a cultural group. Culture is the agent, the natural area the medium, the cultural landscape the result.' In other words, people leave their mark on the landscape through how they build, sculpt, and manage it through processes of construction, farming, landscaping, and conservation. By examining the landscape and its components it is possible to draw conclusions about the societies that made them in the past and inhabit them in the present. Since the cultural turn, cultural geography has broadened its remit to consider *cultural politics and the *cultural economy. Moreover, how it conceives of cultural landscapes has changed, with a more open and fluid understanding of both *culture and *landscape and a wider set of methodologies that recognizes the contested and dynamic nature of landscapes. Cultural landscapes are not simply read as material expressions of a single or dominant culture, but as complex, multifaceted constructions laden with symbolic power. *See also* LANDSCAPE.

References and further reading Olwig, K. (1996), 'Rediscovering the substantive meaning of landscape', *Annals of the Association of American Geographers* 86: 630–53.
Sauer, C. (1925), 'The morphology of landscape', *University of California Publications in Geography* 2(2):19–53.

cultural materialism An approach to understanding *culture that explores its connections with economic activity, social power, and social inequality. Culture is sometimes seen as separate from other spheres of human activity (as in the fine arts or poetry). It is also sometimes seen as a common and positive thing shared by members of a whole community or society. However, writers inspired by *Marxism, most notably British literary critic Raymond Williams writing after the Second World War, argued otherwise. They insisted that what we call 'culture' is one of the many arenas in which dominant social groups seek to express and reproduce their interests and preferences. 'Culture' is thus, Williams and others argued, 'material': it is ultimately linked to the distribution of wealth, resources, and power in the wider society. It is one domain in which, in often subtle ways, dominant and subordinate social groups fight to express their values and goals. In human geography, Denis *Cosgrove and Stephen Daniels introduced cultural materialism to the study of landscape iconography. Later the American Marxist geographer Don *Mitchell wrote a manifesto for cultural materialism that covered both 'high' and 'popular' forms of culture. Mitchell was critical of the apolitical conception of culture advanced by members of the *Berkeley School of cultural landscape geography.

References Mitchell, D. (2000), *Cultural Geography: a Critical Introduction.*

cultural politics The tactics and strategies used by social groups to express and promote their view of the world and challenge alternative viewpoints. All social groups, whether dominant or oppressed, seek to argue for their cultural values and way of life to be accepted by others. Their arguments are inherently ideological and political, seeking to either reinforce or challenge the dominant *hegemony. Such cultural politics might be organized with respect to *race, *religion, *ethnicity, *gender, *sexuality, or *disability.

cultural quarter A concentration of *creative or cultural industries, often linked with urban regeneration schemes. Although clusters of artists, fashion designers, film makers, software writers, and other creative professions have often appeared in cities, from the 1980s there was a call in the USA and Europe for cities to deliberately plan such concentrations as a way of generating economic growth and reviving rundown areas. Key early examples included Manchester and Sheffield in England, and Dublin in Ireland.

cultural relativism The epistemological position that social scientists should seek to understand another culture within the terms of that culture and not their own. At its heart is the belief that all knowledge is mediated through the mind and culture and therefore inherently framed by certain beliefs and values. As a result, knowledge production tends towards *ethnocentrism. Cultural relativism acknowledges and challenges this tendency, arguing that all cultures are equally valid and valuable and should be judged from within their own framing. *See also* RELATIVISM.

cultural turn 1. A shift in geographical thinking to re-engage with questions of *culture, wherein the latter is understood as a dynamic and often conflicted symbolic field, not a unified or unchanging way of life.
    2. A movement within human geography to more broadly engage with cultural and *social theory from across social sciences and humanities (*see* CULTURAL GEOGRAPHY).
    Research on culture within human geography prior to the 1990s, especially in North America, was heavily influenced by Carl *Sauer and the *Berkeley School. They conceived culture as a shared set of customs and practices that were manifest in peoples' material artefacts. These artefacts were seen to express a single, overarching system of cultural beliefs, norms, and practices. Studying these artefacts and their place in the *landscape thus revealed the culture of the people who created them, something seen as especially useful for historical research into previous populations. In contrast to this static, homogenous view of culture, the new cultural geography developed in the 1990s conceived culture as a process—a shifting and unstable system of meanings through which people make sense of the world in different, often conflicting ways. In other words, culture was recast as fluid, flexible, and dynamic; something that constructs society, rather than simply reflecting it. What is more, culture was also seen as a medium through which personal and group *identity is established and an arena in which *power and *resistance are found. In order to develop this notion of culture, geographers began to engage with new critical theories in the humanities and social sciences such as *postmodernism and *post-structuralism. These ideas began to filter out from cultural geography into other subdisciplines such as social, economic, and development geography.

Further reading Cook, I., Crouch, D., Naylor, S., and Ryan, J. (eds.) (2000), *Cultural Turns/ Geographical Turns.*

culture 1. A way of life underpinned by particular values and traditions.
    2. The expression of those values and traditions through writing, music, visual, and performing arts, or through rituals, festivals, and the like.
    3. The intellectual, spiritual, and aesthetic development that distinguishes humans from animals.

'Culture', Raymond Williams famously said, is 'one of the two or three most complicated words in the English language' (1988: 87). This is because the term has been used to mean so many different things in its long history. For some, culture is an overarching phenomenon that characterizes whole societies (as with the *Berkeley School), for others it is plural, constructed, and contested (*see* CULTURAL TURN), and for some it simply does not exist. With regards to the latter, Don *Mitchell has argued, 'There is no culture in the world, only differing arrays of power that organize society in this way, and not that.' For Mitchell, the idea of culture is a screen used by the powerful to advance their own interests and agendas. For example, the argument that high art is one of the pinnacles of cultural creation has long been used normatively to make people believe they should take an interest in such art in order to be considered 'cultured'. In human geography, culture is most often understood in senses **1** and **2**, but in a post-Berkeley School way. Contemporary *cultural geography therefore examines the culture of particular groups and their cultural politics, and how a culture is practised and captured materially and symbolically through cultural artefacts and the various *landscapes in which we live. Much of this research is critical of hegemonic representations of culture and valorizes subcultural and counter-cultural practices.

References Mitchell, D. (2000), *Cultural Geography*.
Williams, R. (1988), *Keywords*.

culture of poverty A set of values and behaviours said to be passed on from parents to children, predisposing them to continue in *poverty. This idea was first proposed by the anthropologist Oscar Lewis in his study of Mexican slum families in the 1950s. It was picked up a decade later in the Moynihan Report on poverty in the USA. Proponents claim the poor internalize a sense of helplessness, dependency, and low self-esteem that prevents them improving their condition. Critics charge that this is no more than blaming the victim, and ignores the role of external, structural factors in causing poverty. *See also* UNDERCLASS.

cultures of nature A term for culturally specific ways of perceiving and valuing the non-human world. The term 'culture of nature' was popularized by landscape architect Alexander Wilson in a book of that name published in 1989. The term subverts the idea that *nature lies outside and beyond *culture because it suggests that the non-human world is always and inevitably understood in culturally particular ways. This means that the idea of a culture–nature distinction is itself a cultural product not an ontological given.

cumulative causation **1.** The process of self-sustaining economic growth in a city or region. The term was widely used in economic and development geography in the 1960s. It referred to positive feedbacks caused when an initial investment (e.g. a new coal mine) creates the conditions necessary for further private and public investment. With luck and judgement these further investments, in turn, can create more economic growth and (possibly) a more complex, networked economy.

2. The process by which migratory movements become self-sustaining over time through socially conditioned decision-making.

cyberspace The virtual space within *Internet technologies wherein interaction occurs. Derived from the Greek word *Kyber* (to navigate), cyberspace means 'navigable space' and was first used by William Gibson in his 1984 sci-fi novel *Neuromancer* to describe how the digital space of networked computers was traversed. The term is taken to refer to the medium and not the technologies that support it, and consists of many different types of virtual domains including the Web, chat rooms, blogs, and online games. While having no materiality and consisting of nothing more than digital data, such domains have a rudimentary geography and can be mapped through a process of *spatialization.

Further reading Dodge, M. and Kitchin, R. (2001), *Mapping Cyberspace*.

cyborg 1. A sentient being that is part machine, part organism.

2. A metaphor used to characterize modern humans. In human geography the latter has found considerable favour because of the arguments made by Donna *Haraway. This influential *Science and Technology Studies scholar argues that people today are so thoroughly dependent on machines, technologies, and other non-humans that they cannot be regarded as purely organic or even purely *human. *See also* ACTOR-NETWORK THEORY; ASSEMBLAGE.

cycle of poverty A situation of persistent *poverty stretching across generations. An individual trapped in such a cycle may lack the resources or opportunities to escape and this disadvantage is passed on to to their children, for example, by inadequate schooling. The solution may involve external intervention from government.

Darby, Henry Clifford (1909–92) A British historical geographer whose studies of landscape change in the centuries leading up to 1800 were among the most ambitious and all-encompassing written by any historian or geographer of his generation. He obtained the first PhD in geography awarded by the University of Cambridge and was later a professor there. He was knighted in 1988.

Darwin, Charles (1809–82) A British botanist and zoologist whose systematic obser-vations of *nature led him to conclude that living species evolve over time in an unplanned manner. Darwin lived during a period when organized religion was still a major force in British and European society. His theory of evolution, presented in *On the Origin of Species* (1859), challenged the idea that life on earth was designed by a powerful deity. Darwin's discoveries had a major influence on academic and wider social thought, one that endures to this day. *See also* DARWINISM.

Darwinism The ideas associated with the work of British naturalist and scientist Charles Darwin (1809–82). Chief among these was the theory of *evolution. Darwin did not originate the theory that species changed incrementally over long periods of time (which was simultaneously advanced by Alfred Russel Wallace), but he did propose a mechanism—natural selection—to explain it. This posits that there are minor, random variations in the offspring of any parent organism. Which of these survive is determined by everything in the local environment, including other organisms, and how far the individual is successfully adapted to it. Thus, chance and contingency account for the development of particular distinctive species' characteristics, rather than destiny, pur-pose, or divine will. Darwin's many writings, which included *On the Origin of Species* (1859), *The Descent of Man* (1871), and an account of his circumnavigation of the globe aboard the vessel HMS *Beagle* (1839), elaborated other important ideas, among them: the interdependency of species in a web of life; the multiplication of species; biogeographical patterns; and the relative role of sex selection. His contribution to scientific methods is also recognized, through his field observations, experimental work, and hypothesis testing on, for example, coral reef formation. Full acceptance of Darwin's specific theory of natural selection did not come until the 1930s, when it was spliced with Mendelian genetics to establish the synthesis of 'neo-Darwinism'.

Darwin's influence on geography was outlined by David *Stoddart under four head-ings: first, the idea of gradual rather than sudden development over time, e.g. the Davisian cycle of erosion; second, ecological relationships between organisms and their environment, e.g. in *urban ecology and the ideas of community, natural area, and succession in *urban geography; third, the idea of selection, struggle, and competi-tion, e.g. in *Ratzel's theory of the state (*see* ENVIRONMENTAL DETERMINISM); and fourth, randomness. Much of this impact was via analogy; for example, the idea that a state is an organism. It is generally agreed that Darwinism had a formative influence on late 19th-century geography, although there is some debate over the relative significance of Darwin's ideas compared with those of Lamarck and others (*see* LAMARCKISM). It is safe to say that modern geography emerged in a Darwinian *paradigm, from which it took ideas of *materialism and evolution.

It is often supposed that Darwin's direct influence waned in the mid-20th century, as physical and human geography drifted apart and the latter turned more to the physical sciences than the life sciences for its ideas, theories, and methods (*see* QUANTITATIVE REVOLUTION; SPATIAL SCIENCE). Biogeography, geomorphology, and quaternary studies continued to demonstrate the significance of Darwinism. But Darwinism's influence, if only indirectly, can be detected in human geography, not just in a revivified *environmental determinism, but also in *evolutionary economics and ongoing debates over bioengineering and the ethics of planetary life. Furthermore, human geographers have used the spread of Darwinism to exemplify the geography of scientific knowledge, most notably in the scholarship of David *Livingstone. The widespread marking of the 200th anniversary of Darwin's birth and the 150th anniversary of the publication of *On the Origin of Species* attests to his status as a global brand. *See also* SOCIAL DARWINISM.

References and further reading Castree, N. (2009), 'Charles Darwin and the geographers', *Environment and Planning A* 41: 2293–98.
Driver, F. (2010), 'Charles Darwin and the geographers: unnatural selection', *Environment and Planning A* 42: 1–4.
Livingstone, D. (1992), *The Geographic Tradition*.
Livingstone, D. (2003), *Putting Science in its Place*.
Stoddart, D. R. (1966), 'Darwin's impact on geography', *Annals of the Association of American Geographers* 56, 683–98.

data The evidence as a basis for analysis, policy, or practice. Data can be quantitative or qualitative. All data are a product of *research design, including specific methods of data acquisition. Quantitative data are numeric and factual in nature, such as *census counts. Qualitative data are textual, visual, and auditory, including letters, *diaries, and other documents, *art, *landscape, *film, *music, *interviews, and *focus groups. Data are often stored in *data archives to enable secondary analysis. *See also* QUANTITATIVE METHODS AND RESEARCH; QUALITATIVE METHODS AND RESEARCH.

data archive A place where paper or digital records of data are deposited, stored, and preserved along with structured *metadata. Archives contain a wealth of information that enables an analysis of different phenomena across time and space. The data held within can be the original documents or processed files. The data might be quantitative in nature, such as surveys and census files, or qualitative such as manuscripts, letters, interview transcripts, and audio and film recordings. Increasingly, archives are seeking to digitize their collections and make them accessible over the Internet. In recent years, archives as institutions of knowledge preservation and production have become the focus of geographical scholarship.

data mining A computational method for analysing large quantities of quantitative *data in order to discover and extract features within the data that warrant further attention. Data mining is considered a pre-analysis phase used to identify patterns such as *clusters, anomalies, or dependencies.

Davis, Mike (1946–) An American historian, social commentator, and critic whose writings have been influential across a range of social science and humanities subjects. Davis's intellectual roots lie in *Marxism, and he has analysed several big issues from an international socialist perspective. His best-known books include *City of Quartz, Ecology of Fear, Late Victorian Holocausts,* and *City of Slums*. He has been an editor of the leading international journal of the political left *New Left Review* and was briefly an editor of *Antipode: a journal of radical geography*. His knack of blending academic analysis with reportage and vignettes has led some to criticize the rigour of his arguments and evidential base.

Dear, Michael (1946–) A British-American human geographer who has made formative contributions to the understanding of cities in the interdisciplinary field of urban studies. A founding editor of the journal *Society and Space*, Dear (writing with Steven Flusty) coined the term the 'LA School of Urbanism' and went on to identify its character in an edited book *From Chicago to LA* (2001). He is perhaps best known for his interest in *postmodernism in the built environment and its effects on the experience of life in several Western cities, but he also carried out important early work on *homelessness. After many years based at the University of Southern California, Los Angeles, he moved to the University of California, Berkeley.

De Blij, Harm (1934–) A Dutch-American human geographer who is a former geography editor on ABC television's *Good Morning America*, a former editor of *National Geographic* magazine, and the author of several books, including *Why Geography Matters* (2007). De Blij's media work has made him one of the few living professional geographers to have a public profile (*see* PUBLIC GEOGRAPHY). Because geography education has a relatively small place in the American educational system, De Blij's recent books have strongly advocated the importance of high-level geographical literacy about the wider world.

debt crisis A situation in which several governments are unable to maintain regular repayments to external lending organizations, such as other governments, international banks, or the *IMF. The term came to prominence in the 1980s when many countries in Latin America accumulated large amounts of debt that outstripped their capacity to pay down. They had borrowed the money in the 1970s in order to invest in infrastructure and new economic activities, hoping these investments would underpin sustained growth in GDP. Through the 1990s indebted governments renegotiated the timing and terms of their repayments, in some cases having portions of national debt written off by external lenders. Since the global financial crisis of 2007, there has been talk among analysts of a 'First World debt crisis', with Greece, Italy, and Portugal in the firing line. These countries have had to instigate austerity programmes at home in order to show external creditors and credit ratings agency that they can continue to repay their debts. In the case of Greece, the programme has been severe and special loan packages have had to be arranged by the *EU to ensure the country did not declare bankruptcy.

debt-for-nature swap An agreement in which part of the external debt owed by a developing country is cancelled in exchange for the funding of *conservation programmes from local sources. In commercial swaps, an *NGO in the Global North might buy some of a country's debt from an international commercial bank and agree to cancel it in return for a conservation investment by the developing country's government. Swaps can also be bilateral, between governments. In 2002 France forgave £25 million of Cameroon's sovereign debt in return for investment in tropical rainforest protection. Most debt-for-nature swaps have occurred in politically stable developing countries in the tropics. Although it is consistent with *sustainable development, critics argue that it is a *neocolonial practice. They say the debts should be forgiven without conditions (*see* DEBT CRISIS).

decentralization The transfer of power from national to regional or local authorities, i.e. down a political or administrative hierarchy. National governments often try to decentralize powers, people, or investments so that specific parts of the wider national *territory might enjoy the benefits. In this sense decentralization is usually strategic or tactical. A national government will aim to satisfy needs or demands coming from places beyond the established centres of economic or political power. *See also* DEVOLUTION.

Declaration of Human Rights A declaration by the United Nations General Assembly of the rights to which all human beings are inherently entitled. The Declaration was adopted in 1948 in the wake of the Second World War. It consists of 30 articles that cover civil, political, social, cultural, and economic rights. The Declaration is enshrined in law through the International Bill of Human Rights, as well as national constitutions and laws. *See also* RIGHTS.

(⊕) SEE WEB LINKS
• Full text of the UN Declaration of Human Rights.

decolonization The process by which a country achieves independence from a former or imperial colonial power (*see* IMPERIALISM). This may be through armed resistance and revolution: for example, Vietnam's struggle to gain independence from France, or by peaceful negotiation, such as Jamaica's independence from the United Kingdom. The term may also describe the break-up of *empires more generally, for example, the dissolution of the Spanish empire in the Americas during the 19th century.

decommodification 1. A process in which a *commodity no longer has a status as commodity (e.g. when it's thrown away).
    2. A political project designed to consciously keep various goods and services from assuming a commodity status and thus being sellable for money in order to realize a profit. The first definition can be applied to all commodities, since commodity status is only ever temporary, involving production or a good or service for sale. The second definition describes recent attempts to find alternatives to capitalism, advocated by activist-critics.

deconstruction A theory, with methodological implications, that emphasizes the incompleteness of the apparently complete categories and concepts used in the West to make sense of the world. Deconstruction is most indebted to the writings of French philosopher Jacques Derrida. One of Derrida's key terms was 'difference', which roughly translates into 'deferral' or 'postponement'. According to Derrida, Western thinking since the European Enlightenment, if not classical Greece, aspires to a false security, as if its favoured terms map onto a world organized into definite 'noun chunks'. Derrida showed that meaning was, in fact, generated by a set of differences internal to language that were relational, such that the meaning of any one thing depended on a 'constitutive exterior', that is, an implied but unspoken or unwritten term. Some human geographers have used Derrida's writings to highlight the conceits and certainties of much human geography research—notably Marcus Doel. Others have deployed his ideas to political ends, as exemplified by J. K. *Gibson-Graham in her influential book *The End of Capitalism (As We Knew It)* (1996). However, arguably most human geographers have deployed deconstruction to analyse the various discourses created and deployed by various elite and lay actors in society. For example, Braun showed how discourses about the non-human world in British Columbia were, despite appearances, implicitly discourses about nature's 'other', namely Euro-American culture. Braun is one of several human geographers who has productively utilized the overlap between deconstructive and post-colonial thinking. Deconstruction is one strand of a wider body of post-structural thinking indebted to *Foucault, *Deleuze, and Guattari among others.

References Braun, B. (2002), *The Intemperate Rainforest*.
Doel, M. A. (1999), *Poststructuralist Geographies*.
Gibson-Graham, J. K. (1996), *The End of Capitalism (As We Knew It)*.

deduction A logical thought process in which statements about unknown or unobservable causes or effects are made on the basis of known facts, processes, or principles. Formally its structure is as follows: if A and B *then* C. Deduction has been formally identified with one of two scientific methods (the other is based on *inference). In practice, deduction is a routine and often unformalized operation that is part of most geographical and non-geographical research.

d

Deep Ecology An environmentalist philosophy, with practical implications, that places the well-being of the non-human world at the centre of human concern, i.e. it is biocentric rather than anthropocentric (*see* ANTHROPOCENTRISM; ENVIRONMENTAL POLITICS). The term was coined by Norwegian philosopher Arne Naess in the 1970s. Deep ecologists are critical of the way modern capitalist societies achieve economic growth by destroying and degrading the natural environment. They are also critical of attempts to make *capitalism more 'sustainable', for example, by *ecological modernization, because they amount to 'shallow ecology'.

defensible space A concept in urban community planning based on augmenting the capacity of residents to feel a sense of responsibility and ownership over their neighbourhood, thereby reducing levels of crime. Formulated by US architect-planner Oscar Newman in the 1970s, it involves physical and design changes to maximize the potential for surveillance by residents, and so increase their sense of territorial ownership. This process is termed 'space syntax' (*see* ARCHITECTURE). Although criticized for trying to use design to solve social issues, the concept persists in efforts to reduce urban crime. *See also* BROKEN WINDOWS THEORY.

deficit model The idea that the general public lacks sufficient scientific and technical literacy to make informed judgements on scientific controversies. The solution is therefore to increase the public understanding of science through better education and communication. The model is criticized for underestimating public knowledge and assuming rational communication is enough to sway minds. It also downplays the role of the scientific community's own interests. *See also* SOCIOLOGY OF SCIENTIFIC KNOWLEDGE.

deforestation The comprehensive removal of *forest cover and the subsequent conversion of land to non-forest uses. Deforestation may not entail the removal of each and every tree; a standard definition is loss of tree crown cover to below 10 per cent of original, although establishing what an original baseline might be is not always straightforward. For those parts of the world without long-run remotely sensed image data, notably in the Global South, fixing baselines is often contentious. The partial removal of tree cover and other forms of impairment, such as caused by air pollution, are referred to as 'forest degradation'. Felling trees is not necessarily deforestation where it is accompanied by subsequent reforestation as part of sustainable forestry.

Although deforestation occurs in all regions, the major concern is with the humid tropics. The main proximate cause of deforestation is clearing land for subsistence or commercial agriculture, followed by commercial logging and for fuel wood; sometimes these occur together. What lies behind these causes is debated. Deforestation has become a key issue for the different explanations of human resource use, from neo-*Malthusianism to *political economy. Among the root causes advanced are population pressure, the absence of private property arrangements (*see* TRAGEDY OF THE COMMONS), political corruption and the power of landed classes, ruling elites and military allies, and market failure. *REDD, or Reducing Emissions from Deforestation and Forest Degradation is the most recent programme designed to address market failure.

The consequences of deforestation are not fully understood, and are likely to vary according to whether the forest is tropical, temperate, or higher latitude. Around a fifth of anthropogenic *greenhouse gas emissions are thought to be caused by deforestation, and the permanent loss of forest cover reduces the level of natural carbon sequestration. There are also important local and regional hydrological effects; the disruption to the hydrological cycle caused by loss of tree cover contributes to aridity. Soil degradation and loss, and habitat and biodiversity loss also result from deforestation. Lastly, there are many socio-economic consequences including population *displacement and loss of livelihood, especially for communities relying on non-timber forest products such as rubber, nuts, and plants.

There is considerable debate over rates of global and regional deforestation. It is clear that it is not a modern phenomenon; widespread deforestation occurred in mediaeval Europe (1050–1250) and the European settlement of the eastern USA. There is some indication that national rates of deforestation decline with higher levels of GNP, a phenomenon termed 'forest transition', but how far this can be generalized is uncertain (*see* ENVIRONMENTAL KUZNETS CURVE).

Further reading Middleton, N. (4th ed. 2008), *The Global Casino: an Introduction to Environmental Issues.*
Williams, M. (2002), *Deforesting the Earth.*

deglobalization 1. The slow-down or reverse of *globalization.
2. A political project opposed to *neoliberal globalization. In the first definition, the term describes how global flows of trade, investment, and migration can decline, as happened for example, from 1914 onwards or, to some degree, from 2008. While most economists would regard this as harmful to standards of living, there are those who actively campaign for it. Walden Bello, a Filipino activist and intellectual, advocates production for domestic markets, the protection of local industries by tariffs, and the replacement of international regulatory bodies such as the *International Monetary Fund by regional entities. He favours de-emphasizing economic growth and making the market subordinate to social, justice, equity, and community. *See also* ANTI-GLOBALIZATION.

degrowth A political and social movement that advocates a downscaling of both production and consumption of goods in order to create more environmentally and socially sustainable communities. Proponents argue that present economic activity and lifestyles are unsustainable given resource constraints, its effects on the environment, and its reproduction of deep social inequity. Instead they advocate the creation of a society that is not obsessed with economic growth and a radical contraction in economic output. *See also* DEGLOBALIZATION.

deindustrialization 1. The progressive closure or downsizing of manufacturing industries in a place, city, or region.
2. The declining share or absolute level of employment in manufacturing industries in a national economy. Industries facing overseas competition, increasing production costs, shrinking markets, and other economic challenges may be forced to relocate some or all parts of a firm. Equally, they may be forced to shut down one or more plants (mines, steelworks, automobile factories, etc.). Locations with a cluster of similar or interlinked firms can suffer a spiral of decline, as happened in the American 'rustbelt' through the 1980s.

Deleuze, Gilles (1925–95) A French philosopher sometimes classified as a post-structuralist, though much of his work was inspired by *Marxism and psychoanalytic theory. Sometimes writing with Felix Guattari, Deleuze's grand analyses of advanced capitalist societies were critical of regimentation and valorized thought and practice that eluded and escaped it. His writings have been a major resource for human geographers writing about *affect, *non-representation theory, and a *more-than-human world.

deliberative mapping A cartographic method of public consultation that seeks to take account of the differing views of experts and citizens with respect to developing and assessing policy options. Those taking part are often divided into panels with similar socio-economic background and expertise that consider an issue both separately and in mixed sessions. Panels use a variety of quantitative and qualitative methods to assess and judge criteria. The aim is to understand and map out the various values and priorities of different groups in relation to a particular issue.

Further reading Burgess, J., Stirling, A., Clark, J., Davies, G., Eames, G., Staley, K., and Williamson, S. (2007), 'Deliberative mapping: a novel analytic-deliberative methodology to support contested science-policy decisions', *Public Understanding of Science* 16(3), 299–322.

demedicalization 1. The reclassification of a condition once thought to be medical in nature to one that is non-medical. **2.** A shift in expertise and control from the medical profession to patients and *complementary and alternative medicine. An example of the former meaning would be the demedicalization of homosexuality, which used to be classed as a mental illness that needed to be treated. In the latter sense, patients gain more control of their own treatment regimes.

democracy A form of government in which members of the whole society, rather than just a few, debate matters of common concern and elect a government which then has a mandate to formulate law and implement policy. The word has ancient Greek origins and translates as 'rule by the people'. Understood literally it means 'self rule', but in practice usually involves adult citizens appointing representatives to rule on their behalf—hence the term 'representative democracy'. Where representatives then elect or form a national government, the result is a 'parliamentary democracy'. But democratic decision-making is not limited to states, and can be found in many sorts of institutions. 'Participatory democracy', which encourages active involvement of all those affected by decisions on a continuing basis, is sometimes fostered by smaller-scale groupings, for example, the radical Occupy movement.

Gatherings or assemblies of individuals (usually men) to make decisions were historically found in many societies and cultures. But as a systematic and institutionalized form of government, democracy slowly replaced autocracy and rule by monarchs and aristocrats in modern Europe, and was (famously) the form of government chosen by the early United States after it gained independence from Britain in the late 18th century. Although such forms of government were routinely denied to colonies and imperial possessions, the emergence of newly independent states after the Second World War gradually increased the number of countries that might be termed democracies. The collapse of the USSR was associated with another wave of democracies. Freedom House, a US-based NGO, calculates that there were 14 democracies in 1924, 40 in 1972, but 117 out of 195 countries in 2011. *See also* ELECTORAL GEOGRAPHY.

Reference Gilmartin, M., (2009), 'Democracy', in Gallaher, C. et al. *Key Concepts in Political Geography*.

demographic dividend *See* YOUTH BULGE.

demographic transition The historical shift from a demographic regime of high and fluctuating *mortality and *fertility rates ('traditional'), to a regime of relatively low and stable mortality and fertility rates ('modern'). Mortality rates decline first, followed by fertility rates; the timing and magnitude of these events affects the subsequent level of population increase. The transition has been observed for much of Europe, North America, and Japan, countries where there is a long run of demographic records. Demographers—notably Frank W. Notestein, Warren Thompson and Kingsley Davis—theorized that the transition would be a universal pattern. There is much debate as to whether other parts of the world are undergoing or will undergo, a similar transition for similar reasons.

The causes of the transition remain uncertain. Marked variations in timing and level among European countries suggest that there are multiple causes. Falling mortality may be caused by improved health care and/or better nutrition. Lower fertility can be associated with greater opportunities for paid labour, lower infant mortality, female emancipation, and/or the increased relative costs of children. It is also unclear whether such population changes are the cause or consequence of other shifts, including economic and cultural changes.

There is also disagreement as to whether the transition is completed in some parts of the world. Continuing declines in mortality and fertility, in many cases to below *replacement level, prompted suggestions of a 'second demographic transition'. But recent research has indicated that fertility levels may in fact be increasing with higher levels of wealth, reversing the previous pattern (Myrskyla et al. 2009). *See also* HISTORICAL DEMOGRAPHY.

Further reading Chesnais, J. C. (1986), *The Demographic Transition: Stages, Patterns, and Economic Implications: A Longitudinal Study of Sixty-Seven Countries Covering the Period 1720–1984.*

Lee, R. D. and Reher, D. S. (eds.) (2011), 'Demographic transition and its consequences', supplement to *Population and Development Review* 37.

Myrskyla, M., Kohler, H-P., and Billari, F. C. (2009), 'Advances in development of reverse fertility declines', *Nature* 460, 741–43.

dependency ratio The ratio between the number of people in a population of working age (normally 15–64) and the rest of the population (0–14 and 65 and over). The figure gives an indication of the relative size of the economically productive and dependent populations. A higher dependency ratio will tend to place more pressure on working-age individuals to sustain the levels of economic growth needed to support both retirees and children who have yet to reach working age.

dependency theory *See* DEVELOPMENT THEORY.

dependent variable *See* VARIABLE.

deprivation The lack or absence of a resource or opportunity regarded as necessary for a basic standard of living. The concept is wider than *poverty, because it may include safety, health, education, employment, and access to services; these factors are often combined in indices of multiple deprivation designed to establish which areas of a country or city are most in need of support. Deprivation may be absolute or relative, i.e. by comparison with a specific group or standard.

deregulation *See* REGULATION.

desakota **region** An area of mixed rural and urban land use in which agricultural and industrial activities are dynamically related by the mobility of workers between them. Households are diverse in terms of their livelihoods, combining agricultural and industrial sources of employment, i.e. they are not readily classifiable by sector. The term was coined by Canadian geographer Terry McGee from the Bahasa Indonesian words for village and town to describe the kind of landscape found in Indonesia and throughout East and Southeast Asia. *Desakota* regions combine high-density rice cultivation with non-farming activities, are generally unplanned, and are linked by advanced transport routes to major cities. Similar kinds of landscapes based on a mosaic of land-use patterns may be found elsewhere in the world, though under different names.

Further reading McGee, T. (1991), 'The emergence of the *desakota* regions in Asia', in Ginsburg, N. et al. *The Extended Metropolis*, 3–25.

description The process of recording in words (written or spoken) the nature or appearance of a phenomenon or event. Description is usually distinguished from *expla-nation and *evaluation. It is a form of *representation. As with all academic subjects, human geography aims to describe the phenomenal world, and the world of the human mind (see GEOGRAPHICAL IMAGINATION), with as much accuracy as possible. In subjects that value *narrative, such as history and historical geography, description is said to fuse into explanation and evaluation.

descriptive statistics The quantitative measures derived from a set of data that describes how values are distributed within that data series. They can include the range, mean, median, mode, percentiles, variance, standard deviation, skewness, and kurtosis. With respect to a data series: *range* is the difference between the minimum and maximum values in a data series; the *mean* is the average value; *median* is the middle value in an ordered series; the *mode* is the value with the highest frequency; the *percentile* is a value on a scale of 1–100 that indicates the percentage of a data series equal or below it; *variance* is a measure of the extent to which the data vary in terms of their distribution; the *standard deviation* is a standardized measure of variance; *skewness* is a measure of the symmetry in the distribution of data values; and *kurtosis* is a measure of the degree to which the distribution of data is concentrated around the mean. These measures can be displayed through graphs, histograms, bar charts, and pie charts to communicate visually the pattern of how data are distributed. Spatial descriptive statistics can be used to describe the characteristics of point patterns, line, areas, and volumes. With respect to point patterns these might include the mean centre, median centre, standard distance (the average distance from points to the mean centre), and standard deviation ellipse (the variance in the distribution of data points).

Further reading Lee, J. (2009), 'Statistics, descriptive', in *International Encyclopedia of Human Geography*.
Kitchin, R. and Tate, N. (1999), *Conducting Research in Human Geography*.

desegregation A social policy intervention that seeks to tackle *segregation, partic-ularly that formed along racial or ethnic lines. Desegregation policies seek to encourage *integration and mixing of different groups by enabling the sharing of space and services. Such policies include the setting of quotas on the mixing of *races within public housing, schooling, and jobs. The term is widely used in the USA, where it may refer to the organized *integration of institutions (e.g. the military), cities, and urban neighbour-hoods or, most commonly, school systems. Court-ordered desegregation of racially divided US school districts dates from 1954 and continues to be contested into the present. Similar issues are found in South African schools. These policies have had varying degrees of success and segregation continues to be a social issue. *See also* MAINSTREAMING; MULTICULTURALISM.

desertification A process of land degradation in dryland areas caused by either human impact (for example, deforestation and over-grazing), and/or natural climatic variability wherein fertile land is transformed into desert. In the 1980s it was identified as a major environmental issue, particularly in sub-Saharan Africa. Desertification reduces the ability of local inhabitants to practise *subsistence agriculture and can exacerbate *poverty and lead to *famine. There remains some debate as to whether the process is anthropogenic or irreversible, and whether there is a single phenomenon of desertification. In 2010 the UN launched the Decade for Deserts and the Fight Against Desertification.

Further reading Middleton, N. (2008), *The Global Casino*.

determinism A perspective on causality that regards effects as the direct outcome of certain dominant or overriding processes, structures, relationships, or institutions. Determinist thinking accents one-way causal relationships. It thus contrasts with approaches that highlight feedback, complexity, chaos, and dialectical change. Early in the history of Anglo-European geography *environmental determinism enjoyed a certain popularity until the 1930s. Since then determinist thinking has been largely eclipsed in the discipline, though some worry that Jared *Diamond and like-minded analysts are reintroducing it in all but name. *See also* ESSENTIALISM.

deterritorialization *See* TERRITORY; TERRITORIALIZATION.

détournement An artistic technique that seeks to satirize, parody, or subvert something through mimicry. It reuses a piece of media such as a popular art work, a piece of literature, a film, or political speech, making a variation that's meaning is antithetical to the original. It was developed in the 1950s by the *Situationists.

Detroit Geographical Expedition and Institute (DGEI) An experiment in an alternative model of higher education arising from the collaboration of young black activists and academic geographers in Detroit 1968–70. In the wake of severe rioting in 1967, many people were searching for new, radical ways to bring about social change. DGEI initially arose from the efforts of William *Bunge, a professor at Wayne State University, and Gwendolyn Warren, a neighbourhood organizer. They organized free college extension courses in urban planning-related subjects for residents of the inner city, thereby reversing the conventional focus on outside experts as the sole authority in such matters. Bunge argued that geographers were often as ignorant about the world on their own doorsteps as 19th-century explorers of the Global South were, hence 'expedition'. *See also* RADICAL GEOGRAPHY.

developing world Those countries which are of low-income but, by implication, can become economically richer. The term is now less commonly used than alternatives such as the *Global South.

development 1. The processes of growth and change, at individual, community, and social levels.
   2. The planned attempts to transform the standard of living among the populations of a poorer country or region, generally by outside forces. In both cases development can also mean a condition or stage, i.e. a country can be described as 'developed' (*see* LESS ECONOMICALLY DEVELOPED COUNTRY). Gillian Hart refers to these two senses as development (little d) and Development (big D). The former is aligned with the uneven and contradictory process of *capitalism (*see* UNEVEN DEVELOPMENT). The latter refers to a complex set of interventions—financial flows, policies, technologies, expertise—directed from richer countries (initially the West but also the USSR and China) to poorer countries from the 1940s onwards (*see* AID). These projects have three main motivations: to close the gap in socio-economic levels between different parts of the world; to effect the social and cultural transformations thought necessary to close the gap; to stabilize countries politically (*see* DEMOCRACY). Development is therefore closely bound up with *globalization and *geopolitics.
   Development is conceived and measured in mainly economic terms, although there is much debate as to whether income alone is an appropriate indicator (*see* DEVELOPMENT

development 102

INDICATORS; HUMAN DEVELOPMENT INDEX; POVERTY). An alternative view, proposed by Amartya *Sen, is to understand development as the individual's freedom to realize their culturally valued goals (*see* CAPABILITIES APPROACH). In his view, freedom is the means and ends of development.

Big D Development began in the 1940s in the context of the US-led rebuilding of economies and societies destroyed by war, *decolonization, and the emerging *Cold War. Inspired by universal ideals, US governments from President Truman onwards encouraged the notion that poorer countries could rapidly catch up with richer ones through a combination of self-help and outside guidance. *Modernization theory was the guiding paradigm setting out the path to progress. Development centred on state-led actions such as agricultural reform, infrastructure, and prestige projects such as dams, which qualified for funds from the *World Bank and other international and national lenders. The USSR encouraged its own socialist state-centred development programmes among its allies and client states. Early expectations that the development gap would be closed by 1970 were disappointed, although some East Asian countries did make significant economic progress (*see* MIDDLE INCOME TRAP; NEWLY INDUSTRIALIZING COUNTRIES). Dependency theorists, notably Raúl Prebisch and Andre Gunder Frank, argued that poorer countries did better when not linked closely with richer ones, which siphoned off their products under conditions of unequal exchange (*see* ECONOMIC COMMISSION FOR LATIN AMERICA; UNDERDEVELOPMENT). In response to the worldwide *debt crisis, development programmes shifted towards *neoliberalism and away from state-led initiatives (*see* WASHINGTON CONSENSUS). Neoliberal policies such as *Structural Adjustment Programmes and later *Poverty Reduction Strategies under the auspices of the *IMF were introduced to stabilize and reform poorer countries' economies, but with mixed results. Critics condemned their narrow focus on markets at the expense of wider social and cultural values, and charged that development thinking was Eurocentric (*see* ANTI-DEVELOPMENT; POST-DEVELOPMENT). In response, the major international development organizations have shifted focus towards softer initiatives, such as encouraging good *governance, building *civil society capacity, nurturing *social capital, and advancing *sustainable development (*see* GENDER AND DEVELOPMENT). Participation is the latest watchword. The *Millennium Development Goals, adopted by the United Nations in 2000 prioritize basic needs such as health and water. In addition, there are new development actors involved. The virtual monopoly on international aid held by the members of the *Development Assistance Committee (DAC), mainly richer *OECD countries, has been broken by the re-emergence of China and India as donors joined by the Gulf states and others (*see* BEIJING CONSENSUS). Non-DAC donors account for around 10 per cent of all overseas development assistance. Prompted by multilateral aid agencies and funded by public support, *Non-Governmental Organizations increasingly manage the flow and disbursement of aid.

On the one hand development thinking and policy is increasingly focused on basic needs, local participation, and wider, less economic meanings of development. There has nonetheless been no significant reform in the institutional framework of development, such as reform of the IMF or the regulations governing trade, *Foreign Direct Investment and *intellectual property rights. Development programmes have also become closely implicated with global security concerns in the wake of the *War on Terror (*see* COMPLEX EMERGENCIES).

Further reading and references Hart, G., (2001), 'Development critique in the 1990s', *Progress in Human Geography* 25; 649–58.

Sen, A. (1999), *Development as Freedom.*

Sheppard, E., Porter, P. W., Faust, D. R., and Nagar, R. (2nd ed. 2009), *A World of Difference: Encountering and Contesting Development.*

World Bank (2009), *World Development Report 2009: Reshaping Economic Development.*

development aid *See* AID.

developmental state A form of government involving direct, concerted, and sustained intervention in national economic development through industrial policies such as export-led growth and labour control. The term is generally applied to East Asian countries such as Japan, South Korea, and Taiwan where, in the late 20th century, technocrats and planners were responsible for strategically shaping those countries' economies rather than just regulating them indirectly.

Development Assistance Committee (DAC) A forum for organizing *aid comprising twenty four member states of the *OECD and three observers, the *World Bank, the *International Monetary Fund, and the *United Nations Development Programme. Formed in 1961, DAC aims to promote development cooperation by setting standards for classifying and accounting for aid, as well as conditions of transparency. DAC members aim to coordinate their aid efforts. Not all major aid donors are members of DAC; China, India, and the Gulf states, for example, make their own arrangements.

development ethics A field of inquiry that reflect on the means and ends of *development in its various forms. However defined, development raises large ethical questions about people's rights, duties, responsibilities, and entitlements. Different visions of what counts as 'development', and how to engender it, implicate different ethical norms and goals. These norms and goals are what development ethicists, such as Amartya *Sen, debate and advocate. Development ethics traces a lineage back to the early political economists, such as Adam Smith, for whom ethical questions were part and parcel of all discussions of economy and government. In the field of development geography ethical questions have been explored frequently, most notably in relation to North-South relations of aid, bank lending, famine relief, and the like. *See also* ETHICS.

Further reading Gasper, D. (2004), *The Ethics of Development.*

development geography *See* DEVELOPMENT THEORY.

development indicators The statistical measures of development. The *World Bank collects data on almost 300 indicators, including measures of economic performance, health, disease, environment, and society. Indices, such as the *Human Development Index, are summary measures calculated from such indicators.

development plan A government plan setting out future development in an area. It charts future *land-use zoning and provides guidance to local interested parties, such as developers, and instructions to local government workers on how development should proceed. The plan is developed through a lengthy process of public consultation, taking account of wider government spatial and sectoral policies. It usually has a fixed lifespan of five to ten years, at which point it is revised through another open process.

development studies An interdisciplinary academic field concerned with the *Global South. Drawing largely from the social sciences, especially economics, it emerged in the 1950s, although more strongly in Europe and Latin America than in the USA. It is institutionalized in degree programmes and publications such as *The Journal of Development Studies* (1964–) and *Third World Quarterly* (1979–). Development studies has not focused on *development more generally, avoiding issues in economically richer countries. It has an applied dimension, as evidenced by 'development economics' and 'development management'. It also has a more intellectual and critical aspect, which has included consideration of what should count as 'development' and thus what *sort* of development should be aspired to.

development theory A group of ideas and models about how best to effect social change and economic transformation (*see* DEVELOPMENT). Chief among them are *modernization theory, dependency theory, *World Systems analysis, *Marxist theories of combined and *uneven development, and, more recently, *neoliberalism. Most such theories are criticized for their *Eurocentrism and the reduction of individuals to solely economic agents. *See also* POST-DEVELOPMENT.

devolution The transfer of power from national to subnational levels by statutory authority, an advanced form of *decentralization. Unlike *federalism, devolved powers can be unilaterally reclaimed by the national government, which thereby retains ultimate sovereignty. France, for example, devolved certain legislative, taxation, and planning powers to elected regional assemblies in the 1980s.

diachronic approach A form of analysis that seeks to describe and explain processes of continuity and change over time. History and geology are diachronic disciplines. *Compare* SYNCHRONIC APPROACH.

dialectical materialism *See* HISTORICAL MATERIALISM.

dialectics An approach to understanding continuity and change in the world that focuses on contradictions between processes and events and their temporary resolution. *Marxist geography has used dialectical thinking extensively in its analysis of *capitalism and its uneven geographies (*see* UNEVEN DEVELOPMENT). David Harvey's book *The Limits to Capital* (1982) is perhaps the most sustained example of dialectical thinking in human geography so far. Dialecticians look for contradictions that are internal to any system. The contradictions are seen to be engines of change, only for the changes to be manifestations of the same contradictions they ostensibly resolve. For example, computer designers and manufacturers may cluster in a place like *Silicon Valley, only for them to look for cheaper or better locations within a few years. The contradiction here is between the economic gains achieved by agglomerating and the future economic gains achieved by dispersal and relocation.

Further reading Harvey, D. (1996), chapter 2 in *Justice, Nature and the Geography of Difference*.

dialogic Something that involves two-way interaction, such as a face-to-face debate between peers. In human geography dialogical approaches to eliciting evidence, such as focus groups, have complemented an earlier commitment to more monological approaches that placed the investigator in the metaphorical driving seat. Dialogical approaches involve the conscious but considered interaction of the researcher and the researched in order to draw out richer, more reflexive, and more considered responses.

Diamond, Jared (1937–) A professor of geography at the University of California, Los Angeles, known globally for his inquiries into how societies use and are affected by their natural resource base. Diamond has a background in the life sciences and is among the the few in contemporary academic geography who addresses very large questions by drawing on very wide bodies of knowledge from across the environmental and social sciences, as well as the humanities. His intellectual ambitions have led some to accuse him of making weak and unsupportable generalizations about human-environment relationships past and present. His most famous books are *Guns, Germs, and Steel* (1997) and *Collapse* (2005). *See also* ENVIRONMENTAL DETERMINISM.

diary A chronological journal of one's thoughts and actions. Diaries are a source of qualitative data important for understanding everyday life. They can either be unsolicited or solicited in nature. An example of the former would be a diary kept by somebody as a personal journal with no intention that it would become a source of data for future studies. Such diaries can be important historical sources for understanding the life of a person at a particular time in space. The latter is a qualitative technique wherein respondents are asked to keep a diary that focuses on a particular aspect of their lives such as journeys which they know will form a source of data for a study. Diaries can be written in a personal journal or online through a blog, be visual recorded through photographs or video, or be audio logs. *See also* QUALITATIVE METHODS AND RESEARCH.

diaspora A human population scattered beyond a home territory, though still interconnected. The term commonly refers to ethno-national or religious groups living outside a homeland, e.g. the Irish or Sikh diaspora, but its usage has become greatly extended in association with *globalization and *postmodernism. A constant theme is that diaspora relates to questions of territory and identity, movement and fixity, and challenges the notion that people's identity has a singular relation to place.

It originally referred to two distinct situations: the settlement of the Mediterranean by Greek cities founding 'daughter' *colonies; and the experience of forced removal and exile of Jews to Babylon in 586 BC. But from being regarded as exceptions to the norm of territorially bounded identities such as *nation-states, diasporas have increasingly been treated as indicative of a more generalized sense of geographically dispersed identity. From association with pain and loss diaspora now often implies creativity and freedom. Many critics argue that the term has become so inflated that it has lost significant meaning.

Stéphane Dufoix outlines several distinct meanings. The most inclusive refers to members of a group or organization scattered about the world, not necessarily with any homeland. This could include professionals, footballers, or students. A more categorical usage is found in sociology and political studies, where various authors have tried to identify types of diaspora according to defined criteria, often for comparative purposes. Robin Cohen identifies victim (e.g. Armenian), labour, and imperial (e.g. Indian and British), trade (e.g. overseas Chinese), and cultural (e.g. Caribbean) variants. These are usually distributed across national borders though linked by meaningful social, cultural, and political relations. Some authors use diaspora in the sense of ethnic minority enclaves within a country, e.g. Koreatowns in the USA. By contrast, anthropologists and cultural theorists are often less concerned with the demographic fact, i.e. whether a group *is* a diaspora, and more with the condition or consciousness of being *in* diaspora. They invoke *non-essentialist ideas of identity such as *hybridity and heterogeneity to explore *deterritorialized meanings of belonging. James Clifford argues that we must pay attention to both 'roots and routes' in identity, and Paul Gilroy writes of the *Black Atlantic* (1994) through metaphors of travel across a dispersed socio-cultural terrain. These authors often refer to cultural expressions such as music (jazz and hip-hop in Gilroy's case), art, fashion, and fiction (e.g. Salman Rushdie's novels). They are less concerned with physical movement and material connections than with imagination. For Avtar Brah, diaspora spaces are paradoxical sites where inclusion and exclusion, belonging and otherness are negotiated. They need not imply crossing state boundaries but might refer to parts of a city.

The expansion of diaspora studies beyond discrete ethno-national groups, including in human geography, has generated much research. Economic studies explore the relationships between diaspora and development, focusing on *remittances. Political studies examine the negative and positive relationships between states and overseas nationals. These might include governments-in-exile, such as founded by Tibetans in Dharamsala, or exile groups (including *refugees) hostile to their home state, e.g. Cuban-Americans. By contrast, certain states have adopted a more positive stance to diasporas and seek ways to include them politically. These diaspora strategies recognize that emigrants can be valuable economic assets (supplying *remittances and expertise) as well as political allies through lobbying foreign governments. States may extend *citizenship rights to overseas nationals, including the right to vote in national elections. Diaspora has thereby escaped its scholarly origins and been incorporated into state practices and institutions; states are in the business of constructing diasporas.

Two main accusations are often levelled at diaspora studies, in addition to the view that the term is hopelessly inflated. The first is that diasporas are sometimes uncritically celebrated for their transgressive dimensions. They represent liberation from place, essentialized identities, or state power. But, as Katharyne Mitchell has pointed out, diasporic culture and politics can be oppressive and encourage absolute loyalties. The second complaint is that diaspora studies are rife with spatial metaphors but are weak on actual geography. Geographical work has therefore insisted on grounding diaspora in specific places and times and avoiding intellectual gestures. *See also* MIGRATION.

References and further reading Carter, S. (2005), 'The geopolitics of diaspora', *Area* 34: 54–63.
Dufoix, S. (2008), *Diasporas*.
Mitchell, K. (1997), 'Different diasporas and the hype of hybridity', *Environment and Planning D* 15: 533–53.
Vertovec, S. and Cohen, R. (eds.) (1999), *Migration, Diasporas and Transnationalism*.

Dicken, Peter (1940–) A professor emeritus at the University of Manchester and economic geographer known internationally for his research into the spatial structure of *transnational corporations. He is the author of *Global Shift* and, with co-workers, has pioneered the concept of *global production networks.

diffusion The spread of phenomenon from a particular location through space and time. The phenomenon might be an innovation such as a new idea, fashion, technology, or product, or it could be a disease or gossip. Studies of diffusion seek to determine the means by which phenomena spread, the factors shaping those means, and to map out the time-space paths taken. While geographers have long been interested in diffusion, the work of Torsten *Hägerstrand was vital in establishing a theoretical platform for such studies. Hägerstrand sought to model processes of innovation diffusion and in particular the channels of communication through which potential adopters learn of new things, and how innovations diffuse across scales from local, to regional, to national, and beyond. In particular, he used *Monte Carlo simulations to determine a 'mean informational field' that specifies the probability that an innovation diffused between neighbouring areas. Since then a number of other mathematical models have been developed to try and explain patterns and processes of diffusion. Others have used more qualitative methods such as case studies and interviews with adopters.

Further reading Hägerstrand, T. (1967), *Innovation Diffusion as Spatial Process*.
Rogers, E. (5th ed. 2003), *Diffusion of Innovations*.

digital cartography The use of computers in the production, distribution, and use of maps. From the 1960s onwards, cartography has become progressively more digital in nature. Cartographic data is now routinely digitally generated (e.g., satellite imagery, *photogrammetry, *GPS, laser ranging tools), stored (database software, hard drives, servers), and processed (CAD, *GIS, and desktop publishing applications). While maps are still produced in paper format, they are invariably printed from a digital source, and increasingly mapping data and cartographic software and functionality is available for use across the Internet (*see* DISTRIBUTED MAPPING) and to location-aware mobile devices. While initial digital cartography was very basic, specialized cartographic and GISs are now highly sophisticated offering a diverse range of functionality for producing maps and undertaking spatial analysis. *See also* CARTOGRAPHY; OPEN SOURCE GIS.

digital divide The inequality between people and places in access to and use of *information and communication technologies, with particular reference to the *Internet. The divide may be social: for example, along lines of income, gender, and age; or spatial: for example, between urban and rural areas, regions of a country, or parts of the world. Access can be limited by virtue of inadequate or non-existent physical infrastructure, lack of sufficient income, or personal characteristics such as illiteracy.

Communication technologies such as wireless telegraphy and the telephone have always diffused unevenly. But the concept of a binary divide between the haves and have-nots of Internet access was popularized in the USA and then international development circles from the late 1990s onwards. It reflected the perceived gulf between the supposed potential of the Internet to enhance market access, political participation, education, and social life as part of the *knowledge economy or Information Age and the observation that, at least to begin with, only the richest and best-educated were connected. National and international programmes to close the divide proliferated, for example, with One Laptop per Child (Graham 2011). Such programmes fitted easily into existing theories of *modernization, premised on the ability of technological investment to help some areas 'catch up' with others.

In more recent years it has been realized that not only is there not a single divide, but that plain access is not the only measure of inequality. As more users generate content (so-called Web 2.0) distinctions emerge between those who can and do supply content and those who are only consumers. People are not all equal online, and cyberspace is not a pure *public space of free communication between unmarked bodies. Quality of access also counts, as speed and reliability become critical. Constant technological innovation redraws the boundaries between the more and less privileged. At a smaller scale, issues of whether women feel safe in internet cafes or if children can find space at home to get online also complicate matters. The social and geographical complexities of the use of digital technologies reach far beyond a simple mappable divide.

Further reading Graham, M. (2011), 'Time machines and virtual portals: the spatialities of the digital divide', *Progress in Development Studies* 11: 211-27.

Digital Terrain Model (DTM) A three-dimensional model of the height of the Earth's surface. The model can either be held as *raster data (a grid with each square assigned a height), or *vector data (a lattice known as a triangular irregular network, TIM). The data for the model are generated through a variety of *surveying and *photogrammetry techniques. A DTM is used in a *GIS as the basis for displaying morphological features and to model issues such as flooding, wind effects, and land use. A related model is the Digital Surface Model (DSM) that includes the heights on features on the ground such as buildings and vegetation, which is used to visualize and model landscapes and urban systems.

disability A physical, psychological, medical, or learning impairment that impacts a person's ability to undertake everyday tasks. Approximately one person in every six (15–18 per cent) of the population in Western societies is disabled in some way by an impairment. Rates in the developing world vary depending on mortality rates, healthcare systems, and prevalence of illness and diseases that can cause impairment. Those people defined as disabled can include those with impairments such as perceptual (e.g., visual and hearing impairments, learning disabilities); illness-related (e.g., multiple sclerosis, AIDS); physical (e.g., cerebral palsy); developmental (e.g., Down Syndrome); psychiatric (e.g., bi-polar, chronic depression, manic-depressive syndrome); mobility (e.g., quadriplegia, paraplegia); and environmental (e.g., asthma, sensitivities to allergens and chemicals in the environment), though not everyone who has such impairments would consider themselves as disabled.

How disability is understood has changed over recent decades. Traditionally, disability was conceptualized in medical terms. Here, the daily problems that disabled people face are seen and treated as being purely functional, the direct result of their impairment. The solution to the problems faced is treatment and rehabilitation aimed at allowing the disabled person to overcome an impairment and to take part in 'normal' daily activities. To many this medical model of disability does not, however, fully represent experiences of disabled people or the role of society in disabling people with impairments. For example, Michael Oliver in *The Politics of Disablement* (1990) argues that the medical model of disability is a theory of personal tragedy, where disabled people are portrayed as the unfortunate individual; the victim of nature or fate. In contrast, the social model of disability argues that the vast majority of daily difficulties faced by disabled people are caused by society failing to accept disabled people for who they are and failing to provide adequate facilities. So, for example, a wheelchair-user seeking access to a building where the entrance has steps cannot enter due to the lack of a ramp not his/her impairment.

Geographers have worked with both the medical and social models of disability, plus other conceptualizations that seek to balance elements of the two. For example, work on visual impairments has sought to develop specific aids such as *tactile maps, develop specialized training that will help visually impaired people *wayfind, and identify ways to alter environments to make them easier to navigate. Such work has been critiqued as reducing the problems faced by disabled people to technical issues that can be solved with technical solutions and of depoliticizing the problems disabled people face by suggesting that structural changes to the environment will lead to lasting solutions for disablement, rather than dealing with the wider exclusionary practices that limit mobility.

In contrast, other research has sought to document and challenge the ways in which society (re)produces disabling environments. Here it is recognized that disabled people are marginalized within and excluded from 'mainstream' society through social and economic relations that discriminate on the basis of impairment and ability. For example, disabled people are not treated with the same respect or value as other people and throughout history have been the victims of discrimination, isolation, segregation, mistreatment, and abuse. Disabled people are often the butt of jokes and bullying, and are often portrayed as ignorant, child-like, hyperdependent, and flawed. In terms of spatial relations, it is argued that the built environment has been organized and planned for the benefit of non-disabled people. In its most extreme form, ableist planning practices create spaces that are explicitly designed to segregate and 'protect' the public from disabled people and vice versa (*see* SEGREGATION; SOCIAL EXCLUSION). For example, people with mental, physical, and sensory impairments have been encouraged and forced to live in different spatial spheres, segregated within schooling, or imprisoned or committed to hospitals or asylums against their will. Even within public spaces, disabled people are often deliberately separated and marginalized to the peripheries, for example, having their own separate toilets, or restricted spaces in theatres and cinemas, or are unable to access public transport. The result is that disabled people are one of the poorest groups in society, underrepresented within the workforce, often unable to find suitable housing, and have restricted access to the public sphere.

More recent work has shifted focus to consider ways to create more enabling geographies by working with disabled people to challenge the ways that they are disabled, and to create more empowering environments and communities in which to live.

Further reading Chouinard, V., Hall, E., and Wilton, R. (2010), *Towards Enabling Geographies: 'Disabled' Bodies and Minds in Society and Space*.
Gleeson, B. (1999), *Geographies of Disability*.
Imrie, R. (1996), *Disability and the City*.
Kitchin, R. (2000), *Disability, Space and Society*.

disaster A catastrophic event with serious consequences. A distinction is sometimes drawn between natural and man-made disasters. Natural disasters originate in geophysical causes, including: geological events (e.g. earthquakes, mudslides, and tsunamis); climatic and meteorological phenomena (e.g. hurricanes and droughts); hydrological processes (floods); and even extra-terrestrial events such as meteorite strikes. Disasters of human origin might include the accidental release of radioactive materials from nuclear power stations, explosions at chemical plants or oil refineries, severe terrorist incidents (Cutter et al. 2004), or warfare. But this distinction is problematic at a number of levels. It is open to question whether the causes of a natural disaster such as a hurricane might include factors of human origin, for example, anthropogenic climate change. With very few exceptions, catastrophic natural events do affect human societies, even in regions of low population density such as Siberia. That an event is a disaster, for example, an extreme forest wildfire, can be a consequence of human actions such as building houses in unsuitable terrain or suppressing high-frequency fires. Moreover, referring to an event as a 'natural' disaster has potentially significant discursive and political consequences. It implies forces outside human control, so-called 'acts of God'. It shifts blame away from the decisions made by politicians, planners, and engineers that might have led to the disaster. Thus explains why one reaction to *Hurricane Katrina was the insistence that 'there is no such thing as a natural disaster' (Smith 2006; Klinenberg 2002). This is not to say that there are not real geophysical forces at work, but that there is no point at which a purely natural element can be separated from a purely social one. Debates about disasters are therefore an important variant of long-standing efforts to understand *nature, and society-nature relations.

In practical research linked with disaster prevention and management, reference is still made to natural disasters. A good recent example is the collaborative project on *Natural Disasters Hotspots: A Global Risk Analysis* undertaken by the World Bank in conjunction with Colombia University and other partners. By mapping the incidence of loss of life and economic damage related to six kinds of geological and meteorological event across grid squares, the project singled out regions where the risk of natural disaster was particularly high. This kind of information feeds into national and regional Disaster Risk Reduction (DRR) strategies (*see* VULNERABILITY).

References Cutter, S. L., Richardson, D. B., and Wilbanks, T. J. (eds.) (2004), *The Geographical Dimensions of Terrorism*.

Klinenberg, E. (2002), *Heat Wave: a Social Autopsy of Disaster in Chicago*.

Smith, N. (2006), 'There's no such thing as a natural disaster, understanding Katrina: perspectives from the social sciences', Social Science Research Council, Washington, DC. World Bank, *Natural Disaster Hotspots: a Global Risk Analysis*.

disaster preparedness A state of readiness in anticipation of *disaster that enables a firm, locale, or country to respond successfully. These may include an assessment of vulnerability, the establishment of appropriate emergency planning strategies, public education, warning systems, and rehearsals or drills.

disciplinary power *See* POWER.

discourse analysis A process, usually formal, in which the language of a person, organization, or community is scrutinized so that patterns and key themes can be identified. Discourse analysis became a major preoccupation of the social sciences and humanities from the 1980s, building on earlier work by continental European linguists and philosophers. It rests on the conviction that language is not merely a window onto the world but the medium through which people actively create order and meaning. In human geography it was key to the *new cultural geography and its focus on various forms of *representation. Rather than take what people say at face value, discourse analysis often aims to read 'between the lines' for implicit or coded meanings. It may also inquire into the material effects of a given discourse. *See also* HEGEMONY; IDEOLOGY; POWER-KNOWLEDGE.

disease An abnormal medical condition that adversely affects the body. Diseases can be infectious or caused by internal dysfunctions, which are either hereditary or stimulated by external factors. Geographers are involved in the study of diseases in three main ways. First, by contributing to *epidemiological studies that seek to determine the causes of particular diseases and their diffusion. Second, by examining how the spatial organization of the healthcare system and access to medicines affects treatments. Third, by investigating how people cope with living with a disease and its effects on their spatial lives. *See also* DISEASE DIFFUSION; HEALTH GEOGRAPHY.

disease diffusion How a *disease spreads across space and time infecting people or animals. Infectious diseases are passed to people by other humans, animals, or other carriers. With increasing mobility a disease, such as Avian flu, can potentially move around the world very quickly causing a *pandemic. A geographical aspect of *epidemiology is to track and trace the routes of such diseases in order to understand how they spread and propagate, and to take preventative measures.

diseconomies of scale The additional costs that are incurred when a firm or a cluster of firms becomes too large. If *economies of scale are cost reductions and efficiency gains achieved when one or more firms grow in size, diseconomies arise because firms face additional costs to do with everything from managing a very large workforce to transporting goods attendant upon becoming bigger in size. The term derives from mainstream economics and has been used by business geographers investigating growth poles and regional development. *See also* AGGLOMERATION.

disinvestment The deliberate withholding of money so that a current set of assets, such as a shopping mall or a steel works, does not enjoy future investment. Disinvestment occurs at the level of single firms or governments, but it also occurs in a more collective, unplanned sense (as when private equity fund managers simultaneously decide that a specific industry or place is too risky to continue to invest in). In analyses of *gentrification, disinvestment in inner urban areas has often been taken as a precondition for subsequent re-investment.

Disneyfication The design and management of places to render them simpler, sanitized, and 'family-friendly' sites to be consumed. The term is derived from Walt Disney, the American animated film-maker who went on to create theme parks in various locations based on his films and characters. Places are stripped of their negative elements and presented on the one hand as safe and serene locations, and on the other hand as authentic, *hyperreal *simulacra, that are sanitized versions of real places. Shopping malls are thus Disneyfied main streets; they seek to look and feel like main streets but without their negative elements, and give the illusion of being safe and secure public spaces while being privately regulated spaces.

Further reading Zukin, S. (1996), *The Cultures of Cities*.

displacement 1. Forced population movement.
2. In *gentrification, the forcing out of long-established and working-class residents of a city neighbourhood by higher-income newcomers.
3. In crime studies, the process by which tougher law enforcement in one area leads to increases in crime in adjacent areas.

Further reading Hyndman, J. (2000), *Managing Displacement: Refugees and the Politics of Humanitarianism.*

dispossession The process of transferring ownership of assets—including land and *natural resources—so that the original owners, users, or beneficiaries no longer enjoy their rights. It may involve coercive, extra-legal, or questionable means. Examples could include a landlord forcing out the occupants of a rental dwelling or a bank seizing an agricultural holding. On a larger scale, national governments have the authority to compulsorily acquire assets in the national interest, as when a new dam is built and an agricultural valley flooded. Many historians describe the loss of land titles by Hispanics in territories that became part of the USA after 1848 due to aggressive litigation as a dispossession. David *Harvey uses the term 'accumulation by dispossession' to refer to the present-day transfer of formerly public and community goods through privatization, *financialization, and the manipulation of economic crisis into private hands (*see* ACCUMULATION).

dissimilarity, index of A measure of unevenness derived from the *Lorenz curve and often used by social geographers to measure residential *segregation. Ranging from 0 to 100, the higher the index, the less a defined social group in a city (e.g. an ethnic minority) is residentially distributed in the same pattern as the rest of the urban population.

distance A measure of separation between two places. A core idea in human geography is that how the world is spatially organized makes a vital difference to how everyday life takes place. Distance is a key concept in understanding spatial organization in quantitative terms. Absolute distance is the measured straight-line separation in defined, standardized units (e.g., centimetres, metres, furlongs, kilometres, miles) between two locations. Effective distance is the length of a route between two locations, such as through a road network, which may be much longer than the straight-line distance. Relative distance expresses the separation between locations through a surrogate such as the cost, time, or effort to travel between locations. Cognitive distance is a measure of how far people think places are separated, which might affect their decision to travel between them.

Further reading Gattrell, A. (1983), *Distance and Space: A Geographical Perspective.*
Pirie, G. H. (2009), 'Distance', in *International Encyclopedia of Human Geography.*

distance decay The negative relationship between distance and the interaction between geographically separated phenomena. It is now well established that, in general, the greater the absolute and/or relational distance (in financial, effort, or temporal terms) between places, the less effect one place has on the other, or the less interaction there is between them. For example, more people travel shorter distances to work or to health services or theatres and so on, than longer distances; the effects of a nuclear accident are more pronounced nearer to a site than further away. Distance decay is the key concept underpinning *gravity models. *See also* DISTANCE.

distanciation *See* TIME-SPACE DISTANCIATION.

distributed mapping A highly dispersed, distributed strategy of sharing cartographic data and tools across the Internet. It is sometimes called 'Online GIS'. Here *GIS software and spatial databases are hosted on a server and made accessible to users across the Internet, enabling them to interact, manipulate, query, and map spatial data. The advantage is that it provides access to both map tools and data for many more people who do not have to invest in expensive software or data licences. A popular example is Google Earth.

distribution, data *See* DESCRIPTIVE STATISTICS.

distributive justice A concept of *justice and attendant policies and laws, in which the redistribution of money, assets, or opportunities from one section of society to another is central. In moral philosophy, political theory, and legal theory, there are multiple definitions of justice; so too of distributive justice. The main idea is that it is unjust if unequal opportunities or outcomes persist over time. While liberals argue that people may become successful through hard work, talent, and sometimes good fortune, many acknowledge that individuals cannot realize their potential if born and raised in conditions that offer few opportunities. *Marxists and other critical theorists go further and argue that modern capitalist, patriarchal, multiethnic societies are shot through with systematic social inequalities that must be redressed (*see* INEQUALITY, SPATIAL). The redistribution of wealth, goods, and services must be social but, human geographers argue, spatial too. Such redistribution can and does take place at range of spatial scales, with the national state usually a key actor because of its considerable tax raising, borrowing, spending, and decision-making power. Redistribution can take a wide range of forms, from regional development grants to local area housing projects to free school lunches for children from low-income households. The question of distributive justice is closely linked to the topic of *uneven geographical development and, in the case of *climate change, uneven contributions to global atmospheric pollution.

diverse economies The description and explanation of economies that are non-capitalist and not, therefore, *market economies. Despite the global dominance of *capitalism, all manner of other economies exist that are separate from or coexistent with it. They range from 'informal economies' to subsistence economies. While many *Marxists argue that these non-capitalist economies are ultimately marginal or at risk of being swallowed up by capitalism, J. K. *Gibson-Graham is among those who regard them as real alternatives that serve important functions for those involved. She has encouraged economic and social geographers to analyse these economies in detail and to assess if they might be reproduced in other contexts. *See also* ALTERNATIVE ECONOMIC GEOGRAPHIES.

Reference Gibson-Graham, J. K. (1996), *The End of Capitalism (As We Knew It)*.

division of labour The specialization of work within and between firms, economic sectors, places, and countries. Rather than each worker performing a wide range of tasks, in most modern capitalist societies he or she typically specializes in performing one mental or manual task. Detailed divisions of labour are also characteristic of informal economies and communist economies (such as Cuba and the former Soviet Union). As described by Adam Smith in *The Wealth of Nations*, by having workers specialize in particular repeated acts of mental or manual labour, capitalist firms have achieved high levels of productivity. The detail division of labour refers to that within a single firm. The social division of labour refers to the economy-wide pattern of work within a country. The *spatial division of labour refers to the geography of this social division. In her book of this name, and using the example of post-1970 Britain, Doreen *Massey argued that Western countries were having their *labour markets remade by large corporations that were using pools of workers in deindustrializing regions to their advantage. In the 1980s, there was talk of a '*new international division of labour' in which these corporations switched parts of their production facilities overseas in order to cut costs. Aside from economic geographers, feminist geographers have been interested in the division of labour in two senses. First, the domestic division of labour in which men enter paid employment and women raise children reproduces certain conceptions of the home and genders space in particular ways. Because that division is changing in many countries, with far more women now in part- or full- time paid employment, its links with the location of jobs and the juggling of domestic responsibilities between men and women has become an important concern. Second, feminist geographers have been interested in the gendering of different jobs, and how the micro-spaces of work can reproduce or challenge gender inequalities. For example, Geraldine Pratt explores the use of Philippine migrant women as childminders in middle-class, white Vancouver households, while Linda *McDowell has explored the gendered performance of work in London's financial services industry.

References McDowell, L. (2009), *Working Bodies*.
Massey, D. (1984), *Spatial Divisions of Labour*.
Pratt, G. (2004), *Working Feminism*.

Doha Round The global trade negotiations facilitated by the *World Trade Organization designed to open up and increase globe trade. The negotiations started in 2001 seek to lower trade barriers by removing or reducing trade tariffs and internal subsidies, especially related to agriculture, and revising trade rules. The negotiations have been fractious with clear divisions in aims and ambitions between developed and *developing nations.

domestic labour The work undertaken in a private household, either paid or unpaid, associated with *social reproduction. It includes *care or nurturing work, such as raising children or tending to elderly, disabled, or infirm persons, cleaning, and cooking. Where such work is done by household members, it is usually allocated to females (*see* GENDER ROLE). Where it is done by others, it may be contracted to companies or individuals (live-out workers) or undertaken by live-in workers. For the latter, the possibilities for abuse and exploitation are high: households are rarely subject to labour laws and, where migrant domestic workers are involved, their migration status can be dependent on their employers' will (*see* FORCED LABOUR). In extreme situations, live-in domestics have no time or space outside their labour. Unpaid domestic work is generally not recorded by standard national accounting systems and is therefore often either ignored or invisible. *See also* GLOBAL CARE CHAIN.

Further reading Cox, R. (2006), *The Servant Problem: Domestic Employment in a Global Economy*.

domino theory A *Cold War geopolitical notion that once one country came under the control of a communist government aligned with the USSR, neighbouring states would follow through a process of spatial contagion. This domino effect was voiced by US President Eisenhower in the 1950s, and later used to describe the danger that if Cambodia fell to communism, then Thailand and Malaysia might follow. The idea possibly neglects the extent to which internal rather than external forces are responsible for political change and overstates the significance of geographical proximity.

Domosh, Mona (1957–) An American feminist historical geographer based at Dartmouth College, USA. Her research has examined the role of the United States in pre-1920s globalization, American empire building, *gender, *class, and the city, and feminist theory and methodology. She is the co-author of *Putting Women in Place* (2001, with Joni Seager) and a standard human geography textbook *The Human Mosaic* (11th ed. 2009 with Roderick Neumann and Patricia Price). She was the founding co-editor of the journal *Gender, Place, and Culture* and has also edited *Cultural Geographies*. Her debate with David Stoddart concerning the role of women in the development of the discipline was an important intervention into the historiography of geography.

Dorling, Danny (1968–) A quantitative human geographer at the University of Sheffield who has persistently drawn attention to the growing socio-spatial divides in well-being, income, educational opportunity, and so on that characterize Britain during the post-1980 era of *neoliberalism. Dorling's detailed analyses of census and other official data sets (often using innovative cartography) has allowed his work to have policy relevance, and he's increasingly visible in public arenas (such as national newspapers) making the case for greater *redistributive justice in the UK and beyond. *See also* PUBLIC GEOGRAPHY.

Further reading Dorling, D. (2011), *Injustice: Why Social Inequality Persists.*

drought A prolonged period of reduced water availability associated with below average precipitation or a significant reduction in groundwater supply. Drought can trigger major food shortages in affected areas (*see* FAMINE). However, there is no automatic link between the two. Indeed, Amaryta *Sen showed that food surpluses, drought, and famine are all complexly related. *See also* DISASTER.

drug A chemical substance that has a physiological effect on the mind or body. Drugs are a key component in healthcare used to diagnose, treat, or prevent diseases, and other health conditions. Certain drugs, such as narcotics, are also used recreationally to stimulate certain sensations which changes usual behaviour. Such recreational drugs are usually illegal outside prescribed medical circumstances and are addictive, although some such as nicotine and alcohol are legal and widely available. Pharmaceutical drugs, and legal and illegal recreational drugs, are large, complex, global industries. Pharmaceutical companies are often multinationals, with a complex spatial organization of research and development, manufacturing, and sales. However, they typically *agglomerate forming *clusters in particular areas. Recreational drugs such as marijuana, heroin, and cocaine form key export commodities for some countries and can have a profound effect on their pattern of land use and development. The drugs have elaborate logistic chains and are smuggled into other countries where they are illegally distributed, sold, and consumed. Given the relationship between drugs and criminality, they are heavily policed and the target of health programmes. Human geographers have researched cultures of recreational drug use but face practical barriers when seeking to research drug supply and use as a criminal activity.

Further reading van Egeraat, C. (2010), 'The scale and scope of process R&D in the Irish pharmaceutical industry', *Irish Geography* 42(1): 35–38.
Sage, C. (1990), 'Drugs and economic development in Latin America: a study in the political economy of cocaine in Bolivia', in Ward, P. (ed.), *Corruption, Development and Inequality*, 38–57.

dual citizenship The possession of *citizenship rights in two countries at the same time, also referred to as dual nationality. There is no internationally agreed convention on the granting or acquisition of such rights, so it is possible for an individual to hold multiple citizenships. *See also* FLEXIBLE CITIZENSHIP.

dual economy A local, regional, or national *economy characterized by the coexistence of and interconnection between two distinct kinds of economic system. The term was coined by development economist J. H. Boeke in *Economics and Economic Policy of Dual Societies* (1953) to describe developing countries in which a largely rural subsistence economy was being articulated with a market economy in which commodities were exchanged for profit (and often overseas rather than domestically). Dual economies persist, despite the spreading influence of *capitalism since Boeke was writing. Today, noncapitalist economies are not only subsistence ones but may be city-based and founded on a diversity of principles, exchanges, reciprocities, obligations, and inequities. *See also* INFORMAL ECONOMY.

dualism A division between two concepts or portions of reality taken to be discrete in either an epistemological or ontological sense. A great deal of Western thought is dualistic because it utilizes antinomies such as nature–culture, urban–rural, and civilized–wild. These antinomies have been supposed to inhere in reality, but critics argue they are impositions on a relationally constituted continuous reality. *See also* ACTOR-NETWORK THEORY; HYBRIDITY.

dual labour market *See* LABOUR MARKETS.

Duncan, James S. (1946–) An American cultural geographer who made formative contributions to the critique of the *Berkeley School of cultural geography and the rise of a *new cultural geography. Duncan suggested that the '*superorganic' conception of *culture bequeathed by Carl *Sauer and his students was problematic and advanced a more politicized idea of *cultural politics in which *landscape became a medium of symbolic struggle between dominant and subordinate social groups. His empirical research on elite urban landscapes in North America and his book *The City as Text: The Politics of Landscape Interpretation in the Kandyan Kingdom* (1990) are regarded as classic examples of contemporary cultural geography.

Dutch disease *See* RESOURCE CURSE.

dwelling 1. A place of residence such as a house, apartment, or tent.
2. The practical activity of being-in-the-world shared by humans and animals. The second sense derives from the attempts by German philosopher Martin Heidegger to undo some of the dichotomies of *modernity by examining the relations between building, dwelling, and thinking. It has been argued that modern Westerners have lost sight of the fact of dwelling. By treating *nature as something separate from themselves (*see* DUALISM) they have, some critics claim, presumed to objectify it as a resource or a threat to be managed through the application of 'value-free' science and technology. The anthropologist Tim *Ingold has challenged the conceit of this objectivist perspective, and called for a rediscovery of our ineluctable dependence upon the living earth. Many human geographers who explore *affect are inspired by Ingold's dwelling perspective. *See also* PHENOMENOLOGY.

Further reading Wylie, J. (2007), *Landscape*.

dynamic equilibrium The ongoing, often non-linear, balancing of phenomena inside a complex system that maintains a relatively stable state. The classic example is the interaction of predators and prey in an *ecosystem. If the population of prey shrinks then the predators starve and also decline. The prey then has a population explosion as the predators usually reproduce more slowly. Once the predators have recovered, the prey reduces quickly again. The relationship between prey and predator is non-linear, leading to lagged fluctuations in population cycles, but are held together in a dynamic equilibrium. In human geography, the dynamic equilibrium concept became widely known as part of the enthusiasm for *systems theory in the 1970s. Today, if the idea has any traction, it is mostly as a metaphor.

Earth Summits Large international conferences that focus on the relationship between humans and the environment and that aim to facilitate *sustainable development through significant inter-governmental action. The first Earth Summit, officially known as the United Nations Conference on Environment and Development, was held in 1992. It was attended by 172 governments and resulted in a number of important policy and legal documents including: the Rio Declaration on Environment and Development, Agenda 21, UN Convention on Biological Diversity, UN Framework Convention on Climate Change, and the Statement on Forest Principles. The second major summit took place in 2012, again focusing on sustainable development and the green economy. Aside from bringing governments into dialogue about global environmental problems, the summits have allowed environmentalists an opportunity to lobby these governments for significant improvements in the human usage of the environment. The summits have also helped to raise public awareness about the scale and severity of environmental problems.

(((⊕))) SEE WEB LINKS
• Earth Summit 2012 (Rio de Janeiro) website.

Earth System Science (ESS) An integrative, holistic approach to studying the interaction between the atmosphere, cryosphere, hydrosphere, lithosphere, biosphere, and heliosphere, but also with ambitions to include a human dimension. ESS values an *interdisciplinary approach that combines the expertise of various specialists in the earth, atmospheric, and environmental sciences. It makes extensive use of *remotely sensed data, models, and high-speed computing. Advocated from the early 1990s onwards, its proponents link it to the need to address global environmental change. It has been vigorously promoted in the USA and, in its grand intellectual ambitions resembles early statements about the nature and aims of physical geography.

Further reading Wainwright, J. (2009), 'Earth system science', in Castree, N. et al. (eds.) *A Companion to Environmental Geography*.

East Asia A subregion of Asia comprising China, Japan, North Korea, South Korea, Mongolia, Taiwan, and Vietnam. The region contains more than 1.5 billion people. Politically and economically, North Korea remains relatively isolated, but the other countries in the region trade with each other and enjoy benign political relations.

Eastern Europe A subregion of Europe that was part of the former Eastern bloc of communist countries until 1989, since when it has become more integrated with the *European Union. Eastern Europe is sandwiched between Russia to the east, and the democratic states of Austria, Switzerland, France, and Germany to the west. It comprises a number of old nation states and some newer ones formed after the end of communist rule in the late 1990s. It is comprised of Bosnia-Herzegovina, Bulgaria, Croatia, the Czech Republic, Estonia, Hungary, Latvia, Lithuania, Macedonia, Montenegro, Poland, Romania, Serbia, Slovakia, and Slovenia. Economically, the region's states enjoyed good rates of economic growth from 1900 until the 2008–2009 global financial crisis. The states that once comprised Yugoslavia were embroiled in political and military conflict during the 1990s, conflict that resulted in attempted 'ethnic cleansing' and genocide by Serbian armed forces. Eastern Europe economies are largely composed of heavy industry, various manufacturing industries, and agriculture, with tourism important in major cities such as Prague and Budapest.

e-business 1. Firms whose principal activities involve the use of information and communication technologies (ICTs).
2. Those elements of any firm that depend centrally on ICTs. In the first definition, we can talk of e-businesses such as online retailer Amazon. These businesses have sometimes changed the economic geography characteristic of their sector, in this case by competing with high-street retailers. In the second defintion, many contemporary firms have key e-business components and these often affect firm geography and its relations with suppliers or consumers.

ecofeminism A political and activist movement that conjoins ideas from *environmentalism with those of *feminism. Ecofeminists argue that the oppression of women and the management of the environment are underpinned by similar patriarchal forces. Just as men seek to dominate women (according to many feminists), so society's relationship with the environment is dominated by a masculinist set of ideas and values that prioritizes culture over nature and leads to the destruction of the natural world. Ecofeminists seek to recast the relationship between the sexes, and between culture and nature, into one that is non-exploitative and harmonious. *See also* MASCULINISM.

ecological fallacy 1. The erroneous belief that aggregate data can be used to infer the characteristics of all the individuals aggregated.
2. The erroneous belief that relationships observed between groups hold for individuals. With respect to the former, aggregate data—when expressed through a single value such as a mean or a classification category on a thematic map—hides the variance within the data set. For example, if we were interested in the age profile of an area, we might use a mean age value to express that profile. If our area has four people, two aged 10 and two aged 60, the average age is 35. Reporting that the average age is 35 gives the impression that there are members of population in that area aged around 35 years old, and yet there are none. Drawing such a conclusion represents an ecological fallacy. A special kind of spatial ecological fallacy is the *modifiable areal unit problem.

ecological footprint An estimation of the amount of land and sea required to supply the *natural resources needed to sustain a given population at its current level of living. It can be calculated for a country, a person, or a city, as it was when originally conceived in 1992. Depending on the level of affluence, individual ecological footprints vary from 1–10 ha, with developed nations in general terms requiring larger footprints. *See also* CARBON FOOTPRINT; CARRYING CAPACITY.

ecological imperialism A deliberate or accidental introduction of new plants, animals, and diseases by European invaders and settlers of the New World, including the Americas and Australasia. The term was coined by historian Alfred W. Crosby to describe how Europeans gained an advantage in conquering new territories and peoples less through the force of arms or technological supremacy, and more through the alteration of indigenous habitats to suit their needs. Above all, the impact of communicative diseases such as measles, cholera, and influenza weakened or destroyed many New World societies.

Further reading Crosby, A. W. (2nd ed. 2004), *Ecological Imperialism*.

ecological modernization A school of thought in the social sciences that regards economic growth and innovation as compatible with the goals of *environmentalism and *sustainable development. The school has German and Dutch origins and is largely optimistic about the prospects of dealing with future environmental problems and threats. Authors such as Joseph Huber and Arthur Mol believe that the current wave of concern about resource scarcity and environmental degradation presents an opportunity for businesses and entrepreneurs. While some commentators regard environmental protection and resource conservation as placing brakes on economic growth, ecological modernizers argue that money can be made by creating novel technologies (such as wind turbines and solar panels). They predict that these technologies will, in time, become affordable and widespread, so benefiting society as a whole. Unlike many *Marxists, ecological modernizers see no necessary contradiction between the 'green agenda' and the logics of *capitalism. Seen from a Marxist perspective, ecological modernizers are either naively hopeful about the future prospects for 'green growth' or else wilfully ignorant of the major environment crises and resource scarcities likely to occur during the course of the 21st century. Few contemporary human geographers advocate ecological modernization or research the validity of the approach, in part because of the dominance of critical (in the sense of left-wing) thinking in the field. *See also* FREE MARKET ENVIRONMENTALISM.

ecology *See* HUMAN ECOLOGY; RESTORATION ECOLOGY.

Economic and Social Research Council (ESRC) A British governmental agency that funds research on economic and social issues, with a particular emphasis on research that has an impact on business, the public sector, and the third sector.

(((∰))) SEE WEB LINKS
• Official website of the Economic and Social Research Council.

Economic Commission for Latin America and the Caribbean (ECLAC) One of five regional commissions of the United Nations, ECLAC seeks to foster economic and social development in Latin American and the Caribbean. It does so by gathering and disseminating economic and social data and information, planning and executing programmes of technical cooperation, and promoting regional and subregional cooperation, and reinforcing economic ties. Founded in 1948, with an initial focus on Latin America, it was expanded in 1984 to include the Caribbean.

(((∰))) SEE WEB LINKS
• Official website of Economic Commission for Latin America and the Caribbean.

economic crisis *See* CRISIS.

economic development The qualitative transformation of a local or national economy beyond economic growth alone. *Development more generally may be understood to include social and environmental elements as well as economic ones. Because modern economies are highly complex there is ongoing debate as to which are the best quantitative measures of economic development.

economic geography A subdiscipline of geography that seeks to describe and explain the absolute and relative location of economic activities, and the flows of information, raw materials, goods, and people that connect otherwise separate local, regional, and national economies. It originated in the late 19th century but, unlike its academic cousin, economics, did not initially favour *theory. In the form of *commercial geography, it tended to be highly *empirical, attending to the relations between a location's natural and human resource base and the character of its economy. The geography of the production of specific commodities was thus based on observation, not deductions from first economic principles. However, this changed from the mid-1950s. Economic geography was, along with *urban geography, at the leading edge of the *Quantitative and Scientific Revolution in Anglophone human geography. Partly inspired by the earlier research of Alfred Weber and Walter *Christaller, a new generation of economic geographers began to look for consistent patterns in the economic landscape that could be explained with reference to producers acting rationally on the basis of their existing resources, the location of their markets, the transportation costs of moving inputs and finished goods, and so on. *Location theory in various forms became a major preoccupation, with economic geographers gathering and analysing quantitative data about all manner of commodity producers in order to identity spatial regularities and departures therefrom. There was an emphasis on describing and seeking to explain spatial decision-making by firms, commuters, labour migrants, and so on. This approach bled into what was called '*regional science', which was linked to government planning and problem-solving.

However, from the early 1970s a new generation of economic geographers began to question quantitative economic geography. As part of the *radical geography movement inspired by the worldwide political protests of 1968, these geographers offered four criticisms of the research pursued by an older generation. First, it was accused of a naive objectivism, or belief that the 'facts' could provide a value-free, unbiased test of a theory. Second, it was criticized for its theoretical assumptions, notably the assumption that economic actors are governed by a universal form of reason (*homo economicus). Third, it was accused of focusing on phenomenal forms not underlying economic processes. Fourth, it was criticized for treating the world's economic geography as if it should (or would) display a spatial order, such that place and regional differences were mere 'noise' to be filtered out in the search for general patterns.

Out of these criticisms emerged a new kind of economic geography indebted to *political economy, especially *Marxism. This research focused on how economic actors had their spatial decision-making structured by the logics of *capitalism, a historically specific system that created its own signature geographies. According to David Harvey in The *Limits to Capital (1982), capitalism rests on a geographical tension between fixity and motion, concentration and dispersal, producing inter-place competition and the compulsion for firms and investors to seek out new opportunities in other regions. Like his *spatial science predecessors, Harvey believed economic activity had a certain spatial order to it, but unlike them, saw this order as fluid and unstable.

Political economic geographers like Harvey saw spatial decision-making by economic actors as structured by definite 'rules' and pressures specific to capitalism, and they also saw economic decision-making as not purely 'rational', but the result of a combination of imperfect reasoning, guess work, and other distinctively human characteristics. They also focused on large firms in order to highlight their considerable importance for jobs, income, taxation, and wider local and national economies. Doreen Massey's *Spatial Divisions of Labour (1984) and Peter Dicken's *Global Shift (1986) were two important contributions here during the 1980s. Dicken's book was among several works that analysed the decline of old industrial regions in North America and Europe and the rise of 'newly industrializing economies' in the Far East and elsewhere. Much of this work was inspired by the neo-Marxist *Regulation Theory of political economy. Aside from examining firm behaviour within a wider capitalist context, there were also important early attempts to understand the geographical concentrations and flows of *money, notably loans by Western banks to developing countries that ended with a debt crisis by the mid-1980s. Stuart *Corbridge's Debt and Development (1993) is an exemplar of this work. Still other political economic research analysed the connections between national states and economic activity, with a particular focus on the attempt of hegemonic countries to maintain their relative economic prowess. John *Agnew and Stuart *Corbridge's *Mastering Space* (1995) is an exemplar of this attempt to link economic and political geography together. Agnew has gone on to explore the economic underpinnings of America's waning political *hegemony (in *Hegemony* 2005).

Much of this research was theoretically innovative and sophisticated, but it tended to avoid quantitative approaches, favouring more qualitative ones. One justification for this was that it is important to understand how and why economic actors do what they do on their own terms. However, quantitative approaches to describing and explaining the changing patterns of economic growth remain important, with certain university geography departments making this a signature of their research (such as the London School of Economics). In California, Michael *Storper and Allen *Scott have used secondary quantitative data sets in their explorations of the roots of sustained regional economic growth. These approaches rarely extend to forecasting economic geographies, remaining focused on current and past patterns of investment and production. Economic geography's relation to mainstream economics has grown closer since the creation of the *Journal of Economic Geography* in 2000. However, the subdiscipline is far more politically left-wing than fifty years ago and today it draws much intellectual inspiration from the critical wings of economic sociology, business studies, the sociology of work, and management studies. The effects of the 1970s critique of location theory endure. Leading economic geographers have been critics of *neoliberalism and have analysed *capitalism from the perspective of ordinary working people (*see* LABOUR GEOGRAPHY), in the process highlighting the key links between production and *social reproduction. Many have also explored how economic geographies are implicated in *culture in various complex ways, thus challenging economists' belief that 'the economy' is something separate in kind. In sum, economic geography today is plural and dominated by no one approach. This makes it a rich environment for practitioners but threatens to weaken the field's external visibility and impact in academia and the wider society.

economic integration The unification and integration of economic policy and trade activities between states by removing or reducing trade tariffs and internal subsidies to business. Historically each state has an economic and tax policy designed to stimulate and protect businesses within its territory. Economic integration, through mechanisms such as the *European Union, seeks to harmonize trade policy and taxation to open-up markets and trading activity. In the case of the EU this has been accompanied by the integration of monetary and fiscal policy across member states. *See also* BRETTON WOODS; DOHA ROUND; WORLD TRADE ORGANIZATION.

economic region A region whose economic system is dominated by or organized around a particular set of industries. Traditionally, they consist of *industrial districts centred on specialized activities such as coal-mining, ship-building, steel-making, and clothing production. More recently economic regions have formed around *knowledge economy businesses, for example, in *Silicon Valley in California and the Cambridge Triangle in the UK.

economies of scale The cost savings that accrue to a firm or a set of firms from increasing in size. For instance, a firm might be able to produce more goods per unit cost with a large, mechanized factory than with a smaller, labour-intensive plant. Geography enters into economies of scale at the firm and inter-firm levels. The precise location and links between parts of a firm affects its cost base, while the same applies to firms whose activities interlink (e.g. where one firm supplies parts to another). *See also* DISECONOMIES OF SCALE.

economies of scope The cost savings per unit of product achieved by a firm when it diversifies its product portfolio. If a firm, using its current workforce, know-how, and technologies, can produce additional product types for little extra cost, then it stands to make additional profits. Often, though not always, *economies of scale and of scope go hand-in-hand.

economy **1.** The art of maximizing the benefits of a given input of effort, money, or other resources.
2. The social relations, technologies, and infrastructures that together permit the production, distribution, sale, and disposal of various goods and services. In the discipline of economics, the neoclassical approach and its derivatives presume that most contemporary national economies in the second sense operate on the basis that the first sense applies. This means that 'rational' economic agents aim to minimize wasted effort, expenditure, etc. and to maximize the returns on their various investments. Economic geographers inspired by *spatial science broadly accepted this presumption and sought to identify the 'rational location' of everything from factories to shopping centres. However, since *Marxism made its mark in human geography forty years ago, an 'economy' has been understood in more complex ways that attend to history, *power, the state, and social conflict. There are various kinds of economy or what Marxists call 'modes of production', and each is seen to have its own means and ends. This insight has opened the door for the exploration of *alternative economic geographies and *diverse economies. More recent work, inspired by Michel Callon, Tim Mitchell, Donald Mackenzie, and others, has questioned whether there is such a 'thing' as economy. Mitchell, for example, tracks how economists make the economy through their calculations, models, and experiments. Mackenzie argues that economic models are an engine of inquiry rather than a camera to reproduce empirical facts, which has significant implications for understanding financial *markets.

Further reading Lee, R. and Wills, J. (eds.) (1997), *Geographies of Economies*.
Mitchell, T. (2005), 'The work of economists: how a discipline makes its world', *European Journal of Sociology* 46(2): 297–320.

ecopark **1.** A centre for recovering and recycling waste materials, thereby producing renewable energy, food, and remanufactured goods. Techniques such as gasification and anaerobic digestion may be used to generate energy.
2. A facility for holiday-makers and tourists run along or designed to demonstrate more environmentally sustainable ways of doing things (see *ecotourism).

ecosystem A community of plants and animals interacting with one another and with their shared physical environment. Organisms and their environment are linked by flows of nutrients and energy. Ecosystems exist at many scales, and they have been regarded as a natural or functional unit of biogeographical analysis. Problems arise, however, when human activities are incorporated into the concept insofar as societies differ from natural systems. Humans can drastically alter the flows of energy and nutrients as well as the mix of species. Ecologists and biographers between the 1920s and 1970s came to regard most ecosystems as orderly and stable in their behaviour, with regular flows of matter and energy binding species into structured relationships of co-dependency. Because the process of natural evolution (first described systematically by Charles *Darwin) is very slow, a set of distinctive species was seen to inhabit any one natural environment—culminating, according to Fredric Clements in so-called 'climax communities' that are well adjusted to the prevailing environmental conditions. Biogeographers for decades sought to understand the character and patterning of ecosystems at various geographical scales, and the effects of human disturbance on them (including the introduction of invasive species). However, a number of ecologists began to study 'erratic' ecosystem behaviour during the 1970s and concluded that it was normal not aberrant. The subsequent approach to ecosystems has emphasized disequilibrium, thresholds, and punctuated development. This has important implications for the practice of environmental conservation because it is no longer so clear what elements of any ecosystem need to be protected or at what geographical scale. Can one *conserve* a *changing* ecosystem? *See also* RESTORATION ECOLOGY.

ecotaxation A form of taxation designed to encourage environmentally sustainable activities through financial incentives. Examples include *carbon taxes and waste or landfill taxes. In Germany the tax system has been reformed to increase the costs of carbon-intense fuels and energy use while at the same time reducing personal income tax. There is some debate as to whether such taxes fall disproportionately on lower-income households.

ecotourism A type of *tourism aimed at minimizing human impact on the landscapes and habitats which form the centre of attraction. It is positioned and marketed as the opposite of mass tourism, by emphasizing the contribution of tourists' spending on environmental conservation and the empowerment of local, often indigenous people. It may also be designed to inform or raise the environmental awareness of participants.

ecumene The inhabited world, or that part of the planet permanently settled by human beings. The term was used by ancient Greeks to refer to what they deemed the civilized world and it is rarely used nowadays.

edge city A concentration of businesses, retailing, and entertainment situated outside a historic city centre, often on *greenfield or formerly residential suburban land. Joel Garreau coined the term in his book *Edge City* (1991) after recognizing that there were more service-sector jobs in the suburbs of US metropolitan areas than in their centres. Edge cities are often located at highway intersections and characterized by high automobile dependency. Garreau identified Tyson's Corner, Virginia, as the archetype, but similar examples are found around the world.

edge effects 1. In ecology the effects on biodiversity of two different types of habitats conjoining.
2. In spatial statistics, the effect of an area's edge or boundary on the observed findings. In both cases, it is acknowledged that the distribution, interaction, and diffusion of a phenomenon observed within a habitat or area often extends beyond its boundary. On the one hand, this means that it is important to take into account the effect of one area on another, and on the other to appreciate that an analysis that focuses only within an area is not capturing the full picture of that phenomenon.

Further reading Yamada, I. (2009), 'Edge effects', in *International Encyclopedia of Human Geography.*

education The organization and dissemination through teaching and instruction of knowledge, reasoning, and skills. Education is formative to the development of intellectual capacities and life skills and, as a result, is formally organized and a compulsory aspect of growing up for children. In most Western countries formal schooling, provided publically or privately, starts at around aged four and progresses until at least aged sixteen, at which point pupils either enter the workplace or continue their education to eighteen or progressing on to higher education or into an apprenticeship. Formal education covers a wide range of subjects spanning the humanities, the social sciences, and the various biophysical sciences, and is designed to give students an academic training, some practical skills training, and an understanding of citizen rights and responsibilities. Individuals can continue to practise formalized life-long learning throughout their lives through professional development.

Critical theorist Henry Giroux has argued that education also occurs outside the formal educational system. What he calls 'public pedagogy' occurs daily via newspapers, television documentaries, soap operas, movies, and other mass media. These media, Giroux argues, do not provide practical training; but they do give people information, ideas, opinions, and cues that can either confirm (or, less commonly, challenge) their existing mindset. Together formal and informal education provide a 'permanent education' for national populations which, in extreme cases, degenerates into propaganda (as it has done in autocratic states or democratic states that have elected highly populist governments).

In the Anglophone world, geography was taught in schools from the first decades of public (or state-prescribed and funded) education in the late 19th century. Aside from teaching youngsters factual information about their own country and the wider world, geography education was one way in which colonialist, imperialist and ethnocentric views were instilled in students. Geography degrees were awarded from the turn of the 20th century. By the 1960s, geographical teaching was well established in Britain at all educational levels, but tended to be small at the university level in other Anglophone countries. By this time, and in the main, geography degrees provided students with advanced skills in literacy, numeracy, and graphicacy—but in ways that tended to reproduce existing socio-cultural values. From the mid-1970s, however, geography degree students in many university departments were exposed to more reflective, often critical, thinking in the form of humanistic, feminist, and *Marxist approaches. Today, pre-university geography is less focused on factual knowledge and far more cognisant of ethical and political issues than in previous decades. Meanwhile, university-level geography is more intellectually diverse, to the point of being entirely fragmented, than a generation ago. Depending on one's view, this makes for an intellectually rich menu for students or one that fails to deliver a considered, suitably structured pedagogical diet.

The contribution of geography to the study of education has mainly been related to five issues. First, there has been a focus on the geography of schooling in terms of the location, resourcing, composition, and access to schools, including for children with special needs, and debates around *mainstreaming. Second, studies have examined the spatial organization of higher education and in particular how the sector is becoming internationalized and commercialized, and being affected by new technological developments such as the *Internet and new forms of pedagogy such as distance learning. Third, there is a concern with how poor access to schooling and educational attainment affects life chances and access to work and feeds cycles of poverty, social polarization, and segregation, as well as how the liberating effects of education can overcome such challenges. Fourth, there is an ongoing interest in pedagogy, and in particular with geographical curricula, how geography is taught at both school and higher education, including the training of geography teachers, and how what is taught shapes pupils' *imaginative geographies. And finally, there is a focus on the status of geography as a school and university subject, especially given pressures to change school curricula and make the discipline more optional.

References and further reading Butler, T. and Hamnett, C. (eds.) (2007), 'The geography of education', special issue of *Urban Studies* 44(7).

Butt, G. (ed.) (2011), *Geography, Education and the Future*.

Erickson, R.A. (2012), 'Geography and the changing landscape of higher education', *Journal of Geography in Higher Education* 36(1): 9–24.

Giroux, H. (2003), 'Public pedagogy and the politics of resistance'. *Educational Philosophy and Theory* 35(1): 5–16.

Egypt A semi-arid Arabic country in northeast Africa, adjacent to the *Middle East, and traversed by the river Nile. Ancient Egypt was famously home to successive pharaohs, it was ruled by the British from the 1880s until the revolution of 1952 when it became a self-governing republic. Under Hosni Mubarak's rule the republican ideal was deformed and a quasi-autocracy created, sparking a people's revolution in 2011. Egypt's population is over 80 million and it has one of the largest and most complex economies in Africa.

electoral geography The geographical study of voting and elections, part of *political geography. Geographers have three main areas of interest. The spatial pattern of voting in multi-party elections and referenda provides a snapshot of political beliefs and priorities, often visible at regional and small scales. Such patterns may be the source of hypotheses about geographical differences within society, or they can be something to explain in terms of underlying social, economic, and cultural factors. Secondly, in addition to broad trends, spatial analysis of voting reveals local anomalies, i.e. places where a party does better or worse than one might expect. For example, it has often been observed that parties do much better than expected where they are already strong, and much worse where they are weak. This suggests a *neighbourhood effect, where voters are more influenced by local factors and local social interactions than national trends. A third area of interest lies in the influence of the territorial organization of elections. Multi-party elections are generally conducted through subnational constituencies or districts, the level at which votes are aggregated to determine winning candidates. The size and shape of these districts can influence the outcome of elections. Because of this, *redistricting, the periodic redrawing of the boundaries of electoral districts in order to accommodate changing population geography, is often a highly contentious issue. Partisan redistricting by a party in power can concentrate opponents' potential voters in a small number of districts with large populations, and spread its own potential voters more thinly among a larger number of districts. The manipulation of the shape of districts to one's advantage is termed *gerrymandering. Where there is an intention to redistrict impartially, geographers have contributed with sophisticated spatial analysis and modelling of voting patterns and social differences. *See also* DEMOCRACY; JOHNSTON, RON; MORRILL, RICHARD.

Further reading Johnston, R. and Pattie, C. (2003), 'Representative democracy and electoral geography', in Agnew, J., Mitchell, K., and Toal, G. (eds.) *A Companion to Political Geography* 337–55.

elites Those individuals who occupy positions of power and/or great wealth. These individuals have a disproportionate influence on decision-making within institutions and firms and are therefore considered key actors in shaping public and private policy and driving implementation. Elites are the focus of attention in much *economic geography and urban development, for example, *regime theory. Researching elites poses particular challenges around access and power relationships.

Further reading McDowell, L. (1998), 'Elites in the City of London: some methodological considerations', *Environment and Planning A* 30: 2133–46.

embeddedness, economic The insinuation of all economic activity into the fabric of everyday social life. Embeddedness challenges the idea that 'the economy' can be studied in abstraction. Instead, the character of local, regional, and national economies is determined by the interplay between economic activities and their social integument. This is most obvious in the case of work because all employment affects and is affected by a worker's wider existence (family life, leisure activities, etc.). The details of embeddedness will vary geographically, despite the supposedly homogenizing effects of *globalization.

embodied knowledge A term for knowledge that is partial, *situated, and developed through experience, contextualized with respect to the *body, circumstance, life history, and locational context. Such knowledge is the counter to the traditional scientific view of knowledge as universal, objective, rational, and of the mind only. Instead it is argued that knowledge is shaped by bodily encounters and processes of *othering, so that the knowledges of disabled, homosexual, black, or female individuals is quite different from the idealized notion of neutral, disembodied knowledge that somehow floats free of encounter and experience. Feminist geographers, in particular, contend that researchers need to be sensitive to the ways in which their own knowledge production is embodied and situated, reflecting on their *positionality.

embodiment *See* BODY.

emergence The properties or changes to the behaviour of a situation or system that arise from the interaction of several otherwise independent elements of that situation or system. Emergence cannot easily be predicted to occur on the basis of existing knowledge of these elements. It is characteristic of complex, unbounded, or open phenomena comprised of layered or interleaving components. *See also* CHAOS, CATASTROPHE, AND COMPLEXITY THEORY.

emerging markets The countries whose economies are said to provide investment opportunities for those willing to take medium or high risks that the investment will fail. These countries are based in the Global South and the former communist bloc. The term originated in the *World Bank in the 1980s and became widely used in the financial services industry based in London, New York, Tokyo, and other established finance centres. The *BRIC countries are among the most successful emerging markets. Political stability is necessary in order to be considered 'emerging'.

emigration A movement out of one country in order to settle in another; hence emigrants are people who leave. In 2010, Mexico had the highest number of emigrants (11.9 million), followed by India and the Russian Federation. Although emigration is a constant process, there are occasions when it achieves levels so high that it transforms societies. In the wake of the Great Famine in the 1840s, emigration from Ireland significantly depleted the country's population.

emissions trading The exchange of the right to emit a certain amount of a pollutant in return for a payment from another polluter. Emissions trading is a form of *free-market environmentalism that, inspired by environmental economics, aims to protect the environment by putting a market value on pollution. Under the *cap-and-trade approach, states prescribe the 'allowable pollution' among a set of firms and then allow the least polluting ones to receive money from more polluting ones as the latter buy pollution credits from the latter. The alternative baseline and credit system enables polluters to reduce emissions below a baseline and offer these 'offsets' for sale to other polluters who may be operating under stricter regulation.

emotional geographies The study of the emotional meanings of and reactions to places and how these shape *sense of place and *spatial behaviour. Everybody experiences a range of emotions from anger, amusement, love, alienation, despair, pride, and so on as they conduct their daily lives. These emotions are important with respect to our sense of self, our attachment to place, our perception of the world, and how we act. Emotional geographies seek to understand the interplay between emotions, identity, and place, as well as the role of emotions in the conduct of producing geographical knowledge. *See also* AFFECT; PSYCHOANALYTIC GEOGRAPHY.

Further reading Davidson, J., Bondi, L., and Smith, M., (eds.) (2007), *Emotional Geographies*.

emotional work Labour in which the display and management of emotions is central to the delivery of a service. Such emotional work might involve smiling, having a pleasant demeanour, flattering or flirting with a customer, and so on. A much-cited example is that of air hostesses, who do not simply look after passengers during a flight, but are expected to produce a certain atmosphere through how they interact with them. Emotional work is thus often gendered and sexualized, especially given the prevalence of women in customer service industries. *See also* BODY WORK.

empire A large territory or set of disparate territories encompassing many different peoples ruled by a single power, and without the consent of all those governed. Empires have existed throughout human history, the earliest being the Akkadian empire in Mesopotamia (modern-day Iraq) 2296–2240 BC. The term is commonly used with reference to the European empires that emerged from the 16th century and which embraced non-contiguous lands across the world (*see* COLONIALISM; IMPERIALISM). More recently, 'empire' is also associated with the writings of political theorists Antonio Negri and Michael Hardt. In their book *Empire* (2000) they describe a form of diffused and decentralized authority that encompasses the civilized world.

empirical A phenomenon that is observable by a person or is otherwise tangible, and so can be considered as evidence of an event, process, or outcome. An 'empirical approach' to research relies heavily on evidence and eschews *metaphysics, speculation, or surmises about intangible causes or effects.

empiricism An approach to research in which it is believed that *data, evidence, and facts can provide an independent basis for testing a *theory, *model, or *hypothesis. Empiricists assume that inference and deduction can occur on the basis of objective information that is observed free from bias.

employment *See* WORK.

empowerment A permanent increase in the capacities of relatively poor or marginalized individuals, households, and communities to shape their own lives and bring about social change. In *development thinking, it can refer either to the increased autonomy of individuals to make choices or, from more critical perspectives, the shift in power from *elites to non-elites, or from dominant to subordinate groups, such as men to women.

enclave economy 1. A foreign-owned export-based industrial zone or complex within but partially autonomous from a national territory. Originally associated with dependency theory (*see* DEVELOPMENT) they were identified within Latin America and later in East Asian *Export Processing Zones. Enclaves provided conditions advantageous to economic development such as strict labour control, financial incentives, or deregulation. More recently, scholars have characterized mining and extractive activities across Africa or financial industries in the Gulf states as enclaves, strongly linked with global flows but only weakly integrated with local areas (Sidaway 2007).

2. An economy associated with a distinct often spatially segregated ethnic group within a larger metropolitan area. Miami's Cuban-American community is a prime example. It usually possesses some vertical and/or horizontal integration of a range of economic activities and, by providing opportunities for ethnic entrepreneurs to flourish, it can encourage eventual *integration. *See also* EXCLAVE.

Reference Sidaway, J. (2007), 'Enclave space: a new metageography of development?', *Area* 39: 331–39.

end of history The idea that there is or will be a conclusion to human conflict, understood in terms of warfare, class struggle, and/or ideology. Versions of the thesis can be found in the writings of both Georg Hegel and Karl *Marx in the 19th century, but more recently it is associated with US political scientist Francis Fukuyama. In *The End of History and the Last Man* (1992) he drew heavily on Hegel's ideas to propose that the end of the *Cold War had led to the final triumph of liberal *democracy as humanity's ultimate form of government and society. Critics pointed to the events surrounding 9/11 to dispute the claim. *See also* CLASH OF CIVILIZATIONS, THE; ETHNIC CLEANSING; WAR.

endogenous growth The economic growth in a place or region that is generated by discoveries, innovations, and decisions occurring within that place or region. It contrasts with exogenous growth as when, for instance, a new oil deposit is found in a hitherto uninhabited area and exploited to serve existing external demand. Endogenous growth is a feature of highly entrepreneurial locations, such as California's *Silicon Valley in the 1970s and 1980s.

energy 1. Power created by harnessing physical and chemical resources to generate heat, light, and the motive force for machinery.
2. The *natural resources, both renewable and non-renewable, from which the power is derived. All organisms utilize energy, the ultimate source of which is the sun (bar minor exceptions). The major transformations in human societies, including *agriculture and the *Industrial Revolution, hinged on finding new ways to exploit the sun's power or to find alternatives to it such as fossil fuels and nuclear power. Finding a long-term solution to the problems of *global warming will require further innovations in energy sources and efficiency to some extent (*see* LOW CARBON ECONOMY).

World energy consumption is rising at approximately double the rate of population growth, although greater efficiency and the spread of recycling and reuse of materials has led to some localized reductions in 'energy intensity', i.e. the amount of energy consumed per unit of GDP. Most of the main sources of energy—oil, coal, gas, nuclear power, hydro-electric power—are consumed within the countries of production. But the development of pipeline technology and very large cargo vessels has increased the volume of energy exports in the past thirty years. Worries about the future of supply, especially of hydrocarbons (oil, coal, and gas), coupled with the geographical unevenness of supply and demand, has created the conditions for a renewed geopolitics of energy in the early 21st century (*see* LIMITS TO GROWTH; PEAK OIL). This harks back to the so-called 'energy crisis' of the early 1970s, when the world price of oil increased fourfold (*see* ORGANIZATION OF PETROLEUM EXPORTING COUNTRIES). There are widespread fears of a 'fuelwood crisis' among some of the two billion or more people depending on wood for heating and cooking.

National energy strategies now focus on the balance of non-renewable and *renewable energy, coupling investment in future supply with attempts to manage and reduce demand. Unequal access to energy supply between different households also remains a problem, manifest in 'fuel poverty'. These strategies are of geographical interest, not simply because of the environmental issues involved, but also because the different kind of energy production can be more or less geographically decentralized. While on the one hand advances in solar and wind power technology facilitate the 'micro-generation' of electricity at the scale of the household, on the other, an expansion of nuclear power would further centralize energy production.

Further reading Bradshaw, M. (2009), 'The geopolitics of global energy security', *Geography Compass* 3: 1920–37.
Mitchell, T. (2011), *Carbon Democracy*.

Enlightenment **1.** A philosophical movement that sought to promote ideas of reason and *rationality and to use them to challenge the teachings and organization of church and state in order to reform society.

2. The historical period 1680–1815 in which Enlightenment philosophy flourished to the extent that it is considered the starting point for *modernity. Enlightenment philosophy argued for intellectual and scientific inquiry, encouraged a public sphere and debate, and forwarded the idea of *democracy. It was underpinned by the notion of *cosmopolitanism wherein intellectual inquiry was seen as shared enterprise and should take place unhindered by religion, rank, or place. Its impact led to radical changes in social, institutional, and governmental structures in Europe and America. Geographers address the Enlightenment in three ways. First, they examine the geographies of Enlightenment thought and practices. Second, they examine how the world was understood geographically in the Enlightenment through exploration, mapping, and travel narratives. Third, they chart the development of geography as a distinct set of knowledge.

Further reading Mayhew, R. (2000), *Enlightenment Geography: The Political Languages of British Geography, 1650–1850.*
Withers, C. W. J. (2007), *Placing the Enlightenment: Thinking Geographically About the Age of Reason.*

entitlement approach A framework for understanding *famine centred on how an individual can use their 'endowments' of land, labour, and assets to obtain food given prevailing conditions of exchange. As set out by Amartya *Sen in *Poverty and Famines* (1981), this approach recognizes that individuals may starve not because there is no food available, but because they lack sufficient entitlement based on their rights and opportunities to grow, buy, work for, or receive food. The approach is criticized for its focus on individuals and narrow conception of rights (Devereux 2001); *see also* CAPABILITIES APPROACH; FOOD SECURITY.

Reference Devereux, S. (2001), 'Sen's entitlements approach: critiques and counter-critiques', *Oxford Development Studies* 29: 245–63.

entrepreneurial city A city governed in ways that encourage private sector solutions to urban challenges rather than dependence on central government support through public expenditure. These include privatization of urban services, financial incentives to commerce and industry, free trade or enterprise zones, tax breaks for the middle- and upper-classes, and zero-tolerance policing. The concept is closely associated with *neoliberal policy initiatives and thinktanks such as the Manhattan Institute. *See also* URBAN ENTREPRENEURIALISM.

Further reading Hall, T. and Hubbard, P. (1998), *The Entrepreneurial City.*

entrepreneurship The activity of making new goods and services that will command a market and so make money. Though *capitalism thrives on competition between firms, many places and countries contain surprisingly few entrepreneurs. Creating genuinely new goods and services that can be marketed internationally is by no means easy. This is why many governments are interested in how one creates an 'entrepreneurial culture' and support fledging entrepreneurs through cheap loans and other mechanisms. Geographically, entrepreneurship is thought to be largely concentrated in the advanced capitalist countries. However, this tends to ignore entrepreneurialism existing in largely rural societies or countries with *informal economies.

entropy **1.** The process by which order naturally descends into disorder over time.

2. A measure of the amount of uncertainty in a probability distribution. With respect to human-environment systems, if a system is not managed then natural processes of entropy lead to the system reverting to *wilderness. For example, in the area around

*Chernobyl where people no longer live and manage the environment, urban landscapes are being colonized by wild plants and animals undoing the order created by society. With respect to social systems, entropy is the process by which social structures disintegrate. A great deal of human activity in terms of cultural practices, social institutions, *governmentality, and the legal system is designed to counteract entropy. In relation to probability distributions, the larger the uncertainty, the greater the entropy. Data sets with high levels of randomness have high rates of entropy. *See* ENTROPY MAXIMIZING MODELS.

entropy maximizing models The statistical models that use what *data are available to generate approximations of missing data in order to identify the most likely spatial pattern given certain constraints. In other words, the models seek to derive estimates of unknown quantities in an area under certain conditions from what is known about that area. The aim is to derive the maximum likelihood of a correct answer given the constraints and the entropy in the data distribution. Entropy maximizing models have been used in human geography to examine travel and voting patterns.

environment The surroundings of something, generally a living organism. Although it is an essentially holistic concept, it has become common to make distinctions between natural or physical and human or sometimes *built environment. But, as Tim *Ingold points out, using the term *global environment implies not something surrounding human beings but something from which we are separated. *See also* ENVIRONMENTAL GEOGRAPHY.
Ingold, T. (2000), *The Perception of the Environment*, chapter 12.

environmental determinism The belief that nature shapes human societies, including their differences from one another, ways of life, cultural beliefs, physiology, and health. In a loose form, environmental determinism has a long history, as one of the three main questions Clarence Glacken (1967: vii) suggests Western people since the classical times have asked of their relationship to nature: 'have [the Earth's] climates, its relief, the configuration of its continents influenced the moral and social nature of individuals, and have they had an influence in molding the character and nature of human culture?' In this form it may often constitute a kind of common sense, a way of making sense of evident human variation. But environmental determinism has also been periodically consolidated as a more coherent doctrine or scientific theory. *Enlightenment thinkers including Montesquieu and Immanuel *Kant speculated on the role of climate in determining racial difference and ranking. In the wake of *Darwinism, leading geographers such as Friedrich *Ratzel, Halford *Mackinder, Nathaniel Shaler, and William Davis formulated the discipline on the causal relationships between physical and human geography. As embodied in the work of Ellen *Semple, notably her *Influences of Geographic Environment* (1911), environmental determinism became the main force shaping US geography in the early 20th century (*see* HUNTINGTON, ELLSWORTH).

But it should be recognized that environmental determinism was not a single, well-defined body of ideas. Its scope ranged from general claims that nature placed limits on human society (*see* MALTHUSIANISM) to more precise claims about the relationship between specific kinds of environment, e.g. deserts, and specific human qualities, e.g. monotheism. Nor did environmental determinism exist in a pure form, isolated from a wider field of ideas about how society and nature were related—which included natural theology, *possibilism, *eugenics, *Marxism, and *scientific racism. Few proponents, Semple included, denied the role of other factors shaping human life. Heredity, or what we would now call genetics, could be invoked either as a rival explanation of human difference or a complementary one. Such diversity and complexity means that the claim that environmental determinism was simply a way of legitimating imperialism abroad and racism at home must be tempered by the fact that it could equally be mobilized in support of anti-imperialism or, in the work of Peter *Kropotkin, anarchist-inspired visions of cooperative life. Nor was it confined to the West; forms of environmental causation can be traced in early 20th century Hindu nationalism, for example.

It is nonetheless right to say that the hold of environmental determinism on academic geography waned from the mid-1900s, as the physical and mathematical sciences displaced the life sciences as the main source of the discipline's ideas and methods. But given that its core propositions were largely untestable and therefore irrefutable, its subsequent periodic resurfacing should come as no surprise. New variants, for example, in the work of Jeffrey *Sachs (*see* NEW ECONOMIC GEOGRAPHY), historian David Landes and Jared *Diamond (*see* GUNS, GERMS, AND STEEL) are being deployed to address the fundamental questions of why some parts of the world are more developed than others. Such work has its critics among human geographers (Radcliffe et al. 2010) but has undoubtedly found a public audience. It can be understood as part of a swing back to the life sciences as a source of ideas for explaining human behaviour and variation alongside socio-biology and *genetics. Moreover, some form of environmental determinism persists as unexamined common sense.

References and further reading Glacken, C. J. (1967), *Traces on the Rhodian Shore: Nature and Culture from Ancient Times at the End of the Eighteenth Century*.
Livingstone, D. N. (2011), 'Environmental determinism', in Agnew, J. A. and Livingstone, D. N. (eds.) *The Sage Handbook of Geographical Knowledge*, 368–80.
Radcliffe, S. et al. (2010), 'Environmentalist thinking and/in geography', *Progress in Human Geography* 43: 98–116.

environmental direct action (EDA) Political activity outside the formal channels of electoral democracy advancing ecological alternatives to conventional practices. EDA may be violent or non-violent, and includes occupations, blockades, demonstrations, sabotage, boycotts, *hacktivism, graffiti, and other types of civil disobedience. The term first became widely used in relation to protests against the construction of roads and airports in the UK, as well as opposition to genetically modified crops, and was particularly associated with the organization UK Earth First! *See also* ACTIVIST GEOGRAPHY; DEMOCRACY; ENVIRONMENTALISM.

environmental ethics The normative principles that guide human use of the environment, addressing the rights and wrongs of various courses of action. *Ethics is a field of moral philosophy with close affinities to theology. But particularly in Western ethics, the concern has been for either how individuals should treat one another or how an individual should conduct him- or herself in society. Relative to non-Western belief systems such as Buddhism or Shintoism, there has been less attention paid to how we should treat animals, plants, and the land as a whole. Historians of environmental ethics often claim that two dominant ethical principles have guided Western societies. The idea of dominion, that humans should have mastery over nature, can be justified by biblical text. A later concept, *utilitarianism, licenses individuals to dispose of their property—including land and animals—for their own designs. Both these principles are *anthropocentric, allowing no scope for the intrinsic right of *nature. Although an alternative ethic can be found in 19th-century conservationists, it was US naturalist and forester Aldo *Leopold who popularized a 'land ethic' in his widely read book *A Sand County Almanac* (1949). He advocated the principle that humans should be members or citizens of nature, not its conquerors. Conduct should be governed by whatever actions preserved the 'integrity, stability, and beauty' of the land, including soil, water, animals, and plants. US historian Roderick Nash outlined in *The Rights of Nature* (1989) the complementary argument that the speech of rights had gradually expanded over time, starting with lords and extending to male property-owners, freed slaves, women, children, and now nature itself. *Deep ecology and the animal rights movement carried forwards these ethical debates which today focus not just on the general relationship between humanity and the natural worlds, but on specific issues such as factory farming, culling wildlife, the use of animals in laboratories, and GM organisms (*see* GENETIC MODIFICATION).

Further reading Robbins, P., Hintz, J., and Moore, S. A. (2012), *Environment and Society.*

environmental geography The geographical inquiries that formally relate some aspect of the human world (society) and some aspects of the physical world (nature) to one another. Environmental geography can be conceived in at least three related ways. It can be regarded as a middle ground between human and physical geography, unifying parts of the discipline that are otherwise moving apart. It can also be regarded as the most recent manifestation of a distinct tradition within geography that attempts to hold humans and the environment together in a single explanatory framework, termed 'the geographical experiment' by David Livingstone. This tradition includes *environmental determinism, *possibilism, human ecology, *cultural ecology, *hazards research, systems approaches, and others. Although possibly neglected in the post-war decades, this tradition has been revived by the increasing interest in global environmental issues and environmental change. An important departure from past versions of environmental geography is that the inquiries are more likely to involve teams of specialists rather than individual generalists. Lastly, it can be thought of as an interdisciplinary field of research spanning the natural and social sciences, but within which the contribution of geographers per se is not necessarily central. In this sense, its component fields comprise *political ecology, research on environment and development, *hazards and *disasters research, *animal geography, Land Change Science, and several more besides. *See also* SUSTAINABILITY SCIENCE.

Further reading Castree, N., Demeritt, D., Liverman, D., and Rhoads, B. (eds.) (2009), *A Companion to Environmental Geography.*
Livingstone, D. N. (1992), *The Geographical Tradition.*
Turner II, B. L. (2002), 'Contested identities: human-environment geography and disciplinary
   implications in a restructuring academy', *Annals of the Association of American Geographers* 92: 52–74.

environmental governance The set of institutions and processes concerned with steering organizations with responsibilities for environment and *environmental policy (*see* GOVERNANCE). By implication, these practices of rule-making and authority is exercised not just by the *state and inter-state agreements but also by a host of non-state actors either opposed to or in concert with states. These include markets (*see* CARBON TRADING; WETLAND BANKING), corporate *certification schemes, *NGOs, municipal networks (e.g. the Cities for Climate Protection programme), indigenous people's organizations, public-private partnerships, and other *civil society associations. The rescaling of environmental governance is a particular focus of current research (Bulkeley 2005).

References and further reading Bulkeley, H. (2005), 'Reconfiguring environmental governance:
   towards a politics of scale and networks', *Political Geography* 24: 875–902.
Himley, M. (2008), 'Geographies of environmental governance: the nexus of nature and neoliberalism',
   Geography Compass, 2(2): 433–51.

environmental health The study of the influence of physical, biological, chemical, and psychosocial environments on human health and ways to correct, control, and prevent any adverse effects. The definition of environment in this context is deliberately broad to include any non-medical factors that affect human health. As such, environmental health investigates the effects of issues such as poor water quality, air pollution, natural hazards, and living conditions on human well-being. A typical example might be to study whether there is a relationship between an industrial plant handling toxic substances and local incidents of cancer, miscarriages, stillbirths, and infertility. *See also* HEALTH GEOGRAPHY.

environmental history The field of study interested in the interaction between humans and the environment in the past. It is a recognized subdiscipline of history with its own associations and journals, as well as a broader interdisciplinary field embracing contributions by human geographers, anthropologists, and others. Although there are antecedents in the work of the *Annales School in France and cultural geography, a distinct environmental history took shape in the USA in the 1960s and 1970s alongside the burgeoning environmental movement. Many of its leading lights are familiar to geographers, for example, William Cronon (who holds a chair of history, geography, and environment at the University of Madison, Wisconsin), Ramachandra Guha, Carolyn Merchant, and Donald Worster. According to Worster, the subject has three main themes. Firstly, it is interested in *nature and how it has changed over time; here, there is a focus on the impact of environmental change on the course of human history (*see* ENVIRONMENTAL DETERMINISM). Secondly, there are studies of how human social and economic organization have impacted on the environment, for example, through soil erosion. Lastly, environmental historians have been interested in cultural ideas of nature, popular and intellectual (*see* TRACES ON THE RHODIAN SHORE). J. Donald Hughes has proposed greater theoretical reflection and plurality in the subject, particularly on the themes of *nature-culture. He also advocates closer attention to the methods and theories of the natural sciences and a more ambitious approach to spatial and temporal scale.

Reference Hughes, J. D. (2008), 'Three dimensions of environmental history', *Environment and History* 14: 391–30.

Environmental Impact Assessment (EIA) A procedure used in *planning to evaluate the possible environmental and social effects of a development project, sometimes including means to mitigate them. EIAs were introduced into US planning by the 1969 National Environmental Policy Act and are now in wide use around the world. Although they are designed to aid rather than replace decision-making, EIAs are criticized for considering only the short-term and failing to take proper account of social and cultural values as opposed to economic costs (*see* COST-BENEFIT ANALYSIS).

environmentalism The beliefs and practices associated with concern for the environment, particularly for the negative impacts of human activity on *nature. Environmentalism covers a very broad range of ideas and actions, although they share the proposition that the environment is something apart from society and under threat from it. A helpful distinction was made by Tim *O' Riordan in *Environmentalism* (1976). He noted two polar types of environmentalism: technocentrism and ecocentrism. Technocentrism implies faith in the ability of human societies to manage or control nature, for example, by finding technological fixes for environmental problems or by pursuing policies of *ecological modernization. Ecocentrism proceeds from the principle that human societies should adapt themselves to the environment rather than the reverse. It embraces the idea that nature has intrinsic value (*see* DEEP ECOLOGY) and promotes small-scale, decentralized, and community-based solutions to environmental problems (*see* BIOREGIONALISM). These two kinds of orientation are themselves quite diverse and are rarely found in pure form; most individuals, organizations, and programmes mix them. The anthropologist Mary Douglas provides a refined version of the same idea by outlining four ways people think about environmental risk: first, individualists regard nature as resilient or endlessly bountiful and therefore generally oppose any attempts to restrain exploitation; second, hierarchists think that nature can and should be managed to avoid serious harm, placing their faith in technical expertise; third, egalitarians regard nature as fragile and prefer social to individual solutions, often favouring a *precautionary principle; and fourth, fatalists conceive nature as arbitrary or capricious and have little faith in management or collective responses (Harrison and Burgess 1984). Useful though these schemes may be, they tend to apply more to Western societies. Where people's livelihoods are closely associated with natural environments such as pastures, forests, and fisheries, there is less scope for a separate or independent environmentalism outside the concern for ways of life as a whole. *See also* ENVIRONMENTAL ETHICS; ENVIRONMENTAL POLITICS.

Further reading Harrison, C. & Burgess, J. (1984), 'Social constructions of nature: a case-study of conflicts over Rainham Marshes', *Transactions of the Institute of British Geographers* 19: 291–310.

environmental justice A political claim that all people and communities have a right to safe, clean, and healthy environments. The environmental justice movement is closely bound up with campaigns against 'environmental racism', which challenges the unjust distribution of environmental harms along lines of *race, *ethnicity, and indigeneity.

In the USA environmental campaigning and awareness has been dominated by large organizations funded by members through subscription, but catering largely to urbanized middle classes and their concern for protecting wildlife, endangered habitats, and wilderness (sometimes called the 'big 10'). But a series of incidents drew attention to the high exposure of low-income, African-American, Hispanic, and Native American communities to environmental harms such as toxic waste dumps, hazardous industrial and agricultural chemicals, and nuclear weapon testing. A campaign against toxic waste facilities in Warren County, Virginia, in the 1980s is credited with launching a distinct environmental justice movement. The movement sought redress through the courts over the unfair geographical distribution of hazardous sites, mapping data from across the USA to demonstrate the systematically unjust nature of their location. The movement developed a wider concern for the ways low-income communities were denied access to decision-making over environmental issues. And it challenged the exclusionary character of mainstream environmental organizations. Attention was drawn to the history of *racism, displacement, and exclusion woven in to US conservation history, beginning with the expulsion of Native American peoples to make way for *national parks in the 19th century. The tardy federal response to the *Hurricane Katrina disaster has also been described as an expression of environmental racism. Environmental justice is associated with a high level of community activism, notable for the role played by women as organizers and advocates. *See also* SOCIAL JUSTICE; SPATIAL JUSTICE.

Further reading Holifield, R., Porter, M., and Walker, G. (eds.) (2010), *Spaces of Environmental Justice*.
Pulido, L. (2000), 'Rethinking environmental racism: white privilege and urban development in Southern California', *Annals of the* Association *of American Geographers* 90: 12–40.

Environmental Kuznets Curve A relationship between economic growth and environmental quality based on the supposition that above a certain level of income, environmental quality improves rather than worsens. It has been observed that in many richer countries, air and water quality gets better with greater economic growth and net deforestation can give way to net afforestation. Evidence for this hypothetical relationship is mixed.

Further reading Ekins, P. (2000), *Economic Growth and Environmental Sustainability*.

Environmental Management System (EMS) A framework and procedure for managing an organization's environmental impact and performance, often based on one or more international standards such as ISO 14001 (*see* INTERNATIONAL ORGANIZATION FOR STANDARDS). An EMS can be adopted by individuals firms, multinational enterprises, local governments, universities, and other organizations.

environmental perception The ways an individual becomes aware of and interprets their surroundings through their senses. The term is widely used in *behavioural geography and is more related to psychological rather than cultural dimensions of sensing and behaviour, though it may extend to cognition, values, and *representation (*see* COGNITIVE MAPPING). Environmental perception can be approached quantitatively, as in Thomas Saarinen's monograph *Perception of the Drought Hazard on the Great Plains* (1969), or more humanistically (*see* HUMANISTIC GEOGRAPHY). Anthropologist Tim *Ingold has advanced a more phenomenological approach based on overcoming the conceptual separation between the perceiver and the world.

environmental policy The frameworks and associated actions taken to manage the relations between society and the natural environment, particularly to minimize the negative impacts of human activity. Many kinds of organization operate environmental policies, including governments, businesses, religious organizations, and civil society bodies. Three broad types of policy tool are in operation across them (*see* GOVERNANCE). Firstly, through legislation governments can enact direct regulation of human activity in the forms of planning restrictions, mandatory levels of waste production, pollution controls, and so forth. Distinct national environmental policies, as opposed to piecemeal legislation, emerged in the 1970s. Secondly, and increasingly, governments can act indirectly through various market mechanisms such as fees, taxes, and incentives (*see* CAP-AND-TRADE; ECOLOGICAL MODERNIZATION). Thirdly, there can be voluntary agreements between relevant bodies, for example, self-certification schemes among resource producers. Geographers have contributed to policy formation in an individual professional capacity, i.e. through expertise, but also through the direct input of geographical associations, for example, to government consultation (*see* APPLIED GEOGRAPHY). *See also* POLICY, GEOGRAPHY AND; PUBLIC POLICY.

environmental politics The political ideas, policies, and practices sharing a concern for the *environment (*see* ENVIRONMENTALISM). They include: firstly, an environmental movement, consisting of *civil society associations (*see* SOCIAL MOVEMENT) and non-governmental organizations from local to global scales; secondly, organized political groupings contesting elections, such as Green parties; thirdly, business initiatives around *Corporate Social Responsibility, certification, and *sustainable development; and fourthly, the actions taken by individuals in response to environmental concerns, for example, ethical consumption. A further category may be more ambiguously environmental: the various movements among marginalized communities outside the developed world concerned with *land rights, *social justice, *displacement, and related social, economic, and political priorities. In these circumstances, there may be no separate 'environment' in the sense used by urban industrialized societies to describe a field of concern at a remove from everyday life (Guha 2000).

Virtually all political positions and beliefs can be crossed with environmentalism, which accounts for the wide spectrum of environmental politics. A distinction is generally made between radical or deep Greens and reformist or shallow Greens. Among the former are included *Deep Ecology, *bioregionalism, *ecofeminism, the *environmental justice movement, and the academic field of *political ecology. Reform orientations include *sustainable development and *ecological modernization. But this distinction conceals the existence of radical political positions that are sometimes described by critics as 'anti-environmental'. Sceptical and contrarian positions do not share concerns for climate change or resource depletion, and often place great faith in human ingenuity precisely spurred on by environmental challenges (*see* WISE USE MOVEMENT).

A second source of variety within the environmental movement and its politics lies in the long history of ideas and organizations. Although it may be unwise to track the precise origins of an environmental concern, two significant developments were the reaction to urban industrialism among 19th-century Romantics and the European colonial encounter with tropical lands (especially islands). Environmentalist organizations and beliefs thereafter consolidated around three main themes. Aesthetic and spiritual concerns for the integrity and beauty of nature inspired early conservationists, whose ideals were shared by enthusiasts for preserving heritage buildings and landscapes (*see* CONSERVATION; HERITAGE CONSERVATION). Economic interests in conserving forest and other environments for future use emerged in colonial forestry and under Gifford Pinchot, who headed US forestry management 1898–1910. Economic calculations were reinvigorated by late 20th-century environmental economics (*see* ECOLOGICAL MODERNIZATION). Finally, the science of ecology developing from the 1940s provided a more scientific insight into core ideas such as the interdependence of humans, organisms, and their biophysical environment. A recognizable environmental movement emerged in the 1960s when ecological insights were combined with existing environmental beliefs, finding a new home in the affluent, generally urbanized, and white middle classes. Green political parties formed in the 1970s in Europe and New Zealand, some achieving national power as coalition partners (in Finland 1995, Germany 1998, Ireland 2007) or establishing a strong presence in local government, for example, in Brazil. Some North American campaigners lamented the 'end of environmentalism' in the 1990s, saddened by the lack of electoral support and the unpopularity of its core message that the public had to cut back on something—e.g. driving—to be 'green'. But elsewhere, *climate change has motivated a renewed level of popular environmentalism.

Reference Guha, R. (2000), *Environmentalism: a Global History*.

environmental racism *See* ENVIRONMENTAL JUSTICE.

environmental security A geopolitical policy discourse relating national and international well-being to climate change and related environmental issues. It arose in military circles after the end of the *Cold War, linking together a number of otherwise disparate threats to peace and stability including so-called water wars, resource conflicts, oil scarcity, and *environmental refugees. Critics, including many human geographers, detect a measure of *environmental determinism in such attempts to ground future threats in environmental, as opposed to more broadly social and political causes. *See also* BIOSECURITY.

Further reading Dalby, S. (2002), *Environmental Security*.

Environment as Hazard, The A book published in 1978 and authored by Ian Burton, Robert Kates, and Gilbert F. *White. Natural *hazards, such as earthquakes, floods, volcanic eruptions, tornados, and hurricanes, are often called 'Acts of God.' While it is true that people have little direct influence over such events, they are in a position to plan appropriately to deal with their consequences. And yet people continue to live on floodplains or on major fault lines or in the lee of volcanoes, and the effects of natural hazards are often amplified by the acts or neglect of people. *The Environment as Hazard* provided an understanding of how people deal with natural hazards, discussing the role of social systems, perceptions of risk, technology, and economic development, and framing the analysis within risk theory. The book was highly influential in policy circles with respect to disaster planning and management, though it was criticized by some for failing to take account of the wider political and economic structural forces shaping development. *See also* BEHAVIOURAL GEOGRAPHY; HAZARDS.

epidemiological transition The transition from the primary cause of death being infectious diseases (e.g., tuberculosis, smallpox, typhus) and *famine to chronic and degenerative illnesses (e.g. heart disease, stroke, cancer). The transition is due to improvements in living standards, public health, and developments in medicine and vaccines. The effect is an associated change in the *demographic transition with falling death rates and a shift in the *population pyramid to a more ageing population.

epidemiology The study of factors shaping diseases and patterns of ill-health. Epidemiology is usually undertaken by medical and public health scientists using statistical methods to try and identify how diseases and illnesses spread and the factors contributing to the diseases/illnesses and their *diffusion. Geographers contribute to epidemiological research by mapping and modelling spatially the patterns of such diseases/illnesses. The aim is to identify possible causes or triggers, routes of transmission, and ways to tackle and prevent health issues. *See also* DIFFUSION; HEALTH GEOGRAPHY; MEDICAL GEOGRAPHY.

epistemic community A group of professionals who create and/or apply knowledge and who share a common set of standards, goals, and values. The term was coined by policy analyst Peter Haas in a study of experts advising governmental officials. It has since been generalized by Noel Castree who applies it to any group—scientists, journalists, medical doctors, criminal lawyers, or wildlife documentarians, say—upon whom we are dependent for knowledge. Given the growing importance of 'lay communities' (e.g. amateur botanists) they too, should be regarded as epistemic communities. *See also* COMMUNITY OF PRACTICE.

Further reading Castree, N. (2013), *Making Sense of Nature*.

epistemology The study of how we know the world and, normatively speaking, how we ought to know the world. Professional epistemologists are found in philosophy departments and inquire into the ways we make reality knowable. All researchers—indeed all lay actors too—have sets of epistemological beliefs. These beliefs are debatable, and in human geography the differences between empiricists, materialists, critical realists, positivists, and others are, in part, epistemological ones.

equality The principle and practice of achieving equal opportunities or outcomes for otherwise different people. Because people live in different places, equality necessarily has a spatial dimension, both within and between nation states. Critics argue that the best way to end inequality is by eliminating its causes, but this usually involves tackling entrenched economic, political, and social practices. *See also* EQUITY; INEQUALITY, SPATIAL.

Equator Principles A management framework for determining, assessing, and managing environmental, social, and financial risk in large infrastructure and industrial projects. The principles are adopted voluntarily by financial institutions where project costs exceed US$10 million. They are designed to ensure that development is socially responsible with negative effects on ecosystems and communities minimized and compensated appropriately.

(⊕) SEE WEB LINKS
• Official website of the Equator Principles.

equity A measure and a goal applied to some or all people and the various institutions that affect their lives. It is a synonym for equality and can apply to the opportunities afforded people in their lives or the outcomes resulting from people's utilization of opportunities. Broadly speaking, socialists favour equality of opportunity and outcome. Liberals, meanwhile, tend to favour the former only and believe individuals must take responsibility for their life fortunes once sufficient opportunities for advancement have been provided to all. Equity can be seen as one measure of *social justice and spatial equity has been a recurrent theme for *Marxist geographers and ethicists in geography since the early 1970s.

error (data) Inaccuracy in data sets that can lead to erroneous conclusions. Errors can include absences, biases, mistakes, and misunderstandings. Errors can be introduced at the data generation stage through sampling or question bias, or inaccurate measurement, or through respondents not understanding the questions. Errors can occur in data analysis through mistakes such as miscoding or misclassification in the data preparation stage. A range of statistical error measures can be used to determine the level of uncertainty or the probability of error in data and its analysis. *See also* DATA.

ESRC *See* ECONOMIC AND SOCIAL RESEARCH COUNCIL.

essentialism The habit of identifying particular attributes of something and claiming they are intrinsic or signature ones that define that thing's character. For instance, it might be argued that differences between men and women are rooted in biology, a sentiment generally criticized by feminist geographers. Environmentalists might say that *nature is essentially too powerful to be treated as a mere tool for the realization of our materialistic aspirations. At its worst, essentialist thinking over-simplifies complex situations or even stereotypes multidimensional phenomena.

estate 1. An area of land or property, usually large in size and sometimes given over to the production of an agricultural crop (*see* PLANTATION).
2. The total assets belonging to an individual or family. Large estates, also called '*latifundia*' in South America, were at the centre of *land reform efforts throughout the 20th century. These often aimed to break estates up and redistribute the land to smaller farmers.

ethical consumption and trade The attempt to make ethical considerations an explicit aspect of commodity consumption and trade, either within or between nation states. Though all economic activity has ethical implications, a distinctive feature of modern *capitalism is that commodities are purchased with little or no consideration given to the human and environmental implications. From the late 1980s, a number of large *NGOs placed a spotlight on the harm inflicted by mass consumption in wealthy Western countries, such as water pollution resulting from pesticides used on farms, or low pay earned by garment workers in '*sweatshops'. Critics argue that ethical consumption and trade holds the false hope that greater social and geographical justice can be achieved by the voluntary actions of millions of 'ethical consumers'. They argue that governments should regulate unethical forms of commodity production out of existence so that consumers do not have to cast ethical 'votes' in the market place.

ethical tourism Travel and vacation activity organized to minimize harm to environments and other cultures, by recognizing and mitigating potential harm. This might include showing respect for local customs, trying to learn and use local languages, using public transport, spending money on locally owned businesses, and minimizing the use of water, electricity, and imported foods. *See also* ECOTOURISM; TOURISM.

Ethical Trading Initiative (ETI) A UK-based partnership of companies, trades unions, and NGOs that aims to improve the welfare of producers and growers of consumer durables in the developing world. Dating from 1998 it has over 100 member companies who subscribe to a code of ethical practice concerning their workers and those of their supply companies.

ethics That aspect of human thought and practice devoted to reflecting on and acting in accordance with value concepts such as justice, *equality, fairness, honesty, respect, rights, entitlements, and care. Often used as a synonym for 'morality', ethics is part of the fabric of daily life but its study and implementation is also a specialist pursuit, as philosophers, legal theorists, and lawyers will attest. Ethics is informal and taken for granted, on the one hand, but also highly codified and subject to enforcement and scrutiny on the other. Geography is constitutive of ethics in at least two senses: first, ethical norms vary globally according to national and subnational histories and customs; secondly, the cross-border links between otherwise different individuals and societies foreground the ethical dimensions of international trade, aid, investment, migration, and so on. For instance, the geographical ethicsit David M. Smith has challenged the moral aphorism 'nearest is dearest' and argued in detail that we should care for others well beyond our shores. Aside from highlighting the ethical relations we have with 'distant strangers', *globalization has also raised questions about how we should compare very different ethical principles, norms, and practices characteristic of different cultures. Can there be a 'global ethics' that supersedes all of the latter? What should we do when different ethical norms characteristic of different societies clash?

Reference Smith, D. M. (1994), *Geography and Social Justice.*

ethics of research *See* RESEARCH ETHICS.

ethnic cleansing The removal by force of one ethnic group from territory claimed or desired by another. Although *genocide, violent dispersal, and confinement have occurred throughout history (*see* HOLOCAUST), the phrase 'ethnic cleansing' was put into common use during the conflict in former Yugoslavia (1990–92) when Serbian forces drove out Muslims in Bosnia and Albanians in Kosovo, resettling their homes and villages with ethnic Serbs. As well as population *displacement, it may involve the destruction or desecration of cultural monuments, places of worship, and other sites of cultural significance.

Further reading Ó Tuathail, G. and Dahlman, C. T. (2011), *Bosnia Remade: Ethnic Cleansing and its Reversal.*

ethnic enclave A neighbourhood or larger territory whose *population is largely *ethnically distinguished from the surrounding area and its inhabitants. Examples include Chinatowns or Jewish quarters that are located in many Western cities, where the majority of residents share the same ethnic identity and the economic landscape is ethnically inflected, with ethnic food restaurants and other businesses.

ethnicity/ethnic group A social classification of people based upon their shared cultural characteristics and heritage. An ethnic identity is defined by the common interests, beliefs, values, language, religion, cultural traditions, historical experiences, and often homeland of a set of individuals. An ethnic group is a collection of people who share a common ethnicity. When more than one ethnic group occupies a *territory they often congregate together to form enclaves and they can form ethnic economies wherein they either employ or service each other or use their ethnicity to trade with other communities, for example, by creating an ethnic restaurant district. There can often be tense relations or conflict between ethnic groups occupying the same territory and this can lead to *ethnic cleansing. Social geographers are interested in patterns of ethnic segregation in towns and cities. The patterns may help to create ethnic identity and solidarity but may also reflect entrenched relations of social inequality and the failed aspirations of 'multiculturalism' and 'social integration'. *See also* ETHNIC ENCLAVE.

ethnocentrism 1. Viewing and understanding the world from the perspective of one's ethnic position, ignoring alternative standpoints.
   2. The belief in the superiority of one's culture and knowledge, with all other cultures measured with respect to it. With regards to the latter, Western science generally views itself as superior and more valid when compared with local and indigenous knowledge. Similarly, Western cultures often view themselves as more civilized and sophisticated rather than simply different from those in developing countries. *See also* EUROCENTRISM.

ethnography A methodological approach that seeks to provide immersive and holistic analyses of social phenomena. Empirical material is usually generated by *participant observation undertaken over an extended period of time (several months or more) and in-depth interviews with a wide range of stakeholders, complemented by other techniques such as a hermeneutic reading of documents and artefacts (such as manuals, email exchanges, visual materials, work spaces, etc.) and time diaries. In essence, ethnography seeks a nuanced understanding of the *lifeworld of a community—its social relations, its rhythms, its cultural norms, its patterns of power and decision-making, its ways of being, and so on—in order to comprehend the many relations between multiple actors and the material world they occupy and how such relations are constituted and continuously unfold. The researcher goes beyond surface descriptions (what is seen and heard), and seeks to gain a deeper understanding of why it is happening by being part of the relations and practices being studied. It is usual for the questions ethnographers ask to change over time, along with their analytical focus, as they engage with and learn more about a community, institution, or subculture.

Further reading Till, K., (2009), 'Ethnography', in *The International Encyclopedia of Human Geography*.

ethnomethodology A sociological approach pioneered by Harold Garfinkel (*Studies in Ethnomethodology* 1967) that seeks to understand the methods through which people make sense of and account for their daily activities. The emphasis is on how people do things in practice and how they construct their world to produce a social order. It is argued that social order is created through interpretive rules and commonsense methods that are nothing more than constructions. In relation to a street parade, an ethnomethologist would seek to understand the way in which those parading produce themselves as parade members by uncovering the interpretive rules and common-sense methods they use in performing tasks and interacting with one another.

Euclidean space *See* SPACE.

eugenics The supposed scientific improvement of population by selective breeding for desired hereditary characteristics. An intellectual movement formed around this idea between the late-19th and mid-20th centuries in Europe and America, in response to alarms about population growth, race, gender, class, and disability. Proponents sought to increase intelligence and general health among the population, and reduce the level of hereditary disease and criminal and immoral behaviour, which was widely thought to have hereditary roots, by advocating sterilization and euthanasia of physically and morally weak individuals. A key figure was Sir Francis Galton, cousin to Charles *Darwin and active member of the *Royal Geographical Society. It attracted many supporters on both left and right, but eugenics was fatally discredited by the excesses of the Nazi regime in Germany. Among its legacies are many statistical tests formulated to describe the distribution of characteristics among populations. *See also* DARWINISM; SOCIAL DARWINISM.

eurocentrism The focus on European culture, history, and politics at the expense of the rest of the world, usually in the belief that Europe is innately superior and that its development has not relied upon exchanges and influences from outside. Further, the values of European societies and intellectual thought are regarded as universal, for example, with regards to *development. US geographer Jim *Blaut in *Eight Eurocentric Historians* (2000) traces this belief from the German sociologist Max Weber to modern historians such as E. L. Jones and the geographer Jared *Diamond, all of whom have tried to explain how and why Europe rose to world economic and political dominance after 1500 based on the continent's supposed qualities. *See also* ETHNOCENTRISM.

Europe The world's second-smallest but third most populous continent, with around 10 per cent of global population. Europe comprises some 50 nation states and principalities. Just over half are members of the *European Union (EU) and most are representative democracies in a political sense. Economically, the countries of northern and western Europe remain the wealthiest per capita (Britain, France, Germany, Holland, Switzerland, Finland, Norway, Denmark, and Sweden). Except for Italy, Spain, Portugal, and the Czech Republic, those countries to the south and east tend to be less prosperous per capita. Because of its huge size and longitude spanning shape, *Russia is only part European. During the *Cold War, Europe contained the major political boundary separating the capitalist West from the communist East. Since the sudden collapse of communism in 1989 all of Europe's former communist states have embraced *capitalism, i.e. private enterprise, the diminution of state control over economy and society, and the sale of commodities for profit. However, their embrace of representative democracy has sometimes been titular, with Russia (among others) being accused of harbouring anti-democratic tendencies among its self-appointed political elite. Europeans have also had to absorb the shock of having organized death occur on their doorstep, namely the civilian atrocities committed by Bosnian Serb soldiers in the mid-1990s, which recalled the Nazi-led genocides of the early 1940s. Both of the 20th-century's world wars (1914–18 and 1939–45) began in Europe with its major powers as antagonists. However, despite this history and enduring linguistic and ethno-cultural differences, Europe is among the most politically stable continents in the world. The EU has done much to foster international understanding between political leaders and their peoples, and has also engineered resource transfers from wealthier to less wealthy regions. Nevertheless, the post-2009 debt crisis in Greece and several other European countries has placed severe strain on European economic solidarity.

European Observation Network for Territorial Development and Cohesion (ESPON) A European Union programme aimed at producing territorial cohesion and the harmonious development of the European territory. Territorial cohesion is one of the three central pillars of the European project along with social and economic cohesion. ESPON draws on the ideas of spatial planning and aims to provide detailed evidence, analysis, and scenarios with regards to territorial development and cooperation across Europe.

European Regional Development Fund (ERDF) A European Union fund designed to address imbalances in *economic development between regions in Europe. The ERDF has three objectives: to modernize and diversify economic structures; create regional competiveness and employment; and foster greater territorial cooperation between regions.

(((●))) SEE WEB LINKS
• European Commission website on the European Regional Development Fund.

European Union (EU) A political and economic union of a number of European nation states (currently 27). It originated in a 1958 economic union of six countries that had been devastated by the *Second World War (1939–45). This European Economic Community (EEC), preceded by a European Coal and Steel Community from 1951, was designed to facilitate trade and investment among its member states by harmonizing customs duties and regulations pertaining to pay, working conditions, and investment. Alongside it, a European Atomic Energy Community was formed to encourage cooperation on developing nuclear energy. The three communities were unified under a single management structure in 1967. Three new members joined in 1973, three in the 1980s, and still more after the fall of the *Berlin Wall in 1989, when many communist countries achieved a new independence. Through the 1980s, members of the European

Community (EC)—as it was by then called—decided to expand the scope of cooperation well beyond trade and nuclear energy. Accordingly, the 1993 Maastricht Treaty—which created the European Union—synthesized a range of agreements and regulations covering everything from citizen rights to a common foreign policy to a common currency (the Euro). It also legitimated the creation of several pan-European institutions, such as a central bank, a parliament, and criminal court. Subsequent amendments to the Treaty, culminating most recently in the 2007 Lisbon Treaty, have been coincident with new members being admitted to the EU. Today, the EU is the world's most comprehensive and complex example of cross-border cooperation between multiple nation states. Advocates claim it has fostered great European solidarity and considerable economic and political stability. Critics claim that the EU is far too removed from the lives of ordinary people and has eroded their political, economic, and civil rights. Some countries, notably Britain, have been selective in their membership of the EU because it is not persuaded that ceding sovereignty in so many areas is to its advantage.

Europe of the Regions A political concept of *Europe as a federated set of cross-border regions rather than simply nation states. Within this federated structure, regions gain a degree of independence and autonomy from nation states and ideas of *regionalism challenge those of nationalism. The concept is seen as an antidote to European integration by providing more localized democracy within the larger federated Europe.

Evans, Estyn (1905–89) The first professor of geography in Northern Ireland, Evans studied the Irish Neolithic period intensively and wrote about the changing relationships between people and land. Born and educated in Wales, he spent most of his career at Queen's University, Belfast, and was a leading voice for landscape conservation in Ulster.

everyday life The ordinary and regular practices that people engage in day in and day out. These practices are the antithesis of spectacular events, political revolutions, or economic crises. They are performed in all those domains that people routinely traverse: the domestic/private, the public, and the commercial. They cover relations of intimacy, friendships, provisioning, work, and leisure. The analysis of everyday life can tell a great deal about prevailing economic practices, cultural norms, gender, and class relations, power inequalities, and much more. For this reason, many human geographers, especially feminist geographers, have scrutinized people's everyday practices as a way of asking questions about the structural and spatial ordering of thought and action in a particular place and time. Although ordinary, everyday life has been extensively theorized, notably by Henri *Lefebvre. *See also* SOCIAL REPRODUCTION.

evidence The role played by *data, facts, and other *empirical indicators in verifying, amending, or falsifying a hypothesis, theory, model, or interpretation. Unlike philosophy (say), geography has been an intensely evidence-based subject since its foundation as a university subject. This reflects its origins in overseas expeditions and its remit to study the varied character of earth surface patterns, processes, and forms.

evolution A process of change internal to an *ecosystem, other living phenomena, society, or social institution. Such change is gradual and unplanned or unanticipated, and results from the 'blind' operation of daily, weekly, monthly, and yearly events. The term has been widely used in academia and society since Charles *Darwin's germinal book *On the Origin of Species* (1859).

evolutionary algorithms A set of algorithms used to solve optimization problems. An example is the travelling salesman problem, wherein the task is to find the optimal solution that minimizes travel between several cities where each city is only visited once. The more cities that are added to an itinerary, the more computationally difficult it is to calculate the optimal solution. Evolutionary algorithms seek to determine as efficiently as possible a population of high-quality solutions, rather than a single global solution, and are used extensively in artificial intelligence systems.

evolutionary economics A form of economic study that draws inspiration from biological evolution to study how economic systems transform over time. Rather than positing that economic actors are rational and there are fixed external and abstract determinants of an economy, evolutionary economics focuses on change within an economy and its various components (e.g., firms, labour, trade), and how these evolve over time through the actions of diverse agents. Its holistic focus therefore seeks to model and explain how resources and innovation shape economic systems and ensure the survival of economic entities and the wider economy.

exceptionalism The view that geography is unlike other sciences in that it possesses no unique object of inquiry but is instead characterized by a unique perspective, the spatial one. In this view, the discipline's role was to describe and explain *areal differentiation. The term entered human geography when Fred K. *Schaefer used it to dismiss the philosophy of the subject advanced by Richard *Hartshorne in *The Nature of Geography* (1939) (*see* CHOROLOGY; NOMOTHETIC). Schaefer argued that geography was like other sciences in its search for spatial *laws.

exchange The process of giving one thing to someone in order to get something in return. Unlike a gift, something given in exchange generally involves strangers or parties who are not friends or relatives. Exchange is an elemental part of all human societies. It takes many forms, but increasingly involves using money as a medium and the exchange of goods and services produced a long way from consumers. For *Marxists, exchange hides worker exploitation because, in capitalist societies, it claims to be equal—yet capitalism is based on capitalists making a profit from their work forces, a profit that is realized when commodities are exchanged. The geographies of modern commodity exchange are exceedingly complex and multiscalar, with some critics arguing that we need to move towards more local and less global geographies. *See also* GIFT ECONOMY.

exchange value The monetary price a good or service can command in a market. All goods and services have a *use value but this is different from the monetary value that buyers will place on it. The latter, in capitalist and many non-capitalist societies, is a means of rendering comparable qualitatively different goods and services, such as a new washing machine and a massage. Money is the medium through which such distinct use values are made exchangeable with any number of others, since the price of one can be quantified relative to the price of another ('One of these is worth three of those'). Increasingly, goods and services are exchanged in and along very long *commodity chains that transcend national borders. Relatedly, money is exchanged for money internationally through currency conversions and overseas lending. For Marxists, capitalist exchange is distinctive insofar as the price a consumer pays for a good or service contains an excess ('surplus value') over and above the monetary cost of producing the good or service in question. This excess accrues to capitalists rather than to the workers who, according to Marxists, ultimately produce all economic value. This said, many forms of exchange value are non-capitalist, though they typically exist at the local scale as islands in a capitalist ocean. For example, Local Economic Trading Schemes (LETS) allow people who are left un- or under-employed by capitalism to swap their labour according to egalitarian principles such as 'one hour of my labour time is worth one hour of yours' (*see* ALTERNATIVE ECONOMIES). Many critical human geographers have examined the new global geographies of commodity exchange and circulation since the 1980s, while others attend to the alternative exchange systems exemplified by LETS as part of a critique of capitalist exchange.

exclave A part of a state's territory that is physically separated from the rest, but surrounded by other sovereign states. For example, Kaliningrad is a district of Russia on the Baltic Sea but cut off from the rest of the country by Poland and Lithuania. It does, however, have independent access to the sea. Ceuta and Melilla are Spanish exclaves entirely surrounded by the territory of Morocco. Such exclaves can be the focus of ongoing territorial conflicts such as the Azerbaijan exclave of Nakhchivan surrounded by Armenia, Turkey, and Iran. *See also* ENCLAVE ECONOMY.

exclusion *See* SOCIAL EXCLUSION.

existentialism A mid-20th-century movement in philosophy, literature, and theatre that prioritized the experiences of embodied individuals who must make their way in a world not entirely of their own making. In Anglophone human geography it was advocated by some humanists from the late 1970s who took issue with the 'abstract individuals' of quantitative *spatial science and of the early research published by *Marxist geographers. *See also* HUMANISTIC GEOGRAPHY.

expatriate A person settled outside their country of origin, often abbreviated as 'expat'. In practice the term is generally applied to professionals, skilled workers, or artists from affluent countries, often transferred by companies, rather than all immigrants in general.

expedition A journey carried out for the purposes of adventure, discovery, *exploration, or scientific research. It may be by land or sea, or more recently, beyond Earth to other planets. Military excursions may also be described as expeditions. Important expeditions that shaped geography include: the voyages of HMS *Beagle* in the 1820s and 1830s (one of which carried Charles *Darwin); John Wesley Powell's expedition to the American west in 1869 (Kirsch 2002): R. F. Scott's doomed Antarctic expedition of 1910: the multinational polar expeditions of the International Geophysical Year 1957–58. Single-purpose expeditions have largely given way to permanent monitoring and observation stations, but geographic expeditions are increasingly aimed at young people from affluent countries for education and adventure.

Kirsch, S. (2002), 'John Wesley Powell and the mapping of the Colorado Plateau, 1869 –1879', *Annals of the Association of American Geographers* 92: 548–72.

experiment An investigation in which an understanding of causes and/or effects is sought by controlling the interaction between two or more variables. Laboratory and field-based experiments have long played a role in physical geography, so too, computer-based ones. Though psychologists have famously used experimental methods, few other social scientists have done so and human geographers have rarely designed experiments to test a hypothesis, theory, or model. In large part this is because they study complex open systems over which it is difficult to exert control. *See also* INTENSIVE RESEARCH.

expertise A high level of skill or knowledge in a particular field or set of tasks. In *governmentality studies, expertise is regarded as a form of practical rationality, an understanding of how to do things. The knowledgeable subjects govern themselves, and are governed through, expertise on matters of health, diet, education, morals, etc. Tim Mitchell, in *Rule of Experts* (2002) sets out how various forms of engineering, surveying, and development expertise helped create the modern state of Egypt.

expert system An artificial intelligence system that draws on the problem-solving expertise of human experts to provide a knowledge base that allows the system to automatically process or suggest answers to similar queries. Expert systems generally output recommendations based on probabilistic reasoning rather than offering definitive answers. Automated online assistants, or predictive texting, would be examples of such a system, where the issue is too complex to be solved without initial expert guidance. In geography, expert systems are used to guide spatial choice and decision-making, for example, in navigation systems to guide route selection or suggest retail recommendations based on location, distance, price, and desired product.

explanation *See* CAUSATION.

Explanation in Geography A text written by David *Harvey (1969), it was a widely read and used monograph in geography that systematically presented the philosophy and methods of *science, and which applied them to the questions and topical concerns of academic geographers. The book became known as a mature manifesto for *spatial science around a decade after the beginning of geography's *Quantitative Revolution.

exploitation 1. Taking systematic advantage of other people in order to appropriate the fruits of their activities.
2. In *Marxist political economy the transfer of economic wealth from wage workers to the owners and shareholders of capitalist enterprises. Marxists regard exploitation as a fundamental feature of *capitalism, wherein the wages that workers receive are, in fact, less than the economic value of the work that they perform in order to produce *commodities for sale. The profits accrued by capitalists thus, according to Marxists, are derived from workers and not from the capitalists' own investments.

exploration 1. The act of journeying from a known territory to a relatively unknown territory, for the purposes of scientific inquiry, geopolitical gain, and/or personal reputation (*see* EXPEDITION).
2. The organized search for minerals or other natural resources in an area, e.g. oil and gas.

Exploration may also be used in a more metaphorical sense to describe any act making something more known or visible in outline. It is often supposed that there was a period during which exploration and discovery were at their height, between the 15th and 19th centuries, associated with European sea voyages to the New World and subsequent *imperialism. But there were many antecedents, for example, in the travels of Chinese admiral Zheng He throughout the India Ocean in the early 15th century. Since the late 19th century various pronouncements have been made that the 'age of exploration' is over, a claim challenged by explorers of oceans and outer space (Naylor and Ryan 2010). Moreover, Felix Driver has identified continuities in the 'cultures of exploration', a set of material, social, literary, and bodily practices still to be found in TV programmes, advertising, and general travel. In his view, the boundaries between exploration, travel, and *tourism are constantly negotiated and not fixed around any specific practices or outcomes. Human geographers have also recently revisited the history of European exploration with a more critical eye on its triumphalism, geopolitical designs, heroic masculinity, and cultural imperialism. *See also* DETROIT GEOGRAPHICAL EXPEDITION AND INSTITUTE.

References Driver, F. (2001), *Geography Militant: Cultures of Exploration and Empire*.
Naylor, S. and Ryan, J. (eds.) (2010), *New Spaces of Exploration*.

exploratory spatial data analysis The use of descriptive and spatial statistics to explore the patterning of spatial data. Typically such methods are used to examine *spatial autocorrelation (things closer to each other are more alike) and spatial heterogeneity (the variance within the data). Such exploration is useful in determining the best approach for examining and analysing the data in more detail. Exploratory methods include producing maps, scatter plots, and other visualizations, and using spatial statistics such as those used to calculate spatial autocorrelation.

export (commodity) A commodity produced primarily for sale and consumption overseas. Even though it may greatly exceed domestic demand, a country may produce very large quantities of a commodity in order to create jobs and income at home. The country can then import commodities it does not produce but nonetheless requires. Critics argue that countries economically dependent on just a few export commodities, like those of the *Middle East, may see the wealth created sequestered by a few capitalists. *See also* RESOURCE CURSE.

Export Processing Zone (**EPZ**) An area of a country where firms can import, process, assemble, and export goods without paying customs duties. Sometimes called 'free trade' or 'foreign export' zones, they have been favoured by developing countries seeking to enhance their foreign exchange earnings, create employment opportunities for their workers, and take advantage of overseas demand for affordable manufactured goods. Over 100 countries currently have EPZs, and they tend to attract manufacturers of clothes, shoes, and other everyday commodities. *See also* MAQUILADORA.

extensive agriculture A type of farming that involves a low input of capital and labour relative to the amount of land employed. The productivity of farming therefore depends more on the natural fertility of soil or quality of pasture, and is generally lower than in cases of *intensive agriculture.

extensive research A term for research that tries to determine the generality or commonality of phenomena and processes by examining a statistically significant *sample in relation to a wider population. It generally uses quantitative methodologies such as questionnaires to ensure a large sample so that the presence or absence of empirical regularities can be established. It contrasts with *intensive research aimed at offering causal explanations. Extensive and intensive methods are used together within a *critical realist approach to research.

external economies The economic advantages accruing to a firm or firms that derive from outside sources. From a firm's perspective the advantages are fortuitous; in their absence a firm would have to bear the costs of producing these internally if it regarded these as especially important. External economies are characteristic of industrial clusters, *agglomerations, and districts. Firms in the same industry, for example, film making or computer game design, may benefit economically from proximity to professionals in other firms. For instance, it may be possible to share advertising or staff training costs with a corporate partner.

externalities The costs or benefits imposed on or enjoyed by an individual, institution, community, or whole society because of the actions of others. 'Negative externalities' are costs, such as atmospheric pollution resulting from unchecked coal burning in a steel factory's power plant, with resulting air-quality impacts on local residents. 'Positive externalities' are benefits, such as those residents derive when a new high-quality state school is constructed in their neighbourhood, with knock-on effects on house prices and their own children's educational experience. Many externalities are geographically specific and localized but, increasingly, many are international in scale, with anthropogenic global warming being the prime example.

extractive industries The economic sector concerned with the discovery and *mining of minerals and *natural resources such as oil, gas, metals and construction materials. It is globally organized by transnational corporations but state-owned corporations are also important, especially in oil and gas. Such industries are frequently the centre of controversy because of the often-harmful environmental impact of their activities.

Further reading Dicken, P. (6th ed. 2011), *Global Shift*.

factor analysis A method of analysis for determining the pattern of relationships amongst a number of variables. Many statistical tests aim to determine the relationship between independent and dependent variables. Factor analysis examines the relationships amongst many dependent variables by constructing a correlation matrix in order to discover something about the nature of the independent variables (factors) that affect them. In particular, it seeks to determine how many factors are needed to explain the pattern of relationship among dependent variables and the characteristics of those factors. For example, we might have two dozen variables concerning why fifty different people moved to a location. These variables might usefully be reduced to a handful of dimensions (e.g., price, reputation, services) that capture the core reasons for the choice of location. Factor analysis would test the relative salience of these dimensions.

fact-value distinction The supposed *ontological difference between how the world is and how people evaluate the world. Since the European *Enlightenment many people have believed that facts are value-free. Meanwhile all value judgements are said to be made about a world whose character is knowable prior to the application of these judgements. The fact-value distinction forms the ontological basis for the epistemological distinction between the 'empirical sciences'(those that rest upon observation and experimentation) and the 'moral sciences' (those that seek to define, justify, and apply key values such as 'rights', 'entitlements', 'fairness', and 'equality'). In geography the distinction separates most of physical geography from the concerns of many human geographers. Within human geography the distinction, in a loose sense, separates those influenced by the *spatial science tradition from those influenced by *humanistic geography, *Marxist geography, *feminist geography, and other approaches in *critical human geography. Most contemporary human geographers recognize that the fact-value distinction is less an ontological given and more an epistemological assumption. Facts cannot be value-free since values are involved in the identification of which facts will be of interest to researchers in the first place. Likewise, any attempt to reason about and apply values will already have been influenced by which facts are taken to be relevant or established.

failed state A state in which one or more of the fundamental conditions of sovereign government are absent (*see* SOVEREIGNTY). These conditions include the presence of a recognized government, that government's monopoly on the legitimate use of physical force, the provision of basic public services, and the ability to represent that country on the international stage. The absence of these conditions is common in countries experiencing civil war, a military invasion, or a major dispute over the location of political borders. The term 'failed state' has been used by political commentators in academia (including political geography), the news media, and current affairs. The global geography of failed states locates them primarily in *Africa and, to a lesser extent, the *Middle East.

fair trade A type of commodity exchange in which consumers voluntarily pay more money for a product to ensure that commodity producers receive enough income to enjoy a decent living standard. Many fair-trade transactions also aim to achieve higher environmental standards in the cultivation of commodities such as coffee, sugar, and bananas. Fair trade was first advocated by non-governmental organizations and charities in the 1980s. Some argue that its growing popularity in Western countries has produced greater fairness in international trade, while others believe that it merely applies sticking-plaster to a global trading system that relies on cheap labour and environmental degradation in developing countries. *See also* ETHICAL TRADING INITIATIVE.

falsification An approach to testing the validity of any *hypothesis or conjecture that entails the search for evidence or reasons that might entail its rejection or modification. The approach was advocated by philosopher of science Karl Popper in the 1930s in relation to natural science and empirical (or factual) knowledge. Popper contrasted falsification with verification (*see* CRITICAL RATIONALISM). The latter involves the search for evidence that confirms a hypothesis or conjecture. Popper argued that falsification is more rigorous because just one piece of negative evidence can challenge 99 confirmatory pieces. The falsificationist attitude is a hallmark of critical thinking, though few contemporary critics in human geography or other subjects subscribe to Popper's strict definition of this attitude.

family A small group of people associated through ties of common descent, marriage, intimacy, and/or co-residence, thereby constituting a meaningful social unit intermediate between the individual and the community or society. Families are generally where children are raised and socialized (*see* SOCIAL REPRODUCTION). A family may reside together in a *household, but the two are not the same. Households may contain unrelated members, while families may be widely distributed. Transnational families, for example, contain members living in more than one country (*see* TRANSNATIONAL COMMUNITIES; TRANSNATIONALISM).

Anthropologists, historians, and sociologists have observed such a diversity of family types and relations, past and present, that there is little evidence for a single normative family arrangement (*see* HISTORICAL DEMOGRAPHY; KINSHIP). Commonly heard arguments that 'the family' is in decline or in crisis are therefore often blind to its historical and geographical variety. Nonetheless, the family is often the object of idealization and governance, as certain family forms (e.g. two married parents plus dependent children, the 'nuclear family') and relations (e.g. *patriarchy or symmetry between men and women) are deemed most natural or conducive to social order (*see* GENDER ROLE). Other forms, for example, single-parent and female-headed families are frequently described as deviant and pathological, even in the absence of conclusive empirical evidence. Governmental programmes, for example, in taxation, *welfare, and *housing, make assumptions about what constitutes a normal family and how it should be the bedrock of the *nation or society. Urban environments, for example, *suburbs, *new towns, and *garden cities, have been constructed around the ideal of a nuclear family with a single wage-earner. *Gentrification, by the same token, has been associated with novel family forms, for example, couples without children, and gay and lesbian families. It is also often assumed that the family is a haven, insulated from the state and the market, the site of egalitarian or symmetrical relations. But as *feminist geographers have uncovered, the family is sometimes equally a site of *power, *inequality, and *violence; it can also be entwined with waged labour (*see* DOMESTIC WORK). *See also* HOME.

Further reading Castells, M. (1997), *The Power of Identity*.

McDowell, L. (1991), 'Life without father and Ford', *Transactions of the Institute of British Geographers* 16: 400–19.

famine A crisis in which large numbers of people in an area cannot obtain enough food to sustain themselves. The situation often leads to excess mortality from either starvation or illness and disease caused by a lack of food. The distinction between the extreme event of famine and chronic hunger or malnourishment can be arbitrary; by some definitions, famines must involve at least 1000 deaths and mortality rates of at least 1/10,000 per day. Even this definition leaves open the question of the relevant spatial and temporal scale. It is not necessarily the case that everyone in an area suffers equally; some social groups, defined, by gender, age, ethnicity, and so forth, may be more vulnerable than others. The geographical analysis of incidence within regions can be also reveal differences, for example, between rural and urban areas. Beyond this, definitions of famine have often proved controversial because of disagreements about cause and whether it is a singular event or a collection of symptoms. In recent years, geographers have focused less on famine specifically and more on *food security and *vulnerability more generally. Even international relief organizations avoid the term, often preferring 'food crisis'.

Famines have been identified in historical records since the 5th century BC. In the 20th century it is estimated that there were some 70 million deaths caused by famine, almost half in China between 1958 and 1962. All the major famines of the last century were located in Asia, the USSR, or Africa, but, aside from the unusual case of North Korea, contemporary famine seems confined to Africa.

Most debate over famine concerns its cause. *Malthusian arguments attributing famine to natural disaster, crop failure, or overpopulation are less commonly made, although some commentators predict catastrophic famines for the mid-21st century induced by shortages of water, food, land, and energy. The idea that Food Availability Decline (FAD) is the prime cause was largely overturned as a result of work by Amartya *Sen. His studies of, among others, the 1943 Bengal and 1973-4 Bangladesh famines revealed that people starved even when food was readily available. In Sen's view they lacked 'entitlement' to food, i.e. the socially sanctioned legal right to food. By this he meant more than income alone, but all the assets a person can make use of. Sen's argument that famine is caused by demand rather than supply-side problems is widely accepted, although not necessarily regarded as complete. *Political economic perspectives seek to address why some people have less entitlement than others, shifting attention to longer-term or structural features such as the incorporation of peasant societies into either imperial or capitalist relations (Davis 2001, Nally 2008). Other analysts stress the role of war and conflict or government failure; UN sanctions on Iraq 1990-2003 arguably brought about famine there. More recent research has argued that, at least in the case of southern Africa, the increased vulnerability of households to famine has been caused by the HIV/AIDS pandemic. The leading geographical contribution to this debate was made by Michael *Watts and Hans Bohle. They conceptualized a 'space of vulnerability' defined by the relations between entitlement, empowerment, and political economy. It seems safe to say that there is no single or universal cause of famine. The 2011 food crisis in Somalia and the Horn of Africa was ascribed to a combination of drought, warfare, poor government, and misguided land redistribution policies, for example. While the term has some emotive power to mobilize aid in emergencies, most researchers are careful to avoid its connotations as an exceptional state related to some natural disaster.

References Davis, M. (2001), *Late Victorian Holocausts*.
Nally, D. (2008), '"That coming storm" the Irish Poor Law, colonial biopolitics and the Great Famine', *Annals of the Association of American Geographers* 98: 714–41.
Sen, A. (1981), *Poverty and Famine*.
Watts, M. and Bohle, H. (1993), 'The space of vulnerability: the causal structure of hunger and famine', *Progress in Human Geography* 17: 43–67.

FAO *See* FOOD AND AGRICULTURE ORGANIZATION.

farming *See* AGRICULTURE.

fascism A radical and authoritarian political ideology that flourished in Europe during the 1920s to 1940s and to varying degrees in other regions of the world, including Japan, China, South America, and Southwest Asia. It was expressed as a political movement and in several governments, and drew its support from across society including industry. Although varying from place to place, fascists shared a number of common ideas: extreme *nationalism, racism, and anti-Semitism, xenophobia, anticlericalism, and a tolerance or promotion of *violence internally and externally in pursuit of national aims. In its ideal, people, state, and party were harmoniously united, while economy and society could be centrally directed. Fascism took root first in Italy, forming the ideology for Mussolini's government (1922–43) and was furthered under Hitler in Germany (until the end of the Second World War) and under Franco (1936–75) in Spain. Although it can be argued that Iraq's Ba'athist regime (1968–2003) sustained fascism after the Second World War, in its core manifestation it did not survive beyond the 1970s. Nonetheless, elements of fascist ideology continued to inform and inspire far-right parties and organizations across the world. In Europe, for example, strongly nationalist politics often adopt the symbols and policies of former fascist regimes (*see* NATIONALISM).

FDI *See* FOREIGN DIRECT INVESTMENT.

fear A distressing emotional response to a real or perceived threat. In geography the study of fear has occurred in two main contexts. First, there are investigations into how fear shapes spatial behaviour with respect to various forms of *crime. In particular, several feminist geographers have examined how the fear of crime, especially physical violence, reshapes the temporal and spatial patterns of individual movement through a city, with a particular focus on age and gender. Here, the perceived threat is just as important as the real likelihood of attack in guiding and limiting spatial choices. Feminists have challenged traditional explanations of fear that suggest it arises due to women's vulnerability, rather than a set of threats, and also the right to be and act in space, rather than to self-regulate their behaviour by avoiding risky places. Related work has focused on the public projection of fear with respect to other vulnerable groups, especially children, and how this has reconfigured their time-space routines. A second body of work addresses the geopolitics of fear in the context of *globalization, national *security, and *terrorism (Pain and Smith 2008). Here, how discourses of fear circulate beyond and between locales, how it is manipulated, and how it is felt, particularly by minority groups and marginalized individuals, are all topics of ongoing study.

Further reading Pain, R. and Smith, S. (eds.) (2008), *Fear: Critical Geopolitics and Everyday Life*. Valentine, G. (1989), 'The geography of women's fear', *Area* 21(4): 385–401.

fecundity The potential of women in a population to bear children. It is related to the proportion of women of child-bearing age (normally 15–49) and prevailing fertility rates.

federalism A political system in which otherwise self-governing localities or regions voluntarily unite into a single polity in which some powers are vested in a central government. A federal state typically involves an agreed and constitutionally defined division of responsibilities, rights, and resources between the territorial components of the federation and central government. The details can vary greatly between federations meaning that federalism is largely titular in some cases because central government is far more powerful than the federated units beneath it. The world's best-known political federation is the *United States of America, but other examples include *Germany, *Brazil, *India, *Nigeria, and *Mexico.

feminism 1. A philosophical viewpoint that seeks to rethink society and the nature of research from a gender-aware perspective.

2. A political movement that seeks to challenge and tackle the issue of *patriarchy and other imbalances of power. Feminism has a history dating back to the *Enlightenment and early calls for equality between men and women. It developed as a major philosophical approach and movement in the 20th century, progressing through waves of thinking and activism. The first wave focused on institutionalized discrimination against women and on women's civil rights, in particular, the rights to vote, education, work, and property. The second wave, from the 1950s on, focused on social relations between men and women, identity, sexuality, the family, and reproductive rights. The third wave, from the 1980s on, started to rethink and criticize feminism itself, recognizing that there is a wide diversity of identities amongst women with respect to 'race', ethnicity, nationality, faith, culture, politics, etc., and that feminism needed to be sensitive to these differences, which could be contradictory or conflicting. Feminism, as a philosophy and a political movement, is thus understood as being diverse in nature. As a result, feminist scholars now refer to feminism*s* in the plural to acknowledge that there are different strands of feminist thought and different kinds of feminist struggles around the world. What unifies them, however, is an ideological commitment to not only examine gender inequalities, but to actively seek to redress such inequalities. As such, there is a focus on power and how it is created, vested, wielded, and reproduced to generate social relations and formations. This includes a critique of how power operates within the academic sphere and through the research process. *See also* FEMINIST EPISTEMOLOGY; FEMINIST GEOGRAPHY.

Feminism and Geography A landmark book written by Gillian *Rose (1993), on *feminist geography that exposed not only the gendered nature of the geographical world, but the gendered nature of geographical knowledge production itself. Drawing on critical social theory, especially *post-structural and *psychoanalytic theory, Rose made a compelling case that geography as a discipline is heavily dominated by men in terms of the gender make-up of staffing, professional societies, and its canon, and practises a *masculinist form of science, seeing the world through a masculine *gaze. Within geography a *power-geometry thus operates, realized through discursive and material practices and structures, and performed through an embodied subjectivity. Feminist geography, Rose argued, offers a counterpoint to such masculinism, offering alternative *ways of seeing, doing, writing, and performing geographical scholarship that produces non-*essentializing geographical knowledge. *See also* WOMEN IN GEOGRAPHY.

feminist epistemology An approach to understanding the world that emphasizes how gender influences the ways we come to comprehend and research reality. It challenges masculinist approaches to knowledge construction (*see* MASCULINISM). The idea that research can be *objective, neutral, and value-free has been shown by feminist critics to be a mask for masculinist reason. All research, these critics have insisted, is always conditioned by the particular norms and values of the researcher and is shot through with relations of *power, usually in subtle ways. They propose an epistemology that acknowledges openly the *positionality of the researcher and *situatedness of knowledge production. Such an epistemology is operationalized through interpretive methods that are applied with a high degree of *reflexivity. Feminist epistemologists have asked what difference it makes to women and the wider society if we value a feminist view on the world.

feminist geography The application of feminist theory and methodologies to understanding human geography. The intent of *feminism is to investigate, reveal, challenge, and change gendered divisions in society. These divisions often manifest themselves as spatial divisions with men and women having different patterns of spatial activity, behaviour, and experiences of place. Feminist geography has thus sought to understand the relationship between *gender divisions and spatial divisions, and to challenge their supposed naturalness and legitimacy. This includes examining gender roles and divisions in the discipline itself with respect to the foci of study, the history, and practice of geography, and the balance of men and women working as professional geographers and career structures (*see* WOMEN IN GEOGRAPHY), and challenging how geographical research is conceptualized and practised.

Feminist geography developed from the late 1970s onwards, building on the second wave feminist movement of the 1960s and *radical geography's challenge to examine and to transform spatial divisions in society. A principal argument was that *gender roles and the uneven and unequal positions and power of women and men in society had up to then been largely ignored by geographers. Early work demonstrated that gender relations were the outcome of and reflected in the spatial structure of society. Men and women experience material *inequalities in terms of access to work, wealth, power, and status that produce different spatial relations with respect to access to *public and *private space and *time-geographies. For example, women are much more likely to experience spatial behaviour restricted to the home and delimited by child-care and domestic duties, and to undertake work that facilitates these duties such as a part-time job located close to home. These inequalities were shown to be reproduced through *patriarchy, which is entrenched in social, political and economic institutions, and popular discourse and the media, and works to maintain a persistent, gendered *power geometry. In subsequent work, feminist geographers highlighted the interrelations between patriarchy, *identity, *embodiment, and spatial *subjectivities, and how their entangling produces gendered, embodied, and *emotional geographies. Importantly, feminist scholarship has also examined the ways in which gendered divisions are historically and geographically differentiated, varying over time, and across space and cultures. Such studies show how gender relations have evolved in particular locales and how they are differently constituted and experienced in different places.

As with feminism more broadly, feminist geography has evolved over time so that it presently consists of a family of theoretical positions, ranging from approaches that are more structuralist in orientation, such as *socialist feminism, that situates women's oppression within the broader framework of class oppression and capital exploitation, through to *post-structuralism that recognizes the plurality and differences amongst women and the contingent, relational, and contextual ways in which gender divisions are reproduced. Moreover, given its focus on power, feminist theory has been extended to understand and explain other forms of spatial division centred on identity and cultural politics. This has led to productive engagements of feminist theory with other social theories such as *post-colonialism, for example. What unites these various approaches is a commitment to exposing gender and spatial divisions, and to tackle such divisions. Unlike many theoretical approaches that seek to be *objective and impartial in the production of knowledge, feminism is explicitly ideological in that it seeks to transform that which it studies (*see* FEMINIST STANDPOINT THEORY).

Part of this commitment is to transform the practices and structures of geography itself. To that end feminist geographers have made critical interventions into the conduct of research in geography, introducing *feminist epistemologies and *methodologies that challenge the *masculinist formulation of science as objective, neutral, and value-free, instead arguing that research always has a *positionality that produces *situated knowledge. They have thus highlighted the masculinist nature of *fieldwork and made the case for more interpretative approaches to research that utilize *qualitative methods. These new epistemologies and methods have been adopted widely across the discipline and applied to a wide range of foci beyond gender.

Further reading Laurie, N., Dwyer, C., Holloway, S., and Smith, F. (1999), *Geographies of New Feminities.*
McDowell, L. (1999), *Gender, Identity and Place.*
Nelson, L. and Seager, J. (2004), *A Companion to Feminist Geography.*
Rose, G. (1993), *Feminism and Geography.*
Women in Geography Study Group (1997), *Feminist Geographies: Explorations in Diversity and Difference.*

feminist standpoint theory An approach that argues that research has traditionally been limited in its analysis and conclusions because it has, in the main, been constructed from the standpoint of men, ignoring the standpoint of women and reproducing patriarchy. Moreover, it is usually the view of white, middle-class, heterosexual, able-bodied men. In contrast, standpoint theory challenges the masculinist bias of rationalist epistemologies and offers an alternative perspective that seeks to understand the world from standpoints that are argued to be preferable, or at least of equal value. *See also* FEMINIST EPISTEMOLOGY; STANDPOINT THEORY.

feminization of poverty The processes which have led to women making up a disproportionate share of people living in *poverty. This disproportion is observable in both developing and developed countries. Not only do women have less access to income, or are paid less for the same labour, they also tend to have fewer opportunities and choices, and to be constrained by prejudices and the organization of society. They are also more likely to form single-headed households, taking on additional duties with reduced access to labour markets.

fertility rate The level of live births in a population, usually expressed as the number of births per thousand people per year. This is also known as the crude birth rate. For comparative purposes it is helpful to employ age-standardized rates, adjusted for the different age structures of the populations compared (*see* TOTAL FERTILITY RATE). Current fertility rates range from 45–50/1000 in some African countries to less than 10/1000 in Japan and parts of Western Europe, so low in fact that some consider it to be a crisis.

feudalism 1. A set of legal and customary relationships surrounding the exchange of land for either military service or rent that flourished in medieval Europe.
2. A type of society centred on such relationships, dominant throughout Europe before capitalism. Some historians suggest that Japan from the 12th to the 19th century can be described as feudal under this broader definition. Others prefer to place feudalism within the general category 'tributary mode of production', societies characterized by the coerced extraction of surplus by one group from another (generally peasants) (*see* ASIATIC MODE OF PRODUCTION).
Such societies did not use the term feudalism themselves. Given that historians have only piecemeal knowledge of the period, there is much uncertainty about how much uniformity there was. There is some consensus around two core features. 'Vassalage' described the relationships among a warrior class. The sovereign granted title to land to other lords in return for their loyalty and military service. In turn, these lords could contract with lesser nobles around the same arrangement. The result was a highly decentralized form of rule. Land could not be bought or sold, i.e. it was not a commodity (*see* COMMODIFICATION). 'Serfdom' was the corresponding condition of tied or unfree labour. Serfs, or peasants, could not own land but were able to work it in return for rent paid to lords in the form of labour, service or, perhaps less commonly, money. They did, however, possess their own tools and livestock. There is disagreement over whether the relationship between lords and peasants was wholly coercive; a complex patchwork of customary rights and dues bound classes together in something approaching interdependence.

Karl *Marx regarded feudalism as a necessary stage before capitalism, and much analysis has centred on the so-called transition between these two types of society (*see* MODE OF PRODUCTION). This kind of reading has gradually fallen out of favour, as more details of how complex and geographically varied the situation was become known.

Further reading Dodgshon, R. A. (1987), *The European Past: Social Evolution and Spatial Order*.

fictitious capital 1. Income that is parasitic on that earned or produced by other people.

2. Income that would be due if non-monetary assets were sold at their paper value.

3. Promised or expected income that will not, despite appearances, be forthcoming.

4. The anticipated future income necessary to pay for current borrowing or investment.

Karl *Marx famously focused on the first and last of these definitions. *Capitalism, he argued, is an economic system predicated on continuous growth. What he called 'productive capital' is dependent on access to land, facilities, and money in order to make, sell, and realize a profit on commodities. Those involved in renting land and property and in lending money are, Marx argued, dependent on productive capital to yield profits in the future in order to pay for assets rented and money borrowed today. *Rentiers and bankers are thus, Marx argued, fictitious capitalists in the first and last definitions. Fictitious capital in the second sense simply refers to the predicted monetary value of non-liquid assets if they were liquidated. This capital is 'fictitious' in a technical sense. In sense three fictitious capital is quite literally fictitious: it is a construct or fantasy, as with a Ponzi scheme in which some investors enjoy high returns while the investment manager pockets the money of other investors while growing the overall number of investors until the house of cards collapses. In *Limits to Capital* (1982), David Harvey showed how finance capital in the first and last definitions was integral to understanding the geographical configuration of capitalism. For instance, by pooling the savings and profits of countless workers and firms, banks possess the monetary assets to pay for major construction projects (in the form of lending to governments and corporations).

fictitious commodity Any commodity whose social and/or ecological value exceeds its monetary value or its practical functions. The neo-Marxist historian Karl *Polanyi famously argued that land, labour (people), and money are fictitious commodities but, strictly speaking, virtually all goods and services produced by capitalist firms can be considered 'fictitious' in Polanyi's sense. For instance, a mahogany dining table is a fictitious commodity in the sense that its monetary cost rests on the fiction that it can somehow account for the entire social and ecological value of the patch of tropical forest from which the wood originally came. Human geographers, following Polanyi, have sought to highlight the problematic 'fictions' involved in treating workers and environment-related goods and services as if they are 'normal commodities'. In *labour geography, researchers such as Andrew Herod have examined employment from the perspective of working people and shown how their wages become the focus for deeply personal questions about lifestyle, place-identity, and much more besides. Similarly, geographers studying *natural resources have shown how the recent turn to *neoliberal management regimes rests on the questionable belief that the non-human world can be 'properly' valued and conserved by adjusting prices and assigning property rights. Clearly, the term 'fictitious commodity' has a *normative edge and has been favoured by those in *critical human geography.

fieldwork The generation of primary data in the field. Fieldwork is often considered to be an essential aspect of geographical scholarship as it involves a first-hand encounter between the researcher and the phenomena, people, and places being studied. It thus provides greater insight and understanding of local conditions and context. It is also a key component of geographical education. This belief in the primacy of fieldwork emerged in the early 19th century, although it was not unchallenged. To some, the chaos of the field was not as reliable as the stability of the museum or library as a site for ordering geographical knowledge (Outram 1996). *Geographical societies funded *expeditions and *exploration that would enable scholars to travel to different parts of the world and interact with societies and environments. Once in the field, the researcher can use the full suite of data generation techniques such as *surveys, *questionnaires, *interviews, *focus groups, *ethnography, and *observation to generate primary data. While fieldwork remains a mainstay of geographic research, Rundstrom and Kenzer argue that it is in decline, replaced by secondary data analysis and so-called 'armchair' studies. This is partly due to cost and resources, but also changes in the nature of geographical scholarship, where *critique has become more common. Moreover, some spatial scientists have questioned the rigour of some fieldwork, suggesting it constitutes little more than adventures in sightseeing.

Historians of geography are revising our ideas about fieldwork. Expeditions and exploration have been critiqued by *feminist and *post-colonial scholars as constituting a *masculinist and domineering form of scientific endeavour in which geographers seek to master new terrains and produce objective knowledge about people and places of which they are not part. The act of observing can be interrogated as an instance of the masculine *gaze. Moreover, the idea that 'the field' is simply a terrain awaiting the investigator is also questioned. A great deal of material and discursive work goes into making certain sites into 'the field' (Driver 2005). This has led to geographers considering the ways in which fieldwork is an embodied, reflexive, and political set of practices that produce *situated knowledge. Moreover, it has led to a consideration of the *ethics of fieldwork and how people interact with local people, for example, learning and using local languages and being sensitive to and respectful of local attitudes and cultures, as well as being cautious of producing an *ethnocentric account. To this end, *activist and *advocacy geography and methods such as *participatory action research seek to produce more *empowering and emancipatory forms of fieldwork.

Further reading Driver, F. (2005), 'Field-work in geography', *Transactions of the Institute of British Geographers*. 25: 267–8.

Nairn, K. (2002), 'Doing feminist fieldwork about geography fieldwork', in Moss, P. (ed.) *Feminist Geography in Practice*.

Outram, D. (1996), 'New spaces of natural history', in Jardine, N. et al. (eds.) *Cultures of Natural History*.

Philips, R. and Johns, J. (2012), *Fieldwork for Human Geography*.

Rundstrom, R. and Kenzer, M. (1989), 'The decline of fieldwork in human geography', *The Professional Geographer* 41(3): 294–303.

film The representation of the world as a continuous set of moving images, often accompanied by a sound track, and almost always with spoken words (for instance, in the form of dialogue between characters). Film consists of a diverse set of related genres including news footage, documentaries, and movies. These genres are themselves internally differentiated (for instance, movies can be cartoon-animation, or can blend special effects with 'real' images and sounds). Film is an important medium of communication, edification, entertainment, and distraction. It commands huge audiences worldwide, though the size of these audiences varies depending on the genre. All film—even 'real life' documentary—is the result of specific directorial and technical decisions about what to show and how. Film expresses and can shape existing social, economic, political, and environmental values, norms, and aspirations. For cultural geographers, film is a lens through which one can see how societies (or specific social groups) represent themselves to each other and to others in conscious and unconscious ways. At the heart of this analysis are debates over *representation and the ways in which film conveys meanings, and how to interpret such meanings. Economic geographers are more interested in the film industry and how it is spatially organized into economic *clusters, and its effects on local economies, and film as an economic *commodity, an important component in the wider *cultural economy. Aside from studying film, geographers are increasingly producing films as part of their investigative methodologies. In terms of data generation, digital video cameras are now cheap and easy to use and many academic studies are generating their own footage as a source of analytical data, recording events, places, and people, and are incorporating such material when communicating their research. The first video-only geographical papers have recently been published.

Further reading Clarke, D. (1997), *The Cinematic City*.
Lukinbeal, C. and Zimmerman, S. (eds.) (2008), *The Geography of Cinema*.

finance The pooling, lending, and investing of *money by various institutions, such as banks, which together comprise the financial system of any country. Finance is of critical importance to firms, governments, and ordinary people. It permits investments or purchases that might otherwise never occur or which would otherwise have to be deferred. The lending or investing of money typically has risks attached to it (*see* DEBT CRISIS). Finance has three main areas: public (government) finance, corporate finance, and personal finance. Economic geographers have largely been interested in the last two, both of which have become highly internationalized because regulations now permit lending and investing between countries to occur more easily than in the past. *See also* FINANCE CAPITAL; FINANCIAL MARKETS.

finance capital **1.** A synonym for *finance.
   2. A sector of any economy (national, regional, or global) whose institutions are in the business of lending and investing money. These institutions have a very uneven global geography, with the City of London and Wall Street the two largest financial centres globally (despite being at the heart of the 2007 financial crisis). However, because these institutions usually operate on a global scale, the money they invest or lend circulates through each artery of the world economy. Finance capital is usually at the cutting edge of capitalist investment because new and often risky commercial ventures in new places require willing lenders or investors. In recent years the distinction between finance capital and productive capital (e.g. a manufacturing company) have become blurred because many companies now engage in producing commodities and in lending money to others (or investing money beyond the perimeters of the firm).

financial crisis A period in which several large banks and other financial institutions become insolvent or even face bankruptcy. Financial institutions are of fundamental importance to the functioning of *capitalism. For almost any firm that makes commodities to start up and prosper, lending is required from banks or shareholders. Likewise, many firms (and also workers and consumers) want to insure against various commercial (and personal) risks by paying a fee. *Financial capital can be seen as a portion of *productive capital that is devoted to lending, investment, and risk assurance. Some finance capital is purely for commercial use or for large institutions, while some is for households and ordinary people (as with credit card debt). However, because no one organization oversees where financial capital goes, and because many financial investments are inherently risky, there is always the possibility that the eventual returns on finance will be low or non-existent. Without proper governmental regulation there is also the possibility that finance capital will cannibalize itself, making money from moving and selling money, rather than from investing money in productive activities. In this situation an imbalance arises between finance capital and productive capital that may lead to a crisis of *capitalism not just of the financial sector of the economy. In the global financial crisis of 2007–2009 many financial institutions went bust, were bought by more solvent institutions, or went into public ownership. Lending also dried up, leading to a crisis of liquidity for many firms and households. Like previous financial crises the geography of the 2007–2009 crisis was uneven, and thus 'global' in a differentiated way. For instance, Canadian finance was not badly affected by the crisis, whereas financial institutions based in Britain and the US (but with worldwide operations) were. *See also* DEBT CRISIS.

financial exclusion A process in which certain sections of any society are denied access to financial goods and services. Typically, the term 'financial exclusion' refers to individuals and households rather than businesses, but it may be extended to geographical areas. The term came to prominence in human geography and other social sciences in the 1990s. During this decade banks, credit card companies, and other money-lenders made money more easily available to ordinary people. This process of financial inclusion notwithstanding, certain people—usually those concentrated in poor inner city or peri-urban neighbourhoods—were considered too risky to lend to (perhaps because they had already had to declare bankruptcy to clear previous debts). Financial exclusion means that the excluded must live day to day on the money they earn or receive in the form of state benefits. Alternatively, they have to seek credit from unregulated lenders including loan sharks charging exorbitant interest rates.

financialization The process whereby *finance capital and financial institutions account for a greater share of all economic activity. Since the early 1980s several countries allowed banks (commercial and retail), credit card firms, building societies, insurance companies, and other financial institutions to expand their customer base. They did this in two ways. First, they offered established financial products to more customers (such as credit cards). Second, they created new financial products and popularized them (such as collateralized debt obligations and credit default swaps). The global financial crisis that began in 2007 shows us that financialization was a high-risk process that was improperly regulated by governments. Critics also point out that because finance capital is parasitic on growth in the 'real economy' (where most products that people buy and use are made), financialization diverts too much money away from investment in productive economic activity. Many countries have not experienced financialization, but those that have—such as the UK—are now considering how economically sustainable it is.

financial markets The markets in which money is bought and sold rather than physical commodities. There are many different kinds of financial markets corresponding to particular forms of money and financial instruments. Notable examples are foreign exchange markets, stock markets, insurance markets, futures markets, and derivatives markets. Though mortgages and credit card debt are both financial market transactions, the term 'financial market' is usually reserved for transactions within the world of professional financiers.

firm A legally recognized entity whose function is to produce goods and/or services for sale to intermediate or final consumers. While many firms are owned and operated by families or just a few people, most large firms have complex ownership and operating structures. Firms have at least three geographies of interest. First, there are spatial concentrations of firms producing specific goods or services (as evidenced by Wall Street in the banking sector). Second, the 'culture' of firms may vary spatially, with certain working habits and management practices specific to a country or region. Finally, many large firms are able to physically relocate, to purchase other firms overseas, or to enter strategic alliances with foreign firms. The increasingly complex nature and organization of firms is a key topic in *economic geography.

Further reading Yeung, H.W-C. (2005), 'The firm as social networks: an organisational perspective', *Growth and Change* 36(3): 307-28.

First Nations The individuals and communities who can trace their biological and cultural heritage back to the *indigenous peoples who inhabited the non-European world prior to the long period of European exploration and colonization. The term 'First Nations' has enjoyed widespread use in Canada and the Pacific Northwest of the US since the 1980s, but is less favoured in Australia and New Zealand (where 'aboriginal' and 'indigenous' peoples are more common terms). Likewise, these and other synonyms are preferred in other continents where First Nations exist, such as Central and South America. Because First Nations peoples often suffered acute discrimination at the hands of immigrant populations, the term has a political charge to it: not only does it signify a person's community membership but also their claims to territory and resources taken away by European settlers since the 17th century. *See also* ABORIGINAL.

first nature 1. The non-human world as it existed prior to the long period of human transformation and destruction of the natural environment.
    2. The few remaining portions of that world, which today exist as metaphorical islands in a sea of 'second nature'. The latter term refers to the many biophysical processes and entities—from domestic animals to plantation forests—that have been deeply and pur-posely altered in order to satisfy human needs and wants. While first nature has long vanished in settled parts of the world, the idea of first nature remains a powerful one in parts of the environmental movement and wider societal discourse (*see*, for example, DEEP ECOLOGY). Many critical human geographers have examined how this idea gets used in struggles over the non-human world. *See also* SOCIAL NATURE; WILDERNESS.

First World A term used for countries that are highly developed with respect to their economy and standard of living. In this context 'developed' refers to either the diversity and complexity of their national economy or the high per capita income enjoyed by citizens. The term originated in the *Cold War and referred to the democratic and capitalist countries allied against the communist bloc. Here, *Second World referred to those sharing a communist ideology, and *Third World was applied to those countries that were politically neutral. Given their general affluence, since the end of the Cold War, the First World has subsequently been regarded as developed nations with liberal democratic political systems and advanced economies. Conversely, Third World has lost its former political meaning and come to signify countries with low levels of eco-nomic *development.

First World War The first of two major wars that took place at the global scale during the 20th century. Starting on 28 July 1914 and ending on 11 November 1918, the war was fought between the Allies (France, UK, Russia, their colonies, and allied countries notably the USA) and the Central Powers (Germany, Austria-Hungary, their colonies, and allies), principally in Europe, but also elsewhere around the world. Over 60 million military personnel were mobilized, and some eight to nine million combatants were killed, with a large number of civilians dying during and immediately afterwards through famine and associated ill health. The war was a major geopolitical event and at its termination three empires ceased to exist (the Russian, Austro-German, and Ottoman). The political map of Europe and what came to be known as the *Middle East was redrawn as territory was either reassigned between nation states or vested in new ones such as Iraq. The war's social, political, technological, and economic legacy was long and large, including sowing the discontent that would lead to the *Second World War (1939–45), the *Cold War, and to later instability across the Middle East.

fiscal crisis The inability of a national or local government to meet its current spending obligations and commitments because of insufficient funds. Government spending has two main sources—taxation and borrowing. When seeking to increase spending quickly it is usually easier to borrow more than it is to raise domestic taxation. Since the mid-1970s many countries have greatly increased the size of their public debt—notable examples being the United States and Japan. If such debt is to be repaid the economies of the borrowing countries need to expand. If they stagnate or fall into a recession not only will current loans have to be rescheduled, but new loans to pay for current spending commitments may not be forthcoming. Therein lie the seeds of a fiscal crisis of the state. In 2011, Greece experienced such a crisis which, typically, led the government to impose austerity measures on the national population.

fixity The condition of being unmoving and unchanging, often contrasted with motion or *mobility in the analysis of geographical landscapes.

flâneur A literary and theoretical urban figure who walks and experiences the city. The importance of the *flâneur* as key participant and observer of city life stems from the 19th-century Parisian poet Charles Baudelaire, and the mid-20th-century social critic Walter Benjamin, notably in *The Arcades Project* (1927–40). The *flâneur* for them represented a figure—understood as male—who had come to terms with the anonymity, alienation, and confusion of urban life, and was taken with *modernity and consumer-driven capitalism. The *flâneur* strolls and consumes the city, and takes delight in its crowds and its varied social geography. As a theoretical figure the *flâneur* represents a way of engaging with and making sense of the city.

Fleure, Herbert J. (1877–1969) A British regional geographer and anthropologist who made notable contributions to geography's profile in universities and schools in Britain during his lifetime. His several books on people-land relationships in Western Europe took issue with *environmental determinism. In his senior role in the *Geographical Association he helped to strengthen geography's pedagogic contributions to the education of young people. He was elected a Fellow of the Royal Society in 1936.

flexible accumulation A *regime of accumulation in which capitalist firms make flexibility in some or all areas of business practice their *modus operandi*. According to many theorists of *capitalism, national economies are often characterized by one or other dominant model of business practice. For example, between the 1930s and 1970s most advanced capitalist economies were dominated by 'Fordist' companies—be they private or publicly owned (*see* FORDISM). Fordist firms mass-produced a narrow range of products by having thousands of workers create and/or assemble standardized raw materials, parts, and components. After the economic crises that hit many developed economies in the 1970s, many firms adopted a more flexible business model. This involved any or all of the following: reducing inventories and moving to '*just-in-time' ordering of raw materials and components; reducing the number of permanent or full-time workers; employing fewer trades union workers; offering a greater diversity of products and giving customers more choice; moving to just-in-time product delivery to wholesalers and retailers. As with any attempt to periodize economic history it is easy to exaggerate the extent to which flexible firms replaced Fordist ones. Mass production and consumption of standardized products are hardly a thing of the past, even as flexibility is now far more insinuated in commodity production than heretofore. *See also* POST-FORDISM.

flexible citizenship A term that describes the way some elites manipulate or take advantage of citizenship rights in different countries or jurisdictions. Anthropologist Aihwa Ong defines it as 'strategies . . . to circumvent *and* benefit from different nation-state regimes by selecting different sites for investments, work and family relocation'. By implication, such people see *citizenship as a resource rather than as a matter of loyalty and belonging. *See also* CITIZENSHIP; DIASPORA; DUAL CITIZENSHIP; TRANSNATIONALISM.

Reference Ong, A. (1999), *Flexible Citizenship*.

flexible labour A range of non-standard employment roles and the workers who perform them characterized by marked variation in working time, tasks, and conditions (*see* WORK). 'Flexibility' tends to be used in a variety of work-related contexts, but it is possible to distinguish a number of core meanings. A flexible worker is someone who can adapt, reskill, and switch tasks in response to rapid changes in the *labour market. Manuel *Castells identifies a new division between 'generic' and 'self-programmable' labour. The former describes workers who can perform one task only, and are vulnerable to substitution by machinery. Although he argues that the economy needs such workers collectively, they are dispensable as individuals. Self-programmable labour, workers with higher levels of formal education or training, can retool themselves for new tasks or switch forms of employment. This contrast illustrates a second meaning of flexibility. For low-wage workers, flexibility might mean being forced to change jobs within more or less similar kinds of employment. But for high-skilled workers, flexibility may mean the ability to dictate the terms of employment by, for example, selling their services to the highest bidder. A third meaning of flexibility relates to the form of employment. Core workers in Fordist economies typically worked a standard number of hours per week, starting and finishing work at the same time (*see* FORDISM). Bureaucracies and large-scale manufacturing depended upon assembling a coordinated and synchronized workforce. But with the rise of *flexible accumulation, work patterns have shifted in at least two significant ways. Firstly, there has been a general increase in the number of part-time, casual, and temporary contracts across economies in the Global North (sometimes called casualization). To some degree this is motivated by the demand for such work from mothers with children. Secondly, companies have moved to allow or require workers to alter their working day by either reorganizing shifts or enabling home- and travel-based work.

The term 'flexible labour market' summarizes some of these meanings. Often associated with *neoliberalism, it describes the spread of non-standard or flexible forms of work and contract. Flexibility can be increased through appropriate regulation. This could mean removing restrictions on sacking employees, justified by the argument that if it is easier to sack someone, it is also less risky and so easier to hire them. Or it could mean obliging companies to offer flexible working terms to new parents. Flexibility is therefore a double-edged sword. For some workers it means greater control over conditions of employment and the possibility of balancing work and family. For others, it means greater levels of insecurity and exploitation. Precarious work (leading to a condition of 'precarity'), is highly insecure and low paid. It is often associated with female and/or immigrant workers, those who are already in the least empowered position in the labour market (*see* INTERPELLATION; SOCIAL POLARIZATION). Trades unions and civil society organizations are campaigning not only for higher wages for such workers, but new regulations to address their vulnerability.

References and further reading Castells, M. (1998), *End of Millennium*.
Trades Union Congress, Commission on Vulnerable Workers (2007), *Hard Work, Hidden Lives*.

Florida, Richard (1958–) An American economic geographer who popularized the terms '*creative class' and 'creative cities', and who advises business and government on how to achieve post-industrial success. Florida is a rare example of a modern geographer who has successfully established himself and his ideas in public debate.

flow/fluidity A metaphor used to describe the movement of money and commodities favoured by many *Marxist geographers and several post-Marxist political economists. They borrowed the metaphor from Karl *Marx to describe the way in which capital accumulation is a process in which flows of money become fixed in the landscape in the form of buildings, roads, and other elements of the built environment. These fixed assets become the arteries through which future streams of money and commodities pass, only to be superseded by new built environments as capitalism melts older solidities into air. *Capitalism thus combines motion and fixity as two—often contradictory—sides of the same coin.

focus group A group discussion to examine a particular issue or phenomenon that is led by a researcher. Rather than conduct one-on-one interviews it is sometimes more productive to conduct a focus group, wherein a collection of individuals can discuss and debate a set of questions of common concern. The strength of the method is the interaction amongst participants, which can identify points of convergence and disagreement amongst the group. The group dynamic is therefore an important component in the method, not a flaw. The role of the moderator is to ignite and sustain that dynamic to derive insight and knowledge. A group will normally consist of four to ten participants who share a common background, job, or interest. By conducting several focus groups it is possible to compare and contrast groups composed of participants with different characteristics.

Food and Agriculture Organization (FAO) A United Nations organization concerned with food security and productivity. Its primary aims are to ensure that people have access to an adequate, nutritious diet and to increase agricultural yields.

((())) SEE WEB LINKS
• Official website of the Food and Agriculture Organization.

food bank A not-for-profit organization that collects and distributes food to individuals and families who are malnourished or hungry. The food bank movement began in the USA in the 1960s and is now found on every continent in the world. Most food banks service an area the size of a city or large town. They take receipt of excess food from food retailers, from farmers, from members of the public, or from a local or national government (who may buy surplus food from farmers as a means of income support). A food bank will dispense food to local organizations working in low-income communities or involved in supporting the poor or homeless. Human geographers have investigated food banks in the context of research into *alternative economies and *neoliberalism.

food desert An area in which residents' access to healthy, affordable food is highly restricted, for example, because of the absence of food retailers in a low-income urban neighbourhood. The metaphor of a desert inverts the idea of an oasis: food deserts, at least in developed countries, are patches of poor nutrition in an otherwise biodiverse metaphorical ecosystem that offers most people a very good diet should they choose to eat well. The metaphor was coined in the early 1990s in the UK and had been used widely in studies of socio-spatial inequality in Western countries. Poor diet is typically linked with low incomes, which are also linked with reduced life expectancy and higher rates of illness.

food security The degree to which access to a sufficient quantity and quality of food to meet one's needs is assured. This means not just that food is available, but that it can be obtained, and that this is a durable situation (*see* ENTITLEMENT APPROACH). Geographically uneven patterns of food supply and demand intersect with social divisions based on *class, *gender, *race, and age in determining whether a *household or individual has food security. Food insecurity can be transitory or, in extreme cases, chronic (*see* FAMINE). It may relate to countries, individuals, or regions within countries; within sub-Saharan Africa the problem of urban food insecurity is growing

In general, world food security has risen over the past 50 years, but there are significant exceptions. For much of the 21st century, demand has risen faster than supply driven by both population growth and changing consumption patterns. It is widely anticipated that the environmental consequences of *climate change and variability will exacerbate this situation. Aside from the factors constraining agricultural productivity in many poorer regions of the world, there are a number of other factors operating at the world level that may be increasing the likelihood of food insecurity. These include growing speculation in financial markets on food commodities and future production; the conversion of agricultural land to non-food crops, for example, biofuels (*see* RENEWABLE ENERGY); the rising cost of fossil fuels and agricultural chemicals derived from them (*see* PEAK OIL); pressure in water supplies from non-agricultural uses; and the decline of biodiversity because of habitat loss.

Governments of countries that are not self-sufficient in key food items tend to take the risk of food insecurity very seriously and have contingency plans in place in case food imports are disrupted. Likewise, if home-grown food items are at risk of disease or weather-related problems then a back-up plan is required. These plans may involve food stockpiles or, more recently, the purchase of agricultural land overseas. These land deals, sometimes criticized as *land grabs, have been undertaken by countries with growing populations and demand, but insufficient agricultural land of their own, including China, South Korea, and Saudi Arabia. Opposition to this practice can take the form of calls for greater 'food sovereignty', i.e. a concentration on meeting national needs before converting land to cash crops for export.

The eradication of famine and *hunger, i.e. the establishment of food security, is the first of the *Millennium Development Goals, and there were major food summits organized by the *Food and Agriculture Organization in 2003 and 2009. There are differing views about how to increase food security. One option is to improve the operation of world food markets, removing national subsidies to production, and encouraging greater trade. Another looks to *genetic modification for a second *Green Revolution in agricultural productivity. *Poverty reduction and agricultural development is a third way forward, advocated by actors within the Global South. The concept of 'food justice' has emerged within *NGOs and community organizations campaigning on this issue; it means that food availability should be treated as a basic *human right and not a matter for markets.

Further reading Battersby, J. (2012), 'Beyond the food desert: finding ways to speak about urban food security in South Africa', *Geografiska Annaler: Series B, Human Geography* 94 (2): 141–59.
Shaw, D. J. (2007), *World Food Security: a History since 1945*.

food tourism A form of *tourism in which a holiday is focused on preparing and/or eating particular sorts of food. Food tourism has become a niche in the wider tourist industry and is especially popular among wealthier Westerners. Typically, it is focused on local, regional, or ethnic foods—many of which derive from organic farming and are prepared according to traditional recipes and techniques. Food tourism is part of a wider desire among some tourists to experience geographical and cultural difference, and is arguably a reaction to *McDonaldization.

footloose industry An industry whose firms face few restrictions on their geographical location. Many industries have locational requirements that tie them to certain places, such as coal mining. Others can choose from any number of possible locations. For instance, a branch plant that assembles vacuum cleaner parts needs access to a sufficiently disciplined workforce and to suitable transportation links, which can be found in many countries around the world.

footprint *See* CARBON FOOTPRINT.

forced labour Any work performed involuntarily and under coercion. The *ILO estimates that there were at least 12.3 million forced labourers in 2009, including child labour, trafficked migrants, and debt-bonded labour (where people work to pay off an onerous debt); most are women and children (*see* TRAFFICKING). Although coercion is implied in the definition, individuals may sometimes appear to volunteer for forced labour or be deceived into it.

Reference International Labour Organization (2009), *The Cost of Coercion.*

forced migration A migration resulting from force rather than volition, including *refugees, *asylum seekers, and *internally displaced persons, but also any other individuals fleeing conflict, disaster, or persecution whether or not they are internationally recognized. The distinction between forced and voluntary migration is not always clear-cut, as in the case of human *trafficking.

forces of production The physical infrastructure of machines, other technologies, and buildings that enter directly into the production of any commodity. The term was coined by Karl *Marx in the late 19th century, who distinguished the forces from the 'relations of production'. The latter are the specific social relations into which employees and employers enter. In a capitalist world, the relations of production are—in a formal sense—free and voluntary. Employers pay a wage to workers who utilize the forces of production to make, distribute, sell, maintain, or dispose of a commodity. Those workers are not forced to work (*see* FORCED LABOUR) nor is their labour tied (as it is in *feudal societies).

Fordism A *regime of accumulation characteristic of North Atlantic capitalist economies from the 1930s until the late 1970s. Named after the automobile manufacturer Henry Ford, the term was popularized by members of the French *Regulation School of economic theory and history, although it was first coined by Italian Marxist Antonio Gramsci. This school argued that *capital accumulation is crisis-prone, with periods of economic stability and growth punctuated by recessions. Beginning just prior to the *Second World War, the prosperity of the American, German, Japanese, French, and British economies was said to be based on the success of a group of Fordist firms and industries. These were very large firms engaged in the mass production of a limited number of commodities for sale to intermediate or final consumers. Mass production was thereby linked with mass consumption. Their activities were supported by national governments which spent a lot of money building a robust welfare system that workers benefited from. Many of these governments also operated Fordist companies directly, as was evident in many of France's nationalized industries. By the late 1970s Fordist firms faced overseas competition and many chose to relocate their facilities abroad. As these firms declined or relocated, jobs were lost and national business taxes contracted. The crisis of Fordism led, according to some, to a new era of *flexible accumulation or *post-Fordism. *See also* TAYLORISM.

foreign aid *See* AID.

Foreign Direct Investment (FDI) A direct investment into production in a country by a company located in another country, either by buying a domestic company and its facilities, entering into a strategic alliance with such a company, or opening a new facility. FDI is dominated by *transnational corporations in all major branches of economic activity, from mining to automobile manufacture to banking. FDI occurs for a wide range of reasons. Investing firms may want to tap new markets, to seek out cheaper sources of labour, take advantage of favourable taxation and customs rules, or buy out local rivals.

forest A large area of woodland. In medieval Europe forest lands were owned by the sovereign and governed by separate laws, usually reserved for hunting and not necessarily covered in trees. The management of woodlands is informed by the interdisciplinary science of forestry, which addresses commercial, conservation, and recreational priorities. Forests are a challenge to capitalist economic systems because trees take much longer to grow to maturity than most investments and they have proved harder to breed selectively than crop plants (Prudham 2005). *See also* DEFORESTATION; REDD.

Reference Prudham, W. S. (2005), *Knock on Wood: Nature as Commodity in Douglas-Fir Country.*

For Space A text written by one of the leading geographers of her generation, Doreen *Massey (2005) makes an impassioned argument for the social sciences to take space seriously in its analysis, and sets out a vision for how the concept of space should be theorized and employed. From her relational perspective, space has three qualities. First, it is always under construction, always in the process of being made. Second, space is the product of diverse interrelations, interactions that occur across a range of scales from global to local. Third, space supports multiplicity, wherein distinct trajectories and heterogeneities can co-exist. Massey makes the case that conceiving of space in this way opens up the possibilities of new heterogeneous, progressive politics and new ways of thinking about how spaces might be.

fortress conservation The creation of protected areas for terrestrial or marine wildlife by the coerced displacement or exclusion of the existing inhabitants. People may be evicted, their land may be seized, and customary rights to water, fishing, hunting, and resources may be curtailed (*see* DISPOSSESSION). Those displaced are described as 'conservation refugees'. Re-entry can be prevented by the use of armed guards and military patrols (Peluso 1993). The forcible relocation of people from lands deemed valuable for nature conservation or *wilderness protection has a long history, including examples in the USA (Yosemite National Park) and colonial empires (British East Africa). But such actions continued even after the end of colonialism, for example, as documented by Dan Brockington in the Mkomazi Game Reserve in Tanzania. Influenced by Western conservation professionals, these countries believed that *nature needed to be protected from people. The metaphor of the fortress captures the strength of commitment to excluding all but tourists or game hunters from areas of natural beauty or distinctiveness. There are signs that the tide is turning against fortress conservation methods, as more community-based approaches that seek to involve and respect the rights of indigenous peoples become more widespread (*see* COMMUNITY-BASED NATURAL RESOURCE MANAGEMENT).

References Brockington, D. (2002), *Fortress Conservation: the Preservation of the Mkomazi Game Reserve, Tanzania.*
Peluso, N. (1993), 'Coercing conservation? The politics of state resource control', *Global Environmental Change* 3: 199–217.

Foucault, Michel (1926–84) A French philosopher and historian of thought whose concepts and findings have had a formative effect on a wide range of social science and humanities subjects, including human geography. His most important books were written during the 1960s and 1970s, and later translated into English and other languages.

A consistent interest was in knowledge—not only what *counts* as 'knowledge' but its changing content over time and its connections with those sanctioned to create and disseminate it. Some of his books examined broad patterns of knowledge, such as *The Order of Things* (1970), while others examined how knowledge was made and mobilized by certain institutions, such *The Birth of the Clinic* (1973), which examined the rise of the 'medical profession'. Foucault took a constructivist and performative view of knowledge: for him not only is it something made with certain criteria in mind (e.g. 'truth', 'well-being', or 'justice', criteria which themselves are constructed) but something that affects the world it ostensibly represents.

Foucault's writings were central to the 'linguistic and cultural turn' in the Anglophone social sciences and humanities from the late 1980s, and the related embrace of *post-modernism in the academy. He is usually considered a post-structuralist, 'post' because he expressed doubts about the structuralist theory that people's thoughts are, at any one moment in history in any given society, governed by a set of immutable rules of *discourse (*see* POST-STRUCTURALISM). Unlike Jacques Derrida's influential post-structural philosophy, the appeal of Foucault's writings was that they grounded some large ideas in concrete examples and archival research into changing European knowledge practices before and since the *Enlightenment. Among these ideas was that of 'power-knowledge': Foucault argued that even 'positive' forms of knowledge—such as psychotherapeutic theory—were tools of social power. *Power, for Foucault, was thus not reducible to violence, intimidation, force, or even the law. Relatedly, he believed human subjects were the effects of power-knowledge. He thereby questioned the humanistic belief that all people have an inner, universal 'essence' that power may occlude or stymie (*see* ESSENTIALISM).

Anglophone human geographers have been deeply influenced by Foucault's writings. Some have used them to inquire into academic geography's own role as a form of power-knowledge, both past and present. Others have taken deeply geographical questions—such as how and why specific ideas concerning social and economic 'development' get transported from the Global North to the Global South—and used Foucault's ideas to question dominant knowledge practices. A third area of inquiry has been space and territory, prompted by Foucault's scattered observations and substantial writings on prisons, clinics, and other institutions, for example, in *Discipline and Punish* (1975/1979) (*see* PANOPTICON). Finally, his ideas about *sovereignty, *governmentality, and *biopolitics—many of which have only recently been translated from French or published from lectures—have generated a significant response from human geographers.

Further reading Crampton, J. W. and Elden, S. (eds.) (2007), *Space, Power and Knowledge: Foucault and Geography*.
Philo, C. (1992), 'Foucault's geography', *Environment and Planning D: Society and Space*, 10: 137–61.

foundationalism An approach to investigating the world that presumes there to be a single, discoverable reality that can be comprehended using a single, coherent philosophy, theory, or method. Foundationalism is a philosophical term and a somewhat pejorative one after the publication of Richard Rorty's *Philosophy and the Mirror of Nature* (1979). Rorty argued that, for far too long, philosophers had been searching for a single metaphorical mirror that, when held up to reality, would reflect it perfectly. In human geography, the *spatial science, humanistic, and *Marxist approaches that vied for intellectual dominance in the 1970s were all later seen as being foundational in this way. By the late 1980s, a set of more intellectually modest anti- or post-foundational approaches held sway, including *postmodernism and *post-structuralism.

fractal analysis An idea developed by Benoit Mandelbrot in the 1950s, fractal analysis seeks to reveal the geometrical order that lies beneath the seeming chaotic, discontinuous, and irregular complexity of the material world. Fractal geometry relates to objects whose spatial form is irregular, but repeats across scale. Fractal analysis measures such a geometry and has been applied to a range of geographic phenomena. Rather than try to identify a stable order in the way cities work, Mike *Batty and Paul Longley use fractal geometry to model and explain the complex and seemingly chaotic evolution and growth of city spaces.

Reference Batty, M. and Longley, P. (1994), *Fractal Cities*.

fragile state A country whose economic, political, and social integrity is weak. The causes of such weakness vary, depending on the country. Chronic poverty, the incidence of natural disasters, corruption among elites, and civil wars are among the many reasons why some countries are unable to function in the way many others do. In recent times, Somalia and Sudan are among those countries considered to be fragile states.

framing The process whereby an institution, group, or individual interpret and represent the world in ways that reflect their own preferences, priorities, and predispositions. The metaphor of a frame interprets this process as one of setting limits to what is discussed or made visible (implying that some things do not make it into the frame). The metaphor also signifies a process of composition where things within the frame are arranged in specific ways relative to one another, with some things foregrounded and made more vivid or noticeable. In these ways framing is a process of social construction, even when those doing the constructing claim that their frames are neutral or truthful. The framing metaphor has enjoyed sustained use in media and communications studies, where it has informed analyses of how 'the news' gets made and reported. In human geography, it has featured in analyses of mass-media representations of, for example, environmental problems or specific countries, but beyond this has not enjoyed much formal use. However, the idea of a frame has featured implicitly in many geographical analyses of expert, elite, and lay discourse, and of various visual representations, such as maps of various kinds. In has thus functioned more as a figure or motif than a formal analytical device. *See also* POSITIONALITY; SITUATEDNESS.

France A West European capitalist democracy whose capital city is *Paris. With a population of 65 million, France is a multicultural country enjoying a high standard of living and considerable political influence within and beyond the *European Union, of which it is a founder member. Formerly an imperial country, its linguistic, cultural, and military influence is felt especially in West and North Africa. Around a fifth of the population was born abroad or are children of immigrants, with Africans forming a substantial part of urban population. France is a major manufacturer of commodities and many French firms are global leaders, such as Renault (cars) and Veolia (utilities). It is also a major exporter of agricultural goods and one of the world's top tourist destinations. With a relatively high level of public spending and direct state involvement in the economy, France is a good example of a *welfare state.

Frankfurt School *See* CRITICAL THEORY.

free market A place where buyers and sellers of any good or service can interact with few, if any, non-market restrictions (e.g. governmental rules or cultural prohibitions). According to *neoclassical economists, a free market obtains when buyers and sellers are free in three senses. First, there is informational transparency such that the nature of a good or service for sale is understood by all parties. Second, the price of a good or service is determined by the balance of overall supply and customer demand in a context where suppliers seek to realize a profit (over and above their costs) and customers have finite budgets with which to purchase wanted commodities. Finally, according to neoclassical economists a good or service can be freely acquired if no undue restraints are placed on market transactions: ideally, any sort of customer demand should be satisfied by a supply of suitable goods or services. In these three ways some regard free markets as a truly democratic choice mechanism for consumers. From the late 1980s, leading capitalist countries (notably the USA) pushed hard for a global free market and helped create the *World Trade Organization to facilitate the more intensive and extensive cross-border exchange of commodities.

free market environmentalism (FME) An approach to managing environmental goods, services, and resources that relies on market mechanisms. These mechanisms include assigning clear property rights where they do not exist, establishing prices where they were hitherto absent, and trading environmental goods, services, and resources as *commodities. Environmentalists have tended to see markets—especially capitalist markets—as anti-ecological. The advocates of FME—the study and refinement of which has been led by environmental economists—argue that markets can be powerful mechanisms for environmental conservation. So long as a regulatory body (such as a national government) can establish suitable parameters within which a market will operate, the argument is that economic actors will pay a suitable price to prevent further environmental degradation. *Carbon trading is just one of many current examples of FME, but its critics argue that this example proves a wider point: namely that FME can only be truly 'ecofriendly' if regulatory bodies set very stringent market parameters. Critical human geographers interested in neoliberal environmental policy have, on the whole, been very critical of FME. *See also* ECOLOGICAL MODERNIZATION.

free trade agreement An inter-government agreement to facilitate the exchange of goods and services across political borders by reducing and harmonizing any trade barriers (such as import duties on certain commodities). Such agreements have become more prominent since the early 1990s, notable examples being the *North American Free Trade Agreement (NAFTA) and the attempts by the *World Trade Organization (WTO) to lower trade barriers between the continents. They are based on the idea of *comparative advantage but critics argue that they risk locking poorer countries into a condition of dependency on wealthier countries for more expensive 'value-added' commodities, like computer games, aircraft, and satnav devices. *See also* TRADE.

friction of distance Due to the effort and cost (in time and money) of moving across space, distance acts as friction against travel. As a result, spatial interactions between near locations greatly exceed those between more geographically separated places. Distance is thus an important factor influencing the interaction between places. The friction of distance is the underlying concept of *gravity models. (See Fig. 3.)

frontier 1. A zone at the edge of a settled, cultivated, or civilized region (*see* ECUMENE).
   2. A region either side of a political *boundary between two *states (*see* BORDER). The idea of a frontier as the outer margin of a settled region can be traced back to ancient empires. The Great Wall of China and Hadrian's Wall marking the northern limit of the Roman empire in Britain, both imply a contrast between a 'civilized' inside and a 'barbaric outside'. Later, during European *imperialism, the term 'frontier' signified the outward-facing limit of colonial *settler societies. Imagining a region as a frontier in this way disregarded the presence of those peoples already dwelling there. According to Taylor and Flint, frontiers in the first sense have everywhere been replaced by frontiers in the second sense, i.e. as a political boundary; there are no unsettled lands into which expansion can occur (*see* WORLD-SYSTEMS APPROACH). Others recognize the persistence of *resource frontiers, while regions such as the oceans and outer space are also frequently described as frontiers in the older, more traditional sense.

Reference Taylor, P. and Flint, C. (4th ed. 2000), *Political Geography*.

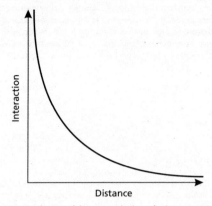

Fig. 3   A graph illustrating the friction of distance with places further apart interacting much less than those closer together

FTSE An index of the value of shares of the top 100 companies listed on the London Stock Exchange (LSE). These companies' worth typically exceeds 80 per cent of the combined value of all LSE-listed firms. The index is calculated in real time and published every 15 seconds.

Fujita, Masahisa (1943–) A Japanese economist based at Kyoto University who has helped pioneer *new economic geography. Fujita obtained his doctorate in *regional science at the University of Pennsylvania, where he also taught for 19 years. He has made major contributions to urban, regional, and spatial economics, and is the co-author of *The Spatial Economy: Cities, Regions and International Trade* (with Paul *Krugman and Anthony Venables, 2001), and *Economics of Agglomeration: Cities, Industrial Location and Regional Growth* (with Jacques-Francois Thisse, 2002).

functionalism The thesis that a phenomenon, either social or natural, exists to fulfil a need or purpose contained within another phenomenon or a wider system. Functionalism was for many years prominent in both sociology and anthropology, where an emphasis on systems and structures led to analyses of 'parts' as the product and medium of 'wholes'. In human geography, functionalism enjoyed limited formal use, despite some early critics of *Marxist geography suggesting that it was a core feature of this approach. One problem with functional thinking is that if phenomena exist to serve functions specified by systems or structures, then how can they be said to have *agency, to resist, or to change? *See also* TELEOLOGY.

functional region A bounded geographical area defined by a set of linkages, interactions, or interdependencies rather than by a single variable such as culture or crop type (known as a formal region), or by an administrative boundary. Functional *regions are sometimes thought of as 'natural catchments' that better define a town's hinterland than administrative boundaries that might not match the geographical pattern of activities. A city and its surrounding *hinterland or *city-region is an example.

fuzzy logic A type of logical reasoning that deals with approximations as opposed to fixed measures. Instead of a binary value either being 0 or 1, in fuzzy logic the value could be between 0 and 1. In this sense, rather than deal with absolute or singular truths, fuzzy logic is said to deal with partial truths or scenarios where more than one truth could apply. For example, warm water is neither hot [1] nor cold [0] but somewhere in between. Many spatial phenomena, including human spatial behaviour, are fuzzy or imprecise, and fuzzy logic is seen as a more appropriate way of building models than using more rigid mathematical formulae.

Gaia The name given by atmospheric chemist James *Lovelock to describe his proposition that the Earth was a single superorganism that achieved a homeostatic or steady state conducive to life through various complicated feedback mechanisms. In his initial hypothesis (1975), which drew in part on early observations of other planets in the solar system, the planet evolved to support life and could not survive without it. Lynn Margulis, a US microbiologist, added important components to the idea. Dismissed at first as either absurd or an example of circular reasoning, scientific investigation of the feedback mechanisms in and between biogeochemical, oceanic, biotic, and atmospheric systems have tended to support the general thesis. As such, Gaian ideas inform *Earth System Science. *See also* HOLISM.

game theory The study of the behaviour of rational decision-makers in strategic situations where individual success in gaming is interdependent upon the choices of others. It uses statistics to identify patterns of conflict and cooperation amongst competing and collaborating actors, and to model and predict the behaviours of actors in certain scenarios. It is used extensively in economics, political science, psychology, and biology. In geography it has mainly been used to examine firm behaviour and political voting.

garden city A planned settlement designed to overcome the limitations of both town and country, by combining the best of both in free-standing, self-sufficient communities with ample parkland and public space. First formulated by British planner Ebenezer Howard in 1898, the concept led to *new towns in the UK, USA, and elsewhere, and informed the idea of garden suburbs. *See also* URBAN AND REGIONAL PLANNING.

Garrison, William (1924–) A pioneer of the *Quantitative Revolution, Garrison was an early adopter of statistical *modelling in human geography and a proponent of *location theory. Based at the University of Washington in Seattle (1950–60), Garrison imported ideas from economics, applying them to locational and transportation problems. A number of his graduate students, the so-called 'space cadets', progressed to successful academic careers and were strong advocates of a more scientific approach in geography. These included Brian *Berry, Duane Marble, Richard Morrill, Michael Dacey, William *Bunge, and Waldo *Tobler. On leaving Washington he held a number of posts in transportation and civil engineering.

gated communities Residential developments designed to provide security and exclusivity to its residents through a combination of physical barriers, surveillance, security personnel, and community self-regulation of architecture and behaviour.

Further reading Le Croix, R. and Webster, C. J. (2008), 'Gated communities', *Geography Compass* 2: 1189–1241.

gateway city A *city that serves as a point-of-entry to a geographical region, usually in terms of migration. New York, Sydney, and Toronto are all gateway cities in that tens of thousands of immigrants arrive in their respective countries via the airports and ports of those cities. But St Louis, Missouri is equally a gateway to the western USA for traffic from the east crossing the Mississippi river.

gay geographies The study of the socio-spatial relations of gay men. Initial geographical research focused on the phenomenon of so-called 'gay ghettos' in certain cities such as San Francisco—areas in which relatively large numbers of gay men lived and socialized. On the one hand, such research sought to understand the formation of such spaces, and on the other cast gay men as important agents of *gentrification. Early studies also traced out the diffusion of the *AIDS virus through homosexual encounters. These studies were later criticized for how they exoticized gay men, treating them as a distinct '*other', and how they were portrayed as occupying distinct social, political, and cultural landscapes that were seen as being at odds with or paralleling the rest of society rather than being constitutive of society. Gay ghettos, for example, had been explained through simple push-pull models of spatial behaviour driven by notions of defence and comfort. More recent research, however, has highlighted the heterogeneity of gay men and their socio-spatial lives. It also argues that the areas in which gay men have concentrated were not simply chosen, but consisted of marginal sites in the urban fabric where *heteronormative conditions were relatively weak. Such gay spaces were and continue to be contested sites, situated in a web of complex *power-geometries. The lives of gay men are thus recognized as being shaped by identity, *cultural politics (including homophobic violence), and the institutional geographies of the state (including the legal system), and not simply the outcome of rational choices. An important aspect of this work has been to trace back through history the geographical strategies used by gay men to meet and socialize and to compare the power geometries affecting gay men across locales. The result has been studies that give a much richer and nuanced account of gay men's socio-spatial lives. *See also* HETERONORMATIVITY; LESBIAN GEOGRAPHIES; SEXUALITY.

Further reading Bell, D. and Valentine, G. (eds.) (1995), *Mapping Desire: Geographies of Sexuality*. Whittle, S. (ed.) (1994), *The Margins of the City: Gay Men's Urban Lives*.

gaze The viewing or framing of a scene or representation through a particular lens. *Feminists, for example, have examined how the male gaze objectifies women as sexually desirable. In so doing, the male gaze produces an asymmetric power relationship between viewer and viewed, with the gaze imposed on women regardless of their wishes. The male gaze thus structures and reproduces relations between men and women. This male gaze is also commonly conveyed in film and television, where the storytelling often projects the world through male eyes, for example, lingering on the female form. In geographical scholarship, the gaze is often associated with the study of *landscape, and how artists and others frame and select how they portray (fix a gaze upon) the world, and how that gaze shapes the gazes of others. For example, Renzo Dubbini details how scientific and artistic developments during the *Renaissance altered how landscapes were perceived and portrayed. Over time, different ways of seeing and depicting the world were created including varying schools of *art, architectural drawings, *maps, *photography, and stereoscopy that shaped how people gazed at and made sense of the world. The concept has also been applied to tourism with respect to how the lenses of tourists are focused with respect to *heritage and tourist attractions.

Further reading Dubbini, R. (2002), *Geography of the Gaze: Urban and Rural Vision in Early Modern Europe*.
Rose, G. (1993), *Feminism and Geography: the Limits of Geographical Knowledge*.

GDP *See* GROSS DOMESTIC PRODUCT.

Geddes, Patrick (1854–1932) A Scottish polymath who is best known for his contributions to town and regional *planning. Born in Ballater, he studied in London before lecturing in zoology in Edinburgh. For thirty years he was the chair of botany in Dundee, finishing his career as the chair of sociology at the University of Bombay. He developed a keen interest in city life and how to plan urban environments so that they aided quality of life and enhanced communities. Understanding social processes and spatial form to be related, he saw town planning as a method for applying sociological insights and was an active contributor to a number of city plans.

G8 (G7) The Group of Eight (G8) was an economic forum, founded in 1975 in the wake of the early 1970s *oil crisis. It originally consisted of six industrialized countries—France, West Germany, Italy, Japan, United Kingdom, and United States. Canada joined the group in 1976 (G7), and Russia in 1997 (G8). The European Union is an ex-officio member. It provided a forum in which member countries could discuss various policy issues, principally the global economy. In 2009 the G8 was replaced by the *G20.

(⊕) SEE WEB LINKS
• Website of the G8 Research Group at the University of Toronto.

gemeinschaft* and *gesellschaft The term *gemeinschaft* is loosely translated as 'community', defined by close-knit bonds, strong emotional ties, heightened sense of place, and homogenous make-up of people. In contrast, *gesellschaft* refers to society defined by mobility, heterogeneity, anonymity, impersonality, and loose associations. These German terms, usually discussed together, are rooted in the thesis of Ferdinand Tönnies on European modernization published in 1887. Tönnies and subsequent researchers have been concerned with the transition from social relations underpinned by *gemeinschaft* to *gesellschaft*, first with industrialization and *urbanization, then *globalization. *Gemeinschaft* is often positioned as an ideal type of social relation which is becoming less and less obtainable because of increased mobility and capitalist forms of social organization. *See also* COMMUNITY; URBANISM.

gender The different roles, qualities, and responsibilities attributed to men and women in society. Whereas sex denotes biological differences between men and women, gender refers to socially constructed characteristics that produce *gender roles based on supposed differences that arise from sexuality and physiology. Gender is a key concept in *feminism and *feminist geography, with research revealing how gender relations are produced and vary over time, place, and culture. Gender as a concept is itself subject to such evolution.

In second-wave feminism, gender was understood as a *social construction, with the position of men and women in society seen as the result of *patriarchy, a set of ideas that cast men and women as having certain characteristics and roles. Such gender relations are reinforced through popular discourse and institutional structures that guide and enforce how society is organized and ordered. So for Simone de Beauvoir in her influential text, *The Second Sex* (1949), women are not born but made; it is not biology or physiology that determines the roles and status of men and women, but social norms and rules. In other words, such thinking challenges the conflation of sex and gender and the notion that the differences between men and women are natural and commonsensical. This is demonstrated by comparing and contrasting gender relations operating in different societies and revealing how social and spatial relations between men and women have changed over time with respect to their roles, responsibilities, duties, activities, and expected behaviour.

This position was challenged by later feminists who noted that it cast gender as socially constructed based on an acceptance of sex and bodily differences between men and women. In other words, bodies were understood as simply male or female, with the sexed body cast as universal. The alternative was to see gender as a system of social organization of sexual difference, recognizing that the *body is not a constant, but it, too, is socially constructed and variable in how it is culturally understood over time and place. Thus gender/sex cannot be separated but rather need to be treated as conjoined, socially constructed through each other.

More recently, post-structural thinkers such as Judith *Butler in her influential book, *Gender Trouble* (1990), have challenged the notion that gender and the sexed body are stable, ontological categories. On the one hand, they have problematized the body as either being male or female, recognizing that some people are born with different patterns of chromosomes and sexual organs, and on the other they have argued that gender is an unstable, fluid category that is productive and *performative in nature. In other words, neither the body nor gender is simply constructed differently within a system of social organization. From this perspective, gender is not made, it is performed; it is not something one is, but something one does. Gender is an embodied practice and what it means to be a man or woman is produced and sustained through acts, gestures, mannerisms, fashion, and lifestyle, contextualized within a system of social organization that shapes how gender is continuously reproduced.

Further reading McDowell, L. (1999), *Gender, Identity and Place*.

gender and development An academic field defined by the belief that gender is essential to understanding *development and that development programmes should be gender-aware. Development intersects with *gender in at least four main ways: the impact of development policies is not gender-neutral, and affects men, women, and children differently; the processes of development reshape gender relations, in often complex ways; the priorities for development may differ by gender; the ability of men and women to actively participate in and share development trajectories is uneven (*see* CIVIL SOCIETY; GENDER ROLE; MICROFINANCE; POVERTY REDUCTION STRATEGIES).

The relations between gender and development have been tackled in different ways by the academic and policy-making communities over time (Momsen 2009). In the 1970s interventions focused on trying to get women more integrated into waged work, under the Women in Development (WID) paradigm. This followed the pioneering work of Esther *Boserup in revealing the extent to which women's labour was central to agriculture, trade, and other economic activities, albeit with very marked regional differences. An alternative Women and Development (WAD) approach emerged from the Global South itself, with more radical overtones. By the 1980s international lenders were switching to a Gender and Development approach (GAD), which took greater account of power relations, the potential for agency, and that gender relations concerned both women and men. The UN *Beijing Conference in 1995 gave impetus to 'gender mainstreaming', in which women's issues were regarded as fundamental to human rights and social justice. The third *Millennium Development Goal addresses gender inequality and the empowerment of women. Its targets reflect the fact that some progress has been made but that substantial *inequalities between men and women remain. They include: eliminating disparities in access to education up to tertiary level and in literacy; increasing women's participation in paid non-agricultural labour; increasing the number of women elected to national assemblies.

Human geographers have done extensive research into gender and development since the 1970s, and such studies have made a significant contribution to *feminist geography (Lawson 2007). Much of this examines how economic and social restructuring have changed livelihoods and gender relations at the *household level, with close attention to the specificities of place. Access to *education and subsequent economic opportunity for both men and women is also a growing focus. There is also interest in: health and healthcare, particularly with reference to *HIV/AIDS; participation and empowerment in microfinance schemes and civil society initiatives; and *migration for work and marriage (*see* GLOBAL CARE CHAIN). Much of this research recognizes the intersections between gender, class, race, and sexuality, as well as the locally specific ways in which gender identities are constructed.

Further reading Lawson, V. (2007), *Making Development Geography*.
Momsen, J. H. (2009), *Gender and Development*.

gender relations *See* GENDER.

gender role The normalized roles that men and women are expected to perform in their everyday lives. Such roles are defined around social and behavioural norms as practised by a society. For example, a common gender role for women is the homemaker and primary child-rearer, with men expected to be the main income earner in order to support his family. Feminist theory, in particular, has highlighted how society actively promotes these normative views and structurally shapes their continued reproduction through everyday discourse and actions, education and the media, and institutional and legal structures and processes, with people socialized and constrained into performing and reproducing particular roles. For example, young children are encouraged to play with particular toys, such as dolls and kitchen sets for girls and action figures and building blocks for boys. At school, girls and boys are pushed towards particular subjects, and in the workplace men and women are directed to certain career paths. Such gender roles often map onto and reproduce a gendered geography. One example would be the common saying, 'a woman's place is in the home.' Indeed, *public space is often cast as the preserve of men, and *private space the preserve of women. Given the rise in female participation in waged labour throughout much of the world, particularly in the Global North, it is often recognized that women may perform a 'dual role;' i.e. carer and wage earner. Surveys demonstrate that among couples where both are engaged in paid employment, women continue to bear a disproportionate burden of household labour (*see* DOMESTIC LABOUR). This gendered division of roles and spaces is often seen as natural and commonsensical, however historical and comparative research reveals that they differ over time and across cultures. Indeed, *feminist geographers have done much to expose how gender roles are constructed and *performed, rather than being *essential and natural. In other words, gender roles are determined and reproduced by society rather than being an innate feature of social relations. *See also* GENDER.

genealogy 1. The study of family history.
2. An approach to the study of modes of thought and practice that inquires into their historical conditions of emergence. Human geographers have been interested in both types of genealogy. For instance, Catherine Nash has critically analysed the ways in which people (re)construct personal identities by using the resources and concepts offered by genealogy websites and television documentaries. With the latter, geographers have drawn on the writings of Michel *Foucault to uncover the history of systems of thought focusing on how ideas and ways of thinking and acting with respect to aspects of society (e.g., policing, madness, schooling) emerge and evolve over time to form a discursive regime that underpins wider public and institutional discourses, policies, and practices (*see* DISCOURSE). Rather than trying to determine the truth of particular forms of knowledge, the genealogical method seeks to contextualize and historicize how knowledge is produced and deployed. To do this it traces out how ideas emerge, their take-up and use, and the debates surrounding them. Genealogy advances Foucault's original method of archaeology, which sought to deconstruct components of accepted knowledge by identifying paradoxes, contradictions, and discontinuities within its formulation, to consider the complex power relations within which knowledge is created and circulates. Foucault's genealogies traced out modern thought with respect to criminality (*Discipline and*

Punish, 1978) and sexuality (*The History of Sexuality,* 1979). In both cases he analysed archival sources to tease apart how discourse, power, and knowledge (medical, academic, moral) are woven together to underpin new forms of governance and new institutional geographies (e.g., prisons, mental asylums, schools). The genealogical method has subsequently been widely employed in the discipline, especially by historical geographers interested in how particular systems of thought underpin various institutional geographies. For example, Chris Philo has inquired into how 'mad houses' came, in their time, to be seen as acceptable institutions for treating the 'insane'.

Further reading Nash, C. (2008), *Of Irish Descent: Origin Stories, Genealogy, and The Politics of Belonging.*

Philo, C. (2007), 'Scaling the asylum: three different geographies of Craig Dunain Lunatic Asylum' in Andrews, J., Topp, L., and Moran, J. (eds,) *Psychiatric Spaces: Architecture, Madness and the Built Environment,* 107–131.

General Agreement on Trade and Tariffs (GATT) A multilateral agreement, first signed in 1947, that sought to encourage free trade among member countries by creating a system of international trade rules, and regulating and reducing tariffs on traded goods. The agreement also sought to provide mechanisms to resolve trade disputes, and in later years harmonization with respect to labour standards, intellectual property, competition, and transparency. The agreement had its roots in the *Bretton Woods negotiations of 1944 and between 1947 and 1994 there were eight rounds of negotiations, which sometimes lasted multiple years, and included over 100 countries. In 1995, GATT was subsumed into the new *World Trade Organization (WTO). The WTO launched a new round of multilateral trade negotiations under the *Doha Round in 2001. *See also* FREE TRADE AGREEMENT; GENERAL AGREEMENT ON TRADE IN SERVICES (GATS).

General Agreement on Trade in Services (GATS) Arising from the Uruguay round of the *GATT negotiations ending in 1994, GATS provides similar international trade rules and regulation but for traded services. It covers all services with the exception of governmental activities and air transport services. *See* also FREE TRADE AGREEMENT; GENERAL AGREEMENT ON TRADE AND TARIFFS (GATT).

generalization The identification and explanation of features that are shared among phenomena of various kind. Colloquially, 'to generalize' means to identify 'signals in the noise'. One makes a statement about one or more phenomena that seeks to capture some enduring, essential, or common characteristic existing through time and/or across space. In the academic world generalization aims to rest on systematic processes of observation, induction, deduction, or abduction and is a form of mental *abstraction. In geography, generalization was long thought by many practitioners to be contrary to the discipline's aims. They regarded the subject as *idiographic, concerned to describe and explain the unique character of places. However, those advancing spatial science disputed this approach and argued that there was a spatial order to the world with the characteristics and patterns of phenomena of the same class existing in otherwise different places. *Locational analysis became the preoccupation of geography's new 'spatial scientists' from the 1960s onwards, such that general patterns and processes were identified for everything from human migration to pathways of disease transmission. Critical realists such as Andrew *Sayer later offered a corrective to this sort of *nomothetic research (*see* CRITICAL REALISM). They argued that while some processes and causal powers are widespread across space and through time, they are realized and have effects in ways that are differentiated and even singular. Though many latter-day spatial scientists still search for generalizations, many critical human geographers tend to favour in-depth case studies of a single place or situation, and how far one can generalize from such studies remains little discussed in the discipline. Noel Castree has called for more rigorous discussion of what case studies can tell us about the world beyond the cases in question.

Further reading Castree, N. (2005), 'The epistemology of particulars: human geography, case studies and "context"'. *Geoforum* 36, 5: 541–44.
Haggett, P. (1963), *Locational Analysis in Human Geography*.
Sayer, A. (2nd ed. 1992), *Method in Social Science*.

General Linear Models A class of *parametric statistical models, including analysis of variance (ANOVA), *regression, *correlation, *factor analysis, that analyse the covariation among variables. The models seek to quantify the relationship between independent variables and dependent variables. As with all statistical models, the data are assumed to meet certain criteria, in this case that the independent variables are not autocorrelated or have collinearity, and the relationship between variables is linear (or can be transformed to be linear).

General Systems Theory An approach that seeks to understand holistically a system through the interactions of its components. It is generally assumed that a system can be understood by breaking it down into individual, independent components, and that the totality of a system can be described by adding all the components together. General Systems Theory, however, posits that both these assumptions are incorrect and what needs to be studied is the interactions between components in order to formulate general principles and laws for how a system is structured and works. In the 1960s it was thought that General Systems Theory would provide a way to unify and model human and physical geography, but the approach was weakly adopted.

Further reading Bennett, R. J. and Chorley, R. J. (1978), *Environmental Systems: Philosophy, Analysis and Control*.

genetic modification The direct manipulation of an organism's DNA by the introduction of either foreign DNA or a synthetic gene; also known as genetic engineering. Humans have been able to alter the characteristic of plants and animals by artificial or indirect selection for thousands of years, but the ability to intervene at the genetic level was possible only from the 1970s (*see* GENETICS). Starting with bacteria, then mice, genetic modifications are now being made to a range of organisms. In 2010, J. Craig Ventner constructed the first synthetic lifeform, a bacterium known as Synthia.

Genetically modified organisms (GMOs) have widely entered the human environment. GM crops account for about 10 per cent of the world's cropland; most of the world's soybeans, and much of its cotton and corn are now modified. GM crops can be designed to resist disease and pests, be resistant to herbicides and tolerate extreme conditions such as drought or high salt levels. They also promise higher yields, although this is subject to some doubt. GM crops are the focus of some controversy. Proponents argue that they could usher in a second *Green Revolution, addressing world *hunger. Opponents raise three kinds of concerns. There are unknown health implications (allergies, for example) of new organisms. Secondly, there will be a gene flow from modified to unmodified organisms, compromising the pure or original stock. Thirdly, GMOs are part of a globalized commercial agricultural industry whose focus on profits and protecting international property rights are incompatible with more communal, local forms of agriculture (*see* AGRIBUSINESS). Opposition to GMOs includes *environmental direct action and state-level regulatory controls: Venezuela and Ecuador have both banned GM seeds and crops.

Genetic modification also raises *ethical and *ontological issues. For many people, the direct manipulation of DNA is trespassing on divine territory. Further, how far should food labelling alert consumers to whether products contain GMOs? As 'transgenic' species, genetically modified mice, monkeys, and crop plants disturb the idea of a clear boundary between what can be considered natural and what is social or cultural (*see* NATURE).

genetics The study of genes and their variation. Genes are the means through which living organisms inherit characteristics from their immediate ancestors (*see* HUMAN GENOME). Modern genetics stems from the work of Gregor Mendel in the 19th century although it was not widely recognized until the early 20th century. As more became known about how genes worked, ideas of scientific *racism were challenged and more credibility was given to Darwin's ideas than those of Lamarck (*see* DARWINISM; LAMARCKISM). Since the 1970s, geneticists have been able to reconstruct both the path of human evolution and how human populations have migrated over the past 100,000 years. This has demolished 19th-century misconceptions about race and human diversity.

Further reading Cavalli-Sforza, L. L. (2001), *Genes, Peoples and Languages.*

genius loci The spirit of a *place, the elements of its character or atmosphere that make it unique. *See also* SENSE OF PLACE; TOPOPHILIA.

genocide In international law, the intent to wholly or partly exterminate an ethnic or national group. The term was defined within a UN Convention of 1948 in response to the *Holocaust. International tribunals have tried individuals for the crime in association with conflicts in the former Yugoslavia (1991) and Rwanda (1992), but there are often disputes over whether an act legally constitutes genocide, e.g. the violence in Darfur, Sudan, in 2003. Critics point out that international courts can only act after the event and there is insufficient protection for people at risk. *See also* ETHNIC CLEANSING.

genre de vie A way of life associated with the interaction of a human community and their local or regional environment. The term featured in the work of French geographer Paul *Vidal de la Blache and his colleagues in the early 20th century. They sought to explain how and why the country's regional (largely rural) landscapes looked as they did and why they differed from one another. By emphasizing the long-term interaction of people and environment, Vidal sought an alternative perspective to *environmental determinism. *See also* CULTURAL LANDSCAPE; REGIONAL GEOGRAPHY.

gentrification The combination of demographic and economic changes accompanying sustained reinvestment in inner urban areas, although it has also been used in rural contexts (*see* RURAL GENTRIFICATION). By implication, the social character of the neighbourhood changes, affecting shops, restaurants, places of worship, and public spaces. Gentrification in its initial narrow sense of the occupation and renovation or upgrading of dwellings in working-class inner city neighbourhoods by the middle-classes, was identified by sociologist Ruth Glass in 1964, based on her observations in Islington, North London. A broader sense of urban transformation was elaborated by Neil *Smith based on the experience of New York, especially the Lower East Side, in the 1980s. Defined more as a return of capital investment than simply a change in the class position of residents, this interpretation encompasses new building, planning, and tax code changes, changes in urban political government, new forms of consumption, and wider cultural shifts linked with *neoliberalism (*see* CREATIVE CLASS).

Gentrification is a key area of urban geographical research, initially perhaps because it conflicted with the expectation that middle-class households would seek new suburban rather than old inner urban residences (*see* CONCENTRIC ZONE MODELS). Empirical work has focused on whether there are distinct stages of gentrification and how it has diffused from a small number of major Western cities in the 1950s (London, Paris, New York, Washington, DC) to urban areas worldwide by the 1990s. A major concern has been its effects on working-class households and whether they are displaced (*see* DISPLACEMENT).

Explanations of gentrification focused first on supposedly temporary demographic factors, such as the delayed family formation of the post-war baby boomers. Once it was recognized as more long-lasting and diversified, the causes were sought in the more general shifts towards a *post-industrial society, including the rise of urban professionals and post-materialist values. In the 1980s gentrification was the focus of a debate between *Marxist accounts that emphasized the return of capital (*see* RENT GAP) and more humanistic explanations in terms of occupational and lifestyle changes. These accommodated the growing evidence that gentrification was more than just a matter of class, but could also be implicated with new gender-related and sexual identities (*see* GAY GEOGRAPHIES). In the 1990s some authors have identified new forms of 'super-gentrification'. Taking Brooklyn Heights as her example, Loretta Lees describes how super-rich individuals linked with global financial industries are taking over already gentrified districts.

Further reading Lees, L., Slater, T., and Wyly, E. (eds.) (2010), *The Gentrification Reader.*

geocoding The addition of locational referents, such as latitude and longitude coordinates, to objects so that they can be accurately mapped and spatially modelled; sometimes called georeferencing.

geocomputation A growing field of study in which computational and statistical techniques are applied to georeferenced and spatial data. With GPS-enabled mobile devices and distributed sensors becoming more common, ever-more georeferenced data is being produced. Geocomputation concerns how to process, analyse, and make sense of that data in order to understand social and environmental issues, exploit it for commercial gain, or aid the users of mobile devices in spatial choice and decision-making. It extends beyond *geographical information systems by concentrating on statistical modelling and visual analytics, rather than data management, descriptive analysis, and mapping. Its core contributory disciplines are geography, mathematics, information, and computer science.

Further reading Longley, P. A., Brooks, S. M., McDonnell, R., and MacMillan, B. (eds.) (1998), *Geocomputation: a Primer.*

geodemographics The profiling of people living in different areas usually for the purposes of marketing, service location planning, and political campaigning. Different kinds of people live in different kinds of areas. Geodemographics links social and territorial data to produce segmented categories of space in order to identify the kinds of people who live in particular places, and their propensity to consume particular goods and services. By combining population, social, economic, and industry data (customer profiling) and analysing them with sophisticated statistical clustering algorithms, it is possible to produce profiled areas at fine spatial scales (such as postcodes). Geodemographics is now a large industry because it inform firms where best to locate their stores to maximize profit, and in which neighbourhoods they should concentrate their marketing efforts, thus saving advertising revenue and generating business. The practice of geodemographics has been criticized because it reductively collapses the infinite complexity of human feelings, desires, motives, emotions, and places into a simple exploitable model. Moreover, it inherently ranks people based on their supposed 'worth' to businesses. This ranking is called software sorting and produces discriminatory practices such as the *redlining of communities deemed unprofitable or high risk by insurers and banks. *See also* RETAILING.

Further reading Goss, J. (1995), 'We know who you are and we know where you live', *Economic Geography* 71: 171–98.

Harris, R., Sleight, P., and Webber, R. (2005), *Geodemographics, GIS and Neighbourhood Targeting.*

geoeconomics The spatial organization of economic activity within and among nation states and the study thereof. More specifically, the term has been used in conscious parallel with *geopolitics. It invokes the idea, first apparent in the 1990s, that with the end of the *Cold War economic issues such as trade dominated international relations in place of strategic or military concerns. It can also therefore be read as a discourse on global economic affairs.

Further reading Sparke, M. (1997), 'Geopolitical fears, geoeconomic hopes', *Annals of the Association of American Geographers* 97(2): 338–49.

Geographical Association, The A British-based organization founded in 1893 that promotes and supports geography as a core part of the school curriculum. It campaigns on the importance of a geographical understanding of the world and supports teachers in their work by producing educational resources.

(((•))) SEE WEB LINKS
• Official website of the Geographical Association.

Geographical Imaginations An influential 1994 monograph by British human geographer Derek *Gregory, surveying a broad landscape of critical social and cultural theory. It showed how questions of *place, *space, and *landscape were central to the exercise of social *power, social *resistance, and social change.

Geographical Information Science (GISc) An interdisciplinary field that examines the fundamental questions posed by *Geographic Information Systems (GIS), constitutes the body of knowledge exploited by GIS, and the research that will enable the development of the next generation of GIS. In short, it is the science underpinning the development of GIS and how GIS analyse the world. It is often considered to be a subfield of information science, though it involves research by scholars in many disciplines such as geography, *cartography, computer science, cognitive science, and *geomatics.

GIS support a variety of operations on geographic information: acquisition, editing, manipulation, analysis, modelling, visualization, publication, and storage. These operations are based on fundamental research into spatial data handling and processing, spatial analysis, *geocomputation, and *geovisualization, as well as how new technologies such as *GPS, the *Internet and mobile networking (e.g., smart phones), and new social and technical phenomena such as *crowdsourcing, *social networking, and *big data offer new opportunities for data generation, sharing, analysis, and use, as well as new GI applications such as *virtual globes, *location based services, *satnavs, and *open source GIS.

The first research agenda for GISc was published in 1988 by David Rhind, former director of the UK's *Ordnance Survey. The key questions he identified concerned the handling of geographic data such as data volumes, how the data might be queried to answer many different questions, how to deal with uncertainty and data error, how to integrate data held by many agencies in multiple formats using different data standards, how to intelligently search for information, and how to automate GIS operations. This was quickly followed in 1989 by the US *National Centre for Geographic Information and Analysis (NCGIA) which identified five research concerns: spatial analysis and statistics; spatial relationships and database structures; artificial intelligence and expert systems; visualization; and social, economic, and institutional issues. Between 1988–96, NCGIA sponsored twenty-one research initiatives around these themes doing much to help establish GIScience as much more than simply the application of GIS to understand the world. This research agenda was subsequently revised, most notably by the University Consortium for Geographic Information Science which represents over 60 research institutions in the United States (McMaster and Usery 2004) thus providing a relatively well-established shared consensus across GISc as to the core questions it seeks to address.

Given the growing use of GIS in their various manifestations, the rapid development of technologies that are location-aware, the wide range of research questions that require investigation, and the investment by *research funding agencies and industry into GISc (e.g., by *Google), GISc is a highly dynamic interdisciplinary field of research that seems set to be that way for some time.

References and further reading Duckham, M., Goodchild, M., and Worboys, M. (eds.) (2003), *Foundations of Geographic Information Science.*
Longley, P., Goodchild, M., Maguire, D., and Rhind, D. (3rd ed. 2010), *Geographic Information Systems and Science.*
McMaster, R. and Usery, E. L. (2004), *A Research Agenda for Geographic Information Science.*
Rhind, D. (1988), 'A GIS research agenda', *International Journal of Geographical Information Systems* 2(1): 23–28.

geographically weighted regression (GWR) A form of regression that is spatially sensitive to local variations within a study area. Linear and multiple *regression posit that the relationship being modelled is consistent within an area. For example, the factors that explain house prices in one neighbourhood hold across the whole city. GWR produces local models within the overall model in order to explain the spatial variation in the salience of different variables that shape a particular phenomenon. Models with Gaussian, logistic, or Poisson forms can be fitted.

Further reading Fotheringham, A. S., Brunsden, C., and Charlton, M. (2002), *Geographically Weighted Regression: the Analysis of Spatially Varying Relationships.*

geographical societies Those associations established to advance geographical knowledge through publications, debates, funding, lobbying, and related promotional and intellectual activities. There are currently three main kinds of geographical society. One is generalist, open to members of the public by subscription, and pitched at popular levels of geography, which may include travel and exploration. The most successful of these is the *National Geographic Society based in Washington, DC in the USA. Through its television channel, publications, films, DVDs, websites, sponsored products, and retail outlets it is said to reach over 360 million people a month. The second kind of society draws its members mainly from educators at secondary level. Examples include the *National Council for Geographic Education in the USA and Britain's *Geographical Association. Through the circulation of materials, conferences, and campaigning, they seek to support and sustain the teaching of geography in secondary schools. The third type of society is more closely associated with researchers and teachers in higher education, an example, being the *American Association of Geographers founded in 1904. It has over 10,000 members and is open to professionals from outside the USA (currently its members are from 60 countries). Before geography became widely established as a subject in universities the main site for geographical knowledge was the society. In fact, societies were often instrumental in encouraging the foundation of university posts and departments.

Geographical societies are organized at a variety of scales. The first specifically geographical society was the *Société de Géographie de Paris, which met in 1821, although earlier general scientific societies did have geographical sections. Paris at the time was a major international centre of science and culture, and the SGP effectively served as a national association. Berlin soon followed suit, with the Gesellscahft für Erdkunde de Berlin 1828. There are fewer local or city-based societies than there were in the late 18th and 19th centuries, but there remain important regional associations, at the US-state level for example. Provincial French societies formed in the 19th century are now more closely associated with individual university departments, however. The trend to national societies was started by the UK *Royal Geographical Society in 1830, following which most countries formed equivalents. By 1900 there were 120 geographical societies in the world, although the majority were in Europe (Heffernan 2011). A distinct international organization was founded in 1922, the *International Geographical Union. Through journals, lectures, teaching materials, support for exploration, media, and campaigning, geographical societies have been a vital part of the history of the subject.

Further reading Heffernan, M. (2011), 'Learned societies', in Agnew, J. A. and Livingstone D. N. (eds.) *The Sage Handbook of Geographical Knowledge*, 111–25.

Geographical Tradition, The A major pioneering work in the history of geography written by David N. *Livingstone (1992), one of the discipline's most accomplished scholars. Livingstone placed geography in a longer time horizon by considering its development since the 15th century. This allowed him to consider its relations to larger intellectual currents, including the *Renaissance, *Enlightenment, and *Darwinism. He also drew on current thinking in the *sociology of scientific knowledge. Blended with an older tradition of geography as the history of geographical ideas derived from J. K. *Wright, Livingstone created a more contextual reading of the subject than was common at the time. It was, however, criticized by feminist scholars who argued that it excluded the contributions of pioneer female geographers (*see* GEOGRAPHY, HISTORY OF).

Geographic Information System (GIS) A suite of integrated software tools for handling and analysing spatially referenced data. The spatial data and their associated attribute data are organized into a relational database and presented to the user as discrete mapping layers which can be overlain, queried, and analysed using a variety of descriptive or analytic techniques, including *modelling. GIS are employed widely by business and government in order to facilitate the mapping, monitoring, and management of an area. While they are often run on desktop computers, increasingly GIS are becoming accessible across the Internet, and thus open to many more users. *See also* GEOGRAPHICAL INFORMATION SCIENCE.

geographies Rather than simply being the plural of geography, the term 'geographies' is used to denote the multiplicity of the world and our situatedness in understanding it. Instead of there being one geography, a *Grand Theory wherein there is only one truth that science seeks to reveal, the use of geographies acknowledges that there are many possible truths—that the world is complex, messy, sometimes paradoxical, and contradictory, and is viewed through different lenses. As such, there are many geographies, and many ways to understand them.

Geographies of Exclusion A 1995 book by David *Sibley that introduced psychoanalytic approaches to geography in order to understand how different social groups are geographically marginalized and discriminated against along lines of *gender, *race, *class, *sexuality, *age, and *disability. In particular, Sibley used object-relations theory to examine how difference is used to produce notions of Self and *Other, and how these differences create and reproduce social and spatial boundaries. In so doing, he explored how some groups of people are deemed 'out of place' in some locales and are pushed to the margins of society.

geography The spatial and temporal analysis of human and natural systems and their interrelation across scales. The study of geography has a long history and can be traced back to classical Greek philosophy and the writings of Ptolemy. Its etymon from the Greek, *geographia*, translates as 'to describe the Earth'. That broad definition still holds today, though there have been many attempts to refine it and give it more precision.

As such, what constitutes the study of geography is a contested terrain. This is perhaps no surprise given the broad scope of the discipline in the 21st century, consisting of both *human and *physical geography, and the wide variety of theoretical approaches used to frame geographical scholarship and the diversity of methods used to examine the geographical world. In The *Geographical Tradition, David Livingstone (1992) contends that geography is elusive to define because it changes as society changes, with what is understood as geography changing over time and space. He concludes that geography 'has meant different things to different people at different times and in different places' (see GEOGRAPHY, HISTORY OF).

To illustrate his argument, Livingstone traces modern geography back to the translation of Ptolemy's Geography into Latin between the late medieval period and the *Renaissance. At this time there were a number of developments with regards to *cartography, *linear perspective, *navigation, *exploration, and science more broadly that put in place principles that are still important in geography today. Geographical thinking progressed through the *Enlightenment and the development of *modernity, with ideas becoming more refined, new ways of thinking being introduced, and new methods of investigation being created. It was during this period, at the start of the 19th century, that the first *geographical societies were formed focused on sponsoring geographical scholarship and collating geographical knowledge. Later in the century, the first university departments were established in Europe and North America, followed by geography being introduced into the school curriculum. At this point, there were already distinct geographical traditions emerging, such as *anthropography in Germany, *regional geography in France, and *environmental determinism in North America.

In the early 20th century, geography had already started to divide into human and physical geography (see PHYSICAL GEOGRAPHY for a discussion on the relationship between human and physical geography), and this division became more pronounced over time. By the time of the *Quantitative Revolution, the stark divisions in how geography was conceived as a discipline were readily apparent, with those such as *Hartshorne in Perspective on the Nature of Geography (1959) arguing that geography was an *idiographic science (that is, it focuses on the uniqueness of place, with an emphasis on description), whereas those favouring a spatial science approach saw geography as a *nomothetic science (that is, its main emphasis was on generalization, with an emphasis on explanation and law-giving).

This plurality of views has continued, with scholars who scrutinize the world through particular theoretical lenses understanding geography in different ways. For example, spatial scientists frame geography as the analytical study of spatial relationships and patterns, and those adopting a political economy lens define geography as 'the study of spatial forms and structures produced historically and specified by modes of production' (Dunford 1981) (see HUMAN GEOGRAPHY). Nevertheless, a broad consensus that geography concerns the interrelationships between people, place, and environment exists, even if the specificity of study is lacking.

References and further reading Bonnett, A. (2008), *What is Geography?*
Castree, N., Rogers, A., and Sherman, D. (eds.) (2005), *Questioning Geography*.
Dunford, M. (1981), *Historical Materialism and Geography*.
Johnston, R. and Sidaway, J. (7th ed. 2013), *Geography and Geographers*.

Geography: A Modern Synthesis A book written by Peter *Haggett (1972) that was a highly influential standard undergraduate textbook; it went through three editions and was translated into six languages. The book provided a synoptic overview of geographical debate, theory, and methods from both human and physical geography, and presented the discipline as an integrated and integrating discipline through its focus on space, scale, and environment. Haggett was a pioneer of quantitative geography, and this approach is very much advocated in the text. This, however, meant the book ignored emerging critiques from *Marxist and *humanistic geographers that were developing at the time. A fourth edition, retitled *Geography: A Global Synthesis*, was published in 2001.

Geography and Gender One of the pioneering texts of *feminist geography was written collectively by nine members of the *Women and Geography Study Group of the (then) Institute of British Geographers and appeared in 1984. Specifically written for undergraduate geographers, it had a dual focus, on the geography of gender but also the role of gender and the position of women, in the discipline and institutions of geography itself. In addition to a section on different epistemological approaches to feminist geography, the book included four chapters analysing the relations between gender, space, and inequality: it addressed urban inequality, work, access to services, and development. Two decades later, the same group produced a self-published CD-Rom entitled 'Geography and Gender Reconsidered'. *See also* WOMEN IN GEOGRAPHY.

Geography and Geographers: Anglo-American Human Geography since 1945 One of the most influential and widely read textbooks on the history and philosophy of human geography, having gone through seven editions. The first five editions were written by British geographer Ron *Johnston starting in 1979, and James Sidaway co-authored the latter two (2004 and 2013). Early editions were framed in reaction to the *paradigm concept, but later versions were more widely situated. The book is based on extensive reading of the subject, its debates, and the contributions of various scholars.

geography, history of The study of geography's past. In a broad sense, this means the study of all forms of geographical knowledge, sometimes termed *geosophy. In a narrower sense it means that study of scholarly or institutionalized geography as identified in *geographical societies, universities, and schools. Interest in the history of the discipline has grown considerably within the past 30 years. This has involved an extension of the period over which geography's history is considered, beyond the late 19th century, when the discipline was institutionalized to include the *Enlightenment and even earlier periods. In English-language history at least, the geographical scope remains largely confined to Europe and North America. Secondly, there has been a proliferation in the ways of approaching and writing history, following trends more widely in the humanities and social sciences. What this means is that there is no agreed and definitive history of geography and nor, according to scholars in this field, could there ever be. Like the meaning of *geography itself, its history is contested.

It is possible to differentiate a number of broadly different approaches to thinking and writing about the history of geography (Livingstone 1995). Encyclopedism seeks to assemble as many facts about geography as possible and arrange them chronologically. A modern example is the Geography in American timeline designed to coincide with the hundredth anniversary of the *Association of American Geographers in 2004. Along the same lines, there is a growing interest in biographical approaches, recording the recollections of eminent and living geographers, and recovering the lives of past scholars. The *Geographers Biobibliographical Studies* (29 volumes) is an example. An alternative contextual perspective does not search for a continuous and essential geography, but assumes that what geography is has varied through time (and place) and can only be understood relative to the circumstances. The exemplar of this approach, David *Livingstone's *The *Geographical Tradition* (1992), understands geography as a socially embedded and historically extended argument or dialogue, i.e. it is unfinished. Although in his view geography has no single 'nature', it does have recurrent discourses, e.g. *cartography, *region, and *space. Another approach is to use some of the stylized models of the history of science, notably Thomas *Kuhn's concept of *paradigm to chart the progress of the discipline and identify its major turning points. A more radical approach, *geneaology, aims to disrupt any sense of clear origins or narrative, focusing instead on ruptures and the appropriation of ideas as acts of power. Robert Mayhew's discussion of Strabo's *Geography* is a fine example. This same scepticism that there is a nature of geography or even a more plural set of discourses constituting a tradition is shared by recent approaches based on the *sociology of scientific knowledge. Trevor *Barnes' numerous writings on the history of economic geography and *spatial science instead highlight the co-production of geographical knowledge between people, instruments, and machines in specific sites. His work, along with Livingstone's also explores the geography of geography, examining the sites, locations, and circulations associated with the production and consumption of geographical knowledge (Agnew and Livingstone 2011).

The history of geography is far from the innocent pastime of antiquarians. Writing geography's history has consequences for the present. Any implication that there is a true, single path of geography (sometimes termed a 'Whig history') by definition excludes those deemed not to be geographers—a criticism levelled at *Hartshorne's *The *Nature of Geography* (1939) (*see* PRESENTISM). The founders of both *radical and *feminist geography sought antecedents in geography's past for inspiration and legitimacy (*see* WOMEN IN GEOGRAPHY). The issues at stake are well illustrated by an exchange of journal papers between Mona Domosh and David Stoddart. Domosh suggested that Victorian women travellers merited inclusion in the history of geography, even though they were excluded at the time from geographical societies by virtue of their sex. Their exclusion resonates with contemporary struggles by women to be accepted within the discipline. Stoddart demurs, observing that he cannot impose upon the past judgements made in the present.

References and further reading Agnew, J. and Livingstone, D. N. (eds.) (2011), *The Sage Handbook of Geographical Knowledge*.
Domosh, M. (1991), 'Towards a feminist historiography of geography', *Transactions of the Institute of British Geographers* 16: 95–104.
Livingstone, D. N. (1995), 'Geographical traditions', *Transactions of the Institute of British Geographers* 20: 420–22.
Mayhew, R. (2011), 'Geography's geneaologies', in Agnew, J. and Livingstone, D. N. (eds.) *The Sage Handbook of Geographical Knowledge*.
Stoddart, D. R. (1991), 'Do we need a feminist historiography of geography—and if we do, what should it be?', *Transactions of the Institute of British Geographers* 16: 484–87.

SEE WEB LINKS
• Geography in American timeline assembled by Donald Dahmann.

geohistory A geographical approach to history. Fernand Braudel's *The Mediterranean and the Mediterranean World in the Age of Philip II* (1972–73) is regarded as an exemplar of geohistory, establishing the long-term relations between humans and their milieu as part of a larger historical project (*see* ANNALES SCHOOL). Historian of geology Martin J. Rudwick uses geohistory to mean the history of the Earth in geological time. Other scholars may use geohistory to mean *historical geography in general.

geoinformatics The combination of spatial data analysis and modelling with *geovisualization to provide visual analytic tools for understanding geographic information. It entwines ideas from information science with *geocomputation. The visual products of *cartography, geodesy, *GIS, and *remote sensing are all considered forms of geoinformatics.

geomatics The scientific study of the measurement and analysis of location and information that is *geocoded. It is closely linked to *surveying and *cartography in terms of being able to accurately collect, display, and analyse such information.

geopolitics The study of the geographical factors in world politics and inter-state relations. The term is also used more generally to describe regional strategic relations, as in 'the geopolitics of the South China Sea'. In the present day it covers much the same ground as *International Relations, although with greater emphasis on geographical factors such as location, resources, and accessibility. Within this broad definition, there are many variants and the differences between them are significant. In part, these stem from the chequered history of the term 'geopolitics', which fell from favour across much of the Anglo-American world after the 1940s.

Its original or 'traditional' form arose towards the end of the 19th century. This 'imperial geopolitics' can be thought of as the application of *Social Darwinism to the state. Combining ideas of permanent national rivalry, the need for state expansion, *environmental determinism, and racist ideas about civilizations, this geopolitics was consciously directed towards informing and aiding statecraft among the European imperial powers, as well as the USA. Admiral Alfred Thayer Mahan (1846–1914) for example, warned the US government about the need to restore naval power in order to secure US trade interests. His ideas on sea power were adapted by Halford *Mackinder, whose *Heartland concept is regarded as the exemplar of this style of reasoning. Inspired by Friedrich *Raztel and the Swedish geographer Rudolph Kjellén (1864–1922)—who coined the term 'geopolitics'—a school of *geopolitik formed in Germany in the 1920s. Because of its close links with the subsequent Nazi regime, American and other geographers repudiated the term 'geopolitics', dismissing it as a pseudo-science of *racism and crude *environmental determinism. Although geographers such as Isaiah *Bowman also addressed strategic relations at the world scale they generally described their work as *political geography. A recognizable version of *geopolitik did, however, thrive among military academies and military dictatorships in South America well into the 1970s. Those scholars who continued to develop and adapt Mackinder's ideas to the *Cold War situation, notably Nicholas Spykman and later Saul Cohen, emphasized spatial themes rather than environmental or racial ones (*see* GEOSTRATEGIC REGION). But within academic geography in general, geopolitics had become a dirty word.

The return of geopolitics was more prominent outside departments of geography and took a clear conservative hue. US foreign policy officials and the intellectuals who sought to influence it, recycled and updated many of the ideas of imperial geopolitics from the 1970s onwards (*see* CLASH OF CIVILIZATIONS; PAX AMERICANA). Among geographers, there were two main responses. On the one hand, some argued for a restored geopolitics stripped of its imperial trappings and more attentive to the changing relations between geopolitical and *geoeconomic relations in an era of globalization. In particular, this line of research recognized non-state political actors, including *social movements and terrorist networks, and new issues such as global environmental change and the global media. A related but distinct response was the formation of *critical geopolitics, which drew more on post-structuralist concepts of *discourse and *representation to interrogate the texts (e.g. speeches, newsreel, policy documents) of politicians and state-centred foreign policy. There are also a number of other strands in current geopolitics. Jennifer Hyndman outlined a 'feminist geopolitics', informed by feminist geographical ideas and focused beyond the scale of the state to consider the politics of social justice, harm, *sexual violence, and the public/private divide (*see* FEAR). 'Popular geopolitics' examines how political geographical ideas circulate through film, television, cartoons, and magazines. 'Anti-geopolitics' describes the challenges to state-centred geopolitics from within civil society, including dissidents, social movements, and allied forms of *resistance. Its aim is to oppose the idea that the interests of the state and its political allies are the same as the interests of communities. Gerry Kearns uses the term 'progressive geopolitics' to refer to the ideas and practices in opposition to conservative geopolitics. It has more faith in international law and *cosmopolitan ideals as ways of regulating the relations between states and people so as to avoid conflict.

Further reading Cohen, S. B. (1991), 'Geopolitical change in the post Cold War era', *Annals of the Association of American Geographers*, 81(4): 551–80.

Dittmer, J. (2010), *Popular Culture, Geopolitics and Identity*.

Dodds, K. (2000), *Geopolitics in a Changing World*.

Hyndman, J. (2001), 'Towards a feminist geopolitics', *Canadian Geographer/ Le Géographe Canadien*, 45(2): 210–22.

Kearns, G. (2009), *Geopolitics and Empire*.

Routledge, P. (2003), 'Anti-geopolitics', in Agnew, J., Mitchell. K., and Toal, G. (eds.) *A Companion to Political Geography*, 236–48.

geopolitik The school of *geopolitics associated with Germany between 1900 and 1940s. Rooted in the tradition of German geography (including *Humboldt, *Ritter, and *Ratzel), and absorbing ideas from British and US political geographers (*see* MACKINDER, HALFORD), it blended *Social Darwinism, *racism, an organic theory of the state, and autarky in search of a science of world politics. Karl Haushofer was its leading practitioner. Closely linked with Germany's expansionism under Wilhelm II and Adolf Hitler, *geopolitik* was strongly challenged by US geographers before and during the Second World War.

geosophy The study of vernacular geographical knowledge in the past and present. US geographer John Kirkland *Wright coined the word in 1947 to outline a kind of history that focused not on what academic geographers wrote and did, but on how ordinary people—farmers, merchants, nomads, and novelists, for example—conceived and imagined their world, whether or not their ideas were later deemed to be true or false. *See also* GEOGRAPHY, HISTORY OF.

geospatial intelligence The analysis of geographical data in order to extract military intelligence, usually using *geocomputational and *geovisualization techniques. Data can be *maps, *remote sensing, *aerial photographs, radar scans, *GPS waypoints, and other forms predominately collected via satellites, planes, or drones, but can include on the ground vehicles and personnel. Increasingly, the data is analysed in real time in order to monitor and assess situations and help direct operations (*see* BIG DATA). Analysis is most often undertaken from a location remote from the territory under observation. The US National Imaging and Mapping Agency, formed in 1996, was renamed the National Geo-Spatial Intelligence Agency in 2003.

geostrategic region A functionally inter-related part of the Earth's surface combining a number of countries. US political geographer Saul B. Cohen identified two such regions in 1973—a 'trade-dependent maritime world' (surrounding the oceans) and a Eurasian continental world centred on the USSR and China. He proposed geopolitical subdivisions within these regions, areas characterized by cultural, economic, or political homogeneity, e.g. South Asia (*see* HEARTLAND, THE). A third regional type, termed a 'shatter belt', was fragmented and contested between geostrategic regions, e.g. the Middle East, sub-Saharan Africa. Cohen has continued to revise this *metageography in light of events.

Further reading Cohen, S. B. (2008), *Geopolitics: the Geography of International Relations*.

geovisualization The visualization and visual analytics of spatial data typically in a digital form. Geovisualization tools can be exploratory, descriptive, or analytic in nature, enabling a user to display, interact with, and analyse *geocoded data. The power of geovisualization is to draw together potentially millions of observations into a single or grouped set of images and to thus be able to examine potential patterns and relationships. Data can be displayed in a variety of ways including *maps, animations, 3-D time-space models, and statistical graphs. Given advances in computation, it is possible to create dynamic, interactive, and interlinked visual toolkits that help users make sense of the data from multiple visual perspectives. An example of such a toolkit is InstantAtlas, that allows the combination of maps, timelines, lists, and graphs to explore large and rich data such as *censuses. *See also* VISUALIZATION.

Further reading Dykes, J., MacEachren, A. M., and Kraak, M.-J. (2004), *Exploring Geovisualization*.

geoweb The use of location as a means of organizing and searching for information on the Internet, rather than simply by keyword. With more and more digital information being georeferenced and ubiquitous *GPS in mobile devices, it is becoming easier to ask 'what is where?' questions of online services. A typical example of the geoweb is *Google Maps. Sometimes it is called the geospatial web. *See also* VIRTUAL GEOGRAPHIES; VIRTUAL GLOBE.

Germany A federal republic, West Europe's largest economy and its largest population (81 million inhabitants). Unified as a single nation state from various separately governed territories in the 1870s, Germany was divided into the Federal Republic of Germany ('West Germany') and the German Democratic Republic ('East Germany') at the end of the *Second World War. The former was aligned with the *West and developed into a highly productive capitalist economy. The latter aligned with the Soviet bloc and was run along centrally planned lines. After the 1989 revolutions in the former Eastern bloc, the country was reunified (*see* BERLIN WALL). Economically and politically it is the most influential state in the *European Union. Its capital is *Berlin, but its sixteen *lander* (or states) have considerable power to make regional level decisions. Germany is an archetypal example of a *welfare state, characterized by a high level of social benefits, strong links between state, finance, and industry at the regional scale and substantial protection of workers' rights. Among Western democracies, it can be considered the antithesis of *neoliberal states such as the USA and Australia.

gerrymandering The redrawing of the boundaries of electoral districts in order to gain an advantage. Assuming that electoral support for political parties has a distinct geographical pattern, partisan interests can attempt to either split up and dilute the supporters of opposing parties or concentrate them in a few areas where much of their strength will be superfluous. The result can be strangely shaped electoral districts. *See also* ELECTORAL GEOGRAPHY; REDISTRICTING.

ghetto A residential district associated with intense social and spatial exclusion. Most analysts recognize two elements: firstly, the large majority of the district's residents belong to a single ethnic group or racialized grouping; and secondly, the majority of that same group found in the city as a whole reside in the district. Originally referring to areas of Jewish concentration in medieval Europe, the term was later widely applied to predominantly African-American neighbourhoods, although it can be used more loosely to describe even affluent concentrations. *See also* ETHNIC GROUP; SEGREGATION; SOCIAL POLARIZATION.

Gibson-Graham, J. K. A pseudonym of Katherine Gibson (1953–) and Julie Graham (1945–2010), two feminist economic geographers who were graduate students together at Clark University in the 1970s. Collaborating for thirty years until Graham's death, Gibson-Graham made a number of important theoretical contributions to *political economy and to the understanding of *capitalism, challenging traditional *Marxist accounts. Her major contribution has been to bring capitalism down to size analytically and politically, creating space for geographers to explore and advocate *alternative economic geographies. Gibson-Graham's influential books include *The End of Capitalism (As We Know It)* (1996) and *A Postcapitalist Politics* (2006).

Giddens, Anthony (1938–) A prolific British sociologist who was a key proponent of *structuration theory, a theorist of *late modernity and, more recently, an advocate of the 'third way', a political path that seeks to go beyond the dichotomy of left and right politics. For much of his career he was based at the University of Cambridge, before taking up the post of director of the London School of Economics. He was an advisor to Tony Blair and is a Labour appointment to the House of Lords. He was a co-founder of Polity Press.

gift economy A mode of exchanging goods, services, or other socially valued things that does not involve the medium of *money and is founded on the principle of reciprocity. In most Western societies, gifting has largely become limited to families and friends and special occasions (such as Christmas or birthdays). However, in several non-Western societies, gifting remains an important way is which strong social bonds are forged among people who are not blood relatives or even close personal friends. Unlike modern market economies—in which the exchange of *commodities via monetary trans-actions usually involves relations between complete strangers—gift economies tend to involve face-to-face relations between people with a view to enhancing *social capital. They are typically also '*moral economies' because gift economies depend on and reproduce such values as trust, obligation, and respect between those involved. Under the principle of reciprocity, a return gift need not be made right away, but it should be made at some time in the future. Therefore, there is an implicit bond between giver and receiver. *Development aid can be understood as a gift, but with conditions attached. If the recipient cannot reciprocate, which is often the case in aid relations, then they are placed in a subservient position; some anthropologists term this 'negative giving' (Mawdsley 2012). Human geographers have also become interested in whether and how gift economies can be revived as a challenge to 'amoral', profit-orientated market economies. Practices such as blood donation and open source software are examples of giving that can feature in larger attempts to create *alternative economic geographies.

Reference and further reading Currah, A. (2007), 'Managing creativity: the tensions between commodities and gifts in a digital networked environment', *Economy and Society* 36: 467–94.
Mawdsley, E., 'The changing geographies of foreign aid and development cooperation: contributions from gift theory', *Transactions of the Institute of British Geographers* 37: 256–272.

gini coefficient A measure of statistical dispersion that assesses the pattern of data in a frequency distribution (also known as the Gini index or Gini ratio). A Gini coefficient of zero is achieved when there is an equal distribution in values (e.g., everybody is earning the same wage). A Gini coefficient of one is achieved when the values are highly skewed (e.g., one person is receiving all the wages). In the case of income then, a higher Gini coefficient indicates that wealth is concentrated in the hands of a relatively small number of people, a low coefficient that wealth is more evenly spread amongst a population. The Gini coefficient is expressed visually through a Lorenz curve (see Fig. 4), where the flatter the curve the more equally a phenomenon is distributed. Many indices of *segregation are related to the Gini coefficient (*see* DISSIMILARITY, INDEX OF).

GIS *See* GEOGRAPHICAL INFORMATION SYSTEM.

global assemblage *See* ASSEMBLAGE.

global care chain A chain of interlinked caring relationships that extends across national borders. The top of the chain is a wealthy household who employs a carer to work in their home, usually to facilitate both parents to work. This carer is often an

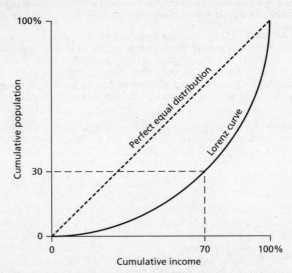

Fig. 4 A Lorenz curve of income distribution showing that 30% of the population earn 70% of income

immigrant who has moved to work for better wages and who may have a family of her/his own that has been left in the country of origin. This family has to be cared for by a local carer, typically a female relative, or by a paid carer whose own family care, in turn, must also be met. Global care chains are transnational in nature, highly gendered, almost exclusively involving women, often structured by race and ethnicity, and have a highly imbalanced *power geometry. Originally referring to paid domestic workers, the concept has been extended to nurses, eldercare workers, and other care professionals.

global city A strategic site for the control and coordination of the global economy, serving as a central node in networks of trade, finance, information, and migration. Although partly interchangeable with the term *world city, the concept of a global city has specific roots in the work of Dutch-American sociologist Saskia *Sassen beginning with *The Global City: New York, London, Tokyo* (1991). Sassen noted the apparent paradox of how the internationalization of economic activity in the form of transnational corporations involved both geographical dispersal and *agglomeration. She argued that internationalization required the greater centralization of corporate decision-making in order to coordinate far-flung activities. Through the related concentration of *producer services such as finance, law, and marketing, global cities developed as the sites of the production of globalized business activities. She also postulated that the concentration of such high-end service firms in select cities would lead to higher levels of *social polarization. Stripped of skilled and mid-level jobs in manufacturing, global cities would be dominated by high-wage occupations on the one hand and low-wage service workers to maintain their lifestyles on the other, supplemented by low-wage manufacturing, e.g. garment sector. These sectors would, in turn, attract migrant labour. Sassen's ideas were refined and broadened over subsequent publications, and generated further research supporting and critiquing her propositions. There were two main strands of research. One addressed the internal social and spatial structure of global cities, testing the polarization thesis. The other explored *world city networks by either tracing the geography of advanced producer service firms or mapping infrastructural networks such as the Internet, shipping, and aircraft movements. The main critiques concerned the tendency to underplay the role of the state and national context, and the over-concentration on economic as opposed to cultural and geopolitical relations. Jennifer Robinson pointed out the bias in research towards a select number of cities in the Global North, leaving out the lives and economies of millions of other urban dwellers. It could be argued that all cities are 'globalizing' to some extent, and that there is more to the economy than finance, law, and media. A broadened research agenda now recognizes value in exploring the myriad ways that cities are linked to one another, including through civil society organizations, and manufacturing commodity chains.

References and further reading Brenner, N. and Keil, R. (eds.) (2006), *The Global Cities Reader*.
Robinson, J. (2002), 'Global and world cities: a view from off the map', *International Journal of Urban and Regional Research*, 26(3), 531–54.

global civil society The totality of voluntary social relationships, communities, and institutions lying between the private realm, the market, and the state, and either acting or constituted at a global scale. Some authors prefer the term 'transnational civil society' to avoid the implication that it is simply a scaled-up national phenomenon. Although there is lively debate on whether such a thing exists, and if so, what it is made up of, in practice it is measured in terms of international *NGOs, global *social movements, transnational advocacy networks, and transnational migrant organizations (*see* MIGRATION-DEVELOPMENT NEXUS; NON-GOVERNMENTAL ORGANIZATION). Critics suggest that it is often less than global, but instead dominated by wealthy, English-speaking Westerners. *See also* ANTI-GLOBALIZATION MOVEMENT; WORLD SOCIAL FORUM.

Further reading Anheier, H., Glasius, M., and Kaldor, M. (eds.) (2001), *Global Civil Society 2001*.
Carr, D. and Norman, E. (2008), 'Global civil society? The Johannesburg World Summit on sustainable development', *Geoforum* 39: 358–71.

global commodity chain *See* COMMODITY CHAIN.

global commons Goods and resources not owned by any particular state, individual, community, or private interest but which can be thought of as belonging to humanity as a whole (*see* COMMONS). Examples include the atmosphere, oceans, Antarctica, biodiversity, and the Internet. How far something is part of the global commons is contested, e.g. does the Amazon rainforest belong to South American countries or to all humanity because of its significance to the planet's health?

global environment The totality of human-environmental and physical-environmental systems conceived at a planetary scale. The term is usually used to describe a terrain of inquiry or a class of challenges either at greater than national and regional scale, or lined by interdependencies that span localities. In this latter sense, global environmental processes are revealed locally but have causes and consequences that can be found at multiple scales. Rather than being thought of as a pre-existing thing, it can be instructive to think of the global environment as an object of inquiry constituted by various overlapping scientific and cultural practices since the 1960s. These include the first pictures of Earth from the Apollo space programme, the growth in planetary-scale data derived from *remote sensing sources, and the creation of international and inter-disciplinary research initiatives such as the *International Geosphere-Biosphere Programme (*see* EARTH SYSTEM SCIENCE). These were given impetus by the recognition of a class of global environmental problems, notably climate change and biodiversity loss. Tim *Ingold reflects, however, that conceiving of the global environment as something apart from human life sets up an unbridgeable opposition with unwelcome ethical consequences.

Reference Ingold, T. (2000), 'Globes and spheres: the topology of environmentalism', in *The Perception of the Environment*, 209–81.

global governance The processes of goal-orientated authority, rule, and coordination operating at a global scale, and the multi-scalar system of institutions and organizations through which these processes operate (*see* GOVERNANCE). In addition to *states and inter-governmental organizations (such as the *United Nations), the system of global governance includes NGOs, transnational corporations, transnational *social movements, standards-setting agencies (e.g. *International Organization for Standardization), and global *certification schemes (*see* GLOBAL CIVIL SOCIETY). Although there is no world government, in the sense of a scaled-up national government, there is an evolving and complex system of rule and authority that can be said to perform many of the functions of a world government. Elements of global governance date back to the 19th century, but as measured by the number of treaties and conventions, intergovernmental bodies, International NGOs etc., it is assuming ever-growing significance.

global inequality The disparities in the standards of living between countries and/or individuals across the world. Interest in global inequality was spurred by two reports in 2005. The UNDP Human Development Report argued that income inequality was growing, stating, for example, that 'the richest 50 individuals in the world have a combined income greater than that of the poorest 416 million'. The UN's Report on the World's Social Situation underlined the growth of health and education inequalities, including between men and women, and the worsening situation. Although it is commonly argued that global inequalities are increasing, not least because of *globalization, it is important to note substantial disagreement among economists. There are considerable difficulties in measuring such things as *poverty, income, and related conditions in internationally standardized ways. In fact, it could be argued that the collection of statistics by national agencies has the unintended consequence of systematically concealing global inequalities (*see* HUMAN DEVELOPMENT INDEX). Further, there appears to be a significant difference between inequality at the country level (which may be increasing) and at the individual level (which may be decreasing). That around a third of the world's population lives in India and China alone means that what goes on in these countries has a disproportionate impact on world measures. Finally, timescale matters. Although it is difficult to do, studies over long periods of time suggest that global inequalities rose rapidly from the early 19th century to the mid-20th century, but thereafter levelled off, though with fluctuations. *See also* DEVELOPMENT; SPATIAL INEQUALITY, WEALTH INEQUALITY.

Further reading UNDP Human Development Report (2005), *International Cooperation at a Crossroads*.

United Nations Economic and Social Affairs (2005), 'Report on the world situation 2005', *The Predicament of Inequality*.

SEE WEB LINKS
• Worldmapper, a collection of world maps illustrating global inequalities.

globalism The view that the entire world is the most salient scale of thought and action due to the dense interconnections and interdependencies that tie *nations together. For some, globalism underpins the argument for some kind of world government. For others, it means nations have to operate with a global mindset to prosper politically and economically. In the latter case there is always a tension between the interests of the nation and the interests of global citizenry. *See also* GLOBALIZATION.

globalization The process whereby people, places, regions, and countries become more interlinked and more interdependent at a planetary scale. It also refers to the outcome of these processes. According to the widely cited definition of David Held and his colleagues in *Global Transformations* (1999) it involves the increased extensity (stretching), intensity, velocity, and impact of relations. By extensity, they mean the length of transborder connections; by intensity, they mean the level of interdependence (or functional integration); by velocity, they mean the speed with which transborder connections can be made or used; and by impact, they mean the degree to which changes in one part of the world rebound on far distant localities. In a world of 'pure' globalization, all people and places would have a myriad of global-scale interconnections that made them highly dependent on distant locations day-on-day, such that major changes in these locations would very quickly have significant positive or negative effects on them.

The term 'globalization' became a buzzword in the worlds of big business, international politics, and news journalism in the 1990s (e.g., *The Economist*). Its rise to prominence coincided with three things of world historic importance. First, the end of the *Cold War and the collapse of communism in the Soviet Union and the former Eastern bloc allowed a host of new countries to join an already highly internationalized capitalist economy. At the same time, *China, while still officially communist, began a steady transformation towards a form of central government-managed capitalism from the late 1970s. Second, from the mid-1980s the *International Monetary Fund and the *World Bank insisted on implementing *Structural Adjustment Policies when lending money to developing countries. These policies made these countries' economies more export-orientated and more open to overseas competition (*see* FREE MARKET). Third, led by the *United States, the major capitalist economies together agreed to reduce barriers to investment and trade. The creation of the *World Trade Organization (WTO) in 1995 was a key part of this process, so too the creation of regionally open economies, like those covered by the *North American Free Trade Agreement and the agreements underpinning the *European Union.

These three things were largely economic in focus. Together they comprised an orchestrated attempt to make political borders and geographical distance less relevant to commodity production, commodity trade, monetary investment, and commodity consumption than previously. They were greatly facilitated by innovations in telecommunications and transportation that increased the speed, increased the volume, but reduced the unit costs of cross-border interaction. The invention of the *Internet, email, and large container ships were just three of many examples of this. For national governments, agreeing to abide by rules enforced by global *governance bodies like the WTO also meant their powers of economic management were diminished. While they could still largely control domestic borrowing and public spending, they were less able to control who invested in their territory or to convince a large firm not to relocate overseas. These connections between economic change and political affairs were repeated in other arenas. The spaces opened up by economically driven globalization were soon used or appropriated by migrants, civil society organizations, and political movements (*see* ANTI-GLOBALIZATION MOVEMENT; GLOBAL CIVIL SOCIETY; TRANSNATIONALISM). The circulation of people, information, and ideas piggy-backed the flows of commodities and finance. The precise nature and implications of globalization were arguably *the* topic dominating Western social science at the turn of the millennium. For some (known by critics as 'hyperglobalists'), globalization was promising to make geography irrelevant in one sense, especially the globalization of *finance capital (for example, Thomas Friedman's *The World Is Flat*, 2005). They envisaged a world in which all nations and peoples would be connected through trade, migration, and tourism. Places and regions could build success according to their competitive and comparative advantages, while workers and consumers worldwide would benefit from cheap imports and ease of access to overseas labour markets and tourist destinations. Contrary to this view, sceptics mined the historical record and pointed out that levels of cross-border economic integration were no greater than during the 19th century era of 'liberal capitalism' that preceded the *First World War (*see* IMPERIALISM). For them, the idea of globalization was hyperbole (Hirst and Thompson, 1996). Despite their differences, these rival positions shared a tendency towards 'all-or-nothing' analysis. By disaggregating globalization into four dimensions, and assessing this quartet for each of commodity production, cross-border trade, financial transactions, labour migration, and so on, Held et al. sought to provide a more discriminating way forwards for analysis. They identified different kinds and degrees of globalization, coexisting with various forms of national, regional, and local insulation from outside forces.

Human geographers, in large part because of their preoccupation with the specificities of *place and *region have long been suspicious of the hyperglobalist arguments even as they take issue with the sceptics' argument that the reality of globalization is overstated. Many have also taken issue with the *rhetoric of *neoliberalism, wherein globalization is represented as a means to spread wealth, reduce poverty, ensure economic efficiency, and produce unhindered economic competition. There has been a major emphasis on describing and explaining the uneven geographies *produced* by globalization, as well as the unevenness perpetuated by *excluding* certain people and locations from globalization (*see* UNEVEN DEVELOPMENT). For instance, using Karl *Marx's theory of capital accumulation, David Harvey (2005) regards globalization as both an attempt to extend the spatial reach of *capitalism and create one of the self-same kinds of spatial inequality that is part of capitalism's DNA. Among other things he points to the hyper-exploitation of Chinese workers attendant upon their country's integration into the world economy, the continued marginalization of sub-Saharan Africa, and the 'First World debt crisis' arising from countries living beyond their means. Along with John *Agnew (2005) and Neil *Smith (2004), he also points to the USA's faltering attempt to use its political *hegemony to retain its increasingly fragile economic prowess. Working at a less macro-economic and geopolitical level, economic geographers investigating *commodity chains and *global production networks have shown how economic *value is created and captured differentially over space. Likewise, urban geographers looking at *world cities and their networks have sought to understand their rise and how they maintain their high economic status. This unevenness partly reflects relations of socio-economic and political *power that render some locations less able to control their destiny than others. It also, relatedly, reflects decisions made by governments, firms, and workers about how best to use their *human agency. For every success, like Singapore, there may be three or four failures, like Liberia. Likewise, where some agents have considerable geographical autonomy (like McDonalds Corporation), others have highly limited options (like poor Mexicans seeking employment over the heavily guarded border with the USA). Accordingly, Doreen *Massey conceptualizes globalization less as a spreading process than as an exceedingly complicated set of relationships, rules, and institutions that connect different localities in different (incomplete) ways, with differential implications for people inhabiting the same locations. *See also* DEVELOPMENT; TIME-SPACE COMPRESSION.

References and further reading Agnew, J. (2005), *Hegemony: The New Shape of Global Power*.
Dicken, P. (6th ed. 2011), *Global Shift*.
Harvey, D. (2005), *A Brief History of Neoliberalism*.
Herod, A. (2009), *Geographies of Globalization*.
Hirst, P. and Thomson, G. (1996), *Globalization in Question*.
Smith, N. (2004), *The Endgame of Globalization*.

Global Justice Movement A network of *social movements united by the search for alternatives to neoliberal or corporate *globalization (*see* NEOLIBERALISM). Emerging from *antiglobalization protests in the 1990s, it is developing novel forms of solidarity and cooperation between the Global North and Global South. *See also* GLOBAL CIVIL SOCIETY; WORLD SOCIAL FORUM.

(((⊕))) **SEE WEB LINKS**
• Official website of the Global Justice Movement.

Global North Those countries found mainly, but not exclusively, in the northern hemisphere, characterized by high levels of *economic development. *See also* FIRST WORLD; MEDC.

Global Positioning System (GPS) A means of pinpointing a location on Earth through triangulation with respect to a constellation of orbiting satellites. The GPS device receives signals from these satellites, which are in a fixed orbit, and by computing the distance to three satellites it is possible to determine the position of the device. This calculation can be undertaken on an ongoing basis meaning that the path travelled by the GPS device can be tracked over time. Originally developed for military use, especially for *geospatial intelligence, given its embedding in *satnavs, mobile phones, and tablets, GPS is now used routinely for civil purposes such as *wayfinding. The technology underpins new emerging industries such as *location-based services.

global production network The entire set of institutions, rules, and relationships involved in making, distributing, and selling a *commodity. The Global Production Network (GPN) approach developed in *economic geography is a *heuristic framework developed within the broader context of *relational (economic) geography. GPN analysis seeks to reveal the multi-actor and multi-scalar characteristics of transnational production systems—and their developmental implications—through exploring the intersecting notions of *power, *value, and *embeddedness. It seeks to build upon and extend work conducted within cognate global *commodity chain and *global value chain approaches. Peter *Dicken's *Global Shift* (2011) is organized around the concept.

Global Shift An influential book by British economic geographer Peter *Dicken, first published in 1992, and now in its 6th edition (2011). Used in teaching but also by researchers, the book explores how *transnational corporations and national governments interact in ways that significantly shape the geography of the global economy, notably through the organization of *global production networks.

Global South The countries of Africa, Asia, Latin America, and the Caribbean, often used in preference to alternative terms such as the *developing world or *Third World. There exists considerable social, economic, and political diversity within the Global South, which includes the majority of the world's countries. *See also* LEDC.

global value chain (GVC) A transnational *commodity chain in which a commodity accrues more value at particular points in the chain. In this sense, the metaphorical links are larger in some parts of the chain than in others. For instance, in a diamond commodity chain, significant value accrues at the moment a diamond is cut by a skilled jeweller. Because value tends to be added at different points in different chains, the geography of wealth may vary significantly between chains. This has led economic and development geographers to inquire into how less wealthy places or countries can introduce higher-value links in the chain to their portfolio of activities. GVC analysis extends the work on *global commodity chains (GCC), and to some extent the term 'GVC' has replaced 'GCC'. In particular, it focuses on the different ways chains can be governed or organized.

Further reading Gereffi, G., Humphrey, J., and Sturgeon, T. (2005), 'The governance of global value chains', *Review of International Political Economy* 12(1): 78–104.

(( )) SEE WEB LINKS

• The Global Value Chain initiative at Duke University assembles information on GVC research.

global village The world's peoples as they are linked through mass communication media. In a book entitled *The Gutenburg Galaxy* (1962) the Canadian thinker Marshall McLuhan used the term to reflect the impact of printing and later electronic communication technology on human consciousness and sensory fields. Such technologies abolished the constraint of distance on communication. The term has been extended to describe the *Internet and its supposed effects on human interaction.

global warming *See* CLIMATE CHANGE.

globe A three-dimensional scale model of the Earth (or other spherical bodies). Globes of Earth usually show the terrain and/or the boundaries of countries and principal cities. Some globes are embossed with relief to show the hilliness of the landscape. Celestial globes show the locations of the stars. The globe as seen from space has become an iconic symbol of shared humanity.

glocalization The dialectical relation between, and the interpenetration of, the global or universal and the local or particular. The term was independently introduced into the social sciences by British sociologist Roland Robertson and Belgian geographer Erik *Swyngedouw in the 1990s, although the former adapted it from Japanese business. In both senses it is a challenge to the idea that *globalization is an all-powerful homogenizing process that will eradicate the differences between people and places. Robertson meant that universalizing and particularizing processes occurred together at the same time and therefore fears that cultural globalization would create deadening uniformity are misplaced (*see* CREOLIZATION; HYBRIDITY). By the same token, however, celebrations of local variety and uniqueness are also mistaken. Swyngedouw, informed by *Marxist geography, employed the term to critique the over-emphasis on globalization as a novel and pervasive force. He insisted that within capitalist *uneven development, local regions shape the operation of global processes even as they are themselves transformed by them. *See* LOCAL-GLOBAL RELATIONS.

References Robertson, R. (1995), 'Glocalization: time-space and homogeneity-heterogeneity', in Featherstone, M. et al. (eds.) *Global Modernities*, 25–44.
Swyngedouw, E. (2001), 'Neither global nor local: "glocalization" and the politics of scale', in Jessop, B. (ed.) *Regulation Theory and the Crisis of Capitalism*, 196–225.

GNP *See* GROSS NATIONAL PRODUCT.

Golledge, Reg (1937–2009) An Australian-born geographer who spent most of his career in the United States, notably at Ohio State University and University of California, Santa Barbara. He was a key proponent of *behavioural geography, an approach that holds to the idea that human spatial activity can only be understood in relation to people's imperfect and partial knowledge of the world. In particular, he championed an analytical version that employed *quantitative methods and drew strongly on cognitive and experimental psychology to analyse and model spatial knowledge, spatial choice and decision-making, and *spatial behaviour.

Further reading Golledge, R. and King, L. (1978), *Cities, Space and Behavior*.

Goodchild, Michael (1944–) A key contributor to and proponent of *GIScience. After an undergraduate degree in physics, Goodchild undertook his doctoral work in geography at McMaster University, Canada. After nearly twenty years at the University of Western Ontario he moved to the University of California, Santa Barbara. He has served as director of the *NCGIA and in numerous research leadership roles. He has made a number of scientific contributions to spatial statistics, notably *spatial autocorrelation, and to *geocomputation more broadly, but is perhaps best known as a disciplinary leader and strong advocate of the utility of GIScience for pure and applied research.

Google A search engine founded in 1996, Google has become one of the most important generators and organizers of information on the Internet. It provides a suite of tools to search, process, and share information, including Google News, Google Scholar, and Google Docs, and a range of communications and *social networking media such as Blogger, Gmail, and Google Plus. From a geographic perspective it provides the most popular online mapping tool, Google Maps, whose API (Application Programming Interface) forms the basis for many mapping *mashups, and Google Earth, a three-dimensional, interactive representation of the planet that enables users to upload and share geographic information.

Gough Map An early medieval map of the whole of Great Britain, thought to date to around 1360. It is named after one of its former owners, Richard Gough (1735–1809). As well as being an important cartographic artefact giving insight into early map making, the six hundred places marked on the map reveal the medieval urban structure of Britain. It is presently held in the Bodleian Library, University of Oxford.

(⊕) SEE WEB LINKS
• Searchable edition of the Gough Map with commentaries.

Gould, Peter R. (1932–2000) An American quantitative geographer who was based at Penn State University for the majority of his career. A strong advocate of *spatial science, he is best known for his books *Spatial Organization: The Geographer's View of the World* (with Ron Abler and John Adams, 1971) and *The Geographer at Work* (1985). He also made a key contribution to *behavioural geography with his co-authored book *Mental Maps* (1974, with Rodney White).

governance The processes of goal-orientated coordination and management involving governmental and non-governmental actors. The term is used in a variety of differing contexts and disciplines, and there is no single definition beyond a core idea. James Rosenau, US political scientist, refers to the emergence of 'governance without government' in international relations. R. A. W. Rhodes, a British political scientist, similarly writes of 'governing without government' in the context of British public policy. They and other authors are pointing to a shift at national and international scales from state-centred government to practices of formulating, coordinating, and delivering organizational goals through greater involvement of civil society (or 'the public') and corporate bodies (the 'market' or 'private sector'). This has two main implications. One is that the *state no longer has a monopoly over public affairs. The other is that the boundary between state and non-state becomes blurred resulting in looser, more flexible, and decentralized systems of policy making. Governance describes a set of changes underway since the 1980s, but as expressed in the phrase 'good governance', it also has a normative dimension. In international *development policy, major lenders and institutions encourage or require states to adopt reformed practices of accountability and transparency, but also involve non-state actors in service provision (*see* POVERTY REDUCTION STRATEGIES).

Within geography there are four main areas of focus regarding governance. First, geographers have sought to theorize the nature of governance and how it operates spatially, particularly with respect to the urban scale and particular spatial systems such as air travel. Such theories include coalition and *regime theory that contend that urban governance is exercised by a alliance of elite actors; neo-Marxist theories, such as *regulation theory, that cast governance as a regulatory aspect of capitalism; *Actor Network Theory in which governance is divested through a range of actors and discursive and material practices; and Foucauldian theory focused on the management and regulation of populations through regimes of disciplining and *governmentality (*see* BIOPOLITICS; FOUCAULT, MICHEL).

Second, there is an interest in *networks as a relatively novel form of governance contrasting with markets and hierarchies. For some researchers, the shift from government to governance is precisely defined by the proliferation of network forms of organization. Researchers on *global value chains classify the different ways that producers, suppliers, and other agents involved in commodity networks are governed (*see* GLOBAL COMMODITY CHAINS).

Third, there is a focus on rescaling governance, meaning the processes through which forms of authority, rule, and decision-making are variously dispersed from the territorially defined nation state (*see* HOLLOWING OUT). With regard to climate policy, for example, this may include not just supra-national bodies such as the United Nations, but also corporations, cities, and networks of cities (*see* ENVIRONMENTAL GOVERNANCE).

Finally, there is a concern with how modes of governance confer different status, rights, and responsibilities on individuals. For example, geographers have examined varying forms of *citizenship and how these shape entitlements and how people are governed, and also how people *resist and seek to change forms of governance and governmentality through acts of civil disobedience and *social movements. *See also* GLOBAL GOVERNANCE.

References Rhodes, R. A. W. (1996), 'The new governance: governing without government', *Political Studies* 46: 652–67.
Rosenau, J. (1995), 'Governance in the twenty-first century', *Global Governance* 1; 13–43.

governmentality 1. A form of state power, distinct from *sovereignty and discipline, combining practices and rationalities of government.
2. A form of power within and beyond the state, concerned with acting on the actions of others or on oneself in order to guide behaviour.

These two definitions are, in fact, closely related and both derive from the writings of Michel *Foucault. Given his own revisions of these ideas and the subsequent contribution of later scholars, there is no single, clear meaning of governmentality. In one sense it refers to a perspective or a way of asking certain questions—notably about *how* things happen rather than *why*. In another sense, governmentality is the subject of analysis, giving rise to a field of governmentality studies.

In terms of the history of how the state works, Foucault developed the concept of governmentality to describe something distinct from the well-established concept of sovereignty and his own ideas about discipline. Arising in 16th-century Europe, it came to dominate the modern state by the 18th century, in what he called 'the governmentalization of the state'. Sovereignty was a mode of power associated with a sovereign's control of *territory, largely prohibitive and with the possibility of violent sanction. By comparison, discipline describes various kinds of *policing and supervision designed to inculcate in individuals a sense of what they must do without a general recourse to violence (*see* PANOPTICON). Governmentality describes the various ways that the state seeks to guide individuals and populations in matters such as health and education (*see* BIOPOLITICS). It is more about regulating processes than things, designed to instil habits or dispositions. The term combines both practices ('government') and forms of thought ('mentality'); he took as his evidence not just the actions of states, but also the many treatises on the 'art of government' from Nico Machiavelli onwards. Foucault regarded governmentality as an essential element of liberal government as it took shape in 19th-century Europe. It also captures the way that neoliberal states seek to govern through appearing to maximize individual freedom and choice. Rather than see freedom and constraint as opposed, as many political theorists do, thinking in terms of governmentality enabled Foucault to treat the actions of states and individuals as aligned. Or, put another way, he conceived of the modern state and the autonomous individual as co-constituted.

This leads to the second main sense of governmentality, as a form of power not limited to the state but found in other sites—the church, family, school, workplace, etc. In this sense it refers to the many practices and associated ideas that not only concern 'the conduct of conduct' but also allow individuals to fashion themselves as certain sorts of subjects. An example might be how food labelling is linked not just to personal, family (and therefore social) health and well-being, but also to educating individual consumer-citizens in virtuous ways of life. There is an ethical dimension to self-government in other words. Because governmentality involves the circulation of rationalities or discursive truths, forms of expertise are also important. These may relate to workplace management or educational reform, but equally include marriage guidance or consumer advice.

Derived from behavioural economics and popularized as 'nudge', 'soft', or 'libertarian paternalism', it can be seen as an example of how these two senses of governmentality are nowadays entwined. It refers to small cues (e.g. the placing of goods in a supermarket) or changes in the default position (e.g. from an opt-in system of organ donation to an opt-out system) that try to advance well-being while sustaining the appearance of consumer choice. This example also suggests the main criticism levelled at governmentality as a concept and an approach. It is not always clear how or indeed whether, it allows for opposition or resistance.

There is a growing field of geographical research using the ideas of governmentality. Foucault's interest in sites beyond the state (e.g. prisons, schools), his close attention to the spatial distribution of bodies, and his frequent reference to cartography and diagrams as essential to the rationalities of government, have informed a wider range of geographical studies.

Further reading Huxley, M. (2008), 'Space and government: governmentality and geography', *Geography Compass* 2/5 1635–58.

Larner, W. (2007), 'Expatriate experts and globalising governmentalities: The New Zealand diaspora strategy', *Transactions of the Institute of British Geographers* 32(3): 331–45.

Rose-Redwood, R. S. (2006), 'Governmentality, geography and the geo-coded world', *Progress in Human Geography* 30(4): 469–86.

government-in-exile A political body that claims sovereign authority over a *territory which by virtue of invasion or occupation it cannot rule. Several European states, including Belgium and Poland, had such governments during the *Second World War. More recent examples include a Tibetan government-in-exile residing in Dharamsala, India and a group claiming authority over the Sahrawi Arab Democratic Republic in North Africa. *See also* DIASPORA.

GPS *See* GLOBAL POSITIONING SYSTEM.

Grameen Bank A *microfinance *NGO established in 1976 in Bangladesh to provide small loans to poor people, mostly women, lacking sufficient collateral to secure funds from commercial banks. The bank emerged from a research project undertaken by Muhammad Yunus and is now 90 per cent owned by its borrowers. The scheme has been emulated in over forty other countries.

SEE WEB LINKS
• Official website of Grameen Bank.

Grand Theory A kind of *theory that aims to be analytically encompassing, epistemologically authoritative, and normatively complete. In human geography, certain kinds of *Marxist thinking are often regarded as exemplars of Grand Theory, typified by David *Harvey's *Limits to Capital*. Such theory is analytically encompassing in that it tries to explain a wide range of social, economic, political, or cultural phenomena with reference to one or more underlying processes or relationships. It is epistemologically authoritative in that its claims are advanced less as hypotheses to be tested than as statements of truth or actuality. And it aims to be normatively complete in that its recommendations for how the world might be changed and improved are presented as if most of the ills of current society will be solved. Throughout the 1990s many human geographers shied away from Grand Theory, even though many Marxist geographers continued to work with some version of it. The move coincided with human geography's engagement with critical theory such as post-structuralism and the discipline becoming more topically and politically plural than ever before. As a way of trying to meld together otherwise different approaches, 'intersectional' forms of theory have been developed. Whether these are a new form of Grand Theory posing as something else is a moot point. Regardless, few in the discipline are any longer willing to be seen to construct grand theoretical edifices designed to describe, explain, and criticize the total metaphorical architecture of modern life.

graphicacy The capacity of people to read, interpret, and produce graphic information (sketches, photographs, diagrams, charts, graphs, maps). Graphicacy is to graphics what literacy is to texts and numeracy is to numbers. Each of these forms of communication has its own symbol and language systems that work to convey information. Given the visual nature of much geographical analysis, graphicacy is considered to be an important disciplinary skill and therefore forms part of the school and university curriculum, notably as mapping skills.

graph theory The mathematical study of the organization of network structures (called graphs). In essence, it analyses how all the nodes in a graph are connected to each other in order to understand the structure of the network and how the network functions. Graph theory is an important component of *network analysis, used to model networked systems such as transport and communication networks, and how goods, services, information, or diseases move or diffuse through them. It underpins how traffic management systems work to regulate flow and how *satnavs work to calculate shortest and quickest routes. It is also used to identify hierarchies of substructures in large networks of interconnections, for example, amongst a large sample of mobile phone users or between webpages. Indeed, graph theory is used by *Google to help rank pages on the basis of the structure and density of interconnections between them.

Further reading Arlinghaus, S. L., Arlinghaus, W. C., and Harary, F. (2002), *Graph Theory and Geography*.

gravity model A *model that correlates the interaction of variables against a cost function such as distance, time, price, or size. In geography, gravity models are associated with Waldo *Tobler's first law of geography: everything is related to everything else, but near things are more related than distant things. In other words, the level of interactions between places declines with increasing distance between them, and is shaped by other cost factors such as the relative size of the places. This relationship is usually exponential, with many more interactions the nearer the places are together. It can be expressed as a mathematical formula and used to predict the expected spatial interaction between locales for different types of movement or contact. *See also* SPATIAL INTERACTION MODELS.

Great Depression A major global economic recession starting in 1929 in the United States, then spreading to other countries, and lasting up until the *Second World War. It was triggered by a severe stock market crash. What followed included mass unemployment, a large reduction in trade, and the radical reduction of personal, state, and corporate wealth and an associated rise in poverty. In some states, notably Spain and Germany, the depression aided the growth of fascist regimes. The severity of collapse led to wide-scale changes to national economic and banking systems with the introduction of structural reform and new regulations.

green belt A designated area surrounding a town or city in which urban forms of development are heavily restricted under planning law. It is intended to prevent *urban sprawl, provide a clear boundary between urban and rural land use, protect agricultural land, provide recreation space, and/or protect landscape. Greenbelts were a key component of the UK's 1947 Town and Country Planning Act and have been deployed in various forms (such as 'green wedges') all over the world.

greenfield development A residential, industrial, or commercial construction on land previously used for agriculture or other non-industrial purposes. Such development is often criticized as it increases urban sprawl and reduces the agricultural capacity of an area. *See also* BROWNFIELD SITES.

green governance The practices and standards adopted by organizations and directed towards achieving greater levels of sustainability. *See also* CORPORATE SOCIAL RESPONSIBILITY.

greenhouse effect *See* CLIMATE CHANGE.

Greenpeace A multi-issue environmentalist international *NGO (*see* ENVIRONMENTALISM). Founded in Vancouver in the early 1970s, it is now organized through relatively autonomous regional offices in over 40 countries, coordinated by an International HQ in Amsterdam. It is funded by individual supporters (said to number 2.8 million) and foundations, maintaining independence from states and corporations. Greenpeace is noted for its *environmental direct action, particularly at sea, but lobbies and campaigns on a broad range of environmental issues. *See also* ENVIRONMENTAL JUSTICE.

(⊕) SEE WEB LINKS
• Official website of Greenpeace.

Green Revolution The diffusion of new high yield variety (HYV) food crops such as wheat and rice with their related agricultural technologies throughout much of the Global South from the 1950s onwards. The new 'miracle seeds' and farming techniques raised food productivity across many regions at a time of *Malthusian fears over population growth. But they could equally be associated with dislocations of rural societies and laying the foundations for modern, global *agribusiness.

Path-breaking research on new crop varieties was conducted in northern Mexico under a joint project between the US Rockefeller Foundation and the Mexican government headed by Norman Baulag, and later in the Philippines at the International Rice Research Institute, also co-financed by the Rockefeller and Ford foundations. Intensive plant breeding and seed bank programmes resulted in, among other things, IR8. This rice variety was of standardized height, and could yield three crops a year under the right conditions. Later varieties of maize, potato, and other food staples were bred for specific ecological niches or to be resistant to specific diseases and pests.

The new varieties were introduced by US and other international aid bodies in the *developing world in the 1960s. The term 'Green Revolution' was intended to contrast this technological fix to food supply problems with the 'red' revolution of communism and land reform. There were immediate gains in those regions most similar to the varieties' sources, notably Asia and Latin America, but less impact in Africa or the non-irrigated parts of India. Planting and harvesting the crops required new and constant inputs of machinery, such as water pumps, fertilizers, and pest control products. The cost of the package needed to support the HYV crops was often beyond many small farmers, leading to fears that the Green Revolution would polarize rural societies. To some extent this happened, for example, in Malaysia (Scott 1985). In 1971 a network of agricultural research stations (CGIAR) was set up under the *World Bank to facilitate use by small farmers and to some degree the worries about growing inequality and labour displacement have been alleviated. From the 1990s onwards these intensive plant breeding programmes have been largely superseded by *biotechnology companies and *genetically modified (GM) crops. At the same time, there is growing awareness of more localized, indigenous experiments with plant growing (*see* INDIGENOUS KNOWLEDGE).

Reference Scott, J. C. (1985), *Weapons of the Weak: Everyday Forms of Peasant Resistance.*

greenwash A false, misleading or exaggerated claim made by commerical businesses about their environmental credentials. A number of *civil society initiatives are aimed at exposing such claims.

Gregory, Derek (1951–) A British human geographer who has made a set of formative contributions to the development of *critical (human) geography. Written while at the University of Cambridge, his first book, *Ideology, Science and Human Geography* (1978), identified several key weaknesses in the then-prevalent *spatial science approach, and charted new directions for research of a more left-wing character. The monograph was entirely theoretical—a long essay, in effect—but his next book was an empirical demonstration of the sort of critical research he advocated. Inspired, in part, by the then lively debates in Marxist history and theory, Gregory sought to explain the late 18th-century change from a domestic to a factory system in the woollen industry of the West Riding of Yorkshire. *Regional Transformation and Industrial Revolution* (1982) showed how working-class people were not only blown by the winds of historical change but, in significant measure, made the metaphorical weather. The book was an important contribution to human geography for two reasons. First, it countered the perception of some critics that *Marxist geography was purely theoretical and given to over-emphasizing the power of economic structures on people's lives. Second, it provided a bridge connecting political economy with *social theory. Unlike the former, the latter focused on significant social relations and institutions beyond those of the formal economy. It allowed Gregory to offer a wider and thicker representation of economically driven change than some then-extant versions of Marxist geography were able to. A subsequent book edited with sociologist John *Urry, *Social Relations and Spatial Structures* (1985) was a further important contribution to the structure-agency debate in human geography.

By the mid-1980s Gregory had helped establish two important publications, one pedagogic, the other related to research. They were the *Dictionary of Human Geography* (now in its fifth edition) and the journal *Environment and Planning D: Society & Space*, respectively. The former was one of several student-focused, research-led texts Gregory went on to co-edit. The latter was to become an important place where new forms of critical human geography could find a home. In 1989 Gregory became a full professor of geography at the University of British Columbia, Vancouver. His next book, *Geographical Imaginations* (1994), was a comprehensive history of academic geography's origins and evolution, with a particular focus on contemporary critical thinking. Gregory showed how political economy, social theory, cultural theory, and science studies all had profound implications for geographical thinking and vice versa.

As part of his research for this book Gregory became fascinated by *post-colonialism and, especially, the writings of Edward *Said. His transplantation from Cambridge to the former colony of British Columbia also sensitized him to the complexities and simplifications involved in all cross-cultural encounters. Gregory proceeded to research the way colonial *power in the 19th century worked through cultural understandings and representations as much as through military power, administrative rules, and the law. He focused on French and British travellers and colonizers venturing to the *Middle East. One fruit of this research was the co-edited book with James *Duncan entitled *Writes of Passage: Reading Travel Writing* (1999). However, the advent of the second Gulf War in 2003, along with the continued conflict between *Israel and *Palestine, led him to switch focus to the current period. His book *Colonial Present* was a meticulously researched inquiry into how the military and intelligence forces of Israel, America, and those states allied in the invasions of *Iraq and *Afghanistan prosecuted their campaigns. Gregory is continuing to investigate the varied modalities of war, past and present, and their geographical integument.

((( ))) SEE WEB LINKS

• Derek Gregory's blog.

Gross Domestic Product (GDP) A measure of national economic activity calculated as the total value added (the difference between net inputs and outputs of industries and services) by all producers deemed resident in a country, plus taxes, and minus subsidies. For international comparisons, GDP is usually expressed in US dollars. GDP does not register non-monetized economic activity found in *alternative economies.

Gross National Income (GNI) A broad measure of national income employed by the *World Bank among others. It is calculated by adding *Gross Domestic Product (GDP) and net receipts of primary income from foreign sources and is usually expressed in US dollars. This measure is increasingly used instead of *Gross National Product.

Gross National Product (GNP) A measure of national economic activity calculated as the total value added (the difference between net inputs and outputs of all industries and services) by all producers based in a country, whether or not the activity actually takes place there. Unlike *Gross Domestic Product it attributes value added based on ownership rather than geographical location, such that it may include, for example, the contribution of transnational corporations to a country's wealth derived from their overseas investments. *See also* GROSS NATIONAL INCOME.

grounded theory A form of theory developed iteratively from empirical observation and *induction. The term was first popularized by the sociologists Barney Glaser and Anselm Strauss in *The Discovery of Grounded Theory* (1967). Reacting against 'top down' *Grand Theory. They used *qualitative data and research methods to progressively develop theories designed to represent (describe and explain) any given situation. Unlike some approaches to research in social and biophysical science, they did not begin with a *hypothesis, *model, or *theory to be tested empirically. Rather, the latter emerges slowly through observation, data collection, and systematic reflection. In human geography, grounded theory has not been developed to the same degree it has in the discipline of sociology. Instead, the term denotes a 'style' of theorizing that pays close attention to empirical specifics rather than glossing over them as often occurs with *Grand Theory. Grounded theory is not associated with any one approach to research; for example, *Critical Realism argues for grounded theory, but one can just as easily find it operationalized by researchers inspired by queer theory or *post-structuralism.

ground truth The process of comparing the remote capture of spatial data with what is actually on the ground. For example, one might compare the pixel data in a *remote sensing image with the land cover in situ in order to verify its veracity. In the case of derived data, such as a remotely sensed image classified into land cover types, ground truthing allows an assessment of the accuracy of the classification algorithm and to tweak it, if necessary. The term has also been used in a critical sense by *critical cartographers to expose how *GIS creates particular, *situated versions of geographic truth that do not fully capture the full diversity of spatial relations on the ground.

Further reading Pickles, J. (1994), *Ground Truth: The Social Implications of Geographic Information Systems.*

growth coalition An association made between business leaders, elected officials, government officers, and other elites in order to promote the pro-business growth of a city, usually by luring outside investment in direct competition with other cities. In *Urban Fortunes* (1987) John Logan and Harvey Molotch also used the term 'growth machine' to describe this form of *urban entrepreneurialism. *See also* ENTREPRENEURIAL CITY; REGIME THEORY.

growth pole A geographical location that attracts industries, investment, and workers. The term was popularized by François Perroux in 1949 and is closely linked to the concepts of *agglomeration economies and positive *externalities. It connotes attraction, like a magnetic force pulling things towards it. *See also* TECHNOPOLE.

growth theory Any *theory that aims to explain the causes of economic growth. A set of growth theories exist and not all of them are complementary. Broadly speaking, most theories are 'mainstream': they regard economic growth as good and aim to identify ways of creating and sustaining it, based on empirical research and more abstract modelling and theorization from first principles. Such theories have their origins in *neoclassical economics, but today have offshoots in the fields of business studies, *economic geography, and *regional science. However, a set of more critical growth theories exist that inquire into the ill-effects of economic growth and which, in different ways, take issue with *capitalism—especially in its *neoliberal form. *Marxist political economy in its various forms is an exemplar of critical growth theory, not least because it focuses on economic instability and the cessation of growth.

In human geography, both mainstream and critical growth theories have been prominent. A particular focus has been on the causes of urban and regional scale growth and decline, rather than national level growth. In the 1980s and 1990s, critics drew heavily on ideas contained in *Regulation Theory. Meanwhile, more mainstream approaches departed from the abstract logics of neoclassical reasoning in order to identify real world processes that were leading new cities and regions to enjoy rapid and sustained economic growth. For instance, Allen J. *Scott made much of *transactions costs and how even the most 'footloose' industries benefit from colocation of firms engaged in the same business.

Further reading Scott, A. (2006), *Geography and Economy*, Oxford: Oxford University Press.

growth triangle A *growth pole based on cooperation between three or more countries. The countries may have complementary tax regulations, labour forces, employment laws, industries, and so on, allowing them to realize cross-border *agglomeration economies, *economies of scale, *economies of scope, and positive externalities. Among the first growth triangles was the SIJORI triangle created in 1989, which covered Singapore, Johor (in Malaysia), and the Riau Islands (in Indonesia).

G20 A state-led economic and financial council of wealthy nations consisting of the finance ministers and central bank governors of nineteen countries from around the world, plus the European Union. These major economies represent around 90 per cent of global GDP, 80 per cent of global trade, and two thirds of the world's population. Founded in 2008 it meets semi-annually to discuss the international financial system and promote financial stability and trade.

(⊕) SEE WEB LINKS
• Official website of the G20 2012 Mexico Summit.

Guantánamo Bay A part of southeastern *Cuba best known as the location of a US naval base established under a 1903 treaty, though challenged by the current Cuban government. The base was used to house Haitian and Cuba refugees in the 1990s and then, following the wars in Afghanistan and Iraq, 'unlawful combatants' suspected of being members of Al Qaeda. Four different camps were opened to detain individuals under maximum security conditions outside the Geneva Convention, which normally covers prisoners of war. Critical human geographers have analysed its exceptional juridical and political status (Reid-Henry 2007). *See also* HOMO SACER.

Reference Reid-Henry, S. (2007), 'Exceptional sovereignty? Guantánamo Bay and the re-colonial present', *Antipode* 39: 627–48.

guanxi Within Chinese society, personalized connections and related social networks characterized by relations of reciprocity, i.e. the giving and receiving of favours. Geographers interested in Chinese and East Asian economies note the significance of such personal relationships in the supposedly impersonal world of business networks. Nonetheless, they also caution against essentializing Chinese business as intrinsically different from systems elsewhere.

guestworker programme An agreement between two states over the supply and conditions of temporary migrant workers. It is expected that migrants will not stay beyond a certain period, although in practice this restriction proves difficult or impossible to enforce. Examples include the Mexico–USA *Bracero Program and the *gastarbeiter* schemes negotiated between West Germany and other countries (including Italy, Turkey, and what is now the former Yugoslavia) from the 1950s to 1970s.

Gulf War A *war that took place between 2 August 1990 and 28 February 1991, noted for its live news broadcasting from the front line, along with the regular release of video footage of battles taken by the allied military. The war commenced with the Iraqi invasion of Kuwait. This was followed by international sanctions and from 17 January 1991, Operation Desert Storm, a US-led offensive against Iraq by a UN coalition force from 34 nations. Although a truce was reached within a week of the ground campaign starting, Iraq was not occupied and it continued to be ruled by Saddam Hussein. The subsequent Iraqi War (20 March 2003–30 April 2003), started on the pretext of halting the development of chemical and biological weapons and support for Al Qaeda, led to fall of the Hussein government and eight years of occupation.

Guns, Germs and Steel A phenomenally successful book (and later TV documentary) by Jared *Diamond (1997) addressing the reasons why Eurasian peoples and societies have achieved such dominance in the world. Drawing on a wide range of evidence, Diamond argues that physical geography and biogeography, rather than innate cultural or racial supremacy are the cause. Critics, including human geographers, fault the book for its *environmental determinism and *eurocentrism.

habitus A set of socially learned habits of thinking and action specific to individuals and the groups (e.g. classes or communities) to which they belong. These habits are acquired slowly over time in the arena of everyday life and become normalized—even though those acquiring these habits rarely, if ever, reflect on why the habits are adopted or whether they are good ones to observe. According to French sociologist Pierre *Bourdieu, a person's habitus is both conscious and subconscious, the 'subjective' result of engagement with the 'objective' conditions of a complex, wider social environment. It encompasses norms, values, preferences, and body practices. A habitus is implicated in processes of social distinction, whereby people seek to differentiate themselves from other members of a society by acquiring and deploying different forms of *capital that go well beyond money. A person's habitus can thus be a reflection of but also a challenge to the prevailing relations of power and inequality that characterize a specific society. All habituses have a geography in at least two senses. First, to the extent that everyday life remains rooted in distinct locations and places, habituses necessarily reflect local cultural norms and the character of face-to-face social relationships. Secondly, habituses are all shaped by messages—denotative, connotative, and symbolic—hailing from distant others via the mass media, government communication channels, and so on. Despite the considerable influence of Bourdieu's thinking on Anglophone social scientists, human geographers have not devoted sustained attention to his exploration of the concept of the habitus.

hacktivism The attacking of computer systems in support of political causes. Hacktivists occupy an ambiguous position between state-backed, organized criminal, and terrorist disruptions of computer systems, but can generally be defined as protesters grounded in *civil society. They target governments, companies, organizations, and individuals by—among other acts—stealing and releasing private data, blocking access to websites, defacing websites, and virtual sit-ins. Hacktivism is often linked to campaigns for free speech and transparency. A high-profile example is wikileaks.

Hägerstrand, Torsten (1916–2004) A Swedish geographer who was an early pioneer of *quantitative geography and introduced a number of key ideas into his discipline. Drawing on the *location theories of *Von Thünen and *Christaller, he realized it was possible to use probability theory to study settlement patterns. Based on analysis of migration flows he identified the inverse relationship of movement to distance and the salience of *gravity models. He produced the first simulations of spatial *diffusion and the associated concept of 'mean information field', which defined the probability of ideas or products being adopted in neighbouring areas. He also recognized the need to examine individual actions and not just aggregate patterns, and developed *time-geography which examined *spatial behaviour through time and space. His ideas were widely adopted across the discipline in the wake of the *Quantitative Revolution. Beyond the academy he took an active role in policy work for the Swedish government, including the formulation of new local government divisions, the reorganization of provisional government, and the national land and water-use plan. He spent most of his career at Lund University, Sweden.

Haggett, Peter (1933–) A British quantitative geographer initially based at the University of Cambridge, but who spent most of his career at the University of Bristol. A strong proponent of *spatial science, Haggett was enormously influential in changing the nature, theories, and methods of human geography through the *Quantitative Revolution, and reshaping British school geography. His strategy was threefold. First, he produced ground-breaking quantitative theory and research, especially relating to *location theory and spatial modelling. Second, he wrote engaging and compelling textbooks, notably *Locational Analysis in Human Geography* (1st ed. 1965) and *Geography: A Modern Synthesis* (1st ed. 1972). Third, he organized formative intellectual events and undertook the disciplinary spadework to shape the wider political and policy agenda concerning geography teaching and research. This included a series of symposia organized with Richard Chorley that led to the influential books *Frontiers in Geographical Teaching* (1965) and *Models in Geography* (1967). His views on geography are expressed in the semi-autobiographical book *The Geographer's Art* (1990).

Hall, Peter (1932–) An influential and prolific British geographer and planner who has written broadly on urban and regional *planning and whose work has shaped planning practice globally. In addition to his scholarly research, he has acted as a planning and regeneration advisor to the British and other governments. His best-known books, each published in multiple editions, include *The World Cities* (1st ed. 1966), *Urban and Regional Planning* (1st ed. 1975), and *Cities of Tomorrow* (1st ed. 1988).

Hanson, Susan (1943–) An urban and economic geographer best known for her research on *gender, economy, and local *labour markets, exemplified by her co-authored book *Gender, Work and Space* (1995, with Geraldine *Pratt). This book showed how women negotiated distance to work, job choice, and family commitments in ways that varied according to their class position and were usually different from men. She has made contributions to the study of urban *transportation and sustainability. Her disciplinary service has been considerable, including being the editor of four leading geography journals. She has spent much of her career at Clark University in Massachusetts, USA.

haptic knowledge An understanding of the world gained through the sense of touch. Touch is integral to the way in which humans interact with the world, the means by which people physically connect with their environment, and interact with others and objects. Through haptic perception, humans come to learn the shape and feel of objects and the space around them. And yet, beyond the development of *tactile maps for visually impaired people, touch is largely an overlooked spatial sense and practice in human geography.

Further reading Paterson, M. and Dodge, M. (eds.) (2012), *Touching Space, Placing Touch*.

Haraway, Donna (1944–) A feminist philosopher of science based at the University of California, Santa Cruz, who has made a number of incisive contributions to debates concerning knowledge production, *technology, *nature, and *culture. Haraway's research into the history of biological discourse showed the profound infusion of science by sexism, racism, and colonialism. Her research also accented the liveliness and agency of the non-human world, such that it cannot be treated as a *tabula rasa* on which humans inscribe their wishes. Her work is at once critical but hopeful, identifying possibilities for more just and humane relations between people and the non-human world. Her principal publications are *Primate Visions* (1989), *Simians, Cyborgs and*

Women: The Reinvention of Women (1991), *Modest_Witness@Second_Millennium. FemaleMan$^{(c)}$_Meets_OncoMouse^{TM}* (1997), and *When Species Meet* (2008). *See also* ACTOR-NETWORK THEORY; CYBORG; MASCULINISM.

Harley, J. Brian (1932-91) A leading cartographic historian and theorist, Harley spent most of his career producing detailed empirical research on the history of mapping and map making. In his later years, however, he became interested in cartographic theory and used the writings of Michel *Foucault and Jacques Derrida to argue that maps were *social constructions, imbued with the values of those who created them. Such values could be revealed using the method of *deconstruction. His work challenged the empiricist view that maps were objective representations of phenomena distributed across the Earth's surface. *See also* CARTOGRAPHY; REPRESENTATION.

Harris, Cole (1936-) An emeritus professor of historical geography at the University of British Columbia whose writings have contributed to revisionist histories of colonization in Canada by pointing to the physical and cultural violence of British colonists towards *First Nations in the Pacific Northwest. His research is theoretically informed but also scrupulously empirical. He was an editor of and contributor to the multivolume *Historical Atlas of Canada* and was made an Officer of the Order of Canada in 2004.

Hartshorne, Richard (1899-1992) A highly influential US geographer who significantly shaped post-*Second World War geography in the United States. Having undertaken graduate work at the University of Chicago, he moved to the University of Minnesota in 1924, then to the University of Wisconsin, Madison in 1940. During the Second World War he served as the chief of geography division in the US Office of Strategic Services. Working in the *regional geography tradition, his research focused on economic and political geography and, after sabbatical trips to Europe in the 1930s, drew on German traditions of geographical thinking, especially the work of Alfred *Hettner. His most influential publication was *The Nature of Geography* (1939) in which he set out his vision of the discipline as the study of the *chorological ordering of phenomena through rational principles. The work became a key theoretical and methodological text for a generation of American geographers until challenged by the *Quantitative Revolution.

Harvey, David (1935-) Perhaps the most famous and influential human geographer living today, Harvey is a Marxist who has shown that capitalism does not simply occupy geographical *space but actively makes and remakes it, thus enrolling material landscapes into the reproduction of social inequality. Harvey spent the 1960s working as lecturer in geography at Bristol University, where he first made his name as a philosopher and theorist of *positivism. His landmark book *Explanation in Geography* (1969) gave the profusion of statistical and numerical methods and techniques in 1960s human geography a robust and consistent intellectual foundation. The book systematically explored the nature of scientific explanation in general; the role of theories, hypotheses, laws, and models; the use of mathematics, geometry, and probability as languages of explanation; the nature of observation, data classification, and data representation; and different forms of scientific explanation. *Explanation* served two purposes. First, it gave Harvey's generation of geographers a heavy-weight justification and manifesto for their project of identifying spatial patterns. Unlike an earlier generation concerned with what Fredric *Schaefer had called *'exceptionalism'—the generation that had educated Harvey and his cohort at the University of Cambridge and elsewhere—the so-called 'spatial scientists' who rose to prominence during the 1960s were concerned to identify geographical regularities within and between places. Secondly, *Explanation* served to align the discipline with the so-called 'real' sciences such as physics and, for some geographers, boosted the discipline's self-image. This was achieved by drawing upon the ideas of philosophers of science.

Explanation, ironically, marked both the high-point and the end-point of Harvey's desire to fashion the foundations of a conventionally scientific geography. He moved to the USA and authored *Social Justice and the City* (1973), a book of equal, if very different, significance to its predecessor. As its title suggests, this volume focused on how to alleviate urban ills such as poverty. Where *Explanation* was strangely detached from its wider socio-political context, namely, the attempts of then British Prime Minister Harold Wilson's Labour government to make Britain a fairer society, and the more distant civil rights and anti-Vietnam protests in the USA, *Social Justice* was thoroughly immersed in it. The book charts Harvey's rapidly changing intellectual and political trajectory. Part 1, titled 'Liberal formulations', contains essays that focus on how existing mechanisms of *urban planning could bring about a more just urban society in Western countries. But Part 2, called 'Socialist formulations', moves beyond the reformism of Part 1 and proposes a revolution in urban affairs predicated on the ideas of political economists like *Marx. One of the book's key essays, 'Revolutionary and counter-revolutionary theory in geography and the problem of ghetto formation', proposed nothing less than a wholesale rejection of the way human geographers studied cities and thought about solving urban social problems at that time (*see* THEORY).

Social Justice established Harvey as a major dissenting voice in urban studies and caused quite a stir on publication. It chronicled Harvey's reinvention as a 'radical geographer', and so took many spatial scientists by surprise. Like Gunnar *Olsson's (1975) *Eggs in Bird/Birds in Egg*, *Social Justice* was deliberately schizophrenic. The book also challenged the prevailing view in scientific geography that 'facts' and 'values' can be kept separate. Harvey called for a geography that could study the world in order to change it along more socially just lines. Finally, *Social Justice* was the first major example of a left-wing style of human geography (or *radical geography). Specifically, it opened the door for the subsequent development of *Marxist geography, of which Harvey was to be a pioneer. Harvey's turn to Marxism meant that he became preoccupied with *capitalism and its workings. Yet he did not entirely abandon earlier themes. In *Explanation in Geography*, Harvey was interested in how social processes produce spatial forms, and he ended the book with the declaration that 'Without theory we cannot hope for . . . consistent, and rational, explanation of events' (Harvey, 1969: 486). These two themes animate his essay publications during the 1970s, which are an attempt to fashion a Marxian theory of how geography is produced by and alters the workings of the capitalist economy. By 'geography' Harvey did not mean the discipline of that name, but the material landscape of towns, cities, and transport networks that act as the 'arteries' of capitalism. To fashion this *historical-geographical materialism Harvey spent the mid-to-late 1970s reading Marx's later works, such as *Capital* and *Grundrisse*. This effort culminated in Harvey's most sophisticated book *The *Limits to Capital* (1982). This text is nothing less than a reconstruction and extension of Marx's theory of capitalism; the extensions are primarily geographical because Marx paid little attention to how geography influences capitalism's operation.

In the mid-1980s, with his reputation as the leading Marxist geographer (indeed, human geographer) established, Harvey returned to the specifically urban issues that were the focus of *Social Justice*. Inquiring into the specific nature and problems of capitalist cities, his two 'Studies in the History and Consciousness of Urbanisation' take the perspectives of *structure and agency respectively (to simplify rather). *The *Urbanization of Capital* unfolds a Marxian theory of how capitalism produces cities with characteristic material properties and contradictions; *Consciousness and the Urban Experience* theorizes how real people respond to having to live in capitalist cities, especially those who lack economic and political power (see *The Urban Experience*,

1989a for an accessible collection of Harvey's writings on cities). Shortly after publishing these two books, Harvey returned to England as Halford Mackinder Professor of Geography at the University of Oxford. Leaving Reagan's America for Thatcher's Britain, Harvey felt himself confronted with an increasingly conservative, anti-Marxist British Left and said so in an outspoken critique of UK urban studies (Harvey, 1987). In retrospect, the late 1980s represented the start of a sharp decline of interest among Anglophone academic leftists in Marxism. While at Oxford, Harvey also wrote his bestselling book *The *Condition of Postmodernity*, a critical analysis of the rise of *postmodernism in several walks of contemporary cultural life (including urban consumption, architecture, and even academia). Returning to Hopkins in 1993 for academic and personal reasons, he then revisited the theme of social justice and linked it to environmental issues in his fifth single-authored book as a Marxist, *Justice, Nature and the Geography of Difference* (1996). Harvey later moved to New York University where he is a professor of anthropology. Two collections of essays followed, one a 'greatest hits' volume (*Spaces of Capital*, 2001), the other about the continued relevance of Marxism to the wider project of creating a better socio-environmental future (*Spaces of Hope*, 2000). As the latter book recounts, Harvey's designation as a 'Marxist' represents something very different today in the Anglophone world compared with the early 1970s. Today, Marxism is seen as rather 'old-hat' among radicals, which makes Harvey's continued commitment to it all the more remarkable given the number of post- and ex-Marxists that litter the intellectual landscape (such as Manuel *Castells and Doreen *Massey). His books *The New Imperialism* (2003) and *A Short History of Neoliberalism* (2005) have given the Marxist approach something of a boost, since they have been widely read. They apply Marxian ideas to make sense, respectively, of America's ventures in Iraq and the rise of US-led *neoliberal policy worldwide. More recently, Harvey's *The Enigma of Capital* (2010) can be seen as an accessible version of Marx's magnum opus, *Capital,* updated for the early 21st century.

Further reading Castree, N. and Gregory, D. (eds.) (2006), *David Harvey: a Critical Reader.*
Woodward, K. and Jones, J-P III (2010), 'David Harvey', in *The International Encyclopedia of Human Geography.*

hazard An event or phenomenon with the potential to cause serious harm, including loss of human life and damage to human-environmental systems. The term 'hazard' is often used interchangeably with *disaster, but the latter generally implies an incident that has actually happened. Hazards refer to possible states and are subject to longer-term analysis. In practice however, hazards and disasters are often researched together.

Distinctions are sometimes made between *natural hazards and non-natural or technological hazards such as chemical spills or nuclear power accidents. This distinction shares the same semantic, political, and ontological problems as the differentiation between natural and anthropogenic disasters (*see* DISASTER; MALTHUSIANISM). Within human and environmental geography, the term 'environmental hazard' is generally preferred, leaving open questions of causality. The analysis of hazards relies upon the related concepts of *risk, exposure, *vulnerability, resilience, and mitigation (Mustafa 2009). In this context, risk is an expression of the probability of an occurrence multiplied by the severity of its consequences. By comparison, exposure is a measure of how many people or how much property is at risk; more populated areas are more exposed. But within a given area at risk not all people are equally vulnerable. Vulnerability is a function of the susceptibility of individuals or households to permanent damage, taking into account their ability to recover (Klinenberg 2002). Resilience is the capacity of an individual, household, or place to be restored to pre-disaster conditions. It can be increased by mitigation, measures to minimize the harm from a hazard which may include physical, technological, or engineering solutions such as coastal defences or early warning systems, as well as social interventions such as public information and *disaster preparedness.

Geographical study of hazards has a long pedigree, and it forms an obvious intersection between human and physical geography. Pioneering work by Gilbert F. *White on US flood hazards from the 1940s onwards introduced the important insight that people's response to hazards and risk was partly a matter of perception. Purely engineering responses, such as levees could result in greater risk if it gave people a false sense of security (*see* BEHAVIOURAL GEOGRAPHY; *ENVIRONMENT AS HAZARD, THE*). Roger and Jeanne Kasperson's later work showed the ways in which risks could even be amplified by media, government, and scientific debate. *Political economy and *political ecology approaches to hazard developed from the 1980s, characterized by greater attention to the social causes of hazards and a finer analysis of how age, class, race, and gender were implicated with vulnerability (*see* ENVIRONMENTAL JUSTICE). Such work also reflected on the uneven, unintended, and often unjust consequences of post-disaster recovery and reconstruction, for example, in the wake of the 2004 Indian Ocean tsunami. The diffusion of *Geographic Information Systems and allied technologies of *geospatial intelligence has greatly extended the national and global mapping and monitoring of hazards. *See also* HURRICANE KATRINA; RISK SOCIETY.

References Klinenberg, E. (2002), *Heat Wave: a Social Autopsy of Disaster in Chicago.*
Mustafa, D. (2009), 'Natural hazards', in Castree, N., Demerit, D., Liverman, D. and Rhoads, B. (eds.) *A Companion to Environmental Geography*, 461–74.

health and development There is a well-developed relationship between health and economic development. *Life expectancy is lowest in the lowest-income countries, with a strong association between ill-health and *poverty, poor sanitation, inadequate hygiene, unsafe water, and poor nutrition. On the one hand, people are more exposed to infectious agents, and on the other are weakened to fight such infections. As a result, *mortality rates are high, especially amongst children and other vulnerable groups. In order to tackle such poor health, a two-pronged approach has been taken by the international community—prevention and cure—to improve living conditions, improve diets, and provide access to vaccines and medicines. These programmes have met with mixed success, with absolute and relative poverty rates generally remaining high throughout the *Third World, and economic development weak in many nations.

Further reading Leon, D. and Walt, G. (eds.) (2001), *Poverty, Inequality and Health.*

health geography The study of the relationship between health and place. In particular, health geography is concerned with wellness and *well-being, the socio-spatial relations of health, the everyday spatial lives of people living with medical conditions and *disabilities, the geographies of informal and formal *care, the spatial organization of health services and industries, including alternative and holistic treatments and health tourism, the effects of health policy and how it differs between locations, and the use of *therapeutic landscapes. It is strongly related to *medical geography, which tends to be more biomedically orientated and to use *quantitative methods, focusing on *epidemiology and the distribution and *diffusion of *diseases and access to medical treatment. Sometimes cast as being 'post-medical geography' (Kearns 1993), health geography is more likely to use interpretative methods and engage with critical social theory in its framing and analysis.

References and further reading Athnamatten, P. and Hazen, H. (2011), *An Introduction to Health Geography.*
Brown, T., McLafferty, S., and Moon, G. (2009), *A Companion to Health and Medical Geography.*
Gesler, W. and Kearns, R. (2002), *Culture/Health/Place.*
Kearns, R. (1993), 'Place and health: towards a reformed medical geography', *The Professional Geographer* 45: 139–47.

health inequality An unequal access to good health and health services. The health status of people varies as a function of, among other things, income and socio-economic standing; those who are wealthy tend to have better living conditions, diets, and access to medicines and treatments. In countries such as the United States, where health care is largely provided privately, funded by health insurance, inequities in access to health services can be acute. Across a population there is also unequal access due to geographic location, with people in rural areas likely to have to travel much further to avail themseves of health care.

Further reading Curtis, S. (2004), *Health and Inequality: a Geographic Perspective.*

Heartland, the A strategically important region covering part of Eurasia. The term originates with British geographer Sir Halford *Mackinder, who first identified a 'geographical pivot of history' in 1904. In two later revisions, he renamed the pivot 'the Heartland', a region largely inaccessible from the sea and then approximately corresponding with Russia (later the USSR) and Central Asia. According to his Heartland thesis (1919), whichever power controlled this region would be in a position to control ('rule') the world as a whole (*see* GEOPOLITICS). It provided a natural fortress from which land-based power could resist sea-based power. He intended the thesis as a warning to Britain and its allies, chiefly the USA, not to underestimate the threat of Germany and/or Russia. Later geopoliticians, such as Saul B. Cohen, adapted the concept and it may have informed the subsequent US strategy of trying to contain the USSR during the *Cold War. Even a century after first proposing the idea, the Heartland thesis and concept receives serious attention within and outside the region itself.

Further reading *The Geographical Journal* (2004) special issue on 'Halford Mackinder the "geographical pivot of history"', 170(4).

Heavily Indebted Poor Country (HIPC) A country identified as needing assistance with managing its external debt burden under the terms of a joint initiative of the *International Monetary Fund and *World Bank launched in 1995. Thirty-six countries receive debt-relief (thirty in Africa), which is conditional on, among other things, the formulation of a *poverty reduction strategy. *See also* MILLENNIUM DEVELOPMENT GOALS.

hedonic pricing A statistical modelling method for breaking down the price of a good into the component parts that determine that price. An example might be a house, the price of which combines many separate factors such as location, form, and number of bedrooms. Although widely used in the analysis of housing markets, hedonic methods have been taken up in estimating the economic cost of ecosystem services where these are not directly measureable. Surrogate or proxy variables are used; for example, the higher price of housing near a city park can be considered to reveal consumers' preferences for the location.

hegemony A form of power exercised through consent rather than coercion and the resulting condition of relatively uncontested dominance. The domination of some people by others is usually thought to involve some level of violence or force. But writing in the 1930s, Italian Marxist Antonio Gramsci argued that the bourgeoisie achieved their power through gaining the consent of those governed; this also accounted for why the working class did not revolt. Later *Marxists, notably Stuart Hall, interpreted hegemony as constructing common sense understandings, i.e. a class or political party (in this case the Conservatives under Margaret Thatcher) achieved hegemonic power by crafting the taken-for-granted nature of, for example, racial difference or inequality (*see* THATCHERISM). Post-Marxists extended hegemony beyond social *class to include the ways that the meanings of social differences, including *gender, *race, and *sexuality, were fixed and linked together to form naturalized hierarchies. A radical democratic politics, according to Ernesto Laclau and Chantal Mouffe, required counter-hegemonic elements. Some geographers, informed by *feminism and *post-structuralism, pursued this line of thinking to uncover how hegemonic understandings of difference were achieved (*see* IDENTITY POLITICS). A separate line of work focuses on a more geopolitical understanding of hegemony, how certain states have historically achieved world domination not simply by military force, but through shaping the rules and institutions of international relations. According to this perspective, past hegemons might include the Netherlands (17th century), Britain (19th century), and the USA (1945–67) (*see* PAX AMERICANA). Agnew and Corbridge argue that hegemony now lies not in a single state, but in an interlocking system of political and economic dominance including both states and non-state actors such as international financial institutions.

Reference Agnew, J. and Corbridge, S. (1995), *Mastering Space*.

heritage The legacy of people, culture, and environments inherited from the past. In its broadest sense, heritage includes natural and built landscapes, physical artefacts, and cultural forms (e.g. music, literature, art, folklore, monuments), intangible culture (values and traditions, customs and practices, spiritual beliefs, language), and biological traits. Heritage is considered important because it connects people with the past and affirms and reproduces cultural identity. *UNESCO has designated a number of world heritage sites considered to be of global significance. *See also* HERITAGE CONSERVATION; HERITAGE INDUSTRY.

heritage conservation The deliberate preservation and conservation of *heritage. This includes the identification, restoration, and protection of significant heritage items from the past (including buildings and landscapes), the collecting, archiving, and display of cultural artefacts and forms, and programmes and policy designed to protect and promote important aspects of cultural identity, such as dialects and national languages.

heritage industry The commodification of *heritage into a consumable commodity, most often as tourist attractions. It is a multi-billion dollar industry and can include museums, heritage sites, *cultural quarters, and artefacts such as books, CDs, and virtual tours. While the heritage industry plays an important role in *heritage conservation and the promotion of cultural identity, it is often critiqued for producing inauthentic, sentimental, nostalgic, patronizing, *hyperreal, and uncritical accounts wherein the past is gentrified and rewritten, often from a *presentist perspective.

Further reading Hewison, R. (1987), *The Heritage Industry*.

hermeneutics The interpretation of *texts or, more broadly, of those media in and through which people convey meaning. Hermeneutics involves the analyst seeking to look beyond their own 'horizon of meaning' in order to truly understand how another person, group, or culture interprets the world. In human geography, the hermeneutic method and sensibility were central to the development of *humanistic geography from the 1970s onwards.

heteronormativity The assumption that normal and natural expressions of *sexuality in society are heterosexual in nature. A heteronormative society is structured morally, socially, and legally to position other forms of sexuality as deviant and to discriminate against non-heterosexuals. The dominance of heteronormativity as an ideological position forwarded by state and church meant that homosexuality was illegal in most countries, though it has been recently decriminalized in many Western states. *See also* GAY GEOGRAPHIES; HETEROPATRIARCHY; LESBIAN GEOGRAPHIES.

heteropatriarchy The supposition that the normal expression of heterosexuality in society is one of a married couple. Such a normative view of heterosexual relations is expressed through everyday discourse, the media, welfare systems, the law, and moral panics with respect to casual sex, promiscuity, one-parent families, illegitimacy, pornography, and prostitution. *See also* FEMINISM; HETERONORMATIVITY.

heterotopia Any real or metaphorical space that permits thought and action that noticeably departs from the conventions of a society. The term was discussed by Michel *Foucault in the late 1960s, and since then many critical human geographers have used it when discussing 'alternative' identities, lifestyles, and political programmes.

Hettner, Alfred (1859–1941) A German geographer who had a considerable influence on the development of German geography and whose ideas shaped American geography in the mid-20th century, notably through the work of Richard *Hartshorne. Hettner completed his doctorate at the University of Strasburg in 1881 on the climate of Chile and Patagonia. He travelled to South America in 1882–84 and 1888–90, principally to study its geomorphology, though on the second trip he discovered the work of Alexander von *Humboldt, leading him to consider the methodological foundations of the discipline. He was made an associate professor at Leipzig University in 1894 and the following year founded the journal *Geographische Zeitschrift*, which he edited for forty years. He moved to the University of Heidelberg in 1899 as its first professor of geography. Over the course of his career he argued for geography to be the comparative science of regions with a unified methodology centred on *chorology to replace the prevalent, fragmented general earth science approach of the late 19th century.

heuristic A device intended to help solve a problem *en route* to a more definitive solution. Using their experience, a person devises a means—for instance, conceptual, computational, or practical—for approximating a more robust solution which may, in turn, follow. In human geography, as in much social science, a heuristic is typically an outline concept, theory, model, or philosophy designed to be refined in the conduct of research.

hierarchical models *Models organized into a hierarchy of layers of successively higher-level units (sometimes called multi-level models). For example, houses are in streets, streets are in neighbourhoods, neighbourhoods are in cities, cities are in states, and so on. In a hierarchical model it becomes possible to describe outcomes for an individual household as a sum of effects for the household, for the street, for the neighbourhood, for the city, and for the state. In other words, the exchangeable collection of effects within and between layers can be taken account of in the model. Once a hierarchical model has been specified, inferences can be drawn from available data for making estimations at any level (e.g., street, neighbourhood, city, etc.). These estimates generally have better properties than sample-based estimates calculated using data only from the layer in question. This makes hierarchical models useful in cases where there is a limited amount of information, especially at the lower layers (the problem of small-area estimation). They are usually applied to model data from large, complex surveys such as *censuses, given their hierarchical data structure.

high-touch work Labour that involves physical contact with the bodies of other people, such as caring, nursing, and *sex work (*see* CARE). By contrast with 'hi-tech' work, it is generally low-status and low-paid, overwhelmingly associated with feminized skills such as caring, empathy, and servicing the needs of others, and undertaken by women. It may involve the 'dirty work' of dealing with the bodily wastes and odours of clients.

hi-tech industry An industry characterized by cutting-edge, usually complex technology, in the process of production and the final product manufactured. The term originated in the United States in the late 1960s but it has no fixed referents for the simple reason that yesterday's hi-tech industries may today seem decidedly low-technology. What is more, the term threatens to create the false impression that more traditional industries—such as mining—lack technological sophistication. Regardless, today's hi-tech industries are usually said to include the following: biotechnology (including agricultural biotechnology), telecommunications, computation and information technology, aerospace, medical instruments and devices, robotics, nanotechnology, and artificial intelligence. Aside from their advanced technical character, if these industries have anything in common it is that they are perceived to be 'clean', in contrast with 'dirty' industries such as steel manufacture. Perceived is the operative word, however, when one takes into account the problems of disposing of the chemicals used in computer manufacture, for example, and of obsolete products in general. Most hi-tech industries begin life with a few start-up companies whose risk of commercial failure is high, and which often seek to attract *venture capital. The social media website Facebook is a notable example of such a start-up venture that has succeeded spectacularly.

In *economic geography and the field of urban and regional planning, hi-tech industries became a significant focus of research activity in the 1980s. Because of the success of *Silicon Valley in California, researchers became interested in which sorts of *places were likely to produce hi-tech start-up firms, subsequently becoming *growth poles for the industries they pioneered. Mainstream researchers focused on the distribution of factors of production, such as labour (in the case of hi-tech, well-educated and usually young entrepreneurs). In public policy terms their analyses often led to prescriptions for what measures might be devised to attract hi-tech start-ups. More critical researchers focused on wider processes of uneven geographical development, in which the decline of some areas—such as America's *Rustbelt of the 1980s—was linked to transfers of *capital to areas with higher economic potential. These researchers took a less booster ish perspective on hi-tech industries. Since the 1980s, economics geographers have focused less on different industries when compared to their forebears. Instead, they have tended to focus on the processes of agglomeration and dispersal (*see* GLOBALIZATION) common to otherwise different industries. Consequently, few economic geographers are today specialists in the spatial dynamics of hi-tech industries. Typically, hi-tech industries are profitable when compared with other industries. Many countries consider them to be a key element of the industrial mix required to create a 'knowledge economy' in which mental rather than manual labour becomes the norm.

Hinduism The predominant religion of the Indian subcontinent and its *diaspora. It is composed of a common but not unified set of theological and philosophical points of view that prescribe morality and ways of being; it does not have a single deity (though most Hindus believe in a Supreme God), a principal prophet, a set scripture, and a rigid set of beliefs. Hindus believe that existence is a cycle of birth, death, and rebirth, shaped by Karma (every action has an equal reaction either immediately or at some point in the future), wherein the soul passes through successive lives with the next incarnation dependent on how the previous life was lived. It is sometimes considered more of a faith than a religion given the absence of an organized church-like structure.

hinterland The region surrounding a city from which it draws resources and to which it provides services. The term originally referred to the area from which exports were funnelled to ports and into which imports flowed. In *Imperial San Francisco* (1999), Gray Brechin uses the Italian word *contado* to describe the territory dominated by a city, implying a less benign relationship. *See also* CITY-REGION.

HIPC *See* HEAVILY INDEBTED POOR COUNTRY.

historical demography The quantitative analysis of populations in the historical past. The main challenge for historical demographers is how to determine demographic variables in the absence of regular and comprehensive population *censuses and/or reliable records of births, deaths, and marriages (vital or civil registration). Such data sources were not begun in Europe until the late 18th and early 19th centuries, and much later elsewhere. To this end, researchers have devised sophisticated mathematical techniques for extracting information on such things as birth, death, and marriage rates from a variety of sources, including parish records, mortality bills, testamentary records, and family or household registers. These techniques were pioneered by Louis Henry in France in the 1960s and later adopted by E. A. (Tony) Wrigley and colleagues at the Cambridge Group for the History of Population, founded in 1964. Chief among these is family reconstitution, a method and procedure for linking marriages, baptisms, and burials throughout a family tree. Such methods reveal important data such as the timing of marriage, the timing and spacing of births, the level of births outside marriage, and so forth. Wrigley and his colleagues, for example, demonstrated that in 17th-century England, variations in fertility, not mortality—as one might expect from demographic transition models—were uppermost in population change (Wrigley and Schofield 1981). Historical demographers have gradually compiled hundreds of local accounts of population change, contributing to a greater understanding of large-scale demographic events, and their often significant geographical variation.

Reference Wrigley, E. A. and Schofield, R.S. (eds.) (1981),*The Population History of England, 1541–1871: A Reconstruction.*

historical-geographical materialism A term for versions of Marxist *political economy that pay close attention to patterns of spatial organization and processes of spatial change, as much as to processes of temporal continuity and change. The term was coined by David *Harvey, in part as a criticism of *Marxism's traditional focus on time rather than space—encapsulated in the term '*historical materialism', long used as a synonym for Marxism *tout court*. Among the most important historical geographical materialists is Henri *Lefebvre.

historical geography A specialism within *human geography that is interested in the geography of the past and its influence on the present. The relations between the academic disciplines of history and geography have generally been close (especially in the French tradition) although not always; geography's preoccupation with *spatial science came partly at the expense of a historical perspective. The traffic of ideas, methods, individuals between the disciplines, the shared subject matter, and the many organized collaborations have made it difficult to discern a distinct subdiscipline of historical geography. A recent attempt to do so by Alan Baker, distinguishes historians' focus on 'period' from geographers' concern for 'place', while acknowledging that both are constructed by 'people' and a complete understanding requires knowledge of all three. In recent years, informed by a trend towards interdisciplinarity as well as a general historical sensibility across human geography, there has been a clear tendency to relax about the field's identity. Despite a relative decline in the number of dedicated postholders and academic courses in historical geography *per se*, self-identified historical geographers regularly express confidence in its health.

The current foci of historical geographical research differ between countries, but in general there are several key themes. Macro-scale studies of world-systems (*see* WORLD-SYSTEMS APPROACH) search for patterns in political, economic, and technological change, often overlapping with economic historians' interest in the development of *capitalism. *Colonialism and *imperialism form another subject area, often informed by *cultural studies into race, gender, and identity. Historical geographies of environment are particularly common in North America, New Zealand, and Australia (*see* ENVIRONMENTAL HISTORY), where the impact of human settlement in modern historical times is a pressing issue. Colonialism and environment are important to understanding and addressing the *land rights of *indigenous peoples. A significant contribution here is *The Historical Atlas of Canada*, in three volumes (1987–93). Historians of science have recently turned to geographical ideas, most notably to uncover the spatiality of science, contributing to a growing body of work on the historical geography of science, including geography and *cartography (*see* GEOGRAPHY, HISTORY OF). In Western Europe and North America the historical geography of capitalism, including its varied regional, urban, and rural manifestations, remains a well-established field of interest (*see* HISTORICAL DEMOGRAPHY). These and other subject areas are approached from the full spectrum of geographical methods and epistemologies. There is an important strand of *feminist historical geography, one intention of which is to dispute the ideas of progressive human betterment by uncovering hidden historical geographies. Because many records and maps are now digitized, *Geographic Information Systems are also deployed in historical geography. For the most part, historical geography focuses on periods and places for which there is some written record. Researchers in this field share with historians the training required to interpret archival documents and an ability to write *monographs.

The present mood of eclecticism and diversity found within historical geography is not necessarily found in the past. What historical geography is has changed over time, and there have been many programmatic statements about it. In the early 20th century, many geographers regarded physical geography as the foundation of historical understanding, for example, Albert P. Brigham in *Geographic Influences in American History* (1903) (*see* ENVIRONMENTAL DETERMINISM). An alternative tradition crystallized in France, where the long-run interdependence of people and environment at a regional scale was examined by both geographers and historians, notably in Lucien Febvre's *La terre et l'évolution humáine* (1922) (*see* ANNALES SCHOOL; POSSIBILISM). In the USA, the *Berkeley School typified a cultural-historical approach, concerned with cultural *diffusion and landscape change. At Wisconsin University, Andrew Hill Clark inspired studies of regional economies from a historical perspective from the 1960s. His British contemporary, Sir Clifford *Darby, did most to formulate a distinct historical geography. Consisting of the study of past geographies, the understanding of the effect of physical geography on history, and the course of landscape change, from his base at the University of Cambridge, he exerted significant influence on a generation of human geographers. The foundation of the *Journal of Historical Geography* in 1975 and *Historical Geography* in 1982 was an important milestone, providing scholars in the field with a greater sense of institutional identity.

References and further reading Baker, A. R H. (2003), *Geography and History: Bridging the Divide*. Domosh, M. and Morin, K. M. (2003), 'Travels with feminist historical geography', *Gender, Place and Culture*, 10(3): 257–64.

(⊕) SEE WEB LINKS

- Website of *Historical Atlas of Canada* Online Learning Project.
- Historical Geography Specialty Group of the Association of American Geographers.

historical materialism An approach to the study of modern society originated by Karl *Marx, with Friedrich Engels, which places the dynamics of economic activity at the heart of the analysis (*see* MARXISM). Marx was critical of the *idealism of 19th-century German philosophers who proposed that new ideas were the engine of social and cultural change and progress. His materialist philosophy proposed that in even the most advanced societies the production of goods and services to meet people's biological and socio-cultural needs remained central to the organization of the entire society. In this sense he had something in common with 'classical economists' such as Adam Smith, but was critical of *neoclassical economists because they represented economic activity as a set of transactions between agents seeking to satisfy their preferences in the context of scarce resources (money, education, non-liquid assets, and so on). Marx regarded neoclassical economics as reductive and simplistic because it focused on individual agents (workers, consumers, firms), it ignored relations of *power between different social groups, and because it depicted economic transactions as largely 'rational', with agents aiming to maximize 'utility' in light of their preferences and resource constraints.

Marx's materialism placed the analysis of *capitalism at its centre. He (and Engels) argued that capitalism is an historically unique economic system that has four distinctive characteristics. First, it is geared towards the incessant search for profit: firms produce commodities as a means to the end of accumulating more wealth than was expended at the beginning of the production process. Second, the search for profits drives technical innovation in both production processes and the commodities produced. Third, though commodity exchange is nominally egalitarian—you pay for what you get, or get paid what you deserve—for Marx and Engels it is the moment when the true origins of profit are routinely concealed. Exchange between individual economic agents, they argued, belies the class inequalities that structure capitalist economic activity. Wage workers are paid less than the value they create when employed by firms, meaning that they are the source of firm profits while being exploited by capitalists—even when it appears they receive a 'fair wage'. Finally, because capitalism is profit-orientated, technologically dynamic yet dependent on wage workers to be profitable, Marx and Engels argued that it is a contradictory system. Periodically, the contradictions become so acute as to lead to widespread economic crises—for instance, by replacing workers with more efficient machinery ('forces of production'), capitalists can cut labour costs (thus dictating the terms of the 'relations of production'), but in the long run they create higher unemployment, meaning fewer consumers can afford to buy the commodities they are selling. As a result firms can go bankrupt, leading to still higher unemployment, and possible social unrest.

Marx and Engels were *historical* materialists in the sense that they accented the temporal dynamism of capitalism, its propensity to squeeze out non-capitalist modes of production over time, and its chronic crisis tendencies. *See also* HISTORICAL-GEOGRAPHICAL MATERIALISM.

historicism 1. An approach to understanding human affairs that focuses on the prior circumstances leading up to an event.

2. An approach to understanding human affairs that regards the present as the predictable outcome of past processes. Historicism in the first sense is a deeply contextual approach to *description and *explanation—the opposite of *reductionism and *essentialism. In the second sense, historicism has been seen by some critics as a signal failing of orthodox versions of *Marxism (*see* TELEOLOGY).

history of geography *See* GEOGRAPHY, HISTORY OF.

HIV/AIDS *See* AIDS.

holism An approach to understanding the human and/or biophysical worlds that places any given phenomena in the much wider context of the multiple relations that together comprise systems (ecological, economic, political, etc.). Holists see reality as more than the sum of its parts because the whole is able to react to changes to the parts. They reject atomism and reductionism (the former seeks to identify the elemental units of a system, while the latter seeks to explain complex or emergent phenomena with reference to the behaviour or potentialities of these units). Holistic thinking has been prominent in a wide range of social sciences, biophysical sciences, and humanities subjects. In human geography it is, historically, most closely associated with *Marxism. Marx considered *capitalism to be a functional system that was in a state of dynamic disequilbrium leading to economic crises that, depending on the circumstances, would lead to capitalism's demise or else a new phase of *accumulation. The relational ontology he advocated prevented him from separating parts from wholes. For instance, Marx regarded money less as a thing or token, and more as the phenomenal form assumed by the ensemble of relationships between capitalists, financiers, and workers.

One criticism of 'strong' (or 'organic') versions of holism is that they over-emphasize the unity or integrity of the system in question. This kind of holism posits that one can analyse any part of a system and soon see the totality of relations and elements that comprise the system in its entirety. It is a kind of holism evident in David *Harvey's most complete analysis of capitalism, *The *Limits to Capital* (1982). However, even Marxists do not treat all elements of the whole as being of equal importance. For instance, they argue that *finance capital is ultimately parasitic upon and responsive to the dynamics of productive (or 'real') capital. However, for some critics a qualification like this does not rescue strong holism from its failings. For example, *critical realists have made the argument that most systems are open not closed: that is, they interact with other systems whose 'logics' might be very different. This can create interference and unexpected (though not necessarily random) effects. Relatedly, Andrew *Sayer also emphasizes stratification and *emergence. The former refers to the layering of social and/or biophysical reality. Lower-level phenomena (such as atoms or individuals) do not directly constitute higher level phenomena (such as a river or a culture), even though they are part of these phenomena. The latter refers to processes or phenomena that are produced as a result of the confluence of ostensibly separate phenomena. For instance, a crowd of individuals can do things and have effects that are simply impossible for individuals alone or small groups. Crowds thus have emergent powers that are irreducible to the individual capacities of the people comprising them. Related to these critical realist insights, some neo- or post-Marxists talked about 'over-determination'. This is an onto-logical maxim that any event, change, or continuity is likely the result of multiple causal processes interacting together. Scrutiny of one or two of these causes is thus unlikely to explain the phenomena under examination. Though many strong holists accept the force of these arguments, some nonetheless insist that what is special about capitalism is its capacity to subsume non-capitalist phenomena to its own logics. Capitalism is thus said to be 'totalizing'.

Other commentators have observed that different systems operate in ways that are ontologically different. This means that while some systems might be amenable to the analysis of 'strong' holists, others may demand a different approach. For instance, pro-ponents of *chaos, catastrophe, and complexity theory argue that some systems can cross thresholds and assume a qualitatively different character, including erratic behaviour that borders on instability. While this may seem like the antithesis of holism, it still holds fast to a relational ontology in which processes and relations assume priority over parts.

hollowing out 1. The relative decline of occupations providing middle-level incomes in a labour market or class structure; a form of *social polarization in which job growth is concentrated in high- and low-wage sectors.
2. The redistribution of functions and capacities from a corporation or state to other bodies. In the case of the *Keynesian *welfare state, this leads to multilevel *governance where the private sector and civil society organizations take over some aspects of welfare provision. Although one implication is that only the shell of the state is left, Bob Jessop

advises that this does not in fact spell the decline of the *state, which retains key powers. *See also* GOVERNANCE; NEOLIBERALISM.

Holocaust The systematic persecution and genocide of the Jews of Europe by the Nazis in Germany and their collaborators prior to and during the *Second World War; sometimes called Shoah or the Final Solution. It is estimated that approximately six million Jews were murdered in concentration and forced labour camps, *ghettos, and by mobile extermination units, along with disabled people, homosexuals, and other political and religious groups deemed undesirable by the Nazi regime. There is substantial geographical research on the Holocaust.

Further reading Gilbert, M. (4th ed. 2009), *The Routledge Atlas of the Holocaust.*

home A place of residence invested with a diverse set of subjective feelings and expectations that distinguish it from other sites, most notably in modern capitalist societies, places of *work. Home is a complex term whose meaning varies historically and culturally. It refers to something both real and imagined, and material and subjective; it is associated with intimacy and personal autonomy on the one hand, but is the object of materialist consumption and state regulation on the other.

A national *census generally asks each individual where their place of 'usual residence' is. This is assumed to be a physical site, a bounded structure of some sort, for example, a shack, apartment, or mansion. It is thought to be a *private space where individuals enjoy a greater level of freedom over their behaviour and expression than in *public space. It may even be *property, allowing the individual to exclude others as they wish. It is usually also assumed to be a place where waged labour does not occur, although there are exceptions. But the concept of home is not captured by this legal, physical, objective definition alone. There is a subjective dimension. A sense of home, a bundle of heightened human emotions relating to oneself or one's intimate companions (human and animal) may be concentrated on a place of residence, or it may be more mobile and dispersed. Migrants and peripatetic peoples reveal the possibility of home being located in more than one place at a time (*see* TRANSNATIONAL COMMUNITIES). What these emotions are is partly a matter of personal circumstances and cultural norms. In the Western ideal of home, these include feelings of familiarity, comfort, intimacy, belonging, or rootedness. But, as *feminist geographers and others have demonstrated, home can also be a place of *fear, *violence, and distress. As an ideal, home is a refuge from waged labour and the site where individuals can constitute themselves as citizens. But in reality, home can equally be the place of inter-personal conflict as well as labour exploitation (*see* DOMESTIC WORK). Its boundaries are porous, open to flow of materials and information, subject to regulations on such things as *sexuality, and the object of *governmentality (*see* LIBERTARIAN PATERNALISM).

Further reading Blunt, A. and Dowling, R. (2006), *Home.*
Hanson, S. and Pratt, G. (1995), *Gender, Work and Space.*

homeland A country or place of origin. An individual's homeland is usually where they were born and raised. But when referring to ethnic or national groups, 'homeland' implies a place of deeply rooted bonds of ancestry and belonging. Hence it is often a focus of *nationalism, not least among populations dispersed in *diasporas. *See also* HOME.

homelessness A condition of being without shelter in situations where this is the social norm. In urbanized societies a secure place of residence is regarded as a necessity or even a right (*see* HOME). Not only is it a place where one can sleep, bathe, eat, raise children, and socialize, but it is also important for well-being in general, and for access to public services such as the post. Homelessness is therefore a major social problem, with many causes (e.g., financial, mental health, fleeing domestic issues) and a number of social consequences for those homeless. The issue is tackled through social policy and charity and housing initiatives that provide shelter and supports, but also through *zero-tolerance programmes that prevent homeless people from living in certain locations such as *central business districts.

Further reading Cloke, P., May, J., and Johnsen, S. (2010), *Swept-up Lives: Re-Envisioning the Homeless City.*
Wolch, J. and Dear, M. (2003), *Malign Neglect: Homelessness in an American City.*

homo economicus A representation of humans that depicts them as rational beings who will choose the best means to achieve their ends given any particular set of options and resource constraints. This representation first assumed importance in *neoclassical economics. In geography, it featured in the economic, urban, and agricultural subdisciplines as part of the transition to *spatial science. The critique of such an assumption is that people often do not act rationally, but rather act in paradoxical or contradictory ways that do not necessarily serve their best interests, and about which it is difficult to generalize and model.

homo sacer A person who is located outside the law, whose life is deemed of no value and who may therefore be killed with impunity. Meaning 'sacred man' in Latin, the term originally referred to certain categories of person under Roman law. In recent years it has been elaborated by Italian political theorist Giorgio Agamben to explore the ways in which sovereign power relegates some persons to states of 'bare life', i.e. exposed to violence. Geographers interested in prisons, immigrant detention centres, and sites of extreme state violence have used and reflected on this concept (*see* GUANTÁNAMO BAY). *See also* BIOPOLITICS.

Further reading Minca, C. (2005), 'The return of the camp', *Progress in Human Geography*, 29: 405–12.

Hong Kong A major metropolis located in East Asia that was a British colony for 156 years until ceded or returned to China in 1997. Its population is seven million, which is highly concentrated to make it one of the densest cities in the world. Though a Chinese city, it retains many customs, rules, and procedures from the period of British rule, and acts as an important conduit for trade between East Asia and the rest of the world.

Hoskins, William George (1908–92) An influential British historian who championed the development of local history. Although he initially trained and worked as an economist, he is best known for his research on landscape history. His key contribution was the book *The Making of the English Landscape* (1955), which was made into a BBC television documentary in 1976, *The Landscape of England*. Both detailed the influence of human activity on the physical landscape over long periods of time. His work has influenced the *heritage and environmental *conservation movements.

hospitality 1. The practice of making guests feel welcome and valued.
2. The individual and collective disposition to acknowledge the claims of others. With respect to *tourism geography, hospitality is an important component of how the tourism industry operates, and how businesses and places market themselves. Hotels, casinos, resorts, spas, and tourist information services form the hospitality service industry. Hospitality has also been considered in geography and moral philosophy with respect to the ethics of care and justice, and responsibilities to proximate and distant strangers and *others, drawing on the ideas of Emmanuel Levinas and Jacques Derrida.

Further reading Barnett, C. (2005), 'Ways of relating: hospitality and the acknowledgement of otherness', *Progress in Human Geography* 29(1): 5–21.

Hotelling model An economic model developed by Harold Hotelling in 1929 that concerns locational decision-making. His famous hypothetical model concerned the location of two ice-cream vendors on a beach and the optimal location for each given an even distribution of sunbathers along the beach's length, which turns out to be midway along its length and close to each other. The example can be extended to two politicians along a political spectrum seeking votes, and so on, and can also be calibrated for associated costs such as travel and product price. The model is used to understand the strategies adopted by competing interests trying to position themselves favourably to attract custom.

hotspot A geographical clustering of cases that differs from the expected distribution of cases. A common example occurs when mapping crime rates. When crimes are plotted on a map it is often the case that some areas will have a disproportionate share of cases. These areas are crime hotspots, where the incidence of crime is higher than elsewhere. It is important that the mapping of such crime incidents is standardized against population and other salient factors, as proportionally one would expect more crimes to occur in areas of high population.

household A group of people sharing a residential unit who pool their income to support one another. More than one household might share a property. Household is often held to be synonymous with a nuclear family unit, but this reflects a *heteropatriarchical view that does not reflect all varieties of household (which could include people living alone, extended families, non-heterosexual families, or a group of unrelated people). The household is an important unit of analysis in the social sciences because it is the basic unit through which economic production, consumption, childcare, and other daily activities are organized and practised. As such, statistics agencies often generate data through household surveys. This data is analysed using a range of statistical techniques, including *hierarchical models, designed to provide an insight into the nature and functioning of households and, through *aggregation, wider society.

housing All forms of permanent and fixed accommodation, chiefly apartments (flats) and houses. The provision of housing of sufficient quantity, quality, and affordability is one of the central problems of all modern societies, whether in the *Global North or *Global South. Housing provides the necessities of shelter, a place to eat, sleep, raise children, and store one's belongings, which has both material and psychological benefits (*see* HOME). But in many contexts it is also a mark of status and a store of wealth itself. The tension between housing as a necessity and an investment is the source of potential conflict. The 2007–2009 global financial crisis was triggered by the so-called '*subprime mortgage crisis', when relatively low-income households in the USA were enticed into taking on house-related loans beyond their means.

Housing is obtained in a number of ways, each of which can be described in terms of a different tenure and housing class. Many people construct dwellings either individually, or with family and community help. Self-built housing, sometimes called *shanty towns, is relatively common throughout much of the Global South. While such people may own their dwellings, they may not necessarily own the land upon which they have built (*see* SQUATTING).

The second main form of tenure is 'social' or 'public' housing, rented by families and individuals from the government or a non-profit organization specializing in accommodation. The collective production and allocation of housing began in the Global North in the early 20th century and was closely associated with the *welfare state and *socialist or *communist governments (*see* COLLECTIVE CONSUMPTION). State housing was also an element of post-war modernization in the Global South, exemplified by Hong Kong and Singapore. But in the late 20th century, some governments inspired by *neoliberal-ism sought to reduce direct investment in social housing and sell off their housing stock either to sitting tenants, NGOs, or private landlords. Where once it might have accom-modated 30–40 per cent of households, social housing in countries such as the UK became associated with low-income and vulnerable households. This process is known as 'residualization' or 'socio-tenurial polarization'. But in other countries the social housing sector remains highly significant, accommodating up to half of the residents of some Dutch cities, for example.

The third way of obtaining housing is through the 'housing market', i.e. the set of agencies, institutions, and regulations by which housing is produced and sold. Under such conditions, housing is not an entitlement but a *commodity. But, unlike most other material commodities, housing is fixed in location. This means that its market or *exchange value is partly conditional on the surrounding environment (*see* EXTERNALI-TIES). Housing type is often organized spatially with similar types of dwelling built in distinct areas; this can sustain its market value and lead to the creation of often localized housing submarkets and particular kinds of classed communities (*see* SUBUR-BANIZATION). Private housing can be rented or owned. Private renting is a common tenure across much of Europe and South America, although it is founded on a potentially exploitative relationship between landlord and tenants (*see* RENT). Where bought, hous-ing is likely to be the largest single market transaction an individual or family makes. It is usual to have to borrow funds in the form of loans and mortgages for this purchase, linking housing into the wider financial system (*see* FINANCIALIZATION). Between 1980 and 2010 housing represented an attractive investment for many ordinary households in wealthier societies, resulting in cumulative personal debt. In the UK, for example, households bought additional properties with low-interest loans in order to secure rental income, the so-called 'buy-to-let' market (*see* SECOND HOMES). Houses can be a long-term investment as well as a source of collateral for short-term borrowing, but this is accompanied by significant risks if the housing market weakens. As a form of *property, housing may be inherited, which has implications for *wealth inequality more generally.

Geographers are interested in changing tenure patterns and the complex links between housing and financial markets, but also study the various forms of discrimination and exclusion around housing (*see* REDLINING; SEGREGATION).

Further reading Smith, S. J. (ed.) (2012), *The International Encyclopedia of Housing and Home*.

How to Lie with Maps A book providing an engaging and well illustrated narrative by Mark Monmonier (1996) that examined the ways in which *maps have long been used for propaganda and ideological purposes to produce particular ways of looking at the world. Moreover, it detailed how all maps inherently tell partial truths due to issues of selectivity, generalization, and the intent of its makers.

hub-and-spoke network A form of network where the majority of paths connect to each other through central nodes. The archetypal example is the route map of an airline, where numerous shorter routes link to connecting nodes, that are themselves linked together. Such a network is highly effective at linking nodes together through a small number of paths, though it may be inefficient in terms of distance travelled. Other examples include communications infrastructure such as the Internet. These networks are often analysed using *graph theory.

***hukou* system** A population registration system used by China's authorities in an attempt to control *internal migration. Codified in 1958, it specifies for each individual whether they are an agricultural or non-agricultural worker, and their local authority of residence. Permission to change from one category to another is difficult to obtain.

As a result, there may be 150 million migrants living in China's cities without legal rights to be there, a so-called 'floating population'.

Further reading Chan, K. W. (2009), 'The Chinese *hukou* system at 50', *Eurasian Geography and Economics* 50: 197–221.

human agency The capacity possessed by people to act of their own volition. According to social theorists, this capacity is never *sui generis*. Instead, all *agency arises from and is relative to the options made available by a person's position in a wider culture, society, economy, and political system. In the influential formulation of sociologist Anthony *Giddens, all agents have their actions enabled and constrained by wider 'structures', while their actions serve to reproduce and, sometimes, to alter these self-same structures. *Structuration is the term he coined to describe this intimate relationship between human action and its broader contexts of operation. Because of the existence of relationships of *power in society, it follows that degrees and kinds of agency are unevenly distributed among individuals. For instance, those in possession of large amounts of *money or who occupy senior positions in national government have ample agency when compared with a homeless person. Relatedly, relatively disempowered agents can decide to club together to create institutions—such as trades unions—that greatly enhance their agency by collectivizing it and pooling their resources.

Human geographers have long been interested in agency, but have understood it in a wide range of ways. Spatial scientists, for example, placed *homo economicus* at the centre of their analysis of the geographical organization of society for many years. Marxist geographers challenged the simplistic, reductionist understanding of society promoted by *spatial science, and accented the processes that govern agency in a capitalist world. Subsequently, humanistic geographers challenged both approaches, aiming to paint a more realistic picture of humans than *homo economicus*, while criticizing the over-emphasis on structures characteristic of early works by *Marxist geographers. In the 1990s, critical human geographers placed considerable emphasis on agency as a political phenomena, as part of their interest in social power, social *resistance, and social change. This, for example, was a notable characteristic of the subfield of *labour geography, which explored the links between agency, *place, and *geographical scale in disputes involving wage workers.

What all these approaches to agency have in common is their *anthropocentrism, consistent with the name of the discipline (*human* geography). From the early 2000s, however, as part of the rediscovery of *nature and environment by human geographers, there has been a strong interest in non-human agency. The biophysical world has been accorded efficacy in respect of human affairs and not only with respect to extreme events such as hurricanes. This is most evident in geographical adaptations of the *actor-network theory created by Bruno *Latour and other *Science and Technology Studies scholars. At the same time, some human geographers have sought to challenge the focus on cognition, speech, visualization, and perception characteristic of most theories of human agency. For instance, those promulgating *non-representational theory have sought to draw attention to how preconscious or subconscious stimuli can affect agency, and how agency involves all the human senses rather than simply touch and command. This can be seen as a partial attempt to renaturalize human agency after decades of over-socialized conceptions of the same.

human capital 1. The value of people as seen from the perspective of *labour markets.

2. The investment people make in themselves in order to enhance their employability and remuneration. The second definition pertains to *human agency, the first to the wider conditions in which agency must be exercised. The term is still commonly used in

mainstream economics, so too parts of economic geography. Here potential and actor-workers are seen as one key 'factor of production' that influences the profits, geographical location, etc. of a firm.

Human Development Index (HDI) A measure of national development combining indicators of health, education, and living standards. It is often used instead of narrow economic indicators of development and was first devised for the *United Nations by Pakistani economist Mahbub ul Haq in 1990 as the basis of the organization's annual Human Development Reports. The exact data used to calculate the index has changed over time, but it does allow for international and temporal comparisons, often revealing discrepancies between a country's economic wealth and its general level of well-being. In 2010, Norway was ranked highest and Zimbabwe lowest out of 169 countries.

((()) SEE WEB LINKS)
• Portal to the Human Development Reports.

human ecology The study of the inter-relations between humans and the natural environment, conceived variously as: a branch of the science of ecology; an interdisciplinary field; geography as a whole. Chicago geographer Harlan Barrows described geography as human ecology in the 1920s, stressing the focus on relations rather than the object of landscape. At the same time, the *Chicago School of sociology described its use of biological concepts such as community and succession to understand city life and organization as human ecology (*see* URBAN ECOLOGY).

human genome The complete set of genes that carries a human being's hereditary information. There are 20,000–25,000 genes in the DNA of a human being. The full genome was revealed by two parallel projects in the early 2000s, one international programme led by US government agencies and one private operation by the Celera Corporation. *See* GENETICS; GENETIC MODIFICATION.

human geography The study of the interrelationships between people, place, and environment, and how these vary spatially and temporally across and between locations. Whereas physical geography concentrates on spatial and environmental processes that shape the natural world and tends to draw on the natural and physical sciences for its scientific underpinnings and methods of investigation, human geography concentrates on the spatial organization and processes shaping the lives and activities of people, and their interactions with places and nature. Human geography is more allied with the social sciences and humanities, sharing their philosophical approaches and methods (*see* PHYSICAL GEOGRAPHY for a discussion on the relationship between human and physical geography; ENVIRONMENTAL GEOGRAPHY).

Human geography consists of a number of sub-disciplinary fields that focus on different elements of human activity and organization, for example, *cultural geography, *economic geography, *health geography, *historical geography, *political geography, *population geography, *rural geography, *social geography, *transport geography, and *urban geography. What distinguishes human geography from other related disciplines, such as development, economics, politics, and sociology, are the application of a set of core geographical concepts to the phenomena under investigation, including *space, *place, *scale, *landscape, *mobility, and *nature. These concepts foreground the notion that the world operates spatially and temporally, and that social relations do not operate independently of place and environment, but are thoroughly grounded in and through them.

With respect to methods, human geography uses the full sweep of *quantitative and *qualitative methods from across the social sciences and humanities, mindful of using them to provide a thorough geographic analysis. It also places emphasis on *fieldwork and mapping (*see* CARTOGRAPHY), and has made a number of contributions to developing new methods and techniques, notably in the areas of *spatial analysis, *spatial statistics, and *GIScience.

The long-term development of human geography has progressed in tandem with that of the discipline more generally (*see* GEOGRAPHY). Since the *Quantitative Revolution in the 1950s and 1960s, the *philosophy underpinning human geography research has diversified enormously. The 1970s saw the introduction of *behavioural geography, *radical geography, and *humanistic geography. These were followed in the 1980s by a turn to *political economy, the development of *feminist geography, and the introduction of critical *social theory underpinning the *cultural turn. Together these approaches formed the basis for the growth of *critical geography, and the introduction of postmodern and post-structural thinking into the discipline in the 1990s. These various developments did not fully replace the theoretical approaches developed in earlier periods, but rather led to further diversification of geographic thought. For example, quantitative geography continues to be a vibrant area of geographical scholarship, especially through the growth of GIScience. The result is that geographical thinking is presently highly pluralist in nature, with no one approach dominating.

Further reading Agnew, J. et al. (ed.) (1996), *Human Geography: an Essential Anthology*.
Aitken, S. and Valentine, G. (eds.) (2006), *Approaches to Human Geography*.
Cloke, P. et al. (eds.) (3rd ed. 2013), *Introducing Human Geographies*.
Daniels, P. et al. (4th ed. 2012), *An Introduction to Human Geography*.
Hubbard, P. et al. (2002), *Thinking Geographically: Space, Theory and Contemporary Human Geography*.
Knox, P. and Marston, S. (6th ed. 2012), *Human Geography: Places and Regions in Global Context*.

Human Geography: a Welfare Approach A book written by David M. Smith (1977), it was a key social geography text that set out a vision for human geography centred around an analysis of social issues and social policy. In particular, the book focused on human welfare in its broad sense and made the case for practising *moral geographies aimed at changing the world for the better. Although inspired by some *Marxist geography, the argument advanced was quite conservative in nature, drawing on economics, classical sociology, and a wide array of geographical theory. *See also* WELFARE GEOGRAPHY.

humanism 1. The search for and cultivation of those shared characteristics that elevate *homo sapiens* above other earthly creatures.
2. A secular doctrine which maintains that humans are not the creations of a deity and which studies people as earthly, fleshly beings who nonetheless possess unique attributes when compared with other living species.
3. An ethical stance dedicated to the cultivation of all that is best about humans, including civility, generosity, creativity, and empathy.
Despite the second definition, humanistic thought has long flourished in most religions and all three meanings can be traced back to at least the European *Renaissance.
In human geography, the humanistic scholars of the 1970s and 1980s were closely aligned with humanism in the second and third definitions above (*see* HUMANISTIC GEOGRAPHY). These scholars were interested in different peoples' *lifeworlds—that is to say, their *subjective understandings, perceptions, and *emotions. Since these lifeworlds arose, in large part, from engagements with local environments, built and natural, humanistic geographers argued that our humanity is, in part, constituted geographically. As some critics later pointed out, most humanistic geographers had an implicitly positive view of 'human nature', thus introducing unproblematized normative assumptions into their writings. Because of the powerful strains of *anti-humanism contained in the

various branches of *post-structuralism, many contemporary human geographers are
loath to use the term 'humanism' in anything but an ironic or critical sense.

humanistic geography A movement within human geography seeking to recentre
the subject on human beings, their experiences, and understandings of the world as
informed by a diverse range of humanist influences. Developing from the *Renaissance,
humanism describes philosophies that emphasize the unique role of human capacities
such as reason, critical reflection, and creativity in explaining social life. Humanistic
geography itself flourished in the 1970s and 1980s, notably in North America. With
hindsight, it can be seen more as a critical reaction to the perceived dominance of
*positivism and *Marxism within human geography than a blueprint for the discipline
as a whole. Although broadly based and not necessarily in agreement with one another,
humanistic geographers held a common aversion to what they saw as the reduction of
human beings within geography. This reduction took two main forms. Within the
positivist-informed schools of *locational analysis and *spatial science, humans were
often described in narrow and abstract terms, for example, as 'economic man' (*see* HOMO
ECONOMICUS) driven solely by profit, cost-minimization, or least effort. Aggregated into
models, the sense of human diversity and potential irrationality was suppressed. Within
*Marxism, or the particular versions of Marxism to which there was objection, reduction
meant the description of humans as workers trapped within economic structures over
which they had no control, and by which they were rendered unthinking dupes. Drawing
upon older traditions of inquiry in *historical and *cultural geography alongside ideas
from philosophies such as *existentialism, *idealism, and *phenomenology, humanistic
geographers instead variously emphasized *agency, *subjectivity, values, and contingency. It contrasted with *behavioural geography, where there was still a normative
expectation of what humans ought to do, e.g. minimize distance travelled, and which
used quantitative methods drawn from psychology.

The leading humanistic geographers included Anne *Buttimer, David *Ley, Edward
*Relph, and Yi-Fu *Tuan, many of whom contributed to the foundational text *Human-
istic Geography: Prospects and Problems* (1978). Their focus was largely on everyday social
life, the close relationships between people and *place, and people and *landscape (*see*
LIFEWORLD). Sometimes criticized for being 'touchy-feely', preoccupied with trivia and
small unrepresentative samples, humanistic geography could, in fact, make use of a
range of rigorous research practices, many of which had their origins in psychoanalysis.
In *A Geography of the Lifeworld* (1979) David Seamon closely interviewed a large number
of volunteers to establish the core characteristics of everyday life: movement, rest, and
encounter. Informed by phenomenology, and prefiguring what was later termed *non-
representational theory he identified the precognitive, non-routine ways in which people
relate to their environments. The earliest uses of *participant observation were by
humanistic geographers, many of whom also critically reflected on themselves as
researchers (*see* POSITIONALITY; REFLEXIVITY). In both methods and interests, humanistic
geography had a far-reaching effect, although the inquiries it influenced were more likely
to be carried out under the headings of cultural, social, or feminist geography.

Further reading Adams, P., Hoelschler, S., and Till, K. (eds.) (2001), *Textures of Place: Exploring
Humanist Geographies.*
Entrikin, J. N. (1976), 'Contemporary humanism in geography', *Annals of the Association of
American Geographers* 66(4): 615–32.

Humanistic Geography: Prospects and Problems A collection of essays edited
by David *Ley and Marwyn S. Samuels (1978) that introduced the ideas of *humanistic
geography to a wide audience while attempting to provide some coherence and authority
to a growing field of scholarship. Many of its contributors were then at the University of
British Columbia, Vancouver, and most were based in North America.

humanitarian intervention The threat or use of military force by one or more states against another for the purposes of safeguarding human life or protecting human rights. According to the principles of the *United Nations, sovereign states are inviolate within their territories, but exceptions have been made where there is deemed to be risk of serious harm to populations, e.g. US intervention in Haiti in 1994 and NATO's campaign in Libya in 2011. Other cases, for example, NATO's operations in Kosovo, then part of Yugoslavia, have not been sanctioned by the UN but have been justified as part of a wider 'responsibility to protect' civilians against states. Russia and China have tried to uphold the rights of sovereign states in such situations, while critics regard humanitarian intervention as a cloak for *neocolonialism. It is not the same as humanitarian aid, which may be without force. *See also* COMPLEX EMERGENCY.

humanities Those subjects and disciplines dedicated to the study of *humanity and its creations, such as fine art, philosophy, history, languages, drama, literature, and music. The term is thought to originate in *Renaissance Europe, where it described a course of study that could be traced back to the Romans and ancient Greeks. Typically, a humanistic education is counter-posed to one centred on science and technology. This reflects a belief that what makes us distinctively human are not the mere facts of our physiology or neurology—whose study human biologists make their own. Instead, humanity's capacity to plan, imagine, dream, speculate, criticize, argue, and change the world to suit its desires is said to compromise its special qualities, ones said to be irreducible to biological imperatives. More generally, humanistic inquiry and learning are contrasted with subjects that seek to measure and control the world, such as economics and civil engineering. The humanities are more interested in *subjectivity, the *lifeworld, and values than in *objectivity, truth, and facts. They have a deeply *hermeneutic dimension.

For many decades, practitioners argued that geography was a humanities subject rather than a science—this despite the discipline's pre-19th-century origins in mapping the earth's surface, surveying territory, and exploring new terrestrial and maritime horizons. As a synthetic subject dedicated to understanding the specificities of different places and regions, some saw academic geography as the art of description and evocation. The geographer's role was to paint a picture of local life so realistic as to transport the reader there imaginatively, if not literally. Such a role, it was said, required the exercise of judgement as much as the accumulation of knowledge. It was a question of skill and experience, not the testing of hypotheses. However, as *spatial science took hold of the discipline, humanistic knowledge took a back seat until revived in a new form by humanistic geographers (*see* HUMANISM; HUMANISTIC GEOGRAPHY). Unlike their early 20th forebears, these geographers wanted to see, feel, and understand the world as others did. However, humanistic geography had lost momentum by the late 1980s as a plethora of critical approaches gained ground, such as *feminist geography. Human geography as a whole came to have a broadly social science flavour, not least because *theory—in a rather formal sense of that term—came to drive the analyses of empirical *case studies. Because of this and a strong interest among critical human geographers in how to create alternatives to *neoliberalism, sexism, racism, and so on, human geography has of late created more space for humanistic inquiry. There has been renewed (or new) interest in everything from public art to cinema to performance to imaginations of the future. This interest speaks of a desire to reveal a more generous sense of the human than offered in recent research, and to explore different ways of being human than those currently available in mainstream society. Because of the new importance of ideas relating to the *more-than-human, we might also see human geography as part of a new movement called the 'post-humanities'.

Further reading Blunt, A. (2003), 'Geography and the humanities' in Holloway, S., Rice, S., and Valentine, G. (eds.) *Key Concepts in Geography*, 73–91.

Daniels, S. et al. (2011), *Envisioning Landscapes, Making Worlds: Geography and the Humanities*.
Dear, M. et al. (eds.) (2011), *GeoHumanities: Art, History, Text at the Edge of Place*.

human resources The goods and services originating from society rather than
*nature. The distinction from *natural resources assumes that society and nature can
be separately identified. There is a sense in which even natural resources, as cultural
appraisals of material substances, are human.

human trafficking *See* TRAFFICKING.

Humboldt, Alexander von (1769–1859) A German naturalist and explorer who is
considered one of the founders of modern academic geography. Having initially trained
as a geologist, von Humboldt used private wealth to travel widely, including a lengthy trip
to South America (1799–1804) to study its flora, fauna, and landscape. He gave many
public lectures, published extensively on aspects of human and physical geography, and
advised governments. His most ambitious work, *Kosmos*, published in five volumes
between 1845 and 1862, sought to provide a synoptic overview of the world. For von
Humboldt geography was a 'total' science, one dedicated to studying the world as a
complex whole. *See also* HOLISM.

hunger A lack of sufficient food to meet a person's necessary requirements for sustained physiological health. Chronic hunger can lead to *famine and starvation. Malnutrition results from not eating the appropriate food, although it may nonetheless be
available. One of the *Millennium Development Goals is the halving of world hunger
levels between 1990 and 2015, but the *Food and Agriculture Organization estimated that
there were 925 million people suffering chronic hunger in 2010. *See also* FOOD SECURITY.

hunter-gatherer A member of a society whose livelihood depends on foraging for
plants and hunting wild animals, rather than arable farming and/or animal domestication. Hunter-gathering was practised by humans for 95 per cent of our existence as a
species until the agricultural revolution. Present-day hunter-gatherer societies include
the Bushmen in southern Africa, the Pila Nguru in Western Australia, and the Sentinelese
in the Andaman Islands. Because throughout history such societies have commonly
consisted of small, usually mobile bands of 30–40 individuals they occupy a significant
position in various, often conflicting theories of human culture and evolution.

Huntington, Ellsworth (1876–1947) An American geographer who spent much of
his career at Yale University. As set out in his books *The Pulse of Asia* (1907) and
Civilization and Climate (1915), Huntington was an advocate of climatic determinism,
arguing that human activity and economic development are overtly shaped by climatic
conditions, particularly temperature and relative humidity (*see* ENVIRONMENTAL DETER-
MINISM). In the latter part of his career he became a keen advocate of *eugenics, serving
as president of the board of directors of the American Eugenics Society from 1934 to 1938.

Hurricane Katrina A large hurricane that severely damaged large tracts of the states
of Louisiana, Mississippi, and Alabama, and devastated the city of New Orleans on
29 August 2005. It was the deadliest storm to hit the United States for 77 years, with
1,836 people dying as a result of the hurricane and subsequent floods, and the costliest
on record in terms of property damage. The bulk of the deaths occurred due to the storm
surge and breaches in flood defences, along with the failure to fully evacuate low-lying
vulnerable areas. In the aftermath of the event there was social unrest, looting,
and violence, and the storm has had long-term social, economic, and environmental
consequences. Critical analysis of the hurricane has highlighted how Katrina was less a
'natural disaster' than a racially differentiated disaster, disproportionately affecting

poorer, non-white people (especially women), raising questions of environmental *racism and *social justice in terms of which groups occupy the most vulnerable parts of the city and who is the focus of disaster management and relief programmes. *See also* DISASTER; HAZARDS.

Further reading Steinberg, P. and Shields, R. (eds.) (2008), *What Is a City? Rethinking the Urban after Hurricane Katrina*.

Hybrid Geographies An influential monograph by British geographer Sarah *Whatmore (2002). Something of a manifesto for a more-than-human geography, the book took inspiration from *Actor-Network Theory and European process philosophy, among other sources (*see* POST-HUMANISM).

hybridity A condition arising from the mixing and transcendence of binary opposites such as nature-society, or colonized-colonizer. Hybrids are therefore non-essentialized forms, irreducible to pure states. Although the term comes from plant and animal sciences, meaning the offspring of different species, it has gained wider currency in association with *postmodernism, *post-colonialism, and other intellectual movements that valorize emergent conditions. In *The Location of Culture* (1994), Homi Bhabha reverses the stigma once attached to racial mixing in colonial circumstances and describes hybridity as novel, creative, and full of potential for change. By comparison, Bruno *Latour refers to hybrid networks of nature-society by way of debunking modernist dichotomies. *See also* THIRD SPACE.

hydraulic society A society in which an elite holds power over a population through its control of *water, usually in the form of large-scale irrigation systems. Karl *Marx and Max Weber both suggested that Asian societies were historically distinct from European in part because of the significance of water power, but the idea was most developed by German historian and geographer Karl Wittfogel in his *Oriental Despotism* (1957). Taking examples from ancient Egypt to modern-day China, he argued that such societies represented a different development path from Western capitalist ones. More recently, US historian Donald Worster controversially applied the concept to the American West in *Rivers of Empire* (1985).

hyper-globalizer A term to describe someone who regards late-20th-century *globalization as a new epoch in human history. As described by David Held and colleagues in *Global Transformations* (1999), the hyper-globalist or ultra-thesis is that economic globalization has eroded the power of the *nation state, effected a borderless economy, and ushered in new forms of social life. It contrasts with a more sceptical position that sees such pronouncements as exaggerated.

hyperreality 1. A situation in which people are unable to distinguish reality from the simulation of reality.
2. A condition in which a *simulacrum appears to be more real than the real thing. In the former case, it is acknowledged that people often experience the world through multiple forms of media that present and filter it; as such one rarely experiences an event directly but through its representation. In a media-saturated world, this representation—the copy—becomes inimical to the real. Taken to its logical extreme, the pastiche copy of an original comes to define what something is expected to be like. For example, Irish bars outside Ireland that were once pastiches of those in Ireland, draw together, emphasize, and rework different design elements to produce a form of hyperreality. This was so much the case that bars in Ireland started to be made more like their simulacra. The term is closely associated with the social theorists Jean Baudrillard and Umberto Eco.

hyperspace **1.** In mathematics, a space that has more than three dimensions.
2. Outside mathematics, used metaphorically to describe any kind of space that cannot be readily mapped into conventional coordinates.

hypothesis A statement about the behaviour of social or biophysical phenomena whose validity can be tested by systematic observation of these phenomena. The term is widely used in the life, earth, and computational sciences, less so in the contemporary social sciences. To qualify as a hypothesis a statement's validity must be uncertain and able to be tested empirically, although theoretical and mathematic tests may suffice as *heuristics *en route* to real world testing. A hypothesis is thus a conjecture made by scientific researchers on the basis of one or more of the following: (i) initial but incomplete observations of a given phenomenon, (ii) inferences from the behaviour of known phenomena that may appear related or similar to those in question, or (iii) deductions made from existing models, theories, or mathematical proofs. All hypotheses begin life as 'working hypotheses' because they inspire investigators to put them to the test. Typically, tests proceed through a mixture of *verification and *falsification. If a hypothesis appears to be partially or approximately true, it can be modified, subject to further testing, and then accepted once researchers concur that enough positive evidence has been adduced. All things being equal, hypotheses that can be tested in controlled laboratory or field conditions, or by a specially designed computer programme, tend to be more robust than those that can only be tested in uncontrolled conditions. Once a hypothesis is said to be true it can often be connected to related hypotheses to form a realistic *model or *theory able to describe, explain, or even predict processes and events in reliable ways.

*Physical geography's branches are all considered to be sciences by their practitioners and one thus finds hypothesis formulation, testing, refinement, acceptance, and rejection a key part of their *modus operandi*. The term is less commonly used in human geography, even amongst those who use numerical data, statistical methods, and geographic information systems (GIS). However, even when the term is not used, one often finds hypothesis formulation and testing *de facto* in much published research.

Both human and physical geographers frequently investigate 'open systems' in which there are dynamic and complex interactions between a myriad of processes, materials, and agents. Given this, some researchers have multiple working hypotheses and may have to use abduction—inferring the existence or operation of a non-observable process or cause from observed phenomena. Through trial-and-error, patience, and logic a researcher can ascertain which working hypothesis warrants refinement and further testing, leading to acceptance as adequate descriptions, explanations, or predictions. Though it is sometimes believed that hypotheses should, once accepted, become 'covering laws' that apply to all cases of the phenomena in question regardless of time or place, this contradicts much geographical practice. Because of the spatio-temporal variability of phenomena across the Earth's surface—human and physical—even supposedly universal processes can have their effects altered by context. This means that hypothesis testing in both human and physical geography yields insights that are intended to be neither purely *nomothetic nor purely *idiographic.

IBG *See* INSTITUTE OF BRITISH GEOGRAPHERS.

ICANN *See* INTERNET CORPORATION FOR ASSIGNED NAMES AND NUMBERS.

iconic architecture A term to describe buildings that are deemed to possess special symbolic and aesthetic value and are widely recognizable by the public. Such buildings may be generic, for example, medieval European Gothic cathedrals or the early 20th-century US skyscrapers; or more commonly specific, for example, the Petronas Towers in Kuala Lumpur or Bilbao's Guggenheim Museum. *See also* ARCHITECTURE; VERNACULAR LANDSCAPE.

iconography The identification, description, and interpretation of the content and meanings in visual *images. Developed initially in art history, the approach focuses on meaning over form, on decoding the ideas and significance of the content of images, including those that are hidden or symbolic. It does this by careful formal reading of the image, disclosing the symbolism at work, and by embedding the analysis in social and historical context. While initially applied to medieval religious paintings, it has been extended to cover all forms of art, as well *maps, *photographs, and architectural drawings. In geography, iconography is most strongly associated with *cultural geography and the interpretation of images relating to *landscapes and *maps. Its application has demonstrated that the meanings of landscape change over time and vary between different groups, and how landscapes are shaped by but also shape human activity and identity. *See also* COSGROVE, DENIS; *ICONOGRAPHY OF LANDSCAPE*.

Iconography of Landscape, The A collection of essays edited by Denis *Cosgrove and Stephen Daniels (1988). Written by scholars from across the humanities and social sciences, it examines the idea of *landscape as a cultural image, a particular way of representing, structuring, or symbolizing surroundings. The essays employ an art-historical method of *iconography—interpreting levels of meaning in human artefacts such as poetry and promotional literature, architectural design, maps, and paintings from different historical periods—to examine the idea, significance, and representation of landscape, and how these inform wider social, cultural, and political issues. The book was important in helping to shift the concept of landscape and the practice of cultural geography away from more traditional notions of cultural landscapes towards a *new cultural geography.

ICT and geography The information and communication technologies (ICT), such as the telegraph, telephone, and *Internet, have been an important focus for geographical research because they are key agents of *time-space compression. By enabling instantaneous communication around the planet in a variety of forms, and the sharing of vast quantities of information, ICTs have had significant effects on the nature and organization of *media, *business, *logistics, cities, and *regions, and promoting the growth of the *knowledge economy. For some, ICTs are leading to the supposed 'death of distance', though work by geographers reveals that place continues to remain a key element of social and economic relations. With the roll-out of new mobile ICTs a new range of geographical effects are occurring, leading to changes in *spatial behaviour and new business models such as *location-based services.

Further reading Castells, M. (1996), *The Rise of the Network Society*.
Graham, S. and Marvin, S. (1996), *Telecommunications and the City*.

idealism Any philosophy which posits that the real world is not knowable in itself but only in the form of representations constructed by situated human actors. Related philosophies that emphasize subjective experience over objective existence are also often said to be idealist. According to critics, some *postmodern and *post-structural theorists are latter-day idealists akin to the famous German idealists Immanuel *Kant and Georg Hegel who were writing in the 18th century. The materialist Karl *Marx was a famous and pointed critic of all forms of idealism, while in human geography Andrew *Sayer's version of *critical realism has sought to separate a defensible epistemological idealism from an indefensible ontological idealism. More recently, attempts to bring *nature back in to human geography's orbit of interest has helped to curb the idealist tendencies of the *cultural turn of the 1990s.

ideal type A form of conceptual *abstraction designed to identify the key characteristics of any given process, system, institution, or policy. The term is associated with German sociologist Max Weber (1864–1920), for whom ideal types were not 'perfect' versions of their 'imperfect' real world analogues, but *heuristics designed to aid research.

identity An individual or shared sense of self. Identity is how people see themselves and express 'who they are inside' to others. Individual identity is expressed through what people say and write, their cultural tastes, how they dress, and their material possessions, the activities they take part in, and the other people with whom they associate, and groups to which they belong. Collective identity is a sense of belonging to the same group, of having the same views, outlook, values, and beliefs (*see* CULTURE). It could relate to a particular aspect of identity such as *sexuality, or a cultural activity such as supporting a particular football team, or a place such as a particular town or nation.

   The notion of an *essentialized identity, that there is a core essence that is innate and natural, something one is born with or inherits, has been challenged by those who understand identity to be *socially constructed or *performative. In the former, identity is both self and externally inscribed, on the one hand shaped by individual choices concerning self-expression, and on the other figured by social and spatial context and how others relate and treat a person. Here, identity is constitutive of *gender, sexuality, *race, *ethnicity, *class, *disability, *religion, *culture, *language, and other social markers, as well as place and *territory (*see* NATIONALISM), that work on a sense of self through discursive and material practices, internally through self-reflection and subconscious processing, and externally through socio-spatial relations and expressions of power. For example, sexuality is constitutive of identity, shaping sexual identification and desire, how one presents as a sexual subject, and how that presentation is figured by the reactions of others to that component of identity; for example, concealing expressions of sexuality in places of strong *heteronormativity and homophobia. Such identifications form the basis of collective identities and provide a platform for organizing *identity politics in the form of *social movements that seek to challenge identity-based discrimination.

In the latter, identity is something one performs, rather than something one is. It is an *embodied enactment that is contingent and relational, reacting to context and situation. From this perspective, sexual identity unfolds through how one acts as a sexual subject, rather than being a category one belongs to. Such a position renders identity fluid, open, and *hybrid. On the one hand, this creates political opportunities by destabilizing the bases of discrimination; on the other, it potentially undermines social movements by emphasizing diversity over coherent, collective identifications. The latter, it is suggested, is dealt with through 'strategic essentialism'; that is diverse identities coming together and acting as if they share a singular identity, using a common voice to strategically tackle an issue.

Identity and identity politics is a core focus of much *cultural and *social geography, which analyses how identities are constructed, represented, negotiated, and contested in everyday life. In particular, there has been much research that has sought to understand the relationship between identity and *sense of place, and the processes of *social exclusion, *othering, and the politics and landscape of difference experienced by individuals and collective groups that lead to *marginalization, *social polarization, and *segregation.

Further reading Atkinson, S., Hopkins, P., and Kwan, M-P. (eds.) (2007), *Geographies of Muslim Identities: Diaspora, Gender and Belonging.*
Keith, M. and Pile, S. (eds.) (1993), *Place and Politics of Identity.*
Woodward, K. (ed.) (2000), *Questioning Identity: Gender, Class, Nation.*

identity politics The political mobilization around cultural identity, as opposed to *ideology or *class. Identity politics can be practised individually, but is usually organized through *social movements. These organizations are built around a common cultural identity such as *race, *ethnicity, *disability, *gender, or *sexuality. Identity politics focuses on issues relating to recognition, rights, and *social justice, as well as inequities and the redistribution of resources. *See also* CULTURAL POLITICS.

ideology 1. Any representation of the world that achieves wide societal acceptance and which serves to advance the interests of one section of society by occluding the asymmetries of *power that disadvantage other sections of society.
2. A system of thought designed to make sense of the world and which may include proposals for the improvement of society or environment.

In the second sense, ideologies are possessed by all people, albeit in usually simplistic and unacknowledged ways. Political parties and organized religions, by contrast, aim to make their ideologies both explicit and popular. In the first sense, ideologies are subject to criticism by those who claim to see them for what they really are. Ideologies in sense two can also be criticized, but the term is usually more descriptive and less normative than sense one.

In *human geography, the term enjoyed a relatively short period of formal usage in sense one in the late 1970s and early 1980s. This was associated with the burgeoning of Marxist thought in the Anglophone academy and numerous discussions about the content and effects of capitalist ideologies on workers and society as a whole (*see* MARXIST GEOGRAPHY). Despite the richness of these Marxian debates (and also feminist debates about the discourses of *patriarchy), human geographers did not advance far with their own discussions and tended to make theoretical claims concerning ideology rather than to test them empirically. These claims took two forms. First, some argued that *spatial science was an ideology, despite its claims to neutrality and its search for truth based on testing theories, *models, and *hypotheses. For instance, Derek Gregory's *Ideology, Science and Human Geography* (1978) argued that spatial scientists' supposed *objectivity was simply a cover for accepting the values and norms of a world in which class inequality, racism, sexism, colonialism, and other ills were rife. Second, some looked beyond human geography to those applied disciplines and professions that sought to manage cities, regions, and natural landscapes. For instance, in an essay on planning in his book The *Urbanization of Capital (1985), David Harvey argued that planners unknowingly designed city spaces so as to facilitate the circulation and *accumulation of *capital. Their professional discourse and practice, Harvey argued, internalized the values and norms of profit-seeking firms, despite these planners being formally separate from such firms. More broadly, Neil *Smith, in his book *Uneven Development, argued that capitalist ideology transcends any one profession, social group, or institution. It is all pervasive, he argued, despite attempts by Marxists and others to highlight its deceptions and maladies.

While human geography's 'cultural and discursive' turn of the 1990s could have facilitated rich discussions of ideology in sense one, researchers preferred to talk of 'power-knowledge', following Michel *Foucault; and later, *hegemony, following Italian Marxist Antonio Gramsci. Meanwhile, Marxist and feminist geographers largely chose not to explore in detail how ideologies played out geographically in different places and nations. As a result, ideology in the first sense is presently not much discussed in human geography, while in sense two it is not a favoured term, with writers preferring alternative concepts, such as 'worldview'. This said, ideology in sense one has attracted the interest of some neo-Marxists investigating *neoliberalism, *Post-Fordism, and other political economic formations, although they rarely use the word in their writings.

Ideology, Science and Human Geography The first book written by Derek *Gregory (1978), it explored the then nascent alternatives to *spatial science. Gregory explored the possibilities contained in 'critical' and 'interpretive' (or *hermeneutic) knowledges geared to social change and mutual understanding respectively. These knowledges subsequently assumed an important place in Anglophone human geography.

idiographic A method relating to the abstraction of the particular or unique elements of a place or object. As a method it contrasts with the *nomothetic, the abstraction of general or shared aspects. Geographers may try to understand Oxford as a unique city, for example, located at a crossing place on the river Thames with a set of particularized conditions and relations; or they may regard it as one of a class of medium-sized cities that can be understood in terms of wider settlement theories. The idiographic approach is associated with *regional geography.

illegal immigration The movement into a country by persons in violation of that country's immigration, visa, and/or residence laws, either through clandestine entry or over-staying, i.e. exceeding the terms of a visa granted for another purpose such as study or tourism. Many analysts prefer the less pejorative terms 'undocumented' or 'irregular' migration, implying that such immigrants are not criminals but may also be victims of poverty, *displacement, and coercive or unjust state practices.

ILO *See* INTERNATIONAL LABOUR ORGANIZATION.

image A visual representation or reflection of an aspect of the world or universe. An image can be two-dimensional, such as a painting or *photograph, or three-dimensional such as a statue or hologram. It can be a single static image or a moving sequence such as a *film. Images can be captured by optical or sensor devices (e.g., an electronic microscope or radar) or be captured by eye and rendered through artistic practice. They can be photorealistic, impressionistic, or some type of *spatialization, including *maps, statistical forms such as graphs, and computer graphics. A volatile image is fleeting and only lasts a short time, whereas a fixed image is one captured onto a medium that holds it over time. *See also* ART; GAZE; VISUALIZATION; WAYS OF SEEING.

imaginative geographies The ways in which other places, peoples, cultures, and landscapes are represented in discourse and action by another group. The imaginative geographies produced—whether conversations, art, media reporting, travel writing, academic articles, intelligence reports—reflect the preconceptions and desires of their creators, and are reflective of the power between these authors and the subjects of their imaginings. The term was popularized by the postcolonial scholar Edward *Said in his influential book *Orientalism* (1978), to describe how the West has constructed a particular, power-laden view of the East, which works both to *other and exoticize the East, but also affirm the Western self. The study of imaginative geographies seeks to unpick the process of their creation and the work they perform in shaping relations between their authors and subjects. *See also* ORIENTALISM.

Further reading Gregory, D. (1995), 'Imaginative geographies', *Progress in Human Geography* 19: 447–85.

imagined community A collective of people who possess a common, imagined sense of political and national unity. The concept was first proposed by Benedict *Anderson in *Imagined Communities* (1983/2006) to think about what constitutes a *nation. Anderson's argument is that at the heart of any nation is a sense of *nationalism; a sense of pride and belonging to a people rooted in place. The nation is an imagined community 'because the members of even the smallest nation will never know most of their fellow-members, meet them, or even hear of them, yet in the minds of each lives the image of their communion' (Anderson, 2006: 6). Even if there is deep internal inequality, a nation persists through deep horizontal comradeship. The nation then is constructed and performed through everyday discourse, the media, ceremony, institutional practices, sports, international politics, war, and so on, to produce a common sense of nationhood. This shared nationhood binds a population at the same time as it separates the community from other nations, and is a powerful enough imagining that people are willing to die for it. However, the sense of imagined community changes over time in response to world events and as new immigrants are absorbed into the collective understanding of the nation.

IMF *See* INTERNATIONAL MONETARY FUND.

immigration The movement of people into one country from another for settlement; hence, immigrants are people who arrive in a country intending their stay to be more than temporary. Definitions and estimations of levels of immigration and who is an immigrant are rarely exact. The UK government describes 'long-term international migrants' as people who, on arrival, state an intention to make the country their usual residence for at least a year. But these intentions may not be realized. Furthermore, this question is asked at only some points of arrival in the form of a sample, the International Passenger Survey. There is no equivalent survey on departure. Not everyone arriving this way is considered a foreigner or subject to immigration control; children born abroad to UK citizens (such as the armed forces) are not counted as immigrants (Anderson and Blinder 2011). The term 'immigrant' is also sometimes inappropriately applied to children born after arrival, also known as the 'second generation'. The '1.5 generation' are those who arrive as children accompanying parents.

Immigration is selective in at least two senses. The particular individuals who migrate may be differentiated by skill, age, gender, race, health, etc. In addition, states increasingly try to select what kinds of people they will admit for different categories of residence, study, and labour (*see* SKILLED MIGRATION). The interaction between these two kinds of selection may result in distinct 'migration channels', in which intermediaries such as recruitment agencies play a role in shaping who can move and how (Findlay and Li 1998). The most common types of immigration are for paid work, family reunification, and study in higher education. Immigration is also spatially selective, in that incomers rarely match the distribution of the resident population. Whereas immigrants from the Old World colonizing the New World in the 19th century often settled in agrarian regions, most modern-day immigrants head for cities, especially larger metropolitan areas (*see* GATEWAY CITIES).

When steamships were the main means of travelling between distant countries, immigration was generally an irrevocable act (although there were exceptions). In the 21st century, however, immigration may be less permanent, and *return migration more common. *See also* DIASPORA; MIGRATION; TRANSNATIONAL COMMUNITIES.

Further reading Anderson, B. and Blinder, S. (2011), 'Who counts as a migrant?', Briefing, The Migration Observatory, University of Oxford.

Findlay, A. and Li, F. L. N. (1998), 'A migration channels approach to the study of professionals moving to and from Hong Kong', *International Migration Review*, 32(3): 682–703.

immutable mobile A phenomenon whose form and function remains stable across different contexts and places. The term was coined by *Science and Technology Studies scholar Bruno *Latour to help describe the agency of non-humans. *Money, books and *maps are important immutable mobiles able to transcend place and time.

imperial city The political, ideological, and commercial centre of an empire or a city that dominates a surrounding region. Rome, Beijing, and London are examples of the former, while Gray Brechin's *Imperial San Francisco* (1999) describes the latter. Human geographers have studied the landscapes of imperial cities, focusing on *monuments, memorials, and statues.

Further reading Driver, F. and Gilbert, D. (eds.) (2003), *Imperial Cities: Landscape, Display and Identity*.

imperialism A system of domination by one geographical area over others in the form of an *empire, sometimes but not necessarily involving settlement or colonization (*see* COLONIALISM). It may also refer to the various habits of mind, ideologies, and discourses sustaining domination, notably *racism but also ideas about *gender, *sexuality, and *class (*see* ORIENTALISM).

Imperialism has taken many different historical forms, but it is generally associated with three waves of European expansion. The first, led by Spain and Portugal, involved the conquest and *dispossession of the Americas from the 16th century onwards (*see* ECOLOGICAL IMPERIALISM). Other European powers, notably France and England, followed them into the Americas and Caribbean. The second, linked more to mercantile capitalism, saw the Dutch and British expand into South and Southeast Asia from the 18th century on. The third phase, sometimes characterized as the Scramble for Africa or 'high imperialism' centred on European occupation of Africa from the 1880s (*see* BERLIN CONFERENCE). In one view, imperialism subsided during the wave of post-1945 independence secured by former colonies in the *Global South. From another perspective, often voiced from the left, imperialism continues in various ways. The term 'neo-imperialism' is often used loosely to describe systems of economic domination, chiefly ascribed to the USA. David *Harvey writes of the *New Imperialism exercised by the USA after the first Iraq War in the 1990s, centred on the control of oil and pursued through economic, political, and military means. Other authors argue that the successful spread of Western and again notably US cultural and consumer products, such as Hollywood films or Coca Cola, constitute a kind of 'cultural imperialism'.

David Livingstone (1992: 160) described geography as 'the science of imperialism *par excellence*', and indeed, many geographers and geographical societies were complicit in European empire-building in the 19th and early 20th centuries. Since the 1970s, however, most geographical work in the academy has been staunchly anti-imperialist in intent. In addition to analysing the larger-scale economic and political patterns of empire, historical geographical work has focused on the quite specific geographies of sites and connections of imperialism to suggest that it was more complex and ambiguous than sometimes thought and that its consequences extend to the present.

Reference Livingstone, D. N. (1992), *The Geographical Tradition*.

Import Substitution Industrialization (ISI) A development strategy based on concerted state intervention in nascent domestic industries as an alternative to buying foreign manufactured goods. The aim was to reduce dependence on exporting primary goods and capture more added-value locally. Associated with the *Economic Commission for Latin America, it was widely advocated in the 1960s and involved import tariffs and government aid to key sectors.

income inequality *See* INEQUALITY.

independent media Those news organizations free from government or corporate control and ownership. The main example is the Independent Media Center or Indymedia, set up during the 1999 Seattle anti-WTO protests and now embracing a global, multi-language, collective of print, radio, satellite TV, and Internet journalists and media outlets.

(⊕) SEE WEB LINKS
• Website of Indymedia.

independent variable *See* VARIABLE.

indeterminism A concept derived from the natural sciences that describes changes where the chances of very different possible outcomes are high. The concept was proposed by physicist Werner Heisenberg in the 1920s and promoted in the 1960s by biologist Jacques Monod. Indeterminism does not imply lack of causation; instead, it posits that the existence of a necessary cause identifiable by a researcher does not imply that any one particular outcome will follow. Indeterminism is a key idea in *chaos, catastrophe, and complexity theory and describes change in open systems of the sort that interests many human (and physical) geographers.

index of segregation *See* SEGREGATION.

India The world's second most populous country and seventh-largest by land area. Located in mainland South *Asia, historically it was home to the ancient Indus Valley Civilization. Four of the world's major religions—Hinduism, Buddhism, Jainism, and Sikhism—also originated there. From the early 18th century, large parts of India came under the control of one of the world's largest trading companies of the era, the British East India Company. Later, it was administered directly by Britain. This period saw the transfer *en masse* of British and other European technologies, rules, laws, and customs. Working with indigenous local and regional leaders, the British transformed Indian economy, society, and culture, though not without periodic resistance. Indian independence was secured in 1947, though it resulted in partition with the creation of the largely Muslim *Pakistan to the north west and north east. India's relations with Pakistan have remained brittle ever since.

India is today a capitalist democracy, but religion and cultural tradition still play an important part in the fabric of everyday life. The country is a federation in which political power is divided and held in check by being distributed between national and regional bodies, and executive and legislative ones. India's economy is one of the world's largest and, in recent years, among the fastest growing. However, because of its large population (roughly 1.2 billion), the per capita wealth is not high, with a relative minority of citizens enjoying good to very high standards of living. After decades of government-led economic protectionism, India joined the *World Trade Organization in 1995, since when it has become more of an export economy whose industries compete on an international stage. In GDP terms, the service sector comprises around half of all economic activity, with industry and agriculture comprising the other half. However, agriculture continues to employ the largest share of the national workforce. India has over 27 cities with a million-plus inhabitants, the largest being *Mumbai with a population of 21 million. The population is urbanizing, but the provision of public services and public health to all citizens remains a challenge.

indifference curve An economic model of consumer behaviour that calculates how people trade off purchase decisions. Given a fixed budget but a range of preferences, the indifference curve, expressed as a graph, shows how a consumer trades off one good for another, relative to the price of the two goods. If a consumer equally prefers two product bundles, then they are indifferent and will receive the same level of satisfaction (utility) from both. The slope of the indifference curve, known as the marginal rate of substitution, is the rate at which a consumer is willing to trade one good for another.

indigeneity *See* INDIGENOUS PEOPLE.

indigenous knowledge The distinct ideas, information, and skills held by *indigenous peoples, usually contrasted with Western scientific knowledge. Although it is not possible to be too prescriptive about either who is indigenous or what counts as indigenous knowledge, there are a number of related characteristics that might differentiate it. Firstly, it is generally context-dependent or local to particular places and regions; the skill in knowing what crops to plant when and where in a changeable environment may not be readily transferred elsewhere. It can therefore be regarded as adaptable to circumstances. Secondly, it is knowledge shared by communities and transmitted orally, i.e. not written down as *codified knowledge. It can be passed on or shared by stories, songs, dances, or through learning by observing and copying others. This does not mean that it is always shared equally; certain skills and information are often the privilege of one gender or age group. Thirdly, indigenous knowledge is holistic, i.e. embedded in lived experience and therefore not readily translated into analytical categories such as economy, ecology, and society. The routine scientific distinction between sacred and secular can also disrupt how such understandings are made. Alternative and related terms include traditional or folk knowledge, indigenous technical knowledge (ITK), and various ethno-knowledges such as ethnobotany.

Interest in indigenous knowledge, or more properly knowledges, is prominent in the fields of development and environment. Long disregarded as primitive or superstitious, since the 1960s professionals, scientists, and *NGO activists working in these fields have increasingly valorized indigenous knowledge. For example, whereas once African pastoralists were widely regarded as poor managers of rangelands, prone to harmful grazing practices based on irrational considerations, they are now more likely to be recognized as wise and skilful, working with the uncertainties of grassland environments. The risk of simply inverting prior disregard by romanticizing indigenous knowledge as superior, timeless, or pristine, is now widely recognized. Even so, when local practices and ideas are incorporated into development or environment thinking, it is often a one-way process. It is added to Western scientific knowledge, the core categories and assumptions of which are unaltered. Multilateral institutions, including the *World Bank and *United Nations Development Programme, now have projects to collect, document, and store indigenous knowledge, with a view to possibly transferring it from one place to another in the form of best practice. Whether oral, context-specific, and embedded knowledge can be documented in this way is open to question. Perhaps a more pressing problem is that the international legal system, particularly on *Intellectual Property Rights (IPR), may offer little protection. IPR assume ideas belong to individuals not groups, and arise from an act of discovery or invention rather than communal processes of shared memory. Following the Convention for Biological Diversity (1992), a system for valuing botanical and related knowledge was put in place, but rights were accorded to national governments rather than indigenous peoples (*see* BIOPIRACY; BIOPROSPECTING). *See also* INDIGENOUS MAPPING; RESOURCE MANAGEMENT.

Further reading Leach, M. and Mearns, R. (eds.) (1996), *The Lie of the Land: Challenging Received Wisdom on the African Environment.*
Watson, A. and Huntington, O. (2008) 'They're here–I can feel them: the epistemic spaces of indigenous and western knowledge', *Social & Cultural Geography* 9(3): 257–81.

indigenous mapping The use of cartography by and for *indigenous peoples. Map-making was historically seen as an adjunct of the colonial and imperial appropriation of the land and resources of indigenous communities. But from the 1960s onwards, pioneered in Alaska and Canada, indigenous groups have increasingly used their own maps in support of land rights claims, especially where documentation is required in court cases. Mapping also has wider relevance. It can document and store *indigenous knowledges about land, resources, and history in order to educate future generations and communicate with outsiders; maps can raise cultural awareness. It can be employed in resource management and land-use planning. Early examples often involved trained outsiders collecting 'map biographies', showing where hunters and trappers gathered their resources from day to day; these could be compiled into community-scale representations. *Participatory Rural Appraisal projects also included mapping exercises. In more recent years, *GIS and *GPS technologies have been adopted to better store and represent indigenous spatial and environmental knowledges. *See also* COUNTER MAPPING.

Further reading Chapin, M., Lamb, Z., and Threlkeld, B. (2005), 'Mapping indigenous lands', *Annual Review of Anthropology*, 34: 615–38.
Peluso, N. L. (1995), 'Whose woods are these? Counter-mapping forest territories in Kalimantan, Indonesia', *Antipode* 27(4): 383–406.
Sparke, M. (1998), 'A map that roared and an original atlas: Canada, cartography, and the narration of nation', *Annals of the Association of American Geographers* 88(3): 463–95.

indigenous people A term to define cultures deriving from or rooted in a particular land or place. The term especially refers to those peoples with significant ancestral and spiritual relations to lands later colonized as *settler societies. *See also* ABORIGINAL; POST-COLONIALISM.

Further reading Shaw, W. S., Herman, R. D. K., and Dobbs, G. (2006), 'Encountering indigeneity: re-imagining and decolonizing geography', *Geografiska Annaler* 88B: 267–76.

individualism An ethic and practice that places self-development and self-responsibility at its centre. It is the antithesis of *communalism. In political and economic philosophy, *neoliberalism is the most recent *ideology to successfully promote individualism as an alternative to *socialism and social democracy. *See also* METHODOLOGICAL INDIVIDUALISM.

individualization A structural characteristic of highly differentiated, democratic societies in which there is an intense focus on individual freedoms and rights. In these societies, it is argued that the individual is becoming the central unit of social life. Individuals are becoming increasingly reflexive and self-steered, rather than being shaped and structured by institutional regulation, and societal and collective norms. In other words, rather than living biographies largely scripted by traditional notions of family, work, gender, class, and so on, people are living more 'do-it-yourself biographies'. As such, the nature of society is changing, underpinned by a greater sense of individualism.

Further reading Beck, U. and Beck-Gernsheim, E. (2002), *Individualization*.

Indonesia A southeast Asian country that is an archipelago of over 17,000 islands and whose capital city is Jakarta. It is the world's fourth most populous country, is a representative democracy, and exports many commodities—especially to its neighbours such as *Singapore. Agriculture remains the largest employer, though industry, including forest products, generates the most *GDP.

induction A form of reasoning in which general conclusions are drawn from the observation of a single class or combination of phenomena. This contrasts with *deduction. Induction is a routine aspect of research in all subjects, as part of a mixture of reasoning devices.

industrial district A place in which there is a concentration of firms whose core business is the same or highly complementary. The term originally referred to the 19th-century *growth poles characteristic of industrializing countries such as Britain. These districts were typically focused on heavy industry or large-scale manufacture, such as coal mining and textiles respectively (*see* MARSHALLIAN INDUSTRIAL DISTRICT). They could exist outside a city or be part of one. Economic geographers have long been interested in the locational characteristics of industrial districts. Many have sought to ascertain whether certain industries are attracted to places with a unique ensemble of production factors. For policy-orientated geographers, this interest has long been linked to a desire to influence the locational decisions of firms in order to direct them to sites of strategic importance, to places suffering economic decline, or to localities that are restructuring economically.

Because of the *deindustrialization of many Western economies from the mid-1970s onwards and the success of *Newly Industrializing Countries, there was a renewed interest in industrial districts among economic geographers. The success of *Third Italy and *Silicon Valley led many researchers to inquire into how new industrial districts could arise in ostensibly deindustrializing countries. Because of the decline of large horizontally and vertically integrated firms in Western economies (*see* FORDISM; FLEXIBLE ACCUMULATION), the focus was on independent firms—often in *hi-tech, 'clean', or creative industries (such as computer games and fashion). Despite ostensibly being competitors, it was discovered that small- and medium-sized firms in the same industry benefit from *untraded interdependencies. This means that even a *footloose industry is likely to have its composite firms commit to one of just a few industrial districts nationally or globally. Industrial districts are sometimes known as industrial clusters. *See also* PORTER, MICHAEL; SCOTT, ALLEN; STORPER, MICHAEL.

industrial geography A subfield of *economic geography concerned with describing and explaining the locations chosen by different industries and these industries' effects on places, regions, and the people who inhabit them, primarily wage workers. An 'industry' is a set of firms that together either extract natural resources, process them, or manufacture new products by altering and assembling various commodities. The subfield dates back to 1910, when George Chisholm (*see* COMMERCIAL GEOGRAPHY) made reference to the *location theory of Alfred Weber when explaining the 'seats of industry'. Through the first half of the 20th century, industrial geography was largely empiricist, its practitioners detailing an industry in one place, region, or whole country without any formal use of *theory or any consistent *methodology. However, from the late 1960s, many economic geographers rediscovered the writings of Alfred Weber, along with the models attributed to *von Thünen, Walter *Christaller, and August *Lösch. These models assumed that economic agents are rational and seek to maximize the returns on their assets. Spatially, this meant that any industry would, given its current assets and the specific 'factors of production' it required, have an optimal location within any given region or country. Industrial geographers in the 1960s began to see how far this *location theory could be used to explain the real world distribution of various industries, though the earlier empiricist tradition lived on well into the 1970s.

By the early 1970s, after tests highlighted the limitation of the theory, industrial geography changed in two ways. First, the new *behavioural geography was used to achieve more complex understandings of how firms' owners and managers make locational decisions. The idea of purely 'rational' actors in possession of all relevant information was criticized. Secondly, industrial geographers came to see firms—especially medium- and large-scale enterprises—as complex entities whose strategic and location requirements were often equally complex and not at all easy to theorize abstractly.

This newer work was, in the main, politically mainstream. However, the rapid deindustrialization of Western European and North American economies after the economic crises of the early and late 1970s, inspired a new kind of research critical of the *uneven development endemic to *capitalism. A number of industrial geographers inspired by Marxism began to look for general processes that could explain deindustrialization in otherwise different industries. In Britain, Doreen *Massey and Ray Hudson were chief among them. However, some otherwise sympathetic critics worried that industrial geography was defaulting back to its empiricist roots. This, along with the virtual erasure of traditional manufacturing and heavy industry in countries such as the USA by the mid-1990s, led to industrial geography's virtual demise. A new round of more theoretically oriented research occurred, led by geographical political economists. It was particularly inspired by French *Regulation Theory and bled into a wider discussion of urban and regional change on both sides of the Atlantic. However, some practitioners retained the earlier commitment to analysing one industry in detail, with the new 'post-industrial' industries attracting attention. For instance, Annalee Saxenian has published extensively on *Silicon Valley and the economic effects of its knowledge workers' migration to the Far East. This kind of research has informed our understanding of so-called *new industrial districts, helping to give empirical support to general explanatory concepts such as *transactions costs and *untraded interdependencies.

industrialization The process whereby a local, regional, or national economy becomes more dependent on various primary, secondary, or tertiary industries. Though agriculture and forestry can become industrialized by introducing advanced machinery, science, and technology into its operations, industrialization typically refers to heavy industry and manufacturing (such as oil extraction and refining).

industrial organization The functional and spatial structure of a medium- or large-size firm, especially a *transnational corporation. Large firms with facilities, assets, and investments in several countries must find ways to structure their operations so as to minimize costs and maximize profits. Their strategies for doing so will vary significantly depending on the industry in which they are involved.

Industrial Revolution A period between the late 18th and early 19th centuries during which key sectors of English industry achieved remarkably higher and sustained levels of productivity. These were associated with technological innovations and working practices that later diffused more widely throughout Europe and North America. This led to a marked divergence between these regions and the rest of the world in standards of living. They also enabled higher rates of population growth alongside rising real wages, contrary to *Malthusian expectations. In addition to transforming the geography of production, these changes produced (and relied upon) a rapid increase in *urbanization. Industrial urbanization was critical in the creation of a new *working class or proletariat, not least because by concentrating workers close together in cities it established the conditions for class consciousness and associated action. Men, women, and children were drawn into waged labour, although the details of how the *division of labour was gendered varied by region and sector.

Revisionist historians in the 1980s demonstrated that the rates of economic growth and technological changes in England between the 1770s and 1830s were far less than once thought. In this sense, there was no sudden or revolutionary change in society, but a much more gradual process. The English economy grew at around 0.2 per cent per year in the late 18th century. But selected key sectors did change rapidly; cotton textiles and metallurgy underwent a burst of technological innovation leading to higher productivity and a dramatic increase in exports. The labour force shifted from agriculture to industry, and despite population growth real wages did not decline and prices did not rise. The population of England was 5.9 million in 1752 but rose to 8.6 million fifty years later. And coal supplanted wood as the main source of energy, breaking society's dependence on purely organic sources.

It is generally recognized that England could not have sustained economic and population growth without the resources of the British Empire. North American land, African labour (in slave plantations), Indian cotton, and Asian markets were essential to prolonging the burst of technological and economic transformation into something longer-lasting.

Further reading Findlay, R. and O'Rourke, K. H. (2007), *Power and Plenty: Trade, War, and the World Economy in the Second Millennium*.

Langton, J. and Morris, R. J. (eds.) (1986), *Atlas of Industrializing Britain, 1780-1924*.

Wrigley, E. A. (1988), *Continuity, Chance and Change: The Character of the Industrial Revolution in England*.

inequality A condition arising from the uneven distribution of a socially valued good (e.g. income, wealth) or attribute (e.g. good health, long life) within a given population; or the absence of *equality (*see* WEALTH INEQUALITY). Inequality should be distinguished from difference and inequity. People may differ according to some attribute, e.g. height. This is not regarded as inequality in itself because there is generally no normative value accorded to height, even though it can be the basis of discrimination. Secondly, not all inequality is deemed unjust or inequitable (*see* EQUITY). Certain individuals may be paid more than others, for example, by virtue of their specific skills, but this may not be widely regarded as unfair or unjust (*see* JUSTICE). Inequality is an inherently normative and therefore contentious issue. It divides those who think more should be done to reduce inequality from those who argue that a degree of inequality can be good for society if it results from entrepreneurs generating income for themselves and indirectly for others. A book by British sociologists Richard Wilkinson and Kate Pickett entitled *The Spirit Level: Why More Equal Societies Almost Always Do Better* (2009) has recently focused this debate.

Inequality is related to, but broader than *poverty because it concerns the distribution of a good across the whole of a society or social group. Most attention is given to income inequality because income is generally the key to accessing other socially valued goods such as health, education, and housing (*see* HEALTH INEQUALITY). Inequality in income is generally measured and discussed in terms of the *Gini coefficient, which summarizes the distribution of income within a society or region. It is much harder to calculate such measures internationally, however (*see* GLOBAL INEQUALITY). Extreme forms of inequality, in which the numbers or proportion found at the top and bottom ends of the income distribution are growing at the expense of the middle, is called *social polarization.

Spatial inequality is the geographical expression of social inequality, recognizing that space is both the medium and outcome of social relations. In its simplest form, spatial inequality is revealed when one maps some attribute, e.g. income or education, aggregated into spatial units. This mapping does, however, conceal differences within spatial units and spatial inequality is scale-dependent (*see* ECOLOGICAL FALLACY; MODIFIABLE AREAL UNIT PROBLEM). As the *World Bank argues (2009), place is one, if not the most important, correlate of individual welfare. According to the World Bank's figures, a child born in a Zambian village will live less than half as long as one born in New York. The New Yorker will earn $4.5 million in their lifetime, the Zambian about $10,000. To the degree that a person's well-being is related to where they live, geographical difference is a large part of inequality. Switching to the processes that might cause inequality, these are clearly social and spatial, relating to the spatial distribution of social and economic resources, patterns of investment, spatial variation in *vulnerability, differences in *accessibility and mobility (*see* SPATIAL MISMATCH), and so forth (*see* SEGREGATION; SOCIAL EXCLUSION).

Geographical approaches to spatial inequality include extensive mapping, especially of income and health inequalities. Explanations of the cause of inequality differ. *Marxist theories concentrate on structural or *class differences, combined with an understanding of uneven development as intrinsic to capitalism (*see* MARXISM). *Feminist theories locate inequalities in *patriarchy, which structures the unequal access to society's goods but also shapes such things as geographical access to work. Liberal theories consider how location influences real income in indirect ways. For example, if it costs more to travel further to work and if one's health and house value are increased by being close to an unpolluted city park, then urban location patterns have an impact on one's overall income. Competition between classes of urban residents can be thought of as contributing to spatial inequality (*see* JUSTICE; WELFARE GEOGRAPHY). More recently, Danny *Dorling has forcefully argued that social inequality is perpetuated by injustice. *See also* WEALTH INEQUALITY.

Reference Dorling, D. (2011), *Injustice: Why Social Inequality Persists.*
World Bank (2009), *World Development Report: Reshaping Economic Geography.*

infant mortality (rate) The number of deaths within the first year of life as a proportion of the number of live births in a given year, usually expressed in the form x deaths per 1,000. Common causes of infant mortality include dehydration (from diarrhoea), pneumonia, malnutrition, and infectious diseases. The mother's general health is also significant, as is the overall state of the health care system. Infant mortality rates are often used as an indicator of the well-being of a society.

inferential statistics A branch of statistics used to make generalizations about a population based upon a sample. To do this, inferential statistics applies a statistical model to the set of sample data. The outcome is either an estimation or the testing of a *hypothesis. In the former case, the sample statistic is used to estimate a population characteristic, called a parameter, for example, calculating the mean or standard deviation. Given that the calculation is based on a sample, it is unlikely that the estimate will precisely match the true population parameter, so it is accompanied by a confidence interval (the likelihood that the estimated parameter matches the population parameter given the representativeness of the sample). In the latter case, a statistical test is used to evaluate, based on the sample data set, the relationship between independent and dependent variables and the validity of a hypothesis. Again this is accompanied by a confidence interval. A wide variety of inferential statistics are commonly used in geography including *Chi-Square test, *correlation, *factor analysis, *regression, *t-test. *See also* DESCRIPTIVE STATISTICS.

informal economy The sum of economic activities that are outside formal regulation, including labour laws, wage policies, health and safety rules, and accounting for tax purposes. Informal work may be carried out in otherwise formal or regulated enterprises. Efforts to analytically and empirically distinguish between formal and informal sectors have proved too complex and self-defeating. It is more meaningful to speak of processes of informalization.

informalization The process by which *work is undertaken in conditions characteristic of an *informal economy, i.e. one in which economic activities are outside formal regulation, including labour laws, wage policies, health and safety rules, and accounting for tax purposes. Because the boundaries between formal, i.e. legal, regulated, and taxed work and informal work are generally blurred, it is often impossible to identify distinct formal and informal sectors. Furthermore, the same task, for example, cutting a person's hair, may be undertaken formally, informally, or even out of friendship. Neither tasks nor enterprises can be classified unambiguously as formal or informal. Informalization is not defined by activity, but by the overall context of state regulation and its enforcement, the power of organized labour, and the opportunism of employers. The processes of informalization include the pressures to subcontract tasks, engage casual labour, and avoid regulations (*see* FLEXIBLE LABOUR; LABOUR FLEXIBILITY). Although informal work is typically thought to occur in cities of the *Global South, many analysts detect informalization more widely. Saskia *Sassen argues that it is a feature of *global cities such as *New York and *Los Angeles, where growing *income inequality, the availability of immigrant labour, and the rising cost of commercial premises have encouraged informalization in both services and labour-intensive manufacturing.

Information Age A historical period in which the creation, circulation, and consumption of information becomes central to the operations of economy and society. Countries that have experienced a post-industrial transition, such as *Japan, are often said to be more information-based than ever before. The idea of the Information Age refers not only to the widespread use of personal computers and mobile devices by citizens with access to the Internet, it also refers to companies that create and deploy information, such as management consultancies, investment banks, and insurance firms. These firms, it is sometimes said, create a more 'weightless economy', i.e. they generate profits from intangible goods such as software. *See also* CASTELLS, MANUEL; INFORMATION ECONOMY.

informational city A new urban reality characteristic of the *Information Age or in Manuel *Castells' original formulation, the informational mode of development. Because of revolutions in work, community, and family, it is marked by *social polarization, flexible working relations, and fragmented communities. For Castells, it is not a type of city but a generalized feature potentially found in all cities.

information and communication technologies (ICT) The suite of systems, devices, and protocols concerned with the production, storage, transmission, and manipulation of data, normally in a digital form. ICT refers to the convergence of computer networks, telephone networks, and other audio-visual networks made possible by the digitalization of information since the 1990s (*see* INTERNET). In general usage, the term ICT has replaced IT, or Information Technology, the sector concerned with computers and computer systems. If there is a difference, it is that ICT accents the technologies (e.g. wireless networks, communications satellites, and *social networking sites) while IT describes the branch of engineering and its associated skills.

information economy An *economy in which the majority of firms rely upon the purchase, creation, manipulation, or deployment of various kinds of information. In some definitions, an information economy marks a new phase in a country's economic evolution away from dependence on primary and manufacturing industry. However, other definitions point to the pervasive reliance upon and use of information across most branches of an economy. Thus, in a country such as Germany, car manufacture has—according to this wider definition—become highly 'informationalized' courtesy of everything from computer-controlled machines to the employment of thousands of accountants and lawyers.

information technology *See* INFORMATION COMMUNICATION TECHNOLOGY (ICT).

informed consent The permission given to a researcher by a respondent to record, analyse, publish, and archive aspects of their life for the purposes of a study. A standard aspect of *research ethics, in a technical sense, informed consent is a legal contract that sets out how a researcher interacts with a participant in their study and how they treat the data they collect. It is informed in the sense that the researcher needs to set out clearly and unambiguously what rights the participant is imparting to them. In some cases, respondents might not be able to impart such consent, such as people with intellectual disabilities or very young children, and the consent of guardians needs to be sought. Moreover, since neither researcher nor participant can fully anticipate how the research will unfold or what will happen to the findings, in this sense, neither party can ever be completely informed.

infrastructure The underlying physical networks of transport, communications, and utilities that enable the flow of people, goods, and services in society. Transport infrastructure includes roads, railways, and airports. Communications infrastructure includes telephone cables, internet broadband cabling, mobile telephone masts, and satellites. Utility networks include water, sewage, and power systems. Public services such as schools, hospitals, emergency services, and local government constitute social infrastructure. Such infrastructure systems are large, complex, and interconnected, and are critical to how places are organized and function.

INGO *See* NON-GOVERNMENTAL ORGANIZATION.

Ingold, Tim (1948–) A social anthropologist who has written extensively on place-making, dwelling, and human-animal relations. In particular he has forwarded an ecological approach concerning how environments are perceived, shaped, and understood by people that prioritizes the study of skilled practices rather than the examination of objects of material culture. His best-known work is *The Perception of the Environment* (2000) that combines *phenomenology and process philosophy to detail how the world and our relationship to it is always in formation. Ingold is a critic of *dualism in *ontology and *epistemology.

Initial Public Offering (IPO) The first-time sale to private or institutional investors of stocks and shares in a private company. Such companies—for example, Google—decide to make IPOs in order to raise additional *capital and to gain quick access to *money.

These liquid assets can be used to pay down existing debt and invest in new products, new processes, or entry into new markets.

inner city The area of an industrial city surrounding the commercial centre and that traditionally housed largely working-class households. Since the economic decline of many Western port and manufacturing cities since the 1950s, the term has acquired more discursive meanings as the site of a complex of social problems: crime, disorder, deprivation, poor health, and dilapidation (*see* SOCIAL EXCLUSION). From the 1960s, many countries embarked on inner-city policies to redress such problems through spatially targeted programmes (*see* URBAN PLANNING; REGIONAL PLANNING). Meanwhile, the actual areas often underwent *gentrification and *urban regneration.

innovation A term for translating a new idea (or invention) into a new process or product that is then implemented or commercialized, or finding new, more efficient or profitable ways to make, market, or sell an existing process or product. Innovation is important because it is potentially transformational and can create additional value to an organization by acting as a catalyst for growth. In the context of a *knowledge society, innovation is seen as a key driver of economic growth.

Innovation Diffusion as a Spatial Process A monograph by Torsten *Hägerstrand (1953) and a key early text in the development of *quantitative and *time geography, translated into English in 1967. Rather than undertake regional analysis, which dominated geographical praxis at the time of its writing, Hägerstrand wanted to scientifically investigate the spatial processes of specific issues. He chose to examine the ways in which six specific cultural artefacts and their effects diffused through a Swedish region (state subsidies for improving pastures, control of bovine tuberculosis, soil mapping, postal money transfer, automobiles, telephones) and how the rate and pattern of diffusion was shaped by planning and policy at national and regional levels. Importantly, he developed experimental, stochastic models to show how different innovations diffused within a population and pioneered the use of *Monte Carlo simulations.

IPO *See* INITIAL PUBLIC OFFERING.

input-output analysis A set of methods for calculating how the related inputs and outputs of a system are affected by their interdependencies. It is usually used for understanding linked sectors in an economy and how the outputs of one industry are inputs to another or how they are recursively interdependent. For example, coal is needed to produce steel, and steel is used in the extraction of coal. An input-output model estimates the relative production needed of both to produce certain outputs. Input-output analysis is used extensively by companies to calibrate their operations, and by governments in terms of calculating their national accounting and undertaking economic planning.

Institute of British Geographers (IBG) A professional organization that represented academic geographers in the UK. It was founded in 1933 as a sister body to the Royal Geographical Society (RGS) to specifically serve geography at the higher education level. The institute included a number of specialist research groups, organized conferences, field trips, seminars, published two journals, and lobbied for the interests of geography within the education system. In 1995, the IBG was merged with the RGS to form a single organization.

institutional economics An approach to the analysis of economic life that focuses on the organizations that comprise the *economy and the institutions (such as government) that seek to shape it. Dating from the 1920s, this approach challenged the *neoclassical economics view that it is possible to abstract from the difference among economic actors in order to identity common processes and tendencies. Institutionalists examine the ways that the history, identity, and composition of different firms are affected by the law, social customs, state regulations, and so on. Institutional economics thus shows all economic actors to be differentiated from one another, to be embedded in distinct milieux, and to be affected by varying ensembles of noneconomic factors. The approach has enjoyed something of a revival in the disciplines of economics and economic sociology, and dovetails well with the empirical (as opposed to purely theoretical) preoccupations of most economic geographers.

institutionalism An approach to the analysis of economy and/or society that focuses on the *modus operandi* and concrete influence of a range of institutions that affect firms, communities, and *civil society. Institutionalism seeks to avoid the analytical antinomies of *holism and *reductionism, *structuralism and atomism, *determinism and voluntarism. It sees economic and social life as complex, changeable, and contingent. The approach intersects well with much research in human geography because it is alive to spatial variability but also to the similarities between otherwise separate locations.

institutional racism *See* RACISM.

institutional thickness The degree to which private companies in a given place, region, or country have their activities supported by non-economic actors and their activities. 'Thickness' refers to a large number of such actors whose activities together offer comprehensive support to firms and so engender strong economic development.

instrumentalism An approach to any relationship, practice, or object that prioritizes ends over means. Instrumentalists will use whatever methods or resources are expedient in order to realize their goals. At best, they are pragmatists able to adapt to the opportunities and constraints of a situation. At worst, however, they can act immorally or with impunity to achieve their ends—hence the critics' motto 'The ends can never justify the means'. In human geography and many other social sciences, for example, modern capitalist society has been criticized for using *nature as a mere means to the end of amassing more wealth and improving standards of living. The result has been both a failure to treat the non-human world as an end in itself and to respect its needs or rights.

integrated transport policy The coordination of transport services so that bus, tram, rail, and road policy and practice are aligned. This includes the harmonization of infrastructure planning and development, the synchronization of timetables, and the development of multi-modal ticketing.

integration (economic) The horizontal and vertical organization and alliances of business firms and trade within and across borders. Alliances can take the form of agreements, cartels, mergers, and trade policy, and enable more efficient and profitable trading by firms. Horizontal integration relates to alliances between competitors, whereas vertical integration refers to the organization of the *supply chain from raw materials to product to customer. A vertically integrated concern is one that brings together various stages of the supply chain or production process under one company or organization. Horizontal disintegration is therefore the opposite. Integration also concerns the combination of regional and national economies into larger economic conglomerations through trade and tariff agreements. *See also* GATT.

integration (social) The blending of social groups wherein all members of society have equal rights and access to work and services, and mutual respect for each other's *cultures. It is often the case that different groups in society live in separate spaces and do not have equal status, with one group discriminated against by others. Social integration concerns creating *equal opportunities and equity, and a society wherein all members can live harmoniously. In *ethnic and *racial terms, this means respecting each other's culture and *religion, and not discriminating on the basis of race. It does not require *assimilation or enforced desegregation. In educational terms, this means the *mainstreaming of disabled children in ordinary, as opposed to special, schools. Much social policy is concerned with producing social, racial, and educational integration, and it is accompanied in law by equality legislation.

intellectual A person whose major occupation is to create ideas and arguments about abstract rather than practical matters. Strictly speaking, the term is not synonymous with 'academic' or 'scholar', since intellectuals need not be professional academics or researchers. Debates on intellectuals focus less on their exact definition and more on their role in society. The Italian Marxist Antonio Gramsci suggested that, although everyone was an intellectual, only a few actually performed that function in society. He distinguished between 'traditional intellectuals' who regarded themselves as elite and independent of society, and 'organic intellectuals' who were rooted in their social class and sought to express their class's interests. More recently, the issue has been whether they speak to their particular profession or, as 'public intellectuals', seek to articulate issues of wider consequence for humanity and/or the non-human world? Notable examples of public intellectuals include Noam Chomsky and Richard Dawkins; within human geography, David *Harvey and Jared *Diamond are the most visible and influential intellectuals outside the discipline (*see* PUBLIC GEOGRAPHY).

intellectual property rights (IPR) The set of legal protections afforded to parties recognized as owning specified ideas or information. These include patents, copyright, and trademark systems. *Property rights are usually thought of in terms of physical assets such as land or buildings. But as far back as 15th-century Italy, regulations protecting ideas emerged and, under the auspices of the modern state and legal system, were subsequently codified. Protection usually means a monopoly over the benefits of an idea over a specified period of time and/or within specified territorial jurisdictions. Although principally national, international systems of IPR date back to the 1880s, when artistic and literary works were covered.

There have been a number of important developments in IPR in the past three or four decades. Although living things were conventionally regarded as outside intellectual property, rulings by the US Supreme Court in the 1980s opened the way for biological entities and interventions to be patented. Cells, genes, and products thereof could be considered property. Secondly, the shift towards a *knowledge or *information economy in much of the *Global North encouraged a more aggressive attitude to protecting rights of all kinds. The unlicensed copying and distribution of material (known as copyright theft), in part made possible by the digitalization of all kinds of products motivated more intensive legislation. This was related to the expansion of transnational corporations, faced with the problem of protecting intellectual property across many incompatible national jurisdictions. Finally, under the *United Nations and the *World Trade Organization, there have been moves to systematize and harmonize intellectual property rights law at the international level (*see* TRIPS). All these developments have proved controversial. The ability of firms to patent 'life' raises significant ethical issues, for example. Moves to coordinate international IPR have often been challenged as a new form of imperialism—Western legal doctrines are imposed on other regions of the world. The notion that an idea is the unambiguous property of one or more individuals clashes with non-Western ways of viewing goods as *commons (*see* INDIGENOUS KNOWLEDGE).

According to Sarah Whatmore, legal decisions over IPR do not simply regulate existing objects, however. Particularly at the microbial and cellular scales, they also constitute new distinctions and relations within 'socio-material fabric'. *See also* LAW, GEOGRAPHY OF.

References Whatmore, S. (2002), *Hybrid Geographies.*

intensive agriculture A type of farming that involves a high input of capital and labour relative to the amount of land employed. The application of chemical pesticides, fungicides, and fertilizers, plus the use of machinery and informational technologies should result in higher productivity. In theory, therefore, intensive agriculture is found where land values are highest, for example, near centres of population or markets. *See also* EXTENSIVE AGRICULTURE.

intensive research The forms of inquiry that investigate the causal relationships among phenomena in order to discover the mechanisms that cause an event to take place. It typically studies in-depth a small group of individuals who share a large number of characteristics and seeks to reveal the structural relations and interactions among group members. The approach generally studies the individuals in their causal contexts using methods such as *interviews, *ethnography, and *observation. It contrasts with *extensive research that tries to determine the generality of causal mechanisms in relation to a wider population. *See also* CRITICAL REALISM.

intercropping The agricultural practice of growing one crop among plants of a different kind, planted either at the same time or in sequence. It acts as a form of pest control and soil conservation.

Interdependent Development A text by Harold C. Brookfield (1975) outlining a significant early critique of *modernization theories of *development that also anticipated themes of *post-colonialism and *environmentalism. Brookfield held positions in South Africa, Canada, the USA, the UK, and Australia, where he was chair of geography at Australian National University. The book was based on two decades of research in Melanesia as well as his thorough understanding of the history of development thinking.

interdisciplinarity The practice of combining knowledge, expertise, and techniques from different disciplines in order to investigate the world or address a problem. Modern universities have long had disciplines as their intellectual foundation. Typically, these have produced specialists possessed of deep knowledge pertaining to a certain category of phenomena (e.g. human anatomy), to the world as seen from a particular perspective (e.g. history), or both (e.g. the political history of modern Africa). Interdisciplines are organized so as to combine a myriad of specialisms and to cross the boundaries between topics, techniques, and methods normally dealt with in separate disciplines. Geography is one such interdiscipline because its practitioners offer their students a combination of training in environmental science, social science, and the *humanities. However, as traditional disciplines have grown in size and diversified, many can arguably be seen as interdisciplines, though questions remain about how far practitioners and students are able to achieve mastery of the full range of knowledges, methods, and perspectives available to them. These questions very much apply to geography whose practitioners are typically specialists in one subfield (e.g. geomorphology or *economic geography). It is rare to find a professional geographer well versed in all of physical or human geography, never mind both. Similarly, many undergraduate geography degrees permit students a wide choice of modules, meaning they can focus on just one or two areas of geography as a whole. Therefore, geography has been said to be a somewhat indisciplined interdiscipline.

These difficulties are symptomatic of the challenges that all interdisciplines face in realizing their potential. It is more common to find this potential realized in problem- or topic-focused research teams that are assembled specially in university research centres, independent research institutes, or research-based foundations, and think-tanks. These teams have become more numerous and visible over the last 25 years, so much so that Michael Gibbons et al. talk of *Mode 2 science' as a new feature of the epistemic landscape. Such knowledge typically arises from attempts to solve real-world problems, such as mitigating the effects of global *climate change. Mode 2 science is not an alternative to Mode 1 (or disciplined-based) knowledge. Instead, it builds upon it pragmatically which suggests that disciplines are still the most important feature of the landscape of human knowledge.

Further reading Gibbons, M. et al. (1994), *The New Production of Knowledge*.
Herbert, D. and Matthews, J. (eds.) (2004), *Unifying Geography*.

Intergovernmental Panel on Climate Change (IPCC) A panel set up by the United Nations Environment Program (UNEP) and the World Meteorological Organization (WMO) in 1988, the IPCC is, in its own words, 'the leading body for the assessment of climate change' and aims 'to provide the world with a clear scientific view on the current state of climate change and its potential environmental and socio-economic consequences'. Rather than commission or conduct its own research, the IPCC surveys and synthesizes independently conducted inquiries by certified experts into climate change. Its fourth report was issued in 2007. Its three working groups focus on different major dimensions of climate change, and these reports aim to be policy relevant but not prescriptive. Working Group 1, which focuses on the science of climate change, has done a great deal to persuade political leaders and the public that anthropogenic climate change is now occurring.

SEE WEB LINKS
• Website of the IPCC.

intermediate technology *See* APPROPRIATE TECHNOLOGY.

intermodal transport A term for transportation by more than one form of carrier during a single journey. This could be a passenger who walks to a station, catches a train, then uses a bus to get from home to work. Or it could be the movement of freight by truck, sea, and rail, wherein a container of goods is transferred between transport modes. Importantly, movement in both cases is efficiently connected and coordinated, and the system is viewed as integrated. *See also* CONTAINERIZATION; INTEGRATED TRANSPORT POLICY; LOGISTICS.

internal colonialism The exercise of *colonialism within, as opposed to beyond, the boundaries of a country. The term was first popularized by Latin American development economists to describe unequal relations within countries. It was widely adopted by African-American and Mexican-American scholars and activists in the 1960s to describe the institutional nature of racism within the USA, particularly in the form of spatial segregation and legal exclusion. Harold Cruse likened ghettos to domestic colonies, while Rodolfo 'Corky' Gonzales compared southwestern USA to a European colony. In the 1970s, political sociologist Michael Hechter applied the concept to Britain's Celtic peripheries.

internally displaced person (IDP) A person who is forced to flee their home but who remains within their country's borders. The cause of flight is generally conflict or other violence, but may also be environmental disaster. Large numbers of IDPs are found in Colombia, DR Congo, Iraq, and Sudan. Some may find refuge in camps, but others relocate to urban areas, often without coming to the attention of authorities.

internal migration A change of residence within national boundaries, usually implying movement between parts of a country rather than at a smaller scale.

international division of labour The *spatial division of labour manifested at the global scale. Though people may be employed in either the private, public, the voluntary (or 'third'), or the informal sectors, the term 'the international division of labour'—coined by economists—pertains mostly to private sector employment. Until the 1960s, the overwhelming majority of jobs in manufacturing and the service sectors were concentrated in just a few countries, namely, the capitalist democracies of Western Europe, North America, Japan, and the Australasia, and secondarily, the communist economies of Eastern Europe and the USSR. The majority of countries in Central and South America, Africa, and Southeast Asia, by contrast, had very high levels of employment in agriculture. However, through a combination of public policies designed to foster indigenous industries and the geographical relocation by Western *transnational companies of assembly plants, a *new international division of labour was created from the late 1960s onwards. A group of developing countries that became known as the *Newly Industrializing Economies (NICs) began to account for a notably larger share of global manufacturing employment. In recent years, they have also seen increases in service sector employment including information-based industries such as banking, insurance, and computer software design.

One view of the reasons for the division of labour between countries is that it reflects both *comparative advantage and *competitive advantage. Firms (both indigenous and overseas) invest in economic activities in country A that are 'rational' given the resources (physical and human) available, the costs of labour, and transportation etc. Meanwhile, firms in country B do the same, and the two countries trade the commodities they are best placed to produce. However, this view is arguably far too simplistic. For instance, it ignores things like trade regulations that one country may impose to protect its own industries from overseas competition. This example speaks to the way such things as asymmetries in political and economic power between countries can serve to shape the international division of labour in ways that depart from the 'rational' employment landscape predicted by *neoclassical economics and its derivatives.

International Financial System (IFS) The group of financial services companies and those bodies tasked with regulating them that operate across political borders. Though a great many financial services companies do not have significant overseas portfolios and are largely subject to national regulations, others—such as Barclays Bank—have branches and investments all over the world. In the wake of the *Great Depression and the *Second World War, the leading capitalist democracies decided to create institutions that could assist private banks and national governments with monetary transactions, debts, loans, and repayments—notably the Bank for International Settlements, the *International Monetary Fund (IMF), and the *World Bank. From the 1960s, there were further efforts to harmonize national policies in order to properly regulate international companies. Today the IFS is a complex configuration designed to ensure orderly flows of money between governments and financial services firms. It failed, however, to prevent the global financial crisis of 2007–, after which some far-reaching reforms to the system were implemented.

International Geographical Union (IGU) Preceded by ten international geographical congresses, the first of which was held in Antwerp in 1871, the IGU was founded in 1922 in Brussels. It links together geographers and geographical societies from around the world and promotes geographical scholarship. Structurally, the organization is divided into three components: a general assembly with delegates appointed by member countries, an executive committee, and thirty-eight commissions that organize international workshops and conferences on particular themes. Every fourth year it hosts a large, international congress.

International Geosphere-Biosphere Program (IGBP) An international programme, launched in 1987, that coordinates international research on global-scale and regional-scale interactions between human systems and the Earth's biological, chemical, and physical processes. It aims to provide scientific leadership and knowledge in order to guide society onto a sustainable pathway during rapid global change. *See also* EARTH SYSTEM SCIENCE; INTERNATIONAL HUMAN DIMENSIONS PROGRAM ON GLOBAL ENVIRONMENTAL CHANGE.

International Human Dimensions Program on Global Environmental Change (IHDP) An integrated social science programme focused on global environmental change and the role of human activity in shaping the Earth's biophysical cycles. Conversely, it also considers how human societies need to adapt their behaviour to minimize further negative effects on the environment and also militate against risks such as *climate change. *See also* INTERNATIONAL GEOSPHERE-BIOSPHERE PROGRAM.

( ) SEE WEB LINKS
• Official website of the International Human Dimensions Program on Global Environmental Change.

International Labour Organization (ILO) A *United Nations body tasked with promoting high standards for the employment of workers worldwide. The ILO is a tripartite organization that seeks to involve the representatives of workers, employers, and national governments in formulating and implementing international labour standards. It is thus an 'honest broker' and a principled advocate for workers, unlike trades unions, which formally represent their members and are thus constitutively partisan.

International Monetary Fund (IMF) An intergovernmetnal organization that works to foster global monetary cooperation, secure financial stability, facilitate international trade, and promote sustainable economic growth. The IMF is based in Washington, DC, and by convention has always been headed by a European. It currently has 186 member countries, whose voting strength is related to their funding contribution. The USA has the most significant influence on the IMF's decisions, but in the wake of the 2007 global economic crisis, the relative power of *BRICs is increasing. It was founded as a reaction to the *Great Depression, wherein trade barriers designed to protect failing economies led to a sharp decline in trade. It also responded to the need for a stable, robust economy post-*Second World War, and was one of the outcomes of the 1944 *Bretton Woods negotiations. Its principal role was to oversee the international monetary system— the system of exchange rates and payments that enabled international trade. It could also lend funds to countries to aid them in the *structural adjustment of their economies. It has therefore been important during economic crises such as the global recession following the 1970s oil crisis, the collapse of the Soviet Bloc, and the global financial crisis of 2007-, in coordinating a financial response and managing debt burdens. The IMF has also been the target of much critique, notably in relation to its *structural adjustment programmes that many argue lead to an increase in poverty in recipient countries.

( ) SEE WEB LINKS
• Official website of the International Monetary Fund.

International Organization for Migration (IOM) An intergovernmental organization founded in 1951 and based in Geneva, the IOM aims to encourage the orderly and humane management of international migration by providing advice to governments and other bodies, to publish reports, compile statistics, and promote policy debate. It is not part of the UN and not all states are members.

SEE WEB LINKS
- Official website of the International Organization for Migration.

International Organization for Standardization (ISO) A non-governmental organization made up of the national standards institutes of 161 countries, and responsible for the development and publication of recognized standards of quality, safety, reliability, efficiency, environmental friendliness, and interchangeability. Standards relate to products and services delivered by the private and public sectors and ensure that they meet certain compliance thresholds.

International Relations (IR) An academic discipline originally concerned with the political relations between states but now embracing non-state political actors at the global scale and drawing on the full range of social sciences. It was institutionalized in the UK after the First World War, and spread to the USA and other Western countries. IR covers much of the same ground as *geopolitics, and the two subjects are frequently taught together. *See also* STATE.

international trade theory A set of models and explanations of the ideal conditions of trade among countries. The two main influences on the theory are David Ricardo's ideas of *comparative advantage formulated in the 18th century, and the Heckscher-Ohlin theory of the early 20th century. The former suggests that countries should specialize in products for which they have cost or efficiency advantages, while the latter proposes that countries should export goods that are based on abundant national resources and import those based on scarce national resources. The 'new trade theory' pioneered by Paul *Krugman models how international trade positively affects the distribution of economic activity but without national differences in factor endowments, i.e. natural resources.

Internet The global network of computer networks through which computational devices (e.g., PCs, laptops, smart phones) can communicate and share information. The networks consist of *telecommunication linkages such as copper, coaxial, and fibre-optic cables and radio and microwave transmission, and are scaled within a hierarchy of networks from local hubs to service providers to regional, national, and international backbone linkages. Although individual networks are diversely owned and have different speeds/capacities they connect and exchange information with each other through communication protocols, in the case of the Internet, most commonly TCP/IP (Transmission Control Protocol/Internet Protocol). Combining computational devices and networks across the globe has radically transformed the sharing of all kinds of information, led to new forms of *media and communication, created new social formations, and reconfigured the *space-economy by enabling radical *time-space compression.

Initially the Internet provided two principal attractions for most people. First, it allowed rapid communication and interaction between individuals located in different places in a variety of forms such as email, bulletin boards, chat, mailing lists, and virtual worlds, including the sharing of files. Second, it enabled people to access a vast collection of digital information that could be searched, retrieved, and read in new ways, including extensive geographic data such as *maps, and to buy goods and services online. Since the middle of the first decade of the new millennium, everyday users could easily and actively participate in the production of the online world, designing, editing, and sharing content, without the need for specialist technical knowledge or programming skills. The Internet started to transition from a place mainly focused on narrow channels of communication and consumption (Web 1.0) to a place of participation, production, and interactivity (Web 2.0), in which people could add value to sites as they used them. Examples of such new media include *social-networking sites (e.g. Facebook), blogs, and microblogs (e.g., WordPress, Twitter), photo- and video-sharing sites (e.g., Flickr and YouTube), wikis (open, collectively authored information resources, e.g., Wikipedia), folksonomies (collective tagging of information, e.g., Del.icio.us and Digg), and *mashups. Recently, the move towards ubiquitous computing—the embedding of software into many different objects and environments and networking them into the Internet—has created a so-called 'Internet of things' that help produce what some have called smart cities (landscapes that are computationally rich). As such, the Internet is spreading far beyond interconnected computers to include all kinds of digital devices (such as cameras, lifts, security doors, televisions).

The Internet is widely understood as a transformative technology, changing societies in a number of ways at a number of scales, altering social and cultural, political and institutional, and economic relations, in part because it alters spatial relations by facilitating radical *time-space compression. For many, the Internet enables the creation of new *social networks and communities that are not encumbered by what people look like or where they live, but rather around what they say, think, believe, and are interested in. The Internet alters how people can discuss and communicate around political issues, how they can organize and protest, how they can engage with politicians and with institutions and state bodies. The Internet is revolutionizing how business is conducted, transforming patterns and modes of work, how companies are organized and function, and facilitating the growth of a *knowledge economy. Data and information are viewed as commodities that can shape and enhance how a company operates, leading to forms of office automation, *telework, and the reconfiguration of company organization including the adoption of *back-offices, that creates efficiencies and increased productivity, competitiveness, and profits. Internet technologies and infrastructures are altering how cities operate, facilitating so-called 'smart buildings', changing how transport systems are monitored and run, and how services are managed and delivered.

Not unsurprisingly then, the Internet has become a focal point for geographical analysis, with research focusing on the actual geography of the Net itself (where the physical infrastructure is located and how it is connected together), and the spatial effects of its use. Such research can sometimes overstate the effects of the Internet, for example, suggesting that it has led to the 'death of distance' or that it creates the means for a truly panoptic form of *surveillance, or that it offers untold benefits to individuals and businesses empowering them through enhanced information and communication which promotes and supports democracy (*see* ARAB SPRING), and new opportunities (*see* TECHNOLOGICAL DETERMINISM). It is perhaps better to view it as being transformative in a broad sense, with some effects being positive, others negative.

In addition, the Internet is increasingly becoming a medium through which research is conducted. The Internet is a key resource through which information such as data, policy documents, news items, academic papers is accessed, connecting researchers to all kinds of digital archives. It is also possible to generate primary data through online surveys and interviews, and to observe social networks and their interactions. *See also* CYBERSPACE; DIGITAL DIVIDE; VIRTUAL GLOBES.

Further reading Dodge, M. and Kitchin, R. (2000), *Mapping Cyberspace*.
Hine, C. (2005), *Virtual Methods*.
Kitchin, R. and Dodge, M. (2011), *Code/Space: Software and Everyday Life*.

Warf, B. (2012), *Global Geographies of the Internet.*
Zook, M. (2005), *The Geography of the Internet Industry.*

Internet Corporation for Assigned Names and Numbers (ICANN) The global coordinating body for Internet addresses. Formed in 1998, ICANN is a not-for-profit public-benefit corporation that develops and maintains the allocation of the Internet's unique address identifiers, i.e. '.org.' '.com.' '.ca', and so forth. It does not control or police the content of the Internet, but it does allow all the computers on all the ICT networks around the world to communicate with each other.

SEE WEB LINKS
• Official website of the Internet Corporation for Assigned Names and Numbers.

interpellation The process by which people are induced to voluntarily subscribe to and desire the logic of systems that work to regulate and subjugate them. It was first used by French Marxist philosopher Louis Althusser to explain why people were willing participants in *capitalism even though it exploits their labour for capital accumulation. His argument was that people are ideologically conditioned to view the benefits, and future potential benefits, seemingly gained from capitalism as enough succour to override any negative consequences of exploitation. In more recent human geography, interpellation is widely used by *feminist geographers to describe the processes by which managers and employers construct the ideal worker in terms of gender, race, skill, appearance, deportment, etc. (McDowell 2009). In interactive service work, where employees have direct contact with customers, there can be a process of dual interpellation; workers must conform to the expectations of both managers and customers. Interpellation is a useful way of understanding heterogeneous workplaces. *See also* MARXISM.

Reference McDowell, L. (2009), *Working Bodies.*

interpolation, spatial A technique for estimating the values at unsampled sites within an area using sampled observations. The method relies on *Tobler's first law of geography, that points near to each other are like each other (*see* SPATIAL AUTOCORRELATION). By using interpolation a data surface can be created to cover the area. For example, we might have the sale price of a number of houses. Using interpolation we can estimate the prices of other houses dependent on their nearness to other houses. *See also* KRIGING.

interpretive approaches The methods of analysis that rely on the interpretive skills of the researcher to turn the data into meaning. Typically, interpretive approaches are applied to qualitative data such as texts (*literature, policy documents, transcripts of interviews) and representations (e.g., *art, *photographs, *films). While these can be analysed in a formalized, quantitative way through methods such as *content analysis, they are more often studied using methods such as discourse analysis or deconstruction that seeks to uncover deeper meanings held within them. How the interpretation is applied is strongly shaped by the theoretical framing of the study (e.g., *feminism, *post-structuralism, *post-colonialism, *psychoanalysis), which set out methodological toolkits for how meaning should be extracted and made sense of. A common critique of interpretive approaches is that the analysis is little more than subjective opinion of the researcher, shaped by their values and ideological bias, rather than being objective, neutral, and value-free. To counter such critiques, those using interpretive approaches often seek to detail their *situatedness in the field and their *positionality *vis-à-vis* the issue under examination. They also employ the same level of rigour and systematization in the application of their methodology and analysis as those using non-interpretative approaches. *See also* HERMENEUTICS; THICK DESCRIPTION.

intersectionality The theory that various forms of discrimination centred on race, gender, class, disability, sexuality, and other forms of identity, do not work independently but interact to produce particularized forms of social oppression. As such, oppression is the result of intersecting forms of exclusionary practices. It is thus suggested that the study of identity-based discrimination needs to identify and take account of these intersectionalities.

Further reading Valentine, G. (2007), 'Theorizing and researching intersectionality', *Professional Geographer* 59: 10–21.

intertextuality The influence of other texts on a text. A text here could be a story, poem, film, painting, and so on. The degree of intertextuality might be quite overt, such as directly quoting from another text, or parodying a particular scene, or it might be more subtle, such as adopting the same style or structure. The theory of intertextuality, taken from the field of semiotics, argues that rather than meaning simply being transferred from writer to reader, it is instead mediated by a set of codes imparted to the writer and reader by other texts. In other words, we bring our knowledge and experience of interacting and producing other texts to bear on writing and reading texts. Interpreting a text from this perspective then consists of *deconstructing its intertextuality, not simply trying to read its meaning.

interval data *See* DATA.

interviews and interviewing A conversational form of data generation. Interviews can be structured (a form of verbal *questionnaire), semi-structured, or unstructured in nature. They are best conducted face-to-face, though they can be done by telephone or via the Internet. A group form of interview is the *focus group. Interviews are a particularly good method for gathering data on people's experiences, opinions, aspirations, and feelings. They can provide a much fuller and richer data set than highly structured *questionnaires, where the questions are more likely to be closed in nature, because the conversational format allows interviewees to expand on their views and allows the interviewer to be responsive to the answers received. On the negative side, interviews are more costly in time terms to undertake and analyse. There is also a greater risk of the interviewer introducing bias through prompting and question phrasing. For interviews to be successful, the interviewer needs to be a good conversationalist with a high level of interpersonal skills as an interview is a complex social encounter that has to be appropriately managed. The interviewer must be able to put the interviewee at ease and develop a sense of trust, ask questions in an interesting manner, be able to listen to the responses and act accordingly, and record the responses without upsetting the conversational flow. It is essential that the interview is adequately recorded to enable appropriate analysis. Generally, interviews are recorded by either audio recording the discussion for later *transcription or the jotting down of comprehensive notes. It is important to gain *informed consent for conducting interviews and to comply with *research ethics.

Further reading King, N. and Horrocks, C. (2010), *Interviews in Qualitative Research.*

investment The conversion of money by a firm or government body into various non-liquid assets with a view to creating immediate or future economic growth. For instance, firms may invest in developing new products or new production facilities in new countries. Governments, by contrast, may invest in major infrastructure projects designed to benefit many firms, as well as consumers and citizens. Most investments involve a meaningful element of risk, and many do not produce the hoped-for results or returns.

Iran An Islamic country and representative democracy located in the *Middle East. Formerly known as Persia, it is highly mountainous, has an arid and semi-arid climate, and is a major oil exporter. Its capital is Tehran, with a population of over seven million—around a tenth of the national population. Despite considerable revenues from oil, the national economy is not among the largest or most complex. Per capita income also remains modest by international standards. Politically, relations with the leading Western democracies remain tense, in large part because Islamic fundamentalism has been important since the Iranian Revolution of 1979. The Iranian government is also implicated with geopolitical developments in other countries of the region and endured a long and bloody war with neighbouring Iraq throughout the 1980s.

Iraq A large country located in the *Middle East and, historically, one of the great hearths of civilization. It became a nation state in 1932 by securing independence from Britain. In 1979 it became a single party state following a *coup d'état* by Saddam Hussein, whose Ba'ath party ruled autocratically for the next twenty-four years. In a quest for additional oil resources Iraq's army invaded Kuwait in 1991 but was repelled by coalition forces led by the United States. Following the terrorist attack on the World Trade Center in 2001, coalition forces invaded Iraq on dubious evidence, leading to the Second *Gulf War. Since then the country's security and law and order has been reliant on enforcement by US forces and their allies. A planned withdrawal of overseas troops will be completed by 2014. The country is on course to be a representative democracy with an export-orientated economy organized along capitalist lines and centred on oil (*see* PETRO-CAPITALISM). However, internecine differences in political aspirations, ethnic identities, religious commitments, and regional loyalties may yet plunge the country into civil war.

irredentism A movement claiming territory in one country should belong to another because of historical, cultural, or legal circumstances; for example, the Republic of Ireland's claims to Northern Ireland or Argentina's claims to the Falkland Islands. Irredentists may advocate annexation of the disputed territory by force.

Isard, Walter (1919–2010) A US economist who laid the modern foundations of *location theory and helped to found the Regional Science Association (RSA) in 1954. Isard was a mathematician by background and, when later an economist, turned his attention to explaining the geographical location of economic activities. He was particularly interested in explaining the causes of sustained regional development, using mainstream economic ideas, mathematics, statistics, and rigorous logic to do so. The term *regional science became a neologism for his favoured approach. Isard envisaged regional science to be able to explain patterns of land use, economic growth, transportation, and so on, across different cities and city-regions. Isard published many books and articles, among the earliest and most notable being *Location and Space-Economy* (1956). In this monograph he translated ideas from the German location theorists Alfred Weber and Johann von Thünen. He also worked at prestigious universities, including Harvard, MIT, and Cornell. This allowed him to gain recognition in the economics profession and have regional science taken seriously as an intellectual pursuit with public policy implications. However, Isard always envisaged regional science as an interdisciplinary, problem-driven field. Several spatial scientists in geography were influenced by Isard's thinking and many became active members of the RSA (*see* SPATIAL SCIENCE).

ISI Web of Knowledge A suite of databases and tools that collate and analyse data concerning the citation of academic research. It has become a highly influential platform in the measurement of academic performance as it purports to measure the impact of research through its use by other academics. *See also* CITATION GEOGRAPHY.

(⊕) SEE WEB LINKS
• Website of the ISI Web of Knowledge.

Islam A major world religion focused on the worship of Allah (Almighty God). It is a monotheistic faith, whose principles and teaching were revealed through the Prophet Muhammad and articulated by the Qur'an, a text considered to be the verbatim word of Allah. Islamic life is structured around the five pillars of Islam, which set out obligatory acts of worship, and Islamic law, which details how everyday life should be practised. There are over one billion followers worldwide.

ISO *See* INTERNATIONAL ORGANIZATION FOR STANDARDIZATION.

Israel A country located in the *Middle East on the Mediterranean coast, it is the world's only country with a majority Jewish population. It came into being in 1948 after Britain withdrew from administering Palestine and was intended to be a *homeland for Jews, many of whom faced discrimination and persecution in their birth countries (*see* GENOCIDE; HOLOCAUST). Israel has defended its borders robustly against perceived and real incursions by its Arab neighbours, such as Egypt and Jordan. It has waged various wars against these neighbours and occupied territories they claim as their own. The United States has long tried to broker peace agreements between Israel and its Arab neighbours, even as it has adopted a largely pro-Israel stance. Israel is a representative democracy with a complex and prosperous economy. Its per capita wealth is among the highest in the region. Its major cities are Tel Aviv and *Jerusalem, and its population is nearly eight million.

IT industry The totality of firms engaged in the manufacture and use of computers, telecommunications equipment, and electronic applications in order to store, retrieve, transmit, and manipulate data. Leading IT firms include Microsoft and Apple. Product development typically requires highly skilled labour, although routine aspects of production (e.g. computer assembly) involve low-skilled labourers often working in factories in *NICs such as Mexico. The industry is central to the existence of many new industrial districts around the world, most famously *Silicon Valley in California. *See also* HI-TECH INDUSTRY; NEW REGIONALISM.

Italy A capitalist democracy located in southern Europe, occupying all of a peninsula extending into the Mediterranean Sea and adjacent islands, and bordered to the north by Switzerland, France, Austria, and Slovenia. Originally the centre of the Roman empire, by the late 19th century is was a collection of principalities and city states rather than a nation state. Unity was achieved in 1861, and a national government put in place subject to periodic elections. The northern part of the country was industrialized far more than the south, creating significant patterns of regional uneven development that persist to this day. In the early 20th century, Italy harboured imperial ambitions, seeking to emulate the overseas ventures of other European states. By 1939, it was a single-party *fascist state and joined Germany in the *Second World War with Britain, the United States, and their allies. After 1945 electoral democracy resumed, though with several periods of coalition rather than majority government. Today, the country is among the wealthiest in the world, and a major exporter of manufactured goods, including motor vehicles, clothes, and wine. It is also a major tourist destination. Its population numbers 60 million and its capital city is Rome.

J

Jackson, Peter (1955–) A social and cultural geographer at the University of Sheffield, England, who has played a key role in establishing *new cultural geography and reinvigorating *social geography. His research has focused predominately on the geographies of *race, *masculinity, and *consumption. Throughout, he attends to the complexities of meaning and the way people construct places, place images, and landscapes so as to express relations of power and resistance. His best-known work is *Maps of Meaning* (1989), which set out a geographical cultural materialism focused on the social and spatial construction of *identity and the playing-out of *cultural politics.

Japan A large country in East Asia located on the western fringe of the Pacific Ocean. It is an archipelago of thousands of islands, but Honshu, Hokkaido, and Kyushu are the largest and contain the majority of the country's 127 million citizens. Japan is largely mountainous and forested and lies along the boundary between continental plates, making it prone to earthquakes. The majority of the country's settlements are located on the coast.

Until the mid-19th century, Japan was an isolated state ruled by a warrior class. By the early 20th century the country had began to industrialize and to trade with the rest of the world. It had also adopted many features of other representative democracies. Its leaders sought to expand their immediate sphere of geopolitical influence by appropriating territory from Russia and China. During the *Second World War it sided with Nazi Germany and its allies, attacking the American naval base at Pearl Harbor in the Pacific Ocean. The Americans subsequently entered the war and detonated two atomic bombs over Hiroshima and Nagasaki leading to Japan's surrender in 1945. The institutions and norms of liberal democracy were promoted from 1947, with the emperor given a more titular role than previously, and Japan was allowed to join the *United Nations in 1956.

A remarkable period of industrial growth followed, sometimes called the Japanese 'economic miracle'. The precondition for this success was strong cooperation between national government, a relatively small number of large firms, and the sizeable workforces employed by these firms (*see* DEVELOPMENTAL STATE). These firms became known as *keiretsu* and had a common business philosophy, entered into strategic partnerships, and had common shareholdings. Rather than trying to maximize shareholder value in the short-term they took a long-term view focused on making high-quality commodities, innovative products, and sustained profits. There were several *keiretsu* and their constituent firms included now famous names such as Honda and Mitsubishi. These *keiretsu* covered a wide range of industries, from automobile manufacture to chemicals and shipbuilding. This ensured economic robustness, protecting Japan from over-reliance on one or two major industries.

During the 1960s and 1970s, Japan progressively liberalized its economy, exporting cars, motorbikes, cameras, stereo systems, and other complex manufactured products to the wider world. Through a combination of quality, affordability, and novelty, these commodities proved to be very successful in foreign markets. In turn, this yielded foreign exchange earnings and profits that enabled further investment, as well as a capacity to import wanted goods and services from overseas. In addition, the custom of saving money rather than taking on debt ensured liquidity was available for firms at low interest rates set by government and private banks. By the late 1980s, Japan had the world's second largest economy and its population was among the wealthiest.

However, Japan suffered a sustained period of low economic growth from the early 1990s, leading to what are sometimes called 'the lost years'. The accumulation of wealth over the previous 30-plus years led private investors to seek out new opportunities to make a profit. A property bubble developed wherein a myriad of developers, owners, and *rentiers borrowed money to construct new buildings and refurbish existing ones. When interest rates rose in 1989 much of the borrowing became unpayable, leading to a drop in property prices, bankruptcies, and many firms losing money. *Keiretsu* and other firms paid off debts from savings and earnings, private investment declined, and government borrowing and spending greatly increased the national debt. Despite all this, Japanese firms remained internationally competitive and unemployment rates did not soar. However, the number of temporary jobs increased, poverty is more widespread, and the benefits enjoyed by a previous generation of workers became far less common. Today, Japan remains among the most economically important countries in the world.

Jerusalem One of the world's oldest continuously occupied cities and a major urban centre of *Israel. Settled over 5000 years ago, it holds a unique place in world history. Jerusalem is holy to three faiths, *Judaism, *Christianity, and *Islam, and the historic centre contains significant sites and places of worship associated with all three (*see* RELIGION; SACRED SPACE). Although Israel regards it as its capital, parts of the city's status is contested in international law. East Jerusalem, annexed by Israel in 1967, is regarded by some authorities as occupied Palestinian territory.

Jevons paradox The proposition that the more efficiently a resource is used the more of it is likely to be consumed. The proposition was first made by English economist William Stanley Jevons in the 19th century. He observed that technological innovations that allowed less of a resource to be used in order to yield the same result did not help to reduce the overall consumption of that resource. The paradox has been referred to in recent debates in human geography and other social sciences over how to decarbonize the global economy (*see* LOW CARBON ECONOMY). For instance, energy-efficient light bulbs may appear to require less power but in the long run could allow societies to use the same amount of coal and natural gas as they would have done in the medium term.

Johnston, Ron (1941–) A highly productive British geographer whose contributions to research and teaching in human geography are, in respect of their breadth, virtually unmatched by any of his contemporaries or successors. Currently Emeritus Professor of Human Geography at Bristol University, he worked at Sheffield University for many years before becoming vice-chancellor of Essex University (1992–5). He has written about a very wide range of issues but is best known for his research in political geography, urban social geography, the history of the discipline, and the use of quantitative methods, and his pedagogic contributions through a range of textbooks. In particular, he is an expert on political voting and *electoral geography, and on the development of geography as a discipline in the 20th century, encapsulated in his book *Geography and Geographers* (1st ed. 1979), now in its sixth edition. As well as publishing hundreds of papers and dozens of books, he was a long-serving editor of the journals *Environment and Planning A* and *Progress in Human Geography*. Johnston has received a great many academic prizes and accolades and was awarded a British OBE in 2011.

journals 1. A regular record of activity and events such as a business diary or parliamentary debate.

2. A regular, scholarly publication of the latest research and thinking within a field. With regards to the former, journals are an important source of historical evidence concerning events at different periods of time. They might include the journals of overseas expeditions or the regimental diaries of troops. In terms of scholarly publication, journals are a key form of scientific dissemination. Aimed at a scholarly audience, each journal focuses on a particular field or specialism and publishes a range of different types of article: research papers, review essays, commentaries, and book reviews. Research papers are generally peer-reviewed and are expected to be original, insightful, and to advance knowledge and debate. They are typically published by learned societies and university and commercial presses for a fee, though there has been a recent growth in open-access journals.

Judaism A monotheistic faith that adheres to the religious and ethical guidelines set out in the Torah (the Law). At the core of the faith is a belief in a covenant between God and the Jews, wherein they are appointed as his chosen people in order to set an example of holiness and ethical behaviour to the world. As a people, Jews have long suffered anti-Semitic discrimination and are scattered across the world, though Israel constitutes a homeland. *See also* DIASPORA; HOLOCAUST.

justice A normative concept and principle that aims to regulate the behaviour of institutions and individuals towards people and the non-human world. It spans the divides across ethical reasoning, political philosophy, and legal theory. There is no agreed definition of justice; it is a contested idea with different definitions assuming the status of enforceable legal principles in different times and places. This legal enforceability underpins the well-known saying that 'justice is served' when a jury or a judge reaches a decision after a court case. However defined, justice is usually regarded as more fundamental than respect, compassion, benevolence, mercy, or charity—all concepts that have, like justice, an essential moral dimension. For example, nowadays slavery is considered profoundly unjust not because it constitutes deep disrespect for the persons enslaved; it is unjust because it abrogates the basic rights all persons are entitled to have upheld by the societies in which they live. These rights are stated in the *United Nations Declaration on Human Rights (1948) and the constitutions of many countries worldwide.

*Rights is one of several elemental concepts that constitute justice in its several definitions. Others include needs, deserts, and entitlements. Each of these concepts can be disaggregated. For instance, property rights are not the same as civil rights or cultural rights. In terms of enforcement, there are three broad categories of justice that cross-cut the different particular definitions just mentioned. Retributive justice describes the range of punishments dealt out to those deemed to have behaved unjustly according to the law. These punishments are differentiated by degree and kind according to the injustices involved. Restorative justice describes various compensations given to victims of injustice, either by those offending against them or another body (e.g. a national government) acting as a proxy for absent or previous offenders. Finally, distributive justice addresses systemic, group-level, or spatial variations in things deemed highly important for all people to live a decent life or at least have the chance of so doing. Examples include monetary wealth, various non-money assets, or access to clean water. While much retributive justice is dispensed to punish individual people or institutions, the other two forms of justice also often involve collectives, such as ethnic minorities or nation states.

Justice is of interest to geographers for at least three reasons. First, lay and legal concepts of justice vary between countries and thus create opportunities for comparison, mutual learning, and the transfer of ideas between contexts. Second, questions arise about whether and how to create greater uniformity in justice within and between nation states. Finally, restorative and distributive justice are intrinsically spatial in that they frequently involve the transfer of resources within and between nation states. Critical reflection on both these forms of justice as presently operationalized also invites us to imagine a future world in which these transfers may be more significant than is currently the situation. The few human geographers who have devoted their careers to analysing justice geographically have been especially preoccupied with the second and third themes. *See also* SPATIAL JUSTICE.

Further reading Smith, D. M. (2000), *Moral Geographies.*

Justice, Nature and the Geography of Difference (1995) A widely read mono-graph by David *Harvey and arguably his most intellectually ambitious work to date. In it he tries to both defend his Marxism against postmodern and post-structural critics and to extend it to incorporate environmental issues. It can be seen as a geographical attempt to marry together the concerns of the three strands of left thinking in the academic and the wider world, namely: the 'social left' concern with work, income, and employment, the 'cultural left' concern with identity and community, and the 'environmental left' concern with ecological degradation and protection.

just-in-time production (JIT) The forms of commodity production based on firms reducing their inventories and thus their carrying costs. Instead of stocking large amounts of components in anticipation of increased demand ('just-in-case') firms either minimize stocks or enter into contractual arrangements with suppliers that require them to carry the costs of stocking. The strategy was favoured by many firms as part of the transition to *flexible accumulation in the major capitalist economies in the 1980s. More generally, firms that make a wide variety of products or many variations on a limited product range will employ JIT production techniques. They can thereby respond to changing market demand quickly without having to pay for and store large volumes of idle inventory. *See also* TOYOTISM.

Kant, Immanuel (1724–1804) A German philosopher who was based in Königsberg (today Kaliningrad in Russia) and was one of the most influential intellectuals of his or any other generation. Today, his work remains a key reference point for philosophers, especially those concerned with metaphysics. However, Kant's body of writing is extremely large, diverse, and complex, making it very difficult to summarize. Considerable disagreements and debates remain about the true meaning and implications of his writings on everything from religion and reason, to astronomy and anthropology.

To simplify, Kant placed the uniqueness and autonomy of humanity at the centre of his philosophical writings. He was especially concerned with whether and how humans could be said to be free from the compulsions and laws that operated on the rest of *nature. He sought a midway between two philosophical positions, namely the materialist view that the non-human world dictated how we understand it, and the sceptical view that there is no way of knowing the world in itself. Kant's idealism proposed that humans were active epistemic, moral, and aesthetic agents who were able to marry their thoughts and feelings about the world to the world's character so as to achieve a degree of harmony with it and practical efficacy towards it. For example, Kant believed that *space and time are not objectively existing things 'out there' but, rather, part of human 'intuition', and thus structured so as to enable us to comprehend and act successfully in the object world.

Kant's philosophical writings may seem a long way from the concerns of modern human geography, and more especially of the geography practised during his lifetime, which was highly practical and concerned with *navigation, *exploration, *surveying, and *cartography as part of Europe's expansion into the so-called New World. However, in the early years of university geography, Kant's ideas made themselves felt. Both Carl *Ritter and Alfred *Hettner, pivotal figures in 19th-century German geography, were informed by Kant's thinking. In his major philosophically informed history of and manifesto for 'real geography', the American geographer Richard *Hartshorne also drew formally upon Kant's writings. In *The Nature of Geography* (1939) Hartshorne argued that 'though any phenomenon studied in geography may at the same time be an object of study in some systematic field, geography is not an agglomeration of pieces of the systematic sciences: it integrates these phenomena according to its distinctive chorographic point of view' (*see* CHOROLOGY). According to his critics, this interpretation codified Kantian idealism in geographical interpretation in two problematic ways. First, it assumed space to be a *container* within which processes and phenomena conjoin differentially on the Earth's surface. Second, to talk of a geographical 'point of view' implied that Hartshorne's favoured unit of chorological analysis—the *region—was a *mental construction*, whose content and boundaries were determined by the analyst. Whether either problem is a direct result of Harthorne's interpretation of Kant is moot, but arguably the first problem persisted in geography through the 1960s and 1970s because *spatial science, like the earlier chorology, also tended to see space as an 'empty' container waiting to be filled with objects of various kinds.

Marxist geographers (including Neil *Smith and David *Harvey) were stridently anti-Kantian in their view of geography as both an object of study and a mode of analysis of the world. Their *materialism led them to see space (and time) as constituted in and through social and ecological processes such that it was both relative and relational, not absolute. This meant that places and regions were material constructions, such that their analysis required respect for their ontological character.

Ironically, though Kant lectured on geography to his students more than any other subject, Anglophone geographers have paid little attention to his lecture notes, focusing more on his scattered philosophical comments on space, time, and reason. A recent translation of these notes has opened the door to a better understanding of why Kant's geography might have contemporary relevance, especially with regard to his notion of *cosmopolitanism and why people of all stripes should be treated as ends in themselves, not merely means for others to achieve their goals.

Further reading Harvey, D. (2000), 'Cosmopolitanism and the banality of geographical evils',
  Public Culture 12, 2: 529–64.
Smith, N. (1989), 'Geography as a museum', in Entrikin, J. and Brunn, S. (eds.) *Reflections on
  Richard Hartshorne's The Nature of Geography*, 89–120.

Katz, Cindi (1954–) An American feminist geographer who is best known for her work on *social reproduction, *children's geographies, and the production of academic knowledge. Based at the City University of New York, Katz has undertaken long-term ethnographic studies in the Sudan and Harlem, using them to develop a sustained theoretical and political project concerning social reproduction, *political economy, and production of space, place, and nature, best illustrated by her book *Growing Up Global: Economic Restructuring and Children's Everyday Lives* (2004).

Kearns, Robin (1959–) A health geographer based at the University of Auckland, New Zealand. Kearns has been instrumental in the development of *health geography as distinct from and complementary to *medical geography, arguing for a more nuanced approach that takes seriously issues of well-being, embodiment, care, *power, and *social justice, as exemplified by his co-authored book *Culture/Place/Health* (2007, with Will Gesler).

Keynesian An economic theory relating to the ideas of British economist John Maynard Keynes (1883–1946) who was noted for his criticisms of *neoclassical economics and his macro-economic theory. Keynes was influential in the formation of the post-war *welfare state in the UK, and the term 'Keynesianism' is often used as a summary description of the social and economic policies underpinning it (*see* REGULATION THEORY). Keynes' most famous work was *The General Theory of Employment, Interest and Money* (1936) written during the Great Depression then blighting the major capitalist economies. Neoclassical economists maintained that, so long as *labour was flexible in its wage demands, there should be full employment in an economy because it was 'irrational' for workers to be long unemployed. However, Keynes pointed out that workers were unlikely to work for pittance wages and, unlikely too, to agree to wage reductions *en masse* when circumstances dictated. At times of economic crisis or recession, when unemployment rises, unsold products pile up, and new investment is weak, Keynes argued that central governments must step in to stimulate what he called 'effective demand' in the economy. This may involve increased government borrowing in the short term. It also implies income support through unemployment and other work-related benefits. Despite his cardinal importance as a political economist, Keynes' writings have had little formal impact on economic geographers, though their insights resonate with some ideas advanced by Karl *Marx and which infuse strands of *Marxist geography. Outside human geography, Keynes' ideas have enjoyed a minor renaissance after the 2008 global financial crisis because he was critical of a *laissez-faire* approach to economic affairs and advocated *regulation and sustaining consumption by public spending.

kinaesthetic learning A learning style in which knowledge is generated by carrying out an activity, rather than listening to a lecture or observing a demonstration. Fieldwork would be one such method of learning, as would tracing fingers over a *tactile map. In a more general sense, it refers to what people learn on an everyday basis as they bodily interact with a place through, for example, *walking. *See also* FLANEUR; PSYCHOGEOGRAPHY.

kinetic elite A term for business and political leaders who are highly mobile, regularly travelling the world in order to conduct deals. They typically travel hundreds of thousands of miles a year, circulating through *airports, hotels, restaurants, and office and factory sites, keeping in contact through the *Internet and mobile phones. They are considered to be key agents of *globalization.

kinship A family relationship, through blood, marriage, or adoption, or other close ties or bonds. Kinship is considered a fundamental element of society, a form of social organization centred on family or very close bonds of association. Its importance is waning to a degree in Western societies with the demise of subsistence living and social care becoming less reliant on family supports, but in other parts of the world kinship retains its salience underpinning care, units of production, and political representation.

knowledge community A virtual *community of practice that uses moderated social media to exchange research material and ideas, discuss topics of mutual interest, and work towards common goals. They evolved from online bulletin boards, mailing lists, and web forums, and now use a variety of forms of Internet communication. An example in the discipline of geography is the Association of American Geographers knowledge community site.

knowledge economy An economy many of whose firms are engaged in the application and production of knowledge. The term is sometimes said to have been coined by Austrian business analyst Peter Drucker in the 1960s. It is often used as a synonym for the term *information economy, but some regard this as an erroneous conflation. Where information constitutes the 'pieces' out of which knowledge is, in large part made, knowledge—some commentators insist—is the linking of these pieces into meaningful chains, and often arises out of practical experience (in which *tacit understanding plays an important role). Hence, a knowledge economy is seen here as one in which firms and workers do more than create, manipulate, or apply information. Instead, it is one in which knowledgeable workers use their know-how to create knowledge-products, such as the reports produced by management consultancy firms or the marketing strategies devised by advertising companies. This said, one thing the idea of a knowledge economy has in common with that of an information economy is that it is often seen as both evolutionary and positive. It is said to be a stage that formerly industrial economies pass through, and a good one too, insofar as it requires a better educated workforce who operate in offices (not mines or fields) and are generally well paid. As with all transition models, however, this view of economic change is too simplistic to be credible.

knowledge transfer The movement of knowledge from one institution (or a part of one) to another (or to a different part of the same institution), including the embedding of this knowledge once it has reached its destination. Knowledge transfer (KT) is more than the mere communication of knowledge, which is why sending an email within or across institutional boundaries will rarely suffice. Knowledge is sticky for at least two reasons.

First, it often resides in the heads and infrastructures of particular groups of people. Second, much knowledge is *tacit and thus hard to verbalize, and may be better communicated by demonstration. KT is thus an active process, requiring thought and effort, and it is not guaranteed to succeed. It can take many forms, including mentoring new employees, work shadowing by those seeking to acquire new knowledge, and training events organized by those seeking to impart knowledge.

Because many advanced capitalist economies are now so dependent on the production and application of knowledge, KT has become an important concern of firms and economic policy makers. It has even, in part, inspired the development of an academic-cum-practical subject called 'knowledge management'. Economic geographers have taken a particular interest in the analysis of KT because of its spatial aspects. For instance, ostensibly separate firms who compete in similar markets but who are geographically proximate have been shown to exchange a great deal of information and knowledge, often in a very informal way. Alternatively, transnational firms with complex, distanciated operations frequently need to ensure timely transfer of knowledge between their organizational units.

Aside from analysing KT, many academic researchers are engaged in it actively. Indeed, one of the several criteria by which academics are judged professionally by their peers is KT. It involves relating the key insights of academic research to relevant stakeholders, or providing them with professional training relating to new techniques, standards, or goals. Some geographers engage in KT, but KT is most common within academic life in professionally orientated disciplines such as nursing, urban planning, or engineering.

Kondratieff waves The long-term cycles of economic growth and decline described by the Russian economist Nikolai Kondratieff in 1925. Kondratieff based his idea on observations of the evolution of industrial capitalism in 19th-century Europe and North America. He noticed that four-part cycles stretched over roughly 50 years, beginning with take-off, a sustained period of high productivity and profits, then a progressive decline, ending with a depression or recession. As a description of periods of economic history Kondratieff waves are approximate to the point of being crude, and—to the extent that they are real—invite many different explanations as to their causes. In light of the environmental challenges posed by the *Anthropocene, many hope for a new Kondratieff wave based on a set of powerful new 'clean technologies'.

kriging A method of spatial *interpolation. It uses linear least squares algorithms, employing the known values of nearby locations to estimate the values at unobserved locations. It is employed extensively in industries such as mining, using the locations of known deposits to predict the location of new deposits.

Kropotkin, Peter (1842–1921) An influential Russian anarchist geographer writing during the early years of geography's institutionalization as a university subject. Born into wealth, Kropotkin first entered the military, then the civil service. A leading figure in the Russian Geographical Society, he had a passion for exploration and wrote reports on China, Siberia, Finland, and the Arctic. He was active as a political organizer among the working class, importing ideas to Russia from socialist and anarchist organizations in Western Europe. Arrested for subversion, he escaped to Britain in 1876. He travelled widely in Europe, but was arrested in France and while in jail wrote his account of 'What geography ought to be'. He argued that geography should teach knowledge about other people and places in order to create mutual respect rather than to serve imperial control. He spent most of the rest of his life in Britain as a prominent intellectual in geographical and biological sciences. His ideas were revived with the development of *radical geography in the discipline in the late 1960s and 1970s. *See also* ANARCHIST GEOGRAPHY.

Krugman, Paul (1953–) A Nobel prize-winning economist who helped establish the *new economic geography, especially through his book *Development, Geography, and Economic Theory* (1995). His work mainly concerns patterns of international *trade, international finance, and spatial economics. In addition to his academic work he has sought to write for a wider audience and has developed a profile as a *public intellectual, writing a regular *New York Times* column. Krugman is critical of much mainstream economic thinking and his politics cleave to social democracy rather than *neoliberalism.

Kuhn, Thomas (1922–96) An American historian of science and sometime philosopher who initially trained as a physicist. He started his career at Harvard University before moving to the University of California, Berkeley, then Princeton University, and finally MIT. He is most noted for his highly influential book *The Structure of Scientific Revolutions* (1962). In it, Kuhn argued that science evolves in bursts and spurts through a series of *paradigms. These are agreed ways of understanding and researching the world that periodically are challenged by new ways of thinking. Kuhn challenged the idea that scientific progress is linear and based purely on the exercise of reason and *logic. His notion was adopted in geography to explain the *quantitative revolution of the 1960s and subsequent challenges to it. The notion of paradigms and their formation is highly contested in understanding the history of the discipline. Today, the idea is considered of little use when recounting the most recent period in the evolution of human (and physical) geography. However, Kuhn is—despite himself—considered to be a founding thinker of *Science and Technology Studies, a field that has influenced human geographers strongly over the last decade.

Kuznets cycle A period of growth lasting 15–25 years characteristic of capitalist economies as described by Russian-American economist Simon Kuznets in the 1940s. Through detailed empirical research into long-run national economic data, Kuznets identified cycles of growth that he linked—in the case of the United States—with waves of mass immigration, a resulting construction boom, an increase in new business start-ups, and an enlargement of the paid workforce. His empirical inquiries also led him to identify the 'Kuznets curve'. Here economic growth leads to heightened social inequality in the first place, followed later by a decrease in equality as wages rise and more workers are incorporated into the industrialized economy of cities (*see* ENVIRONMENTAL KUZNETS CURVE). As with *Kondratieff waves, Kuznets cycles and curves are largely of interest to economic historians and forecasters. However, economic geographers are interested in them because of their spatial differentiation. While the global economy as a whole might be said to experience cycles or curves, it is more common to find different regions experiencing these non-synchronously.

Kwan, Mei-Po (1962–) A GIS specialist, presently a visiting professor at the University of California, Berkeley, who has drawn on feminist theory to develop a more critical form of *GIScience. While her empirical research addresses questions in urban, transportation, health, and economic geography, especially through examining spatio-temporal characteristics of people's daily activities, Kwan's theoretical and methodological contributions have been to apply social theory to GIS, to help create qualitative GIS, and to develop new methods of 3D *geovisualization and *geocomputation.

Kyoto Protocol A commitment to manage *greenhouse gas emissions adopted under the *United Nations Framework Convention on Climate Change (UNFCCC) in 1997. Under its terms, 41 industrial countries (known as Annex 1) were committed to reducing their emissions by an average of 4.2 per cent by 2008–2012 from a baseline set in 1990. They could do so via *emissions trading, the Clean Development Mechanism, and other methods (*see* CARBON OFF-SETTING). The protocol also created an adaption fund, by which developed countries would help vulnerable developing countries, reporting and accounting regulations, and a compliance mechanism. The US government did not ratify the protocol and led moves to adopt a successor agreement centred on a worldwide *cap-and-trade system applying to more countries. Criticized from many quarters, progress towards meeting the stated targets was slow. A successor to the protocol has yet to be agreed and implemented.

labour control regime An ensemble of techniques and norms designed to ensure stable habits of work among paid workers. Because capitalist firms rely so much on their workers to do what they are paid for, erratic work habits or workers prone to striking can be very costly for these firms. A control regime cross-cuts otherwise different firms in the same industry, and possibly several industries, in the same region or country. Typically, national or local state bodies help firms to construct and sustain it—for instance, by offering generous maternity leave to working mothers or by obliging the unemployed to find work within a specified period. The most successful labour control regimes interpellate workers so that they come to accept the norms of the regime as their own (*see* INTERPELLATION). After the long period of economic crisis and restructuring experienced by Western countries after 1974, and the rise of *Newly Industrializing Countries, economic geographers began to analyse regional and national differences in the character of labour control regimes. *See also* HEGEMONY; LABOUR GEOGRAPHY.

labour flexibility **1.** The degree to which workers can adapt to changes in their workplaces or in external labour markets.
2. The deliberate use by firms of permanent and/or temporary workers in order to maximize their adaptability to changing market conditions or firm strategies.

The first definition is worker-centred (*see* FLEXIBLE LABOUR), while the second definition is firm-centred.

It used to be said of industrial blue- and white-collar workers that they had a 'job for life'. However, in many countries dynamism within firms and *labour markets means that workers must now be adaptable over the course of their lifetimes. Firms often assist workers by providing formal training opportunities and placements. But now many workers also independently retrain two or more times during their working lives in order to secure paid employment. To some extent the possession of good transferable skills eases the transitions between different jobs, but it can be a challenging and protracted transition when medium- or highly-skilled jobs are involved. It is thus more common to find a social worker retraining as a school teacher than a medical doctor retraining to become a helicopter pilot, for example.

The second definition refers to attempts by firms to make their workforces more responsive to changing economic conditions. For instance, during the crisis of *Fordism and the move towards *flexible accumulation, many firms reduced the number of 'core' workers while expecting them to multi-task more than previously, and hired in far more temporary workers whom they could pay less and also avoid paying benefits such as pension contribution. Critics thus saw the move to a flexible labour force as exploitative, benefiting capitalists at the expense of their workers.

labour geography A sub-discipline of human geography dedicated to understanding the relations between *work, *place, *space, and geographical *scale. Though employment and workers have long been central to the fields of industrial relations, business studies, labour economics, and labour sociology, these fields rarely accented the geography involved. Andrew Herod has made a useful distinction between 'a geography of labour' and a 'labour geography'. The former, Herod argued, is a kind of analysis in which work and workers are examined from the outside, with little or no appreciation for the lived experiences of employment. It was characteristic of the *location theory favoured by many economic geographers influenced by the *spatial science approach in the 1960s and 1970s; so too those who examined the geographical decision-making of firm owners and managers. It was also characteristic of much *Marxist geography and geographical political economy more widely, wherein 'labour' was an abstraction assigned to a specific social *class, and seen to be largely controlled and exploited by capitalists (see, for example, Doreen Massey's *Spatial Divisions of Labour).

In contrast to all this, a 'labour geography' places workers at the centre of the analysis, and concerns itself with their thoughts, feelings, and actions—especially insofar as geography enters into them. It takes seriously the diverse interests, identities, needs, and aspirations of workers, and has focused largely on paid workers operating within a capitalist *mode of production. Above all else, it is interested in the *agency of labour, that is, workers' capacity to configure geography so as to protect and advance their interests. Aside from Herod, leading labour geographers include Gordon *Clark, Jamie *Peck, Geraldine *Pratt, and Jane Wills. Their work straddles economic, political, social, population, and cultural geography, and it has exerted an influence outside human geography, as showcased in the edited collection *Handbook of Employment and Society: Working Space* (McGrath-Champ et al., 2010).

Labour geographers have advanced the understanding of work and workers in several significant ways. First, they have analysed the different, sometimes overlapping but often discrete local labour markets that almost all workers must enter to find employment. They have attended to how geography influences which markers can be entered. For example, Pratt and *Hanson's *Gender, Work and Space* (1995) explored how women in different class groups negotiated parental responsibilities, the need or desire to work, and the spatial constraints imposed by a lack of time in order to make decisions about where, locally, they could work, and who, therefore, they could work for (*see* SPATIAL ENTRAP-MENT). Second, they have analysed the geography of employment law and labour regulations. While such laws and regulations can assist workers (e.g. by guaranteeing maternity benefits for female workers), it can also work against them (e.g. by failing to specify a minimum wage they should be paid). The geography of all this matters, because it is in workers' interests to have the most favourable laws and regulations applicable at the national scale, if not the supra-national scale. Diverse local or regional arrangements within a country can produce a very uneven geography of labour law and regulation. How does this occur, why, and how can it be changed where it occurs? This three-part question has preoccupied labour geographers such as Clark and Herod.

Thirdly, all workers are placed-based and most—aside from those willing and able to migrate—are place-*bound*. This can render workers vulnerable when their employers wish to relocate a facility or push for things like a wage freeze or compulsory redundan-cies. Labour geographers have thus inquired into what local, regional, national, and international scale strategies workers employ to assist in their disputes with employers. A significant focus of interest has been '*upscaling', where a local work force gets supports from workers elsewhere. Until the 1980s, national level upscaling in most Western democracies was almost guaranteed because of the strength of trades unions. However, today it often proceeds with little or no trades union support, as evidenced by the dockers' strike in Liverpool, UK, from 1995 to 1998. What is more, immigrant workers can face special difficulties in defending their rights in places far from home, lacking the organizational means to come together locally to pressure employers to treat them fairly. Finally, labour geographers have inquired into new alliances between workers and new *social movements (NSMs). These alliances arise in part because work is umbilically connected to workers' social and biological reproduction, in part because NSMs are more politically important than trades unions in many places around the world. How, it has been asked, does 'social movement unionism' utilize geography to advance its participants' interests? Jane Wills, for example, has both examined and actively supported the London campaign to ensure a living wage for indigenous and immigrant workers, regardless of gender, ethnicity, sexual orientation, etc.

As is doubtless clear from the above, labour geography is an overtly political field most of whose members are social democrats, feminists, socialists, anti-racists, and critics of homophobia. Despite this, there is an unexplored political tension with *environmentalism. Most contemporary jobs in a capitalist world, not to mention the lifestyles that workers' wages support, are deeply destructive of ecosystems. What would a more normatively 'green' labour geography look like? This question remains to be explored. In the meantime, labour geography flourishes, its now numerous practitioners exploring all aspects of work and geography from the insider (worker) perspective.

Further reading Castree, N., Coe, N., Ward, K., and Samers, M. (2004), *Spaces of Work.*

Lier, D. (2007), 'Places of work, scales of organising: a review of labour geography', *Geography Compass* 1: 814–833.

Rutherford, T. (2010), 'De/Re-centring work and class?: a review and critique of labour geography', *Geography Compass* 4: 768–777.

labour market The metaphorical place where aspiring workers and employers meet, such that the supply of labour intersects with demand for it. As *neoclassical economics would have it, at any one time labourers get what they deserve in terms of jobs, wages, and working conditions. For instance, if there is an over-supply of unskilled farm workers in an agrarian region then many will be under-employed and very low paid, with the rest unemployed and reliant on charity, family, or government aid. Although labour markets can be differentiated according to the kinds of work/jobs involved, the degree of skill required to undertake/fill them, and so on, the neoclassical view treats labour like any other commodity market in which demand and supply curves intersect to determine the price an employer pays and the wage that a worker receives.

This view analyses labour markets in an abstract way, screening out the complexities of and concrete relationships between firms, workers, and various relevant institutions (such as trades unions). It also tends to ignore their geography, as if it was of little interest or consequence. The first weakness was addressed by a group of heterodox economists, political economists, and economic sociologists from the 1950s onwards, many of whom advocated *institutionalism as an approach, and the *embeddedness of many firms, most workers, and various regulatory institutions that affect the character of labour markets. For instance, it was shown that many labour markets are internal to firms, meaning that otherwise well-qualified workers outside the firm were not given the chance to apply for vacancies. Relatedly, these researchers identified dual labour markets, wherein a 'glass ceiling' prevented low-skilled workers advancing to medium- or high- skilled jobs. Connected to this, feminist and anti-racist scholars showed how discrimination in labour markets mirrored the discrimination that women and ethnic minorities faced in other walks of life, often despite legislation designed to prevent such discrimination (*see* SEGMENTED LABOUR MARKET THEORY).

Building on these critical alternatives to the neoclassical view, from the 1980s onwards, a number of labour geographers began to analyse the geography of labour markers and why it matters; Gordon *Clark and Jamie *Peck were among the pioneers. Most labour markets, they showed, are ineluctably *local*. Firms must typically employ workers located within easy transportation distance, while workers typically seek out employment on their doorstep. This binds firms and workers into a relationship of local dependency. Firms have many *sunk costs and, in the case of medium- and large-size enterprises, these costs must be paid over the long term and also underpin sustained economic success. Firms rely on a supply of the right quantity and quality of labour locally to ensure commodity production continues day-in, day-out, and can be adjusted to variations in external market conditions and firm strategy. Meanwhile, workers require locally available work in order to earn wages and ensure their own and their families' material and emotional well-being. Because of their local dependency, many firms contribute to the places and communities from which their workforce is drawn (e.g. by contributing money to local charities or schools). Workers may, depending on the character of the *labour control regime, organize collectively to improve their wages, benefits, and working conditions. In short, local labour markets are all about social relationships that can, depending on the circumstances, be cooperative or conflictual, good natured or tense.

Since the end of the 20th century, many labour markets have become more stretched out (or distantiated). This reflects the increased importance of knowledge and information technology in the affairs of many firms. For instance, many travel writers, sales managers, and copy editors can work for firms located in other countries and use a personal computer, email, or Skype to work from home. This allows many workers to live in a favoured *place, without having to relocate to the home-base of their employer. It also frees firms from many of the constraints associated with purely local labour markets. At the same time, large-scale migrations since around 1980 have affected the character of many local labour markets. Major countries of immigration, such as Australia, Canada, and members of the *European Union, have attracted both highly skilled and low-wage workers, especially to metropolitan regions. The skill differences intersect with divisions related to 'race', ethnicity, gender, and citizenship status to produce complex and dynamic local labour markets.

Further reading McDowell, L. (2009), *Working Bodies*.
Peck, J. (1996), *Workplace*.

labour power The capacity of a person to work, in return for which they receive a wage or other things in exchange. The term is closely associated with *Marxism and Karl *Polanyi's notion of a pseudo-commodity (*see* COMMODITY). For Marx and Polanyi, workers do not sell themselves in a capitalist system—this, after all, would be tantamount to voluntary enslavement. Instead, they sell their capacity to perform work for others for a definite period of time in return for definite sums of money or other things. For Marx, wage workers are unique commodities in a capitalist system because they produce the economic value appropriated by the capitalist class in the form of profit (*see* LABOUR THEORY OF VALUE).

labour process The conduct of work wherein people use their minds, limbs, machines, and other tools to make, move, market, sell, repair, or dispose of commodities. The term is associated with *Marxism. Marxists maintain that the labour process in capitalist firms is typically not controlled by wage workers. Instead, owners, senior managers, and skilled technicians determine the functional and spatial organization of commodity production. Most wage workers, they maintain, are slotted in to a firm's labour process—often leading to unskilled, low paid, and unrewarding work for those involved.

labour productivity The amount of goods or services produced by a wage worker in a given amount of time. Economists and economic geographers frequently use it as a comparative measure when describing the economic performance of different regions and countries. Despite the implication that only human labour is determinant of productivity, technology and the logistics of production are crucial inputs to labour productivity.

labour theory of value A theory, central to *Marxist political economy, that regards the exercise of *labour power as the origin of wealth in capitalist societies. Karl Marx argued that value is not something intrinsic to commodities. All value, he maintained, is relative because it involves relationships between human agents and the material world. People imbue things with *value, rather than things being valuable in themselves. While values are plural and contested—for instance, one person may value baby seals, while another values fur coats—Marx argued that *capitalism produces a particular kind of economic value that is created exclusively by living labourers. To understand what Marx meant we need to distinguish between the *forces of production and the social relations of production. The former, such as mechanical saws used in the logging industry, contribute significantly to the number and kinds of commodities a capitalist firm is able to produce. The latter involves capitalists employing workers to use the forces of production to produce new goods and services in return for a wage. In theory, few people would need to work again if machines and various smart technologies could undertake the work that people must currently perform. However, Marx argued that such a scenario is antithetical to capitalism's future existence. If the forces of production were the real source of all economic value, Marx insisted, then the innovation inspired by inter-firm competition would, logically, lead to a largely work-free world in which firms would compete technologically first and foremost. But because workers produce economic value, not the forces of production, capitalists must continue to employ people and push them to be productive. One illustration of why Marx thought this to be true is that, in the long run, replacing wage workers by machines and technologies will under-mine the consumer markets that capitalists rely upon to sell their commodities and realize a profit. Only by abolishing the wage relation between workers and employers could a relatively work-free world in which science and technology freed people from labour come about.

What, then, is 'economic value' in capitalism? For Marx it is a social relation of exploitation between workers and employers that assumes the phenomenal form of commodities, pre-eminently *money. This idea that relations between people become crystallized into things is a central one in Marx's later political economic writings. Money is the ultimate form of value in a capitalist world because it is *the* means whereby other forms of value can be acquired via a process of exchange. This means it is a form of value able to commensurate all other values (ethical, religious, aesthetic, cultural, etc.) to the extent that these values can be articulated in market exchanges. Marx argued that money is the material expression of a real but invisible process whereby the collective labour of wage workers is appropriated by the capitalist class. Though workers appear to receive a wage that pays for the value created by their workplace endeavours, Marx tried to show why this is not the case (*see* EXPLOITATION). His argument was that, through the 'blind' process of inter-firm competition, capitalists pay workers less than the value they create. What he called the 'socially necessary labour time' required to produce various com-modities constituted a moving and contingent average that some firms managed to better, thus generating economy-wide surpluses that were pocketed by capitalists after each round of commodity sales. This average was constituted and driven down by inter-firm competition. Profits thus arose not because consumers paid 'over the odds', so much as because worker salaries were, in aggregate, less than the value of the goods and services they created.

Marx tried to prove his theory by using a mixture of logic and evidence. Even so, the theory has come in for considerable criticism, even among Marxists. There are a number of technical and evidential problems that have led some to conclude it is wholly erroneous. More orthodox Marxists take it as axiomatic, however. Chapter 1 of David *Harvey's book *The *Limits to Capital* is the most complete presentation of the theory in the discipline. Meanwhile, most mainstream economists today regard the theory as either irrelevant to their core concerns, or else flawed. Even some in the Marxist fold—notably, several so-called 'analytical' Marxists—argue that Marx's key insights do not require the labour theory of value to be compelling.

laissez-faire An approach to economic affairs that advocates non-interference by governments or other non-economic actors. It is an extreme form of economic *liberalism and a core tenet of *neoliberalism.

Lamarckism The ideas associated with French naturalist Jean-Baptiste Lamarck (1744–1829), above all the proposition that an organism could pass on to its offspring characteristics acquired during its lifetime. Darwin's later counter explanation, that random mutations among offspring and *natural selection explained evolution, was not widely accepted until the 1930s. Thus, between 1880 and 1920 neo-Lamarckian ideas flourished, not least among geographers trying to trace the relative impact of environment and heredity on human cultures (*see* ENVIRONMENTAL DETERMINISM). These were often highly selective of Lamarck's original thinking. The study of epigenetics—the study of heritable changes in gene expression by mechanisms other than changes in the underlying DNA sequence—has revived serious interest in Lamarckian ideas.

land art An *art movement that emerged in the late 1960s in which art works are situated in and constructed out of the material in natural *landscapes. The materials used include wood, soil, rocks, and water, and sometimes processed material such as concrete. The work is left unattended and exposed to the processes of entropy.

Land Degradation and Society A book edited by Piers *Blaikie and Harold Brookfield (1987), it was an important early work in what was to be called *political ecology. Blaikie and Brookfield argued that social erosion or more generally, land degradation, was not just an issue for the physical and biological sciences but that social scientists and historians had vital contributions. The book surveyed land degradation past and present, as well as under *colonialism and *socialism.

land grab The acquisition of large areas of agricultural land by overseas firms, governments, or individuals, largely in countries of the developing world. This process accelerated, especially in Africa, after a spike in world food prices 2007. In search of future profits and also their own country's future *food security, outside investors purchase land (and, where possible, proximate water resources) in order to grow food or biofuels in the years to come. Many critics of land grabbing fear that it may compromise the future agricultural development and food security of developing countries.

landless movement A number of organizations protesting and campaigning for greater access to land and *land rights. It describes the *Movimento dos Trabalhadores Sem Terra (MST) in Brazil, the Landless Peoples Movement (LPM) in South Africa, and other popular opposition groupings in India, and elsewhere.

landmark A distinctive geographic feature that can be seen clearly from a distance and by which the viewer can establish their location. It may be natural or human-made, and is often of interest to tourists. *See also* NAVIGATION; WAYFINDING.

land reform The state-led reorganization of agricultural land-holding. It is generally designed to either consolidate small farms into larger ones or redistribute land from one social group to another. In both cases there may also be a change in the conditions

land rent theory 274

of *land tenure. An example of the former is the reorganization of French farms after 1945 in order to create more viable and productive enterprises. Examples of the latter include the redistribution of land from large owners to smaller peasants in Egypt, as well as the forced collectivization of farming in China, both in the 1950s.

land rent theory Any theory that aims to describe or explain the distribution of income earned between different parcels of urban, peri-urban, or rural land. Land is an important factor of production, as well as the stage upon which people's everyday lives are played out. Yet its monetary worth when sold or rented is not determined exclusively by its intrinsic qualities. Like all valued phenomena, its worth is *relative* in socio-cultural, spatial, and historical terms. For instance, a highly fertile parcel of land 300 km away from a major city may be worth far less than a moderately fertile one 50 km away. Land rent theories, of which there are several competing ones, seek to account for variations in rent (real or potential income earned) at any one time at a given geographical scale. They presume there to be an underlying logic applicable to otherwise different parts of the world.

land rights The title to land and associated resources. Disputes over land rights can arise for many reasons, but human geographers have been interested in at least four kinds of situation: first, the assertions by *indigenous peoples against *settler societies (*see* COLONIALISM; DISPOSSESSION); second, the campaigns by landless groups for greater access to agricultural land (*see* LANDLESS MOVEMENT; LAND REFORM); third, the efforts by urban *squatters to obtain secure land tenure; and fourth, the organized opposition to land evictions for dams and development projects. In several countries, notably Australia, Canada, and New Zealand, legal and political struggles over indigenous rights have been significant and ongoing since the 1970s. *See also* RIGHTS.

Further reading Howitt, R. and Jackson, S. (1998), 'Some things do change: indigenous rights, geographers and geography in Australia', *Australian Geographer* 29(2): 155–73.

landscape 1. The arrangement or pattern of 'things on the land' and the terrain, shape, and structure of land.
  2. The social and cultural significance and meaning of such patterns and terrains.
  3. A picture or art work representing an area. Landscapes can be *wilderness, managed countryside, rural and urban settlements, and relate to common or private land. Their maritime equivalents are seascapes.

Landscape has long been of interest to geographers in terms of its form and the natural and human processes that shape it, how people experience it, and how it is packaged as a commodity to be valued and used, its meanings, and its role in shaping a sense of place and place attachment, how it is represented, and what those representations seek to convey, and how it is an outcome and the medium of social relations.

In the early part of the 20th century, there were two predominant approaches to landscape. The first is *environmental determinism, exemplified by Ellen *Semple, which argued that different natural landscapes shaped the constitution, organization, and social relations of human societies. The other approach, centred on the concept of *cultural landscape, explored how people leave their material imprint on the landscape through their activities such as farming and construction, exemplified by Carl *Sauer and the *Berkeley School; it drew on the older German tradition of *landschaft (*see* VERNACULAR LANDSCAPE).

These approaches flourished until the second half of the century. During the period of the *quantitative revolution in the late 1950s and 1960s, landscape effectively disappeared to simply become the surface on which human activity occurred. Within the *behavioural geography that followed, landscape was understood through the lens of perception and cognition, with attempts to measure how people come to know and evaluate landscapes, and how they navigate their way through them (*see* ENVIRONMENTAL PERCEPTION, LANDSCAPE EVALUATION, WAYFINDING). *Humanistic geographers, in contrast, adopted more *existential and *phenomenological approaches to landscape that sought to understand people's lived experiences, senses of place, and the meanings ascribed to them.

In *new cultural geography, the idea of landscape was refashioned in two ways. First, it was posited that landscape could not be read simply as material expressions of culture, but rather needed to be understood as complex, multifaceted constructions laden with symbolic power (*see* CULTURAL MATERIALISM). To understand landscapes requires a focus on meaning over form and the decoding of their hidden or symbolic meanings within social and historical context (*see* GAZE; ICONOGRAPHY; WAYS OF SEEING). This approach was exemplified in the work of Denis *Cosgrove, especially his book *Social Formation and Symbolic Landscape*. Second, it was argued that much more attention needed to be paid to the materiality of landscape and its formation through ideologically informed human action. How the landscape is shaped is a reflection of culture and capital, property rights and law, power, and social and economic processes. As such, the built and managed landscape produces and is a product of social relations. Landscape is thus the outcome and an active component of the wider *political economy bound up in *capitalism's *creative destruction and *uneven development.

More recently, landscape has been theorized through the lens of *post-structuralism, which posits that it needs to be understood relationally and as always in the process of becoming; its meaning, production, and how it is experienced is never fixed but rather emerging contingently and contextually. Landscape is *performative, having no *ontological security, instead emerging through practices and encounters. For example, John Wylie has detailed the emerging *affective response to landscape as it is traversed (*see* WALKING).

References and further reading Matless, D. (1998), *Landscape and Englishness*.
Mitchell, D. (1996), *The Lie of the Land: Migrant Workers and the California Landscape*.
Mitchell, W. J. T. (ed.) (1994), *Landscape and Power*.
Wylie, J. (2007), *Landscape*.

landscape archaeology The study of how people shaped, used, and left their mark on the natural *landscape in the past. In contrast with other forms of archaeology that largely focus on human societies, studying habitation, and artefacts, landscape archaeology concentrates on the wider *cultural landscape and patterns of land use and alteration.

landscape ecology The study of ecological systems and the relationship between different types of environments (urban, agricultural, natural, aquatic) within a landscape. It seeks to provide a holistic analysis, blending perspectives from the natural and social sciences in order to understand the effects of different processes, including those that are performed by people, on the ecological make-up of an area. *See also* HUMAN ECOLOGY.

landscape evaluation A set of methods for assessing, describing, and classifying *landscapes. The methods can be either quantitative—involving inventory-taking and scaled judgements, or qualitative—consisting of subjective responses or preferences to aesthetics or scenic quality. The data produced are used principally in planning and design.

landschaft A German word for *'landscape', in geography the term is associated with the continental European school of *Landschaftsgeographie*, wherein the discipline is cast as 'landscape science'. Developed by German geographers in the late 19th century, it focused on classifying and analysing landscapes of particular *regions. While some practitioners focused purely on the environmental processes that shaped landscape, others recognized the effects of *human agency in producing *cultural landscapes.

land tenure The legal or customary relationship of people to land, defining the rights and responsibilities of those involved. There are many diverse forms of tenure, in the past and in the present. Private ownership vests exclusive rights to land and its resources in an individual or corporate body. Communal ownership involves shared rights within a community (*see* TRAGEDY OF THE COMMONS).

Land Use and Land Cover Change (LULAC) An analysis that focuses on the processes and dynamics of land use and land cover change across the earth's surface. The results are used to model biomass and ecosystems, and provide inputs with respect to climate change, hydrological, and other environmental models. It specifically examines the effects of human activity on land cover, including deforestation, pollution, changing patterns of agriculture, and conservation and environmental programmes, and how land use is shaped by and shapes social, economic, and environmental processes. *See also* INTERNATIONAL GEOSPHERE-BIOSPHERE PROGRAM; INTERNATIONAL HUMAN DIMENSIONS PROGRAM ON GLOBAL ENVIRONMENTAL CHANGE.

land-use survey The *surveying and mapping of the use and management of each plot of land and building. Traditionally, the survey work would have been undertaken through surveying *fieldwork, making detailed measurements and classification of land cover, and its purpose. It is now typically undertaken through the spectral analysis of *aerial photographs and *remote sensing images, with the findings integrated into *Geographical Information Systems for use in *planning and *governance. *See also* LAND-USE ZONING.

land-use zoning The classification of land within a development plan. Land parcels are zoned based on their existing land use and their intended future use. Typically land-use parcels are bundled together to form relatively large areas of contiguous zoning to provide a coherent pattern of land use. The development plan is used to guide planning and land-use changes. *See also* LAND-USE SURVEY.

language Verbal and written systems that enable communication, either between people or with computers. A dialect is a local version of a larger language group. The study of the spatial distribution of languages and dialects has been a feature of geography since the 19th century. Studies have sought to map language use, the relationship between cognate and different languages, and the diffusion and contraction of different languages over time. Work within cultural and political geography has examined the role of language in the formation of cultural and regional *identity, its role in *cultural politics, and the role of language policy and nationalist politics in shaping language use. For example, in the context of the United Kingdom, the Welsh language is an important marker of Welsh identity and Welsh nationalism and is supported by pro-Welsh-speaking education, service delivery, and media policy. More recently there have been two new engagements by geographers with language. The first concerns the rise of English as the *lingua franca* of international publication and the effect this has on geographical knowledge production. It is suggested that the Anglophone domination of publication is changing the nature of geography within different national systems and language groups by driving the adoption of theory and empirical foci dominant within Anglophone geography. Second, through the engagement with post-structural theory and the linguistic turn in philosophy, geographers have become much more interested in the role of language in constructing both the world and our theories about it. Here, there is an explicit engagement with how language, *discourse, and *representation work in practice to produce understanding and shape thinking with respect to the world.

Further reading Jones, R. (2009), 'Language', in *International Encyclopedia of Human Geography*.

Larner, Wendy (1963–) A New Zealand geographer based at the University of Bristol, UK. Her research focuses on political economy and the contested and contradictory processes of globalization, *neoliberalism and post-welfarist governance, and cultural economies, notably the fashion industry. She is the author of the book *Fashioning Globalisation* (2013) and is an editor of the journal *Antipode*.

late modernity A phase of *modernity characteristic of advanced capitalist societies. According to social theorists such as Anthony *Giddens, it marks the intensification of earlier tendencies definitional of *modernity. These include the expansion in the reach of science and technology, the supercession of industry by informational, knowledge, and service industries, the speeding up of innovations in commodities and production processes, and so on. However, as Ulrich Beck and Giddens explain, some features of late modernity are relatively new, such as *reflexivity about the problems modernity itself creates that threaten to undermine it. *Climate change is one such problem. *See also* RISK SOCIETY.

Latin America A continent stretching from the subtropical zone of the northern hemisphere south across the equator to the cool temperate zone of the southern hemisphere. It has two parts, namely South America and Central America, the thin cord of land (plus islands) connecting South America to *North America. The continent comprises twenty countries, of which the largest is *Brazil. They are bordered by the Atlantic Ocean to the east, the Pacific Ocean to the west, and the Caribbean Sea to the northeast. Latin America's long western seaboard marks the conjunction of tectonic plates, making it earthquake-prone and very mountainous. It also contains the world's largest continuous area of tropical and subtropical forest, much of it concentrated in the *Amazon drainage basin. Because it spans many lines of latitude and contains high mountains, Latin America's climates and ecosystems are highly diverse. Indeed, the continent is the focus of international attempts to protect *biodiversity. Its population is now approaching 600 million, with Brazil and *Mexico by far the largest demographic contributors. The continent has many large cities, with six having more than six million (Bogotà in Columbia, Lima in Peru, Rio de Janeiro and *São Paulo in Brazil, Mexico City, and Buenos Aires in Argentina). Three countries were considered to be Newly Industrializing Countries (NICs) when that term was coined 35 years ago, namely Argentina, Brazil, and Mexico. While several countries are prosperous and politically stable (e.g. Costa Rica), several remain troubled by civil war, violence resulting from the international drug trade, and corruption among political, military, and economic elites. Colombia and Mexico are perhaps the two countries that have made most headlines in this regard in recent years.

Historically, Latin America had many indigenous peoples organized into different societies. Many of these societies were culturally and technically sophisticated when compared with other ancient civilizations, such as that of Ancient Egypt. The most famous are the Maya, Inca, and Aztec civilizations, each of which left architectural legacies that are today considered to be part of world heritage, such is their historic significance and cultural value. In the 15th century Mediterranean explorers discovered the east coast of Latin America and thereafter Spain and Portugal proceeded to annex territory and establish settlements. Both countries waged war on Latin America's indigenous peoples, while Catholic missionaries sought to convert many to the teachings of the Bible and the edicts of the pope in Rome. European colonists, which later included

France (by the 17th century), also brought new diseases to Latin America, many of which proved lethal to populations that had never experienced them before. The colonists established agricultural plantations and farms, built new towns and cities, and transported European customs, laws, traditions, and languages across the Atlantic with a transformative effect. At the time, these effects were thought to 'civilize' and modernize life on the continent, but critics point to the physical and cultural violence enacted by colonizers. By the early 19th century, the Spanish and Portuguese empires were being eclipsed by those of Britain and France. Descendents of the original colonizers and mixed-ancestry (*mestizo*) residents began to agitate for independence from Lisbon and Madrid. By 1825 most of Latin America consisted of independent nation states.

A century later most Latin American countries still had largely agricultural economies, exporting significant volumes of produce to Europe. However, in order to increase wealth and levels of social development many national governments incentivized the development of industry. The *First World War, the *Great Depression of the 1930s, and the *Second World War all affected Latin America's export markets significantly. Consequently, after 1945 many governments implemented strong import-substitution policies, using trade barriers to protect home-grown manufacturing against foreign competition. These policies were relatively successful, and Latin America was able to industrialize strongly while still earning foreign revenue from the export of beef, oil, wood, and other basic commodities. However, most of its countries borrowed heavily from Western banks during the 1960s in order to build modern infrastructure, improve public education, and so on. When interest rates on loans rose during the 1970s and 1980s a *debt crisis occurred. This led to economic stagnation in many countries and, with Chile as the exemplar, most Latin American governments abandoned protectionist trade policies and, encouraged by the *International Monetary Fund and *World Bank, embraced *free trade and *structural adjustment. By the 1990s, the public finances were in much better shape in many countries, partly because of government austerity packages, and partly because of strong export earnings arising from successful competition with foreign economies. However, some countries continued to be plagued by debt problems, notably Argentina (which experienced a serious recession 1999–2002).

Partly because of the economic instability of the 1980s, partly because of public dismay with right-wing (often autocratic) governments, the new millennium saw a turn to the left in Latin American politics—Brazil, Venezuela, and Bolivia being notable examples. Many left-wing new *social movements sprang up, while *civil society in many countries became more politically vocal; for instance, the *World Social Forum originated in Brazil. Though economic growth rates are positive in many countries, Latin America remains one of the most unequal continents in terms of average incomes. *Poverty is a serious problem, with many citizens living in barely adequate housing (*see* SHANTY TOWN). The field of Latin American studies is devoted to studying the continent, and overlaps with *development studies, which itself is partly constituted by *development geography.

Latour, Bruno (1947–) A French sociologist of science and technology and a philosopher of modern life whose many publications have been influential far beyond his home discipline of *Science and Technology studies (STS). Latour was trained as an anthropologist and, among his early works, co-authored an ethnographic study of scientists at California's Salk Institute. *Laboratory Life* (Latour and Woolgar, 1979) shared and developed the social constructionist perspective of early STS. It argued that scientific 'facts' do not await discovery but are, in fact, manufactured by scientists who believe they are using reason and the *scientific method. However, Latour's next book, *Science in Action* (1987), began his journey towards a broader form of constructionism that was far more 'symmetrical' than his earlier *social* constructionism. Latour's increasing familiarity with how scientific discoveries and inventions occurred led him to question the presumption that 'the social' exists separately from the things it supposedly 'constructs'. By the time of *We Have Never Been Modern* (1991), Latour argued that the basic ontological coordinates of Western thinking were deceiving their users. Dualisms such as nature–culture, society–environment, and objectivity–subjectivity were, he argued, serving to conceal how reality is enacted daily and how, from time to time, new phenomena emerge like the Higgs-Boson particle. He proposed that all phenomena are, in some measure, 'socionatural', that agency extends far beyond *human agency, and that all agents (or 'actants' as he called them) are part of wider networks, meaning their agency is both enabled and constrained by their relations with other actants. In this light, he proposed that the world is continuously constructed by all manner of phenomena that are brought into relations of interdependency. 'Composition' is, perhaps, a better metaphor to describe Latour's world of actor-networks than construction, for it implies an active coming together of diverse agents, capacities, and materials. While humans are significant composers, Latour insists that much effort is required to make 'matters of fact', and that non-humans are crucial participants in even the most artificial devices. On this basis, Latour has proposed a new political constitution in his book *Politics of Nature* (2004). He proposes to allow non-humans to become, or to inspire, 'matters of concern' in an expanded constituency of citizens that exceed the human.

Latour's writings are deeply geographical in a number of ways and it is no surprise that this architect of *Actor-Network Theory has been influential in human geography, especially among British researchers. First, by questioning the idea that only humans can be said to possess 'agency', he has inspired many to look beyond earlier debates over what determines action within and between places. Since the late 1990s, many human geographers have shown that non-humans are crucial participants in enabling and constraining human agency. Many have also talked about non-humans as political phenomena, or as entitled to being given a 'voice' politically. Second, by questioning the idea that 'the human' is an ontologically discrete thing, Latour's work has invited some geographers to think about the 'divide' that splinters academic geography into putative physical and human halves. They have argued that the 'two ontologies' supposition that allow geographers to study society and nature separately is questionable and have called for new forms of analysis that 'rematerialize' human geography, and 'resocialize' physical geography. Finally, because actor-networks often stretch over considerable spans of time and space, they have led some to question established concepts of geographical *scale in human geography. The processes and relations so central to the composition of reality are argued not to be 'contained' by various socially constructed scales arrayed hierarchically (local, national, etc.). Instead, they are seen to be more like a complex mesh that is extended and stringy, and replete with gaps, areas of density, and areas of thinness. The analysis of such geographies of connectivity is called *topology.

Among several criticisms of Latour's thinking, two stand out. First, he has been accused of a general levelling of agency among diverse actants. He has been said to go too far in the direction of cutting human agency down to size. Second, he has been charged with lacking any theory of social structure or power. Actor-networks in *capitalism, for example, can be said to be organized by overarching processes of profit-seeking, inter-firm competition, and compulsive technical innovation. Latour was based at the École Nationale Superieure des Mines from 1982 until he took up a new position at Sciences Po Paris in 2006.

Further reading Laurier, E. (2004), 'Bruno Latour' in Hubbard, P., et al. (eds.), *Key Thinkers on Space and Place*.

law The system of rules recognized within a community that governs the conduct of its members and which can be enforced through sanctions. The law or complete body of individual laws is generally codified through documents and supported by specialized institutions and/or professionals, for example, a judiciary. To the extent that states have monopolized power through the exercise of *sovereignty, one major type of law is national or 'civil', stemming from a legislature. But not all law is national in this way. Sharia law, the moral code and religious law of *Islam, circulates independently of particular states although it may also be fully or partially incorporated into national legal systems. It is an example of 'common' law, deriving from the cumulative decisions of judges or persons recognized as having legal authority in some way. The complexity of law therefore, especially in so-called common law jurisdictions that lack a written constitution, stems from the combination of codified rules and specialized interpretations.

The significance of interpretation, or more generally the importance of the practice of law, is one reason why the relationship between law and geography is not straightforward. Before the 1980s, the very explicit studies of geography and law tended to involve either descriptively mapping different legal regimes or systems, or assuming that they had an effect on the landscape. For example, geographers interested in water noted the difference between the riparian rights derived from Latin law and the more inclusive system of Islamic water law. Different countries or in the case of the USA, states within countries, had different water laws that affected how water was distributed and used (*see* WATER). But from the 1980s, influenced by the emergence of *Critical Legal Studies on the one hand, and the retheorization of *space within human geography on the other, a new field of 'legal geographies' developed. By contrast with earlier work it recognized the mutual constitution of law and space, i.e. the spatiality of the law and the formation of legal spaces. Secondly, the field acknowledged the centrality of *power in the relations between law and space. Rather than regard the law as the neutral precursor or foundation of political life (as it is sometimes made out to be), law was understood as a partly autonomous mode of power in its own right, and as a form of power that mediated others, e.g. political and economic. This did not mean, however, that law could be understood as the automatic projection of already-established power, the state or capital, for instance. Rather, there was scope for negotiation and contest throughout the legal process. Thirdly, the new legal geographers paid more attention to the practices of law and law enforcement, particularly their unevenness in space (*see* POLICING). The aim was to demystify the legal process by accounting for its actual operation.

Among the key areas of legal geographical inquiry are *race and the racialization of space, marginalized groups in the city such as the homeless, the operation of property rights, labour activism, border policing, and indigenous people's *land rights. The role of lawyers themselves is also coming under scrutiny, and law firms are one of the advanced *producer services that interest researchers into *global cities and the globalization of *services in general.

Further reading Blomley, N. K., Delaney, D., and Ford, R. T. (eds.) (2001), *The Legal Geographies Reader*.

Law of the Sea An international treaty signed in 1983 and in force from 1994 governing the world's seas and oceans (more formally the United Nations Convention on the Law of the Sea). It superseded a hodgepodge of existing customs and agreements by establishing a 12 nautical mile *'territorial sea' around each country with a coastline, and a 200-mile Exclusive Economic Zone covering fishing and mineral rights. Although intended to encourage peaceful, cooperative, and sustainable use of the world's seas and oceans, it has not prevented disputes over maritime boundaries, island sovereignty, or ice-covered waters. The islands of the South China Sea is one area of contention, and the Lomonosov ridge, which Russia claims is part of its continental shelf in the Arctic Ocean, is another.

law (scientific) A written or mathematic statement that describes the behaviour of a specified phenomenon (usually natural) regardless of the time or location of its behaviour. To behave in law-like ways, a phenomenon must possess stable qualities that cause it to act or react the same even when situated in very different time-space coordinates. This is why scientific laws are usually thought to be universal across all the phenomena in each class to which a given law pertains. Most laws tend to be succinct and descriptive, unlike the theories that may be required to explain the causal processes that give rise to law-like behaviour. Most laws also tend to apply to non-human phenomena, notwithstanding the regular behaviour exhibited by the human body and mind.

Famous laws include the conservation of energy (which states that energy switches states but remains quantitatively stable), and the law of gravity (which states that all earthly objects fall to Earth unless helped up by a force equal to or greater than the Earth's gravitational force). These laws refer to processes or causal powers intrinsic to aspects of the biophysical world. However, some laws—more commonly found in the social sciences, including human geography—are statistical and describe correlations (more formally known as 'constant conjunctions') or repeated patterns. For instance, the *rank-size rule has proven to be remarkably consistent between otherwise different countries worldwide. All known (or supposed) laws are based upon repeated observations of the phenomena described by them.

In the 1960s, many geographers (human and physical) became energized by the idea that the Earth surface phenomena of different kinds might display law-like behaviour (i.e. their spatial form in two or three dimensions might be shown to be regular, suggesting underlying universal processes or causal powers). For instance, Peter *Haggett in his book *Locational Analysis in Human Geography* (1965), codified the spatial forms that everything from human migration patterns to settlement systems to disease diffusion might assume on the surface of the Earth. However, empirical research subsequently revealed two things. First, many geographical laws were hard to verify in more than approximate terms. Second, even 'laws' that seemed empirically valid—such as Waldo *Tobler's first law of geography—lacked an underlying explanatory theory and were highly abstract to the point of being almost vacuous. Consequently, by the 1970s most human geographers were doubtful that laws could be found, though many still believed that the spatial form of Earth surface phenomena often exhibited regular patterns that were well worth investigating (e.g. low longevity among city dwellers is typically found in low income, ethnic minority neighbourhoods). Meanwhile, critical realists argued that, while many phenomena exhibit law-like behaviour, they only do so under artificial conditions created by real or thought-experiments. In the real world, these phenomena must interact with all sorts of others in open systems (social and biophysical) so that their behaviour is continuously modified. Critical realists thus argue that *intensive research on different cases is as valid as *extensive research into the existence of general spatial patterns among cases. *See also* GENERALIZATION.

LDC *See* LESS ECONOMICALLY DEVELOPED COUNTRY.

LEADER programme A European *rural development programme in operation since 1991. LEADER, an acronym of '*Liaison Entre Actions de Développement de l'Économie Rurale*' (meaning 'links between the rural economy and development actions'), is a *local development approach that encourages local actors and communities using public and private finance, to initiate small business development. Its aim is to diversify the rural economy and to provide a viable, sustainable alternative to the agriculture sector.

lean production A form of commodity production that responds efficiently to market demand. It is sometimes known as *just-in-time (JIT) production and was famously associated with the Toyota automobile company (*see* TOYOTISM). During the 1960s, the firm began to eliminate waste, reduce inventory, and train its workers to be more flexible, thus moving towards a production process where commodities were almost 'made to order', while still being mass produced. *See also* FLEXIBLE ACCUMULATION.

leapfrogging The process of skipping one stage of technological development and adopting another, supposedly a more efficient and less polluting one. An example might be the rapid diffusion of mobile telephony without first investing in fixed line systems.

learning regions Any region in which the formal or informal transfer of knowledge between firms, universities, or other significant institutions enables mutual learning, leading to economic or other benefits (*see* KNOWLEDGE TRANSFER). Although some see fast, cheap transportation and communication as responsible for the 'end of geography', learning regions belie this view. Physical proximity of knowledge-based organizations—such as computer software companies—has been seen to facilitate knowledge transfer and exchange in ways not easily done via long-distance communication. Much of this leads to '*untraded interdependencies' that are beneficial to all involved, and which reveal the continued *embeddedness of all economic life, even in the *Information Age. *See also* CREATIVE CLASS.

least-cost location A location at which the total costs for a business operation are at their lowest. The location is calculated by finding the locale where labour, site, materials, and distribution costs are minimized with respect to suppliers and markets. *See also* VON THÜNEN MODEL.

lebensraum The geographical area needed by an organism for its development. If the *state can be regarded as an organism, as it was by Friedrich *Ratzel, then it means the territory and resources required by that state to flourish. As taken up by Nazi Germany, the doctrine of *lebensraum* licensed expansion eastwards into Poland and other lands (*see* GEOPOLITIK).

LEDC *See* LESS ECONOMICALLY DEVELOPED COUNTRY.

Lefebvre, Henri (1901–91) A French sociologist and philosopher whose myriad writings have had a profound impact on geographical thinking. Lefebvre wrote extensively on urban and rural life, and the effects of processes of modernization, industrialization, and surburbanization on everyday social relations. His key contribution, particularly through his book, *The *Production of Space* (1974, translated into English 1991) was to spatialize Marxist theory, transforming Marx's periodization of *capitalism into a history and *political economy of space. In so doing he argued that the main tension in society is not class struggle, but spatial conflict, especially in cities.

Left, the A term that encapsulates the radical political positions informed by *socialism, *feminism, *Marxism, *post-structuralism, *anarchism, and related convictions united, if at all, by a commitment to lasting social change and greater equity between people. The Left's core principles include greater redistribution of power and wealth, the spread of *democracy and human rights, the recognition of difference, *multiculturalism and anti-racism, pacifism and anti-imperialism, although their relative priority is debated. Within human geography, the journal *Antipode* has been a vehicle for the Left's discussions and interventions. *See also* CRITICAL GEOGRAPHY; RADICAL GEOGRAPHY.

leisure The time and activities outside *work and away from the workplace during which one undertakes activities for pleasure based on personal choice. To some degree leisure is subjective, i.e. a state of mind or experience that is personal or related to particular habits, beliefs, and cultures. It may enhance the opportunity to realize creative or playful feelings, as well as cultivate non-routine bodily actions. Objective assessments generally classify certain activities as leisure, but these can include activities also under-taken in relation to work, e.g. walking or reading. What counts as leisure is therefore also a matter of context. Leisure overlaps with, but can be roughly distinguished from *recreation, generally an outdoor activity undertaken within the vicinity, and *tourism, activities taking place further from home and usually commercialized. In practice, studies of leisure, recreation, and tourism are closely related.

The scholarly study of leisure has tracked its historical development from a mainly elite phenomenon in the late 19th century to a mass activity in the 20th century. In 1850, for example, the average working week in the USA was around 70 hours and time outside work was taken up with recuperation and family life (*see* REPRODUCTION OF LABOUR). Only the rich could afford the non-productive consumption of time. Growing affluence, shorter working weeks (now nearer 40 hours in the USA), and paid holiday time greatly expanded the scope for leisure of the average Westerner in the post-war period; by one estimate, the average American has 125–140 days a year available for leisure. Research in the 1950s and 1960s focused on the growing range of leisure activities, but was mindful of the limitations of access. Not everyone had the money, time, or means of travel to access all leisure opportunities. Using time-budget surveys, researchers generally distinguished between active and passive forms. In the 1980s, as *radical geography took hold, more attention was paid to the gender inequalities in leisure time and experience; calculations of the average working week often assume work means only waged labour outside the home, omitting the demands of household-based work (*see* DOMESTIC LABOUR). *Sexuality, *disability, and *race are also potential constraints. The role of commercialization in leisure was also critiqued. Leisure could be viewed as securing and reproducing disciplined and healthy bodies fit for work. More recent geographical research has further explored the relations between the *body and leisure, focusing on practice and *performativity, as well as the connections between *consumption (e.g. shopping, listening to music) and leisure.

Further reading Hall, C. M. and Page, S. J. (3rd ed. 2005), *The Geography of Tourism and Recreation: Environment, Place and Space.*

Leopold, Aldo (1887–1948) A prominent American conservationist and wildlife man-agement specialist. He started his working life with the US Forest Service. He published the first textbook on wildlife management and ecology in 1933 and in the same year took up a professorship at the University of Wisconsin, Madison. His best-selling book *A Sand County Almanac* (1949) examined people's relationships with the natural world, and his writings have informed *environmental ethics and had a lasting legacy on environmental and conservation movements. *See also* ENVIRONMENTAL POLITICS; WILDERNESS.

lesbian geographies The study of the socio-spatial relations of lesbian women. Initially, much of the research on the geographies of *sexuality focused on gay men. Lesbian women, it was thought, were much less visible in the landscape, lacking a bar culture or concentration into so-called gay ghettos, and therefore lacked an explicit geography. Recent work though has revealed the complex spatiality of lesbian women and the geographical strategies used for managing their lives. Adopting approaches from *feminist geography and *queer theory, lesbian geographies examines the spatial lives of lesbians and how they are shaped by *heteronormativity and *heteropatriarchy. Research has highlighted the ways in which lesbian women seek to negotiate their sexuality in different spaces and contexts, build spaces in which to socialize and live, construct networks of friendship, and organize politically. *See also* GAY GEOGRAPHIES; QUEER THEORY.

Further reading Valentine, G. (ed.) (2000), *From Nowhere to Everywhere: Lesbian Geographies.*

Less Economically Developed Country (LEDC) A low-income or economically poorer country; the term is generally applied to countries of Africa, Asia, and Latin America. The inclusion of the adjective 'economically' is designed to dispel the notion that such countries are somehow backward or primitive relative to others. LEDC has replaced earlier terms such as Least or Less Developed Country over the past 30 years. The World Bank categorizes countries according to their per capita *Gross National Income (GNI) into four groups (see Table 1).

Table 1 World Bank categories by GNI

	Gross National Income per capita 2007	Number of countries 2007
Low-income countries	$1025 or less	32
Lower middle-income countries	$1026–4035	54
Upper-middle-income countries	$4036–12,475	54
High-income countries	$12,476 and above	70

Source: World Bank, Washington, DC

levels of measurement The different ways that delimit the form of quantitative data and how it can be analysed. There are four main ways. Nominal data are categorical in nature, with observations recorded into discrete units (e.g., apartment, terraced, semi-detached, detached houses). Ordinal data are observations that are placed in a rank order, where certain observations are greater than others (e.g., miniscule, tiny, small, medium, large, massive). Interval data are measurements along a scale that possesses a fixed but arbitrary interval and an arbitrary origin (e.g., temperature along the Celsius scale). Addition or multiplication by a constant will not alter the interval nature of the observations. Data can either be continuous (e.g., time or length) or discrete (e.g., counts of a phenomenon in nature). Ratio data are similar to interval data except the scale possesses a true zero origin, and multiplication by a constant will not alter the ratio nature of the observations (e.g., exam marks on a scale of 0–100).

Ley, David (1947–) An urban social geographer based at the University of British Columbia who has spent most of his career researching and theorizing urban transformation. His first book, *The Black Inner City as Frontier Outpost* (1974), was a key text in the development of urban *social geography and *humanistic geography. He has also made important contributions to understanding *gentrification, notably through his book, *The New Middle Class and the Remaking of the Central City* (1996), and the transnational migration of elites (*Millionaire Migrants* 2010). In all his research, Ley has been interested in how different social groups interpret and use cities, particularly at the neighbourhood scale.

liberalism A worldview with several different branches that emphasizes the freedom of individuals to think and act according to their own volition. Liberals of all stripes are *normative in the sense that they oppose anti-liberal arrangements such as autocracy, dictatorship, communalism, and *slavery. Liberals are sometimes known as libertarians. Because untrammelled freedom threatens to impinge on the freedoms of others, virtually all self-styled liberals recognize that some balance must be struck between people's autonomy and constraints on that autonomy. Liberalism's origins lie in Ancient Greece, where *democracy was invented, and—much later—in the Reformation and then

*Enlightenment Europe, where the slow decline in the importance of monarchical rule, religion, and tradition inspired many to create novel ideas and practices. The French Revolution of 1789 was a key event in liberalism's history, despite its intentions soon being undermined by the regime of Napoleon Bonaparte. The criticism of slavery in Europe, North America, and elsewhere, leading to its abolition, was also a key contributor to liberalism's rise—as was the gradual decline of European empires. By the late 19th century liberalism had been elaborated as a worldview by the likes of John Stuart Mill, and its core tenets were embodied, however imperfectly, in several political parties bearing its name (such as the British Liberal Party). In the early 20th century liberalism faced some serious challenges, notably *fascism and *communism—both of which stressed submission of the individual to central government goals.

In the 21st century, liberalism—in its various concrete forms—can be said to be a core feature of virtually every electoral *democracy worldwide, except those where 'democracy' is merely a front for quasi-autocratic rule (as in *Russia). In simple terms, there are three domains where liberals argue for the cultivation of freedom: in the market (people should be free to buy and sell as they wish); in the public domain (people should be free to think, act, and vote as they wish when it comes to public affairs); and in the private domain (people are entitled to privacy and to do what they wish in the private domain, subject only to the rule of democratically determined laws). In all three cases freedom can never be absolute, but liberals argue that it should be maximized within bounds set by deliberations among those (or their representatives) who enjoy freedom. It is important to note that liberals need not be committed to maximizing freedom in all three domains. For example, some may argue that market freedoms should be curtailed by government intervention to protect the public interest or disadvantaged social groups. Meanwhile, they may be strong advocates of public and private freedom. Because freedom is relative, there is no universal definition offered by liberals of what a truly 'free person' is.

We can examine liberalism's relationship to human geography as both constitutive of the subject and as a real phenomenon that human geographers debate and analyse. In both cases, liberalism has been remarkably under-examined given how rich its history is and how important its ideas are to recent Western and world history. In the first case, human geography can be said to be a 'liberal' discipline in a number of different ways. Like other disciplines it has long valued the academic freedom of its members to research and teach what they wish. What is more, since the late 1980s human geographers have used this freedom to create unprecedented levels of intellectual diversity—a multitude of topical, methodological, and conceptual concerns can be found in the discipline, making it much more tolerant of heterodoxy than, say, economics. Thirdly, much of the *critical human geography that is now taught and published is critical of a previous kind of liberalism said to characterize human geography. In his criticism of what he called 'liberal formulations', David *Harvey's first book as a Marxist—*Social Justice and the City (1974)—argued that *spatial science and the *regional geography of the time were both 'liberal' in a very restricted way. By failing to criticize the structural inequalities characteristic of capitalist societies, Harvey accused them of being complicit with their perpetuation. Critical geographers have since examined forms of *inequality other than *class, in the process amplifying Harvey's concern that researchers and teachers criticize the limited freedoms available to the majority of people in the modern world.

Turning to liberalism as an object of analysis, many critical human geographers (e.g. Mitchell and Peck) have been examining the varied spatial forms assumed by *neoliberalism. They are generally dismissive of the freedoms delivered by neoliberal policies, arguing that the realities of heightened social inequality in neoliberalized countries belie the neoliberal rhetoric of enhanced freedom. At the same time, other critical human geographers have been examining the links between various forms of real and virtual *space and different forms of democracy. Partly inspired by the anti-capitalist movements that began in the late 1990s worldwide, they have been interested in how freedom of speech and the right to protest can better be used to challenge powerful institutions and actors (*see* RESISTANCE). Through all this, most human geographers have not, surprisingly, engaged deeply with the rich and complex traditions of liberal political theory. This reflects the discipline's slowness to engage more generally with political theory, having been concerned with economic theory in the 1960s, political economy in the 1970s and 1980s, cultural theory in the 1990s and, more recently, *Actor-Network Theory and other practice-orientated approaches.

Further reading Barnett, C. and Low, M. (2004), *Spaces of Democracy*.
Mitchell, K. (2004), *Crossing the Neoliberal Line: Pacific Rim Migration and the Metropolis*.
Peck, J. (2010), *Constructions of Neoliberal Reason*.

libertarianism *See* LIBERALISM

libertarian paternalism
The use of insights from behavioural economics and psychology to guide people's choices in ways that supposedly make them better off; also termed soft paternalism. In theory, its methods retain the importance of consumer choice (*libertarianism) but also generate socially desirable ends (paternalism). The idea was developed by Richard Thaler and Cass Sunstein, authors of *Nudge: Improving Decisions About Health, Wealth and Happiness* (2008). They recommended altering the default option on such things as organ donation, switching from opt-in to opt-out, or unobtrusive changes to the environment such as placing healthy foods at eye level in canteens. Critics question the ethics of the clandestine manipulation of behaviour and stress the wider context of decision-making. What happens, they ask, to those who consistently fail to make the 'right' choices, e.g. by continuing to smoke cigarettes? Are they stigmatized? Geographers interested in *governmentality find a great deal of scope to explore the ramifications of the concept and its policy application.

liberty
The theory and practice of freedom. Liberty is a core value of almost all democracies worldwide, and there is a rich history of arguments for it going back to the *Enlightenment. Because modern societies are functionally differentiated into the political, public, private, and market realms, the idea and practice of liberty needs to be disaggregated to attend to the specificities of these realms. *See also* LIBERALISM.

licensing agreements
An agreement made between a firm holding a patent, copyright, trademark, or some other *intellectual property right with another firm, where the latter is licensed to make, sell, or use the former's commodities or image.

lifecourse approach
A way of understanding the relations between key events and life transitions (e.g. birth, employment, marriage) in individual biographies. These may involve places of work and residence, as well as mobility. Bailey suggests a key focus is on the time-space synchronization of family members' lifecourses, e.g. dual-career households. It can also be a way of understanding how events or places early in life affect later well-being, e.g. health or economic inequality. *See also* BIOGRAPHICAL APPROACHES.

Reference Bailey, A. J. (2009), 'Population geography: lifecourse matters', *Progress in Human Geography* 33: 407–18.

life expectancy
The number of years a person can expect to live on average estimated from existing *mortality rates. Given that the risk of death is often highest in the year or so after birth, life expectancy is commonly measured from a person's first

birthday. Life expectancy ranges from 30–40 years at birth in poorer countries to over 70 years in richer ones and over 80 among some sub-groups.

life history *See* BIOGRAPHICAL APPROACH.

life table A means of summarizing the relationship between age and mortality for a given population. For each age the table shows the probability of an individual dying within the next year of their life, calculated using existing age-specific *mortality rates. Life tables are used to compare different populations and in life-insurance calculations.

lifeworld The individual and collective horizon of daily existence in which perceiving subjects move through a world of objects and processes that comprise their space of thought and action. The concept is most closely associated with the *phenomenology of German philosopher Edmund Husserl (1859–1938). Husserl wished to stress the *hermeneutic character of human existence, against the view that the world existed outside an objective given. In many respects his writing continued Immanuel *Kant's transcendental *idealism insofar as he saw reflective consciousness of reality as the key dimension of human existence.

Likert scale A bipolar scaling method for capturing value judgements along a spectrum of positive to negative statements. It is often used on *questionnaire surveys, with respondents presented with a series of scaled options, wherein they have to select the option that best matches their view. For example, possible answers might range on a scale from 'strongly agree' through to 'strongly disagree'.

Limits to Capital A book by David *Harvey (1982) that arguably presents the most complete and sophisticated theoretical analysis of the relationship between *capitalism and geography. The limits referred to in the title have a double meaning: they mark both the limitations of Marx's master work *Das Kapital* (published in three volumes), and the systemic limits of capitalism as a *mode of production. Harvey extends Marx's analysis to incorporate geographical issues and, in so doing, shows how geography is hard-wired to capitalism's crisis tendencies.

limits to growth A perspective on human population and resources use that advises radical steps to avoid catastrophic consequences. Although it shares much in common with long-standing *Malthusian and neo-Malthusian positions, the argument crystallized around a report by the Club of Rome published in 1972. *The Limits to Growth* was authored by US environmental scientist Donella H. Meadows and three colleagues. Its innovation was to mathematically model variables at the world scale and explore feedback mechanisms among them. In addition to population and food production, which Malthus himself considered, they added resource depletion, *pollution, and *industrialization. The models indicated that unrestrained consumption would lead to an overshooting of the planet's *carrying capacity at some time in the not-too-distant future. The report generated a great deal of debate and became a touchstone for a more pessimistic view on population, environment, and development. Its models were criticized for their simplicity and unrealistic assumptions. Many economists doubted its reasoning, suggesting that the normal operation of the market would forestall any overshoot and encourage substitution of one resource by another or technological fixes. Some of the original authors updated the report in 2004 and confirmed their initial findings with more sophisticated modelling. *See also* PEAK OIL.

linear perspective A method for creating the illusion of three-dimensional depth in a two-dimensional image. It uses a horizon and a system of converging orthogonal lines to produce a 'vanishing point', thus generating the impression of distance and space. The system was developed and formalized by Italian artists in the *Renaissance period.

linear programming A mathematical method for seeking the optimal locations or configuration of systems (such as maximum profit or lowest cost) against a set of constraints represented as linear relationships. The method works iteratively, converging on an optimal solution from an initial feasible solution by calculating the intersections of the linear cost functions. It was initially devised to address resource allocation problems, but has been used to calculate optimal locations in the planning of health, transport, and education systems.

liquid modernity A period characteristic of advanced capitalist societies in which everyday life is experienced as highly fluid and in which individuals and institutions become adept at change, adaptation, and reinvention. The term was coined by Polish social theorist Zygmunt Bauman, who argues that earlier periods of modern life, while dynamic, were far more 'solid'. Today, by contrast, social, cultural, technical, political, environmental, and economic change is faster than ever before, presenting many individuals with a range of choices about where and how to live. For Bauman, liquid modernity is a period in which the stresses and opportunities of life have become individualized, in part because of the success of *neoliberalism as an alternative to social democracy, communalism, or *Keynesian welfare capitalism.

literature A term that describes written material such as novel, stories, poetry, and essays. While it can include non-fiction works, it typically refers to works of imagination. Geographers have long been interested in literature. Prior to the 1970s, it was viewed principally as a source of geographical data relating to local and regional identities and landscapes. During the 1970s and 1980s, with the *humanistic turn, geographers turned to novels and prose to examine the subjective experience of place. In both cases, the *texts were often taken at face value, analysed using *content or *discourse analysis, and used instrumentally to confirm or illustrate established geographical knowledge. Such approaches were critiqued in the late 1980s and 1990s by geographers drawing on literary and social theory, especially *post-structural, *psychoanalytic, and *post-colonial varieties. They sought to *deconstruct literary texts, as well as travel writing and scientific journals, in order to understand the ways in which *geographical imaginaries are produced and consumed. Such readings did not view texts as simple mimetic representations of the world, but as complex, *intertextual documents. In parallel, the spatial turn in the humanities has seen literary theorists engage and employ key geographical concepts such as place, space, and landscape in their readings of texts. *See also* REPRESENTATION, ICONOGRAPHY.

Further reading Brosseau, M. (1994), 'Geography's literature', *Progress in Human Geography* 18: 333–53.
Kitchin, R. and Kneale, J. (eds.) (2002), *Lost in Space: Geographies of Science Fiction*.

Liverman, Diana (1954–) An environmental geographer based at the University of Arizona and the University of Oxford whose research focuses on the human dimensions of global environmental change. In particular, she has contributed to debates on human vulnerability and adaptation to *climate change, including *food security and climate justice, and on the political economy and political ecology of environmental management in the Americas. Among her many publications she co-edited the *Companion to Environmental Geography* (2009), which showcases recent geographical research into human-environment relations.

Livingstone, David N. (1953–) A historical geographer specializing in the produc-tion of geographical knowledge and the spatialities of science based at Queen's University, Belfast. His book *The *Geographical Tradition* (1992) was an important intervention into how the histories of geography as a discipline are produced. He argued for non-*presentist, non-progressive, contextual accounts that reveal the situated mess-iness and contested nature of geographical endeavours. Since then, much of his writing has attended to the multiple strands of geographical thinking within and outside aca-demic geography, with a particular focus on the different spaces in which knowledge is made and through which it circulates. *See* GEOGRAPHY, HISTORY OF.

Local Agenda 21 An international framework for action on *sustainable development by local government agreed at the 1992 *Rio Earth Summit. It set out a series of actions such as combating poverty, changing consumption patterns, promoting health, adopting more sustainable settlement patterns, protecting fragile environments, conserving bio-diversity, controlling pollution, and strengthening the role of civic society and marginal-ized groups in local governance. As a framework, it does not prescribe any specific actions. Thousands of local governments around the world have therefore been able to incorporate it into new or existing schemes with varying degrees of efficacy.

local food networks A term used to encompass social organizations designed to encourage more locally bounded, self-sufficient, and sustainable practices of food pro-duction, distribution, and consumption. Also termed *alternative food networks, they are consciously opposed to global and corporate food systems operating through major retailing systems and involving the long-distance movements of foodstuffs. Farmers markets are an example. Ideally, such networks also educate consumers to not only buy more locally, but to become more aware of where their food comes from, and how it is produced.

Further reading Goodman, D., DuPuis, M., and Goodman, M. (eds) (2011), *Alternative Food Networks.*

local-global relations A descriptive term for the variety of ways of considering local (small-scale) and global (large-scale) processes and phenomena in relation to one another. J. K. Gibson-Graham set out six ways in which the local and global might be combined by way of critiquing and overcoming their binary separation. First, local and global can be thought of as alternative perspectives on the same thing, i.e. as interpretive frames without any particular content. Second, they can be understood relationally, i.e. local and global derive their respective meaning from not being global and local. Third, local and global refer to shorter or longer networks (*see* ACTOR-NETWORK THEORY; SCALE). In this sense, something global does not stand above something local, encompassing it, but is simply a longer network. These three conceptions are different perspectives. The fourth and fifth approaches suggest that the local and global are the same. Either everything global is really local, e.g. a transnational corporation is actually a multi-locale entity, or everything local is really global, i.e. each place is another entry point into planet-spanning connections and flows (*see* PLACE). The sixth and final position is that local and global refer not to locations but to processes, i.e. of *localization and *global-ization operating simultaneously (*see* GLOCALIZATION). J. K. Gibson-Graham's intention is to dispel the common idea that global = powerful/active/masculine and local = weak/passive/ feminine, although in practice it proves difficult not to fall into this binary trap. *See also* TRANSNATIONALISM.

Reference Gibson-Graham, J. K. (2002), 'Beyond global vs. local' in Herod, A. and Wright, M. (eds.) *Geographies of Power* 25–60.

locality 1. A place.

2. A theorized conception of place associated with three localities programmes funded by the UK *Economic Research Council in the 1980s. These cooperative research initiatives sought to identify and explain Britain's social and spatial restructuring through in-depth case studies on, and comparative analysis of, selected places and regions. Partly inspired by Doreen *Massey's *Spatial Divisions of Labour* the projects sought to balance and combine understanding of local, national, and global processes. In so doing they generated much conceptual debate, not least over how exactly to identify a locality.

Further reading Cooke, P. (ed.) (1989), *Localities: the Changing Face of Urban Britain*.

localization 1. The processes by which economic and other activity is embedded in places, either in contrast to, in opposition to, or as a related aspect of, *globalization.

2. Resistance to globalization based on increased local control and economic self-sufficiency. In economic geography, 'localization economies' are cost savings arising from the physical clustering of firms in the same sector (*see* AGGLOMERATION ECONOMIES). *See also* DEGLOBALIZATION.

local knowledge The *tacit and explicit knowledge possessed and used by people who share the same *culture. Typically, this knowledge is acquired from sustained proximity (face-to-face interaction), but now that long-distance migration is such a common feature of modern life, it can also 'travel' and enter different cultural milieux. The term is closely associated with the American cultural anthropologist Clifford Geertz and his book *Local Knowledge* (1983). Geertz argued that too much social science had been enamoured with the ideas of *objectivity and *abstraction. The former presupposed that the social and cultural worlds inhabited by people could be represented in a neutral way by an impartial observer. The latter presupposed that there is an underlying order shared among otherwise different societies and cultures. Against these presuppositions, Geertz insisted that difference and diversity continued to characterize human existence on Earth, even after the supposedly unifying effects of *globalization have been taken into account. He further argued that to understand these differences it was important for the investigator to immerse him- or herself in the *lifeworlds of those they are investigating (*see* THICK DESCRIPTION). Such immersion involved the 'interpretation of interpretation', a *hermeneutic sensibility acquired through patience and sustained *fieldwork. Geertz questioned the idea of a universal human reason, arguing instead that people actively make the world meaningful in different ways because they are, fundamentally, interpretive beings.

Geertz's ideas were among several emanating from a broadly defined cultural theory that helped to change the character of Anglophone human geography in the 1990s. Coincident with the rise to prominence of *postmodernist thinking, Geertz's ideas helped to bring about a 'cultural turn' in which many geographers became interested in the varied forms and effects of language, symbolism, meaning, and *representation. Though few emulated his commitment to serious *ethnographic research in overseas cultural environments, his idea of local knowledge appealed to geographers seeking to escape the influence of *Grand Theory in human geography. Ironically, Geertz would probably not have approved of the large interest among human geographers in the signs and symbols created by powerful institutions and actors. He may not have approved either of the rather exclusive focus on graphical or pictographic representations, such as maps and official documents. Through the 1990s, there was less interest in how lay actors make the world meaningful, except, perhaps, when engaged in social *resistance. Even so, many human geographers of the period, especially 'new cultural geographers', were inspired by Geertz's focus on cultural difference and the interpretive nature of human existence. This inspiration also came from Edward *Said's work, and gave impetus to the growth of *post-colonialism in human geography.

local state Institutions of government at subnational levels, including elected local government and regional assemblies, as well as the regional offices of national government bodies. This might include health and education agencies, utilities, and courts. The local state was extensively theorized by British human geographers in the 1980s (*see* LOCALITY). They asked how much autonomy did it have from the national state and how far could it engage in productive activity rather than just deliver public services?

locational advantage The advantages accrued by a firm through being located at a particular site or within a jurisdiction. These can include access to raw materials, key markets, low wages, special taxes or tariffs, and the benefits of *agglomeration. Such advantages help firms minimize their costs and maximize their profits. *See also* LEAST-COST LOCATION; LINEAR PROGRAMMING; LOCATIONAL ANALYSIS.

locational analysis The study of the pattern and structure of location and the flows between sites. It operationalizes *location theory. Locational analysis is closely associated with the development of quantitative geography in the discipline from the late 1950s onward (*see* QUANTITATIVE REVOLUTION). The focus of analysis was to explain statistically the spatial logic and processes underpinning the siting of different kinds of locations (e.g. settlements, factories, schools, etc.), the relationships and linkages between these sites (e.g. competing factories), networks (e.g. road systems), and areas (e.g. market catchments), and to produce predictive models that would detail what might happen in geographic and economic terms if the locational structure was altered (e.g. by adding a new factory in an area). By applying statistical methods to analysing spatially referenced data, the aim was to determine generalizable laws that could be applied universally to understand and model the locational pattern and structure of society. In other words, there was an attempt to reposition geography as the 'science of locations'. Initially, locational analysis drew heavily on German theorists such as von Thünen, *Christaller, Weber, and Lösch, who each provided early models of the space economy, but was then developed further, principally by geographers in America (especially at the universities of Washington, Ohio, Northwestern, and Iowa), and Britain (especially at the universities of Cambridge and Bristol) (*see* LÖSCH MODEL: VON THÜNEN MODEL). Since then, the sophistication of *spatial analysis and models has increased significantly, aided by the development of computing that can undertake complex calculations on large data sets. While most early analysis focused on economic activity and the movement of people and goods, locational analysis has been applied to every kind of human activity and used widely in public policy and industry to determine the optimal locales for sites. The approach is not without its critics, who argue that it is highly reductionist and fails to take adequate account of *human agency or the wider *political economy in its analysis. *See also* LOCATIONAL ANALYSIS IN HUMAN GEOGRAPHY; SPATIAL ANALYSIS.

Further reading Abler, R., Adams, J. S., and Gould, P. R. (1971), *Spatial Organization: the Geographer's View of the World*.

Fotheringham, S., Brunsden, C., and Charlton, M. (2000), *Quantitative Geography: Perspectives on Spatial Data Analysis*.

Locational Analysis in Human Geography A key text in the development of quantitative geography written by Peter *Haggett (1965). It provided a synoptic overview of geographical modelling and statistical analysis focused on the concept of location. The book was divided into two parts: 'Models of Locational Structure' that examined movement, networks, nodes, hierarchies, and surfaces; and 'Methods in Locational Analysis' detailing the collecting, description, region-building, and testing of spatial data. Importantly, the book brought together the earlier ideas of German theorists such as von Thünen, *Christaller, Alfred Weber, and Lösch, with those being developed in the United

States at the time by Michael Dacey, William *Garrison, William *Bunge, and Brian *Berry. *See also* HAGGETT, PETER; LOCATIONAL ANALYSIS.

location based services (LBS) A term describing digitally provided services that are delivered in situ and in real time and are sensitive to present location. Such services might include direction-giving via a *satnav device, or information about nearby restaurants, their menus, prices, and diner ratings, or local weather forecasts or traffic reports, delivered by a smart phone. The information is provided through devices that know their location through embedded *GPS.

location quotient A measure of the concentration of activity in a sub-area relative to the overall area. It is calculated as a simple ratio. For example, if the market share for a supermarket is 35.4 per cent for the country, but 54.2 per cent for a specific region, the location quotient would be $54.2/35.4 = 1.53$. A quotient over 1.0 indicates that the activity is more concentrated in a sub-area relative to the whole area, a quotient under 1.0 indicates that it is less concentrated. Mapping the location quotients for all sub-areas provides a holistic picture of the pattern of concentration.

location theory A set of theories and models that seek to account for the location of different activities and the interconnections between them. In particular it focuses on the spatial organization of economic activity, for example, theories that seek to explain the optimal location for a factory given the source of raw materials and the market. Prior to the *quantitative revolution such theories tended to be largely restricted to German economics, for example (*see* LÖSCH MODEL; VON THÜNEN MODEL).

As quantitative geography became established, the development of location theory and the search for spatial laws that explained social and economic phenomena became a core preoccupation. The existing German work was imported into the discipline and new theories and models were developed that utilized *gravity models and *network analysis, and which drew theoretical strength from neoclassical economics (*see* CENTRAL PLACE THEORY; HOTELLING MODEL; UTILITY THEORY). As research developed and the shortcomings of neoclassical economics, which prioritized time over space and posited rational behaviour, were recognized, new formulations were forwarded such as *satisficing behaviour. In this formulation, location theory became the cornerstone of geography's claims to being a *spatial science wherein the geographical world could be *modelled, explained, predicted, and *simulated. The validity of such location theory is empirically tested through locational analysis.

By the late 1960s and early 1970s, these principles of location theory were already starting to be challenged by *radical and *humanistic geographers who argued that they failed to adequately account for either *structure or *agency in the spatial organization of society and economy. *Political economists and *Marxists, in particular, sought to create location theories that understood the spatial organization of industry as the outcome of the forces of *capitalism and how these create and exploit *uneven development and the *spatial divisions of labour. Here, location was posited to reflect the complex interrelation of economics, politics, and ideology and spatial organization could not be modelled independently of the wider structural forces shaping social and economic relations.

Nevertheless, more quantitatively orientated formulations of location theory have persisted in *economic geography and *regional science, becoming ever more sophisticated in nature. Moreover, mainstream economists such as the Nobel Laureate Paul *Krugman have become interested in the location of economic activity, developing what has been termed '*new economic geography', reinvigorating the creation and use of location theories more broadly.

Further reading Krugman, P. (1995), *Development, Geography and Economic Theory.*
Smith, D. M. (1981), *Industrial Location: an Economic Geographical Analysis.*

lock-in A situation arising when one standard or technology becomes so widely adopted that the costs of either switching or abandoning it become prohibitively high. The concept appears in *evolutionary economics and by extension in human geography, where it is invoked to explain how certain economic arrangements may persist even though they are not the most efficient (*see* PATH DEPENDENCY).

logic The study and use of reason. Philosophers study logic in a formal sense, while most other social sciences and humanities scholars tend to use it as part of their everyday research and teaching. Though often associated almost exclusively with *the scientific method, logic is used in all areas of academic life, albeit often unreflexively. Logic is at work when a researcher makes valid inferences, deductions, retroductions, or forecasts on the basis of known facts, specific assumptions, or well-defined rules. Some logic proceeds by identifying what follows necessarily from the latter, but often by identifying what possibly or probably follows. Human geographers of all stripes regard themselves as logical thinkers, but the intellectual differences among them mean that various informal and formal definitions of logic are at work that might benefit from the sort of explicit scrutiny philosophers give the subject.

logical empiricism A philosophy of science with several strands whose core tenet is that any statement that cannot be tested empirically cannot be a part of science. Sometimes known as *logical positivism, it arose in the 1920s and 1930s when groups of philosophers and mathematicians based in Berlin and Vienna decided to demarcate *science from non-science. Theirs was an attempt to free human knowledge from what they regarded as the distortions of prejudice, superstition, autocracy, religious belief, and political *ideology. They argued that even *logic was not scientific in itself because, in its 'pure' form, it produced mere tautologies (such as $1 + 1 = 2$). For logic to yield scientific knowledge, they argued, it had to be used to examine the validity of empirically testable statements that might, for instance, be phrased as *hypotheses. The logic empiricists disagreed over how best to test such statements, with some arguing for the utility of *verification (the accumulation of positive evidence), others for the utility of *falsification (the focus on negative instances that broke perceived rules). However, they were all *realists in the sense that, for them, science could yield knowledge that accurately represented a reality existing independently of humans.

By the early 1960s, logical empiricism was a large and complex movement connecting universities in Western Europe and North America. Elements of it influenced the turn to *spatial science among a new generation of geographers in the 1950s and 1960s. However, it was not until 1969 that a systematic presentation of the movement was provided for the benefit of the geographical community. David Harvey's *Explanation in Geography* (1969) showed how geographical phenomena of all kinds could be examined scientifically. In truth, his presentation rather flattered geographers, making it appear that their engagements with logical empiricism and their use of the *scientific method was more systematic than in actuality. Through the 1970s, those human geographers seeking to make their subject a science can be better understood as honouring the spirit but not the full letter of logical empiricism. In part, this is because their concerns were more empirical than philosophical. Few were willing or able to read the heavyweight tomes authored by the likes of Rudolph Carnap or Karl Popper. In any case, within philosophy logical empiricism had been largely eclipsed by the 1970s and remains something of an historical curiosity, best remembered for its idealized presentation of what 'real science' should look like. Today, very few human geographers make formal use of logical empiricist ideas, even as many remain committed to the ideals of *science.

logical positivism A philosophy of knowledge whose central idea is that the world is only knowable on the basis of observation and evidence. It is associated with a group of scholars active in the early 20th century known as the Vienna Circle, after the city in which they lived (*see* LOGICAL EMPIRICISM). Their thinking derived from the 19th-century French polymath Auguste Comte. In French *positif* means 'imposed on the mind by experience'. Comte was thus an opponent of *idealism in its various forms, such as theology and *metaphysics. He argued that the social sciences can create an objective understanding of society akin to that achieved for *nature in the biophysical sciences. He thus, like the logical empiricists, believed in the unity of the scientific enterprise. It is doubtful whether geographers ever formally embraced all the tenets of logical positivism, despite Derek *Gregory implying as much in his influential book *Ideology, Science and Human Geography* (1978). Today, it is discussed in geography, principally in histories of the discipline, especially those presented in undergraduate textbooks.

Further reading Kitchin, R. (2006), 'Positivistic geography and spatial science', in Aitken, S. and Valentine, G. (eds.) *Approaches in Human Geography* 20–29.

logistics The organization and management of the movement of goods and services within a system. Traditionally, it referred to the branch of the military tasked with procuring, maintaining, and transporting material, personnel, and facilities throughout an army or navy so that it could function effectively. It now refers more broadly to logistical arrangements of all industries, coordinating transportation within the organization, from suppliers and to customers.

logit regression A form of *regression used when the dependent variable is binary in nature. For example, in the case of trying to determine whether a person moves house or not, the dependent variable is move/stay (1/0), and the independent variables might be the cost of the rent or the desirability of the neighbourhood. The logit regression measures the probability of the dependent variable outcome equalling 1 (moving) given the independent variables. Based on the results, it is possible to predict outcomes under differing conditions.

Further reading Gelman, A. and Hill, J. (2007), *Data Analysis Using Regression and Multilevel/ Hierarchical Models*.

log-linear modelling A *general linear method for analysing the relationship between two or more *categorical data variables. It is an extension of the two-way contingency table used in *chi-square, enabling the analysis of contingency tables that involve three or more variables by comparing the natural logarithm of the cell frequencies. No distinction is made between independent and dependent variables, thus only association between variables is calculated. If one or more variables are treated as explicitly dependent and others as independent, then *logit regression should be used instead. *See also* NOMINAL DATA.

logocentrism A belief, said to be typical of Western thinking, that thought precedes speech and speech proceeds writing. The term was coined by a German philosopher Ludwig Klages in the 1920s. According to one old definition, a *logos* is a foundation or generative process. Logocentrism is typical of the dualism that structures Western thinking. Such thinking presumes the world to be cleaved into discrete parts, with some acting as causes, others as effects. However, as post-structural critics have pointed out, this presumption is problematic—even on its own terms. It belies the relational character of all forms of *representation—even those, such as pure thought, presumed to be originary. It also creates a problematic hierarchy in which action and practice are seen to be somehow derivative of conception, perception, speech, and writing. Human geographers critical of logocentrism have devoted much energy to showing how *place, *space, *landscape, and *nature are all, in part, constructions or compositions that do not simply reflect the straight-line transmission of human designs into realized plans.

London The capital city of the United Kingdom, as well as the largest, with a population of just over eight million. The greater London region contains some thirteen million people. For nearly a century (from 1825) it was the world's largest city. Situated on the Thames River, inland from the North Sea, London was a Roman settlement some two millennia ago and by the 18th century was a thriving city of politics, commerce, science, and cultural innovation. Economically, the city has long benefited from being the seat of national government, but it has also been a significant port and banking centrre. Today, it is by far the largest metropolitan economy in the UK, by some measures the largest in the *European Union, and is generally placed at the apex of *world city networks (*see* GLOBAL CITY). Three notable features of its economy are: its financial institutions such as international banks and insurance companies; tourism; and higher education.

The so-called Square Mile in the City, encompassing globally important financial institutions, creates thousands of well-paid jobs and enormous tax revenues, though was central to the causes of the 2008 global financial crisis. Perhaps 400,000 London workers are employed directly in the tourist industry, with tourists spending some £17 billion in 2010. Five airports, including two very large airports (Gatwick and Heathrow) bring visitors to the city, as well as connecting residents to the rest of the world. London's economy is so large and physically extensive it has spread beyond the city's administrative *borders into adjoining boroughs. London has several world-class institutions of higher education, most of them colleges of the University of London. They educate hundreds of thousands of students, some 30 per cent from overseas.

London is governed by a metropolitan authority led by an elected mayor, though its constituent boroughs each have their own elected councils that provide a range of public services. It is a *superdiverse and *cosmopolitan city in terms of ethnic origin, and around a third of the population was born abroad. Because it has been such a large *growth pole for so long, land and property prices are very high, though a relative shortage of residential accommodation exacerbates the problem. The national government is seeking ways to increase housing supply, though it may impinge on the *green belt around the city. The city suffers from traffic congestion, despite having one of the world's oldest underground train systems, known as 'the Tube'. To help keep private vehicles out of the city, London introduced a congestion tax in 2003. The city also hosted the summer Olympic Games for the third time in its history in 2012.

Longhurst, Robyn (1962–) A New Zealand feminist social geographer based at the University of Waikato. Her research examines the relationship between *embodiment and geography by examining issues of *gender and *sexuality, and she has critiqued the *masculinist epistemology and ontology of the discipline. Her books include *Bodies* (2001), *Maternities: Gender, Bodies and Space* (2008), and *Space, Place and Sex* (2010, with Lynda Johnston). She has also been an editor of the journal *Gender, Place and Culture*.

longitudinal data analysis The tracking over time of a selected population, making repeated observations of the same variables with respect to the population. The analysis usually tracks a cohort of interest (e.g., a set of people, companies, locations), collecting measurements at different time periods (e.g., every day, once a year, once every five years). It can also apply to whole populations such as with a population *census. Longitudinal analysis is very useful because it enables the study of change over time, but avoids the cross-level fallacy that might arise from using cross-sectional data (sampling a different set of people from the same population at each time period, *see* ECOLOGICAL FALLACY). There are a number of different methods for analysing longitudinal data that seek to take account of whether the data are continuous or discrete in temporal terms, or events (significant life changes) are repeatable or non-repeatable, or single or multiple, or the form of data collected (nominal, ordinal, interval, ratio, *see* LEVELS OF MEASUREMENT). The approach has mostly been used in geography to study population change, residential mobility, and *migration. *See also* BIOGRAPHICAL APPROACH; COHORT ANALYSIS.

Further reading Singer, J. and Willett, J. (2003), *Applied Longitudinal Data Analysis: Modelling Change and Event Occurrence*.

Lorenz curve *See* GINI COEFFICIENT.

Los Angeles A city in California, USA (population 3.8 million) but also an abbreviation for a larger metropolitan region including the cities of Long Beach and Santa Ana and numerous other municipalities (population 12.8 million). LA's remarkable ethnic diversity, diversified and productive economy, hazard-filled physical environment, and creative cultural life have ensured constant attention from human geographers. Often regarded as the antithesis of Chicago, the archetypal modern city, Los Angeles was associated with a school of urban theorists from the 1980s onwards including Ed *Soja, Allen J. *Scott, Jennifer *Wolch, Michael *Storper, and Michael *Dear.

Lösch model An extension of *Chistaller's *Central Place Theory, developed by the German economist August Lösch, used to identify the locational organization of activity around major central places for particular services or industry. Whereas Christaller identified the ordered structure of places from the top down wherein places are located where they maximize profit, Lösch starts from the bottom up, identifying the smallest unit of analysis (expressed as a lattice of hexagons) wherein the need to travel for any good is minimized and profits held level. The Lösch model then scales up, overlaying the market areas for difference values of k (a constant distance) to include the most number of places.

Lovelock, James (1919–) A British scientist, inventor, and *public intellectual best known for his *Gaia thesis that views the Earth as a single, living biological organism composed of a complex interacting system of living and non-living parts. Formulated while working for NASA in the 1960s, Lovelock's notion of Gaia postulates that the biosphere has a self-regulatory effect on the environment and its ability to sustain life. Lovelock's writings are highly contested within the scientific community and beyond, but they have nonetheless had a profound impact on thinking about the Earth and people's relationship to it, contributing to debates on environmental *sustainability, *food security, and *climate change, and shaping the arguments of environmental movements. He remains a controversial figure, mostly recently arguing for the expansion of nuclear power to substitute for the use of fossil fuels in providing energy. He has also suggested that the planet is over-populated with *homo sapiens*.

low carbon economy An economic system in which the emission of carbon dioxide and other *greenhouse gases is systematically minimized. Although most human societies have been low producers of CO_2 and many traditional communities still are, the term is generally used to refer to the future aspirations of carbon-intensive industrialized societies. A 'decarbonized' or zero carbon economy is one in which the emission of CO_2 is a bare minimum and all power is produced by *renewable energy. Some activists regard this as a realistic possibility for countries in the Global North within the foreseeable future. A related concept is 'carbon neutrality', which refers to the net emissions of a concern. Any CO_2 generated can be offset through buying credits in a carbon market (*see* CARBON OFF-SETTING; CARBON TRADING).

Transition to a low carbon economy is motivated by the aim of mitigating the impact of anthropogenic climate change. It would necessitate a range of technological, regulatory, and behavioural changes across all sectors of society and at a range of spatial scales. According to the UK government's Low Carbon Transition Plan (2009) there needs to be three main interventions. First, the energy efficiency of buildings and industries should be greatly improved, for example, by altering the regulations governing new construction. Second, there would have to be a decarbonization of power and heat generation and transport, i.e., a move towards more renewable energy and/or *nuclear power. Third, technologies for carbon capture and storage (CCS) must be developed. These catch emissions at the point of production, transport, and store them long term in suitable geological structures. Alongside government and industry initiatives, there is a range of municipal and voluntary actions motivated by the goal of lowering CO_2 emissions. These include the Transition Town movement, a network of community groups whose aim is to make their communities more resilient to impending climate change. Strategies include reducing dependence on fossil fuels and imported or non-local food. *See also* CARBON TAX; ECOTAXATION.

Lowenthal, David (1923–) A historical geographer whose research focused on the relationships between *culture and *landscape, *perception and environment, *heritage and *conservation. In particular, he was concerned with the features that made places and landscapes valued, exploring the connections between past societies and landscape, and the uses of the past and the way that people shape landscapes to conform with shared narratives that express cultural values, as exemplified by his books *The Past Is a Foreign Country* (1985) and *The Heritage Crusade and the Spoils of History* (1996).

Lynch, Kevin A. (1918–84) An American urban planner who spent most of his career teaching and writing at the Massachusetts Institute of Technology (MIT). His book *The Image of the City* (1960) was influential in *behavioural geography and the understanding of spatial cognition. In it, he devised a standardized framework for understanding the *mental maps possessed by city dwellers based on paths, edges, districts, nodes, and landmarks. *See also* COGNITIVE MAPPING.

Maastricht Treaty A treaty signed by twelve European Community member countries in February 1992, and coming into effect in November 1993; it created the *European Union and laid the blueprint for economic and monetary union. The treaty added two new pillars to the European Community: the Common Foreign and Security Policy, and Justice and Home Affairs. It provided the people of the twelve member countries with European citizenship and the right to move, live, and vote in local and European elections in other member countries. Importantly, it set out the criteria for the creation of a single currency, the Euro. It has subsequently been amended by the treaties of Amsterdam, Nice, and Lisbon.

Mackinder, Sir Halford (1861–1947) A British geographer who helped to establish geography as an academic subject in British universities and to forge links between university and school geography. Mackinder set up the *Geographical Association and was later its chairman. His lecture, 'On the scope and methods of geography' in 1887, persuaded the *Royal Geographical Society to fund a post for him in geography at the University of Oxford. His academic writing largely concerned *geopolitics, and was especially concerned with how Britain's imperial ambitions could be peacefully secured. Mackinder was a diplomat and director of the London School of Economics when not being a professional geographer.

mainstreaming The integration of disabled children into the ordinary school system and the phasing out of specialized schools. The prevalent mode of *education for disabled children has been to educate them in a socially and spatially segregated school system due to their special needs. Mainstreaming argues that this *segregation further disables these children by removing them from the rest of society and stymies their social development. Mainstreaming disabled students increases educational attainment, increases self-esteem, and improves social skills, as well as reducing the stigma of disability by exposing all children to a classroom of varying abilities.

mall An abbreviation for shopping mall, a large complex of retail businesses housed in a single-roofed structure with access for pedestrians but not vehicles; dedicated car parking is provided adjacent to the shopping area. Also known as shopping centres, malls are regarded as exemplary sites of consumption, socialization, and identity. Critics, however, claim that malls are not true *public spaces, because they are usually corporate-controlled and heavily regulated; protest marches and labour actions are generally banned, for example. *See also* RETAILING.

Malthusianism A doctrine holding that unrestrained population growth will inevitably lead to catastrophe, as growing numbers exceed the available resources. The idea is derived from the work of the economist Thomas Malthus (1776–1834), although not all of its manifestations are faithful to his argument. In *An Essay on the Principle of Population* (1798) Malthus deduced a natural law of population, namely that the geometric growth in population conflicts with the arithmetic growth in food. Although he described this as an ever-present tendency, given that various checks—including moral restraint, disease, and famine—would forestall crisis, later interpretations took the principle to be a prediction of necessary overpopulation and consequent suffering. Malthus framed his argument in opposition to the prevailing ideas of human perfectibility arising from the French Revolution and the *Enlightenment. Hence they have been characterized as pessimistic.

Malthus's ideas were debated and contested at the time, but a revived Malthusianism took shape from the 1950s onwards in response to the rapidly growing world population. Often termed 'neo-Malthusianism', such views stressed the necessity for robust population planning and fertility control in order to avert looming disaster. Malthus himself had scorned the use of contraception. These arguments crystallized around the 1974 World Population Conference in Bucharest, but were also expressed in popular books such as *The Population Bomb* by Paul R. Ehrlich (1968) and the Club of Rome's report *The Limits to Growth* (1972). Famines in northern Africa in the 1970s and 1980s seemed to confirm their fears.

By the 1990s population projections were anticipating a deceleration of world population growth and eventual stabilization by the mid-21st century. Malthusianism faded in academic and policy circles, but rising world food prices from 2007 raised the spectre of Malthusian crisis again. In *Collapse*, for example, Jared Diamond ascribes the Rwandan genocide to Malthusian causes.

Further reading Woods, R. (2nd ed. 1989), 'Malthus, Marx and population crises', in Johnston, R. J. and Taylor, P. (eds.) *A World in Crisis? Geographical Perspectives*, 127–49.

Man's Role in Changing the Face of the Earth A landmark publication in understanding human-environment relationships in inter-disciplinary and historical perspectives, appearing in 1956. It was based on a symposium held in Princeton, sponsored by the Wenner-Gren Foundation and National Science Foundation and chaired by Carl *Sauer. Written by over fifty contributors, and edited by William L. Thomas Jr, its three sections address environmental history, the human impact on the environment, and future prospects for population and resources.

manufacturing The deliberate transformation of raw materials or goods in order to create a new *commodity. Manufacturing is normally distinguished from *extractive industries (such as *mining), *agriculture, and service industries. It covers a wide range of activities, from heavy manufacturing (e.g. steel production) through to assembly production (e.g. car manufacture). A great deal of contemporary manufacturing produces composite commodities, that is to say, commodities comprised of numerous separately manufactured parts (e.g. a personal computer).

map hacking The combination of different mapping tools and spatial data to create new cartographic applications. Presently there exists a huge number of online open mapping tools, as well as a growing set of *open data that is georeferenced. By hacking the tools and data together it is possible to create new and interesting ways to explore a particular issue. *See also* BIG DATA; MASHUP; OPEN DATA.

map interactivity The ability to interact with maps beyond simply being able to read them. With the advent of *GIS and online mapping, maps can now be queried through interfaces that allow users to choose the level and form of *abstraction, *generalization, and design, and to be able to query the underlying data. Such interactivity enables greater exploration of the mapped data.

Mappa mundi A medieval European map of the world. Just over one thousand such maps still survive and are made up of four types. The first type are T-O maps of the known, inhabited parts of the world at the time, with the landmass displayed as a circle divided into three continents (Africa, Asia, and Europe) by a T. The second type are quadripartite maps that add a fourth land mass, the *antipodes. The third type are zonal maps that divided the world into parallel zones of climate and habitation. The fourth type are more complex maps. The maps are schematic in nature, lacking scientific principles of construction, and were not designed to aid navigation but rather illustrate knowledge and aid storytelling. One noted example is the Hereford *Mappa mundi*, a T-O map residing in Hereford Cathedral, England dating to 1290.

Further reading Harley, J. B. and Woodward, D. (eds.) (1987), *The History of Cartography, Volume I: Cartography in Prehistoric, Ancient, and Medieval Europe and the Mediterranean.*

mapping *See* CARTOGRAPHY.

Mapping Desire A text by David Bell and Gill Valentine (eds.), published in 1995, that helped to establish the study of the geographies of *sexuality. Drawing on critical social theory, *queer theory, and emerging debates in cultural geography concerning identity, cultural politics, and citizenship, the book provided a wide-ranging overview of the spaces of sex and the sexing of space with respect to gay men, lesbian women, bisexuals, and transsexuals. *See also* GAY GEOGRAPHIES; HETERONORMATIVITY; LESBIAN GEOGRAPHIES.

map projection A method for converting the three-dimensional nature of the world into a two-dimensional representation as a map. A *globe is the only form of mapping wherein the transformation from world to representation is consistent in terms of scale and distance. All other mappings involve the use of projections. In essence, a projection is a means of flattening the globe. This flattening process involves a set of mathematical transformations designed to translate the spatial relationships onto a planar form—a plane, cylinder, cone, and miscellaneous based on no particular geometric form. Inevitably, in the translation process some spatial elements are distorted, and most map projections seek to maintain one key component such as size of area, shape, distance, and direction. For example, conformal projections preserve small shapes and directions but distort areas, and equal area projections preserve areas but distort shape. *See also* CARTOGRAPHY; MERCATOR PROJECTION; PETERS PROJECTION. (See Fig. 5.)

Further reading Snyder, J. P. (1997), *Flattening the Earth: Two Thousand Years of Map Projections.*

maps Spatial representations of the Earth's surface that depict selected aspects of it. Conventionally, a map is understood as a two-dimensional representation of the geographic landscape depicted as if seen from directly above, drawn using a consistently applied reduction in scale, *map projection, abstraction, *generalization, and symbol sets. While maps are understood to be formalized expressions of scientific principles and endeavour, it is now accepted that other spatial representations of the Earth's surface should also be considered as maps (such as sketches and visual art as in Australian Aboriginal songline maps). Traditionally published as paper maps, the geospatial data underpinning their creation is now more likely to be displayed as interactive maps (*see* MAP INTERACTIVITY) and *globes via a computer or mobile device screen (*see* VIRTUAL GLOBE). Indeed, many national mapping agencies are scaling back their printed map production in favour of digital media.

Maps are important because they provide a means of organizing large amounts of often multidimensional information about a place in a way that facilitates human exploration and understanding. Indeed, maps are important tools for organizing spatial knowledge, facilitating navigation, and controlling territory. They are instrumental in the work of the state, in aiding *governance and administration, and in assisting trade and the accumulation of capital. As such, maps are rhetorically powerful images that frame

(a) Cylindrical projection

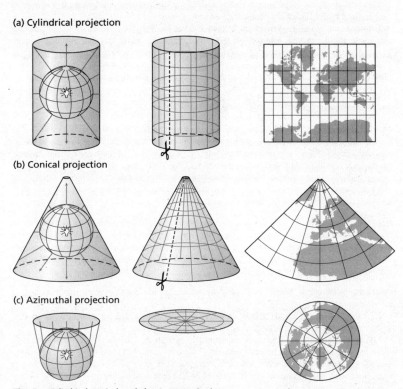

(b) Conical projection

(c) Azimuthal projection

Fig. 5   Cylindrical, conical, and planar map projections
(adapted from http://earth.rice.edu/mtpe/geo/geosphere/topics/mapprojections.html)

our understanding of the human and physical world, shaping our conception of places, and constructing our sense of spatial relations. Map-makers thus not only represent space, but create it through their message. For example, *propaganda maps seek to shape the geographical imagination of citizens. In other cases, maps can precede and make the territory they seek to portray. For example, the first maps of Siam delineated the geographical features and boundaries of a nation that did not yet exist, providing a model for it rather than depicting it (Winichakul 1994). Here, maps acted as key resources in defining and shaping national identity.

Lately, some cartographic theorists have argued for understanding maps not as *representations, but as performances or elements of a continuous process of world-making (Kitchin and Dodge 2007). Drawing on strands of *post-structuralism they argue that maps do not have ontological security but are always in a state of becoming, brought into being through embodied, social, and technical practices to solve relational problems such as plotting, planning, and navigating. Maps, they contend, emerge through a mix of creative, reflexive, playful, tactile, and habitual practices; affected by the knowledge, experience, and skill of the individual to perform mappings and apply them in the world, and shaped by the context of their reproduction.

However one conceives of maps, they are a key geographical medium for portraying and exploring the spatial relations of the world. *See also* CARTOGRAPHY.

References and further reading Crampton, J. (2010), *Mapping: a Critical Introduction to Cartography and GIS.*

Kitchin, R. and Dodge, M. (2007), 'Rethinking maps', *Progress in Human Geography* 31(3): 331–44.

Pickles, J. (2004), *A History of Spaces: Cartographic Reason, Mapping and the Geo-Coded World.*

Winichakul, T. (1994), *Siam Mapped: a History of the Geo-Body of a Nation.*

Wood, D. and Fels, J. (2009), *The Nature of Maps.*

maquiladora A Mexican *Export Processing Zone, mostly found along the US–Mexico border. In *maquiladoras* firms can import goods, process, assemble, and transform them, and then export them overseas without paying customs duty. They have earned Mexico prodigious amounts of foreign currency since the 1960s, but have been criticized for offering Mexican workers low wages and poor working conditions. The name *maquiladora* derives from the Spanish and means 'miller's portion', referring to the share a miller received for grinding other people's grain.

marginalization The social and economic process of individuals or groups being pushed to the margins or excluded from society. These processes can work discursively and materially, and operate implicitly or explicitly, to stigmatize and discriminate against people, and to deny them equal positioning and rights in society. *See also* CULTURAL POLITICS; EQUITY; MORAL GEOGRAPHIES.

market economy 1. An economy in which goods and services are exchanged for money.

2. An economy in which goods and services are exchanged for money with as few governmental rules and regulations as is necessary.

All capitalist economies are market economies in the first sense. The second meaning is far less generic than the first and closely associated with both the 'classical liberalism' of 19th-century Britain and America and early 21st-century *neoliberalism. According to both doctrines, goods and services provided by the central state are only desirable if they absolutely cannot be delivered by market means. Some argue that these goods and services include 'strategic' ones underpinned by major infrastructural investments, such as rail transportation and water supply. However, some advocates of a market economy argue that even these can be delivered by private providers and sold to consumers both affordably and to a high standard. In this sense these advocates argue that the 'interventionist state' needs to be 'rolled back' so that the market economy in sense two can flourish. A key belief here is that the entrepreneurial activities of commodity producers competing with each other are, together, more 'intelligent' than the centrally planned activities of state bodies that try to deliver goods and services to citizens. Even so, the market economy in sense two requires active governmental regulation to avoid problems such as 'externalities' (e.g. atmospheric pollution due to uncosted industrial emissions) and monopolies (where one firm dominates over others in an economic sector). This regulatory function requires government to act as 'night watchman' or 'referee' rather than provider of goods and services.

Critical social scientists, including many economic geographers, have argued that a market economy in sense two produces inequality and injustice. For instance, research into the privatization of water supply previously delivered by the state suggests that low-income individuals are virtually excluded from the new market in H_2O. One of the major foci of the anti-capitalist protests at the turn of the millennium was the market economy. It has been suggested that by extending the market, the ethical and moral norms that govern 'proper' economic behaviour are eroded. Karl *Polanyi called this 'disembedding' and argued that, if left unchecked, a market economy would create a 'stark utopia' in which many people and the non-human world become so much detritus.

Markov chain analysis A probabilistic method for modelling random outcomes along a chain of events with known rules. The probability of an event occurring at each step along the chain takes account of the previous step and a known set of rules. For example, with respect to movement, a person might turn left, right, or continue forwards, but this movement might be constrained by rules such as if the last move was left then the probability the next move is left is 0.3, forwards 0.4, and right 0.3, with similar rules for if the last move was right and forwards. In this way, a random path (chain) is developed against a set of rules. The typical use of Markov chains in geography is in the modelling of migration, changing population distributions, and the growth of firms.

Markusen, Ann (1947–) An American professor of economic geography at Minnesota University who has published influential policy-relevant research into the engines of regional growth and local economic development. An economist by training, she has studied the rise, location, and fall of major American industries, such as IT and defence.

Marshallian industrial district A spatial *cluster of firms in the same industry benefiting from pooled resources such as labour, transport, power supply, and business knowledge (*see* UNTRADED INTERDEPENDENCIES). The economist Alfred Marshall first described such *industrial districts in the textile sector of northwest England. Firms were closely integrated with one another in the district, but had few formal linkages outside it other than marketing their products. Modern districts can source labour and inputs from further afield and are therefore bound together more by knowledge-sharing practices. The term 'neo-Marshallian district' captures the difference between the older manufacturing and newer knowledge economies; clusters of media companies are an example.

Marston, Sallie (1962–) An American geographer based at the University of Arizona, her research has examined the intersections of the *state, politics, *culture, and political identity and she has made significant interventions into debates over the concept of *scale. She is a key pedagogic force in North American geography through her two co-authored textbooks, *World Regions in Global Context: Peoples, Places, and Environments* (4th ed. 2011) and *Human Geography: Places and Regions in a Global Context* (5th ed 2010).

Marxism A body of thought and action that is critical of *capitalism and which aims to supersede it with a more socially and environmentally just alternative. Marxism has many different strands and originates with the copious writings of Karl *Marx (1818–83). His most famous and influential book was *Capital*, volume 1 (published in 1867). Marx lived during the early decades of industrial capitalism in Europe and North America. He was interested in how and why so much wealth was created on the basis of so much human hardship and suffering. His analyses suggested that owners of the means of production appropriated the economic value of their workers, who have only their capacity to labour to 'sell' in order to earn enough money to live. Marx argued that working-class people form a 'class in itself' that, by becoming conscious of its exploitation by capitalists, will become a 'class for itself' and overthrow capitalism in an act of social revolution (*see* CLASS). Marx argued that his diagnosis of capitalism's ills was rigorous and not based on merely moral condemnation of capitalism: a revolution, he argued, is ever possible because of capitalism's internal contradictions, which become especially manifest in moments of economic crisis (*see* DIALECTICS). Marx's work, along with that of other socialist thinkers, inspired numerous trade unions and workers international bodies at the turn of the 20th century, with the most prominent being concentrated in Western and Eastern Europe.

Capitalism both expanded geographically and changed (albeit not fundamentally) after Marx's death. This led a new generation of Marxists to analyse it anew. Some wondered why revolutions had not occurred in leading capitalist states such as Britain, while they had done in pre-capitalist societies such as Russia (in 1917–18). With the rise of the 'welfare state' in much of Europe after the Second World War, members of the Frankfurt School of *Critical Theory argued that capitalists, using the powers of the national state, had successfully pacified working-class people by improving living standards and opportunities for self-improvement. This partially inspired a philosophical turn in Marxist thinking, evidenced in France by existentialists such as Jean-Paul Sartre and structuralists such as Louis Althusser. When Atlantic capitalism entered a period of major economic crisis in the mid-1970s, many Marxists again saw opportunities for revolutionary change, only to find that *neoliberalism was the medicine prescribed to cure the economic and social ills of the period of *Fordism.

A signal feature of Marxism after 1945 was its prominence in the social sciences and humanities, including geography (*see* MARXIST GEOGRAPHY). While this allowed Marxist thought to flourish in quantity and quality, it also cut it off from grass-roots politics and working-class activists. By the mid-1980s Marxist thought in the Western academy was on the wane, all the more so after the *Cold War ended in 1989. Today, its major academic advocates are ageing (such as David *Harvey), with only a minority of younger acolytes keeping the flame alive (such as Don *Mitchell). Ironically, the financial crisis of 2008–09 and its aftermath showed the continued relevance of Marxism despite its apparent lack of current popularity.

Marxist geography An approach to the analysis of geographical questions and phenomena informed, to a greater or lesser degree, by the concepts and findings of academic *Marxism. This approach is principally interested in those aspects of the world that are affected by *capitalism. From the early 1970s, it influenced human geography significantly, beginning with the economic, development, urban, and political subdisciplines, then cultural geography and *political ecology too. Arguably, the founding text was David *Harvey's *Social Justice and the City* (1973), or at least the second part entitled 'Socialist formulations'. Thereafter, Marxist geographers built the theoretical foundations of the approach, turning then to empirical research, only to return to theoretical issues as the approach matured and diversified—in part through internal critique—during the 1980s and 1990s. By the time of human geography's '*cultural turn', Marxism was said to be in a state of intellectual and political crisis. A new generation of human geographers were much less interested in Marxist geography than their forebears, though an older generation—like Harvey and Neil *Smith—worked hard to show the continued relevance and importance of the approach.

Marxist geography arose in a particular historical context. The worldwide rebellions against political economic authority of 1968 coincided with geography's domination by a *spatial science approach that seemed to some to be increasingly problematic (*see* RADICAL GEOGRAPHY). Despite its claims to *objectivity and its search for spatial patterns based on the systematic analysis of *evidence, critics argued that it flattered to deceive. Its explanations were seen to be mere descriptions shorn of any theory of causality, and were also charged with lacking historical context. What is more, critics claimed that it failed to acknowledge the *values it implicitly promoted e.g. that socio-spatial inequality might be ameliorated once it is understood, but not eliminated (since, for Marxists, elimination involves ending capitalism, something spatial scientists never considered). Critics called for a more overtly political form of human geography in which the *fact-value distinction could not be readily maintained anymore.

By the late 1960s, Marxism was a major component of the Western social sciences, (*see* WESTERN MARXISM). Despite the numerous strands of Marxism that had developed subsequent to Karl Marx's death in 1893, Harvey and his first students (notably Smith and Richard *Walker)—who virtually invented Anglophone Marxist geography—preferred to ignore them and read Marx's later writings in the original, rather than interpretations of them. The result was pioneering works of *theory, notably *The Limits to Capital* (1982) and *Uneven Development* (1984). These books argued that capitalism creates a geography in its own image and that this geography then affects the dynamics of capital *accumulation. Far from being a mere 'effect', the cause of which is capitalism, Harvey and Smith showed that *place, *space, *landscape, and even *nature are both effects and causes, outcomes and agents, simultaneously. Theirs was a *dialectical understanding of reality, in which parts and wholes, relations and entities are indissoluble. Specifically, they demonstrated that capitalism: (i) must invest huge amounts of *money in the creation of built environments within places, but also between them; (ii) is necessarily expansionary geographically, seeking out new investment opportunities externally, even as it restructures its existing internal geography; (iii) creates new scales to contain and enable economic activity, including the global *scale, meaning that scale is produced; (iv) encounters geographical barriers to further growth because of the costs 'sunk' into current infrastructures; (v) switches money (a form of *capital) into major new investments in new locations as a way of staving off economic *crisis; and (vi) sets regions and places against one another because of their common implication in the accumulation process (*see* UNEVEN DEVELOPMENT).

By the late 1980s, Marxist geography had become less abstract and more intellectually pluralistic. For example, development geographers began to engage with *world-system analysis and dependency theory, both of which arose from particular (re)interpretations of Marx's political economy. Meanwhile, geographers interested in human-environment relations made loose use of Marxism in creating political ecology. At the same time, economic geographers trying to make sense of the end of the Fordist-*Keynesian era of Western economic dominance, drew on 'mid-range' theory that could connect abstract arguments to the empirical complexities of history and geography (*see* REGULATION THEORY). Away from economics, '*cultural materialism' extended Marxism's insights to the realms of cultural forms (such as architectural design, *landscape, and aesthetics more broadly: for example, see the early writings of Denis *Cosgrove).

Despite its vibrancy, by the mid-1990s Marxist geography was also under attack from erstwhile sympathizers on the political Left, a contributory factor being the sudden collapse of communism ('actually existing Marxism') between 1989–91 in Eastern Europe and the former *Soviet Union. The critics voiced at least two main concerns, using the insights of *feminism, *postmodernism, and *post-structuralism. First, it was argued that Marxism focused far too much analytical attention on the economy and far too much political attention on class struggle. What, it was asked, about those realms of life irreducible to the rhythms of capital accumulation? What about the politics of gender, age, disability, sexuality, and ethnicity? Second, it was argued that Marxism, ironically, tended to exaggerate the dominance and power of capitalism. It is not simply that we live in a more-than-capitalist world, the critics argued; it is also that the capitalist part is less secure and totalizing than the Marxists portrayed it (see J. K. *Gibson-Graham's germinal book *The End of Capitalism* (*As We Know It*)). David Harvey wrote two major rebuttals to Marxism's critics—*The Condition of Postmodernity* (1989) and *Justice, Nature and the Geography of Difference* (1996). A third complaint about Marxist geography, that it failed to acknowledge the environmental crisis of late capitalism, was countered by renewed work on *nature and its *commodification (*see* CRITICAL GEOGRAPHY; SWYNGEDOUW,

ERIK). Marxist geography has refused to fade way, however. Real-world developments seem to have confirmed the power of Marxist arguments. Not only is anti-capitalist sentiment widespread globally (*see* ANTI-GLOBALIZATION MOVEMENT); *neoliberal capitalism has also been producing dynamic and highly uneven new geographies of growth and decline, above all the global financial crisis of 2007 onwards. Harvey continues to keep the flame of Marxism burning bright by publishing book after book, including reissues of *The Limits to Capital*. A new, albeit small, generation of Marxist and Marxist-inspired geographers continues to produce lively and theoretically informed work, much of it to be found in the journal *Antipode*. *See also* HISTORICAL MATERIALISM; MASSEY, DOREEN; PEET, RICHARD.

Further reading Swyngedouw, E. (1999), 'Marxism and historical-geographical materialism: a spectre is haunting geography', *Scottish Geographical Journal*, 115(2): 91–102.

Marx, Karl (1818–83) A thinker, writer, and activist whose many words and deeds inspired *Marxism and a revolutionary politics committed to creating a communist world (*see* COMMUNISM). Marx claimed to have identified the fundamental 'laws' governing the dynamics of *capitalism. He argued that the justifications of why capitalism was 'good' or 'necessary' were merely an ideological smoke-screen designed to institutionalize social inequality and injustice. Marx collaborated with another German intellectual, Friedrich Engels, but his most famous works were sole authored, notably the several volumes of *Capital* (which, bar the first, were published after his death). *See also* MARXISM; MARXIST GEOGRAPHY.

masculinism The processes and ideologies that prioritize the experiences of men and reproduce power structures that are advantageous to them. A critique of geography by *feminist geographers is that the discipline has traditionally been masculinist in orientation and practice. *See also* FEMINISM AND GEOGRAPHY; ROSE, GILLIAN; WOMEN IN GEOGRAPHY.

masculinities The study of men and men's status, roles, and identities in society. Given that geography has been critiqued by feminists as being highly *masculinist in nature, the primary focus on the intersection of gender and geography has been concentrated on women, mapping out their roles and spatialities, and how they are shaped by gendered power relations. This has recently been countered by analysis that examines the geographies of masculinity. Such analysis recognizes that men are not an amorphous group and, like women, are expected to perform certain *gender roles and enact particular spatialities with respect to family and social life, work, and state (e.g. military service at times of war). Men, while mainly dominant to women, are subject to uneven and unequal *power geometries along lines of *class, *race, *sexuality, ability, stature, and so on, and have varying *identities, ambitions, opportunities, lifestyles, and geographies. Masculinity is therefore understood as a social, historical, and political construct that varies within society and across place and time. *See also* FEMINISM; IDENTITY POLITICS; PARENTING.

Further reading van Hoven, B. and Hörschelmann, K. (2005), *Spaces of Masculinities*.

mashup An internet-related term that refers to the combination of two different sets of data and program tools to create a new web-based application. For example, a mashup might take data from web services, such as craigslist, Flickr, or open government databases (such as a land registry), and plug them into other applications, such as Google Maps, to produce a new way of visualizing or interacting with the data. Such mashups allow the inventive combining of dynamically produced data through new web technologies. *See also* OPEN DATA.

Massey, Doreen (1944–) A leading British geographer who has made formative contributions across a spectrum of topics and subfields in international human geography. She is Emeritus Professor at the Open University, where she spent most of her career after studying at the universities of Oxford and Philadelphia. Her academic contributions fall into three areas. First, she was a leading critic of economic geographers in the 1960s and 1970s who had been inspired by *spatial science and the *Quantitative Revolution. She argued that a fixation on the assets and attributes of declining regions was a form of 'spatial fetishism' that underplayed the wider social and spatial processes that explained how and why any given region was no longer 'successful'. Inspired by Marxist *political economy, she went on to explain uneven regional economic development with reference to investment decisions made by corporations. Her book *Spatial Divisions of Labour* (1984) suggested that regions were increasingly being judged by firms in relative terms, as rival locations for 'mobile capital'.

Secondly, Massey has challenged the traditional idea that places are simply geographically delimited points on the surface of the Earth whose character can be understood by investigating what occurs at these points. Her idea that we need a 'global sense of place' emphasizes that what constitutes a *place is, in significant measure, dictated by its external relations with other places near and far. Relatedly, she has talked about the 'geometry' of power, which is the uneven distribution and effects of the capacity to exert power over others. For Massey, all places occupy specific locations in wider sets of sociospatial relations which themselves contain distributed power unequally, such that some places come to matter more than others. Massey's research into how best to conceive of place today intersects with her writings on the geography of ethical concern and moral responsibility. She has challenged the maxim that 'nearest is dearest' by showing how human well-being today is the precondition and result of interdependency between otherwise different places.

Finally, Massey has sought to reconceptualize the foundational categories of *space and *time—or, as she prefers to say, time-space—in order to make room for mutual understanding and respect among humans. Her mid-career work on the gendering of space and her later work on the 'spatialization of time' both endeavour to 'unfreeze' stereotypes and essentialisms about 'other' people and places. Massey has received numerous prizes and awards in recognition of her research and has exerted an interdisciplinary influence that extends well beyond human geography.

Further reading Massey, D. (2005), *For Space*.

material culture *See* CULTURE.

materiality The stuff of the world, both animate and inanimate (and including the human *body). Though physical geographers have remained centrally interested in materiality—or more formally, 'process and form'—human geographers tended to background it and focus more on human cognition, perception, and intentionality, and on social relations. However, in recent years there has been a 'new materialism' in human geography, especially evident in Britain. The emphasis has been on how materiality is central to various forms of human experience and action. *See also* AFFECT; NONREPRESENTATIONAL THEORY.

McDonaldization The process by which the core business principles of the US food company McDonalds diffuse globally and become culturally embedded. According to US sociologist George Ritzer these principles are efficiency, calculability, predictability, control through the substitution of technology for people, and what he calls the irrationality of rationality, which includes the dehumanizing experience of working under such conditions. *See also* GLOBALIZATION.

McDowell, Linda (1948–) A British human geographer who has made significant contributions to economic, cultural, and urban geography informed throughout by an active engagement and retheorization of *feminist geography. She is Professor of Human Geography at the University of Oxford. McDowell has done much to bring questions of personal and social identity into the study of *labour geography and economic geography more generally. This has been achieved through a series of monographs examining Britain's working life from different but complementary angles, including *Capital Culture* (1997) on financial industries, *Redundant Masculinities* on low-skilled young males (2003), and *Hard Labour: the forgotten voices of Latvian volunteer workers* (2005). The themes of work, space, gender, class, and the body are brought together in *Working Bodies* (2009), which challenges the idea that working life has entered a new, less exploitative epoch.

MDS *See* MULTIDIMENSIONAL SCALING.

Mecca A city in Saudi Arabia said to be the birthplace of the prophet Muhammad and the place where the Qur'an was written. For this reason Mecca is a holy city for Muslims and the site of annual pilgrimages. Because of its long religious significance, Mecca is today a highly cosmopolitan city, dominated by people who hail from all parts of the wider Muslim world.

MEDC *See* MORE ECONOMICALLY DEVELOPED COUNTRY.

media The mass communication of information through newspapers, magazines, books, radio, television, and film. More recently, such media has been complemented by new forms of *social networking media wherein individuals can communicate with many others through internet-based platforms such as blogs, Twitter, and Facebook. The media industry is an important agent in shaping how information is gathered, synthesized, and communicated to audiences. By providing information through its lens, media project a particular *gaze on various issues and places, and thus help to mould public understanding and opinions. Given the advances in *information and communication technologies it is now possible for news and analysis to be transmitted live around the world. Modern mass media has had a profound impact on the *time-space compression of information (*see* GLOBALIZATION). Before technologies such as the telegraph, information travelled at the speed of transportation (usually by foot, horse, or ship) and was much more localized in nature. In the age of global twenty-four-hour news channels it is often instantaneous, with a much greater reach. In spite of this, the geographic focus of attention for such channels is usually quite circumscribed and there are still localized media markets that concentrate on issues relevant to that area. Geographical analysis of the media concentrates on the geography of the media industry, the infrastructures of communication, deconstructing how places and people are represented in different media forms, and the effects of the media on society.

Further reading Adams, P. C. (2009), *Geographies of Media and Communication: a Critical Introduction.*

medical geography The study of *epidemiology, ill health, and health-care systems from a geographical perspective. With respect to epidemiology the focus of analysis is the spatial distribution and diffusion of diseases in order to better understand their causes, transmission routes, and effects of treatments. Typically, the analysis is quantitative in nature, spatially modelling, statistically testing, and mapping disease patterns. In relation to chronic and lifestyle diseases such as heart disease and diabetes, or environmental health related illnesses such as cancers or asthma, analysis focuses on identifying particular *hotspots and determining the main factors underpinning their prevalence.

Research on health-care systems focuses on the siting, distribution, and access to health resources and treatments, mapping and modelling how effective the system is with respect to serving a population and tackling particular health issues. Medical geography is highly related to *health geography, but differs in that it tends to focus on mapping and modelling medical conditions and the means of treatment, whereas health geography tends to focus more on wellness and well-being, alternative and holistic treatments, health policy from a more sociological rather than medical perspective, and is more likely to use qualitative methods and employ social theory. Medical geography is usually practised in interdisciplinary teams linking together medics, health specialists, and geographers.

Further reading Meade, M. S. and Earickson, R. (2000), *Medical Geography*.

medieval geography The geographical study during the European Middle Ages, a period stretching from the end of the Roman empire in 476 CE to the conquest of Constantinople, the capital of the Byzantine empire by the Ottoman empire (1453 CE). Although the word 'geography' was not in widespread use during this period, there were important advances in *cartography and *exploration, although these were overshadowed by the much greater scientific output of the Islamic and Chinese worlds.

Further reading Lilley, K. D. (2011), 'Geography's medieval history: a forgotten enterprise?', *Dialogues in Human Geography* 1(2), 147–62.

Mediterranean A sea located between southern Europe and North Africa, and connected to the Atlantic Ocean and Black Sea. It translates from Latin to mean 'in the middle of land'. Historically it was fringed by a number of ancient civilizations, notably Egyptian, Greek, and Roman. Today the sea is surrounded by many nation states, of which the most developed is Italy, with others much poorer (e.g. Libya). The historical meeting point between Christian and Muslim peoples, this religious difference is most graphically played out on the borders of Israel.

mega-city A very large urbanized area with a population of ten million or more, although lower thresholds (e.g. five million) have also been used. The enumeration of urban populations is inexact, but a common estimate is that there were twenty-one cities of over ten million in 2011, headed by Tokyo.

megalopolis A very large urbanized region consisting of multiple cities or urban centres, functionally linked by transport and communications in which each place has some degree of economic specialization. French geographer Jean Gottmann used the term in 1961 to analyse the region of the US eastern seaboard from Boston to Washington, DC. But earlier writers had used it in more negative ways, as a synonym for uncontrolled urban expansion.

Meinig, Donald (1924–) An American geographer who has made notable contributions to understanding the historical geography of the United States and the cultural geography of *landscape. Meinig's paper on the Mormon culture region (1965) is regarded as a classic study. His four-volume work *The Shaping of America* (1986–2004) is grand in analytical ambition and draws on a vast array of archival sources. He is Professor Emeritus at Syracuse University in the USA.

memorials and monuments These are events, such as public holidays or parades, or structures, such as statues or buildings, created to honour and remember a person or an event. Such memorials and monuments are often strategically placed in the landscape and are highly symbolic, using emotive *iconography to create affective responses, such as a flush of *nationalism.

Further reading Johnson, N. (1995), 'Cast in stone: monuments, geography and nationalism', *Environment and Planning D: Society and Space* 13: 51–65.

memory The remembering of the past. Whereas history is the documented recording of what happened in the past, memory is how that history is connected to the present. And while history is largely an academic endeavour pursued by a few, memory is everyday and practised by everybody; it can be individual or collective, and public or private in nature. The result is that the historical record and memories relating to a specific event can be quite different. Indeed, memory is selective, ideologically framed, contested and negotiated, and not simply remembered. Memory is an important component of reproducing cultural and *national identities providing raw material for legitimating and sustaining *imagined communities. For example, the memory of the *Holocaust is an aspect of present-day Jewish identity, and the memory of the 1840s potato famine in Ireland along with British colonization is a core part of Irish identity. Memory is highly discursive, communicated through books, plays, song, but also has a materiality expressed through museum displays, *memorials and monuments, *heritage sites, and specific places. With regard to the latter, the 9/11 attacks in the US are symbolically attached to Ground Zero, for example. Through memory, places become imbued with meaning. *Cultural geography has long sought to understand the link between memory and place, and the way in which our understanding of landscapes is shaped by our own and collective memories. *See also* HISTORICAL GEOGRAPHY; ORAL HISTORY.

Further reading Lowenthal, D. (1985), *The Past Is a Foreign Country*.
Schama, S. (1995), *Landscape and Memory*.

mental health The mental well-being of people. Mental health issues are diverse and affect people in different ways and can lead to proscribed *spatial behaviour, opportunities, and lived experiences of a place. There is a distinct pattern to the institutional geographies of mental health, for example, through the spatial organization of mental health facilities and the incarceration of some sufferers in asylums. *See also* CARE; DISABILITY; HEALTH GEOGRAPHY.

Further reading Milligan, C. (2001), *The Geographies of Care*.

mental map The geographical knowledge a person possesses held within long-term memory. This knowledge can be expressed in a variety of ways, for example, in producing a sketch map or ranking preferences for places, or *wayfinding between locations. Mental maps is a core concept in *behavioural geography, a key source from which people make spatial choices and decisions. The term has a variety of synonyms, the most common of which is cognitive map. *See also* COGNITIVE MAPPING; ENVIRONMENTAL PERCEPTION.

Mercator projection A *map projection created by the Flemish cartographer Gerardus Mercator in 1569 (see Fig. 6). It is specifically designed to aid navigation as straight lines on the map represent lines of constant geographical direction. By drawing a line between two locations and measuring the angle between that line and the meridian, the bearing for moving between the two places is provided. This supplied sailors with very useful information, but came at the cost of massive distortion of areas towards the poles (areas that ships rarely sailed at the time). The result is that the areas of land masses in different parts of the map bear little relation to each other. For example, Greenland and Saudi Arabia have approximately the same land area (2,175,600 km^2 and 2,149,690 km^2 respectively), yet Greenland appears to be considerably larger on a Mercator map. Given the popularity of the Mercator projection, this has led to a common misconception about the relative sizes of countries, especially those in higher and lower latitude vis-à-vis mid latitudes. *See* PETERS PROJECTION.

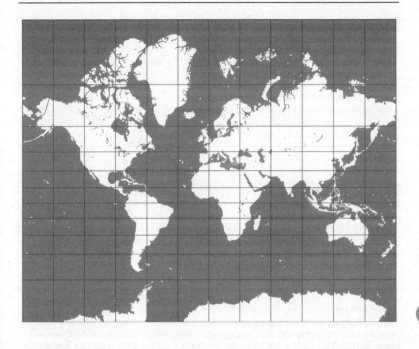

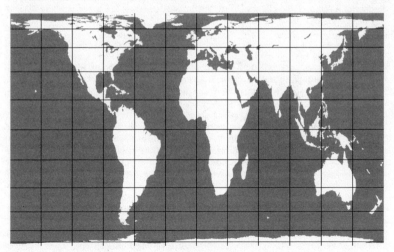

Fig. 6   Mercator projection versus Peters projection

Mercosur A *free trade agreement, created in 1991 through the Treaty of Asuncion, that links together five Latin American countries: Argentina, Brazil, Paraguay, Uruguay, and Venezuela. It coordinates macroeconomic and sectoral trade policy and removes tariffs between partners to create a common market.

(⊕) SEE WEB LINKS
• Official website of Mercosur (in Portuguese and Spanish).

MesoAmerica A historical region stretching from central modern-day Mexico south to Costa Rica and thus covering a large part of Central America. As far back as 7000 BC a number of sedentary pre-Columbian societies developed, growing crops such as maize and squash. Over time these societies developed similar customs, rituals, and social stratifications. Archaeologists classify them as a 'civilization' of considerable durability and complexity. These societies were badly affected by the arrival of Spanish colonists from the 16th century onwards and went into long-term decline. *See also* INDIGENOUS PEOPLE.

metadata A term to describe data that provides information about other data. Metadata helps a user of a dataset understand its composition and how it should be used and interpreted. Metadata usually details data definitions, when the data was collected, by whom, for what purpose, using what standards, if it has been modified, and how. It is an essential component of all databases.

metageography The taken-for-granted spatial organizing frameworks through which knowledge is organized. A metageography simplifies the world into basic *ontological categories that share supposed commonalities. Such a process tends to *essentialize the character of each category. An example of a metageography is the division of land masses into *continents where the people living within are assumed to have certain characteristics (e.g. to share a European culture, or an African way of life). Sometimes, places elsewhere in the world are ascribed to another metageography, for example, Singapore as part of the Global North. Such categorizations are inherently ideological and form an *imaginative geography.

Further reading Lewis, M. W. and Wigen, K. (1997), *The Myth of Continents: a Critique of Metageography*.

metaphor The characterization of something with reference to something else to which it is not otherwise related. Metaphors are used commonly in both lay and expert *discourses. In human geography they have played several roles. First, and most commonly, they have been used conventionally as communicative tools. For instance, economic geographers have long talked about 'rounds' or 'waves' of investment, while Marxist geographers are apt to talk about 'circuits' of capital. Secondly, however, they have been treated as research foci in their own right. It has been argued that metaphors sometimes need to be closely scrutinized because of the partial and particular ways in which they represent the world to listeners or readers. For example, Cindi *Katz and Neil Smith drew critical attention to the overtly geographical metaphors used during human geography's 'cultural turn' during the 1990s. During this turn much emphasis was given to marginalized, subaltern, or oppressed people, and the talk was of the 'positionality', 'locatedness', and 'situatedness' of all perspectives on reality. Katz and Smith suggested that these metaphors, ironically, reproduced the outdated notion that the world's geography is a terrain of discrete places and sites rather than a tangle of intersecting and interfering processes, relationships, and flows. In a similarly critical vein, Trevor *Barnes deconstructed the metaphors favoured by economic geographers in their analyses of investment flows, regional economic growth, and regional restructuring. Though all language is in some measure metaphorical, there is a difference between utilizing metaphors unthinkingly, tactically, and reflexively.

References Barnes, T. J. (1992), 'Reading the texts of theoretical economic geography', in Barnes, T. J. and Duncan, J. S. (eds.), *Writing Worlds*, 118–35.

Katz, C. and Smith, N. (1993), 'Grounding metaphor', in Keith, M. and Pile, S. (eds.) *Place and the Politics of Identity*, 67–83.

metaphysics A branch of philosophy concerned with the fundamentals of existence. A 'metaphysical statement' or argument can concern *ontology, *epistemology, or both. To be more specific, it can relate to the nature of causality, existence, space, time, death, life, continuity, change, and other foundational subjects. Human geographers have made many metaphysical arguments as part of their research, even if they rarely use the word metaphysics. For example, *critical realism is predicated on several metaphysical claims about the *nature of the human and non-human worlds.

methodological individualism An approach to investigating what people think, say, and do that treats individuals as the fundamental unit of analysis. The analyst may look for patterns among otherwise different individuals but will not, in the first instance, focus on groups or the social relations that may structure individual thought, speech, or practice. In human geography, methodological individualism was implicit in much early *spatial science and in *behavioural geography.

methodological nationalism The assumption that nation, state, and society are the same entity, and that this entity is the natural unit of both social organization and social science inquiry. It can be extended to imply that the epistemological frameworks of social sciences are nationalized (for example, political science is conceived as distinct from international relations, sociologists study national-level societies), such that transnational phenomena are hidden from view.

Further reading Wimmer, A. and Glick Schiller, N. (2002), 'Methodological nationalism and beyond', *Global Networks,* 2(4) 301–34.

methodology How a study is conceived and operationalized. While methods are the specific techniques used for data generation and analysis, methodology is the wider approach and organization through which those methods are employed. It provides the justification for the types of questions asked, how they are asked, and how they are analysed and interpreted, as well as practical issues such as how data is sourced and the *sampling framework used. The methodology adopted by a researcher is informed by their wider *ontological, *epistemological, and *ideological beliefs as these define what is the most appropriate and valid way to make sense of the world. In other words, methodology is not simply about the practicalities of undertaking a study, but is a deeply philosophical endeavour.

Metropolis Subtitled 'from division of labour to urban form', Allen J. *Scott's (1988) book helped restore an understanding of cities not as places where people simply live, but as places where they also work. His focus on the processes of *agglomeration economies, the organization of production, *labour markets, and the *division of labour therefore contrasts with the *Chicago School tradition of *urban ecology. In addition to classic cases such as Birmingham's gun and jewellery industries, he drew on his own extensive research into Los Angeles' garment and high-tech industries.

Mexico The largest country in Central America by population and GDP but which, despite its relative wealth, is infamous for its ongoing problems with drug supply and corruption in the military, police, and politics. Bordered by the United States to the north, Mexico is a major tourist destination and the largest single source of migrants into the

USA (*see* NORTH AMERICAN FREE TRADE AGREEMENT). However, the presence of powerful drug cartels and the illegal smuggling of drugs into the USA have caused considerable problems (*see* NARCO-STATE). Chiapas in southern Mexico, was also the site of a famous peasant uprising in the 1990s by the *Zapatistas, who reacted to attempted *neoliberal reforms of agriculture and trade rules.

Mexico City The capital city of Mexico and one of the world's largest conurbations. Its population is said to exceed twenty-one million and it generates around one-fifth of Mexico's GDP. It has long suffered from air pollution problems due to excessive road traffic.

microfinance A term for financial services aimed at very low-income individuals and communities who would be otherwise excluded from banking, savings, and credit arrangements. A common form is micro-credit, based on poor people pooling their savings and taking it in turn to access them (*see* GRAMEEN BANK). Microfinance institutions are often caught between being co-opted into mainstream finance on the one hand, for example by stock flotation, and dependence on state largesse and private donors on the other. *See also* ALTERNATIVE ECONOMIC GEOGRAPHIES.

microsimulation A method of modelling that operates at the level of individual units such as people, households, companies, or vehicles. Each individual unit has associated data relating to them such as age, sex, employment status, household composition, firm characteristics, and vehicle type. A *model with defined rules is then applied to these units to simulate how they would behave under certain conditions. In geography, microsimulation is used to model movement and spatial choice and decision-making. In cases where individual data are unavailable, then statistical methods can be applied to the aggregate characteristics of the wider population (for example, as reported in a census) to estimate likely individual data. *See also* AGENT-BASED MODELS.

Middle East A subcontinental region including parts of Southwest Asia and North Africa. There is no agreement on the boundaries of the region, nor which countries lie within it. A narrow definition, for example, in the *CIA World Factbook*, does not include parts of Africa, Central Asia, or Pakistan, although it does add Armenia and Georgia. The broadest definitions include Cyprus, *Egypt, and Central Asian states bordering China. By common agreement, the Middle East does include the countries of the Arabian Peninsula and the eastern Mediterranean region, notably Israel, Syria, Jordan, Lebanon, and *Iraq. *Iran and Turkey are also generally classified as part of the region. Confusion over its geographical boundaries is understandable given that the term 'Middle East' originates with 19th-century British government foreign policy. In the early 19th century, following its invasion of Egypt, the French described the Ottoman empire (including what became Turkey) as the 'Near East', i.e. adjacent to Europe. Britain preferred 'Middle' to describe what was then Persia (later Iran) as distinct from 'Far East', i.e. China and its region. From the beginning therefore, Middle East was identified by forces outside the region for purposes of *geopolitics (*see* ORIENTALISM). With the destruction of the Ottoman empire in 1922, the discovery of oil in the region, and the foundation of the state of *Israel in 1948, the region's significance to outside powers was extended. Geographical expertise on the Middle East, for example, in the form of *Area Studies, was not unrelated to efforts to secure regional peace and stability on the one hand, and access to oil and gas on the other. A network of associations, journals, courses, publications, and experts continues to sustain the idea of the Middle East, although at least now with more direct participation of scholars from the region. An alternative designation that covers part of the region (though also extending beyond it in northwest Africa), the Arab World is equally problematic for its use of an ethnic or linguistic marker to define territory.

There are a number of reasons why geographers and related scholars are interested in the region. It includes widespread arid environments and examples of how societies have successfully adapted to aridity, notably through irrigation and related legal codes. The area surrounding the rivers Tigris and Euphrates, termed Mesopotamia (mostly within present-day Iraq), was one of the hearths of plant and animal domestication as well as the foundation of cities and the development of writing. *Judaism, *Christianity, and *Islam originate from the region, and their sacred sites and cities, including *Mecca and Jerusalem, remain highly significant. In more recent years, the politics of war, violence, and statehood, including the conflict between Israel, Palestinians and neighbouring states, and the invasion of Iraq, have become important. The rise of the Gulf States, notably the United Arab Emirates, Bahrain, and Qatar, as centres of global financial capital and property speculation, represents an important shift in the world's economic geography. *See also* GULF WAR.

((()) SEE WEB LINKS

• The *Arab World Geographer/le géographe de monde arabe* journal.

middle-income trap A condition faced by some developing countries when, following a period of rapid economic growth that lifts them out of low-income status, progress stalls. According to the World Bank, three-quarters of the countries classified as middle-income in 1960 had not become higher-income by 2009. Many Latin American states are said to fall into this trap, perhaps because of the failure to achieve a reasonable distribution of wealth. China and other countries with per capita GDP of around $4000 are also argued to be at risk.

migrant A person who changes their place of usual residence by moving across a political or administrative boundary, for example, between countries or regions within the same country. The term is not generally applied to short-distance *residential mobility. Defining who is a migrant is not exact. An international migrant, for example, may be classified as foreign-born, foreign-national and/or someone who has moved to a country for at least a year. Some surveys and official sources treat *refugees as migrants, but others do not. *See also* MIGRATION.

Further reading Anderson, B. and Blinder, S. (2011), 'Who counts as a migrant?' Briefing, The Migration Observatory at the University of Oxford.

migration The movement of groups and individuals from one place to another, involving a change of usual residence. Migration is usually distinguished from *mobility in general by conventions of spatial and temporal scale. For example, by convention international migration requires crossing a national boundary for an actual or intended period of at least one year. *Residential mobility, by contrast, may consist of a short-distance move between properties in the same city.

Typologies of migration differentiate between *internal and international migration, and the two forms are usually studied separately. Looked at historically, however, the movement of people long predates nation-states; *homo sapiens* left Africa some 150,000 years ago. Geographers are interested in inter-regional, rural-urban, and urban-rural movements, especially in societies with low birth and death rates where migration is often the major cause of population change (*see* COUNTER-URBANIZATION). In 2008, about 3 per cent of Americans moved to another county, for example, and in China, it is estimated that there were 140 million migrants, mostly from rural to urban areas (Fan 2008).

The major focus of current geographical work, however, is international migration. It is estimated that there were 215 million people living outside their country of birth in 2010, around 3 per cent of the world's population. But this surprisingly low number has disproportionate effects on the places and countries linked by flows, economically, socially, culturally, and—increasingly—politically. This type of migration is further classified by time, differentiating temporary (or short-term), permanent (or long-term), and circular (including seasonal) forms. Whereas permanent migration was once considered the norm—especially during the era of colonial settlement in the 19th century—it is now recognized that growing numbers of people are implicated in migrations at a variety of spatial and temporal scales. *Transnational migrants may live in two places at once, or at least shuttle between them on a regular basis in addition to sustaining meaningful interconnections. Further distinctions are often made between legal and *illegal immigration.

Beginning with the work of *Ravenstein, geographers and others have sought to explain and model migration. An elementary dichotomy between *forced and voluntary migration has proved difficult to sustain analytically, not least because of the rise in human *trafficking. Can children accompanying adults, for example, be said to choose to move? The *globalization of human flows has not only drawn in more counties and regions into the world migration pattern, but it has also eroded once-basic division between sending (or home, origin) and receiving (or host, destination) countries. Many are now both; the Russian federation is in the top three *emigration and immigration countries. Rather than explain migration in terms of 'push' factors at an origin and 'pull' factors at a destination, the metaphor of a revolving door may be more appropriate. In a widely cited textbook, Castles and Miller (2009) discuss three broad kinds of explanation: first, *neoclassical economics, focusing mainly on the individual level (*see* TODARO MODEL); second, historical-structural, including *world systems theory; and third, *migration-systems theory, including a concentration on the role of social networks (see also Massey 1999 for a more elaborate list of theories). The observation that migration flows along distinct 'corridors' (e.g. Mexico–USA, Turkey–Germany) fits with this theory. But, compared with the 1960s and 1970s, when geographers applied various *spatial interaction models (*see* GRAVITY MODEL) to migration, there is now less discipline-specific research on the causes and consequences of migration.

Geographical research on migration is far-reaching, covering both historical past and the present (King et al. 2010). Once considered a peripheral subject in social sciences, the study of migration is increasingly deemed central. Paradoxically, given the changes in personal and social mobility associated with globalization, it is ever harder to distinguish migration from the greater register of flows (King 2002); are backpackers migrants? There is a clear trend towards studying migrants, their experiences, biographies, families, emotions, etc., as contrasted with the demographic fact of migration. Migration is generally a selective process, by age, skill, gender, race, class, and health, and it may also be implicated with critical *lifecourse events. Recent research foci have included the impact of climate change, the *migration-development nexus, children's migration, international student migration, and the heightened security and surveillance directed at moving bodies of all kinds. *See also* IMMIGRATION; IOM.

Reference and further reading Castles, S. and Miller, M. J. (4th ed. 2009), *The Age of Migration*.
Fan, C. C. (2008), *China on the Move: Migration, the State and the Household*.
King, R. (2002), 'Towards a new map of European immigration', *International Journal of Population Geography* 8: 89–106.
King, R., Black, R., Collyer, M., Fielding, A., and Skeldon, R. (2010), *The Atlas of Human Migration*.
Massey, D. S. (1999), 'Why does immigration occur?' in Hirschman, C., Kasinitz, P., and Dewind, J. (eds.) *The Handbook of International Migration: the American Experience*.
Samers, M. (2009), *Migration*.

(⊕) SEE WEB LINKS

- The Migration Policy Institute provides up-to-date information and analysis of world migration issues.
- The Southern African Migration Project gives information on the region's migration issues.

migration-development nexus The links between *migration and *development, specifically in the context of migrant-sending countries in the Global South. Assuming prominence in academic and international policy circles in the 2000s, the term reflects a change in how migration is assessed. Instead of being regarded as a loss and harmful to economic prosperity, migration is increasingly viewed as an opportunity for development via its *transnational impacts. *See also* BRAIN DRAIN; REMITTANCES.

Further reading *Population, Space and Place* (2009), Special issue on Rethinking the migration-development nexus. 15(2).

Migration Systems Theory A theory of human *migration that combines macro-, meso-, and micro-level factors to produce more inclusive explanations. It is premised on the observation that most international migration occurs within systems, or countries linked by geographical, economics, colonial, or other historical relations, for example, migration within southeast Asia.

Further reading Castles, S. and Miller, M. J. (4th ed. 2009), *The Age of Migration*.

milieu A French word meaning 'environment' or 'surroundings'. In the early decades of academic geography there was great interest in how different milieux were created and what effects they had on people and their use of the natural environment. However, with the advent of *modernity, the relatively stable, slow-changing milieux of pre-industrial societies gave way to more dynamic social, cultural, economic, and political formations. The term is now used more as a simple noun or a *metaphor rather than designating a substantial research concern in human geography.

militant particularism The practice of pursuing general goals by way of opposi-tional actions, such as strikes, undertaken at separate locations. The term was coined by British Marxist Raymond Williams and appropriated by David Harvey in his book **Justice, Nature and the Geography of Difference*. Like Williams, Harvey argued that any general project of emancipation must necessarily be realized with reference to specific groups of people struggling against particular injustices in specific places with their own history and character. This sets up a potential tension between what appears politically neces-sary or progressive at one geographical scale—the global, and another—the local.

military geography A subdiscipline of geography specializing in the application of geographical knowledge to military problems in times of war and peace. It overlaps with military science, and is most established in US military academies and associated institutions (*see also* GEOSPATIAL INTELLIGENCE). Military geographers are interested in the full range of geographical knowledge, physical and human, especially now with advanced geospatial technologies. Understanding the role of geographical factors in military planning also involves analysing past operations, and there are affinities with military history. Geographers have a long-standing and close relationship with military activities (*see* WAR), but the field of military geography fell out of favour as a result of the Vietnam War. It has recovered, and there is now a speciality group of the American Association of Geographers in this area. In addition, there are geographical studies of the military; for example, the changing distribution and impact of military bases. These are generally more critical, focused on the way that militarism constructs space, places, and landscapes. *See also* CRITICAL GEOPOLITICS.

Further reading Galgano, F. and Palka, E. J. (eds.) (2010), *Modern Military Geography: from Peace to War*.
Woodward, R. (2004), *Military Geographies*.

military-industrial complex The set of interdependent relationships between government and defence industries including contracts for equipment and services, moves of personnel between the two sectors, and policy dialogue. It is said to constitute a single powerful entity spanning capital and the *state, with a vested interest in defence spending and the continuation of warfare. According to Trevor *Barnes, the *Cold War military-industrial complex embraced many geographers.

Further reading Barnes, T. (2008), 'Geography's underworld: the military–industrial complex, mathematical modelling and the quantitative revolution', *Geoforum* 39: 3–16.

Millennium Development Goals A set of eight *development goals adopted by the *United Nations in 2000 with specific targets set for 2015. The goals are: eradicating extreme poverty by halving the numbers living on less than $1 a day; achieving universal primary education; promoting gender equality and empowering women; reducing child mortality rates by two-thirds; improving maternal health; combating HIV/AIDS, malaria, and other diseases; ensuring environmental sustainability, for example, by halving the number of people without access to water; and developing a global partnership for development.

(⊕) SEE WEB LINKS
• Official website of Millennium Development Goals.

mining The activities associated with the extraction of *natural resources from the ground. Extraction is either by subsurface tunnelling or drilling, or by removal of the surface materials through quarrying, open-pit mining, or strip-mining, i.e. the systematic removal of large amounts of surface material. Although mining employs relatively few people relative to other sectors such as manufacturing and services, and generally constitutes a small share of the economy (with exceptions), it is the source of the raw materials for the production of manufactured goods (*see* EXTRACTIVE INDUSTRIES). Furthermore, mine workers have played an important role in labour history and national politics throughout the world.

Three kinds of resources are mined: *energy resources such as hydrocarbons and uranium; metallic minerals such as copper, iron ore, and gold; non-metallic minerals such as construction materials, precious stones, and various industrial minerals (e.g. potash, salt). Mining techniques vary greatly by type of resource and location. The actual extraction of resources adds less value than the subsequent processing (e.g. refining and smelting). Hence countries where minerals are extracted strive to retain processing industries, creating tensions between producers, consumers, and the transnational corporations that control much of the mining industry. Mining itself is often highly localized because the location and access to deposits is constrained by geological factors. It tends to concentrate workers in specialized communities where there are few other sources of work, and is often controlled by large, often multinational, enterprises (*see* ENCLAVE ECONOMY). World commodity prices for minerals are often volatile, making mining employment precarious. These factors might explain why mining communities have been at the forefront of organized labour and socialist politics, from the US Appalachians to Zambia's Copperbelt. Sociologists have often looked to mining districts as exemplars of working-class community life, noting their strong association with ideals of masculine labour. *See also* RESOURCE WARS.

Further reading Dicken, P. (6th ed. 2011), *Global Shift*.
Mitchell, T. (2011), *Carbon Democracy*.

minor theory *See* THEORY.

Mitchell, Don (1965–) An American *Marxist geographer who has made original contributions to the understanding of *landscape, *cultural geography, and the politics of public space. A student of Neil *Smith, Mitchell sought to rematerialize the study of landscapes. Focusing on California's agricultural revolution of the 20th century, he saw the landscape as the physical result of unequal social relations between wage workers and their employers. Relatedly, he has criticized conceptions of *culture that lose sight of the economic forces that today structure cultural activity (*see* CULTURAL MATERIALISM). Finally, Mitchell has shown how notionally 'public' spaces are, in fact, available only for selective use and (with Lynn Staehli) has challenged the socio-political exclusions written into these spaces (*see* PUBLIC SPACE).

mixed methods research The use of both *quantitative and *qualitative methods within a single *methodology. By using such an approach, researchers hope to gain both breadth and depth in their understanding of an issue. Sometimes quantitative data is used to frame and contextualize the qualitative element of the research. For example, in the case of migration research, one might first conduct an analysis of migration patterns by examining census data, followed by interviews with a small sample of migrants in order to gain a deeper understanding of the reasons for and experiences of migration. Alternatively, the converse could be enacted, with qualitative data being used to inform a larger quantitative study. For example, in-depth interviews with a small sample of migrants could be used to design a survey that is then administered to thousands of migrants. In both cases, quantitative and qualitative methods are used in concert to enhance insights.

Further reading McKendrick, J. (1998), 'Multi-method research: an introduction to its application in population geography', *Professional Geographer* 51: 40–49.

MNC *See* TRANSNATIONAL CORPORATION.

mobile GIS *See* GIS.

mobility The movement and circulation of people, goods, and information locally or across scales. Mobility has long been a concern of geographers because it is a fundamental spatial process interconnecting people and places. Indeed, how human societies function is dependent on movement and circulation: to gather food and sources of energy; to work and trade; to send and retrieve messages and information; and to seek new opportunities. People move through their own efforts or via private or public *transportation. Component parts and finished goods are shipped between source, factory, and shop. Information circulates through word of mouth, the postal system, the *media, or the *Internet. *Capital circulates through the financial system and through the physical exchange of money for goods and services. Utilities such as water, electricity, and gas flow into areas through extended infrastructures, and waste flows out. The elements of nature flow through environmental systems. As a result, Doreen *Massey has argued, *places are not simply bounded locations but are constituted from the various flows that move and circulate through them daily.

Consequently, there is a rich tradition of geographical research that has examined mobility, including the daily patterns of *spatial behaviour including: *commuting; *migration flows and experiences; the spatial *diffusion of ideas, information, diseases, products, and so on; the organization and functioning of *supply chains and *logistics; the *tourism industry; the modes, systems, use, and regulation of *transportation and their effects on everyday life; and the circulation of information and capital. Geographers have also examined the role of mobility in shaping *identity and *citizenship related to *diaspora, transnationalism, and immigrant communities. All these studies are framed by a range of different theoretical and methodological approaches. For example, *quantitative geographers have sought to explain migration using *spatial interaction models or how a disease spreads using *network analysis. *Behavioural geographers have documented spatial behaviour using *time-geography, creating and analysing 3D *visualizations of movement through time and space. *Feminists have examined how the daily movement of women is more constrained, more closely tied to the home and domestic duties. *Political economists have detailed how the circulation of capital creates *uneven development and shapes the *space economy.

In recent years a number of geographers and sociologists have argued that mobility should become the core focus of analysis, rather than simply being considered a component part of social relations (*see* MOBILITY TURN). Grounded partly in *post-structural thinking, it is contended that the world needs to be understood as fluid and always in motion, rather than as largely sedentary linked by some interconnections and movement (*see* SEDENTARISM). Mobility, however, whether of people or goods, is also understood as always involving immobility, the structures, and individuals who make movement possible.

References and further reading Adey, P. (2009), *Mobility*.
Cresswell, T. (2006), *On the Move: Mobility in the Modern Western World*.
Hanley, R. (2003), *Moving People, Goods and Information in the Twenty First Century: Urban Technology, the New Economy, and Cutting-Edge Infrastructure*.
Massey, D. (1993), 'Power geometry and a progressive sense of place', in Bird, J. et al., *Mapping the Futures: Local Cultures, Global Change*, 60–70.

mobility turn/mobilities paradigm A shift in thinking within the social sciences that prioritizes the concept of *mobility. Such thinking, rather than understanding the world as largely fixed with some movement between locations, views the world as fluid and always in motion. It argues that rather than examining people, society, and economy as if rooted in places, there is a need to recognize that life consists of mobile practices. In other words, people are mobile subjects who constantly move about to interact, work, consume, and so on, and need to be comprehended as such. The turn draws together all forms of movement and circulation and theorizes them holistically and relationally, rather than as separate, discrete forms of action associated with particular activities. Here, there is an emphasis on practice, and the meanings, subjectivities, and spaces of movement in all its diverse forms (writing, walking, dancing, driving, travelling, exploring, emigrating, and so on).

Further reading Cresswell, T. and Merriman, P. (eds.) (2011), *Geographies of Mobilities: Practices, Spaces, Subjects*.
Urry, J. (2008), *Mobilities*.

model An abstract, generalized, and structured representation of a system and its operation. Models seek to represent the various elements that comprise a system, the interrelationships between these elements, and the processes that make the system work and produce particular outcomes. They are extremely common in the physical and natural sciences, and are also routinely developed and used to understand and regulate human systems. For example, climate models are used in forecasting weather and transport models are used in traffic management. Model building became a feature of geographic scholarship through the *quantitative revolution and the development of *spatial science. Geographers devised conceptual models of human and environmental systems and sought to formalize these as statistical or mathematical models through empirically testing the relationships between elements. The aim was to produce models that could explain how a system operated, which could then be used to predict and simulate particular outcomes under certain conditions. It was thus hoped that models could provide valuable inputs into *planning and *policy formulation and help shape how society was governed and managed. A range of models was developed, especially with regards to *locational analysis, land use, and *transportation, *migration, and urban development. However model building did not become paradigmatic in the discipline as hoped by early proponents. Critics argued that models were often too abstracted, generalized, and simplified in nature to capture or explain the full complexity of how human systems operate. Nonetheless, model building is still an important component of human geography and *geographic information science, with significant progress being made in the complexity, sophistication, and testing of models due to advances in computation and the availability of spatial and temporal data. *See also* GEOCOMPUTATION; *MODELS IN GEOGRAPHY*; URBAN MODELLING.

Further reading Wilson, A. G. (2000), *Complex Spatial Systems: the Modelling Foundations of Urban and Regional Analysis.*

Models in Geography A book edited by Richard J. Chorley and Peter *Haggett (1967), this 816-page, two-volume set was a key text in the development of the *Quantitative Revolution. It sought 'a model-based paradigm to replace the classificatory paradigm of orthodoxy geography' that could be applied to both human and physical geography and thus unite them in common study. The book brought together many leading and emerging quantitative geographers of the time to provide a synoptic overview of the state of play with respect to *modelling in the discipline.

mode of production The particular combination of the *forces of production and social relations of production that define the way goods and services are made in a society. The concept is closely associated with the writings of Karl *Marx, his collaborator Friedrich Engels, and their many Marxist successors. Marx and Engels were materialists who believed that one had to focus on human engagements with physical reality and human practices (rather than ideas) in order to understand society. In the first instance all humans must meet their biological and social needs by appropriating or transforming natural resources. The forces of production describe the technologies invented for such acts of appropriation and transformation. However, to fixate on these alone to characterize the economy of any society is to risk *technological determinism, according to Marx and Engels. The forces of production produce goods and services—more generally, commodities—in the context of definite relations of production. These are the relations between those involved in the process of commodity production. The character of these relations affects not only what forces of production get adopted at any one time, but also how they affect the *labour process and who enjoys what share of the economic outputs produced. Marx and Engels famously argued that, in capitalist societies, the relations of production are such that capitalists control the forces of production, while workers can only utilize them, having nothing else to sell but their *labour power. According to the *labour theory of value, this permits capitalists to appropriate the surplus value created by workers, since the forces of production in themselves cannot produce *value of a capitalist kind. However, capitalism is so organized as to create a contradiction between the forces and relations of production (*see* DIALECTICS). While it is rational for capitalists to make their workers work ever more efficiently and to substitute technology for living labour, this can ultimately lead to a crisis of capital accumulation because unemployment increases and capitalist commodity markers dry up through lack of sufficient demand.

Some argue that Marx and Engels posited a progressive view of history in which societies would pass through stages, culminating in a post-capitalist mode of production that permitted a fairer distribution of economic wealth (*see* COMMUNISM). Regardless, such a view has proven unfounded, with *capitalism now the globally dominant mode of production—despite the myriad social and environmental problems it creates. Two foci of geographical analysis (and historical analysis) have been: the way different modes of production articulate with each other; and the way all modes of production are necessarily embedded in norms, customs, relations, and habits that exceed the economic realm. Both things require attention to local, regional, and national contexts and to the *path-dependency of all modes of production when one gets down to the fine detail. In short, the concept of a mode of production—while helpful—is too analytically abstract to tell us what we need to know to understand the economic characteristics of any given location on the Earth's surface.

modernism An early 20th-century movement in literature and the arts that self-consciously sought to break with tradition and questioned the idea that there was a single 'right' way to think, perceive, or act. The movement's ethos was well summarized by poet Ezra Pound in his 1934 injunction 'Make it new!'. The movement reflected and sought to contribute to the considerable technological, economic, and political dynamism of the time, of which the *First World War (1914–18) was the most devastating example. It was avowedly *avant-garde and not closely related to the daily lives of ordinary people. It was also emphatically urban, flourishing in *London, *Paris, and *Berlin, among other places. At the time modernism flourished academic geography remained a rather sleepy, conservative subject not much influenced by the radical ideas of the modernists. However, sixty years later, *postmodernism could be said to have partly reprised modernism, with undoubted effect on the discipline. What is more, some geographers have studied modernism, especially in relation to its vision of what urban life could and should be all about. David *Harvey, for example, suggests that modernism reflected a *fin-de-siecle* crisis of capital accumulation and a round of intense *time-space compression. While modernism undoubtedly had politically radical elements in it, in *The *Condition of Postmodernity* (1989) Harvey argues that its postmodern successor merely uses the modernist celebration of difference, irreverence, and montage as a vehicle for a new round of urban development and capitalist economic growth.

Modernity An historical period and associated experience connected to the spread of capitalism and characterized by perpetual change and innovation. Compared with the relative stability of life in 'traditional' or precapitalist societies of various kinds, modern life as experienced from the 1800s onwards is notably dynamic. According to Marshall Berman's argument in *All That is Solid Melts into Air* (1982) this new experience of space and time was captured by the artistic movement of *modernism, most notably in poetry and novels about the modern city. The acceleration of social life, the intensification of visual and other sensual experiences, and the rapid change in the built environment were among the effects of modernity. Although on the surface it might look like modernity was driven by technological changes such as industrial production or railways, underpinning this dynamism was *capitalism, which, according to *Marxists, necessitates the constant reconfiguration of the built environment without regard for pre-existing communities or traditions, It also infuses—some say colonizes—non-economic domains (such as art and literature) so that they become increasingly commodified (*see* COMMODIFICATION). This means that the dynamism of modernity can be found in putatively non-economic realms that might otherwise change more gradually. As a critique of modernity and its capitalist basis, some are calling for greater slowness (*see* CITTASLOW) and a *relocalization of much commodity production and consumption. *See also* LATE MODERNITY.

modernization theory The notion that poorer countries could and should catch up with richer ones by following the correct principles, thereby following a single, identifi-able path of *development. Modernization refers to the complex of social, political, technological, and economic changes associated with industrialization (both capitalist and socialist), and the move away from traditional ways of life (*see* MODERNITY). A distinct modernization theory only emerged after the *Second World War, in the context of post-war reconstruction, *decolonization, the *Cold War, and the US New Deal programmes to address the *Great Depression. It formed the matrix of early development policy, and had economic, demographic, cultural, social, and technological dimensions. All were founded on the idea that societies can be classified on a single metric defined by poles of tradition and modernity. Thus, traditional societies were rural, centred on subsistence farming by family labour and governed by kinship ties, tribal rule, or chiefdom. By contrast, modern societies were urban, centred on wage labour in industry, and organized by states.

A key economic idea, advanced by Walt W. Rostow, was that a country could pass through *stages of growth from 'traditional' to 'high mass consumption' by following the correct national growth strategies. Demographers, such as Kingsley Davis, identified a corresponding set of stages of population change, from high unstable to low and stable levels of birth and death rates (*see* DEMOGRAPHIC TRANSITION). In sociology, Talcott Parsons reasoned that societies would invariably become more complex, specialized, and differentiated over time, converging on a common end point. A variant of this idea was that poor societies were culturally deficient and people needed to learn new values (*see* CULTURE OF POVERTY). Human geographers made important contributions to mapping modernization through technological and infrastructural developments, such as *ports, highways, and *telecommunications.

Modernization theories were challenged from left and right politically. *Neoliberals distrusted the focus on the state. Others disputed the implicit *eurocentrism of a single path of development, noting that Western countries had become richer precisely at the expense of poorer ones (*see* UNDERDEVELOPMENT). Modernization theories understated the degree to which all countries are interdependent. There were reasonably successful instances of the application of modernization thinking, for example, India's five-year plans, but also disasters, such as China's Great Leap Forward 1959–62.

mode 2 science A novel sort of science said to be far more common than a generation ago and possibly definitive of science in the 21st century. According to Helga Nowotny and colleagues in *The New Production of Knowledge* (1994), 'mode 2 knowledge' is typically problem-driven and multidisciplinary, with the external environment (rather than academic disciplines) setting the agenda for research. It contrast with 'mode 1 knowledge', which is that emergent from 'classical' scientific inquiry since it is shaped by discipline specific academic groups pursuing their own blue skies or applied concerns. In human geography an interest in mode 2 knowledge has accompanied research into 'citizen science' and participatory environmental decision-making.

modifiable areal unit problem An *ecological fallacy issue created by drawing inferences concerning individuals based on their spatial aggregation. When mapping data such as those contained in a population census, the results are aggregated into zones and displayed as a *choropleth map. The modifiable areal unit problem consists of two related issues. First, the form of the zones can make a difference to the pattern observed. For example, in Figure 7, shifting the grid square boundaries leads to a different pattern being displayed and therefore a different conclusion about the variable being mapped. Second, the scale of the zones used can alter the pattern observed because as smaller areas are aggregated into larger ones, high concentrations in some localized areas become merged with low concentrations elsewhere, providing an average value that does not reflect either location. The problem is not easily addressed and caution needs to be exercised when drawing conclusions from spatially aggregated data.

Further reading Openshaw, S. (1984), 'Modifiable areal unit problem', *Concepts and Techniques in Modern Geography* 38.

money Any socially accepted token that can act as a means of commodity exchange and/or a store of economic value. Money has existed almost as long as societies have been exchanging goods and services internally or with other societies. What *counts* as money has always been a matter of convention—for example, certain sea shells in one

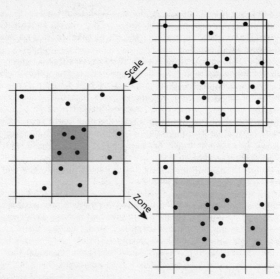

Fig. 7 The scaling and zoning components of the modifiable areal unit problem (source: Kitchin and Tate 2000: 178)

society, gold coins in another. This reflects the fact that money is not useful or valuable because of its physical form, but because of the social functions it is designed to serve. A good illustration of this fact is that the paper notes used in almost all countries worldwide are not especially costly to produce. Their face value is usually much higher than the costs incurred in their production by a government-controlled mint. One thing different forms of money usually have in common is that they are small and lightweight, making them readily transportable.

Money, it has famously been said, 'makes the world go around'. For millennia it has allowed people to exchange goods and services that are qualitatively diverse, to hoard or accumulate wealth, and to spread out their purchases in time and/or space (because money is portable and its value usually endures over time). Money, in its various concrete forms, can make commensurate (or render comparable) otherwise incommensurable commodities. It is extraordinarily liquid because it can be converted (by payment or rent) into almost any physical commodity existing in a society. Unlike other commodities (e.g. a washing machine), it does not lose value through being used or by being held unused for a long period of time—unless price inflation or a currency devaluation occurs. Money is thus very special in the world of commodities, and is sometimes considered the most abstract or 'universal' commodity of all. With some exceptions, such as nearly all members of the European Union, all countries today have their own national money (or currency), but each of these can usually be converted into other currencies via the daily exchange rate. Because of the sheer size and stability of their economies, some countries' currencies are considered especially valuable—such as the Chinese renimbi, the US dollar, the European Union euro, or the Japanese yen.

Human geographers began to study money seriously from the 1980s onwards. Much of the research has been macro-economic, concerned with the geographical dynamics of money. At the level of pure *theory, David Harvey's The *Limits to Capital is arguably the most complete exploration of money in *capitalism (*see* FINANCE). Harvey showed that money is integral to the expansion of the capitalist *mode of production, and to *time-space compression, because it is the means whereby the ceaseless search occurs for new investment opportunities and profits. Its physical mobility and ability to exchange itself for non-money commodities is key here. Harvey also showed that *finance capital is both essential for, but parasitic upon, the survival of capitalism, because it concentrates and redistributes the monies accumulated by firms, investors, and savers without itself creating the economic *value specific to capitalism (*see* LABOUR THEORY OF VALUE).

Also working at a macro-economic, but less purely theoretical level, other economic geographers have examined the global geographies of monetary flows and their conse- quences. For instance, Stuart *Corbridge provided an early study of the *debt crisis afflicting the developing world from the early 1980s. Meanwhile, others have examined monetary flows into *emerging markets, or changing exchange rates and attacks on national currencies by operatives within the global financial system (both of which were evident in the Far East Asian financial crisis of 1998). Much of this research has utilized insights from *political economy in order to highlight the role of powerful financial actors (e.g. commercial banks and hedge fund managers) in determining the value and location of money globally. Gordon *Clark is among the few to focus squarely on one set of such institutions (pension fund managers).

Some human geographers have tried to explain the reasons why existing global financial centres—notably, *London and *New York—have been able to retain their historic dominance and to build upon it. These centres are important creators of jobs and tax revenue for their local and national economies. Relatedly, other geographers investigate how offshore financial centres or *tax havens are able to escape the regulatory systems put in place elsewhere in order to capture tax revenue and ensure stability and fair play in the global financial system.

Access to money, and especially credit, is a critical component of daily life in capitalist societies. It has been argued that daily life has been 'financialized', permeated by loans, credit cards, hire purchase, and so on (*see* FINANCIALIZATION). Yet many at the lower end of the *labour market, the unemployed, and the homeless lack such access. This has led some to inquire into how and why retail banks and building societies have withdrawn services in low-income neighbourhoods, allowing loan sharks to fill the vacuum (*see* FINANCIAL EXCLUSION). However, this vacuum has often also been filled by government agencies, charities, and new social movements that seek to create alternative trading and exchanging systems (*see* ALTERNATIVE ECONOMIC GEOGRAPHIES). So-called local economic trading systems (LETS) often use forms of money that stand outside the mainstream, such as time credits linked to the exchange of locally available forms of labour (e.g. an unemployed gardener works for an unemployed mechanic, and vice versa, for a locally agreed time exchange rate).

Further reading Corbridge, S., Martin, R., and Thrift, N. (eds.) (1994), *Money, Power and Space*.

Monk, Janice (1937–) An Australian-American geographer who helped to pioneer feminist approaches in human geography. Monk not only published some of the early research into women and the structuring of geographical space, she has also done much to make academic geography more hospitable to female students and academics. With Vera Norwood, she edited *The Desert Is No Lady: Southwestern Landscapes in Women's Writing and Art* (1997).

monograph An academic book that focuses on a specific topic, presenting and analysing the subject matter at an advanced level and in some detail.

Monte Carlo simulation A statistical method that enables the calculation of an approximate solution to a mathematical problem or model that is too complex or resource-intensive to solve analytically. It works through random statistical sampling to calculate probabilities of an outcome occurring based on certain conditions. For example, we might want to calculate the probability of traffic flows between a large set of cities based on their size and distance under certain circumstances. From a *gravity model calibrated to a sample of known interactions, the probability of all other interactions can be computationally calculated. Usually several thousand such Monte Carlo runs are undertaken to provide a robust set of estimations of probable interaction.

moral economy The norms governing how economic relations should operate in peasant societies. As discussed by historian E. P. Thomson in England and anthropologist James C. Scott in Southeast Asia, these norms include the rightful distribution of goods, land, and labour, following principles of collective reciprocity, kinship, and locality as opposed to individual profit-seeking and private ownership. It is argued that all economies are embedded in cultural values.

moral geographies The geographical dimensions of moral principles and practices. Morality describes a family of principles and practices, such as *justice, responsibility, and *care. It can be studied 'positively' and normatively. In the first case, morals existing today and in the past are described and explained. In the second case, arguments for different morals are made in which it is supposed they amount to moral progress or improvement. The study of morality (or ethics) has long been central to the discipline of philosophy, as well—more practically—to those applied subjects (such as medicine) in which moral issues are an unavoidable concern. However, much philosophical discourse on the topic is ageographical: it pays little attention to and abstracts from questions of *place, *space, *landscape, and distance—though considerable attention has been devoted to *nature, *environment, and how to treat outsiders or strangers. Moral geographers seek to understand why and how moral reasoning and moral action are affected once one takes geography seriously. However, few have made the subject their life's work, with the notable exception of David M. Smith and Robert Sack. Smith's monograph *Moral Geographies: Ethics in a World of Difference* (2000) remains the most comprehensive and systematic discussion of morality by a human geographer, followed closely by Sack's *The Real and the Good* (2003).

To investigate 'moral geographies' is to do more than study the different moral principles, codes, and practices prevailing in different places and countries around the world. In the first place, many societies project moral values onto particular sites or landscapes, as if the values are intrinsic to the latter. For instance, the French market town of Lourdes is credited by many Roman Catholics with being a holy place. Another example is urban planning, wherein many designers of the built environment have believed they can create a more moral society through urban design. As David *Livingstone has shown, even the climate and weather have been moralized, as if they engender particular moral orders among people. Secondly, moral reasoning and action have long extended beyond the boundaries of one's own *community. Since at least the 16th century, long-distance relations among different societies have grown in number and significance, such that geographical interdependency is an important fact of modern life. This raises questions about how far we should care about the plight of other people, questions that receive practical responses in the form of such things as emergency *aid after a natural disaster has occurred on the other side of the world. The counter-question also thus arises: is 'nearest always dearest'? Third, moral questions arise about how we should treat strangers or outsiders who wish to live in our home places or countries. The modern world is characterized by large-scale movements of people, temporarily or permanently (*see* MIGRATION). For instance, should asylum seekers be given refuge and, if so, under what terms and conditions?

In the fourth instance, many places and territories are the subject of fierce disagreements between rival parties, such as those between *Israel and *Palestine. Morally speaking, important questions arise about who should be entitled to claim these places and territories as their own, and how a compromise might be reached rather than an impasse. Fifth, geography matters to the quality of people's lives: where they are born and raised is a question of 'moral (bad) luck', since they have no say in the matter. Issues of 'redistributive justice' (*see* JUSTICE) then arise. Should those enjoying moral good luck (e.g. wealth and happiness) seek to channel some of their considerable resources to compensate for the lack of the same elsewhere in their own country and abroad? Finally, this links to the moral dimensions of *development, which have been accented by many development geographers. Development is not a single 'objective' thing measured in terms of a society's increased GDP or life expectancy. Instead, it is a morally contested concept in which different definitions of what constitutes development clash (*see* SEN, AMARTYA).

Despite the number and importance of these moral issues, human geographers have only just begun to explore these in sufficient detail. For instance, environmental ethics have barely received any attention, despite it being a major focus of moral philosophers for at least forty years. There is also the additional issue of academic geography's own morals. Many human geographers have inquired into how the knowledge they produce contains its own moral values, many of which may be implicit/hidden, and many of which may be questionable.

moral landscape 1. A metaphor for the prevailing moral norms structuring a person's daily, weekly, and yearly passage through a society.

2. The way that any specific *landscape actively communicates moral norms or challenges to those norms by counter-cultures, subcultures, or other oppositional groups. For example, David Matless shows how specific conceptions of rural landscapes were key media for the communication of what it meant to be 'properly' English in the early 20th century.

Reference Matless, D. (1998), *Landscape and Englishness*.

morbidity A state of disease or poor health. Morbidity rates either refer to prevalence, i.e. the number of people suffering from a given condition at any one time, or incidence, the number of sufferers during a period, i.e. year.

More Economically Developed Country (MEDC) A high-income or economically richer country; the term is generally applied to countries outside Asia, Africa, and Latin America.

more-than-human 1. A term used critically to remind human geographers that the non-human world not only exists but has causal powers and capacities of its own.

2. A term used positively to highlight the absolute dependence of humans on a vast and complex array of non-human entities, only some of which are subject to human control. In both cases the more-than-human accents a relational worldview in which parts cannot be dissociated readily. Clark has criticized human geographers for fixating on non-human entities that are non-threatening and/or able to be managed. He calls for a greater recognition of the enormous power of the Earth to disrupt and destroy human plans and creations.

Reference Clark, N. (2011), *Inhuman Nature*.

Morrill, Richard (1934–) An American human geographer whose work on a range of topics was inspired by and contributed to the rise of *spatial science in the 1950s and 1960s. Morrill helped to make the department of Geography at Washington University, Seattle, a major international centre for theoretically driven attempts to locate general patterns of location and movement among diverse phenomena. A long-time social activist, he has also contributed to research and policy on electoral redistricting.

mortality rate The number of deaths in a given area per year per 1000 people, also known as the crude death rate. To compare populations, it is usual to employ age-standardized rates, i.e. adjusted for the different age structures of the populations. In general, more youthful populations will have lower mortality rates. In *pre-industrial societies the rate could be as high as 40/1000, and in poorer countries today it may be over 25/1000; the unstandardized rate in richer countries can be 5/1000 or less.

Moscow The capital city of Russia and of the former Union of Soviet Socialist Republics (the USSR). During the *Cold War, Moscow was a metonym in the West for communism, totalitarian rule, and the threat of nuclear war. Since the break-up of the USSR in 1989 Moscow has become a major international city as well as the seat of the Russian prime minister, president, and parliament. It is Russia's largest city with almost twelve million inhabitants and is said to be home to more billionaires than any other city in the world.

Movimento dos Trabalhadores Rurais Sem-Terra (MST) A landless workers' movement in Brazil that seeks land reform and civil rights for rural farmers and peasants dispossessed of land. During the military dictatorship, lasting from 1964 to 1985, land ownership was concentrated into *latifundia*, large privately owned, landed *estates. With close links to the Catholic Church, MST was founded in 1984, and draws on the liberation theology espoused by Paulo Freire that seeks to educate the poor so that they can seek *social justice.

((()) SEE WEB LINKS
• Website of *Movimento dos Trabalhadores Rurais Sem-Terra* (in Portuguese).

multiculturalism 1. The condition of living in socially and culturally diverse locales, wherein there is the proximate co-existence of people from different ethnic, racial, and religious backgrounds.
   2. Institutionalized policies that seek to balance equality, fairness, and justice, and the rights of individuals and groups for self-expression and cultural difference. Multiculturalism recognizes that in modern nation states, due to global patterns of migration, there exists a heterogeneous set of people who do not share racial or ethnic affiliations, cultural and religious beliefs and practices, or belong to the same *imagined community. Indeed, many towns and cities are demographically diverse in their make-up, and while many communities live relatively harmoniously, there are often strong patterns of residential *segregation, especially along racial lines, and tensions between groups. Initially, the response to demographically plural societies was *assimilation, wherein new groups were expected to take on the same values and practices of the existing population. Multicultural policy, in contrast, recognizes the right to cultural autonomy and seeks to promote shared understanding and acceptance of difference. The policy is under attack in many countries due to the perceived failure to address tensions between groups, reduce racism, or prevent 'race riots'.

Further reading Mitchell, K. (2004), 'Geographies of identity: multiculturalism unplugged', *Progress in Human Geography* 28: 641–65.

Multidimensional Scaling (MDS) A method for converting distance estimates between a set of locations into a two or more dimensional configuration showing the relative position of locations. The distances can be either all metric (metric MDS) or all interval/ordinal (non-metric MDS). The purpose of the technique is to discover a pattern or structure from the collection of individual distance estimates that can be statistically compared with the real world configuration in order to assess people's *mental maps.

Multi-Fibre Agreement (MFA) An international trade agreement from 1974–2004 that imposed quotas on developing countries when exporting textiles to the developed world. It was designed to prevent developing countries flooding overseas markets with low-cost textiles, which would have undermined overseas markets' textile industries almost overnight. As part of the free trade agreements brokered by the *WTO, the MFA expired in late 2004.

multifunctionality An activity that performs a number of different functions. Agriculture is often said to be multifunctional in that it produces more than food and fibres, but also manages the land and environment, maintains a rural economy and lifestyle, and stems out-migration and age-dependency imbalances. Such activities are not simply externalities, the by-products of agriculture, but are deemed key functions hence the subsidization of the sector.

multi-level models *See* HIERARCHICAL MODELS.

multi-method *See* MIXED METHOD RESEARCH.

multinational corporation *See* TRANSNATIONAL CORPORATION.

multi-sited ethnography *See* ETHNOGRAPHY.

multitude The global population that sustains *empire through its labour, consumption, and creative forces, but which can potentially overthrow it. The term derives from the work of Michael Hardt and Antonio Negri (*Multitude* 2004) and is the equivalent of the masses or proletariat in earlier, more mainstream *Marxist political projects, although it extends beyond class to include dimensions of race, gender, and sexuality.

multivariate analysis An approach that seeks to consider the effects of many interdependent independent variables on a dependent variable, or to establish the level of interdependence between independent variables. Such analysis might include *principal components analysis, multiple *regression, or ANOVAs.

Mumbai The largest city in India in terms of population and economy, it was called Bombay during the period of British rule in India. Its population today exceeds twenty million. It is a major financial centre and also home to the headquarters of many national and international firms in India.

Mumford, Lewis (1895–1990) An American critic and author best known in human geography for his writing about cities and urban life. An early believer in the power of technology and ingenuity to improve the quality of human life, his later work was more pessimistic. A consistent theme was the divorce between technology and large-scale, top down planning on the one hand, and a concern with the needs and wants of ordinary people, on the other.

music The sounds, usually produced by musical instruments or voices, that are played in a harmonious sequence. Music thus consists of 'organized sound' as defined by French composer Edgard Varèse. It is often accompanied by lyrics that are sung. Music is performed and listened to in all cultures. It serves as entertainment, a marker of lifestyle and tastes, accompaniment to rituals and other cultural practices such as dance, and to enact *memory. It is also a cultural product that is consumed by audiences via CDs, audio files, radio, and concerts. A wide variety of different music genres exists, supported by a large music industry that has a distinct *space economy. As a cultural practice, music forms an important aspect of cultural *identity. Academic research has examined the geographies of music, how music varies between and helps produce places, the spatial organization of the music industry, the *cultural politics expressed through music, and the spatiality of musical performance.

Further reading Leyshon, A., Matless, D., and Revill, G. (eds.) (1998), *The Place of Music*.

NAFTA *See* NORTH AMERICAN FREE TRADE AGREEMENT.

nanotechnology The technologies that manipulate or create materials and devices at the nanometre scale of 1–100 nm. A nanometre is a billionth of a metre, equivalent to the atomic or molecular scale of matter. Thus, nanotechnology builds structures using individual atoms and molecules. A rapidly growing area of research, it is anticipated that nanotechnology will be a major new industry producing new, more durable, and efficient materials for manufactured goods.

narco state A nation state whose government, judiciary, and military have been effectively infiltrated by drug cartels, or where the illegal drug trade is covertly run by elements of the government. It can also refer to a region under the control of organized crime for the purposes of producing or trafficking drugs where legitimate political authority is absent. 'Narco state' is more a journalistic phrase than an entity under international law. It has been used to describe Colombia, Guinea-Bissau, Suriname, and Mexico at various times.

nation A large group of people said to be bound together by a shared history, culture, language, religion, and/or *homeland. A primordialist view of nations, promulgated by *nationalism, suggests that there are natural or essential expressions of human identity and collective life. The contrasting and now more common view, *social construction, is that nations are cultural and political communities in part brought about by nationalism, i.e. they are examples of *imagined communities. Although the terms 'nation' and '*state' are often used interchangeably (as in the United Nations), they refer to different things. Where nations are social collectives, states are legal and political entities with organized institutions. *See also* DIASPORA; NATION STATE.

National Center for Geographic Information and Analysis (NCGIA) A US-based university consortium founded in 1988 that focuses on basic research and education in *Geographical Information Science and its related technologies. Through its programme of research and workshops it has shaped the development and teaching of GIS within academia.

(⊕) SEE WEB LINKS
• Official website of the National Center for Geographic Information and Analysis.

National Council for Geographic Education (NCGE) A US-based, non-profit organization, founded in 1915, to enhance the status and quality of geography teaching and learning in schools and universities. As well as advocacy work, NCGE supports research on geography education and develops geography curricula, resources. and learning materials.

(⊕) SEE WEB LINKS
• Official website of the National Council for Geographic Education.

National Geographic The monthly magazine of the *National Geographic Society (NGS) first published in 1888. *National Geographic* pioneered the use of photo-journalism with respect to issues of geography, culture, archaeology, natural science, and environmental conservation. It is presently circulated in 34 languages to 8.5 million subscribers worldwide.

National Geographic Society (NGS) Established in 1888, the NGS is the largest geographical society globally with a membership of 8.5 million. Its mission is to increase and diffuse geographic knowledge while promoting the conservation of the world's cultural, historical, and natural resources. It publishes the highly influential magazine *National Geographic, as well as a range of related travel, nature, and educational magazines, and has its own television channel.

((⊕)) SEE WEB LINKS
• Official website of National Geographic Society.

national identity *See* NATIONALISM.

nationalism A political ideology and associated movement intended to realize or further the aims of a *nation, most notably for independent self-government in a defined territory. In a broader sense, nationalism also refers to sentiments of attachment to or solidarity with a national identity or purpose (*see* IMAGINED COMMUNITY).

Nationalism as a type of political mobilization has at least two contrasting aspects. It is historically linked with efforts by peoples to secure independence from larger political entities such as empires, and formed a key ingredient of anti-imperial struggles in the Americas from the late 18th century, and later, more widely in the *Global South in post-1945 anti-colonial movements. This form is echoed by contemporary independence campaigns across much of Europe, from the Basque country to Scotland (*see* INTERNAL COLONIALISM). A second aspect is more top-down, expressed in the many ways states have tried to forge national belonging by combinations of coercive and persuasive measures such as national days, common school curricula (including for geography), commemorative ceremonies, and standardized languages. There is much interest among geographers in how *cultural landscapes, including monuments, symbolize national identity. Michael Billig coined the term 'banal nationalism' to describe the routine and everyday ways that national identities are enacted, for example, through nationalist symbols on bank notes. Geographical education can also play a part in instilling a sense of national identity, not least through *cartography.

As a sentiment, nationalism may take more or less benign forms, from supporting a national sports team to harbouring aggression towards others, for example, competing nations or persecuted minorities. In both senses, therefore, nationalism has positive and negative characteristics.

Further reading Storey, D. (2001), *Territory: the Claiming of Space*.

national parks Areas protected for their *conservation significance and the aesthetic value, designated by national governments. Such parks are often deemed to be of national and symbolic significance. Permanent settlement is prevented in some cases, e.g. the USA. In others, human activity is permitted but managed to minimize impact, e.g. in the UK. Yellowstone National Park in the USA was the first national park (1872). *See also* WILDERNESS.

national spatial strategies The long-term *spatial planning frameworks designed to guide development at a national scale. In Europe, such spatial strategies have their roots in the European Spatial Development Perspective (EDSP) adopted by member states in 1999. Each state was to produce a spatial strategy that set out how different parts of the country would grow in a way that was sustainable and would produce *agglomeration effects for settlement patterns and the economy. These strategies generally favoured *polycentric urban development within regions. *See also* EUROPEAN OBSERVATION NETWORK FOR TERRITORIAL DEVELOPMENT AND COHESION.

Further reading Duhr, S., Colomb, C., and Nadin, V. (2011), *European Spatial Planning and Territorial Cooperation.*

nation-building The process by which *nationalist forces, including the state, political parties, and elites attempt to construct a unified national identity. By implication, *nations do not spring from deeply rooted historical affinities, but have to be forged from myriad local, linguistic, ethnic, class, and other identities. Nation-building took place in late 19th-century Europe and post-colonial Africa, for example. In recent years the phrase has been used to refer to efforts by outside forces to establish workable political and *civil society institutions in countries recovering from invasion and occupation, notably Afghanistan and Iraq. *See also* IMAGINED COMMUNITIES.

nation-state 1. A self-governing country, often regarded as the basic unit of political territory in the modern world.
  2. The combination of a *nation with a *state to form a close association between a people and a political territory.
  In the first sense, it is often synonymous with the term 'state', distinguished from subnational forms of government. In the second sense, it may refer to an ideal or aspiration of *nationalism, whereby a people acquire self-government over a territory (*see* SELF-DETERMINATION). In reality, very few modern-day countries are coterminous with nations. Even so, the idea that nations, states, and societies are one and the same, and that they form the basic building blocks of the world's political geography, is a powerful concept (*see* METHODOLOGICAL NATIONALISM). *See also* WESTPHALIAN MODEL.

NATO The North Atlantic Treaty Organization is a military alliance between 28 states, mainly in North America and Western Europe, founded in 1949, and headquartered in Brussels, Belgium. Its members are committed to collective self-defence, initially with the threat of the USSR in mind (*see* COLD WAR). Since 1989, however, NATO has engaged in military operations unrelated to the immediate defence of member states, in the former Yugoslavia (1994), Afghanistan (2003), and Libya (2011).

natural experiment The systematic observation of certain phenomena in one or more places where the conditions affecting the behaviour of the observed phenomena cannot be controlled by the experimenter. Unlike laboratory or computational experiments, where the researcher can control the parameters, natural experiments involve observing open systems where a myriad of processes, causal powers, and interacting effects are operative. The term derives from observations of disease diffusion in urban neighbourhoods, but today describes any attempt to determine the relationship between interacting variables in real world situations. Because human (and physical) geographers typically study open systems, especially at the local and regional scales, natural experiments are a common feature of their research. The philosophy of *critical realism provides a conceptual toolkit for analysing natural experiments under the rubric of *intensive research.

natural growth rate In economics, the rate at which national income would have to grow to maintain a constant rate of employment.

natural hazard An event or phenomenon with the potential to cause serious harm, including loss of human life and damage to human-environmental systems, and which originates in the natural environment (*see* HAZARD). They are distinguished from technological hazards such as accidents at nuclear reactors. The actual effect of geological, meteorological, and hydrological factors is always contingent upon social factors. For this reason, the term 'environmental hazard' is now more common. *See also* DISASTER.

natural increase The number of births minus the number of deaths in a population. The rate can be negative if *mortality levels exceed *fertility, depending also on the level of migration.

naturalism A view that most of reality is comprised of natural processes and entities existing regardless of human thought or action, and the further view that the natural sciences are best equipped to study them. Naturalism is the enemy of religion or supernaturalism because it questions the existence of a transcendent power or force that governs earthly phenomena. It also seeks to impose analytical limits on the applicability of *social construction in the social sciences and humanities, including human geography. Almost all physical geographers are naturalists, while most human geographers see naturalism as inapplicable to the world of people insofar as people 'escape' their own mental and bodily nature by way of language, symbolism, culture, and social relations of various kinds.

natural resources The biophysical materials and processes that meet human needs and wants. They can be distinguished from human resources such as labour, knowledge, and technology. A narrow definition of natural resources includes all those substances and effects produced by biological, geological, or other environmental processes that serve as factors of production, i.e. inputs into the economy. These include minerals, timber, soil, and fish, but also less tangible things such as wind and sunlight (*see* RENEWABLE ENERGY). A broad definition recognizes that nature provides a wide range of indirect resources necessary to sustain life. These 'ecosystem services' include the role of oceans and forests in carbon sequestration, clean air and water, and environmental sinks for waste products. Further still, one might count the spiritual or aesthetic value of the natural environment as a resource for human well-being and happiness. An important qualification in all of these cases is that natural resources are only defined as such by potential users, i.e. a quality in *nature becomes a resource only relative to socio-cultural appraisal and technological capacity (*see* SOCIO-NATURE). Uranium is not a natural resource unless a society knows about nuclear fission. A mineral deposit may not be a resource if it lies beneath land valued for its spiritual significance and integrity. Furthermore, the 'naturalness' of natural resources is disturbed by the creation of transuranic elements (generated only by nuclear reactors) and transgenic species (the result of *genetic modification).

A conventional distinction is made between renewable and non-renewable natural resources. Renewable resources are those whose use does not deplete them or alter their availability, i.e. they are not finite or exhaustible. Non-renewable resources are those whose availability is finite, although these include resources that can be reused and recycled such as metallic minerals. In fact, even renewable resources can be depleted if their rate of consumption exceeds their rate of regeneration. Soil, for example, is a renewable resource but can be depleted or degraded by excessive exploitation. Renewable resources are also sometimes termed 'stock', and non-renewable 'flow', resources.

The geographical study of the distribution of resources was an important theme in 19th- and early 20th-century geography (*see* COMMERCIAL GEOGRAPHY). Knowledge of resources, including land for agriculture, was vital to classical economists. But in the second half of the 20th century both economics and *economic geography disregarded the resource base, generally assuming it to be given and inexhaustible. Renewed interest in resources came with the various critiques of neo-*Malthusianism and its tenet that resource scarcity placed limits on human well-being and endeavour (*see* LIMITS TO GROWTH; TRAGEDY OF THE COMMONS). Often grounded in *Marxism, these critiques often underplayed the significance of the biophysical or material dimensions of resources. More recent work, in what is termed 'critical resource geographies', considers not just the social, cultural, and political construction of resources, but also how their natural properties, in turn, structure their exploitation. Scott Prudham, for example, has explored how the biophysical qualities of Douglas Fir woodlands have shaped the timber industry in the Pacific Northwest. The time it takes the trees to grow and the way they grow directly influences the wider social relations of production (*see* COMMODIFICATION). *See also* RESERVES; RESOURCE MANAGEMENT; RESOURCE WARS.

References and further reading Bakker, K. and Bridge, G. (2006), 'Material worlds? Resource geographies and the "matter of nature"', *Progress in Human Geography* 30: 5–27.
Montgomery, D. R. (2007), *Dirt: the Erosion of Civilizations*.
Prudham, W. S. (2005), *Knock on Wood: Nature as Commodity in Douglas-Fir Country*.

nature: **1.** The non-human world, especially those parts untouched or barely affected by humans ('the natural environment').

2. The entire physical world, including humans as biological entities and products of evolutionary history.

3. The power or force governing some or all living things (such as gravity or the conservation of energy).

4. The essential quality or defining property of something (e.g. it is natural for birds to fly and fish to swim). As a shorthand, we can (respectively) call these meanings 'external nature', 'universal nature', 'superordinate nature', and 'intrinsic nature'. Human geographers have, in recent years, questioned the 'givenness' of nature described by these conventional definitions.

Depending on the context of usage, the idea of nature can function as a noun, a verb, an adverb, or an adjective; it can also be characterized as object or subject, passive or active. For instance, we can talk of a 'nature reserve', 'natural beauty', a 'naturally destructive' hurricane, or the 'natural order' being restored. 'Nature' is both an ordinary word used in everyday discourse, and also part of the lexicon of scientists and other credentialized *experts. Several meanings of the term 'nature' can be in play simultaneously. For example, consider the sentence 'You can only understand the nature of Human Geography by understanding the different ways that human geographers have studied nature'. Here the fourth meaning of 'nature' is used to describe the quality of an academic subject, only then to mean an object of study (in potentially all four senses of the term) in the second part of the sentence. What is more, the term can be used in evaluative as well as non-evaluative ways. In the bestselling book *The End of Nature* (2nd ed. 2003), the American environmentalist Bill McKibben suggests that both non-human nature and human nature are together progressively disappearing. This, he argues, is because modern societies are destroying that which evolution bequeathed us—by both design and accident. On the basis of this non-evaluative observation, McKibben then criticizes the modern way of life: for him, 'nature' is that which we should seek to protect, nurture, and sustain. Like many others, he espouses a nature-centric morality implying that nature = good, therefore less nature = bad. This overlaps with a widespread assumption that what is natural is 'normal' and what is unnatural is 'abnormal', 'artificial', 'fake', or in some other way unsuitable. In summary, the term nature and its multiple meanings are promiscuous in the English language. This becomes even more evident if we consider its 'collateral concepts'. These are terms whose meanings are closely related—and sometimes synonymous with—the meanings of 'nature'. For instance, widely used words such as 'biology', 'sex', 'genes', 'intelligence', and 'race' are often proxies for the term 'nature'.

It is easy to get lost in the complexity of meaning and the range of contexts in which the term 'nature' and its collateral concepts get used. A consistent feature is that when people talk about nature they believe they are making *ontological statements of a cognitive, moral, or aesthetic kind. That is to say, they believe they are making statements about a biophysical reality that exists independently of the words, concepts, and terms used to make linguistic sense of it. In this respect, we are apt to assume that 'nature' is a 'mimetic concept' whose meanings capture in words actual existing phenomena that exist 'out there' (or 'in here' if we're discussing our own physiology and neurology).

When academic geography began to divide into two major halves, nature—as an object of study—largely became the preserve of physical geographers. After the Second World War, human geographers became ever more focused on social, cultural, economic, and political issues, and tended to bracket-out issues of nature, environment, and biology. From the 1980s, human geographers rediscovered the topic of nature by way of a seemingly paradoxical insistence that it was not as natural as it seemed. This rediscovery has taken three forms.

First, Marxist geographer Neil *Smith proposed the counter-intuitive idea that nature is socially produced in his book *Uneven Development* (1984). According to Smith, capitalism has remade nature head-to-toe over the last two centuries, meaning that such things as genetically modified crops are only the latest in a very long line of material transformations of the non-human world. Nature has become a mere means to the end of profit-realization, and in the process it has been physically reconstituted into an anthropogenic 'second nature'. Though not formally referenced to his book, a brilliant 1991 monograph by William Cronon illustrated Smith's arguments in bracing detail. *Nature's Metropolis* tells the epic story of how the rise of Chicago during the 19th century was umbilically connected to the formation of entirely new agricultural landscapes throughout the mid-West of the USA.

If Smith directed human geographers' attention to the economic and political processes that were behind the physical remaking of nature, others were more minded to pay attention to our ideas and beliefs about nature. The suggestion was that people in the West routinely mistake their culturally constructed representations of what we call 'nature' for a world believed to be somehow intrinsically 'natural'. This challenging idea built on the insight of cultural critic Raymond Williams (1976) that when we talk about nature, we are really talking about ourselves—even though we rarely realize it. Many so-called '*new cultural geographers' have shown that all sorts of spoken, written, and visual representations of 'nature'—including scientific ones—at some level reflect the cultural norms, values, and prejudices of those doing the representing. The politics of *representation questions the commonsense idea that a thing we call 'nature' by convention can be appealed to as an absolute foundation to legitimate social beliefs or related social actions (see Bruce Braun's *The Intemperate Rainforest*, for example).

Notwithstanding their intellectual differences, the two approaches to 'nature' summarized above have one key thing in common: they presume an ontological distinction between 'society' and a world of non-social things (trees, elephants, rivers, etc.). A third approach, that of human geography's so-called 'new materialists', challenges the society-nature dualism that animates the other two. It favours a non-dualistic ontology in which the world is envisaged as comprising entities and relationships that have no discrete, *a priori* identities. This means that 'society' and 'nature' are simply the terms we have invented to pigeon-hole certain things that cannot, in fact, be so cleanly separated. Geographer Sarah *Whatmore (2002) has been a leading proponent of the idea of *hybridity, arguing that the so-called 'natural world' is neither entirely 'produced' by capitalism nor entirely 'constructed' in accordance with culturally particular beliefs. Building on *Actor-Network Theory (ANT), Whatmore has questioned the presumption that certain spaces (cities, for example) are less 'natural' than others (such as wilderness areas). She argues that what appear to be qualitatively different kinds of space are, in fact, the complex and internally differentiated result of interlinked 'actor-networks'. These networks contain and combine all manner of things—people, machines, species—and it is impossible to accord any one part of a network ontological priority over the rest. Whatmore's ideas have found an echo is so-called *non-representational theory (NRT). NRT argues that our engagement with what we call 'nature' goes well beyond language, cognition, and conscious thought to encompass the pre-conscious, touch, taste, smell, and hearing. This implies that we are all continuously immersed in multisensory engagements with our surroundings, such that it is invidious to distinguish the so-called 'social' world from the so-called 'natural' world. Likewise, it is invidious to distinguish between the geographical analogues of these two terms. This said, Nigel Clark has recently argued that human geography's 'new materialisms' focus too much on the world of everyday human experience and, like the approaches they criticize, have lost sight of nature's power and volatility, its capacity to destroy us. Clark has called for a new *rapprochement* between the humanities and social sciences and the earth sciences given the future challenges presented by the *Anthropocene. *See also* ACTOR-NETWORK THEORY; ASSEMBLAGE; FIRST NATURE; HYBRIDITY; MATERIALISM; NON-REPRESENTATIONAL THEORY; PRODUCTION OF NATURE; REPRESENTATION; WILDERNESS.

Further reading Castree, N. (2011), 'Nature', in Agnew, J. and Duncan, J. (eds.) *A Companion to Human Geography* 179–96.
Castree, N. (2013), *Making Sense of Nature.*
Clark, N. (2011), *Inhuman Nature.*
Whatmore, S. (2002), *Hybrid Geographies.*
Williams, R. (1976), *Keywords.*

Nature of Geography A landmark work in the philosophy of geography by Richard *Hartshorne (1939), one of the leading US geographers of the 20th century. Written largely while at the University of Vienna, Hartshorne synthesized the work of European geographers from Immanuel *Kant onwards to define geography as a logical and systematic science, the study of *areal differentiation. It was published as two issues of the *Annals of American Association of Geographers* but twenty years later Hartshorne produced a shorter summary, *Perspective on the Nature of Geography.*

Further reading Entrikin, J. N. and Brun, S. D. (eds.) (1989), *Reflections on Richard Hartshorne's 'The Nature of Geography'.*

Nature's Metropolis An award-winning monograph by American historical geographer William Cronon (1991) that demonstrates the umbilical connection between the country and the city in the rise of Chicago at the turn of the 20th century. Cronon's aim was to question the urban-rural dualism common in Western thought by demonstrating how the prodigious growth of one city (Chicago, a manufacturing and distribution centre) was profoundly dependent on the large-scale transformation of its extended hinterland into a farming landscape.

navigation The practice of travelling from one place to another following a prescribed route. Such navigation requires the accurate monitoring of position and direction. It is a key maritime and aerial skill for sailing or flying efficiently across oceans and continents, in order to arrive safely at a destination. Prior to the development of modern technologies such as *GPS, navigators would use techniques such as dead reckoning, taking celestial measurements, or identifying key landmarks to plot their progress.

near-shoring The transfer of business by a company to others in countries adjacent to its own. Near-shoring is a form of subcontracting or *outsourcing in which a firm seeks to reduce costs by having one or more of its operations conducted by independent firms elsewhere. Unlike off-shoring, where far-flung countries may be involved, near-shoring may allow a firm to deal with a new business partner in the same time-zone, speaking the same language, possessed of the same culture, and so on.

negative correlation *See* CORRELATION.

neighbourhood An urban residential area, generally small enough to be covered easily on foot. It is sometimes assumed that neighbourhoods are also communities defined by social interaction or defined by geographical boundaries such as major roads, parks, or rivers, but this need not be the case. The degree to which inhabitants of a neighbourhood identify with the area or interact with others is an empirical question. Nonetheless, neighbourhoods have formed the basis of much urban social geographical research, notably in the tradition of the *Chicago School. *See also* GENTRIFICATION; URBAN GEOGRAPHY.

neighbourhood effect The influence on an individual's behaviour and attitudes that can be attributed to interaction with others in a neighbourhood. For example, how an individual votes in elections might be partly explained by such factors as income, age, and gender, but it may also reflect the local social milieu. It can be assumed that people who live near one another communicate and interact more with one another than with others further away. This effect is, however, difficult to measure in practice.

neoclassical economics A school of economic analysis, which, to cite Lionel Robbins famous definition, 'studies human behaviour as a relationship between ends and scarce means which have alternative uses' (1932). Neoclassical economics was created in the late 19th century as an alternative to the classical economics of Adam Smith and (more radically) Karl *Marx. It was codified by the University of Cambridge economist Alfred Marshall in the early 20th century. It remains the dominant approach in Anglo-American economics, and was for years the *paradigm informing *economic geography. It is methodologically individualist, taking it as axiomatic that all economic actors, possessed of certain means and with particular ends in mind, will make rational decisions about what to do at any given moment in time. It employs mathematics and statistics and seeks to connect micro-economic behaviour with macro-economic trends. Despite being heavily criticized for a century, it is remarkably resilient. Although it has relatively little presence in current economic geography, it holds more sway in the *new economic geography practised today by some economists.

Reference Robbins, L. (1932), *An Essay on the Nature and Significance of Economic Science.*

neocolonialism *See* COLONIALISM.

neoconservatism A political ideology mainly associated with the USA. Neoconservatives stress the importance of traditional moral, religious, and family values in opposition to the kinds of personal hedonism and anti-establishment attitudes associated with the 1960s *counterculture. Mass media and popular culture are important fields of political intervention. They do not share *neoliberalism's faith in the *free market, which can corrode conservative values. In foreign policy terms, neoconservatives have not been afraid to project US military might in pursuit of advancing democracy, most notably in the Iraq War (2003).

neo-Darwinism *See* DARWINISM.

neogeography The new forms of geographical knowledge enabled by Web 2.0 technologies wherein geographical data are sourced through the collective actions of many
individuals, and processed and displayed through online resources. Neogeography produces geographical outputs that have not been produced by professionals, but rather
through *crowd-sourcing. These data range from place tags on virtual globes, to up-
loaded GPS traces of locations, to georeferenced communication that can be mapped
and combined with other data to create large, dynamic, open data sets.

Further reading Graham, M. (2010), 'Neogeography and the palimpsests of place', *Tijdschrift voor
Economische en Sociale Geografie* 101(4): 422–36.

neo-imperialism *See* IMPERIALISM.

neoliberalism A worldview (or philosophy of life), a wide-ranging policy programme,
and a set of concrete policy measures in which individual freedom is given priority.
Neoliberalism is a late 20th- and early 21st-century phenomenon and traces its roots to
the earlier *liberalism advocated by such thinkers as Adam Smith and John Locke.
Building on these thinkers' ideas, the economists Friedrich von Hayek and Milton
Friedman authored manifestos advocating a return to liberal values and policies: namely,
The Road to Serfdom (1944), *The Constitution of Liberty* (1960), and *Capitalism and
Freedom* (1962). They had little impact upon public policy until the 1970s, when dictator
Augusto Pinochet invited neoliberal economists to reorder Chile's economy and society.
Subsequently, neoliberal ideas were introduced in Britain (under Margaret Thatcher's
leadership), the USA (under Ronald Reagan's leadership), and New Zealand. Thereafter,
they enjoyed a global influence because of America's leading role in the *International
Monetary Fund (IMF), the *World Bank, and the *World Trade Organization (WTO).

Three things make neoliberalism new ('neo') when compared to its 18th-century
forebear. First, it was crafted as an explicit critique of post-war 'managed capitalism',
be it in the former communist bloc, the Western social democracies, or the many
'developmental states' of the Global South. Secondly, on principle it takes a very dim
view of the state, public goods, and common resources, except insofar as any of them
can aid the cause of individual freedom and liberty. Finally, it has travelled far and
wide geographically courtesy of various institutions and networks in which American
neoliberals have played a highly active role.

'Neoliberalism' is very much a critics' term: it is virtually never used by those whom the
critics describe as neoliberals. It can be disaggregated into a worldview (a body of
normative goals and aspirations amounting to a philosophy of life, or something close
to one), a political discourse (a set of values, norms, and ambitions professed by those
who control, or realistically seek to control, the formal apparatuses of government), and
a set of public policies (regulations and procedures that make both the worldview and
the policy discourse flesh in some way). As a short-hand, we can think in terms of the
'three ps': philosophy, programme, and practice.

As a worldview neoliberalism has two signature characteristics. First, it sees the state
(national and local) as existing to maximize the independence of both real and institutional individuals: anything less would be a travesty of 'true freedom', according to
neoliberals. Second, neoliberals see money-mediated markets as the best mechanism
for coordinating among the diverse needs and wants of free people. This is because
markets are deemed to be highly 'intelligent', as well as 'efficient': price signals, it is
claimed, enable providers and users of goods and services to achieve many of their
desires, given whatever restraints of resource availability happen to be in place for those
involved.

As a policy discourse, the neoliberal worldview is typically understood by analysts to
include the following five proposals for significant change: *privatization (i.e. assigning

clear, legally enforceable, private property rights to hitherto unowned, state-owned, or communally owned aspects of the social, cultural, and natural worlds); *marketization (i.e. rendering alienable and exchangeable things that might not previously have been subject to a market calculus lubricated by monetary transactions within and between nation states); state roll-back or *deregulation (i.e. the withdrawal or diminution of state intervention in certain areas of social, cultural, and environmental life in order to enable firms and consumers to exercise 'freedom of choice'); market-friendly reregulation (i.e. a reconfiguration of the state so as to extend the frontiers of privatization and marketization); and the use of market proxies in the residual state sector (i.e. making remaining state functions and services more market-like in their operation through the use of measures such as internal markets, cost-recovery, and budget-capping).

Critics of neoliberalism argue that there has been a notable gap between the ideals and the realities. For instance, in *A Brief History of Neoliberalism* (2005) David *Harvey argues that the neoliberal worldview has been a rhetorical cover for policies that have increased the freedom and liberty of the few at the expense of the many. In addition, some former neoliberals (such as Nobel Prize economist Joseph Stiglitz, 2002) have broken ranks and criticized the dogmatic application of policies in places such as Argentina. Neoliberal policies have generated widespread social opposition among those negatively affected by them, such as the Zapatistas in southern Mexico. Finally, the 2007–09 global financial crisis was seen by some to have driven a stake into neoliberalism's heart. The latter's support for 'free-market' finance is widely regarded as the root cause of the serial bank failures, government rescue packages, and subsequent economic recessions witnessed across the world. Some commentators thus believe we are entering a 'post-neoliberal period'.

The assessment above presumes that neoliberalism is a single coherent thing. But one should not confuse neoliberalism as philosophy, programme, or policies, even though they are all necessarily related. However, very few analysts of neoliberalism see it in these simplistic terms, which is why the process-term 'neoliberalization' has been favoured by many. This describes an ongoing, unfinished process of proposing, revising, testing, applying, and further altering neoliberal ideas and policies. As Neil Brenner and Nik Theodore (2002) have argued, 'actually existing neoliberalism' is not the same as the neoliberal worldview.

These arguments suggest that what is called 'neoliberalism' in the singular is, in reality, a complex historical-geographical formation marked by unevenness and variety: that is to say, a set of interconnected 'neoliberalizations' in the plural. Neoliberal ideas may well have 'gone global' from the mid-1980s courtesy of the USA and its influence in key institutions like the IMF, but this has not comprised a tidy process of downwards and outwards diffusion from neoliberalism's North Atlantic heartlands. Instead, there has been path-dependency, contingent couplings, unplanned adaptations, organic mutations, and a good deal of social resistance to new liberal policies. Varying combinations of coercion, consent, contestation, and compromise describe the spatio-temporal evolution of neoliberal projects in different parts of the world. Accordingly, if we are now 'post-neoliberal', the question of exactly how and to what degree will need to be answered on a case-by-case basis. *See also* INTERNATIONAL MONETARY FUND; PRIVATIZATION; THATCHERISM; TRAGEDY OF THE COMMONS; THE WORLD BANK; THE WORLD TRADE ORGANIZATION; WORKFARE.

Further reading Anderson, P. (2000), 'Renewals', *New Left Review* 1: 1–21.

Brenner, N. and Theodore, N. (2002), 'Cities and the geographies of "actually existing neoliberalism"', *Antipode* 34(3): 349–79.

Crouch, C. (2011), *The Strange Non-Death of Neo-liberalism*.

Mudge, S. (2009), 'What is neoliberalism?', *Socio-Economic Review* 6(4): 703–31.

Stiglitz, J. (2002), *Globalization and its Discontents*.

Neo-Marshallian industrial districts *See* MARSHALLIAN DISTRICTS.

neo-Marxism *See* MARXISM; MARXIST GEOGRAPHY.

neopatrimonialism The use of state resources to forge and sustain patron-client relations. Max Weber distinguished 'patrimonialism', a traditional form of authority based on charismatic power, from the modern form of legal-rational authority he saw as expressed by the bureaucratic state. The 'neo' indicates that, far from being displaced by modern government, such relations of influence and favour can thrive alongside and within it. In one view, the use of state resources by elites to buy loyalty among the public is corruption, or bad *governance. In another, it is an effective way of the poor to be directly linked to the state and obtain the support and goods they need.

Netherlands A small west European democracy with a North Sea shoreline and shared borders with Belgium (to the south) and Germany (to the east). Sometimes known as Holland, it is low lying, with most of the country barely above sea level, and 20 per cent below it. Amsterdam is the largest city, with The Hague as the political capital. Dutch is the official language among its seventeen million inhabitants. The standard of living is high, and the economy highly export orientated. Rotterdam is a major European port and Schiphol an important European airport. Several Dutch companies, such as the airline KLM and the science publisher Elsevier, are global leaders in their industries. The Netherlands has a good social welfare system and its political culture contrasts with the *neoliberalism prevalent in the USA and Britain.

net migration *See* MIGRATION.

network A set of *nodes and the paths linking them together. Networks are both an object of analysis and a method of analysis (*see* ACTOR-NETWORK THEORY; SOCIAL NETWORKS). They are also an increasingly common metaphor for transformations in modern life (*see* NETWORK SOCIETY). Networked forms of organization are differentiated from others such as hierarchies (e.g. an army) and markets, which are more decentralized. There are three basic geometrical kinds that can be used to describe different sorts of organization: firstly, a chain, in which nodes are linked in a sequence (e.g. a *supply chain); secondly, a hub or wheel, in which one central node is linked to others (*see* HUB-AND-SPOKE); and thirdly, an all-channel network in which any node can be connected to any other. The latter can be investigated by *network analysis.

Further reading Thompson, G. F. (2003), *Between Hierarchies & Markets: the Logic and Limits of Network Forms of Organization.*

network analysis The analysis of the characteristics of a network. In geography, networks are typically infrastructure such as the road system or electricity grid, but they also include social networks such as friendships and business transactions. Analysis focuses on the network typology and how it is structured in order to reveal its functional properties. These include connectivity, regional and nodal measures, as well as how networks evolve, how vulnerable and resilient they are under different conditions, and how networks can be optimized to improve performance. *See also* GRAPH THEORY.

Further reading Curtin, K. M. (2007), 'Network analysis in geographic information science: review, assessment, and projections', *Cartography and Geographic Information Science* 34(2): 103–11.

Network Society A new mode of socio-technical organization centred on *information and communication technologies (ICTs) that is reshaping the post-industrial economic and social landscape. As theorized by Manuel *Castells in *The Network Society* (1996), it is globally connected through ICTs, prioritizing the growth of the *information economy, and creating spatial and temporal fluidity that encourages corporate restructuring. He argues that this fluidity represents the move to a 'space of flows' characterized by mobility and *time-space compression, with this space-economy replacing the 'space of places', the traditional modern economy centred on location, and the overcoming of time by space (e.g., based on friction of distance).

neural networks A form of modelling that mimics the structure and functioning of the brain to perform a particular task. Knowledge within the model is created through a learning process shaped by learning rules. A learning rule is a procedure for modifying weights and biases of a network until a certain task is achieved. Learning can be supervised, where the model is trained to match inputs to certain outputs, and unsupervised, where the network self-organizes to teach itself to identify patterns in the data. In geography, neural networks are most often used to mine large spatial and non-spatial data sets, and to recognize patterns and classify data, especially in remote sensing.

new cultural geography A form of cultural geography that arose in the late 1980s and that understands culture more as a process than manifest in material artefacts. Hence, it can be distinguished from an earlier cultural geography, exemplified by the *Berkeley School. Engaging with social and *critical theory, new cultural geography reframed the analysis of landscapes and artefacts, and extended the focus to include identity and representation. *See also* CULTURAL TURN.

new economic geography A body of research into the *space economy that derives its core ideas from mainstream economics, specifically latter-day versions of neo-classicism (*see* NEOCLASSICAL ECONOMICS). As a discipline, economics has almost always been indifferent to geographical variation, abstracting from local, regional, and national economic differences in order to identify general principles, forces, and processes. In the 1960s and 1970s, many economic geographers tried to apply mainstream economic thinking in order to theorize and model the space economy, in so doing extending rather than challenging its principal tenets (such as the rationality of economic actors, *see* HOMO ECONOMICUS). However, thereafter, the relations with economics grew more distant, as *political economy and *institutionalist approaches came to dominate, though *regional science continued to pose geographical questions in the language of conventional economic thinking. From the early 1990s, the leading US economist Paul *Krugman (1991) argued that more economists needed to take the concerns of economic geographers seriously, especially their preoccupation with *agglomeration, inter-place competition, and the switching of investment between regions. Krugman wanted to develop formal economic theories and models from economic first principles that could account for the geographical 'lumpiness' of all economic activity while maintaining the economic rigour of his profession and its use of both mathematic reasoning and quantitative-statistical evidence. This new economic geography (NEG) is sometimes known as 'geographical economics' to distinguish it from the majority of research conducted by economic geographers.

In some respects NEG has been a great success. Many more economists have followed Krugman's lead and become interested in spatial agglomeration and how places continue (or fail) to enjoy economic success (Krugman, 2011). At the same time, economic geographers and economists have been able to converse more with one another, not least because the *Journal of Economic Geography* was founded in 2005 to encourage exchange. Furthermore, the term 'new economic geography' has been increasingly displaced by the broader description of 'geographical economics'. Although the boundary between the work of economists and geographers has become more blurred, many human geographers remain critical of NEG, regarding it as a throw-back to 1960s location *theory. *See also* PORTER, MICHAEL.

References and further reading Brakman, S., Garretsen, H., and Marrewijk, C. (2009), *The New Introduction to Geographical Economics*.

Krugman, P. (1991), *Geography and Trade*.

Krugman, P. (2011), 'The new economic geography, now middle-aged', *Regional Studies* 45, 1: 1–7.

New Imperialism, The A book by Marxist geographer David *Harvey (2003) that helped to revive the concept of *imperialism among left-wing intellectuals and activists. Imperialism was thought to be a thing of the past, something that ended in the mid-20th century when the former colonies of Britain, France, and other Western European hegemonies achieved independence. However, after the invasion of *Iraq by America and its allies in 2003, Harvey argued that a new kind of imperialism was being initiated based not on political control of overseas territories, but on economic control and the exertion of political influence, all spear-headed by military force. Harvey argued that America was seeking to compensate for its declining economic importance by using its continued military dominance to project its interests overseas, not least by ensuring continued access to oil in the *Middle East.

New International Division of Labour (NIDL) The spatial pattern of paid employment following the *deindustrialization of Western economies during the 1970s and 1980s, and the rise of *Newly Industrializing Countries. This new pattern saw a number of low-skilled product assembly jobs move to the *Global South, especially Southeast Asia and parts of Central and South America. Meanwhile, jobs related to product design, research, and development typically remained in the *Global North. The NIDL was, initially, driven by mostly Western multinational corporations relocating parts of their operations in order to reduce costs and access new overseas markets. *See also* DIVISION OF LABOUR; INTERNATIONAL DIVISION OF LABOUR; SPATIAL DIVISION OF LABOUR.

Newly Industrializing Countries (NICs) A group of countries mainly in East Asia (also known as 'Tiger Economies') and Latin America that experienced rapid rates of economic growth in the 1960s and 1970s, moving them out of the category of low-income countries, otherwise referred to as the *Third World or *developing world. Some, for example, Singapore and South Korea, continued to develop into high-income countries, while others stalled under the weight of the *debt crisis and subsequent problems (*see* MIDDLE-INCOME TRAP). NICs, or Newly Industrializing Economies (NIEs) did not follow a single path. Asian economies—Hong Kong, Taiwan, South Korea, and Singapore— focused on export-led growth, attracting *Foreign Direct Investment into sectors such as garments and consumer electronics. Some argued that this demonstrated the wisdom of free trade and market-friendly policies, but others suggested that in each case the state played a powerful role (*see* ASIAN MIRACLE; DEVELOPMENTAL STATE). Brazil, Mexico, and Latin American NICs specialized more in *import-substitution industrialization, protecting domestic industries by trade tariffs.

Further reading Knox, P. et al., (5th ed. 2008), *The Geography of the World Economy*.

new regionalism A descriptive and normative term referring to new economically successful regions and to the region as the geographical scale at which economic policy and planning is best fitted. With the end of *Fordism and attempts to find new growth models from the late 1970s onwards, many Western capitalist countries began to experiment with giving cities and regions more autonomy in determining their own futures. This involved a move from government to *governance, wherein many non-state actors were invited to participate in establishing and steering local economic trajectories. At the same time, many national governments also entered into new cooperative agreements with near neighbours, spawning a new regionalism internationally, as well as subnationally. Unlike the old pattern of economically successful regions, one reflective of the *Cold War and strong national government control over industry, the new regionalism in the *Global North is based largely on 'clean' industries such as financial services and computer games design.

new retail geography *See* RETAILING.

new social movements *See* SOCIAL MOVEMENTS.

new town A planned urban settlement, often in a new location distant from existing settlements. New town designs are often informed by utopian ideals and intended to meet social needs, for example, by constructing well-serviced *neighbourhood communities. But they have also served to manage metropolitan decentralization, for example, in Cairo and London.

new urbanism A movement among urban architects, designers, and planners to encourage a more human-scale in settlement planning, including mixed-use neighbourhoods, restoration of pedestrian movement over automobiles, accessible public space, and high-quality design of houses and neighbourhoods. An early example of these principles was Seaside, Florida, built in 1981.

New Working Class Studies An interdisciplinary field in the social sciences and humanities devoted to understanding the experiences of working-class people and the effects of their class position on their lives. Because of the considerable influence of *Marxism on Western social science and the humanities after 1945, the working classes were a major focus of analysis, and thought to be the key political agents able to instigate progressive social change. However, after 1968, various criticisms of Marxism led to a new *identity politics in which the rights of, and oppressions experienced by women, ethnic minorities, immigrants, homosexuals, and other 'different' people were emphasized. In part because of the new round of critiques of capitalism arising from the late 1990s *anti-globalization movement, in part because it was realized that identity and class politics are intertwined, there has been a renewed interest in working-class lives. In human geography, this is evident in the vibrancy of *labour geography.

Further reading Russo, J. and Linkon, S. L. (eds.) (2005), *New Working Class Studies*.

New World, The A highly influential text in political geography composed in the wake of the First World War and published in 1921. Its author, Isaiah *Bowman, set out to describe region-by-region the threats and opportunities posed by the post-war world from the US perspective, advocating a measure of liberal interventionism in world affairs in contrast with more isolationist tendencies in US foreign policy. The US Army adopted the book as a basic geographical text at the outset of the Second World War.

New York A US city in a state of the same name. New York has over eight million inhabitants packed into five boroughs (the Bronx, Brooklyn, Manhattan, Queens, and Staten Island), and is the most densely populated city in the USA. The wider New York metropolitan region contains nineteen million people. The city was founded by Dutch colonists nearly 400 years ago as a trading post, with British colonists taking control in 1664 and renaming the city after the Duke of York. It remained a British stronghold during the American Revolutionary War (1775–83), but then became the first capital of the young United States. During the late 19th and early 20th centuries, waves of European migrants came through New York, many staying to make it America's most multilingual, ethnic, and religious city. A major port, New York's economy was large, diverse, and successful prior to the Great Depression of the 1930s, bouncing back strongly after the Second World War. Despite its government going technically bankrupt in the 1970s, New

York's recent history is one of economic success. The city is a major centre for banking and finance, other *producer services as well as the arts and popular culture (*see* GLOBAL CITY). It contains *iconic architecture (e.g. the Empire State Building and the Statue of Liberty), and iconic sites (such as Central Park and the former location of the World Trade Center). These attract over fifty million tourists a year. The city is home to the United Nations, and *Wall Street/lower Manhattan remains one of the most powerful centres of *finance capital in the world.

New Zealand An island country located in the South Pacific Ocean with two main land masses and several smaller islands. Prior to the arrival of European explorers in the mid-17th century, New Zealand was occupied by Maori peoples. New Zealand became a free-standing British colony in 1841 and subsequently attracted emigrants from the United Kingdom. This led to conflicts with the Maori, who were *dispossessed of land. New Zealand became *de facto* independent in 1907, *de jure* independent in 1947. Benefiting from its ties with Australia and Britain as part of the British Commonwealth, New Zealand's economy prospered until the 1970s when it suffered an acute recession. This led it to liberalize its economy, which remains highly export-orientated. Its population is just 4.4 million, and its capital city is the port of Wellington on the North Island. New Zealand is a representative democracy and the first country in the world to grant women equal voting rights with men.

NGO *See* NON-GOVERNMENTAL ORGANIZATION.

Nigeria A West African country with coastline on the Atlantic Ocean to the south, and bordered by the Republic of Benin in the west, Chad and Cameroon in the east, and Niger in the north. It is Africa's most populous country with an estimated 170 million inhabitants. Prior to Britain assuming control of Nigeria in 1901, it was a region in which different indigenous groups controlled different territories, some having already interacted with Europeans over the previous three centuries (e.g. as part of the West African slave trade involving Britain, the United States, and the Caribbean). Campaigns for independence came to fruition in 1960, since when Nigeria has been self-governing. The country has suffered civil war and periods of autocratic rule, though since 1999 representative democracy has been restored. The three largest and most influential ethno-linguistic groups in Nigeria are the Hausa, Igbo, and Yoruba, their historically uneasy co-existence a function of the political borders created by the British. The Nigerian economy is the second largest in Africa measured by GDP, with oil exports being a major revenue generator (*see* PETRO-CAPITALISM). It is among the least indebted countries in Africa. Its capital city is Aduja, its largest Lagos.

Nijkamp, Peter (1946–) A prolific Dutch regional economist based at Vrije Universitat, Amsterdam. He has published widely on issues of economic development, *labour markets, *transportation, *planning, and the *space economy, and methodological issues especially relating to *spatial science and *modelling. He is also an accomplished research administrator, being active at a national and European level, and has acted as an advisor to a number of governments and international agencies.

NIMBY An acronym for Not In My Back Yard used to describe the attitude of local opponents to developments such as housing, windfarms, landfill sites, and industry in sensitive locations. The term and its associated form, NIMBYism, is usually pejorative. It is implied that opponents think only of their own local needs and preferences rather than national priorities.

node A point along a network segment or an intersection or hub. Within network analysis, a node is a specific location, such as a station, or a town, or an individual, that is linked to others by pathways. They are points of fixity and intersection, where types of activity occur before being distributed through the network. *See also* GRAPH THEORY; HUB-AND-SPOKE NETWORK; NETWORK ANALYSIS.

nomad A member of a society whose livelihood depends on constant movement with no permanent place of residence. There are three main forms of nomadism: pastoral nomads who tend herd animals in grassland regions; *hunter-gatherers; and peripatetic peoples who make a living among otherwise *sedentary peoples through their crafts or skills, a mode of existence widespread across South Asia. Nomadic practices can also be combined with arable farming and more sedentary ways of life. In recent decades the term has also been applied to highly mobile individuals in general, e.g. high-skilled transient migrants. Further, some *postmodern theorists regard nomadism as a form of wandering or rootlessness, indicative of a new condition of social and cultural life.

nominal data *See* LEVELS OF MEASUREMENT.

nominalism In philosophy, the doctrine that everything that exists is particular such that the identification of categories or universals into which particulars can be grouped is no more than semantic artifice. Thus, things denominated by the same name share nothing except that fact according to nominalists. In human geography, nominalism has come to mean a particular form of *social constructionism in which words, language, discourses, or symbols are said to have an entirely contingent relationship with the real world phenomena to which they refer. Strong nominalists are idealists and have been criticized by materialists and realists for their denial of the existence (or efficacy) of processes and events existing independently of human sense-making practices. *See also* POSTMODERNISM.

nomothetic A method of relating to the abstraction of the general or universal elements of a place or object. As a method or approach, it contrasts the *idiographic, the abstraction of particular or unique elements. As formulated by various German historians, sociologists, and philosophers at the end of the 19th century, these two approaches were deemed equally valid and complementary alternatives. Within mid-20th-century geography, however, there was a tendency to regard only nomothetic approaches as properly scientific. These were regarded as ways of finding laws in geography, for example, spatial laws (*see* SPATIAL SCIENCE). Idiographic approaches were caricatured as descriptions. Not until the 1980s was the careful historiographical work undertaken by geographers to clarify this misunderstanding.

Further reading Entrikin, J. N. and Brunn, S. D. (eds.) (1989), *Reflections on Richard Hartshorne's 'The Nature of Geography'.*

non-consequentialism An approach to moral reasoning and practice that deems an action to be right or wrong by virtue of its relation to ethical principles or arguments, not by virtue of its real world consequences. For instance, failing to help the victims of an earthquake would be seen as morally wrong by non-consequentialists because it is inhumane and careless at the level of principle, not because of the particular number of victims affected in any given case. Much moral reasoning in human geography has, so far, been non-consequentialist, deriving ethical norms from first principles and reasoned arguments. *See also* MORALITY.

non-governmental organization (NGO) A non-profit, legally constituted organization that operates on behalf of citizens independently from any government. The term 'NGO' was first used by the *United Nations (UN) in 1945 to differentiate participation rights with respect to intergovernmental agencies and international private organizations. NGOs referred to the latter, which the UN recognized and consulted, but which did not having voting status. Since then, NGOs have proliferated globally and are a well-established and important part of civil society. Typically, they represent the interests of citizens against the interests of the state and private businesses and are diverse in nature, usually organized with respect to specific issues such as *human rights, access and provision of services, and political, social, economic, and environmental issues. In some cases, NGOs actively campaign on particular issues seeking transformation through legal and policy changes; in other cases NGOs become service providers, part of what some call the 'third sector'. NGOs can be local, regional, national, or international in their scope, seeking to influence and shape agendas at their respective scale. To be recognized as an NGO by the UN, the organization must be voluntary and non-profit making, not be tied to any political party, not linked to any criminal organization, be non-violent in its activities, and, in cases where an NGO receives state funding, government officials are generally excluded from its membership and management boards to ensure its independence. Given the rise of public-private partnerships, the relationship between state and NGOs is blurring with the emergence of government-organized NGOs (GONGOs), especially in developing countries, and quasi-non-governmental organizations (QUANGOs). *See also* CIVIL SOCIETY.

non-parametric statistics A suite of statistical procedures and tests for analysing nominal or ordinal level data, that is, noncontinuous data such as categories. The tests make no assumptions about the probability distributions of the variables being tested. *See also* LEVELS OF MEASUREMENT; PARAMETRIC STATISTICS.

non-place A location or route whose appearance is not sufficiently unique or meaningful for people to consider it to be a *place. The term was popularized by French anthropologist Marc Augé. Motorways, chain hotels, airports, and supermarkets are all 'non-places' for Augé because they appear the same or similar regardless of where they are situated in time and space. *See also* PLACELESSNESS.

non-profit organization *See* NON-GOVERNMENTAL ORGANIZATION.

non-renewable resources *See* NATURAL RESOURCES.

non-representational theory An approach to the means and ends of human geographic inquiry that takes issue with a focus on *representation, cognition, and perception at the expense of the unconscious, *haptic knowledge, and practical dimensions of human existence. The approach (hereafter NRT) was first explicitly advocated by British geographer Nigel *Thrift in a series of publications, including a book of the same name (2007), in which he drew upon a wide range of pre-existing work across several disciplines. Despite its name, NRT is not a *theory in the conventional sense of the term. Instead, it comprises a set of tenets designed to orientate research in human geography and the wider social sciences. These tenets all presuppose the insufficiency of research preoccupied with conscious thought and the translation of such thought into verbal, written, or graphic signs and symbols.

Thrift argued that too much research in human geography inspired by the insights of *postmodernism and *post-structuralism was so preoccupied. For him, this was problematic in several ways. First, it overlooked the role of the unconscious or pre-conscious in governing what people think, feel, and do. Second, it also failed to attend to the important role of emotions in people's lives, such as love, stress, anxiety, and excitement. Third, it paid insufficient attention to embodiment because it focused on the mind (its contents and products). Yet embodiment, Thrift argued, affects thought and feeling continuously; for instance, to inhabit a pregnant, disabled, or obese body is to think and feel in ways that are likely to be very dissimilar. Finally, Thrift and other proponents of NRT argued that more emphasis on practice was needed. Practice, they argued, is not simply the product of conscious reasoning nor a direct reflection of what a person is feeling. Instead, it is often habitual, often unthinking, often improvised, often spontaneous, and often reacts back on thought and feeling iteratively (*see* PERFORMATIVITY). In sum, NRT regards human existence as *equally* mental and physical, as embodied and practical. As such, dualisms (e.g. mind versus body, representation versus reality) are unhelpful in our analysis. It is a holistic approach that aims to understand people as complex, situated actors operating in very specific circumstances and fashioning particular time-space pathways in conditions not entirely of their own making. Life is seen as a series of 'presentations' or doings, ones responsive to but also able to affect mind and body.

The approach has significant methodological, topical, and ethical-political implications for research in human geography. First, it suggests the need to expand the toolkit of *qualitative research methods used in the discipline. To date, these have sought to elicit and take seriously the perceptions, opinions, understandings, and values of various people. They have largely failed to observe people's practice (what they do, rather than what they say, or even what they say they do). Second, NRT extends the range of legitimate topics of geographical interest. Things such as walking, dancing, climbing, and travelling are all deeply geographical insofar as they involve movements in and through places, landscapes, borders, and environments. Third, where much political thinking in human geography has been systematic, rationalist, and directed towards achieving a clearly defined end (e.g. the emancipation of women in *feminist geography), NRT is interested in a politics of openness where novelty, surprise, and creativity might be cultivated. It is suspicious of muscular forms of political reasoning and of encompassing moral systems or ethical norms. It accents the diverse and changeable forms that political and ethical action takes and could take in the future. The implication is that academic disciplines such as human geography exist to 'enliven' the world by multiplying the possibilities in it, rather than seeking to impose analytical or normative order.

In its early incarnations, NRT made considerable reference to continental European philosophers and lacked an empirical base. However, many scholars have now published detailed case studies of *affect, *embodiment, and human practice. Even so, some critics regard it as a largely philosophical approach that is over-reacting to the perceived limitations of previous research. These critics have voiced two specific concerns. First, they argue that representations—their content and effects—still matter enormously in everyday life. Think of maps, newspapers, websites, or books like this dictionary. Second, they argue that NRT pays insufficient attention to the social relations that govern people's lives, including relations of power. Embodiment, emotion, and action, the critics argue, are all structured by (indeed often used in the direct service of) powerful rules, norms, and institutions. In fairness to some advocates of NRT, they seek to incorporate both criticisms into their approach and dispute the suggestion that theirs is an anti-representational doctrine uninterested in inequality, suffering, or injustice. Many prefer the description 'more than representational' to admit the continued significance of representation. NRT seems set to continue to evolve and remain a vibrant approach in human geography. *See also* AFFECT; ASSEMBLAGE; PHENOMENOLOGY.

Further reading Adey, P. (2010), *Mobility*.
Lorimer, H. (2005), 'Cultural geography: the busyness of being "more than representational"', *Progress in Human Geography* 29: 83–94.
Thrift, N. (2004), 'Summoning life', in Cloke, P., Crang, P., and Goodwin, M. (eds.) *Envisioning Human Geographies*, 81–103.

non-response The rate of non-completion amongst a sample in a survey. For example, if 1000 questionnaires were distributed and 100 were not completed and returned, the non-response rate will be 10 per cent. The rate of non-response can create a bias in the results if a large proportion of people holding certain views fail to respond as the data will not reflect their views, thereby skewing the answers of the sample.

normal distribution The expected probability distribution of data around a mean given normal conditions. Much continuous data, such as people's height or wealth, is normally distributed, with most people being close to the mean and incidents falling away the further one moves from the mean (see Fig. 8). As such, when graphed a normal distribution appears as a bell-shaped curve around the mean. The rate of variance from the mean is measured as the *standard deviation, with small deviations leading to a steep distribution curve and a high deviation to a relatively flat curve. Non-normal distributions result in curves that are noticeably skewed.

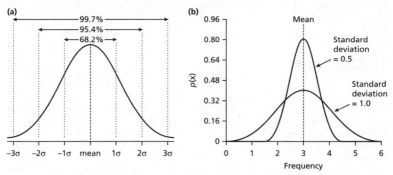

Fig. 8 (a) a normal distribution (b) a distribution for the same mean but different standard deviations (source: Kitchin and Tate 2000: 103)

normative theory Any *theory that states standards, values, or concrete proposals that involve criticism of present arrangements and thus calls for change in order to create a better future. A great deal of scholarship in the social sciences and humanities is normative. Most political and moral theory is explicitly normative (it prescribes standards and values); so too most applied social science (e.g. town planning) because it translates normative reasoning into practical measures. However, much scholarship is implicitly normative (it criticizes the present without explicitly justifying the standards or values underpinning the criticisms, or discussing what feasible future alternatives are implied by these criticisms).

In human geography, much of the research that inquires into morality, *ethics, and *justice is explicitly normative. It utilizes one or other normative theories (e.g. liberal or socialist) when examining a geographical issue such as inequalities in human life expectancy or the global environmental effects of Western lifestyles. However, arguably there is far more research in human geography that is implicitly normative, and whose criticisms of the present-day world need to be more rigorously justified and whose preferred futures need to pass the test of feasibility (are they mere utopias?). This is the view of Andrew *Sayer, who, with Elizabeth Olson, had enjoined self-styled 'critical human geographers' to incorporate normative theory more fully and more overtly into the research they conduct. Sayer and Olson argue that a problematic fact-value dichotomy in social science has led these geographers to under-emphasize normative arguments and proposals, as if their criticisms follow 'obviously' from facts. Sayer and Olson conclude that a 'normative turn' is now required, extending well beyond the efforts of moral geographers such as David M. Smith (*see* MORAL GEOGRAPHIES).

Further reading Sayer, A. and Olson, E. (2009), 'Radical geography and its critical standpoints', *Antipode* 41, 1: 180–98.

North America A continent located in the northern hemisphere and bordered to the north by the Arctic Ocean, to the east by the Atlantic Ocean, to the west by the Pacific Ocean, and to the south by South America. Its population is approximately 530 million, most of whom are citizens of the *United States and *Canada. *Mexico is generally considered part of North America, as are sometimes the countries of the Caribbean, *Central America, and Greenland.

North American Free Trade Agreement (NAFTA) A free trade agreement between Canada, Mexico, and the United States that came into effect in 1994. NAFTA first reduced and later eliminated trade and investment tariffs between the three countries, creating the world's largest trading block by size and population.

(((⊕))) SEE WEB LINKS
• Secretariat of the North American Free Trade Agreement.

North–South divide A cartographic metaphor for spatial and social *inequality, as well as an often imprecise geographical description for regional differences. The distinction between Global North and South as a summary description of world economic inequality was popularized in the 1980s by the *Brandt Commission. But the notion of a north–south divide has also been applied to Africa and the European Union, Italy, France, and many countries of the African Sahel such as Chad and the Ivory Coast. The term is frequently used in the UK to distinguish between a supposedly wealthy, productive, but unfriendly South and a poorer, more dependent, but friendlier North. The roots of this division are apparent in early 19th-century fiction, when in fact the north was the forward-looking and productive region but the discourse of north–south resurfaces particularly during times of recession. In 1980, the Black Report uncovered serious regional health inequalities, and later research has established marked differences in educational attainment (Dorling 2011). But inequalities within regions are almost always greater than between them.

Reference Dorling, D. (2011), *Injustice: Why Social Inequality Persists*.

nuclear power The energy and heat generated by the controlled reaction (fission) of uranium inside a nuclear reactor. By heating water or another coolant and using the resultant steam to drive turbines, it can generate electricity. This is often described as a source of clean or *renewable energy because it does not depend on fossil fuels and does not produce as much excess CO_2 as other forms (*see* ENERGY; LOW-CARBON ECONOMY). For this reason, nuclear power is often invoked as a technical solution to *global warming. Some 14–15 per cent of the world's electricity is already generated from nuclear power, and in some countries, notably France, it is the major source of electricity. The main obstacles to wider adoption are cost, including the unknown costs of the treatment and long-term secure storage of the radioactive by-products of nuclear fission, and public acceptability. The catastrophic failure of the nuclear power reactors in Fukushima, Japan, in March 2011, led not only to the suspension of generation by that means in Japan, but also Germany's announcement that it would phase out nuclear power by 2022. Further, the use of nuclear technology to produce weapons concerns many peace activists. Although the Non-Proliferation Treaty (1970) is supposed to prevent crossover between civilian and military uses of nuclear science, it has proved difficult to enforce.

Nuclear power was developed in the 1950s and for some commentators it marked the beginning of a new era. There have been both optimistic and alarmist responses. In formulating his idea of the *risk society, Ulrich Beck regarded nuclear power as the chief example of a *hazard produced from within techno-science. In the past, science shielded society from harm; now it produces it. The disastrous accident at the Chernobyl plant in Ukraine in 1986, which blighted the surrounding area, caused 100,000 people to be evacuated, and released a plume of radioactive material across Western Europe, illustrated the difficulties of managing and anticipating risk (*see* DISASTER). There is limited geographical research on nuclear power. British geographer Stan Openshaw used advanced spatial analysis to both critique official accounts of where plants could be located and examine the potential relation between them and the clustering of childhood leukaemia. In the USA, a serious nuclear accident at Three Mile Island, Harrisburg, Pennsylvania in 1979, stimulated interest in the geographical problems of evacuation. Among the problems were that some people over-react, i.e. flee from areas outside the designated evacuation zone and add to the traffic on roads, but some under-react, and decline to leave altogether.

Further reading Blowers, A. and Openshaw, S. (eds.) (1987), *Nuclear Power in Crisis.*

null hypothesis *See* HYPOTHESIS.

n

O

obesogenic environments The spatial arrangements and lifestyles that encourage high energy intake and sedentary patterns of behaviour, thus fostering obesity. Such environments, through their dispersed spatial organization, encourage vehicular travel rather than walking or cycling, reducing active exercise. Conversely, one way to reduce obesity is design environments that encourage active lifestyles.

Object-Based Image Analysis (OBIA) A method for analysing *remote sensing imagery to identify meaningful image-objects in the landscape and to assess their spatial, spectral, and temporal characteristics. The technique has been made possible by the advent of high-resolution images and sophisticated pattern recognition algorithms that segment images.

objectivity 1. In scientific inquiry the principle that facts should be able to speak for themselves.
2. More generally, an ethic of impartiality in which a person analyses or judges things without bringing their own values, preferences, or prejudices to bear.
In the second sense, objectivity has been practised for centuries, but in the first sense, objectivity is a product of the *Enlightenment and part of science's challenge to both religion and superstition. Human geographers generally aim for objectivity in the second sense, which is to say that they refrain from dogmatism and seek to analyse arguments, concepts, and the world in reasoned ways. In the first sense, objectivity was a key feature of *spatial science, and lives on in its latter-day variants. Objectivity here involves using a mixture of abduction, *deduction, *induction, and *logic to describe, explain, and/or assess evidence and/or the scientific claims of other researchers. The world of objects is observed and allowed, as it were, to 'object' to any particular *hypothesis designed to characterize it. However, critics argue that all supposed 'objectivity' is inevitably reflective of the values, goals, and experiences of researchers, as *Science and Technology Studies reveals. *See also* OBSERVATION.

observation 1. The general act of observing the self or the world.
2. The systematic act of observing the characteristics or behaviour of any phenomena of interest to an analyst. Observation in the second sense is a signature feature of all academic research, exemplified in the mid-19th century by Charles *Darwin. In *science, observation is fundamental because it permits the analyst to test a *hypothesis through a mix of empirical *verification and *falsification. Observation is part of human geographers' *modus operandi*, not least because geography is the study of visible phenomena on or near the Earth's surface. However, the reliance on *vision involved (*see* OCULAR-CENTRISM) has been criticized by some because, they argue, it creates a problematic distance between the observer and the observed. While this distance is supposed to ensure *objectivity, critics claim that it can lead to misunderstanding because of a failure to engage with or get close to that being analysed. *See also* PARTICIPANT OBSERVATION.

Occidentalism The negative images or stereotypes of the *West, originating from other world regions. Coined in the 1980s, it was intended as an inversion of the better-known concept of *Orientalism.

Further reading Bonnett, A. (2004), *The Idea of the West*.

Oceania A region of the South Pacific Ocean comprised of numerous peninsulas, islands, archipelagos, and atolls. The term dates from 1812, and since then has been applied inconsistently, sometimes including the coastal area of *Southeast Asia, *Australia, *New Zealand, and everything in-between and to the east, but sometimes excluding the former. Excluding Australia and the region to its immediate north, Oceania has been said to comprise the island groups of Melanesia, Micronesia, and Polynesia. Including the former, Oceania's landmasses are enormously varied in size. The region's climate and ecosystems are tropical and subtropical in the main, becoming temperate in southern Australia, Tasmania, and New Zealand. Most of Oceania's territories are self-governing, but several islands are administered by the United States, Britain, and France.

ocularcentrism A mode of apprehending the world that emphasizes *vision and phenomena perceptible to the human eye. Science can be said to be ocularcentric because it is deeply committed to *observation as a means of registering the real and testing hypotheses. The same can be said of geography, both physical and human, because its *raison d'être* is to describe, explain, and (sometimes) predict the arrangement of phenomena on the surface of the Earth. A number of *feminist geographers, among others, have criticized this ocularcentrism because it has allowed geographers to objectify the world (*see* GAZE). In other words, reliance on vision, they argue, places an often damaging distance between observer and the observed, which can fatally distort the former's understanding of the latter.

OECD (Organization of Economic Cooperation and Development) An organization spanning thirty-four countries that promotes social and economic development. The OECD has its roots in the Organization for European Economic Cooperation (OEEC), a body established in 1947 to oversee the US-financed Marshall Plan for the reconstruction of Europe after the *Second World War. The addition of the USA and Canada led to the rebranding as the OECD in 1961. The OECD generates comparative economic data and measures global trends in development, using these to formulate policy advice that advances a vision of market economies backed by democratic institutions.

(⊕) SEE WEB LINKS
• The official website of the OECD.

offshoring The movement of a business activity undertaken by a company in one country to the same or another company in a different country. Offshoring can involve a firm's core business (e.g. manufacturing shoes) or its support services (e.g. accounting). It became common from the 1970s onwards as Western multinational companies sought to reduce their costs and/or enter new overseas markets. The process is ongoing and involves firms worldwide. *See also* NEAR-SHORING.

oil crisis An economic crisis in the early 1970s caused by the embargo of oil exports by the *Organization of Petroleum Exporting Countries (OPEC) in response to Western foreign policy in the Middle East. The embargo lasted from October 1973 to March 1974, but was followed by higher global oil prices. Given the importance of oil to national economies worldwide, its induced scarcity had dramatic effects on productivity and led to rises in inflation, suppressing economic activity, and inducing recession. The effects of the crisis persisted for many years and arguably speeded up processes of post-industrialization. *See also* PEAK OIL.

Olsson, Gunnar (1935–) A Swedish geographer who has divided his career between Sweden and the United States. Initially he trained as a quantitative human geographer, but by the early 1970s had become disillusioned with its certainties and exactitudes. Instead he turned to linguistic philosophy in order to critique positivist epistemology, as best exemplified by his book *Birds in Egg/Eggs in Bird* (1980). In order to try and get beyond the limits of language he has undertaken experimental writing and abstract sculpture to examine the questions 'what is truth?' and 'how does knowledge become taken for granted?'.

Olympic Games An international festival of *sport held every four years. Summer Olympics and Winter Olympics feature different sports and are staggered such that one follows the other at two-year intervals. These are accompanied by Paralympics for athletes with physical disabilities and by Youth Games. The modern games date from 1896. From small beginnings they have assumed enormous significance as anchors of the globalization of sport, sporting-related industries, and transnational capital in general, but also as moments for national competitiveness and geopolitical rivalry. The events in Moscow (1980) and Los Angeles (1984) were widely boycotted because of *Cold War tensions. Geographers are interested in all aspects of the Olympics, with particular attention paid to their role in *urban regeneration and *city marketing.

ontology A set of beliefs and arguments about what exists or is real. While some ontologies refer to 'timeless' phenomena, such as gravity or matter, others refer to historically or geographically contingent phenomena, such as gender relations or racism. Knowingly or not, all people have an ontology, though only philosophers devote their careers to presenting and debating them in fine detail. All academic disciplines are characterized by ontological entities believed to exist, and which are the focus of much conceptual debate and empirical research. In human geography, these include *landscape, *scale, *space, *place, and *region. Indeed, human geographers have done much to detail the ontological characteristics of these, albeit in non-metaphysical ways that attend to their social construction rather than *a priori* character. More generally, most human geographers have accepted that the biophysical world is ontologically different and distinct from the social world made by people (though the existence of this supposed ontological divide has recently been questioned). This broad consensus notwithstanding, human geographers divide between those whose ontology is largely Cartesian (*see* CARTESIANISM), and those whose ontology is largely relational (*see* ACTOR-NETWORK THEORY; HOLISM). The former presume the world to be cleaved into distinct parts (e.g. categories of people or zones) which then enter into or withdraw from relations structured by rules, norms, or goals. The latter, by contrast, presume the world to be a meshwork of relations such that 'things' cannot be defined *a priori* or in isolation from the contexts in which they exist. Broadly speaking, those schooled in approaches whose roots lie in *spatial science have a Cartesian ontology, while those schooled in *Marxist geography, many strands of feminist geography, *non-representational theory, and ANT are relationalists for whom things and relations, causes and effects, the local and the global are but sides of the same coin. *Critical realism's rich ontological vocabulary, though no longer influential in human geography, sought to beat a middle path between these otherwise opposed ontological terrains.

All ontologies involve epistemological commitments on the part of ordinary people as well as researchers. An *epistemology comprises a set of beliefs and arguments about how we can reliably acquire knowledge about those things we take to exist or be real. For example, an *empiricist maintains that only perceptible evidence ('facts') can give us knowledge of reality, meaning, in turn, that anything that cannot be inferred, deduced, or abducted directly from evidence cannot be said to exist. Many Marxists, by contrast, regard much perceptible evidence as misleading, such that it conceals relations and processes whose reality must be revealed by *abstraction because they are phenomenally invisible. Many rightly argue that ontology and epistemology are not readily separable. For example, critics of *postmodernism in human geography argued that it reduced the latter to the former in ways tantamount to *idealism.

In the main, human geographers have been better at stating their ontological beliefs than defending them against challenges from rival ontological perspectives. This pattern was established in the 1970s when humanistic and Marxist geographers largely talked past each other in their attempts to focus on human experience and intentionality on the one side, and the spatial dynamics of capital *accumulation on the other side. It also reflects the fact that most human geographers see philosophical reasoning as a means to other ends, ends pertaining to the theories, models, research methods, locations, and topics they are ultimately interested in. Among the few contemporary exceptions to this is Swedish geographer Gunnar *Olsson.

OPEC *See* ORGANIZATION OF PETROLEUM EXPORTING COUNTRIES.

open data The data that is freely available to everyone to use, analyse, display, and distribute for any purpose. Traditionally, social, economic, environmental, and spatial data have been generated and held by governments and companies, who own and control the data copyright, and restrict its use and purposes (*see* INTELLECTUAL PROPERTY RIGHTS). While much data continues to be generated by these agents, the philosophy of data sharing has been transformed to make the data freely available. From a government perspective, it is acknowledged that data has already been paid for by the taxpayer and that restricting access through payment limits its use and the potential to create additional value. *See also* BIG DATA; CROWD-SOURCING; OPEN SOURCE GIS.

open source GIS A *GIS software that is free to use, but also provides access to the source code enabling users to modify and extend the programs. Open source GIS is part of the wider open-source initiative that sees a move away from expensive, proprietary software developed by commercial vendors to free-to-access software. It is accompanied by a similar shift to *open data, wherein data is made freely available for analysis.

opportunity costs The costs of any activity measured in terms of the *value of the next best alternative not chosen. Opportunity costs arise when a person or organization has several options available and is seeking to determine which one is best when all the options cannot be pursued at the same time. The costs involved are relative, arising from a comparison of the benefits of pursuing option A as compared to not pursuing option B or C. Opportunity costs is a key idea in economics because *money, given its ability to purchase a huge range of different goods, services and assets, allows people to quantify the costs of otherwise incommensurable options according to a single measure. In economic geography, opportunity costs are relevant to the locational decision-making of firms regarding everything from whether and where to offshore or outsource, to deciding which new markets to enter overseas. *See also* OFFSHORING; OUTSOURCING.

optimization problem The problem of finding the best solution from a set of all possible solutions. In geography, optimization problems usually refer to finding the best location for a facility that maximizes benefits and minimizes negative effects. This might include trying to determine the best place to live or to locate a factory or a shop. *See also* CENTRAL PLACE THEORY; HOTELLING MODEL.

oral history The collection of living people's testimony about their own experiences. Oral history is concerned with first-hand knowledge of people, events, and places. Interviews are recorded, transcribed, and placed in historical context. Oral history complements archival and documentary research by providing the recollections and observations of participants. Where oral histories focus on the biographies of individuals, as opposed to places or events, they are often referred to as life histories. Testimony is often archived to preserve the past and provide future material for historical research. *See also* BIOGRAPHICAL APPROACHES.

ordinal data *See* LEVELS OF MEASUREMENT.

Ordnance Survey The British state mapping agency, first established in 1791 by the Board of Ordnance to undertake surveying and mapping of Britain. The agency has been at the forefront of state and commercial surveying and mapping developments, including new digital map data and products. It has also played an important role in British colonialism, with mapping a key strategy in conquest and administration.

(⊕) SEE WEB LINKS
• Website of the Ordnance Survey.

organic intellectual *See* INTELLECTUAL.

Organization of Petroleum Exporting Countries (OPEC) An inter-governmental organization created at the Baghdad Conference in 1960, that seeks to coordinate and unify petroleum policies among member countries, and stabilize prices and oil supply. The five founding members were Iran, Iraq, Kuwait, Saudi Arabia, and Venezuela, later joined by Qatar, Indonesia, Libya, United Arab Emirates, Algeria, Nigeria, Ecuador, Angola, and Gabon. OPEC gained prominence in the early 1970s with the *oil crisis, which led them to take a more powerful position in the global oil market and increased the political power of member countries. OPEC's ability to control the oil market has lessened in recent years with the discovery of significant oil deposits in non-member countries, but it remains a significant force.

(⊕) SEE WEB LINKS
• Official website of the Organization of Petroleum Exporting Countries.

Oriental Despotism The proposition that Asian societies that developed based on large-scale organized irrigation systems were not capable of achieving the kind of democratic government thought to typify the *West (*see* ASIATIC MODE OF PRODUCTION; HYDRAULIC SOCIETY). Versions of the thesis can be found in the works of Karl *Marx and Max Weber, and were elaborated by German-American geographer Karl Wittfogel in 1957.

Orientalism 1. An aesthetic 18th- and 19th-century movement in art, literature, and architecture that sought inspiration in 'oriental' motifs and themes.
2. The study of countries and regions in 'the Orient'.
3. A discourse of knowledge about the Orient produced by colonial and Western powers from the 19th century onwards.
It is the latter understanding of Orientalism as a discourse that geographers have recently engaged with. Developed by the Palestinian-American cultural critic Edward *Said, and rooted in *post-structural theory, especially that developed by Michel *Foucault, Orientalism refers to the ideas, thoughts, and depictions of the East articulated by Europeans and North Americans that cast the West as being intellectually and culturally superior to the East. This in turn reproduces and legitimizes Western hegemony and its

policy towards and presence in the East (*see* COLONIALISM). In essence, Orientalism is a regime of knowledge and *power that constructs *imaginative geographies of the East through a process of *othering in which Eastern culture is portrayed as underdeveloped, inferior, irrational, threatening, and exotic. These imaginative geographies do not simply describe and teach, but also work to produce the Orient by shaping cultural encounters, Western policy, and interventions. Said's book, *Orientalism* (1978), was enormously important in the development of *postcolonial theory that sought to document and explain the relationships between colonizer and colonized, and his notion of imaginative geographies has been widely adopted within cultural and political geography, most notably by Derek *Gregory. Despite widespread academic critique, Orientalist discourse remains prevalent in popular understandings of 'oriental culture', cultural encounters with people originating in these countries, foreign policy strategies, and interventions directed by the West towards 'oriental states' in the East.

Further reading Gregory, D. (2004), *The Colonial Present*.
Mitchell, T. (1988), *Colonising Egypt*.

O' Riordan, Tim (1942–) A British environmental scientist who has made major contributions to analysing *environmental policy, environmental appraisal and evaluation, *environmental governance and decision-making, and *sustainable development. His best-known book is *Environmentalism* (1st ed. 1976) which provided an overarching survey of environmental ideologies, politics, policy, and practice.

Other, the A person or group of people who are perceived to be different in some fundamental way from oneself and the group one perceives one belongs to. Otherness refers to defining characteristics of the Other, and othering is the process whereby otherness is mobilized to produce in- and out-groups within society and to justify the way in which Others are treated. For example, disabled people are often perceived and treated differently from able-bodied people, cast as the Other on the grounds of their impairment. Others are often defined by race, ethnicity, gender, and sexuality.

Further reading Sibley, D. (1995), *Geographies of Exclusion: Society and Difference in the West*.

Ó Tuathail, Gearóid (Gerard Toal) (1962–) An Irish political geographer who has been a key proponent of *critical geopolitics, currently at Virginia Tech. Using a *poststructural lens, through a series of detailed empirical studies of the Balkans and Caucasus region he has examined and theorized the political discourses and manoeuvrings that sustain and justify the practices of *power, including *ethnic cleansing. His best-known work is *Critical Geopolitics* (1996), which proposed a new approach to understanding geopolitics that took issue with realist and political economy approaches.

outsourcing The process of contracting-out a business activity, which an organization may have previously performed internally, to an independent firm where the process is purchased as a service. Outsourcing covers commodity manufacture and business services, though not necessarily both in the case of any one firm at any one time. The term became popular in business circles in the 1970s, as large vertically- and horizontally-integrated companies began to downsize and aimed to cut their operating costs. Outsourcing overseas is part of the wider phenomenon of *offshoring. Outsourcing can give firms a cost advantage and greater strategic flexibility than if they provide a business service themselves. *See also* SUPPLY CHAIN.

overdetermination An observed change or continuity in the behaviour of one or more phenomena that has several causes simultaneously, none of which may be sufficient alone but some of which are necessary. The term was coined by the psychoanalyst Sigmund Freud in 1913 when discussing the content of his patients' dreams. In social science it was popularized by *Marxist philosopher Louis Althusser in the 1960s in his critique of orthodox *Marxism. Althusser searched for concepts able to recognize what he saw as the dominance of the capitalist *mode of production in the modern world, without resorting to a crude economic determinism that discounted all sorts of important non-capitalist relations, customs, institutions, and processes. In human geography, the term was used by the neo-Marxist economic geographers Julie Graham and Kathy Gibson before *postmodernism and *post-structuralism inspired them to become the post-Marxist J-K *Gibson-Graham. In their hands, it was an attempt to rescue *Marxist geography from an over-emphasis on the supposed power of *capitalism to (re)shape the world's human (and non-human) geography. However, Glassman maintains that Gibson-Graham's attempt to rescue a Marxian concept of causality in the analysis of open systems goes too far, declining into an incoherent 'everythingism'.

Reference Glassman, J. (2003), 'Rethinking overdetermination, structural power, and social change', *Antipode 35*, 4: 678–698.

overlay The process of draping layers of map information on top of each other. Such a process exposes how categories of data intersect and can reveal important patterns of convergence and divergence. In his classic study The *Structure and Growth of Residential Neighborhoods in American Cities* (1939), Hoyt overlaid areas of low rent, high percentage of buildings needing major repairs, older building stock, and high percentage non-white population, which revealed a very strong overlap of these areas, suggesting a strong correlation between variables. Overlay is an important function in all *GIS packages used to reveal spatial overlap and patterns.

Further reading Ahlqvist, O. (2009), 'Overlay', in *International Encyclopedia of Human Geography* 8: 48–55.

overpopulation *See* MALTHUSIANISM.

ownership *See* PROPERTY.

Paasi, Anssi (1955–) A Finnish political geographer who has made a number of insightful contributions to the theorizing and study of *borders and *regions. The principal aim of his research is to explain how regions become recognizable territories that people identify with, developing the notion of the institutionalization of regions in which territory is socio-spatially constructed along with an associated socio-spatial consciousness, as exemplified in his book, *Territories, Boundaries and Consciousness* (1997).

Pacific Rim A number of countries and parts of countries that share a Pacific Ocean coastline. The term has become common in geopolitical and *geoeconomic discourse since the late 1980s because of the growing importance of *China, *South Korea, *Singapore, *India, *Russia, and *Australia on the world stage.

Pakistan An Islamic republic located in South Asia and bordered by *India to the east, *Afghanistan to the west and north, *Iran to the southwest, and *China in the far northeast. Roughly the size of Britain and France combined, it has ocean access via the Arabian Sea. Historically, Pakistan was home to the Bronze Age Indus Valley (or Harappan) civilization. Created as a result of the British India Independence Act of 1947, Pakistan remains a largely Muslim country. There were initially two geographically separated parts, West and East Pakistan, but following civil war in 1971 the latter became independent as Bangladesh. Politically, periods of military rule have been punctuated by civilian rule and, as a democracy, it remains somewhat fragile. Economically, it is a developing economy, with significant exports of wheat, clothing, and textiles. It spans several climatic zones (arid, tropical humid, and sub-tropical humid), and its northeastern parts reach into the Himalayan mountains. Relations with neighbouring India remain tense, while it assisted the USA and its allies in the so-called 'war on terror' in *Iraq and neighbouring Afghanistan from 2003.

Palestine A disputed territory in the *Middle East, located between the shores of the eastern Mediterranean Sea and the River Jordan. After the state of *Israel was created in 1948, millions of Jews (most from Europe) migrated to Palestine, while many Muslims moved outside Israel's new borders into adjacent territories. Israel's existence, never mind its exact boundaries, was immediately contentious, with many Arabs perceiving the new Jewish state as appropriating their *territory. Subsequent friction between Israel and its neighbours led to armed conflict and expansion into adjacent areas, notably the West Bank and the Gaza Strip. The expansion has been contested by Palestine liberation fighters, leading to Israeli retaliations and international attempts to mediate through diplomacy. Modern-day Palestine comprises the West Bank and Gaza, both administered by the Palestinian Authority which, though internationally recognized in many respects, is not a fully *sovereign state.

pandemic The condition when an infectious disease moves from being a local epidemic to a global phenomenon affecting millions of people. There have been many such pandemics, for example, the Black Death in the 14th century, Spanish Flu in the early

20th century, and HIV/AIDS at the end of the 20th century. In each case, millions of people were infected, with a great many dying due to associated illnesses. Geographers are interested in documenting the spatial processes of diffusion that create pandemics. *See also* DIFFUSION; EPIDEMIOLOGY.

panel study A form of longitudinal study that tracks a cohort of individuals over a period of time. The panel shares some characteristic, such as all having the same medical condition or being born on the same day. Data is collected at defined periods, such as every three months or every five years, depending on what is being studied. Often a range of panels are established to enable within- and across-panel analysis. *See also* COHORT ANALYSIS; LONGITUDINAL DATA ANALYSIS.

Panopticon A model design for a building enabling individuals to be continually observed in isolation from one another and in ignorance of whether they were actually being observed at any particular moment. Philosopher Jeremy Bentham conceived of the plan in 1791, intending it to be used for prisons but also other sites, such as hospitals and poor-houses, in which individuals were under surveillance. The basic design involves a central point of observation around which individual cells are organized and through which light can pass, so revealing the cell's inhabitant. This enlightened form of observation not only contrasted with the use of restraint or darkness as means of punishment, but, according to Bentham, it also encouraged self-discipline. Though a few examples were actually built, the Panopticon is better known through the work of Michel *Foucault, and his book *Discipline and Punish* (1978). It illustrated his concept of disciplinary power.

paradigm A way of thinking about and practically interrogating the world common to a substantial proportion of researchers in a given discipline at any one moment in time. The term was made famous by historian of science Thomas *Kuhn, in his highly influential book *The Structure of Scientific Revolutions* (1962). This text described changes in the natural sciences (e.g. physics) since the *Enlightenment. Though Kuhn's definition of the term was inconsistent, interpreters understood him to say that disciplines tend to be dominated by a single paradigm until a new one revolutionizes thinking. 'Normal science', as he called it, involves most researchers in a discipline working on a standard set of issues, posing recognized questions, utilizing accepted methods, and usually arriving at conclusions that add to knowledge incrementally. However, periodically, paradigm-shifting research is conducted, be it purely conceptual or formal, or more empirical (e.g. a century ago Albert Einstein's theory of relatively posed a fundamental challenge to the Newtonian paradigm in Western physics). Because a new paradigm in effect 'speaks a different language' from the old one, Kuhn argued that its success depends on enough researchers having the courage to jump on the new bandwagon rather than play it safe.

The paradigm concept, as developed by Kuhn, has proven influential in how academics think about change in their various disciplines. In the 1960s, Richard Chorley and Peter *Haggett referred to it in their path-breaking collection *Models in Geography* (1967), which sought to develop the new *spatial science that was then superseding an older regional, descriptive, and *idiographic form of geographical inquiry. Later, in his book *Geography and Geographers* (1979), Ron *Johnston also made use of it to characterize human geography's multi-paradigm status, with spatial science, humanistic and Marxist geography all, as he saw it, vying for dominance in the 1980s. However, subsequently geographers found the paradigm concept unhelpful, perhaps because it was too rigid to account for the numerous intellectual currents and cross-overs that became evident from the early 1990s.

Even so, Kuhn's legacy lives on in more indirect ways through his considerable, though unintended influence on *Science and Technology Studies (STS), which has had quite an impact on parts of human geography. Despite himself, Kuhn's book suggested that scientific progress is not entirely rational, nor is it simply based on what the evidence tells scientists. Instead, science proceeds through competition and alliances among all-too-human researchers. Additionally, Kuhn's paradigm idea suggested that the world does not determine how scientists see it. Instead, paradigms act as filters or lenses that both reveal and conceal aspects of reality in different ways. These insights have been used by some recent historians of geography, notably Trevor *Barnes, to recount human geography's post-war history as a story of politics and power-plays among situated researchers who were constitutionally unable, despite the ideals of *science, to rise above their immediate contexts so that 'pure reason' and *objectivity could determine which ontologies, epistemologies, theories, models, hypotheses, or research methods they favoured.

paradoxical geographies A theoretic understanding of the production of *space arguing that spatial processes are often unrepresentable, unknowable, and contradictory in nature given that they are enacted by multiple actors and actants, often without conscious thought, who have varying aims or purposes. As a consequence, spatial relations are not easily explained but are paradoxical in nature: complex, entangled, and rhizomic. Drawing on *post-structuralism, this viewpoint argues that it is thus impossible to derive a *Grand Theory of the world as it inevitably fails to capture the evident paradoxes. Rather, all that is achievable is relational understanding of the production of space created through views from particular positions. See also SITUATED KNOWLEDGE.

Further reading Rose, G. (1993), *Feminism and Geography: the Limits of Geographical Knowledge.*

parametric statistics A suite of statistical procedures and tests for analysing interval and ratio level data, that is, continuous data such as scales. Unlike *non-parametric tests, parametric statistics take into account the probability distributions of the variables being tested. Common parametric statistics include *correlation and *regression.

parenting The rearing of children, usually by the children's parents. Parenting concerns general care, well-being, education, and socialization. Feminist research has highlighted the way in which parenting is gendered, with women expected to take a more active role and to socio-spatially structure their daily lives to provide childcare. This creates a form of spatial entrapment that limits women's lives to mirror those of their children and domestic living. Where parents become separated, the spatial lives of both children and parents becomes more complex as parenting gets stretched across two domestic sites.

Further reading Aitken, S. C. (1998), *Family Fantasies and Community Space.*

Pareto optimality A situation in which it is impossible to make some people better off without making others worse off. The concept is associated with Italian economist Vilfredo Pareto (1848–1923), and has long been a key idea in *neoclassical economics. Pareto was interested in how to allocate resources (e.g. money) among different individuals, groups, or institutions, either in one *place or else distributed across a larger *territory. Rather than any one party receiving the totality of the resources, Pareto argued that an optimal distribution ensured that all parties benefited equally, relative to their current resources. A change to a different allocation that makes at least one individual better off without making any other individual worse off is thus called a Pareto improvement. Geographically, Pareto optimality obtains in models of the *space economy that analyse the 'rational' allocation of resources by a government, firm, or investor seeking the best location/s in which to realize its ambitions (e.g. social welfare, decreased costs, or increased profits).

Paris The capital of *France and the country's largest city, with some twelve million people occupying the wider metropolitan area. It is a very important city for business, politics, culture, the arts, architecture, education, and fashion, both within the *European Union and globally. Paris is also highly multicultural, though ethnic minorities are mostly concentrated in public housing, rental accommodation, and low-income neighbour-hoods. The city is home to important international organizations such as UNESCO, the OECD, the International Chamber of Commerce, and the European Space Agency.

Park, Robert (1864–1944) An influential American sociologist who was a key figure in the *Chicago School of urban sociology. From 1887 to 1898, Park worked as a journalist before moving into the academy. After studying in Germany he returned to the United States where he took up a post at Tuskegee Institute, Alabama, before moving to the University of Chicago where he worked from 1914 to 1933. Park's research interests centred on *human ecology, collective behaviour, and race relations, especially in cities. He theorized urban environments as Darwinian ecosystems in which people collabo-rated and competed, leading to spatial divisions in social organization, and he helped put in place a framework for the systematic and holistic study of society.

participant observation A methodology in which the researcher seeks to observe events and the behaviour of people by taking part in the activity him- or herself. The idea underpinning this approach is that to fully understand a community or activity, rather than *interviewing people or observing from a distance, one has to become a member of the community and perform an activity. There are two forms of participant observation. The first is the participant as observer. In this form, the observer reveals their intentions to the observed group from the start of the project. The observer then attempts to build trusting relationships with the host community. This stance has distinct advantages because the observer can ask the community members to explain certain events to them and record events as they happen. If trusting relationships are not developed then the project will suffer greatly. The danger with such an open approach is that the community will modify its behaviour due to the presence of the researcher. The second form is covert observation wherein other participants have no knowledge that they are being studied. This research approach raises a number of *ethical questions concerning deception. It is usually justified, however, by arguing that the group would not have agreed to take part otherwise or would have acted differently if they had know about the researcher's presence. In both cases, the researcher seeks to remain an impartial and neutral observer. *See also* ETHNOGRAPHY.

participatory action research A methodology that seeks to involve the people upon whom a research project is focused as active participants in that project and to actively create change through action. Participatory action research (PAR) aims to shift the position of 'the researched' to one of co-researchers, involving them in every stage of the research process, from ideas to data generation to analysis and interpretation to writing the final report. PAR is thus an attempt to address the problems of representive-ness and unequal power arrangements between researcher and researched within social research and to create a *moral geography of social action through studies with and by research subjects. Here, the role of the academic becomes enabler or facilitator: the academic takes a supportive position and seeks to inform and impart knowledge and skills to the research subjects who co-direct the project. This strategy seeks to ensure that research focuses on the issues most relevant to a particular group and to empower the co-researchers by providing them with the tools and skills to contribute to a debate and effect change. The research is action-orientated in the sense that it seeks to actively tackle an issue of relevance to the participants. At the heart of the PAR philosophy is the belief that the best people to inform policy makers of the problems and potential solutions that people face are the people themselves—they are the 'experts' of their own experiences. An example of a PAR project would be one in which disabled people design and undertake an access survey of a town and then use the findings to campaign for changes to the built environment. *See also* ACTION RESEARCH; PARTICIPATORY RURAL APPRAISAL.

Further reading Kindon, S., Pain, R., and Kesby, M. (2007), *Participatory Action Research Approaches and Methods: Connecting People, Participation and Place.*

participatory democracy *See* DEMOCRACY.

Participatory Rural Appraisal (PRA) An approach to international aid in developing countries that aims to include rural people in the planning and management of development programmes directed at transforming their lives. PRA seeks to combine established knowledge with the views and opinions of local residents to foster development that is in tune with their aspirations. It empowers them and confers ownership of programmes to them. The approach is used extensively in rural aid programmes. *See also* PARTICIPATORY ACTION RESEARCH.

partition The division of a political territory to produce two or more territories for the purposes of separate government. In the past century, partition was often undertaken by imperial powers in the context of dismantling empires and/or attempting to address ethno-nationalist rivalries. The partition of British India into Pakistan (West and East) and India in 1947 created two independent sovereign states, although it did not avert the loss of hundreds of thousands of lives and the displacement of ten to twelve million individuals. *See also* FEDERALISM.

partnerships A mode of governance wherein different parties negotiate an agreed settlement with respect to social and economic conditions over a set period of time and work together for mutual benefit. A partnership usually brings together a mix of government, civil society organizations (*NGOs, *trades unions, church representatives, etc.), and employers, who trade issues such as work conditions, salaries and benefits, productivity targets, to create a social contract and stable political landscape, labour relations, and delivery of services.

pastoral A form of art, music, poetry, or literature that evokes a rural way of life in which humanity and nature are in harmony. Traceable as far back as Hesiod's poems in the 7th century BC, this style flourished in the *Renaissance and continues to this day as a romantic evocation of the countryside, often in opposition to the city.

pastoralism A form of *agriculture involving care for domesticated herd animals, from small-scale herding to extensive cattle ranching. Pastoral *nomads follow their herds in search of pastures. Where this requires seasonal movement between upland and lowland areas, it is termed 'transhumance'. *See also* TRAGEDY OF THE COMMONS.

path dependency A situation arising when a system or organization follows one possible path such that others become progressively more difficult to adopt. In the analysis of technological change and innovation, it can be used to explain why suboptimal arrangements persist despite alternatives. The often-cited example is how the standard QWERTY keyboard used in most computers continues to be used despite its inefficiencies. It was originally adopted to slow down operators of manual typewriters. In economic geography, especially where informed by *evolutionary economics or *institutional economics, the concept is invoked to explain how economic *clusters persist through time and how new geographical configurations are influenced, though not determined, by prior conditions.

patriarchy A system of social relations that produces inequalities that favour the interests of men over women, or otherwise empower men in general over women. *Feminist analysis reveals how this inequitable system is embedded in social, political, and economic institutions, how the domestic sphere is organized, and is reflected in and reproduced through popular discourse and the media. The result is various forms of discrimination and restricted access to *power, resources, goods, and services. Patriarchy is expressed spatially with respect to access to public space and workspaces and spatial entrapment in the home. *See also* MASCULINISM.

Further reading McDowell, L. (1999), *Gender, Identity and Place: Understanding Feminist Geographies.*

Patterned Ground: entanglements of nature and culture This book edited by Stephan Harrison, Stephen Pile, and Nigel *Thrift (2004) explored the intersection of three key concepts in human geography—landscape, nature, and culture—through 108 short essays. The author of each essay was asked to write about one element in the landscape about which they were particularly passionate, drawing out its wider significance, and how people understand it and its relationship to the world. In so doing, the book provided new ways to think about everyday parts of the landscape and their interrelation.

Pax Americana The concept of a period and region relatively free from conflict and characterized by order under the auspices of the military and political power of the USA. In Latin, *pax* means 'peace', hence the phrase means American Peace. The idea has been invoked at various times, including after the US Civil War (1865 onwards), the turn of the 19th and 20th centuries, and after the *Second World War. In more recent years, it is associated with the idea that the USA can and should be the 'world's policeman', enforcing peace by force if necessary.

peace The absence or converse of *war and conflict. Derek *Gregory argues that the distinction between war and peace has, however, become increasingly dissolved temporally and spatially as an international regime characterized by war between states gives way to one featuring war within states and the semi-permanent state of emergency implied by the War on Terror. Nick Megoran notes that geographers have paid more attention to war than peace, which deserves more attention in its own right.

Reference Gregory, D. (2010), 'War and peace', *Transactions of the Institute of British Geographers* 35, 154–86.
Megoran, N. (2010), 'Towards a geography of peace: pacific geopolitics and evangelical Christian Crusade apologies', *Transactions of the Institute of British Geographers* 35, 382–98.

peak oil The moment when extraction of crude oil reaches its highest level, after which rates permanently decline because of geophysical limits to the resource's availability. The idea that oil extraction can be depicted as a bell-shaped curve with a single highpoint was first spelled out by Shell Oil geologist M. King Hubbert in 1956. He estimated the peak based on current rates of discovery and estimates of ultimate recoverable reserves. Such models are based on a number of contentious assumptions to cope with uncertainties of supply, demand, and technology. Whether there has been or will be a peak, and if so, when, are ongoing matters of debate.

Further reading Bridge, G. (2010), 'Geographies of peak oil: the other carbon problem', *Geoforum* 41: 523–30.

Pearl River Delta A highly urbanized coastal region in *China where the Pearl River flows into the South China Sea. Located in Guangdong province, the region has experienced prodigious levels of economic growth, physical development, and population inflow since the Chinese government began to open the national economy to world trade from 1979 onwards. The delta area contains many thousands of manufacturing companies producing nearly one third of all of China's export commodities and almost 10 per cent of national *GDP. The population is estimated to be well over 60 million, concentrated in several large cities, notably Guangzhou, Shenzhen, and *Hong Kong. Though a large middle class has benefited from the region's economic success, many workers live in relative squalor. The region is also notorious for air, water, and land pollution.

peasantry A class of small-scale family farmers who have direct access to land rather than work land for wages or under conditions of slavery. Peasants rely on family members to provide enough to sustain themselves and, when conditions allow, sell some products at markets. They may own the land, rent it or be bound to labour on behalf of landowners. The peasant household is a single, relatively self-supporting unit of production, consumption, and reproduction. There is usually a well-defined division of labour by gender and generation or age. Peasant households can be communally bonded and may also be relatively egalitarian. But peasants are generally incorporated into wider societies under conditions of structural inequality and power. Under feudal conditions, for example, peasants did not own the land but worked it in return for services and a share of their product yielded to a land-holding class (SEE FEUDALISM). In communist societies, peasants farmed land owned by the state. Historians and anthropologists are interested in the forms of peasant rebellion and resistance throughout the world (Scott 1985).

Until the last third of the 20th century, most people in the world could be classified as peasants. Because *modernity is associated with industrialization and urbanization, it was commonly assumed that the peasantry would disappear over time, swallowed up by larger, capitalist farming enterprises and conditions of waged labour (*see* AGRARIAN QUESTION). They very often appear as victims of modernity, whether through colonial taxation and labour regimes, or forced collectivization of Soviet agriculture, for example. Although this may be true of Europe (Berger 1979), peasants comprise significant proportions of the population of China, India, Africa, and other countries of the developing world. Furthermore, there are signs of a resurgence in peasant farming in areas of Eastern and central Europe under post-socialist conditions. Geographers are interested in how peasant communities are incorporated or not into more urban and capitalist societies.

References Berger, J. (1979), *Pig Earth*.
Scott, J. F. (1985), *Weapons of the Weak: Everyday Forms of Peasant Resistance*.
Shanin, T. (ed.) (1988), *Peasants*.

Peck, Jamie (1962–) A British economic geographer who is a key theorist of the changing geographies of *capitalism, especially the rise of the *entrepreneurial city, *neoliberalism, and more flexible *labour markets. Peck's research interests primarily concern *political economy, economic regulation and transformation, policy making and statecraft, and employment relations, with a particular emphasis on charting the ideology, discourses, practices, and effects of *neoliberalism. His key works include *Workplace: The Social Regulation of Labor Markets* (1996), *Workfare States* (2001), and *Constructions of Neoliberal Reason* (2010). He is at the University of British Columbia, Vancouver, Canada.

peer review The evaluation of a research paper, book manuscript, or grant application by people in the same field in order to assess the quality of the argument made and its contribution to advancing that field. It is the standard approach for evaluating the quality and utility of academic work. Usually three or more peers are asked to judge a work with respect to a set of criteria. Most often this is a double-blind process, meaning the reviewers do not know the identity of the author and the author does not know who reviewed the work.

Peet, Richard (1940–) A British-born *radical geographer who has been based at Clark University in the US since 1967. Although trained as a mainstream economic geographer, in the late 1960s and early 1970s Peet argued for geography to become more socially *relevant, seeking to tackle social issues not just study them; his own research focused on issues of *poverty and *inequality. At this time he was at the vanguard of the development of Marxist-inspired structural accounts of socio-spatial relations in the discipline. During the 1980s and 1990s his attention shifted to theorizing international underdevelopment and global *capitalism, and the role of large intergovernmental agencies in sustaining and reproducing capitalist relations. Recent works have been critical of the leading global institutions designed to regulate *capitalism, notably *Unholy Trinity: The IMF, World Bank and WTO* (updated 2009).

people's geography A radical geographical idea to construct geographical knowledge grounded in people's everyday lives and struggles, and opposed to the ways geography serves the interests of the powerful. David *Harvey voiced the concept in his 'historical materialist manifesto for geography' in 1984. It was taken up by US geographers meeting in New York in 1999 in the form of the People's Geography Project, an attempt to popularize the insights of *critical geography for the US public.

(((∰))) SEE WEB LINKS
• People's Geography Project at the University of Syracuse, USA.

perestroika A late 1980s political movement within the Soviet communist party that contributed to the collapse of the Soviet empire and the end of the *Cold War. Formulated in 1986 by the Soviet premier Mikhail Gorbachev, *perestroika* was a programme of economic, political, and social restructuring designed to reform and open up Soviet institutions and create a market economy. New freedoms for public assembly, free speech, and private ownership undermined the authoritarian regime and led to democratic movements in Eastern Europe. By the summer of 1991, the Soviet Union had broken up into independent states.

performance The acting out of different identities and roles. Erving Goffman, in his classic text *The Presentation of Self in Everyday Life* (1959), argued that individuals perform their identity in very conscious ways, seeking to present themselves to the world in a particular fashion. Using the analogy of the theatre, an individual is an actor on a stage who, using costumes and props, interacts with other actors and presents to an audience. While the actor wants to control how he or she is perceived, such control is elusive and the performance is open to interpretation. Focusing on performance enables an analysis of how people seek to create particular spatialized identities and spaces. In contrast, the theory of *performativity focuses on the unconscious performance of identity and production of space.

performative mapping An approach to cartography that understands map-making and map-use as performative and embodied. Traditionally, cartographic theory has concentrated on the maps produced, their accuracy and readability, and technical innovation. Performative mapping recognizes that maps are produced and used through a diverse set of practices—surveying, drafting, digitizing, scaling, generalizing, rolling, folding, marketing—contextualized by the politics and situation of those producing and using them. It argues that cartographic theory needs to shift from concentrating on representation, to focusing on practices and processes, and how maps are made in embodied and contextual ways.

Further reading Kitchin, R. and Dodge, M. (2007), 'Rethinking maps', *Progress in Human Geography* 31(3): 331–44.

performativity The unconscious, unintentional, citational performances of identity. A key concept in post-structural theory, especially through the work of Judith *Butler, performativity captures the notion that identity is something one does, not something one is. *Gender, in these terms, is not a natural, essentialized identity, but rather is performed as an everyday, commonsensical, taken-for-granted, embodied practice (*see* ESSENTIALISM). Gender and what it means to be a woman or man is produced and sustained through acts, gestures, mannerisms, clothing, and so on. In this sense, identity is continuously remade through repeated, iterative, stylized performances. These performances are citational, in that they cite established roles and identities, with identity constantly being brought into being, albeit in an image of itself, thus giving the impression of coherence and stability. Performativity differs from *performance in that it is the unconscious, habitual routine acting out of identity, rather than framed within conscious thought and decision-making. The power of performativity is that it undermines and denaturalizes the notion of essentialized categories. For example, sexual identity is recast as something one does, troubling the binary of heterosexual-homosexual, and destabilizing the assumptions underpinning *heteronormativity. Such ideas have led to development of *queer theory, which has been an important theoretical approach in understanding the geographies of sexualities, and have also influenced ontogenetic ways of thinking about the production of space.

Further reading Bell, D. and Valentine, G. (eds.) (1995), *Mapping Desire*.
Butler, J. (1990), *Gender Trouble: Feminism and the Subversion of Identity*.
Rose, G. (1999), 'Performing space', in Massey, D., Allen, J., and Sarre, P. (eds.) *Human Geography Today*, 247–59.

periphery *See* CORE-PERIPHERY.

Peters projection An equal-area map projection that more accurately displays the relative size of countries. One of the most commonly displayed map projections, the *Mercator projection (see Fig. 6), distorts the size of areas across the map in order to keep lines of direct navigation straight. It vastly increases the size of areas in the upper and lower hemispheres relative to areas around the equator, giving the impression that Greenland and the African continent are approximately the same size, when, in fact, the latter is fourteen times larger in land mass. The Peters projection displays both land masses at their relative size. Presented in 1973, its creator Arno Peters argued that the Mercator projection made countries at the equator appear smaller and therefore less important and that his new projection rectified such a perception. Many charities and international organizations subsequently adopted the projection for displaying their maps. The projection is identical to one published by James Gall in 1885, and the projection is now often referred to as the Gall-Peters projection.

petrocapitalism A form of capital accumulation founded on the extraction, distribution, and consumption of petroleum. The term may refer to the larger globalized economy that depends on oil and gas for energy, industrial products, and profits, and which is coupled with a geopolitical state of affairs in which control over oil resources and their distribution is paramount. It may also describe a particular country whose dependence on oil exports shapes not just its economy, but also its political institutions. Michael *Watts has written extensively about Nigeria in these terms, arguing that oil rents drive its political economy in ways not fully captured by the related idea of *resource curse. *See also* LOW CARBON ECONOMY.

petty commodity production The small-scale production of goods and services for trade based on individual or family labour, i.e. unlike the production of commodities under *capitalist relations of waged labour.

phallocentrism The conscious and unconscious symbolic representations of male power, often through phallic imagery. The concept originates in *psychoanalytic thought and has been used to examine how expressions of *masculinity are used in texts and landscapes to reinforce and reproduce *patriarchal power structures.

Further reading Lico, G. R. A. (2001), 'Architecture and sexuality: the politics of gendered space', *Humanities Diliman* 2: 30–44.

phenomenology An approach to the study of people and the world that highlights the active and varied ways in which sense-making occurs. Though the term derives from *Enlightenment philosophers such as Immanuel *Kant, phenomenology is most associated with the 20th-century writings of Edmund Husserl, Martin Heidegger, and Maurice Merleau-Ponty. Reacting to the ideas of *objectivity and absolute truth, these philosophers emphasized the *hermeneutic dimensions of human existence. If a 'phenomenon' is something made manifest in human experience, then phenomenology is the study of how people structure their experience of other people and the non-human world. It is ostensibly antidualistic, seeking a way past the antinomies of subject–object, idealism-materialism. Despite this, many early humanistic geographers interpreted phenomenology in a rather subjectivist way, in reaction to the rational humans of *spatial science, the cognitive humans of *behavioural geography, and the abstract humans of much early *Marxist geography. Phenomenology offered a philosophically rich language with which they could describe the complexity and variety of human experience, including its affective and practical/tactile elements. However, critics worried that, in some humanistic geographers' hands, it created desocialized representations of human agents and failed to grasp the tangle of contingent relations that enabled and constrained subject-positions and action (*see* STRUCTURATION). After *postmodernism influenced human geographers, interest in phenomenology declined, it being seen as too much of a *Grand Theory. However, aspects of the approach have enjoyed a revival of sorts courtesy of *non-representational theory, especially in recent work on *landscape.

philosophy of geography The ideas about the foundational concepts in geographical thought and their study by systematic and critical means. Among these concepts are *nature, *space, *time, and *place, all of which are shared more widely with other fields of inquiry. The academic discipline of philosophy itself is concerned with rigorous inquiry into the fundamental aspects of reality, existence, logic, and reason. It is usually divided into distinct philosophical fields, many of which are relevant to human geography. *Epistemology addresses theories of knowledge, its methods, validity, and conditions. *Ontology reflects on the nature of being, i.e. what can be said to exist? *Ethics, sometimes included within moral and political philosophy, inquires into the principles that guide or ought to guide human conduct (*see* IDEOLOGY). The philosophy of science, which cuts across these areas, considers the conditions under which we may consistently produce valid and reliable knowledge, and the limits to this process. Questions of *methodology, therefore, also come under philosophical scrutiny. Philosophy shapes the kinds of questions one might legitimately ask, how those questions are operationalized, how data are gathered, analysed, and interpreted, and it frames positions and debates about issues such as research ethics, *positionality, validity, and the politics of research. All academic researchers proceed on the basis of various philosophical beliefs or assumptions just as we do this in our everyday lives, even if this is done unconsciously or unreflexively. Philosophical matters cannot simply be put to one side or subsumed within methodological decisions. The decision whether to opt for qualitative and/or quantitative methods should be informed by philosophical consideration.

There has been continuous but fitful exchange between human geography and philosophy over the centuries, dating back to classical Greece. Immanuel *Kant, for example, was an important figure in philosophy who also lectured on aspects of geography; Kantian ideas influenced subsequent German and American geographers (*see* HARTSHORNE, RICHARD; RITTER, CARL). But, with some exceptions, after the rise of modern institutionalized geography in the late 19th century, there was no sustained engagement by geographers in philosophy until the 1960s. Thereafter, there were explorations of *positivism, *Marxism, *phenomenology, *existentialism and *critical realism, *feminism, *post-structuralism, all of which may be termed 'philosophies of geography'. The journal *Ethics, Policy and Environment* incorporates the short-lived journal *Philosophy and Geography*, and continues to publish articles on explicitly philosophical topics.

Two paired sorts of philosophy have, in their various permutations, proven influential in human geography, and especially its ontological grounds. On the one hand, research streams that derive from spatial science tend to see the world as comprised of parts or units that interact, or fail to interact (*see* CARTESIANISM; REDUCTIONISM). On the other hand, the majority of research influenced by continental European philosophy (e.g. *Marxist geography and *non-representational theory) sees the world as comprised of relations in which causes are also effects, and in which there is no such thing as elemental 'units' of analysis that can be abstracted ontologically from systems, processes, or networks (*see* ASSEMBLAGE; HOLISM). *Critical realism is a middle ground between these positions.

A second distinction can be made between philosophies that are avowedly constructionist and those that are more *materialist. The majority of human geographers have embraced a 'two-worlds' *ontology, in which the world of humans is seen to be qualitatively different from the world of rocks, rivers, and rainforests. However, they have disagreed about the ontological properties of the former, with some (such as critical realists) emphasizing the causal powers of social relations, rules, and institutions, and others placing more emphasis on language, symbolism, and *representation. The latter, in effect, have upended the philosophical distinction between *epistemology and ontology, by emphasizing the material realities 'constructed' by historically and geographically contingent discourses, images, and icons created by various human agents. More recently, this debate over the real nature of 'the social' has been complicated by *Actor-Network Theory and *non-representational theory, among others. These approaches highlight the indissoluble links between what we call 'society' and what we call '*nature'. Human geographers have also shown a growing interest in ethics, especially insofar as it relates to nature and place, and a range of broadly *post-structuralist philosophers including *Butler, *Foucault, *Deleuze, Brian Massumi and Jane Bennett.

Despite their heightened philosophical awareness, human geographers have only engaged with a small portion of the wider body of thought published by professional philosophers. They have also, in some respects, come to rely less on philosophical discourse to persuade their colleagues to change the focus or manner of their research. Many philosophically inclined human geographers have accepted that no one philosophy can trump all others, and that philosophy is but one discourse among many (rather than a privileged one that underpins all the rest). While this has contributed to fostering intellectual diversity, it has also rather Balkanized *epistemic communities within the discipline. There is, today, less philosophically based debate and critique among alternative positions. Ironically, freed from the burden of having to defend and modify their philosophical positions because of external criticism, many human geographers are using philosophical discourse as an ostensibly secure foundation for empirical research or argumentation (this, arguably, has been the fate of *post-structuralism in human geography). Though more philosophically literate than their predecessors, today's human geographers may need to better connect their abstract arguments with the practicalities of *methodology and the conduct of either *intensive- or *extensive research.

Further reading Aitken, S. C. and Valentine, G. (eds.) (2006), *Approaches to Human Geography*.
Graham, I. et al. (2010), 'Theorizing our world' in Gomez, B., and Jones III, J. P. (eds.) *Research Methods in Geography*, 9–25.
Johnston, R. and Sidaway, J. (7th ed. 2013), *Geography and Geographers*.
Kitchin, R. (2013), 'Explanation/Understanding', in Cloke, P., Crang, P., and Goodwin, M. *Introducing Human Geographies*.

photogrammetry The science and technology of making measurements using photographs. Aerial photographs contain various positional errors due to angle and curvature of the Earth which means they cannot be used directly to accurately measure distances, areas, or directions. Photogrammetry seeks to either derive accurate information from an aerial photograph, or to transform it by removing the errors. The information within the *aerial photography can then be used to construct accurate maps of the area in question. It is thus an important mode of *surveying for remote or inaccessible areas.

photography The process of recording static images via a lens or a light sensor. Traditionally, photographs were generated by exposing light-sensitive material to various forms of light (e.g., visual, x-ray, infrared) and chemically processing this material to produce a print or slide. More recently, digital cameras use light sensors to capture visual data. Given that geography is often said to be a very visual discipline, observing people, landscapes, and natural environments, photography has been a key method of generating and recording fieldwork. Photographic archives provide important repositories for the historical analysis of people, place, and events. Photographs are generally either used to provide visual support for a discourse (e.g., photographs of urban landscape to illustrate an argument about gentrification) or can form the raw data for analysis. In the latter case, analytic methods such as *deconstruction and *content analysis are applied to the image, and associated images, to tease out meaning and provide derivative data. In some cases, such as landscape perception studies, photographs are visual prompts for generating data about sense of place or evaluations of different types of locales. Auto-photography is a *biographical method of data collection wherein research respondents are provided with a camera to record a visual diary about their everyday life or particular aspect of it. The data are often analysed in conjunction with other data such as *interviews or *ethnography. *See also*: ART AND GEOGRAPHY; CINEMA; PHOTOGRAPHY AND GEOGRAPHY; REPRESENTATION; VISUALIZATION.

Further reading Rose, G. (2006), *Visual Methods: an Introduction to the Interpretation of Visual Materials*.
Sidaway, J. D. (2002), 'Photography as geographical fieldwork', *Journal of the Geography of Higher Education* 26: 95–103.

photography and geography From its inception in the 19th century, *photography has been a key technology in the development of geography as a discipline. Photographs enabled the systematic recording of landforms, people, their *cultures, and their *landscapes, and provided a new means to document and display information, and a new source of data for analysis. Like *maps, photographs helped make the distant and unvisited familiar and knowable by producing images that were easily transported and interpreted, and a means of cataloguing, categorizing, and making sense of the world (e.g., people, fauna, flora, places). Photography thus contributed to the projects of *exploration, *colonization, and modernity. Photographs provided the evidence to support civilizing and modernizing initiatives and a means to visually chart the effects of change and progress by recording vistas of the same places over time. In the 20th century, *aerial photography and *photogrammetry enabled the production of more accurate and detailed maps, especially of remote areas. As time has advanced, photographic archives have become important sources of data for historical analysis, especially when they are accompanied by additional *metadata. In recent years, with the advent of online sharing and storage of photographs through applications such as flickr and *Google Streetview, it has been possible to create bespoke geographic analysis of photographs, especially when they are *geocoded, pulling together hundreds of images of the same place and events.

As recent work by critical geographers has highlighted, it is important to note that photography is not a neutral activity. There is a politics to how an image is composed and framed in terms of what is included and excluded, how it is presented, and how it is interpreted with regards to meaning. Photographs are used to support and endorse written discourse and ideology, and provide data towards theory building. Photographs are thus understood as a particular form of *representation, structured through a way of seeing, and shaped by the technology of their production, and the values and training of the photographer. Somewhat paradoxically, photographs are often thought to be scientific, rational, and objective, *and* subjective, experiential, and artful: they capture the essence or truth of the world (the camera does not lie), but taking a photograph is reliant on the choices, judgements, and skill of the photographer. Moreover, it is increasingly becoming easier to alter images through packages such as Photoshop. What this means is that a photograph cannot be read simply at face value, but must be carefully interpreted within a contextual frame. *See also* FILM; GAZE.

Further reading Ryan, J. (1997), *Picturing Empire: Photography and the Visualisation of the British Empire*.
Schwartz, M. and Ryan, J. (eds.) (2003), *Picturing Place: Photography and the Geographical Imagination*.

physical geography The study of the spatial and environmental processes that shape the natural world. Physical geography studies a number of interrelated environmental spheres such as the atmosphere (air), biosphere (ecosystems), hydrosphere (water systems), lithosphere (rocky shell of the Earth), and pedosphere (soils), the processes that drive their operation and development, how they interact with each other, how the activities of people impact upon them, and how they impact on people. It is divided into a number of areas of subspecialism including biogeography (plant and animal species), climatology and meteorology (climate and weather), geomorphology (landforms), glaciology (ice), hydrology (water), oceanography (oceans), palaeogeography (past physical geography), and pedology (soils). Research is often interdisciplinary across the natural and physical sciences. and generally uses the scientific method common to these other disciplines.

The relationship between *human and physical geography has varied over time, across different geographic and national traditions, and with respect to the issue under examination. In the 19th and early 20th centuries, human and physical geography were integrated in the *anthropography of the German tradition, the *regional geography of the French tradition, and the *environmental determinism of the North American tradition. In all three cases analysis examined human-environment systems and interactions within geographic areas. Over time, as the nature of geographical inquiry changed with the introduction of new approaches to geographical scholarship, and subdisciplinary fields grew in importance, the relationship between human and physical geography has altered.

In some cases, human and physical geographers presently interact in very loose ways or not at all. For example, it is relatively rare in social geography that any reference is made to the work of physical geographers. Instead, social geographers are much more likely to interact with sociologists, anthropologists, and health specialists. Similarly, physical geography analysis of the characteristics and dynamics of glaciers will seldom draw directly on human geography, with collaborations more likely to be with hydrologists or atmospheric scientists. Indeed, in many countries, human and physical geography are separate academic departments located in different faculties (usually social sciences and natural/Earth sciences respectively). It is also the case that human and physical geographers often attend different scientific meetings and belong to different scientific bodies.

It can sometimes be the case that human and physical geographers are examining the same issue, but are doing so in such different ways, using dissimilar conceptual lenses and methodological tools, that they seemingly have little to say to each other. For example, a human geographer might be studying the formation of a rural *landscape from the perspective of *political economy where how the land is shaped is understood as being structured by *capitalism and its social relations. A physical geographer might examine the same landscape with respect to how specific human interventions and practices shape the physical processes that constitute the landscape. Each has a very different understanding of what is meant by landscape and *nature, the processes that are at work, and how to study and analyse those processes.

In other cases, human and physical geographers do work very closely together, especially with regards to environmental issues such as *environmental management, *biodiversity, *conservation, *resource management, *natural hazards, human impact on *ecosystems, *climate change, and *climate policy (*see* ENVIRONMENTAL GEOGRAPHY; SUSTAINABILITY SCIENCE). In these instances there is an attempt to create a more holistic analysis of the interrelationship between people and environments, and how human and environmental systems interact and shape each other in complex and diverse ways. For example, in the area of climate change, physical and human geographers are working together to, on the one hand, understand how human activity influences the climatic system, and on the other hand to understand what climate change might mean for human populations and the adaptations that might be required to deal with more severe weather and sea-level rise. These kinds of working relationships are well encapsulated by the work of the *International Geosphere-Biosphere Program (IGBP) and *International Human Dimensions Program on Global Environmental Change.

Physical geography is being pulled in two directions. On the one hand, in recent years there have been several calls for human and physical geography to be more integrated, making the discipline stronger, and providing a more holistic analysis. The challenge for such integrationists is to find a means to facilitate stronger amalgamation given the differences in approaches and methods, and the pressures towards subdisciplinary specialism. On the other, much of the scientific work of physical geographers, especially in modelling, is drawn towards *Earth Systems Science and closer integration with other natural sciences in interdisciplinary projects.

Further reading Castree, N., Rogers, A., and Sherman, D. (eds.) (2005), *Questioning Geography*.

Harrison, S. et al. (2004), 'Thinking across the divide: perspectives on the conversations between physical and human geography', *Area* 36(4): 435–42.

Holloway, S. et al. (eds.) (2nd ed. 2009), *Key Concepts in Geography*.

Massey, D. (1999), 'Space-time, "science" and the relationship between physical geography and human geography', *Transactions of the Institute of British Geographers* 24(3): 261–76.

Rhoads, B. (2004), 'Whither physical geography?' *Annals of the Association of American Geographers* 94(4): 748–55.

Strahler, A. (5th ed. 2010), *Introducing Physical Geography*.

place 1. A fixed point on the Earth's surface.
2. A locus of individual and group identity.
3. The scale of everyday life.

Until the 1970s all three meanings of place were understood via a 'mosaic' metaphor that implied that different places were discrete and singular. However, in the wake of *globalization, it became necessary for human geographers to rethink their ideas about place. This is not to imply that places are becoming the same, as if globalization is an homogenizing process. Rather, the challenge has been to conceptualize place difference and place interdependence simultaneously. The 'inside' and 'outside' of a place is no longer clear cut. The metaphors of 'switching points' and 'nodes' better enable us to see places as at once unique and connected, and mediate between older *idiographic and *nomothetic approaches. As will be explained, these metaphors currently find favour among most human geographers writing about place. Despite definition three possibly implying that all places are of a similar area (e.g. 100 square kilometres), human geographers have never sought to offer an absolute measure of what distinguishes a place from, say, a *region. This is because what constitutes a place is partly a function of changing technologies and infrastructures (e.g. roads, railways). In turn, these affect people's perceptions of what is near or local, and what is far.

In its early years as a university subject, many geographers devoted some or all of their careers to studying one or more places. Typically, theirs was a holistic analysis that covered both human and physical geography and which presumed there to be unique or even singular characteristics that distinguished one place from another (*see* AREAL DIFFERENTIATION). With the post-1950 *Quantitative Revolution in geography this sort of place analysis, also conducted at the regional scale, was largely eclipsed. Places began to be seen as instances of general processes because the new ontological presumption was that a certain spatial order was operative within and between otherwise different and distant localities. This presumption was also made by the early Marxist geographers, despite their concern to criticize *spatial science. They were initially interested in the 'laws of motion' of *capitalism that governed towns, cities, and rural landscapes worldwide. However, within a decade these new approaches to place came in for criticism. First, it was argued that place similarity is not synonymous with place sameness: only by abstracting too much from the specifics of places could general patterns be identified, so said many critics. For instance, in a particular twist on this argument, Edward *Relph argued that the spread of homogenous, featureless modern architecture across Western cities was creating a damaging *placelessness. Secondly, it was argued that the *hermeneutic and affective dimensions of place experience were being ignored in the rush to privilege general theories and models. Humanistic geographers especially emphasized the second meaning of place, arguing that attention must be paid to how people value and interpret the places they inhabit, or have inhabited in the past. These valuations and interpretations, they argued, matter greatly to people and may vary considerably according to age, nationality, ethnicity, gender, and so on.

Despite the validity of these arguments, some critics worried that they reintroduced the *idiographic obsessions of many early 20th-century geographers. They also argued that humanistic geographers were presuming some essential 'humanity' (*see* HUMANISM) possessed by all people, thus ignoring the malleability of identities wrought out of changing sets of social relations, customs, and norms. By the 1990s, these concerns had translated into a new body of research into how place residents represented the 'realities' of place to themselves and others. Their representations and signs (e.g. graffiti) were seen to express and reproduce/alter the various subject-positions they occupied by virtue of how they were *interpellated by socially available discourses of various kinds. Place identities were thus understood to be implicated in *power, *resistance. and struggles over whose definitions of place would win out. Work by the likes of British geographers David Sibley and Tim Cresswell looked specifically at those who transgressed the behaviour normally permitted in certain places. Places, they argued, were more than a mere stage upon which fully formed subjects acted out their lives. Instead, places were part of the process of subject-formation and the regulation of behaviour, a process that involved social relations of cooperation and antagonism between people inhabiting the same locality. As most Western countries have become highly multiethnic and polycultural over the last twenty-five years, the complexities of individual, group, and place identity have multiplied, so too, the challenges of accommodating different representations of what any given place should look and feel like. Coincident with this research into place and the politics of identity has been research into place as the scale enabling and constraining everyday life. This research has focused less on identity, discourse, and symbolism, and more (or as much) on human agency and practice. Inspired by Anthony *Gidden's theory of *structuration, Derek *Gregory and Allen *Pred drew attention to how situated actors made local geographies, but not under conditions they could freely choose or entirely control. Relatedly, the British 'localities studies' funded by the Economic and Social Research Council sought to paint a picture of how international capitalism and national government were together redefining the local coordinates of life for Britons. At the same time, studies of local *labour markets by Jamie *Peck and others attended closely to the opportunities and constraints confronted by wage workers by virtue of their place-bound existence. Since this research in the 1980s and 1990s, a focus on place as the arena in which everyday life is played out has become a signature of many human geographers' research. For instance, this is highly apparent in the subfield of *labour geography.

Meanwhile, empirical interest in place, as set out in definition one, has continued apace in a number of ways. For instance, research by British geographer Daniel *Dorling has mapped the often significant local differences in the indicators used to measure the quality of human lives (e.g. longevity, educational achievement levels, unemployment levels). Writing in a more normative register, David M. Smith has used evidence of such spatial inequalities to make moral arguments that the least well off should receive significant amounts of aid and assistance from those whose good fortune it is to be born and raised in wealthy places (*see* MORAL GEOGRAPHIES).

Cross-cutting the last 30 years of research on place have seen new metaphors used to inform human geographers' descriptive and explanatory endeavours. Dissenting from the 'mosaic' view evident a century ago, today's human geographers prefer metaphors such as 'circuits and switching points' and 'networks and nodes'. Places are seen as 'glocal', their past, present, and future the result of local action responding to, but also influencing much wider sets of relationships, rules, and processes. As Doreen *Massey famously argued many years ago, we need a 'global sense of place' because our era is one of what Erik *Swyngedouw calls 'glocalization' rather than a placeless globalization. Though not the only ones preoccupied with place in the contemporary social sciences and humanities, human geographers are major contributors to understandings of the character and significance of place.

References Cresswell, T. (1994), *In Place/Out of Place*.
Dorling, D. and Shaw, M. (2002), *Health, Place and Society*.
Gregory, D. (1982), *Regional Transformation and Industrial Revolution*.
Massey, D. (1994), 'A global sense of place', in *Space, Place and Gender* 146–56.

Pred, A. (1984), 'Place as historically contingent process', *Annals of the Association of American Geographers* 74, 2: 279–97.
Smith, D. M. (2000), *Moral Geographies*.
Swyngedouw, E. (2006), *Glocalizations*.

Place and Placelessness The title of a book by Edward *Relph (1976), it was a key text in the elaboration of the concepts of *place and *sense of place, and in the development of *humanistic geography, especially the use of *phenomenology. The book examines the relationship between people and place and, in particular, people's attachment to particular locales and how that shapes their lives. Placelessness, Relph details, is a condition of alienation wherein an individual feels little attachment to a place caused by the homogenizing effects of capitalism and mobility.

place attachment The sense of belonging, loyalty, or affection that a person feels for one or more places. Despite hyperbolic claims that ours is an age of human mobility where *routes* matter more than *roots*, most people on the planet spend the bulk of their lives in just one or two locations. These places are sites of formative experiences, as well the loci of family, friendships, work, and leisure. For these reasons, people typically build strong attachments to places. The strength of feeling may be such as to spark conflict when two or more parties lay claim to a place or *territory, as is currently the case with *Palestine. More usually, place attachment stops people from migrating or else draws them back periodically once they have left. It remains an important component of individual and collective memory.

placelessness The condition of an environment lacking significant places and the associated attitude of a lack of attachment to place caused by the homogenizing effects of modernity, e.g. commercialism, mass consumption, standard planning regulations, alienation, and obsession with speed and movement. Shopping malls, highways, post-war US suburbs, and edge cities are typically described as placeless, although cultural geographers have argued that they can be sites of meaning-filled engagement and identity. *See also* GENIUS LOCI; NON-PLACE; PLACE AND PLACELESSNESS; RELPH, EDWARD.

place marketing The construction and dissemination of selected representations of a *place designed to have a positive effect on outsiders who could potentially invest in, visit, or move to the place in question. Place marketing is typically undertaken by local government agencies, perhaps working with local businesses. It is a form of strategic advertising designed to attract new public or private investments, tourists, and new residents to a particular locality. Place marketing became widespread in Western countries after the long period of post-1970 *deindustrialization and the various economic recessions of the 1970s and 1980s. Towns and cities tried to be more *entrepreneurial, taking measures to set *accumulation on a new path. Place marketing cannot afford to misrepresent a place. Instead, it has to put a positive spin on current assets, while drawing attention away from local problems and weaknesses.

Further reading Kearns, G. and Philo, C. (eds.) (1993), *Selling Places*.

place names The names attached to different locations on the Earth's surface, be they inhabited or not., Place names often tell a story of human movement and settlement past and present. Human geographers have long been interested in place names for two reasons. First, for historical geographers, old place names are important clues in understanding patterns of migration, conflict, colonization, and cultural assimilation in previous centuries. Secondly, for political and cultural geographers, many contemporary place names are bound up in the dynamics of conflict about who has rights to a specific location or wider *territory. *Toponyms are thus more than 'mere names' because they both evidence and become embroiled in disputes over the movement of different ethno-cultural groups. *See also* TOPONYM.

planning The production and implementation of plans that organize and regulate land use and social and economic development in an area. Planned development has long been a feature of how societies have built, managed, and governed environments. Plans are devised to coordinate and integrate the development of infrastructure, utilities, buildings, and green environments, and their occupancy and use. Such organized planning came to the fore in 19th-century Europe as part of the project of modernity. For example, the Haussmann Plan, implemented between 1853–70, was designed to modernize medieval Paris, transforming the city's streets and their layout, the design of buildings, city facilities and utilities, and creating public parks and monuments. Ebenezer Howard's ideas for creating *garden cities were utopian plans in which development would be spatially organized to balance social and economic needs with nature, and led to a number of new towns developed on its principles in Britain and North America. Over the course of the 20th century the creation of plans for all development became a routine aspect of government work and led to the profession of planning.

Professional planning works across a number of scales and domains (e.g., *urban and regional, transport, landscape, environmental, *spatial planning), with planners working for the public (state agencies, local authorities) and private sector (representing the interests of developers). Typically the work is divided into forward planning and the creation of *development plans that set out future land-use zoning and anticipated new infrastructure and buildings, the evaluation and awarding of planning permissions, and the overseeing of on-going development work, including the regulation of development that is unauthorized or fails to meet permission conditions or building standards. Planners often work with architects, engineers, and economic consultants to develop and assess plans, their viability, sustainability, and likely local impacts.

Planning as an academic discipline seeks to train planners with respect to the technical, operational, and legal aspects of the profession and develop planning theory and methods to guide planning practice. Planning theory seeks to provide a conceptual framework for how planning is conceived, its aims, and how it is undertaken. Its nature varies culturally and historically across the world, but in Britain, planning generally falls into one of three schools that are not mutually exclusive (Huxley 2009). First, there is planning as the production of technical expert knowledge in the form of general principles for the effective physical and aesthetic design and building of new developments that balanced social and economic concerns. Second, there is planning as a form of rational policy making or scientific advice for political decision-makers charged with addressing a particular issue, such as the provision of housing or regeneration. Versions include the use of systems theory which seeks to create sustainable development by balancing various factors within a planning model and procedural theory that prescribes an order, criteria, and weights for assessing planning issues and identifying solutions. Both sought optimal solutions based on scientific procedures and measurements, but did not handle politics or power very effectively. Third, there is planning as a form of participatory democracy in which the public and stakeholders work with planners to produce a plan. From this perspective, planning is a process of managed consultation and mediating conflicting views about how a plan is devised and implemented. These theories focus primarily on the process of planning. In recent years, there has been more critical focus applied to planning itself and its aims, objectives, practices, ideology, ethics, and role in producing places and communities. Such critical planning theory analyses the intersection of planning and power within the profession of planning and in how planning operates discursively and materially to create landscapes.

References and further reading Hall, P. (3rd ed. 2002), *Cities of Tomorrow*.
Healey, P. (1997), *Collaborative Planning*.

Huxley, M. (2009), 'Planning, Urban', in the *International Encyclopedia of Human Geography*.
Parker, G. and Doak, J. (2012), *Key Concepts in Planning*.
Taylor, N. (1998), *Urban Planning Theory since 1945*.

plantation **1.** A large arable estate or farm, usually associated with colonial exploitation of tropical and subtropical regions and focusing on one main crop, e.g. sugar or tobacco.

2. A colonial settlement. From the early 17th century onwards, some regions of the Americas became so specialized in this form of agriculture, based on imported slave labour, that they can be referred to as 'plantation societies'.

plaza An urban *public space. 'Plaza' is a Spanish word (the Italian equivalent is 'piazza') used to refer to a large open space or square, usually found at the centre of a city, bordered by the church or cathedral, city hall, and law courts. Plazas were central to Spanish colonial cities in Latin America. In recent decades they have become important places for regenerating cities in other regions based on attracting large numbers of people back to city centres, especially at night. More broadly, plaza is used to describe a commercial shopping centre.

plural societies Societies which are made up of a diverse collection of people belonging to different linguistic, ethnic, and racial groups. They are different from *multicultural societies in that members of each group occupy different spaces, with their own institutions, and only meet in the marketplace to trade or in shared public space. It was originally used to describe some states in the developing world—for example, Southeast Asia and the Caribbean—usually created under colonial rule. Here, different ethnic groups undertook specific labour and occupied particular places and positions in the social hierarchy. The concept has been extended to developed countries where a pluralist organization of labour and space has arisen.

point pattern analysis The analysis of the spatial distribution of data expressed as points on a map. Points might represent the location of crimes or factories or incidents of a disease. Point pattern analysis seeks to describe the distribution of points and to determine if there is any significance in their arrangement or how to optimize their location. The most common kind of analysis is to assess the level of *clustering.

Poisson distribution The probability distribution that results from a Poisson experiment, an experiment in which the results can be discretely categorized and is proportional to the size of the region (e.g. length, area, volume, length of time). For example, if a boat delivers on average ten visitors a day, the Poisson distribution details the probability that nine, eight, seven, etc. visitors will visit on any future day. The distribution is skewed and has the property that the variance is equal to the mean.

Poisson regression models A type of *generalized linear model that is used to analyse count data and contingency tables, where the independent variable is assumed to have a *Poisson distribution. *See also* LOG-LINEAR MODELS; REGRESSION.

Polanyi, Karl (1886–1964) A Hungarian political economist and historian best known for his book *The Great Transformation* (1944), which examines from a historical perspective the symbiotic relationship in the development of states and markets under *capitalism. The state, he reasoned, was required to regulate society for capitalism, and capitalism in turn helped foster social change. In so doing he demonstrated that the economy and its transformations cannot be understood in isolation from the wider context of culture, politics, institutions, and society, and that economic theory must be adapted to the particular circumstances of a society and should not be applied universally. As such, he highlighted how and why economies vary across space and time. *See also* EMBEDDEDNESS.

policing The regulation of populations and territories by dedicated government bodies for the purposes of maintaining social order, safety, and health; more specifically, policing refers to law enforcement, crime prevention, and detection. Geographers have a long-standing interest in researching *crime, but since the 1990s have also studied police agencies themselves, for example, through ethnography. How and where the law is actually applied (or not) is more geographically differentiated than it might appear (*see* LAW). *See also* GOVERNMENTALITY.

policy, geography and 1. The study of how policy shapes the production of space and the related geography of policy formulation.

2. How geographers engage with policy debates. There is a long tradition within geographical scholarship of examining *public policy, deconstructing its agendas and aims, and documenting its effects on the world. For example, much research has focused on the formulation and implementation of local and national government and supranational (e.g., *European Union) policies with respect to environmental, economic, social, and cultural issues. This work seeks to detail the ways in which policy is formulated within a contested political landscape, how it is applied and resisted in practice, how it reshapes or alters social and economic relations, and how policy ideas can circulate between locations (*see* POLICY TRANSFER). Such studies reveal the complex ways in which policy is made and implemented, and opens up avenues for thinking about alternative policy interventions. For example, in their book, *Urban Renaissance: New Labour, Community and Urban Policy* (2003), Rob Imrie and Mike Raco critically examine the policies of the-then Labour government in the UK, detailing the thinking behind these and the effects the policies had on people living in British cities through a number of case studies. Other studies have compared and contrasted policy interventions in different jurisdictions; for example, Andrew Power in *Landscapes of Care* (2010) has examined policy with respect to family care-giving in several Western nations and how different formulations of the welfare state give rise to very different levels of support for care-givers. In *A Handbook for Globalisation and Environmental Policy* (2012) the full scope of environmental policy is detailed from governmental considerations, to the role of private companies, to public participation in policy formulation. And in *Mobile Urbanism* (2011) several authors examine the ways in which policies designed to shape cities, such as *business improvement districts, or tackling drugs, or strengthening *social capital, travel between locations, with policy makers in one place importing ideas and praxis from another.

How geographers engage with policy beyond studying it is a live debate within the discipline framed as one of *relevance. On the one hand are those who believe that a crucial role for geographers is to contribute to policy research by producing research that is of strategic use to policy makers and to become active in the process of formulating policy itself. In this way, geography can make an explicit contribution to the production of geographies, rather than simply studying such geographies. Sometimes labelled *applied geography, there is a rich history of geographers undertaking consultancy-style research, working with governments, state agencies, and the third sector to document an issue and suggest recommendations to address it. Such work has been undertaken across every form of geographical scholarship from environmental management to economic development to social exclusion, with geographers providing key insights into how an issue might be tackled. Key geographical technologies such as *GIS and *remote sensing are often routinely used in policy research, especially relating to planning and environmental issues. The critique of such work is that geographical praxis becomes subservient to the desires of policy makers, which are often quite conservative with a limited agenda, and it limits academic freedom to report findings openly. The argument thus follows that policy work is better left to professional consultants who apply knowledge, rather than produce new knowledge. This view has been countered recently by those such as McGuirk and O'Neill, who maintain that it is possible to make policy interventions while retaining critical, open scholarship.

On the other hand, there are those who believe that geographers' primary role is to study and understand the world, and to communicate that knowledge through teaching and writing. Here it is argued that the production of fundamental knowledge is a core endeavour of higher education, providing understanding, insight, and enlightenment which has value in and of itself. It is up to others to take and apply these ideas to policy formulation, if applicable. Geographers thus might contribute to *public policy debates, presenting analysis and critique, but should not be compelled to work directly to policy makers. The critique of this position is that by simply studying the world and failing to engage directly with policy makers, geography misses out on the potential to make a critical intervention into how an issue is tackled by government. *See also* PUBLIC GEOGRAPHY.

Further reading Imrie, R. (2004), 'Urban geography, relevance, and resistance to the "policy turn"', *Urban Geography* 25: 697–708.

McGuirk, P. and O'Neill, P. (2012), 'Critical geographies with the state: the problem of social vulnerability and the politics of engaged research', *Antipode*, 44.4, 1374–94.

Martin, R. (2001), 'Geography and public policy: the case of the missing agenda', *Progress in Human Geography* 25: 189–210.

Peck J. (1999), 'Grey geography?', *Transactions of the Institute of British Geographers* 24: 131–36.

policy transfer The movement of policies and the administrative arrangements that support these from one domain or location to another. The idea is that sub-optimal programmes and institutions learn from successful policy and programmes elsewhere. It is often bound up in the rhetoric of best practice, efficiencies, and productivity, and the harmonization of policy across territories, such as the European Union. Often tied to the industry of management consultancy, the business of policy transfer has become an important shaper of institutional governance and agent of globalization.

Further reading McCann, E. and Ward, K. (eds.) (2011), *Mobile Urbanism: City Policymaking in the Global Age.*

political ecology An approach to investigating human-environment relationships that emphasizes the economic and political processes affecting access to and use of land and resources. Unlike an earlier approach called *cultural ecology, political ecology questioned how far the behaviour of users of land and resources could be explained with reference to the biophysical characteristics of the latter. Though they eschewed *environmental determinism, cultural ecologists paid close attention to the various ways those who lived off the land and water—especially in the *Global South—adapted their ways of life to prevailing biophysical opportunities and constraints. However, the attempted *modernization of developing world economies after 1945, along with their greater integration (through trade and investment) into the world economy, altered the living conditions of many peasants, small holders, and shifting cultivators in rural areas. From the late 1970s, political ecologists—who were based mostly in human geography, anthropology, and rural sociology in the first instance—sought to attend to these new agro-rural dynamics. They rejected suggestions made in the 1970s that a raft of new environmental problems in the developing world, such as *desertification, were the products either of over-population or ignorant land users. Instead, they emphasized the new sets of national and international relationships that local land and resources users were enmeshed in. These relationships were seen to create new incentives and pressures that could result in what cultural ecologists would have called 'maladaptations' (i.e. land and resource uses that could produce environmental degradation).

In human geography, three now-classic studies founded political ecology. They were Piers Blaikie's *The Political Economy of Soil Erosion in Developing Countries* (1985), Blaikie and Harold Brookfield's *Land Degradation and Society* (1987), and Michael Watts' *Silent Violence* (1983). The first two outlined some core principles on which political ecology would be based. These were as follows: (i) the household or individual land user was the unit of analysis, not a local *culture or community; (ii) this unit must be understood in a wider political and economic context, extending up to the global scale such that a 'chain of explanation' could be constructed from something like global commodity markets to a farmer's decision on which crops to grow in any given year; (iii) this context often involves asymmetries in power in that a rural household or land user cannot control things such as international market demand or trade barriers that nonetheless directly impact on their livelihoods; and (iv) local ecology and resource characteristics, in themselves, cannot ultimately explain the decision-making of peasants and farmers in rural parts of the developing world. Watts' study was perhaps the first sustained application of political ecology to explaining an empirical case, that of rural life in northern *Nigeria before and during the period of British colonialism (which ended in 1960). Watts utilized neo-Marxist ideas such as proletarianization, incorporation, and marginalization. The first referred to the historic loss of control over the means of production and reproduction by peasants in northern Nigeria courtesy of the British. The second referred to peasants' forced inclusion in a capitalist *market economy in which producers had either to sell one or other agrarian commodity in return for money, or else sell their *labour power in return for a wage. The third concept referred to the way loss of control over land, natural resources, and/or the conditions prevailing in distant commodity markets rendered many rural inhabitants vulnerable to poverty, which could then oblige them to make 'irrational' decisions in a bid to survive (e.g. over-grazing the same area of pasture).

Despite sounding like a tightly defined approach, political ecology was intellectually open from the start, albeit cleaving to the left-critical side of social science in general and human geography in particular. Since the mid-1980s it has grown considerably and diversified, with Peet and Watts' (2nd ed. 2004) *Liberation Ecologies* providing a snapshot of the approach in its maturity, and Robbins' (2011) eponymous textbook a summary of it for the benefit of degree students. As it has evolved, three things have stood out. First, more attention has been paid to the biophysical characteristics of land and water as they interact dialectically with land and resource users themselves subject to political and economic pressures and opportunities. This is a corrective to the earlier over-emphasis on the latter, as if *nature no longer mattered. Second, more attention has been paid to political issues than in the 1980s, with the *agency and *resistance of peasants, farmers, farm workers, and *indigenous peoples much more a focus than previously. Finally, the diversity and complexity of the local and extra-local relationships in which land and resource users are embroiled has also received more attention. For instance, the differences and the interplay between gender and class relations has been explored by feminist political ecologists (see, for example, Rocheleau et al. (1997), *Feminist Political Ecology: Global Perspectives and Local Experience*). All this has produced more rounded research, but also been coincident with political ecology becoming ever more intellectually plural and normatively diverse. For instance, despite its roots in the study of rural areas in the Global South, there is now an urban political ecology whose practitioners not only study cities but also ones in the Global North. The enrichment provided by political ecology's lack of orthodoxy must be weighed against its potential inability to amount to more than the sum of its increasingly unrelated parts.

Further reading Robbins, P. (2nd ed. 2011), *Political Ecology: a Critical Introduction*,.

political economy The trans-disciplinary study of economic and political processes founded on the assumption that they are necessarily related or integrated. Although the term originates in 17th-century moral philosophy, within human geography in the past few decades it has been more or less synonymous with *Marxism and related approaches (*see* HISTORICAL MATERIALISM; MARXIST GEOGRAPHY). These include Marxist geography *sensu strictu*, *world-system analysis, *regulation theory, and dependency theory (*see* DEVELOPMENT THEORY). The many forms of analysis that adopt or extend elements of Marxism are often termed 'neo-Marxist', and these, too, could be described as political economy. Some of the work of Manuel *Castells on the *Network Society and Anthony *Giddens in sociology might also be described this way, given the prominence they accord to understanding societies through their relations of production. These approaches differ but they share: a critical approach to *power, *capitalism, and the *state; an emphasis on historical and structural forces of compulsion more than individual human *agency (*see* AGENCY-STRUCTURE); a focus on the social relations of production reproduction, and consumption. It is common to contrast political economy approaches to *post-structuralism, where greater emphasis is given to practice, meaning, and discourse, although there is much fertile ground between them.

Political Economy of Soil Erosion in Developing Countries, The One of the foundational studies in what was to be later termed *political ecology. Based in part on his field research in Nepal, its author Piers *Blaikie (1985) argued that soil erosion was not caused by mismanagement or overpopulation as *neo-Malthusian theories would believe, but by the position of peasant farmers in a wider political economy.

political geography A subdiscipline concerned with the study of the spatial dimensions of politics. Although sharing many of the theories, methods, and interests as *human geography in general, it has a particular interest in *territory, the *state, *power, and boundaries (including *borders), across a range of scales from the *body to the planet. 'Politics' refers not simply to the formal organization of political life through government, elections, parties, etc., but all aspects of social life involving *governance or where some degree of contentiousness or conflict may arise. Interpreted more broadly, therefore, political geography can encompass all those ideas about the relationships between geography and politics extending beyond academic contexts (*see* ANTI-POLITICS).

p

Political geography has meant and studied different things in different contexts. In the late 19th century it was partly synonymous with human geography as a whole. Friedrich *Ratzel is credited with the first use of the term in his book *Politische Geographie*, in which he aligned non-physical geography with the study of the state in space. *Mackinder similarly distinguished political and physical geography. The work of geographers in France, Germany, Britain, and the USA in exploring the geographical foundations of state power is now more commonly classified as *geopolitics. Anxious to distance themselves from the German school of *geopolitik* because of its close links to the Nazi regime, prominent US geographers such as Isaiah *Bowman and Richard *Hartshorne described their work as 'political geography'. But, actual empirical research in the field dried up, perhaps because of the taint of geopolitics, and theoretical advance halted. The main exception was work on boundaries and boundary disputes, which was a preoccupation of French and German geographers before the *Second World War and of interest to British geographers in the subsequent phase of *decolonization. In terms of theory, a notable exception was the work of French geographer Jean Gottmann who, like Hartshorne, tried to understand the relations between the modern state, territory, and *identity. His recognition of the significance of *iconography and the state idea prefigured later contributions.

In the 1960s, political geography was reframed in terms of political studies from spatial perspectives, with elections, boundaries, and subnational administrative organization among its subject matter (*see* ELECTORAL GEOGRAPHY; SPATIAL SCIENCE). A core problem for example, was the effect of international boundaries on spatial interaction. The impact of the cultural and political upheavals across the world in the late 1960s was twofold. On the one hand, impelled by *radical geography and informed by *Marxism, *feminism, and *socialism, swathes of human geography became politicized, i.e. were more attentive to conflict and difference and prepared to challenge the existing order. In one sense, most if not all, human geography could be described thereafter as political. The specific area of a self-described political geography itself enjoyed a revival. The former focus on the state gave way to an interest in the world scale; for example, in Peter *Taylor's development of the *world-systems approach, as well as the urban scale, in the work of Kevin *Cox, Ron *Johnston, David *Harvey, and others. Issues of *class, and later *race, *gender, and *sexuality came to the fore. In France, Yves Lacoste founded the journal *Hérodote* (1976) to introduce French geographers to some of the radical ideas of the country's new generation of social and political theorists. The leading journal *Political Geography Quarterly* (later renamed *Political Geography*) was founded in 1982, marking the recovery of the field. Thereafter, political geography generated and responded to the same currents as human geography in general, including *postmodernism, *post-structuralism, and *post-colonialism (*see* CRITICAL GEOPOLITICS). To the long-standing interests in the state, *power and boundaries, modern courses and texts in the field include sexual politics, *citizenship, *social movements, *civil society, *globalization, and *environment. Indeed, globalization has reopened older debates about the relations between territory, identity, and boundaries. Wars in the Balkans, Afghanistan, and Iraq, and the related 'war on terror' have prompted a greater interest in violence, both state and non-state (*see* TERRORISM; WAR). *Political ecology marks the overlap between political geography and a concern for *nature, resources, and the environment. Given the significance of *climate change, *food security, and oil resources, political geographers have in some ways revived the preoccupations of their 19th-century predecessors for the physical environment, although without the trappings of environmental determinism.

Further reading Agnew, J. (2002), *Making Political Geography*.

Jones, M., Jones, R., and Woods, M. (2004), *An Introduction to Political Geography: Space, Place and Politics*.

Painter, J. and Jeffreys, A. (2009), *Political Geography: an Introduction to Space and Power*.

political system The set of institutions, organizations, and constitutional arrangements that form a government or *state. The world's main political system is currently the *nation state, but past examples include *empires, leagues, and city states and, in more anthropological terms, tribes and clans.

pollution 1. Substances or energy entering an environment at levels that cause harm to either living organisms or buildings and other structures.

2. The contamination of some state, place, or space by impurity.

The first sense covers the impairment of air and water quality by chemicals, particles, noise, and light; it is usually understood as anthropogenic. The second sense derives largely from the work of anthropologist Mary Douglas, whose book *Purity and Danger* (1966) examined the rituals and significance of purity in different societies.

polycentricity A region or country characterized by several places or cities of a similar size and importance, even if they vary in terms of their economic or social characteristics. These different localities may develop various interdependencies organically over time, but their functional integration can also be facilitated by national or local government planning. For instance, the *Randstad* in the *Netherlands is polycentric because Amsterdam, Rotterdam, The Hague, and Utrecht are all fairly close by car or rail, and there are significant levels of interaction between them all.

polyphony A textual strategy for including multiple voices in a text in order to disrupt and destabilize the authorial voice. It is used as a political strategy to provide a more balanced representation of the phenomena under investigation. It can include texts that are written by multiple authors, each writing with their own voice and expressing their own opinions, and texts that include multiple voices within the narrative, such as the reporting of interview-based or ethnographic research.

popular geography The varieties of geographical knowledge produced and circulated outside institutions of higher education and specialized or technical inquiry. Popular geography can be contrasted with academic geography; it is aimed at a mass audience. Examples include the magazine *National Geographic*, television programmes on travel and exploration, and school geography.

population density The number of people per unit of area, for example, per square kilometre. Mongolia has 1.77 people per km^2 and Singapore over 7000 per km^2. It should not be confused with overcrowding, which is a measure of the average number of people per room in a dwelling or area.

population geography The geographical study of population, including its spatial distribution, dynamics, and movement. As a subdiscipline, it has taken at least three distinct but related forms, the most recent of which appears increasingly integrated with *human geography in general. The earliest and most enduring form of population geography emerged from the 1950s onwards, as part of *spatial science. Pioneered by Glenn Trewartha, Wilbur *Zelinsky, William A. V. Clark, and others in the USA, as well as Jacqueline Beujeau-Garnier and Pierre George in France, it focused on the systematic study of the distribution of population as a whole and the spatial variation in population characteristics such as *fertility and *mortality. Given the rapidly growing global population as well as the baby boom in affluent countries such as the USA, these geographers studied the relation between demographic growth and resources at an international scale, and population redistribution nationally (*see* DEMOGRAPHIC TRANSITION). An exemplary contribution might be Zelinksy's mobility transition model (1971) linking migration and demographic change. They used secondary data sources such as censuses to map and describe population change and variation, including such trends as *counter-urbanization. Such work could often be distinguished from population studies in general by its use of smaller scale data, below national level. *Population projections at national and regional scales could be used to inform public policy debates on resource allocation. The increasing availability of more sophisticated spatial data, including more flexible *census geographies, inter-censual surveys, and more detailed cross-tabulations such as the US Public-Use Microdata Samples encouraged more advanced modelling, simulation, and projection techniques (*see* GEODEMOGRAPHICS). This broad population geography has always been international and therefore comparative in scope, particularly under the auspices of the IGU Commission on Population Geography. To some extent, however, progress in the *Global South has been held back by the poor availability of high-quality spatial data (Hugo 2006). Regular international conferences in population geography began in 2002.

  A second variant of population geography is narrower in focus, akin to spatial demography. Geographers working in this field stressed the importance of keeping close to demography, its theories and methods, and therefore concentrating more on the core demographic variables of fertility, mortality, and, to a lesser extent, migration. They applied mathematical techniques to describe, infer, and also explain population patterns past and present. A volume edited by British geographers Bob Woods and Phil Rees (1986) *Population Structures and Models: Developments in spatial demography* typifies this approach. Woods' own specialism was the *historical demography of infant mortality in Victorian Britain. Spatial demography has a strong historical component, not least among French and British geographers. By detailing the spatial (and temporal) variation in mortality, fertility, nuptuality, etc., geographers were able to disrupt many of the generalizations of population change and identify the significance of place.

Many population geographers from the 1980s onwards expressed anxiety that they were marginalized from mainstream human geography and its embrace of social theories from *Marxism to *feminism, and *postmodernism (Findlay and Graham 1991). Not enough research was being done on key issues such as famine, gender, and environment. They also sensed that other human geographers were overlooking the significance of population to wider processes. A 'retheorization' of population geography (White and Jackson) gradually took shape, involving more methodological diversity and theoretical plurality. New methods, such as *lifecourse analysis, helped integrate biographical and individual-level studies into the field. In recent years there has been greater attention paid to gender, religion, age, disability, generation, sexuality, and race, variables which go beyond the vital statistics of births, deaths, and marriages. Furthermore, population geographers have begun to critique the standard census categories of the field, recognizing the *social construction of childhood, *whiteness, femininity, etc. Representative of this more theoretical approach is James Tyner's (2009) *War, Violence and Population: making the body count.* Tyner argues that population geography should pay more attention to war and violence, using examples from the Vietnam War, Cambodia's killing fields, and the Rwandan genocide. Grounded in *post-colonialism and *post-structuralism, he deploys Foucault's concepts of biopower and disciplinary power to uncover the logics behind such violence.

This more recent form of population geography is increasingly aligned with human geography as a whole. One consequence has been the relative neglect of studies of fertility, mortality, and *morbidity, the latter becoming the preserve of medical geography. Of the core demographic topics, *migration continued to be the most central to population geographers; most of the papers in the main population geography journals, *Population, Space and Place* (launched in 1995 as *The International Journal of Population Geography*) and *Espace, Populations, Sociétés* (founded 1983), concern migration and related topics such as *transnationalism.

All three forms of population geography outlined here continue side by side. Spatial and historical demography is making increasing use of data sources from outside Europe. Popular textbooks such as *Population Geography: Problems, Concept and Prospects* (Peters and Larkin 2010) teach new generations the basics of the subject. By contrast, Adrian Bailey's (2005) *Making Population Geography* presents a broader, more theoretically informed perspective. Recent conferences and journal special issues have focused on climate change, neo-Malthusianism, children's geographies, vulnerability, and difference, although migration continues to predominate.

References and further reading Findlay, A. and Graham, E. (1991), 'On the challenges facing population geography', *Progress in Human Geography* 15: 149–62.

Gober, P. and Tyner, J. (2003), 'Population geography', in Gaile, G. L. and Willmott, C. J. (eds.) *Geography in America at the Dawn of the 21st Century*, 185–199.

Hugo, G. (2006), 'Population geography', *Progress in Human Geography* 30(4), 513–23.

Population, Space and Place (2004) special issue on 'Fifty Years since Trewartha', 10(4), 277–355.

White, P. and Jackson, P. (1995), 'Retheorising population geography', *International Journal of Population Geography* 1(2): 111–23.

population projection A mathematical calculation of the size and structure of a future population based on current levels of fertility, mortality, and migration.

Projections are hypothetical scenarios, not estimates or forecasts (which may assume changing levels of fertility, etc.). Given the uncertainties involved, demographers increasingly make probabilistic projections, e.g. that it is 80 per cent probable that the world population will lie between 7.4 and 10.4 billion by 2050 (Lutz et al. 2001).

Reference Lutz, W., Sanderson W., and Scherbov, S. (2001), 'The end of world population growth', *Nature* 412 (6846): 543–45.

population pyramid   A diagram showing the age and sex structure of a population. It is typically shown as a histogram, with the size of each five-year age group for males and females separately arranged either side of the vertical axis. The shape of a healthy population's diagram should be a pyramid, but it is also a way of illustrating the loss of cohorts, for example, by war, or exceptional gains, for example, a youth bulge.

populism   A political discourse suggesting that the interests of the mass of the people are opposed to the interests of an elite. Populist ideas and rhetoric have been mobilized by both left- and right-wing political movements, most recently in the Occupy Movement, among whose slogans is the claim that the interests of 99 per cent of people are contrary to the super-rich one per cent. Simplistic references to place and country can feature in populist discourses.

port   A coastal or inland location with a harbour where people and cargo can be transferred between land and boats. The location provides shelter from storms and optimal access to fishing grounds, shipping routes, and markets. Given their importance to international trade, many ports have become the focal points around which large cities have developed. Deep water ports are key nodes in international flows of goods, able to handle the largest of ships. *See also* CONTAINERIZATION; GATEWAY CITY; TRANSPORT GEOGRAPHY.

Porter, Michael (1947–)   A US economist based at the Harvard Business School who specializes in analysing company strategy and the competiveness of regions and nations. He has contributed to *economic geography through his writings on location, competition, *innovation, and the role of clustering and *agglomeration on economic development. His work has extended beyond the academy to influence the decisions of business, government, and the community sector.

positionality   The recognition and declaration of one's own position in a piece of academic work. *Feminist critique of traditional science questions the extent to which it can be *objective, neutral, and value-free. Instead, it posits that all research is produced within a contextual framing and is situated with respect to the position of the researcher. Rather than concealing the positionality of the researcher and the work, feminists argue that their positionality should be reflected upon and declared so that the politics and power framing of a study and the standpoint of the researcher, is known, enabling those engaging with the research to be able to better evaluate its merits. *See also* MASCULINISM; REFLEXIVITY; SITUATED KNOWLEDGE.

Further reading Rose, G. (1997), 'Situating knowledges: positionality, reflexivity and other tactics', *Progress in Human Geography* 21: 305–20.

positivism   A philosophy that seeks to define the basis on which true knowledge of the world can be created. Historically, it is associated with the writings of Frenchman August Comte (1798–1827) and is part of the *Enlightenment belief that neither religion, superstition, nor metaphysics can tell us anything truthful about the material reality we inhabit. In the early 20th century, Comte's ideas were finessed and blended with others to form the *logical positivism of the Vienna Circle (*see* LOGICAL EMPIRICISM). In its various post-Comtean forms, positivism exhibits the following features: (i) a belief that all knowledge must be founded on systematic *observation of the world; (ii) a belief that some combination of *verification and *falsification can allow such observation to test hypotheses (testable statements about the world); (iii) suspicion that non-observable forces or processes exist, even if their perceptible outcomes do not always suggest their existence in any obvious way; (iv) the conviction that facts and values are separable; and (v) a belief that utilization of a common scientific method can, in time, yield complete knowledge of the human and biophysical worlds.

Though they rarely used the word, there is little doubt that many geographers in the 1960s and 1970s strongly embraced several of its principles. *Spatial science in its various concrete forms was implicitly positivist, while David Harvey's *Explanation in Geography* justified its utilization in geography without mentioning the term. Today, one might say that a positivist sensibility pervades a good deal of human geography, and most parts of physical geography. However, positivism came in for sustained and heavy criticism by many human geographers from the mid-1970s onwards, leading some to declare themselves non- or post-positivist. It was argued that while observation is crucial for all research, facts do not speak for themselves independently of the values and *paradigms of observers. It was suggested that there is no 'real world' out there that can be appealed to in order to distinguish true from false statements because *representation and reality are linked in recursive and dynamic ways (*see* HERMENEUTICS). Furthermore, critics argued that many real but invisible processes give rise to visible events, and that we need to understand their substance, not merely their results. Finally, critics questioned the idea that a single, putatively value-free method of inquiry could somehow accommodate the diversity of ontologies, epistemologies, theories, and concepts created by researchers. Because of all this, positivism is not only less popular in human geography than 40 years ago, but something of a closet philosophy among its continued adherents in the discipline.

Further reading Kitchin, R. (2006), 'Positivism', in Aitken, S. and Valentine, G. (eds.) *Approaches to Human Geography*.

possibilism The idea that humans can choose, within certain limits, how they interact with the physical environment. It contrasts with the idea of *environmental determinism, wherein natural forces shape society strongly. Possibilism is closely associated with the work of French geographers in the period 1870–1920, notably Paul *Vidal de la Blache. *See also* PROBABILISM.

Further reading Livingstone, D. N. (1992), *The Geographical Tradition*.

post-colonialism An intellectual movement, based largely in the humanities, concerned to firstly move beyond conventional understandings of colonial rule, and secondly, to understand the operations of colonial *power in the present, sixty years after the start of a wave of decolonization which largely, thought not totally, dismantled the major European *empires. Post-colonialism is thus 'post' in two distinct senses, one having to do with broadening the concept of *colonialism, the other having to do with extending its temporal applicability beyond the 1950s and 1960s when the former European colonies (e.g. Algeria) gained their independence.

Human geographers were attracted to post-colonial thinking after the publication of Edward *Said's (1978) book *Orientalism*. Though it took time for them to appreciate the book's importance, once *postmodernism and *post-structuralism caught human geographers' collective attention they began to reconsider both the character of colonialism and their own discipline. They began to see 19th- and early 20th-century colonialism in *Africa, *Asia, and elsewhere as a *cultural*, as much as political, bureaucratic, and military process. Discourses about and representations of Europe and the 'Orient', the West and

'Darkest Africa', were shown to be essential components of the process of exerting control over far distant territories and peoples (*see* ORIENTALISM). New critical histories of academic geography were also written that revealed the subject's unwitting complicity in colonial thinking, reproducing in university research and teaching the 'common sense' prejudices against less 'civilized' societies characteristic of the Victorian and Edwardian periods.

Rather than work with a broad-brush conception of colonialism, human geographers revealed the multiple concrete colonialisms operative a century ago, and explored the varied experiences of different colonizers (according to things such as their class, gender, religious convictions, and so on). Colonialism was shown to be more differentiated and hesitant than commonly believed, and more than something relating to distant lands. It also affected colonizing societies themselves, as Jane Jacobs demonstrated in *Edge of Empire* (1996), which tracks the past and present colonial relations between London and Australia, and Catherine Nash in her work on Ireland's post-colonial landscapes. Work on European travellers' experiences of the colonies also revealed the subtle, but often stark ways in which non-Western sites and societies began to challenge Europeans' confident sense of self, initiating a more generous sense of what the world had to offer.

Historical geographies of European colonialism and travel aside, many human geographers have also been post-colonial critics in the second aim above. Though today's major world powers advocate all countries' right of self-determination, their rhetoric is rather belied by their various attempts to exert control over countries deemed to be strategically important to their interests. As in the era of formal colonialism, this control has economic and military dimensions, even if direct political rule is no longer feasible or desirable. However, as Derek *Gregory (2004) shows in *The Colonial Present*, modern versions of many colonial era cultural prejudices structure the thinking and actions of governments, intelligence personnel, and military professionals.

Despite its vibrancy, post-colonial thinking in human geography has not escaped criticism. Some have claimed it is too bookish, focusing on colonists' representations, and not enough on the actual practices of colonial rule. Others question whether ostensibly post-colonial researchers can truly step outside the cultural parameters laid down by their Anglophone forebears. On the plus side, not only has post-colonialism inspired human geographers to focus their eyes beyond the West—something that arguably has not happened enough since the 1960s—it has opened the door for scholars educated outside the West to have their voices heard in the discipline in ways scarcely conceivable even twenty years ago.

Further reading Blunt, A. and Wills, J. (2000), *Dissenting Geographies*.
Crush, J. (1994), 'Post-colonialism, decolonization, and geography' in Godlewska, A. and
    Smith, N. (eds.) *Geography and Empire* 333–50.
Nash, C. (2004), 'Postcolonial geographies', in Cloke, P., Crang, P., and Goodwin, M. (eds.)
    Envisioning Geographies 104–27.

post-development the critique and rejection of the idea of *development as contained within the theories and policies advocated by the governments, institutions, and mainstream theorists of the *Global North. Post-development thinking seeks neither reform of nor alternatives to dominant development ideas, but questions their very foundation in *eurocentric norms and racial hierarchies.

Post-development ideas and practices emerged from *social movements and scholars. A host of urban popular movements, indigenous rights organizations, peasant farmer and *landless movement groups flourished from the 1980s, often in reaction to *International Monetary Fund-imposed *structural adjustment programmes. Though diverse in origins and politics, they challenged prevailing assumptions that their communities were indelibly poor, marginalized, and/or deficient in some way, and therefore needed external assistance (e.g., *Chipko Movement, *Movimento dos Trabalhadores Rurais Sem-Terra, *Zapatistas). They espoused values other than those of economics, including frugality, participation, non-violence, *indigenous knowledge, *deep ecology, and gender equality.

Academic expressions of post-developmentalism often draw from such movements, but they are also influenced by *post-colonialism and *post-structuralism, and above all the ideas of Michel *Foucault. The Colombian anthropologist Arturo Escobar, for example, examined the discursive construction of Colombia as a poor country in *World Bank documents and missions from the 1940s on. In *Encountering Development* (1995) he argued that the development actors of the *Global North discovered, constructed, and globalized mass poverty in Asia, Africa, and Latin America. Countries such as Colombia came to be defined as poor in opposition to the North, constituting the poor and their territories as an object of government. By the same token, agents of the Global North assumed the role of experts.

Critics of post-development thinkers suggest that they *essentialize development programmes and ideas, failing to recognize the diversity among them, and how they have changed. They are also charged with romanticizing local and grassroots politics, while under-estimating the degree to which their critique of the state and championing of localism, in fact, fits with the very *neoliberal ideas they seek to oppose.

Further reading Lawson, V. (2007), *Making Development Geography*.

post-Fordism A new economic, political, and social regime thought to replace the long post-1945 period of *Fordism in the major Western democracies. Beginning in the mid-1980s, post-Fordism (sometimes equated with *flexible accumulation) was characterized by a sea-change in economic, governmental, and societal arrangements. Economically, firms began to employ more flexible workers and technologies, moved to *just-in-time production, and favoured out-sourcing and short contracts with suppliers, distributors, marketers, etc. Politically, the *welfare state was progressively restructured by national governments in order to reduce public spending and place the onus on citizens to provide for themselves. At the same time, national trades unions lost power and members. Finally, society began to change towards a less solidaristic 'help-thy-neighbour' ethic, best represented by *neoliberalism. Economic geographers have done much to trace the uneven geographies of post-Fordism, in the process challenging the simplistic idea of an historical sea-change experienced equally by all Western countries.

Further reading Amin, A. (ed.) (1994), *Post-Fordism: a Reader*.

post-humanism A family of approaches advocated by some human geographers and others in the *humanities, that questions the supposed separation of humans from a wider *assemblage of relations, processes, and phenomena. For centuries, Western scholars have thought humanity to be different in kind from the rest of *nature, able to modify its surroundings in order to realize its own needs, wants, and desires. However, notwithstanding the evident uniqueness of *homo sapiens*, post-humanists remind us that we are not only biophysical entities made of flesh and blood (like other living creatures), but remain reliant on and daily affected by a plethora of non-human substances and actors (e.g. metals, domestic pets, and water). Post-humanists reject the historical argument, famously made by Francis Fukuyama in *Our Posthuman Future* (2002), that we are now becoming post-human by virtue of new technologies such as genetic modification. Their point is that we have *always* been (and remain) post-human: we are constitutively 'impure' and worldly. Geographically, post-humanists question attempts to purify *place, *space, or *territory, as if they can be—or be seen to be—either wholly social or wholly natural. The ethical implication of this is not to reject *anthropocentrism in favour of ecocentrism, but to attend more closely to the moral connections between humans and non-humans arising from their ontological imbrication. This muddies the waters supposedly separating *environmental ethics and human ethics.

Further reading Braun, B. (2004), 'Querying post-humanism', *Geoforum* 35, 2: 269–73.

post-industrial society A society in which the majority of jobs are knowledge-based and involve mental rather than manual labour. The term was popularized in the early 1970s by the American commentator Daniel Bell. He suggested that advanced capitalist societies would evolve such that heavy industry and manufacturing would give way to economic activities based more on the possession and application of knowledge (*see* KNOWLEDGE ECONOMY). His was a progressive vision that, while partly prescient, did not foresee (i) the large number of routine/mundane jobs characteristic of post-industrial economies, and (ii) the large number of post-industrial jobs that would 'flee' the West and be created in countries such as *India. What's more, looking at countries such as *Australia and *Canada, one can see the persistence of a great many heavy industries and associated forms of manual labour. As with all epochal concepts, Bell's risked oversimplifying a far more complex story of historical-geographical change in Western countries.

Postmodern Geographies A book by Edward *Soja (1989), sub-titled 'the reassertion of space in critical social theory', it was a major early work in the postmodern turn (*see* POSTMODERNISM). Soja, a geographer and urban theorist at the University of California, Los Angeles, pulled together a number of reflections on space by social theorists from *Marx to *Foucault and *Lefebvre to challenge the *historicism of much contemporary theory. He also used *Los Angeles to think through these ideas, associating him with the 'Los Angeles School' of urban theorists.

postmodernism A broad movement across the arts, humanities, and social sciences that questions or opposes many of the presumed certainties of *modernism. Chief among these were: the authority of the scientific method and claims to objectivity; the sense of progress according to common ideals such as *equality and *justice based on universal principles; a refusal to be bound by the conventions of modern style and *representation; and the intrinsic orderliness of social life and reality more generally. What underpins these is a profound and principled scepticism about the existence of universal modes of explanation resting on secure *ontological foundations (*see* FOUNDATIONALISM; RELATIVISM; UNIVERSALISM). In its place, postmodernism offers contingency and uncertainty. As well as being a movement, postmodernism can be thought of as a period or turning point in intellectual, cultural, and social life. The postmodern movement developed in the 1970s and flourished in the 1980s and 1990s, taking different but loosely related forms in art, architecture, dance, literature, philosophy, social theory, and also human geography. Although many of the issues it raised were not resolved, there is a general sense that the postmodern tide has flowed and passed. A further distinction can be made between postmodernism as an expression, for example, in the arts, and 'postmodernity' as the experience or condition being expressed (*see* MODERNITY). In David *Harvey's well-known book *The *Condition of Postmodernity*, for example, he describes a novel experience of space and time aligned with shifts in the capital accumulation process from the mid 1970s (*see* FLEXIBLE ACCUMULATION).

Postmodernism erupted into human geography and generated considerable debate and disagreement. The contours of this debate can be illustrated by the contrasts between some of the main protagonists. Harvey regarded postmodernism not as a fundamentally new state of affairs, but as another modulation of the long-running ambiguities of modernism itself, i.e. between order, fixity, and stability on the one hand, and transience, disorder, and contingency on the other. In his view, *Marxism still provided the adequate means for making sense of the world and the prospect of universal explanation remained. By contrast, in their various writings, Michael *Dear and David *Ley were far less convinced that nothing fundamental had changed and less persuaded by the certainties offered by modern forms of explanation such as Marxism or *positivism. In their interpretations, postmodernism represented a realignment of social forces away from the centrality of class towards something much more plural and open. Differences of gender, race, and sexuality were equally important for progressive politics. Many *feminist geographers also made this point, critical of Harvey for underplaying the importance of difference. To Ley and Dear it was also a potentially liberating moment because older political models were bankrupt. Dear, to take a small but telling example, enjoins readers of his book *The Spaces of Postmodernity* (with Steven Flusty, 2002) not to read the chapters in the printed order. Ed *Soja, like Dear, a resident of *Los Angeles, refused to choose between modernism and postmodernism, preferring to work with the tension between them. Soja's emphasis in *Postmodern Geographies* is on the reassertion of space in social theory as the defining feature of the age (*see* SPATIAL TURN). In a similar fashion, Derek *Gregory emphasized the continuities with modernism but regarded the encounter between human geography and cultural studies as the central element of postmodernism.

The greatest impact of these debates was in rethinking *urbanism and the nature of cities (*see* URBAN GEOGRAPHY) and in adding impetus to the momentum of *cultural geography. The nature of human geographical debates over postmodernism can be gauged from the readings collected by Dear and Flusty in *The Spaces of Postmodernity*.

References Gregory, D. (1994), *Geographical Imaginations*.

Ley, D. (1987), 'Styles of the times: liberal and neo-conservative landscapes in inner Vancouver, 1968–1986', *Journal of Historical Geography* 13 (1): 40–56.

post-normal science A form of *science, and research more generally, that must cope with evidential uncertainty, values disputes, high stakes, and the urgent need for action. According to science analysts Silvio Funtowicz and Jerome Ravetz 'normal science' (*see* PARADIGM) occurs where investigators' findings are well evidenced and, in value terms, relatively uncontroversial, often leading to practically effective inventions or policies. By contrast, the topics of interest to post-normal science are ones where there are real doubts about what current evidence signifies, where the implications of science's discoveries are significant, where pre-emptive action to avert major ecological or social problems may be required now, but where large disagreements arise over whether and how such action should occur. Until very recently (and perhaps still) the science of global climate change was post-normal. To the extent that they research climate change and its likely impacts, along with other significant developments such as genetically modified organisms, human geographers are involved in producing post-normal research.

post-politics *See* ANTI-POLITICS.

post-productivist agriculture A suite of changes to farming practice in the developed world since 1945 involving, among other things: a shift from a focus on maximizing output to the quality of farm goods; the diversification of farm activities away from agriculture, for example, tourism; the encouragement of sustainable, including organic farming; the reduction in direct state support for farming in order to sustain national levels of food production. The effects of post-productivism go beyond farming to include new relations of rural governance.

Further reading Wilson. G. A. (2001), 'From productivism to post-productivism . . . and back again?', *Transactions of the Institute of British Geographers* 26: 103–20.

post-socialism A period and condition following the collapse of communist governments in East and Central Europe from 1990 onwards (*see* COMMUNISM; SOCIALISM). The term post-communism is also used. Socialist states were characterized by one-party government (the communist party), state-ownership of the major industrial sectors, central price controls, and high levels of collective provision of welfare and housing. To varying degrees, the countries of the region adopted multiparty democracy, market economies, and privatized industries, resulting in generally mixed economies. But, to describe this process as a 'transition' would be misleading (*see* TRANSITION ECONOMY). Despite some optimistic expectations, the institutions of liberal democracy could not be swiftly grafted onto socialist societies and economies. Initially at least, living conditions across much of the region fell. Furthermore, households in marginal regions and circumstances sometimes had to revive older, pre-communist practices of making a living. Multiparty democracy allowed authoritarian and nationalist parties to compete for power. Secondly, it is not clear that such counties are converging on a Western European model of liberal capitalism. Rather, new institutions are being combined with pre-existing ones in novel and often complex ways. Finally, there is considerable diversity across the region. Some former communist states have become members of the *European Union, while others continue with recognizably socialist ways.

Further reading Pickles, J. and Smith, A. (1998), *Theorising Transition: the Political Economy of Post-Communist Transformation.*

post-structuralism A body of writing, originating largely in post-1960 France, that takes issue with the core arguments of *structuralism. It continues to exert a large influence on the social sciences and the humanities. In a generic sense, structuralism is any theory or piece of research that emphasizes the *power of relations, rules, norms, or processes that any one person or institution is helpless to control. However, post-structuralists such as Gilles *Deleuze, Jacques Derrida, Michel *Foucault, and Julia Kristeva were critical of a specific kind of structuralism influential in mid-20th-century academic life. This structuralism, advocated by linguist Ferdinand de Saussure and anthropologist Claude Levi-Strauss, posited a real but invisible set of rules and concepts that gave rise to ostensibly different forms of signification (e.g. speech, rituals, paintings) (*see* SEMIOTICS). Post-structuralists were suspicious of this claim that the evident diversity and dynamism of human life was reducible to a few timeless regularities intrinsic either to the human mind or arising organically (though not necessarily) from human social evolution. At the level of philosophy, some (notably Derrida) showed that in order to give the appearance that 'structures' were enduring, structuralists were forced to deny the implications of their own analysis: namely, that all putative structures (e.g. the 'rules of language') have no secure or timeless foundation that will guarantee their permanence or security. At the level of history, others (notably Foucault from the late 1960s) began to research the varied and changing knowledges that new *epistemic communities were constructing from the 18th century (e.g. medics, psychiatrists). These knowledges were shown to be *sui generis*, not mere epiphenomena of invisible, cast-iron structures.

In turn, these contributions crystallized several themes that have come to characterize post-structural thought. The first is that discourses, significations, and representations are material; indeed, they seek to materialize (or disclose) the world in different ways that deserve to be understood for their intended effects. The second is that these discourses, significations, and representations are irreducible to any root cause, underlying principle, or universal rules. To search outside them for some secure foundation is to forever beg the question of what the foundation itself is founded on. The third is that all signification must be understood in its context or contexts: there is no 'essential' meaning intrinsic to any given speech, act, book, newspaper, film, etc. The fourth is that 'the human' does not precede signification. Instead, people are interpellated in different ways in different webs of signification (*see* INTERPELLATION). We thus need to talk of identities and subject-positions in the plural (*see* HUMANISM). Finally, the implication of all this for research is the 'death of the author' since all inquiry is not reducible to the sovereign intentions of a fully formed, discrete human agent.

Initially, in the 1990s, many human geographers were greatly taken with the first three themes. The discourses and representations of everyone from professional cartographers to urban planners to geographical information scientists became the focus of forensic analysis designed to 'deconstruct' their apparent innocence, coherence, and legitimacy. This was usually linked with Foucault's insight that social *power was not simply concentrated in a few institutions or agencies (e.g. central government or the police), but instead dispersed among a plethora of epistemic communities—many of which seemed benign or even benevolent (e.g. charity workers, philanthropists, and development professionals). Indeed, human geographers shone a sceptical light on their own knowledge claims, pursuing the fifth theme above in historical work into the rhetorics used by their spatial science and Marxist forebears (Barnes 1996). Looking outside their own discipline, human geographers attended closely to the ways in which signs in and about certain sites (e.g. public squares), places, landscapes, and territories were as material as the things to which they referred, and were vehicles for conveying authority and resistance. By the turn of the millennium, far more attention was given to the latter as researchers looked closely at the oppositional discourses of, for example, the *anti-globalization movement. Far more attention was also paid to how subject-positions were enacted in speech, dress, and comportment in the micro-spaces of everyday life (e.g. workplaces, homes). The work of US post-structuralist Judith *Butler was of particular inspiration here (*see* PERFORMATIVITY).

By this time critics had already sharpened their knives and wielded them. For example, Andrew *Sayer—a 'strong realist' (*see* REALISM)—accused human geography's post-structuralists of *nominalism and *idealism. While it is true that some had presumed—without always demonstrating empirically—the efficacy of signification, more savvy practitioners were clear that theirs was not an anti-realism that delinked language, discourse, and representation from its wider conditions of existence. Inspired by the writings of Gilles Deleuze and Felix Guattari, recently many post-structuralist geographers have been examining how the world is composed by assembling, stabilizing, and undoing various materials, agents, and forces. Their 'radical empiricism' looks for nothing above, beneath, or beyond the 'assemblages' concocted by differently empowered social actors (including their discourses), and it recognizes the agency of non-humans. Normatively, this work is committed to exploration, becoming, and invention in order to challenge attempts to govern thought and practice by freezing and fixing current arrangements. As such, post-structuralism today has affinities with *Actor-Network Theory and *non-representation theory (*see* POST-HUMANISM). Only time will tell if it will continue to be paradigmatic for so many human geographers in the future. *See also* ASSEMBLAGE; DISCOURSE ANALYSIS; HYBRIDITY.

References and further reading Barnes, T. (1996), *Logics of Dislocation*.
Doel M. A. (2004), 'Poststructuralist geographies: the essential selection', in Cloke, P. et al. (eds.) *Envisioning Human Geographies* 146– 71.

poverty The lack of sufficient means to enjoy a standard of living considered normal and acceptable in a given society. There are broadly two ways in which one might interpret what 'means' are. One is simply income; poverty is the lack of sufficient income to acquire what one's society considers either necessary (for example, in terms of food, shelter, and clothing) or adequate. The second takes account of broader factors, based on the ability to access safely whatever an individual needs to live the life that they choose according to their values. This is often termed the *capabilities approach to poverty and development (*see* ENTITLEMENT APPROACH). The first set of ideas is utilitarian and the second more concerned with welfare as a whole (*see* DEPRIVATION).

Poverty can be absolute or relative. Absolute poverty is based on the idea that there is a minimum nutritional requirement to life, for example, 2400 calories a day or the money necessary to obtain that amount of food. This defines a 'poverty line', i.e. a threshold below which a household or individual is regarded as poor and above which they are deemed not poor. This is invariant. It is often argued, however, that in richer parts of the world few if any people fall below this kind of threshold. But most people would not go on to claim that there is no poverty in, say, Australia or Canada. Relative poverty is an expression of how far below the average income a household or individual lies. For example, across the European Union, households with less than 60 per cent of median income are classified as poor. Over time, the level of income defining poverty therefore changes, most likely because the median goes up. But also, the degree of relative poverty is a function of *inequality. The more unequal a society's income distribution is, the greater the probability that households will be poor. Generally speaking, countries in the *Global South emphasize absolute measures and those in the *Global North collect data on relative measures. Poverty can also be chronic, i.e. lasting an individual's lifetime or a significant part thereof, or transitory, i.e. short-term (*see* CYCLE OF POVERTY). Individuals close to a poverty line may find themselves fluctuating in and out of poverty, for example, due to seasonally affected harvests or employment insecurity.

Definitions of poverty are closely related to how it is measured, and vice versa. One option would be to simply ask people if they are poor—a subjective measure. But, it often turns out that people even just below median income describe themselves as 'poor', which probably overstates things. Furthermore, there are people who actively choose a life of poverty out of religious conviction. For comparative purposes, objective measures are preferred. Income definitions of poverty are generally measured in two ways, either the amount of money needed to obtain a nutritionally adequate amount of food (sometimes adjusted for urban and rural locations), or the amount needed to also acquire clothing, shelter, health, and education ('consumption'). A common measure calculated by the *World Bank is the daily income needed for adequate consumption which was estimated at US$1 a day in 1985 and now stands at US$1.25 (recalibrated for inflation). This is taken as the poverty line. In international comparisons this value is adjusted for Purchasing Power Parity (PPP) to allow for the different cost of basics in different countries. Individuals and households with incomes below this value are described as living in 'extreme poverty'. In 1990, 1.9 billion people (43 per cent of the world's population) were so defined; in 2008, 1.29 billion (23 per cent) were classified as extremely poor. Further indicators based on these measures can be calculated. The 'poverty gap' is the mean shortfall from the poverty line, expressed as a percentage of the poverty line. It shows the depth of poverty. The poverty severity index further quantifies the level of inequality among those below the poverty line. Welfare definitions of poverty are generally realized by more broad-based indices (*see* HUMAN DEVELOPMENT INDEX). The Oxford Poverty and Human Development Initiative (OPHI) calculates a Multidimensional Poverty Index based on ten indicators including whether a household has electricity, a dirt floor, clean water within 30 minutes by foot, children at school, and so forth. A household is deemed poor if it is deprived on more than three of the indicators. On this index, 90 per cent of Ethiopians are classed as poor, whereas only 40 per cent have incomes of less than $1.25 a day. What such comparisons show is that having income or not is not a reliable indication of whether a household can or cannot get what it needs.

There is considerable interest in the spatial patterns of poverty based on both income or welfare measures, at international and smaller scales. More, however, is known about the geography of poverty than the geography of wealth. Mapping poor countries, i.e. those with low average incomes or high percentages living in poverty, is not, however, the same as mapping poor people. The OPHI points out that over twice as many of the world's poor people live in middle-income countries as low-income ones. Within countries, it is common to differentiate rural and urban poverty. Most poor people in the world live in rural areas, where lack of land or work generates poverty. At smaller scales, intra-urban variations in poverty have preoccupied social reformers since the 19th century. Intriguingly, Scott Orford, Danny Dorling, and colleagues discovered that geographical patterns in London's relative poverty were fairly similar at the end of the 19th and 20th centuries. In the 1980s the concept of 'poverty concentration' was identified. W. J. Wilson described how in US cities, the proportion of people living in poor neighbourhoods who were poor was increasing. This meant that poor urban Americans were less and less likely to meet non-poor people in their immediate neighbourhoods (*see* NEIGHBOURHOOD EFFECT; UNDERCLASS). There are also important social differences; poverty levels almost everywhere tend to be higher for women than men, and the elderly or children than adults (*see* RACISM).

Measuring and mapping poverty is generally accompanied by efforts to explain and reduce it. The causes of poverty are manifold and there is no consensus. Some theories stress geographic factors such as climate or geographical isolation on the one hand (*see* ENVIRONMENTAL DETERMINISM), or location on the other (*see* INNER CITY). Others locate causes in socio-economic conditions, either at the individual level or in terms of family and community (*see* CULTURE OF POVERTY). Human geographers tend to favour more structural explanations as formulated in *development theory. Considerable effort is expended at the international level to reduce poverty through, among other things, the *Millennium Development Goals (*see* DEVELOPMENT; POVERTY REDUCTION STRATEGIES). Civil society campaigns, such as Make Poverty History or Canada's End Poverty Now, have also sprung up since the 1990s. These efforts suffered a setback as a result of the 2007 global economic crisis.

Further reading and references Orford, S. et al. (2002), 'Life and death of the people of London: a historical GIS of Charles Booth's inquiry', *Health and Place* 8(1): 25–35.
Sachs, J. (2005), *The End of Poverty.*
Wilson, W.J. (1987), *The Truly Disadvantaged.*

SEE WEB LINKS
- World Bank Poverty and Equity data.
- Official website of the United Nations Development Programme.
- Oxford Poverty and Human Development Initiative.
- Official website of Make Poverty History campaign.

poverty reduction strategies The development programmes centred on alleviating *poverty in *LEDCs. Following criticism of *Structural Adjustment Policies and their mixed record of success, from the late 1990s international lenders adopted new approaches in line with the *Millennium Development Goals. Although still firmly within *neoliberal parameters favouring the state over the market, the conditions attached to low-interest loans from the *World Bank and *International Monetary Fund now included a requirement to show consultation between government and communities, and higher levels of public participation in setting priorities (*see* HEAVILY INDEBTED POOR COUNTRY). Countries were asked to draft their own individualized poverty reduction strategy papers based on wider consultation, although the speed with which they were done often prevented meaningful public input (*see* CIVIL SOCIETY).

Powell, Joseph (1940–) A historical geographer who has spent his entire career at Monash University in Australia. Joe Powell is noted for his research on the development of Australia since 1788, especially relating to pioneer settlement, *environmental management, *regional planning, and landscape modification, as exemplified by his book *An Historical Geography of Modern Australia* (1988). He has also acted as a disciplinary leader and has been active in charting the historiography of Australian geography.

power The ability or capacity to either act oneself or direct the action of others; it may be exercised by individuals, groups (such as classes), institutions, or any organized entity that can be considered an agent. Power is variously thought to be the precondition for action but also as its outcome; it can be overt or covert, for example, when setting an agenda that omits contentious issues. At one extreme it may involve force or coercion, but at the other it may operate through consent or will (*see* HEGEMONY). Power may be expressed through actions but equally through *representation and *discourse (*see* CRITICAL GEOPOLITICS).

Within human geography the principal conception of power is of a substance or resource that is possessed more by some agents and entities than others, chiefly the *state, but also *capital (for example, in the form of *transnational corporations). *Patriarchy, understood as a form of collective power that enables men as a class to dominate women (and children) as a class, also fits this description. In John Allen's terms, it is 'power over others' and in that sense is normally thought of as something negative or constraining. It is located in certain normally centralized sites, although it may be dispersed and delegated (*see* DECENTRALIZATION; DEVOLUTION). Some states may hold more power than others. In early political geography, state power was related to the occupation and control of territory and its resources, and the state's imperative was to maximize its power at the expense of others (*see* GEOPOLITICS; SUPERPOWER). This conception of power is clearly state-centric but insofar as it is visible and located it can be challenged (*see* RESISTANCE; SOVEREIGNTY). But the same idea of power ('over') applies to individuals; researchers have power over the subjects of their research, for example (*see* REFLEXIVITY). Much *feminist geography is also concerned with gendered power beyond the state, for example, located in workplaces and households.

One alternative concept, although not especially common in current human geography, locates power in all forms of social interaction. John Allen describes it as 'power to' do something in concert with others. Conceived thus, it both facilitates and constrains (*see* STRUCTURATION). It can be helpful to think of power in this way, because all people deploy power in some form or another, and it need not always be negative.

The main alternative to 'power over' comes from feminism and *post-structuralism. These share a sense of power as dispersed (not centred), and less immediately obvious. Michel *Foucault, for example, thought of 'disciplinary power' as something that circulates rather than adheres to specific sites. Working through techniques rather than through ideology or culture, it produces disciplined bodies, i.e. individuals fit to work, consume, love, learn, and function in society. Elaborated as *governmentality, Foucauldian scholars examine how individual conduct is steered through a combination of techniques, informed by *expertise, but also by the desire to regulate oneself. Other versions of more dispersed, networked, or fluid conceptions of power are found in the work of Gilles *Deleuze and Hardt and Negri (*see* EMPIRE; MULTITUDE). What these and the Foucauldian perspective share is the idea that power is productive or generative rather than negative and constraining. As Allen describes, power includes not just oppression and domination, but also seduction, negotiation, persuasion, and inducement. It is also always relational, i.e. entwined with *resistance, which itself can take many forms. *See also* EMPOWERMENT.

Further reading Allen, J. (2003), *The Lost Geographies of Power.*

Allen, J. (2003), 'Power', in Agnew, J., Mitchell, K., and Toal, G. (eds.) *A Companion to Political Geography* 95–108.

Painter, J. (2008), 'Geographies of space and power', in Cox, K. R., Low, M., and Robinson, J. (eds.) *The Sage Handbook of Political Geography* 57–72.

power-geometry The geographically uneven relations of *power that give institutions, communities, and individuals different kinds and degrees of *human agency—even within the same *place. The term was coined by Doreen *Massey in a critique of David *Harvey's notion of *time-space compression. Massey argued that this concept is too generalized, presuming all people to be subject to the collapse of time and space driven by the incessant restructuring of *capitalism. The concept of a power-geometry highlighted the differential relations of inter-place, international dependency, force, and constraint that bind people in heterogeneous ways—depending on who and where they are on the surface of the Earth. Despite the metaphor of geometry suggesting a certain solidity to power relations, Massey emphasized their dynamism as they interacted in often unexpected ways (*see* OVERDETERMINATION).

Reference Massey, D. (1993), 'Power geometry and a progressive sense of place', in Bird, J. et al. (eds.) *Mapping the Futures*, 60–70.

pragmatism A philosophy contending that what counts as knowledge is determined by its usefulness to human agents situated in changing historical and geographical circumstances. Originating in the late 19th century in the United States, pragmatism rejects the idea that philosophy is a privileged form of knowledge because it can disclose once-and-for-all the foundations of all human knowledge. Consequently, for pragmatists a statement said to be 'true' is not accepted by people because it mirrors reality in language, but because enough people find they can agree on its content and practical implications. Revived by Richard Rorty and others from the 1980s, pragmatism has had a wide influence on the contemporary humanities and social sciences, including human geography. It attends to the way knowledge gets made, the rhetorics used by its creators to claim epistemological legitimacy, and the grounds for agreement and debate among interlocutors. Human geographers have drawn on pragmatist ideas in order to examine their own construction of knowledge, as well as that of those they study. For instance, Trevor *Barnes has used it along with *post-structuralism to show how spatial scientists in the 1960s developed their new *paradigm, while John Allen uses it to examine how social *power relations are enacted.

References Allen, J. (2008), 'Pragmatism and power, or the power to make a difference in a radically contingent world', *Geoforum*, 39, 8: 1613–24.

Barnes, T. (2008), 'American pragmatism: towards a geographical introduction', *Geoforum* 39, 8: 1542–54.

Bridge, G. (2005), *Reason in the City of Difference*.

Pratt, Geraldine (1957–) A feminist geographer based at the University of British Columbia, best known for her books *Gender, Work and Space* (with Susan *Hanson, 1995) and *Working Feminism* (2004), and also for her long-term collaboration with the Philippine Women's Centre of BC, researching the lives of Filipino women who move to Canada. She has made a number of contributions to understanding female labour, transnational *migration and family, and feminist praxis with respect to collaboration, participation, testimonial theatre, and political organizing. She was an editor of *Environment and Planning D: Society and Space* and a co-editor of the fourth and fifth editions of the best-selling *Dictionary of Human Geography*.

praxis The conversion of knowledge into practical action, especially knowledge whose goal is to challenge prevailing political and moral arrangements. The ancient Greek philosopher Aristotle contrasted '*praxis*' with '*theoria*', or the pursuit of knowledge for knowledge's sake. In the mid-19th century, Karl *Marx reprised this more pointedly when, in his *Theses on Feuerbach*, he stated that 'philosophers have only interpreted the world in various ways; the point is to change it'. Since Marx penned these famous words, praxis has normally been taken to mean change-making action informed by a deep and conscious understanding of the contradictions and problems of the contemporary world. From the early 1970s, *radical geography called for forms of praxis more transformative than those associated with the reformist policies issuing from research in *spatial science and its offshoots. Subsequently, an emphasis on transformative action has characterized elements of *critical human geography. *See also* ACTION RESEARCH; ACTIVISM.

precarity *See* FLEXIBLE LABOUR.

precautionary principle A principle in operation in situations where there is no scientific consensus on a matter, but where there is good reason to think that a course of action will lead to serious harm; then the presumption is that the course should not be followed. The principle gives greater weight to the responsibility to protect the public, ecosystems, or species against harm, than to the need for strong scientific proof. It is embodied in some legal codes across the world, and is often invoked in cases such as anthropogenic climate change, food safety, and species extinction.

Pred, Allan (1936–2007) A US geographer who was based at the University of California, Berkeley for the whole of his academic career, though he spent much time in Sweden in his later years. He wrote three important trilogies. The first (1962–67) focused on the emergence and spatial dynamics of the American urban system and was very much in the tradition of *spatial science and *location theory. The second (1986–90) examined the development of everyday consciousness in the unfolding of *modernity in 18th- and 19th-century Sweden but through the perspective of social theory. The third (1995–2004) detailed the everyday spatialities of capitalist societies using contemporary Sweden as a case study. His work thoroughly engaged geography with history and made contributions to *time geography and debates on *structure and agency; he was one of the first geographers to experiment with different styles of academic writing, polyphony, and textual playfulness.

prediction A statement about future events, based on repeated observations of similar past events and/or the results of *models or simulations derived from known principles and processes. Though prediction is a feature of several areas of physical geography, it is today less common in human geography, where it was once associated with attempts to understand scientifically future patterns of spatial agglomeration and dispersal. Prediction can be important to *applied geography. For instance, it might be necessary to predict traffic patterns related to a proposed out-of-town shopping mall so as to cost necessary road improvements attendant with the mall's construction.

pre-industrial city An urban settlement characteristic of the period before the *Industrial Revolution, namely feudal societies (*see* FEUDALISM). Although such cities were very diverse, Gideon Sjoberg proposed that they shared similar social and morphological features. These included elite residences at the centre surrounded by lower-class neighbourhoods where households were grouped by occupation, ethnicity, or extended family, thus inverting the *concentric zone model of industrial cities.

presentism The practice of writing history from the uncritical perspective of the present. In the case of the history of geography, this can imply that the present is the inevitable culmination of past events. Or it may suggest that there is one true path from the past to the present, a path taken by disciplinary heroes, rendering others as 'deviant'. Finally, it can take current definitions of geography and project them onto the past regardless of what was believed at the time. David Livingstone discusses presentism and its alternatives in *The *Geographical Tradition* (1992).

principal components analysis (PCA) A method for identifying patterns (principal components) of similarity and difference in a complex dataset. PCA uses orthogonal linear transformations to convert a set of possibly correlated variables into a set of uncorrelated components. The first principal component accounts for the most variance in the data set, with subsequent components accounting for the next largest amounts. Once the principal components are determined, PCA can be used to reduce the number of dimensions within a dataset without much loss of information, making it useful for techniques such as image compression.

privacy The ability or sometimes right of individuals and groups to withhold information about themselves or remove themselves from public view. Different cultures and legal systems have varying ideas about privacy. For example, governments differ as to what they require citizens to reveal in census returns. The issue has become particularly pressing in the digital age as it is less easy to manage the generation and circulation of personal information. *See* PRIVATE SPACE.

private space The areas of the geographical environment that are restricted in their occupancy and use. Such spaces are not open to all members of the public and include private residences and other privately owned properties such as commercial premises. The *home is a key private space and is often considered a sanctuary from the openness of public space, though as feminists note it can also keep issues such as domestic violence out of the public sphere.

privatization The assignation of legal title to a named individual, group, or institution, giving them more or less exclusive rights to dispose of that which is named by the title. The term is commonly used to describe the transfer of ownership from state, community, or public bodies to private individuals or companies (*see* PROPERTY). Examples include land, water, utilities, transport, and schools, but it may also describe the process of granting intellectual property rights to goods formerly available to all, such as seeds (*see* TRIPS).

probabilism The idea that humans can choose how they interact with the physical environment, but not freely; nature makes some choices much more likely than others. Put this way, it is a compromise between *environmental determinism and *possibilism, although in practice all three positions differ more by emphasis than by principle.

probability models A set of models that seek to determine statistically the probability of a condition occurring. There are a wide variety of probability models used in geographical inquiry that draw on different areas of mathematics. Common models include the suite of *general linear models and *Bayesian statistics. *See also* CORRELATION; LOG-LINEAR MODELS; MARKOV CHAINS; POISSON REGRESSION MODELS; REGRESSION; SPATIAL INTERACTION MODELS.

producer services The business *services provided by one firm to another as part of the latter's process of producing commodities (*see* OUTSOURCING). Producer services include such things as accountancy, marketing, advertising, market testing, and commercial lending. The term 'advanced producer services' (APS) described firms that provide very high-value services based on their professional and often global expertise. Under *globalization, the number of producer service firms worldwide has grown significantly, but despite the latitude provided by *information and communication technologies, there is a distinct propensity for producer services to cluster in global or *world cities (*see* SASSEN, SASKIA).

production The process of combining and transforming materials in order to make something new, usually a *commodity. It has long been common to define production in relation to goods manufactured by industries, such as steel and mobile phones. However, a good deal of contemporary commodity production pertains to 'weightless commodities', e.g. *intellectual property rights. Though commodities are produced in various *modes of production, in contemporary *capitalism the signature characteristic of production is the sheer volume of commodities and the speed of their *consumption, such that new ones must quickly be produced to replace those already sold.

production of nature The idea that *nature is increasingly produced as an artefact of *capitalism through processes of material transformation, rather than something that precedes or exists outside capitalist relations. The argument was advanced by Neil *Smith in *Uneven Development* (1984). He suggested that biophysical processes of all kinds were being subsumed within capitalism.

Production of Space, The A work of *theory by the French Marxist intellectual Henri *Lefebvre, written in 1974 and translated into English in 1991, since when it has attracted considerable interest among *Marxist geographers and post-Marxist critics such as Ed *Soja. Lefebvre's central argument was that each *mode of production produces *space in its own image. He challenged the Newtonian idea that space is *a priori*, a universal container in which events occur. For Lefebvre, 'produced space' both reproduces modes of production but can also be the site of their contestation and dissolution. The 'politics of space' concerns the political work space in its physical and symbolic aspects, but also the way oppositional groups use space to change the world. In the latter respect, Lefebvre was much influenced by *Situationism.

professionalization of geography The adoption of new managerialism in higher education and its effects on pedagogy and research. This has included the use of performance metrics to evaluate productivity and quality, the branding of the discipline as useful to policy makers and industry, the transformation from amateur to professionally run geographical societies, and the introduction of professional accreditations such as 'chartered geographer'. It is argued that such professionalization has altered the practice of geographical inquiry, how forms of scholarship are valued, and how the discipline is organized and operates as a community of scholars.

propaganda maps A form of persuasive *cartography in which a *map is drawn in such a way as to convey explicitly a particular political message. Propaganda maps have been used extensively in territorial disputes to convince people to see the world in the way desired by the map creator. The cartographer can use design, symbolism, and cartouches, scale, generalization, and *map projection to convey a message. *See also* HOW TO LIE WITH MAPS.

property 1. A thing or things (which can be material or intangible) that belong to a person, persons, or legally constituted entity, e.g. corporation.
    2. A social relation centred on the uses of something or things.
    Property concerns three broad questions: what sorts of things can be owned (or not); how can they be owned; and who can own them? Land, vehicles, and machinery can be property, but so can personal image rights, musical recordings, and gene sequences. Since what can be owned, how they can be owned, and who can own them constantly change, issues of property lie at the centre of conflict, *law, and *ethics.

Within the Western tradition of *liberalism, a basic distinction is made between things owned by the *state or community (public) and everything else (private). The term 'quasi-public' is sometimes used to describe land or space that is privately owned but appears as if it is public, e.g. a shopping mall (*see* PRIVATE SPACE; PUBLIC SPACE). The essence of private property, which includes personal possessions, is that the owner is regarded as sovereign, i.e. they enjoy full use of the property. It is alienable, i.e. the owner can sell it or dispose of it, and the owner can exclude others from the use of it. Indeed, the ideal of a property-owning and therefore secure individual is at the centre of the concept of *liberalism. In this ideal, the state can only interfere with property rights under exceptional circumstances defined by law (*see* SOVEREIGNTY). From an alternative perspective, however, the ability to secure exclusive use of some good is the foundation of injustice and exploitation. For *Marx, the private ownership of capital (including money and machinery) was the basis for the class division in *capitalism. The origins of liberal property, where one party enjoys rights not available to another, often lie in acts of *violence (Blomley 2003). In practice, private property is hedged by conditions, including the requirements to recognize the use others enjoy of their property (Mitchell 2004). The development of private land ownership is closely linked with *cartography and map-making. Without maps there can no clear indication of who owns what. The legal provisions concerning material property have been progressively extended into intangible goods through systems of patent and copyright. These *intellectual property rights are increasingly important in a *knowledge economy.

This Western system is not universal, although it is bound up with *colonialism and the spread of *capitalism. An alternative set of property arrangements is the *commons, wherein a community enjoys the right to use a good and exclude others, but not the right to sell it (*see* COMMON POOL RESOURCES; COMMON PROPERTY RESOURCES; DISPOSSESSION; TRAGEDY OF THE COMMONS). Across the world, there are numerous clashes and disputes arising from attempts to convert commons into private or state-owned property (*see* PRIVATIZATION).There are also things with no clear owners, such as the atmosphere, seas, Moon, and, under the provision of international treaty, Antarctica (*see* WILDERNESS). These are sometimes called '*global commons'.

References and further reading Blomley, N. K. (2003), 'Law, property, and the geography of violence', *Annals of the Association of American Geographers* 93: 121–41.
Mitchell, K. (2004), *Crossing the Neoliberal Line: Pacific Rim Migration and the Metropolis*.

protest An act or statement registering objection, either expressed individually or organized collectively. There are many forms of protest, including writing letters to representatives, signing online petitions, attending rallies, boycotting products, setting fires (incendiarism), and taking direct action (*see* ENVIRONMENTAL DIRECT ACTION). The repertoire of protest varies historically and geographically. For example, in India *satyagraha* describes the practice of non-violent protest that also involves a quest for truth. Internet-based protests are adding to and extending more traditional forms of objection (*see* HACKTIVISM). Geographers' interest focuses on four main areas. First, especially in historical geography, mapping the distribution of protests can reveal something of the underlying geography of social, cultural, and political change. Second, there is interest in the actual geography of protest events, including the detailed disposition of protestors and authorities as well as the relative role of on- and off-line actions (*see* SOCIAL MOVEMENTS). Thirdly, geographers have studied protest camps and occupations, where activists seek to appropriate strategic sites. A good example was the UK-based Greenham Common Women's Peace Camp outside an RAF airbase where nuclear weapons were located (1983–2000). Finally, some forms of protest are mobile, and possibly transnational, as protestors travel from place to place in caravans or freedom rides. *See also* ANTI-GLOBALIZATION; CIVIL SOCIETY; GLOBAL JUSTICE MOVEMENT; RESISTANCE.

proximity The physical closeness or co-location of individuals or institutions. While some cases of proximity are inconsequential for those involved, others yield significant benefits (e.g. financial or affective). For instance, economic geographers have examined the several beneficial *untraded interdependencies that many firms in the same industry develop by virtue of having physical access to each other in a particular *place or *region. Alternatively, because of trade barriers they might otherwise face, some firms might decide to locate some of their operations in a foreign country in order to exploit a new consumer market.

proximity analysis The study of the effect of nearness of locales on their relationship to each other. A form of *location analysis, it is a very commonly used function in GIS, especially in examining the effects of one type of feature, such as airport and noise pollution, on another, such as residential houses, and to assess the optimal location for new facilities based on the proximity of the target market and other similar facilities. *See also* GEODEMOGRAPHICS.

proxy data A form of data that can stand in for other missing or unobtainable data. Proxy data are commonly used in the historical analysis of climate change where it is not possible to physical measure the climate at different points in the Earth's past. Instead it is possible to proxy the climate conditions by examining tree ring growth or the layering and plant make-up of peat bogs. Several sources of proxy data are often combined, for example, several census variables relating to income, housing, education, and health might be combined to infer levels of social deprivation.

pseudo-commodity *See* COMMODITY; COMMODIFICATION.

psychoanalytical geography A form of geographical analysis that draws on the theories of psychoanalysis to examine how the relationship between self, society, and space is mediated through the psyche and the unconscious mind. Here, there is an attempt to apply the ideas of leading psychoanalytic theorists such as Freud, Lacan, Jung, Klein, Kristeva, Douglas, and others, developed in clinical settings, to seek to understand how people relate to, behave in, and seek to order and manage places. In particular, psychoanalytical geographies have examined feelings of being in place/out of place, affective response to environments, the negotiation of material and symbolic geographies of everyday life, and processes of *othering and exclusion of some groups by others from a place. In relation to the latter, David *Sibley in his seminal work *Geographies of Exclusion* (1995) argued, drawing on object-relations theory, that the urge to exclude others from one's proximity is connected to unconscious desires to maintain cleanliness and purity. Here, abject fear of the self being defiled or polluted is projected onto others (usually defined by bodily appearance (e.g., disabled, black, female) or body codings (e.g., dress, style) who are depicted as deviant or dangerous. Social boundaries between groups are thus maintained largely unconsciously, enacting processes that create spatial separation. The application of psychoanalysis has been met with some scepticism within the discipline, critiqued as being acultural, ahistorical, and empirically unverifiable. Nonetheless, a number of geographers continue to draw on its ideas and methods. *See also* PSYCHOANALYTIC METHODS.

Further reading Philo, C. and Parr, H. (2003), 'Introducing psychoanalytic geographies', *Social & Cultural Geography* 4(3): 283–93.

psychoanalytic methods The techniques designed to reveal aspects of the unconscious mind. In general, geographers have little used standard psychoanalytical methods of free association, transference, and analytic listening. This is mainly to do with the geographic rather than subject-based focus of their analysis. Instead, they have used techniques such as identification and empathy operationalized through interviews, 'playing' with materials, and 'mapping' and 'tracking' of material objects, and the ideological work they do in conveying particular unconscious messages about people and place.

Further reading Kingsbury, P. (2009), 'Psychoanalytic methods', in *International Encyclopedia of Human Geography*, Vol 8, 480–86.

psychogeography An artistic strategy that seeks to explore the effects of the geographical environment on emotions and behaviour. It was developed in the 1950s in France as a way of reflecting upon urbanism and urban life. The main technique used is the '*dérive*', a form of wandering that relies on chance and coincidence, accompanied by continuous observation. The idea is to transverse routes through a city that would not normally be taken, for example, using a map of Paris to navigate London, to observe from a fresh perspective the organization and structure of cities and peoples' lives within them. *See also* FLANEUR; SITUATIONISM.

Further reading Coverley, M. (2010), *Psychogeography*.

Ptolemy (*c.* AD 100–170) A Greek philosopher resident in Egypt whose writing shaped thinking on astronomy, geography, and mathematics in European and Islamic science for centuries after his death. His treatise *Almagest* forwarded a geocentric model of the universe wherein the sun, planets, and stars circled the Earth. His book *Geography* described the known world of the Roman empire, set out a system of latitude and longitude for recording location, and a rudimentary map projection for representing that information. As such, his work provided an initial framework for systematic *cartography.

public buildings The structures owned by public bodies such as governments to which members of the public have general access. These include city halls, museums, libraries, and hospitals, but not, for example, barracks and prisons, where access is restricted.

public geography The interventions by geographers that are addressed to or produced with non-academic audiences, and which emphasize the importance of social values in matters of debate. The term 'public geographies' is also often used to imply that there are not only many publics, but also many ways in which academic geographers and non-academics may engage constructively.

The idea of a public geography arose in the 2000s in response to a presidential address to the American Sociological Association by Michael Burawoy (University of California, Berkeley). Aiming to recover a greater purpose for sociology he made a distinction between two kinds of audience (academic and extra-academic) and two complementary kinds of knowledge, instrumental and reflexive. The former is about solving problems, the latter is a dialogue about ends and value premises. When combined, they define a division of labour (see Table 2).

Table 2 Defining a division of labour

	Academic Audience	Extra-academic audience
Instrumental knowledge	Professional	Policy
Reflexive knowledge	Critical	Public

'Public sociology' is distinguished from 'policy sociology' by its concern for values rather than problems. By extension, public geography is not the same as *applied or policy-relevant geography, because these are largely about solving problems, e.g. coastal defence or efficient transport (*see* POLICY, GEOGRAPHY AND). Burawoy's vision sits along-side others in a spectrum of public geographies. What these might entail is elaborated by Kevin Ward. It could involve making geographical research more accessible by using various forms of popular media. It can include making geographical knowledge together with members of the public, i.e. recognizing the values of lay *expertise (*see* PARTICIPATORY ACTION RESEARCH). It might also mean giving greater recognition to lay or extra-academic geographical knowledge in its own right. *See also* ACTIVIST GEOGRAPHY; PUBLIC INTELLECTUAL.

References Burawoy, M. (2005), 'For public sociology', *American Sociological Review* 70: 4–28.
Ward, K. (2006), 'Geographies and public policy: towards public geographies', *Progress in Human Geography* 30(4): 495–503.

public goods The facilities and assets that are available for free or at a nominal cost to all citizens of a country. Public goods are usually provided and maintained by local or national governments. These are usually important contributors to everyday life, with implications for the successful functioning of economy, culture, and the natural environment. Some public goods are 'pure' in that everyone benefits equally (e.g. universal vaccination programmes). Others are less universal and readily accessible only by a section of the national population (e.g. a national park), though still accessible to all in principle. Some public goods are so spatially specific that a politics attaches to the decision about where best to locate them. For instance, in the interests of greater geographical *justice, a national government may decide to build a new motorway in a remote and poor region rather than improve the motorway system in a wealthy but traffic-congested region.

public intellectual *See* INTELLECTUAL.

public policy A course of action developed, adopted, and pursued by a government (local, regional, national, or supranational), and implemented and enforced by its agencies, in order to address an issue of public interest. Public policy seeks to achieve certain aims and objectives by setting out a strategy and associated tasks, along with the means of evaluating success. Policy is a statement of the preferred path forwards and has no legal status, though enabling legislation is often passed that ensures it can implemented and enforced. Policy could concern any aspect of everyday life, for example, *health, *education, *welfare, *transport, *consumption, *regional development, and the *economy. Public policy is inherently political and contested. Its formulation is usually preceded by public debate as to how best to address an issue, wherein different vested interests seek to shape the agenda and proposed course of action. Once enacted, policy often works in the interests of some groups or places at the expense of others, and there may be on-going attempts to amend or scrap published policy. Policies are often reviewed and refreshed after a set number of years, and are also abandoned and replaced, especially with a change in government which has been elected with a different mandate. Given the key role policy plays in shaping society, nature, and space it has been a key area of interest for geographers. *See also* POLICY, GEOGRAPHY AND; POLICY TRANSFER.

public space The areas of the geographical environment that are accessible to and shared by all members of the public. Such spaces include streets, parks, and wilderness. Retail spaces such as shops and retail parks blur the distinction between public and private spaces. While they are open to the public, they are privately owned and regulated. Moreover, public spaces in general are increasingly subject to regulation and surveillance that restrict how the space can be used. Work by feminists and others questions the extent to which public space has ever been truly public and open, noting that access to such spaces has long been differentiated along lines of gender, race, class, ability, and sexuality. *See also* PRIVATE SPACE.

Public Understanding of Science (PUS) The various ways in which members of national publics perceive and respond to the claims of *science. Contemporary science, in its various pure and applied forms, is far more publicly visible than ever before. In part, this is because *technoscience is such a key part of contemporary *capitalism (as evidenced by plant, animal, insect, microbial, and human *biotechnology). In part, it is because scientists, many of whom are publicly funded and aware of the ethically contentious nature of their inquiries, have sought to enlighten and excite publics about the benefits of science. Insofar as science remains central to the formulation of a great many public policies—such as the global Kyoto Protocol on greenhouse gas emissions—it is important that publics understand their strengths and limitations. Scientists and their professional organizations, such the British Royal Society, are increasingly concerned to explain and justify their endeavours to members of the public. This impinges on physical geography insofar as it is considered to be a science, while several human geographers have inquired into how the environmental sciences are perceived publicly, and how they should be governed in the public interest. *See also* DEFICIT MODEL; SOCIOLOGY OF SCIENTIFIC KNOWLEDGE; SCIENCE AND TECHNOLOGY STUDIES.

Further reading Demeritt, D. (2006), 'Science studies, climate change, and the prospects for constructivist critique', *Economy and Society* 35, 3: 453–79.

publishing The preparation, production, and distribution of printed work such as journals, books, and maps. In recent years this has included digital versions of these products. The publishing industry is diverse, ranging from small to international presses. It is the key means through which academia shares pedagogic and research ideas and knowledge.

p

qualitative data and research A term for non-numeric information, including text, images, and sounds, including *literature, *diaries, policy documents, *interview transcripts, *photographs, *art, video, *films, and *music, and its associated inquiry. While these data can be converted into quantitative data through classification, much of the richness of the material is lost through such a translation process. Consequently, qualitative data analysis generally works with the original materials, seeking to tease out and build up meaning and understanding using analytical techniques such as *content analysis and *deconstruction. Qualitative data in the social sciences is often generated through *interviews, *focus groups, *observation, *ethnography, and *participatory methods, or is accessed through *archive collections, and generally consists of *case studies focused on particular individuals, communities, and places. Qualitative research became important in the discipline in the 1970s with the development of *humanistic and interpretative approaches, and the use of philosophies such as *phenomenology, *existentialism, and *idealism. It was seen to provide data that was much richer and contextual than *quantitative data, which seemed to atomize individuals. It was thus felt that qualitative methods provided greater insight into people's lives and the meaning of place. Qualitative methods have remained an important component of geographical research, providing a rich armoury of techniques for examining socio-spatial relations.

Further reading DeLyser, D., Herbert, S., Aitken, S., Crang, M., and McDowell, L. (2010), *The Sage Handbook of Qualitative Geography.*
Hay, I. (2010), *Qualitative Research Methods in Human Geography.*

quality of life An overarching concept concerning the general well-being of individuals and communities. Unlike 'standard of living', which principally concerns income-levels, quality of life is more multidimensional considering factors such as health, access to services and employment, social belonging, deprivation, recreation and leisure, and levels of crime and social unrest. Quality of life has become a key political discourse in many Western countries and in international aid programmes, with the aspiration of improving conditions for all sections of society, especially those living in poverty. While difficult to measure and assess, there have been a number of attempts to create quality of life indexes as a way of evaluating and monitoring the effectiveness of such policies and programmes.

quantitative data and research A term for numeric information and its use in systematic inquiry. The information gathered is either extensive and relates to physical properties of phenomena (such as length, height, distance, weight, area, volume), or representative and relates to non-physical characteristics of phenomena (such as social class, educational attainment, social deprivation, quality of life rankings). In geography, a combination of extensive and representative quantitative information can be gathered to explain social and economic issues. Quantitative data have different *levels of measurement that determine what kinds of analysis can be undertaken. Analysis is performed either through *descriptive statistics or data visualization, including *maps, or *inferential statistics (using *parametric or *non-parametric tests), or the data are used as the inputs to predictive and simulation *models. Quantitative data in the social sciences is mostly generated through *surveys and *questionnaires, much of which are derived through instruments such as *censuses, household surveys, passenger surveys, or political polling, or are extracted from large databases such as those held by government departments, health, and financial institutions. More recently it can be generated using sensor and scanner technologies. Quantitative data is a key input into *geographic information systems, enabling sophisticated mapping of areas. The use of quantitative data and methods of analysis became a key focus of concern in geography in the 1960s with the *Quantitative Revolution and the attempt to transform the discipline dominated by descriptive regional studies to a science of spatial laws. While quantitative geography is not as dominant as it once was, it is still a potent and vital part of the discipline, especially with regards to policy and *applied research. *See also* BIG DATA; SPATIAL SCIENCE.

Further reading Fotheringham, A. S., Brunsdon, C., and Charlton, M. (2000), *Quantitative Geography*.
Haggett, P. (1984), *Geography: a Modern Synthesis*.
Harris, R. and Jarvis, C. (2010), *Statistics for Geography and Environmental Science*.

Quantitative Revolution The widespread adoption of abstract *models, *inferential statistics, physical science analogies, and allied *quantitative data and research methods by both physical and human geographers in the 1950s and 1960s (*see* SPATIAL SCIENCE). Proponents of these new theories and methods often had a strong sense of how they departed dramatically from the previous concerns of geographers for more descriptive, non-quantitative, or *ideographic approaches. Some interpreted it as a *paradigm change and it serves as a useful episode for understanding ideas about the history of geography (*see* KUHN, THOMAS).

Further reading Barnes, T. J. (2004), 'Placing ideas: genius loci, heterotopias and geography's quantitative revolution', *Progress in Human Geography* 29:565–95.
Burton, I. (1963), 'The quantitative revolution and theoretical geography', *The Canadian Geographer/Geograph Canadien* 7:151–62.

queer theory A set of interrelated post-structural theories that understand *sexuality as non-essentialist and fluid (*see* POST-STRUCTURALISM). Such a positioning recognizes that sexuality is not fixed as either straight or gay, but that there is a diversity of sexual identities. Differences and *power geometries operate within sexual communities; for example, men who occasionally have sex with other men but who do not identify as gay, or women who adopt a hyperfeminine image that conforms with *heteronormative femininity. Queer theory has its roots in the writings of Michel *Foucault and Judith *Butler amongst others, such as Eve Kosofsky Sedgwick and Michael Warner. In *The History of Sexuality*, Foucault argued that how sexuality is understood within societies is historically and spatially contingent. He traced out a *genealogy of sexual behaviour, discourse, and law, demonstrating that what has been considered normal, natural, and proper sexual relations has changed over time and space. Sexuality from this perspective is a social regulatory framework maintained through discourses of heteronormativity and *patriarchy. Judith Butler, drawing on Foucault, argued that sexual identity is something that one performs, rather than something one is (*see* PERFORMATIVITY). This notion destabilizes and denaturalizes the ontological foundations of sexuality by arguing that it is not innate and fixed, but performative and fluid.

Queer theory was introduced into geography by David Bell and colleagues in 1994 in their paper 'All hyped up and no place to go'. They argued that the production of space is sexed, with different locales subject to different normative expectations of what sexual activity might take place there and what sexual subjects should occupy that space. Over the following years, queer theory has shaped geographical thinking on sexuality and *gender, in particular, with a number of studies documenting historical and contemporary queer geographies in a diverse set of locations in the developed and developing world. It has also influenced how geographers have theorized spatial *identities more broadly, especially through the concept of performativity. Further, it has influenced thinking with respect to other core concepts. For example, Gillian *Rose draws on Judith Butler to rethink the concept of *space, arguing that space is brought into being through performativity. *See also* GAY GEOGRAPHIES; LESBIAN GEOGRAPHIES.

Further reading Bell, D., Binnie, J., Cream, J., and Valentine, G. (1994), 'All hyped up and
    no place to go', *Gender, Place and Culture* 1(1): 31–47.
Brown, G., Lim, J., and Browne, K. (eds.) (2007), *Geographies of Sexualities.*
Rose, G. (1999), 'Performing space', in Massey, D., Allen, J., and Sarre, P. (eds.) *Human Geography
    Today* 247–59.

questionnaire A form of *survey that generates factual information about an issue. A questionnaire usually consists of a series of questions designed to generate quantitative data that can later be statistically analysed. A common example is a *census. Question types include asking respondents for factual information, selecting a suitable category, detailing multiple choices, selecting an answer along a scale, preferentially ranking alternatives, and open questions. The latter are kept to a minimum as they are difficult to code subsequently.

race A social construction focused on supposed biological or ethnic differences that is used to produce material consequences for people of supposedly different races. Race is not easy to define as it is often cast in *essentialist, natural, or biological terms, or confused with *ethnicity and *culture. In general terms, race is a collection of ideas and practices through which people have been categorized, most usually relating to skin colour and facial features. This categorization affects how people are treated and shapes their lives in a myriad of ways. Categorization is often essentialist in nature, with the assumed traits of people linked to their supposed race which thus legitimates their treatment. Such thinking gained scientific weight with the rise of *social Darwinism and *eugenics in the 19th century wherein social traits and biological heredity were formally linked, with races placed into an ordered hierarchy of intelligence and cultural sophistication. The notion that there are different races, with different characteristics, has underpinned the widespread practice of *racism, and a range of political and economic projects, enforced through violence, such as *colonialism, *slavery, *apartheid, and the *Holocaust, wherein certain peoples were deemed of less worth and had less rights than others. As such, race has been mobilized to produce different geographies such as segregated neighbourhoods and *ghettos, restricted access to work, and circumscribed *mobility (*see* SEGREGATION). In recent years, geographers have examined how race is spatially constructed, producing particular *power geometries, and have also examined the extent to which the discipline of geography has been complicit in the reproduction of racist ideologies, especially through its involvement in colonial projects. *See also* ORIENTALISM.

Further reading Anderson, K. (1991), *Vancouver's Chinatown: Racial Discourse in Canada, 1875–1980*. Schein, R. (2002), 'Race, racism and geography', *Professional Geographer* 54: 1–5.

race to the bottom A process of competitive deregulation between countries, provinces, or cities designed to attract relatively mobile investment (*see* REGULATION). The term is often used by critics to describe *neoliberal policies such as cutting corporation taxes, controlling labour organizations, and removing environmental protections in order to make regions supposedly more attractive to global capital, for example, through *outsourcing.

racism A set of social relations that is used to discriminate against people based on their assumed *race. Given their political power, wealth, and historical precedent, racism is usually expressed as discrimination by white populations against 'non-white' people. Racism can be both overt, explicitly expressed through discourse and law, and materially through forms of violence, and covert in nature, working in more implicit and subtle ways to disenfranchise people through the restriction of life opportunities. Racism was initially based on the notion that there were distinct biological differences between supposed races. As this idea has been increasingly challenged, it has been replaced by cultural racism that posits that there are cultural differences between groups that explain their relative social position, and these differences mean that they are incompatible with each other. Both biological and cultural racism is expressed spatially through processes that work to limit access and mobility and increase *segregation, including *white flight. In recent years, a number of geographers have examined the spatial processes of racism and the geographies that they produce. They have also examined the hegemonic *whiteness of the discipline of geography, and its role in perpetuating racist ideologies. In much the same way as *feminists have challenged the *masculinist nature of geography, they have called for geography's theories and praxis to become anti-racist in formulation.

Further reading Nayak, A. (2003), *Race, Place and Globalisation*.
Peake, L. and Kobayashi, A. (2002), 'Policies and practices for an antiracist geography at the millennium', *Professional Geographer* 54: 50–61.

radical geography A term for geographical research and teaching aimed at combating oppression, domination, and exploitation, and supporting social *justice, greater *equality, and emancipation. Radical geographers seek more than just reform and are convinced of the need to effect long-lasting social transformation. Although these convictions and ideals have always been present in human geography to some degree, the term 'radical geography' emerged in the late 1960s and early 1970s in response to specific events and movements. These included anti-war protests against US involvement in Vietnam, the US civil rights movement, and its fight against racism, feminism, and women's liberation, *environmentalism, and anti-colonialism. In 1968, a critical year, there were significant protests and civil unrest in France, USA, Mexico, Britain, Czechoslovakia, and elsewhere. An important moment was the foundation of the journal *Antipode* by staff and graduate students at Clark University, Massachusetts in 1969. *Antipode*, now subtitled 'a radical journal of geography' continues to publish. In 1974, the Union of Socialist Geographers was formed in North America (*see* SOCIALIST GEOGRAPHY). Initially arising from a mix of socialism, social democracy, and liberalism, radical geography was soon also influenced by *Marxism, *anarchism, and feminism. Of these, Marxism and feminism formed the core of radical geography, so much so that when subsequent generations turned to a wider range of political philosophies and ideas, e.g. *post-colonialism and *post-structuralism, they increasingly adopted the term '*critical geography'. The optimism of the 1960s generation of radical geographers may have been dimmed by the reversals of left-wing causes in the 1980s and 1990s (*see* NEOLIBERALISM; REAGANISM; THATCHERISM), but the flourishing of the *anti-globalization movements after the 1999 protests against the *World Trade Organization summit (the so-called Battle of/in Seattle), and the subsequent global recession revived radical spirits. *See also* ACTIVIST GEOGRAPHY; ADVOCACY GEOGRAPHY; DETROIT GEOGRAPHICAL EXPEDITION AND INSTITUTE.

Further reading Castree, N. et al. (eds.) (2010), *The Point Is to Change It: Geographies of Hope and Survival in an Age of Crisis*.
Peet, R. (ed.) (1977), *Radical Geography*.

RAE *See* RESEARCH ASSESSMENT.

rail transport The movement of people and goods by locomotive-pulled carriages along rails with a uniform gauge. While track-based movement of carriages has a long history, especially in mining, the first commercial, self-powered trains began operation in the early 19th century. Given its relative speed and capacity compared with canal or road transportation, the railways grew rapidly, becoming a significant agent of *time-space compression and opening up places to economic and demographic growth. While still important for *commuting and freight transport, the rail network has shrunk in many places as it has been superseded by *road and *air travel. *See also* TRANSPORT GEOGRAPHY.

rainforest A type of forest found in regions where long-term average rainfall exceeds 1750 mm per year. Most such regions are in the tropics, but there are also areas of temperate rainforest, for example, in the Pacific Northwest of North America, Japan, and southern Australia. Rainforest regions occupy central or even iconic positions within current environmental debates because of their high levels of biodiversity and role in the planet's hydrological and climate systems.

random sample *See* SAMPLING.

rank-size rule A commonly observed regularity in the settlement structure of a country, wherein the rank of a city in the country's hierarchy of settlements is linearly related to its population size. Zipf's law further states that the population of any city X is equal to the population of the largest city divided by the rank of the city X.

raster data Spatial data that are stored and displayed in a matrix of cells organized into rows and columns. Each cell is assigned a value representing the data contained within it. Typical raster data include satellite imagery or digital photographs, where information is stored as pixels. Raster data is useful because it has a simple data structure, it is good for representing surfaces, and it is amenable to advanced spatial and statistical analysis, and to overlaying data. *See also* VECTOR DATA.

ratio data *See* LEVELS OF MEASUREMENT.

rational actor Any individual or organization whose principal motivation is to ensure the most for the least when confronted with more than one option about what to do and when possessed of finite resources (e.g. time or money). Pure rationality—which is the precise calculation of benefits resulting from costs, leading to one course of action—is rare in life, meaning that the idea of a rational actor is something of an *ideal type, useful for operationalizing models, theories, or predictions about human behaviour.

rational choice theory Any theory predicated on the idea of the *rational actor who makes clear decisions after calculating the precise costs and benefits of possible alternative courses of action. Such theories have been widespread in the social sciences since the late 19th century, primarily in economics. In human geography, rational choice theories were characteristic of the turn to *spatial science in economic and urban geography in the 1960s. Attempts were made to describe people's locational decision-making (e.g. where to migrate to, or what to grow where) when they had certain ends, limited resources, and more than one way of realizing their ends. Subsequently, *behavioural geography sought to represent human decision-making in more complex ways taking account of cognitive processing and individual psychology. *Humanistic geography sought to challenge rational choice theory more fundamentally still, by questioning the idea that all people shared a common set of drivers underpinning their behaviour in *place or across wider territories. Others pointed out that any proposition about human nature (*see* HUMANISM) is *normative because it implicitly assumes that if the proposition does not hold in reality, the problem lies with the individuals in question. Three decades on, and the idea of rationality lives on in various models and theories. However, it is typically linked to a greater appreciation of the complexity and unpredictability of the systems in which individuals find themselves when seeking to determine a course of action (*see* COMPLEXITY THEORY).

rationalism 1. The belief that humans are primarily *rational actors.
2. The belief that mental reasoning is or should be more important than emotion or blind-faith in human decision-making.

Rationalism can be traced back to the philosophers of the *Enlightenment such as René Descartes and Immanuel *Kant. It was a reaction to the centuries of authority exerted by organized religion, monarchs, and the nobility in European societies. Rationalists argued that people should utilize their minds—notably *logic—when determining what is true and false, right and wrong, safe and dangerous, and so on. Though *humanism in its various forms extends beyond rationalism, it encompasses it. In human geography, rationalism became axiomatic in the 1960s and 1970s courtesy of the *location theory then *de rigeur* in economic and urban geography (*see* REGIONAL SCIENCE). Since then, more complex understandings of human thought and decision-making have been favoured when seeking to explain behaviour within and between places. Rationalism in the second sense is now thought to be unduly *normative, while the first sense is far too reductionist to describe what motivates real world actors.

Ratzel, Friedrich (1844–1904) A German geographer who is credited with being the founder of modern *political geography. He originated the notion of *lebensraum* and was instrumental in the development of *anthropogeography. He initially trained as a zoologist, then worked as a travelling reporter for a newspaper, including a lengthy trip to North America (1874–75). From 1875–86 he worked at the Technische Hochschule at Munich teaching geography before taking up a professorship at the University of Leipzig. He produced the two volumes, *Anthropogeographie* (1882 and 1891), examining the relationship between the environment and human societies. The first volume formed the basis of *environmental determinism. This was accompanied by the three volumes of *Völkerkunde* (*The History of Mankind*) in 1885–88, and *Politische Geographie* in 1897 which provided the foundations for *geopolitik. His notion of *lebensraum* was reworked by National Socialism (the Nazi party) to justify the drive for territory to the east of Germany.

Ravenstein's Laws A series of generalizations about (internal) *migration formulated by German-born geographer and cartographer E. G. Ravenstein (1834–1913) based on statistical data from the British Isles. The most well-known laws are: migrants generally move to improve their economic circumstances; every migration flow generates a counterflow; the majority of migrants move a short distance; longer-distance migrants tend to go to bigger cities; urban dwellers migrate less than rural persons; females move shorter distances than males.

reading, geography of An argument that where a text is read has an important bearing on how it is read and interpreted. Reading, it is contended, is not a neutral activity but is shaped by local cultural knowledges and politics. Consequently, how a scientific idea is understood can vary between locales. David Livingstone illustrates such a spatially inflected reading of Darwin's theory of evolution, detailing how the theory was interpreted in different ways in America, New Zealand, and Russia.

Further reading Livingstone, D. N. (2005), 'Science, text and space: thoughts on the geography of reading', *Transactions of the Institute of British Geographers* 30: 391–401.

Reaganism The political ideas associated with US President Ronald Reagan (1911–2004) who held office between 1981 and 1989. He was also governor of California 1967–75. His administrations' policies included minimizing government, reducing taxes, privatization, anti-union legislation, and sustaining or increasing military expenditure. Commentators saw similarities between these ideas and those of UK Prime Minister Margaret Thatcher (*see* THATCHERISM), describing them both in terms of *neoliberalism.

realism An ontological belief that there is a world existing external to any one human observer and actor's knowledge of and beliefs about that world. Realists are highly critical of *idealism and maintain that while beliefs about the external world vary enormously, that world is not reducible to any one of them. This then raises the question of whether the external world is ever knowable 'in itself', or only comprehensible in terms of contingent epistemic practices which reveal the interests, goals, and norms of situated human agents (e.g. academics and religious leaders). 'Strong realists', commonly found in the environmental, engineering, and biomedical sciences, maintain that some knowledges are able to 'cut reality at the joints' and accurately represent in words and images its ontological character. 'Semantic realists' remain agnostic on this matter, but argue that our various representations of the world are real to the extent that they influence our actions in and on the non-human world.

Almost all human geographers are realists in the minimal sense that they believe there is more to the world than what humans think, say, or do. However, a particular version of strong realism took hold in the 1960s and 1970s, whose philosophical tenets were known as *positivism (see LOGICAL POSITIVISM). Though few human geographers subscribed to all of these tenets, they were realists in the specific sense that they believed (i) the world of human behaviour could be studied objectively, free from any bias on the part of the researcher; (ii) this world exhibited spatial patterns and regularities reflective of common processes of human decision-making (see RATIONAL CHOICE THEORY); and (iii) these patterns and regularities could be detected empirically by gathering and interpreting evidence, allowing reality to, as it were, 'speak for itself'.

By the early 1980s, other strong realists took issue with the realism characteristic of *spatial science and its derivatives. Andrew *Sayer's influential book *Method in Social Science* (1984) criticized positivism for being too 'shallow' in its ontology of the real (see CRITICAL REALISM). He argued first that reality is *stratified*, such that perceptible events are but the outcomes of invisible causes and process that, while entirely real, can only be represented through abstraction and theory-building not by direct observation. Second, he questioned the positivist belief that only 'constant conjunctions' suggest persistent or widespread causal processes at work. For Sayer, the number of times something occurs (e.g. A and B happen together frequently, while C and D do not) has nothing to do with how important, generalized, or persistent the processes causing it are. In 'open systems' of the sort that interest human geographers, Sayer argued, *overdetermination is normal, meaning that enduring, general, and important processes may manifest themselves in heterogeneous rather than consistent ways. It follows that different phenomenal events may, in fact and counter-intuitively, reflect the existence of the same root causes. Finally, Sayer distinguished society from *nature, arguing that the discourses and representations of social actors affect the social worlds they ostensibly arise from. While society is irreducible to signs and symbols, Sayer nonetheless recognized that the latter are real and efficacious. As *pragmatism argues, what people believe about reality is real to the extent that enough other people have similar thoughts and act on them. This means that the job of social research is not necessarily to correct people's 'defective' understanding of reality, but to illuminate how and why certain understanding becomes influential (see also HEGEMONY; IDEOLOGY).

In the 1990s, realists like Sayer and the 'shallow realists' he criticized were opposed to the wave of *nominalism that swept through human geography courtesy of *postmodernism and *post-structuralism. Though the differences were, in retrospect, drawn a little too sharply, human geography's 'cultural and linguistic turn' seemed dismissive of the realist belief that the social and natural worlds are more than what prevailing discourses, signs, and representations take them to be. Realists were seen as too committed to the idea that the world can be studied in more-or-less accurate ways, free from observer bias, or undue prejudice. Meanwhile, the nominalists were seen to contradictorily emphasize the reality of signification while downplaying the reality of those institutions, cities, landscapes, etc. to which the signs referred. We can see with hindsight that different versions of realism were in play, with that of Sayer and his followers arguably the more thought through and sophisticated. Since the late 1990s, human geographers have generally refrained from exploring the philosophical basis of their preferred forms of realism in print, in part because of a waning belief in the discipline that one form will be seen as so logically compelling as to vanquish all the others (*see* GRAND THEORY; PHILOSOPHY).

realism (IR) The position held within *International Relations that *states are the only meaning and legitimate actors in world politics, and that they act according to their respective national interests and not out of any *cosmopolitan or international values. Whereas relations between people within states may be governed by laws, relations between states are not guided by principles.

recession A significant slow-down in economic activity when compared with recent trends. By convention, national data on economic growth are released every three months, i.e. every quarter. Two successive quarters of negative growth is regarded as a recession. An unusually sustained period of negative growth may be termed a depression, but there is no consensus on this (*see* GREAT DEPRESSION). Though recessions are normally identified at the level of national economies, strictly speaking, they also occur locally or regionally. This means a national economy need not be in recession for one of its constituent territories to be (and vice versa). Because all capitalist economies are by definition growth-orientated, recessions are perceived as problematic because aggregate profits fall, demand declines, unemployment rises, wages freeze, government spending declines, or (alternatively) government borrowing rises to maintain levels of public expenditure. Human geographers have long been interested in the relative locations of recessions and how afflicted economies can recover from them. In addition, macroeconomic theory—such as David *Harvey's *The *Limits to Capital*—has explored how sometimes unsynchronized, sometimes widespread recessions in different parts of the world are part of capitalism's DNA, rendering them vulnerable to being eclipsed even as they offer new opportunities for renewed *accumulation. *See also* CRISIS.

Reclus, Élisée (1830–1905) A French geographer who sought to develop a global geography that was universal, historical, dialectical, and political. He is best known for his monumental work *Nouvelle Geographie Universelle* which was produced as nineteen large volumes between 1876 and 1894. He wrote many other works including the six volumes of *L'Homme et la Terre*. After opposing Napoleon III's *coup d'état* of 1851 he was forced into exile for five years, travelling to North and South America. In 1871 he played an active role in the Paris Commune and when the city fell he was exiled to Switzerland where he became involved in revolutionary politics and *anarchism. In 1890 he returned to France and in 1894 accepted a position at New University in Brussels, Belgium. He was a pioneer of social and urban geography, examining issues of class, race, gender, power, social domination, urbanization, and ecology, with his ideas explicitly shaping the work of urban planners such as Patrick *Geddes and Lewis *Mumford.

recoding A process of assigning data a new code within a different classification scheme. Recoding is often undertaken to enable comparisons between locations. For example, the parameters of social class are defined differently in the Irish and Northern Irish census. By recoding the data in one jurisdiction to fit the parameters of the other, an all-island analysis becomes possible.

recreation The activities undertaken for pleasure and enjoyment outside of waged employment. There is no definitive classification of what activities constitute recreation, although distinctions are often made between those carried out at home (*leisure) and away from home (including *tourism), and between active pursuits such as climbing and more passive pursuits such as going to the cinema. *Sport is often distinguished by its greater degree of formal organization and competitiveness, but sports can equally be informal.

Further reading Hall, C. M. and Page, S. J. (3rd ed. 2005), *The Geography of Tourism and Recreation: Environment, Place and Space.*

recycling The processing of waste products for re-use. In an effort to attain higher levels of *sustainability, households are encouraged to: reduce their consumption of water, electricity, and packaging; re-use goods such as bottles; and recycle goods and materials usually through organized networks of collection and processing. These may be local, but are increasingly global in extent, raising issues of environmental harm and social equity. *See also* WASTE MANAGEMENT.

Further reading Gregson, N., Crang, M., Ahamed, F., Akter, N., and Ferdous, R. (2010), 'Following things of rubbish value: end-of-life ships, "chock-chocky" furniture and the Bangladeshi middle class consumer', *Geoforum* 41: 846–54.

REDD An acronym for Reducing Emissions from Deforestation and Forest Degradation, REDD is an *environmental governance framework devised within the ongoing negotiations of the *United Nations Framework Convention on Climate Change (UNFCC). Negotiations began in 2005 and are continuing. Thus REDD is an evolving set of mechanisms and agreements. It is now more usual to refer to REDD+ ('plus'), in recognition of the extension of the framework to include wider issues of forestry management and poverty reduction (*see* SUSTAINABLE DEVELOPMENT).

REDD was initially devised to meet two aims. Land-use change accounts for 10 per cent or more of global greenhouse gas emissions, so reducing the rate of deforestation (the permanent removal of tree cover) and forest degradation (i.e. changes which impair forest ecosystems short of complete removal) would theoretically cut emissions. Secondly, by valuing forests in quantifiable terms, REDD would incentivize their protection. It is claimed this will have additional benefits in terms of maintaining biodiversity. Under the framework, governments and other donors in the *Global North pay communities and governments in the *Global South not to cut down trees or degrade forests. Provided that forest communities receive all or part of the funds donated, it may also help with poverty reduction.

In outline, REDD+ is a win-win proposition. But there are criticisms. As with any *development policy, it is not certain who benefits and where the money goes. By allowing deforestation in one place to be offset by tree-planting in another, it may actually encourage it. One charge is that indigenous communities are being displaced by such schemes. Finally, there is a difficulty in verifying and quantifying something that does not happen. How can avoided deforestation be established? For these and other reasons, REDD+ has not yet been included with the wider Clean Development Mechanism for mitigating greenhouse gas emissions.

redevelopment The demolition of a part of the built environment and its replacement by new buildings. This is often a contested process because it may involve displacement of existing businesses and/or residents, and the destruction of buildings valued for their community, architectural, or historic qualities. *See also* GENTRIFICATION; URBAN REGENERATION.

redistribution The reallocation of goods and resources among members of a society or social group. Anthropologists have described many societies in which some central authority, for example, a chief, collects a share of the product of that society's members in order to reserve it for themselves (tribute), or provide occasions of spectacular collective consumption. In capitalist societies, redistribution is achieved through complex systems of taxation, benefits, credits, and cash transfers, often referred to as part of the *welfare state. It can be argued to serve economic, social, and ethical purposes, maintaining levels of social solidarity. *See also* INEQUALITY.

redistricting The redesign of the size and shape of districts used in elections, for example, US congressional seats. Given that the geography of population changes over time, for example, through *suburbanization, most democracies periodically reassess the organization of electoral districts to avoid excessive variations in the number of voters in each one. This process can be conducted impartially, or in a partisan fashion (*see* GERRYMANDERING). *See also* ELECTORAL GEOGRAPHY.

red-light district An area, usually in a city, associated with the sex industry (*see* SEX WORK). It may include a concentration of prostitution and adult entertainment venues.
Further reading Hubbard, P. (2011), *Cities and Sexualities*.

redlining The practice whereby financial institutions clandestinely designate certain areas of a city as high-risk in terms of lending, with the result that residents of such areas or prospective buyers are effectively blocked from obtaining loans. Redlining is often associated with racial discrimination and is generally illegal.

reductionism The belief that complex events or multifaceted phenomena can be explained with reference to the properties or capacities of their constituent units. In the physical sciences, these units can often be isolated and examined, while in the social sciences and humanities it is common to use *abstraction to conceptualize them since experimental control is almost impossible when studying 'open systems' (such as a local economy in decline). In human geography, reductionism was favoured by spatial scientists seeking to construct general theories and models of how people behave when deciding where to live/work/invest/move. Complex phenomena such as the economic and demographic growth of a city like Boston, were seen to reflect broadly rational decision-making by individual actors possessed of knowledge and resources, and presented with several locational options. However, subsequent research pointed to the indissoluble links between parts and wholes in social life, such that the latter helps to govern the former rather than being a product of the parts combined (*see* HOLISM). Attention was also paid to *emergence, chaotic behaviour, and the crossing of thresholds, meaning that the combined effects of the behaviour of parts is not deducible from the analysis of any one part. The critique of reductionism can be found in the analytical and quantitative parts of human geography, and also in the relational, post-*positivist parts (*see* RELATIONAL GEOGRAPHY).

REF *See* RESEARCH ASSESSMENT.

reflexivity An act of self-reflection that considers how one's own opinions, values, and actions shape how data is generated, analysed, and interpreted. Reflexivity has become an important methodological consideration in the social sciences, especially through the influence of *feminist critique on the *masculinist rationality of much research, and the growth of *qualitative methodologies. The premise underpinning reflexivity is that the researcher inherently shapes and biases a research project, either through the choices they make with respect to theory and methodology, or through the very process of conducting research. With respect to the latter, while an *ethnographer might seek to be an impartial observer of a community, their very presence may affect how that community behaves. In other words, the observations of the ethnographer are not independent of his/her participation. To be reflexive is to consider and self-critique how the assumptions, choices, and actions of one affects what is observed. For many, this also means declaring any issues raised through such a reflexive process in any dissemination of the research, so that readers can take account of how the project was *situated.

Further reading Mauthner, N. S and Doucet, A. (2003), 'Reflexive accounts and accounts of reflexivity in qualitative data analysis', *Sociology* 37: 413–31.

refugee A person forced from their home and seeking refuge, usually in another country. Refugees within countries are termed *internally displaced persons (IDPs), and they usually outnumber those who have crossed international boundaries. In international law, the United Nations Convention Relating to the Status of Refugees 1951 (amended 1967) defines a refugee as:

'A person who owing to a well-founded fear of being persecuted for reasons of race, religion, nationality, membership of a particular social group or political opinion, is outside the country of his nationality and is unable or, owing to such fear, is unwilling to avail himself of the protection of that country; or who, not having a nationality and being outside the country of his former habitual residence as a result of such events, is unable or, owing to such fear, is unwilling to return to it.'

Refugees conventionally described individuals fleeing oppression imposed by their home country governments, e.g. Jews in Nazi Germany. The United Nations High Commissioner for Refugees (UNHCR) also includes people forced from home by conflict, e.g. from the Darfur region of Sudan. The UN recognizes as a separate category those Palestinians who fled or were forced from the land currently constituting the state of Israel; they are administered by a separate agency, the UNRWA. In recent years, humanitarian agencies and academics have popularized the idea of *environmental refugees displaced by natural disasters, e.g. by Hurricane Katrina from New Orleans.

People forced from their homes to another country may seek refugee status by applying to the host government (*see* ASYLUM).

Work by geographers on refugees has concentrated on such things as the contribution of refugees to post-conflict resolution, attempts by governments to disperse refugees within national territories, and efforts to deter asylum-seekers by procedural practices. *See also* DIASPORA; FORCED MIGRATION; MIGRATION; TRANSNATIONAL COMMUNITIES; STATELESS PERSONS.

Table 3 Refugees by category

Category of forced displacement	Total (millions)
Refugees under UNHCR mandate	11.4
Refugees under UNWRA mandate	4.6
Total number of refugees	16.0
Conflict-generated IDPs	26.0
Natural disaster IDPs	25.0
Total number of IDPs	51.0
Total number of refugees and IDPs	67.0

Source: UNHCR *2007 Global Trends*, June 2008

regime of accumulation A historically specific but relatively long-lived means by which capital *accumulation is ensured. The term derives from the French neo-Marxist school of *Regulation Theory. At its broadest, it defines: (i) a dominant ensemble of industries whose production methods and intended markers share similar characteristics; (ii) a set of national government measures designed to support these industries; and (iii) a complex set of rules, norms, and institutions designed to ensure stable and positive relations between firms, the state, and wage workers. The latter two encompass what is known as the 'mode of social regulation', without which commodity production would be impossible (*see* EMBEDDEDNESS, ECONOMIC). After 1945, many economic geographers and historians believed that a *Fordist-*Keynesian regime of accumulation prevailed in Western Europe, North America, and Japan. After the successive economic crises of the 1970s, this regime began to crumble as many large firms relocated overseas, unemployment rose, government spending was cut, government borrowing increased, and national trades unions were reined in by liberal and conservative politicians. Even so, *path dependency meant that there were few clean breaks with the past, and thus the geographies of *Fordism's successor—known variously as *flexible accumulation or *neoliberalism—are complex and uneven.

regime theory A theory of urban governance and development which contends that successful cities are driven forwards by coalitions of actors working in concert with each other. In contrast to more structural accounts of urban development, such as *regulation theory, regime theory prioritizes the agency of city actors to enact change. However, in contrast with coalition theory, regime theory recognizes that power is not simply held and wielded by city elites, but is negotiated and dispersed, and that policy and action emerges from the meshing of interests across governmental and non-governmental actors. Diverse groups thus compensate for their individual lack of power by combining to form a more powerful collective regime to produce the capacity needed to achieve agreed aims. *See also* GROWTH COALITION.

Further reading Stone, C. (1989), *Regime Politics: Governing Atlanta*.

region A relatively bounded area regarded as meaningful for geographic analysis by virtue of either one or more distinctive features or a high level of functional integration. Although the term has been applied to areas at many different scales, from part of a dwelling to a substantial portion of the Earth's surface, it has two main senses in common usage. First, it refers to an area of subnational extent, a definition also used in government and planning (*see* REGIONAL PLANNING; REGIONALISM; REGIONALIZATION). Second, it describes a number of contiguous countries, often also called a 'world region', e.g. the *Caribbean. Beyond this, there is wide disagreement about what regions are, and their importance within geography. These centre on three main questions. First, are regions real things or just mental constructs? For some geographers, especially in the *spatial-science tradition, regions are simply convenient ways of classifying objects on the surface. For others, they have an identity or personality independent of geographers' knowledge of them. Second, regions can be thought of as naturally or socially defined. Andrew Herbertson sought to combine climatic and other physical geographical features into 'major natural regions'; *bioregionalism proposes that humans should live within the natural limits of their regions. But for most current human geographers, regions are understood as *socially constructed or produced, part of a multi-scalar process (*see* SCALE). Finally, regions can be thought of as integrated and relatively bounded, or discontinuous, divided, and porous. The first view suggests regions can either be 'formal', i.e. characterized by the uniformity of some feature such as climate or language, or *'functional', i.e. integrated by interaction or linkages (*see* CITY-REGION). The methodological problem has always been how to identify a region's boundaries according to either of these approaches. An alternative formulated by John Allen, Doreen *Massey, and Allan Cochrane, is to treat regions as *assemblages, marked by heterogeneity and openness.

Further reading Allen, J. et al. (1998), *Rethinking the Region*.
Herod, A. (2011), *Scale*.

regional development An economic policy aimed at combating *regional inequalities by stimulating economic growth within regions. Promoting and incentivizing regional development has long been a goal of national governments and transnational bodies such as the *European Union through its structural funds programmes. Such programmes aim to encourage inward investment and grow local businesses to provide long-term, viable employment opportunities. It does this by selective investment in key infrastructure and providing grant aid to businesses.

Further reading Pike, A., Rodriguez-Pose, A., and Tomaney, J. (2006), *Local and Regional Development*.

regional geography The study of parts of the Earth's land surface ('*regions') in order to: find out how and why one part differs from or is similar to others; and understand how the various features of the area, physical and human, relate to one another in their specific combination. Defined thus, it is a synthetic or integrative approach that contrasts with general or *systematic geography, the study of classes of object such as cities or rivers. Although regions can, in principle, vary in extent from a room to the globe, in practice there have been three main kinds of regional geography in the past fifty years. World regional geography is a mainstay of geographical education at all levels up to undergraduate study. Typically it involves learning about Africa or North America and all the different countries therein (Johnson et al. 2009). A second form, though in relative decline, is the specialized study of a country or larger region with the intention of bringing together human and physical geography. Oscar Spate's *India and Pakistan* (1954) (subtitled *a General and Regional Geography*) was a comprehensive geographical account of these two countries (or one country before 1947) with chapters on geology, soil, farming, industry, etc. The third kind of regional geography is the study of subnational regions, a tradition founded in France and Germany, where it retains some importance. In whatever form, regional geography has undergone many changes. It has variously been placed at the heart of the discipline, as one important approach among others, and at the declining margins of geography.

The origins of a regional approach geography can be traced back to the classical Greek concept of chorographic knowledge (*see* CHOROLOGY). In its later *Renaissance manifestation, this meant the orderly study of portions of the Earth's surface as distinct from the study of the Earth as a whole ('geography') and its relations to other bodies ('cosmography'). From the 17th century onwards it became common to differentiate 'special' or 'regional' geography from 'general' or 'systematic', notably in the work of German geographers Carl *Ritter and Alexander von *Humboldt. As geography became institutionalized in European and North American universities, its regional element took two broad forms. On the one hand, typified by Andrew Herbertson's 'natural regions' (1919) there were attempts to classify and divide the planet's surface into large regions in which climate, soils, and vegetation were similar. These regions could then form the basis for a more scientific understanding of differences between human societies. On the other hand, there were more bottom-up approaches that inquired into the uniqueness of particular regions. The Vidalian tradition of French geography, whose exponents specialized in regional monographs of parts of France, typified this approach (*see* VIDAL DE LA BLACHE). By integrating the study of place, work, and family, these geographers established what one might call the 'personality' of a region. Both kinds of knowledge, but especially the detailed understanding of particular areas, were harnessed by the combatants in the *Second World War as vital to successful operations (*see* MILITARY GEOGRAPHY). Geographers at the Universities of Oxford and Cambridge collaborated on an (unfinished) series of *Admiralty Handbooks* describing the features of those parts of the world where warfare was anticipated. After the war, this kind of geographical knowledge was pursued in *Area Studies. Although Richard *Hartshorne had placed the regional *method* at the centre of his study of *areal differentiation, both human and physical geographers found less and less utility in the study of regions. George Kimble summarized a widely held view in the 1950s when he declared that the 'region' was an 18th-century concept, fit for studying the relatively sedentary life of peasant agriculture, but not suited to understanding the flows and dynamics of an urban, industrial world (*see* SPATIAL SCIENCE). Within *Anglo-American geography, regional geography faded from academic courses.

A 'new regional geography' was announced in the 1980s. As defined by Anne Gilbert it had three components, though none involved physical geography. The first, rooted in *Marxist geography, concerned the *uneven development of capitalism and the associated production of *scale (*see* LOCALITY; *SPATIAL DIVISIONS OF LABOUR*); regions were one outcome and a medium of multi-scalar processes ranging from the *body to the world. The second sought to understand how all social life is set in time and space contexts drawing on ideas from *time-geography and *structuration (*see* CONTEXTUALITY). The third attended to the rise in regional identities and particularly its association with regional culture (*see* PLACE). Elements of the first and third approaches persist, although the Marxist influence has waned. Current economic geographers are interested in whether knowledge, innovation, and creativity have a particular affinity for regional-scale clusters. Following a more 'relational approach' they assess the relative significance of local qualities and global networks (*see* RELATIONAL GEOGRAPHY). In this and other ways, although regional geography is not necessarily studied in traditional ways, there is an ongoing concern for regions and processes of regionalization. *See* REGIONAL SCIENCE.

References and further reading Agnew, J., Livingstone, D., and Rogers, A., (eds.) (1996), *Human Geography: an Anthology.*
Gilbert, A. (1988), 'The new regional geography in English- and French-speaking countries', *Progress in Human Geography* 12: 208–28.
Herod, A. (2011), *Scale.*
Johnson, D. L. et al. (10th ed. 2009), *World Regional Geography.*

regional inequality A difference in the standards of living and opportunities for work between regions. It is often the case that some regions within a nation state are relatively wealthy compared with other regions, having a greater share of well-paid employment and provision of services. Other regions, usually in peripheral locations, lag behind. *Regional development policy is one strategy employed to try and narrow such inequalities between regions.

regional innovation systems A networked approach to economic development, centred on the premise that innovation creates new products, ways of doing things, and value, and seeks to build and take advantage of connections between public and private sector actors in a region to stimulate economic growth. By linking together and partnering companies with higher education institutes and development agencies, there is a sharing and scaling up of expertise, knowledge transfer, and translation effects. The region is considered to be the ideal scale for such a system as it has a sufficient density and abundance of actors, institutions, and firms to provide a platform that can be built upon.

regionalism 1. A political mobilization designed to further the interests of a subnational region, for example, towards greater autonomy from a *nation state or independence (*see* SECESSION).

2. The strategies of economic policy and regulation directed towards enhancing economic integration at subnational scales. *See also* REGIONAL POLICY.

regional multiplier The stimulation of economic growth in a region by growth itself. As industries in a region grow, they produce a demand for materials, goods, and services that help other local industries grow, which in turn produces further demand and also attracts further investment into the region. Moreover, there are *spillover effects from increases in wages and lower unemployment that lead to a greater circulation of capital. As such, there is a *cumulative causation effect, with momentum becoming self-perpetuating. The multiplier effect also works in reverse, so that as economic growth slows or businesses shut, the effects ripple throughout the local economy.

regional planning A form of *spatial planning conducted at the regional scale that seeks to plan and coordinate the development of residential settlement, transport and utility infrastructure, and economic development. It is usually overseen and governed by a regional planning agency that seeks to balance national objectives with local conditions. By planning at this scale a more synoptic approach can be employed that takes into account the characteristics and needs of different locales. Regional planning is a key component of *regional development and it is shaped by *regional policy.

regional science A discipline combining elements of economics, economic geography, and *quantitative spatial analysis. It emerged after the *Second World War when a group of economists led by Walter *Isard organized meetings of the Regional Science Association (RSA) independently of the more established American Economic Association. Isard believed mainstream economics gave insufficient attention to space and location, matters of increasing significance in the post-war transformation of the US landscape. For much of the 1960s and 1970s, regional science ran in parallel with human geography, sharing a focus on *spatial science. It did not embrace *political economy, meaning the two fields became increasingly separated. The Regional Science Association International runs the *Journal of Regional Science*, and organizes annual conferences.

regression A statistical technique for identifying the relationship between a dependent *variable and one or more independent variables. Part of the family of *general linear models, it can be thought of as an extension of *correlation. Whereas correlation describes the linear relationship between two variables and is symmetrical in nature (the correlation between A and B is the same as B and A), linear regression enables an analysis of how one variable varies with respect to another and to predict the nature of that relationship. For example, it can be used to answer a question such as 'given x, how well can we predict y'; 'given educational attainment, how well can we predict future earnings?'. Regression is a very commonly used method of *quantitative data analysis in human geography and takes a number of forms. Its simplest form is linear regression, which regresses one variable with respect to another. If these two variables are plotted on a graph, with the dependent variable on the y axis, and the independent variable of the x axis, regression constructs a line of best fit through the scatter of points, expressed as $y = a + bx$, where a is the intercept, the point at which the line crosses the y axis (i.e., the value of y where $x = 0$), and b is the slope that denotes the increase in y corresponding to a unit increase in x (see Fig. 9). From this equation it is possible to predict the value of y for any value of x. The difference between the observed value (the points in the scatter plot) and the predicted value (the line) is the residual value. If the observed point rests on the line then its residual value is 0. The residuals represent unexplained variation in the relationship between the variables. The residual values can be used to provide a goodness-of-fit measure, R^2. An R^2 value of 1 would indicate a perfect positive correlation between variables and a value of -1 a perfect negative correlation. A value of 0 would suggest no correlation at all. The level of confidence in the R^2 value is calculated by performing a *significance test. Multiple regression extends the analysis to simultaneously

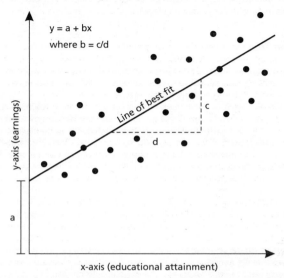

$$y = a + bx$$
$$\text{where } b = c/d$$

Line of best fit

y-axis (earnings)

c

d

a

x-axis (educational attainment)

Fig. 9   A linear regression of earnings (*y*) based on education attainment (*x*) expressed as y = a + bx

consider a number of independent variables and to calculate their relative importance in predicting *y*. Other forms of regression include *geographically weighted regression, *logit regression, *Poisson regression, and step-wise regression.

regulation A mechanism designed to control relations between or the behaviour of specific institutions, groups of institutions, or sections of a society. Self-regulation is common in the professions, such as the law and accountancy. More generally, national, regional, or local government create and enforce regulations. For instance, the British Conservative government in 1989 did this when privatizing water and sewerage services in England and Wales. New private providers not only had to act in accordance with new regulations but also report directly to national regulatory bodies designed to ensure such things as fair prices for consumers and adequate investment in future infrastructure. 'Regulatory capture' occurs where institutions or social groups whose behaviour is supposedly being regulated by the state (or some other independent organization) define the latter's agenda. Deregulation describes the supposed lifting of controls, for example, in removing the monopoly of state utility companies (*see* PRIVATIZATION). Deregulation is a key component of *neoliberalism.

Human geographers are deeply interested in the spatial configuration of regulation, especially in the economic, political, and environmental domains. First, similar regulations implemented in different places may produce different results, creating space for policy-relevant comparative research into why. Second, regulations are symptomatic of prevailing political philosophies (e.g. *neoliberalism). Examining the performance of regulation in different countries or places can thus tell us much about the links between the claims of the philosophies and the actualities of practice. Finally, since 1990 a great many global regulations have been agreed and adopted by a plethora of countries (e.g. members of the *World Trade Organization). Examining the differential effects of these common regulations at the national scale is important when assessing whether it was right to replace previous domestic regulations.

Regulation Theory A neo-Marxist branch of *political economy that seeks to understand how capital *accumulation can occur on a relatively stable basis given that recessions and depressions are endemic to the capitalist *mode of production. Regulation Theory is closely associated with the French neo-Marxists Alain Lipietz, Michel Aglietta, and Robert Boyer. This trio accepted Karl *Marx's abstract analysis of *capitalism as an economic system that was growth-orientated, technologically dynamic, and prone to periodic crises. However, they were concerned to ground this analysis in the lessons of history, and were also influenced by *institutionalism in economics and sociology. Accordingly, they looked at the characteristics of post-1945 Western capitalism, which arose from the embers of the economic crisis of 1929 and the 1930s, and the *Second World War (1939–45).

The Regulation Theorists noticed three things about what became known as the Fordist-Keynesian *regime of accumulation. First, the bulk of commodity production and national GDP was generated by a group of very large vertically and horizontally integrated firms in industries such as coal mining, steel manufacturing, heavy engineering, car manufacture, and ship-building. Secondly, these firms employed huge workforces and paid them relatively well, which helped to maintain demand in the domestic economy. Third, these workforce's interests were upheld by well-resourced national trades unions, while national governments funded robust welfare programmes and provided many public goods (such as universal education to age 16). In sum, according to the Regulation Theorists what regulated capitalism's tendencies towards 'boom-and-bust' between around 1950 and 1973 was a social contrast between capital, workers, and the national state. All agreed to support and assist each other, and to avoid conflict through communication and negotiation.

Regulation Theory proved to be highly influential in economic and urban geography in the 1990s, for at least two reasons. First, the previous two decades had seen the Western economies undergo massive economic restructuring, with attendant social effects. Second, early work by Marxist geographers was highly theoretical, and there was a perceived need to test (and enrich) such theory with reference to empirical *evidence. Consequently, and in part through the efforts of British sociologist Bob Jessop, many human geographers set about investigating whether and how the Fordist-Keynesian regime was being replaced in Western countries and its subnational variation. They examined how elements of the previous regime were held onto even after the crises of the 1970s and 1980s. This led to much comparative reflection on the pros and cons—as well as the possibilities of adopting—different political economic regimes (sometimes known as *varieties of capitalism).

Though few in economic and urban geography now make formal use of the language or findings of Regulation Theory, its influence endures. It can be credited with making many human geographers aware that all economies must be analysed in their wider political and cultural contexts. It is thus opposed to the 'clean lines' characteristic of the models, equations, and graphs favoured by many economists, and not a few geographical economists (*see* NEW ECONOMIC GEOGRAPHY). Ongoing work by Jamie *Peck, Neil Brenner, and others into our putatively 'post-neoliberal' world is also conducted in the regulationist spirit. It inquires into what institutions, norms, and measures are now being searched for to ensure economic growth and social stability in these turbulent times. Despite its focus on regulation and how capitalism is able to survive despite itself, Regulation Theory is not politically reformist. True to its Marxist roots, it retains an interest in how capitalism can be eliminated, however remote this possibility currently is.

Reilly's law A formulation of the *gravity model applied to the retail sector first forwarded by William J. Reilly in 1931. The law posits that larger cities will attract people from much further away due to their greater spheres of influence created through a larger choice of goods and services. The retail *hinterlands of places are determined by calculating their catchment break points, the point at which the population on one side will go to one city and those on the other side to another city, dependent on their relative attractiveness. *See also* CENTRAL PLACE THEORY; FRICTION OF DISTANCE; SPATIAL INTERACTION MODELS; TOBLER'S FIRST LAW OF GEOGRAPHY.

relational database A method for storing large quantities of related data in inter-connected tables. Each table shares at least one common field with another table enabling information to be extracted and combined across the tables. The common fields that permit spatial data analysis is address information.

relational geography A family of approaches to understanding human geographies that strongly emphasizes the co-constitution and mutual entanglement of otherwise different (and often far distant) phenomena. Early examples of these relational approaches (in the 1970s and early 1980s) were *Marxist geography and, despite critics' claims that it fixated on *subjectivity, a good deal of *humanistic geography. More recently, research inspired by *Actor-Network Theory, *non-representation theory, and the *post-structuralism of *Deleuze and Guattari is deeply relational, so too, the ongoing work of Marxists. Despite their important differences of detail, relational approaches share a common antipathy to *Cartesianism and its stringent commitment to *analysis. Cartesian thinking—represented by much *spatial science in the 1960s, and *behavioural geography in the 1970s—takes an atomist view of reality, regarding the world as composed of discrete units (e.g. firms or flood plains) that interact (or not) in various ways. Contrary to this, relational thinkers insist that the world of 'things' (people, institutions, trees, animals, etc.) has no meaningful existence outside various more-or-less stable, more-or-less enduring relationships and processes. Relational thinkers thus reject *reductionism in explanation, see *causation as lacking a single locus, and regard *materiality as something dispersed among a great many interconnected phenomena. In many ways, relational thinkers reprise geographers' early 20th-century commitment to synthesis since they are deeply interested in how things 'hang together' at the Earth's surface at a range of geographical and temporal scales.

Today, two forms of relational thinking are prominent, though they are manifest in several research streams in human geography. One form accents overarching processes and relations that unify, but also are affected by all manner of different phenomena in different places (*see* HOLISM). David *Harvey's Marxism is emblematic of this form. The other form attends more closely to the experiences and actions of individuals, with a significant emphasis on difference and the possibilities of 'becoming' out—with the current norms, habits, and rules prevailing in any given society. If the first form leans towards the *nomothetic—looking for a certain order underpinning otherwise varied and separate situations—then the second leans more towards *idiography. The second has also arguably been more successful than the first at deconstructing the dualism between mind and body, so that mental processes and sensations are seen as thoroughly bound up with human corporeality (*compare with* RATIONAL ACTOR).

If relational thinking has a weakness it is that it threatens to elide different relations into a baggy 'everythingism' of description and explanation. As *critical realists such as Andrew *Sayer argued thirty years ago, it is important to distinguish between 'necessary' and 'contingent' relations, and 'internal' and 'external' relations if we are to truly understand how the world is 'overdetermined' (*see* OVERDETERMINATION). The spirit, if not the letter, of Sayer's argument lives on in recent work by economic and social

r

geographers known as 'intersectional analysis', where relations of gender, class, and ethno-racial inequality are studied in their complex combinations in context.

relational space Any *space that is produced by, rather than existing as the *a priori* container of, processes and relationships. The acclaimed physicist Isaac Newton proclaimed space (and time) to be absolute, something given in *nature. The philosopher Baruch Spinoza, by contrast, suggested that space is created by biophysical and humanly designed processes and systems. While Newton's approach licenses aspatial forms of analysis where intellectual *abstraction from *place, *landscape, or *territory is seen as unproblematic, Spinoza's invites us to see space (and time) as both effect and cause, outcome and precondition. In human geography it was, ironically, the Newtonian view that prevailed when the discipline first self-consciously sought to make itself into a *science (in the 1960s). Prior to this, some later commentators argued that *idealism about space had prevailed insofar as many early 20th-century geographers imposed their own geographical categories onto the world when writing about places and regions (*see* IDIOGRAPHIC). David *Harvey, in his initial Marxist work *Social Justice and the City* (1973), was the first to strongly advocate relational space as a proper focus of geographical inquiry. His argument was that people produce various spaces according to the character and aims of various processes, so that these spaces are constitutive not mere epiphenomena. Harvey also argued that while all locations have absolute qualities at any one given moment in time, they nonetheless cannot be understood outside their relations with other locations. These relations can make them temporally nearer or further apart, wealthy or poor, stable or unstable, and so on.

Further reading Harvey, D. (2006), 'Space as a keyword', in Castree, N. and Gregory, D. (eds.) *David Harvey: a Critical Reader* 270–94.

relative space An understanding of *space wherein the relative location of bodies is determined with respect to other bodies. Relative space contrasts with absolute space, wherein location is understood with respect to an independent frame of reference such as a coordinate system. The dimensions of absolute space are fixed and immovable, whereas relative space is a movable dimension. The difference between absolute and relative space has been a long-running debate in physics. For example, while Newton posited the existence of a universal absolute space, Leibniz thought that space made no sense except as the relative location of bodies.

relativism The epistemological proposition that all statements about the world—cognitive, ethical, or aesthetic—are relative to the world views of those making the statements. Relativists take issue with two other epistemological propositions that, at various times, have proven to be socially influential. The first is that because all humans have the same neural hardware and are creatures of natural evolution, they must possess a shared disposition to see the world in the same (or a very similar) way. The second is that while some statements about reality are erroneous or false, others are true by virtue of how they are arrived at. It follows that by utilizing the same method as truth finders do, all people would—with sufficient time and resources—come to understand their beliefs about the world as in need of correction. Relativists challenge both propositions on the grounds that they ignore, or see as a problem, the evident diversity of human understandings past and present.

Relativism comes in both 'positive' and 'normative' forms. In the first, the analyst is concerned to take seriously the often incommensurable ways that different communities or societies make sense of the world. As part of this, they may also self-consciously point to their own situatedness and socialization as researchers, meaning that their representations are as relative as those whose representations of reality are the focus of the research (*see* SITUATED KNOWLEDGE). Relativism of the second kind is more judge-mental and rejects the argument that there is some universal epistemic basis on which we can determine whose knowledges or beliefs should take priority over all others. This kind of relativism was promoted by many advocates of *postmodernism in the social sciences and humanities, in part to challenge the confident claims of those who pur-ported to be the voices of *science, truth, and reason. Some of these advocates were sociologists of science (such as Bruno *Latour), who treated scientists much like an anthropologist would treat a foreign 'tribe': namely, as an alien culture worthy of having its own peculiar norms, concepts, and rituals understood on their own terms.

'Strong' relativism is a favourite target of critics, but is rarely actually maintained or advocated. It amounts to the claim that all perspectives on reality are equally valid, meaning that we should refrain (i) from trying to distinguish better from worse perspec-tives; and (ii) staging debates between rival perspectives for fear of disrespecting one or other of them by exposing them to potential attack. However, a less muscular form of relativism—common across the social sciences and humanities—makes more humble, but nonetheless important claims, namely that: (i) different perspectives on the world exist for good reasons and deserve to be understood in their own terms before we start to judge them from our own standpoint; (ii) our own perspectives are thus partial and do not exhaust the range of ways that people perceive and value the world; and (iii) enrichment and mutual learning can arise when respectful debates occur between people who are aware of the partiality and specificity of their own sense-making prac-tices. One version of this less muscular relativism has been promoted by philosophical pragmatists such as Richard Rorty (*see* PRAGMATISM). They reject the reality-representa-tion dualism that underpins so much debate between 'realists' (*see* REALISM) and relativists. Instead, they see all knowledge as *practical*: that is, as created to produce certain effects using certain rhetorical idioms ('truth', 'justice', 'logic'). The diversity of perspectives extant in the world, pragmatists argue, simply reflects the range of goals that knowledge and beliefs are designed to serve. To search for absolutes such as 'truth' is thus a futile quest.

Human geography (like its physical counterpart) was once deeply committed to the idea that, while the knowledges of real-world actors may be relative, that of its practi-tioners should not be. In the 1960s and 1970s there was considerable discussion about the *scientific method and a strong belief that phenomena arranged at the Earth's surface possessed a certain orderliness waiting to be discovered. However, this particular kind of realism was challenged, and by the 1980s it was firmly on the back foot. On the one side, the early Marxist and feminist geographers argued that *spatial scientists' knowledge was relative, despite its claims to *objectivity. They put forward their own avowedly relative alternatives designed to emancipate working-class people and women. On the other side, humanistic geographers' less avowedly political research highlighted the *hermeneutic aspects of human existence, and pointed to the variety of '*lifeworlds' created by people (old and young, women and men, rich and poor, etc.). After *postmodernism and *post-structuralism made their presence felt in human geography, these early cases for rela-tivism became more generalized, morphing into a celebration of epistemic diversity both in the world 'out there' and also 'in here' (i.e. within the discipline itself). However, this celebration was not uncritical. It was largely designed to make space for 'alternative' perspectives on the world that had for too long been excluded.

Since the turn of the millennium the commitment to relativism has remained strong in human geography, even though many latter-day spatial scientists remain confident that their inquiries are more objective than many of their colleagues. However, it has come at a certain price. Arguably, the volume and quality of debate among geographers of different epistemic persuasions is not all it could be. There is a need for more 'engaged pluralism' so that the merits of dissimilar understandings of reality could be more widely considered, leading to changes in the disciplinary matrix. This could be consistent with the pragmatists' argument that the goal of knowledge should be edification and the improvement of life, not some absolute criteria such as truth. *See also* PHILOSOPHY OF GEOGRAPHY.

relevance Originating in the late 1960s, there has been an ongoing set of debates concerning how relevant geographic research should be for people's everyday lives. The debate started as a reaction to what was perceived as politically sterile and peopleless quantitative geography that, on the one hand, focused on mundane and abstract issues, and on the other sought to understand the world but did not seek explicitly to change it. For *radical geographers, human geography thus largely ignored the huge social and geopolitical events of the times, such as urban unrest, the Vietnam and *Cold Wars, and poverty in the *Third World, and did little to address these issues. They called for more relevant research that focused not on abstract problems, such as modelling the spatial processes that underpinned migration patterns, but on concrete social, political, and economic issues that people faced daily. With a few exceptions, such as Bill *Bunge who pioneered the development of *activist forms of geographical praxis, this turn to relevance was largely an intellectual exercise for the next two decades (*see* DETROIT GEOGRAPHICAL EXPEDITION AND INSTITUTE). In the early 1990s, the relevance debate was taken in two directions. The first was an instrumentalist and *neoliberal drive to make geographic scholarship more relevant to the needs of the state and economy. Arguments were made that human geography should be more applied in focus, aiding states with *policy formulation, and working with industry to stimulate and guide development. Accompanying this was a drive to promote *geographic information systems as a key spatial technology and skill set for industry and the public sector. The second was a turn to *advocacy and *activist forms of geography that sought to work on behalf of and with communities to improve their lives. Both of these turns sought to move geographical praxis beyond intellectual contributions to knowledge production, to work more directly with the potential consumers of geographical knowledge. *See also* APPLIED GEOGRAPHY; PARTICIPATORY ACTION RESEARCH.

Further reading Fuller, D. and Kitchin, R. (eds.) (2004), *Radical Theory/Critical Praxis: Making a Difference beyond the Academy?*

reliability The repeatability or consistency in obtaining the same finding from the administering of a research instrument. Golledge and Stimson describe three kinds of reliability: (i) quixotic reliability, where a single method of observation continually yields an unvarying measurement; (ii) diachronic reliability, the stability of an observation through time; and (iii) synchronic reliability, the similarity of observations within the same time period. Reliability is important because it is generally accepted that the more consistent a finding, the more weight can be attributed to it. For example, if a result is consistently found, it is often referred to as a *law.

Further reading Golledge, R. and Stimson, R. (1997), *Spatial Behaviour*.

religion An organized and institutionalized system of faith, worship, spiritual practices, and sacred teachings. Such systems include large, widely practised faiths such as *Christianity, *Islam, *Judaism, *Hinduism, and their various denominations, as well as a myriad of other smaller faiths and related systems such as paganism. Each of these faith systems is prevalent in particular parts of the world and has associated *sacred spaces, routes of pilgrimage, and calendars. A long scholarly tradition, stretching back to the 16th and 17th centuries, has been to map the distribution and diffusion of religions. This work was often undertaken by religious orders to determine which areas had been converted and where to send missionaries. Other work sought to identify and locate places mentioned in religious texts, such as the Bible, and to explore the divine creation and ordering of landscapes and nature and people's relationship to these. In the early 20th century, through the influence of the *Berkeley School, geographical research examined the nature of sacred spaces and the production of *cultural landscapes shaped explicitly by religious values, practices, and *architecture. Such research continues, but has been joined by a wider range of approaches and foci of study.

One body of work concentrates on the production and consumption of *sacred spaces such as temples, churches, and other holy sites such as wells, and their role in shaping wider communal relations. Here, on the one hand research focuses on the personal and collective experience of such locales, and on the other, on the wider politics relating to them. With respect to the former, there is an attempt to understand the immanent and transcendent communion that takes place at these sites, how they produce personal meanings, sense of identity and spirituality, and the way in which such spaces develop their sacred meanings. Such work is often rooted in the traditions of *humanistic geography and its emphasis on sense of place and identity. For example, Lily Kong has examined how, for those practising a faith, religious sites contribute to a sense of community rooted in place in Singapore. Such sites are often also symbolic expressions of power and contested spaces. Here there might be conflict between different religious groups occupying the same areas or there may be tension between a secular state, industry, and religious authorities, for example, over the siting, regulation, and maintenance of cemeteries, or the promotion of religious sites and festivals for tourism.

Another body of work has focused on the development of *secularism (the separation of church and state) and secularization (the diminishing role of religion in society) in some parts of the world on the one hand, and on the other hand the growth of religious fundamentalism and its effects on broader social and political relations. In much of Europe, the roles of the church and state are clearly divided, and church-going rates are in decline, though religious groups still seek to influence public policy but with diminishing effect. In contrast, religious dogma within the US Bible belt increasingly pervades social and political discourse, influencing policy, including school curricula. Similarly, religious fundamentalism is strongly tied into civil society and political systems in the Middle East and elsewhere. Such beliefs, often in conjunction with nationalism, can fuel religious conflict between people of different faiths leading to terrorist activities, civil wars, and genocide (*see* HOLOCAUST). For example, sectarianism in Northern Ireland between Protestants and Catholics has led to a complex geography of residence, work, and leisure, and conflicts over space in the province. In the former Yugoslavia, religion and nationalism led to civil war, genocide, and ultimately to its break-up into separate new states. Religion has also played a role in Al Qaeda's attacks on the West and is at the core of the 'war on terror'. The study of religion has therefore become an increasing aspect of geopolitics research.

Finally, religion can also play a part in the ways in which geographical research is conducted. Certainly the spiritual beliefs of Yi-Fu *Tuan influenced the humanistic approach he developed, which drew extensively from religious philosophy. Similarly, *Christian geographers bring to bear their beliefs, moral values, and faith to shape their geographical agenda, praxis, and ethics.

Further reading and references Agnew, J. (2006), 'Religion and geopolitics', *Geopolitics* 11: 183–91.

Holloway, J. and Valins, O. (2002), 'Placing religion and spirituality in geography', *Social and Cultural Geography* 3: 5–9.

Kong, L. (1993), 'Negotiating conceptions of sacred space: a case study of religious buildings in Singapore', *Transactions of the Institute of British Geographers* 18: 342–58.

Park, C. (1994), *Sacred Worlds: an Introduction to Geography and Religion*.

relocalization The civil society strategies to increase the resilience of localities by increasing the degree to which food, energy, and other goods are produced locally. Such schemes are strongly linked with efforts to move towards a *low-carbon economy and may also involve encouraging alternative local currencies.

Relph, Edward (1944–) A Welsh-born geographer based as the University of Toronto, best known for his book *Place and Placelessness* (1976) and his advancement of *humanistic geography. His prime contribution has been to focus a philosophical lens on the concept of *place, seeking to produce a *phenomenology of places. In so doing he has examined the complexity of places as they are experienced and made by people, studying and theorizing *sense of place, the meanings of place, *place attachment, and *place identity.

remittances Money sent from one part of the world to another, usually by migrants to family and friends in their places of origin. Remittances are thought to be significant because of their role in *development. In 2010, around US \$440 billion was remitted internationally, 74 per cent to developing countries (the major destinations are India, Mexico, and China and the main source of origin is the USA). In addition to these formal figures, there are informal and unrecorded flows. Remittance flows may provide an alternative to *aid and *Foreign Direct Investment because they are often directed at households, including many in poorer rural districts. There is debate over whether their net impact is positive. Some studies suggest remittances sustain a third or more of households in poor areas, providing for basic living needs as well as education. Others argue that they increase local social and spatial inequalities, drive land and price inflation, and encourage dependency on overseas earnings at the expense of local development. Many governments are seeking to channel remittances into development projects and into the formal banking sector, away from informal money transfer routes. In recent years, new technologies have facilitated cheaper money transfer schemes, such as MPesa in Kenya, which uses mobile phones. Remittance flows are central to the *migration-development nexus. Some researchers recognize non-monetary or 'social' remittances, including norms, practices, identities, and *social capital that impact either positively or negatively on the place of origin. These might include ideas about health care, contraception, gender, or democracy as well as *social networks, transferred either in person or via letters, emails, videos, etc.

Further reading *World Bank Migration Remittances Factbook* (2nd ed. 2011).

remote sensing The capture, processing, and analysis of reflected or emitted radiation from the Earth's surface and atmosphere. Data is generally captured from high above the planet in the form of *raster arrays, including images, using sensors attached to orbiting satellites, with the data relayed back to base stations (*see also* AERIAL PHOTOGRAPHY; PHOTOGRAMMATERY). The data is used to analyse the Earth's surface and atmosphere from local to global scales, and to monitor change over time. Remote sensing can be both passive and active in nature. Passive systems simply measure naturally reflected or emitted radiation, capturing reflected solar radiation in the form of ultraviolet, visible, near-infrared (NIR) wavelengths; reflected and emitted radiation in the mid-infrared; and emitted radiation only in the far-infrared (e.g., thermal energy) and microwave wavelengths. Active systems, such as radar (radio detection and ranging) and lidar (light detection and ranging), measure the reflection of their own generated electromagnetic radiation.

The arrays of data generated are composed of pixels that cover a plot of known size. Each pixel details the radiation level detected for that plot. The level measured is the result of two main factors: atmospheric conditions and surface coverage. Electromagnetic radiation is scattered, absorbed, and refracted as it passes through the atmosphere, from the sun to the Earth and when it is reflected back. The radiation absorbed and reflected back from a plot is influenced by surface-cover type and its roughness, with different wavelengths affected in diverse ways depending on the coverage. For example, water absorbs radiation in the NIR and longer wavelengths, whereas vegetation absorbs visible wavelengths, especially in the green portion of the spectrum, and reflects the NIR wavelengths. By accounting for atmospheric conditions, and given that different kinds of surface cover absorb, scatter, and reflect wavelengths of radiation along the electromagnetic spectrum in different ways, it is thus possible to draw some conclusions about the land-cover type of each pixel.

The veracity of those conclusions is also shaped by the array resolution. This has four dimensions. Spectral resolution refers to the number of wavelength bands recorded and the sensitivity of the sensor with respect to those bands (panchromatic is composed of a single band and multispectral includes several bands, for example, IKONOS satellite records four bands). The spatial resolution refers to the size of the plot covered by each pixel and determines the smallest object that can be identified. For example, very coarse sensors such as the AVHRR, which detects cloud cover and surface temperature over a very wide area (useful for modelling the weather), have a resolution of 1.1 km^2, whereas Landsat has a coverage of 30 m^2 (enabling the detection of roads and rivers), and IKONOS has a coverage of 4 m^2 for multispectral data and 1 m^2 for panchromatic data (enabling the detection of small buildings, vehicles, footpaths, etc.). Radiometric resolution refers to the data range for each pixel, for example, radiation measured along a scale of 255 possible values (8 bit scale) or 2047 possible values (11 bit scale). Temporal resolution refers to how frequently a particular portion of the Earth is re-sensed, given the satellite's orbit.

Remote sensing data can be analysed in a number of ways. The first step is to usually clean the data, such as georeferencing the array and correcting for atmospheric or sensor effects. Next, the data can be analysed visually or by using techniques such as feature extraction, classification, comparison (over time), or data fusion (merging data types). Each of these techniques has a number of forms, suitable for different kinds of remotely sensed data, that have been developed over time to improve the ability to extract information.

The value of remote sensing is that it provides a temporally and spatially consistent set of surface and atmospheric data for the entire planet, enabling changes in land cover, such as *deforestation or ice sheet coverage, to be tracked. Its application to social and economic issues has largely been restricted to issues of mapping and planning, though there have been attempts to estimate population and economic activity from settlement patterns and land cover. More recently, it has been used to identify war atrocities, such as the destruction of a village. The data also forms an important input into *GISs, providing terrain overlays.

Further reading Campbell, J. and Wynne, R. (5th ed. 2011), *Introduction to Remote Sensing*.
Gibson, P. and Power, C. (2000), *Introductory Remote Sensing Principles and Concepts*.
Lillesand, T., Kiefer, R., and Chipman, J. (6th ed. 2008), *Remote Sensing and Image Interpretation*.

Renaissance An intellectual and cultural movement that began in late-medieval Italy and continued for several centuries across Europe, which had wide influence on literature, art, philosophy, politics, and science. The movement developed in tandem with the invention of the printing press and changes in forms of education, so that new ideas started to migrate more freely and to be conjoined. With respect to science, theories started to be built on repeated observation, and in art and cartography, *linear perspective was developed. As such, a single universal system of measuring and representing the world was produced. The Renaissance is thus often understood as a bridge between the medieval period and the *Enlightenment and *modernity.

Further reading Mayhew, R. (2002), 'Geography, print culture and the Renaissance', *History of European Ideas* 27(4): 349–69.

renewable energy An *energy generated from replenishable sources to produce heat and electricity. The main sources are solar radiation, wind, tides, water, and geothermal activity. Biomass can also provide renewable energy if the rate of consumption does not exceed the rate of regeneration. Wood and animal dung burned for heating, and plants grown for biofuel are examples. *See also* LOW-CARBON ECONOMY; NUCLEAR POWER; NATURAL RESOURCES.

renewable resource *See* NATURAL RESOURCES.

rent The money charged by the owners of assets for others to use them. Many of these assets are geographically fixed and have a long life. This is obvious in the case of parcels of land, but applies also to infrastructure (e.g. roads), houses, factories, and office buildings. Collectively, the owners of rentable assets are called the *rentier class, whose ownership rights underpin the income stream they receive from allowing others to use their assets. The geography of rent is highly uneven. For instance, a parcel of fertile agricultural land close to a city may command five times the rent of a similar parcel less close to a major city. Mainstream economics explains this geography with reference to the 'law' of supply and demand. Taking the existing distribution of ownership and resources as a given, it explains high rents in place X as the result of many potential renters haggling over relatively scarce assets. This view, with suitable modifications to render it more realistic, was adopted by several economic, urban, and agricultural geographers in the 1960s and 1970s (*see* BID-RENT CURVE). However, *Marxist geographers subsequently pointed out that rental markets involve social relations between classes whose interests are opposed. For instance, landlords may wish to maximize their profits, while tenants will wish to inhabit good-quality accommodation for a price that does not account for most of their income. This led to a focus on how the rentier class and its institutions (e.g. estate agents and construction companies) seek to manage the scarcity of rentable assets in order to ensure favourable economic returns at the expense of workers, small business owners, and others.

rent gap The difference between the current rent derived from a plot of land and the rent that could be extracted under another use. In his analysis of *gentrification, Neil *Smith argues that progressive disinvestment in inner city properties so reduced their rental return to owners that it created the conditions for dramatic reinvestment through residential turnover.

rentier class That strata of a society whose members own assets that they loan (*rent) to others in order to receive an income stream that, in normal economic conditions, should exceed the costs of buying, maintaining, or improving those assets. Rentiers thus profit from ownership *per se*, rather than from producing commodities which they sell. They sell rights of use to their assets rather than the assets as such. Many assets are mobile (e.g. rental car), but others are locationally fixed (e.g. commercial office building). While the rentier class provides assets vital for the well-being of any country's economy and society, critics see it as both parasitic and exploitative: parasitic because its profits ultimately derive from *money created in the 'real economy', and exploitative because it benefits from others (e.g. young workers) lacking the means to own their own assets (e.g. a house). *See also* PETRO-CAPITALISM; RESOURCE CURSE.

replacement level The *total fertility rate at which a population would remain constant in size. In richer countries the level is around 2.1 births per woman of child-bearing age, but it can be higher where mortality rates are greater.

representation The act of capturing in words, images, or other communicative media the characteristics of things taken to exist or occur outside these media. The term 'representation' is both a verb and a noun: it refers to a process and its various products. It involves acts of substitution and translation in which different people make sense of the world in various ways and then concretize those sense-making acts in forms that can be shared with others. As cultural critic Michael Shapiro once put it, despite frequent appearances to the contrary, 'Representations do not "imitate" reality but are the practices through which things take on meaning and value...' (1988: xi). These practices can be visual (a book, a film, a map, a comic strip, a photograph); they can be oral and aural (a lecture or guided tour); they can be quantitative (e.g. a graph of mean atmospheric temperatures or a computerized Global Circulation Model) or qualitative (e.g. the words and pictures in an issue of the *National Geographic* magazine); they can be tactile (e.g. an interactive museum display); they can purely linguistic; they can involve some combination of discourse and (ostensibly) wordless communication (such as instrumental music); they can be obviously 'physical' (e.g. a sculpture); they can invite silent consumption (e.g. reading an ecotourism brochure when planning a holiday); they can be communicated using a rhetoric of certainty and precision, or be hedged around with qualification and caveats.

Some representational forms are relatively durable and can 'travel' through space and time (e.g. a book or a picture) (*see* IMMUTABLE MOBILE). Others are relatively durable over time but fixed in space, and so must physically attract consumers and users (e.g. the Eden Project in southwest England, which physically represents various ecosystems in miniature). Still others are transient or relatively ephemeral (e.g. the daily news on the radio, a billboard advert, or a documentary on the Discovery Channel). Some representations command small audiences, others very large ones that are spread across several countries or continents. Many representations are inconsequential, but not a few are hugely influential in the short term or longer term.

Clearly, this definition of 'representation' is ecumenical. As David Runciman and Monica Vieira note in *Representation* (2008: vii), 'representation' 'encompasses an extraordinary range of meanings and applications, stretching from mental images...to legal processes to theatrical performances'. This range notwithstanding, all representations *refer* to things near or far. They are commentaries on something that they themselves are not—objects, events, arguments, and so on. They are exercises in communication about the world, and they can work in all of the registers of understanding, evaluation, and affect. They are the means by which and the media through which meanings are attached to various portions of reality, and those portions of reality themselves delimited (or, perhaps, called into question and recategorized).

There is necessarily a *politics* to representation because people are not mere receptacles for information that passes through their eyes or ears, only to be 'correctly' processed by their brains. Instead, in speaking *about* something, they are speaking *of* it in ways that may reflect their own values or goals (*see* RELATIVISM). We often think these two aspects of representation to be separate, but they are not. The first—which we might associate with a journalist or an academic, say—involves making something present to us spatially (here) and temporally (today) via words, images, and so on. Consider a daily newspaper: we are enjoined to think and feel about that which might not otherwise be in front of us, near to us, or visible to us. The second aspect of representation we tend to associate with democratic political systems and most legal systems. We elect senators or MPs to represent our views and desires in our absence (hence the term 'representative democracy'); delegates and consuls are appointed to act on behalf of whole countries or their leaders; and (if in court) lawyers are our appointed defenders or prosecutors. Together, they *stand for* our interests and wishes because they *stand in* for us physically and rhetorically. Here we appreciate why the two senses of representation—'epistemic' and 'political'—are intimately connected. For they *both* involve substitution. Representers of various kinds are doing exactly what the word implies: they are making sense of the world for themselves and us, and thus acting as representatives (whether they occupy the political-legal sphere or not). In some form these representatives are interposing themselves between us and that to which they refer.

From the late 1980s, many critics in the social sciences and humanities fomented a 'crisis of representation' by questioning the commitment to *realism so dear to scientists and many other researchers. Some of these realists had themselves already questioned how realistic the representations of others were, as in the Marxist critique of *spatial science as *ideology. Their successors, however, were more sceptical about realism in any form. The argument was that representation is not what it appeared to be because it said as much about the predilections of the representers as the characteristics of the phenomena being represented. Influenced by *postmodernism and *post-structuralism, human geographers set about 'deconstructing' the content and rhetoric of various discourses and images, including those of cartographers, urban planners, and local politicians. They showed the world to literally be geo*graphed,* made manifest through a plethora of contingent representations—many of which claimed considerable epistemic authority because of who constructed them. Duncan and Ley's (1993) edited collection *Place/Culture/Representation* was a prominent example. However, by the turn of the millennium concerns were expressed that human geography was being 'dematerialized' because the physical world of bodies, buildings, and barnacles had been left behind in the obsession with representations of that world. Since then greater attempts have been made to attend both to the effects (and non-effects) of representations, and all the other registers in which people influence and are influenced by the world (*see,* for example, NON-REPRESENTATIONAL THEORY). *See also* HYPERREALITY; SIMULACRUM.

References and further reading Castree, N. and Macmillan, T. (2004), 'Old news: representation and academic novelty', *Environment and Planning A* 36, 3: 469–80.
Shapiro, M. (1988), *The Politics of Representation.*

reproductive labour The generally unremunerated *work involved in sustaining individuals fit for the waged labour process and ensuring the supply of future workers by raising and caring for children. In *capitalist societies, profit is realized through productive (normally waged) labour. But capitalists cannot produce workers themselves, and rely upon families to do so. In practice this normally means women, who assume responsibility for cooking, cleaning, and child-rearing within the household. Although thought of as highly localized, reproductive labour can be implicated in transnational relations (*see* GLOBAL CARE CHAINS). *See also* DOMESTIC WORK.

research assessment The measurement of the quality and impact of research. In an education system increasingly shaped by *neoliberal policy, the assessment of research has become increasingly common. A combination of *peer review and a range of performance indicators are used to evaluate the standard of the research, its impact on other research projects, and the wider literature, principally through citation metrics, and value for money. The results of such exercises are used in the allocation of resources between and within institutions. Consequently, assessment exercises have had a major impact on the higher education landscape, changing institutional cultures and organization, reshaping the working practices and conditions of academics, and creating a new geography of knowledge production as resources and labour are concentrated into particular sites and disinvested in others. In a world of increasingly mobile academic talent, such assessments have also led to the development of English as a global *lingua franca* of academic *publishing.

Further reading Castree, N. (2006), 'Research assessment and the production of geographical knowledge', *Progress in Human Geography* 30: 747–82.

research ethics A set of ethical and moral rules that guide research practice (*see* ETHICS). In human geography, research ethics generally concern the extent to which the researcher acts ethically with respect to the participants in their research project, and to what ends they employ their findings. In sciences, such as biology, it also includes animal welfare. Given its roots in philosophy, how to be ethical is a debated issue and there are varying views as to how researchers should act ethically. Many research funders issue guidelines setting out how they expect the researchers they fund to act, generally advocating a professional approach that prioritizes issues such as privacy, confidentiality, anonymity, and dignity. In general terms this means gaining consent for participation, not coercing people to take part, not withholding information about the true nature of the research, not asking them to do something that might diminish their self-esteem, not exposing participants to physical or mental stress, and treating participants with respect, and protecting their privacy and anonymity.

research funding The funding dedicated to the production of new knowledge. Such funding is usually allocated through a competitive process and is administered by government funding agencies, state agencies, philanthropic organizations, private industry, and voluntary and community sector bodies. Funding typically covers staff costs, equipment, travel, dissemination, and knowledge transfer. Many governments consider research and development (R&D) critical for producing a knowledge society and aim to spend three percent of GDP on R&D as a way of producing specialized talent and commodifiable knowledge.

reserves **1.** Areas designated for special purposes and otherwise protected from general use or exploitation, for example, for nature *conservation (*see* NATIONAL PARKS).

2. The stock of a nonrenewable *natural resource, the magnitude of which is known with a high degree of certainty, which can be exploited with prevailing levels of technology, and where it is economically viable to do so.

3. The amount of any commodity that is available for use if and when needed, e.g. a central bank's gold reserves, which guarantee the paper money it issues.

The definition and identification of reserves is important in the extraction of minerals, including energy minerals such as coal, gas, and oil. In calculating the amount of any natural resource that might be available for human use there are two main considerations. The first is the degree of geological certainty about its magnitude, distribution, and quality. The existence of resources can be known with varying levels of confidence— either measured, indicated, or inferred. The second is the economic feasibility of exploiting the resource at the available level of technology, e.g. in maritime oil drilling. There may also be issues of legal and political access; for example, is oil found in ancestral lands where exploitation is proscribed? Feasibility varies in potentially unpredictable fashion. If, for example, the world price of crude oil rises, some mineral deposits that were formerly too expensive to exploit may become more accessible. But, the price of oil is also in part a function of expected supply, in turn dependent on reserves. Reserves are therefore that subset of a resource which is known with a very high degree of certainty, and which it is profitable to exploit at the time. This category is often further divided into proven, i.e. measured, and probable reserves, including inferred deposits. The substantial uncertainties and feedbacks involved in estimating reserves make it very difficult to determine how much of any given mineral there actually is and how long its supply will last. *See also* PEAK OIL.

resistance The opposition to domination in words, thoughts, and/or actions. In human geography, resistance generally has political connotations. It can describe a range of overt actions, including strikes, occupations, *protests, direct action, and more organized forms such as *social movements (*see* ENVIRONMENTAL DIRECT ACTION). But resistance can take more subtle forms, including non-compliance with instructions, daydreaming, absenteeism, and myriad small acts described as 'weapons of the weak' by anthropologist James Scott. Within human geography, theoretical debates on resistance centre on whether it should be understood in a binary fashion as a reaction to domination, or whether, following the ideas of Michel *Foucault, resistance and domination need to be seen as more entangled with one another (*see* POWER).

Further reading Featherstone, D. (2008), *Resistance, Space and Political Identities*.
Sharp, J., Routledge, P., Philo, C., and Paddison, R. (eds.) (2000), *Entanglements of Power*.

resort life-cycle model A series of hypothetical stages through which a tourist resort passes, according to Canadian geographer R. W. Butler. The stages—exploration, involvement, development, consolidation, and stagnation—describe the process by which resorts rise and fall. Early exclusivity gives way to mass provision and low returns, leading to a situation where either decline will set in or the resort will have to reinvent itself somehow. *See also* TOURISM.

Reference Butler, R. W. (1980), 'The concept of a tourist area cycle of evolution', *The Canadian Geographer/Géographer Canadien* 24: 5–12.

resource allocation The strategic distribution of resources (e.g. money, time, equipment) among groups or individuals within a large organization or, less typically, a region. *See also* RESOURCE MANAGEMENT.

resource curse The apparent paradox that an abundance of a *natural resource is associated with declining national standards of living rather than prosperity. It is specifically associated with dependence on a single natural resource for export, for example, oil or natural gas. The first recognition that resources might be a curse came in the 1990s, when it was noted that oil-rich countries were not growing as quickly as others. Subsequent economic analysis found strong support for the idea, although it is still debated. Empirical confirmation usually takes the form of correlations between resource availability and national economic performance, disregarding the historical geography of resource use. Several reasons can be advanced for the effect, both economic and political. The economic causes are that reliance on one natural resource crowds out investment in manufacturing and agriculture, making them less competitive, while making the national economy over-reliant on a single commodity whose value in world markets might be volatile. Other sectors can suffer from labour shortages. This has the added disadvantage that in general, *manufacturing industries are associated with greater gains in labour productivity than natural resource industries. These economic problems are sometimes termed the 'Dutch disease' because of the negative effects of natural gas exports on the Netherlands in the 1960s. The political causes include government complacency and failure to plan for the long term, as well as the corruption arising when elites try to monopolize the income (rents) from the resource. In addition, resource dependency can be the result of prior colonial occupation, under which exploitation was not designed to benefit the local population but to enrich the colonizing power. In extreme circumstances, the resource curse can supposedly lead to *resource wars, further undermining the stability and prosperity of a country.

resource economics A branch of economics concerned with the supply and consumption of *natural resources and in particular, how markets can optimize their use.

Resource economists also try to establish the appropriate price for environmental goods and services when they are not directly bought and sold (*see* HEDONIC PRICING).

resource frontier A region distant from the main economic and population core of a country whose economy is dominated by the extraction of *natural resources such as minerals, oil, furs, and timber. Such frontiers often experience great economic volatility as one resource is exhausted to be replaced by another in a cycle of boom and bust. The lands and livelihoods of *indigenous peoples are frequently dispossessed in resource frontiers, as outside forces take control. *See also* AMAZON; FRONTIER.

Further reading Tsing, A. L. (2005), *Friction: an Ethnography of Global Connection.*

resource management The various knowledges and practices involved in securing the orderly supply of *natural resources in space and time. It can take many forms with different degrees of organization. *Indigenous knowledge is regarded as a holistic and context-related way of managing resources. Community-based forms are also grounded in traditional practices, but have been revived as a reaction to state-led or top-down approaches (*see* COMMON PROPERTY RESOURCES; COMMUNITY-BASED NATURAL RESOURCE MANAGEMENT; COMMUNITY FORESTRY). The principal agent of resource management is the state, sometimes in concert with other states in international regulatory systems. The notion that states should manage resources, as opposed to simply secure their availability by territorial expansion and *dispossession, arose in the early 20th century. Pioneered by Gifford Pinchot in the USA and by colonial officials and administrators elsewhere, this new perspective recognized that certain resources were potentially scarce but could be better managed to guarantee future supply. *Conservation management sought to make resources such as timber available over the long term. From the 1980s, conservation management was joined by a new focus on *sustainable development in recognition that there were social and inter-generational equity issues involved in not exploiting resources as rapidly as possible. More recently, ideas of adaptive resource management have taken account of the inherent uncertainties involved in the availability of resources such as fish and pasture land. Governed by non-equilibrium conditions, such resources may fluctuate wildly in supply without prior warning, this requiring constant monitoring and evaluation.

resource periphery A region located at some distance from economic core areas where the dominant form of development is in primary industries such as mining, oil, and gas production, fishing, and logging (*see* EXTRACTIVE INDUSTRIES). According to Hayter et al. these often arise out of the processes of European imperialism and colonialism, placing them on the margins of the global economy. Like *resource frontiers, they are often characterized by boom-and-bust cycles. They also combine the problems associated with primary industry with those of environment, indigenous rights, and geopolitics. *See also* CORE-PERIPHERY.

Reference Hayter, R., Barnes, T. J., and Bradshaw, M. J. (2003), 'Relocating resource peripheries to the core of economic geography's theorizing', *Area* 35:15–23.

resources *See* NATURAL RESOURCES.

resource wars The armed conflicts associated with the competition for *natural resources (*see* WAR). It is an imprecise term, but has been popularized by Michael Klare, who argues that future conflicts will not be driven by ideology, as they were in the *Cold War, but by the race to gain access to oil, water, and land. Climate change and resource depletion are argued to intensify the prospect (*see* PEAK OIL). In one sense, almost all wars are about resources, if one includes territory as a resource. This was true for the inter-state rivalries of the imperial era, but also during the *Cold War itself, when access to oil became paramount. The Iraq War (2003–11) has also been ascribed to oil, even though the main combatants did not justify it as such. But critics of the concept of resource war argue that it is too simplistic to explain conflict by reference to any one factor (*see* ENVIRONMENTAL DETERMINISM).

It may be more helpful to distinguish between 'resource conflicts' and 'conflict resources'. Resource conflicts arise within and between states over access to and control of natural resources. Examples given are the so-called 'diamond wars' in Sierra Leone and Angola during the 1990s. These conflicts are often associated with separatist movements, for example, the Cabinda province in Angola (*see* SECESSION). Conflict resources are commodities that are used to sustain conflicts whose cause is unrelated to resources. Oil, timber, drugs, diamonds, etc. can provide the funds to buy arms and so perpetuate violence. In practice it is often difficult to determine how far resources are the specific cause of conflict and the link might be indirect. A country weakened by the *resource curse, for example, may not be able to prevent grievances from becoming armed conflicts.

References and further reading Klare, M. T. (2002), *Resource Wars: the New Landscape of Global Conflict.*

Le Billon, P. (2008), 'Diamond wars? Conflict diamonds and geographies of resource wars', *Annals of the Association of American Geographers* 98(2): 345–72.

response variable In a statistical model, explanatory variables are the inputs to the model, whereas response variables are the outputs to the model. For example, a *dependency ratio is the response variable generated by a model that calculates the ratio between three explanatory variables: the number of people aged between 15 and 64 divided by the combined number of people aged between 0–14 and 64-plus.

restoration ecology The science of repairing degraded *ecosystems and habitats. If successfully applied, the result is 'ecological restoration'. Mainstream or conservation ecology is the science of understanding ecosystems in order to maintain them. Restoration ecology goes a step further in seeking to reverse what might be considered as harmful changes. This might mean removing non-native species and reintroducing native ones, including reforestation. For example, it has often been proposed that large areas of the US Great Plains could be cleared of cattle and stocked with buffalo, a native species, instead. Other interventions include the dismantling of dams, thus draining their reservoirs and restoring the natural hydrology. Removing the channels that straighten rivers is another form of restoration; allowing the channel to shift and water to occupy floodplains is thought to provide better long-term flood protection in many cases. There are also projects for wetland restoration, for example, in the Great Fen scheme in Cambridgeshire, England. One great difficulty with such schemes is knowing precisely what habitats and landscapes were like before significant human intervention. Another is that change and disequilibrium are often inherent in ecosystems, making them difficult to manage once restored. Ecological restoration is often a combination of scientific and historical knowledge, informed by modern-day environmental ethics.

Further reading Graf, W. L. (2001), 'Damage control: restoring the physical integrity of America's rivers', *Annals of the Association of American Geographers* 91(1): 1–27.

restructuring The significant alteration undergone by a local, regional, or national economy, usually over a period of years. Capitalist firms are always liable to restructure themselves functionally and spatially in order to outdo their competitors. However, there are times when large numbers of firms located in the same territory are forced to relocate, close, lay off many workers, search for new markets, or offer new goods and services than those previously offered (*see* DEINDUSTRIALIZATION). Restructuring is usually caused by the 'hidden hand' of the capitalist market (*see* CRISIS). However, once initiated, firms, workers and governmental bodies can together make significant choices about how to restructure the *space economy contained in their *borders.

retailing The commercialized sale of goods to members of the public. The retail industry or sector includes all those businesses concerned with the sale, marketing, and distribution of goods to consumers. Retailing is therefore an important element of the more generalized process of *consumption, and even more widely, of the circulation of commodities within capitalist societies (*see* CAPITALISM; COMMODITY). Although long regarded as a principally local or national activity, retailing has become extensively globalized since the 1980s. Retail companies such as Wal-Mart, Carrefour, and Tesco, now number among the largest *transnational corporations. At the other extreme, there are countless alternative retailing spaces such as charity shops, car boot sales, and garage sales which are less formally organized but often subsidiary.

The geographical study of retailing, or 'retail geography' has taken two broad forms. One approach draws upon the concepts of spatial analysis to link retail location and consumer behaviour, often through sophisticated modelling (*see* GEODEMOGRAPHICS; WILSON, ALAN). Its roots lie in the study of spatial patterns of services (*see* CENTRAL PLACE THEORY). But since the 1990s there has been a 'new' retail geography, informed by *political economy and cultural studies, and taking a more critical and less applied stance. This includes the study of corporate restructuring in the retail sector under different national regulatory environments, as well as the globalization of retail supply chains (*see* COMMODITY CHAINS). It takes account of the rise of forms of *ethical consumption and trade, and recognizes the growing significance of online retailing (*see* E-BUSINESS). *See also* CONSUMPTION; MALL; RETAIL PARK.

Further reading Wrigley, N. (2009), 'Retail geographies', in *The International Encyclopedia of Human Geography*.

retail park A concentration of large retail premises usually found on the outskirts of towns or cities, generally only accessible by car. Unlike a shopping *mall, the retailers are not gathered into a single-roofed structure. They are also known as power centers in the USA.

reterritorialization The process in which economic activities are geographically configured during a period of *restructuring. The term was favoured by geographer-cum-sociologist Neil Brenner. Like many others, Brenner argued that *globalization was producing a round of deterritorialization as many places, cities, and regions fell into decline due to their industries going bankrupt or relocating overseas. However, he also made the less obvious point that the spatial configuration of new economic spaces was unlike the old. Because of new forms of government *regulation, Brenner argued that economic activity was being rescaled upwards and downwards (*see* SCALE). For instance, many cities were forming functional economic regions as a matter of deliberate policy, whereas before, even cities within the same region would often be competing.

Reference Brenner, N. (1999), 'Globalisation as reterritorialisation', *Urban Studies* 36, 3: 431–51.

retirement community A planned residential development for retired families and individuals. Some may be age-restricted, for example, to persons over the age of 55. While such communities are increasingly common in the warmer parts of wealthier countries, they are also emerging in regions of the *Global South. Perhaps the most well-known is Sun City, Arizona, started in the 1960s.

retirement migration The relocation of one's place of permanent residence following withdrawal from full-time waged employment. Retirees may migrate to areas of the same country where the climate and environment are more to their liking, or property prices are lower. Alternatively, they may move abroad, as for example, the increasing trend of Americans to relocate to Mexico and Panama.

retroduction A form of logical reasoning that uses evidence to impute the existence of a causal mechanism that could reasonably have produced the observed effects, even if not themselves directly observable. It is sometimes called abduction and is used widely in the social and biophysical sciences. A classic example is Isaac Newton's discovery of gravity. While imperceptible, the effects of gravity are not. Newton asked: what must exist if apples are to fall from trees and people to remain rooted to the ground?

reurbanization The planned or unplanned revival of former urban centres and neighbourhoods by the increase in the number of people living and working in them. It is a counter-trend to *suburbanization and has been widely observed in North America and Western Europe. Planned reurbanization may include infilling or adapting older buildings, or new higher-density redevelopment schemes.

revealed preference analysis A method for measuring consumer behaviour. Rather than trying to assess the psychology of the consumer, revealed preference analysis is based on the actual behaviour of the consumer through their purchasing habits. In other words, rather than taking at face value what consumers said they would do, it measures what they actually did, seeking to determine the reasons underpinning that choice.

rewilding *See* RESTORATION ECOLOGY.

RGS *See* ROYAL GEOGRAPHICAL SOCIETY.

rhetoric The various devices used by one person to persuade another to believe what they say. Though often used pejoratively as a synonym for how populists and demagogues seek to control publics, to be 'rhetorical' is not necessarily to utter dramatic or over-blown statements. For instance, scientists use words like 'truth' and 'objectivity' in order to convince non-scientists that their knowledge claims reflect the material realities of the phenomena they study. Different genres of *representation utilize different rhetorical repertoires. Since human geography's *cultural turn in the late 1980s, practitioners have become acutely aware of their own and others' use of rhetoric. It has obliged them to attend closely to the politics of how knowledge is communicated to others.

rhizome A metaphor favoured by *post-structuralists Gilles *Deleuze and Félix Guattari to describe non-hierarchical, decentred relationships in which there are many points of connection and many routes of travel. Botanically, a rhizome is a mass or tangle of roots that allow a plant to expand underground in a non-hierarchical fashion. In *A Thousand Plateaus* (1980) Deleuze and Guattari argued that too much *critical theory—like the social world it studied—was analytically systematic and politically prescriptive. They argued for greater attention to the gaps and blind-spots of existing institutions, laws, and relationships. Rhizomatic analysis and politics, for them, was about multiplying the possibilities for alternative ways of life. In human geography, the rhizome metaphor has featured in non-*Marxist forms of relational thinking (*see* RELATIONAL GEOGRAPHY).

rhythmnanalysis An approach to everyday life that focuses on the effects of rhythms on people and the places they occupy. It was developed by Henri *Lefebvre in *Rhythmanalysis: Space, Time and Everyday Life* (2004), and focuses on the cyclical and linear rhythms that structure the body and everyday behaviour. Cyclical rhythms are repetitious, such as night into day and day into night, or the times of meals. Linear rhythms might be the flow of traffic along a road.

rights Goods, services, or modes of treatment to which a person is entitled by virtue of the society to which they belong (*see* CITIZENSHIP). Despite arguments that some rights are natural, the fact that these arguments are having to be made suggests that all rights are, instead, conferred. Indeed, what *counts* as a right varies historically and geographically, and all rights require active enforcement if they are to be more than nominal. There is necessarily a relative dimension to all rights, even supposedly universal ones (*see* RELATIVISM). For instance, the right to modesty and privacy ensured by being expected to wear a burka in some Muslim societies might be seen in Western societies as a denial of women's rights to dress freely. Likewise, even the United Nations Universal Declaration of Human Rights (1948) enshrines conceptions of rights that not all societies concur with or are willing to observe. Debates over which rights a society will legally enforce can become extremely heated, as shown in the *United States in the stand-off between pro- and anti-abortionists. When a person's (or a non-human's) rights have been denied or offended against, the apparatus of the law (e.g. courts and solicitors) is usually turned to in order to ensure redress. Even though rights are attached to individuals, their enjoyment and enforcement are necessarily social. For instance, for me to enjoy freedom of speech I need to be careful not to silence you, even though I may dislike profoundly what you have to say. It is usual to distinguish *civil*, *political*, and *social* rights. The first covers things such as *privacy and *security of *property ownership, the second things such as voting rights, and the third things such as the right of children to receive a formal education. Such rights are often bound up in notions of citizenship, the rights conferred on citizens of a state.

Rights are of geographical interest in several important respects. First, national differences in the legal definition of rights, and their degree of enforcement, remain considerable. As the world's nation states enter into ever-closer relations of trade and investment, pressure has grown to create greater homogeneity in things like the rights of wage workers or *refugees (*see* INTELLECTUAL PROPERTY RIGHTS). This not only invites comparative analysis of different 'rights cultures'; it also invites analysis of how certain rights definitions become hegemonic by being enshrined in international law. Second, arguments over who should enjoy which rights frequently make reference to geographical metaphors as well as more literal rights geographies. For instance, Geraldine *Pratt's research into how Vancouver activists sought to defend the rights of immigrant Filipino care-workers shows how complex references to universal/global, national, and private spaces were used. Finally, these representations of geography aside, the material exercise and enjoyment of rights necessarily has a locational basis to it. In recent years, human geographers have been especially interested in how civil rights in public spaces (such as plazas and urban parks) are being contested between citizens, the police, and ruling politicians (Mitchell, 2003). This interest feeds into more general arguments about civil rights to speak and act in larger spaces, such as cities (Harvey 2012).

References Harvey, D. (2012), *Rebel Cities*.
Mitchell, D. (2003), *The Right to the City*.
Pratt, G. (1999), 'From registered nurse to registered nanny', *Economic Geography* 75, 2: 215–36.

Rio de Janeiro The former capital of *Brazil and its second largest city, with just over six million inhabitants. A coastal metropolis known for its hills and vistas, it is a major centre of production, trade, and education. More overseas tourists visit it annually than any other city in the southern hemisphere. It will be a host city of the 2014 Football World Cup and the site of the 2016 Olympics and Paralympics.

Rio Earth Summit The United Nations Conference on Environment and Development was held in *Rio de Janeiro, Brazil, in 1992 (*see* EARTH SUMMITS). It led to the formation of the *United Nations Framework Convention on Climate Change (UNFCCC), the Convention on Biological Diversity, and Agenda 21, an action plan for *sustainable development. But no agreement was reached on deforestation, the other pressing issue discussed.

riparian conflict The disputes arising between governments, landowners, or other parties over access to shared surface water resources, usually rivers. Either one party is upstream of another and so can compromise the quality and quantity of water received by users downstream, or two parties occupy either side of a river which, in turn, forms the boundary between them. *See also* RESOURCE WARS.

risk The real or perceived probability of an undesirable event occurring. The difference between these probabilities is not clear cut because even the most precise and 'objective' risk calculations are only as good as the assumptions made, past evidence analysed, and methods used. Depending on a person's situation, some risks are small and others large, some trivial and others of considerable significance. Situations often arise where risks are low but the consequences of a risk event profound, meaning that it is important to insure against the event despite its occurrence being unlikely. Equally, situations arise where people are at risk and do not know it until after the fact. For example, communities who suffered *environmental injustice in the United States in the 1970s and 1980s long lived in ignorance of their exposure to polluted water, soil, and air. While some risks are typically localized (e.g. flooding near a river), others may apply to a whole society (e.g. lung cancer due to most adults smoking).

In the period prior to *modernity, the risks that most people faced were arguably natural. Their inability to control, or adequately protect themselves from powerful environmental processes (such as heavy rainfall, high winds, or extreme cold) meant that most risks to well-being had an external origin. However, over the last 150 years *manufactured risks* have proliferated (*see* RISK SOCIETY). For example, consider the risks to human life created by nuclear weapons, nuclear power stations, and mass vehicular travel. Once recognized as risks, it may be possible for people to insure against these manufactured threats. Because these threats have identifiable origins in society (e.g. tobacco firms), people for whom a risk becomes a reality may also seek legal redress (e.g. monetary compensation).

Human geographers have long been interested in the risks to people's health and livelihoods posed by the natural environment. Since the 1940s, they have made at least two seminal contributions. First, Gilbert *White and his colleagues at Chicago University argued that risk perception is as important as the objective possibility of a risk event occurring. His work on communities inhabiting flood plains showed that lay actors were often dimly aware of the objective threats (*see* HAZARD). This research fed into a subsequent stream of inquiry into environmental perception which progressively took issue with the simplistic models of human agency then prevalent in geography. Even when presented with all the 'facts' about their real situation, people were shown not always to be 'rational' in their management of risk. Second, in the 1970s geographers investigating natural disasters in the *Global South undertook pioneering research into 'social *vulnerability' and 'social resilience'. Among them was Piers *Blaikie, most notably in his co-authored book *At Risk* (1994). Noticing that more people were being killed by events such as earthquakes than ever before, they dismissed the idea that 'over-population' was the root-cause (i.e. too many people living in high-risk areas). Instead, they argued that social inequality—a result of hierarchical social relations and the maldistribution of resources—was rendering millions vulnerable to the effects of 'natural' risk events. The solution, they argued, was not simply a question of physical engineering (e.g. bigger levees on rivers), but also a question of ensuring vulnerable communities had the resources to make themselves resilient to risk events. For instance, if people build strong *social capital locally they can receive much-needed help from neighbours if their homes have been destroyed by a hurricane. The key insight here was that risk is relative, not always absolute: a high-impact risk event for one community in one *place can have a local impact on a more resilient community in exactly the same place.

Risk Society A new type of society in which people are not only exposed to numerous risks but aware of this exposure in more-or-less informed ways. The term was popularized by German social theorist Ulrich Beck in a 1986 book of the name. Beck argued that manufactured risks were, in the West at least, eclipsing natural ones. After 1945, most leading capitalist countries had insured individual citizens against falling foul of *risk events by collectivizing the costs. For instance, national insurance payments in Britain paid for a person's unemployment benefit when they were made redundant. By the 1980s, however, Beck detected changes in the character of manufactured risks and societal responses to them. First, some potential risk events were transnational and stood to affect hundreds of millions of people (e.g. the thinning of the stratospheric ozone layer). Second, some of these events were only predictable in a very approximate way, such that the details were almost incalculable (e.g. the local effects of global *climate change). Third, the magnitude of some potential risk events was so large as to make them almost uninsurable financially. Fourth, people were more aware of risks than their forebears because of heightened media reporting of risk. Finally, because risk experts had manifestly failed to accurately calculate some risks, public faith in their capacities decreased. According to Beck, a new 'subpolitics' had developed that challenged the faith of national governments and business in the power of science and technology to prevent risk events occurring. The environmental movement, led by *Greenpeace and other *NGOs, was an example of subpolitics because most of its work was conducted outside the formal channels of representative democracy (e.g. voting at elections, forming a political party). *See also* NATURAL HAZARDS.

Ritter, Carl (1779–1859) A 19th-century German geographer considered one of the founders of modern geography. He was appointed as the first chair of geography in Germany at the military academy in Berlin in 1820 and founded the Berlin Geographical Society. Rather than practise a conventional compendium style of geography, providing summations of the geography of a *region, Ritter sought to understand the interdependencies between physical and human geography, and the development of an area over time using an *inductive approach. The first volume of *Die Erdkunde* (Earth Science), his massive unfinished treatise was published 1817, with the last volume published in 1859. His work was highly influential in the development of geography internationally and his approach was widely adopted in France, Russia, and North America.

river basin The area of land drained by a river and its tributaries. It forms a basic geographical unit in the management of water resources. Advocates of *bioregionalism propose organizing human activity more within the boundaries of river basins in order to minimize the transfer of water between them, so living more within ecological limits.

road pricing A mechanism wherein vehicle users are charged directly for using roads. It includes road tolls and congestion charges, which are paid in excess of any vehicle tax. Road pricing is designed to either generate revenue or discourage road usage. It can involve a fixed rate or a variable charge depending on the time of day. Revenues contribute towards the cost of building and maintain the road infrastructure. Charges and tolls also seek to reduce peak-hour traffic in order avoid congestion, encourage the use of public transport, and reduce pollution.

road transport and travel There have been dedicated roads for the *transportation of people and goods for many centuries. Roads provided vital routes for trade, warfare, and pilgrimage. Until the early 20th century such roads were travelled by horse and carriage, or on foot. With the introduction of engine-powered vehicles, the road network developed at pace, and was accompanied by advances in road-building technologies, materials, and supporting infrastructure such as bridges, tunnels, traffic lights, and signage, as well as systems of governance and laws with respect to drivers (e.g., licensing, testing), vehicles (e.g., road worthiness and pollution standards), and roads themselves (e.g., speed limits). Over time, the nature of roads has become increasingly hierarchically ordered from narrow laneways to multiple lane motorways, with some locations bypassed to lower congestion and speed up travel. The result is many nations have a dense network of roads linking residences and businesses together, and car ownership is prevalent in most Western countries and rising rapidly in others. A very large proportion of freight is transported along roads and a significant proportion of public transport is road-based using buses and taxis. Road travel is a significant daily mode of *spatial behaviour and a key factor in *logistics, business operations, and how places function.

Further reading Merriman, P. (2007), *Driving Spaces: a Cultural-Historical Geography of England's M1 Motorway*.

rogue state A term circulating within US foreign policy circles in the 1990s to describe those countries the USA deemed a threat to world peace and stability. They were identified on the basis of several criteria: developing weapons of mass destruction; sponsoring terrorism; abusing human rights; supporting organized criminal activities (*see* NARCO STATE). North Korea, Libya, Iraq, Afghanistan, Somalia, and Cuba are among the countries described this way but critics point out that the USA may itself pose the greatest threat to stability through its military interventions and its 'war on terror'.

Rose, Gillian (1962–) A British feminist geographer based at the Open University. Her book *Feminism and Geography* (1993) had a major impact in the discipline, critiquing the *masculinist nature of geographical scholarship. As well as being a champion of *feminist geography, Rose has been important in introducing *post-structural and psychoanalytic thought to the discipline, and contributing to epistemological and methodological debates with respect to *positionality, *situated knowledges, and *visual methods.

Royal Geographical Society (RGS) One of the world's largest geographical societies, which supports the production and advancement of geographical knowledge about the world and promotes the discipline of geography. It was founded as the Geographical Society of London in 1830, starting as a dining club at which current scientific issues and ideas were informally debated. It was granted a Royal Charter in 1859. The organization took an active role in funding explorations to different parts of the world and in the colonial expansion of the British empire. Through its focus on education it sponsored the incorporation of geography as both a school and university discipline. With the rise of professional geographical scholarship, a group of society Fellows started the Institute of British Geographers (IBG) in 1933. The RGS and IBG merged in 1995. Throughout its history it has provided funding for field research and expeditions, organized lectures and conferences, developed a collection of resources including an extensive set of maps, and published various works including the journals, *The Geographical Journal*, *Transactions of the Institute of British Geographers*, and *Area*.

rural depopulation The decrease in population size in rural areas due to out-migration. The process of rural depopulation has been occurring in Western societies since the industrial and agricultural revolutions. On the one hand, the demand for labour in agriculture has been declining with increasing mechanization, on the other, employment opportunities, especially for better-paid work, has been higher in urban areas. While there is counter-migration to many rural areas, driven principally through lifestyle choice, it does not match the levels of out-migration (*see* COUNTER-URBANIZATION; RURAL GENTRIFICATION). The process of rural depopulation is particularly acute at present in many developing countries as rural dwellers move to the cities to take advantage of new opportunities. Such depopulation has a *cumulative causation effect, reducing local demand, and making it less attractive for inward investment. *See also* TODARO MODEL.

rural gentrification The *gentrification of small villages and towns in rural areas, as well as the restoration of individual dwellings. Traditionally, gentrification has been considered a highly urban process, particularly relating to large towns and cities. The same processes of gentrification, such as the reinvestment of capital, social upgrading of a locale by incoming higher-income groups, landscape change and upgrading, and displacement of indigenous low-income groups, take place in some rural locations. These locations are usually within *commuting distance of larger settlements, or are home to large higher-skilled employers such as higher education institutions, or have developed into vibrant cultural centres, or desirable tourist or retirement destinations.

rural geography The study of people, places, and landscapes in rural areas and the processes and practices through which *rurality is produced and contested. Given the focus on a type of area and the processes that produce them, rural geography is very broad in its scope, ranging from studies of environmental management and policy, to various economic, political, and social formations and processes, to cultural analyses of rural life and how it is understood by urban dwellers. The study of the rural has long been a core focus of the discipline, right back to the *anthropogeography of Fredrich *Ratzel and the study of the relationship between people and their natural environments, and in the development of *regional geography. In the latter, the rural was understood to be a functional component of a region's economy, characterized by the local *landscape, land-use, and local *cultures. Research sought to document rural life, forms, and patterns of *agriculture, local *cultural landscapes, relations with nearby urban centres, and to classify and map rural areas within and across regions. The rural was understood as a particular kind of geographical area, with a social organization and ways of life distinct from urban areas, yet the urban and rural and their interrelation constituted the region.

The designation of the rural as a distinct focus of geographical study is more recent, having developed as a subdisciplinary field over the past fifty years. This was, in part, a reaction to the growing interest in urban issues, which remains a more studied terrain, but also due to the fracturing of the discipline into subfields in the wake of the *Quantitative Revolution. As with other core component fields of the wider discipline, such as urban, economic, and social geography, rural geography was defined largely by the focus on which the lens of study was directed, rather than the nature of the lens itself. Consequently, rural geography has been examined through a range of philosophical viewpoints from positivism through humanistic approaches, political economy, feminism, to poststructuralism, each providing a particular way to conceive the rural, rurality, and the processes that produce them. This has led to a number of long-running debates within rural geography, notably the problems of defining rural areas (as distinct from urban or suburban) and what constitutes *rurality.

As Michael Woods (2009) details, what unites the various approaches is a concern with a number of consistent areas of study. These include: *agricultural geography, and the study of farm landscapes, businesses, and households, and agricultural trade and policy; *resource management and *conservation; land use and *planning; economic development, including restructuring to develop new industries given the decline in nonagricultural and primary industry employment, and the reliance on farming subsidies; infrastructure, including the provision of transport and utility services; recreation and tourism, and the use of the countryside for *leisure; population, *migration, and settlement patterns, especially given processes such as depopulation and *counterurbanization; *poverty and deprivation amongst rural communities, and the forms of social welfare used to tackle these issues; social structure, social difference, and experiences of rural life, recognizing that there are a multiplicity of social groups living in rural areas, and that there are issues concerning *race, *gender, *sexuality, and *disability, with particular *cultural politics operating; rural culture and wider popular and media discourses about rural areas and rurality; and politics and *governance, and how political processes and the machinations of the state and civil society shape rural society and economy. These various concerns have been examined, and compared and contrasted, across and between developed and developing nations.

References and further reading Cloke, P. and Little, J. (eds.) (1997), *Contested Countryside Cultures*.
Cloke, P., Marsden, T., and Mooney, P. (eds.) (2006), *Handbook of Rural Studies*.
Little, J. (2001), *Gender and Rural Geography*.
Woods, M. (2005), *Rural Geography: Processes, Responses and Experiences in Rural Restructuring*.
Woods, M. (2009), 'Rural geography', in *The International Encyclopedia of Human Geography*.

rural idyll An idealized, romanticized construct that presents rural areas as happier, healthier, and with fewer problems than urban areas. The rural is cast as an idyllic place to live, portrayed as having beautiful landscapes, more neighbourly communities, and a better *quality of life. As such it is a place to aspire to escape to from the 'urban jungle'. As with all constructs it suppresses reality, with rural areas often being far from idyllic for the people living there. *See also* PASTORAL.

rurality The various factors that make a place rural in nature and distinctive from other kinds of spaces. Traditionally, such factors include landscapes dominated by *agriculture or *wilderness, remoteness, and dispersed population patterns. Much recent literature has considered the extent to which rurality is changing, especially given processes of *counterurbanization, or indeed is subject to spatial processes different from that experienced in other spaces.

Further reading Cloke, P., Marsden, T., and Mooney, P. (2006), *Handbook of Rural Studies*.

rural-urban continuum A concept that posits that there is no sharp division between urban and rural life, but that settlements exist along a continuum from very rural through to highly urban. The urban does not simply stop and the rural start, but they bleed through into each other. Moreover, it is possible to find spaces in a city that are rural-like, and places in rural areas that are quite urban. As such, it is problematic to talk of places as simply rural or urban, rather one needs to consider how they entwine and overlap. *See also* RURALITY; URBANISM.

Russia The world's largest country and heart of the former *Soviet Union, occupying much of the Eurasian landmass. Its considerable economic wealth is based primarily on the extraction, processing, and export of natural resources, such as gas, oil, and coal. The 2010 population was 143 million, with just under 10 per cent concentrated in the capital city Moscow. Nominally Russia is a representative democracy, but there have been persistent problems of corruption and intimidation with the political system since the

Soviet Union dissolved in 1991. Despite the country's wealth, social inequality is very high, with life expectancy among lower-income people very low by Western standards. Despite the end of the *Cold War and the political restructuring of the Soviet Union, Russia continues to exert considerable political influence with respect to former satellites but also on the world stage, being a permanent member of the *United Nations Security Council. *See also* TRANSITION ECONOMY.

rustbelt An area of the United States which, during the 1980s, suffered a sustained period of *deindustrialization and underwent significant economic *restructuring. The area encompassed the states and cities of the Midwest, the northeast, and the upper South. Before and after the *Second World War, the area had thrived, producing medium to heavy commodities for sale to intermediate and final consumers (such as automobiles and steel). Many cities in the area are undergoing *degrowth. *Compare* SUNBELT.

S

Sachs, Jeffrey (1954–) An American economist, presently the Professor of Sustainable Development and director of the Earth Institute at Columbia University, New York. He has published widely on issues such as *economic development, *poverty and debt, health, *globalization, and sustainability. He has advised numerous governments, notably those in South America in the 1980s dealing with hyper-inflation, Eastern Europe in the 1990s in the transition to market economies, and Africa in the 2000s concerning poverty and development. He is a special advisor to the *United Nations on the *Millennium Development Goals. His ideas concerning economic development have been widely adopted, though they are also the target of critique as being overtly *neoliberal in orientation and *environmentally determinist.

sacred space The places and sites that have special religious significance and spiritual qualities (*see* RELIGION). These include churches, temples, sites of miracles or specific holy events, holy wells, and *monuments. Such sacred spaces are often the focus of pilgrimage, with members of a faith travelling to a site, often along a set, well-worn route, to pray or take part in a particular ceremony or event, or to seek spiritual healing. Sacred spaces are understood by believers to hold transcendent spiritual qualities, locations where one can be closer to the divine and in which one can be contemplative and celebrate one's faith. Geographers have been interested in charting the *spatiality of such religious sites and pilgrimages as part of a broader project concerned with the geography of religion.

Further reading Hopkins, P., Kong, L., and Olson, E. (eds.) (2012), *Religion and Place: Landscape, Politics and Piety*.

Said, Edward (1935–2003) A leading *post-colonial scholar and literary theorist, born in Jerusalem but whose academic career was based in Columbia University, New York, from 1963 until his death. Said was a Palestinian and involved himself in the affairs of the Arab-Israeli conflict throughout his life. The author of over twenty books, his work was explicitly geographical in nature and his ideas concerning *colonialism and *nationalism have had much resonance in the discipline, especially those of *Orientalism and *geographical imagination.

sampling The method of selecting a subset of data from the total population of potential data. Sampling is used because the total population of potential data might be very large and it is unfeasible in terms of time and resources to harvest it all. Instead a sample of data is made that seeks to be free of bias and as representative of the whole population as possible. There are many different sampling methods, each designed to cope with a particular limitation such as difficulty of identifying potential respondents. If the data are to be analysed using probability-based statistical methods then a scientific approach to sampling has to be undertaken. A systematic sample involves the methodical selection of cases from a sampling frame, where, although the initial start point is randomly selected, the subsequent selection of points is at a regular interval (e.g. every tenth house). A random sample avoids any interviewer/sample bias as every unit in a population has the same probability of independent selection. There are a variety of other designs based on the simple random sample, which include the stratified random sample (the sampling frame divided into subgroups or strata, which are then each sampled using the simple random method), and the multistage random sample (the sampling frame divided into hierarchical levels or stages, wherein each level is sampled using a simple random method which selects the elements to be included at the next level). A judgemental sample (also known as a purposive sample) is the most subjective sampling method. Sampling elements are selected based on the interviewer's experience that they are likely to produce the required results. A quota sample selects those elements to be included in the sample on the basis of satisfying a predefined quota but is not random or stratified in nature. Another non-random sampling method is a snowball sample, wherein initial contacts provide details of other people who might fulfil the sampling requirements. With regards to sample size, it is often thought that 'more is better', with larger samples producing a more representative dataset than smaller ones.

Santos, Milton (1926–2001) A prolific Brazilian geographer who wrote over fifty books and had a large influence on the discipline in South America. Having initially studied law, Santos worked as a journalist and political advisor to the state and national government between 1949 and 1964. He was imprisoned by the military dictatorship in 1964 and was exiled on release. He worked at a number of universities in France and later in Canada, Venezuela, Tanzania, and the United States. He returned to Brazil in 1972, teaching at the University of São Paulo, then the Federal University of Rio de Janeiro, before returning to São Paulo. While his writings are wide-ranging, he paid particular attention to *poverty, *capitalism, and *globalization, and argued that geography needed to be understood holistically rather than through a subdisciplinary lens.

São Paulo The largest and most populous city in *Brazil and South America; the population of the municipality is over eleven million but there are over twenty million people living in the sprawling urban region on which it is centred. Founded by Portuguese colonists in the 16th century, it is now Brazil's main economic and financial centre.

Sassen, Saskia (1949–) A sociologist well known for her work on the mobility of *labour and *capital, *globalization and *global cities, presently based at Columbia University, New York, and the London School of Economics. Although born in the Netherlands, she grew up and studied in Argentina, France, Italy, and the United States with her own global movements becoming the catalyst for her focus on the macro-processes shaping the global capitalist economy. Her books *The Global City* (1991) and *Cities and the World Economy* (1994) have been particularly influential in shaping debates about the relationship between cities and globalization.

satisficing behaviour A decision-making strategy by individuals and firms that seek satisfactory returns rather than optimum profit or growth. The aim is to meet an acceptable, predetermined threshold of growth, based on a rational understanding of the market, rather than trying to achieve a more abstract notion of maximizing profit. In geographical terms, this means siting a company in a location that generates sufficient profits that satisfies expectation and other criteria, rather than trying to find an elusive optimal location that will maximize turnover and profit. *See also* LOCATION THEORY.

satnav A *wayfinding device that uses a combination of a *Global Position System (GPS) and a *map database to determine present location and the route to a destination. The term is an abbreviation for satellite *navigation system. Satnavs are usually mounted in cars, though they can be handheld, and guide a traveller along a route using a visual map display and verbal instructions.

Sauer, Carl O. (1889–1975) An American cultural geographer who was a major figure in the discipline in the mid-20th century. Born in Missouri, he had part of his schooling in Germany before returning to America to undertake his university studies. He graduated with a doctorate from the University of Chicago in 1915 having studied with Ellen Churchill *Semple, though he rejected her *environmental determinism. He taught at the University of Michigan until 1923 when he moved to the University of California, Berkeley. He remained there until he retired, founding what became the *Berkeley School of cultural geography. In 1925 he published *The Morphology of Landscape*, the work for which he is best known. Drawing extensively on German geography, he argued for the need to understand the role of human activity and culture in shaping the *landscape, going against the prevalent orthodoxy in American geography at the time which argued that human activity was shaped by the environment (*see* ENVIRONMENTAL DETERMINISM). His arguments were underpinned by extensive and detailed empirical fieldwork, often carried out with colleagues from across the social and natural sciences. The agency of people to shape the world and alter environments and ecological systems through their management of land and resources was the predominant focus of his career. His work was enormously influential in American human geography, but also had a major impact across disciplines.

Further reading Denevan, W. M. and Mathewson, K., (eds.) (2009), *Carl Sauer on Cultural and Landscape: Readings and Commentaries.*

Sayer, Andrew (1949–) A British sociologist who worked initially at the University of Sussex before moving to the University of Lancaster in 1993. His work has been divided into two main strands, both of which have had an influence in geography. First, he has examined the relationship between *social theory and *political economy through the study of such issues as the division of labour and the circulation of capital. Second, he has explored the relationship between philosophy and method, forwarding a *critical realist approach best exemplified by his book *Method in Social Science* (1984).

scale 1. The nested hierarchy, in terms of size or area, of different objects or zones.
   2. A precise, scientific means of measuring phenomena at the Earth's surface (*see* SCALES, ANALYTICAL). Scale is a key concept in geographical inquiry, with geographers interested in the ways in which different processes and activities take place at and translate across different temporal and spatial scales, and how analysis conducted at different scales provides different levels of detail and insight into phenomenon. In human geography, attention has mostly been focused on spatial scale. It has traditionally been understood to consist of analytical and hierarchical scales. Analytical scales, mostly closely associated with cartography and the scaling of a *map, consist of precise, geometric properties that provide an *objective set of definable measurements useful for making absolute and relative comparisons. Hierarchical scales are nested sets of categories that fit inside each other. A typical geographical example is a hierarchy of zones working up from the body to the home, the street, the neighbourhood, the district, the region, the nation, and the continent to the global.
   Recent thinking has challenged the ontologically pregiven, essentialized nature of analytic and hierarchical geographic scales, instead arguing that scale is *socially constructed, and that geographic scales such as the local, regional, national, and supranational, are themselves implicated in the constitution of social, economic, and political processes. Scale, it is suggested, is produced and transformed by different actors and processes, varying in form and meaning over time and space (*see* SMITH, NEIL). There is thus a 'politics of scale' or a 'scalar politics' that is fundamental to the ways in which we conceive, organize, and produce *space, and this is open to change as structural forces such as *globalization, *capitalism, and *neoliberalism reshape the scale at which actions

occur producing *uneven development (*see* RETERRITORIALIZATION). Overlooking this politics of scale can limit geographical analysis as it fails to appreciate how spatial processes often work horizontally and vertically, cutting across hierarchical structures (such as political units) that carve space up into discrete scalar units. It is thus argued that geographers need to 'understand how particular scales become constituted and transformed in response to particular socio-spatial dynamics' (Marston 2000, 225) and how phenomena can become rescaled.

Scale seems to be crucial to human geography's identity but also difficult to conceptualize. For example, an ATM machine is physically located on a high street, but it is connected in real-time to a bank's server located several hundred miles away. When a person withdraws money at what scale is the transaction occurring? Locally, nationally, both simultaneously, or across a *network? One way forward may be to dispense with it altogether, adopting a 'flat ontology'. *Actor-Network Theory, where hierarchical scale is replaced by the notion that networks are either longer ('global') or shorter ('local') is one version. Another, advanced by Marston et al. (2005) is that all use of scale vocabulary invariably undermines progressive politics because higher levels (i.e. global) are always conceived as having more *power than local levels. They argue for a focus on interconnected but dissimilar sites instead. These views have found limited support. Instead, and influenced by more *post-structuralism, various human geographers now think of scale in terms of practices, performances, or craft. Kaiser and Nikiforova, for example, detail how scales are performed in the Estonian border town of Narva through everyday practices. Narva, Estonia, Europe, and the former Soviet Union are not hierarchically arranged but made present in varying combinations through border checks, flags, school books, etc. Kaiser and Nikiforova argue that as long as people make sense of the world through the category of scale, it serves a purpose in geographical analysis. *See also* MODIFIABLE AREAL UNIT PROBLEM.

References and further reading Herod, A. (2010), *Scale*.
Kaiser, R. and Nikiforova, N. (2008), 'The performativity of scale: the social construction of scale effects in Narva, Estonia', *Environment and Planning D: Society and Space* 26: 537–62.
Marston, S. A. (2000), 'The social construction of scale', *Progress in Human Geography* 24(2): 219–42.
Marston, S. A., Jones III, J. P., and Woodward, K. (2005), 'Human geography without scale', *Transactions of the Institute of British Geographers NS* 30: 416–32.
Sheppard, R. and McMaster, R. (eds.) (2004), *Scale and Geographic Inquiry*.

scales, analytical The scales of scientific measurement that enable the precise recording and display of observations. Such scales relate to distance, temperature, speed, volume, and so on, using predefined units of known qualities and granularity (intervals along a continuum). Such scales are often hierarchically organized based on granularity, for example, millimetres, centimetres, metres, kilometres, etc. Conducting analysis at different scales can lead to scale dependence issues such as the *modifiable areal unit problem, a common issue for data displayed at varying areal scales. *See also* LEVELS OF MEASUREMENT.

Scandinavia A region of northern Europe comprising of Denmark, Sweden, and Norway, although Iceland, Finland, and the Faeroe Islands are sometimes also included. The first three countries have strong linguistic, cultural, and historical similarities.

Schaefer, Frederic (1890–1952) A German economist whose posthumously published 1953 essay is sometimes said to have initiated geography's scientific or *Quantitative Revolution. After working with geographers at the University of Iowa, Schaefer challenged Richard *Hartshorne's then-influential vision of 'areal differentiation' (*see* IDIOGRAPHY) as geography's *raison d'être*. He wrote that 'Geography has to be conceived as the science concerned with formulating the laws governing the distribution of certain features on the surface of the earth' (p. 227). In response, Hartshorne updated his 1939 work *The *Nature of Geography*, only to find that a younger generation preferred to follow Schaefer's lead.

Reference Schaefer, F. K. (1953), 'Exceptionalism in geography: a methodological examination', *Annals of the Association of American Geographers* 43, 3: 226–249.

science A mode of inquiry, along with the resulting knowledge, that aims to 'cut reality at the joints' and thereby represent objectively the characteristics of the human and/or non-human worlds. Scientific inquiry not only aspires to be methodical and reflexive (*see* SCIENTIFIC METHOD; REFLEXIVITY), it is also usually thought to focus only on phenomena whose existence can be proven empirically, by gathering and interpreting *data or *evidence. However, the manipulation of abstract phenomena by pure reason (*see* LOGIC) is also considered science (as in the case of mathematics). By basing its knowledge largely on factually testable theories, models, or hypotheses, science sought to distinguish itself from religion, metaphysics, and superstition during the European *Enlightenment period. Indeed, when the English philosopher William Whewell suggested the term 'scientist' in 1840 he was referring to a specialist in producing knowledge arising from rigorous reasoning about what systematic observations might signify (*see* ABSTRACTION; INDUCTION; DEDUCTION; RETRODUCTION). Within twenty years, English zoologist Charles *Darwin published a magisterial work of science, *On the Origin of Species* (1859), one that posed a significant challenge to existing beliefs that a deity had created the earth and its creatures according to its own design. By the end of the 19th century science in its various branches—mathematics, physics, geology, etc.—had, in the West at least—managed to separate itself from organized religion and other external influences. Strong institutions emerged to defend science and advance its practitioners' interests (such as the British Royal Society). The successful defence of the idea of academic freedom allowed amateur and professional scientists to satisfy their curiosity or else undertake applied research linked to the industrial and military ambitions of their nation states. By 1900, science could boast a string of path-breaking theories and practical inventions.

The huge growth of scientific knowledge in the 19th-century West was coincident with the ontological dualism between *nature and society being taken ever more for granted. Natural scientists (such as Darwin) studied the non-human world and their evident success raised the questions: can societies be studied scientifically?; do they possess the qualities of orderliness and predictability seemingly so characteristic of nature?; indeed, as partly natural creatures themselves, to what extent are people's social actions governed by their biology? These were large questions, with three important theorists answering the first two positively, namely *Marx, Durkheim, and Weber. In different ways they argued that 'the social' was ontologically distinct from nature (though not unrelated to it), yet possessed a certain integrity that could be revealed through careful inquiry. Because societies were too physically large to be analysed experimentally through laboratory or field experiments, the three men gathered large bodies of evidence about social discourses and practices and sought to detect patterns therein. They concluded that universal laws of society did not exist, but that historically and geographically specific rules, process, and norms did—ones created, yet not controlled, by people (*see* STRUCTURATION). Meanwhile, neoclassical economists began their project of analysing all economic behaviour as if universal processes and relations *did* exist. Their abstract models, theories, and equations paid little heed to the specificities of time or space, proceeding from ontological assumptions (e.g. that humans are rational) to make logical inferences, deductions, and predictions using mathematics. *see* RATIONALISM.

Late 19th-century geography modelled itself as a 'science' of society-environment relations. In Halford *Mackinder's (1887) influential vision, it would be a 'bridging' subject. However, his vision was much affected by Darwinian science, and coloured by the atmosphere of '*Social Darwinism'. The latter proposed that different sections of society, and different 'branches of the human race', were dissimilar because they had adapted in different ways to their prevailing environments. Several of Mackinder's successors sought to describe 'the varieties of man' within and between nations with reference to climate, natural resources, etc. Some of this work came perilously close to *racism and chauvinism dressed up as objective analysis (*see* ENVIRONMENTAL DETER-MINISM). If the early geographers had taken more inspiration from the laboratory sciences or the kind of social science promoted by Marx, then their discipline may have built much stronger intellectual foundations than the weak ones constructed by the 1930s. By this time, too much 'geographical science' amounted to unconvincing speculations about the relations between exhaustively described natural environments and the peoples who inhabited them. It seemed immured in *place and *region, and largely ignorant of emerging international issues such as the 1929 Wall Street Crash and subsequent *Great Depression.

After 1945, a new generation of geographers sought to make their subject more rigorous empirically, and more able to rival the theoretical and practical achievements of subjects such as economics and physics. Specialists in human and *physical geography emerged who studied only certain phenomena at the Earth's surface rather than the totality of human and physical phenomena combined. Their presumption was that the world's geography was not a patchwork of differences (*see* IDIOGRAPHIC) but of com-monalities (*see* NOMOTHETIC). As part of their *rhetoric, these geographers talked much of science, though it is doubtful many adhered to a detailed understanding of what the term meant (*see* POSITIVISM). However, one of the first 'spatial scientists', Frederic *Schaefer, had been involved with the *Vienna Circle of *logical positivism in the 1930s. Later, David *Harvey showed in *Explanation in Geography* (1969) how the scien-tific method could apply to geography, while new textbooks formalized the scientific approach for geography degree students (*see* SPATIAL SCIENCE). But, with the rise of *humanistic and *radical geography, the ambitions of this explicitly scientific approach were checked.

Since the 1980s the number of human geographers who would describe themselves as scientists has shrunken markedly, especially in contrast with physical geographers. However, this does not signify a profound scepticism about or indifference to science. On the contrary, human geographers continue to adhere to the generic scientific goals of rigour and honesty in inquiry (*see* VALUES). A minority still also believe in the possibility of value-free knowledge (*see* FACT-VALUE DISTINCTION). Some have also examined the way science gets enacted by environmental scientists, inspired by the *Science and Technology Studies insight that all scientific knowledge is fabricated rather than a window through which to see reality. In part, this work has been historical, attending to the sites where science was conducted during the *Enlightenment and its routes of travel so as to influence a wider society (*see* GEOGRAPHY, HISTORY OF). Still others have examined how contemporary environmental science is understood by the public, espe-cially when it comes to momentous issues such as global *climate change (e.g. Carvalho and Burgess, 2005) (*see* PUBLIC UNDERSTANDING OF SCIENCE). This recent work marks a shift from criticizing the idea of 'science' in human geography to analysing the way science (past and present) operates in a wider societal context.

References and further reading Carvalho, A. and Burgess, J. (2005), 'Cultural circuits of climate change in UK broadsheet newspapers, 1985-2003', *Risk Analysis*, 25 6: 1457–69.
Castree, N. (2004), 'Is geography a science?', in Castree, N. et al. (eds.), *Questioning Geography* 57–79.
Harvey, D. (1973), *Social Justice and the City*.
Mackinder, H. (1887), 'On the scope and methods of geography', *Proceedings of the Royal Geographical Society* 9, 3: 141–74.

Science and Technology Studies (STS) An interdisciplinary field which, though diverse in approach and theory, has a shared concern for critical inquiry into the status, ideas, claims, and practices of scientific and technological activities. There are three main principles of STS. First, *science is understood not as a finished accumulation of knowledge, but as a process as thoroughly social as any other. Proponents therefore doubt claims that scientific knowledge arises from direct encounters with the natural world; the boundaries between natural and social objects tend to be blurred (*see* NATURE; SOCIO-NATURE). The idea that the status of science is founded on its application of strict standards, norms, and methods is also questioned. Secondly, technology is understood as something not separate from society, i.e. proponents reject the contrasting views of *technological determinism and its opposite, the social determination of technology. Thirdly, science and technology must be understood together, a position that differentiates STS in general from the closely related *sociology of scientific knowledge (*see* TECHNOSCIENCE).

There are many schools of thought within STS including *Actor-Network Theory as well as *feminist epistemologies and cultural studies of science (*see* HARAWAY, DONNA; LATOUR, BRUNO). The latter seek to uncover not just the cultural meanings associated with scientific practice, but also the influence of racism, sexism, and *ethnocentrism on science (*see* MASCULINISM). *Ontological positions vary from *realism to *constructivism, and *materialism to *relativism. STS methods include detailed historical analysis but also *ethnographies of laboratories and scrutiny of experiments themselves. There is particular focus on the role of instruments and devices, but also the apparently more mundane practices of writing and drawing diagrams (*see* IMMUTABLE MOBILE). In terms of research, STS has a strong focus on technoscientific controversies, including the role of *expertise, the *media, and *rhetoric. Examples include *nuclear power, human reproduction, and organ transplantation, *AIDS research, and the *Challenger* space shuttle disaster. Controversies are closely linked with the *public understanding of science, and STS scholars (including geographers) have contributed to various experiments in overcoming some of the supposed barriers between the public and scientific experts (Lane et al. 2011).

The main criticisms of STS are that it undermines the credibility of science just at the time when it is most necessary, for example, with respect to debates over *global warming (Demeritt 2006) (*see* SCIENCE WARS). Furthermore, even sympathetic commentators question whether its insights actually facilitate better scientific practice. Much of the work is non-normative, i.e. silent on how things ought to be done. Proponents of STS have acknowledged these problems and are looking to more positive interventions.

References and further reading Demeritt, D. (2006), 'Science studies, climate change and the prospects for constructivist critique', *Economy and Society* 35: 453–79.
Lane, S. et al. (2011), 'Doing flood risk science differently: an experiment in radical scientific method', *Transactions of the Institute of British Geographers* 36(1): 15–36.
Sismondo, S. (2010), *An Introduction to Science and Technology Studies*.

science park A planned area dedicated to realizing the commercial potential of scientific activity through concentrated effort in research and development. Also termed *technopoles or technology parks, they are often linked with a nearby university. The classic example was Stanford Industrial Park created by Stanford University in 1951, which contributed to the emergence of *Silicon Valley. Other examples include Hsinchu Science Park in Taiwan and Cambridge Science Park in the UK.

Science studies *See* SCIENCE AND TECHNOLOGY STUDIES.

Science Wars A series of debates and exchanges largely between US intellectuals in the 1990s. At issue was the status of science. On one side were ranged various commentators who, drawing on *post-structuralism, *postmodernism, and the *sociology of scientific knowledge, were sceptical about claims that science proceeded through objective, disinterested, or value-free inquiry. On the other side, were defenders of *realism. Perhaps the most controversial exchange concerned an article written by physicist Alan Sokal and published by the journal *Social Text*. After publication, Sokal announced that the article was a hoax, consisting of nonsense; he argued that it showed critics of science did not understand what they were talking about.

scientific method A procedure for investigating the material world utilized by scientists. Various philosophies of *science, such as *logical positivism, have sought to codify the procedure, which is not to be confused with the specific techniques of data gathering and analysis used by individual scientists. In *Explanation in Geography* (1969) David *Harvey did the same for geographers by distinguishing the inductive and deductive routes to explaining the form, location, or behaviour of material phenomena on the Earth's surface (see Fig. 10). However, subsequently doubts arose about whether there was a single method that all scientists could reasonably follow all of the time. Examination of the research practices of scientists—revealed by *Science and Technology Studies from the early 1970s onwards—suggested a messier procedure than prescribed by science philosophers. In practice, 'the scientific method' is better understood as a plethora of procedures observed by self-styled 'scientists' according to their expertise (*see* PARADIGM).

Scientific Revolution A period of intense, significant, and innovative development across the sciences between the early 16th and late 17th centuries, largely centred on Western Europe. Although *science is arguably always in progress and there may be more than one revolution, historians generally agree that this phase was of particular importance and impact. In astronomy, for example, Copernicus, Kepler, and then Galileo, developed the idea that the universe was centred on the Sun, not the Earth. In the 17th century Isaac Newton formulated the theory of universal gravity, the laws of motion, and, in parallel with Wilhelm Leibniz, devised calculus. William Harvey established the circulation of blood within the body.

These and other discoveries shared at least two common features. Firstly, they reflected the conviction that experience, including personal observation, counted for more than scriptural or monarchical authority. Experimentation was encouraged and made possible by the invention of a great variety of new instruments, such as Antoni van Leeuwenhoek's microscope and Robert Boyle's air pump. Secondly, they manifested a mechanical philosophy; a view of the universe as a clockwork mechanism whose workings could be identified. To this end, scholars integrated mathematics with natural philosophy, although in so doing they did not necessarily reject all traces of magic, astrology, or alchemy.

Among the background factors which made the revolution possible were the voyages of discovery and exploration, especially in the Americas, and the Reformation, the widespread challenge to the Catholic Church and to authority in general. Practical problems of measurement and navigation informed scientific progress, not least in the field of *cartography. Although scholars did not necessarily recognize the same disciplinary boundaries as we have today, there were conceptual advances in geography and *chorology. The 17th-century German geographer Bernhard Varenius codified the distinction between general and special geography, for example (*see* REGIONAL GEOGRAPHY; SYSTEMATIC GEOGRAPHY). Modern historians of geography are also interested in the Scientific Revolution because it exemplifies the role of space and place in scientific practice. The modern laboratory emerged as a separate and distinct scientific site, while the circulation of letters, documents, and instruments within international networks of scholars accelerated the pace of discovery.

Further reading Livingstone, D. N. (1992), *The Geographical Tradition*.
Livingstone, D. N. and Withers, C. W. J. (eds.) (2005), *Geography and Revolution*.

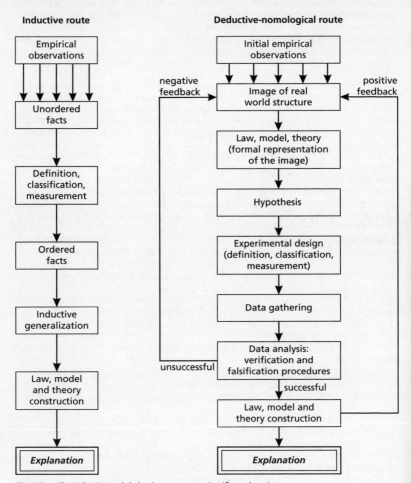

Inductive route

Empirical observations

↓ ↓ ↓ ↓ ↓

Unordered facts

↓

Definition, classification, measurement

↓

Ordered facts

↓

Inductive generalization

↓

Law, model and theory construction

↓

Explanation

Deductive-nomological route

Initial empirical observations

↓ ↓ ↓ ↓ ↓

negative feedback → Image of real world structure ← positive feedback

↓

Law, model, theory (formal representation of the image)

↓

Hypothesis

↓

Experimental design (definition, classification, measurement)

↓

Data gathering

↓

unsuccessful ← Data analysis: verification and falsification procedures

↓ successful

Law, model and theory construction

↓

Explanation

Fig. 10 The inductive and deductive routes to scientific explanation

Scott, Allen J. (1938–) A distinguished economic geographer who has worked in Britain, France, Canada, and the United States, and is presently based at the University of California, Los Angeles. His research has largely focused on the location and spatial and institutional organization of industry, *agglomeration, *city-regions, and economic change under *capitalism. His most recent work has examined the role of creative industries and the *cultural economy, exemplified by his book *The Cultural Economy of Cities* (2000).

search behaviour The process of searching for and evaluating solutions to *spatial choice and decision-making problems. For example, in navigating an area, individuals search for a route that satisfies some demand, such as the quickest or shortest route; or in selecting the location of a new factory, the owners will search for an optimal site. *See also* BEHAVIOURAL GEOGRAPHY.

secession The process in which a region gains independence from the state of which it was formerly a part, or becomes part of another state. Secession may be relatively peaceful, as in the departure of Eritrea from Ethiopia (at least initially) or involve violence. Attempts by people living in Biafra to secede from Nigeria in the 1960s led to civil war in 1967–70. Secessionist movements are currently found in almost every region of the world.

secondary data analysis Analysis of data sets that have been generated by another researcher or agency. Such data might be produced by government statistical agencies, such as a *census, or be held in a *data archive. There are three main reasons for analysing secondary data. First, the data might not be available in any other form and it is impossible or not feasible to generate a comparable data set. This is particularly the case with historical data sets. In some cases, the data collection task would be difficult for one researcher alone: data surveyed at the national scale, for example. Second, secondary data enables the replication of analysis, allowing different researchers to corroborate analytical findings. Third, generating raw data is time-consuming and costly so utilizing secondary data represents a considerable saving of resources. Although there are many benefits to analysing secondary data, there are also drawbacks. For example, the research design, the questions asked, and the *sampling frame used have been created for the purpose of the original project, not the specific focus of the present project; the data might have restrictions on access and use; have weak documentation and *metadata; or have issues of data quality due to how it has been collected or processed. Much *quantitative geography involves the analysis of secondary data, especially official statistical data sources. Increasingly, secondary data held in qualitative data archives is also being analysed.

second home A property owned and maintained by a household in addition to its main place of residence, commonly in the form of a 'holiday home' or 'weekend retreat'. Such properties are often concentrated in low-density, high-amenity rural areas, and are often thought to compromise the ability of local families to find housing or even lock local economies into patterns of seasonal dependence. But where second homes are purpose-built they may be less controversial. Further, the idea of multiple residences corresponds with changing patterns of lifestyle, mobility, and meanings of home.

Second World A term used to define the Soviet Union and allied communist countries in eastern Europe. It is a term deriving from the *Cold War. *See also* FIRST WORLD; THIRD WORLD.

Second World War A major global conflict and geopolitical event that took place between 1939 and 1945. There were two main blocs of warring nations, the Allies, consisting of the United Kingdom and *Commonwealth nations, France, the United States, Russia, and other states, and the Axis powers, consisting of Germany, Italy, Japan, and other states. Within this global war, a number of civil and regional wars took place. While the conflict had a global reach, the main theatres of war were Europe and East Asia. Over 100 million people were mobilized into armies and over 50 million people, including civilians, died through the administering of 'total war' and the *Holocaust. Beyond the size, scale, and effects of the war, it had a number of long-term effects, reshaping the political map, setting the stage for the *Cold War that followed, providing the impetus for new supranational political agencies (e.g., *United Nations, *IMF, *World Bank), and military alliances (e.g., *NATO), and ushering in the nuclear age.

secularism The principle of division between state and organized *religion. Commonly linked with the *Enlightenment and rise of *modernism, secularism argues for the right of individuals to not have religion or its rules imposed on them through the apparatus of the state. While many democratic states are notionally secular, with religious orders modernizing and practising religious believers declining in number, the influence of religion is strong in many others where religious orders continue to play an important role in shaping policy and running education, health, and welfare systems. The term 'secularization' describes the diminishing role of religion in the governance of society and people's everyday lives.

security The condition and associated feeling of being free from danger or threat. This may be at a personal level, which among other things depends upon one's immediate environment (*see* FEAR). Or it may be more collective, as in 'national security' or 'global security' (*see* RISK). Threats can be real or imagined, imminent or in the future. Governments concerned with new threats to security, such as climate change, terrorism, biohazards, etc., do not just engage in technological or organizational responses (*see* BIOSECURITY). They also generate new discourses of fear, security, possible futures, which may in turn construct *imagined geographies of safety and danger. The proliferation of *surveillance systems, private security guards, public information on security, and the attendant anxieties about personal safety have, according to some, led to a 'securitization' of everyday life. In a series of publications, for example, Cindi *Katz has critically revealed the links between parents' concerns for children's well-being and the state's preoccupation with security.

Reference Katz, C., (2008) 'Me and my monkey: what's hiding in the security state?', in Pain, R. and Smith, S. J. (eds.) *Fear: Critical Geopolitics and Everyday Life*, 59–72.

sedentarism **1.** The habits and routines associated with relatively low levels of activity and movement, leading to health-related problems such as obesity.
2. The cultural, moral, and legal preference for fixed and stable residence, and the corresponding denigration or demonization of more mobile forms of life, such as *nomadism. In this second sense, the values of localness, rootedness, and *place are positively regarded, and *mobility is deemed deviant. Sedentarization is the forced settlement of nomadic peoples; for example, the indigenous peoples of America's Great Plains were settled by the US Army in the 19th century.

segmented labour market theory The idea that *labour markets are not unified but split, generally into two sectors, primary and secondary. The primary sector includes large capital-intensive firms with well-developed structures of reward and career progression. The secondary sector comprises lower-skilled and lower-paid employees with less job security (*see* FLEXIBLE LABOUR; LABOUR FLEXIBILITY). Female and ethnic minority workers are said to be trapped in the secondary sector.

segregation The separation of social groups into particular roles and/or spaces. For example, people of a certain *class or *ethnicity might be limited in what work they can undertake or where they can live based on the social group to which they belong. This leads to distinct segregated geographical patterns in terms of *labour markets and residence, that have knock-on consequences in terms of living conditions and life opportunities. Segregation occurs through the market and choice, and through discrimination and policy. For example, people of a certain wealth can choose to live in particular districts or within *gated communities which are beyond the means of other social groups. In other cases, people are segregated through discrimination, enforced through emotional and physical violence, leading to their concentration in the less desirable parts of towns and cities. For example, homophobic discrimination was a key driver in the formation of so-called *gay ghettos in Western cities. Such discrimination can be enforced through policy. For example, *apartheid laws in *South Africa enforced segregation across all aspects of life, and policies of *redlining in the US mortgage market have limited where certain social groups can buy property. Segregation, which can also be thought of as the opposite of *assimilation, explicitly undermines *social cohesion within a society and can lead to social unrest. The measurement of residential segregation using quantitative indices has been an important strand within *social geography (*see* DISSIMILARITY, INDEX OF).

selection bias A bias introduced into a study through a poor *sampling strategy that skews the findings in a particular direction. Such bias leads to erroneous conclusions about a phenomenon because it weakly represents the true nature of a population.

self The reflective and reflexive ability of human beings to take themselves as objects of their own thought. That is, a person being conscious of and understanding their own existence, and the ways in which they are distinguished from others. The notion of self is expressed through *identity, character, abilities, and attitudes. The self is sometimes divided into 'I', which is the spontaneous essence of a person, and the 'me', how people see themselves through the eyes of others. The self evolves over time as a person develops and comes into contact with new ideas, situations, people, and places. The self is key to the notion of *agency and *self-determination, that is, the ability to make decisions and act freely in the world, though it is recognized that self is also expressed through the unconscious, and how one pictures oneself, desires oneself to be, how one presents oneself, and how one is seen does not necessarily align. Geographers tend to be interested in the relations between self and others, self and society, and self and place. The first concerns the process of *othering and how one differentiates oneself from and treats others, often drawing on ideas from *psychoanalysis. The second concerns the ongoing *agency-structure debate and the extent to which people have free will to act autonomously. The third focuses on the relationship between individuals, the *environment, their *sense of place, and their *spatial behaviour, examined in particular through the lens of *humanistic and *behavioural geography.

self-determination The principle in international law that a people should be able to decide how they are governed; for example, whether they have an independent nation-state or remain part of a larger entity such as an empire.

self-directed photography *See* AUTOPHOTOGRAPHY.

semiotics The study and interpretation of signs and symbols. According to its founder, Ferdinand de Saussure, a system of communication such as language should not be understood through historical inquiry, but through its structural qualities (*see* STRUCTURALISM). Words (sounds and inscriptions) gain their meaning in relation to other words, not by direct and immediate connection to some object. A sign has two parts, signified and signifier. The signified is the idea or mental image (e.g. a piece of furniture with four or more legs supporting a horizontal surface); and the signifier is the mark or symbol associated with it (e.g. the word 'table'). But the connection between the two is not fixed forever and can change. This means that interpreting signs is always social and conditional, and that communication is as much the transformation of meaning as its transmission. *See also* HERMENEUTICS; TEXT.

semi-structured interview *See* INTERVIEWS AND INTERVIEWING.

Semple, Ellen Churchill (1863–1932) One of the leading geographers of her generation, a renowned educator and first woman president of the *American Association of Geographers (in 1921). Educated at Vassar College, she later studied under Friedrich *Ratzel at the University of Leipzig in the 1890s. German universities did not admit women to degree programmes at the time and she had to obtain special permission to attend. Returning to the USA, Semple made her reputation with detailed research on communities in the mountains of Kentucky, demonstrating the social and cultural effects of geographical isolation. Inspired by Ratzel's *anthropogeography, she wrote two major books: *American History and its Geographic Conditions* (1903), and *Influences of the Geographic Environment* (1911). The latter became one of the most successful textbooks of its day and one of the major texts in Anglo-American geography. Although her work is now often dismissed for its unmistakable *environmental determinism, its influence at the time was considerable. Affiliated with the universities of Chicago (1906–24) and then Clark (1921–29), Semple was active as a visiting lecturer across the USA and as far afield as the University of Oxford, UK. The latter part of her career was spent travelling in and researching the Mediterranean, culminating in *The Geography of the Mediterranean Region* (1931). Semple's regional expertise contributed to the US preparations for the peace negotiations at the end of the First World War.

Sen, Amartya (1933–) An Indian economist and Nobel prize winner best known for his work on *poverty, *famine, *welfare and development economics, and social choice theory. He has taught at the University of Delhi, London School of Economics, Universities of Oxford and Cambridge, and Harvard University. His overriding focus has been in redressing economic and social *inequality and to improve human *well-being. His work has shaped international thinking with regards to development, especially through his books *Poverty and Famines* (1982) and *Development as Freedom* (1999). *See also* CAPABILITIES APPROACH; ENTITLEMENT APPROACH.

sense of place The specific feelings, perceptions, and attitudes generated in people by the particular qualities of a locality, or the events that they experience there. If a *place looks and feels too much like others, it may be regarded by some as 'placeless' (*see* NON-PLACE; PLACELESSNESS). A sense of place thus only arises if a locality is thought of as distinctive in terms of its built and/or natural environments, and/or its site/location; this is a necessarily subjective appraisal. It is perfectly possible for people to develop a sense of place in otherwise placeless locations because of their particular experiences there. Several *humanistic geographers in the 1970s and 1980s sought to understand how people valued their home-places in different ways (*see* VALUE; VALUES). This was sometimes linked to normative criticisms of the homogenous urban landscapes being created by architects and planners in Western and communist countries during the post-1945 period (*see* RELPH, EDWARD). However, these criticisms sometimes rested implicitly on a pre-modern romance for cohesive *community able to shut out the *creative destruction of *modernity. Tim Cresswell showed how the sense of place enjoyed by some often came at the expense of others perceived as 'outsiders' who threatened the integrity of place. Relatedly, others argued for creating senses of place that foster diversity and tolerance among people living in the same locality. For instance, David Ley's research into how overseas immigrants are received in the neighbourhoods of Vancouver accents the capacity for tolerance among co-existing strangers. This has become a major issue worldwide because recent mass migrations have produced highly multicultural places that combine indigenous and non-indigenous groups.

References Cresswell, T. (1996), *In Place/Out of Place: Geography, Ideology and Transgression.* Ley, D. (1995), 'Between Europe and Asia: the case of the missing sequoias', *Ecumene* 2, 2: 187–212.

sensorium The sum of all information available to a person at any one time through their senses and their mind. Within any situation, a sensorium is the total field of perception and cognition, the basis upon which people can sense, interpret, and act in the world. This can include the world immediately around us, but also that channelled through the media. *See also* SENSUOUS GEOGRAPHIES.

sensuous geographies The study of individual interactions with the geographic world through the senses, principally sight, hearing, touch, smell, and kinaesthesia. The main argument made by those studying sensuous geographies is that it is through the senses that people experience and come to know the world. It is therefore important to understand how the senses filter and work together to mediate and shape the information available to a person and how they interact with environments. Of particular interest are the senses other than sight, which is considered the primary spatial channel. Often situated within humanistic or behavioural geography, research has particularly focused on *haptic (touch) and hearing geographies, and how those missing a sense, such as the visually impaired, come to understand the world and develop spatial knowledge. *See also* SENSORIUM.

Further reading Paterson, M. and Dodge, M. (eds.) (2012), *Touching Space, Placing Touch.* Rodaway, P. (1994), *Sensuous Geographies: Body, Sense and Place.*

services The economic activities centred on the processing of intangible or 'weightless' goods. Collectively termed the service or tertiary sector, they can be contrasted with *manufacturing (the production of tangible goods), *agriculture, and *extractive industries (both of which supply raw materials). Services include: industries, e.g. *retailing, education, and accountancy; and occupations or professions, e.g. clerk, teacher, and architect. Service workers may therefore be found in manufacturing and other non-service industries, e.g. janitors at a car assembly plant. Service workers and firms are also integrated with other sectors in *global production networks. In the *Global North typically around three quarters of the waged workforce are classified as service employees, and even in the *Global South, somewhere between a third and half of all workers are in the service economy. In the Global North, therefore, the term 'services' encompasses such a large and diverse part of the labour force and economy that it has questionable analytical value. Given such diversity, it is usual to distinguish among different types of service work. Public services are provided or largely funded by government and, in principle, open to all sometimes without direct payment (*see* WELFARE STATE). Private services are commercially based. This distinction is blurred however, as many public services are contracted out to commercial or voluntary firms. A second distinction is between *producer services, where other firms are the customer, and consumer services, which are directed at individuals. The former include advanced producer services (APS) or knowledge-intensive services (KIS), which are based on specialized and high-value expertise, e.g. advertising, finance, and law. The term 'advanced business services' (ABS) is also used to describe the same thing and in turn, it can be divided into financial services and professional business services such as logistics and headhunting. Within consumer or customer services an important distinction can be made between those provided at a distance, e.g. call centres, and those that require the co-presence of provider and customer, e.g. sales assistant, waiter, or manicurist. In *Working Bodies* (2009), Linda McDowell argues that this 'interactive service work' is increasingly important in the UK, and by implication other countries of the Global North. Because the service is provided directly and in person, the conduct and appearance of workers in these jobs is often minutely policed (*see* BODY WORK; EMOTIONAL LABOUR).

Recent geographical work on services has focused on industries, occupations, and workplaces. The globalization of services, termed the 'second global shift' by John Bryson, involves new arrangements of *outsourcing and *offshoring. India, for example, is emerging as a major provider of business services. The geographical organization of service-sector transnational companies such as those involved in law and logistics is another significant topic (Dicken 2011). Researchers of *world city networks are interested in how advanced producer services connect key places in the world economy. The circulation and lifestyles of the high-skilled migrants among *global cities links with this research. There are also studies of the significance of small- and medium-sized service companies and their inter-firm relations for generating localized economic growth. From a worker perspective, the important questions are how the rise of the service economy since the 1970s in the Global North has been implicated with social changes, above all the increase in female waged labour. One argument is that the onus placed on personal skills in service work advantages women at the expense of men. Whether the *knowledge economy represents a shift towards less exploitative work conditions, or whether it conceals new divisions around *gender, *race, *class, and bodily appearance, is an important debate (*see* FLEXIBLE LABOUR; INTERPELLATION). Labour economists debate whether the growth in service sector jobs causes a polarization of wages and conditions. Within the Global South, alongside concerns for the gendered nature of service work, there is research on the impact of *neoliberal reforms on public sector service employment. Once regarded as a high-status and relatively secure job, the restructuring of government employment has intensified insecurity among well-educated youths in many countries.

Further reading Bryson, J. (2007), 'The second global shift', *Geografiska Annaler*, series B 89: 31–43. Dicken, P. (6th ed. 2011), *Global Shift*.
Jeffrey, C. (2010), *Timepass: Youth, Class and the Politics of Waiting in India*.

settlement geography   **1.** The study of settlement patterns and structure.

2. The study of the forms and processes of human habitation through the construction of dwellings and occupation of the land. The first sense recognizes that humans live in a range of places, from small villages to metropolitan regions that bridge the distinction between urban and rural. But since the 1960s, the decline of regional geography and the separate development of *urban geography and *rural geography has resulted in the term 'settlement geography' falling out of use in Anglo-American geography. The second sense reflects a more historical and cultural approach to the ways human societies have populated the land.

settler society   A form of colonial society based around widespread settlement by the colonizing power, rather than just resource extraction (*see* COLONIALISM). Settlement was often accompanied by the violent destruction and dispossession of existing indigenous societies.

sex/gender distinction   The term 'sex' refers to the biological differences between men and women (e.g., chromosomes, hormonal profiles, internal and external sex organs) whereas *gender refers to the characteristics that society delineates as masculine or feminine. As such, sex as male or female is invariant across cultures, whereas *gender roles—what it means to be a man or woman—can vary significantly.

sex tourism   Travel to another location for the purposes of buying sex. Travel usually occurs from a place where prostitution is illegal to one where it is legal, little policed, or significantly cheaper, and can take place within a country or between nations. It is also infused with cultural ideas of sexuality and exoticism. The travel is either organized within the tourism sector, or from outside using its structures and networks. It is thought to be worth several billion dollars a year and contributes to the practice of sex *trafficking of women and children to work as prostitutes. *See also* SEX WORK.

sexuality A person's sexual orientation or preference. Sexuality is a key component of individual *identity, shaping intimate relationships and reflected in behaviour and fashion and bodily appearance. Traditionally, sexuality was understood to be rooted in people's biological make-up. In recent years, this *essentialized, natural conception of sexual identity has been challenged, replaced with the notion that sexuality is *socially constructed wherein it is recognized that sexual identity and practices are shaped by political and moral discourse about the 'proper' way to enact sexual relations. Since the early 1990s, geographers have examined how space is sexed and how sexuality is shaped by socio-spatial processes. Such research has detailed the ways in which dominant *heteronormative and *heteropatriarchial discourses produce (hetero)sexual-ized spaces such as the bedroom, the beach, bars, massage parlours, *red-light districts, while demonizing other spaces such as supposed *gay ghettos. Most research to date has focused primarily on dissident sexualities such as *sex work or *sex tourism, and *gay and *lesbian geographies, examining the daily lives of people who express a particular sexual orientation or particular communities or places. A further strand of work has critiqued geography as a discipline for its generally patronizing, moralistic, and straight approach to sexual relations, and challenged geographers to adopt more liberal attitudes and more sophisticated understandings of sexuality.

Further reading Bell, D. and Valentine, G. (1995), *Mapping Desire: Geographies of Sexuality.*
Chauncey, G. (1995), *Gay New York: the Making of the Gay Male World, 1890–1940.*
Ingram, G. B., Bouthillette, A-M., and Retter, Y. (1997), *Queers in Space: Communities, Public Places, Sites of Resistance.*

sexual violence A sexual act obtained or attempted to be obtained through threat, coercion, or kidnapping for sex trafficking, or unwanted sexual comments or advances. Sexual violence covers a wide range of acts, from inter-personal encounters to more organized and systematic violation. At one level, it includes rape or attempted rape, which can take place regardless of the relationship status between perpetrator and victim (e.g., being married), and in a variety of settings, including the home. In a more organized form, the International Criminal Tribunal for the former Yugoslavia ruled in 2001 that rape and sexual enslavement are crimes against humanity. This was a response to the deliberate use of rape as a means of terror by Serbian forces in Bosnia during the war in the former Yugoslavia. Apart from physical violence, coercion might consist of intimidation or blackmail or take place when the victim is unable to give consent (e.g. drugged). The *fear of sexual violence has been demonstrated to constrain the *spatial behaviour of women. *See also* TRAFFICKING.

Further reading Pain, R. (1991), 'Space, sexual violence and social control', *Progress in Human Geography* 15: 15–431.

sex work The selling of sex for money or favours. Sex work can take a number of forms from stripping to massages to prostitution. It predominately consists of men buying sexual services from women, but also includes child prostitution, men selling to men, and men selling to women. Just as it is varied in its forms, it varies with respect to working conditions, risks, and rewards. Sex work is framed with moralizing discourses and regulated through legislation and *policing that differs between places. In some countries sex work is legal, or legal in certain restricted places, and in many others it is illegal. A prime strategy to contain sex work is to constrain it spatially to certain sites such as *red-light districts, where it can be effectively monitored and regulated. These sites are usually located where they are tolerated, not where they can attract the most custom. *See also* SEX TOURISM.

Further reading Hubbard, P. (1999), *Sex and the City: Geographies of Prostitution in the Urban West.*

shadow state A system of governance existing parallel to or concealed within the formal, organized, and legitimate state. The term has been used in two different contexts. In Western democracies the shadow state describes the collection of voluntary and non-profit organizations that provide services to the public and are publically funded, but are not themselves formally part of the state (*see* NEOLIBERALISM). In the context of post-colonial Africa and the countries of the former Soviet Union, the shadow state arises from the way state officials gain power and wealth through alliances with non-state actors such as warlords, criminal gangs, and transnational companies.

shanty town A settlement consisting of structures built by residents often using salvaged materials and without observing the relevant building regulations. If the residents do not have legal title to the land, the term squatter settlement may also be used (*see* SQUATTING).

sharecropping A form of agriculture in which a tenant farmer gives a share of their crop to the landowner instead of monetary payment. Although more common in the feudal past and, for example, in US cotton farming after the Civil War, this arrangement continues in modern agricultural regions, in California, for example.

Sheppard, Eric (1950–) A British-born economic geographer based at the University of Minnesota for much of his career, moving to the University of California, Los Angeles in 2012. His work has focused on trade and the uneven geographies of *globalization, the spatial dynamics of *capitalism, processes of *urbanization, and the politics of *neoliberalism, undertaking comparative research across developed and developing nations.

shifting cultivation The use of plot rotation by farmers to maintain soil fertility. A plot of land is typically farmed until its soils become depleted or weeds become rife, and then left to recover ('in fallow') while activity switches to another plot. One form of shifting cultivation found throughout tropical forest lands and in the cultivation of dry rice in tropical uplands is 'slash-and-burn'. Land is cleared by burning, leaving the wood ash as a fertilizer, cultivated, and then abandoned. Critics regarded such practices as wasteful, but others recognize it as a successful adaptation to tropical environments.

shift-share model A statistical model for calculating changes or shift in employment within a set of areas, and to identify areas that have a higher proportion or share of jobs in a particular sector and thus exhibit competitive advantage. Employment growth in an area is related to regional share plus the shift in numbers employed, and the model seeks to determine differential effects, such as competitive and local factors, and pro-portionality effects such as industry mix, composition, and structural factors. *See also* LOCATION QUOTIENTS.

shipping The movement of goods and passengers via *waterways and sea-going vessels. Shipping has long been important for trade and migration, becoming increas-ingly more so with developments in vessel-building and seaworthiness, and associated technologies of mapping and navigation. From the late medieval period, shipping enabled *colonization and nascent processes of *globalization, and has played a key role in military conflicts. Some 90 per cent of world trade in materials and goods goes by sea. *See also* CONTAINERIZATION; PORT.

shortage economy The lack of sufficient consumer goods and industrial inputs arising not from occasional failings but from the structural conditions of economic organization. It was said to be endemic to the centrally planned economies of communist countries in Eastern Europe and the *Soviet Union. In the absence of the market signals associated with *capitalism, critics argued that such economies were prone to both short- and long-term mismatches between supply and demand. Black markets or *alternative economies sometimes filled the gap.

Sibley, David (1940–) A British social geographer who was based at the University of Hull for much of his career. After completing a PhD at the University of Cambridge in geographical *modelling, he spent several years outside the academy world working with English gypsies. This work provided the basis for his book *Outsiders in an Urban Society* (1981). Over the next twenty years he sought to theorize outsiders, *marginaliza- tion, *social exclusion, and the *production of space, drawing on social anthropology, *feminist, and *psychoanalytic theory, best exemplified by his book *Geographies of Exclusion* (1995).

significance test A statistical test used to determine whether a null *hypothesis is rejected or not. The test establishes whether there is a relationship between variables and the extent to which such a relationship might have occurred by chance. In effect, the test provides a level of confidence in the null hypothesis.

Silicon Valley A region south of San Francisco, California, famous for its concentra- tion of *hi-tech industries. It is centred on Santa Clara Valley (also a county) but spills over into the neighbouring counties of San Mateo, Marin, and San Francisco. The 'silicon' part of the name refers to silicon-based integrated circuit, or micro-processor, the vital component of modern computing that was invented in the region. Major companies such as Hewlett-Packard, Apple, eBay, and Google have their headquarters there, and the region is a dense cluster of innovation, high-skilled immigration, and *venture capital.

Further reading Saxenian, A. (1996), *Regional Advantage: Culture and Competition in Silicon Valley and Route 128*.

simulacrum An image, representation, or effigy of someone or something; a copy. In conventional usage a simulacrum is thought to be an imperfect or false likeness, not as good as the real thing. But according to Jean Baudrillard, a simulacrum replaces or supersedes the real. In *Simulations* (1983) he develops his argument that the *postmod- ern age is so saturated by signs, information, or meanings that the boundaries between representation and reality have collapsed. In the age of the simulacrum, simulacra no longer refer to some reality, they are reality itself. An example can be found in Ian MacDonald's novel *River of Gods* (2004), in which artificial intelligences play soap stars who are deemed more real than living persons. *See also* HYPERREALITY.

simulation A model that seeks to simulate real-world processes and what might happen under different scenarios. In human geography, most simulations are computer-based, using a range of data to simulate how a system works. The computer game 'SimCity' is an example of an urban simulation that models how a city will grow and develop under the conditions of the players choosing, based on known urban processes. *See also* AGENT-BASED MODELLING.

Singapore A city state in *Southeast Asia located on one large island and many smaller ones separated from Malaysia by the narrow Straits of Johor, and from Indonesia by the wider Singapore Strait. A British trading post and colony in the early 1800s, it declared independence in 1963 as part of Malaysia, but two years later became fully independent in its own right. With a population of over five million, this tropical country was one of the Four Asian Tigers (*see* ASIAN MIRACLE; NEWLY INDUSTRIALIZING COUNTRIES) and has become a major centre of global trade and finance. Because of its export and import activities, it is frequently measured as one of the world's most globalized countries.

situated knowledge The idea that all forms of knowledge reflect the particular conditions in which they are produced, and at some level reflect the social identities and social locations of knowledge producers. The term was coined by historian of science Donna *Haraway in *Simians, Cyborgs, and Women: the Reinvention of Nature* (1991) to question what she regarded as two dangerous myths in Western societies. The first was that it is possible to be epistemologically objective, to somehow be a neutral mouthpiece for the world's truths if one adopts the 'right' method of inquiry. The second myth was that *science and scientists are uniquely and exclusively equipped to be objective. Haraway was not advocating *relativism. Instead, she was calling for all knowledge producers to take full responsibility for their epistemic claims rather than pretending that 'reality' has definitively grounded these claims.

Situationism The ideas and practices associated with the Situationist International, a small but influential *avant-garde movement active in Western Europe 1957–72. They blended *Marxism, surrealism, and other intellectual currents with particular reference to urban space and *urbanism. Although they shared the Left's critique of hierarchical power relations, they also sought revolutionary change in everyday life and its spaces. The most well-known figure, Guy Debord, wrote *La société du spectacle* (1967) in which he critiqued the colonization of everyday life by commodities. This was an early reaction to the growing influence of advertising, television, and the media in society. Countering commodification included reappropriating city spaces from commercial domination. To this end, Situationists resisted urban redevelopment, experimented with new ways of mapping the city, and encouraged distinct and autonomous ways of moving through its streets. The *dérive*, or drift, for example, was an exercise in consciously navigating through the city while resisting the routine pedestrian flows favoured by planners. Another technique, *détournement*, sought to subvert advertising and branding by manipulating slogans and images, a practice continued by the radical Canadian anti-capitalist organization Adbusters. Although select and short-lived, the influence of the Situationists can be felt in *psychogeography and many radical and experimental ways of trying to change urban life.

Further reading Pinder, D. (2005), *Visions of the City*.

sketch maps A hand-drawn map of an area produced from memory. Sketch maps are a frequently used method of data generation in *cognitive mapping research for determining how much a person knows about an area and its spatial relations. It takes a number of forms including a basic version where the respondent is simply asked to draw a map of an area, a normal version that asks the respondent to include certain features, and a cued version that provides a portion of the map with the respondent asked to complete it. Sketch mapping has been demonstrated to have a high degree of reliability, but suffers because it relies on the graphic skill of the drawer.

skid row An urban area in which there is a high concentration of hostels, rooming-houses, or single-occupancy dwellings catering to low-income and transient populations, including homeless individuals (*see* HOMELESSNESS).

skilled migration The movement between countries of high-skilled or trained individuals for permanent or temporary settlement; sometimes termed 'skills migration'. Since the late 20th century, many states have devised specific immigration visas to attract individuals with skills specifically in shortage in the economy, or high levels of skill and education generally.

slavery A form of *forced labour in which a person is owned, controlled, and commanded by another, usually for the purposes of work. Definitions in international law tend to be narrower than those used by anti-slavery campaigners, which may include various types of exploitation such as bonded labour, forced marriage, child labour, and *human trafficking. Domestic servitude, in extreme cases, can be a form of slavery (Anderson 2000). *See also* DIASPORA; RACE.

Reference Anderson, B. (2000), *Doing the Dirty Work? The Global Politics of Domestic Labour*.

slow city movement *See* CITTASLOW.

slum An urban area where there is a concentration of poor-quality housing, either because of long-term neglect and disinvestment or because residents are too poor to build to better standards (*see* SHANTY TOWN). Slum residents are likely to be low-income and experience over-crowding, poor facilities, and vulnerable or hazardous environments. Outsiders may stigmatize slum-dwellers, associating their housing conditions with moral failings (*see* CULTURE OF POVERTY). But across the world, slum-dwellers are organizing to improve conditions and demand greater rights to the city.

(((⊕))) SEE WEB LINKS
• Official website of Slum Dwellers International.

small- and medium-size enterprise (SME). A business classified as not being large according to the relevant criteria such as size of labour force but sometimes also turnover. Different countries uses different cut-offs, varying between 250 and 1500 workers. In the UK, for example, over 90 per cent of enterprises have fewer than 250 employees. SMEs are thought to be important sources of innovation.

Smith, Neil (1954–2012) An influential Marxist geographer who made significant contributions to theories of nature, scale, and urban development. He did his PhD research into gentrification under the supervision of David *Harvey at the Johns Hopkins University, Baltimore. Though younger than Harvey, Smith underwent a similar academic and political transformation to that of his supervisor. This entailed a rejection of the kind of geography taught to him as an undergraduate—a so-called 'new geography' (or *spatial science)—and an older *regional geography.

Like Harvey, Smith built carefully and creatively upon the late political-economic writings of Karl *Marx. He has made germinal contributions in four areas, three beginning with his book *Uneven Development* (1985) published two years after he graduated from Hopkins. First, he is responsible for the *rent gap thesis on studies of *gentrification and urban redevelopment. In opposition to theories that posit urban professionals as welcome 'pioneers' returning to blighted inner-city neighbourhoods, Smith's thesis focused on the *political economy of gentrification, suggesting that only when the gap between actual and potential ground *rent is sufficiently high do waves of gentrification occur. This thesis thus pointed to the class dynamics of land use and the power of *rentiers and investors to govern the uses of urban space. Highly political questions thereby arise about who has a 'right to the city'.

Second, Smith popularized the counterintuitive idea of the *production of nature. His claim is that in a capitalist world *nature is no longer natural but, instead, actively produced at a discursive and material level in the service of capital accumulation. This 'denaturalizing' move usefully focused some geographers' analytical attention on the processes that remake nature (e.g. commercial agriculture), and it also posed a challenge to those whose politics is founded on ideas of a non-social nature with supposedly intrinsic capacities and values.

Third, Smith presented a powerful Marxian account of *uneven geographical development. Unlike some other theories, Smith did not look to 'natural differences' in geography for an explanation. Instead, he argued that capitalism produces and needs uneven geographical development: it is part of the system's operating hardware, as it were. This means that it is a socially constructed phenomena and thus, in theory, entirely preventable. Finally, *Uneven Development* also advanced the challenging idea that geographical *scale is socially produced and a tool of power—thus being more than simply a mental category we use to divide up the world. Smith argued that capitalism (including the capitalist state) actively organizes commodity production, distribution, exchange, and consumption at certain scales at certain historical moments. These constructed geographical scales become containers, constrainers, and enablers of different sorts of activities undertaken by different groups—producers, rentiers, politicians, financiers, trades unionists, and so on. Geographical scale, for Smith, thus enters into the very fabric of capitalist life and struggles to alter and transcend it.

Smith advanced his work in all four areas both empirically and theoretically over a thirty-year period. He has also authored a critical biography of Isaiah *Bowman, a political geographer who was influential within the Franklin D. Roosevelt administration in the USA (1933–45). In *American Empire* (2003) Smith shows that geographical knowledge can alter the world it ostensibly describes, meaning it is both political and *performative. He was also a founder member of the International Critical Geography Group (ICCG), which seeks to bring together left-wing scholars and activists of various stripes who are committed to radical reform of the current world order and, better still, revolutionary change. In *Endgame of Globalisation* (2005) he sought a more public profile for his otherwise academic writing, making him a public geographer of sorts. *See also* CRITICAL GEOGRAPHY; MARXIST GEOGRAPHY; PUBLIC GEOGRAPHY.

Smith, Susan J. (1956–) A British social geographer who was based at the University of Edinburgh 1990–2004 and presently works at the University of Cambridge, where she is Mistress of Girton College. She has made significant contributions to the geographical study of *race and racism, notably through her book *The Politics of Race and Residence* (1989), housing markets, *inequality and *segregation, and *soundscapes. She was editor-in-chief of the *International Encyclopedia of Housing and Home* (2012).

snowballing *See* SAMPLING.

social area analysis A quantitative technique for understanding urban social structure, especially residential patterns. The method uses area-based census data on occupation and schooling; fertility, women at work, and single-family dwellings; and ethnic population concentration, to construct three indices that are combined to categorise residential areas. In this sense, it was a forerunner of *geodemographic analysis, which uses more sophisticated analytical techniques to define area types. The technique was used to explain residential social structure as the product of economic development and urbanization processes.

social capital The resources and ability of a social group to act collaboratively to effect positive change. In its broadest sense it concerns the collective use of social resources to the benefit of a community, but it was first used more narrowly with respect to its effects on improving economic performance. The premise is that those societies where social networks and relations, and regional and civic institutions, are strong, with well-established bonds of mutual trust, reciprocity, and civic engagement, tend to fare better economically through enhanced collaboration and cooperation. Through sharing and working together, rather than simply competing, all firms in an area benefit mutually. Society is also less individualized, has fewer social problems, and has higher levels of democracy. The argument thus follows that for an underperforming region to becoming economically competitive and more socially cohesive, it must enhance its social capital by reviving and creating institutions and activities that produce networks of trust and reciprocity. This means bringing the state, business, and civil society together in new ways to encourage and support civic engagement and social interaction. Aligned with the notion of *creative cities, enhancing social capital became an important policy device in the late 1990s, and early 2000s to try and stimulate economic growth.

Further reading Putnam, R. (2000), *Bowling Alone: the Collapse and Revival of American Community*.

social class *See* CLASS.

social cohesion The extent to which there are bonds of trust that bind people together into a society, as opposed to mistrust and antipathy that cause division and tension. Maintaining and enhancing social cohesion is a key aim of many governments, as well as supranational political bodies such as the *European Union, because when social cohesion weakens it can lead to unrest and conflict between groups. Policies such as *multiculturalism, for example, seek to foster social cohesion by building mutual respect and interaction.

social construction The process whereby phenomena that appear to exist independently of society are shown, counterintuitively, to be understood in socially contingent ways, or even to be materially altered by society. Social constructionist arguments can apply purely to knowledge or also to the biophysical world. They became increasingly significant in human geography from the early 1970s, as the ideal of *objectivity and the presumption of a single reality both came under attack. Social constructionist arguments were used to contest claims and actions undertaken in the name of a 'truth' or 'facts' existing 'out there' in the world. The ostensible differences between 'subjective' and 'objective' knowledge (e.g. 'opinion versus truth') were challenged by showing that *all* knowledge bears the mark of its originators (*see* SITUATED KNOWLEDGE). Social constructionists also pointed to the plurality of ways in which people make the world meaningful to themselves, such that distinguishing between the contents and referents of any knowledge or *discourse is problematic. This meant that the philosophical distinction between *epistemology and *ontology began to seem unstable. This instability was heightened when some showed that the society-nature dualism was false by virtue of how modern societies physically transformed the non-human world even as they still used terms like 'natural environment' and *wilderness when describing it (*see* NATURE).

However, since the late 1990s several critics have pointed to a logical flaw in social constructionist arguments. The 'social' relations, values, and processes doing all the 'constructing', it has been argued, must *themselves* be constructed from something else and cannot construct the world *entirely* as they please—otherwise reality would be wholly reducible to human wishes and desires. There have been two responses to these criticisms. Some have sought to qualify and refine constructionist arguments, drawing back from some of the 'strong' ontological claims made in the 1990s (Demeritt 2002). Others have abandoned the metaphor of 'construction' in favour of metaphors such as 'composition' and 'assembly'. These point to the co-constitution of multiple realities by a myriad of human and non-human actors (Whatmore 1999). Even so, the embers of constructionism remain aglow in human geography, with some arguing vocally that they deserve to be reignited (e.g. Castree 2013). Whether one is a constructionist or not, the perpetual ontological question arises about what the 'real' units or relations are doing the constructing, composing, or assembling. In this respect, the debates over social constructionism and its alternatives defy resolution.

References Castree, N. (2013), *Making Sense of Nature*.
Demeritt, D. (2002), 'What is the "social construction of nature"? A typology and sympathetic critique', *Progress in Human Geography* 26, 6: 766–89.
Whatmore, S. (1999), 'Hybrid geographies', in Massey, D. et al. (eds.) *Human Geography Today* 3–21.

social Darwinism The application of Darwin's ideas to understanding human society and in particular the idea that the relations between states and classes are characterized by an ongoing struggle and the 'survival of the fittest' (in the words of sociologist Herbert Spencer). More a term of approbation than a scientific theory, social Darwinism blended ideas of unrestrained economic competition, *eugenics, and *scientific racism.

social distance 1. The similarity or closeness of social groups.
2. The number of links in a social network that separate individuals or groups. Social distance provides a measure of *social cohesion or *segregation by measuring the level of interaction or intermixing of individuals and groups. It is sometimes measured through levels of intimacy, for example, the degree of intergroup marriage or whether members of another group would be welcomed in a family or a workplace. The less the intimacy or interaction, the greater the social distance.

social economy A part of the economy made up of organizations that are neither public (government) nor private (business), but are in-between, including non-profit, voluntary, and charitable activities. It can include social enterprises, i.e. those not principally motivated by financial gain. These includes cooperatives, credit unions, and other *alternative economies.

social exclusion The *marginalization and exclusion of individuals and groups from full participation in normal, everyday activities and resources such as *housing, *work, social services, and the political sphere. Social exclusion can be the product of active discrimination and the denial of rights due to discursive (e.g. legislation) and material (e.g. violence) processes centred on cultural (e.g. disability, sexuality, gender) and ethnic identity, or be the product of poverty and weak mobility due to a lack of individual resources to secure participation. In general, social exclusion is multidimensional in nature, with a number of factors working in concert to disenfranchise certain groups of people. It can create alienation and feelings of powerlessness, *social polarization and *stratification, and undermines *social cohesion. The processes of social exclusion work spatially, with people being excluded from particular places creating patterns of *segregation. In policy terms, social exclusion is countered through programmes of social inclusion that seek to provide all members of society with the opportunities, resources, and rights necessary to participate fully in economic, social, and cultural life, to enjoy a standard of living and well-being that is considered normal in the society in which they live, and to have a greater participation in decision-making which affects their lives.

Further reading Gough, J., Eisenschitz, A., and McCulloch, A. (2005), *Spaces of Social Exclusion*.
Sibley, D. (1995), *Geographies of Exclusion*.

Social Formation and Symbolic Landscape A key text by Denis *Cosgrove (1984) in the development of new cultural geography that provided a compelling history of the idea of landscape in Western thought. Examining both landscapes and their representation through art, the book challenged the *Berkeley school of landscape interpretation through the application of Marxist ideas concerning social order and *ways of seeing shaped by context and power. Landscape and how it is portrayed and viewed, Cosgrove argued, is reflective of processes of social formation at the time of its creation, and cannot be understood in purely aesthetic ways free of this context.

social geography The study of social relations, social identities, and social inequalities from a spatial perspective. In particular, social geography is concerned with the spatial variation and the spatial processes constructing social aspects of everyday life. Prior to the *cultural turn, social geography was principally concerned with social *inequalities and conflicts, *social justice, welfare, community relations, and the social construction of place, especially with respect to urban societies. For example, in his book *A Social Geography of the City* (1983), David Ley reviewed the everyday geographies of cities including the formation of social networks, patterns of *housing, residential differentiation, and neighbourhood change in cities, patterns of *poverty, social deprivation, *social polarization, and *segregation, *quality of life, and what makes for a livable city, and the nature of power and politics and the role of state institutions in shaping socio-spatial relations. In so doing he detailed how urban places are socio-spatially produced, leading to distinct social relations and spatial patterns. Related studies examined how neighbourhoods are formed and operate as social worlds, the conflicts that can arise between communities sharing urban space, patterns of criminal activity, and the social uses of space for *consumption, *work, *leisure, and *recreation, the location, access, and use of social institutions such as schools, prisons, and social and *health services, and how people developed distinct *senses of place. The approaches used were typically a mix of *humanistic, *behavioural, and *radical geography, with spatial patterns explained as the result of spatial choice and decision-making or structural forces rooted in *capitalism. A particular concern was the notion of social justice and the welfare of citizens; that is, geographical analysis sought to highlight inequalities and the processes that produced them with the aim of providing insights that might be used to tackle them and create a more just and fair society (*see* WELFARE GEOGRAPHY). In this sense, social geography aimed to produce a *moral geography of the city. Over time, rural geographers sought to extend these foci to communities in the *countryside.

While these issues remain of key interest to social geographers, with the *cultural turn, social geography became increasingly interested in the role of *identity and *cultural politics in shaping the geography of social relations and inequalities. At the broad level, there has been an engagement with social theory, such as *feminism, *post-colonialism, *post-structuralism, and *psychoanalysis, to think through the processes of *othering and *social exclusion that operate with respect to identity, and how these shape and constrain access and opportunities across everyday life. These approaches emphasize a focus on the relations of *power in explaining socio-spatial processes. *Maps of Meaning* (1989) by Peter Jackson was a seminal contribution to this endeavour, detailing the way in which *ideology with respect to identity is mobilized through *discourse and material practices to reproduce unequal and uneven social geographies. While *class, *race, and *ethnicity had already been the foci of some attention, from the early 1990s they were examined in more detail, and were joined by studies that concentrated on *gender, *sexuality, *disability, age, and how socio-spatial processes expressed as *racism, *patriarchy, *heteronormativity, *heteropatriarchy, ableism, and ageism, work to create particular geographies for women (*see* FEMINIST GEOGRAPHY), *lesbians, and *gay men, disabled people, and *children, *youths, and the elderly (see AGEING). What these studies have clearly shown is that the social geographies of urban and rural life are not simply determined by choice or capital, but are also shaped by broader cultural and identity politics creating particular *power geometries. In recent years, social geographers have continued to develop and apply new ideas to understand social relations and divisions, often overlapping with *cultural and *critical geography.

Further reading Del Casino, V. (2009), *Social Geography*.

Knox, P. and Pinch, S. (6th ed. 2010), *Urban Social Geography*.

Pain, R., Barke, M., Fuller, D., Gough, J., MacFarlane, R., and Mowl, G. (2001), *Introducing Social Geographies*.

Valentine, G. (2001), *Social Geographies*.

socialism A political ideology prioritizing the collective ownership of the means of production and distribution, and so challenging private and individual forms of *property. There are many varieties of socialist thinking and practice. A distinction can be drawn between the principle of state ownership, expressed in the form of nationalized industries and social housing, for example, and more community-based forms, such as mutual aid associations. Unlike communists, socialists see a continuing role for the *state. *See also* SOCIALIST GEOGRAPHY.

socialist city An ideal urban form corresponding with the state socialist societies of the Soviet Union and the communist bloc. Though possibly never fully realized, its principles informed urban planning in these countries. These principles included: state rather than market control over housing and land use; planned residential development in high-density, well-serviced neighbourhoods; public rather than private transport and minimal commutes; extensive green space; limited city size, and balanced urban hierarchies. Socialist cities would attempt to avoid the kinds of social and spatial inequalities associated with capitalist cities.

socialist feminism A form of *feminism that situates women's oppression within the broader framework of class oppression and capital exploitation, and not solely the outcome of *patriarchy. Drawing on Marxist analysis, a principal argument is that the division of labour in capitalist societies relies on women supporting men's position in the labour market, thus subjugating them and making them financially reliant on men. Liberating women from such social and economic positioning requires the broad transformation of society that would occur with the adoption of socialist principles. *See also* SOCIALISM.

socialist geography A subgroup of geographical research and teaching informed by *socialism. There are antecedents in the work of *Peter Kropotkin, late 19th-century French geographer Élisée *Reclus, and British socialist Frank Horrabin (1920s), but an organized socialist geography emerged in Canada in the 1970s. The Union of Socialist Geographers first met in Vancouver in 1975, and their newsletter continued until 1981. There is a the Socialist and Critical Geography Study Group of the American Association of Geographers.

social justice *See* JUSTICE.

Social Justice and the City A text written by David *Harvey (1973), it was one of the first books written by an Anglo-American human geographer to develop *Marxist geography. The first half sets out a liberal perspective on urban social processes and their implications for social *justice. The key idea is that cities add to the distributional imbalances behind *inequality. The second half refutes this argument, using Marxism to locate the problem not in distribution, but in the capitalist *mode of production.

social movements Organizations that undertake purposive collective action generally outside formal political channels and directed towards bringing about social change (*see* CIVIL SOCIETY). Social movements therefore differ from organized political bodies such as parties or trades unions, although such entities may originate from social movements. Their purpose may be to change institutions, values, or both. They may aim to transform society, as in the US civil rights movement, or reform just one element of policy, for example, the abolition of nuclear power. Some social movements, often infused with religious sentiment, seek redemption for individuals and society as a whole, in which case they may not be averse to violence; Japan's *Aum Shinrikyo* is an example. Others are expressly organized around alternative values and lifestyles, concerned as much with individual self-realization as societal change; gay liberation is an example.

A distinction is often drawn between 'old and new' social movements, reflecting the emergence of a clutch of new political mobilizations from the 1960s onwards. Rather than organized around labour rights, civil rights, or national self-determination, new movements centred on non-workplace issues such as environment, peace, and *feminism (see ENVIRONMENTAL POLITICS). Furthermore, they were thought to employ novel modes of organizing, based on grassroots networks and media-aware tactics. But it can be argued that the distinction is overdrawn while some movements, for example, around human rights, span old and new. More recently, it has become common to recognize global or transnational social movements, exemplified by Islamism, *environmentalism, and the *global justice movement (see GLOBAL CIVIL SOCIETY). Geographers are interested in how such movements either link or transcend places, and sustain novel forms of networked association. See also URBAN SOCIAL MOVEMENTS.

Further reading Castree, N., Featherstone, D., and Herod, A. (2008), 'Contrapuntal geographies', in Cox, K. R., Low, M., and Robinson, J. (eds.) *The Sage Handbook of Political Geography*, 305–21.

social nature A non-dualist conceptualization of the relations between, and the insep-arability of, *society and *nature. The term was popularized by several human geogra-phers in the 1990s who sought to highlight the social characteristics of those phenomena we routinely take to be natural. Academic geography has been organized around the society-natural dualism for several decades, while this dualism continues to animate everyday thinking (e.g. city dwellers may go *wilderness camping in order to 'get back to nature'). The idea of social nature suggested that the dualism was socially created (not reflective of an ontological divide). It further suggested that references to what we call *nature, along with nature's material properties, were shot through with social values and goals. It was associated with several approaches to the analysis of nature that shared a loose family resemblance. In retrospect, work on social nature was a way station to more recent 'post-natural', '*post-humanist' research that goes beyond a focus on *represen-tation in order to rematerialize our understanding of people-environment relations.

Further reading Castree, N. and Braun, B. (eds.) (2001), *Social Nature: Theory, Practice and Politics*.

social network A group of individuals linked together through social relationships. Individuals can belong to multiple, overlapping or interlinked social networks, each defined around different kinds of relationships or activities, for example, *kinship, friendship, sporting or hobby activities, political affiliation, and ethnic or sexual identity. The links between individuals can be weak or strong, and be maintained through different forms of communication and interaction such as face-to-face meetings, tele-phone conversations, letters, emails, and *social networking sites. Networks are under-stood to be self-organizing and emergent in nature. Social network analysis seeks to analyse the nature, form, and dynamics of such networks, how networks are built, maintained, and evolve over time and across space, how ideas and practices diffuse through a network, and the role of individuals within the network. Generally, the network is conceived as a collection of hub (individuals) and spokes (relationships), and its visual representation is called a sociogram. Much social network analysis is quantitative in nature, drawing on *graph theory, and seeks to model how a network functions and how it might develop under different conditions; for example, in a network dominated by one key individual, what happens if they are removed? Analysis typically takes place at three levels: the micro, focusing on particular actors and relationships; the meso, focusing on localized parts of a network; and the macro, concerned with the entire network.

Further reading Kadushin, C. (2012), *Understanding Social Networks*.
Scott, J. (2000), *Social Network Analysis*.

social network analysis (SNA) *See* SOCIAL NETWORK.

social networking sites *Internet sites that enable people to communicate, build social networks, and share their thoughts and media files (e.g., photos, sound files). There are a number of different forms including blogs, microblogs such as Twitter, Facebook, shared gaming spaces, multi-user virtual worlds, media and code sharing services such as YouTube, Flickr, and SourceForge, peer-to-peer file-sharing via protocols like BitTorrent, and social tagging and bookmarking. Social networking grew rapidly in the mid-2000s with the rise of Web 2.0, allowing people with few computing skills to communicate easily and to connect to people with shared interests. On the one hand, it facilitates interaction between established friends and family, and on the other it allows users to develop new social networks across the globe. Its growth was aided by the development of smart phones and the mobile Internet. There has been much debate about the extent to which online social networks constitute meaningful communities, and about whether they reduce the salience of geographical location. Geographical analysis highlights that social networking tends to enhance and supplement real-world relationships, rather than replacing them.

social physics The application of the insights of physics to understanding aggregate human behaviour. John Q. Stewart and William Warntz systematically codified these ideas in the 1950s, suggesting, for example, that social interaction could be modelled by analogy with gravitational equations. More recently, John Urry has suggested that there is a 'new social physics', drawing on ideas of *complexity, *networks, and small worlds to bridge the natural and social sciences.

Reference Urry, J. (2004), 'Small worlds and the new "social physics"', *Global Networks*, 4: 109–30.

social polarization The splitting of a society into two distinct groups that are different ends of a spectrum, such as rich and poor, or white and black. It can also refer to divisions within a city (*see* GLOBAL CITY). In Marxist terms, social polarization on an axis of wealth divided people into bourgeoisie (the owners of production) and proletariat (the workers for production). Such polarization was ameliorated by the rise of the middle class. Social polarization is often *racialized with black members of society in Europe and North America much more likely to be poor. In all cases, polarization weakens *social cohesion and leads to patterns of *segregation.

social reproduction The processes and mechanisms by which a society maintains and transforms its social order, formations, and relations across time and space. In other words, the means by which a society reproduces itself on a continuous basis without descending into anarchy and chaos. Such processes include social norms, policy and legislation, and institutions, which work discursively and materially to maintain the status quo. This status quo is continually under pressure through resistance and transgression, and as a result the rules and norms of society gradually transform. In certain circumstances, such as invasion by a foreign power, a political coup, or revolution, the condition of social reproduction can be radically reconfigured.

Social Science Research Council (**SSRC**) An independent, non-profit, international research funding agency founded in 1923, with its headquarters in New York,
and offices in China, Egypt, Japan, and Vietnam. Its principal funding programmes
concentrate on conflict and peace building, development, and social change, the public
sphere, knowledge and learning, and strengthening global social science, with the
majority of its funding being allocated to 'context-specific' or 'place-based' projects.
It actively promotes interdisciplinary research and work with practitioners and policy-
makers.

(())) SEE WEB LINKS
• Official website of the Social Science Research Council.

social sciences An overarching term for academic disciplines that focus on the
nature of society and human action, behaviour, and relationships. Core component
disciplines include anthropology, demography, economics, human geography, law,
political science, psychology, *sociology, as well as fields such as applied social studies,
communications, health studies, migration studies, and social policy. While each of these
disciplines includes historical analysis, history as a discipline is more usually considered
a part of the arts and *humanities. The social sciences grew as disciplines, becoming core
to university curricula, in late-19th-century Europe. While they have primarily been
concerned with the creation of fundamental knowledge about society, each has engaged
in more applied and policy work, seeking to transfer knowledge into reshaping society in
productive ways. While there is much overlap between them, each discipline is distinguished by its specific focus, its key concepts and philosophical underpinnings, and its
dominant methodologies and approach. For example, economics focuses on economy,
finance, and economic processes, and its dominant methodology is econometrics. In his
presidential address to the world congress of sociology, Immanuel *Wallerstein claims
that the forces of globalization have so reshaped the world as to render these older
disciplinary boundaries archaic, unnecessary, and obstructive. Incubated within nation
state-societies, the foundational social science disciplines cannot make sense of a global,
borderless, or transnational age. Further, increasing importance is presently being placed
on interdisciplinary research, drawing together expertise, ideas, and methodological
competences across social science disciplines, and also with the natural sciences, and
arts and humanities (*see* INTERDISCIPLINARITY). This has resulted in a fracturing of core
social science disciplines and led to the creation of specific fields of study, new departments, or units in academic institutions, and new professional bodies, such as migration
studies or *geocomputation. *See also* METHODOLOGICAL NATIONALISM; SPATIAL SCIENCE.

References and further reading Backhouse, R. E. and Fontaine, P. (eds.) (2010), *The History of the
    Social Sciences since 1945.*
Johnston, R. J. (2003), 'Geography and the social science tradition', in Holloway, S., Rice, S., and
    Valentine, G. (eds.) *Key Concepts in Geography*, 51–72.
Wallerstein, I. (1999), 'The heritage of sociology, the promise of social science', *Current Sociology*, 47(1),
    1–37.

social space **1.** An area occupied and used by a community that is perceived to belong
to them by both the group and others, and which holds significant meaning and *sense
of place.
  2. The spatial organization of social and symbolic relations in terms of ties, transactions, and networks amongst a community that might be spread out across boundaries.
  With respect to the first sense, a community is understood to be a relatively homogeneous group in terms of demographic and socio-economic characteristics, shared values,
and place identity. In effect, social spaces consist of neighbourhoods or parts of them,
and *ethnic enclaves are an example. In many cases, the social spaces of different

communities intersect, potentially leading to tension and conflict. In relation to the second sense, social space concerns the social interactions and institutional arrangements that facilitate a community operating both locally and transnationally, including spaces such as the cultural exchanges and events, the *Internet, and mass *media. A family or a community or *diaspora group can be understood as a social or societal space. This second definition, which derives from the sociology of Georg Simmel, recognizes that the relation between social and geographic spaces is contingent. Ludger Pries, for instance, suggests that after a couple of centuries during which social spaces became contiguous with the geographic space of the modern nation state, now various transnational social spaces are forming (*see* TRANSNATIONALISM).

Further reading Pries, L. (ed.) (2001), *New Transnational Social Spaces*.

social stratification The way in which societies are stratified into levels of status depending on various demographic and socio-economic characteristics. *Class, for example, is a form of social stratification, with people stratified on the basis of wealth and social status into working class, middle class, and upper class. Studies of social stratification examine why such strata exist, how they are maintained, and the conditions and opportunities for people in each strata. From a geographical perspective, social stratification is associated with *segregation and distinct residential patterns, with members of a strata living in the same areas.

social theory A large and diverse body of ideas concerned with what *society is and how it works. Social theories usually acknowledge the complex determinations between *power, *ideology, and economic forces in constituting social life as a recognizably coherent and relatively enduring phenomenon. In contrast with sociology, social theory has pretentions to formulate grander or more *essentialist explanations. Manuel *Castells, Anthony *Giddens, and Ulrich Beck might all be described as social theorists. Human geographers began to pay serious attention to social theory in the 1980s. Derek *Gregory, for example, placed social theory alongside cultural studies and *political economy as the three main influences constituting *postmodern geography. The chief geographical aim was to inject space into otherwise aspatial social theories (*see* SPATIAL TURN). The journal *Environment and Planning D: Society and Space* was founded in 1983 to stimulate this exchange.

Further reading Benko, G. and Strohmayer, U. (eds.) (1997), *Space and Social Theory*.
Gregory, D. and Urry, J. (eds.) (1985), *Social Relations and Spatial Structures*.

Sociétié de Géographie de Paris The world's oldest dedicated geographical society founded in December 1821. The society's magazine was first published in 1822 as *Bulletin de la Société de Géographie*, renamed *La Géographie* in 1899, and *Acta Geographica* from 1947, with a gap in publication 1940–46. The society has an extensive library, map, and photograph collection. *See also* GEOGRAPHICAL SOCIETIES.

society An aggregation of individuals connected by inter-personal relations, generally considered larger than and distinct from a family, kinship group, or *community. What a society is and how far it can be considered to possess causal influence has been a major preoccupation of sociologists, though far less so human geographers. For the former, a key question is whether events (e.g. riots) or actions (e.g. suicide) can be explained by reference to individual motivations and agency, or some extra-individual entity, i.e. society (*see* METHODOLOGICAL INDIVIDUALISM; STRUCTURATION). Among human geographers, society has three main senses. The first treats society as something left over when economy, polity, and culture are removed, i.e. it is a residual term. The second, shared by anthropology and history, refers to generic types of human association, e.g. hunter-gatherer societies, pre-industrial societies, or slave-owning societies. In current social theory, examples include *knowledge society and *network society. The third equates society with nation and/or state, as in the phrase, Canadian society. In so doing, a supposedly distinct social form is linked with a territory (*see* METHODOLOGICAL NATIONALISM; TERRITORIAL TRAP). Geographers, like sociologists, assume that society is therefore a meaningful unit of analysis in much the same way as the national economy. How far this is or has ever been the case is open to question. On the one hand, social ties often extend across political boundaries (*see* TRANSNATIONALISM) and on the other, political boundaries move while people stay put: the break-up of the USSR is an example. Within sociology there have been various challenges to the concept of nation/state/ society, including *world-system analysis and *Actor-Network Theory. ANT is rooted in the sociology of association, concerned with explaining how people and things are held together, rather than assuming at the outset that they are. In *Sociology Beyond Societies* (2000) John *Urry has further called for a switch from the study of society as a set of bounded institutions, to exploring globalization through concepts of network, flow, and region (*see* MOBILITY TURN).

sociology of scientific knowledge (SSK) The sociological inquiry into scientific ideas through close scrutiny of the practices of science rather than just its finished output. Emerging in the late 1960s, mainly in the UK, scholars in this field rejected the conventional approach to the sociology of science as exemplified by US sociologist R. K. Merton. Merton focused on scientists as a community rather than their ideas. A group of historians at the University of Edinburgh, Scotland, formulated an alternative approach, often termed the 'strong programme'. The 'weak' programme treated false or wrong ideas in science as the result of social factors but true ideas as the outcome of nature. A theory was true because it corresponded with reality. The strong programme was more agnostic about scientific truth and adopted the principle of symmetry, i.e. false and true beliefs were explained in the same manner. Moreover, proponents rejected the notion that scientific beliefs were simply the result of external interests, such as *religion, *capital, or the power of the *state. They did not distinguish between internal and external or contextual factors but sought continuity between scientific and other social processes. The 'Edinburgh School', including David Bloor and Barry Barnes, specialized in historical studies of science, whereas the parallel 'Bath School' concentrated more on first-hand research in laboratories themselves. The sociology of scientific knowledge is one of the roots of *Science and Technology Studies and is now often subsumed within it. Within human geography, Trevor *Barnes has developed its insights further.

Further reading Barnes, T. J. (2001) '"In the beginning was economic geography"—a science studies approach to disciplinary history', *Progress in Human Geography*. 25: 521–544.
Sismondo, S. (2nd ed. 2010), *An Introduction to Science and Technology Studies*.

socio-nature The indissoluble connections between what we call *nature and what we call *society. Like *social nature, it reflects a non-dualist way of thinking. Erik *Swyngedouw argued that analysing 'nature' and 'society' in abstraction from one another gives us a false picture. Inspired by Karl *Marx's metaphor of 'metabolism' and Bruno *Latour's notions of 'ontological symmetry' and 'actants', Swyngedouw favoured the neologism 'socio-nature' to focus attention on the 'missing middle' between society and nature. This was not a return to *environmental determinism, but it did challenge the claims about nature being simply a *social construction. Unlike some research in which the term *social nature was favoured, that utilizing the term socio-nature paid attention to the material agency of the non-human world. *See also* PRODUCTION OF NATURE.

Reference Swyngedouw, E. (2003), 'Modernity and the production of the Spanish waterscape, 1890–1930', in Bassett, T. and Zimmerer, K. (eds.) *Geographical Political Ecology* 94–112.

SOE *See* STATE-OWNED ENTERPRISE.

soft capitalism A form of *capitalism animated by the intense and widespread circulation of theories of capitalism. As explained by Nigel *Thrift in *Knowing Capitalism* (2005), capitalism has become 'more knowledgeable' in the past thirty years. The economy relies more on ideas and self-consciously new thinking, generated by the intersection of academia and business through business schools, publications, lecture tours, etc. (*see* CULTURAL CIRCUIT OF CAPITAL). Thrift argues that capitalism can therefore only be understood through *cultural economy.

software The lines of code, consisting of instructions and algorithms, that process digital data and tell computer hardware what to do. Software is diverse in nature, including hard-coded applications with no or limited programmability (e.g., embedded on chips), specialized applications (e.g., banking systems), generic user applications (e.g., spreadsheets), and operating systems (e.g., Linux), that run on a variety of hardware platforms (anything that has a digital component). Geographers have been interested in how software shapes spatial processes and the *spatiality of everyday life, and the geography of software development. Recent research has highlighted how software is essential to the functioning of modern cities; how it is deeply embedded into the systems and infrastructure of the built environment, and in the management and governance of urban societies. Software-enabled technologies and services augment and facilitate how cities are planned and understood, how urban services and utilities are managed, and how urban lives are lived. Modes of analysis such as *geodemographics utilizes computational power to 'software-sort' individuals, processing data about them to decide what services and treatment they might receive based on where they live (*see* BIG DATA). The production of software itself has a particular space economy to its creation and circulation. Its operations are organized and structured both sectorally and spatially to enable efficient production, and minimize costs and maximize profit, concentrated into centres such as Silicon Valley, Bangalore, Boston, and Dublin.

Further reading Graham, S. (2005), 'Software-sorted geographies', *Progress in Human Geography* 29: 562–80.
Kitchin, R. and Dodge, M. (2011), *Code/Space: Software and Everyday Life*.

Soja, Edward (1940–) An American urban geographer and planner based at the University of California, Los Angeles. He has been a key advocate of the *spatial turn in the social sciences, arguing for the development of spatially orientated, *postmodern social theory. His key contributions to this project are the books *Postmodern Geographies* (1989), *Thirdspace* (1996), and *Postmetropolis* (2000), which draw upon and extend a range of theoretical influences, but most particularly the ideas of Henri *Lefebvre.

soundscape The audible landscape in which people live. Given the overwhelming dominance of the visual and textual in mediating and describing the social and physical landscape through which everyday life takes place, it is sometimes easy to forget that it is accompanied by other non-visual data that are sensed and shape experience. A soundscape is the noises, speech, and *music that fill space and time, and are encountered daily, providing a soundtrack to human life. Soundscapes are important because they provide strong affective cues and contour emotional responses to places (*see* AFFECT). Certain soundscapes are associated with particular locales, such as the noise of traffic, construction, and crowds with urban spaces, the deep rumblings of planes taking off and landing with airports, and that of animals, the weather, and silences with wilderness. Soundscapes are temporal as well as spatial, ebbing and flowing throughout the day, or only occurring for specific events such as festivals or funerals.

Further reading Smith, S. J. (1994), 'Soundscape', *Area* 26: 232–40.

South *See* GLOBAL SOUTH.

South Africa The southernmost country in *Africa and the continent's largest economy. It has a complex history. From the 17th century, Dutch, British, and other European settlers fought with one another and with African peoples, notably the Xhosa and Zulu for control of the region and its mineral resources (gold and diamonds). Independence from Britain was secured in 1910 but thereafter the country was governed by its white minority until 1994 (*see* APARTHEID). South Africa is an important regional power and its industries employ thousands of immigrant workers from neighbouring countries.

Southeast Asia A region of Asia bordered by *India to the west, *China to the north, and *Australia and Papua New Guinea to the south. The region's countries are conventionally distinguished between a mainland group (also known as Indochina) and an island group, of which *Indonesia is the largest. This group was also termed the East Indies from the 16th century. *See also* ASSOCIATION OF SOUTHEAST ASIAN NATIONS.

South Korea A country in *East Asia occupying the southern half of the Korean peninsula; it was formerly known as the Republic of Korea. It is one of the world's largest economies, and a major exporter of manufactured goods (*see* NEWLY INDUSTRIALIZING COUNTRIES). Until the 1940s the peninsula was a single country, Korea, but following occupation by Japan, and then after 1945 by the *Soviet Union and USA, it was divided into two governments. From 1950–53 the two sides, the communist north (backed by the Soviet Union and China) and the south (backed by the United Nations), fought. The cessation of hostilities entrenched the division, which is still marked by a tense military stand-off.

sovereignty A supreme authority over a political body, usually the territory of a *state and its resident population. Sovereignty is a legal and political concept. It implies that the sovereign entity, which may be a person (e.g. monarch) or a political institution (e.g. elected assembly), possesses the sole legitimate power to makes laws, mint money, raise taxes, imprison criminals, etc. As such, sovereignty has two dimensions. One is internal or domestic; a sovereign power, such as a government, has the right to command its citizens resident in the territory under its authority in ways that no other body, including no other state, can do. This is what distinguished the weakest state from the most powerful transnational corporation. The other is external; sovereignty arises from a system of states and is based upon mutual recognition (*see* WESTPHALIAN MODEL). A state is only sovereign insofar as other sovereign authorities recognize and treat it as such. There are many instances of entities that claim to rightfully govern a territory which are nonetheless not recognized as legitimate authorities by other states; Northern Cyprus, is one example.

Sovereignty is a highly contentious concept within political science, *international relations, and *political geography. Much of the debate is normative, considering not just what sovereignty ought to be but where it ought it lie, i.e. who should exercise sovereign power? From the 17th century onwards, thinkers such as Thomas Hobbes and John Locke have argued over the proper distribution of powers and rights within and between territorial jurisdictions. Does sovereignty lie with the monarch or the people? Is it absolute or conditional? In this regard it is also important to distinguish between sovereignty as an ideal, or *de jure*, and effective or *de facto* sovereignty. Sovereignty as supreme authority has rarely, if ever, existed. Bodies making claims to sovereign authority have always been challenged. States, for instance, do not always possess effective rule over 'their' territories, even if other countries treat them as if they do (*see* COMPLEX EMERGENCIES; FAILED STATES; NARCO-STATES). Moreover, from a *post-structuralist perspective, sovereignty can be understood as a social construction. The issue is not what sovereignty is, but how discourses and practices of sovereignty generate the effects of state power.

Geographers have approached sovereignty principally through its relations with states and *territory. In its ideal form as supreme authority, state sovereignty necessitates the systematic demarcation of land, sea, and air. No two entities can be sovereign over the same space, requiring the delineation of agreed *boundaries (*see* BORDER). But as an effective quality, sovereignty can be pooled, unbundled, and distributed in complex ways (*see* EUROPEAN UNION). Aihwa Ong, for example, uses the term 'graduated sovereignty' to describe the process by which states accord differential rights to spatial zones, citizens, and non-citizens. John *Agnew proposes a distinction between different 'sovereignty regimes' according to their degrees of central state authority (strong or weak), and extent of territoriality (consolidated or open). The classic form of sovereignty has a strong state and its power is consolidated within a given territory. By contrast, under *imperialism, state power is often weaker and sovereignty is generally threatened from within and without (*see* SECESSION). This decoupling of sovereignty and territory can be further extended by the proposition that modes of sovereign authority also circulate through networks or in networked entities.

In addition to discussions of the general relations between sovereignty and space, geographers are also interested in two ongoing debates. One concerns whether the state or nation state is losing its sovereignty in the face of *globalization, the rise of US *hegemony, and/or the formation of supranational bodies exemplified by the European Union (*see* HOLLOWING OUT). One error sometimes made in this debate is the assumption that sovereignty in its ideal form ever actually existed or was universal. In these arguments, sovereignty is also sometimes confused with wider notions of power and influence. Geographical studies of state borders, for example, generally contest the idea that state power is waning. In a second area of inquiry, the opposite assumption is made. In the wake of some of the more extreme actions taken as part of the war on terror, notably the prison camp at *Guantánamo Bay or, more generally, the detention of asylum-seekers in offshore locations, there is growing interest in the idea of sovereignty not as the source of law but as the power to suspend law. Following the ideas of German jurist and philosopher Carl Schmitt, Giorgio Agamben has explored the idea of the 'state of exception', often associated with national states of emergency. This can be extended to spaces of exception, sites where legal protections are withheld (*see* HOMO SACER).

Further reading Agnew, J. (2005), 'Sovereignty regimes: territoriality and state authority in contemporary world politics', *Annals of the Association of American Geographers* 95(2): 437–61.
Dahlman, C. (2010), 'Sovereignty', in Gallaher, C., Dahlman, C. T., Gilmartin, M., Mountz, A., and Shirlow, P., *Key Concepts in Political Geography*, 28–40.
Ong, A. (2006), *Flexible Citizenship*.
Pratt, G. (2005), 'Abandoned women and the spaces of the exception', *Antipode* 37: 1052–78.

sovereign wealth fund An investment fund owned and controlled by a national government and usually used to acquire assets overseas to generate long-term returns. The major funds are based on budgetary surpluses derived from high export earnings, notably from *natural resources such as oil. The returns from funds are used either to counteract the volatility of export earnings from primary commodities or to meet anticipated demands in the future, such as pensions. Norway, Abu Dhabi, and *Singapore operate large sovereign wealth funds, which some argue can redress the problems of *resource curse.

Soviet Union An abbreviated name for the Union of Soviet Socialist Republics (USSR), a multinational and *federal state formed in 1922 and dissolved in 1991. The territory once governed as the USSR now consists of the Russian Federation (or *Russia) and fourteen other sovereign *nation states located in the Baltic Sea region, *Eastern Europe,

the Transcaucasian region, and Central Asia. The USSR covered one sixth of the Earth's
land surface and stretched across eleven time zones from the Baltic Sea to the Bering
Straits, separating it from Alaska, USA. Much of this land was part of the Russian Empire.
But when the Tsar (emperor) was overthrown by revolution in 1917 following a period of
civil war, the Communist Party succeeded in establishing unified rule. The USSR was
governed according to state socialist and *communist principles, including a centrally
planned economy, forced industrialization, and the collectivization of agriculture (*see*
STALINISM). Although allied to the USA during the *Second World War, relations between
the two superpowers worsened after the war resulting in the *Cold War. By the 1980s
secessionist movements were flourishing, notably in the Baltic states, and the tearing
down of the *Berlin Wall in *Germany triggered a series of events leading to dissolution.
Foreign geographers' interest in the Soviet Union was partly motivated by strategic
concerns, but also by the fact that it represented the largest and most thorough attempt
to construct a modern industrial society along non-capitalist lines (*see* CAPITALISM).
This had ramifications for the way cities were organized, land and resources were
used, housing and goods were allocated, and the environment was managed. *See also*
POST-SOCIALISM.

Further reading Brown, A. et al. (eds.) (1982), *The Cambridge Encyclopedia of Russia and the
Soviet Union.*
Pallot, J. and Shaw, D. (1981), *Planning in the Soviet Union.*

space 1. The geometric container in which life takes place and matter exists.
   2. The spatial ordering and arrangement of the world produced through social relations and practices. Like many key conceptual terms, space is understood in a myriad of
different ways. For physicists, space is the geometrical dimensions of the universe
through which objects move and interact. Here, space is understood as a container
and its dimensions and the trajectory of objects moving through it can be understood
through Euclidean geometry and mapped. Prior to the 1950s, geographers implicitly
understood space in this way, but research focused on spatial processes rather than the
nature of space itself. Space was absolute and *essentialized in nature and spatial
processes were *teleological and measureable. The ontology of space was beyond question, it was simply the spatial dimensions in which life took place. With the advent of the
*Quantitative Revolution in the 1960s, geographers started to much more explicitly cast
space as a geometrical system of organization which could be measured objectively
and scientifically and which actively shaped social relations in ways that could be
*modelled and *simulated. Geography was thus recast as a *spatial science that sought
to detail spatial relations and produce spatial laws about *spatial behaviour.
   During the 1970s the concept of absolute space was complemented by that of cognitive
space (*see* COGNITIVE MAPPING). This perspective argued that while the space in which
people live is absolute in nature, it is not perceived or cognized as such. Rather, to be able
to operate in the world and undertake complex spatial choices and decisions, people rely
on spatial understandings of places and their ability to remember and think about spatial
relations. Consequently, human spatial behaviour, and therefore most spatial processes
of note are based on cognitive space—space as mentally constructed. Here, space is
ontologically abstract, representational, and intangible; it is a product of the mind.
   Also developing from the 1970s onwards were relational ontologies of space, first
articulated within human geography by radical geographers. They argued that spatial
science was highly reductionist and that absolute notions of space emptied space of
its meaning and purpose, and failed to recognize the diverse ways in which space
is produced (*see* PRODUCTION OF SPACE). Space, it was argued, was not a given, neutral,
and passive geometry, essentialist and teleological in nature; rather it was relational,
contingent, and active, something that is produced or constructed by people through

social relations and practices. Space is not an absolute geometric container in which social and economic life takes place, rather it is constitutive of such relations. Such thinking posited that the spaces people inhabit—the built environment, transport systems, the countryside—do not simply exist, pre-formed and awaiting meaning. Rather, they and the spatial relations they engender are produced—made, shaped, managed, and given meaning by people; they are the products of diverse material and discursive practices that in turn actively shape social relations. This relational understanding of space is perhaps most fully developed by Henri *Lefebvre in his book *The Production of Space* (1974/1991).

From the early 1980s, *feminist geographers have argued our understanding of space is highly *masculinist, wherein space is cast as something that can be rationally and scientifically understood and mastered. In contrast, Gillian *Rose in *Feminism and Geography* (1993) argued that space is never fully knowable as we can never achieve an all-encompassing, exhaustive god's eye view of the world, only views from particular positions that are differentially shaped. She forwards the notion of *paradoxical space which recognizes that the production of space is complex, *situated, often unrepresentable, and contradictory, producing multidimensional and messy spaces. Moreover, space can be used or thought of in a metaphorical sense; for example, the production of city space is seen as akin to a text that is written and read (city as text), as an organic and living entity (city as body), as a massively complex assemblage of nuts and bolts (city as machine), or as a network of flows and fluxes (city as network).

Some geographers have argued that it makes little sense to think of space without including time as they are mutually constitutive. They suggest we should think not about time or space but of *time-space. Such a conceptualization has its roots in the work of Torsten *Hagerstrand and his notion of *time-geography, but is now usually infused by post-structural thought that understands time-space as multiple, relational, contingent, dynamic, and paradoxical.

More recently, ontogenetic conceptions of space have been forwarded. These shift the focus of the debate concerning the ontology of space from 'what space is' to 'how space becomes.' Space, they argue, is not ontologically secure—a fixable, definable, knowable, pre-determined entity; rather, space is always in the process of becoming; it is always in the process of taking place. Here, space gains its form, function, and meaning through practice. From this perspective space can be understood as a verb rather than a noun, 'spacing' as opposed to 'space'.

Space, far from being simply the container in which everyday life takes place, is open to various different conceptualizations. All of these different ways of thinking about space are presently being used by geographers. For example, absolute conceptions of space still predominate in spatial science and *GIScience, and relative conceptions of space are popular with radical and feminist geographers.

Further reading Crang, M. and Thrift, N. (2000), *Thinking Space*.
Gatrell, A. (1983), *Distance and Space: a Geographic Perspective*.
Kitchin, R. and Dodge, M. (2011), *Code/Space*.
Massey, D. (2005), *For Space*.

Space and Place   A text by Yi-Fu *Tuan (1977), who was at the forefront of developing and promoting *humanistic geography. *Space and Place* was his second much cited, seminal contribution to the debate, after *Topophilia*, intersecting geography with ideas from philosophy, art, psychology, and religion. The focus of Tuan's analysis is a person's experience and attachment to *place, and concepts such as *home, neighbourhood, and *nation, and the ways in which people feel and think about space, and the role of time. For Tuan, space is open, free, ineffable, and taken for granted, the landscape in which things take place, whereas place is space once it is known and has personal meanings attached. For him, place is security and space is freedom, where we are attached to the one and long for the other.

space-economy The *economy as understood in spatial terms. There are two uses of the term in human geography. One originates with the pioneering *location theory of von *Thünen and *Lösch, updated by Walter Isard in the 1950s as part of *regional science. The space-economy is the object to be explained by location theory, i.e. the spatial distribution of economic activities and their linkages. Using the term implies that economic ideas in isolation are insufficient. This meaning has lapsed, and the term 'spatial economy' is now more widely used, e.g. in *Fujita, Krugman, and Venables' book *The Spatial Economy* (1999). The other use (often without a hyphen) is within *Marxist geography, where it captures the idea that the capitalist landscape and capitalist processes of accumulation and circulation are dialectically related (*see* CAPITALISM). This is elaborated by Eric *Sheppard and Trevor *Barnes in their book *The Capitalist Space Economy* (1990).

space-for-time substitution A technique for using different aged sites to infer a temporal trend where a continuous record is absent. It is used in studies of ecology and archaeology to construct a chronosequence of development or events, noting the vegetation or artefacts at different locations and then, assuming that the sites are subject to the same conditions and processes, hypothesizing the factors underpinning transitions from one phase to another. It is also called ergodic reasoning.

space of exception *See* SOVEREIGNTY.

space of flows The dominant spatial logic of the *network society according to Manuel *Castells. As set out in *The Rise of the Network Society* (2nd ed. 2000) this abstract concept has three material layers: circuits of electronic exchanges; nodes and hubs, e.g. *global cities; and the spatial practices of the dominant managerial elites, including their exclusive social networks and the sites that sustain their privileged lifestyle, e.g. *gated communities or VIP lounges in airports (*see* KINETIC ELITE). There is a disjuncture between the space of flows and the 'space of places', where non-elites reside; Castells' example is Belleville, a Parisian working-class immigrant district.

Spain A country in southwest Europe sharing the Iberian peninsula with Portugal. The Balearic Islands in the western Mediterranean, the Canary Islands in the Atlantic Ocean, and two small *exclaves in North Africa are also part of Spain. Between the 15th and 19th centuries the Spanish empire included other parts of Europe, Asia, and, above all, large swathes of the Americas. For much of the 20th century it was governed by the *fascist regime (1936–75) of General Franco but joined the *European Union (then Community) in 1986. Madrid is the capital and Barcelona the other major metropolitan area. Spain's regions have strong independent identities and the political system is quasi-*federal. Decades of political stability and prosperity have been threatened by the consequences of the 2007 global economic crisis, to which Spain is highly exposed.

Spate, O. H. K. (1911–2000) A British regional and historical geographer best known for his role in the development of Australian geography as the foundation professor of geography at the Australian National University, a position he took up in 1951. His first teaching post was at the University of Rangoon (in what was then Burma, now Myanmar). After service in the *Second World War, Spate took up a post at the London School of Economics specializing in the study of South Asia, before moving to Canberra where he broadened his focus to the study of the *Pacific Rim.

spatial analysis The mapping and statistical analysis of spatial properties and patterns. Spatial analysis grew in popularity in the 1960s with the rise of *quantitative geography and *location and *network analysis. With the development of *GIS, spatial analysis has become a mainstream policy tool for making sense of spatial data and for aiding companies to plan their activities. *See also* CENSUS GEOGRAPHY; GEOCOMPUTATION; GEODEMOGRAPHICS; SPATIAL SCIENCE; SPATIAL STATISTICS.

spatial autocorrelation A measure of the similarity or interdependence of an object in space with surrounding objects. Spatial autocorrelation is intuitively necessary in geographic space, since without it, the distribution of phenomena would be independent of location, and thus random. Clearly, the spatial distribution of phenomena is not random. As *Tobler's First Law of Geography denotes, things near to each other are more likely to be alike than those further apart. For example, in a city *segregated by religion such as Belfast, a Catholic's neighbour is more likely to be another Catholic than a Protestant. The fact that many geographic phenomena are autocorrelated—that is the same or similar to its neighbours—provides a problem for classical statistics that assume independence of observations in its *sampling and analysis. Consequently, a number of statistical techniques have been developed to measure and model patterns of spatial dependency in data, which include the *variogram and methods of *fractal analysis.

Further reading Goodchild, M. (1986), *Spatial Autocorrelation*.

spatial behaviour How humans act spatially in terms of making spatial choices and decisions. Spatial behaviour is the core focus of *behavioural geography and concerns the analysis of people's time-space activity patterns, how people *wayfind and select routes, how they make decisions about movement and *migration, and how they make location choices such as where to live and shop. Such research is also interested in how people acquire spatial knowledge and how this shapes their spatial behaviour. Some studies have extended this work to examine the spatial behaviour of *animals. *See also* CHOICE MODELLING; COGNITIVE MAPPING.

Further reading Golledge, R. G. and Stimson, R. (1997), *Spatial Behaviour: a Geographic Perspective*.

spatial covariation A measure of the degree to which two spatial variables are interdependent, so that as one changes, the other changes as well. Spatial data are often covariant because things near to each other are often similar in nature. As a consequence, *spatial statistics have to account for high degrees of covariance between what would ideally be independent variables. *See also* SPATIAL AUTOCORRELATION; TOBLER'S FIRST LAW OF GEOGRAPHY.

spatial data infrastructure (SDI) A framework for the storing, exchange, and use of geospatial data and associated *metadata related to a region or nation. The SDI aims to pull together the plethora of spatial data sets related to an area, to provide a common set of data standards and formats, and to make data available for analysis, along with suitable *GIS tools. Many national governments have national SDIs under development, and organizations such as the *European Union are seeking to implement supranational SDIs through its INSPIRE programme.

SEE WEB LINKS
• European Commission site on the INSPIRE directive.

spatial data mining The *data mining of spatial databases to identify interesting and useful spatial patterns. Given the size and complexity of many spatial databases, data mining methods apply techniques such as *cluster analysis to determine patterns within the data and to extract data of particular interest. Learning-based data mining methods, such as *neural networks, seek to train the programme how to identify similar patterns elsewhere in the data sets.

spatial diffusion *See* DIFFUSION.

spatial division of labour The distribution of different stages of economic activity across space, leading to the specialization of work within particular places at a range of scales (*see* DIVISION OF LABOUR; INTERNATIONAL DIVISION OF LABOUR). Although the term is most closely associated with Doreen *Massey and her book about regional differences in the UK, *Spatial Divisions of Labour* (1984), it is widely applicable at international and local scales. A simple example at the international scale is the way that command-and-control functions of *transnational corporations cluster in *global cities, research and development activities locate in regions of highly skilled labour, while simple component manufacturing takes place in low-wage regions in the *Global South. At a smaller scale, a study by Kristin Nelson showed how employers moved to the suburbs of the San Francisco Bay Area in order to tap the local supply of middle-class white women prepared to work part-time. In other words, the geographical reorganization of economic activity creates a spatial division of labour but also relies upon it. In this sense, the spatial division of labour is one facet of the general territorial relations between *capital and labour which have the potential to be conflict-ridden (*see* LABOUR GEOGRAPHY).

Reference Nelson, K. (1986), 'Labour demand, labour supply and the suburbanization of low-wage office work', in Scott, A. J. and Storper, M. (eds.) *Production, Work, Territory* 149–71.

Spatial Divisions of Labour, The A ground-breaking book by Doreen *Massey (1984); informed by Marxist geographical understandings of *uneven development and intended to demonstrate the significance of *space, it considered the relationships between the spatial restructuring of *capital and labour in the UK. Massey argued that the reorganization of production across rather than within regions generally weakened the power of labour but had different effects according to specific regional contexts. There was an updated second edition in 1995.

spatial econometrics A form of econometrics (the statistical analysis of economic data) that takes account of spatial interaction and structure. It thus inflects econometrics with spatial statistics. Spatial econometrics is typically used within economics, geography, and *regional science to analyse the nature of the *space-economy, and the location, flow, and movement of goods and services.

spatial economics The study of problems of location and resource allocation over space using the theories, concepts, and models of economics. Although its subject matter overlaps considerably with *economic geography and *regional science, it relies more on modelling. *See also* NEW ECONOMIC GEOGRAPHY.

spatial entrapment The inability of a worker to access employment outside a geographically limited *labour market area. Low-paid, low-skilled workers are especially vulnerable to spatial entrapment, as are women with domestic responsibilities who cannot stray too far from home each day. Spatial entrapment can prevent workers getting a job, or limit them to poorly paid jobs, or ones with inferior terms and conditions. Attempts by workers to overcome entrapment can involve excessive journey-to-work times and monetary costs. *See also* SPATIAL MISMATCH.

spatial fetishism The assignment of causal power to space *per se* in determining human action. In other words, space is understood to explain social and economic relations. Examples include the propositions that 'urban form shapes the nature of a community' and 'the core exploits the periphery'. Such a position, often implicitly and explicitly adopted within *quantitative geography and *spatial science, has been critiqued by many human geographers who argue that space is the product of social and economic processes that unfold spatially, not vice versa.

Further reading Gregory, D. and Urry, J. (eds.) (1985), *Social Relations and Spatial Structures.*

spatial fix The channelling of liquid *capital into various forms of fixed capital in order to postpone or provide a solution to a crisis of over-accumulation of the kind endemic to *capitalism. The term is associated with Marxist geographer David *Harvey. He noticed that in the lead up to and aftermath of a major economic crisis 'capital switching occurs'. *Money is diverted into expensive, long-lasting infrastructures such as roads and airports. These investments slow down the turnover time of capital in one part of the economy, only to speed it up when they subsequently help to produce new rounds of commodity production. The 'fix' is thus only ever temporary, and new built environments may later need to be destroyed so that surplus capital can be sunk into building newer ones. *See also* UNEVEN DEVELOPMENT.

spatial identity The *identity or perceived image of a place, as opposed to identities of individuals who live there. Each place has characteristics that make it unique and which help shape a *sense of place and how it is viewed and perceived. This spatial identity changes over time, evolving with material changes to the environment, and discursive portrayals of the place in the *media and through *place marketing campaigns. *See also* GENIUS LOCI.

spatial interaction The interdependent movement and flow of people, goods, services, information, and finance between locations. Rather than simply being about movement *per se*, spatial interaction seeks to place such movement in context, and to recognize the interdependence of interactions; that is, flow has consequences at origin, destination, and along the route. *See also* MOBILITY; SPATIAL INTERACTION MODEL.

spatial interaction model (SIM) An application and extension of the *gravity model to model flows of people, goods, and services between places in a network. SIMs calculate likely movements, such as migration, between nodes based on their distance apart and the relative weight of the node with respect to some phenomena, such as population size or the characteristics of the migrants. A range of different statistical methodologies have been applied to the technique including *generalized linear models, *Poisson regression, maximum likelihood, and *neural networks. Spatial interaction models are widely applied in *demography, *transportation, and *regional science to compute likely flows under different scenarios.

Further reading Fotheringham, A. S. and O'Kelly, M. (1989), *Spatial Interaction Models.*

spatiality A term that denotes socially produced space, rather than space conceived in absolute terms. That is, spatiality recognizes the roles people play in creating space and the interaction between space and human action. Spatiality denotes the idea that rather than space being a backdrop to social life, it is constitutive of social life; social and spatial relations are mutually constituted. *See also* PRODUCTION OF SPACE; SOJA, EDWARD.

spatialization A process that converts data which have no geographic referents into a map-like form. Spatialization provides a means of *visualizing, *navigating, and comprehending such non-spatial data. It works by applying a spatial topological structure through the application of concepts such as hierarchy and proximity (nearness/likeness). Such spatializations are often applied to large amounts of non-spatial information, for example, creating a map of thousands of webpages by grouping pages with similar semantic content in the same part of the spatialization.

Further reading Dodge, M. and Kitchin, R. (2000), *Mapping Cyberspace.*

spatial justice Whereas social *justice tends to focus on the inequalities between people, spatial justice focuses on the disparities between places. Given the uneven spatial distribution of resources and rights, with some places better served than others, spatial justice seeks a fairer redistribution. Spatial justice also recognizes that some places receive a disproportionate share of harmful practices that exposes the local population to risks, such as the siting of a polluting industry, which it seeks to ameliorate.

spatial memory The ability to remember spatial information concerning locations and layout. Spatial memory has been studied extensively in cognitive psychology, *behavioural geography, and neuroscience. In geography, it most often takes the form of *cognitive mapping studies.

spatial mismatch The proposition that high rates of joblessness are partly caused by the geographical separation of areas of labour supply and demand within a metropolitan area, coupled with inadequate means of transport to connect the two. US economist John Kain suggested the idea in the 1960s to account for how racial residential segregation limited employment opportunities for African-Americans. Trapped by discriminatory housing markets in inner urban areas, they were either unable to access jobs in the suburbs or were unaware of them in the first place.

spatial monopoly A market monopoly with respect to an area, where a single company or *cartel monopolizes access to a particular good or service within that locale. Spatial monopolies can arise through competition, where a trader successfully out-trades its competition, forcing them out of an area, or through a distance function where consumers travel to the nearest supplier, providing that supplier with a natural catchment free of competition, or through collusion where rival companies agree to carve up the market into sole areas of trading.

spatial ontology The classification of phenomena into different spatial categories. A spatial ontology is essential for making *maps and using *GIS and is created by dividing the world up into different features and zones (e.g., land use classes, administrative boundaries), which are often ordered hierarchically, and detailing the relationships between them (e.g., intersects, touches, crosses, within, contains, overlaps), according to logical principles. If different spatial ontologies are used within or between jurisdictions it can make comparison difficult (e.g., if two different land use classifications are employed). Within *critical GIS there is a recognition that spatial ontologies are not pre-given, but rather there are diverse ways of constructing them that may lead to multiple interpretations (see ECOLOGICAL FALLACY; MODIFIABLE AREAL UNIT PROBLEM).

Spatial Organization: The Geographer's View of the World A book written by Ron *Abler, John Adams, and Peter *Gould (1971), it was an influential introductory textbook to quantitative geography that forwarded the notion of a scientific, human geography (see SPATIAL SCIENCE). The book positions geography as a science of spatial *laws and *theories, and through its five parts examines issues of measurement, relationships and classification, spatial structure, and processes with regards to *spatial interaction, *diffusion, and decision-making, finishing with a chapter on the future of geography. The book was a standard text, particularly in North America, introducing students to *spatial analysis.

spatial planning The geographical expression, implementation, and coordination of public policy across sectors and scales. Typically *planning has been practised as a relatively discrete set of domains (urban, regional, transport, environmental planning) and mostly concerned with *land use. Spatial planning seeks a more holistic approach that aims to combine and translate sector-based policy (economic, social, transport, energy) into a spatial form, recognizing that how a policy is geographically integrated and implemented will make a difference to its success. It does so by creating a spatial plan that expresses where and in what form policy will unfold, coordinates and aligns initiatives to avoid duplication of effort or divergent policies being adopted, and sets out the governance framework for delivery. These plans are multi-scalar, with local plans nesting inside regional plans, that nest inside national plans, and sometimes cross jurisdictions. As such, spatial planning seeks to create long-term, sustainable frameworks for social, territorial, and economic development, both within and between countries by integrating policy between sectors such as housing, transport, energy, and industry, and to improve national and local systems of development. Many governments have recently devised national spatial plans, especially in Europe, where the adoption of the European Spatial Development Perspective and the creation of European Spatial Planning Observation Network, that links together spatial planning across member states, have been important. This is being supported by the development of national *spatial data infrastructures to provide the necessary spatial data and tools to create evidence-informed spatial plans.

Further reading Dühr, S., Colomb, C., and Nadin, V. (2010), *European Spatial Planning and Territorial Cooperation*.

SEE WEB LINKS
- Official website for ESPON European Observation Network for Territorial Development and Cohesion.

spatial science **1.** An approach to human geography centred on the analysis of spatial patterns and processes through quantitative methods, with the ultimate aim of establishing spatial laws.

2. A collective term for *GIS, *cartography, *remote sensing, *photogrammetry, *surveying, geodesy, and related disciplines concerned with scientific spatial analysis, sometimes also termed 'spatial sciences'.

The first sense generally refers to a period in the history of geography between the late 1950s and early 1970s when spatial analysis was the discipline's cutting edge. It is also synonymous with the *Quantitative Revolution. The second sense is often used to imply a set of academic and technical interests separate from but also complementary to geography. It is widely used in the USA and Australia in this sense.

Understood as a period in geographical history, spatial science is generally interpreted as a reaction to the dominant approach of mid-20th-century Anglo-American geography that focused on *regional geography using a range of descriptive tools. It was given impetus by the perceived failings of geography to provide adequate scientific knowledge during the *Second World War, by the growing intervention of the post-war state in *spatial planning, and the general investment into the physical and mathematical sciences during the *Cold War (*see* REGIONAL SCIENCE). Whereas geography before the war was strongly influenced by the life sciences, as were *social sciences in general, from the 1950s concepts and models from physics, mathematics, geometry, and the new cybernetic sciences assumed importance. Many of the new ideas in geography took the form of direct analogies, e.g. the *gravity model (*see* REILLY'S LAW).

If there was a guiding scientific epistemology it was *logical positivism, although it cannot be said that it was thoroughly applied. This held out the prospect of the progress of science through the formulation of universal laws. It was anticipated that spatial laws, which would be the preserve of geographical inquiry, might lead to explanations of spatial interaction, spatial diffusion, and spatial patterns. In the spirit of *modernity, explaining spatial patterns and processes was a precondition for better planning, of transport networks, industrial location, the siting of public services, etc. (*see* MODELLING).

*Locational analysis, which partly rested on the revival of ideas dating back to the 1830s, was a significant field of research and modelling (*see* LÖSCH MODEL; VON THÜNEN MODEL). The search for spatial regularities was aided by the development of spatial *models, the application of geometry to spatial patterns, and the wider use of *inferential and *spatial statistics. The ability to understand and use these techniques differentiated a generation of younger geographers from the colleagues, adding to the sense of profound change.

The immediate outcome of spatial science was mixed. It undoubtedly revived geography as a university discipline and influenced a generation of school geography teaching. Whether spatial laws were or even could be discovered was less certain, though *Tobler's first law of geography provided a start. To some, it was questionable whether there could be specifically *spatial* laws when space was not independent of time and matter (*see* SPATIAL FETISHISM). The preoccupation with space in isolation was described as 'spatial separatism'. Nor was it all-pervasive. Spatial science developed in various universities, though by no means all geography departments. The universities of Iowa and Washington, Seattle were at the forefront, along with the universities of Chicago and Northwestern University, Illinois. Outside the USA, Bristol and Cambridge in England and Lund in Sweden were important centres (*see* ABLER, RONALD F.; BERRY, BRIAN J. L.; GARRISON, WILLIAM; HÄGERSTRAND, TORSTEN; HAGGETT, PETER; ISARD, WALTER; SCHAEFER, F. K.; ULLMAN, EDWARD). *Trevor Barnes has examined the historical geography of spatial science with considerable detail and sophistication.

If spatial science in one sense endured relative decline with the rise of *radical and *humanistic geography, its core methods and insights were carried forward, and later extended by the growth of spatial sciences in general, aided by significant advances in computation, spatial data handling, and modelling (*see* GEOCOMPUTATION, GEOVISUALIZATION, GEOGRAPHICAL INFORMATION SCIENCE).

Further reading Barnes, T. J. (2001), 'Lives lived and lives told: biographies of geography's quantitative revolution', *Environment and Planning D: Society and Space* 19: 409–29.
Barnes, T. J. and Farish, M. (2006), 'Between regions: science, militarism, and American geography from World War to Cold War', *Annals of the Association of American Geographers* 96: 807–26.
Johnston, R. J. and Sidaway, J. (6th ed. 2004), *Geography and Geographers*.

spatial statistics The statistics that examine the nature of spatial variation by extending statistical analysis to spatial forms. In general, spatial statistics are used to describe and interpret four main spatial forms—points, lines, areas, and volumes—as well as calculate *spatial interaction and spatial *autocorrelation, and other spatial processes.

Further reading Bailey, T. and Gatrell, A. C. (1995), *Interactive Spatial Data Analysis*.

spatial structure The spatial arrangement of and relationship between phenomena. Human geography is often interested in the nature of a place's spatial structure, how it is organized, and the spatial processes that have led to that arrangement, and conversely how spatial structure shapes socio-economic processes. While *quantitative geographers seek to measure and chart the geometries of spatial structure and model the processes that created it, other geographers are interested in how spatial structure is both the medium and outcome of socio-spatial and political-economic processes. *See also* LOCATION ANALYSIS; PRODUCTION OF SPACE; SPATIAL ANALYSIS; SPATIAL FETISHISM.

spatial turn A heightened engagement with the concepts and ideas of *space that spread across the *social sciences and *humanities from the 1990s onwards. Although this is an instance of *interdisciplinarity, the growing interest in space among sociologists, historians, cultural theorists, etc., was not simply a newfound interest in human geography as a whole. Edward *Soja, the US geographer and planner, recognized and championed a spatial turn in the 1990s. In his view, it was a necessary corrective to the dominance of historical thinking, or historicism, in social theory. He noted how many thinkers not normally associated with geography, including Manuel *Castells, Michel *Foucault, Henri *Lefebvre, and John Berger were or had engaged with ideas of space and *spatiality. Insofar as there has been a spatial turn, it is likely to be related to a number of ongoing developments including *postmodernism (and notably postmodern *urbanism), globalization, and mobility. Geographical conceptions of space often proved to be less metaphorical and immaterial than the ideas previously circulating in cultural and social studies. For example, the idea of *deterritorialization could be refined by greater awareness of geographical inquiries. An interest in *networks of all kinds also established some common ground. Finally, advances in digital mapping and spatial data analysis also found new audiences. Franco Moretti, for example, mapped the plots of literary works in his *Atlas of the European Novel 1800–1900* (1999).

Further reading Warf, B. and Arias, S. (eds.) (2008), *The Spatial Turn*.

Special Economic Zone (SEZ) An area of *China designated for development and the attraction of *foreign direct investment (*see* EXPORT PROCESSING ZONE). In 1979, four SEZs were established, in Shantou, Shenzen, Xiamen, and Zhuhai, each located on the country's southeast coast. They offered tax concessions, exceptions to import duties, and infrastructure to international investors. SEZs were successful in kick-starting China's export-led economic boom, and were followed by similar smaller zones throughout the country.

spectacle An arrangement designed for visual impact. There are at least three main uses of the term in human geography.

1. One describes distinct or extravagant events, e.g. the opening ceremony of an *Olympic Games, a *carnival parade, or even possibly a riot.

2. A second usage refers to how certain urban quarters have been planned to appeal to the consumption desires of the middle classes by their concentration of restaurants, museums, and entertainment venues (*see* URBAN REGENERATION). The chief examples of such urban spectacles are *waterfront developments, e.g. Sydney's Darling Harbour.

3. The third meaning of spectacle comes from *Situationism. In *La Société du Spectacle* (1967) Guy Debord describes how social life has been so thoroughly colonized by commodities that social relations are always mediated by images (*see* COMMODITY FETISHISM).

spillover An unpriced and indirect effect of economic activity, also known as an *externality. Economic geographers assert that where firms are located close to others, their productivity rises as a result of proximity. Knowledge spillovers are the basis of *Marshallian districts, although they are difficult to identify empirically.

Spivak, Gayatri (1942–) An Indian post-colonial literary theorist who has championed deconstruction, post-colonial feminism, and *subaltern studies. After graduating from the Presidency College of the University of Calcutta, she moved the United States to undertake graduate work. She took a post at Columbia University, New York in 1992. Her work on the subaltern, *positionality and the *ethnocentricity of Western knowledge production has been particularly influential.

spontaneous settlement A term sometimes used to describe how low-income urban residents rapidly construct dwellings on whatever land becomes available. The assumption that no planning is involved may be incorrect however. *See also* SHANTY TOWN; SQUATTING.

sport(s) A form of organized and rule-based *recreation involving a degree of skill, physical exertion, and competition between teams or individuals. By some definitions, mental activities such as chess are classified as sports, but in common understanding they involve some form of kinetic bodily activity. This is often in association with specialized equipment or prosthetic devices (cycles, running shoes, oars, etc.) or in concert with animals, e.g. horse racing. Sport is both a passive, i.e. spectator, and active, i.e. participant activity, and the degree of regulation varies from casual play to internationally codified and sanctioned rules. A small number of sports are played across the world; the 2010 Vancouver winter Olympic games featured 15 sports and there were 36 at the 2012 London summer Olympics. But there are thousands of others that are more national or local.

There is an intrinsic relation between sports and human geography. Much sport is a form of competition in and for space, with territorial positions, relative locations, and distance being key elements. Organized sports are generally bounded in some way, in arenas, tracks, stadiums, and related surfaces. Moreover, sports involve bodies moving in and so making space and its qualities; Derek McCormack notes how the quality of a field is transformed once it is populated by moving football players. But, strangely, the geographical study of sport has been more established outside academic geography than within. Early authorities in the geography of sport include US geographer John F Rooney, who wrote *A Geography of American Sport* (1976), and British geographer John Bale. Including work done in sports studies more widely, sport has, however, been studied from most of the perspectives recognizable to human geography. The origin and diffusion of organized sports, from folk beginnings though nationally organized leagues and regulations in the 19th century to the current era of globalization, forms an important theme. The links between organized and competitive sport, nationalism and the urban working classes from the 1880s onwards are informative. The role of empire in diffusing games was significant, the more so when former colonies began to defeat imperial masters, as happens with cricket. Internationalizing sports also revealed important differences in regional culture and style, for example, in the contrasting way baseball is played in Japan and the USA. The regional aspect of sports is also apparent in the uneven production of athletes; Texas, for example, produced a disproportionately high number of collegiate (American) football players in the 1970s according to Rooney.

Place and location are also important concepts in understanding sports. Organized sports are associated with specific sites and teams with specific locations. Fans are attached to places through allegiance to sports teams, sometimes vicariously through satellite television and the Internet. There are studies of how home advantage and environmental variation affects performance, but also of how, why, and with what consequences sports teams often relocate their bases within or between cities. This can be extended into what John Bale describes as the *imaginative geographies of sports, the ways in which perceptions of places and even countries are shaped by relations to sport. Another area of study is therefore the impact of sports and sporting activity on individual and community well-being. These effects can be positive, but also negative; for example, the impact of noise and disturbance around match days (*see* EXTERNALITIES). Some sports, for example, golf and alpine skiing, have potentially significant environmental impacts. Finally, there is growing interest in the individual sporting body, and the *emotional, *affective, and *performative dimensions of participation. Although not framed as sports geography, Justin Spinney's account of cyclists on Mont Ventoux, France, suggests what kinds of directions could be further pursued.

References and further reading Bale, J. (2nd ed. 2003), *Sports Geography*.
Giulianotti, R. and Robertson, R., (eds.) (2007), *Globalization and Sport*.
McCormack, D. P. (2008), 'Geographies for moving bodies: thinking, dancing, spaces', *Geography Compass*: 1822–36.

Spinney, J. (2006), 'A place of sense: a kinaesthetic ethnography of cyclists on Mont Ventoux', *Environment and Planning D: Society and Space* 24(5): 709–32.

squatting The occupation of property or land without recognized legal entitlement, and without meeting the requirements of land and building regulations. In rural areas, squatting may be a strategy by the landless or rural poor to obtain land for cultivation. In urban areas, squatters may take over abandoned or empty buildings. In many European cities, squatters organized forms of communal residence, notably Christiana, a settlement on the site of an old barracks in Copenhagen, Denmark that began in 1971. More commonly, squatting is found in cities across Asia, Africa, the Caribbean, and Latin America, where up to half or more of a city's dwellers may not have secure title to their dwellings.

SSK *See* SOCIOLOGY OF SCIENTIFIC KNOWLEDGE.

stable population A population with unchanging rates of fertility and mortality, leading to a constant age distribution and growth rate.

stages of growth model A model of economic *development proposed by Walt W. Rostow in the early 1960s, based on the idea that there are five key stages of growth in a country's development, from traditional society to high mass consumption. He suggested that during a critical 'take-off period' of ten to thirty years, a society could be rapidly transformed with the appropriate policies on infrastructure, investment, and savings. *See also* MODERNIZATION THEORY.

Stalinism The political ideas and practices associated with Joseph Stalin (1879–1953), who ruled the Soviet Union between 1923 and 1953 as General Secretary of the Communist Party. Stalin's rule featured the extensive use of judicial and non-judicial violence against opponents, in the form of killings, purges, incarceration, and forced population movement. The party dominated political and public life. He prioritized heavy industry in the economy and forced through the collectivization of agriculture, leading to great suffering. After his death the Soviet Union's new leaders repudiated many of his methods and acts.

standpoint theory A critical epistemological position that challenges conventional understandings of objectivity and neutrality in science. Although it is now largely identified with feminism, the roots of standpoint logic go back further, including into Marx's work (*see* FEMINIST STANDPOINT THEORY; MARXISM). Sandra Harding has suggested there are five main propositions. Firstly, the structure of societies has epistemological consequences; one's material life limits what one can know about the world and oneself. Secondly, in hierarchical societies (which almost all are), the understandings possessed by the ruling and the ruled will be diametrically opposed. Slave-owners, for example, understand the world in ways opposed and different to how slaves see things. Thirdly, rulers' understandings are nonetheless made real and operative, not least through the natural and social sciences. Fourthly, to challenge these understandings takes intellectual work by those dominated. As Harding puts it, standpoint is 'an achievement, not an ascription'. Finally, this work has the possibility of liberation or social transformation. Harding is keen, however, to distinguish this kind of 'strong objectivity' from the various forms of relativism characteristic of *postmodernism. That is to say, standpoint theorists do believe that some accounts of the world are better than others.

Further reading Harding, S. (2003), 'Standpoint methodology', in. Turner, S. P. and Roth, P. A. (eds.) *The Blackwell Guide to the Philosophy of the Social Sciences*, 291–310.

state **1.** A political organization larger than a household or kinship group, capable of exercising coercion over a given territory.

2. A political community organized under a central government within a defined territory, commonly referred to as a country, e.g. Malawi (*see* NATION STATE).

3. A component unit of a federal government, e.g. Kansas (*see* FEDERALISM).

The state is among the most pervasive but also elusive concepts in human geography. Some clarification can be achieved by distinguishing between a historical perspective, interested in how the state has changed over time, and a more systematic focus on the modern state, how it functions, and what forms it takes. Historians recognize state-like forms of political organization as far back as the 10th century in various regions across the world. They seem to have emerged in response to the need to organize resources for warfare. City states flourished from the 14th century, notably in Europe, where they were associated with the control of trade and economic activity. At the same time, certain dynastic rulers succeeded in commanding larger territories, the basis of the modern nation state. City and nation states co-existed with *empires (*see* IMPERIALISM). Between the 17th and early 19th centuries, these larger national states became the norm in Europe and, especially after 1945, the near universal form of political and territorial organization. The main point to take from this perspective is that the modern nation state, sometimes assumed to be the normal or natural way that societies are governed, is a relatively recent innovation (Brenner 1999).

A second perspective considers the state as a set of institutions with key functions. For liberal theorists, such as John Locke, the state is an impartial arbiter of social life; individuals willingly cede some of their rights to a central authority, which in return guarantees a measure of protection and common welfare (*see* SOVEREIGNTY). Liberals might differ over how much power that state should wield; neoliberals favour less intervention, supporters of the welfare state desire more (*see* NEOLIBERALISM). Marxists, by contrast, regard the state—at least under *capitalism—as an instrument by which the owners of capital (the bourgeoisie) dominate the working class, although there are debates as to how far the state itself can be an arena of class struggle (*see* MARXISM; POLITICAL ECONOMY). The main function of the state is to enable capital accumulation on the one hand and secure the reproduction of labour force by, for example, investing in health and education on the other. Radical feminist perspectives emphasize the state's role in sustaining the conditions for *patriarchy, for example, through the provisions and rules for taxation and social benefits (Chouinard 2004). By contrast to these approaches, social constructionists focus on how certain practices—for example, the policing of international boundaries—produce the structural effect of the state (Mitchell 1991). Finally, a concern for what the state does leads to typologies of different kinds of state (Coe et al. 2007). Neoliberal states, such as the USA, combine liberal democracy with reliance on the *market economy, whereas welfare states, such as Germany, have a more extensive system of social support based on the values of *social cohesion (*see* DEVELOPMENTAL STATE; FAILED STATE; NARCO-STATE).

There has been and continues to be wide-ranging debate about the state among human geographers. Andrew Herod notes three distinct ways of thinking about the state geographically. Within the *geopolitik tradition, Friedrich *Ratzel and later Rudolph Kjellén conceived of the state in organismic terms. The state as an organism needed resources (land) to grow, thereby driving territorial expansion and the growth of larger states at the expense of smaller ones (*see* LEBENSRAUM). These ideas gave way to more functionalist, systematic conceptions of the state as spatial container of society, politics, culture, and economics. As expressed in the work of Richard *Hartshorne, Jean Gottmann, and others, the state was understood as the basic unit of territorial control. Its role was to organize people and resources materially and ideationally by, for example, constructing integrative transport systems. Later geographers critiqued this container idea for naturalizing the relationship between the state and territory (*see* METHODOLOGICAL NATIONALISM; TERRITORIAL TRAP). Herod's third geographical idea of the state recognizes the limitations of the container idea, and uses concepts of *network and *assemblage to conceive of it in more dispersed, less coherent forms. This is accompanied by a decentring of the state within *political geography more generally. *See also* BORDERS; GOVERNMENTALITY; HOLLOWING OUT; STATE APPARATUS.

References and further reading Brenner, N. J. (1999), 'Beyond state-centrism? Space, territoriality and geographical scale in globalization studies', *Theory and Society* 28: 39–78.
Chouinard, V. (2004), 'Making feminist sense of the state and citizenship', in Staeheli, L. A. and Kofman, E. (eds.) *Mapping Women, Making Politics*, 227–43.
Coe, N., Kelly, P., and Yeung, H. W-C. (2007), *Economic Geography*.
Herod, A. (2011), *Scale*.
Mitchell, T. (1991), 'The limits of the state: beyond statistical approaches and their critics', *American Political Science Review* 85: 77–96.

state apparatus The set of institutions and organizations through which the *state governs to: establish the conditions for successful economic growth; foster social cohesion by providing for the well-being of the population, e.g. through a welfare state; and secure its own legitimacy in the eyes of the populace.

stateless persons People who are not considered by any state as nationals and who therefore lack *citizenship rights of any sort. The UNHCR estimates that there are twelve million stateless persons, who are not necessarily refugees. The situation may arise either when a state ceases to exist (e.g. Palestine) or when a state refuses to recognize people as citizens, for example, Bihari and Urdu speakers in Bangladesh.

state-owned enterprise (SOE) An industrial organization fully or partly owned by government and not in private hands. There are many different forms of SOEs but two in particular are important. Many *OPEC countries created National Oil Companies (NOCs) to control oil production and secure its revenues; the world's *extractive industries sector includes a significant SOE presence. *China's economy is also dominated by SOEs, which account for around half of all output.

stepwise regression A form of *regression where it is possible to build a regression model in steps, either adding or removing variables and recomputing the regression coefficients. It is especially useful for dealing with a large number of potential independent variables and in fine-tuning a model. It is possible to start with all the potential variables in the model and to drop out variables that have little effect, or to start with no variables and add new ones based on a calculation of which variable would have the largest potential effect if added. Variables are either added or removed based on an F-test, a form of *t-test. *See also* GENERAL LINEAR MODELS.

Stern Review, The A report by British economist Nicholas Stern into the economic consequences of global warming, published in 2006. *The Stern Review on the Economics of Climate Change* was commissioned by UK Chancellor of the Exchequer Gordon Brown and provided the most comprehensive summary of the subject to date. Stern described global warming as a 'market failure', necessitating decisive and immediate action, contrary to the views of other economists (e.g. Bjorn Lomborg) who argued that postponing a response would cost less in the long run.

stochastic processes A process that develops somewhat randomly over time. A stochastic model is one in which one or more variables has a random quality, meaning that each time the model is run a different outcome is obtained, despite some elements of the model possibly being predictable. Nearly all human and natural systems cannot be perfectly determined because they do contain some element of chance or randomness, and in this sense they are stochastic in nature. *See also* MARKOV CHAIN ANALYSIS.

Storper, Michael (1954–) An American economic geographer based at the University of California, Los Angeles; his work concerns the spatial dynamics of production and work in advanced capitalist economies and the effects of the processes of *globalization, with a particular focus on territorial and regional production complexes and flexible specialization, as exemplified by his book *The Regional World: Territorial Development in a Global Economy* (1997). He has been a long-term collaborator with Allen *Scott and Richard *Walker.

Structural Adjustment Policies A set of programmes and regulatory actions designed collaboratively by the *World Bank and the *International Monetary Fund, and intended to restore economic health to *LEDCs in the wake of the debt crisis. They were distinguished from earlier aid programmes by the greater level of conditions attached to loans and funds, and the fact that these conditions had the aim of increasing the role of markets over states in economic and social policy (*see* DEVELOPMENT; NEOLIBERALISM).

SAPs, as they were known, were first introduced in Jamaica in 1979 and by the time the IMF and World Bank changed course in the late 1990s, they had been built into agreements with countries throughout Africa, South and Central America, South Asia, and Eastern Europe. Governments had little choice but to agree because private lenders were deterred by their level of debt. Conditions undermined national sovereignty to a degree. There were three kinds of policies: (i) deflationary actions to control the money supply, suppress inflation, restrain wages, lower public spending, cut subsidies to food and fuel, and balance national budgets; (ii) sectoral policies to focus resources on export-orientated growth and *comparative advantage, for example, agriculture and extractive industries; (iii) institutional reforms to encourage trade liberalization, privatization, and deregulation. The expectation was that short-term pain would lead to long-term gain, but it was often the poorer households that suffered the brunt of more expensive food, fuel, and healthcare. The middle classes were vulnerable to public sector job cuts, while exporters faced intense competition from abroad. Women were particularly exposed to the effects, caught between reduced public support for services, higher prices, and shortages of employment. In many countries there was unrest and food riots. Critics argued that the 'one-size-fits-all' approach of the programme was misguided; what might work in a middle-income country such as Peru would not necessarily work in a low-income country like Mozambique. By the mid 1990s even its proponents recognized that there were problems with the approach, and that adjustment was taking longer than anticipated; the emphasis shifted to *poverty reduction strategies.

structural equation modelling A statistical technique for modelling a system where some of the variables are endogenous in nature (that is, influenced by other variables in the same system), and some are exogenous (that is, determined outside the system). For example, there is a bi-directional relationship between health service demand and leisure facility demand, with one effecting the other to some degree. The *model might also include exogenous variables affecting both, such as socio-economic and demographic status, or one of them, such as treatment cost or leisure cost. Structural equation modelling uses a set of simultaneous and linear equations to model the relationships between these variables to determine the relative explanatory power of each.

structuralism An approach to describing and explaining human thought and practice that emphasizes the determining role of overarching rules, principles, or processes (*see* AGENCY-STRUCTURE DEBATE). During the mid-to-late 20th century, structuralism was very influential in the Western *social sciences and *humanities, including linguistics, psychology, and anthropology, though less so in human geography. Structuralist ideas are largely grounded in the linguistic theory of Ferdinand de Saussure, the anthropology of Claude Levi-Strauss, and the Marxism of Louis Althusser (*see* SEMIOTICS). Structuralists oppose most varieties of *humanism in two ways. First, they dispute the idea of a universal 'human nature' that transcended *time and *place. Second, they challenge the idea that individuals can be said to exist separately from a wider historically and geographically specific context. It was often said of structuralists that they were 'anti-humanist' because they regarded people as products of 'structures' (like the rules governing language use or the social relations of the capitalist economy). Individuals were only 'free' insofar as they could operate within the parameters laid down by the prevalent *culture, economy, and so on.

Human geographers have never engaged closely with the work of the leading theorists of structuralism. However, the early work of Marxist geographers introduced the spirit (if not the letter) of structuralism into human geography. Two important works of abstract *theory *The Limits to Capital* (1982) by David *Harvey and *Uneven Development* (1984) by Neil *Smith both highlighted the 'systemic' qualities of *capitalism, notwithstanding the empirical variety assumed by this *mode of production in different times and places. This produced a reaction among humanistic geographers who wished to emphasize the relative autonomy of thinking and feeling individuals. In the 1980s, a rapprochement between the apparent causal determinism of Marxist structuralism and the apparent voluntarism of *humanistic geography was attempted (*see* STRUCTURATION). Human agency was seen to be more than a narrowly circumscribed effect of structural forces, but also significantly controlled by them. These debates mostly subsided in the 1990s, when *post-structuralism exerted considerable influence on human geographers. Despite its prefix, this approach—in practice—could itself be rather structuralist. There was a major focus on the social power of various discourses, representations, and symbols that interpellated a range of social actors (*see* INTERPELLATION). The sources and effects of human agency were often obscure. This, along with the anti-capitalist protests of the late 1990s, inspired some human geographers to focus on social resistance to power, drawing on the metaphor of 'networks' as opposed to the more structuralist metaphor of 'system'.

structuration The processes by which social life is constituted and reproduced through the interaction between and mutual formation of agents and structures. Theories of structuration seek to answer one of the most enduring puzzles in *social theory (*see* AGENCY-STRUCTURE DEBATE). The puzzle is how to reconcile two seemingly opposed ideas about causation in society. On the one hand there are theories that ascribe causality to the intentions and actions of individuals, which can be aggregated to explain larger events such as war or recession. An example is *rational choice theory, which underpins much of *neoclassical economics. These agent-centred accounts contrast with more structural explanations of social life. These seek causality in large-scale and often hidden forces, or structures, which work behind the backs of individuals. Many variants of *Marxism are an example, in that they often regard *capital as a sort of super agent determining the lives of individuals and over which they have no real control. Both these propositions seem intuitively correct. We think of ourselves as intentional agents but we also sense that things happen for mysterious and deep-rooted reasons. Karl *Marx wrote that 'Men [sic] make their own history, but they do not make it as they please; they do not make it under circumstances chosen by themselves, but under circumstances directly found, given and transmitted from the past' (1852). Structuration theories attempt to work through the implications of this observation. Nigel Thrift, in an early survey of the concept in human geography, identified different theories in the work of Anthony *Giddens, Pierre *Bourdieu, and Roy Bhaskar, a founding thinker in *critical realism.

Although there are differences in emphasis, all three develop what Giddens called 'the duality of structure'. In contrast to *structuralism, whose various forms presuppose sets of rules (structures) which generate events or the actions of agents, structuration considers how agents may themselves transform structures in a recursive relationship. Human geographers, notably Derek *Gregory and Allan *Pred, made concerted efforts to realize the possibilities of structuration theory through empirical research. They followed Giddens' lead in trying to incorporate space and time into the theory (*see* TIME-GEOGRAPHY). But, although these theories might have provided solutions at an *ontological level, it was found that they were difficult to operationalize in research. As soon as one cuts into some social reality, it invariably leads to the separation of macro- and micro-level phenomena, reinstating the distinction between structure and agency.

References Marx, K. (1972), 'The eighteenth Brumaire of Louis Bonaparte' in Tucker, R.C. (ed.)
The Marx-Engels Reader.
Thrift, N. (1983), 'On the determination of social action in space and time', *Environment and Planning D: Society and Space* 1: 23–57.

structure-agency debate *See* AGENCY-STRUCTURE DEBATE.

STS *See* SCIENCE AND TECHNOLOGY STUDIES.

studentification The domination of residential neighbourhoods by student households, and the associated social, cultural, and environmental changes. In the UK the rapid expansion in student numbers in the 1990s was not matched by an increase in university accommodation, pushing thousands of students into multiple-occupation dwellings in areas surrounding campuses. Many communities resisted this process, concerned by the impact on rents and environmental quality. Some geographers, for example, Darren Smith, have analysed studentification as a precursor of *gentrification.

Further reading Smith, D. P. and Holt, L. (2007), 'Studentification and "apprentice" gentrifiers within Britain's provincial towns and cities: extending the meaning of gentrification', *Environment and Planning A* 39(1) 142–61.

Subaltern Studies A collective of scholars originating from South Asian with the common objective of revising historical accounts of the region, notably by trying to understand history from the perspective of the oppressed. In a general sense, Subaltern Studies refers to a wider body of work influenced by or sympathetic to the aims of the original group. The term 'subaltern', meaning someone of inferior rank by virtue of their class, race, or gender, was taken from Italian Marxist Antonio Gramsci. Founded in the early 1980s, they challenged the then dominant interpretations of Indian history, which, they argued, overstated the role of elites in securing independence and were insufficiently critical of *nationalism. Among the important early contributions was *Elementary Aspects of Peasant Insurgency in Colonial India* by the group's founder, Ranajit Guha. As their work became more widely known in the late 1980s, they influenced work on the field of *post-colonialism. By this time many of the collective's scholars had moved outside South Asia, among them Gayatri *Spivak and Partha Chaterjee. Spivak, however, challenged the school's proposition that historians could recover the voice of the oppressed. In 'Can the Subaltern Speak?' (1988), she examined the problem of how the oppressed could find expression without being drawn into the language and ideas of the oppressor.

Further reading Guha, R. (ed.) (1997), *The Subaltern Studies Reader, 1986–1995*.

subject 1. The locus of thinking, feeling, and acting.
  2. A field of specialized knowledge.
  3. A person ruled by, or owing allegiance to, a monarch (*see* SOVEREIGNTY).

Most debate centres on the first of these definitions. In this sense, the subject is another word for actor or agent, i.e. the supposed origin of social relations. A central preoccupation of philosophy and *social theory, the subject is conceptualized in manifold ways. A broad distinction can be drawn between *humanist and *structuralist or *post-structuralist conceptions. Humanist philosophies, which inform *humanistic geography, regard the subject as a unified entity capable of thought, sensation, and action, self-aware and therefore the origin of social relations. The subject is often further conceived as a *rational economic actor. Within this, there are important differences of emphasis. Feminism, for example, stresses the gendered characteristics of the subject, and is less persuaded that it is universal, i.e. the same everywhere (*see* INTERSECTION-ALITY). *Identity politics develops the idea of difference, i.e., that the subject is differentiated by *race, *class, *gender, *sexuality, and so forth. Structuralism, which informed *Marxist geography, is more suspicious of the idea of a knowing subject. With varying degrees of emphasis, structuralist and post-structuralist philosophies regard the subject as the outcome or effect of power and/or knowledge (*see* AGENCY-STRUCTURE DEBATE; INTERPELLATION). The subject is not the sole origin of social relations but in some version, is the bearer of such relations, and in others, such as *Actor-Network Theory, shares the capacity to act with non-human and technological entities (*see* CYBORG).

subjectivity The influence of personal feelings, beliefs, desires, and interests on the conduct and outcome of action, including academic research and teaching. A subjective judgement is therefore in contrast to an objective one, insofar as the latter requires that the facts should be able to speak for themselves (*see* OBJECTIVITY). There are five main reactions to subjectivity in human geography. One regards it as an inevitable but undesirable feature of scientific inquiry, which should be minimized as far as possible (*see* VALUES). This deems objectivity to be the foundation of reliable and publicly acceptable knowledge. The opposite position, which valorizes subjectivity as the irreducible feature of human knowledge, was advocated by *humanistic geographers. They were dismissive of claims on behalf of objective knowledge, a view shared widely among the *sociologists of scientific knowledge who uncovered the constant presence of social, political, and personal factors in scientific inquiry. A variant on this, closely associated with *feminist geography, advocates *positionality in research, i.e. the conscious and critical reflection on one's own position in society and personal qualities. In some accounts, this is also termed 'strong objectivity', because it explicitly confronts the way in which social and power relations influence the production of knowledge (*see* FEMINIST STANDPOINT THEORY; STANDPOINT THEORY). A fourth response is to think in terms of inter-subjectivity rather than subjectivity, i.e. acknowledging that interpretations are shared rather than idiosyncratic. Finally, *structural and *post-structural theories are sceptical of the idea of the subject as the origin of action or meaning. They stress various kinds of subjecthood or subjectification, processes by which the effect of subjectivity is produced without individual agency.

subprime mortgage crisis A series of events and underlying conditions that began in the US housing market and eventually led to the 2007 global economic recession. In the US financial industry, a subprime mortgage is a high-risk loan made to a property purchaser. The loan is deemed high risk because it is made to someone who is likely to find it hard to repay by virtue of their circumstances, income, or credit history. The interest rates are therefore high. When, in the mid-2000s, house prices began to fall and borrowers began to default in large numbers, the effects cascaded throughout the US and then the global financial system. This was because the debts had already been traded between financial institutions through complex arrangements (known as securitization) such that it could not be easily determined which banks and lenders were most exposed to the bad debts. *See also* CRISIS; HOUSING.

Sub-Saharan Africa That part of the continent of Africa south of the Sahara desert. When used in regional classification by international agencies such as the *World Bank it includes all African countries except those bordering the Mediterranean and Western Sahara (North Africa). Sometimes, however, Sudan and South Sudan are classified with North Africa because they, too, are majority Arab countries.

subsidiarity The principle that governmental responsibilities and actions should be exercised at the lowest level of authority possible. In a federal system this might mean, for example, that primary education is the responsibility of the most local form of government, sales tax is set at the state or provincial level, and defence is a matter for the federal government (*see* FEDERALISM). The aim is to exercise authority as close as possible to the affected population, so maximizing the degree of *democracy. Many debates within the *European Union about the distribution of powers hinge on subsidiarity.

subsistence agriculture A type of farming that produces enough to meet the consumption needs of a farming family, but no surplus product for sale in markets. Such cultivators are governed more by the desire to minimize risks than maximize yields. Most pre-industrial agriculture was subsistence-based, and it is widespread in Sub-Saharan Africa. But subsistence farmers everywhere face being drawn into the relations of commodity production and integrated world food markets.

suburbanization The expansion of the built environment beyond the limits of long-standing urban cores, most notably with the spread of automobile ownership in affluent countries from the mid-20th century onwards. As well as being a physical change, suburbanization is often understood as a set of social and cultural transformations involving new relations of class, gender, religion, and race. Though led by residential change, industries, services, and retailing have followed (*see* EDGE CITY).

sunbelt A region of high economic growth based on industries other than traditional or heavy manufacturing, e.g. *services, *hi-tech, and *tourism, and also characterized by a relatively warm climate. The original Sunbelt was the south and southwest states of the USA, as contrasted with the northern and eastern states of the Snowbelt, Frostbelt, or *Rustbelt, which were once the heart of the country's manufacturing strength but by the 1970s were suffering from *deindustrialization. Climate may have been one factor encouraging regional economic change, but others were more important, e.g. labour costs, business regulations, and cost of land. Southern France and the Mediterranean coastal region between Valencia (Spain) and Genoa (Italy) have also been described as sunbelts.

sunk costs The investments made by a firm that cannot be easily recovered and therefore discourage relocation. These include the costs of setting up plant and machinery, the cost of doing business, and the costs of moving. These are fixed and not related to output.

Further reading Clark, G. L. and Wrigley, N. (1995), 'Sunk costs: a framework for economic geography', *Transactions of the Institute of British Geographers* 20: 204–23.

superdiversity The unusually high mix of ethnic groups in certain cities and countries; also termed 'hyperdiversity'. Popularized by Steve Vertovec, it refers to situations where migrants and ethnic minority groups constitute a high percentage of a population; their national origins are highly diverse; and there is a mix of migration statuses and associated rights. *See also* ASSIMILATION; INTEGRATION; COSMOPOLITANISM.

Further reading Vertovec, S. (2007), 'Superdiversity and its implications', *Ethnic and Racial Studies* 30: 1024–54.

superpower A state so dominant in international affairs that it is able to exert power and influence across the world in political, economic, cultural, and/or military terms. The term has been applied to the British empire, the Soviet Union, and the USA, which since the end of the *Cold War, is arguably the only superpower.

supply chain The system linking assembly firms, suppliers, distribution facilities, and labour in the movement of a product or service from source to consumer. The combination of improved transport and information technology associated with *globalization greatly reduced the costs of establishing and managing global supply chains, enabling new firms and regions to compete in the world economy (*see* OUTSOURCING). Supply chains need no longer be localized. But there are risks; political unrest and natural disasters, such as the 2011 Japanese earthquake, can disrupt supply chains and halt production. *See also* COMMODITY CHAINS.

surplus value The difference between the economic value expended in commodity production and that received by capitalists once commodities have been sold. According to Karl *Marx, value in *capitalism is produced exclusively by wage workers. Capitalists, as a class, pay their workers less than the value they create in the production process. However, this is not evident in the wage relation because workers are encouraged to regard their pay as commensurate with their education and skills. The difference between the costs of commodity production and the returns on commodity sales (i.e. profit) is, according to *Marxists, a function of workers' being systematically under-paid for the work they do. This *labour theory of value has been challenged strongly by many economists, though few in human geography have sought to criticize it forensically.

surveillance The monitoring of people and systems in order to regulate their behaviour. Surveillance has been a common feature of every society, used to observe the lives and activities of members in order to effect law and order, ensure that taxes are paid, and secure the loyalty of subjects. The nature and depth of this monitoring has varied over time and space, shaped by the mode of state governance, and development of surveillance techniques and technologies. For example, as Western states moved from a feudal to modern society they adopted a new mode of *governance that sought to create a uniformity of social services across societies (e.g., law enforcement, public health, access to education) that required the systematic management and regulation of population. Such management was implemented through the application of wide-scale public administration, such as population *censuses, health records, class attendance and exams, crime records, the civil registration of births, deaths, and marriages, that scientifically and rationally captured, catalogued, and classified people, and facilitated the imposition of uniform and universal regulations. Such information provided a detailed knowledge of a population, enabling new professional elites (e.g., civil servants, teachers, doctors, police officers, health inspectors, welfare officers, and so on) to govern more effectively and efficiently by identifying, disciplining, and punishing those who transgressed societal norms and rules (*see* BIOPOLITICS). The presence of such surveillance also worked to instil self-regulation, that is, people altered their behaviour to expected norms because they were aware that their behaviour was potentially being observed. Surveillance is not limited to use by the state. For example, businesses also monitor the work of their employees to ensure efficiency, productivity, and competitive advantage, and to reduce risk and workplace fraud and crime.

Along with new systems and techniques of administration, surveillance has been facilitated by new technologies that facilitate observation. The most famous example

surveys

from the 19th century was Jeremy Bentham's *Panopticon, a building designed so all its occupants could be seen from a single location (a central tower surrounded by open rooms) designed to aid prison officers to monitor and control a large number of inmates with as few staff as possible. Other important developments included unique mechanisms of identification such as fingerprinting and photography, and forms of documentation like passports and social security numbers. These provided scientific means of authentication and accreditation, and provided a means to cross-reference records. In the 20th century, such technologies included covert forms such as wire taps on phones, and overt forms such as CCTV (closed circuit television). By the end of the century, CCTV had become routinely deployed in public space, especially shopping streets and malls, and within private buildings, to monitor for and deter anti-social and criminal behaviour. In addition, security and surveillance in certain locations, such as airports, became heightened, including baggage being screened by x-ray machines.

In the 21st century, surveillance capabilities are being embedded into all kinds of technologies such as computers and mobile phones which monitor their own use, communicating data back to service providers who seek to extract commercial value from such information (*see* BIG DATA). The power of surveillance to shape behaviour is also no longer enacted externally, but also internally. For example, the scan rate of a shop till operator might have been monitored by a control room using a CCTV camera, whereas such monitoring is now built into the scan technology used by operator, tracking precisely in real-time the scan rate, enabling the shop owner to effectively police worker productivity.

The result of advances in surveillance technologies is a vast amount of information generated about people daily so that they are accompanied by a growing 'data shadow'. The formation of this data shadow clearly raises questions concerning privacy, confidentiality, individual freedoms, and civil liberties, and how society is governed and managed. However, despite advances in surveillance tools and systems of organization, it is important to note that they are not fully panoptic in scope and remain open to vertical (within an activity) and horizontal (across activities) fragmentation. For example, within an activity, observation, judgement, and enforcement have often been undertaken by different agencies who communicate imperfectly; and across activities, different organizations, for legal, institutional, or technical reasons, have not easily been able to exchange or compare information. Indeed, the extent of fraud, deviance, and crime throughout contemporary Western societies is clearly indicative of the fragmentary nature of surveillance.

Further reading Dodge, M. and Kitchin R. (2005), 'Codes of life: Identification codes and the machine-readable world', *Environment and Planning D: Society and Space* 23(6): 851–81.
Graham, S. and Wood, D. (2003), 'Digitizing surveillance: categorization, space, inequality', *Critical Social Policy* 23(2): 227–48.
Hannah, M. (1997), 'Imperfect panopticism: envisioning the construction of normal lives', in Benko, G. and Strohmayer, U. (eds.) *Space and Social Theory* 344–60.
Lyon, D. (2007), *Surveillance Studies: an Overview.*

surveying The practice of measuring locations and boundaries. Using precision instruments, surveying provides exact measurements of the absolute location of places and their relative position to each other, and traditionally has provided the raw data for map-making by plotting the positions of objects, the paths between them, and the boundaries of parcels of land. *See also* CARTOGRAPHY; GEOMATICS.

surveys A method of data generation which seeks to produce data on a specific subject from individual members of a particular sample population. Surveys consist of a family of related forms ranging from face-to-face surveys, postal surveys, to telephone and internet surveys, and can use a number of different *sampling strategies. In general, surveys use *questionnaires to generate quantitative data from which they can calculate statistical information, though they might include some open questions. Beyond academia, consumer, market, and policy-led research rely almost exclusively on large-scale surveys to generate data about all aspects of people's daily lives. A *census, administered by a national statistics organization, is a good example. Survey data is typically analysed using *descriptive and *inferential statistics.

sustainability The property of a system or process that allows for both its use and long-term regeneration. In fisheries and forestry, the term 'maximum sustained yield' refers to the highest amount of fish that can be caught or trees that can be felled without compromising the ability of the fish population or woodland to be replenished over time. Over-use leads to eventual depletion of the resource, but under-use causes wastefulness. The term is now used interchangeably with *sustainable development, progress in which is assessed by sustainability indicators at national and international levels.

sustainability science An interdisciplinary field of inquiry into the fundamental character of nature-society interactions at local and global scales, and directed towards identifying the causes of and solutions for major environmental challenges. Its practitioners intend to apply whatever knowledge is relevant to addressing problems, from the humanities to engineering.
Kates, R. W. et al. (2001), 'Sustainability science', *Science*, vol. 292 no. 5517, 641–2.

sustainable community A settlement or part of a settlement either planned for or aiming towards *sustainability, i.e. a balance of economic security, environmental quality, and social well-being.

sustainable development The human exploitation of *natural resources that balances economic growth, environmental *sustainability, and social equity from the present and into the long-term future. Until the 1980s, it was commonly supposed that economic and environmental aims were intrinsically opposed. The former required resource exploitation and the inevitable side effects of waste and pollution, resulting in the depletion of natural systems. But, organized around a series of international conferences and agreements, the proposition took hold that the two aims could be reconciled and combined with social objectives if the appropriate steps were followed. Although there is no consensus on the exact meaning of sustainable development, it generally indicates a balance between three sets of goals: biological systems, their genetic diversity (*biodiversity), resilience, and productivity; social systems, including *empowerment, social cohesion, and cultural diversity; and economic systems, growth, *equity, and efficiency.

The breadth of meaning implied enabled diverse interests to subscribe to the goal of sustainable development, to some degree covering over their political differences. From a social point of view, it suggested moves towards equity in the present and in the future, i.e. between generations. Ecologists could stress the intention to maintain the productivity of agricultural systems (*see* AGRI-ENVIRONMENT SCHEMES). Development specialists saw the prospect of improving the quality of life for the poor but not at the expense of their environments upon which they depended. Economists could think of the level of consumption that could be sustained over long periods without serious degradation to natural stocks. In this calculation, *social capital in the form of technology and expertise could substitute for any lost natural capital. This breadth and inclusivity has its critics, some of whom find the term so broad as to be meaningless. In particular, there is a tension between those who approach sustainable development as a technical matter, involving measurements, standards, indicators, and appropriate policies, and those who view it more politically, concerned for the causes of unsustainability and the real divisions between various interests (Mansfield 2009). Others worry that adding social goals will compromise ecological imperatives.

The concept of sustainable development has been refined through a series of international agreements, beginning in 1980 with the World Conservation Strategy published by the International Union for the Conservation of Nature (IUCN) (*see* EARTH SUMMITS; RIO EARTH SUMMIT). It received wider attention as a consequence of the 1987 World Commission on Environment and Development, or *Brundtland Report, which defined it as 'development that meets the needs of the present without compromising the ability of future generations to meet their own needs'. Ensuring environmental sustainability was one of the *Millennium Development Goals (2000), which included targets for forest cover, CO_2 emissions, solid fuel used, and energy consumption. The 2002 World Summit on Sustainable Development in South Africa added more targets for biodiversity loss, fish stocks, water efficiency, and chemical pollution. But the resources to implement these goals were, in the view of many in the development community, lacking. Furthermore, critics allege that sustainable development has become synonymous with a set of *neoliberal measures that cannot deliver long-run social equity.

Further reading Mansfield, B. (2009), 'Sustainability', in Castree, N. et al. *A Companion to Environmental Geography*, 42–49.

Sneddon, C. (2000), 'Sustainability, in ecological economics, ecology and livelihoods: a review', *Progress in Human Geography*. 24(4): 521–49.

Sustainable Livelihoods Approach

A framework and set of principles to address the problems of the (largely) rural poor in the *Global South. Rather than focus just on low income as a source of poverty, it takes account of a wider range of personal, household, and contextual factors. It was inspired by the Amartya *Sen's *capabilities approach and developed at the Institute for Development Studies, Sussex, UK in the 1990s. According to its main proponents, Robert Chambers, Gordon Conway, and Ian Scoones, a 'livelihood' is made up of the capabilities, assets (material and social), and activities needed for an individual or household to make a living. It is sustainable if it can withstand shocks or stress, such as a disaster, if it can be maintained or enhanced, if it can be passed between generations, and if it can be supported by the available natural resources. The approach has two elements. There is a set of principles, which are fairly flexible rather than prescriptive, and include such things as encouraging partnership and recognizing dynamic situations. There is also a framework for thinking about the problems, which considers livelihood assets in the general political and economic context on the one hand, and the *vulnerability context on the other. It takes account of livelihood strategies. This approach was developed by the UK's Department for International Development and has motivated further research and analysis. But it also has its critics, who note its under-developed concept of political power. *See also* DEVELOPMENT.

Further reading Chambers, R. and Conway, G. R. (1992), *Sustainable Rural Livelihoods*.

De Haan, L. and Zoomers, A. (2005), 'Exploring the frontier of livelihood research', *Development and Change*, 36(1): 27–47.

sweatshop

A pejorative term for a workplace characterized by low-wage, labour-intensive production coupled with intense and/or unlawful labour exploitation. Although often used with reference to the garment industry, it is also applied more generally.

Swyngedouw, Erik

(1956–) A Belgian geographer and political economist who undertook his graduate work in the United States. He was based at the University of Oxford from 1988 to 2006, when he moved to the University of Manchester. His work, which is deeply informed by *Marxism, examines issues of *capitalism, economic development, *urbanization, *glocalization, and resources, notably water supply, with a recent focus on the *post-political.

Sydney The most populous city in *Australia and in the wider region of Australasia (about 4.6 million). It is the capital of the state New South Wales, but not of the country as a whole. The Sydney region has been inhabited for around 30,000 years, and it was here that British explorers landed in 1770, and set up a colony eight years later, dispossessing the *indigenous Cadigal people. Sydney is now a major global financial, business, and cultural centre; around a third of its population is foreign-born.

symbolic capital A form of *cultural capital that refers to the resources available to people based on honour or prestige, that elevates their status and provides them with a privileged position. For example, a member of a royal family possesses the symbolic capital of the crown, drawing value from this status which affects how others treat him or her. Similarly, other entities such as *monuments can possess symbolic value and utility, making them key symbolic landmarks, which in turn raises an area's status, for example, the Eiffel Tower in Paris. *See also* ICONIC ARCHITECTURE.

symbolic ethnicity An *ethnicity that is predominantly displayed through symbolic and cultural practices and events, rather than lived as an everyday experience. Coined by sociologist Herbert Gans, it is sometimes also called 'optional ethnicity' as the individual chooses whether to display ethnic roots and doing so incurs few social costs. It is often used to describe generational descendants of migrants who express elements of their heritage, such as third- and fourth-generation migrants of Irish descent celebrating St Patrick's Day or taking part in Irish dancing or music.

symbolic interactionism A form of *social constructionism, holding that people react not to some physical reality but to their interpretation of reality based on interaction and communication with other people and things in general. It derives from the work of US philosopher and sociologist George Herbert Mead (1863–1931) and was later elaborated by Herbert Blumer. It was among the philosophies informing *humanistic geography.

symbolic violence The harm arising from the almost unconscious ways structures and hierarchies are internalized by subjects and therefore rendered normal. The term comes from Pierre *Bourdieu, who was concerned with the ways that domination proceeds tacitly, embedded in everyday social habits. Slavoj Žižek also discusses symbolic violence in *Violence* (2008), arguing that it is located in the signification of language itself, i.e. the very ways in which we talk to one another sustain relations of domination.

synchronic approach Analysis of the relations between phenomena at one point in time rather than through time (*see* DIACHRONIC APPROACH).

system An arrangement of interdependent or interacting things operating in a more or less unified way. A system is presumed to be bounded or closed to some degree, so distinguishing its internal relations from external ones. It has a structure or discernible pattern of relations between components and an associated characteristic behaviour. It is often assumed that a system has a function or purpose, i.e., it is either designed or self-organized to achieve some ends (*see* TELEOLOGY). Beyond these general features, the term 'system' is employed so widely across the natural and *social sciences that it can refer to many different things. Within geography, there were concerted efforts to construct a unified subject around the study of physical and human systems in the 1970s and 1980s. *See also* CHAOS, CATASTROPHE, AND COMPLEXITY; GENERAL SYSTEMS THEORY.

systematic geography The study of geographical phenomena organized by class or type rather than by region, i.e. the complementary and alternative approach to *regional geography. From the 1950s, geographers increasingly specialized in systematic topics such as urban, agricultural, and economic geography rather than specific regions of the world.

systems theory *See* GENERAL SYSTEMS THEORY.

S

tacit knowledge A knowledge that is very difficult to communicate through formal means such as writing because it is personal, implicit, and/or context-dependent. Such 'know-how', it is argued, can only be transmitted through direct experience and personal interaction, in contrast with *codified knowledge. Tacit knowledge therefore does not travel readily and 'sticks' to particular sites, e.g. a trading floor, restaurant kitchen, or sports training centre. Transmission requires personal proximity. Economic geographers are interested in the effect of places in the circulation of tacit knowledge and its role in generating *innovation (*see* CLUSTERS). Empirical research, however, casts doubt on the simplistic distinction between locally fixed tacit knowledge and globally mobile codified knowledge.

Further reading Bathelt, H., Malmberg, A., and Maskell, P. (2004), 'Clusters and knowledge: local buzz, global pipelines and the process of knowledge creation', *Progress in Human Geography* 28: 31–56.

tactile map A *map that can be read through touch. The maps have raised areas that represent various features such as buildings and roads, and various forms of raised shading are used to represent land use. Braille is used for labels. Given that most people with visual impairments have some form of vision, a tactile map typically also uses strongly contrasting colours such as black and white. A variety of materials can be used to create the maps, including special paper where coloured areas rise on the application of heat. In recent years, tactile maps have been supplemented with *haptic soundscapes that combine touch and sound.

Taiwan An island state located 180 km off the southeast coast of mainland *China (more formally called the People's Republic of China). Taiwan is also known as the Republic of China (ROC), and, notably in international sporting events, Chinese Taipei (Taipei is the capital). In 1912, Chinese nationalists assumed power in the Chinese mainland, replacing the former Chinese empire with the Republic of China. In 1949, they were defeated by the forces of the Chinese Communist party. Under its leader Chiang Kai-shek, the ROC and its supporters decamped to the island of Formosa, later renamed Taiwan. Both the ROC and PRC claim to be the rightful government of both mainland and island, and there is considerable diplomatic and military tension between them. Most international bodies and states recognize the PRC rather than Taiwan (*see* SOVEREIGNTY). Taiwan is a multiparty democracy and its economy is one of the four Asian Tigers (*see* NEWLY INDUSTRIALIZING COUNTRIES).

tariff A tax applied to imports. In general, the higher the value of the imported good, the higher the tariff. Tariffs not only raise revenue for government, but by making imports more expensive than they would be otherwise, they can be used to increase the relative competitiveness of domestic producers of the same goods. It is therefore a protectionist measure. The systematic reduction of tariffs is one of the aims of the *World Trade Organization. *See also* TRADE.

tax haven A jurisdiction in which corporate and individual taxes, as well as business regulations, are designed to be relatively attractive to investors and financial traders (*see* FINANCE). They are often also termed 'offshore financial centres', although many are not islands, for example, Switzerland and Panama (*see* OFFSHORING). International bodies including the *OECD and *IMF are concerned that such places encourage tax evasion and money-laundering, and both exert pressure on these to reform.

Further reading Palan, R., Murphy, R., and Chavagneux, C. (2010), *Tax Havens: How Globalization Really Works*.

Taylor, Peter J. (1944–) A British political geographer based at Newcastle University between 1968 and 1995, then subsequently at Loughborough University. He has written widely on *political geography, especially with respect to *electoral geography, *the world-systems approach, and the territorial state and the global economy. He has also contributed to the analysis of *world cities, especially through the research of the Globalization and World Cities (GaWC) network that he founded.

Taylor, W Griffith (1880–1963) A British-born Australian geographer who helped establish the discipline in Australia and Canada. Taylor's family emigrated to Sydney when he was three years old. He was educated at the University of Sydney and the University of Cambridge. After an exploration trip to Antarctica he initially worked as an environmental researcher. He gained a position at the University of Sydney in 1921 as the founding head of the geography department. His flirtations with *environmental determinism and *social Darwinism proved controversial, and he resigned in 1928 and moved to the University of Chicago. In 1935, he moved to the University of Toronto as the founding professor of the geography department, retiring in 1951. In the same year he was appointed the first honorary president of the Canadian Association of Geographers and also moved back to Australia, where in 1960 he was the founding president of the Institute of Australian Geographers. Unusually, he had also served as president of the Association of American Geographers in 1940, the first non-American to hold the post.

Taylorism The organization of work according to the principles of Frederick W. Taylor (1856–1915) and his doctrine of 'scientific management'. As applied to manufacturing industries in his native USA, Taylorism was based on deconstructing any production process into a sequence of simple actions and then coordinating them by means of managerial intervention in order to achieve the highest productivity in the least time. It constituted an advanced *division of labour and, as critics pointed out, led to the de-skilling of individual labourers (each of whom repeatedly executed one standardized action), and the loss of control over the labour process to managers. Some writers used the term 'bloody Taylorism' or 'bloody Taylorization' to describe the intense application of these principles in conjunction with labour *exploitation in *Newly Industrializing Economies. *See also* FORDISM; TOYOTISM.

technological determinism A reductionist, theoretical position in which technology is understood to determine, in fairly linear simple cause-and-effect ways, the social, cultural, political, and economic aspects of people's lives. Here, technology is seen as independent, active, and determining, and society is dependent, passive, and reactive. From this perspective, technical advancements are the key drivers of social and economic change. For example, technological determinists argue that new technical developments such as rail, telegraph, cars, telecommunications, elevators, and computers are key factors determining the shape and functioning of modern societies. Moreover, they would suggest that social, economic, and environmental issues can be solved purely through technological solutions. The counter-argument is that technology and its uses are *socially constructed, have different effects across space and time, and social problems cannot simply be solved by technology but also need social and political solutions.

technopole A planned *agglomeration of firms specializing in *hi-tech industry, with a significant presence of research and development and innovative activity. This broad description includes: science cities dedicated only to research (e.g. Akademgorodok in Siberia); technology parks associated with universities and/or government initiative (e.g. Sophia Antipolis, France); and centres within larger metropolitan regions (e.g. Silicon Roundabout, London). It can also describe unplanned concentrations, e.g. *Silicon Valley.

technoscience The activities that transcend or erase the conventional distinctions between science and technology on the one hand, and pure and applied science on the other. Introduced by Bruno *Latour, it implies that scientists and engineers build networks composed of heterogeneous elements such that their outcomes cannot be reduced to something called science or engineering, for example (*see* ACTOR-NETWORK THEORY; SCIENCE AND TECHNOLOGY STUDIES).

telecommunications The technologies of communication that enable the instantaneous transfer of information between distant places. The first such technology was the telegraph, invented in the early 19th century, with the first commercial transmission in 1844 using Morse code. The telegraph enabled massive *time-space compression and distanciation, enabling messages that would have been carried by horse to be transmitted within seconds, speeding up the spread of news. Telegraph lines quickly spread across North America, Europe, and other parts of the world, linking together urban centres. It rapidly became a key political and economic technology, for example, enabling London to manage the British *empire from a distance and to quickly react to developments. From the late 19th century, the telegraph was supplemented with the telephone that enabled verbal telecommunication, and in the early 20th century radio enabled mass broadcast. In the late 20th century, the transmission of messages was extended to microwave and satellite technology, enabling mobile communication, and the *Internet was developed that enabled the communication of diverse media forms. Along with developments in *transportation, given how telecommunications connect people and places, radically shrinking the effects of *space and *time, they have been key agents in *globalization. Moreover, they have become vital infrastructure for urban and economic life, especially given the rise of the *knowledge economy.

Further reading Graham, S. and Marvin, S. (1995), *Telecommunications and the City*.

telecommuting/telework The utilization of *telecommunications to perform work outside the workplace, for example, at home, in a cafe, or during a journey using fixed-line or mobile *Internet. Given the cost and time of *commuting, and the relatively cheap price of *telecommunications, telecommuting has grown rapidly, particularly for those working in the knowledge economy who process and manage information. The logic of its use is to move the work to workers, rather than vice versa, while also enabling more flexible working hours and companies to hire skilled staff that do not necessarily live close to their offices.

teleology A form of explanatory reasoning that assumes that causes and effects are preordained. Put another way, it is the belief that processes are subject to design or intention, and therefore there is only one way in which they can unfold. In religious thinking, teleology is implied by the belief in a divine creator but there are also versions in secular thought. Some interpretations of natural evolution suppose that it has a direction, for example, towards superior forms of life. This was not *Darwin's view. This idea that the Earth is designed and that geographical processes such as erosion reveal this design has been a common theme in thinking about *nature, not least in 19th-century natural theology (Glacken 1967). Elements of this view persisted in William Davis's concept of the cycle of erosion formulated in the 1890s and Frederic Clements' related idea of the climax community, towards which *ecosystems arrived through a process of succession (devised in the early 1900s). In human geography, the *stages of growth theory of development can be understood as teleological, based as it was on a definite sequence of stages towards a known end. Certain readings of Marx's ideas of historical change through a series of *modes of production, *feudalism, *capitalism, *socialism, and *communism, are also teleological (*see* MARXISM). There are several objections and refutations to teleological ideas. They seemingly leave no scope for human *agency, contingency, or chance; the course of history is inevitable and fixed. As theories, teleological propositions are untestable and so unverifiable, a criticism levelled at the cycle of erosion. In scientific terms, they are counter-intuitive because they place effects before causes.

Reference Glacken, C. J. (1967), *Traces on the Rhodian Shore*.

temporality A term to describe having qualities related to *time. Although there are many varied uses of the term within philosophy, history, anthropology, and the social *sciences, it generally indicates that time is multiple, heterogeneous, and/or social rather than fixed and natural. *Compare* SPATIALITY.

terms of trade The ratio of export prices to import prices for any country or region. If country A specializes in exporting manufactured goods and country B specializes in primary exports such as agricultural goods or mineral resources, then over time, the terms of trade will change in favour of country A. This is because the price of manufactured goods tends to increase faster than the price of primary products. Country B must export more coffee or copper to purchase the same amount of computers over time. Critics argue that the organization of international *trade and the way prices are established for different products are fixed by countries in the *Global North to their advantage (*see* UNEQUAL EXCHANGE).

terra incognita A Latin phrase meaning 'unknown land' used by *Renaissance cartographers to indicate uncharted territory. It is now used metaphorically to describe unfamiliar or unexplored terrain of any kind. *Mare incognitum* is the equivalent term for seas.

terra nullius A Latin phrase meaning 'land belonging to no one', which was enshrined as a principle in European law from the 18th century onwards. It meant that European countries could, in their view, legitimately claim sovereignty over lands deemed unoccupied or without an existing sovereign authority. Such lands were, in fact, inhabited, but Europeans often deemed their inhabitants too primitive and incapable of forming political authority, signing treaties, or using land productively. The doctrine was invoked by Britain to legitimate its possession of Australia (*see* COLONIALISM; DISPOSSESSION).

territorial cohesion The alignment of policy across regions and nation states to create mutually beneficial competitiveness and *sustainable development. Territorial cohesion is one of the three pillars of the European Union, along with social and economic cohesion (*see* SOCIAL COHESION). The aim is to create an integrative approach to development that ensures that all regions benefit from the European project and to make the European Union globally competitive. A mechanism for delivery is *spatial planning.

(⊕) SEE WEB LINKS

• European Commission website on Regional Policy, including territorial cohesion.

territoriality The control of people and resources achieved through the control of space or *territory. In one view, associated with ethology and socio-biology, human beings are driven by instinct to organize themselves around and lay claim to territories, in much the same way as other species. Territorial disputes, whether between neighbours over a fence or states over an international boundary, are therefore rooted in natural tendencies. Traces of this organismic approach to territoriality can be found in the work of *geopolitics (*see* GEOPOLITIK; RATZEL). The more widely accepted view, among human geographers at least, is that territoriality has social and cultural origins. The first major geographical theory along these lines was formulated by French geographer Jean Gottmann. He argued that the close association of a people and their space was a response to two basic needs, for security and defence on the one hand, and for opportunities to lead the good life, i.e. pursue economic activities, on the other. Gottmann's thinking focused on the modern state. Robert Sack, a US geographer, developed a more extensive concept of 'human territoriality' as a universal, though not instinctual feature of social life. Reasoning through examples at a range of scales, Sack argued that human territoriality was the primary geographical expression of social power. It rested on three moments: classification by area; the communication of the boundaries of the area (s); and enforced control over access to the area. A simple example might be a parent's instruction to a child not to enter the garage. In this case, rather than instruct the child not to go near or touch sharp and other dangerous objects, the parent identifies the garage as a space the child should not enter. This has the effect of reifying or depersonalizing power, i.e. the injunction seems to come not from the parent but from the property of the garage itself. Gang turfs, native reserves, and even *national parks are all larger-scale expressions of the same set of processes (*see* FORTRESS CONSERVATION). The principal form of human territoriality is the state's organization of political territory (*see* SOVEREIGNTY; STATE). Territoriality can, of course, be resisted, by trespass, occupation, and other forms of appropriating space.

Further reading Gottmann, J. (1973), *The Significance of Territory*.

Neumann, R. P. (2004), 'Nature-state-territory: toward a critical theorization of conservation enclosures', in Peet, R. and Watts, M. (eds.) *Liberation Ecologies*, 2nd ed., 195–217.

Sack, R. J. (1983), 'Human territoriality: a theory', *Annals of the Association of American Geographers* 73: 55–74.

territorialization The organization of human activities by fixing them in spatial *territory. The *state is the main agent of territorialization, organizing administrative boundaries for defence, elections, education, health care, policing international boundaries, gathering statistics according to spatial units, and enforcing property laws. 'Deterritorialization' describes the many processes operating in the other direction, as it were, i.e. to lessen the relationships between human activities and their territorial bases. A prime example is the *globalization of the financial industry, but it might also describe the supposed decline in people's attachment to places and more generally the idea that the nation-state's powers are waning (*see* HOLLOWING OUT). In some accounts of globalization, this process is its defining characteristic. But on closer analysis it turns out that while one form of territorialization, associated with the state, might arguably be weakening, other forms are not. Sometimes therefore the term '*reterritorialization' is used to describe the processes by which economic or other activities are rearranged in new spatial configurations not necessarily corresponding with established state-centred geographies.

There is a second, more metaphorical use of the term 'deterritorialization'. As employed by theorists Gilles *Deleuze and Felix Guattari it refers to the dissolution of older forms of thought (associated with the state) and the emergence of new, more fluid, or mobile epistemologies (what they term nomadic thought).

territorial justice *See* JUSTICE.

territorial sea The belt of coastal waters along a state's coastline regarded as *sovereign territory. Within the territorial sea, states have the right to regulate and police activities, and the proprietary right to control and exploit natural resources. Under the 1982 United Nations Convention on the Law of the Sea this belt extends 12 nautical miles (22 km) from the coastal baseline, taken at the mean low-water mark. Where states are separated by less than 24 nautical miles, the extent of their territorial sea is the mid-point between them. While sovereign territory is subject to the laws of that state, ships of other nations are allowed free passage. *See* CONTIGUOUS ZONE.

territorial trap The conceptual error of: (i) regarding states as fixed units of territorial sovereign space, unchanging through time; (ii) separating domestic (inside) from foreign (outside) political spaces; (iii) treating the territorial state as a container of society. The idea was developed by US geographer John *Agnew as a critique of the assumptions made by mainstream or realist international relations. *See also* METHODOLOGICAL NATIONALISM; STATE; TERRITORY; TRANSNATIONALISM.

Reference Agnew, J. A. (1994), 'The territorial trap: the geographical assumptions of international relations theory', *Review of International Political Economy* 1: 53–80.

territory **1.** A bounded part of the Earth's surface claimed and occupied by a particular individual, group, or institution, including states.
2. A division of a country directly administered by a federal government, and therefore lacking the self-government characteristic of a *state, e.g. Australia's Northern Territory.

Within human geography, most interest is in territory in the first of these two senses. The term 'territory' is deployed in a number of different ways within human geography. It is mainly used with reference to the modern or sovereign *state. The state is defined as an entity that lays claim to and/or controls a contiguous territory marked by clear boundaries and recognized in international law. By extension, a *nation is often understood as a collective identity with a shared territory. In this sense territory has three dimensions. It is material, as in a stretch of land or sea. It has a functional element, meaning that some polity organizes the territory for particular ends. Lastly, there is a symbolic element that links the territory to social identity. People express attachments to territory in other words. The idea that states, societies, and nations necessarily coincide within well-defined territories has been extensively critiqued (*see* METHODOLOGICAL NATIONALISM; TERRITORIAL TRAP). Territories need not be associated just with states; gang turfs are an obvious example of a territory.

A second approach to territory regards it in more processual terms, not as a static object with a fixed set of characteristics (*see* TERRITORIALITY). Anssi *Paasi describes the social processes through which territory is institutionalized. These include the construction and communication of boundaries by *cartography and other practices, and their symbolization through naming, the use of flags, and related social practices. Administrative practices institutionalize territory. In this sense, territory is always an ongoing accomplishment and can, under certain circumstances, be dissolved, for example with the break-up of the former Soviet Union.

The third main approach to territory is informed by *Foucault's analysis of sovereignty and *governmentality. Rather than seek general properties of territory, British geographer Stuart Elden has argued that it must be grasped in its historical and geographical specificity. His *geneaological perspectve focuses on the changing techniques for measuring and controlling terrain over the past several centuries (*see* GENEAOLOGY). *See also* PROPERTY.

Further reading Elden, S., (2010), 'Land, terrain, territory', *Progress in Human Geography*, 34(6): 799–817.
Paasi, A. (2008), 'Territory', in Agnew, J., Mitchell, K., and Toal, G. (eds.) *A Companion to Political Geography*, 108–122.
Storey, D. (2001), *Territory: the Claiming of Space*.

terrorism A premeditated act of violence and intimidation directed against civilians and intended to achieve clear political aims. Beyond this simple definition, there is much dispute over what terrorism actually means. Most official or government definitions restrict terrorism to organized non-state actors such as insurgents and revolutionaries. Critical scholars, however, suggest that states also use terrorist methods and tactics. This is certainly true from an historical perspective. Stalin's Great Terror in 1930s USSR was designed to achieve mass repression, for example (*see* STALINISM). Furthermore, who is or is not a terrorist is often a matter of politicized judgement. It is often said that one person's 'freedom fighter' is another person's terrorist, depending on one's sympathies and allegiances; Nelson Mandela was regarded as a terrorist by the South African authorities. With the proliferation of '*new wars' and *shadow states, where the lines between crime, violence, and authority are disrupted, it may be increasingly difficult to differentiate state from non-state actors in the way many official definitions imply. Whoever the perpetrator, state or non-state, organized group, or lone individual, acts of terror generally share a number of characteristics. They are often, but not always, without warning, directed at public sites such as marketplaces, places of worship, and transport hubs, and intended not simply to cause harm but to spread fear among the widest possible audience. Terrorist acts have a communicative aspect. They include assassination and bombing but also torture and abduction, rape and organized *sexual violence, and the destruction of homes and significant sites. Geographical work on terrorism has therefore considered locational aspects, as well as managerial responses, drawing parallels with *hazards. But other geographers have approached terrorism more critically, exploring the political, economic, and geopolitical roots of fear and violence more generally.

Further reading Gallaher, C. (2009), 'Terrorism.', in Gallaher, C., Dahlman, C. T., Gilmartin, M., Mountz, A., and Shirlow, P., *Key Concepts in Political Geography*, 247–59.
Gregory, D. and Pred, A. (eds.) (2007), *Violent Geographies*.
Hoffman, B. (1998), *Inside Terrorism*.

((())) SEE WEB LINKS
• US Department of State List of Foreign Terrorist organizations.

text A term to describe printed or written material. Text can refer to the entire body of such material or to a particular manifestation, as in textbook. When speaking in terms of text, one is normally thinking about the content or what is communicated, rather than the material object of, say, a book. Within human geography, these literal meanings have been extended by more metaphorical uses. Anything that can be treated as an organized set of signs or symbols might be described as a text (*see* SEMIOTICS). For example, the architecture of buildings or the features of a *cultural landscape can be regarded as possessing textuality, the properties of a text. A map, likewise, has textual properties. In this sense, they can be read.

There are two main kinds of analysis of texts within human geography. One, typified by *content analysis, focuses on the systematic and often quantitative scrutiny of written texts looking for patterns, word frequencies, and word associations (*see* CONTENT

CLOUD). The other form of analysis presupposes that textual meanings are variously unstable, layered, or hidden in some way, and therefore require interpretation. *Hermeneutics, *deconstruction, and *discourse analysis are examples of these more qualitative approaches to texts, trying to probe their means of *representing the world (*see* ICONOGRAPHY). These approaches feature strongly in *cultural geography, although critics warn of focusing too much on the texts at the expense of the practices and context of their use. One path has led to a greater interest in texts as material objects, either in their circulation (*see* IMMUTABLE MOBILE; READING) or through 'materialist hermeneutics' which address how technologies and formats of printing and book production shape geographical knowledge. A second path, characterized by new work on critical *cartography, treats texts such as *maps in a more processual way, reflecting on their manifestation through practices, e.g. standing in a city street attempting to use a map to locate oneself. (*See also* LITERATURE).

Further reading Barnes, T. and Duncan, J. (eds.) (1991), *Writing Worlds: Discourse, Text and Metaphors in the Representation of Landscape.*

Dixon, D. P. (2010), 'Analyzing meaning', in Gomez, B. and Jones III, J. P. (eds.) *Research Methods in Geography*, 392–407.

Mayhew, R. (2007), 'Materialist hermeneutics, textuality and the history of geography', *Journal of Historical Geography* 33: 466–88.

textuality *See* TEXT.

Thatcherism The political ideas associated with Margaret Thatcher (1925–), prime minister of the UK (1979–90) and leader of the Conservative Party (1975–90). During her three terms of office she prioritized private enterprise, low taxes, control of money supply, deregulation, the privatization of utilities and state-owned companies, and restrictions on workers' rights. These policies were pursued with conviction rather than by consensus. Sociologist Stuart Hall described Thatcherism as a kind of 'authoritarian populism', a liberal stance on the economy laced with conservative social values. *See also* NEOLIBERALISM; REAGANISM.

The Earth as Transformed by Human Action A multi-authored volume (1993) that aimed to document at global and regional scales the main changes to the Earth's biosphere over the past 300 years. Inspired by *Man's Role in Changing the Face of the Earth* (1956), it began with a symposium at Clark University in 1987 and thereafter sought to provide a definitive account of global environmental change. The team of editors was headed by Billie L. Turner II. *See also* ENVIRONMENTAL GEOGRAPHY; SUSTAINABILITY SCIENCE.

thematic map A *map that focuses on one specific theme, rather than providing a general *topographical map that combines various kinds of data. For example, a thematic map might concentrate on displaying the spatial distribution of population, health, transportation, climate, soils, geology, and so on. A good example is *choropleth maps that usually display just a single variable.

Theoretical Geography A text that was among the first significant books associated with *spatial science. Author William *Bunge (1962) argued that geography was a science, that its aim was to find spatial laws, and that geometry and mathematical *cartography were the means of finding them. He was one of the first geographers to explicitly identify a theoretical project as distinct from but complementary to empirical inquiry (*see* THEORY).

theory A coherent though revisable set of concepts and statements designed to explain the way some aspect of the world works. Theory typically addresses 'how?' and 'why?'

questions (pertaining to causality), rather than only 'what?' questions (pertaining to the number and characteristics of real world phenomena). In the biophysical sciences, a theory is often the result of piecing together separate *hypotheses that have withstood the tests of *falsification and *verification. In the social sciences, including human geography, theory is typically the result of a less formal testing of concepts and hypotheses— especially the *Grand Theory associated with the likes of Karl *Marx, Ulrich Beck, Anthony *Giddens, or Jurgen Habermas. These writers proposed theories intended to represent in knowledge the major sets of institutions, social relationships, and processes that structure thought and action in people's everyday lives. They offered a metaphorical view from 'on high', making visible the totality obscured when one is forced to live life 'on the ground' (*see* HOLISM). The 'test' of such theories' validity could not be a set of laboratory or even field experiments because societies are complex systems spaced out across territory and changeable over time. Only some combination of inference, deduction, *retroduction, and abstraction would identify the combination of invisible and translocal forces that make societies more than the sum of their members' separate discourses and practices.

Between the 1960s and 1990s the well-springs of theory in human geography came from economics, political economy, and sociology respectively. The *location theory characteristic of *spatial science tried to explain what it took to be orderly patterns of location and movement on the Earth's surface. It made reference to the 'rational' decisions made by individual actors possessed of finite resources they could nonetheless deploy in a range of ways to achieve one or more ends (*see* RATIONAL ACTOR; REDUCTIONISM). In the 1970s, Marxists focused less on individual decision-makers, and more on the historically specific overarching processes capable of both unifying and differentiating the global *space economy (*see* MARXIST GEOGRAPHY; MODE OF PRODUCTION; REGULATION THEORY). Their theories were intended to represent the injustices and contradictions of an economic system that location theory simply took for granted as correctable 'side effects' of otherwise rational human behaviour. In the 1980s, sensing the problems of fixating on *capitalism to the exclusion of all else, attempts were made to theorize relations, processes, and institutions that were widespread but irreducible to *class or capital *accumulation. The philosophy of *critical realism, influential during this decade, was an attempt to show theorists how to study complex 'open systems' in which a myriad of contingently related phenomena were in play.

From the mid-1990s human geographers' engagement with theory changed in two key respects. First, a new suspicion about the claims of 'meta-theory' (otherwise known as *Grand Theory) arose because of the arguments made by *postmodern philosophers. There was a new preference for 'minor theory' that was more circumscribed in its epistemological ambitions and more aware of its 'local' origins. Second, a less formal and 'muscular' sort of theory issuing from the *humanities began to catch human geographers' eyes. Such theory typically focused less on the major components comprising contemporary societies (e.g. economy, state, *community, nation state, the public sphere, or the household). Instead, attention was paid to *discourse, *representation, and *visuality in an attempt to show how a myriad of social actors in all walks of life create and respond to messages whose meanings are as material as the things they refer to. Geographical research under the umbrella of *post-colonialism is a good example of this switch to using cultural theory. Some critics felt that, for all its virtues, this research lost sight of the enduring importance of large-scale economic and political forces in structuring life locally and globally (as evidenced by the impacts of the financial crisis that began in 2007). Others felt that the theoretical concepts in play—such as Michel *Foucault's ideas of 'power-knowledge' and *governmentality—were too generic or semantically slippery. However, still others were able to blend cultural, social, and economic theory in productive ways in order to show the interpenetration of realms long thought to be separate (e.g. love and gift-giving, on the one side, and money-making on the other). For instance, some research into the geographies of *neoliberalism drew on both neo-Marxist and Foucauldian ideas to show the relations between changing practices in business and government and new subject-positions into which ordinary people were being interpellated. Alternatively, by using cultural theory against Marxist *political economy, J-K *Gibson-Graham tried to reveal present and future alternatives to *capitalism.

In recent years, many human geographers reacting to the limitations of theory in its various forms have taken a more philosophical turn. They have looked for a language that can sensitize us to the world's variety and complexity, its fissures and openings. For them, even in a 'minor' key, theory in human geography has been too certain in its claims, too fixated on the moves of the powerful, or the reactions of those engaged in organized *resistance. *Non-representational theory is a good example in that it is very much not a theory in the conventional sense, but rather a set of intellectual tools to be worked with performatively to present novel or surprising *affects. For a previous generation of theorists this is to give up on theory altogether. For them, the challenge remains deriving theory from and testing it against the complications of everyday life, while making it part of the politics of progressive change. Because human geographers, like most academics, have been progressively professionalized, questions arise about whether and how theoretically informed research can connect to real world organizations agitating for a better world. Questions also continue to arise about the *eurocentricity of much of the theory that human geographers find de rigeur. Does such theory merely serve to entrench the interests of those living in one part of the globe, even as they proclaim an interest in the *Global South? (*see* POST-DEVELOPMENT).

Further reading Harvey, D. (1973), 'Revolutionary and counter-revolutionary theory in geography', in *Social Justice and the City*.

Katz, C. (1996), 'Towards minor theory', *Environment and Planning D: Society and Space* 14, 3: 487–99.

McDowell, L. (2nd ed. 2002), 'Problems of/for theory', in Johnston, R. J. et al. (eds.) *Geographies of Global Change*, 296–309.

therapeutic landscape A place that is beneficial to one's health. The study of therapeutic landscapes examines the relationship between place and *well-being, and how different kinds of places beyond medical facilities either enhance one's health or harm it. Such landscapes include the home, spas, temples, holy wells, retreats, and gardens, and they aid well-being in physical and psychological ways, especially in reducing stress or separating people from unhealthy situations such as drug-taking or domestic violence.

Further reading Williams, A. (ed.) (2007), *Therapeutic Landscapes*.

thick description An approach to and objective of *ethnography that regards culture in terms of complex layers of meaning not immediately accessible to outsiders. From this perspective, the aim of the ethnographer is not to find structural patterns in cultural life, nor to explain cultural behaviour through identifying causes. Moreover, it goes beyond the 'thin description' of enumerating facts and details. Closely associated with the anthropologist Clifford Geertz, thick description involves the analysts' interpretation of others' interpretations of what is going on. There is no escape from interpretation to some bedrock reality. Geertz's view of culture is similar to other *interpretive approaches, centred on finding meaning (*see* HERMENEUTICS; TEXT). To do so requires the ethnographer to attend not to just what is said, but how things are said, and how speech is accompanied by various gestures and non-verbal forms of communication. But ethnography is more than just decoding. In Geertz's view, it should be more like the work of a literary critic, who adds something. In human geography, Geertz's ideas informed the *cultural turn and were developed at length by James S. *Duncan in his book *The City of Text* (2005) about the Kandayan kingdom of Sri Lanka.

Reference Geertz, C. (1973), *The Interpretation of Cultures*.

Third Italy, the A number of adjacent provinces in the central northern part of Italy noted for their clusters of design-related craft industries. The region includes Tuscany, Umbria, Emilia-Romagna, and neighbouring provinces. Within the region there are clusters of *small and medium–sized enterprises specializing in high value-added industries such as jewellery, fashion accessories, knitwear, and ceramics. It is called Third Italy as distinct from the *Fordist centres of mass production in the north and the less-developed south, implying that the area is an exemplar of a new form of industrial organization (*see* AGGLOMERATION; FLEXIBLE ACCUMULATION).

thirdspace A concept and argument centred on the proposition that it is necessary to think beyond the dualisms which characterize conventional understandings of space. As formulated by Edward *Soja and influenced by Henri *Lefebvre, thirdspace is neither solid material space nor imagined mental space—the usual dualism used to differentiate meanings of the term—but something both and more than these. Soja describes third-space as a creative combination and extension of existing ideas, regarding this way of thinking as opening up possibilities for emancipation.

Further reading Soja, E. W. (1996), *Thirdspace: Journeys to Los Angeles and other Real-and-Imagined Spaces*.

third space An indeterminate, fluid, mutable, liminal space that is neither dominated by one group or another. It was developed as a concept within post-colonial studies by Homi Bhabba in *The Location of Culture* (1994) and refers to a space positioned in between the colonizer and colonized characterized by *hybridity in which translation and negotiation can happen. Here, the conjunction of colonizer and colonized space produces a third space that is productive of new possibilities, creating new cultural meanings and inclusionary politics.

Third World The economically poorer countries of the world, largely found in Asia, Africa, Latin America, and Oceania. Regarded as arbitrary or even pejorative, since the late 1990s the term has gradually been replaced by alternatives such as *Global South or *Less Economically Developed Country.

The idea of a *tiers monde* or Third World was first popularized by French demographer Alfred Sauvy in the 1950s. In the context of the *Cold War and *modernization theory, Sauvy identified a group of countries aligned neither with the capitalist West ('First World') nor the Soviet communist bloc ('Second World'). The question he posed was which path these countries would follow, capitalist or communist, and how would this shape the unity of the world? As the promise of development anticipated by modernization theories failed to appear by the end of the 1960s, 'Third World' came to stand for a more negative state of affairs: *poverty, *deprivation, high population growth rates, and poor *infrastructure. Separated from its original, more optimistic context, the term became a catch-all description that overlooked the enormous variety of *culture, society, and history within the countries so described. It was subject to criticism both from the right because of its associations with aid-dependency, and the left in the form of *post-development theories.

Following the collapse of the USSR, the idea of a Second World also ceased to have much contemporary relevance. Nonetheless, the term lives on, for example, in the international studies journal *Third Word Quarterly*, although here it is often expressed in the plural to imply diversity.

Further reading Chari, S. and Corbridge, S. (eds.) (2008), *The Development Reader*.

Thrift, Nigel (1949–) A highly productive and influential British geographer whose writing has spanned the breadth of human geography. He worked at the Australian National University, the University of Wales, Lampeter, and the University of Bristol before becoming Pro-Vice Chancellor for Research at the University of Oxford in 2003 and Vice-Chancellor of Warwick University in 2006. He has served as the managing editor of *Environment and Planning A*, and *Environment and Planning D: Society and Space*, and has been a key figure in the British Research Assessment Exercise. Thrift is a theorist of some note and he has contributed to a number of debates across the discipline and the social sciences more broadly. He has been a key catalyst in introducing social theory to geography and fostering the *spatial turn. In the early part of his career his work focused on economic development, *political economy, *structuration theory, *new regionalism, and *time geography. From the early 1990s he has continued his work on time geography and economic geography, especially through a focus on the geographies of finance and *soft capitalism (*Knowing Capitalism* 2005), but these engagements have been inflected with post-structural theory. More broadly he has turned his focus to issues of *identity, *subjectivity, *representation, and *power and has been a key architect of *non-representational theory which shifts attention to practices, *performativity, and embodied knowledge (*Non-Representational Theory* 2007). His empirical attention focused on engagements with technology and understanding cities, in *Cities: Reimagining the Urban* (with Ash Amin 2002).

Tiananmen Square A very large public square in *Beijing, *China. It is adjacent to the Forbidden City, location of the imperial palace of China's ruling dynasties from 1368 to 1912. First built in the 17th century, the square was greatly enlarged in the 1950s. It is the site of many important national events, including Mao's declaration of the formation of the People's Republic of China in 1949 and, more recently, mass demonstrations in favour of greater political reform in June 1989. These were suppressed by the military leading to civilian casualties; the crackdown drew protests from around the world.

time A fundamental dimension manifest in the sequential ordering of events and existence into past, present, and future. Within human geography, a distinction is generally made between the idea of time as an invariant or universal dimension, something which together with *space forms the backdrop to events and matter (i.e. absolute time), and time as a socially constructed quality. The key insight derived from understanding time socially is that we should not confuse the apparently objective and universal sense of time as measured by clocks and calendars with time more generally. Understood socially, time can take on different meanings in different cultures and be experienced in multiple ways. In this sense, time has a history. This can best be appreciated by considering how, between medieval and industrial periods in Europe, the meaning, experience, and objective qualities of time changed. From being principally related to seasonal cycles and religious calendars, time was increasingly organized around the requirements of coordinating industrial labour. Sociologist Max Weber regarded the clock as the key technology of *capitalism. Without it employers and employees could not agree on when waged labour should start and stop. First the hour and then the second became common measures of time and therefore of labour. Time becomes commodified. As detailed by Nigel *Thrift, the coordination of multiple local solar times into first national and then international systems in the form of time zones in the course of the 19th century was critical to the circulation of goods and people. A common feature of many current grand or epochal theories of change is that this modern industrial time is being broken down and reconfigured either by increased acceleration (e.g. *time-space compression) or by the enhanced simultaneity afforded by *information and communication technologies. In *The Rise of the Network Society* (1996) Manuel Castells terms the decomposition of sequential order 'timeless time', corresponding with the *space of flows. He and others also propose that different people inhabit different temporalities, contrasting the accelerated life of *kinetic elites with the greater stasis of low-income communities. Moreover, key biological or natural constraints may be overcome by technological intervention, for example, in extending the human reproductive age or the appearance of fresh produce in supermarket shelves.

With a few exceptions, human geographers have usually treated time and space separately, and given priority to space (*see* HISTORICISM; SPATIAL TURN). Within *historical geography there have been recurrent debates on whether to approach time as a series of snapshots or more as a process. *Time-geography considers time as a resource on a par with space and work in this tradition often highlights the problems of coordinating tasks in time and space. Geographers interested in work are increasingly interested in the struggles between employees, employers, and regulatory authorities over working hours and *flexible labour arrangements. For example, operatives in India's call-centre industry must be awake in the European daytime, often at great personal cost, while live-in domestic workers may find that they have no time of their own.

References and further reading Crang, M. (2011), 'Time' in Agnew, J. and Livingstone, D. (eds.) *The SAGE Handbook of Geographical Knowledge*, 331–43.
Glennie, P. and Thrift, N. (2009), *Shaping the Day: a History of Timekeeping in England and Wales 1300–1800*.
May, J. and Thrift, N. (eds.) (2001), *Timespace: Geographies of Temporality*.
Nadeem, S. (2009), 'The uses and abuses of time: globalization and time arbitrage in India's outsourcing industries', *Global Networks* 9: 20–40.

time-geography A conceptual framework and associated approach to human geography that highlights how *time and space are resources in social action. Developed by Torsten *Hägerstrand and his colleagues at Lund University, Sweden, in the 1970s and 1980s, it is one of the most significant attempts to construct an original and foundational human geographic approach. Some of the initial limitations to time-geography based on data availability and computational power have now been overcome, and it is enjoying a revival.

Time-geography combines *ontological thought with a better-known notational system, which can also serve as a method. Hägerstrand had a holistic vision of geography as integrating human and physical elements in their specific contexts. He regarded time and space not as absolutes but as related to matter (*see* SPACE). This led him to seek a materialist perspective on social life emphasizing humans' corporeality and their constraint by time-space. Humans can be considered goal-orientated beings, intent on accomplishing 'projects' such as buying milk from a shop or organizing a conference. To realize any project necessitates movement, which always involves a trade-off between space and time resources. Walking to a shop uses time. An individual's sequence of movements and stationary activities in pursuit of a project can be described as a space-time path. This in turn is subject to certain 'constraints': of capability, e.g. the need to eat and sleep; of 'coupling', the need to be at the same place at the same time as someone else to achieve something; and of authority, the regulatory field within which an individual has to operate, e.g. laws governing the opening hours of shops. From these basics Hägerstrand devised a specialized vocabulary (e.g. 'domain', 'station', 'bundle'), and a system for representing time-space paths in diagrams. For example, given all the constraints one could draw a time-space prism defining the limits of what was possible for an individual. A simple example might be a hunter-gatherer whose search for food is defined by the speed at which they can walk (which translates into distance), and their need to return to their encampment by nightfall.

It was perhaps no coincidence that time-geography was elaborated in Sweden. Swedish geography and social sciences in general has a strong applied component (*see* APPLIED GEOGRAPHY). The notational system could provide a framework for thinking through the consequences of planning and policies for people's well-being and ability to coordinate their tasks. For example, given the timetabling of public transport and the opening hours of peri-natal clinics, how possible is it for expectant mothers to attend them? How can parents take two children to school and nursery and arrive at their own workplaces on time? Geographers interested in transport and *accessibility were therefore attracted to time-geography (*see* TRANSPORT GEOGRAPHY). Dealing with large numbers of movements proved problematic until later advances in *geocomputation and *visualization. US geographer Mei-Po Kwan, for example, has produced innovative work combining surveys, *travel diaries, and official statistics to explore the relations between race, class, and gender on the one hand, and everyday movement through the city on the other. But time-geography was not confined to planning applications. Anthony *Giddens tried to incorporate its ideas into his social theory of *structuration. Allan *Pred realized its possibilities in this direction through his extensive research on rural and urban change in 19th-century Sweden.

Time-geography was criticized for reducing movement and encounter to an abstract geometry, although this misses the connections between the notation system and the underlying ontology. Its diagrammatic depiction of movement contrasts with later work on moving bodies informed by *non-representational theory. Feminist geographers, notably Gillian *Rose, objected to the unmarked body depicted in the diagrams, i.e. bodies stripped of difference. The idea that individuals can move through space overlooks many of the obstacles blocking passage. But, Hägerstrand's basic interest in the phenomenology of movement, rest, and encounter as constitutive elements of everyday life has appealed to geographers interested in *mobility (*see* MOBILITY TURN/PARADIGM). Given the apparent increase in the number and complexity of the tasks of coordinating work, family, and social life faced by contemporary urban dwellers, it seems likely that time-geography will continue to flourish.

Further reading Kwan, M. P. (2004), 'Geovisualization of human activity patterns using 3D GIS: a time-geographic approach', in Goodchild, M. F. and Janelle, D. G. (eds.) *Spatially Integrating Social Sciences* 48–60.
Neutens, T., Schwanen, T., and Witlox, F. (2011), 'The prism of everyday life: towards a research agenda for time geography', *Transport Reviews* 31(1): 25–47.

time-series analysis The statistical analysis of time-series data (data that has been repeatedly collected at set time periods) and forecasts based on that analysis. Time-series analysis is used to understand spatio-temporal change, that is, how variables change across time and space, and is reliant on *longitudinal data. A variety of techniques can be used, including spectral analysis that seeks to distinguish the long-term trend, cyclical and oscillating functions, and random or irregular functions; cross-spectral analysis that compares sites; and the expansion method that examines patterns of growth over time. Time-space forecasting models that use *regression techniques are employed to predict future spatial patterns given past trends. Time-series analysis has been extensively applied in *medical geography and *epidemiology research to examine the diffusion of diseases. *See also* TIME-GEOGRAPHY.

time-space The dyadic conjoining of *time and *space that recognizes that they are mutually constituted and it therefore makes little sense to conceive of them separately. The argument is that everyday life takes place in both time and space—everything happens at some time in some place—therefore thinking about time and space as separate categories tends to lead to one being prioritized over the other. This has negative consequences because, as May and Thrift note, prioritization of time produces a 'debilitating historicism' that reduces space to a neutral backdrop and a prioritization of space leads to debilitating 'spatial imperialism' that overemphasizes space at the expense of time. Time-space extends beyond the idea of four-dimensional time-space (a four-dimensional version of absolute space: three space axes plus time), however, to recognize a multiplicity of time-spaces that are relational, contingent, dynamic, and paradoxical. *See also* PARADOXICAL SPACE; PRODUCTION OF SPACE; RELATIONAL SPACE; SPACE.

Reference May, J. and Thrift, N. (eds.) (2001), *Timespace: Geographies of Temporality*.

time-space compression The phenomenon that places seem closer together and more interconnected due to improvements in transport and communications technologies. Time-space compression consists of two related processes. First, time-space convergence is the rapid shrinkage in the time it takes to travel or communicate between places. Places that used to take months to travel between by boat or by horse, with speed dictated by natural physiology and wind, can now be travelled in hours due to advances in technology (e.g., cars, planes) and infrastructure (e.g., canals, rail, roads, airports). A similar process of convergence has occurred with communications through the development of *telecommunications, to the degree that communication and the sending of information is now undertaken in real-time. As a consequence, the *friction of distance dissipates in shaping interactions through the 'annihilation of space by time'. Second, time-space distanciation is the interpenetration and integration of places, so that separate and self-contained systems become increasingly interdependent. That is, people in one location can profoundly shape what is happening elsewhere, for example, managers in a *multinational company's headquarters in one city making decisions that affect workers in another. Similarly, people, goods, services, and information from many diverse locations flow in and out of places daily, creating what Doreen *Massey has termed a 'progressive sense of place', meaning that the character of a place is shaped as much by processes from outside intersecting with it as those acting within it (*see* POWER-GEOMETRY). Time-space compression is understood as a key process underpinning *globalization, creating a world that is shrinking in relative size, is speeded up, is relatively inexpensive to traverse, and is ever-more interconnected and interdependent. For David *Harvey, it is not simply a technologically driven process (*see* TECHNOLOGICAL DETERMINISM) but rather transport and ICT developments are being driven by the need to reduce the turnover time of capital. In other words, time-space compression is produced in order to facilitate *capitalism and the accumulation of profit.

Further reading Allen, J. and Hamnett, C. (eds.) (1985), *A Shrinking World?*
Harvey, D. (1989), *The Condition of Postmodernity*.
Massey, D. (1993), 'Power-geometry and a progressive sense of place', in Bird, J., Curtis, B., Putnam, T., Robertson, G., and Tickner, L. (eds.) *Mapping the Futures: Local Cultures, Global Change* 59–69.

time-space convergence *See* TIME-SPACE COMPRESSION.

time-space diary A method for recording an individual's location, travel path, and activity at different times. Respondents are asked to keep a diary in which they record their spatial behaviour, charting their movement across the landscape, including their time of arrival and departure at locations. They might also be asked to record other associated data, including who else they met or the purpose of their trip. In the age of *big data, large time-space diary data sets that are automatically generated, is increasingly possible. For example, the Oyster Card system in London records the origin and destinations of journeys across the city. Time-space diary data are used to model human *spatial behaviour and as inputs into *time-geography analysis and *transportation models.

time-space distanciation *See* TIME-SPACE COMPRESSION.

time-space forecasting models The statistical models that try to predict the evolution of a system over both space and time. In essence, the models seek to predict how a geographical area will develop over time given its past history, present conditions, and the spatial processes at work. Weather models are an obvious common example, but also planning and regional models that seek to forecast the likelihood of an area flooding or predict how a region might perform under different economic scenarios.

tipping point A concept popularized by the economist Malcolm Gladwell (2000), it is the threshold at which a phenomenon, object, system, or process is displaced from a state of stable equilibrium into a new status that is dissimilar from the first, and which is difficult to reverse. Preceding a tipping point there is a build up of small, incremental changes that, in and of themselves, make little difference to the status quo. Once a tipping point is reached, change tends to be rapid. An example of a tipping point is the replacement of one technology with another. For example, car travel reached a tipping point, and largely superseded rail travel, when cars became cheap enough that the majority of households could afford one. It is presently argued that climate change is reaching a tipping point at which global warming will be impossible to reverse. It is an important concept in *complexity theory where the identification of when a system is liable to become unstable and undergo a critical transition is a key problem.

Further reading Gladwell, M. (2000), *Tipping Point.*
Scheffer, M. (2010), 'Complex systems: foreseeing tipping points', *Nature* 467: 411–12.

TNC *See* TRANSNATIONAL CORPORATION.

Tobin tax A tax on currency exchange transactions proposed by Nobel-prize winning economist James Tobin in 1972. Its aim was to slow down speculation in currency markets, so reducing their volatility. Variants on the idea, including levies on transactions in shares, bonds, and derivatives in order to fund development, featured in campaigns for a so-called 'Robin Hood tax' in the wake of the 2008 world financial crisis. Collectively, such ideas are known as Financial Transactions Taxes (FTT).

Tobler's first law of geography The proposition that 'everything is related to everything else, but near things are more related than distant things' set out by Swiss-American geographer Waldo Tobler in 1970. In essence, it implies that all forms of social interaction are subject to distance decay.

Todaro model An economic *model of rural-urban *migration that seeks to explain growing *urbanization, particularly in developing countries. Also known as the Harris-Todaro model, it seeks to account for migration from rural areas to cities even when the opportunities for employment in urban areas are low, arguing that migration is seen as an individual investment, increasing the probability of obtaining better employment with a higher wage. This is especially the case if industrial wages are substantially higher than agricultural wages. Unemployment acts to create equilibrium, regulating the flow of migrants. Migration in these terms is a rational economic behaviour.

Tokyo The capital city of *Japan and part of Greater Tokyo, generally reckoned to be the largest or one of the largest metropolitan regions in the world. With around thirty five million inhabitants, the Tokyo region is also the world's most concentrated area of consumer purchasing power. It is an archetypal *global city, a centre for multinational finance, services, and manufacturing industries.

topographic map *See* TOPOGRAPHY.

topography The examination of the Earth's surface and its salient physical and cultural features. A topographic map portrays the topography of an area. The shape of the Earth's surface is usually detailed through contour lines, with features such as rivers, roads, and different kinds of buildings also included, along with place names, a scale, and legend. The underlying data for the map creation is produced through *surveying and *photogrammatery, and is usually generated by national mapping agencies. *See also* AERIAL PHOTOGRAPHY; GEOMATICS; TOPONYMS.

topology A branch of geometry that analyses connectivity and relative location. In geography, topology generally refers to the location of nodes and their connectivity to other nodes to form *networks and is usually analysed using *graph theory. In visualizing the topology of a network, it is the mapping of the connections that is key, rather than the precise location of nodes and routes. For example, the London Tube map is a map of topology rather than *topography.

toponym A term for a place name, while toponymy is the study of place names, in particular their origins and what they can reveal about the history or nature of a place. In much of the world there is often either no agreed name for places or their names are contested for political, cultural, and historical reasons.

Further reading Nash, C. (1999), 'Irish place-names: post-colonial locations', *Transactions of the Institute of British Geographers* 24: 457–80.

Topophilia A much-cited book by Yi-Fu *Tuan (1974) that examines the relationship between people and environment from a *humanistic geography perspective. *Topophilia* literally means the love of place, with Tuan using the concept to explore the affective bonds between people and settings, and *environmental perception, attitudes, and values (*see* AFFECT). Tuan weaves together arguments from philosophy, especially *phenomenology, religion, art, and psychology to consider *place attachment and how people relate on an *emotional and perceptual level to the places that they inhabit.

total fertility rate (TFR) The average number of children that would be born to a woman over her lifetime, assuming existing *fertility rates. It is calculated by summing the age-specific fertility rates of women throughout their supposed child-bearing ages, normally 15–49. The TFR of a population is imagined rather than actual figure, because it involves major assumptions about what would happen to a cohort of women over time, but it is useful for demographic comparisons.

tourism A term to cover travel to places away from one's home environment undertaken principally for *leisure but also for business. Tourist activities generally involve spending money in a new location and do not involve remuneration from within the place or country visited. Definitions of tourism by international organizations such as the World Tourist Organization recognize anyone who spends at least one night but no longer than one year somewhere other than their country of residence as a tourist. Tourism is often distinguished from *recreation because it takes place further from the home and is more commercialized. It overlaps with *leisure, but includes business travel. In *The Tourist Gaze* (1991) John Urry argued persuasively that the core feature of tourism was the desire to *gaze upon what was different or unusual. Much of tourism can be understood in terms of the arrangements of places and landscapes to be viewed, and the cultivation of techniques of viewing and circulating images, e.g. photography, video, postcards, etc. But tourist activities do more than please the sense of sight, and often involve multiple embodied experiences, e.g. kayaking, dining, and sunbathing. Tourism is a form of and has its origins in travel, but a distinction is often made between the two; travel is described as a more specialized, niche, or selective activity, while tourism is associated with organized popular or mass activities. In part, the difference is one of marketing or discourse.

Although tourism now includes an increasingly diverse range of activities, perhaps too many for convenient classification, it is often described as the world's largest industry. The World Travel and Tourist Council estimates that tourism accounts for 11 per cent of world GDP and 8 per cent of all waged work (200 million employees). But tourism as it is now understood is a relatively recent phenomenon. Most historical accounts trace its origins to the Grand Tour, undertaken by elite young European men between the 17th and 19th centuries. They would travel within Europe to see and learn about cultural matters, notably the fruits of the *Renaissance and Greek and Roman classical civilizations. Health spas, seaside towns, and mountain resorts also became fixtures for the wealthy traveller. The 19th century saw the development of journeys to *wild places inspired by romantic ideas or picturesque or sublime landscapes: England's Lake District was a leading attraction (*see* WILDERNESS). The spread of road and rail travel in the 19th century allowed the urban working classes to enjoy annual trips to seaside resorts such as Long Island, New York, ushering in the first organized tourist industry. But it was not until the combination of greater affluence, more leisure time, and air travel after the *Second World War that modern mass tourism took off. Until the late 20th century, however, it remained open largely to Westerners, and Europe itself accounted for the majority of international tourist journeys. The *globalization of tourism in the past two or so decades has involved almost every country becoming both an origin and destination of tourist travel to some degree. Close to a billion international tourist visits are now made annually, with China established in the top five for destinations and origins, alongside the USA and European countries. Singapore, Kuala Lumpur, and Dubai also count among the top tourist urban destinations.

The geographical interest in tourism has developed strongly since the 1980s, although there are studies dating back to the 1930s. It draws upon the same range of methods and perspectives as the rest of *human geography, although there are important overlaps with *environmental geography (for example, in coastal and marine environment management) and a strong element of *applied geography. Given that tourism hinges precisely on the differences between one place and another, it is intrinsically geographical. The main areas of research are on factors of supply and demand, but also on social, economic, and environmental impact (*see* RESORT LIFE-CYCLE MODEL). There are separate studies of urban and rural tourism, as well as a concern for regional differences (Hudman and Jackson 2003). The different forms of tourism and their related bodily and sensuous experiences—heritage visits, *ecotourism, package holidays, adventure travel, and backpacking among them—are also well studied. In unpacking the experiences of tours, however, it becomes apparent how many of its core characteristics—difference, exoticism, *cosmopolitanism, leisureliness—are increasingly found more widely and even close to home. The interests of tourist studies in *mobility, pleasure, and difference are, in this regard, central to much of current human geography.

References and further reading Hall, C. M. and Page, S. J. (3rd ed. 2005), *The Geography of Tourism and Recreation: Environment, Place and Space.*
Hudman, L. E. and Jackson, R. H. (4th ed. 2002), *Geography of Travel and Tourism.*
Sheller, M. and Urry, J. (eds.) (2004), *Tourism Mobilities.*

(⊕) **SEE WEB LINKS**

• Website of the Recreation, Tourism and Sport Specialty Group of the Association
  of American Geographers.
• Official website of the World Tourism and Travel Council.

townscape A concept used in *urban geography based on the combination of town
plan, land use units, and architectural forms. This approach was pioneered by Anglo-
German geographer M. R. G. Conzen and carried on by scholars at the University of
Birmingham.

Toyotism A business model pioneered by Japanese auto manufacturer Toyota in the
1960s, prefiguring *flexible accumulation. It includes *just-in-time production, giving
greater autonomy to work teams, constant monitoring and improvement of processes,
and constant quality control, all of which are designed to reduce waste or unnecessary
effort. It differs from *Taylorism and *Fordism by placing more onus on multiskilled and
proficient labour working in teams.

Traces on the Rhodian Shore A book by Clarence J. Glacken (1967) and subtitled
'Nature and Culture in Western Thought from Ancient Times to the End of the Eighteenth
Century'. It was a landmark study in the history of geographical ideas and remains one of
the most important sources for understanding how the ideas of nature and culture have
changed over time. Glacken (1909–89) was chair of the Department of Geography at
the University of California, Berkeley when it was published. *See also* BERKELEY SCHOOL;
ENVIRONMENTAL HISTORY.

trade The buying and selling of goods and services. In the modern world this is
generally achieved through the medium of *money, implying the existence of markets
(*see* MARKET ECONOMY). The direct exchange of goods and services is termed barter, but
is far less significant now than in the past. In capitalist societies, trade is the link between
production and *consumption, and immense efforts go in to making it possible through
regulation (*see* FREE TRADE AGREEMENT; GENERAL AGREEMENT ON TRADE AND TARIFFS;
WORLD TRADE ORGANIZATION).

   In both *human geography and economics, the study of trade within countries has
conventionally been separate from the study of international trade. Economists, and
particularly those working in *new economic geography or geographical economics, are
interested in *international trade theory. This reflects a long-standing belief that trade
between countries is the source of prosperity, a doctrine known as mercantilism. Conventional trade theories stem from the concept of *comparative advantage, which
encourages countries to specialize in certain exports. From 1979 onwards, however,
*Paul Krugman produced a series of models explaining international trade without
presupposing national differences in factor endowments. He showed how trade between
countries with the same endowments takes place based on differences rooted in the
purely economic decision-making by firms. His insights generated a stream of inquiry
into the relations between trade, specialization, and agglomeration. Among other things,
these models seek to explain the apparent paradox of why falling transport costs between
adjacent countries results in more, not less, trade.

   A more common theme in human geographical research is the mapping of international trade flows as a sign of the growing integration and changing patterns of economic
activity. Trade flows are an important subject for economic historians, too, as they are
intertwined with the development of *imperialism and the foundation of globally
*uneven development. As Peter Dicken observes in *Global Shift* (2011), international
trade grew faster than output between 1960 and 2007, suggesting that more of what is
made or extracted is exported. He summarizes the changing patterns in merchandise

trade, which reveal the growing tendency for trade to flow within regions such as the European Union and North America as well as between them. In most cases, a country's major trading partners are still its neighbours. Dicken also maps the *balance of trade, showing the distribution of trade surpluses and deficits by country. These may be the basis of trade disputes if there is a suspicion that they are based on unfair conditions.

Finally, world trade arrangements are the subject of political argument. On the one hand, advocates of free trade and *globalization continue the mercantilist claim that removing barriers to trade will, in the long-run bring prosperity to all. Opponents, notably in the *anti-globalization movement, argue that structural imbalances in the *terms of trade between the *Global North and *Global South lead to *unequal exchange and perpetuate uneven development (*see* IMPORT SUBSTITUTION INDUSTRIALIZATION).
See also DOHA ROUND; FAIR TRADE; FINANCIAL CAPITAL; FOREIGN DIRECT INVESTMENT; NORTH AMERICAN FREE TRADE AGREEMENT.

References and further reading Brakman, S., Garretsen, H., and van Marrewijk, C. (2009), *The New Introduction to Geographical Economics*.
Findlay, R. and O'Rourke, K. H. (2007), *Power and Plenty: Trade, War, and the World Economy in the Second Millennium*.
World Bank (2009), *World Development Report: Reshaping Economic Geography*.

traditional ecological knowledge (TEK) What *indigenous people know and understand about their immediate environments, including botanical classifications (sometimes termed ethnobotany), ecological relations, environmental change, and the values that infuse them. A challenge for environmental scientists is to document such knowledge as both baseline understandings of environment and to translate these into forms compatible with international property rights.

trafficking A trade in illegal goods or in violation of states' trade laws. Drugs, arms, body parts, nuclear material, endangered species, and other commodities may be trafficked, but geographers have focused mostly on human trafficking. This is defined by the United Nations as 'The recruitment, transportation, transfer, harbouring, or receipt of persons, by means of the threat or use of force or other forms of coercion, of abduction, of fraud, of deception, of the abuse of power or of a position of vulnerability or of the giving or receiving of payments or benefits to achieve the consent of a person having control over another person, for the purpose of exploitation.' It is often distinguished from smuggling, which is presumed to involve some consent on behalf of the migrant. In practice, the distinction is difficult to maintain. Human trafficking is often associated with international organized crime, as well as with *slavery, bonded, or *forced labour; it is linked with the *sex trade. Accurate figures are hard to come by, but official estimates suggest around 90 per cent of victims are women and children. One of the dilemmas posed by human trafficking is whether it should be treated as a crime or a *human rights violation.

Whether a particular transaction is trafficking may not be clear. States' regulations of goods vary and international agreements on such things as the trade in arms are hard to enforce, not least because states or their agencies themselves may be engaged in illegal trade. Abraham and Van Schendel distinguish between legal (i.e. considered legitimate by states) and licit (what people regard as legitimate); the two need not be the same.

Reference Van Schendel, W. and Abraham, I. (eds.) (2005), *Illicit Flows and Criminal Things*.

(⊕) SEE WEB LINKS
• Official website of the United Nations Office on Drugs and Crime.

Tragedy of the Commons An allegory or *model of how unfettered use of a resource or good by individuals leads inexorably to over-exploitation, degradation, and/or pollution. The idea is closely associated with Garrett Hardin, whose widely cited paper employed the example of pastoralists. Assuming that the pasture was a *commons, i.e. land not owned by individuals but collectively, Hardin reasoned that there would be no means of preventing each individual pastoralist from increasing the size of their herd. The gains of so doing would accrue to the individual, but the costs—in this case the use of pasture—would be shared by all. As each pastoralist adds animals, so the total number grazing the pasture increases, leading to its inevitable degradation. Furthermore, even if pastoralists were aware of the dangers, they would not be able to prevent the tragedy. No individual would willingly forego the chance of adding to their herd, assuming that their fellow pastoralists were unlikely to be equally self-sacrificing. In other words, Hardin suggested that self-restraint was inconceivable. The tragedy also applied to putting things into the environment, for example, factories polluting the atmosphere.

Hardin presented the allegory as a warning of the risks of uncontrolled population growth, arguing against the idea that each family had the right to determine how many children it wanted. But it has been extended to resource management questions more generally, to suggest that where goods and resources are either held in common (commons) or outside property relations ('open access resources') they will inevitably be diminished. There are two possible solutions, according to this line of thought. One is private ownership of the commons, such that each individual bears the costs and benefits themselves. The other is central or state control, setting up and enforcing rules for using the good. The tragedy of the commons therefore appealed to those wishing to extend privatization and marketization as solutions to environmental problems, from traffic congestion to over-fishing.

Critics of the model point to the many examples of successfully managed commons past and present, arguing that the assumption of individual pursuit of maximum gain does not hold universally (Ostrom 1990). They differentiate between commons, where communities may effectively exclude outsiders and restrain themselves without the need for state sanction, and open access resources, where outside users cannot be prevented from accessing the resource. Furthermore, there are many examples of how the extension of state control over commons through nationalization, has led to greater resource exploitation—known as 'the tragedy of incursion' (McCoy and Anderson 1987). Private ownership may also lead to degradation where short-term profit-making is the priority. Not all common resource use leads to tragedy, and environmental despoliation has causes other than those located in property relations.

References and further reading Hardin, G. (1968), 'The Tragedy of the Commons', *Science*. 162 (3859) 1243–48.
McCoy, B. J. and Anderson, J. M. (eds.) (1987), *The Question of the Commons*.
Mansfield, B. (2001), 'Property regime or development policy? Explaining growth in the US Pacific groundfish fishery', *Professional Geographer* 53(3): 384–97.
Ostrom, E. (1990), *Governing the Commons*.

transactional analysis A method for analysing the mode of organization and transactions that occur between firms within an industrial sector. It calculates the number of firms within an industry and the number of exchanges between them and the rates per firm. A low level of transactions suggests that companies are vertically integrated, relying on internal company transactions to reduce transaction costs, whereas a high number of external transactions suggests a more horizontal mode of organization that utilize *agglomeration economies of scale through subcontracting, and is suggestive of the formation of industrial clusters. The clustering effect takes place in order that transaction costs are not increased through transportation costs.

transaction cost The amount that undertaking an economic exchange costs a company. It is a function of the costs of obtaining the relevant information, finding and checking on customers, fixing the terms of the transaction, and securing payment. In order to reduce transaction costs a company may try to internalize these by, for example, *vertical integration or pooling them through *agglomeration with other companies (*see* UNTRADED INTERDEPENDENCIES).

transcription The translation of a taped *interview to a written text. The process of transcription is usually verbatim, recording everything that was said. It is usually supplemented with *metadata such as details of the person talking, the time, date, and place, and also with annotations and *thick description such as contextual information that will aid its analysis. Once transcribed the text can be analysed using *qualitative techniques such as *content analysis and *deconstruction.

transfer price The amount a *transnational corporation charges itself for economic transactions between countries but within the same company. Unlike prices set externally by the interaction of independent buyers and sellers, transfer prices are fixed internally. They can therefore be used to circumvent or exploit different national taxation systems.

transition economy A country classified as moving from central planning to market-oriented economic principles, for example, China, the successor states to the USSR, and the socialist economies of east and central Europe. The term was widely used by international organizations such as the *OECD and *World Bank in the wake of the collapse of the USSR with the expectation that formerly socialist countries would converge on the liberal democratic model of private property, markets, trade liberalization, and minimal state provision of services. But as a description of countries such as Cambodia, Poland, and China, it risks grouping together very diverse cases. Furthermore, the concept of transition implies a single path of development towards a known destination, overlooking the possibility of alternative trajectories. Some analysts therefore prefer the term transformation. *See also* POST-SOCIALISM.

translation **1.** The expression of the sense of one language by another.
2. In *Actor-Network Theory, the process by which the interests of various actors are aligned to bring them together into an actor-network.

translocal *See* TRANSNATIONALISM.

transnational capitalist class An elite that controls global rather than national circuits of capital accumulation and whose interests transcend those of nation states. Various theorists have arrived at this concept in different ways, though most agree that the transnational capitalist class (TCC) is not simply the aggregation of diverse national capitalist classes. Indeed, their interests may be opposed. The most influential thesis on this class was set out by Leslie Sklair in *The Transnational Capitalist Class* (2001). He proposed that there were four main fractions: (i) the owners and controllers of *transnational corporations and their local affiliates, including the main salaried employees of corporations alongside non-executive directors; (ii) globalizing bureaucrats and politicians, including those championing *neoliberal globalization; (iii) globalizing professionals who perform ideological and technical roles, for example, by operating global benchmarking and certification systems; (iv) consumerist elites (merchants and media), who propagate what Sklair calls the culture-ideology of materialism. The TCC is regarded as a recent phenomenon. William Robinson and Jerry Harris trace the emergence of this class to the decline in Keynesianism (*see* KEYNES, J. M.) and the rise of neoliberalism from the 1970s.

Statements about the transnational capitalist class are best regarded as propositions awaiting further research. One line of inquiry seeks to identify the structural basis of a class by examining interlocking directorates. These are formed when one individual sits on more than one board of directors. *Network analysis can identify key individuals. Testing for the presence of a distinct class consciousness or set of behaviours is much more difficult. If such an elite really exists as a class, one might expect high rates of inter-marriage among their children or other common forms of socialization. Geographers have begun to show an interest in the super-rich, also known as high net worth individuals, but almost by definition, their lives are often shrouded in secrecy.

References and further reading Beaverstock, J., Hubbard, P. J., and Short, J. (2004), 'Getting away with it? Exposing the geographies of the global super-rich', *Geoforum* 35(4): 401-07.

Carroll, W. K. (2009), 'Transnationalists and national networkers in the global corporate elite', *Global Networks*, 9(3): 298-314.

Robinson, W. and Harris, J. 'Toward a global ruling class? Globalization and the transnational ruling class', *Science and Society* 64 (1): 11-54.

transnational communities Social groups that sustain meaningful and ongoing relations across the borders of nation states. Although there are potentially many kinds of transnational community, the exemplar and the case that has received the most attention relates to migrant *transnationalism. First, explicitly identified by anthropologists and sociologists working in the Americas and Caribbean in the 1990s, such communities have been recognized all over the world. There is some debate about the extent, novelty, and significance of these communities and it is generally agreed that transnational practices, e.g. sending *remittances, have a long history. Further, empirical studies have found that the number of individuals engaging in intense transnational activity may be limited, although their impacts can be significant. Thomas Faist suggests a helpful way to delimit transnational communities. 'Transnational families or kinship groups' are held together by relations of reciprocity, for example, through the exchange of gifts, visits, remittances, or marriage. 'Transnational circuits' are based on exchange relations undertaken by mobile traders through trading networks. 'Transnational communities' are characterized by relations of solidarity beyond kinship, based on shared values, beliefs, symbols, and experiences. A common expression of solidarity is the way migrants form associations to raise money or aid for projects in their place of origin; these are often termed 'hometown associations', and they are regarded as increasingly significant vehicles for *development (*see* MIGRANT-DEVELOPMENT NEXUS).

Further reading Faist, T. (2000), *The Volume and Dynamics of International Migration and Transnational Social Spaces*.

Page, B., Mercer, C., and Evans, M. (eds.) (2009), special issue on African transnationalisms and diaspora networks, *Global Networks* 9(2).

Yeoh, B. S. A., Huang, S., and Lam, T. (eds.) (2005) 'Transnationalizing the "Asian" family: imaginaries, intimacies and strategic intents', special issue on Asian Transnational families. *Global Networks* 5(4).

transnational corporation (TNC) A firm that can organize and control activities in more than one country at a time (*see* FOREIGN DIRECT INVESTMENT). The term is often used interchangeably with 'multinational corporation' (MNC). A distinction is sometimes made between firms operating in two countries (transnational) and more than two (multinational); in this definition, a company with operations in Canada and the USA would be trans- but not multinational. Another differentiation is made between *firms that operate in many countries but have one clear home country (multinational), and those which have few attachments to any one particular country (transnational) (*see* TRANSNATIONAL CAPITALIST CLASS). The latter definition would rule out most companies generally regarded as transnational.

The United Nations Conference on Trade and Development (UNCTAD) publishes a Transnationality Index measuring the ratios of foreign to total employment, assets, and sales. On this index, there are very few corporations that are genuinely global. In fact, most TNCs are rooted in home countries, which also shape their ways of doing business, including organizational structures and management recruitment (Morgan et al. 2004). Japanese *keiretsu*, for example, differ from Korean *chaebol* in their patterns of organization and ownership. *Keiretsu* companies are structured around long-term stable relationships between affiliated enterprises, whereas *chaebol* are typically centralized within the control of a single family. Even where their operations are dispersed, they are usually locally embedded, i.e. adjusted to local regulations, cultures, and working practices. Although they are reckoned to account for one third or more of all international trade and a tenth of world *GNP, TNCs directly employ only 1–3 per cent of the world's waged labour force. The vast majority of TNC employees are located in the *Global North. Therefore, it is more accurate to describe TNCs as multilocational rather than global. Transnational corporations are private enterprises, but large multinational operations include *State-Owned Enterprises, especially in *extractive industries.

The geographical research on TNCs is usefully summarized by Peter Dicken in *Global Shift* (6th ed. 2011). He examines the different institutional and spatial organization strategies of such companies and how they manage *global production networks.

Further reading Morgan, G., Kristensen, P. H., and Whitley, R. (eds.) (2004), *The Multinational Firm.*

( ) SEE WEB LINKS
- Weblink to the United Nations Conference on Trade and Development World Investment Report includes the Transnationality Index.

transnationalism The sustained and meaningful flows, networks, and relations connecting individuals and social groups across the borders of nation states. If 'international' processes are exchanges between governments or nation states, for example, diplomacy or trade, then transnational processes are exchanges between various non-state actors, e.g. businesses, *civil society organizations, organized criminal gangs, labour unions, and migrant communities (*see* SOCIAL MOVEMENT; TRANSNATIONAL COMMUNITIES; TRANSNATIONAL CORPORATIONS). Sometimes the term 'transnational' is used in place of global. If there is a difference, it is that transnationalism is more limited in scope than *globalization, referring mainly to social relations (rather than flows of money, goods, or information), and without the implication that the phenomenon described is universal. Baseball, for example, which is played within a small number of countries, might be described as transnational while football/soccer is global. These distinctions are not rigid. It is not always clear, for example, when an organization is 'non-state' (*see* STATE). Furthermore, it is not usual to describe regular and shorter-distance cross-border movement, for example, by commuting workers between neighbouring countries, as transnational. By the same token, ongoing long-distance exchanges within countries, for instance, between cities and villages in China, is not termed transnational. An alternative term is '*translocal' and 'translocalism', highlighting that meaningful social connections are often sustained between specific places. Translocalism captures the sense of individuals who can be said to live in two places at the same time. The emphasis is therefore in contrast with the vaguer concept of *deterritorialization, which is sometimes said to result from heightened individual *mobility. Perhaps the most significant area of research in this field is on migrant transnationalism (*see* DIASPORA; MIGRANT).

Further reading Brickell, K. and Datta, A. (eds.) (2011), *Translocal Geographies.*
Vertovec, S. (2009), *Transnationalism.*

transparency Openness and clarity in how research was conducted and for what purpose. Transparency in the aims, objectives, methods, and outcomes of research is

important to enable readers to understand and replicate a study, and to establish trust
and accountability in the research findings and their interpretation.

transport(ation) geography The study of the spatial distribution and effects of
transport modalities and *infrastructure, and the movement of people and goods through
transport systems. Transportation is an essential aspect of everyday life, *work, and
*trade, facilitating all kinds of flows and interactions between locations and across scales,
and mediating *spatial behaviour and the development of local and regional *space-
economies. The study of transport has long been a part of geographical inquiry as a core
component of *regional geography. Here, research focused on the connections and
interactions between locales, and the effects of transportation on trade, development,
and geopolitical stability, both historically and in the contemporary period of study. For
example, the development of the northwest of England and the growth of the city of
Liverpool was recognized to be based on its status as a deep water *port. The city
developed as a trading hub, connected to its *hinterland by road, canals, and rail, and
to the rest of the world through shipping, becoming a vital conduit for Britain's *Industrial Revolution and *colonial expansion. When the importance of shipping declined in
the late 20th century, the city and wider region's fortunes similarly suffered.

During the 1960s and the *Quantitative Revolution, transport geography developed to
become a distinct subfield in the discipline as geographers sought to develop spatial laws
and models with respect to the spatial organization of transport systems and the spatial
interactions that occurred through the network. The application of *network analysis,
*graph theory, and *model building led to the creation of land-use transportation models
for use in *urban and regional planning. Particular attention was applied to the functioning, infrastructure, and roles of different modes of transportation such as *road, *rail,
*waterways, and *shipping. In the following decade, ideas from *behavioural and *time-
geography were used to examine and model individual and household travel activity
patterns and *spatial choice and decision-making with respect to modalities and routes.

These quantitative, modelling-based studies were complemented from the 1980s
onwards by work that examined the *political economy of transport, focusing in particular on issues of infrastructure ownership, regulation, and accessibility, and wider
transportation policy such as creating *intermodal transport systems, and issues of safety
and security. These studies examined the wider structural issues shaping how transportation operated, for example, the effects of deregulation and privatization of public
transit. In addition, there was a growing focus on differential access and costs across
people and places to forms of transport, for example, the exclusion of many disabled
people from public transport, and the reliance on the car in rural areas due to infrequent
bus services along limited routes. Issues of sustainability also came to the fore, especially
in the context of the rising dominance of car travel, dependence on oil, environmental
pollution, and the contribution of transport to climate change. With the growth of *new
economic geography in the 1990s, there was an increasing interest in the role of transportation in trade, especially *logistics and supply chains, and its role in fostering
*globalization through significant *time-space compression.

At the same time, *cultural geographers started to consider the representation and
materiality of travel; how it is discursively produced through *discourse such as images,
adverts, policy documents, and *travel writing, and how journeys are experienced as
*embodied encounters with the world, though this work has had little impact on trans-
port geography itself. Similarly, transport geography's interest in certain forms of movement, such as *migration or *tourism, has largely been restricted to the travel mode, and
flows and patterns of travel, rather than a wider engagement with either phenomenon.

The latest challenge to how transport geography is studied comes from the new
*mobilities paradigm, which posits the notion that movement and flow is not simply

one facet of social and economic relations, but rather is constitutive of human societies and what it means to be human. Mobility is positioned as a key lens through which to examine social relations. From this perspective, transportation is a narrowly conceived and limited aspect of mobility and transportation geography needs to adapt to think more broadly about human mobility and the role of transportation systems in social and economic life. Given its quite narrow and applied policy focus, the extent to which transport geography will widely engage with the new mobilities paradigm is uncertain.

Further reading Black, W. R. (2003), *Transportation: a Geographical Analysis*.

Knowles, R., Shaw, J., and Docherty, I. (eds.) (2008), *Transport Geographies: Mobilities, Flows and Spaces*.

Rodrigue, J.-P, Comtois, C., and Slack, B. (2006), *The Geography of Transport Systems*.

Shaw, J. and Hesse, M. (2010), 'Transport, geography and the "new" mobilities', *Transactions of the Institute of British Geographers* 35: 305–12.

transportation problem The puzzle of minimizing *transport costs between a set of origins and destinations. For example, a company supplying many stores needs to find the least-cost route between them in terms of travel and time costs. Similarly, a team managing a city's traffic flow seeks to establish an optimal pattern of movement that minimizes congestion and delays. In transportation modelling, this problem is explored under different scenarios, such as altering travel costs (e.g. fuel prices) or the network configuration (e.g. adding/removing roads or altering store locations).

transport costs The costs of transporting people, goods, and services between locations. Transport costs are often a key part of a company's operating costs and therefore are a consideration in decisions concerning where to locate operations with respect to suppliers and market. The importance of transport costs to location decisions varies by type of product and can be compensated for by other factors such as tax rates and grants. Costs are not simply the price of vehicles and fuel, but also associated administration and time. *See also* INDUSTRIAL GEOGRAPHY; LOCATIONAL ANALYSIS.

travelling theory The ideas and theories that travel, from person to person, discipline to discipline, situation to situation, place to place, and from one period to another. The concept, coined by the post-colonial scholar Edward *Said in *The World, the Text and the Critic* (1983), concerns the circulation of knowledge, how specific ideas move and mutate, being understood and used in different ways across place, context, and time. As such, Said argued that theories have no fixed meaning, but take on different forms depending on where, when, and how they are used. For Said, the mobility of theory is welcome because it can unblock intellectual and cultural formations, and open up new political possibilities.

travel-to-work *See* COMMUTING.

travel writing Written accounts of a journey from one place to another, or accounts that provide information to fellow travellers. Travel writing covers a whole range of trip types, such as expeditions, excursions, migrations, pilgrimages, and tourist trips, and can take different forms such as a travel diary, an *autobiographical or biographical account, or a travel guide, and the text is often accompanied by illustrations and *photographs. The narrative focuses on people, their culture, and the places, landscape, and environment, usually set within a broader social, political, and historical context. It differs from academic, geographical writing in that it is often written from a personal perspective and for a non-academic audience, and differs from local histories and books about places through its focus on movement and exploration. Geographers have become interested in travel writing because it provides insights into the nature of *mobility, how places are represented and consumed, the popular geographies of location and movement, and the cultures of exploration, travel, and *tourism, from the perspective of people who are not academics or applying academic methods. As such, there have been a number of studies that have examined travel writing written by different kinds of travellers, of various locations, at different historical periods. For example, a number of scholars have examined the travel diaries of British travellers to Africa and India during the 19th-century colonial expansion. These accounts not only provide insight into the places travelled to and through, but also the travellers themselves.

Further reading Duncan, J. and Gregory, D. (eds.) (1999), *Writes of Passage: Reading Travel Writing.*

trend surface analysis A technique that uses least-square *regressions to convert a series of point observations into a surface to reveal the general spatial pattern of the data. For example, a trend surface can be fitted to pollution measurements from a set of monitoring stations to reveal how pollution trends spatially across an area. Usually, the surface is displayed using isolines, providing a set of data contours. In addition, the regression residuals, the difference between the observations, and the best fit surface can also be mapped to reveal anomalies. *See also* INTERPOLATION; KRIGING.

Triad The three macro-regions of North America, *Western Europe (or the *European Union), and Japan (sometimes with *Southeast Asia) which, it is argued, dominate international trade and production. Instead of *globalization, which implies the wider diffusion of economic activity, in his book *Triad Power* (1985), Kenichi Ohmae predicted triadization, concentrating activity in and between the three regions. Although there was some empirical support for the concept, subsequent events, notably the rise of the *BRICS, means that it is now less recognized.

triangulation **1.** The use of more than one method of data generation and analysis to provide a more detailed and balanced picture, and to cross-validate results.

2. A method in surveying to measure the location of a feature. Triangulation is a common practice in empirical research to ensure a richness of suitable complementary data and to enhance confidence in the reliability and soundness of the findings and conclusions. In surveying, the precise location of a point can be determined by intersecting the sightlines, measured as angles, taken from three points of known location. *See also* MIXED METHODS.

TRIPS (Trade-Related aspects of Intellectual Property Rights) Agreement
An international agreement incorporating *intellectual property rights into international trade, signed in 1994 and administered by the *World Trade Organization. The agreement sets minimum standards for national legal systems to recognize such things as copyright, patents, and trademarks. It identifies what can be protected, for example, computer programs, and establishes procedures for enforcement and resolving disputes. Countries of the *Global South have a transition period before they are required to implement the appropriate views on TRIPS. There are opposing views on TRIPS. On one side, international businesses argue that IPR are necessary to reward and stimulate innovation. If, for example, a pharmaceutical company cannot stop unlicensed copying of a new drug then, so the argument goes, it will have no incentive to invest in costly research and development. The counter view is that TRIPS gives an unfair advantage to Western countries and transnational corporations who have already established themselves at the expense of potential new sources of innovation in the Global South. The two main areas of contention have been medicines and seeds. The high cost of HIV/AIDS (*see* AIDS) treatment medicines has encouraged unlicensed copying which is unlawful under the agreement. Further, as argued forcefully by Vandana Shiva among others, patenting biological entities such as seeds is a form of *biopiracy, granting more reward to Western

scientists and companies than to the indigenous peoples whose common knowledge is vital to understanding their qualities (*see* INDIGENOUS KNOWLEDGE).

Further reading Shiva, V. (2001), *Protect or Plunder?*

(()) SEE WEB LINKS
• World Trade Organization TRIPS gateway.

tropical geography The geographical study of tropical regions and the resultant accumulation of geographical knowledge. The idea that the tropics constituted a distinct region for inquiry emerged from the 15th- and 16th-century voyages of discovery by Europeans, but was systematized in the 20th century by French, German, and Dutch geographers in particular. The most significant work was *Les Pays Tropicaux* by French geographer Pierre Gourou which went through several editions and translations. Later critics suggest that much of tropical geography was suffused with *racism, *imperialism, and *environmental determinism. *See also* TROPICALITY.

tropicality A mode of constructing and representing the tropics as a site of geographical knowledge. Like *Orientalism, it is an instance of *imagined geographies. European explorers, travel writers, and scholars (including geographers) conceived of the tropics as possessing common natural and cultural characteristics that differentiated them from the supposedly normal temperate realms. These representations could be deeply contradictory, for instance, imaging the tropics as fecund and luxuriant on the one hand, but degenerate and debilitating on the other.

Further reading *Singapore Journal of Tropical Geography* (2000), special issue on 'Constructing the Tropics', 21 (1).

trust The conviction that someone or something is reliable and/or truthful. In economic geography, questions of trust arise when non-routine transactions are conducted at a distance. In the absence of face-to-face contact, which is the conventional means of establishing trust, partners rely on reputations or institutional contexts. Building trust is an important way of reducing risk and uncertainty, but how far it requires personal meetings as opposed to long-range communication is an important empirical question. In the historical geography of science, the issue of trust is central to the successful circulation of scientific truths. How can the results of an experiment or the observations of an explorer be trusted by others not present? Historians have charted the development of conventions for establishing trustworthiness, which in practice often involved judgements based on social class or moral character rather than just facts.

t-test A statistical method for evaluating whether the means of two groups of data are significantly different from each other. The test assumes that the data for each group follows a *normal distribution. The test can be applied to unrelated and related data sets. For example, given a data set of the distance travelled to work by men and women, an unrelated t-test would be used to test whether the means differs. A related t-test would be used if the data were the distances travelled by the same men at two different times. The test calculates a t-statistic based on comparing the data distributions and, based on the size of the samples, a p-value that provides the probability that the means are different from one another. In cases of more than two groups, an *analysis of variance (anova) test is used.

Tuan, Yi-Fu (1930–) A Chinese-American geographer who has been a key proponent of *humanistic geography. Born in Tientsin in China, he was educated in China, Australia, the Philippines, and the UK before moving to the University of California, Berkeley in 1951 to undertake graduate work. After initial work at the University of New Mexico and the University of Toronto, Tuan moved to the University of Minnesota in 1968 and on to the University of Wisconsin, Madison in 1983. He retired in 1998 but has continued to write.

His two books *Topophilia (1974) and *Space and Place (1977) were highly influential in challenging spatial science, instead forwarding geographical scholarship centred on humanism and metaphysics using ideas from *phenomenology and *existentialism. His writing consequently drew on his personal experiences, including his childhood experience as well as his understanding of Chinese culture and *cultural landscapes, and a wide range of sources including philosophy, religion, and art to explore themes of *place, *home, *space, attachment, the meaning of existence, and how to live the 'good life'— one that is fulfilling and ethical. His work is highly reflective and often autobiographical, questioning how one knows oneself through knowing the world,. The author of over twenty books, his writing has been widely read across the social sciences and humanities.

Further reading Adams, P. C., Hoelscher, S., and Till, K. E. (eds.) (2001), *Textures of Place: Exploring Humanist Geographies.*

Turner, Frederick J. (1861–1932) A US historian best known for his 'frontier thesis' (first expressed in 1893) and 'sectional hypothesis' in which he posited that the American landscape was sectioned into discrete regions defined by economic, political, and cultural relations, not political state boundaries, and that the overriding force shaping American history and identity was the western movement of the frontier rather than more traditional social and economic forces such as class and capital accumulation. Initially based at the University of Wisconsin, he moved to Harvard in 1910, retiring in 1924. His best-known works are *The Frontier in American History* (1921) and *The Significance of Sections in American History* (1932).

Tyndall Centre for Climate Change A unique experiment in trans-disciplinary research and institutional partnership created in 2000 by three UK research councils in order to advance research on climate change. Named after 19th-century Irish physicist John Tyndall, the centre has its headquarters at the University of East Anglia, Norwich, England, but has partner institutions in seven other UK Universities as well as Fudan University, China. The centre's aims include research but also influencing national and international *climate policy and communicating with businesses and the public.

uncertainty A condition in which the possible consequences or effects of an action are known, but not the relative likelihood of their occurrence. It can be distinguished from *risk and *error. Risk is a quantified uncertainty, i.e. the probability of each outcome is calculated. Error is the difference between a measured and a true value. Modelling and visualizing uncertainty is an important challenge in processing geographical information.

Further reading Goodchild, M. F. (2009), 'Uncertainty', in *The International Encyclopedia of Human Geography*.

underclass The poorest and most socially excluded sections of society who are thought to be persistently trapped in a *cycle of poverty. Members of the underclass are said to usually suffer multiple deprivations, such as high unemployment, low income, and dependence on welfare, poor-quality housing, lack of transport and mobility, and higher rates of poor health. They may be spatially constrained into certain locations that provide few local job opportunities, have poor and underperforming social infrastructure such as childcare and schools, and high crime rates, drug use, and anti-social behaviour; geographers study this phenomenon as 'concentrated poverty' (*see* SEGREGATION). In the USA, the term 'underclass' usually carries racial connotations—African-Americans are said to constitute its largest fraction and *racism compounds other forms of *social exclusion. It is a controversial term, and many critics suggest that it lumps together too many variables to be analytically useful; to some, it is more a term of stigmatization than analysis (*see* CULTURE OF POVERTY). For this reason, it is used less since the heyday of debate in the 1990s. W. J. Wilson, one of the leading experts on the topic in the USA, switched to the term 'ghetto poor' for example. *See also* CLASS; INEQUALITY; POVERTY; SEGREGATION; SOCIAL POLARIZATION; WORKING CLASS.

Reference Wilson, W. J. (1996), *When Work Disappears: the World of the New Urban Poor*.

underdevelopment A condition in which the resources of a region are not being realized to their potential. From the perspective of post-war *modernization theory, underdevelopment was defined by an absence of certain factors found in more 'developed' areas (*see* DEVELOPMENT; DEVELOPMENT THEORY; STAGES OF GROWTH MODEL). Underdeveloped regions and countries relied on non-commercial agriculture, had inadequate infrastructure, and were characterized by low levels of education, poor health, and the preponderance of traditional ideas over modern, rational economic thinking. In this view, the aim of development was to transform such regions. Critics of this view, notably the dependency school, regarded underdevelopment as less the lack of some qualities, and more the outcome of active processes of development elsewhere (*see* ECONOMIC COMMISSION FOR LATIN AMERICA). Walter Rodney, a Guyanese historian, wrote *How Europe Underdeveloped Africa* (1972) through *colonialism, *slavery, and the extraction of resources. A decade later, US historian Manning Marable extended the argument in his book, *How Capitalism Underdeveloped Black America* (1983). In both cases, underdevelopment was not a state but a dynamic process. The term is not widely used any more. *See also* UNEVEN DEVELOPMENT.

underpopulation A situation in which there are too few people to realize the economic potential of an area or support its population's standard of living. It has sometimes been argued that countries such as Australia, Canada, and Mongolia have too few people to make best use of their resources of food, minerals, and energy.

unemployment *See* LABOUR; WORK.

UNEP *See* UNITED NATIONS ENVIRONMENTAL PROGRAMME.

unequal exchange A structural condition of trading relations such that one partner receives more than they ought to and the other less than if trade was between equals. The idea can be found in *Marx's work but was developed by dependency theorists in the 1970s, notably Andre Gunder Frank and Samir Amin (*see* DEVELOPMENT THEORY). Structural imbalance can arise either because core capitalist countries dictate the rules of international trade, or because exporters of agricultural goods are always disadvantaged relative to exporters of manufactured goods, who can better realize productivity gains.

UNESCO (United Nations Educational, Scientific and Cultural Organization) Founded in the immediate aftermath of the *Second World War, UNESCO works to create a culture of peace through intellectual and cultural programmes of activity. It is a branch of the United Nations and has 195 member states. Its central aim is to promote dialogue and respect between peoples, promote *democracy, *human rights, *education, and *sustainable development, alleviate *poverty, and prevent *war. Some of its programmes include: World Heritage Sites, Biosphere Reserves, Geoparks, Endangered Languages, and City of Literature.

SEE WEB LINKS

• Official website of the United Nations Educational, Scientific and Cultural Organization.

uneven development The processes by which varied levels of *development through both time and across *space are produced, as well as the outcome of these processes. Although conceptualized in different ways, the main implication is that standards of living either are not or will never be equal everywhere. This contrasts with economic theories based on spatial equilibrium, such as *neoclassical economics and *modernization theory.

There have been three main phases of theorizing uneven development. The first was a response to the late 19th- and early 20th-century period of *imperialism. Whereas many commentators, Karl *Marx included, had assumed that capitalism would diffuse globally resulting in even development, this proved not to be the case. Marxist theorists, notably Lenin, Luxembourg, and Trotsky, debated whether and how *socialism could be achieved if Marx's vision of a global working class was not to prove correct any time soon. At issue was whether capitalism needed imperialism for its expansion or whether imperialism was an obstacle to capitalist development. Trotsky theorized that development was 'combined and uneven', rejecting the dominant idea that development proceeded through stages and suggesting that capitalism could develop through internal variation rather than external expansion (*see* STAGES OF GROWTH MODEL).

A second phase arose in response to the failings of post-war development, both in theory and in practice (*see* MODERNIZATION THEORY). Centred on the ideas of dependency theory, critics of Western-style capitalism argued that countries of the Global South were structurally locked into conditions of disadvantage and inequality (*see* DEVELOPMENT THEORY; UNDERDEVELOPMENT; UNEQUAL EXCHANGE). However, critics argued that this theory was too rigid and failed to account for the rise of the *Newly

Industrializing Countries. It could also not account for the major economic set-back
suffered by some of these countries in the late 1970s because of the international debt
crisis. By the early 1980s, two things were clear. First, the precise patterns of unevenness
were dynamic. For instance, all the leading capitalist states of the 20th century were
experiencing profound *deindustrialization, restructuring, high inflation, and rising
unemployment from the mid-1970s onwards. Second, whatever the enduring causes of
these patterns, there was a great deal of contingent causation bound up with the
decisions made by political leaders.

These observations ushered in a third phase of theorizing uneven development, in
which human geographers were more prominent. In *Uneven Development* (1984),
Marxist geographer Neil *Smith took issue with the opposed suggestions that (i) development could ever be even; and (ii) uneven development was accidental and contingent
(e.g. a product of the uneven distribution of natural resources on the Earth's surface). He
also had no truck with the idea, common in the 1970s, that *underdevelopment was
caused by overpopulation. Smith showed that uneven development is *intrinsic* to the
capitalist *mode of production, both an effect and a cause of further spatio-temporal
change. Capitalism must create *agglomerations, *growth poles, and *telecommunications networks in order to make commodities, but by allowing the circulation of *capital
in search of further profits this existing geography of production, distribution, and
consumption is threatened. The tendency of capital to concentrate geographically stands
in tension with a tendency to equalization which, in turn, produces new patterns of
differentiation. Moreover, the dynamism of the process meant that spaces 'see-sawed'
between levels of development, through cycles of investment, disinvestment, and
reinvestment.

Support for Smith's arguments can be found at the international scale in the *fin-de-
millennium* geographies associated with *neoliberal *globalization and the end of communism (1989–91), including China's planned transition to capitalism (*see* GLOBAL
INEQUALITY). There is also overwhelming evidence in the *Global North that uneven
development is a subnational phenomenon. Even highly 'developed' countries contain
regions, cities, and neighbourhoods where levels of development are comparatively low
(*see* GENTRIFICATION; RENT GAP). Many economic, political, social, and development
geographers remain deeply interested in describing, explaining, and seeking to ameliorate patterns of uneven development at a range of spatio-temporal scales. For instance,
research into *global production networks examines the distribution of economic value
along international commodity chains, while that into *industrial districts focuses on how
and why some places become growth poles.

Further reading Corbridge, S. (1986), *Capitalist World Development*.
Smith, N. (1986), 'On the necessity of uneven development', *International Journal of Urban
and Regional Research* 10: 87–104.

UNFCCC *See* UNITED NATIONS FRAMEWORK CONVENTION ON CLIMATE CHANGE.

UNHCR *See* UNITED NATIONS HIGH COMMISSIONER FOR REFUGEES.

unions A common abbreviation for trades unions or labour organizations. Modern
unions date from the mass industrialization of the 19th century, when they formed
according to either crafts (e.g. plumbers), sectors (e.g. mining), or geographical regions.
They campaigned for better wages and working conditions, notably over the length of the
working day. Particularly in Western Europe, labour organizations were instrumental in
the creation of socialist and social democratic political parties. In some countries, such as
the USA, unions were organized locally though coordinated by national federations while
in others, e.g. France, labour formed strong national organizations. Although international links were present in the early 20th century, it is only in the past two or three

decades that national unions have collaborated at regional and global scales in order to match and confront globalizing capital: the International Trade Union Confederation was formed in 2006, bringing together formerly separate organizations. Geographical interest in unions barely existed before the 1990s, although historical geographers mapped their role in early industrialization and, in the USA, their effect on the regional and political landscape (*see* LABOUR GEOGRAPHY). Since then, the main foci have been: the relations between labour organization and different national systems of regulation; the agency of organized labour in shaping economic geographical patterns; the role of space, place, and transnational networks in organizing protests and other labour actions; and how unions have allied with other associations, especially at local and urban scales, in the cause of social *justice. In the USA, the Justice for Janitors campaign is a good example and more widely, the various living wage campaigns have attracted geographical interest. Finally, geographers have increasingly collaborated with local, national, and international labour organizations in framing research projects.

Further reading Herod, A. (ed.) (1998), *Organizing the Landscape: Perspectives on Labour Unionism.* Wills, J. and Waterman, P. (eds) (2001), *Place, Space and the New Labour Internationalism.*

United Kingdom A country in northwestern Europe occupying most of the land area of two large islands known as the British Isles. Its full title is the United Kingdom of Great Britain and Northern Ireland, although it is often abbreviated to UK. Great Britain includes England, Wales, and Scotland. Northern Ireland is part of the UK but has shared the island of Ireland with the Republic of Ireland since the island's *partition (1920–22). Scotland, Wales, and Northern Ireland (but not England) have elected assemblies, although their powers and responsibilities differ. Scotland, which was a separate country though sharing the same monarch as England and Wales until the Act of Union in 1707, has its own parliament whose powers extend further than the other assemblies. In addition, there are several smaller territories in or near the British Isles that are not part of the United Kingdom, but which are 'crown dependencies', i.e. possessions of the British monarch. These are Guernsey, Jersey, and the Isle of Man. There are fourteen 'British Overseas Territories', the remnants of the former British *empire (*see* COMMON-WEALTH OF NATIONS). The capital of the UK is *London; Edinburgh is the capital of Scotland, Cardiff of Wales, and Belfast of Northern Ireland.

The UK is one of the most populous countries in Europe (population 63 million) and among the ten largest economies in the world. Since the 1950s service industries, notably finance, tourism, and creative industries have replaced manufacturing as the core economic sectors. The UK's economy is highly globalized, with significant levels of inward and outward *foreign direct investment. Around one in eight of the population was born abroad. The UK is one of six permanent members of the United Nations Security Council and its military forces are routinely engaged in many parts of the world.

United Nations An international organization founded in 1945 in the wake of the *Second World War as a vehicle to try and maintain international peace and security, develop friendly relations among nations, and promote social progress, better living standards, and *human rights. It replaced the League of Nations, an organization that was founded in 1919 at the end of the *First World War. Initially consisting of 51 member countries, it now has 193 members, and its main headquarters are located in New York. There are six main UN bodies to which a range of agencies, bodies, and committees report. The General Assembly is the main deliberative organ of the UN and is composed of representatives of all member states. The *United Nations Environment Programme (UNEP), *United Nations High Commissioner for Refugees (UNHCR), United Nations Children Fund (UNICEF), and *World Food Programme (WFP) are all programmes that report to the General Assembly. The Security Council has primary responsibility for the maintenance of international peace and security and is composed of five permanent members—China, France, Russian Federation, the United Kingdom, and the United States—and ten non-permanent, elected members. Decisions on substantive security matters require nine votes, including the concurring votes of all five permanent members. This is the rule of 'great power unanimity', which provides them with the power of 'veto'. The Economic and Social Council coordinates the economic, social, and related work of the United Nations, including a number of bodies such as the Commission on Population and Development, Commission for Social Development, Commission on the Status of Women, and Commission on Sustainable Development, plus five regional economic commissions. The Trusteeship Council was founded to supervise eleven Trust Territories to prepare them for self-government and independence, and was suspended in 1994. The International Court of Justice is the principal judicial organ of the United Nations and settles legal disputes between states and gives legal advice to the UN. The Secretariat carries out the day-to-day work of the UN. In addition, the UN has a number of specialized agencies that have their own charter, governing structure, and finances including the *World Health Organization (WHO), *United Nations Educational, Scientific and Cultural Organization (UNESCO), *International Monetary Fund (IMF), and *World Bank. Collectively, all these UN bodies work on a variety of issues including peacekeeping, conflict prevention, humanitarian assistance, *sustainable development, environment and refugees protection, disaster relief, promoting *democracy, gender equality and the advancement of women, governance, international health, and expanding food production and scientific knowledge.

(⊕) SEE WEB LINKS
• Official website of the United Nations.

United Nations Environmental Programme (UNEP) An institution of the United Nations responsible for encouraging, facilitating, and coordinating policy on environmental matters worldwide. Created in 1972, it has multiple roles but generally works in partnership with national governments and other international and intergovernmental organizations; it co-funded the *Intergovernmental Panel on Climate Change. UNEP, which is based in Nairobi, Kenya, also collates environmental statistics and publishes reports.

United Nations Framework Convention on Climate Change (UNFCCC) An international agreement made at the *Rio Earth Summit in 1992 to cooperate over responses to anthropogenic climate change. The convention led to further negotiations, the 1997 *Kyoto Protocol, and subsequent agreements struck at the annual Conference of Parties (COP); COP18 was in Doha in 2012.

United Nations High Commissioner for Refugees (UNHCR) (*Haut Commissariat des Nations Unies pour les réfugiés*) Organization founded in 1950, based in Geneva, and the UN's main *refugee agency.

(⊕) SEE WEB LINKS
• Official website of the United Nations High Commissioner for Refugees.

United States Geological Survey (USGS) A US state agency, established in 1879, that undertakes scientific research and the mapping of environments and ecosystems. The USGS's work is not confined to geology, but also includes hydrological, biosphere, and meteorological research, along with natural resources and hazards. It also works with other agencies in managing natural environments and planning new, and altering existing, developments. It is a key source of geographical data and scientific and technical expertise.

(⊕) SEE WEB LINKS

• Official website of the United States Geological Survey.

United States of America (USA) The world's most powerful country in a political and military sense, and also—although there is now some debate about this—in an economic sense too. Also commonly referred to as 'America' or the United States, it is a federal republic comprising fifty states and a district (the latter encompasses its capital city Washington). Most of these United States are contiguous, located between Canada (to the north) and Mexico (to the south), and fringed by the Atlantic Ocean (to the east) and the Pacific Ocean (to the west). The present-day USA was colonized by British, French, and other immigrants from the 17th century onwards, who settled along the eastern coastal regions and began a long process of engaging with and displacing existing *First Nations peoples. In 1776 some of these settlers declared and won their independence from Britain through armed struggle. Over the next century the geographical expansion of settlement led to the addition of many more states and territories, eventually reaching the Pacific coast. However, the process of political unification was interrupted by a civil war between a number of northern states opposed to slavery, and a number of southern states which utilized slaves (mostly imported from Africa) to sustain a largely agricultural export economy. The formation of the USA over nearly two centuries also entailed the killing, *dispossession, and cultural denigration of *indigenous peoples, not to mention major ecological transformations of the physical *landscape (such as the decimation of bison herds and wolf populations).

From the 19th century onwards, millions of mostly European (but also Chinese, Japanese, Indian, and Mexican) immigrants entered the country. This further diversified the country's already multinational, multifaith, multiethnic, and multilingual population. It also entrenched values of liberty and freedom because most immigrants had to make their own way in life with limited support from either the federal government or any one of the many state governments. By 1945 the USA had the world's largest and strongest economy, with particular strengths in manufacturing and agriculture. America also had the world's largest and most powerful military forces and, for the next thirty years, engaged in a *Cold War with the *Soviet Union. This 'war' saw the USA use its monetary and military muscle to influence political leaders across the world, especially in new nation states that might otherwise be persuaded to embrace *communism over *capitalism, and *socialism over social democracy and liberalism. Globally, the period of American *hegemony began to dwindle at the turn of the 21st century. The country became heavily indebted, with its economy less able to provide the money necessary to meet the considerable costs of government and public service provision, or the lifestyle demands of households and consumers. Highly expensive wars fought in Iraq and Afghanistan from 2003, coming after the so-called First Gulf War a decade earlier, displayed America's continued military might but worsened its national debt. At the same time, increasing levels of social *inequality in the USA meant that a small section of the population commanded extant wealth, while many others fell into *poverty—especially after the global *financial crisis of 2007–09.

The USA has symbolized many things in its history. For some it remains a beacon of freedom and a champion of the individual against *the state. For others, it exemplifies the virtues of *capitalism and the *free market, while still others argue that its current economic failings demonstrate the folly in trusting the latter to deliver continued economic growth and prosperity. America has also been seen as an *imperial power, both during and since the Cold War—belying its own proclaimed commitment to peoples' freedom of choice.

Further reading Meinig, D. (1986–2004), *The Shaping of America: a Geographical Perspective on 500 Years of History*, 4 volumes.

universalism The belief that certain principles, concepts, truths, and values are undeniably valid in all times and places and, by extension, the characteristics of phenomena are invariant (*see* ESSENTIALISM; GRAND THEORY). Universal knowledge is therefore the opposite of local, particular, and *situated knowledge. It is transcendental, placeless, and untouched by context.

Universalism is a core tenet of major world religions, but in a more philosophical and scientific sense it is associated with the *Enlightenment. Though recognizing classical antecedents, various European thinkers declared that it was possible to make scientific, moral, or other statements that were universal (*see* SCIENTIFIC REVOLUTION). Furthermore, this was a desirable goal of any mode of inquiry. Such truths were stable, i.e. they would be true anywhere, because they were also objective or impartial, arrived at by rational and disembodied means. They did not bear the imprint of privilege or hierarchy (although it seemed that only men were deemed capable of recognizing universal properties). A good example in human geography is the *modernization theory of *development, which prescribes a single sequence of stages and actions to move between them based on the experience of selected Western countries (*see* POST-DEVELOPMENT).

There are many challenges to universalism, and much of *post-structuralism *feminism, and *post-colonialism is founded on a principled rejection of the idea. In essence, the criticism is that what is purported to be universal turns out to be truths produced by and for a relatively privileged class of white Western males (*see* STANDPOINT THEORY). Furthermore, as Edward *Said argues, the notion that the Western mind is capable of finding universals is predicated on the prior denigration of non-Western or other cultures (*see* ORIENTALISM). It also effaces connections between cultures (*see* EUROCENTRISM) and regards alternatives as inferior or incomplete.

Further reading Lawson. V. (2007), *Making Development Geography*.

university An institution combining research and higher education, with the power to award degrees for undergraduate and/or postgraduate study. The first universities were founded in the early medieval period and were often extensions of cathedral schools. The modern university, organized around the ideal of academic freedom and the teaching of a wide range of disciplines, originated in early 19th-century Germany. Universities are a ubiquitous feature of the educational landscape of all modern states.

untraded interdependencies The intangible benefits gained by firms when they cluster together in *agglomerations. Some of the gains from agglomeration are traded, i.e. can be costed or quantified. An example might be lower transport costs for supplying parts. Others are less obvious, for instance, the support of chambers of commerce or the benefits of increased face-to-face interaction, also known as 'buzz' (*see* TACIT KNOWLEDGE). Geographers argue that these are important even if they cannot be given a cost.

upscaling 1. The process of reconstituting activities or phenomena at a higher or larger geographical *scale, especially with reference to *governance.

2. Transferring the understanding of processes gained at smaller or experimental scales to larger scales, notably in physical geographical study, e.g. catchment studies.

urban ecology 1. The study of urban social life and land-use patterns using insights and concepts drawn from the ecological science of plants, animals, and their communities.

2. The scientific study of ecological processes in cities. Lying at the intersection of *human ecology and sociology, urban ecology in the first sense was consolidated by the *Chicago School in the years after the First World War. The leading proponents were Robert *Park and Ernest W. Burgess. Much of their diverse work centred on three kinds of study. First, urban ecologists explored sites (e.g. churches and dancehalls) and communities (e.g. ghettoes) as social worlds. Second, they mapped forms of social disorganization (e.g. diseases, alcoholism) in order to reveal underlying patterns and processes. Third, they considered the relations between peoples and communities in the city in terms of interdependence, often drawing on organic metaphors such as competition and adaptation. These ideas greatly influenced urban and social geographers from the 1960s onwards.

urban entrepreneurialism A form of *urban governance focused on promoting economic growth through enabling the private sector to flourish, in contrast with urban managerialism, which concentrates on the provision of public services. The term was popularized by David *Harvey to describe the shift he observed in western cities taking place in the 1980s. *See also* ENTREPRENEURIAL CITY.

urban exploration The adoption of the practices and discourse of *exploration in the context of cities. The inquiries made by social reformer William Booth into 19th-century British cities, published as *In Darkest England and the Way Out* (1890) are an early example. Much of the work of the *Chicago School of *urban ecology, especially their ethnographies of places, drew upon ideas of exploration. In geography, the *Detroit Geographical Expedition and Institute in the 1970s was explicitly framed in exploratory terms. In more recent years, urban exploration or 'urbex' refers to the practice of lone individuals or small groups entering derelict and often inaccessible buildings, sites, and environments with a view to photographing scenes, recalling lost histories and memories, evoking childhood experiences of entering dangerous buildings, and related emotions and affects.

Further reading Garrett, B. L. (2010), 'Urban explorers: quests for myth, mystery and meaning', *Geography Compass* 4, 1448–61.

urban fringe An area between urban and rural landscapes often overlooked by the separate strategies of urban and rural planning.

urban geography The study of cities and city life from a geographical perspective (*see* CITY). Although urban geography is one of the most popular and productive parts of human geography, a precise delineation of the field is understandably difficult. Attempts to find the essential characteristics of urban places or urban life, for example, by contrast with the rural and rural life, have proved inconclusive (*see* RURALITY; URBANISM). In much of the world, the distinction between urban and non-urban is blurred or meaningless, as those characteristics once associated with cities such as waged labour, electricity, or the preponderance of secondary relations (i.e. with strangers) become more widespread. In one sense, therefore, the vast majority of human geographical work may be described as urban by default. Considering urban settlements in historical perspective also complicates the search for essential urban qualities. Furthermore, the geographical study of urban life is informed by and contributes to studies in allied disciplines; one of the main journals in the field is simply called *Urban Studies*. A final complication is that the city as a spatial form can be regarded as both the cause and the consequence of social relations. From one perspective, exemplified by the *Chicago School of *urban ecology, cities shaped social effects among their inhabitants. By contrast, many Marxist-inspired geographers in the 1970s thought of cities as the projection of less visible economic processes; inquiry should focus on the processes rather than the outcome. In this regard, David *Harvey's contributions have been critical in pointing a way forward.

Despite some ambivalence about the term 'urban geography', over the past sixty years urban geographers have developed some distinct and ongoing themes (Hall and Barrett 2012). Perhaps the most important has been the study of the internal social and spatial structure of cities, in part inspired by ideas from the Chicago School. *Urban morphology considers the spatial layout and appearance of cities in different historical and national contexts. It can be extended by typologies of different kinds of urban area, for example, *edge city, exurb, or suburb. Most focus has been on the social differentiation of urban areas by *class, age, *race, *gender, and *sexuality, as well as its causes and consequences (*see* COMMUNITY; GENTRIFICATION; SEGREGATION; SOCIAL AREA ANALYSIS; SOCIAL GEOGRAPHY). A second long-standing theme considers cities as systems or networks, linked by flows of people, goods, money, and information (*see* CENTRAL PLACE THEORY; URBAN SYSTEM; WORLD CITY NETWORK). The third area of inquiry has considered the diversity of cities in historical and international contexts, again frequently through typologies (*see* INDUSTRIAL CITY; PRE-INDUSTRIAL CITY; POST-INDUSTRIAL CITY). Here, an important development in the past two decades has been the recognition that *normative models or ideas derived from a narrow set of mainly Western cities are not universal (*see* DESAKOTA REGION). Finally, urban geography has led and responded to the general shifts in theory and ideas found in *human geography as a whole. Particularly during the 1980s, the urban focus of *Marxist geographers brought urban geography to the centre of the discipline. Thirty years earlier there had been only a handful of texts described as urban geography. The *postmodern turn was also profoundly urban, not least because many of its leading proponents lived and studied in *Los Angeles. Urban geography currently accommodates, on the one hand, *non-representational theory, evinced in *Cities* by Ash Amin and Nigel Thrift (2002) and, on the other hand, the application of sophisticated modelling and innovative data analytics of the Centre for Advanced Spatial Analysis, University of London. It remains a very broad and productive field, as shown by two of the leading journals, *Urban Geography* and the *International Journal of Urban and Regional Research*.

References and further reading Hall, T. and Barrett, H. (2012), *Urban Geography*.
Latham, A., McCormack, D., McNamara, K., and McNeill, D. (2009), *Key Concepts in Urban Geography*.
Knox, P. and Pinch, S. (6th ed. 2010), *Urban Social Geography*.

(⊕) SEE WEB LINKS

- Website of the Centre for Advanced Spatial Analysis (CASA), London.
- Website of the Urban Geography Specialty Group of the Association of American Geographers.

urban governance The set of institutions and procedures by which cities are governed. These include formal urban governments, which may be elected, alongside business, non-governmental, and other organizations. This recognizes the fact that over the past few decades, city government has become increasingly integrated with a wide range of other bodies, so blurring lines of responsibility and accountability. *See also* ENTREPRENEURIAL CITY; URBAN ENTREPRENEURIALISM; URBAN MANAGERS.

urbanism The distinct qualities of life and experiences associated with living in cities. This narrow sense of the term is deep rooted in urban sociology. But in more recent decades, as *urbanization processes seemingly erode differences between rural and urban environments, 'urbanism' has been used to refer to a more general condition of life. Hence some geographers refer to 'postmodern urbanism' to describe the enhanced sense of fluidity and contingency supposedly characteristic of the late 20th-century city (*see* POSTMODERNISM).

The idea that city-dwelling has particular qualities has been around as long as cities themselves, but the modern systematic attempt to discover what distinguishes urban life dates from the late 19th century onwards. Poets and artists began to express a new urban sensibility (*see* FLÂNEUR). In their wake, European sociologists approached urbanism in two broad ways. Some emphasized the diversity and complexity of city life in contrast with rural living. Louis Wirth defined 'urbanism as a way of life' arising from the size, density, and heterogeneity of city society; these included a multiplication of people's jobs and a greater likelihood of not knowing others. Some others, for example, Georg Simmel and Ferdinand Tönnies, stressed how the city simplified social relations around new forms of rational calculation (*see* GEMEINSCHAFT AND GESELLSCHAFT). Simmel, for example, argued that the intense circulation of money had social and psychological effects, reducing and supplanting other forms of value. The result, 'anomie', described an alienated and anonymous form of urban life. But in contrast, surrealist and other *avant-garde artists and writers sought the continued presence of desire, fantasy, and myth among urban dwellers, casting doubt on the pervasiveness of rationality. Attempts to establish empirically the specific quality of urban as distinct from rural life generally proved elusive, however. If there were distinguishable social and psychological states, they were as likely to be found in so-called rural as urban areas (*see* URBAN VILLAGE). *See also* NEW URBANISM; RURALITY.

Further reading Bridge, G. (2009), 'Urbanism', in *The International Encyclopedia of Human Geography*.

urbanization The absolute and/or relative growth in the number of people living in urban settlements, with reference to a single country, region, or the world as a whole. To this basic demographic fact many analysts have proposed related economic, social, and cultural transformations, many of which can also be described as *modernization (*see* URBANISM). But attempts to identify simple linear relationships between urban growth and such factors as industrialization or the decline in face-to-face interaction have been frustrated by the great variety of changes associated with urbanization worldwide.

Urbanization of Capital, The A companion text (published in 1985) to *Consciousness and the Urban Experience* setting out David *Harvey's thinking on the geography of capitalist accumulation, rent, class, and urban politics. In it, he spells out how *capitalism produces a *built environment suited to its needs at one moment in time, only for it to subsequently become a barrier to further capital accumulation necessitating its periodic reconfiguration.

urban managers A group of professional bureaucrats who administer the allocation of public goods such as social housing and so influence the social and spatial form of cities. The equivalent term in the private sector is 'urban gatekeeper'. Geographers' interest in such individuals arises from the recognition that the actual allocation of urban public goods may not always conform to formal regulations because of the influence of informal bureaucratic practices. *See also* HOUSING; URBAN GEOGRAPHY.

urban modelling The production of *models about the form and functioning of cities. Geographers and sociologists have long been interested in the ways in which urban areas are structured, work, and evolve. The *Chicago School of urban sociology, through the work of Ernest Burgess and Homer Hoyt, produced initial theoretical models of the urban morphology of cities, detailing how they were divided up into discrete zones and the relationships between them (*see* CONCENTRIC ZONE MODELS). These models were quite simplistic and static, and in the 1960s geographers started to produce more complex theoretical models of how the urban system worked and to empirically test these models using a variety of data inputs including *census, economic, and transport data. In particular, there was an attempt to create land-use transportation models that sought to explain for planning and policy purposes the relationship between *land use and its spatial arrangement with movement and access within a city-region. As computing has become more powerful, and data sources more readily available, urban modelling has steadily become more sophisticated, leading to a suite of different model types, such as macroeconomic, social physics and social interaction, and microeconomic, that are static or dynamic in their working assumptions and unfolding. Most urban models are now complex computer *simulations, with the theoretical model organized in an array of related algorithms that process relevant data. These simulations effectively become urban laboratories in which it is possible to calibrate and test the ability of a model to mimic real-world outcomes and to then predict urban development in the future and the effects of different interventions in urban planning (such as the building of a new road). The most common urban models are presently *agent-based models that generally use *cellular automata.

Further reading Batty, M. (2005), *Cities and Complexity: Understanding Cities with Cellular Automata, Agent-Based Models and Fractals.*
Wilson, A. G. (2000), *Complex Spatial Systems: the Modelling Foundations of Urban and Regional Analysis.*

urban morphology The shape of cities in terms of their form, function, and layout, for example, street patterns. The study of urban morphology was pioneered by Lewis *Mumford who was interested in how cities changed over time. Later exponents focused on spatial models of city form (*see* CONCENTRIC ZONE MODEL) and the detailed investigation of *townscapes.

urban planning The strategic conception and realization of schemes and principles for the organization of land use and the built environment at urban and city-region scales. Given that many countries are intensively urbanized with settlements linked together in *city-regions, it is increasingly common to link urban (sometimes called town planning) and regional planning together, often within a *spatial planning framework.

Practically all interventions in the built environment are planned in the sense of being intended and designed, and the systematic, principled, and long-term objective of city planning arose in 19th-century Europe in response to the physical and social problems of industrial cities (*see* GARDEN CITY). From the outset, it involved the production of often-detailed plans or diagrams, to imagine and coordinate the activity. From the 1940s onwards, both capitalist and socialist states planned wide-ranging restructuring of cities and urban systems, assisted by the growth in professional planners (*see* BUCHANAN REPORT; GREEN BELT; NEW TOWNS; PLANNING; URBAN REGENERATION). From the 1980s onwards, communities and private sector capital were incorporated into the urban planning process, albeit unevenly. The integration of national, regional, and urban planning was exemplified by France, which from 1963, set out a series of comprehensive schemes. The merits of such spatially targeted planning were challenged in the 1980s, as *neoliberal governments preferred to trust the private sector, taking a less interventionist and more enabling approach.

Further reading Fainstein, S. and Campbell, S. (eds.) (3rd ed. 2011), *Readings in Planning Theory.*
Hall, P. and Tewdwr-Jones, M. (5th ed. 2011), *Urban and Regional Planning.*

Urban Question, The First published in French as *La Question urbaine* (1972, English trans. 1977) this book by Spanish sociologist Manuel *Castells revolutionized the study of urban issues through its elaboration of *Marxist political economy. Castells critiqued the idea of the universal category of 'urban' that underpinned almost all previous work on cities. *See also* SOCIAL JUSTICE AND THE CITY; URBAN GEOGRAPHY.

urban regeneration A term for the various strategies to restore profitability and/or repopulate areas of the city deemed to be in decline. Also termed 'urban renewal' or 'reconstruction', it describes a broad range of interventions in the built environment and in communities facilitated by the state, the private sector, public-private partnerships, or less commonly, by community-level agencies. In essence, urban regeneration promises physical, material, or spatial solutions to social and economic problems. Given that it almost always involves land at least already partly occupied and in commercial use (i.e. *brownfield sites), urban regeneration projects are generally contentious. The main issue is whether people or profit comes first. For example, major changes in the built environment often lead to the *displacement of long-time residents. Where new jobs arise, it is not always certain that they will be taken up by people living nearby. And where there are financial risks involved, especially in major property and infrastructure schemes, the question arises of who will bear them—the public or private sector?

Arguably, the first large-scale reconstruction of an existing urban area was undertaken by Georges-Eugène Haussmann in Second Empire Paris between 1852 and 1870 in which a large swathe of medieval Paris was cleared to create a more ordered and modern layout, including better utility infrastructure, public parks, and monuments. The major wave of renewal in Western Europe and North America took place from the 1950s onwards, centred on slum clearance, public housing projects, and motorway construction. From the 1970s, the regeneration of post-industrial cities whose manufacturing cores had contracted became a priority. Regeneration schemes have taken a variety of forms, depending on the political, economic, and technological context. But in general they either involve the replacement of the existing built environment with new uses ('hard renewal'), often led by property firms, or the rehabilitation of buildings accompanied by measures to preserve areas characterized by their heritage value ('soft renewal') (*see* GENTRIFICATION). The former is more likely to generate concerted local opposition. In recent decades, regeneration has increasingly been focused on sports or arts-related projects such as stadiums, galleries, and museums (*see* CULTURAL QUARTER; OLYMPICS). *See also* WATERFRONT DEVELOPMENT.

urban renewal *See* URBAN REGENERATION.

urban social movement A type of organized collective protest that not only takes place within a city or cities, but is concerned with some aspect of urban life, for example, housing, services, or other forms of *collective consumption. It is distinct from work-place-based struggles and therefore *social class may not always be the principal mobilization. The study of such movements was inspired by Manuel *Castells, whose book *The City and the Grassroots* (1983) sought to define specifically urban forms of protest based on the comparative analysis of various historical cases.

urban sprawl The spread or increase of low-density, automobile-dependent built environment around existing urban areas, generally with the implication that this process is unplanned or uncontrolled. Such sprawl is usually viewed negatively, not least because the resulting high transport and energy costs add to pressure on the environment. By comparison, compact cities with higher density and shorter distances between residence and workplaces are thought to be more energy- and time-efficient. *See also* EDGE CITY.

urban system A set of towns and cities that can be considered linked together by various forms of social and economic interaction. It may be national, regional, or global in scope (*see* WORLD CITY NETWORK). Thinking about cities in this way is an alternative to considering them each as isolated entities. *See also* POLYCENTRICITY.

urban village 1. A *neighbourhood whose residents are from one main ethnic group, but where this concentration arises more from the group's choice than external constraint or *social exclusion, i.e. in contrast to a *ghetto.

2. In urban planning and design, a well-defined, medium-density, mixed-use area where pedestrians are prioritized over automobiles. It is closely associated with *new urbanism.

urbicide The destruction of whole cities or parts of the built environment for political and military ends. There are many examples of victorious armies destroying their enemy's cities, for example, the Roman obliteration of Carthage in 146 BC. But many analysts argue that in recent decades cities have become a particular focal point for violence, part of the urbanization of *war (Graham 2010). Examples include the targeting of specific buildings and districts by Serbian forces in Croatia and Bosnia during the 1990s war, the demolition of Palestinian neighbourhoods by Israeli forces, and the assault on Baghdad by the US military during the Iraq War.

Further reading Graham, S. (2010), *Cities under Siege; the New Military Urbanism*.

Urry, John (1946–) A British sociologist who has spent his career at Lancaster University. His research has been characterized by its productivity, variety, the extent to which his ideas have evolved over time, and his engagement with spatial thought. He has written on *locality studies, *regionalism, *tourism, *leisure, the spatial dynamics and relations of *capitalism, and the *production of space, all of which are concerns shared by human geographers. Most recently he has been one of the main proponents of the *mobilities turn. Key books include *The Tourist Gaze* (1990), *Sociology beyond Societies* (2000), and *Mobility* (2007).

use value The practical utility of an object, usually a purchased commodity such as a shirt or washing machine. Use values are usually incommensurable. For instance, one cannot use a picture frame to write a dictionary, nor a pen to frame a painting. However, this does not mean that use values are entirely objective (i.e. intrinsic to manufactured objects). Only because certain uses become socially recognized and valued are objects able to become perceived as 'useful'. Marxists distinguish use values from *exchange value (price), *value (linked to but not the same as price—*see* LABOUR THEORY OF VALUE), and sign value (the symbolic work performed on others by the commodities one owns). While most commodities require various physical locations in order to be used, these locations are themselves possessed of use value (e.g. an airport or a train station).

USSR *See* SOVIET UNION.

utilitarianism An ethical theory holding that the worth of an act depends upon its consequences, namely whether it maximizes good, understood as happiness, pleasure, or satisfaction. According to *Enlightenment philosopher Jeremy Bentham, the correct course of action is one that leads to the 'greatest good for the greatest number'. This position, which was developed by John Stuart Mill in the 19th century, assumes that happiness can, in fact, be measured and calculated across a population, which many critics dispute.

utility theory A way of explaining behaviour that assumes each person makes choices that provide them with the highest possible level of satisfaction or utility. This state is termed utility maximization. It is a core idea in *neoclassical economics, the aim of which is to explain an individual's preferences and describe the associated demand curve, i.e. how much of something a consumer will purchase at varying levels of cost. In *migration geography, place utility is the satisfaction an individual derives from a particular location.

utopia An imagined place or state of perfection. The opposite is dystopia. Utopianism, the belief that ideals can be achieved, has informed much urban *planning and inspired the foundation of alternative communities (*see* COMMUNE).

Further reading Harvey, D. (2000), *Spaces of Hope*.

u

Valentine, Gill (1965–) A productive British social geographer best known for her work on gender, sexuality, and children geographies. Based at the University of Sheffield for a number of years, she then moved to Leeds University, before returning to Sheffield to take up a senior management position. She has made important contributions to understanding the social production of space, the *intersectionality of identities, *citizenship, and *consumption, as well as debates concerning research methods. She has been an editor of the journals *Social and Cultural Geography* and *Gender, Place and Culture*.

validation The process of establishing the legitimacy of a proposition or argument. It can be distinguished from *verification, which establishes truthfulness. In modelling terms, only close systems such as the mathematical components of models can be verified. But models that use parameters for data that are only approximately known cannot be verified, only validated. A valid model (or statement) has no known or detectable flaws and is internally consistent.

Further reading Oreskes, N. et al. (1994), 'Verification, validation, and confirmation of numerical models in earth sciences', *Science* 263(5417): 641–46.

value 1. The worth or importance attached to something.

2. A moral or ethical belief guiding a person's words and deeds in everyday life.

3. The number observed for a particular variable in statistical analysis.

The first two meanings overlap but are not synonymous. For instance, a person can value something highly (e.g. diamonds) without recourse to any moral or ethical principles. Likewise, value in the first meaning can derive from a person's aesthetic reaction to something (perhaps they find it beautiful), while value in sense two is irreducible to peoples' aesthetic responses. However, both meanings pertain to the process of judging things rather than simply seeking to describe their qualities or explain their behaviour. Philosophers have long debated whether values are independent of facts or whether facts—despite usually being seen as 'neutral' (value-free)—actually contain the values of those who produced them and those who observe them (*see* FACT-VALUE DISTINCTION). This debate has implications for research and teaching because if neither is simply about relaying facts then even the 'purest' or 'hardest' sciences must justify the value-based choices they unwittingly make when analysing and interpreting data. Value in the third sense pertains to what are taken to be facts (empirical events that can be phenomenally observed). Statisticians calculating means, medians, standard deviations, correlations, and so on, use the word 'value' to describe the numerical scores achieved by the variables they study (e.g. level of formal education, income level, and longevity). However, these statisticians' observed values are argued by some to themselves reflect contestable value-judgements about what is worth observing in the first place.

Human geographers have long been interested in their own and/or other's values in all three senses. David *Harvey's book **Social Justice and the City* (1973) argued that, despite its apparent value-neutrality, the *spatial science then dominant in the discipline served to reproduce (not question or challenge) the existing capitalist, patriarchal, and racist social order. For him, the *rhetoric of *science was window-dressing for a counter-revolutionary *ideology. At about the same time, the *humanistic geographer Anne *Buttimer argued that geographers should be explicit about their own values and interested in studying those of real world actors. In *Values in Geography* (1974) Buttimer placed acts of valuation at the centre of human experience, arguing that disagreements and debates over which values to embrace are not to be avoided in the hope that 'objective analysis' can answer important human questions. Humans, Buttimer argued, have the unique capacity to construct and confer values; they are meaning-making creatures unlike all others.

Subsequent research travelled in three directions. First, Buttimer's humanistic successors began to inquire empirically into the varied ways different individuals and social groups value the built and natural environments they inhabit (an example being Burgess and Gold's *Valued Environments*, 1982). Largely, they rejected the idea that other's values could be represented in a value-free way, and argued that interpretation was a skill or craft, not a science (*see* HERMENEUTICS; THICK DESCRIPTION). Some of this research had policy implications because it challenged the idea of many planners that a traditional cost-benefit analysis could help governments decide how to proceed when a major new development (e.g. a new airport) was in the pipeline. Because of value incommensurability—that is, the clash between rival conceptions of *how* to value and *what* to value—it was shown to be difficult to compare on a single scale the costs and benefits of a proposed development from the perspective of the various people who would be affected by it. Second, a less ground-level analysis of value was provided by Marxists. They argued that value is not only a social phenomenon (one irreducible to individual hearts and minds), but often 'blind', too, in that it arises 'spontaneously' from the decisions made by millions of human agents operating in sets of social relations, according to various subject-positions, and with various enticements thrown at them (e.g. through product advertising). In a complex argument, Marxist geographers claimed that the 'real' value contained in commodities derived from the efforts of wage workers (*see* LABOUR POWER; LABOUR THEORY OF VALUE). Value was thus 'objective' and material, not merely subjective, even though the personal value consumers placed on the commodities they purchase necessarily has a subjective component. In a capitalist world, the Marxists argued, the owners of the means of production seek to appropriate *surplus value from workers, but must cultivate diverse needs, wants, and desires in consumers in order to do so.

This Marxian research proposed that we can only change our values by acting politically to change the nature of social relationships and institutions. However, this focus on *praxis arguably neglected the importance of moral and ethical reasoning. One cannot (and should not) act to change societal values without first giving good reasons why those values are wanting. A third stream of research inquired into the different reasons used to justify different sorts of values, especially values that were avowedly moral or ethical in character (like 'love thy neighbour' or 'to each according to their abilities'). Moral geographers, notably David M. Smith, began to make *normative arguments about geographies of ethical action. For instance, if one values all human life equally, but if the means to live well are grossly maldistributed, then it follows logically and practically that one should provide adequate *aid to far-distant strangers—even ones whose values one disagrees with (*see* MORAL GEOGRAPHIES).

In terms of their own values, there is an acute awareness across human geography that unadulterated *objectivity in research and teaching is impossible. But this value pluralism still leaves two problems. First, the spectre of moral *relativism looms large, in which one person's values are as good and justifiable as another's. Second, there is also a danger of moral indifference, wherein supposed incommensurability is an excuse not to debate or try to understand other values.

values The principles by which individuals or social groups are supposed to conduct themselves and/or which denote what is considered important. In different ways, a geographic education has often been conceived as a means of transmitting values such as patriotism, internationalism, anti-racism, and respect for nature. More narrowly, the conduct of scientific inquiry is often supposed to be informed by values or norms. R. K. Merton, for example, described the norms of science as: communalism, i.e. a commitment to sharing insights; *universalism, i.e. the necessity of appraising work without regard for race, gender, or difference; disinterestedness, or the absence of personal gain; and organized scepticism, i.e. the willingness to subject all propositions to rigorous scrutiny. *See also* ETHICS.

variable An attribute, factor, or feature than may vary, e.g. age, income, or distance. In trying to explain why a phenomena or relationship varies, a distinction is made between independent variables—those theorized to cause the variation, and dependent variables—those in which variation is thought to be caused. For example, health might be considered a dependent variable and age, education, and geographical location might be relevant independent variables.

varieties of capitalism An approach to *capitalism that recognizes significant differences in its manifestation based on how capitalist economic organization is embedded in different sorts of states. In *Varieties of Capitalism* edited by Peter A. Hall and David Kosice (2001), advocates of this idea examine how institutional and socio-cultural differences among states lead to four main kinds of capitalism: *welfare states, *neoliberal states, *developmental states, and *socialist states.

Further reading Peck, J. (2007), 'Variegated capitalism', *Progress in Human Geography* 31(6): 731–772.

variogram A statistical method that quantifies the spatial or temporal correlation of a set of location observations. It is a representation of the variability between pairs of data at certain distances and directions, describing the degree of spatial dependence and patterning in the data. It is used to detect the nature of patterns in *spatially autocorrelated data.

vector data Geographic data that is stored and presented in map form as a set of linked coordinates, for example, nodes connected by lines. By linking the lines together, polygons can be formed. *GIS systems typically handle two types of data: *raster (pixels) and vector. Vector data tends to be more complex and detailed than raster data, but it is also more difficult to analyse statistically. *See also* VECTOR MAP.

vector map A map composed of *vector data. For example, *topographic maps are vector maps made up of points, lines, and polygons that represent the surface of the Earth and its various features.

venture capital Investment in new economic enterprises ('start-ups') usually in return for a share of the enterprise's equity. Innovative products or processes are generally risky investments, but since the 1940s a sector of venture capitalists has emerged specializing in assisting new firms. It has been shown that the geographical distribution of venture capital is a major influence on the geography of *entrepreneurship. *Silicon Valley is the classic example of how venture capital contributes to patterns of economic location.

verification The process of establishing the truth or otherwise of a proposition or theory. In *logical positivism, the verification principle states that only statements capable of being empirically verified are meaningful as far as science is concerned, i.e. propositions about *ethics have no status. *Compare* VALIDATION.

vernacular landscape A landscape that reflects the occupancy, culture, and activities of the people who live there and their ancestors. It is sometimes considered an authentic landscape in that it contains localized forms of architecture, land division, and use, and shows how people live their everyday lives, in contrast to more homogeneous, globalized forms of *modernist architecture and planning that have the same look and feel. *See also* CULTURAL LANDSCAPE; LANDSCAPE.

vertical geopolitics The extension of *critical geopolitics by adding a third, vertical dimension, i.e. airspace and subterranean space. The term was coined by British geographer Stephen Graham in response to the war on Iraq as well as actions undertaken by the Israeli government in the Palestinian territories. Graham noted the increasing significance of, on the one hand, air power and aerial supremacy to the conduct of war, and on the other, how resort to bunkers, tunnels, and other underground structures was becoming a defensive reaction.

Reference Graham, S. (2004), 'Vertical geopolitics: Baghdad and after', *Antipode*, 36(1) 12–23.

vertical integration The internalization of the production process within a single firm. Considered a key characteristic of *Fordism, an example might be how all stages of making a car, from building components to assembling the vehicle and then selling it are controlled by a single company. The opposite practice, vertical disintegration, occurs when elements of the production process are out-sourced or subcontracted, regarded as a feature of *flexible accumulation or *Post-Fordism.

Via Campesina, La An international confederation of peasant organizations dedicated to defending the rights of small- and medium-scale producers, women farmers, indigenous agriculturalists, the rural landless, and migrant farm workers. Founded in Belgium in 1993, it has member organizations in 70 countries in both *Global South and *Global North. Its focus is the advance of 'food sovereignty', the right of peoples to healthy, culturally appropriate food grown locally and under sustainable conditions. It therefore opposes *agribusiness and *neoliberalism.

Vidal de la Blache, Paul (1845–1918) A founding father of French geography as a modern academic discipline. Appointed to the chair of Geography at the University of Paris Sorbonne) in 1898, he was able to exert tremendous influence over the way the subject was approached and taught across the country. His effect on academic appointments as well as the way of approaching geography established '*la tradition vidalienne*' (the Vidalian tradition) into the next generation of French geographers.

For much of the 19th century, geography languished in schools and universities. Defeat in the Franco-Prussian war (1871) persuaded the national government to reform teaching, including geography. From his position at the University of Nancy, Vidal (as he is often referred to) began to encourage a coherent geographical approach, although it followed the lines laid down by the pre-eminent German geographer Carl *Ritter. With strong affinities to history, Vidal's geography centred on the close relationships between people and their natural environment at the regional scale (*see* REGIONAL GEOGRAPHY). He developed the concepts of **milieu* (natural setting), **genre de vie* (way of life), and *paysage* (*landscape) to explore these relationships.

Vidal avoided the stronger sense of *environmental determinism found in some German, US, and British geography, preferring to emphasize how the natural environment

provides possibilities for human development. Later, this approach was termed *possibilism. His ideas were spelled out in *Tableau de la géographie de France* (*Portrait of French Geography*) in 1903 and were elaborated in *Principes de géographie humaine* (*Principles of Human Geography*) published in 1922 and completed by his son-in-law Emmanuel de Martonne.

Vidal's stress on the long-term regional interdependence of people and environment, the integrated character of regions, and the corresponding integrity of a France composed of regions suited his geography to nationalist causes. Nancy was in Lorraine, part of which was occupied by Germany after 1871, and the last major work of his life, *France de l'Est* (1918) addressed this part of the country.

Further reading Martin, G. J. (4th ed. 2005), *All Possible Worlds.*

Vienna Circle *See* LOGICAL POSITIVISM.

violence The intentional use of physical force to cause harm or physical injury, either actual or threatened. Violence may be directed towards oneself (e.g. suicide), towards others (inter-personal violence), or by one collective against another, including in the form of political violence (*see* CRIME; SEXUAL VIOLENCE; TERRORISM; WAR). Although violence is often thought of as direct or immediate, Norwegian sociologist Johan Galtung conceptualized 'structural violence' as the systematic prevention of individuals' potential by government action; racial discrimination is an example (*see* RACISM). US political theorist Iris Marion Young similarly examined 'systematic violence'—including physical attacks, sexual and racial harassment, and intimidation—as an obstacle to justice. *Violent Geographies: Fear, Terror and Political Violence*, edited by Derek Gregory and Allen Pred (2007) marked an important contribution to geographical understanding of political violence. *See also* SYMBOLIC VIOLENCE.

virtual geographies The spatial dimensions, socio-spatial processes, and *spatiality of *Internet media. It is sometimes posited that beyond game spaces that mimic geographic space in their visual dimensions, the Internet has no space, no virtual geographies. It is a medium that is principally composed of text and two-dimensional images. However, the virtual domains of the Internet are replete with the vocabulary of place: nouns, such as rooms, lobbies, highway, frontier, cafes; and verbs, such as surf, inhabit, build, enter. The virtual is often built out of the ideas and language of place. The employment of these geographic metaphors provides domains with a familiar landscape that engenders a form of *spatiality and a conception of navigation. Within online chat rooms, for example, this spatiality provides a common sense of reality that contextualizes and grounds communication and provides a nascent sense of place for inhabitants. In some cases, the process of *spatialization can be used to create a virtual geography where no obvious one exists, for example, producing a map of database contents. In the case of virtual worlds or games spaces, such as massively multiplayer online role-playing games (MMORPG), for example, World of Warcraft, the virtual geographies are more explicit and it is possible to chart and map their spatial geometries and spatiality, and the processes of virtual place-making. *See also* VIRTUAL GLOBE.

Further reading Dodge, M. and Kitchin, R. (2000), *Mapping Cyberspace.*
Shields, R. (2004), *The Virtual.*

virtual globe The digital geospatial databases and mapping systems of the entire Earth. Virtual globes are online *GISs that allow users to examine and query the spatial structure of the world, to 'fly over' the landscape, undertake spatial queries such as computing distances and routes, to overlay other layers of spatial data, or annotate with place markers, and to create *mashups with other data sets. *Google Earth and Bing Maps are two examples, where it is possible to interact with a digital, scalable, and seamless geographic database of the planet, including maps, remotely sensed and other data. In the case of Google Earth, it is possible to zoom from a great height into an area and in many locations to see the three-dimensional landscape of urban structures, and to drop into a 360-degree street view that can be used to navigate the terrain. Prior to Google Earth, it was expensive to gain access to such complex geovisualizations and GIS capabilities, and it required specialist skills and knowledges. As such, virtual globes have been important in opening up geographic data, data *visualization, and analytic techniques to a generalist audience, and in allowing that audience to share geographic data.

Further reading Tuttle, B. (2008), 'Virtual globes: an overview of their history and future challenges', *Geography Compass 2950* 1478–1505.

virtual reality Visual, interactive, computer-generated environments in which the user can move around and explore. Virtual reality presently takes two forms. The first is totally immersive environments in which users wear head-mounted goggles to view a stereoscopic virtual world. When the user moves, the virtual world is continuously updated providing the illusion that (s)he is fully immersed in a 3D, interactive space. The second form is screen-based and allows the user to interact with a responsive 'game-space'. Both forms have three essential attributes: they are inclusive, they are interactive, and the interaction is in real time.

vision The physiological act of seeing, as distinct from *visuality, which recognizes that what we see and how we see is culturally and technologically conditioned. Denis *Cosgrove considers the centrality of vision to geography in *Geography and Vision* (2008), including *maps, *landscape, diagrams, *globes, prints, *photography, and *art.

visuality Culturally constructed *ways of seeing. If *vision is a largely physiological human attribute, i.e. the ability of eyes to see, then visuality concerns the ways vision is shaped by cultural, social, and technological conditions.

Further reading Rose, G. (3rd ed. 2011), *Visual Methodologies*.

visualization The visual *representation of data to aid understanding and analysis. Spotting patterns and trends in tables of data is often difficult to achieve through the visual scanning of rows and columns. One method to make sense of such data is to use *descriptive and *inferential statistics. Another is to convert the data into a visualization that graphically displays the data and the relationships between different classes of data. This might include the production of scatter plots, graphs, histograms, and pie charts. Such visualizations reveal and describe patterns in the data and facilitate the effective communication of complex information between people. They do this by exploiting one of the most powerful human information-processing abilities, the conjunction of the eye-brain vision system with spatial cognition skills. The mind's ability to effectively process visual data enables preliminary conclusions to be drawn about what such patterns might mean and in what ways the data might be analysed statistically.

While general statistical visualizations are very commonly produced in geographical analysis, geographers are often more interested in creating geographic visualizations that reveal the *spatial* relationships between data and facilitate a spatial understanding of a phenomena or process. In order to achieve such a geographic visualization the underlining data have to be *geocoded or a process of *spatialization needs to be applied to the data; that is, it must be possible to attribute the data to a location.

The example, *par excellence*, of a geographic visualization is the *map, which plots the locations of phenomena on to a two-dimensional plane to reveal the relative positioning of places across the surface of the Earth. With developments in computing and *ICTs, maps are commonly produced and circulated in a digital form, especially within *GISs. GISs allow the routine production of geographic visualizations, in map and other geographic visualization form (such as terrain models and 3D city landscapes) and statistical forms. They also facilitate exploratory spatial data analysis by enabling various layers of spatial data to be overlain on base maps and the user to interact with and query those layers, including the application of spatial statistics. Moreover, with the addition of time data it is possible to produce temporal maps, or other forms of spatio-temporal visualizations (such as 3D graphs), that reveal change over time, and these can be sequenced into an animation. The power of such geographic visualizations is becoming ever more accessible to the general public through online, *open source GIS, and *virtual globes such as *Google Earth.

As representations, visualizations are rhetorically powerful, framing how we understand the human and physical world, shaping the comprehension and sense of place, spatial processes and spatiality. This power can be exploited to convey a particular message such as with *propaganda maps. In this sense, visualizations create rather than simply reveal knowledge and there is a politics of visualization at work in terms of how they are framed, what is included and excluded, and how they are contextualized by supporting text and other visual representations. Nevertheless, they are a vital component of a geographer's methodological toolkit. See also GEOINFORMATICS.

Further reading Dodge, M., McDerby, M., and Turner, M. (2008), *Geographic Visualization: Concepts, Tools and Applications.*
Dorling, D. (2012), *The Visualisation of Spatial Social Structure.*

visual methods *See* VISUALIZATION.

von Thünen model
An economic *land-use model developed by Prussian landowner and economist Johann Heinrich von Thünen (first published in 1826) that explained the ideal spatial pattern of agriculture through farm product prices, yield per unit of land, land rent, and distance from the market. The model was one of the first explanations of the *space-economy that recognized the importance of the *friction of distance. The *model posits that given land rent varies with respect to transportation costs, the rate of decline in land rent from the market differs by the type of produce grown, with heavy goods that have high transportation costs demanding lower rents nearer to the market to be profitable. A family of land-rent slopes can be created for each different type of produce, and by plotting these on a graph, and noting the intersections of the slopes, it is possible to determine what produce would be best grown at different distances from the market. The model is generally used as a norm or ideal against which actual patterns of agricultural land-use is compared. While the model is quite simplistic—it treats the market as an isolated node as opposed to being connected into a network of competing locations and ignores the actual decision-making processes of farmers—it provided a useful starting point for the development of more complex *locational analysis models after its rediscovery during the *quantitative revolution. See also LAND RENT THEORY.

voting *See* ELECTORAL GEOGRAPHY.

vulnerability
The susceptibility of individuals, households, and places to serious harm. The source or cause of harm might be social or environmental. Vulnerability is a function of *risk, the probability of a harmful event and the level of exposure to it, coupled with personal characteristics such as income, gender, age, and mobility. Not all individuals equally at risk are equally vulnerable. Vulnerability takes on slightly different meanings in different contexts (Wisner 2009). In *hazard and *disaster research it reflects the different levels of potential harm resulting from an event such as a flood or earthquake. In Chicago's 1995 heatwave, for example, those most vulnerable and therefore most likely to die were elderly African-American men living alone in high crime areas

(Klinenberg 2002). In climate change studies, vulnerability is a property of certain kinds of environment, such as coral reefs or mangroves. But in public health terms, vulnerable populations are often identified by their behaviour, for example, unprotected sexual intercourse. In development studies, vulnerability is understood in a more rounded way, as a feature of household livelihoods in their economic, political, and ecological contexts. Geographical work involves not just mapping and identifying vulnerability, but tracking its causes in economic and political structures.

References and further reading Adger, W. N. and Brown, K. (2009), 'Vulnerability and resilience to environmental change', in Castree, N., Demerit, D., Liverman, D., and Rhoads, B. (eds.) *A Companion to Environmental Geography* 109–22.

Klinenberg, E. (2002), *Heat Wave: a Social Autopsy of Disaster in Chicago.*

Wisner, B. (2009), 'Vulnerability', in the *International Encyclopedia of Human Geography.*

V

Walker, Richard (1947–) A US radical and economic geographer based at the University of California, Berkeley. He is best known for his work on the logic of *capitalism as an economic, political, and social system and its geographical evolution, regional development (*The Capitalist Imperative*, with Michael Storper, 1989), and an enduring focus on California as a centre of capitalist production (*The City and the Country*, 2007). He was a long-term editor of the radical geography journal *Antipode*, and practises being an academic activist in the Bay Area.

walking Travelling by foot at a relatively slow pace. Walking can be a method for understanding everyday experience of *landscapes through an *embodied, multisensory experience. In the latter case, walking is understood as a *performative act through which one traverses an environment. In the act of walking one reflects on one's position in relationship with, and *affective connections to, the world. Walking thus opens up the possibility to explore self-landscape and subject-world relations. These reflections are captured through *autoethnography. *See also* FLÂNEUR; NON-REPRESENTATIONAL THEORY.

Further reading Wylie, J. (2005), 'A single day's walking: narrating self and landscape on the South West Coast Path', *Transactions of the Institute of British Geographers* 30: 234–47.

Wallerstein, Immanuel (1930–) A US sociologist and founder of the *world-systems approach. After appointments at Columbia University in New York and McGill University in Montreal, he spent most of his career at the Fernand Braudel Center for the Study of Economies, Historical Systems, and Civilization at Binghamton University in Vestal, New York. World-systems analysis has influenced geographical thinking in political geography, *world city networks, and *global commodity chains. His best-known work is the *Modern World-System* (1974–2011), of which the first four volumes have been published.

Wall Street The most important US financial district and a globally pre-eminent centre of financial industries. It is clustered around Wall Street in Manhattan, *New York and the New York Stock Exchange, the world's largest, is located there. 'Wall Street' is also used to describe US financial industry more generally, wherever it is located. *See also* FINANCE CAPITAL; FINANCIAL MARKETS.

war A sustained state of armed conflict. Forms of warfare have differed throughout history, and many modern commentators suggest that in a globalized era it is increasingly difficult to distinguish war from more general circumstances of violence. A rough periodization of war might characterize the 19th century in terms of war between states fought by professional or conscripted armies, and the first half of the 20th century in terms of wars between coalitions of states using mass armies backed up by organized war economies. The *Cold War involved less overt and direct conflict between major powers but more proxy wars in the *Global South. From the late 20th century onwards, war between states has declined but intra-state wars have multiplied. Drawing on examples from the *Balkans and the Transcaucasian region, Mary Kaldor suggests these 'new wars' blur the boundaries between warfare, organized crime, and human rights violations (*see* COMPLEX EMERGENCY). These new wars are a consequence of the erosion of the state's autonomy and its monopoly of legitimate violence. Although these may be low-intensity, they are rarely local. Transnational flows of arms, volunteers, remittances, and humanitarian *aid link them to the rest of the world. Derek *Gregory suggests that the temporal and spatial boundaries of war are being dissolved, taking the 'war on terror' as his example. War and *peace, in other words, are not alternate states. Warfare is not an occasional aberration but a constant state of affairs that suffuses society in complex ways (*see* MILITARY-INDUSTRIAL COMPLEX). Instances of cyberwarfare confirm this point of view (*see* HACKTIVISM).

Geography and war have a long and close association, particularly through *cartography and military mapping and the production of *propaganda maps. Geographical knowledge of battlefield conditions, such as terrain and weather, is vital to the conduct of war. More generally, geographers have supplied systematic geographical intelligence for longer-term planning, especially at the regional level. During the Second World War, for example, around 670 members of the American Association of Geographers worked directly for war-related government agencies (Toal 2011). In 2004 the US government renamed the National Images and Mapping Agency, and it is now called the National Geospatial Intelligence Agency (*see* GEOSPATIAL INTELLIGENCE); it is responsible for integrating cartographic, geodetic, and remotely sensed data to support not just warfare, but also disaster response.

References Gregory, D. (2010), 'War and peace', *Transactions of the Institute of British Geographers* 35(2) 154–86.

Kaldor, M. (2nd ed. 2006), *New and Old Wars*.

Toal, G. (2011), 'Battlefield', in Agnew, J. and Livingstone, D. (eds.) *The Sage Handbook of Geographical Knowledge*, 217–27.

Washington consensus The ten economic policy recommendations listed by economist John Williamson as agreed upon in 1989 by the main financial institutions in Washington, DC (the US Treasury, the *World Bank, and the *International Monetary Fund). The phrase was seized upon by critics as shorthand for *neoliberalism or market-centred economic reforms, despite Williamson's protestations. The package of measures included liberalization of trade and *Foreign Direct Investment, *privatization of state enterprises, *deregulation, secure property rights, tax reform, and the redirection of public spending from subsidies towards pro-poor programmes in health, education, and infrastructure. Talk of the Washington consensus faded in the late 1990s and by the onset of the 2008 global economic crisis its 'death' was widely declared. Various authors, notably US economist Joseph Stiglitz, have pronounced on a post-Washington consensus that balances state and market while aiming to be more sustainable and democratic. *See also* BEIJING CONSENSUS.

Washington, DC The capital of the *United States of America and seat of its federal government, including the official residence of the president (the White House), the Capitol, which contains the two houses of Congress—the Senate and the House of Representatives—the country's legislature, and the Supreme Court. DC, sometimes used as an abbreviation for the capital, stands for District of Columbia, an area under direct federal jurisdiction and not part of any US state.

waste 1. Any good or material for which a user has no further purpose.

2. Energy generated as an unwanted by-product of a production process.

Materials are not intrinsically waste because their value is contingent on many factors such as cost, level of technology, and regulatory standards. What is of no value to one user may be useful to another, including another in a different location. Geographers have tended to focus on the linear path from production to consumption, leaving whatever happens next as a matter of pollution, waste disposal or, in economic terms, externality (*see* EXTERNALITIES). But the re-use and *recycling of materials creates new circuits of value, for example, around e-waste, i.e. disposed computers. Although over 90 per cent of waste is handled within the country of origin, a small, significant component is traded. This is mostly between *MEDCs, although China has become an important centre for waste recycling and recovery of materials for industrial use. Such flows have led to a geographical focus on waste mobilities.

Further reading Davies, A. R. (2012), 'Geography and the matter of waste mobilities', *Transactions of the Institute of British Geographers* 37: 191–6.
Dicken, P. (2011), *Global Shift.*

water A liquid that is essential for life on the planet. Water is a chemical compound of oxygen and hydrogen (in the form H_2O). Although a liquid at most ambient temperatures and pressures, it can take a solid form (ice) and a gaseous state (water vapour, including clouds). It is a near ubiquitous substance, present at the cellular level to the world's oceans. Only a fraction (2.5 per cent) of all water is freshwater, suitable for direct human consumption, and of that, almost 99 per cent is found in ice or groundwater. Surface water, in rivers, lakes, and marshes is, from this perspective, extremely scarce. Projections of future water scarcities based on growing demand have fuelled the idea that the 21st century will be characterized by a series of 'water wars' (*see* RESOURCE WARS; RIPARIAN CONFLICT).

Although water is a basic necessity for human life, it is estimated that around one billion people do not have adequate access to supplies of suitable quality water. In part, access to water is a matter of geography; it is unevenly distributed in space and time relative to human societies' needs. But access is also governed by law, custom, technology, economics, and society (*see* ENTITLEMENT APPROACHES). Water can be variously regarded as: a gift of God, freely available to all (as in Islamic water law); a communal or public good to be shared within a defined community; a state-managed resource subject to large-scale engineering (*see* HYDRAULIC SOCIETY); and a *commodity, to be bought and sold on the market. In any given society, the system of 'water rights', i.e. lawful access to water, is important in determining supply and demand. In the past two or three decades, there has been a global shift away from communal and public modes of water rights towards greater *privatization and *commodification (*see* NEOLIBERALISM). It is argued that state-run water management often fails to recover costs or reach the poor. In many places however, notably Bolivia and South Africa, regional and urban communities have resisted this process, objecting to both privatization and the involvement of *transnational corporations.

Further reading Bakker, K. (2009), 'Water', in Castree, N., Demeritt, D., Liverman, D., and Rhoads, B. (eds.) *A Companion to Environmental Geography* 515–32.
Swyngedouw, E. (2004), *Social Power and the Urbanisation of Water: Flows of Power.*

SEE WEB LINKS
• Official website of the World Water Council.

waterfront development A term for urban regeneration schemes centred on recovering areas formerly associated with riverside industrial uses such as docks, power generation, and processing industries. Once at the heart of industrial cities, waterfront areas were increasingly abandoned from the 1970s onwards, creating the conditions for reinvestment. The standard development cleaned up the industrial pollution and introduced new consumption-based activities such as shopping, museums, and entertainment. Early pioneers included Boston, Baltimore, Sydney, and Glasgow. *See also* URBAN REGENERATION.

waterway A navigable body of inland water, such as a river, canal, or lake. For a waterway to be navigable it must have a weak current, sufficient depth and breadth, and be free of rapids or obstacles, or have a means of bypassing them. Waterways have long provided a key means of *shipping people and freight. Prior to the development of rail and automobiles, the development of canal networks formed a key means of moving freight in bulk across a landscape, and were a key technology in the Industrial Revolution, enabling the shipping of raw and manufactured materials. In many places, such as continental Europe, inland shipping is still an important mode of transportation.

Watts, Michael J. (1951-) An Anglo-American human geographer best known for his work on the political economy of food security, famine, and agrarian change based on field research in northern Nigeria (*Silent Violence* 1983) and developing the field of *political ecology through work on food commodities and industrial agriculture, and also on *petrocapitalism in the Niger delta. As a member of the California collective Retort, he co-wrote *Afflicted Powers* (2005), an analysis of military *neoliberalism in the wake of the 9/11 attack on the Twin Towers. Watts has taught geography and development studies at the University of California, Berkeley since 1979.

wayfinding The task of traversing between two locations using environmental or spatial cues such as direction signs or a map. The ability to wayfind is a key spatial competence, and how people undertake the task is a core research question in studies of spatial cognition and *behavioural geography. *See also* COGNITIVE MAPPING; NAVIGATION; SPATIAL BEHAVIOUR.

way of seeing An idea developed within visual culture by John Berger who argues that how a scene is visually represented and how people learn to see and interpret the world, is contextually and ideologically framed. In other words, a picture never simply presents an image and a viewer never simply perceives it. Instead, a visual *representation needs to be understood as being produced from within a particular perspective and cultural context. Moreover, how a viewer interprets the image is shaped by their *positionality. In this sense, a piece of art or a photograph is not a neutral, value-free representation, but is imbued with various meanings that need to be *deconstructed. *See also* NEW CULTURAL GEOGRAPHY; GAZE.

wealth inequality An unequal distribution of financial assets between people. It differs from income *inequality in that the latter refers to salary, whereas wealth concerns all assets of value including savings, property, and equities. The distribution of wealth is highly uneven across societies, with a small percentage of the population owning a large proportion of the assets, and the majority owning comparatively little. For example, Wolff notes that in the United States, which has one of the most iniquitous distributions of wealth in the world, 61.9 per cent of all wealth was held by just 5 per cent of the population in 2007, with the poorest 40 per cent of the population owning just 0.2 per cent of assets. Wealth inequalities exist across different axes of identity such as gender, race, and disability. For example, women are much more likely to have fewer financial assets than men. Moreover, the wealth inequality between nations has been widening, extending the wealth gap between the developed and developing countries. It has been argued that wealth inequalities, and the transference of wealth from the poor to the rich through inappropriate credit lending, was one of the causes of the 2007 global finance crash. It is also suggested, through the 'spirit level' thesis, that if wealth was more evenly distributed, society as a whole would benefit as social and health costs would be reduced.

Reference Wolff, E. N. (2010), *Recent Trends in Household Wealth in the United States: Rising Debt and the Middle-Class Squeeze—an Update to 2007.*

Weberian A term relating to the ideas and works of Max Weber (1864–1920), the German social theorist generally regarded as one of the founders of modern social science (alongside Karl *Marx and Emile Durkheim). He is best known for his theories that rationalization is the core element of Westernization and for analysing how Protestant religion lies at the heart of *capitalism. Although less influential than Marx in human geography, his ideas on class, status, and *power were important in the study of urban social geography during the 1970s and 1980s.

welfare geography An approach in human geography concerned with spatial *inequality and social *justice. Although the term is now rarely used, there was a distinct and innovative body of work on these themes centred on the contribution of British geographer David M. Smith in the 1970s and 1980s. It can best be understood in its historical context. Welfare geography developed partly out of *locational analysis,*spatial science, and *behavioural geography, but possessed a stronger normative dimension; it was concerned with what distributions of, say, public spending in health or elderly care ought to be, and not just with what they were. It took ideas from 'welfare economics', the study of the effect of public policies on the distribution of welfare within societies, but again added a more *normative angle. Welfare geography placed more emphasis on justice than efficiency. It was also distinct from *Marxist geography, with which it shared many ideas, in its focus on the distribution and consumption of social goods more than their production. In other words, it took as given how a society generates wealth, and concentrated instead on what is done with it. Smith summarized the approach as 'who gets what, where, and how'. He drew upon his extensive research into inequality in the UK, USA, and South Africa to examine such issues as differential levels of geographical access to medical care, variations in policing activity, and the impact of racial discrimination on quality of life (*see HUMAN GEOGRAPHY: A WELFARE APPROACH*). Most of the concerns of welfare geography continue to be the subject of research, although not generally under that heading.

welfare state **1.** A type of *state in which a high level of collective provision through state benefits co-exists with a market economy.
   2. That part of the state concerned with the collective provision of state benefits.
   The first sense helps distinguish some states in the *Global North from others. Welfare states, such as Sweden, Germany, and France, maintain relatively high levels of social support through, for example, subsidized housing, state pensions, free health care, and unemployment benefits. They are typically governed through social democratic parties, which place a high value on *social cohesion. Sometimes the term 'Keynesian welfare state' is used, implying that it is informed by the economic ideas of J. M. Keynes (*see* KEYNESIAN). These states contrast with neoliberal states such as the USA and Australia, where market forms of provision predominate, for example, in the form of private pensions (*see* NEOLIBERALISM). But even neoliberal states have welfare states in the second sense, i.e. the institutions that provide and regulate whatever public provision remains.

well-being The state of feeling content and healthy, of experiencing a good *quality of life. Well-being is not simply concerned with people's mental and physical health, but also their social wellness and satisfaction with their lives. Achieving personal well-being is a key aspiration for individuals, usually characterized by good health, prosperity, strong family relations and friendships, job satisfaction, sufficient social supports, freedom of expression, nice living environment, and low stress and worries. Such aspirations are not easy to attain and much government policy seeks to enhance its citizens' well-being by enhancing their quality of life.

w

Werlen, Benno (1952–) A Swiss geographer currently at the Friedrich-Schiller-University of Jena, Germany, noted for his contributions to *social geography and the relations between social theory and space. His most widely admired work is *Society, Action and Space*, published in German in 1987 and translated into English in 1992. He is executive director of the *International Geographical Union's initiative to persuade the *United Nations to create an International Year of Global Understanding.

(⊕) SEE WEB LINKS
• Website for Global Understanding.

West, the The countries and peoples associated with Europe by geographical location, ancestral relation, or political alliance in contrast with other world regions or civilizations. It is therefore also a synonym for the wealthier and politically powerful countries of the world aligned with the USA. The use of this cardinal direction to describe a portion of humanity probably dates back to the division of the Roman Empire between Rome and Byzantium in the 7th century AD. Later it was deployed in contrast with the Orient, Asia, or the East (*see* ORIENTALISM), and associated with Christendom, the region dominated by Christian rulers. During the *Cold War the main referent shifted to the USSR and the West embraced those parts of the world colonized and settled by Europeans (e.g. Australia) as well as political allies (e.g. Japan) alongside North America. After the end of the Cold War, commentators who subscribed to the view that humanity could be divided into civilizations often contrasted the West with either Islam or 'the Rest' (*see* CLASH OF CIVILIZATIONS, THE).

Western Europe 1. In geographical terms, the western half of *Europe and the countries within it.
2. In political terms, those European countries allied with the USA and opposed to the Soviet-led Eastern bloc during the *Cold War. The two definitions do not overlap. For example, Austria and Switzerland are generally described as lying within Western Europe, but they were not US allies. *See also* BERLIN WALL; EASTERN EUROPE; THE WEST.

Western Marxism Currents of Marxist thought circulating outside and mostly independently from Soviet *Marxism and its associations with the communist state of the USSR. Especially after the 1950s, Western Marxists were more likely to be university academics and stress Marx's more abstract philosophy than engage with economic analysis.

Westphalian model The system of sovereign states formalized in Europe by the Treaty of Westphalia 1648 (*see* STATE; SOVEREIGNTY). This provided for the ruler of each territory to be recognized as sovereign by other rulers, a situation also dependent on the recognition of agreed political *boundaries. The Westphalian model therefore describes an ideal international treaty based on nation states.

wetland banking A form of mitigation banking by which the loss or impairment of wetland in one location is compensated for by the creation, restoration, or enhancement of an equivalent area of wetland in another location. As a result, there should be no net loss of wetland but developments can proceed that might involve draining ground.

Further reading Robertson, M. M. (2004), 'The neoliberalization of ecosystem services: wetland mitigation banking and problems in environmental governance', *Geoforum* 35:361–73.

Whatmore, Sarah (1959–) A British cultural geographer who has made significant theoretical advances in developing a *more-than-human approach, notably in *Hybrid Geographies* (2002). Currently Professor of Environment and Public Policy at Oxford

University, she has also explored ideas of *science, the public, and *expertise through projects on flood-risk modelling and urban biogeography, both of which engage with the common ground between human and *physical geography.

white flight The movement to the suburbs by middle-class households from the majority white population supposedly in reaction to the growing demands and presence of racial and ethnic minorities in city centres, and the related fears about crime and schooling. The term was widely used to describe the situation in US cities from the 1960s onwards, but is widely regarded as simplifying a more complex set of processes.

White, Gilbert F. (1911–2006) An American environmental geographer best known for his work on environmental hazards. A Quaker, he was a conscientious objector during the Second World War, though he worked in France aiding refugees. He returned to work at Haverford College, Philadelphia, a Quaker institution, before taking up a post as Professor of Geography at the University of Chicago in 1955. He moved to the University of Colorado, Boulder in 1970 where he stayed until retirement. White was an enormously influential geographer who helped to shape approaches to hazards in general and floodplain management in particular. *See also* ENVIRONMENT AS HAZARD, THE.

whiteness The normalization of white people's social norms and cultural practices as the natural and proper way of society. Here, 'white' is used as a synonym for people of European origin who have a light skin colour. As Linda Peake (2009) details, whiteness is understood, from an academic perspective as a historical and geographically specific *social construct that has been afforded a privileged position at the top of a racialized and embodied system of social stratification. In other words, a higher cultural valuation has been attached to people who are classed as white. This positioning has been developed over a number of centuries, often drawing on spurious scientific evidence that sought to demonstrate the intellectual and cultural superiority of white people. For many white people, whiteness is an implicit, unconscious expression, although for some, such as white supremacists, it is an explicit ideology. For anti-racists, whiteness is a problem because it works to discriminate against non-whites, either implicitly or explicitly, and to suppress other cultural forms.

Further reading Bonnett, A. (2000), *White Identities*.
Peake, L. (2009), 'Whiteness' in the *International Encyclopedia of Human Geography*.

wilderness An area devoid of human habitation, cultivation, or significant use. The meaning of wilderness has, however, changed through time. Before the 18th century, wilderness was regarded as inhospitable, even dangerous, the abode of wild beasts, and the antithesis of cultivated and civilized land. In more modern times, wilderness describes an area designated as free from human exploitation. Antarctica, for example, was established as a continent in which there would be no permanent human settlement under the terms of a 1959 international treaty. The 1964 US Wilderness Act similarly provides for the creation of areas 'untrammelled by man', where humans are only 'a visitor who does not remain'. The motivations for establishing wilderness include its supposed aesthetic and spiritual value as a refuge from the strains of modern industrial life, its role in sustaining biodiversity or a 'natural laboratory' for scientific research, and its value for recreation. In recent years, the idea of 'rewilding' has taken hold. This can describe various forms of ecological restoration (*see* RESTORATION ECOLOGY), for example, dismantling dams or reversing the channelization of rivers. 'Pleistocene rewilding' involves the reintroduction of species found in a region until driven to local extinction or near-extinction by the arrival and expansion of human societies some ten to thirteen thousand years ago. Where the species, normally megafauna, are fully extinct, extant relatives may be substituted as proxy species. Such schemes to reconstruct 'nature as it was', are criticized for their lack of authenticity, however.

It is debateable whether wilderness in the sense of untouched nature currently exists or even has ever existed. There is much ambivalence over the use of the term. One objection is that in the *Anthropocene nowhere on the planet is free from human influence; anthropogenic *climate change is pervasive in its effects. A second objection is that, given how the term has changed historically, it makes more sense to think of the *idea* of wilderness rather than a biophysical reality. It is a social and cultural construction, as much imagined in art and literature as on the ground. Moreover, it is an idea with anti-human connotations. William Cronon, the US historian, has suggested that the 'trouble with wilderness' is that it sets up an impossible ideal. If the only truly good nature is nature from which humans are absent, he argues, how then are we to live? Further, by valuing wilderness so highly there is a risk of overlooking the more mundane environments closer to home and equally deserving of value. The final objection is that many areas now designated as wilderness were once inhabited. In *settler societies and in colonized Africa, indigenous peoples were regularly displaced by force to make way for protected reserves (*see* FORTRESS CONSERVATION). During the European settlement of the New World, the myth of pristine nature developed with serious consequences lasting until the present.

For these reasons, many human geographers are reluctant to use the term 'wilderness' in its naïve meaning. Yet, it thrives in popular understanding and continues to be invoked by many environmentalists. One alternative is to refer to 'wildness', a quality that might be found anywhere and does not rule out some human presence. Another is to adopt a topological approach to 'wild' things, examining how, for example, so-called wild animals are caught up in multiple socio-technological networks. In Sarah *Whatmore's argument, wildness is not found in bounded territories, but in hybrid forms. *See* ENVIRONMENTAL POLITICS; ENVIRONMENTALISM.

Reference and further reading Cronon, W. (1995), 'The trouble with wilderness', in Cronon, W. (ed.), *Uncommon Ground*, 69—90.
Martin, P. S. (2007), *The Twilight of the Mammoth: Ice Age Extinctions and the Rewilding of America*.
Whatmore, S. (2002), *Hybrid Geographies*.

wildness and wilding *See* WILDERNESS.

Wilson, Sir Alan (1939–) A leading figure in mathematical geography who pioneered the use of entropy in *spatial interaction models, and demonstrated the practical and commercial use of urban and regional modelling (*see* URBAN MODELLING). Wilson had a background in mathematics, statistics, and physics before he was appointed to the University of Leeds, UK, where he became Professor of Urban and Regional Geography in 1970 and was later vice-chancellor. As well as advancing *spatial science he co-founded the spin-off company GMAP (with Martin Clarke), which provided consultancy to businesses based on spatial modelling. He also co-founded the journal *Environment and Planning A* (1969). After serving as director-general for higher education at the UK's Department for Education and Skills he joined the Centre for Advanced Spatial Analysis at the University of London.

wine An alcoholic beverage made from fermented grape juice. Because the variety and quality of wines owes much to often small-scale variations in soil, climate, aspect and other features of the land (known collectively as *terroir*), as well as to custom and expertise, human geographers have studied intensively the geography of wine. The cultivation of grapevines is termed 'viticulture'. Wine is a major agricultural product and export of France, Italy, the USA, Australia, and many other countries.

Wise Use movement A loose coalition of US rural dwellers, landowners, resource-based industries, and think tanks united by their support for individual property rights and opposition to federal government land ownership and environmental regulation. Originating in the American Southwest in the 1970s and 1980s, this coalition has confronted mainstream environmental organizations which, in their view, seek to curtail individual freedom and responsibility for the environment by extending public owner-ship of land and restrictions on its uses.

Wolch, Jennifer (1953–) An American professor of geography and urban planning noted for her work on urban homelessness and the service-dependent poor (*Landscapes of Despair* 1987, with Michael *Dear, and *Malign Neglect* 1993), urban sprawl and sustainable urban planning, and *animal geographies (*Animal Geographies* 1998, edited with Jody Emel). Wolch was founder and director of the Center for Sustainable Cities at the University of Southern California and is currently dean of the College of Environ-mental Design, University of California, Berkeley.

Women and Geography Study Group (WGSG) The WGSG was established in 1980 as a study group of the Institute of British Geographers (IBG) (now *RGS-IBG). The group actively promotes the study of gender from a geographical perspective and the undertaking of geographical research through a *feminist approach. It also actively cam-paigns on gender inequalities in the discipline. Writing as a collective, the WGSG has produced two books: *Geography and Gender* (1984) and *Feminist Geographies* (1997).

(⊕) SEE WEB LINKS
• Website of the Women and Geography Study Group.

women in geography **1.** The study of the role and status of women in the discipline of geography.
2. The focus on women and women's lives in geographical analysis. A number of empirical studies have repeatedly shown that the gender balance of professional geog-raphers is biased in favour of men. While the balance at undergraduate and postgraduate level is approximately even in most Western countries, men are more likely to progress into university teaching positions, and are much more likely to hold senior appoint-ments. *Feminist critique of the discipline thus notes that geography is highly masculine, with a noticeable glass ceiling operating with respect to career paths and promotions. Moreover, the history of geography tends to erase the contributions of women to the discipline, instead charting paternal lines of descent. These imbalances, feminists argue, have led to geography being *masculinist in its foci and practices, with geographical research concentrating on arenas dominated by men, such as work and public spaces, adopting approaches that largely silence women's voices, and for the most part ignoring arenas dominated by women such as the home and also the everyday lives of women. In order to address these erasures and imbalances, feminist geographers have sought to highlight and challenge the masculinist nature of the discipline, to campaign for gender equality in appointments and career progression, to promote alternative *ways of seeing, knowing, and doing, and to produce new historiographies of the discipline, recovering and upholding the pioneering work of women geographers. *See also* WOMEN AND GEOGRAPHY STUDY GROUP.

Further reading Domosh, M. (1991), 'Towards a feminist historiography', *Transactions of the Institute of British Geographers* NS 16: 95–104.
Maddrell, A. (2009), *Complex Locations: Women's Geographical Work in the UK 1850–1970*.
Women and Geography Study Group (1984), *Gender and Geography*.

Wood, Denis (1945–) An American geographer noted for his influential and critical work on *cartography. *The Power of Maps* (1992) challenged the idea that *maps represented reality, and instead treated them as forms of argument. He developed this theme in later publications, including *The Nature of Maps* (2008) with John Fels. Wood's background in art and design helped him interpret maps in a new, more radical light.

work A purposeful, social, and transformative activity understood by those undertaking it as differing from *leisure or play. There is no objective, unambiguous, and universal definition of what precise activities constitute work. Work is a social construction and what work is varies between cultures and by context. A limited definition might be activities that lead directly or indirectly to one's subsistence, but much of what is understood as work in societies of the *Global North is far removed from *subsistence. Another definition might be remunerated labour or paid employment, but this omits the many activities necessary for *social reproduction that are frequently not paid, notably household or *domestic labour (*see* REPRODUCTIVE LABOUR). But if one decides that work is an activity that maintains society in general, then it is hard to see what does not count as work. Furthermore the same activity, say running, might be undertaken for leisure or, if one is a professional athlete, for work. Nor can work be defined by motivation; looking after a child might be done for money, but equally for love. Children's play often mimics or anticipates work that will be undertaken as an adult. Whereas in the Global North, work is an activity often associated with particular sites or workplaces that are regarded as separate from *home, in rural agricultural societies there is often no such distinction. And for urban dwellers carrying out *informal work in the cities of the *Global South, there may be no one site associated with work. Although in industrial capitalist societies work is often defined by time, i.e. contracted hours and days of employment, in other contexts there is no clear distinction. Live-in domestic workers may find that they have no time of their own and that their services are potentially demanded without limit.

Organized states of the Global North generally classify work according to the administrative practices of taxation, employment, and benefit regulations. Individuals above the age of compulsory education are deemed as economically active if they are engaged in or looking for paid employment. They are economically inactive if they are not in this situation, e.g. students in full-time education. Economically active people not currently employed but looking for paid employment are classified as unemployed. Activities undertaken within employment for which remuneration is recorded are deemed as work for the purposes of taxation. Volunteer labour is not, in this sense, work. These complex calculations lie behind the estimates of such measures as *Gross National Income (GNI), used to describe levels of economic development.

For most adults some form of work is necessary, although more affluent societies recognize a conventional age at which an individual might retire and cease paid labour. But given the enormous variety of forms and conditions of work it is no surprise that it holds an ambiguous position (McDowell 2009). Work can be the source of income, status, pleasure, identity, and friendship, but equally the cause of alienation, unhappiness, poor health, and social stigma. Whereas in the 1960s and 1970s some commentators anticipated a decline in paid work and an associated rise in leisure time as machines and computers replaced people, for many in the Global North this has not happened. Women, for example, increasingly have to cope with waged work and household labour. Recent geographical study addresses the 'work–life balance', i.e. how individuals and families attempt to combine the demands of both on their time. From the perspective of *time-geography, this can be understood in terms of how households use resources of time and space within the constraints established by, for example, the geographical distribution of work and housing, and the functioning of transport systems (Jarvis 2006). *See also* LABOUR GEOGRAPHY; LABOUR MARKETS; UNIONS.

Further reading Jarvis, H. (2006), *Work-Life City Limits*.
Krint, G. (3rd ed. 2005), *The Sociology of Work*.
McDowell, L. (2009), *Working Bodies*.

working class A group of people who work for wages and who have a relatively low degree of supervisory power or autonomy within the workplace. Typified by skilled and semi-skilled manual workers in 19th century urban industrial economies, sociologists have struggled with the concept in more modern, *post-industrial contexts. The diversification of forms of *work, especially with *services, and the kinds of worker, notably the increase in waged women workers, has blurred former distinctions between working and middle class. *See also* CLASS.

World Bank An international body, composed of 188 member states, whose mission is to reduce poverty and facilitate development and trade by providing finance and technical aid to countries, especially those in the developing world. It was established in 1944 as part of the *Bretton Woods Agreement, with its initial mandate to aid postwar reconstruction. The bank consists of two institutions: the International Bank for Reconstruction and Development (IBRD) that aims to reduce poverty in middle-income and credit-worthy poorer countries, and the International Development Association (IDA), that focuses exclusively on the world's poorest countries. These two institutions are part of a larger body known as the World Bank Group that includes the International Finance Corporation (IFC), the Multilateral Investment Guarantee Agency (MIGA), and the International Centre for the Settlement of Investment Disputes (ICSID). The World Bank is deeply implicated in *development, although its policies and approach are often vigorously opposed (*see* POVERTY REDUCTION STRATEGIES). Critics, most notably the *non-governmental organizations sector, argue that its policies often do more harm than good because they consist of 'shock therapy', that is, rapid and significant change in a short space of time. Moreover, despite moving away from *structural adjustment policies, it promotes *neoliberal governance that widens *wealth inequalities, rather than closing them. *See also* INTERNATIONAL MONETARY FUND.

(∰) SEE WEB LINKS
• Official website of the World Bank.

world city An urban region with an exceptionally high concentration of economic activity and functioning as a major node in global networks of trade, financial, information, and related flows. As such, its form, function, and significance cannot be understood purely within its respective national context, but must be located within the broader framework of the world-system or *globalization. The term is usually ascribed to Scottish planner and urbanist Patrick Geddes in 1915, but was first popularized by Peter *Hall in his book *The World Cities* (1966). Hall added population concentration and political power to business concentration in his definition, listing *London, Paris, Randstad-Holland, Rhine-Ruhr (Germany), *Moscow, *New York, and *Tokyo as world cities. But the concept owes its modern success to Jonathan Friedmann, a US planner based at the University of California, Los Angeles. In two key publications in the 1980s, Friedmann developed the 'world city hypothesis'. His insight was that certain cities could only be understood in terms of the world-system as conceived by Immanuel Wallerstein (*see* WORLD-SYSTEMS APPROACH), and in particular the emergent *New International Division of Labour. Although Los Angeles may have been a laboratory for his ideas, Friedmann set out a number of propositions about the social and spatial form of world cities more generally, thereby opening up a generative research agenda. This was soon combined with a second major conceptual innovation, *Saskia Sassen's idea of a global city, to produce a significant research field (*see* GLOBAL CITY; WORLD CITY NETWORK). Although the terms 'global' and 'world city' are often used interchangeably, or in combination (world/global city) there are important differences between Friedmann's and Sassen's approaches. The former is more faithful to World-System Analysis, while the latter focuses more on *producer services as the driver of global city status. Both ideas continue to inspire empirical and theoretical research. The Globalization and World Cities group and network (GaWC) based at Loughborough University, UK, is the major centre of these activities.

Further reading Friedmann J. (1986), 'The world city hypothesis', *Development and Change*, 69-83.

(⊕) SEE WEB LINKS
- Globalization and World Cities Research Network (GaWC), Loughborough University, England.

World City Network A metageographical arrangement consisting of three components: (i) a set of *world cities; (ii) the links between them; (iii) the transnational service firms that have office locations within some or all of these cities. The firms, in such fields as law, finance, and advertising create an interlocking network among the cities through their multiple branch-office locations. The concept was developed by Peter J. *Taylor and elaborated by colleagues in the Globalization and World Cities Research Network based at Loughborough University, UK.

World Commission on Environment and Development *See* BRUNDTLAND REPORT.

World Food Programme (WFP) A programme founded in 1961 as a branch of the United Nations, the WFP's mission is the eradication of *hunger. In particular, it responds in emergency situations, such as conflict or *natural disasters, to provide food to people. Through its various programmes it seeks to protect livelihoods, reduce chronic hunger and malnutrition, and strengthen the capacity of countries to source food. Its headquarters are in Rome, Italy. *See also* FOOD AND AGRICULTURE ORGANIZATION (FAO).

(⊕) SEE WEB LINKS
- Official website of the World Food Programme.

World Health Organization (WHO) The directing and coordinating authority for health within the United Nations system. It was established in 1948, shortly after the creation of the *United Nations, and presently consists of 194 member states; its headquarters are in Geneva, Switzerland. WHO is responsible for shaping the global health research agenda, setting evidence-informed policy options, tackling the spread of diseases, promoting public health initiatives, providing technical advice to countries, and measuring health trends. It produces a number of reports and public health data sets.

(⊕) SEE WEB LINKS
- Official website of the World Health Organization (WHO).

World Social Forum An annual gathering of *civil society organizations, activists, and campaigners united by their opposition to *neoliberal globalization (*see also* ANTI-GLOBALIZATION MOVEMENT; GLOBAL JUSTICE MOVEMENT). First held in Porto Alegre, Brazil in 2001, it has also taken place in Mumbai, Nairobi, and Dakar as well as other Brazilian cities. It is normally timed to coincide with the meetings of the World Economic Forum in Davos, Switzerland.

Further reading Mertes, T. (2004), *A Movement of Movements*.

world-systems approach A holistic method of analysis into historical and geographical social change over the timescale of centuries. It is sometimes referred to as world-systems analysis or framework. This approach derives from the writings of US scholar Immanuel *Wallerstein who spent most of his academic career at Binghamton University, USA. Wallerstein blended together elements of dependency theory (*see* DEVELOPMENT THEORY: ECONOMIC COMMISSION FOR LATIN AMERICA), *Marxism and the *Annales School to create a way of thinking that anticipated much of what was later described as *globalization. His starting point was to classify three different modes of production by their core relations of *exchange and associate each with a type of society. Thus, the reciprocal-lineage mode was associated with mini-systems; the redistributive-tributary mode in which surplus was extracted from one class by another was connected to world-empires; and the capitalist mode of production gave rise to world-economies. World-empires, such as the Inca or Roman empires, and world-economies, namely the modern *capitalist world economy, are described as 'world-systems'. This does not mean that everything in the world is part of them. Rather, they are worlds that contain all the essential processes of social change. For Wallerstein, these world-systems are the starting point for understanding social change, not the societies we imagine as coterminous with states. The approach is therefore critical of *methodological nationalism and differs from, say, *international relations, which takes the state as the building block of the international order. There is a geographical component. The capitalist world-system contains both core processes (i.e. high added value) and peripheral processes (low added value). These tend to cluster together, creating distinct core and periphery areas, but any given area may contain a mixture of both. Regions where core and peripheral processes are balanced are termed semi-peripheral. These types of regions do not necessarily coincide with states, although they are frequently mapped that way.

Wallerstein developed his analysis of the Modern World-System through four volumes between 1974 and 2011 (ending the account in 1914). Others have also contributed, and there is a journal devoted to world-systems research. One important line of inquiry, initiated by Gary Gereffi, has led to *global commodity chain analysis. Among geographers, the major contribution has been from Peter J. *Taylor and Colin Flint, notably in their co-authored textbook *Political Geography* (6th ed. 2011). Taylor, in particular, has added a more sophisticated geographical analysis of the state, placing it within a theory of *scale, and extended the concept into *World City Networks. *See also* HISTORICAL MATERIALISM.

(⊕) SEE WEB LINKS
• *Journal of World-Systems Research.*

World Trade Organization (WTO) An international organization established in 1995 as the successor to GATT (General Agreement on Trade and Tariffs), the WTO deals with the rules of trade between nations. Its headquarters are in Geneva, Switzerland. Its main function is to negotiate international trading agreements that are ratified by its 155 member states, and enable the producers, exporters, and importers of goods and services to trade as smoothly and freely as possible. It also operates dispute resolution services, provides data and reports on world trade, and promotes the liberalization of trade. *See also* DOHA ROUND; INTERNATIONAL MONETARY FUND; WORLD BANK.

(⊕) SEE WEB LINKS
• Official website of the World Trade Organization (WTO)

Wright, John Kirtland (1891–1969) Following a PhD in history from Harvard University, Wright spent most of his career at the *American Geographical Society, where he was librarian, director, and then research associate of the society (1920–56). He made major contributions to the history of geography and cartography, emphasizing the significance of geographical ideas and the imagination (*see* GEOSOPHY).

Further reading Wright, J. K. (1947), 'Terrae incognitae: the place of imagination in geography', *Annals of the Association of American Geographers* 37: 1–15.

writing A form of communication by means of the inscription of letters, words, and/or symbols. Geographers are interested in writing for at least three main reasons. Firstly, the invention of writing (and later printing) was an important moment in *time-space distantiation, i.e. the stretching of social relations across both space and time. Secondly, written communications have played specific roles in the constitution of *globalization as a set of practices, as Miles Ogborn has argued in the case of the East India Company's trading network. Thirdly, different tropes of writing have been evident in geography's intellectual history, i.e. there have been different styles of communicating geographical knowledge (Withers 2011).

References Ogborn, M. (2002), 'Writing travels: power, knowledge and ritual on the English East India Company's early voyages', *Transactions of the Institute of British Geographers* 27(2): 155–71.
Withers, C. W. J. (2011), 'Geography's narratives and intellectual history', in Agnew, J. and Livingstone, D. (eds.) *The Sage Handbook of Geographical Knowledge* 39–50.

WTO *See* WORLD TRADE ORGANIZATION.

xenophobia A fear of or antipathy towards foreigners and strangers, their cultures, and their customs. It is related to *racism, but is more centred on *ethnicity and *nationality. An example is English antipathy towards the French and French culture. Such xenophobia can be expressed individually, but is also represented and reproduced through the wider culture. *See also* OTHERING.

Yeung, Henry Wai-Chung (1968–) An economic geographer born in China, who gained his PhD at Manchester University before joining the National University of Singapore where he is now a professor. He is exceptionally active in the development of economic geography through conference organization and journal editorship, and has made significant theoretical contributions to a relational perspective on the subject. His writings advance conceptual understanding of the *firm, Chinese business networks, *global production networks, and transnational entrepreneurship, and contribute to geographical understanding of the Asia Pacific region.

youth 1. The period in the human life cycle encompassing adolescence and young adulthood.
   2. A member of a group defined by this period. Standard definitions of youth regard it as a biologically defined period with social and legal consequences, although these vary between societies, e.g. the age at which a person can be legally married. Typically, the age range 16–30 is used in international data collection. It is often assumed to be a transitional period, leading to adulthood. But many of the things generally assumed to be signs of adulthood, such as stable employment, relationships, a place to live, are not always available to all. Whether an individual makes the transition to adulthood is partly a function of socio-political circumstances. For example, across much of India and Africa, young educated men and women are unable to find work and face a prolonged spell of suspension between childhood and adulthood. What constitutes the experience of youth in one place and time may not be the experience of youth in another; in other words, there can be important differences between cohorts. After the *Second World War, with rising wealth Western youths became a target market for particular goods and services; the 'teenager' emerged as a distinct social category. The growth of distinct youth cultures has sometimes been accompanied by moral panics concerning behaviour and attitudes, which are framed as rebellious and resistive to expected social norms. As the work of geographers has shown, these youth cultures are often associated with certain spaces, such as the park, the street corner, the youth club, and nightclub, and are rooted in place and shaped by local practices, cultures, and identity politics, such as *religion and *race.
   Kenichi Ohmae suggests that youth consumption patterns, now diffused beyond the West currently drive much of *globalization. An alternative interpretation sees the rising pressure to consume coinciding with the decreasing ability to do so, because of global unemployment and under-employment. The result is widespread dissatisfaction and alienation among youths. Whereas in some countries the increase in the numbers and proportion of young people has coincided with economic growth, in others it has not (*see* YOUTH BULGE). Youth frustrations with poor prospects and the monopoly on political power held by older generations have been identified as causes of a growing number of social and political movements in the Global South, including the *Arab Spring.

Futher reading Jeffrey, C. and Dyson, J. (eds.) (2008), *Telling Young Lives: Portraits of Global Youth.*
Ohmae, K. (1995), *The End of the Nation-State.*
Skelton, T. and Valentine, G. (eds.) (1997), *Cool Places: Geographies of Youth Cultures.*
United Nations Population Fund (2011), *State of World Population 2011,* chapter 2 Youth.

youth bulge The relatively large increase in the numbers and proportion of a country's population of youthful age, conventionally 16–25 or 16–30. When infant mortality rates fall but fertility rates do not, at least in the short term, there will be a surge in the number of births relative to preceding years. As this cohort ages it enters the age at which waged employment is the norm. If economic conditions are favourable, as they were in much of East Asia, the result is a 'demographic dividend', an expansion of labour that contributes to economic growth. But under less favourable conditions, a 'demographic bomb' can result in young people being unable to find employment. It has been argued that this is one factor behind youth political unrest, notably in North Africa and the Middle East in 2011.

y

Zapatistas An abbreviation for the Zapatista Army of National Liberation, or in Spanish, *Ejército Zapatista de Liberación Nacional* (EZLN), a popular uprising in Chiapas, southern Mexico. The movement was announced in 1994 on the day Mexico signed the *North American Free Trade Agreement, and it combines demands related to indigenous peoples' rights, gender equality, participatory democracy, and opposition to globalization (*see* GLOBAL JUSTICE MOVEMENT). The Zapatistas had a galvanizing effect on protests worldwide, and drew much attention from sympathetic scholars because of their innovative networking and use of the *Internet.

Zelinsky, Wilbur (1921–) A US cultural and population geographer who studied for his PhD at the University of California, Berkeley under Carl *Sauer and has been based in Pennsylvania State University since 1963. In addition to extensive work on the cultural geography of the USA, including religion, folk culture, and place names, he is best known for the mobility transition model. This describes the relationships between changes in personal mobility and the modernization of society, positing general shifts from inter-rural to inter-urban migration on the one hand, and rural-urban to urban-rural on the other.

Reference Zelinksy, W. (1971), 'The hypothesis of the mobility transition', *Geographical Review* 61: 219–49.

zero tolerance The practice of *policing and law enforcement without scope for discretion. An offence receives the relevant sanction automatically without taking into account circumstances or extenuating factors. The idea conforms to the *broken windows theory of criminality, whereby if minor infractions are punished then crime levels can be reduced. It was rolled out in New York in the 1990s and has been emulated elsewhere, although there is much debate over its effectiveness.

Zimbabwe A country in south central Africa that was known as Southern Rhodesia during British colonial occupation from the late 19th century. In 1965 the white settler minority made a unilateral declaration of independence (UDI) to block rule by the majority black African population. Not until 1980 was Zimbabwe's independence secured through armed conflict and then negotiation. Since then, the issue of land redistribution from white settlers to, among others, the veterans of conflict has caused deep divisions and further unrest.

zoning In land-use planning, the division of land into distinct tracts and their classification according to permitted use. Land can be zoned for commercial, residential, recreational, or industrial purposes, and any change of use must be sought through application to the planning authorities. Zoning regulations are therefore an important way in which *urban managers can attempt to shape how cities develop. By setting the minimum lot sizes for residential development, or stipulating whether residences can be single- or multiple-occupancy, they can also influence the social geography of cities.

Appendix 1 Journals in Human Geography and related fields

General

ACME: an International E-Journal for Critical Geographies Open access online journal, 2002–

Annals of the Association of American Geographers A journal of the Association of American Geographers, Taylor & Francis, 1910–

Antipode: a Radical Journal of Geography Wiley-Blackwell, 1969–

Applied Geography Elsevier, 1981–

Applied Spatial Analysis and Policy Springer, 2008–

Area A journal of the Royal Geographical Society, 1969–

Australian Geographical Studies Journal of the Institute of Australian Geographers, 1963–2004

Bulletin of Geography: socio-economic series Versita, 2000–

Canadian Geographer/Le Géographe canadien Journal of the Canadian Association of Geographers, Wiley–Blackwell, 1950–

Chinese Geographical Science Springer, 1991–

Dialogues in Human Geography Sage, 2011–

Environment and Planning A Pion, 1969–

Environment and Planning D: Society and Space Pion, 1983–

Erdkunde: Archive for Scientific Geography Independent journal, University of Bonn, Germany, 1947–

Fennia: International Journal of Geography Open access online journal, Geographical Society of Finland, 1889–

Focus on Geography Journal of the American Geographical Society, Wiley, 1950–

Geografiska Annaler Series B. Human Geography Journal of the Swedish Society for Anthropology and Geography, Wiley–Blackwell, 1919–

Geografisk Tidsskrift–Danish Journal of Geography Journal of the Royal Danish Geographical Society, Taylor & Francis, 1900–

Geoforum Elsevier, 1970–

Geografie Czech Geographical Society, 1895–

Geographical A journal of the Royal Geographical Society, 1935–

Geographical Journal A journal of the Royal Geographical Society, 1831–

Geographical Research Journal of the Institute of Australian Geographers, formerly *Australian Geographical Studies*, 2005–

Geographical Review Journal of the American Geographical Society, Wiley, 1916–

Geographia Polonica A journal of the Polish Academy of Sciences, 1964–

Geography Journal of the Geographical Association, 1927–

Geography Compass Wiley-Blackwell, online journal, 2007–

GeoJournal Springer, 1977–

Geoscape: alternative approaches to Middle-European Geography Jan Evangelista Purkyne University, 2006–

Human Geographies University of Bucharest, 2007–

Human Geography: a New Radical Journal Independent online journal, 2008–

International Research in Geographical and Environmental Education Taylor & Francis, 1992–

Journal of Geography Journal of the National Council for Geographic Education, Taylor & Francis, 1902–

Journal of Geography and Regional Planning Open access, Academic Journals, 2008–

Journal of Geography in Higher Education Taylor & Francis, 1977–

National Geographic Magazine Journal of the National Geographic Society, 1888–

New Zealand Geographer Journal of the New Zealand Geographical Society, Wiley-Blackwell, 1945–

Norsk Geografisk Tidsskrift – Norwegian Journal of Geography Journal of the Norwegian Geographical Society, 1926–

Professional Geographer A journal of the Association of American Geographers, Taylor & Francis, 1949–

Progress in Human Geography Sage, 1977– formerly *Progress in Geography* (1969–76)

Review of International Geographical Education Online journal, 2011–

Scottish Geographical Journal Journal of the Scottish Geographical Society, formerly *Scottish Geographical Magazine*, Taylor & Francis, 1885–

Tijdschrift voor Economische en Sociale Geographie Journal of the Royal Dutch Geographical Society, Wiley-Blackwell, 1967–

Transactions of the Institute of British Geographers A journal of the Royal Geographical Society, Wiley-Blackwell, 1933–

Regional focus

African Geographical Review Journal of the African Specialty Group of the Association of American Geographers, formerly *East African Geographical Review* (1963–2000), Taylor & Francis, 2000–

Annals of Arid Zone Journal of the Arid Zone Research Association of India, 1962–

Arab World Geographer Independent journal, 1998–

Arctic, Antarctic and Alpine Research Journal of the Institute of Arctic and Alpine Research, University of Colorado, Boulder, 1961–

Arctic Journal Journal of the Arctic Institute of North America, 1948–

Asian Geographer, Taylor & Francis, 1981–

Asia Pacific Viewpoint Victoria University of Wellington, Wiley-Blackwell, 1960–

Australian Geographer Journal of the Geographical Society of New South Wales, Taylor & Francis, 1928–

Canadian Geographic/géographica Journal of the Royal Canadian Geographical Society, 1930–

Eurasian Geography and Economics formerly *Soviet Geography* (1960–91), *Post-Soviet Geography* (1992–95), *Post-Soviet Geography and Economics* (1996–2002), Bellwether, 2009–

Irish Geography Journal of the Geographical Society of Ireland, Taylor & Francis, 1944–

New Zealand Geographer Journal of the New Zealand Geographical Society, Wiley-Blackwell, 1945–

Polar Geography, known as *Polar Geography and Geology* (1980–94), Taylor & Francis, 1900–

The Polar Journal, Taylor & Francis, 2011–

Polar Record Cambridge University Press, 1931–

Singapore Journal of Tropical Geography Department of Geography, National University of Singapore, Wiley-Blackwell, 1980–

South African Geographical Journal, Journal of the Society of South African Geographers, Taylor & Francis, 1917–

Cartography and GIS

Annals of GIS Journal of the International Association of Chinese Professionals in Geographic Information Sciences, Taylor & Francis, 1995–

Cartographica Canadian Cartographic Association, University of Toronto Press, 1965– Cartography

Cartographic Journal British Cartography Society, Maney, 1964–

Cartography and Geographic Information Science Cartography and Geographic Information Society, formerly *American Cartographer* (1974–89), and *Cartography and Geographic Information Systems* (1990–98), 1974–

Computers, Environment and Urban Systems, Elsevier, 1975–

Geocarto International, Taylor & Francis, 1986–

Geographical Analysis, Wiley-Blackwell, 1969–

Geo-spatial Information Science, Wuhan University, Taylor & Francis, 1998–

Imago Mundi: the International Journal for the History of Cartography, Taylor & Francis, 1935–

International Journal of Geographical Information Science, formerly *International Journal of Geographical Information Systems*, Taylor & Francis, 1987–

Journal of Geographical Systems, Springer, 1999–

Journal of Maps, Online journal, Taylor & Francis, 2005–

Social and cultural geography

Children's Geographies Taylor & Francis, 2003–

Cultural Geographies formerly *Ecumene* Sage, 1994–

Emotion, Space and Society Journal of the Society for the Study of Emotion, Affect and Space, Elsevier, 2008–

Gender, Place and Culture: a Journal of Feminist Geography, Taylor & Francis, 1994–

Journal of Cultural Geography Taylor & Francis, 1979–

Population, Place and Space formerly *International Journal of Population Geography* (1995–2003) Wiley–Blackwell, 2004–

Social and Cultural Geography Taylor & Francis, 2000–

Social Geography Online open access journal, Copernicus, 2011–

Space and Culture Sage, 1997–

Economic Geography

Annals of Regional Science Western Regional Science Association, Springer, 1967–

Cambridge Journal of Regions, Economy, and Society Cambridge Political Economy Society, Oxford University Press, 2010–

Economic Geography, Clark University, 1925–

European Planning Studies Taylor & Francis, 1993–

European Urban and Regional Studies Sage, 1994–

International Regional Science Review Sage, 1975–

Journal of Economic Geography Oxford University Press, 2001–

Papers in Regional Science Wiley-Blackwell, 1955–

Regional Studies Journal of the Regional Studies Association, Taylor & Francis, 1967–

Environmental Geography

Environmental Hazards, Taylor & Francis, 1999–

Global Environmental Change Elsevier, 1990–

Journal of Geography and Natural Disasters Open access online journal, 2011–

Urban Geography

Housing Studies, Taylor & Francis, 1986–
International Journal of Urban and Regional Research Wiley-Blackwell, 1977–
Urban Geography Bellwether, 1980–
Urban Policy and Research Taylor & Francis, 1982–
Urban Studies, Sage, 1964–

Historical Geography

Journal of Historical Geography Elsevier, 1975–

Transport Geography

Journal of Transport Geography Elsevier, 1993–

Political Geography

Geopolitics formerly *Geopolitics and International Boundaries*, Taylor & Francis, 1996–
Journal of Borderlands Studies Journal of the Association of Borderlands Studies, Taylor & Francis, 1986–
Political Geography formerly Political Geography Quarterly, Elsevier, 1982–
Space and Polity Taylor & Francis, 1997
Territory, Politics, Governance A journal of the Regional Studies association, Taylor & Francis, 2012–

Other

Journal of Rural Studies Elsevier, 1985–
Health and Place Elsevier, 1995–
Landscape and Urban Planning formerly Landscape, Elsevier, 1986–
Landscape History Journal of the Society of Landscape Studies, Taylor & Francis, 1979–
Landscape Research Journal of the Landscape Research Group, Taylor & Francis, 1985–

Appendix 2 Geographical Societies

Major national and regional geographical societies (with date of foundation)

International and regional

International Geographical Union/Union Géographique Internationale, 1922
Commonwealth Geographical Bureau, 1970
The European Geography Association, 1988
Pan American Institute of Geography and History/Instituto Panamericano de Geografía
e Historia, 1928

National

Argentina	Sociedad Argentina de Estudios Geográficos, 1922
Australia	Institute of Australian Geographers, 1958
	The Geographical Society of New South Wales, 1927
Austria	Österreichische Geographische Gesellschaft, 1856
Bangladesh	Bangladesh Geographical Society, 1955
Belgium	Société Royale Belge de Géographie, 1876
Brazil	Sociedada Brasileira de Geografia, 1883
Canada	The Royal Canadian Geographical Society, 1929
	Canadian Association of Geographers, 1951
China	The Geographical Society of China, 1950
Colombia	Sociedad Geográfica de Colombia, 1903
Croatia	Croatia Geographical Society, 1897
Czech Republic	Česká Geografická Společnost, 1894
Denmark	Royal Danish Geographical Society, 1876
Egypt	The Egyptian Geographical Society, 1875
Estonia	Estonian Geographical Society, 1955
Finland	Geografiska Sällskapet i Finland, 1888
France	Société de Géographie, Paris, 1821
	Comité National Francais de Géographie, 1920
Georgia	Georgian Geographical Society, 1924
Germany	Die Gesellschaft für Erdkunde zu Berlin, 1828
	Deutschen Gesellschaft für Geographie, 1995
	Der Verband der Geographen an Deutschen Hochschulen, 1991
Ghana	Ghana Geographical Association, 1958
Hungary	Hungarian Geographical Society (MFT), 1872
India	Geographical Society of India, 1926
	National Association of Geographers, India, 1980
Ireland	Geographical Society of Ireland/ Cumann Tíreolaíochta na hÉireann, 1934
Israel	Israeli Geographical Association, 1959
Italy	Societá Geográfica Italiana, 1867
Jamaica	Jamaican Geographical Society, 1966
Japan	Association of Japanese Geographers, 1925
Korea	Korean Geographical Society, 1945

Latvia	Geographical Society of Latvia, 1923
Mexico	Sociedad Mexicana de Geografía y Estadística, 1833
Netherlands	Royal Dutch Geographical Society, 1873
New Zealand	New Zealand Geographical Society, 1944
Nigeria	Nigerian Geographical Association, 1938
Norway	Norsk Geografisk Selskap, 1889
Peru	Sociedad Geográfica de Lima, 1888
Poland	Polish Geographical Society, 1918
Portugal	Sociedade de Geografia de Lisboa, 1875
	Associação Portuguesa de Geógrafos, 1987
Russia	Russian Geographical Society, 1845
Saudi Arabia	Saudi Geographical Society, 1984
Serbia	Serbian Geographical Society, 1910
Slovak Republic	Slovak Geographical Society, 1946
Slovenia	Association of the Geographical Societies of Slovenia, 1922
Spain	Asociación de Geógrafos Españoles, 1975
	Real Sociedad Geográfica, 1876
South Africa	Society of South African Geographers, 1994
Sweden	Swedish Society for Anthropology and Geography, 1877
Switzerland	Swiss Association of Geography/Verband Geographie Schweiz/
	Association Suisse de Géographie, 1970
Tanzania	Geographical Association of Tanzania, 1967
Tunisia	L'Association des Géographes Tunisiens, 1977
Turkey	Turkish Geographical Society, 1942
Uganda	Uganda Geographical Association, 1961
United Kingdom	Geographical Association, 1893
	Royal Geographical Society, 1830
	Royal Scottish Geographical Society, 1884
United States	American Geographical Society, 1851
	Association of American Geographers, 1904
	California Geographical Society, 1946
	Geographic Society of Chicago, 1989
	National Geographic Society, 1888
Zambia	Zambian Geographical Association, 1967
Zimbabwe	Geographical Association of Zimbabwe, 1966

Appendix 3 Medals and Awards

Lauréat Prix International de Géographie Vautrin Ludaka ('Vautrin-Lud prize')

Awarded by the International Festival of Geography, Saint-Dié-des-Vosges, France. First awarded 1991. (Human geography recipients only listed.)

1991	Peter Haggett
1992	Gilbert F. White and Torsten Hägerstrand
1993	Peter Gould
1994	Milton Santos
1995	David Harvey
1996	Paul Claval and Roger Brunet
1997	Jean-Bernard Racine
1998	Doreen Massey
1999	Ron Johnston
2000	Yves Lacoste
2001	Peter Hall
2003	Allen J. Scott
2004	Philippe Pinchemel
2005	Brian J. L. Berry
2007	Michael Goodchild
2008	Horacio Capel Sáez
2009	Terry McGee
2010	Denise Pumain
2011	Antoine Bailly
2012	Yi-Fu Tuan

Lauréat d'honneur

Awarded by the International Geographical Union. (Human geography recipients only listed.)

1976	Innokenti P. Gerasimov, Chauncy D. Harris
1980	Shinzo Kiuchi
1984	Torsten Hägerstrand, Michael J. Wise
1988	Jacqueline Beauheu-Garnier, Oscar H. K. Spate, Gilbert F. White
1992	Peter Haggett, Jerszy Kostrowicki, Akin Mabogunje
1996	Harold Brookfield, Yola Verhasselt
2000	Leslie Curry, Yi-Fu Tuan
2004	Paul Claval, Maria Teresa Gutiérrez de McGregor, Robert Kates, Mohammad Shafi, Alan Wilson
2008	Mohammed S. Abulezz, György Enyedi, Hartwig Haubrich, Leszek Kosinski
2012	Larry Bourne, Janice Monk

Anders Retzius Medal in Gold

Awarded by the Swedish Society for Anthropology and Geography. (Human geography recipients only listed.)

1969	David Hannerberg
1973	Torsten Hägerstrand
1976	William William-Olsson
1978	Wolfgang Hartke
1985	Akin Mabogunje
1989	David Harvey
1991	Allan Pred
1994	Peter Haggett
1997	Peter Gould
2000	Erik Bylund
2003	Doreen Massey
2006	Gunnar Törnqvist
2009	Allen J. Scott
2012	Don Mitchell

Association of American Geographers

Major Honors awarded since 1996. (Human geography recipients only listed.)
*Lifetime Achievement
+Distinguished Scholarship

2012	*Kevin Cox, +Richard Walker
2011	*Susan Cutter, +Diana Liverman, +Mei-Po Kwan
2010	*Ronald J. Johnston, + James S. Duncan, +Daniel A. Griffith
2009	*Audrey Kobayashi, +David F. Ley
2008	*Lawrence A Brown, +Paul L. Knox
2007	*Reginald Golledge, *Peirce Lewis, +Nigel Thrift
2006	*Christopher 'Kit' Salter, +John Agnew, +William E. Doolittle
2005	*John Fraser Hart *Allan R. Pred, +Jennifer Wolch
2004	*Philip W. Porter, +Edward J. Malecki
2003	*Susan Hanson, +Peter J. Taylor
2002	*Gilbert F. White, +Arthur Getis
2000	*Janice J. Monk, +Neil Smith
1999	+Michael P. Conzen, +Eric S. Sheppard
1998	*Norman J. W. Thrower, +Gerard Rushton
1997	+James M. Blaut, +Michael R. Greenberg
1996	*Harold M. Rose, +Michael F. Goodchild

Royal Geographical Society with the Institute of British Geographers (Human geography recipients only listed.)

Founder's Medal

1977	Michael J. Wise
1980	William R. Mead
1988	Peter Hall
1992	Alan Wilson
1997	Tony Wrigley
1998	Robert Bennett
2000	Brian Robson
2001	William Graf
2003	Mike Goodchild
2006	Derek Gregory
2009	Alan Baker
2010	Diana Liverman
2011	David Livingstone

Patron's Medal

1973	E. H. Thompson
1980	Preston James
1984	Pierre Gourou
1986	Peter Haggett
1995	David Harvey
1997	David Rhind
2002	David Keeble

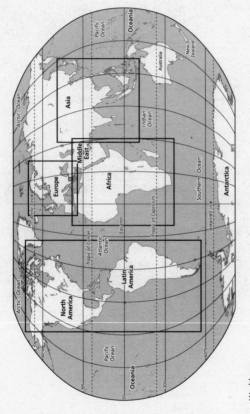

World map

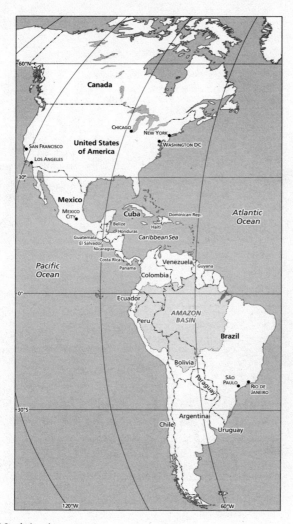

North and South America

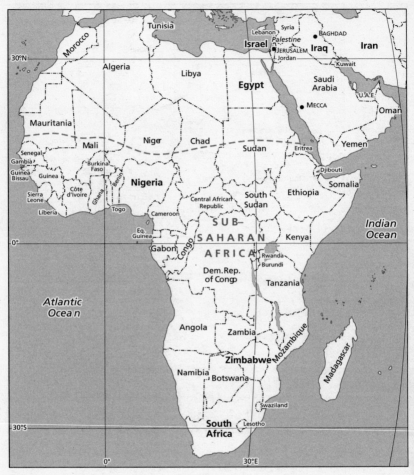

Africa

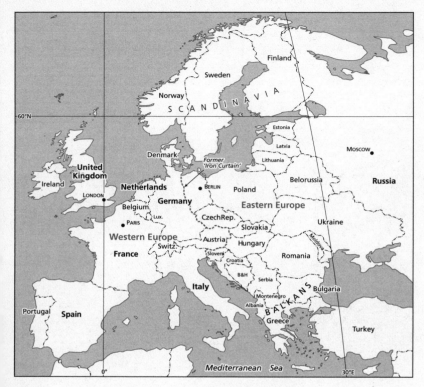

Europe

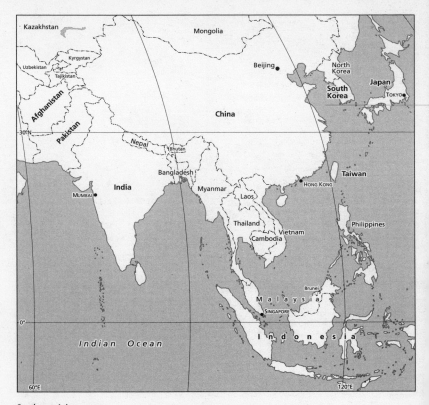

Southeast Asia